Date Due

APR 0 5 1989		
MAR 2 6 1994		
APR 2 9 1996		
FEB 0 3 1998		
FEB 1 6 1999		
MAR 0 2 1999		
JAN 2 0 2001		
MAY 1 8 2010		

BRODART, INC.   Cat. No. 23 233   Printed in U.S.A.

ILLINOIS

A Descriptive and Historical Guide

ILLINOIS

A Descriptive and Historical Guide

NEW REVISED EDITION

HARRY HANSEN, *Editor*

*Originally Compiled by the Federal Writers Project
of the Works Progress Administration
of the State of Illinois*

AMERICAN GUIDE SERIES

ILLUSTRATED

HASTINGS HOUSE • *Publishers* • New York

Library of Congress Cataloging in Publication Data

Main entry under title:

Illinois; a descriptive and historical guide.

  (American guide series)
  "Originally compiled by the Federal Writers' Project of the Works
Progress Administration of the State of Illinois."
    1. Illinois—Description and travel—1951-   —Guide-books. 2. Auto-
mobiles—Road guides—Illinois. 3. Illinois—History. I. Hansen, Harry,
ed. II. Federal Writers Project. Illinois. Illinois; a descriptive and historical guide. III. Series.

F546.I275   1974   917.73'04'4   74-8910
ISBN 0-8038-3381-4

Published simultaneously in Canada by
Saunders of Toronto, Ltd., Don Mills, Ontario

Printed in the United States of America

A Word About the New Revised Edition

This is the second revised edition of *Illinois, A Descriptive and Historical Guide,* commonly referred to as the Illinois State Guide of the American Guide Series. It was compiled and written originally by the Federal Writers Project of the Works Progress Administration during the depression years "as part of a nation-wide plan to give employment to professionally trained writers, journalists, and research workers." Henry G. Alsberg was director of the Project, 1935-39, and set the pattern for the series, and John T. Frederick was director for Illinois and editor of the first edition. Harold L. Hitchens was editor of the first revision in 1947.

Although the Federal Writers Project has been described in numerous essays and articles, its full history was not available until 1973, when Jerre Mangione published *The Dream and the Deal, 1935-1943* (Little, Brown & Co.). This book, written by an established author who worked at the Washington headquarters of the Project, is a circumstantial account of the Project's superb accomplishments despite the handicaps of political opposition to a subsidy for the arts, and administrative difficulties caused by distances between editorial offices, path-breaking assignments, and the artistic temperament.

John T. Frederick was an instructor in the School of Journalism of Northwestern University, who had acquired a reputation as an appraiser of young writing talent while editing *The Midland,* a noncommercial literary magazine that he published in Iowa. He also conducted a radio program, "Of Men and Books." The Illinois project, as Mangione writes, proved a stepping stone in the careers of a number of writers who became nationally important. He cites especially Richard Wright, who was enabled by the Project to work on his stories. Other workers were Arna Bontemps, who was writing *Drums of Dusk;* Nelson Algren, who already had written *Somebody in Boots;* Saul Bellow, just out of college; Sam Ross, a novelist in embreyo; Jack Conroy, specialist in folklore; Isaac Rosenfeld, Lionel Abel, Margaret Walker, Frank Yerby, Willard Motley, Katherine Dunham, George Victor Martin, Stuart Engstrand and many others, with Studs Terkel getting his first radio experience on the associated radio program of the Project. There was intense political opposition in Congress to the whole WPA program and many conservatives were convinced that subsidizing writers and artists was a wasteful boondoggle. But Jerre Mangione tells how veterans of the Project told him that it virtually saved them from starvation. One writer said: "The salary wasn't much, it averaged about $84 a month, but it fed us and gave us a feeling of hope and self-respect." And another said: "We knew that as long as we stayed on the raft we wouldn't drown."

Eight years later, in 1947, a revision was undertaken by Harold L. Hutchins, with the help of Miss Helen Rogers, Assistant State Librarian, and the Illinois Agricultural Extension Service. The principal articles were amended and the running text of the cities and towns was updated.

In 1947 the State was at the threshold of the vast readjustment in political, educational, social and economic affairs. This included the accelerated shift of transportation from rails to airplanes and trucks; the immense expansion of educational facilities through Federal Aid, and the roadbuilding program of the Federal Government, with its impact on makers of highway materials and employment. In the offing were those tense periods of social protest, agitation for civil rights, and arguments over foreign military involvement, and the rush of population from farms to the central cities and from the cities to the suburban towns. With the erection of the first Chicago skyscraper in many years, a new era of massive construction opened for Illinois.

To incorporate reports of these changes in *Illinois, a Descriptive and Historical Guide* has been the responsibility of the present compilers. They have retained much of the material written for the original edition. They have used the population figures published by the Bureau of the Census in 1970 and supplemented them by later reports of 1971 and 1972. They are immensely grateful to the many organizations and individuals who helped so generously, and especially to the officials of the State of Illinois and the City of Chicago, and the Illinois State Historical Society.

Contents

Part III Tours

Maps

Illustrations

NEW AND OLD LANDMARKS *between pages 162 and 163*

TRANSPORATION AND COMMERCE *between pages 288 and 289*

General Information
for Recreation and Touring

Sources of Information. The State of Illinois has extensive services to give the public specific information about business, industry, touring, and opportunities for recreation. It is especially efficient in providing historical information about towns and highways that give access to landmarks and sites associated with exploration and settlement during 300 years of western expansion, and thousands of years of aboriginal habitation. The principal services of information are located in Springfield, although there are branches in some of the large cities. The Division of Tourism of the Department of Business & Economic Development is one source; it issues a biennial *Calendar of Events* and has folders describing the *Lincoln Heritage Trail* and the *Hiawatha Pioneer Trail.* It cooperates with the Regional Tourism Promotion Councils, which get out descriptive folders for specific areas. Another branch of this Department is the Illinois Information Service, which issues illustrated booklets describing aspects of life in Illinois. Address 222 S. College St., Springfield 62706. Much information of great usefulness to tourists is provided by the Division of Education, Department of Conservation, State Office Building, Springfield 62706. One of its sections is the Division of Parks and Memorials, which lists locations and facilities and invites the public to ask for free publications entitled *Migratory Bird Regulations, Illinois Fishing Waters, Animal and Bird Synopsis, Film Catalogue, Illinois Fishing Guide, Camping Sheets,* and digests of *Fishing Regulations, Hunting and Trapping Regulations, Boat Regulation & Safety Act,* and the *Snowmobile Registration & Safety Act.*

One of the finest helps provided free by the State is the Official Highway Map, which is published annually and gives all the new and established roads. Copies may be had by writing to William F. Cellini, Division of Highways, 2300 S. 31st St., Springfield 62706, or the Secretary of State's Office, Room 115, State Capitol, Springfield 62706.

Motor Vehicle Laws: Residents required to have driver's licenses; non-residents' licenses honored if their state grants a like privilege to Illinois motorists; visitors from states not requiring driver's license are allowed to operate a motor vehicle for only 90 days in any calendar year; minimum age for drivers, 16 years. Financial Responsibility Law requires every motorist involved in an accident causing death, bodily injury, or property damage to others in excess of $100 to report the accident, and show he is able to pay possible damages by depositing security or proving he was covered by liability insurance or bond. Law does not apply to owners of parked cars or cars used without permission. Penalty for failure to report or deposit security is suspension of driver's license and all car registrations; or suspension of all non-resident privileges. Speed laws: maximum speed outside built-up areas is 55 mph. since operation of restrictions due to energy crisis. Otherwise 70 mph. on Interstate roads. In urban areas, maximum speed is 30 mph., but local ordinance may reduce it to 20 mph.; outside urban areas local ordinance may lower the maximum speed to not less than 35 mph.; maximum speed in school zones is 20 mph.; most trucks are limited to 55 mph. Parking lights may not be used in lieu of headlights for driving at dusk. Passing a school bus from either direction when it is stopped to load or unload children is prohibited. Turns must be signaled by hand or lights.

Watchfulness by the authorities to insure safe driving includes action against drunken driving. An amendment to the Vehicle Code in 1972 stipulates that anyone who drives a motor vehicle within the State thereby implies consent to tests of breath to determine alcoholic content when arrested for driving under the influence of liquor or drugs. Refusal to submit to such a test entails three month's suspension of the driver's license.

Fishing Regulations: Game fish defined as black, rock Warmouth, yellow or white bass, blue gill, crappie, pickerel, pike, trout and whitefish. For open seasons and daily and possession limits for the various species, see *Illinois Fishing Regulations,* issued by the Department of Conservation and effective for two years beginning July 1 of each odd-numbered year. *Licenses:* hook and line (50 hooks or less), resident, $2.25 (persons 65 or older, veterans with service-connected disability, and the blind, 50 cents); non-resident ten-day permit, $2.25, annual, $4.25; all obtainable from county, city, village, township, and incorporated town clerks; all licenses expire on January 31 unless otherwise specified. *Prohibited:* taking of game fish except by hook and line attached to rod or held in hand; to use in the taking of any fish a spear, gig (except as specified for rough fish), snare, treated grain, firearms, explosives, electrical devices or chemicals of any kind, wire basket, wire seine or net, or artificial light, except when used strictly for illumination.

Hunting Regulations: It is unlawful to kill at any time Reeves pheasant, ruffed grouse, prairie chicken, eagle, white squirrel, badger, and otter. No species of owl may be taken. Owners and tenants of land may destroy any protected wild animal or bird when it is destroying property, after obtaining written permission from the Department of Conservation. Open seasons and daily kill and possession limits for quail, cock pheasant, Hungarian partridge, deer, rabbit, black, grey, or fox squirrel, grey and red fox, skunk, opossum, mink, muskrat, raccoon, and beaver are listed in *Illinois Hunting and Trapping Regulations* issued annually by the Department of Conservation. Muskrat, mink, and beaver may be taken only with traps. Common domestic pigeons and crows may be taken at any time. Migratory game birds (ducks, mergansers, coots, geese, doves, woodcocks, and jacksnipes) are covered by Federal regulations. *Licenses:* resident hunting, $3.25; non-resident, reciprocal with State of resident, with a minimum of $15; resident trapping, $3.25; obtainable from officials listed for fishing licenses. *Prohibited:* taking of any song, insectivorous, or non-game birds protected by law; destruction of houses or dens of wild game protected by law; killing of wild game from any automobile or other vehicle or by the use of lights; hunting or trapping upon the lands of another without first obtaining permission from the owner or tenant; use of a silencer or other muffling device on a gun; use of a ferret; feeding and baiting; use of any mechanical device, smoke, or gases to dislodge an animal from its den; use of a shotgun larger than ten-gauge and capable of firing more than three consecutive shots; use of a shotgun load with shot size larger than BB to take any species of wild game; to take any species of wild game, except white-tail deer, with a shotgun loaded with rifled slugs.

Liquor Regulations: Sale of liquor and restrictions vested in local authorities, subject to Federal regulations. Sale of liquor prohibited in some cities, towns and communities by local option.

Miscellaneous Laws: Picking wild flowers in State parks and similar areas, destroying shrubbery or trees, prohibited. Camp fires, where permitted, must be thoroughly extinguished before leaving.

Poisonous Snakes and Plants: Many species of snakes are found in Illinois, but only four are of the poisonous variety; the swamp rattlesnake throughout the State except in the Ohio River valley, the timber rattler in the southern and western portion, the copperhead in the southern third, and the cottonmouth moccasin in the extreme southern end of the State. Poison ivy, a climbing shrub with three broadly ovate, notched leaflets is common in most sections, occasionally found climbing around trees or growing in shrubs. Poison sumac, an upright shrub 6 to 18 feet high, is common, especially in the swamps of Lake County.

SPECTATOR SPORTS AND CONTESTS

Spectator sports flourish in all parts of Illinois. Crowds jam the stadia for baseball, collegiate and professional football and basketball. The Chicago Cubs of the National League play in Wrigley field, Chicago, which can seat more than 37,000. The White Sox of the American League are at home in White Sox Park, Chicago, which holds 46,000. In 1970 and 1971 there were more than 1,600,000 admissions at the two parks. Four other Illinois cities have professional baseball clubs in the Midwest League; the Danville Brewers, the Decatur Giants, the Quad Cities (Rock Island-Moline) Angels, and the Quincy Cubs. The Chicago Bulls are members of the National Conference of the National Football League. A huge audience has grown up for basketball, which starts with high school contests all over the State and gets into the colleges and professional teams. The University of Illinois and North-western University have teams in the Big Ten. De Paul University and Loyola University play contests with the Basketball Independents. The Chicago Bulls are members of the Western Conference of the National Basketball Assn. Hockey is also on exhibition and the Chicago Black Hawks play members of the National Hockey League.

Chicago has two other major amphitheaters: the Chicago Stadium, seating up to 18,000, and the International Amphitheatre, capacity 9,500.

COUNTY FAIRS AND FESTIVALS

The county fair is a thriving institution in Illinois, attracting more visitors every year. The big show is the State Fair at Springfield in August, which has everything for a million spectators and draws people from the whole Midwest. Some county fairs get going as early as June. They started as exhibitions of what the land produced, and that included not only fowl and livestock, but garden fruit packed in mason jars and table cloths and quilts that the women of the household had stitched together. Today the county fair has all that, and much more. It has homecoming days, old settlers' days, fiddlers' contests, and even electric bands, for the guitar has replaced the accordian that the immigrants brought.

With the growth of interest in Illinois beginnings and the stimulation of the Illinois Sesquicentennial celebration, county fairs turned to pageants and staging of historical episodes. Hinsdale put on *Plank Road to Railroad*. West Chicago produced *In Old Turner Junction: Story of a Railroad*. Golconda had a Pope County pageant starting with Sarahsville. Arcola reached into the recent past to show *Horse Farming Days*. Other towns have discovered special reasons for fairs and celebrations. Charleston can boast that it has the oldest county fair at the site of the fourth Lincoln-Douglas debate. Lincoln has never forgotten that A. L. dedicated its site with watermelon juice, and sometimes reenacts that. Hoopeston puts on a sweet corn festival and Murphysboro an apple festival, with apple pie baking contests. The conventional county fair will always have the 4-H Clubs, and prizes for the best breeds. And some fairs will hire carnival companies to add to the din.

Nostalgia accounts for the survival of some appurtenances of fairs. How else explain the popularity of the steam-operated threshing machine? Once it provided the big event of a farmer's harvest season. Today the steam engine, with its piercing whistle and its clanking wheels, recalls the time when all hands turned out to feed the thresher from dawn to dusk. The American Thresherman Assn. helps keep it going.

RECREATION

Illinois' distribution of population, with half of the people centered in one great metropolitan area, affects the pattern of recreation as well as commercial and industrial activity. The concentration of population in the northeast portion of the State demands a more thorough development of nearby facilities than of those downstate where there is not the pressure of large masses seeking a place to play and relax.

Fortunately the whole shoreline of Lake Michigan in Illinois lies close to Chicago. The extensive dunes region over the line in Indiana, and the smaller dunes area north of Waukegan have been developed as recreational centers. Illinois Beach State Park, between Waukegan and Zion, preserves 1,651 acres of beach land with its natural features and offers 3½ miles of swimming beach, picnicking and camping sites, and accommodations in a modern hotel-lodge. Inland from the lake, near the Wisconsin line, is the Chain o'Lakes region, the only considerable group of natural lakes in the State. Chain o'Lakes State Park of 960 acres and the adjoining Chain o'Lakes Conservation Area of 3,253 acres provide fishing, boating, camping, hunting, and other recreations.

Near at hand are the facilities of the Forest Preserve District of Cook County, with a total area of over 63,000 acres of forest, meadows, and water, roughly bordering the city on the west. Within them are hiking trails, bridle and bicycle paths, playfields, and nature centers, and special features, from golf courses and swimming pools to ski and toboggan slides.

Chicago is the State's most concentrated recreational and entertainment center. Whereas city dwellers seek the countryside for their leisure periods, many down-staters flock to the metropolis, attracted by its galleries, theaters, beaches, and tremendously varied commercial recreation. Chicago's chief recreational attraction is Lake Michigan, and a maximum extent of the shore line has been developed for the people's use. Public beaches ranging from tiny street-end beaches to those that extend for almost a mile, dot the lakefront throughout its 20 odd miles. All of them are patroled and many have public bathhouses. In summer the eastern horizon is specked with the white of sails and hulls; eight harbors, from Montrose on the north to Jackson Park on the south, accommodate the numerous craft—catboat to yacht—that make sailing and cruising a major Chicago pasttime.

Also of major importance is the Chicago park system, comprising 429 parks and playgrounds under the control of the Chicago Park District. Four of the larger parks, Lincoln, Grant, Burnham, and Jackson, stretch in a green belt along the lake front. Their public recreational facilities, while include beaches, bridle paths, bowling greens, tennis courts, and golf courses, are supplemented by the privately-endowed Field Museum of Natural History, Shedd Aquarium, Adler Planetarium, Museum of Science and Industry, Art Institute, Chicago Historical Society, and Chicago Academy of Sciences. The Chicago Zoological Park, better known as the Brookfield Zoo, in the near western suburbs, attracts thousands of sightseers annually, not only for its trained porpoises and Children's Zoo, but for its excellence and completeness. These are the showplaces most frequently seen by visitors to Chicago, but the remainder of the park system, permeating the whole of the city, has been extensively developed for neighborhood use. Fieldhouses, gymnasiums, swimming pools, and tennis courts are scattered throughout Chicago; classes and competition in sports ranging from archery to wrestling and in such diverse hobbies as model airplane building and photography are conducted on a year-around basis.

There are 180 major picnic areas, with simple picnic facilities. All groups of 25 or more must obtain picnic permits by personal application at Room 929, County Bldg., 118 N. Clark St., Chicago. Smaller highway picnic sites may be used by families without permission.

There are public swimming pools, open in summer, 1-10 p.m. Cermak Pool, Ogden Ave. west of Harlem Ave., in Lyons; Whealan Pool, Devon Ave. east of Milwaukee Ave., Chicago; Green Lake, Torrence Ave. and 159th St., Calumet City. Persons 12 yrs. and over, 50c; under 12, 10c and free on Monday, Wednesday, Friday, 2:30-5:30.

Boating tobogganing, ice skating, at designated places. Consult general information folder available at Forest Preserve District hq, 536 N. Harlem Ave., River Forest, Ill. 60305.

Golf Courses. Billy Caldwell, Caldwell Ave., southeast of Central Ave., Chicago, Burnham Woods, 142nd and Burnham Ave., Burnham. Edgebrook, 6,000 N. Central Ave., Chicago. Indian Boundary, Forest Preserve Dr. between Belmont and Cumberland; Meadow Lark, 31st St., west of Wolf Rd. Chick Evans, Golf Rd. west of Harms Rd., Morton Grove. Pipe o' Peace. 131st St. and Halsted, Riverdale.

Nature Centers. Trailside Museum, Chicago Ave. and Thatcher Ave., River Forest. Closed Thursday. Little Red School House, 104th Ave., south of 95th St. Closed Friday. River Trail, Milwaukee Ave. near River Rd. Closed Friday. Sand Ridge, Paxton, Ave. north of 159th St., Calumet City. Closed Friday.

Bicycling became the popular exercise for the 1970's. Schoolboys found the bicycle a pleasing toy while young men eager for speed adopted the motorcycle. In between were adults who took up cycling as recreation. True enjoyment is in pedaling and following trails where neither the motorcycle nor the motor car obtrudes. The agitation for available paths and safe routes won the support of Chicago's Mayor Richard J. Daley, who tried a bike himself. This led the park authorities to place markers designating safe bicycle routes and advising caution on motorists, in Lincoln, Grant, Jackson, and Washington Parks and connections.

Illinois Prairie Path, originally designated for hiking and horseback riding in 1966, was opened to bicycles. It starts in Elmhurst, proceeds to Wheaton, and branches off to Batavia Junction and Dunham Road. It traverses woods and meadows and is provided with resting places.

ILLINOIS STATE PARK SYSTEM

Outside of the Chicago area, the major factor in recreation is the State park system. More than 100 State parks, memorials, and conservation areas, chosen for both scenic beauty and historical interest, are maintained throughout the State. These areas range in size from one-tenth acre at Fort Edwards State Memorial at Warsaw to 5,637 acres of the combined Pere Marquette State Park and adjoining Pere Marquette Conservation Area. Among the more important and widely used parks are Starved Rock in LaSalle County, Lincoln's New Salem in Menard County, White Pines Forest in Ogle County, Mississippi Palisades in Carroll County, Pere Marquette in Jersey County, Giant City in Jackson-Union Counties, and Illinois Beach in Lake County.

Although the great pageant of the steamboats is long gone, there has been a revival of small river excursion vessels. At Lincoln's New Salem State Park, a replica of the old stern-wheeler *Talisman*, the first steamboat to venture on the Sangamon River in Lincoln's time, offers hour-long trips during summer and fall. An excursion boat is based at Starved Rock State Park on the Illinois River, a small one is usually to be found at Pere Marquette State Park on the Mississippi, and another one at Hamilton, across from Keokuk, Iowa.

But if the big boats have vanished, quite the opposite is true of the small pleasure craft. Ranging from elaborate houseboats to small outboards, rowboats, and canoes, they occupy the rivers and their adjacent backwaters and lakes. Each river town has its growing marina, its harbors, docks, and clubhouses, while on summer week-ends the broad, placid pools above the dams are crowded with small craft.

A state of few natural lakes, Illinois has utilized well those it has, and has created others. Lakes Springfield, Bloomington, and Decatur, all impoundments behind dams, are extensively used as recreation centers. A dozen State recreational areas have been developed around other man-made lakes.

Part I
ILLINOIS

The General Background

The Land Itself

SEEN FROM THE AIR, the land of Illinois reveals graphically the agricultural importance of the State. Carved by intensive cultivation into an intricate mosaic of squares and rectangles, the level prairie resembles nothing so much as a vast stretch of modernistic linoleum. In the grainfields no land is wasted; pasture adjoins field, farm fits snugly against farm, and between them is nothing but the straight line of a fence or hedgerow.

Lying between the Great Lakes and the Mississippi, Illinois enjoys a drainage system extraordinarily complete and extensive. Water from 23 states crosses its surface and flows along its boundaries, eastward through Lake Michigan to the Atlantic Ocean and southward in the Mississippi to the Gulf. Although its topography presents no striking contrasts of surface contour, the State is separated into seven gentle but distinct basins, bearing the names of Lake Michigan, the Illinois, the Rock, the Kaskaskia, the Big Muddy, the Wabash, and the Ohio Rivers. The arteries and branches of these six great rivers serve 87.2 per cent of the 56,665 square miles of the State's surface. The largest, the Illinois, runs from northeast to southwest and drains an area 250 miles long and 100 miles wide, comprising 43 per cent of the State.

The conception of Illinois as an unrelieved table-top admits pleasant and unexpected contradictions. A portion of the hilly Wisconsin driftless area projects into the northwest corner; there, at Charles Mound, is the highest spot in the State, 1,241 feet above sea level. An extension of the Ozark Range, with several hills exceeding a thousand feet in altitude, crosses southern Illinois. The Mississippi and its tributaries, especially the Illinois, have carved long ranges of bluffs, the more rugged portions of which have been enclosed in State parks.

Elsewhere is prairie, but its original extent and appearance have been greatly altered. The earliest settlers found almost half the State in forest, with the prairie running in great fingers between the creeks and other waterways, its surface lush with waist-high grasses and liberally bedecked with wild flowers. Here occurred the transition from the wooded lands of the East to the treeless plains of the West. Since this was the pioneer's first encounter with the prairie, Illinois came to be known as the Prairie State, although westward lay lands more worthy of the title than the semi-wooded surface of Illinois.

The pioneers admired the grasslands, but clung to the wooded waterways. At the time of early settlement the fertility of the prairie was not known nor was it available until the invention of plows capable of breaking the tough sod. The waterways furnished timber for fuel and building, a convenient water supply, and protection for the settlers' jerry-built cabins from prairie fires and windstorms. Fires invariably swept the grasslands in the late summer, when the Indians burned off the prairie to drive out game. When the settlers at last began to surround their homesteads with several plowed furrows as a fire check.

The fame of the great stretches of treeless grasslands spread eastward, even to England, and magazines carried articles of description, speculating upon their origin (which is still unexplained) and the possibilities of their cultivation. Dickens, while visiting St. Louis in 1842, especially requested that he be shown the "paroarer," as he noted it was pronounced locally. A rumbling, ancient coach took him out to Looking Glass Prairie, near Belleville, and he returned to write:

> .... there lay, stretched out before my view, a vast expanse of level ground; unbroken, save by one thin line of trees, which scarcely amounted to a scratch upon the great blank .... a tranquil sea or lake without water, if such a simile be admissible .... and solitude and silence reigning paramount around .... I felt little of that sense of freedom and exhilaration which a Scottish heath inspires, or even our English downs awakens. It was lonely and wild, but oppressive in its barren monotony.

Lumbering activities and the pioneer's early preference for the woodland reduced the forests from their original extent, 42 per cent, to little more than 5 per cent. What is now commonly thought of as prairie is often the increment gained from the clearing of woodlands. Given over now almost wholly to farms, the prairies are constantly in flux as the landscape alters with the agricultural season. April transforms the Illinois country into a vast patchwork quilt of fresh color. Spring planting brings out tractors that furrow the land with geometric nicety. By summer the contours of the prairie are soft and round with ripening crops. July ushers in three months of intense industry. Harvesting machines gather the yield of the fertile land, trucks and trains loaded with grain begin to move toward the cities. When autumn comes, the prairies, gashed by plows and stripped of their harvest, have a worn, desolate aspect that is heightened by the somber browns and yellows of the season. The prairies are dull throughout winter save for intermittent snowfalls, and then, in late March, the land stirs, splotches of green appear, and farmers turn again to the soil.

The level aspect of Illinois topography has its explanation in the State's glacial history. As late as 13,000 years ago—a tick of the clock in geological time—there was still to be found in Illinois the last of the great ice sheets that had crept down from the North and with a leveling action comparable to that of a road-scraper, effaced hills and valleys carved by centuries of erosion. Ninety per cent of the State's surface was covered by ice; the only unglaciated areas are Jo Daviess County in the extreme northwest, Calhoun County in the west-central section, and the seven southernmost counties. In these areas the rugged terrain, sharply dissected by valleys, indicates the probable appearance of the whole of Illinois before the ice age. Elsewhere, save for sporadic outcrops, the uneven relief lies beneath a mantle of drift averaging 75 feet in depth.

The four ice-sheets that invaded the United States are definitely known to have reached Illinois. The next to last of these covered so great a portion of the State that it has been named the Illinoisan by geologists. Occurring approximately 150,000 years ago, it pushed south to the northern edge of the Ozark Range, and there, halted by increasing melting and the barricade of hills, piled up rock debris 20 feet deep on the hillsides. This was the greatest southern penetration of any of the North American glaciers.

The Wisconsin Glacier, which moved into Illinois 70,000 years ago and receded 57,000 years later, covered only the northeast quarter of the State, but because of its geological lateness its effects are more obvious to the layman. The great central portion of the State which was covered by the older Illinoisan sheet, but not overlaid by the Wisconsin, is much more nearly even in relief and mature in drainage. The terminal moraines—ridges of drift piled up where the glacial front stopped—are low and inconspicuous. Those of the last glacier, however, are among the largest known to geologists. Sharply defined and extensive in length, they comprise the chief topographical relief of the northeast portion of the State. The major ones are named for cities that have been built upon them; the Shelbyville, Bloomington, Marseilles, and Valparaiso moraines are four of the most important.

Marked with the characteristics of recent glaciation, the land bordering Lake Michigan near the Wisconsin state line is poorly drained, with many lakes and marshes formed by the melting Wisconsin glacier. Thus was created the lake region of Illinois, major recreational area for the metropolis of Chicago. At the time of recession the waters of the glacier were impounded between the Valparaiso moraine and the receding edge of ice, forming Lake Chicago, ancestor of Lake Michigan. The site of Chicago lay deep beneath the surface of this ancient lake, and deposition from its waters accounts for the table-top flatness of the city today. In successive stages the water receded north and east.

Glaciation and climate largely explain the agricultural distinction of the Illinois country. The average growing season varies from 160 days in the north to 211 days at Cairo, in the south. The drift laid down by the ice had been gathered from so great a variety of bedrock that an ample percentage of essential minerals was assured. Much of the State is veneered with a layer of loess, the finer particles of drift that were sorted out by the melting water from the glaciers, deposited in the valleys, picked up by the wind and spread across the land. Enriched by prairie grasses during the course of thousands of years, it possesses an even texture which, with the regularity of the terrain, makes Illinois particularly suitable for mechanical cultivation.

Buried beneath the glacial drift, the rock strata of Illinois effect little influence upon the topography, but their minerals yield to the State an income placing it eighth in the country in mineral output. All of the substructure that has been explored by deep wells is sedimentary in nature, except for red granite and other igneous rock found at depths of 1,000 to 8,000 feet in the northern half of the State. The entire

State is underlain with igneous rock, mother-rock of all formations, but sedimentation has buried it to a depth of probably more than 12,000 feet in the southern part.

Of the five geological eras, the third, the Paleozoic, was by far the most important both geologically and economically. Beginning some 600 million years ago, its was characterized by repeated submergences and uplifts. What is now Illinois was then covered by a series of shallow seas. In great cycles, the seas advanced, covered the land for millions of years, and then retreated to expose the surface again to weathering and erosion. The strata laid down during each submergence differ, depending upon the depth of the sea and the nature of the land at its shore line.

The oldest period of the Paleozoic Era was the Cambrian, during which thick layers of sandstone and dolomite were deposited over the entire State. These rocks outcrop only locally in northern Illinois; otherwise, they slant upward from the south to come to the surface in Wisconsin. Rainfall in the latter area, seeping through the soil to the sandstone layers, follows them to northern Illinois, where it enters the wells of many municipalities.

The second period of the Paleozoic Era was the Ordovician, which saw a series of submergences of long duration. Its first deposits, the Prairie du Chien group, included a limestone which was the basis of Utica's natural cement industry, important in the last century but now abandoned. One of the middle Ordovician deposits is a layer of St. Peter sandstone, which outcrops in Ottawa and nearby in a remarkably pure form that has achieved national industrial importance as a source of silica sand, used in glass-making and a hundred other processes. St. Peter sandstone also forms the picturesque bluffs that comprise Starved Rock State Park. Platteville limestone, also a middle Ordovician deposit, is used in making Portland cement. Later in the period a layer of Galena dolomite was laid down. It bears the lead which gave Galena its name and its early mining boom, and the zinc ores that are still mined in that region. Related to this formation is the Kimmswick limestone, which is the oldest of the petroleum-bearing formations in Illinois.

The third period, the Silurian, laid down several strata of dolomite and limestone, which are quarried extensively near Chicago and Joliet for road material and other uses. The next period, the Devonian, also is important for limestone. Both Silurian and Devonian rocks yield oil. Among the Mississippian deposits are the sediments that have supplied most of the State's oil.

Near the end of the Paleozoic Era occurred the Pennsylvania period, when Illinois' great coal beds were deposited. The beds are a small portion of the Pennsylvania deposits, but they have yielded a continuous supply of fuel for the industrial development of the State. The land at this time was low and marshy. A favorable climate encouraged the growth of giant trees and ferns that subsequent eons compressed into the coal veins that underlie two-thirds of the State.

Despite a half-century of extensive mining operations, not more than 3 per cent, it is estimated, of Illinois' coal reserve has been tapped.

Following the close of the Pennsylvanian period, the greater portion of Illinois remained above sea level. Except for brief invasions of extreme southern Illinois during the Cretaceous and Tertiary periods of the Mesozoic and Cenozoic eras, the work of the seas was done. Now rain and wind attacked the surface to erode and crease it with great valleys and ridges. Then, following a vast climatic change, snow fell in the northern region, year after year, deeper in the winter than the brief summer sun could melt.

So began the glacial period. Even as the curtain descended upon the State's geological drama, the ice sheets appeared, effaced the ruggedness, and retreated—so recently that Indian legends make awed mention of the Ice God that once came down from the North.

Before the White Man

WHEN THE FIRST WHITE SETTLERS came to the Illinois country they found large mounds of earth rising up out of the prairie, usually near navigable rivers. Because these mounds were sometimes shaped like beasts and often contained utensils and remains of burials, they were said to have been erected by people who antedated the Indians and became known as Mound Builders. But archaeological research has determined long since that the mounds were built by Indians and many were used for burial purposes for hundreds of years.

More than 10,000 mounds are scattered throughout Illinois. Because it was situated at the confluence of the great rivers various mound-building cultures shuttled back and forth across the State. Here are found obsidian from Yellowstone, Catlinite from Minnesota, copper from Michigan and Minnesota, mica from the Alleghenies, and shells from the Gulf of Mexico. And in the mounds of other States are found the kind of flint mined only in the ancient quarry in Union County, Illinois.

Archeologists have found two major culture patterns in the State, of which the Woodland is the older and more basic. One phase of this culture is represented by the effigy mounds in northwestern Illinois; this came down from Wisconsin. Another is the Hopewell phase which probably had its origin farther east. The other major pattern is known as the Mississippi culture, and is divided into Upper, Middle, and Lower phases; it runs up along the Mississippi, the Illinois, and other rivers, as far north as Astalan, Wisconsin.

Woodland pottery is crude and unevenly colored; textiles and shell work are absent; and only its stone work is definitely well-fashioned. Houses of the period were circular and temporary. The mounds themselves are round, are generally smaller than those of the Mississippi culture, and were not used as substructures. The dead were usually buried in the mounds in flexed positions; a few of the remains found had been cremated. In the Hopewell phase of this culture—so-called because it probably came to Illinois from the vicinity of the famous Hopewell mounds in Ohio—copper and mica ornaments occur. One of its chief characteristics is the frequent use of log tombs, over which the mounds were built.

In the more recent Mississippi culture, the pottery work is well-fired from carefully prepared clays; it is evenly colored and of many forms. Shell work is highly developed. Finely woven textiles are frequent. The dwellings were square or rectangular, of a permanent or semi-permanent nature, and the mounds were often used as substructures for these houses. In the cemeteries near the mounds the dead were buried in extended positions, together with projectile points, pottery, charms, and amulets.

One of the richest archeological areas in the Middle West is at the junction of the Spoon and the Illinois Rivers in Fulton County. Expeditions from the University of Chicago under Professor Fay-Cooper Cole found as many as three cultural manifestations of the two basic patterns existing in the same mounds. In the 800 mounds in Fulton County, six different cultural manifestations have been discovered, with the Middle Mississippi and the Hopewell phases often existing side by side, although different in time. Thus, though the religious practices and beliefs among the mound builders apparently differed, they continued to use the same spots for their burials.

In the same area, near Lewistown, on a high bluff overlooking the two rivers, is the Dickson Mound. Here a great museum has been erected, in part of which the remains of Indians buried centuries ago are exposed. *See Tour 16.*

Fifteen miles southwest of Joliet is the Fisher Group, where three successive occupancies were disclosed; under the original surface were skeletons with medium and long skulls, interred in a flexed position, and unaccompanied by relics; in the middle levels were found burials of a short-headed people; with them were many pottery vessels, and artifacts of stone, bone, and shell. The upper levels held mixed types and mixed artifacts. In one of the smaller mounds of this group occurred skeletons of a short-headed people, extended on their backs with their heads to the west; in these graves were iron, brass, and silver utensils and trinkets, of white man's manufacture, indicating that some of the mound builders lived here down to historic times.

In the American Bottom, near East St. Louis, are the mounds of the world-famous Cahokia Group. *See Tour 19A.* Here the mounds of the Middle Mississippi phase were used as substructures for ceremonial buildings. The pottery is highly developed and sometimes, in form and design, indicates southern connections. Near the center of the area, which contains eighty-five smaller mounds, stands the largest earthwork in the world, the Cahokia or Monks' Mound. A truncated pyramid, rectangular in form, with a broad terrace or apron extending from the south side, it covers 16 acres. Its greatest height is 100 feet; the east-west width is 710 feet, and the north-south length, including the terrace, 1,080 feet.

Also belonging to the Middle Mississippi phase are the four Kincaid Mounds near Metropolis, in Massic County. The largest, a truncated pyramid, rises 32 feet above ground, and covers 2 acres at its base. The nearby village site comprises more than 100 acres.

One of the newest of excavations is the Koster site, 6 *m.* south of Eldred, where remains of a large Indian settlement lasting through centuries before the white man came have been uncovered. *See Tour 22.* Eldred is on Illinois 108, 3 *m.* east of the Illinois River and Kampsville, which is on the opposite bank in Calhoun County and connected with a free ferry. Collegians at the excavation provide guides. There is a small exhibit of artifacts at Kampsville.

Effigy mounds, belonging to the Woodland culture, occur in the northwestern part of the State. They possibly represent totems or clan symbols; usually no burials are found in them. Near Galena is a mound shaped like a serpent, which strikingly resembles the famous Serpent Mound of Ohio. At the junction of Smallpox Creek with the Mississippi is the effigy of a bird with outspread wings. Also belonging to the Woodland culture are seventeen conical mounds on the bluffs overlooking East Dubuque and the Mississippi River, the largest of which is 70 feet in diameter and 12 feet high.

Thousands of small mounds, usually called bluff mounds, line the Illinois River. In culture they are of two types, for here again the Woodland and the Middle Mississippi, separated by considerable lapses of time, are found in the same area. Among other larger mounds of the State are the Montezuma Mounds near Pearl and the Beardstown Mounds in Cass County.

Of the historic Indians, the Illinois Confederacy was first in importance and one of the oldest. It was of Algonquian linguistic stock, and consisted of six tribes—the Cahokia, Kaskaskia, Michigamea, Moingwena, Peoria, and Tamoroa. Once the Illinois Confederacy occupied most of the Illinois country, but the early Jesuits found that there had been vast movements of all the tribes of the region due to wars with the Iroquois. Closely related to them, if not at one time actually a part of the Confederacy, were the Miami, who dwelt for a time in the region south of Chicago.

The Indians in the Confederacy called themselves Iliniwek (superior men), and indeed were physically well-built. They were friendly and talkative, but most of the early explorers reported them rather shiftless and treacherous. In war they were excellent archers; they also used a war club and a kind of lance with dexterity; but their proud title of superior men was not earned in war, for they were often defeated by the Iroquois and the northern lake tribes, sometimes by smaller numbers than their own.

Father Allouez first met a party of Illinois at La Pointe, Wisconsin, in 1667, when they came to trade. Three years later he found them at the Mascouten village on the upper Fox River, from which point they were setting out to join their tribes then living on the west side of the Mississippi. It was also on the Iowa side of the river that Father Marquette first encountered the Kaskaskia tribe that proved so friendly; on his return he met the same band at its ancestral village on the Illinois River near Peoria. Father Hennepin estimated that they numbered 6,500 in 1680; Father Sebastian Rasles gave an estimate of 9,000 in 1692. The Kaskaskia village on the Illinois near Lake Peoria was an important gathering place for all the tribes. When La Salle visited the town in 1680, it had 460 lodges, each housing several families. He reported that the annual assemblies of the tribes were attended by 6,000 to 8,000.

The lodges of this town topped the banks of the Illinois for more than a mile. Corn, beans, and pumpkins matted the adjacent meadows, and maize, planted in the spring, was given special attention by the squaws. When the maize crop was gathered, it was usually stored in pits, often under the houses. Pumpkins were sliced into discs and dried. When the work of harvesting was over, the tribes began to file westward for the serious task of obtaining enough meat to last through the winter and early spring. The men stalked and killed the game; the women dried the meat and carried it back to the village. The Indians' diet was further supplemented by wild fowl, nuts, roots, berries, and fish, which they speared in the lakes and streams.

The usual totems of the Illinois tribes were the crane, beaver, white hind, and tortoise, although the Kaskaskia sometimes used the feather of an arrow, or two arrows fitted like a St. Andrew's cross. Each village had several leaders, each of whom controlled from 30 to 50 young men. A reed mat with the feathers of various birds wrapped in it was carried on the warpath by the leader.

The Illinois, according to one account, did not immediately bury their dead; bodies were wrapped in skins, and attached by the foot and head to a tree. After the flesh had rotted away, the bones were gathered up and buried. The *De Gannes Memoir,* probably written by the nephew of Tonti, declares that the Illinois buried their dead in shallow trenches lined with planks. Both kinds of graves have been found in Illinois. Grave gifts for the deceased, to accompany him on his journey to the "land beyond the milky way," consisted of an earthen pot, his bow and arrows, a handful of corn and tobacco, and often a calumet pipe.

The *De Gannes Memoir* further states that men frequently had several wives. As all persons in the village addressed one another in terms of kinship, the sisters, aunts, and nieces of a man's wife were *nirimoua,* and they in turn called him by the same name; if a brave were a successful hunter, he could marry all the women thus related to him. When a man died, his wife was prohibited from marrying for a year; the penalty for breaking this tribal law was death, after which the offender's scalp was raised over the lodge of her husband's family. Many shamans, or medicine men, lived among the tribes, and attempted to cure illnesses by chants and ceremonies which they professed to have learned through visions; once a year they held a colorful dance at which they gave a preview of their nostrums and powers. In their leisure time, the warriors played a brutal form of lacrosse, or gambled at a game of matching odd and even with sticks. So earnestly did the players engage in the latter that they often gambled away their female relatives.

According to the *De Gannes Memoir* and the reports of Father Hennepin, the Illinois built their cabins like long arbors, and covered them with a double mat of reeds, which the women gathered from the rivers and wove into rectangles sometimes 60 feet long. Each house had four or five fires and accommodated eight to ten families. Some of the villages were enclosed within palisades; others were set in the open with a good view of the surrounding country.

About 1680 the Iroquois descended upon the Illinois tribes, wiped out the principal villages, and pursued some of the conquered bands down the Illinois River to the Mississippi. There they attacked the Tamoroa, and took 700 of their women and children prisoners. In 1682 La Salle built Fort St. Louis at Starved Rock and gathered about it 3,000 warriors of the various Algonquian tribes in a confederation against the Iroquois; 1,200 of these were Illinois. Twenty years later, we find the Illinois dispersed again; Peoria, Cahokia, and Kaskaskia were centers for the tribes of those names; the Tamoroa were associated now with the Kaskaskia, and the Michigamea lived near Fort de Chartres on the Mississippi. In 1729 Illinois warriors helped the French subdue the Natchez, and later fought in the Chickasaw War. Though they became involved in the Conspiracy of Pontiac at the conclusion of the French and Indian War in 1763, they had by then taken over many vices of the white man and had lost much of their vigor. When Pontiac was killed by a Peoria Indian near Cahokia in 1769, his tribes—the Chippewa, Ottawa, and Potawatomi—descended from the north and east upon the Illinois and almost annihilated them. A widespread legend relates that a band of fugitives took refuge on Starved Rock, where they were besieged by the Potawatomi and killed. *See Tour 14A*.

In 1778 the Kaskakia numbered 310 and lived in a small village three miles north of Kaskaskia. The Peoria and Michigamea lived a few miles farther up the river and together numbered 170. By this time all had become demoralized by liquor. In 1800 there were only 150 Illinois surviving. In 1833 they sold their holdings in Illinois and moved west of the Mississippi; by 1855 the consolidated Peoria, Kaskaskia, Wea, and Piankashaw, living on an Indian reservation in Oklahoma, numbered 149, with much admixture of white blood.

In the seventeenth century, enemies other than the Iroquois came to make war on the Illinois and settle on their land. The Sauk and Fox moved down from Wisconsin to the northwestern part of the State and claimed all the territory between the Mississippi and the Rock Rivers. Originally they had lived along the St. Lawrence; subsequently, harassed by the Iroquois, they moved to Wisconsin. Father Allouez set up a mission among them at Green Bay in 1669. After defeating the Mascoutens near the mouth of the Iowa River, they formed an alliance with the Potawatomi and forced the Illinois to move southward. Their defeat during the Black Hawk War in 1832, when they resisted the encroachments of the white men, caused their ultimate removal from the State.

By the time the French explorers came, the Winnebago sometimes drifted down from Wisconsin into northern Illinois, the Kickapoo had moved into the area at the foot of Lake Michigan, and the Mascouten, friendly to the Illinois, lived in the great grassy plains east of the Mississippi. Along the Wabash dwelt the Piankashaw, and around the southern and western shores of Lake Michigan stretched the hunting grounds of the Potawatomi, a particularly warlike tribe, who, in the Conspiracy of Pontiac, annihilated the garrison at St. Joseph, and in 1812 committed the Fort Dearborn massacre. Associated with the Potawatomi were the Chippewa and Ottawa, among the most energetic and powerful tribes of the Northwest; they lived on both sides of the Wabash. At one time the Shawnee dwelt in the southeastern part of the State.

As white civilization advanced westward, the Indians found their forests despoiled and their rivers polluted. Corrupted first with liquor and disease, then used as pawns in colonial politics, they were herded to reservations in the West. In 1832, the year the Sauk and Foxes were driven from Illinois after the Black Hawk War, the Winnebago ceded to the United States all of their territory lying southeast of the Wisconsin and Fox Rivers. In 1833, at a grand council of chiefs in Chicago, the Potawatomi, Ottawa, and Chippewa also ceded their holdings, and prepared to move across the Mississippi to Indian reservations, together with the Illinois.

The State and the People

ILLINOIS IS A SOVEREIGN STATE in the American union, the central industrial-commercial core in a highly productive agricultural region. Its political boundaries separate it arbitrarily from the adjacent states of Indiana and Wisconsin, and its natural boundaries from Iowa, Missouri and Kentucky. On the map it is an oblong 380 feet long and 205 feet wide, comprising 53,748 *sq.m.* of land and 652 of water, or a total of 56,400 *sq. mi.,* tapering to the convergence of the Ohio and Mississippi Rivers at the south. It provides the connecting links in water transport from the Atlantic Ocean to the Gulf of Mexico by means of the Chicago and Illinois Rivers. Its land is a plateau averaging between 600 and 700 ft. above sea level, and its highest spot is Charles Mound in Jo Daviess County, 1,235 ft.

In 1970 the U. S. Bureau of the Census recorded a population of 11,113,976. Of this total 83.04 percent live in urban areas. There were 9,045,753 people living in the nine Standard Metropolitan Statistical Areas, or 81.39 percent of the total. The nine SMSA areas were Bloomington-Normal, 104,389; Champaign-Urbana, 163,281; Chicago, 6,978,-847; Rock Island-Moline-East Moline-Davenport (Ia.), 362,638, (Illinois part, 219,951); Decatur, 125,010; Peoria, 341,979; Rockford, 272,063; St. Louis-East St. Louis, 2,363,017, (Illinois part, 536,110); Springfield, 120,704.

There are 102 counties in Illinois, of which 13 are counted as completely rural because they have no incorporated areas with more than 2,500 people.

The State slogan is Land of Lincoln, adopted in 1955. The official flower is the native violet; tree, the oak; bird, the cardinal, chosen by school children. The General Assembly made fluorite the official mineral. The State seal was adopted in 1868; it carries an eagle and the motto *National Unity, State Sovereignty.* In July, 1970, the State flag was altered to resemble the Great Seal and carry the word *Illinois.*

In recording the population of Illinois with reference to nativity and descent, the Census of 1970 used a base figure of 11,109, 450 for its total, compared with 10,081,653 for 1960. The original 1970 figure is 9,526 short, according to a later correction, which made the State's total 11,113,976. Making allowances for this variant, the census summary reported 9,617,500 native white residents, of whom 7,734,197 lived in cities and towns, and 1,491,950 native non-whites. In 1960 there were 8,337,076 native whites and 1,058,539 native nonwhites; thus 1970 showed a ten-year gain of 1,280,484 whites and 433,411 non-whites. There were 1,421,745 Negroes, of whom 1,399,102 were urban dwellers, and there were 364,397 persons of Spanish language, 351,182 of them urban. Farm and country life appealed chiefly to whites; there were 1,365,928 whites in the countryside and 500,983 on farms, whereas only 19,385 Negroes were counted as rural nonfarm people and only 3,298 were on farms. As for the Spanish-speaking people in Illinois, 11,377 were rural nonfarm, and 1,868 were farming.

In classifying the "country of origin of foreign stock" the Census shows the diminution of certain foreign stocks once uppermost in Illinois, and the increase in others. Foreign stock means persons of foreign birth and of foreign or mixed parentage. The northern European stocks showed declines; there were 415,545 persons of German stock in Illinois in 1960, but only 312,070 in 1970, more than 100,000 fewer. The missing had died or moved out of the State. This was also true of the other large stocks: United Kingdom, Ireland, Italy, the Scandinavian countries, and Czechoslovakia. But there were increased stocks from Greece, Cuba, Asia, Mexico and South America. In 1960 3,141 were of Cuban stock; in 1970, 19,649; Asia (China, Japan, etc.) in 1960 had 37,542; in 1970, 71,738. The other Americas had 11,644 in 1960, 31,276 in 1970. The people of Mexican parentage numbered 63,063 in 1960 and 107,268 in 1970, accounting for a large addition to "people of Spanish language."

The first appearance of Negroes on Illinois territory is ascribed by historians to the French. The French had established religious missions at Cahokia in 1699 and Kaskaskia in 1703, and settled at Prairie du Rocher in 1725. Fort de Chartres was begun in 1718, and as the commandants came up from Louisiana it is probable that they brought blacks as personal servants, although for manual labor they recruited Indians. The Illinois territory became part of the district of Louisiana in 1717. In 1720 Phillipe Francois Renault, director general of mines for the Company of the West, brought up an undetermined number of miners and slaves to exploit the minerals of the region. He is supposed to have reached the Fever River area, where the Indians had been turning out lead. Renault is said to have received 25 slaves a year for five years. In 1732 165 slaves were counted in the Illinois country and there were 436 in 1752.

Out of 1,098,569 Negroes, counted by the Bureau of the Census in 1970, all were native-born except 5,331. There were 612,251 born in Illinois and 379,427 born outside the State; of the latter 344,436 came to Chicago from the South. The number in school, aged 3 to 24, was 365,555; of this total 231,513 were in elementary schools and only 15,809 attended nonpublic schools; 84,538 went to high school, 6,061 of them to nonpublic schools. College was attended by 22,310.

Fundamental figures of population, work force, unemployed, earnings and income vary from month to month, but the changes are usually few. Trends are best identifiable when the figures for years of activities are compared. The Department of Labor in June, 1972, made the following summaries on the basis of its reports. Citing the final figure for the population of Illinois given by the Census of 1970 as 11,113,976, it listed the resident population two years later, including resident armed forces, at 11,251,000. On this basis the civilian work force of Illinois in 1972 was 5,129,400, with 4,879,100 employed and 245,000 unemployed. The largest number, 3,071,900, was in non-manufacturing, including government employment, while manufacturing claimed 1,279,-200. Agriculture, once the State's reason for existence, had only 159,000 in its work force.

In manufacturing the average weekly earnings were $173.48; the average hourly wage was $4.21, and the average weekly hours were 41.2.

The total personal income of Illinois residents in 1971 was placed at $53.4 billions, which is more easily grasped when cut down to per capita income of Illinois residents, $4,775.

The Census of 1970 reported the number of veterans of the military services living in Illinois as 1,544,901, of whom 1,392,561 were white (43.6%), 144,984 Negro (37%), and 25,344 Spanish-speaking (24.1%). Of those who served in Vietnam 201,924 were white, 24,123 Negro, and 5,859 Spanish-speaking. Korean veterans were 230,380 white, 33,065 Negro, and 6,181 Spanish-speaking. Veterans of World War II in Illinois were 149,678 white, 64,681 Negro, and 7,542 Spanish-speaking. World War I veterans were 76,816 white, 6,981 Negro. Veterans who had served in noncombatant branches of the military were 201,232 white, 14,266 Negro, and 4,973 Spanish-speaking residents.

The big movement of Mexicans and people of Mexican and Spanish descent into Illinois began in the 1920s, according to a study by Mark Reisler in the *Journal* of the Illinois State Historical Society. In 1900 no state in the Midwest had more than 500 Mexicans; in 1910 there were 672 in Illinois; in 1920 this had grown to 3,854. In Chicago the Mexican population rose from 1,224 in 1920 to 19,362 in 1930. By 1940 Metropolitan Chicago, which included the industrial area around East Chicago, Indiana, had about 35,000.

The Mexicans moved north because the ordinary worker, if employed, earned 57c a day in Mexico and in the North about six times as much. The American quota system restricted immigration from Europe and let down the bars to Mexico. The railroads needed unskilled labor for track maintenance. According to Reisler 80 percent of the track workers on the Burlington and 30 percent on the New York Central were Mexicans. During the steel strike of 1919 Mexicans were hired to replace strikers and were laid off when the strike ended.

"During the relatively prosperous 1920s, steel companies sent agents to American border towns, and sometimes into Mexico itself, to recruit workers. By 1926 more than 6,000 Mexicans were employed in the Chicago area steel industry." Mexicans also were hired for unskilled jobs in the meatpacking industry. Steel plants paid 45c to 50c per hour; packinghouses, 42½c to 47c per hour; railroads 35c to 41c per hour.

In a little over fifty years of the 20th century the Negro population of the United States more than doubled, rising to 21,500,000 between 1910 and 1966. Their numbers in the central cities increased five-fold. In 1910, 91% of the 9,800,000 Negroes were in the South and 27% in cities of 2,500 or more. By 1966 the numbers outside the South had risen from 880,000 to 9,700,000. The 12 largest central cities contained two-thirds of the Negro population outside of the South and one-third of the total number in the country (*Kerner Commission*).

Government

TWO IMPORTANT ACTS that affected the welfare of every citizen of the State of Illinois took place in time to be applied when the 1970 decade began. They were the collection of a graduated State corporate and individual income tax, and the adoption of a new Constitution, which revised offices and procedures.

Fortyseven years had passed before the voters of Illinois authorized a new Constitution to displace one adopted in 1870, which imposed handicaps on the governing of a dynamic, progressive, modern State when not revised to meet the changing needs of the times.

The first constitution of 1818 was suitable for the rudimentary State, but its seams were soon split by social and economic expansion. Thus, in 1848, a second constitution was adopted. It, in turn, became inadequate, and a constitutional convention was called in 1862. The constitution as framed was rejected. Another convention met in December, 1869, and framed a new constitution, which was ratified July 2, 1870. The third constitution was written primarily to serve an agrarian state, and as industries and railroads developed many of its provisions proved too restrictive. But despite agitation to revise it a convention was not called until 1918.

In the intervening years so many powerful political and economic forces had developed in Illinois that the issues before the convention were almost irreconcilable. The split between the industrial colossus that was Chicago and the rural communities downstate was sharp. Experience in governing the conglomerate area in the northeastern part of the State had built up demands for more home rule and better tax procedures, but also support for several measures that shocked the more conservative counties—the initiative and referendum and direct primaries, strongly supported by the Progressives. The convention met from December 12, 1920, to October 10, 1922. The resultant instrument provided for an individual and corporate income tax, public ownership of utilities, Bible

---

STATE AND MUNICIPAL POLICE

The State police and highway patrol employees numbered 2,200 in 1972. Of the 1,666 police 594 were civilians. The Chicago police force of 14,549 had 13,053 officers, of whom 119 were female, and 1,677 civilians. The number of officers and civilians in the police forces of Illinois cities were: Peoria, 258 (204 officers, 54 civilians); Springfield 179, (133 and 46); Evanston, 166 (129 and 37); Joliet, 151 (118 and 33); Skokie, 130 (88 and 42); Aurora, 120 (106 and 14); East St. Louis, 117 (101 and 16); Cicero, 103 (97 and 6).

18

reading without comment in the public schools, civil rights for Negroes, and a measure of home rule. By this time the liberals of the Chicago metropolitan area had turned against the project and with the help of the newspapers advocated its defeat. When put to a vote on December 12, 1922, it was rejected by 921,398 to 185,298, and the State staggered on under the Constitution of 1870.

Fortyseven years later the State was able to call another convention. By that time the need for revision was great. The sixth constitutional convention met in Springfield Dec. 8, 1969. It consisted of 116 members, two elected from each senatorial district. A new constitution was adopted Dec. 15, 1970, effective July 1, 1971. It was voted for in sections by 2,017,717 electors, of whom 1,122,425 voted for it, and 838,168 against.

The Constitution of 1970 enlarged the bill of rights by guaranteeing freedom from discrimination on the basis of race, color, creed, national ancestry, and sex in the hiring and promotion practices of an employer or in the sale or rental of property. It also guarantees women the equal protection of the laws and prohibits discrimination based on physical or mental handicaps. It lowers residency requirements, provides for uniform election laws, and for a bipartisan board to supervise their administration. The former difficulty of getting amendments accepted—of 36 proposed between 1878 and 1970 only 15 were adopted—was remedied by reducing the majorities required for adoption.

The 1970 Constitution provides for an annual balanced executive budget, a uniform system of accounting for local governments, and an auditor general appointed by the General Assembly. Income tax must be at a nongraduated rate, and the rate for corporations must not exceed the rate for individuals by more than 8 to 5. It exempts the homestead tax and omits food from the sales tax. Borrowing for general obligations needs a three-fifths approval from legislature or voters; revenue bonds require only a simple legislative majority.

The State Constitution requires the General Assembly to abolish all ad valorem personal property taxes on or before Jan. 1, 1979. Revenue lost thereby subsequent to Jan. 2, 1971, must be replaced by the State. The Illinois Supreme Court ruled in 1971 that the provision abolishing the tax was unconstitutional because it violated the equal protection clause of the 14th Amendment. The U. S. Supreme Court in turn upheld the abolition of the personal property tax on individuals. The personal property tax annually produced about $400,000,000, of which school districts were the principal beneficiaries, receiving about 60%.

The possibility of harm to the environment was recognized in the new Constitution, for it provides that individuals may bring legal action if their rights to a healthy environment are curtailed; the General Assembly, however, must decide on reasonable regulations.

The State has the primary responsibility for financing educational institutions and services. The new Constitution ordered establishment of the State Board of Education and Governor Dan Walker signed a bill making it an official policy-making body beginning Jan. 1, 1975. The Board will design guidelines for public and private schools, pre-school through Grade 12 and vocational education. It will choose the State Superintendent of Education, who will serve no longer than three years.

Two special projects were defeated by the voters. They rejected the proposal to abolish the death penalty, by 1,218,791 against 676,302, and defeated the proposal to lower the voting age to 18, by 1,052,924 against 869,816.

The elected executive officers of the State government are the governor, lieutenant governor, treasurer, attorney general, secretary of state and comptroller. With the exception of the treasurer, who serves a two-year term, they hold office for four years. The superintendent of public instruction will no longer be an elected office after 1978; instead a State Board of Education will be authorized, which will appoint a chief State education officer. Beginning in 1978 all elected executive officers will be chosen in the even-numbered years in which a President of the United States is not elected. The governor and lieutenant governor will be jointly elected, removing the possibility of their being of rival political parties. A significant responsibility of the governor is the power to appoint most of the key officials in the agencies under him and thereby to exercise administrative control over those agencies. The governor has the power to call special sessions of the General Assembly, to grant pardons, commutations, and reprieves for all offenses against the State, and to veto legislation, including separate items or sections of appropriation bills. He may also reduce appropriations. His annual salary is $45,000.

Illinois was the first State to adopt a civil administrative code. By means of this measure, enacted in 1917, more than a hundred State agencies were consolidated into departments administered by directors whom the governor appoints with the consent of the senate. The governor also appoints the members of certain boards and commissions beyond the scope of the code, notably the Illinois State Civil Service Commission, and, with the advice and consent of the senate, he selects three judges who hear and determine claims against the State.

The General Assembly or Illinois legislature consists of a senate and house of representatives. Senators serve four years, representatives two years. The State is divided into 51 senatorial districts; the separate voters of each elect one senator and three representatives.

The General Assembly met biennially until the Constitution of 1970 ordered it to convene annually. The lieutenant governor presides over the senate; the speaker of the house is nominated at the caucus of the major party, and is formally chosen by vote of the house of representatives. The powers of the legislature are distinct and more comprehensive than those of the judicial and executive branches. To override a veto, both houses must muster a two-thirds vote of their total membership.

The State judiciary consists of the Supreme Court, the Appellate Courts, and the Circuit Courts. The Supreme Court has seven justices, elected to serve 10 years. They elect one of their number Chief Justice, to serve three years. The Supreme Court has authority over all courts and may exercise original jurisdiction in cases relating to revenue, mandamus, prohibition, or habeas corpus. The Appellate Courts hear appeals from the Circuit Courts. They have five districts. Cook County, the first district, has five divisions. The remaining 101 downstate counties are divided into four districts, each having one division. Elgin is the seat of the Second District; Ottawa of the third; Springfield of the fourth, and Mount Vernon of the Fifth. The only trial court is the circuit court. The State is divided into 21 judicial circuits. In each circuit one of the circuit judges is selected by the circuit and associate judges as chief judge.

The Constitution provides that Supreme, Appellate and Circuit Judges shall be nominated at primary elections and by petition and elected at general or judicial elections.

Under the Illinois Constitution, the county forms an extension of State powers. As with cities and incorporated villages, the county exercises those powers authorized under the enactment of law by the General Assembly, the State's governing body.

Repeated efforts to impose a State sales tax in order to meet the heavy expenditures of the Depression were thwarted by the State Supreme Court on the grounds of unconstitutionality. In 1933 Governor Henry Horner obtained a 2 per cent sales tax from the Legislature and approval by the Court. He invalidated the property tax in consequence. About 1,000,000 persons were reportedly without means of subsistence in Illinois in 1933. The Legislature voted a bond issue for $30,000,000 to be sustained by the tax on gasoline. A year later it added 1 cent to the sales tax for emergency relief and established unemployment insurance. In 1935 the State voted aid to dependent children and pensions for old age and blind persons. Twelve percent of the State income tax reverts back to counties and cities. Effective in 1970, and affecting taxes collected in 1971, a major portion of personal property previously assessed was exempted.

The State has adopted anti-pollution controls to save the land and the health of the people. An Environmental Protection Act enacted in May, 1970, established standards and enforcement, along with monitoring and surveillance of conditions near industries. New laws provide suits for infringement with penalties of $10,000 and $1,000 a day until elimination of the abuse; thereafter jail sentences may be imposed. A proposal for a bond issue to combat pollution failed of enactment in 1969, but by Nov. 3, 1970, the voters were more alert to the dangers and voted a $750,000,000 bond issue to improve treatment of sewage by municipalities and sanitary districts. The State pays 26 percent of the cost of local projects and the Federal Government an equivalent share.

By 1967 the racial clashes and demonstrations had reached such intensity that members of the Federal Government sought an explanation for the disaffection among black Americans. President Lyndon B. Johnson in July, 1967, appointed the National Advisory Commission on Civil Disorders to find answers to: What happened? Why did it happen? What can be done to prevent it from happening again? Because he made Governor Otto Kerner of Illinois chairman it became known as the Kerner Commission.

After seven months of study the Kerner commission in February, 1968, issued a report of 1,400 pages, 250,000 words, saying white racism was principally responsible for the explosive mixture caused by discrimination, poverty and frustration among the blacks, based on segregation in employment, education, and housing; that white society condoned the black ghetto, and America was moving toward two societies, one white, one black, separate and unequal. The report qualified this conclusion, however, and said this movement could be reversed, and recommended legislation to bring about reforms.

Although the Kerner Commission had no connection with the State of Illinois its findings gave encouragement to those fighting for civil rights. The latter won many concessions during the 1960s, but often more than persuasion was needed to move officials. The State of Illinois had a fine record for helping the indigent ever since the depressed 1930s. The State Assembly acted on unemployment insurance, needy old age and dependent children, and outlawed discrimination in the public services. Municipalities increased open housing, especially after seeing their slum areas go up in flames. Boards of education made efforts to obey the mandates of the U. S. Supreme Court, but had to be prodded by decisions of the Federal District Courts. A new cardinal of the Catholic Archdiocese of Chicago backed reforms with his authority. The Federal Government became lavish in its grants of aid to schools, libraries, and organizations for helping the poor and the minorities, but made nondiscrimination a condition of its largesse.

THE DEPARTMENT OF PUBLIC HEALTH is one activity of the State that touches the welfare of every community and citizen. The Department was organized in 1877 with a staff of three and a budget of $5,000, plus $1,000 for contingencies. Nearly a century later the Department employs approximately 1,100, mostly professionals, and administers State and Federal funds in excess of $43,000,000. In the 1970-71 fiscal year the State appropriated $18,000,000 and the Federal Government $25,500,000. One of its major activities is to promote county and multiple-county health departments, which are separate from city and local district health organizations.

Among many activities the Department in recent years has expanded the Bureau of Environmental Health, which provides for inspection of drugs, devices and cosmetics in the Division of Food and Drugs, and of retail food processing; the Division of Milk Control, which tests milk, cheese, butter, ice cream and other products manufactured in the 177 dairy plants in Illinois; the Division of General Sanitation, which includes regulation of migrant camps and trailer parks, and the Division of

Radiological Health. This last division is growing annually for it deals with radiation in medical diagnosis and therapy, in industry, and in nuclear power reactors. Radiological health is the science of eliminating risk from the use of radiation. New instruments are in use to measure radiation levels around nuclear power reactors and strict accountability of the medical profession is exacted to regulate the amount of radiation received by patients. In 1970, 7,750 facilities used radiation for medical purposes and had 11,476 x-ray machines, while 507 industrial plants used it in various forms. Surveillance by the Department of Public Health also covers the burial of radioactive wastes, which is done in a 20-acre site in Bureau County owned by the State.

HEALTH CONDITIONS IN ILLINOIS
Report of the Illinois Dept. of Public Health

In 1970 there were 205,203 births and 110,474 deaths among Illinois residents, as compared to 195,699 births and 111,107 deaths in 1969. Most of the increase in births can be attributed to the marked increase from 138,705 births in 1945 to 196,007 in 1947. On the basis of the 1970 census population the birth rate was 18.5 per 1,000 and the death rate 9.9, the same as the all-time low in 1961. The infant death rate, 21.5 per 1,000 live births, was below the 1969 rate of 22.4.

Among the 205,203 births there were 71,761 first-born; of these 15,164 were illegitimate. From the age of one year to about 35 years accidents are the leading cause of death. Over age 35, heart disease leads. For all ages the leading causes of death in 1970 were heart disease (47,690), cancer (19,145), cerebrovascular disease (10,974), accidents (5,177), and influenza and pneumonia, (3,457). Motor car accidents accounted for 2,448 deaths. Of 904 deaths of school children, aged 5 to 14, accidents accounted for 430, leukemia took 63. There were 764 motor vehicle accidents, 346 homicides and 136 suicides in the 15 to 24 year age group. Among all ages there were 1,026 suicides, or 9.2 per 100,000 population; the rate has been declining since the high of 18.5 in 1932. Drugs accounted for 338 deaths.

Tuberculosis accounted for 2,138 new cases and 285 deaths. There were 5,204 cases of syphilis. Gonorrhea "is rapidly becoming an epidemic disease." There were 42,464 cases in 1968, 50,337 cases in 1969, and 51,668 cases in 1970.

Three Hundred Years of History

FRENCH AND BRITISH

THE FIRST EXISTING RECORDS of white men in Illinois were made by Father Jacques Marquette. On May 17, 1673, he and Louis Jolliet, with five *voyageurs,* left Mackinac, paddled over parts of Lakes Huron and Michigan into Green Bay, thence up the Fox River, crossed at the portage, and went down the Wisconsin. On June 17 they entered the Mississippi. On the west side of the river, in what is now Iowa, they encountered and exchanged friendly greetings with the Kaskaskia tribe of Illinois Indians. The adventurers passed the mouth of the Missouri, saw the famous Piasa or Thunder Bird painted on the cliffs near the present city of Alton, and reached the mouths of the Ohio and Arkansas Rivers. There, having concluded that the Mississippi flowed not into some western ocean, but into the Gulf of Mexico, and fearing Spaniards and hostile Indians, the Marquette party turned back late in July, 1673.

They returned by way of the Illinois River, which Marquette described in his *Journal:* "We have seen nothing like this river for the fertility of the land, its prairies, woods, wild cattle, stag, deer, ducks, parrots, and even beaver." And Jolliet later reported that the valley was "the most beautiful and most suitable for settlement."

Near Starved Rock they encountered the same tribe of Kaskaskia, now returned to their ancestral village site (about nine miles below the town of Ottawa), and their friendliness so won Father Marquette that he promised to return and set up a mission among them. From the Des Plaines River they took the ancient portage trail to the Chicago River, thence to Lake Michigan, and up to Green Bay. Here Marquette, ill from the hardships of the voyage, was left behind, and Jolliet went on alone to Montreal, where, almost in sight of the town, his canoe overturned and his carefully kept *Journal* was lost. Nonetheless he gave enthusiastic verbal descriptions of the new country, of its fertility and ease of cultivation; he spoke of its marvellous transportation facilities, and showed how, with a canal built through "but half a league of prairie" a boat could sail from Lake Erie down the Mississippi to the Gulf of Mexico.

On October 25, 1674, with two *voyageurs* as companions, Father Marquette set out from Green Bay to keep his promise to the Kaskaskia. The voyage proved a hard one, and not until December 4 did the party reach the mouth of the Chicago River. Because of the severe cold and the recurrence of his old illness, Marquette stopped "two leagues" above the mouth of the river for the winter. With the spring his strength returned, and in Easter week, 1675, he established the first mission in the Illinois country at the Great Village of the Illinois, calling it the Mission of the Immaculate Conception of the Blessed Virgin. But then, weakened again by illness, he decided to return to St. Ignace (Mackinac). He was canoed up the eastern shore of Lake Michigan by his two faithful companions; finally, when he was unable to go farther, they landed near the river named for him in the present state of Michigan. There, on May 18, 1675, he died.

Robert René Cavelier, Sieur de La Salle, the French explorer, came later to the Illinois country. In 1679, after the sinking of his *Griffon* on Lake Erie, he erected a fort at the mouth of the St. Joseph River, ascended that river, portaged to the Kankakee, and canoed up the Illinois River to Lake Peoria, where he made friends with the Peoria tribe of the Illinois. About two miles below the lake, on the south side of the river, he built Fort Crève Coeur in January, 1680. In his absence the men mutinied and plundered the fort, and raiding Iroquois burned the Peoria village. Upon his return to the Illinois Country in 1682, La Salle, with Tonti, built Fort St. Louis at Starved Rock as a key to the vast empire of forts and commerce he had conceived. But his enemies at court prevailed, and he was soon recalled. Returning to France, he received permission from the king to establish a colony at the mouth of the Mississippi; On March 20, 1687, on a branch of the Trinity River, he was shot from ambush.

Tonti, La Salle's lieutenant, obtained in 1690 the privileges previously granted La Salle. In 1691-92 he moved Fort St. Louis from Starved Rock to Pimitoui, on Peoria Lake. For ten years he devoted himself to bringing in settlers, missionaries, and trade supplies. When he died in 1704, a chain of forts stretched from Montreal to Mobile.

The Mission of the Holy Family was established at Cahokia (*see Tour 8*) in 1699 by priests of the Seminary of Foreign Missions. In 1703 the Jesuits moved the Mission of the Immaculate Conception to the Indian village of Kaskaskia, sixty miles below Cahokia, a short distance from the mouth of the Kaskaskia River. These two towns of the American Bottom, Cahokia and Kaskaskia, soon became the centers of French life in the Illinois country. In 1720, after the collapse of the Mississippi Bubble, the commandant of the Illinois country completed Fort de Chartres, 17 miles north of Kaskaskia. The name Illinois was first officially used when the seventh civil and military district of the French province of Louisiana was so designated.

Meanwhile British colonists were advancing on French territory. New York fur traders reached the Great Lakes by way of the Mohawk Valley; Carolina frontiersmen pushed around the southern end of the Appalachians into the lower Mississippi Valley; the English continued their Hudson Bay fur trade. Land speculation grew among the English colonists.

In 1747 the Ohio Land Company was organized, and in 1749 was granted 200,000 acres of land near the forks of the Ohio on condition that the territory be fortified and a hundred families settled on the land within seven years. Thus began the struggle which, at the end of the French and Indian War, found England in possession of all French territory on the North American continent.

The English occupation of the Illinois country did not begin at once. Pontiac, chief of the Ottawa, rose against the British in 1763, and captured all but three of the newly acquired forts in the Lakes Region. He was not defeated until the following year, and it was not until October 10, 1765, that the French flag was lowered and the British raised at Fort de Chartres. Here, on December 6, 1768, was held the first court under English jurisdiction in the Illinois country.

There was widespread sympathy in Illinois for the Colonial cause in the American Revolution. In 1776-77 powder purchased from the French and Spaniards was run up the Mississippi and Ohio Rivers from New Orleans to Wheeling, West Virginia. As the war progressed, the strategic position of the Illinois country as a link with Spanish and French allies, and as a base for attack on the British at Detroit, became apparent.

The task of seizing this country was undertaken by George Rogers Clark in 1778. Authorized by the Governor of Virginia, he floated down the Ohio River with a band of 175 men. From Fort Massac he set out overland for Kaskaskia. On July 4, 1778, Clark entered the village, and was greeted warmly by the inhabitants. Father Gibault, at Clark's request, traveled to Vincennes, won the allegiance of the people there, and persuaded them to sign the Oath of Vincennes. Hearing of Clark's success, the Virginia Assembly decreed on December 9, 1778, that Illinois was to be a county of Virginia. But six days later Vincennes was lost to the British under the command of Governor Hamilton of Detroit.

Seeing the entire territory threatened, Clark set out for Vincennes with 17 men. It was February; the rivers and bottom-lands were flooded; for miles the men waded in water up to their waists. At Vincennes Clark succeeded in detaching the townspeople from the garrison, and on February 25, 1779, Hamilton capitulated. The next year, when the British attacked the Illinois towns, Clark came to the aid of Cahokia and helped beat them off. As the war drew to a close, military operations ceased except for the periodic Indian raids instigated by the British.

FROM TERRITORY TO STATE

To organize the vast territory Clark had secured for the United States, the Ordinance of 1787 was passed. It created the Northwest Territory as a Federal territory to consist of the present states of Illinois, Indiana, Michigan, Ohio, and Wisconsin; slavery was prohibited, except as a punishment for crime; a territorial government with limited suffrage was set up; provision was made that any area with 60,000 persons could organize as a state and apply for admission to the Union.

Trouble with the British and their Indian allies continued. In 1794 Anthony Wayne defeated their combined forces at the Battle of Fallen Timbers in Ohio. By the Treaty of Greenville the Indians ceded tracts of land at strategic places, including the mouth of the Chicago River, a post at Peoria and another at the mouth of the Illinois.

Against this growing threat of the white man rose Tecumseh, and his brother, the Shawnee Prophet. They organized the Indians of the Northwest Territory, ordered white men barred from Indian villages, and forbade the selling of any more land to them. The Battle of Tippecanoe November 7, 1811, though won by whites, deterred Tecumseh little, and the Indians remained active throughout the War of 1812, aiding the British in gaining possession of most of the Northwest Territory. Detroit was captured; the garrison and inhabitants of Fort Dearborn were massacred by the Indians on August 15, 1812. The end of the war brought the Northwest Territory back to the American republic, but trouble with the Indians continued until the Black Hawk War.

Illinois remained part of the Northwest Territory until 1800. In that year, by an Act of Congress approved May 7 but not effective until July 4, 1801, it became part of Indiana Territory. In 1809, by an Act approved February 3, the Territory of Illinois was created, which included within its bounds the present state of Wisconsin. Illinois became a territory of the second class on May 21, 1812; during all of this territorial period Illinois was governed by Ninian Edwards. Finally, on December 3, 1818, shorn of the Wisconsin Teritory, it was admitted as a State of the Union, although its population was only 40,258, far short of the 60,000 stipulated by the Ordinance of 1787.

A State constitution was ratified without being submitted to the people, and Shadrach Bond, elected without opposition, became the first State governor of Illinois. The first capital was Kaskaskia; two years later Vandalia succeeded it. Through the efforts of Nathaniel Pope, territorial delegate from Illinois, the northern boundary of the State, fixed by the Ordinance of 1787 at an east-west line placed at the tip of Lake Michigan, was moved 51 miles north, to a line along the longitude 42° 30', and as a result Illinois obtained a shoreline on the Great Lakes. The reason given was that "additional security for the perpetuation of the union" would be afforded if Illinois were identified with the northern states.

SETTLERS RUSH INTO ILLINOIS

Through the gateway at Shawneetown, down the main highway of the Ohio River, settlers converged upon the young State from many directions—from North Carolina, Tennessee, Virginia, Kentucky, Maryland, Pennsylvania, New York, and the New England states. In flatboats and keelboats loaded with horses, cattle, and furniture, they came. Some, too poor to pay for this kind of transportation, struck out across country and braved the wilderness.

Because of a widespread belief in the superior fertility of woodland, because of the toughness of the prairie sod and the pioneer's constant need for timber, the first settlers built their cabins along the river bottoms and in the groves. But as population increased the desirable sites became scarce, hardy adventurers pushed out into the prairies, and thus discovered the almost limitless richness of the great treeless regions.

Despite hardships, they kept coming, first the advance guard of lone-wolf trappers and hunters, then the poor squatters, followed by farmers with stock and capital, and finally young men of education seeking their fortunes in land and trade. Socialistic and religious colonies organized elsewhere and migrated here: Birkbeck's English colony at Albion (1818), the Quakers on the Fox River (1835), Swiss wine-grape growers along the Ohio, Bishop Chase and his Jubilee College at Robin's Nest (1839), later the Swedish Janssonists at Bishop Hill (1846), and the Mormons (1839) and Icarians (1850) at Nauvoo.

The frontier towns were busy centers of trade but the great curse of the expanding frontier fell on these towns and farms: they lacked capital. The produce of the West poured down the Mississippi—only to accumulate on the wharves at New Orleans. The small sums of money that dribbled through to the West went directly back east to pay debts. The Federal banking system, inadequate in its credit mechanisms, and the State banks, unstable and uncontrolled, made merchants and farmers distrustful of all banking systems. The State banks at Edwardsville and Shawneetown failed in the early twenties. Soon all bank notes were so suspect that barter of tangibles was quite commonly preferred to any kind of paper money. But there was only a small market for produce, and debt-ridden farmers, unable to dispose of their goods and too numerous to be dispossessed, filled the State.

Not far behind the first settlers came the frontier church. A Methodist circuit-rider, the Reverend Joseph Lillard, stopped at New Design in 1793. The first Baptist church was founded there three years later; the denomination was strengthened by the coming of John Mason Peck and his establishment, the Rock Spring Seminary, in 1827. The Methodists, with their circuit-riding preachers, began to arrive in 1801; they taught simplicity in dress and living, and sowed the beginnings of the anti-slavery movement in the State. In 1796 came the Presbyterians with the Reverend John Evans at their head; insisting on a learned clergy, they quickly established their denominational colleges. Despite its early missionary work and the adherence of the French settlers, the Catholic church grew more slowly; not until 1844 was the separate diocese of Chicago established.

The question of public education was debated bitterly. The largest part of the population had been drawn from the South, which had developed no public schools. Those from the North thought education a function of the church. Finally in 1825 a law allowed localities to levy school taxes. It was repealed soon after and it was not until 1845, after a campaign waged by the workers and farmers that a free education law was again passed, and even ten years elapsed before many communities took advantage of it.

The population of the State grew from 55,211 in 1820 to 157,445 in 1830. With this growth came a tremendous shift in the distribution of population. Opened in 1825, the Erie Canal brought swarms of immigrants by way of the Great Lakes, repeating the process of settlement that had been occurring through the Ohio River Valley for half a century. Fort Dearborn, rebuilt in 1816, was the nucleus of a settlement incorporated as the town of Chicago in 1833, and as a city in 1837.

The canal enabled Chicago to surpass Shawneetown on the Ohio as the port of entry into the young State. In 1832 a land boom throughout the northern part of Illinois increased Chicago's population from 150 to 2,000 within the year. Seventy-five buildings were erected in the spring of 1834, and that year immigrants came in such numbers that they had to sleep on floors because of inadequate accommodations. Provisions were scarce; flour sold for $20 a barrel; between 1835 and 1836 the price of lots jumped from $9,000 to $25,000. In 1835, 255 sailing ships arrived at Chicago; in 1836, 40 steamboats and 383 sailing ships docked. By 1837, the year of its incorporation as a city, Chicago had a population of 8,000, with 120 stores, 20 of which were wholesale concerns. Chicago soon became a wheat center; in 1841 it paid $1 a bushel while the Peoria market was paying only 40¢. Lines of 30, 40, even 80 wagons came as far as 250 miles loaded with wheat for the new metropolis; their loads completely overtaxed the capacities of the 150 vessels docked at Chicago in 1841.

THE BLACK HAWK WAR

A tragic chapter in Illinois history was the Black Hawk War of 1832, in which the settlers whipped up animosity against the Indians to push them out of the State. The Sauk and Fox once claimed all the land west of the Fox and the Illinois, and east of the Mississippi Rivers. In 1804, while five of their chiefs were in St. Louis arranging for the release of one of their tribesmen charged with murder, they were plied with drink. In return for an annuity of $1,000 a year, and the right to live and hunt in the area so long as it belonged to the Federal government, they deeded the land away. In 1816, 1822, and 1825, the agreement was renewed. The tribes continued to live at their great villages, the Sauk on the north side of Rock River near the present city of Rock Island, and the Fox three miles away on the Mississippi. Miners heading for the newly discovered lead mines at Galena saw their fertile lands, and by 1825 white settlers began to move in upon them. Realizing the inevitability of a conflict, Keokuk, the peace-time chief of the tribes, decided to move across the Mississippi into what is now Iowa.

But Black Hawk, a war chief less friendly to the settlers, persuaded by British and Indian friends that $1,000 a year was manifestly inadequate payment for this vast region, decided to remain on the land. The majority of the tribe left for Iowa, but friction soon developed between those who remained and the settlers; Black Hawk ordered the whites to stop planting in the cornfields of the tribes Governor Reynolds proclaimed Illinois in a "state of actual invasion" by the Indians and called for volunteers. When the volunteer army approached the Indian village on June 25, 1831, Black Hawk ordered it abandoned, and under cover of night the Indians moved across the Mississippi into Iowa without a struggle.

In the spring of 1832, Black Hawk and 400 braves, together with their women and children, crossed the Mississippi, apparently intending to go to the Winnebago in Wisconsin, and raise a corn crop with them. Their mission was misunderstood, and troops again took the field. Under Major Isaiah Stillman, they came upon the Indians encamped. Black Hawk sent three braves with white flags to explain that no hostilities were intended. In the excitement accompanying the negotiations, shooting began; three Indian tribesmen, including one of the truce-bearers were killed. In the ensuing Battle of Stillman's Run, the white men were ingloriously routed.

Guerrilla warfare began, with the Indians proving elusive in the forests. In July, his forces weakened by hunger, Black Hawk decided to surrender. He wanted to return his people to Iowa, but again his offer of truce went unheeded. Many of the warriors were killed at the Battle of Bad Axe, August 2, 1832, where the white men turned savage and committed indescribable acts of cruelty, even scalping the Indians. As survivors tried to cross the Mississippi on rafts, a gunboat opened fire, killing or drowning most of them. Those who managed to cross to the west side of the river were set upon by the Sioux, the traditional enemies of the Sauk and Fox. These events, together with the peace pow-wow held in Chicago in 1833, in which the Potawatomi and their allies ceded all their land in Illinois and moved west of the Mississippi, removed the last of the Indians from the State.

CANAL AND RAILROAD BOOM

A feverish campaign for internal improvements spread in the 1830s; by the end of the decade the movement had brought the State to the verge of bankruptcy under a staggering debt of $14,000,000. In 1837 a flood of measures had been passed by the legislature, providing for the building of railroads, canals, and turnpikes, and the improvement of rivers and harbors. A canal charter had been granted in 1825; in 1827 Congress had given 224,322 acres to the State. The Illinois and Michigan Canal was begun in 1836. The Wabash, Illinois, Kaskaskia and Rock Rivers were to be deepened and improved. A great Illinois Central Railroad from the western terminus of the canal at La Salle to the mouth of the Ohio River at Cairo was proposed, with two east-west lines, the Southern Cross from Alton to Mount Carmel, and the Northern Cross through Springfield and Quincy.

At the same time the question of removing the State capital from Vandalia arose; Alton, Jacksonville, Peoria, Springfield, and others, wished to succeed it. They also wanted the benefits of the internal improvements. Consequently, in the session of 1837, the Sangamon County delegates, called the "Long Nine," because all its members—including Abraham Lincoln—were exceptionally tall men, arranged a trade. They voted internal improvements for these towns in return for votes for Springfield as the capital.

Over-speculation, aggravated by the nation-wide panic of 1837, impeded the improvements. The State awoke to find that, for the debt it had assumed, it had only 24 miles of railroad—the Jacksonville and

Meredosia section of the Northern Cross, later extended to Springfield—and only a small section of the Illinois and Michigan Canal. Not until 1848 was the Canal completed to become an avenue for Michigan lumber to the treeless prairies and opened an artery into Chicago which diverted to the north much of the trade that had formerly gone to St. Louis.

The State-owned Northern Cross, the first railroad pulled by a steam locomotive west of the Allegheny Mountains and north of the Ohio River, made its initial run late in 1838, using thin strips of iron mounted on wood for its rails. As the engine required great quantities of water, passengers were often recruited for carrying water from the nearest source; they were also expected to help the crew load wood. Traveling was not only slow but dangerous. The inadequate rails became unspiked at the ends and curled up into "snake heads," which pierced the floor boards of the cars. Another cause of serious accidents was the theft of rails; iron was scarce in the prairie country, and farmers quickly conceived many uses for them, chiefly as sled runners. Occasionally engines in need of repairs had to be hauled home by teams of horses. The expense of operating the Northern Cross proved so great that the State finally leased the property to private concerns. Subsequently two locomotives were sold to a man who conceived the idea of running them as trackless steam wagons across the open prairies, a scheme that failed.

Generally, throughout the 1840's, the stagecoach ruled the Illinois roads. A short-lived craze for planked roads reached the State from Russia through Canada. Although these roads were sturdily and evenly built the expense of construction and maintenance proved so high that few brought profit to the companies that laid them. By 1850 the plank roads were being dismantled, and the railroad boom once more gripped Illinois.

In the 1840s Hancock County became the scene of violent clashes between the conservative Illinois farmers and the Mormons who had settled in Nauvoo. Joseph Smith, prophet of the Mormon Church of Jesus Christ of Latter-day Saints, and his followers had been forced out of Missouri and platted a town on the Mississippi in Hancock County. Here Smith's religious pronouncements and the Mormon's overbearing trade practices brought clashes with the conservative farmers and led to calling out the militia and the murder of Smith and his brother while they were in protective custody in the Carthage jail. *See article on Nauvoo.* In the subsequent tension the Mormons agreed to leave Illinois and beginning Feb. 11, 1846, Brigham Young led the first contingent westward to Utah.

ILLINOIS IN MEXICAN WAR

In the spring of 1846 the fight over the annexation of Texas brought on a declaration of war against Mexico by President James K. Polk, who called for three regiments of volunteers from Illinois. The Illinois legislature had voted for annexation and Polk's call was answered with enthusiasm. A fourth regiment was formed under command of Edward D. Baker, Representative in Congress, who had agreed not to run for reelection so that his fellow-Whig, Abraham Lincoln, might try for the seat. Another Whig leader, John J. Hardin, who also had stepped aside reluctantly in Lincoln's behalf, enlisted and was killed at the front. These Illinois troops fought at Buena Vista and Cerro Gordo —one Illinois village was named for the latter—but as enlistment was for only one year they were replaced before the fall of Mexico City.

Lincoln was elected to Congress in the fall, 1846, and by the time the 30th Congress met in December, 1847, the fighting was over and the Whigs were pinning responsibility for an unjust war on Polk. With other Whig members Lincoln voted against an endorsement of the war as "just and necessary" presented by another Illinois Representative. Lincoln went home to find himself criticized as a Benedict Arnold. By agreement he did not run for reelection, but he campaigned for General Taylor, the Whig nominee, and as the slavery issue heated up he voted "forty times" for the Wilmot Proviso prohibiting slavery in new territory, and for abolition of the slave trade in the District of Columbia.

A new constitution was adopted in 1848. The population of the State increased from 157,445 in 1830 to 851,470 in 1850. The new constitution provided for popular election of all State officials and popular referendum on questions of policy. As a compromise the township system of the North and the county system of the South were both legalized.

A HOUSE DIVIDED, 1848-1870

Illinois now entered the transition stage during which Chicago developed from a mud-rutted town of 29,963 in 1850 to a city of 296,977 in 1870. The State had 10 incorporated cities in 1850: Chicago, Alton, Springfield, Beardstown, Pekin, Quincy, Peoria, Bloomington, Galena, and Rock Island. Their difficulties were many: houses were scarce, rents high, the streets so bad they became quagmires in rainy weather. One of the issues of the day was the hog nuisance; the streets, squares, and parks were public hog-pens. Nor were there public utilities until the middle fifties, when the more progressive communities began to install water systems and gas for street lighting.

Twenty years after the rush to the lead mines at Galena in the late 1820s, at which time a group of tent-cities containing more than 10,000 people had sprung up, the gold rush to California swept through Illinois. In 1849 more than 15,000 men and boys left the State for the western fields. The exodus subsided in 1850 as a result of discouraging letters and editorial warnings, but in 1852, with new stories of gold discoveries, the rush was revived. With the opening of the fertile lands of Kansas and Nebraska to settlement in 1854, still another migration took place. In the gold rush to Pike's Peak in 1859, additional thousands left the State. The whole of the fifties was characterized by this draining of Illinoisans to the West.

In ever greater numbers immigrants arrived from Europe. French Icarians under Cabet set up a communistic colony at Nauvoo in 1849. Portuguese came to Springfield and Jacksonville; Scandinavians to Chicago, Rockford, Galesburg, Victoria, Andover, and Moline. The Bishop

Hill colony was settled by Swedish Janssonists in 1846. But by far the most numerous were the Germans, fleeing their country after the defeat of their Revolution in 1848, and the Irish, driven out by potato famines and British oppression. By 1860 there were 130,804 Germans in Illinois, living chiefly in Chicago, Belleville, Galena, Quincy, Alton, Peoria, and Peru, perpetuating their rich culture in music societies, literary clubs, and *Turnvereine*.

The railroad fever of the 1850s greatly affected the people of Illinois. Farms were mortgaged, counties and municipalities subscribed to stock, Eastern capitalists poured millions into the enterprises. Many of the politicians in the State, from Governor French and Senator Douglas to township officials, speculated in land and railroad stock, and became wealthy. Senator Douglas persuaded Congress to grant 2,707,200 acres of land, scattered over 47 counties, for the long-awaited Illinois Central Railroad, and in 1851 articles of incorporation were granted by the legislature to a group of Eastern financiers, headed by Robert Rantoul of Massachusetts, on condition that the State be paid 7 percent of the gross receipts annually. In September, 1856, the railroad was completed. The Galena & Chicago Union was able to pay dividends of 20 percent after its first year.

In 1858 George M. Pullman, a cabinet-maker, began to convert old railroad passenger cars to the uses of long-distance travel for the Chicago & Alton line. When his sleeping-cars proved successful, he founded the Pullman Palace Car Company in 1867, and in 1880 built the town of Pullman for his employees; it has since become part of Chicago. The refrigeration of beef in railroad cars was perfected in Chicago in 1857; nine years later fruits were likewise transported. The first steel rails made in this country were rolled in May 1865, at the Chicago Rolling Mills. In 1873 the Joliet Iron & Steel Company began to produce Bessemer steel. In 1874, 1,398 miles of steel rails were laid in the State.

LINCOLN AND DOUGLAS AS LEADERS

In the struggle that split the Union and led to the Civil War, Illinois furnished the two opposing national leaders. Stephen A. Douglas and Abraham Lincoln. The State itself was soon as divided as the nation. As early as 1796 and again in 1802, memorials from the Illinois country had been addressed to Congress asking for repeal of the prohibition against slavery in the Ordinance of 1787. In 1824 a movement to amend the State constitution to allow the introduction of slavery was defeated. The kidnapping of free Negro residents in the State was countenanced for two generations, and the "black laws" of 1819 were still in effect. In 1837 the State legislature, excited by the spread of Garrison's abolitionism, passed a resolution excluding abolition papers from the State and making the circulation of abolition petitions to Congress illegal. In the same year, November 8, the valiant abolitionist newspaper editor of the Alton *Observer,* Elijah P. Lovejoy, while defending his fourth press from destruction by Alton mobs, was shot dead. Lovejoy's fight was continued by such men as Benjamin Lundy and his *Genius of Universal Emancipation* at Hennepin. Anti-slavery societies grew. In 1840 the Liberty Party was formed in Illinois, and by 1846 it had gained a majority of 13 northern counties.

Yet in 1853 an act drawn by John A. Logan providing that free Negroes who entered the State could be sold into servitude was passed by the legislature. This bill aroused the anger of Democrats and Whigs alike. Even so, the Democrats might have maintained their power in the State if Douglas had not in 1854 sponsored the Kansas-Nebraska bill enabling settlers in the new territories to choose between free soil and slavery, with an amendment thereto repealing the Missouri Compromise of 1820, which had prohibited slavery forever in the Louisiana Purchase above the line of 36° 30'. From the opposition to this bill, in the form of a coalition of disapproving Democrats, Whigs, and Free Soilers, came the germ of the Republican Party in Illinois. After a mass meeting in Rockford on March 18, 1854, and another at Ottawa on August 1, a State Republican convention was held in Springfield on October 4 and 5. In the elections of 1854 the State was almost equally divided; the northern or Yankee half voted solidly anti-Nebraska, while the southern or downstate half voted with the solid South. Looking now toward the national elections, the Republican Party of Illinois was organized at a convention in Bloomington, May 29, 1856, with some leaders in the Democratic Party of the State taking active parts. The first Republican governor, William H. Bissell, was elected that year.

The Dred Scott decision hastened the coming of the Civil War. When the United States Supreme Court in 1857, held that the Missouri Compromise was unconstitutional, and that Congress had no power to pass a law forbidding a master from carrying slaves into the territories, it posed a serious question. Could slavery be excluded from the territories by any means? Douglas contended that it could, because the people could withhold the protective local legislation essential to its existence. Yet even this doctrine had its faults, for soon he found himself at odds with President Buchanan and the slavery Democrats over popular sovereignty as manifested in the case of Kansas, then seeking admission to the Union. At the same time Douglas was losing ground. The sensational contest in 1858 between Lincoln and Douglas was fought on the issue of free soil or popular sovereignty.

On the evening of his nomination for the senatorship by the Republican convention, at Springfield, Lincoln declared: "A house divided against itself cannot stand. I believe this government cannot endure permanently, half slave and half free." Forecasting another decision like that in the Dred Scott case, but applying to the States as well as territories, he said, "Such a decision is all that slavery now lacks of being alike lawful in all the states." The famous Lincoln-Douglas debates at Ottawa, Freeport, Jonesboro, Charlestown, Galesburg, Quincy, and Alton carried on the controversy. In the last debate, at Alton, on October 15, 1858, Lincoln summed up his position in memorable words: "That is the issue . . . It is the eternal struggle

between two principles—right and wrong—throughout the world . . . .
The one is the common right of humanity, the other is the divine right
of kings. It is the same principle in whatever shape it develops itself.
It is the same spirit that says, 'You toil and work and earn bread, and
I'll eat it.' " Douglas won the election in 1858; Lincoln won the presi-
dency two years later.

With Lincoln in the White House and war declared, southern Illinois was spotted with sympathy for the Confederacy. At meetings
such as that held at Marion in Williamson County, there was wild
talk of setting up "Egypt" as a separate State aligned with the South.
Douglas rushed back to Illinois from Washington to bring his followers to the support of the Government. But his strength sapped by
years of political battles, he died on June 3, 1861. Discontent with
Lincoln was soon manifest, and in the fall of 1861 at the elections to the
constitutional convention, the Democrats outnumbered the Republicans
more than two to one. The Emancipation Proclamation and the arbi-
trary arrests for disloyal utterances during the war were responsible
for the existence of a strong party of protest.

The Democratic Party nominated George B. McClellan, major
general USA., for President Aug. 31, 1964, in a "wigwam" on the Chicago lake front. The convention was packed with bitter opponents of
Lincoln; anti-war protesters, and advocates of an immediate cessation of
fighting and a calling of a convention of the states to repair the Federal
Union. The hero of the convention was Clement L. Vallandigham,
former Representative from Ohio, who had been exiled to the Confederate lines by Major General Burnside for incendiary speeches against
the war, and who had returned via Canada. Governor Horatio Seymour
of New York presided at the convention. It contended the war was a
failure. Three days later Lincoln announced the taking of Atlanta by
General Sherman. In the November election Lincoln polled 2,216,067
votes and 212 electoral votes; McClellan 1,808,725 and 21.

In four years Illinois contributed more than 250,000 men to the
Union forces. In 1864 Lincoln received a 30,736 majority vote in
Illinois, and at his untimely death his most savage critics in the State
paused to pay homage to him; the Chicago *Times,* suppressed once for
disloyalty during the Civil War, declared that the public had come to
"realize something of the magnitude of the concerns involved in his
lease of existence."

The war over, Illinois began to take stock: it had contributed
heavily in money and men; 5,857 had been killed in action; 3,051 had
died of wounds, and 19,934 of disease. Now, with its railroads and
fertile farm lands, its factories and mines, its people from all over the
world, the State settled down to the problem of construction.

In 1870 a State convention, almost equally divided between the
Democratic downstate and the Republican north, formed a constitution
that was ratified. It granted the franchise to Negroes, but not to women;
one delegate remarked during the debate that the adherents of women
suffrage were "long haired men and short-haired women." It also pro-

vided that the Illinois and Michigan canal was never to be leased or sold without referendum, established a system of cumulative voting for State representatives, created enlarged courts in Cook County and necessary legal powers to govern metropolitan Chicago, and increased the responsibility of the State for the support of educational institutions.

The new industrialism brought disorder. Newspapers cried out against lawlessness. It was said that in Cairo one man a week was killed, while Chicago was a haven for gamblers, confidence men, and murderers. Springfield, declared the *Illinois State Register,* was infested with "an unwholesome debris of bullies, strumpets, vagrants, and sneak-thieves." But by far the greatest calamity of the decade was the Chicago Fire of October 8-9, 1871, as a result of which 250 people lost their lives, thousands were left homeless and destitute, and the financial loss was estimated at $200,000,000.

Discontent was growing among the farmers. They objected strenuously to excessive charges by middlemen, exorbitant freight rates, and the high price of manufactured goods. Illinois was still a farm State, with six-sevenths of its terrain under cultivation as late as 1880. The invention and manufacture of farm implements had made considerable progress but the average farmer was still struggling with mortgages.

The farmers organized the Order of Patrons of Husbandry, founded in 1868, the forerunner of the Grange movement in Illinois. The original purpose—buying machinery for members at a discount—broadened in the early seventies when hundreds of new grants organized, with a peak of 761 in 1873 and 704 in 1874.

With the Grange movement came political pressure that forced the passage in 1871 of railroad acts that stipulated that charges for long hauls were never to be less than for short hauls, that storage fees were to be uniform, and that no road was to charge a greater mileage rate on one section of its line than on any other. The second State railroad commission in the country was created, but the railroads refused to recognize the rates set. When the railroad act was held unconstitutional by the State Supreme Court in 1873, the farmers forced the passage of another act.

CHICAGO BECOMES MEAT PACKING CENTER

During this period of general expansion great impetus was given to coal mining, farm implement manufacture and meat packing. Three names are associated with the packing industry: Philip D. Armour, Nelson Morris, and Gustavus F. Swift. Before he came to Chicago, Armour had been first a partner in Jacob Plankington's packing house in Milwaukee, one of the largest in the country, and later became head of his own concern. When tremendous shipments of cattle and hogs began to pour into Chicago in 1865, the legislature incorporated the Union Stock Yards on 345 swampy acres south of the city limits. Foreseeing the rich future of the Middle West as a packing center, Armour, with his brothers, moved the headquarters of Armour & Company to Chicago from Milwaukee in 1875. Before Armour's rise, a young Bavarian named Nelson Morris had procured contracts for provisioning

Union troops during the Civil War, and had amassed a fortune. In 1875 Gustavus F. Swift, a Cape Cod Yankee, who had owned a large dressed-beef business in New England, opened a big slaughterhouse in Chicago. Swift subsequently revolutionized meatpacking by the use of railroad refrigeration, for shipping fresh meat to the East.

The Knights of Labor met in Chicago in June, 1884, and called for an eight-hour day, incorporation of labor unions, prohibition of work by children under 14, an employers' liability act, and a mechanic's lien law. Sympathy with the labor program became so great that in the next two years politicians became "friends of labor," as in the preceding decade of agrarian revolt they had been "friends of the farmer."

The fight for the eight-hour day continued unabated; the Knights of Labor formed a hundred new lodges throughout the State each week early in 1886. Even the press began to favor the eight-hour day, saying it was theoretically sound, so long as labor asked only for eight hours' pay, but warned against allowing the movement to "degenerate to a demand for the 8-hour day with 10-hour pay." The fight would probably have been won but for the Haymarket bomb of May 4, 1886. The strike collapsed in June.

Farmers joined with the Illinois State Labor Association at Decatur in April 1888 to form the Illinois Labor Party, which disintegrated rapidly through lack of harmony. The Democratic nominee for governor, John M. Palmer, took a stand for labor, denouncing the Pinkerton corps of private detectives who, he said, had been hired by the industrialists to break the strikes of the preceding year. He was repudiated by the conservative voters and members of his own party.

But the road was paved for the farmer-labor-Democratic coalition, which in 1892 elected Judge John P. Altgeld to the governorship. Altgeld personified the whole spirit of the revolt of the farmers and workers in the steel plants and other industries. His administration was conspicuous for its consideration for the workers and was strongly attacked by the industrial leaders who had been fighting the eight-hour day. Altgeld appointed Florence Kelley, who had been associated with Jane Addams at Hull House, factory inspector; he inaugurated the indeterminate sentence and the parole system, built hospitals for the insane at Bartonville and Peoria, improved the State school system, gave liberal grants to the University of Illinois, pardoned the three anarchists who had survived the Haymarket trial in a message that condemned the proceedings as unfair and illegal, and objected to the sending of Federal troops into the State by President Cleveland during the 1894 Pullman strike. Of all his acts the pardoning of the socalled anarchists was most strongly condemned, even though some leading men had expressed the view that the men had been tried unfairly.

John P. Altgeld's campaign for a second term as governor failed in 1896, partly because his radical labor policies had alienated business and industry, and partly because he was running on the Democratic ticket with William Jennings Bryan, whose attacks on the monetary system had alarmed all adherents of the gold standard and split his party. Bryan,

Illinois-born lawyer who had represented Nebraska in Congress, led a strong section of Democrats who wanted money made easier under a silver instead of a gold standard; his speech before the Committee on Resolutions at the Chicago convention of 1896 had the "cross of gold" peroration that made him the logical nominee for the Presidency. In the subsequent election William B. McKinley was elected with 271 electoral votes, while Bryan received 176. The victory of John R. Tanner as governor brought the Republicans back in the State House and in three succeeding terms Richard Yates and Charles S. Deneen continued the party in power.

Unable to win with Populism, some workingmen turned to more radical politics. In 1901 the Socialist Party of the United States was organized in Chicago by Eugene Victor Debs, Seymour Stedman, and other radicals. The party grew; by 1915 there were 44 Socialists holding political offices in the State including one mayor, 18 aldermen, and two State legislators. In 1916 William Cunnea, law partner of Clarence Darrow, ran on the Socialist ticket and was almost elected State's Attorney, losing on a recount. Another radical organization was the Industrial Workers of the World; organized in 1905, with Chicago as its center; its slogan of One Big Union spread throughout the West. Chicago, too, was to see the demise of the I. W. W. when 100 leading members were tried before Federal Judge Kenesaw M. Landis on charges arising out of their opposition to World War I.

In Chicago in 1919 the Communist Party was organized by the left wing of the Socialist Party, which split on the question of support of the Russian Revolution.

A strong element for political reform developed during the administration of President Theodore Roosevelt (1901-1908), who had a large following in the Republican Party in Illinois. Corrupt practices connected with the election of senators by the State Legislature brought powerful demands for their direct election, by popular vote, which was finally effected by an amendment to the U. S. Constitution in 1913. Illinois voted Republican in 1908 when William H. Taft was elected President. In 1912 Roosevelt led a campaign against the renomination of Taft and won a large majority of Illinois delegates in the presidential primaries. At the Republican National Convention in the Wabash Ave. Coliseum the Republican Old Guard threw out enough of the Roosevelt delegates to renominate Taft. Roosevelt, who had directed strategy from his headquarters in the Congress Hotel, announced a bolt from the Republican Party. In September the Progressive National Party met formally at the Coliseum and nominated Roosevelt for the Presidency. This split the Republican vote and elected Woodrow Wilson President and Edward F. Dunne, Democrat, Governor of Illinois.

In the first twenty years of the new century Illinois was one of the most progressive states in the Union in the field of social legislation. After the passage of the first mining law in 1872, it continued to provide for the safe operation of mines by enacting supplementary legislation in 1899, 1910, and 1913. Child labor legislation was adopted in 1891; a law fixing the maximum hours of labor for women was passed

History

THE OLD STATE CAPITOL AT SPRINGFIELD, AS REBUILT

RESTORED HOUSE OF GENERAL ASSEMBLY, OLD STATE CAPITOL,
WITH DESK USED BY LINCOLN

ONE HUNDRED YEARS AFTER
LINCOLN-DOUGLAS DEBATE AT
KNOX COLLEGE. TABLET COM-
MEMORATING EVENT OF
OCTOBER 7, 1858

LINCOLN-DOUGLAS MEMORIAL IN QUINCY PARK
COMMEMORATING DEBATE OF OCTOBER 13, 1858.

LINCOLN'S SPRINGFIELD
HOME WHEN ELECTED
PRESIDENT.

LINCOLN MONUMENT AND
TOMB IN OAK RIDGE
CEMETERY, SPRINGFIELD

MANSION HOUSE OF JOSEPH SMITH, MORMON PROPHET, NAUVOO

HOTEL NAUVOO, HISTORIC LANDMARK IN NAUVOO

GREEK REVIVAL MANSION OF THE HISTORICAL SOCIETY OF
QUINCY AND ADAMS COUNTY. BUILT 1835 BY JOHN WOOD,
LATER ILLINOIS GOVERNOR

RENDLEMAN HOUSE, NOW MUSEUM OF THE MISSISSIPPI, CAIRO

OLD IRON FURNACE, SHAWNEE NATIONAL FOREST,
NEAR HARRISBURG

LINCOLN TRAIL STATE PARK IN CLARK COUNTY

MOUNTAIN SHEEP AT THE BROOKFIELD ZOO

A BUSY DAY AT THE BROOKFIELD ZOO

GARDENS OF THE BROOKFIELD ZOO

PINE CREEK, WHITE PINES
FOREST STATE PARK,
IN OGLE COUNTY

as early as 1893; the first workmen's compensation acts of 1911 were improved in 1913 and 1917. Many other measures were adopted; governmental reforms were undertaken, among which were the establishment of civil service, and the act of 1910 providing direct primaries in the State elections. After the 1907 local option law was adopted, dry areas spread throughout the State, until Illinois became at least technically "dry" by the Volstead Act.

Illinois played its part in World War I. By June 1917, less than three months after the declaration of war, 351,153 Illinois men were in uniform. Illinois was one of the three states to furnish an entire National Guard Division. Officially designated the 33rd, it was popularly called the Prairie Division, and saw action at St. Mihiel, Verdun, Chateau Thierry, and Meuse-Argonne. At the conclusion of the war the 33rd came home to be welcomed, but missing were more than 5,000 men from the farms, offices, and factories of the State.

After the war Illinois, along with the rest of the nation, enjoyed an extraordinary period of construction and speculation. Politics, prohibition, crime, and the high cost of living filled the headlines of the newspapers. Governor Len Small launched an extensive program of building hard roads throughout the State. His political ally was the colorful William Hale Thompson, serving his second term as mayor of Chicago, who called himself Big Bill the Builder. In the wide-open town gangsters ran the illegal beer and liquor trade. There followed the reform administration of Mayor Dever in 1923 but in the next election in 1927 Thompson was returned for a third time. In 1931 Anton Cermak was elected mayor of Chicago. Then came the Democratic landslide of 1932, which turned the Republicans out of office. Henry Horner, judge of the probate court of Cook County for five years, was elected Governor. Mayor Cermak was fatally wounded on February 15, 1933, when an assassin made an attempt on the life of President Franklin Roosevelt in Florida. Democratic policies again triumphed in 1934 when 22 additional Democrats were elected to the State House of Representatives.

With the rest of the nation, Illinois participated in the slow, incomplete economic recovery that marked the 1930s. In 1936, Governor Horner was re-elected, and the State supported a second term for President Roosevelt. An oil boom in southern Illinois, numerous strikes, and a generally slack condition in industry marked the latter part of the decade. The 1938 elections gave Republicans control of the State House of Representatives. Edward J. Kelly, who had succeeded Cermak as mayor of Chicago, was re-elected in 1935 and 1939. His closely knit Democratic organization was largely responsible for carrying the State for Roosevelt.

ILLINOIS ENTERS WORLD WAR II

By a small margin Illinois went for Roosevelt in 1940, but downstate Republican votes were sufficiently numerous to give that party complete control of the State, with Dwight H. Green as Governor. The demands created by the European War and the growing likelihood of American participation stimulated State industrial and agricultural activity. The Illinois National Guard was called into Federal service, her men answered the induction calls, and on December 7, 1941, when the Japanese blow was struck at Pearl Harbor, Illinois entered the struggle.

On October 16, 1940, the first registration day of the draft, 1,008,316 male residents of the United States were registered in Illinois. Of this number, 544,294 lived and registered in Cook County (Chicago and suburbs), and 464,022 in the other counties of the state. By April 1946 the state's total registration reached 2,967,677, of which number some 2,000,000 men were between the ages of 18 and 35 inclusive. The net contribution was the actual war service of 900,000 Illinois men and 19,000 Illinois women in the armed forces of their country. This constituted 11.5% of the state's population, while on the national scale 9.2% of America's entire population served in the armed forces.

At the height of the war effort, on January 1, 1945, Illinois had 845,700 men and 17,200 women inducted, enlisted, or commissioned in the armed forces. In June 1945, one month after V-E Day, with a partial demobilization already under way, Illinois was represented in the service by 750,000 men and women, or about 6% of the U. S. armed forces.

The War Department's records show that between November 1, 1940, and June 30, 1945, a total of 603,000 Illinois men and 13,462 Illinois women served in the Army. For approximately the same period the U. S. Navy had a total of 235,252 Illinois men and women in its service; the Marine Corps, 37,524, and the Coast Guard 10,178.

Among its men and women in the Navy, Illinois suffered 8,879 casualties, including killed, wounded, and missing. Of those in the Army, 18,601 were casualties, including 10,921 killed in action.

Throughout the war Illinois workers produced war supplies valued at about 8% of the national total. The number of employed civilian workers in the state rose from 2,870,000 in March, 1940, to 3,260,000 in March, 1944. This increase occurred despite the withdrawal of some 700,000 to duties with the armed forces.

From 1942 through the end of war in August, 1945, Illinois manufactured goods for war use valued at an estimated $27 billion. From 1941 to August, 1945, the value of all products made in Illinois was $53 billion, or more than 8% of the nation's total. Of all the communication equipment produced in the United States 20% came from Illinois, while other principal war manufacturers were ordnance, aircraft engines, and ships (including ocean-going vessels of small, special types built at Seneca on the Illinois River). By 1946, the Chicago-Calumet industrial area had an annual production capacity of 18,594,000 net tons of steel, or some 500,000 tons more than Pittsburgh.

War bond sales in Illinois represented 6.5% of the nation's total: from May 1, 1941 to December 31, 1945, the purchases of war bonds by private (non-bank) investors amounted to $11,966,000,000, out of the national total of $174 billion.

For an account of the civil rights demonstrations and effects of the school desegregation orders of the United States Supreme Court, 1954-1970, see *Education* and *Chicago*.

Agriculture, Coal and Oil

A GRICULTURE remains one of the primary activities by which the people of Illinois make a living, helping to fill the nation's breadbasket and providing a huge amount of food for people overseas. This has been the situation since settlers first turned the rich black soil that had been maturing since the Glacial Period. Concomitant with using the soil for growing crops and pasturage, agriculture stimulated the great era of invention of labor-saving machinery, and made Illinois the producing center of mechanical farm apparatus, leading to the mechanization of farms and export of farm machinery to all parts of the globe.

Illinois holds first place among the states as a producer of soy beans, its crop amounting to one-fifth of the nation's annual output. It led all others in value of the 1967 corn crop, when its 1,091,500,000 bu. of corn topped the $1 billion mark for the first time. It held second place in corn production in 1970, its 20,229,000 planted acres making a close competitor to Iowa's 20,790,000, and surpassing the great grain states of Kansas, Missouri, Minnesota, Indiana, Nebraska and Texas.

Almost half of the cultivated area in Illinois is planted to corn. Since the end of World War II nearly all planting has been of hybrid corn, with smaller stalks but higher yield. The upward trend in yield persists as a result of improved breeding, increased use of plant food, and application by farmers of methods recommended by State and college research agencies.

Reports prepared by the Assessors' Annual Farm Census of the State Department of Agriculture show that farms with livestock and poultry decreased sharply in the 1960-70 decade, continuing a trend that began after World War II. In 1970 the farm census numbered 124,900 units, 3 percent fewer than the 128,700 of 1969. The average size of farms was 235 acres, compared with 229 acres in 1969. Ten years earlier, in 1960, there were 159,900 farms averaging 190 acres per farm. Over 1,100,000 acres have been lost to farming in the last decade. Losses by urbanization, highway building, lakes and other non-farm uses have been partly offset by reclamation of strip mines and drainage of river bottoms.

Farm employment keeps going down, too, but here mechanization has been a factor. In 1950 the annual average of farm employment was 280,200; in 1960, 200,300; in 1965, 163,500; in 1970, 131,400.

In recent decades there has been a slight drop in the number of cattle, hogs, pigs, sheep and lambs on Illinois farms, but the inventory value shows a steady increase. On January 1, 1970, for instance, the inventory value of livestock and poultry totaled $879,000,000, up 13

41

percent over the year before. Inventory of hogs increased 18 percent and sheep 7 percent. Total value of all chickens, excluding broilers, increased 20 percent.

Illinois is second only to Iowa in hogs weaned, seventh in beef cattle fed and in the top twenty in dairy and egg production. On January 1, 1971, there were 649,000 cattle on feed, and 11,881,000 pigs, giving the State second place.

Comparative figures show that the average value per head of all cattle was $180 on January 1, 1970; $159 in 1969, and $150 in 1968. Hogs and pigs were worth $40.60 per head in 1969, $31 in 1968, and $28.40 two years earlier. Sheep moved up from $18 a head to $20. This is reflected in the steady rise in retail meat prices.

The consumption of beef continues to increase in spite of the surge in prices. In 1972 the per capita consumption of beef in the United States was placed at 115.5 lbs. by agricultural authorities. Domestic beef supplies increased only 3%. The cost of production, especially of corn, has caused farmers who formerly raised beef cattle to turn to corn and soybeans. Grain farmers, who raised cattle as a side line, feeding them surplus corn, found it more profitable to sell all their corn on the open market. The demand for beef by foreign countries has further affected the domestic supply and if more American shippers take advantage of the higher prices offered by European countries beef will be in short supply at American dinner tables. To satisfy those who will take no substitute for top sirloin steaks, the meat industry has adopted new methods of enlarging the supply. Feed lots operated by corporations on a massive scale have had an important part in increasing production. Feed lots handling 8,000 head are the most profitable and are located chiefly in the Plains and western states; in Illinois the feed lot operation is smaller and the State's share in total U. S. production is smaller.

Milk-cow farms fell from about 46,000 in 1960 to 12,000 in 1970, and the numbers dropped 47 percent to 245,000 head. Poultry farms dropped from about 51,000 to 8,000 and numbers went down 54 percent. Cash receipts realized by farmers from the sale of livestock and livestock products realized $1.3 billion in 1969, 50 percent of the total, up from $1.2 billion.

Crop reports for the 1960-70 decade show an exceptional yield in all categories in 1967, and it may be some time before this record is duplicated. Valuation moves higher, due primarily to the inflated market. Five crops generally account for 98 percent of total value in a typical year: Corn, 60 percent; soybeans, 28.7; all hay, 4.4; wheat 3.2, and oats 1.4.

Corn production ran as high as 100 bu. per acre in 1967, when 10,788,000 acres were harvested. In succeeding years there were fewer acres and output ran from 89 to 98 bu. per acre. Soybean production was an exception, gaining annually; 6,600,000 acres was a record high for plantings, with a yield of 33.5 bu. per acre in 1969. But the floods of the early 1970s forecast more limited production until the land returns to normal. Winter wheat yields from 37 to 39 bu. per acre;

here, too, 1967 was its big year of the 1960-70 decade, with total production of 72,000,000 bu., whereas the 1969 yield was down to 48,100,000 bu. Oats show little change, with yields around 60 bu. per acre.

Illinois is a selective apple and peach state, valuing its apple crop at more than $6,000,000 and its peach crop at around $1,700,000 in a good year.

A large amount of Illinois farm land is sown in hay and pasture crops. In 1970, 3,378,000 tons of all kinds of hay were produced on 1,260,000 acres. In the production of hay, Illinois ranks 15th in the nation. Alfalfa and clover-timothy hay make up 97 percent of the hay crop. For many years the nation's leading producer of red clover seed, Illinois was first among the States in 1970 with 6,480,000 lbs., less than half of the 1965 total.

Morris Birkbeck, who came to Illinois in the second decade of the 19th century and organized the first agricultural society, was the first of many who publicized the richness of Illinois land and the ease of acquiring it. Land was available at as little at $1.25 an acre, to be paid for out of the earnings of the farm. The liberality of land policy was evident in the treatment of canals and railroads. The first settlers depended on rivers to transport their surplus. Peoria early assumed importance as a shipping point for grain and cured meats, and other towns along the Illinois, the Mississippi, and the smaller rivers of the State contributed their flatboat loads of wheat, hams, whiskey, salted beef, beans, and tobacco. As settlements pushed back from the rivers, these channels became inadequate. The Illinois & Michigan Canal was supported with gifts of public lands. Hard on the heels of the canal diggers came the railroad builders, to the immense stimulation of farming. The canal and the railroads aided expansion, for in order to sell land given them by the State and to create business for themselves as carriers they resorted to extensive programs to attract settlers. The railroad building of Illinois had been pretty well completed—so far as tapping farm products was concerned—within the decade following the Civil War. In the early 20th century came the movement for good roads. Today, with more than 95,000 miles of good roads connecting all farming areas with their markets, trucks are the principal means of transportation.

The instrument that more than any others helped the farmer to break the hard soil of Illinois was the steel plow. In 1837 John Deere perfected a steel plow at Grand Detour and next year built eight more. In 1847 Cyrus Hall McCormick came to Chicago and by 1856 was building mechanical reapers at a rate of 15 a day. After World War I the tractor enabled the farmer to enlarge the cultivation of acreage, and after that the corn-picker, the combine, and other devices made farming a completely mechanized operation.

The General Office of the Illinois Department of Agriculture is located in the Junior Livestock Building on the Illinois State Fairgrounds in Springfield. It coordinates the activities of 10 divisions: county fairs, markets, meats, poultry and livestock inspection, plant industry, soil and water conservation and warehouses, feeds, fertilizers and standards, agricultural statistics, apiary and grain inspection.

Among the many activities intended to support and improve farming in Illinois are the county fairs that come under the authority of a Division of the State Department of Agriculture. The Department reports that although vast changes in entertainment have come about in the last few decades state and county fairs remain a favorite form of recreation for more than 100,000,000 Americans, or nearly half the population of the United States. "In the 1969-70 fiscal period," says the Division, "attendance at Illinois county fairs topped State attendance figures for professional football, baseball, and major league hockey."

County fairs are financially supported by the General Assembly, which appropriates money from the Fair and Exposition Fund, which is derived from a tax on parimutuel betting at metropolitan race tracks. In one year, 1969, 100 agricultural and industrial fairs were held in Illinois. Of these fairs, 24 participated in the Agricultural Premium Fund and six filed under the Fair and Exposition Fund. A total of 92 fairs took part in the fairgrounds rehabilitation program and were reimbursed with $395,898. They spent $740,322 for fairground improvements. An enrollment of 79,727 4-H club members were reimbursed $395,206 for premium payments and had total state aid of $383,615. In 1970 fairs had an attendance of 3,762,869, had receipts of $4,556,886 other than rehabilitation and State aid, and paid $2,545,624 in premiums.

Control of pesticides and herbicides was strongly augmented when it became unlawful on January 1, 1970, to sell or use DDT for outdoor pest control. Chemical producers, distributors, and retail outlets were notified, and inspectors were sent to retail outlets to see that supplies were removed and destroyed. The Weed and Herbicide Section of the Division of Plant Industry oversees the use of pest controls. Anyone applying pesticides professionally must have a license from the Department of Agriculture. The University of Illinois cooperates by conducting periods of training for persons engaged in the commercial application of pesticides.

In August, 1969, marihuana was declared a noxious weed. Ragweeds are considered noxious within cities and villages; Canada thistle is noxious in northern and eastern Illinois. Johnsongrass is the most serious noxious weed in southern Illinois and has been moving north, causing severe losses to farmers. Numerous group meetings are held regularly in rural areas to plan weed eradication and especially the control of marihuana.

Besides the grain that Illinois ships to foreign parts there is regular export of plant material and seeds. The Department of Agriculture reports that the greatest segment of foreign export material consists of grains and other field crop seeds. The amounts of some are exceptionally large: in one year 2,118,167 lbs. of seed corn, 1,239,960 lbs. of soybean seeds, were shipped abroad. Another Illinois product sent to distant destinations was horse radish, of which 83,000 lbs. were certified for shipment in 1970.

Statistics are supposed to be dull, but they do contain surprises. Take the subject of cheese production. Illinois takes sixth place nationally in cheese production, which is 4.1 percent of the United States total, but it takes first place in the production of domestic Swiss, or one-third of the national output; second place in Munster, third in Italian cheese, and third in cottage cheese. Yet in milk production it ranks 11th, or only 2.5 percent of the national total.

Everyone presumes to know where the most roses are grown—in New York State? Or Texas? But the Illinois Department of Agricultures cites figures to show that Illinois raises the most roses commercially, and for extra measure, the most gladioli.

City people customarily think of farming in terms of wheat and corn crops, cattle and pigs. Rarely do they consider beekeeping as an essential adjunct to farming. The Illinois Department of Agriculture offers food for the imagination when it says that farmers and producers depend on bees for pollenization of more than 80 crops, and that in 1969 honey bees added more than $50,000,000 to the value of agriculture because the State had been protecting pollenization. This was performed by the Division of Apiary Inspection, which checks more than 28,000 hives annually to eradicate disease.

One of the tasks of the State inspectors is to provide more opportunities for supporting honey bees. Many socalled waste places can be planted to sweet clover, red clover, and alfalfa, in order to increase pollen. Inspectors also locate diseased colonies and keep them from spreading. The State has laws prescribing the kinds of containers. When areas have to be sprayed to eradicate various forms of parasites the Division cooperates with the Illinois State Beekeepers Association to protect apiaries against harm. Bees suffer also from poison sprays and from severe winters.

COAL AND OIL

Before the coming of the railroads coal mining was unimportant in the State. As there was no means of large-scale transportation of the bulky commodity except by water, mining before the 1850's was confined to the vicinity of rivers. But in the middle 1850's the industry in Illinois suddenly expanded; locomotives began to use coal instead of wood, and the railroads were showing a marked interest in coal transportation. Another factor was the introduction in 1873 of Bessemer furnaces, using bituminous coal, into the steel plants of Illinois. Related to the coal mining industry was the smelting of lead and zinc from Missouri in Illinois coal towns. Illinois was the third coal producing State in the nation in 1917, with 810 mines, which produced more than 86,000,000 tons of coal.

Coal continues to be a profitable natural resource and mining has shown some improvement in recent years. In 1970, for instance, 64 mines produced 64,884,103 tons, the largest since 1945, with an increase of 51,519 tons over the previous year. Out of this total more than half—33,268,533 tons—came from strip mining, which reached 33,300,-000 in 1972 and is regularly uncovering new acreage. Illinois has mined more than 4.25 billion tons of coal since 1833 and there is still a large reserve.

The largest coal producer in the United States is the Peabody Coal Co. mine No. 10 near Taylorville. In 1954 it produced 2,645,923 tons. Peabody mine No. 17 near Pana is the second largest producer in Illinois and the sixth largest in the United States.

Perry County led in production in 1970, accounting for 8,389,000 tons solely from strip mining, whereas Franklin County was second with 8,334,000, entirely from underground mines. Other counties, in order, were Jefferson, with 8,400,000 tons chiefly from underground; St. Clair, 6,100,000, from strip; Fulton 6,000,000 from underground, Williamson, almost equally divided between underground, 2,400,000 tons, and strip 2,500,000. Other counties with mines were Christian, Randolph, Gallatin, Montgomery, Peoria, Saline, Knox, Douglas, Kankakee, Vermilion, Jackson, Johnson, Stark, Pope, and Mercer.

Thus 22 counties were producing coal in 1970: 29 underground mines brought 31,615,000 tons and 35 strip mines 33,268,000 tons. Of the 10,214 employees 6,785 worked underground, 3,429 in strip mining. The railroads carried the biggest shipments, 47,000,000 tons, while barges carried 8,000,000.

Every year had its fatalities: in 1967, 20; in 1968, 15; in 1969, 12; in 1970, 15. More than 500 are injured annually. No animals have been used underground since 1966.

Damage to the soil by strip mining was partly halted when the State Assembly enacted a reclamation law on Jan. 1, 1962, by the terms of which mine operators must help restore the ravaged land. By 1970 strip mining had effected 159,311 acres and 98,539 acres were considered reclaimed under supervision of the Illinois Department of Conservation. The major source of water pollution by strip mining comes from waste disposal areas. The principal method of reclamation consists of grading peaks and ridges to a minimum width of 18 feet and seeding them with grass and legumes from an airplane. Some reclaimed lands are ready for use by farm machinery and row production. Few areas have been developed for forest or recreational areas, although there has been some tree planting. Land affected by mining or other industries can be reclaimed, but stone quarries produce a more difficult problem.

Reclamation plans are submitted by operators by December 1. If their surety bonds are forfeited the Department of Conservation performs the necessary reclamation procedure. Research on treatment for difficult spoil banks and waters is being conducted by the Cooperative Wildlife Research Unit of Southern Illinois University with Mid-West Coal Producers Institute, Peabody Coal Co. and the Department of Conservation. Thus new ways of encouraging vegetation on ruined lands are constantly being tested in the field.

Efforts of the State and local communities to adopt pollution control have affected the use of bituminous coal, natural gas and petroleum. Coal has been losing its primacy to oil and gas, but fossil fuels are used to produce electricity, and the dependence on electricity is a key to modern technical advance. The largest producer in northeastern Illinois is the Commonwealth Edison Co., which provides enough electricity for the consumption of approx. 50,000,000 kilowatt hours a year, more than double that produced in 1960. It pioneered with the installation of Dresden Nuclear Power Station near Morris, Illinois, and has been expanding since. Officially it had in 1972 a commitment of $2½ billion to nuclear power, the largest of any privately-owned utility company in the country. It then began experimenting with the breeder-reactor type of nuclear energy. The breeder reactor has the unique ability to produce more fuel than it consumes.

In 1972 the Commonwealth Edison Co. joined a cooperative effort of the utility industry headed by the U. S. Atomic Energy Commission to build at Oak Ridge, Tenn., an experimental breeder-reactor of 300 and 500 megawatts at an estimated cost of $500,000,000. Commonwealth Edison committed $13,400,000 and agreed to furnish key management. Two Chicago-based organizations, the Breeder Reactor Corp. and the Project Management Corp., have charge of funding, contracting, and operational details.

Seven nuclear power reactors are producing electricity in Illinois and eight others have been authorized by the Atomic Energy Commission. Three large units at the Dresden station, Morris, are operated by the Commonwealth Edison Co., which has two larger units at Zion. Two more at the Quad Cities station, Cordova, are operated by Commonwealth Edison and the Illinois Gas & Electric Co. Eight others are to be opened during the present decade in Seneca, Byron, Braidwood, and Clinton.

Illinois is a great oil refining State and the largest refineries are concentrated in the Chicago metropolitan area, which includes the great industrial part of northwest Indiana. The State is crossed by many miles of pipelines, which carry crude petroleum and natural gas from wells hundreds of miles away. A pipeline is a facility in transportation; it differs from other agents in that the carrier remains stationary and its contents move. One of the biggest suppliers of Illinois refineries is a 40-inch pipeline that comes into southern Illinois from the Gulf Coast and supplies refineries all the way to Chicago. While a huge amount of petroleum comes from midwestern wells, crude is also piped in from Canada; the biggest line to reach Chicago from that source is a 34-inch pipe. Some big refineries are the Mobil Oil plant at Joliet, planned to produce 160,000 bbl. a day; Texaco at Lockport, producing 72,000 bbl. a day, and Union Oil at Lemont, 140,000 bbl. a day.

The Natural Gas Pipeline Co. of America, which is owned by the Peoples Gas Co., recently expanded its big storage facility at Mahomet, Ill. It stores gas in underground rock formations. It also liquifies pipeline flow gas by reducing it to a temperature of minus 260 degrees. The Natural Gas Pipeline supplies more than three-fourths of all the natural gas used in Chicago. It supplies Peoples Gas, Northern Illinois Gas Co., and North Shore Gas Co.

Crude petroleum is being pumped out of Illinois soil in decreasing amounts. The 34,874,000 barrels of 42 gallons each realized in 1972 were practically only one-half of the return twenty years earlier.

Fewer new industries are locating inside the city of Chicago than in the suburbs. In 1972 only one new plant started in Chicago, while 12 opened in the suburbs. Of firms locating in the metropolitan area from outside two came into the city and 36 into the suburban area. Of firms already established, four firms moved from the suburbs into the city, and 40 moved from the city to the suburbs. Another movement is the opening of branches, showing the continued expansion of established houses to reach new markets both inside Chicago and inside its suburbs.

When a going concern invests large sums in expansion of its plant it indicates continuing confidence in the economy. In the great industrial area that includes six Illinois counties and two Indiana counties, of which Chicago is the central point, heavy industry is still expanding. First place in investment in new construction is accorded to primary metals, which include steel and pig iron production, primary and secondary smelting of non-ferrous metals, and ferrous and non-ferrous castings. The largest annual amount ever invested in this industry was more than $527,000,000 in 1969. The chemical industry had the second largest investment in new plant facilities. Chemicals cover a vast variety of products, from detergents to vitamins and rust preventives. Third largest investment was in petroleum refining and by-products, followed by electrical machinery, fabricated metals, food processing, and transportation equipment.

By Air, Rail, Land, and Water

I

ILLINOIS is the perfect example of a technical turnabout in an industrial economy. In 25 years it has passed from the greatest railroad center in the world to the greatest depot for passenger air traffic. The railroads still retain a big haulage of heavy manufactured products and agricultural commodities, but even those categories are being reduced by trucking. This has been made possible by the superb system of hard-surfaced highways, in which State roads have been widened and straightened, and the Federal Interstate System has provided expressways that eliminate traffic congestion and permit speedy passage between distant points. The highways provide the routes for the thousands of trucks that carry goods from producer to consumer, portal to portal. Although the railroads are still essential for moving heavy manufactured products out of industrial areas, like Chicago, Peoria, and Rock Island-Moline, trucks are able to carry comparatively lighter loads to all points in Illinois in one day, and retail chain stores 200 and more miles from their supply depots can replenish their stocks overnight.

Road mileage in Illinois (130,187 in 1971) is the fourth longest in the United States, exceeded only by Texas, California, and Kansas. In 1972, 5,643,853 vehicles moved over the roads; licenses to drive reached 6,003,609. License plates are green and white and carry the legend *Land of Lincoln*. In 1972 the State collected nearly $400,000,000 from its gasoline tax of 7.5c.

Federal aid for public transit systems dates from 1964, when the first Urban Mass Transportation Act allocated $375,000,000 for this purpose. The inadequacy of this amount was quickly realized, for additional amounts were appropriated in the next few years. The Federal Government, in the Urban Mass Transportation Act of 1970, authorized the expenditure of $3.1 billion in seven years. In 1971 the General Assembly of Illinois voted to set aside $900,000,000 to remedy the ills of transportation in Illinois, $200,000,000 of the amount for the improvement of mass transit systems for four years. The State also organized a Department of Transportation to supervise improvement in public transit systems.

In the Chicago area railroads still play a major role in transportation. By 1972 they held records for interregional freight traffic, which a study by the Chicago Assn. of Commerce evaluated as follows: rail, 54%; trucking, 22.4%; water, 12.2%; pipeline, 11%; air, .08%. But if interurban traffic were included in the count, trucks quite likely would double their percentage of hauling. Yet Chicago remains the great midwestern terminal for long-haul rail shipments.

In 1972 there were more than 132 railyards that marshalled 40,000 freight cars daily. Cars that formerly carried 58 tons now have a capacity of 80 tons. Piggyback loads were begun in 1935; now 21 yards handle this form of freight.

Great readjustments in administration and operation of railroads are still being made in Illinois. The Chicago & North Western Railway was finally sold by Northwest Industries to the Chicago & North Western Transportation Co., formed by its employees. It is the first railroad to be owned wholly by the employees and the largest corporation so owned. About 1,000 of the railroad's 13,500 employees bought stock. The corporation assumed a debt of around $400,000,000. A 5.25% fare increase was authorized by August, 1972, but was considered inadequate to meet the costs of commuter service. The railroad cited costly competition by the Jefferson Park Rapid Transit line of the Chicago Transit Authority.

All railroads in Illinois are affected by the settlement of the long controversy over the employment of firemen on diesel locomotives, which had run ever since diesels were introduced. The railroads asked the elimination of firemen from diesels on the ground that they are not needed. The United Transportation Union fought the proposal by declaring the firemen were needed in reserve for the engineers. About 18,000 firemen's jobs were involved. The settlement retains the men now employed but stipulates there will be no replacement when attrition gradually removes them.

A prime example of the diversion of railroad capital to other investments is the Illinois Central Railroad, which was organized in 1851 and from 1856 on influenced the location of numerous towns and industrial sites along its right-of-way in Illinois. As the passenger business outside of commuting declined the corporation formed Illinois Central Industries with five divisions: railroading, consumer products, real estate, industrial products, and financial services. Consumer products include soft-drink bottling, hosiery, and motor car mufflers. Industries include a foundry, electronics, and metal fabrication. Financial services include life insurance and savings and loan institutions. Real estate has as its principal task the selling of rights to build over the right-of-way, and especially the development of Illinois Center, south of East Wacker Drive, north of Grant Park, comprising 83 acres of the former freight yards of the railroad, already the site of the 80-story Standard Oil Building, the Regency-Hyatt hotel and tall office structures. The consolidation of the Illinois Central with the Gulf, Mobile & Ohio, as the Illinois Central Gulf was a logical result of shrinkage in railroad income. The merger was completed in 1973 after a Federal Court decided in its favor and thereby invalidated the protests filed by competing railroads.

II

When the great railroad system of Illinois lost its passenger traffic to the air lines and buses, and much of its consumer freight to motor trucks, the local accommodation train between small towns was displaced by bus lines. Trucks, with their portal-to-portal handling of goods, proved most useful for intracity and regional transport. Air cargo, relatively minor, was beginning to be used for quick deliveries across sectional lines.

The Federal Interstate Highway System, officially the National System of Interstate and Defense Highways, is a network of rural and urban expressways that gives easy and unobstructed passage for motor cars from the Atlantic Coast to the Pacific, and from the Gulf of Mexico and the southwestern border to Canada. It was begun in 1956 under the direction of the Federal Highway Administration in cooperation with the Highway Departments of the states. The states determine the location of the routes and their construction and are responsible for maintenance and operation. The Federal Government pays 90 percent of the cost of building from funds derived chiefly from the tax on motor fuel. These funds have become so large that they constitute a vested interest on the part of those who profit primarily from them—road building contractors, cement manufacturers, motor vehicle and road machinery manufacturers, and such related agencies as real estate developers and motor car associations. Efforts of the municipalities to obtain part of the huge fund for remedying the many liabilities of urban traffic for a long time met with solid opposition in the national House of Representatives. It was not until 1973 that some small concession was made to other agencies.

Good roads became a subject for legislation in the early 1900s, when Representative Homer J. Tice, William G. Edens, and the Chicago Motor Club began agitating for roads that the automobiles could use. In 1911 the State Assembly imposed license fees on cars, the proceeds to be applied to road building. Later it authorized counties to appoint superintendents of highways and pay one-half the cost of roads, the State to assume the other half and maintenance. The great expansion of motor car use led Governor Lowden in 1918 to get authority for a $60,000,000 bond issue to improve 4,300 miles of roads. During Len Small's term a bond issue for $100,000,000 was issued to maintain 9,900 miles.

Although Chicago had plenty of funds to finance new factories and all the technical expertness needed, it did not develop a great motor car industry. When numerous reports from abroad proved that the internal combustion engine could be harnessed to a vehicle many mechanics in Illinois shops began constructing automobiles. But Robert P. Howard writes in *Illinois, A History of the Prairie State,* that the 160 highly competitive companies in Chicago and downstate wound up as failures. Illinois did make a contribution to the motor car age. One of the cars it produced was the Woods Electric, a high-seated buggy of black trim and glass, which proved most popular with women who favored a sedate and unhurried ride. It was powered by batteries and steered by a tiller, and its speed was little better than a horse's trot. The yellow-colored taxicab was Chicago's—or rather John D. Hertz's—gift to the world, and the Checker cab came from Joliet. The Velie, Moline, and

Stevens were marketed from Moline. Charles and J. Frank Duryea left
a bicycle shop in Peoria to build a gas car in Springfield, Mass., and in
1895 Frank won first prize offered by Herman Kohlsaat's *Chicago
Times Herald* for a sustained ride of 40 miles, from Jackson Park to
Evanston and back, which he covered in nine hours.

Trucking is one of the biggest industries of Illinois. With the aid
of the good roads that join every city, village and crossroads hamlet in
the State thousands of trucks fan out from the manufacturers and
processors every day. Huge carriers that have taken over a large slice
of haulage that used to go to the railroads carry products to eight major
interchanges: Bloomington, Danville, Decatur, Peoria, Springfield,
Rockford, Rock Island, and Quincy. They connect with transcontinental
lines in the East St. Louis-St. Louis gateway. It is estimated that 1,200
places in Illinois are dependent solely on truck service. One-day
delivery from Chicago is normal except to the extreme southwestern
part of the State. In three days Illinois carriers can reach every important key city in the United States. Supermarkets in parts of five states
can replenish their stocks overnight. In 1970 the Illinois trucking industry employed 340,000, who earned $2.6 billions. There was a registra-
tion of 660,450 trucks in the State, but this figure included many local
vehicles not engaged in intrastate hauling.

III

Illinois was closely associated with the development of aeronautics,
in theory as well as practice. An outstanding contributor to the technology was Octave Chanute, a civil engineer, born in Paris in 1832 and
brought to America as a child. He became associated with midwestern
railroads and chief engineer of the Chicago & Alton. In 1883 he located
his office in Chicago. He studied the findings of Otto and Gustav Lilien-
thal, published his theories of flight and took part in testing gliders on the
sand dunes of Indiana. During 1893 he presided at the International
Conference on Aerial Navigation at the World's Columbian Exposition.
Wilbur and Orville Wright conferred with Chanute in Chicago in 1901
and, according to John Clayton, in *The Illinois Fact Book and Historical
Almanac,* this helped the Wrights to decide to build a biplane and
gave them other technical guidance that they used profitably in the
first successful flight of a heavier-than-air machine in 1903.

Chicago is served by three airports that have recorded an amazing
expansion. Continuous rebuilding to meet the massive demands of commercial aviation is an unending procedure at Chicago's three airports:
O'Hare International Airport, largest in the world; Chicago Midway
Airport, gaining preeminence for domestic scheduled airlines, and Merrill C. Meigs Field, for nonscheduled and commuting planes, located
on an island off Chicago's front yard. On the drawing boards are the
experimental draughts of another major field, intended to continue
Chicago's leadership in aviation into the 21st century.

All that anybody knew about Orchard Place in 1942 was that it
was a plot of undeveloped Cook County prairie, with some trees, scattered

houses, and dirt highways west of the Mannheim Road. But the War Production Board of the USA spotted it as suited for a huge airplane factory it needed in its emergency, and bought 1,790 acres so that Douglas Aircraft Company could start turning out C-54 military transports at great speed. To serve its purposes Douglas covered huge areas of good soil with concrete for flooring of plant buildings and runways, and raised immense wooden structures. One of the biggest ever built was the assembly shed, seven-eighths of a mile long and covering 1.7 million square ft. The concrete floor was reinforced and used for airplane parking by the 928th Troop Carrier Group of the US Air Force Reserve. In two years Douglas completed 665 warplanes in its assembly shed. It was razed in May, 1967.

When the pilots began using the Douglas field its call letters became ORD, after its local name, Orchard Place. In 1945 came V-J Day and Douglas' occupation was gone. In March, 1946, the U. S. Government transferred to the City of Chicago 1,080 acres, because the city had discovered that its 640 acres at the Municipal Airport in Cicero were wholly inadequate to care for the thousands of carrier planes and millions of passengers that were threatening to swamp the services. The traveling public, which had made Chicago the greatest railroad terminal in the world, was transferring its favor to flying and taking to planes in huge numbers.

In 1949 the new field became the CHICAGO-O'HARE INTERNATIONAL AIRPORT. It was named to honor Lieut. Commander Edward H. O'Hare of the U. S. Naval Air Force, familiarly known as Butch O'Hare, who was killed in action on the Pacific in 1942. Attacked in the air by nine hostile bombers O'Hare shot down six before his own plane was hit. He was awarded the Medal of Honor of the U. S. Navy after his death.

The field was opened to commercial air traffic in 1955. In 1963 President John F. Kennedy formally dedicated it, and the fine Interstate highway was named the John F. Kennedy Expressway. The facilities at the airport now exceeded all previous records for size and multiplicity of accommodations. Runways were measured by miles, passengers by millions. In addition to 11 major domestic scheduled airlines 11 foreign lines opened new opportunities for travel. A three-story circular restaurant, the Seven Continents, stood at the intersection of the domestic and international sections, each a quarter of a mile long. There was a control tower 81 ft. tall, which guided takeoffs and landings that reached nearly two a minute. And out of the air came a startling parade of aircraft—scheduled and nonscheduled, helicopters, military planes, executive planes.

The Department of Aviation of the City of Chicago made the following summary of operations at O'Hare in 1970: Total operations, 641,390, of which 565,072 takeoffs and landings were domestic scheduled planes, 21,821 foreign, 4,702 helicopters, and 49,795 nonscheduled. Passengers arriving and departing numbered 29,689,015. By the end of 1972 O'Hare had served 34,233,462 passengers.

Direct service to foreign places has made Illinois the hub of Midwestern commercial aviation. Pan American World Airways has made a success of the one-week in Europe bargain tours, and operates ten nonstop flights to Jamaica weekly. Braniff has direct service to Hawaii and South America. The Chicago to Paris flights of Air France and special ski flights to the French Alps have proved most popular. Air Wisconsin, which operates in Wisconsin, Illinois, Iowa and Minnesota, has had as much as a 30 percent gain in air cargo, a service favored by light industries. The freight section of aviation is growing. At O'Hare a big Cargo City is on the drawing boards. In the first six months of 1973 air freight at all airports reached 774,411,000 lbs., a 15.7% rise over 1973. TWA reported handling 300 tons of air freight daily. British Airways, a combination of BOAC and BEAC, established a world record on July 25, 1973, for the most freight carried in a single 747 passenger aircraft between Chicago and London, more than 75,000 lbs.

O'HARE INTERNATIONAL TOWER, the big hotel operated in connection with the airport, was opened in June, 1973. This huge structure has a curved facade of tinted windows facing the Control Tower and the inner court of the main building of the airport. Designed by Skidmore, Owings & Merrill, it has 979 guest rooms, 63 conference rooms, and 20 halls for conventions or banquets. It is completely self-contained and by means of moving sidewalks and underground communications makes possible quick registration and check-out of guests by computer. Besides all the technical advantages it has special features, such as the Gaslight Club, a French bistro, a Swiss hütte, an English pub, a Balkan grill and a Japanese restaurant.

What is called the largest parking garage in the country was opened to cars in December, 1972. The steel and concrete structure of six levels, which was planned to accommodate 9,150 motor cars when full, has elevators to take customers to a tunnel that enables them to reach the airline terminals and the airport hotel. At the end are moving sidewalks, 230 ft. long, that carry pedestrians and their baggage at 120 ft. a minute and can transport 10,000 persons per hour. The initial cost of parking was 50 cents for four hours or portion thereof, with a limit of $3 for four hours, and a city tax of 15 cents. There are 4,600 spaces for parking on the open lots around the airport, all some distance away from the terminals.

The most arresting business structure in the neighborhood of O'Hare International Airport is the headquarters of UNITED AIR LINES, on Algonquin Road in Elk Grove Township, completed in 1961. It was designed by Myron Goldsmith, architect-engineer of Skidmore, Owings & Merrill, who had been a student of Mies van der Rohe at the Illinois Institute of Technology in the late 1930s and now occupies Mies' chair there. The headquarters consists of two low two-story buildings that have prestressed concrete framing and extraordinary bays, 66 by 60 ft., with the glass pane set back from the outer structural members. United recognized the potential strength of the O'Hare project before it opened and is the leading airplane operator there. It employs more than 6,000 at O'Hare.

The REGENCY HYATT HOUSE, a big 12-story structure, stands forth in the open area like a huge monument, about one mile southeast of the Airport buildings. Opened in June, 1971, it was one of the most elaborate, as well as costly, of the Hyatt chain, the tab for the 750-room hotel coming to $30,000,000. Designed by John Portman, Jr., it is built around a hollow square with rooms opening on corridors that are actually balconies overlooking the lobby. Bridges lead to the 12 centrally located elevators, all glass-enclosed. The Hyatt House chain is owned by the Pritzker Family of Chicago, which is locating another unit on East Wacker Drive in the new Illinois Center.

CHICAGO MIDWAY AIRPORT is the oldest and today the second largest airport in Chicago. It was called Chicago Municipal Airport when opened May 8, 1926, at Cicero Ave. and 63rd St. Its planes had neither range nor speed; they were piston engine propeller craft, and for a decade or so a load of 20 passengers was considered normal and 40 a risk. But planes were continually undergoing technical changes and the field was adding acreage until by the end of the 1930s it had 640 acres for runways and terminal buildings. After the close of World War II, when air transportation was growing in full fury, Midway Airport, as it came to be called, was a confused, cramped, difficult field. In 1955 more than 9,000,000 passengers arrived and departed at Midway and the city of Chicago was working frantically to get ready the big field west of the Mannheim Road.

The authorities had expected O'Hare to assume about one-half of the Midway load and then accommodate the rising tide, but something happened that changed the prospects of Midway. This was the coming into service in March, 1959, of the big jets that needed almost a mile of runway to become airborne. Midway lacked the facilities; moreover it had no easy connections with O'Hare for travelers who were changing planes. The transcontinental carriers were not willing to asume the expense of using two airfields and resisted efforts to schedule flights from Midway. Business lagged, funds were cut; it seemed incredible, but Midway was closing down.

The return of Midway Airport to the status of a major operation had a slower start than expected because of the economic recession in the late 1960s. But the need to lighten traffic at O'Hare led the city to intensify efforts to make Midway efficient and attractive to airlines and customers. The city expended $11,000,000 in 1968 on enlarged runways and other facilities; it persuaded various airlines to transfer to Midway their interconnecting flights to cities within a radius of 800 miles of Chicago, and it publicized the advantages of Midway for domestic flights. Even when Midway seemed hardly comparable with a giant such as O'Hare, it was regaining its place as one of the great air depots of America. By the end of 1970 it had completed the year's record, 182,348 operations, including scheduled, nonscheduled and helicopter flights, and carriage of 1,437,481 passengers. These were fewer than the year before, but air cargo—mail, express and freight—increased 500 percent, from 5,500,000 lbs. to 32,402,000 lbs.

The third unit of the Department of Aviation is MERRILL C. MEIGS FIELD, located on Northerly Island off Chicago's lake front, south of Achsah Bond Drive and the Adler Planetarium. The island was built by landfill for the Century of Progress Exposition and was named for a former newspaper publisher whose family long had been associated with Chicago. It is a port for general aviation—unscheduled, executive, and commuter planes, and has proved of great usefulness because of its proximity to the Loop and McCormick Place. Meigs Field, like O'Hare and Midway, reflects the economic situation. After a steady increase in operations during the 1960 decade it drifted from its peak. In 1968 it had 91,432 takeoffs and landings and served 275,062 passengers; this dropped in 1970 to 80,031 flights and 258,207 passengers. Meigs Field is known for its excellent installations and its potential usefulness for commuting planes.

There are 19 airports, major and minor, in the Chicago Metropolitan Area, which includes Joliet. The total number of commercial airports in the State is 157. There are 86 heliports, many in the service of hospitals.

The Illinois Department of Aeronautics recently initiated an air age educational program for the schools, as well as soil conservation airlifts in connection with the Dept. of Agriculture. It is responsible for developing a state-wide airport system, issuing air charts and navigational aids, and promoting aviation safety.

IV

Water transportation is an important aid to commerce in Illinois. Up and down the Mississippi, the Ohio, and the Illinois Rivers move numerous towboats pushing long combinations of barges carrying petroleum and gas to the tank farms that appear on the outskirts of river towns; heaps of soft coal for the plants of the power and light companies; tons of grain to be stored in huge elevators and transshiped to other barges and trucks. Heavy machinery is moved from the interior of the State over the Illinois River at rates less expensive than if shipped by rail. Over the Illinois River annually move 30,000,000 tons of manufactured goods and commodities.

Nostalgia for the days of the steamboats does not include a desire to revive their business records. Modern barge traffic far exceeds the tonnage carried by the stern-wheelers of a century ago. Towboats of from 1,000 to 5,000 hp operated by diesels guide immense loads. The prospering of barge traffic at the ports of Illinois along the Upper Mississippi has become possible since the organization of the Inland Waterways Corporation, which started the Federal Barge Line in 1927. The first towboats were 600 hp craft, pushing 500-ton barges because heavier vessels would scrape the river bed or pile up on snags. The barge service really began to thrive when the Federal Government made possible a 9-ft. channel by constructing 26 locks and dams between Minneapolis and Alton in 1938. In the ensuing upsurge of commerce Rock Island became the most important river port in Illinois.

Port of Chicago. The two major shipping depots of the Port of Chicago are the NAVY PIER, at the foot of Grand Ave. and CALUMET HARBOR and LAKE CALUMET. The Pier can accommodate six ocean-going vessels at one time and has 385,000 sq. ft. of space under its roof. Its facilities are operated by the North Pier Terminal Co. and the Great Lakes Storage & Contracting Co.

The Port of Chicago is one of 40 ports opened to the ships of the Soviet Union by the American-Soviet shipping agreement of October, 1972. Grain intended for the Soviet Union was allocated to three shipping lines, one-third for Soviet ships, one-third for American ships, and one-third for ships of other flags. Before these arrangements were completed 42% of the grain intended for the Soviet Union was shipped from Chicago in 40 third-flag vessels, the total amounting to 626,000 tons. The first ship flying the flag of the Soviet Union to enter the Port was the *MV Dubossary,* which arrived April 23, 1973, and berthed at the Calumet Grain Co. elevator in Lake Calumet to load 9,000 long tons of Illinois soybeans.

The Port has registered a steady rise in tonnage and value in recent years except for the period of recession. In 1968 the Port had exports of 2,174,347 tons, valued at $389,552,966. The report for exports in 1969 was better: 2,350,015 tons valued at $275,101,227, but imports were lower, 1,716,893 tons valued at $375,091,474. Returns in subsequent years have varied with the state of the economy.

Ship arrivals from overseas are increasing in numbers, tonnage varies. In 1972 overseas import tonnage was 1,441,378 tons, a drop of 1 percent from 1971. Container cargo was on the increase, 6,932 tons in 1972, compared with 5,652 tons in 1971. The Port maintains a tight security system with motorized and radio-equipped foot patrols, inspection of ships manifests and cargo before unloading begins and check of all vehicles on leaving. The Port has no major thefts and pilfering is usually confined to edible goods.

The inland waterways continue to handle increased tonnage. This is also true of shipping on the Great Lakes. More than 30,000,000 tons of limestone are shipped annually on the Great Lakes.

Lake Calumet is an important transfer point between lake and ocean ships and river barges. Its paved dock area can accommodate up to 17 vessels. It has two grain elevators with a total storage capacity of 13,500,000 bu. and three transit sheds and warehouses with 500,000 sq. ft. of available space. The total grain capacity of Chicago facilities is 58,270,000 bu. (The country's largest capacities are in Minneapolis-St. Paul, 125,159,000 bu.)

The city strictly enforces ordinances for keeping harbor waters clean. Regulations control the disposal of sanitary and galley wastes from ships and compliance from foreign ships is reported as excellent. Chicago also takes part in a long-range effort to clean up lake waters, which remain a major problem that needs interstate action.

Larger ore boats are being built for the ore traffic. Two new "super" boats are the *Roger Blough* of the U. S. Steel Corp. and the *Stewart Corp* of the Bethlehem Steel Corp. The *Corp* is 1,000 ft. long, 105 ft. wide, and carries an average of 60,000 tons of ore on voyages between Taconite, Minn. and Burns Harbor, Ind.

Labor History and Employment

Labor organization in Illinois dates from the 1850s. Among the thousands drawn west in the labor vacuum created by the construction of the Illinois and Michigan Canal (1836-1848) and the Illinois Central Railroad (1851-1855) were emigrants from European cities where workers' unions were common. When the canal and the railroad were completed, some laborers turned to homesteading, others were employed in newly opened coal mines, and others found jobs in urban industries. Among the latter were Germans who introduced principles of group action that had been evolved in their homeland. Clubs and societies were organized among the tailors, waggoners, and carpenters of Chicago. These so-called mechanics' unions participated in the successful movement to obtain free public schools (1855).

Shortly after the Civil War began, English miners from St. Clair County, Illinois, met in St. Louis and established the American Miners' Association "to mutually instruct and improve each other in knowledge, which is power, to study the laws of life, the relation of Labor to Capital, politics, municipal affairs, literature, science, or any other subject relating to the general welfare of our class." Branches of the A.M.A. were formed in Ohio, Indiana, and Maryland, but, owing to membership losses in the post-Civil War depression, the organization became inactive after 1868.

The decline in real wages incident to the Civil War contributed to the formation of a score of trade unions at Chicago in 1863. Strikes that year among the coal miners were answered with the La Salle Black Law which, as summarized by Earl R. Beckner in *A History of Illinois Labor Legislation,* "prohibited any person from preventing any other person from working at any lawful occupation on any terms he might see fit and from combining for the purpose of depriving the owner or possessor of property of its lawful use and management." During the two decades in which the Black Law was enforced, violaters were punished by fines and imprisonment. However, later attempts to revive the statute were frustrated by the courts.

The enactment of the La Salle Black Law spurred organized labor to consider political action. Formation of an independent party was forestalled, however, through appeasing measures, advanced in 1864 by the two major parties. In the following year the eight-hour day advocated by Ira Steward (1831-1883), a Boston mechanic, absorbed the workingman's attention. Eight-hour Leagues were organized throughout the State in 1866 to support those candidates for the General Assembly who endorsed the eight-hour working day. A sympathetic legislature was elected, and, in 1867, Illinois was the first

State to declare that "eight hours of labor . . . shall constitute and be a legal day's work, where there is no special contract or agreement to the contrary."

This, however, was immediately offset by the development of a solid array of special contracts and agreements to the contrary. And, in a joint ultimatum employers warned they would discharge all employees unwilling to work ten hours a day. Defiant Chicago workers called a general strike on May 1st, the day on which the law was to be effective. Two days later, following disorders between strikers and non-strikers, Mayor John B. Rice of Chicago intimated that the La Salle Black Law would be invoked. Thus admonished, the strikers returned to work; the eight-hour law was a dead issue.

To complicate matters a practice destined to provoke a long time controversy was instituted in 1871 when arrangements were made to least convict labor to private employers under the so-called "contract system." As a result of competition between the products of free and convict labor the wages of coopers, shoemakers, stonecutters, and, later, clothing and furniture workers were reduced. In 1884, for example, the work of shoemakers who received an average annual wage of $355 was duplicated by 766 convicts who were paid an average annual wage of $159. Although the contract system was countenanced by the General Assembly because of State revenues thus derived, many persons opposed it as a vicious mechanism for lowering the workingmen's standard of living.

The use of child labor also served to depress the wage level. Remedial legislation was opposed on the contention that initiative would be blighted; widows would be deprived of their sole support; and families would lose the added revenue required to augment the father's income. Notwithstanding these objections, the General Assembly in enactment of the general mining law of 1872 adopted a provision forbidding mine operators to employ children under 14 years of age; two years later the age limit was set at 12 years. An act of 1877 prohibited the employment of children under 14 years of age in "begging, peddling, acrobatics, gymnastics, singing [non-religious], playing musical instruments [non-religious], obscene exhibitions, or occupations that endangered life and health." Neither of the foregoing laws was thoroughly enforced.

In the hard times that followed the panic of 1873 labor unions, including the Sons of Vulcan (iron-puddlers) and the Knights of St. Crispin (shoemakers), underwent heavy membership losses. The subsequent upswing of business was marked by the formation of a socialist party in Chicago, four candidates of which were elected to the General Assembly (1878), and the renewal of labor organization on all fronts. Local assemblies of the Knights of Labor were chartered at Peoria, Chicago, and Springfield in 1877. In the same year delegates from 17 trade unions met at Chicago and formed a Trade Council which, renamed the Trade and Labor Assembly in 1879, was the forerunner of the Chicago Federation of Labor.

As production increased and profits mounted, workmen made determined efforts to raise wage scales that in many instances remained at depression levels. Strikes and lockouts occurred throughout the State. In the nation-wide railroad strike of 1877, militiamen were detailed to Peoria, Chicago, Decatur, Galesburg, and East St. Louis. Shortly afterwards the General Assembly passed a law prohibiting any person or persons from impeding or obstructing the operation of railroads or any other business under penalty of fines and prison.

A major objective of organized labor was attained in 1879 with the creation of the Illinois Bureau of Labor Statistics. Despite its limited authority and an insufficient appropriation, the bureau performed valuable services, furnishing data frequently used to substantiate abuses that otherwise might have been ascribed to mere chronic complaint on the part of workingmen. The General Assembly of 1879 also enacted the Armed Workmen Law, requiring all military organizations other than the State militia to be licensed by the governor. The law was meant to disband such groups in Chicago as the Labor Guards, the *Jaeger Verein,* the Bohemian Sharpshooters, and other military societies which bewildered workers had forced in reaction to over-zealous police.

The first half of the 1880-90 decade saw renewed demands for the eight-hour day, the emergence of the Black International at Chicago, and the rapid growth of unions throughout the State. The Knights of Labor, its prestige enhanced by a series of successful railroad strikes, had enrolled an Illinois membership of 52,461 in 1886. The Federation of Organized Trades and Labor Unions, forerunner of the American Federation of Labor, experienced comparable gains. At the fourth convention of the federation, held in Chicago on May 7, 1884, the 25 delegates endorsed a general strike for the eight-hour day, beginning on May 1, 1886. Local assemblies of the Knights of Labor enthusiastically concurred in the movement, although T. V. Powderly, Grand Master Workman, sought to undermine their zeal by secretly disavowing the general strike.

The Black International, organized by anarchists at Pittsburgh in 1883 and immediately centralized at Chicago, injected martial temper into the Illinois labor movement. The conduct of the handful of converts won to its doctrine of violence and terrorism during the depression of 1884 was such as to support resentment aroused by the newspapers concerning the purposes of the International but the Central Labor Union, organized at Chicago in 1884 under the International's sponsorship, made rapid gains among butchers, carpenters, cigar makers, metal workers, cabinet workers, hodcarriers, and lumberyard workers. Members of the *Lehr und Wehrverein,* which, though formed in 1875 had been unaffected by the Armed Workmen Act, allied themselves with the International and drilled secretly in preparation for open strife. Among the anarchists' propaganda agencies were the *Fackel,* the *Vorbote, The Alarm,* the *Boudoucnost,* and the *Arbeiter-*

Zeitung. The editor of *The Alarm,* the only English language paper in the group, was Albert Parsons, a veteran of the Confederate Army. The militant Central Labor Union and the conservative Trade and Labor Assembly united their 40 affiliates behind the general strike for an eight-hour day. Alarmed Chicago employers met in April, 1886, and agreed, if necessary, to crush the eight-hour demand by hiring hordes of strikebreakers. About 100,000 workers, of whom 58,000 were in Chicago, struck on May 1. No immediate disorders occurred.

Two days after the strike began, August Spies, co-editor of the *Arbeiter-Zeitung,* spoke on the eight-hour day at a rally of striking lumber-shovers. The meeting was held near Cyrus H. McCormick's reaper works, where three months earlier 1,500 employees had been locked out and replaced with strikebreakers under the protection of 300 Pinkertons. As Spies neared the end of his address about 200 of his listeners moved off to the reaper works where they beset homeward-bound strikebreakers. A detachment of police suddenly appeared at the scene of the disturbance. Curious to know what was happening, the remainder of Spies' audience started toward the reaper works. Evidently mistrusting the approaching crowd's intent, the police fired into its ranks, killing six and wounding others.

THE HAYMARKET TRAGEDY

Infuriated by the tragedy Spies issued a call for a rally on the evening of May 4 "to denounce the latest atrocious act of the police." The meeting took place, not at the Haymarket, but two blocks away on Desplaines Street between Lake and Randolph Streets. The night was overcast and but 3,000 assembled; among them was the senior Carter Harrison, then mayor of Chicago. Referring to the dead of the previous day, Spies opened the meeting with a talk on "Justice"; Albert Parsons spoke next on the eight-hour day. As Samuel Fielden, popular labor orator, began the final address, rain fell and the crowd dwindled to about 500. Mayor Harrison, relieved by the moderate tone of the rally, strolled to the Desplaines Street police station and told Inspector John Bonfield that "nothing is likely to occur that will require interference." When the mayor departed, Bonfield marched 200 policemen to the gathering and ordered its dispersal. Fielden remonstrated: "But officer, this is a peaceable meeting." And, at that moment a dynamite bomb exploded, killing eight policemen and wounding about 65 others. The number of civilian dead was not determined, nor was the identity of the bomb-thrower ever learned.

Spies, Parsons, and Fielden were arrested, along with five other labor leaders, George Engel, Oscar Neebe, Michael Schwab, Louis Lingg, and Adolph Fischer. The legal philosophy that prevailed was expressed by State's Attorney Grinnel, who, in his concluding address to the jury on August 11, 1886, said: "These men have been selected, picked out by the grand jury and indicted because they were leaders. They were no more guilty than the thousands who follow them. . . ."

Seven were sentenced to death; the eighth, Oscar Neebe, received 15 years imprisonment. An appeal was made to the Illinois Supreme

Court which, in a 273-page opinion, affirmed the lower court. On the eve of the execution Governor Oglesby commuted the sentences of Schwab and Fielden to life imprisonment; that same night Louis Lingg escaped the gallows by exploding a fusecap in his mouth. Spies, Engel, Parsons, and Fischer were hanged on November 11, 1887. Six years later Governor John P. Altgeld (1847-1902), aware that he was inviting political oblivion for himself, pardoned Neebe, Schwab, and Fielden. The *Pardon Message,* an 18,000-word document, charged gross irregularities in the trial procedure and scored the conduct of the presiding Judge, Joseph E. Gary.

In the wake of the Haymarket tragedy and the unfortunate association of anarchy and unionism thereby lodged in the public mind, organized labor's progress was halted and demands for an eight-hour day were temporarily relinquished. Branded as anarchistic on the basis of Fielden's membership in Local Assembly No. 1037, the Knights of Labor underwent decline. The major cause of the Knights' rapid extinction was, however, the skilled workers' increasing preference for trade separatism. Thus, while the power of the Knights' "one big union" waned between 1889-1894, membership in the craft unions of the Chicago Trade and Labor Assembly was more than tripled.

Genuine recognition of the rights and problems of labor occurred in the administration (1892-1896) of Governor Altgeld. A law enacted in 1893 forbade employers to prevent employees from forming, joining, and belonging to lawful labor unions; the Illinois Supreme Court, however, held this to be unconstitutional in 1900. A State Board of Arbitration, empowered to investigate and make public its recommendations for settling industrial disputes, was established in 1895 and maintained thereafter until its duties were vested in the Industrial Commission (1917).

In 1893 the Legislature enacted laws vital to the employment of children and women. They prohibited the employment of children under 14 in factories and limited the working day of women to eight hours and the week to 48 hours. The laws were badly enforced. After a series of court actions brought by manufacturers the Illinois Supreme Court pronounced the laws unconstitutional.

Employees of the Pullman Palace Car Company, who occupied houses in the company town of Pullman, had their wages cut during the hard times of the 1890s. When they protested to George M. Pullman, the owner, and asked restoration of wage cuts of 25 to 40 percent, he discharged the leaders. Thereupon the Pullman employees walked out. Most of them were members of the American Railway Union, which Eugene Debs had organized in 1893. Pullman refused to arbitrate and the union stopped handling Pullman cars. Railroad executives of the General Managers Assn. ordered dismissal of all employees who refused to move Pullman cars. There were no laws against hiring strikebreakers, and Pullman and the railroads hired 2,000 extra men to operate the cars. By attaching mail cars to Pullmans the owners could show that stopping Pullman cars also meant interference with the U. S. mails.

This involved the Federal government, and the strike reached a swift ending. About 3,400 men, later described by Police Superintendent Brennan of Chicago as "thugs, thieves, and ex-convicts," were sworn in as U. S. deputy marshals at the request of the General Managers Association. Clashes between strikers and deputies took place. On July 2, the Federal Court at Chicago issued an injunction ordering Debs and the American Railway Union to cease and desist from interfering with the mails, interstate commerce, and the operation of railroads. Two days later President Cleveland detailed four companies of infantry to Chicago. Governor Altgeld immediately informed the President that "Local officials have been able to handle the siutation. . . . The Federal Government had been applied to by men who had political and selfish motives for wanting to ignore the State government. . . . As Governor of Illinois, I protest against this, and ask an immediate withdrawal of Federal troops from active duty in this State."

Governor Altgeld's request was not heeded. On July 6 Federal troops attempted to start railroad traffic in Chicago but made no progress. The strikers tried to block trains with their massed bodies; rails were torn up and hundreds of boxcars fired. Governor Altgeld mobilized five regiments of militiamen, some of whom shot and killed seven strikers on July 7. On that day Eugene Debs was arrested and the strike was practically broken although it continued sporadically throughout the summer. The executives of the American Federation of Labor, in special session at Chicago, advised the strikers to return to work on July 12. Found guilty of violating the Federal court injunction, Debs was imprisoned at Woodstock, Illinois, for six months.

The Pullman strike and the Haymarket tragedy are notable, though sordid episodes in the history of American labor strife. Similar events of Chicago origin and nation-wide consequence include the formation of the Industrial Workers of the World in 1905 by Eugene Debs, Daniel De Leon, Vincent St. John, and "Big Bill" Haywood; the strike of 40,000 clothing workers in 1910, led by Sidney Hillman, a one-time resident of Jane Addams' Hull House; and the post-World War organization of steel-workers under the leadership of John Fitzpatrick and William Z. Foster. The latter movement culminated in the general steel strike of 1919, which was broken following issuance of a court injunction and the use of Federal troops. The clothing workers' strike, although lost, contributed to the development of the Amalgamated Clothing Workers of America, now strong with 261,000 members (1973). The Industrial Workers of the World received a death blow at Chicago, the city of its birth, when, in 1919, more than 100 of its leaders were tried before Federal Judge Kenesaw Mountain Landis and found guilty of criminal syndicalism.

The growth of the United Mine Workers of America in the Illinois coal fields has its roots in the successful coal strike of 1897, by which the miners won the eight-hour day, a 20 per cent increase in pay, abolishment of the company store, and recognition of their union. Repudiation of this agreement by the Chicago-Virden Coal Company in 1898 was the immediate cause of the so-called Virden riot (*see Tour 17*), a violent outbreak ending for the first time in victory for an A.F. of L. affiliate in a major strike. The Herrin massacre (*see Herrin, Tour 4*) occurred in the coal strike of 1922, which was ended by State and Federal troops. In 1929 the miners struck again and were again defeated. Three years later, a split in the ranks of the United Mine Workers of America led to the formation of the Progressive Miners of America. For several years thereafter the two unions fought bitterly throughout southern Illinois; later their feud was continued in the Federal courts.

Rapid strides were made in labor legislation enacted in the succeeding thirty years. Following Altgeld's courageous precedent, subsequent governors, with the support of organized labor, attacked the evils of unbridled industrialism and sought to impart fair play in dealings between employer and labor. In some instances the courts retained conservative views. A change in attitude may be dated from 1909, however, when following the decision of Judge Richard S. Tuthill of the Circuit Court of Cook County in which he ruled the recently enacted Ten-Hour Working Day Law for Women unconstitutional, he was vigorously berated on every side. Judge Tuthill's decision was reversed by the Illinois Supreme Court on April 12, 1910. The brief for the defense was prepared by Louis D. Brandeis, who had volunteered his services.

The State-Use Law of 1903 barred the products of convict labor from the open market, thereby silencing one of the workingman's chief complaints; night work by children under 16 years of age and the employment of children under 14 was also prohibited that year. An Occupational Disease Act was passed in 1911. The Illinois Mining Code, revised in 1879 and 1899, was given teeth in 1911 when inspectors were empowered to shut down the mines of operators who repeatedly failed to comply with safety regulations. The Workmen's Compensation Act became law in 1913. The use of injunctions to restrain peaceful picketing was prohibited in 1925. By an amendment of 1929, State certification was required for the employment of children over 14 and under 16 years of age. A minimum wage law for minors and women was enacted in 1933; three years later the working day of women, with the exception of nurses, cannery workers, and telephone and switchboard operators, was limited to eight hours.

The strongest union organizer of this period was John L. Lewis, an Illinois miner who had acquired a firm hold on District 12, the Illinois section of the United Mine Workers of America, and became president of the latter. By his ability to get concessions from the Peabody Coal Company he managed to offset the attempts of the Progressive Miners of America to control the field. In 1935 Lewis extended his campaign to organize industrial workers and by forming the Committee for Industrial Organization with the help of the Amalgamated Clothing Workers, the International Ladies Garment Workers and other groups forged a powerful spearhead for unionizing workers elsewhere, especially in the steel mills of South Chicago and Northern Indiana. In two years the Carnegie-Illinois Steel Co. of U. S. Steel signed a contract with the CIO giving workers benefits such as the 40-hour week and vacations with pay, and other mills followed suit.

Fansteel Manufacturing Co. of North Chicago resisted the demands of the workers, who staged a sitdown strike in February, 1937. With heat cut off the strikers capitulated after nine days. The company discharged the leading strikers and when ordered by the National Labor Relations Board to rehire them let the issue be carried to the United States Supreme Court, which upheld the company.

Republic Steel in South Chicago also resisted the unionization in the spring of 1937, and the steel workers called a strike May 27, 1937. Mayor Kelly of Chicago limited the pickets to 10 men at the main gate, all others to remain two blocks away. On Memorial Day the strikers disregarded the mayor's instructions and started a march across fields to the plant. They were met by Chicago police with a barrage of bullets and tear gas and 10 strikers were killed. In the uproar that followed the police were exonerated by a coroner's jury, but pictures taken by a newsreel camera showed the police attacking unarmed men and caused the LaFollette Civil Liberties Committee of the U. S. Senate to denounce the action.

Representatives of four railway operating unions met in Chicago Dec. 10, 1968, to form the United Transportation Union of 280,000 members, effective Jan. 1, 1969. They announced that "the shrinking railroad industry no longer makes it possible for the traditional individual union to meet demands of the times." The merging unions were the Brotherhood of Railway Trainmen, 185,000; the Brotherhood of Locomotive Firemen and Enginemen, 69,750; the Order of Railway Conductors and Brakemen, 13,700; and the Switchmens Union of North America, 12,000. The Brotherhood of Locomotive Engineers declined to join.

The Illinois Department of Labor, which has its main office in Springfield and a large office in Chicago is responsible for the enforcement of laws affecting the welfare of the State's work force of approx. 5,000,000 workers. It administers laws of occupational safety and health, wage payment and wage collections, regulation of private employment agencies, intrastate conciliation and mediation, the six-day week law and the eight-hour day for women, child labor, industrial home work and the minimum wage. Through the Bureau of Employment Security the Department administers programs founded by the U. S. Government, including unemployment insurance, and job placements as part of the State Employment Service and the Manpower Training Program. In helping workers to collect wages it increased its limit on amounts to $1,000.

The total number of non-agricultural wage and salaried employees in Illinois averaged 4,281,000 in fiscal 1972 and 4,322,500 in 1973. Not subject to the Division of Safety Inspection are employees of the Federal Government (109,800), local government (409,300), interstate railroads (54,900), and coal mining (10,100), so that the Division is actually responsible for 3,697,700 employees.

The minimum hourly wage in 1971 was $1.40 for those 18 years old and over; and $1.15 for those under 18. In 1973 the minimum wage for those 18 and over was $1.60, for those under 18, $1.25.

Safety of construction workers is also a responsibility of the State Department of Labor under the law. Construction is a $4 billion industry in Illinois, Chicago accounting for more than one-half. During a typical year, 1971, 844,566 permits for residential housekeeping units were issued.

When the state first began to enact laws against discrimination in employment it specified only discrimination because of race. The Fair Employment Practices act has been amended since to prohibit discrimination between employees on the basis of race, color, religion, sex, national origin or ancestry, and paying less for these reasons for substantially equal or similar work.

About 900,000 women are regularly employed in Illinois. They are protected against discrimination in employment by a minimum wage law, which specifies: "No employer shall discriminate between employees on the basis of sex by paying lower wages to employees of the opposite sex for the same or substantially similar work on jobs the performance of which requires equal skill, effort, and responsibility, and which are performed under similar working conditions, except where such payment is made pursuant to (1) a seniority system; (2) a merit system; (3) a system which measures earnings by quantity or quality of product; or (4) a differential based on any other fact or other than sex."

The State's first flat minimum wage law was enacted in 1971. Beginning in 1972 workers 19 years old and older were paid a minimum of $1.40 an hr., and those under 19, $1.15. Beginning in 1973 workers over 19 received $1.60; under 19, $1.25. The 1973 Legisture increased rates to $1.75 an hour for adult employees and $1.40 an hr. for those under 18, effective 1974. Higher minimum wage rates up to $2.10 were voted effective in 1976. Unemployment compensation has been liberalized; weekly benefits run from $60 for an individual with no family obligations to $105 for one with four or more dependent children. The maximum amount of wages subject to a tax is $4,200.

Wages and fringe benefits are the main issues in labor-management disputes that reach the Conciliation and Mediation Services of the Labor Department. Mutual agreements are worked out by the collective bargaining process, with the Service helping when needed. Disputes have tapered down in the last decade, remaining in the 700-800 bracket; 25% occur in the principal industries, construction and retail trade, and only 1% in transportation.

By the start of the 1970-1980 decade the Labor Department was making special efforts, through a number of bureaus and divisions to connect the unemployed with jobs and answer the specific demands of employers. In mid-1972 there were an estimated 5,133,300 persons in the Illinois work force, of whom 249,000, or 4.9% were unemployed. The agricultural work force was down to 159,000, showing not only the shift to other occupations but the effect of mechanization on manpower. The Chicago metropolitan area had 3,350,000, with 155,000 or 4.5% unemployed; Peoria-Pekin had 158,075, with 10,100 or 6.4% unemployed; Moline-Rock Island-Davenport had 159,325, with 8,785 or 5.5% unemployed; Rockford, 126,725, with 6,550, or 5.2% unemployed; East St. Louis, 182,650, with 15,275 or 8.4% unemployed. The average jobless rate in Illinois at this time was 4.7%, whereas the national rate was 5.8%.

The Illinois State Employment Service has a staff in which all races are represented; its chief function is placement of workers with employers, but it also is engaged in counseling, testing, training, job analysis and applying State laws and Presidential directives. Almost $600,000 per month has been saved in welfare costs by transfering recipients of aid to families with dependent children to jobs. The Work Incentive Program provides opportunities for training. The Federal Emergency Employment Act provides subsidized employment in State, county and municipal governments such as hospitals. The Service also administers the Model Cities Program and the Concentrated Employment Program, which applies to disadvantaged persons in depressed areas.

The Employment Service cooperated with the Illinois Department of Public Aid in applying the Food Stamp Program. This program was begun in 1964, and in 1972 the Service applied the work requirement provisions, which require able-bodied members of a household to register for employment. The manpower Development and Training Program provides institutional training; the Federal Government pays 90% of the cost and the State pays 10%. A trainee in a school gets an allowance; the employer of the on-the-job trainee is reimbursed for special costs. The Service noted that the big increase in institutional trainees, 50% in 1972, was attributed to Vietnam veterans. During fiscal 1972 more than $15,000,000 was paid out in these training programs in Illinois, and since the program began in 1963 nearly $16,000,000 had been paid out at that time. Nearly one-third of those in training elected health services, such as practical nursing. English as a second language was available to Spanish-speaking persons.

Veteran Job Fairs are devices for helping veterans find employment. The recruiting of veterans by big and little corporations goes on at widely publicized events. The Chicago job fair of May 9-10, 1972, was held in the Chicago Amphitheatre and resulted in 4,000 men being placed in jobs. Rehabilitation and placement of disabled and handicapped veterans are part of the program. There is an Older Worker Program, which includes vocational training, and a program for youths 21 years old and younger. A new element was added to the youth employment program when approximately 20,000 were Vietnam veterans. The Employment Service provides for counseling and training in correctional institutions for prisoners about to be released or paroled.

The Federal Labor Department announced Oct. 10, 1972, that nine building contractors and 15 building trades unions of Chicago had agreed to yearly goals for hiring 9,820 workers of minority races by 1976. The Manpower Administration of the Labor Dept. had allocated $1,700,000 to the Chicago Urban League for operating a training program for the unskilled. Contractors who did not join the agreement were to be denied Federal contracts.

Education: Public Schools and Libraries

ILLINOIS has been a major objective of massive immigrations for nearly 200 years. This means that the public school system, largely Anglican in its beginnings, has had to absorb large cultural accessions from foreign lands, first from northern Europe, then from the Mediterranean areas, then from eastern European states, and finally from Spanish-speaking areas. Foreign cultures often have been given recognition; there have been special courses in German, Polish, and Bohemian (Czech), in Illinois schools. But the elasticity of American schools, and the desire of immigrants to conform, have contributed to the viability of the American system, which remains uniform in all parts of the United States.

Illinois schools and libraries expected to operate with smaller budgets when the U. S. Dept. of Health, Education & Welfare in 1973 impounded funds voted by Congress. The State joined nine other states in contesting the action in the U. S. District Court in Washington, D. C. The court held for the states in November, a decision which, if sustained, returns $17,000,000 to Illinois alone.

PUBLIC JUNIOR COLLEGES

Expansion of the junior college system is one of the prime achievements of public education in Illinois. The junior colleges open opportunities for students on full-time and half-time bases, offering academic courses that can lead to transfer to four-year colleges and universities, and occupational subjects for students who need technical skills. The usefulness of the vocational courses is shown by the enrollment, 60 percent of the total.

The junior colleges are the responsibility of the Illinois Junior College Board of Springfield. There are 38 public college districts with 47 campuses in operation (1973). The number of students enrolling is around 200,000. The colleges are governed by a local board of trustees in cooperation with the Springfield board. In order to make courses easily accessible the colleges conduct courses evenings and Saturdays for students employed during the day. Studies that can be continued in four-year colleges include agriculture, architecture, biological and physical science, business and management, communications, engineering, fine and applied arts, foreign languages, and health professions. Courses of occupational use, preparing the student for employment, include accounting, office management, data processing, nursing, dental assistance, physical therapy, mechanical techniques in aviation, electronics, automobiling, welding, forestry, sanitation, and public service skills. The college makes provision for adult and continuing education.

The seven City Colleges of Chicago are a part of the public junior college system. There are three Illinois Eastern Junior Colleges, at Robinson, Olney, and Mt. Carmel, and two Black Hawk District Colleges, at Moline and Kewanee. Operating revenue in the fiscal year 1971 was $133,844,859; local taxes provide 46.62%; state funds, 35.60%; Federal funds, 2.24%; student tuition, 13.74%, other sources, 1.80%.

DESEGREGATION

For more than a decade the principal issue in the public school system of Illinois has been bringing together the various ethnic elements in a common educational effort. While the bulk of the State has instituted desegregation of the public schools, there remains strong sentiment against busing children from their own neighborhoods to achieve integration. The reluctance of many communities to change ingrained ways of living has slowed the national programs, but the threat of court action and promise of fiscal aid from the Federal Government to school districts have helped to bring about compliance.

In November, 1971, Michael J. Bakalis, State Superintendent of Public Instruction, asked for immediate steps to desegregate schools in accordance with the decision of the United States Supreme Court of 1954 and the Illinois Armstrong Act of 1963, which asked desegregation "as soon as possible." Before publishing his guide lines, or Action Goals, Supt. Bakalis initiated a public discussion of the issues, calling six regional public hearings, following this with the Chicago Conference, which drafted objectives for reform and legislation.

Despite these appeals, desegregation remained a slow process. As late as the spring of 1973 a bitter controversy was waged in Rockford, where white parents objected violently to the forced busing of their children to schools outside of their own neighborhoods. Supt. Bakalis warned the citizens of Rockford that they had no choice; while it was hoped they would find a reasonable solution voluntarily, communities had no option to choose between segregated and nonsegregated schools, because "the legal right to a nonsegregated education has been firmly established in this country." It is the responsibility of the school boards, not parents, says he, to insure that students are assigned to schools in a non-discriminatory manner. In his annual State of Education Message in 1973 Bakalis said: "Desegregation of Illinois schools has met with varying degrees of success. In Chicago racial segregation in the schools has increased. The number of all-black schools has increased and proportionately more white students are attending mostly white high schools. Park Forest, on the other hand, has shown what can be done. The school board of that community has exhibited a deep sense of responsibility and has involved the total community in the development of a desegregation plan—a plan which is working and has earned general community support."

Supt. Bakalis wrote: "Many of our classrooms in this State are more racially and culturally isolated than those in the deep South. The number of minority students attending all-minority schools in Illinois is on the increase, not decrease. Just three years ago (1970) one of seven black students in Illinois attended a predominantly white school, while one of four did so in Mississippi. More than one in three black students in Illinois attend an all-black school, while in Mississippi the ratio is one in ten. Illinois and Michigan have the dubious distinction among the 50 states of having the highest percentage of minority students attending segregated schools. And this racial separation in our schools is not limited to just Cook County, but exists in many of the State's large metropolitan areas." *Illinois Education News, March, 1973.*

Elementary School District 130 of Blue Island was one of the first to be guided by the State Superintendent's Action Goals. To help overcome racial segregation the district set aside special days for parents from schools dominated by one race to visit schools of the other race; recruited teachers to reflect the racial mix of the district; planned field trips and outdoor recreation between districts to bring different races toegther in activities; developed interracial choral groups and PTA fund drives.

After School District II of Kankakee was warned by the U. S. Dept. of Health, Education & Welfare that it must desegregate its schools or face a compliance order the district reorganized and today asserts it has a racially balanced system. A 20 percent increase in pupil transportation was necessary. Teachers were reassigned and black teachers were recruited. Musical productions and athletic contests became biracial. Community participation was encouraged.

The successful plan for desegregation in Park Forest was carried out in the Beacon Hill section, where nine elementary schools were reorganized so that four became centers for primary grades 1-3, and five for intermediate grades, 4-6.

BILINGUAL EDUCATION

Recognition of the diverse ethnic elements in American culture has been strongly emphasized since the agitations of the 1960s. The Illinois Office of Public Instruction has a Bilingual-Migrant Section that encourages study of the cultural contribution of ethnic groups, primarily Spanish-speaking Mexican-Americans, who are encouraged to use two languages freely. The Illinois office has initiated programs for the study of ethnic influences by elementary and secondary schools and colleges in order to benefit under the 1972 amendment to the Federal Education Act, which authorizes the U. S. Commissioner of Education to grant aid to public and private institutions that develop ethnic heritage studies.

One of the major problems of public education is providing for the Spanish-speaking people of Illinois, who number more than 500,000. The drop-out rate is 70% and many pupils "are functionally illiterate in both English and Spanish." There are not enough bilingual teachers and almost no bilingual counselors, social workers, or school psychologists. Parents often prefer to have their children employed than to use time to get a high school diploma. An effort is being made with the cooperation of the Illinois Migrant Council, the Spanish-speaking Peoples Commission and other groups to provide for needs on a bilingual basis. Another objective is to open State colleges to at least 50 Latin-American high school graduates or dropouts who do not have academic credits, and also to provide counseling, tutoring, and other aid.

State aid for bilingual language programs was increased in 1972 to $2,370,000, of which $1,400,000 was allocated to Chicago schools and $970,000 to downstate schools. This was a rise from the appropriation of $850,000 in 1971. The program is directed to Spanish-speaking students, Puerto Rican and Mexican, of whom there are more than 100,000. Illinois educators agitated to receive a larger slice of Federal aid before curtailment of national appropriations went into effect. Under the pre-1973 allotment Illinois received $2.50 per Spanish-speaking students whereas Pennyvania, with about 15,000 students, received $41.55 per student.

Since 1968 Illinois has kept a record of the schoolwork of migrant children as part of a national program under the Elementary and Secondary Education Act. When such children move from one school to another the Record Transfer System makes the child's education continuous. Special attention is given to the child's health and nutritional and psychological needs. Older students move toward vocational training. There are 29 schools in Illinois with special programs for migrant children, one of the most successful in Princeville, near Peoria, which offers an eight-week summer program from 8:30 a.m. to 2:30 p.m.

FINANCING

The State and Federal Governments combine to finance continuing education. The State provided $7,500,000 in 1972 to pay for the education of recipients of public assistance. There are special classes for adults and youth whose schooling has been interrupted. Provision is made to pay persons who teach special programs, such as those for the hard-of-hearing and blind or partially sighted pupils. The State allocated $1,500,000 for Americanization and general educational development. The adult basic education programs under the Federal Act of 1969 were financed from a grant of $2,271,708. Curtailment of some of the Federal aid will necessitate adjustment of expenditures for specific objectives in the school system.

Federal aid to education comes in the form of grants for specific purposes. Thus Eastern Illinois University of Charleston received $255,893 to develop teaching plans and materials for "integrating the concepts of career development with subjects taught at kindergarten and lower grade levels, including language arts, mathematics, science and social studies." The program calls for testing at the Buzzard Laboratory school at Eastern, in four Illinois school systems, and one out-of-state having Mexican-American or American Indian students.

State and local appropriations for the public schools increased every year from 1966-67 through 1971; State aid went up from $368,600 to $1,059,700, or 187 percent, while local aid rose from $1,014,100 to $1,732,100, a rise of 71 percent. State appropriations for schools are around one-third of the total appropriations; in 1972 the slice for education was lower, at 31.9 percent, whereas highways and airways received 25.7 percent, and health and welfare, 30.6 percent.

Changes in financing education in Illinois have been proposed in recent years to meet the objections of property owners who consider the present tax inequitable. The finance task force of the Governor's Commission on Schools recommended that part of the school tax on property owners be shifted to the State. The chief objection to the tax is that it makes the quality of the schooling depend on the wealth of the district, when it should depend on the wealth of the State as a whole. State support of public schools covers about 38 percent of what is needed. The Federal Court in Illinois decided the State had no constitutional duty to attempt to equalize education for the slums and the suburbs. The U. S. Supreme Court made a decision with a similar effect.

To obtain State aid every public school must provide certain programs demanded by the State legislature. They include: *Lunch* for any child classified as needy; *physical examination and immunization* against measles, smallpox, polio; instruction about *narcotics and alcohol; consumer education,* grades 8-12, how to buy and use one's personal resources; *conservation* of natural resources, wildlife, care of pets; *civic responsibility,* principles of representative government, voting, history; *driver training,* grades 9-12, obligatory for license, 15-18; *transportation* for every child living 1½ miles from the school; *bilingual instructions* in schools with 10% or more students from homes where English is not spoken, and special facilities and programs for each *handicapped* child.

The State of Illinois makes special provision for the education of the handicapped, for adults and youths whose schooling has been interrupted, for deaf children, gifted children, and others who need help. About 60,000 children are handicapped in various ways and need special education. Programs for continuing education have been made available to inmates of State correctional institutions. Adult education is considered a prime necessity. About 500,000 citizens take part in courses of private business and vocational schools.

The importance of proper driving on the highways is recognized by the State, which has a schedule for reimbursement of school districts that teach driving. For the pupil who completes the classroom instruction the State pays $10; for the pupil who completes practice driving, up to $40. In 1972 the districts were paid $8,200,000 for this special course.

ENROLLMENT

In the ten years from 1962 to 1972, total public school enrollment in Illinois increased from 1,889,657 to 2,373,776. In the elementary classification attendance rose from 1,391,776 to 1,678,517; in the secondary schools it rose from 497,881 to 695,259. The State office made the following comment in 1973: "Indications are that in 1970-71 primary enrollment peaked at 1,684,132 and will decline to less than 1,600,000 by 1976-77. Secondary level enrollment, on the other hand, will peak in 1976-77 at 778,130 and will follow the decline in elementary enrollments."

Enrollment of pupils in independent, private, and parochial schools has been descreasing. In the 1967-68 fiscal year, for instance, enrollment in nonpublic schools dropped from 558,196 to 440,000. Cost of operation and higher tuition charges have been among the causes.

The Office of Superintendent of Public Instruction has three locations: the State Office Building, Springfield, 188 W. Randolph St., Chicago, and the Southern Illinois Office, Mt. Vernon, Jefferson County. In order to disseminate information about educational programs and methods the Community Relations unit of the Office of Public Instruction uses two vans stocked with publications, visiting schools, shopping centers and other places where they can be useful.

LIBRARIES AND LIBRARY SYSTEMS

For the public libraries of the State the 20 years between 1950 and 1970 have been a period of tremendous expansion. With funds made available by the Federal Government and the State, the libraries were able to do a major job of rebuilding and rehabilitation. The installation of library systems enabled local libraries to draw on the reservoirs of books in their areas. There was money available for bookmobiles, which enlarged the radius of communication; pilot programs to test public response at specific locations, and special services, such as the audiovisual, motion picture and microfilm processes. Illinois libraries are supported by a tax levied on the real property within the taxing area. A levy of .15 percent of the fair value of all taxable property in the area as equalized or assessed is permitted without a referendum. By referendum the levy may be raised to as much as .40 percent (Act of 1970).

In numbers of libraries and books Illinois ranks with the five top states. Numbers are important, for they indicate the extent of organization for reference purposes, but specialization shows the fields of professional usefulness. From the home base of the American Library Assn. in Huron Street, Chicago, the vibrations of energy go forth to the libraries of the nation. This helps not only the librarian's traditional task but spreads a spirit of inquiry and watchfulness to help the free action of the mind. The ALA has made itself the guardian of access to free expression guaranteed by the United States Constitution.

At the start of 1973 there were 510 public libraries in Illinois, 490 (96%) of them members of the 18 library systems. Twenty eligible libraries were not members of a system, these including Aurora, Cicero, Collinsville, Highland Park, LaSalle, Mattoon, and Streator. There also were 22 association and endowed libraries that could not enter a public system because they were not tax-supported. In 1972 the libraries of Illinois had more than 3,000,000 registered borrowers, more than 17,000,000 books, received 46,000 different periodicals, had 43,000,000 transactions, had $44,600,000 in receipts, paid $5,311,000 for printed materials (chiefly books) and paid $23,900,000 in wages and salaries.

The ILLINOIS STATE LIBRARY, located in the Centennial Building, Springfield stands at the head of the public libraries of the State. The secretary of state is State Librarian and the library has a director, an advisory committee of professionals and citizens, and an editor for its publication, *Illinois Libraries*. The library has the responsibility of extending the usefulness of established libraries and assisting in the organization of new centers to bring library services to the 2,000,000 residents of Illinois who do not have tax-supported libraries. The library serves the needs of officials of the State government, administers the Illinois Library System Act, allocates Federal funds, coordinates the resources of public, academic, school, and special libraries, and develops information centers. In 1972 it had a stock of 555,027 volumes, 690,720 Federal documents, and 70,000 State documents. Plans for a separate building were in the making.

The State Library has specific duties to perform for the General Assembly. It looks up information on any question asked by a member of the Assembly. If the member telephones his wants, the library will deliver the material needed as quickly as it is located and pick up used items on a twice-a-day schedule. Court decisions, legislative history of bills, legislation of other states, innumerable reports and articles are provided; if they are not available in Illinois the library has access to the book stocks of other states. The library issues a *Legislative Information Bulletin* listing new publications and has a service that catalogues articles in periodicals and provides photocopies as requested.

One of the great reference libraries of the country is the ILLINOIS STATE HISTORICAL LIBRARY, located in the reconstructed Old State Capitol in Springfield. It is administered by the State Historian under direction of a board of three trustees appointed by the Governor. It is incredibly rich in books, newspapers, letters, and documents associated with Illinois personalities and events. A recent count, now exceeded, reported more than 124,000 bound volumes and 3,299,404 manuscripts, among them 1,284 original manuscripts of Abraham Lincoln. In addition to the Lincoln collection, which has as a high point one of the five copies of the Gettysburg Address in Lincoln's handwriting, it has the original manuscript of Edward Everett's address at Gettysburg; extensive material on the Black Hawk War; microfilm files of Illinois newspapers from the earliest times; papers of Illinois Governors, and extensive collections dealing with the Civil War, the Mormon settlement at Nauvoo, and the Negro in Illinois. The *Illinois Blue Book* says the library has "some 600 volumes written by the early travelers in Illinois, several hundred histories of the State, and histories of every county, many towns, their institutions, churches, schools. . . . The map collection begins with those of the early days when information was supplied by explorers and extends to those that include the latest changes made by the State highway department."

The library system of the University of Illinois is larger than that of any state university, and is the third among American universities, exceeded in size only by Harvard and Yale, and fifth among all American libraries. On June 30, 1972, the collections had 7,898,273 items, including 5,479,914 volumes and pamphlets, prints, films, microtexts, manuscripts, music scores, maps, aerial photographs, broadsides, and sound recordings. The items were distributed as follows: Chicago Circle, 1,006,518; Medical Center, Chicago, 223,310; Urbana-Champaign, 6,668,445.

Among college libraries of recent construction the Joseph Regenstein Graduate Library at the University of Chicago and the University Library at Northwestern University in Evanston are the most impressive. The Regenstein, opened in the fall of 1970, has room for 3,500,000 volumes. In design its exterior of heavily scored blocks of limestone is far removed from the neo-Gothic with which the university began its life in 1892, while its internal arrangements embody the most satisfying and tested arrangements for classification and accessibility of books and provision for study. There are ten libraries in the university system. The new University Library of Northwestern University has been built on the James Roscoe Miller campus, which was dredged out of Lake Michigan. It has approx. 1,300,000 volumes and is one of eleven libraries in the university with a total of more than 2,000,000 books.

The John Crerar Library, 35 W. 33d St., Chicago, on the campus of Illinois Institute of Technology, long has been accorded first rank for its scientific reference works. With more than 1,100,000 volumes on its shelves, it is known for the following collections: Senn Medical, Chanute Aeronautics, Du Bois Raymond Psychology, Meisner Physiology, Pribram Bacteriology, Brum History of Medicine, Martin Gynecology, Gurlu Pediatrics. It has the papers of James B. Herrick and Ludwig Hektoen and has been designated the Midwest Regional Medical Library. The library was opened in 1895 with a bequest from John Crerar, a Chicago manufacturer.

The Archive-Library of the American Medical Assn., 535 N. Dearborn St., dates from 1868, has more than 100,000 archival items and 55,000 books, with a large section on the history of medicine.

The Newberry Library of Chicago has rich collections in American history and literature, and by careful administration through many years has acquired rarities in other fields such as printing, Portuguese discovery and colonization, music, and American Indians. *See article under Chicago, North Side.*

The Murray-Green Library of Roosevelt University, although installed only in 1945, already has more than 220,000 volumes, many of them dealing with social, political and labor subjects.

The Chicago Bar Association has one of the largest law libraries in Illinois—145,000 volumes at 29 S. Lake St. The Law School library of Loyola University at 41 E. Pearson St., Chicago, has 53,000 books. The Law Library of De Paul University, 25 East Jackson Blvd. has 57,000 volumes. The American Assn. of Law Libraries has its offices at 53 West Jackson Blvd.

Religious Organizations in Illinois

Missionaries were among the earliest pioneers in what is now Illinois. Father Jacques Marquette, a French Jesuit priest, accompanied Louis Jolliet on his expedition to the Mississippi in 1673. Two years later Marquette established the first mission to spread Christianity among the local Indians. Other missions were subsequently established by other French-Canadian priests at Cahokia and Kaskaskia. Protestantism came after 1763, when the entire country between the Ohio and the Mississippi was lost by France to England. The first Catholic baptism on the present site of Chicago had to wait till 1822, and the first Catholic church in that settlement till 1833. The diocese (now Archdiocese) of Chicago was formed by Pope Gregory XVI in 1843; ten years later the diocese of Quincy, now of Springfield, was established as its offshoot. In 1877 the diocese of Peoria was organized; in 1887 the diocese of Belleville and in 1908 the diocese of Rockford. Other diocesan organizations are Joliet and St. Nicholas-Ukrainian, Chicago.

According to the *Official Catholic Directory for 1973* the Chicago diocese is the largest in Illinois with 2,489,320 communicants in Cook and Lake Counties. Chicago had six colleges and universities with 27,377 students; Catholic students in all schools, parochial or public, numbered 425,077; 24 hospitals had 8,552 beds and 1,195,303 patients annually, of whom 929,606 were outpatients.

Belleville diocese had 26,000 Catholics in schools; 8 hospitals with 189,296 patients. Joliet diocese had 77,395 students, 2 hospitals with 149,247 patients and a Catholic population of 323,626. Peoria diocese had 55,434 students, 16 hospitals with 299,608 patients and a Catholic population of 222,608. Rockford had 46,530 students, 4 hospitals with 113,728 patients a year and 207,116 members. St. Nicholas-Ukrainian, Chicago, had 2,228 students and a membership of 20,812.

Although the English brought their Anglican services with them as they supplanted the French and their missionaries in 1763, the first Illinois diocese of the Protestant Episcopal Church was organized as late as 1835. Called the Diocese of Illinois, it included the entire state, but was divided in 1877 to form two more dioceses, those of Quincy and Springfield. In 1884 the original diocese was renamed the Diocese of Chicago. It now comprises the northern third of Illinois.

The earliest Congregational Church was opened at Sandy Creek, Newton, in 1809. By the 1830s there were churches at Batavia, Jacksonville, Peoria, Princeton, and Quincy. When abolition of slavery became a controversial issue Philo Carpenter led a faction opposed to slavery out of the Chicago organization and formed several congregations on an anti-slavery basis. In 1957 the General Council of the Congregational Christian Churches joined the Evangelical and Reformed church in the United Church of Christ. The National Association of Congregational Christian Churches continued to maintain headquarters in Milwaukee.

Lutherans came to Illinois in the 1840s, when the influx of German immigrants started in earnest, and in the 1850s, when Norwegians and Swedes followed these pioneers. The first German Lutheran church in Chicago was built in 1846; the first Norwegian Lutheran parish was formed there in 1848; and the first Swedish Lutheran group met in 1853. Over a period of years the Lutherans of the Missouri Synod built a number of colleges that are still flourishing. They now have 528 churches and 352,243 communicants in Illinois of which 238 churches and 197,301 members are in the Northern Illinois District. Valparaiso University is supported by the Lutheran University Assn. of the Synod. The Lutheran Church in America was organized June 28, 1962, by the American, Augustana, Finnish, and United Evangelical Lutheran Churches. One of the regional offices is located at 327 S. La-Salle St., Chicago. The Lutheran Church in America is the largest of the Lutheran denominations.

The first Methodist in Illinois was Captain Joseph Ogle, who migrated from Virginia in 1785, settling at New Design in what is now Monroe County. In Chicago the Methodists were the earliest religious group to meet for services, though not the first to build a permanent church. The muddy village was the site of a mission in 1828 when a minister arrived from Peoria to head the Fox River Methodist Mission. Chicago's Methodists met with him and his successors for services in a log cabin, a schoolhouse, and a tavern before their first church was erected in 1845. The different Methodist groups have a record of combining to create stronger organizations. In 1939 three large groups, including the southern church, disaffiliated at the time of the Civil War, joined in The Methodist Church. In 1968 this body combined with the Evangelical United Brethren and formed the present United Methodist Church, which enrolls more than 10,500,000 members. Northwestern University, Evanston, was founded by Methodists and supported by the church. The African Methodist Episcopal Church is also well represented in Illinois.

Captain Ogle's son-in-law, James Lemen, also a transplanted Virginian, was the first Baptist in Illinois, settling at New Design in 1786. The first Baptist preacher migrated to Illinois country from Kentucky in 1787. In May 1796 the first Baptist church was established at New Design. By the fall of 1807 there were six Baptist churches in the Illinois part of the Indiana Territory. Chicago's first Baptist church was organized in 1833, followed by the second in 1844, and several more in the 1850s. In 1892 the University of Chicago began under Baptist auspices but the rule that a majority of the board must be Baptists has been relaxed long since. The National Baptist Convention, USA, with a national membership of more than 6,400,000, is strongly represented by a large Negro membership in Chicago and East St. Louis.

The first Presbyterians came to Illinois from South Carolina in 1802. They were a group of Scotch-Irish who settled in Rand County, east of Kaskasia, but the honor of building the first Presbyterian church in Illinois was claimed by the people of White County in 1816. The first Presbyterian sermon was preached in Chicago in 1833, and by mid-century the city had four Presbyterian churches. The largest Presbyterian organization today is the United Presbyterian Church in the USA, the result of several mergers and now having more than 3,000,000 members. The organization has 491 congregations in Illinois, 182,257 members above the age of confirmation, and 756 clergymen.

Many other denominations established churches in Illinois in the 19th century. The emigration of Mormons from Nauvoo did not remove all the followers of Joseph Smith's doctrines. The Reorganized Church of Jesus Christ of Latter-day Saints, with headquarters in Independence, Mo., continued to support congregations in Illinois; later the Utah church became well-established in the State and both support memorials in Nauvoo. The Christian Science Church has numerous congregations in Illinois. There is substantial representation of the Greek Orthodox Church and other Eastern European organizations in South Chicago and other industrial areas in Illinois. Wilmette is headquarters of the Baha'i Faith. Mennonites have church headquarters in Rosemont. Adventists, Jehovah's Witnesses, and other organizations are firmly organized.

According to the seventh edition of the *Directory of American Jewish Organizations* there were 299,355 orthodox and reformed Jews in Illinois in 1970; 285,000 in Chicago, 3,000 in Rock Island, 1,800 in Peoria, 1,400 in Springfield, and 1,000 in Champaign. There is an orthodox synagogue at 16 S. Clark St. in the Chicago Loop. Temple Sholem, 3480 Lake Shore Dr., has the largest reform congregation, 2,189, and Temple Emmanuel, 5959 N. Sheridan Road is next with 900. There are large congregations in the North Shore cities of Skokie and Waukegan.

National offices of ten religious organizations are located in Illinois, most of them in the Chicago area. They are: National Spiritual Assembly (Baha'i Faith), Wilmette; Conservative Baptist Assn. of America, Wheaton; Baptist General Conference, Evanston; North American Baptist General Conference, Forest Park; Church of the Brethren, Elgin; Independent Fundamental Churches of America, Westchester; Mennonite Church, Rosemont; General Assn. of Regular Baptist Churches, Des Plaines; Serbian Eastern Orthodox Church, Libertyville; Serbian Eastern Orthodox Church in U. S. and Canada, Midwest Diocese, Chicago.

Houses and Towers

ILLINOIS is the focal point for an understanding of the modern architecture of the western world. Actually Chicago is the laboratory, for it has led in solving the problems generated by building skyward. Here construction changed from brick to steel, and the steel skeleton provided opportunities for utilizing space up to and beyond 1,000 feet above ground level, eventually leading to the construction of the world's tallest commercial building.

Before that time Chicago, like the rest of the western world, had built variations of French Renaissance and English Gothic, and architects with diplomas from Paris had filled Illinois with columns and pediments, broad staircases and marble entablatures, domes and cupolas.

The fourth Vandalia Capitol, built in 1836 and now restored as the Courthouse, was an echo of the Federal style. The first Capitol at Springfield, lately restored and rebuilt to its original condition, was a successful use of Graeco-Roman design in native limestone. When John H. Van Osdel dug up the blueprints he had buried in the light of burning Chicago, his duplicates of pre-fire structures offered no innovations in design. The Cook County Courthouse, sharing a city block with the City Hall, was typical of the French mode—small columns and large ones, walls that advanced and drew back with ledges for pigeon roosts. But in the 1890s there came a clamor for more stories, taller buildings, served by elevators, and architects began to see that hanging pillars on the sides of buildings was justified neither by appearance nor by use.

The early settlers of Illinois built with the materials at hand. Log cabins provided the first shelter. These the French inhabitants built with the logs vertical, as can be seen in Cahokia, while the English placed their logs horizontally, notching them at the corners and chinking the cracks with clay and straw. Throughout the early history of the State log structures served as houses, barns, schools, churches, and taverns. As soon as the settlers could get sawed lumber they began to build frame houses. One of the first of the chain of innovations that came out of Illinois was the balloon frame, so called because of its lightness and strength. Applied by George W. Snow in Chicago in 1832, this method, still in use, replaced heavy braced frames of large timbers by lighter studding closely spaced and held together by sheathing under the clapboards. These frame houses were built in the Greek Revival style then popular in the East and South. The more pretentious houses had porticos, but even the humblest had Greek characteristics in their cornices, doorways, and molding profiles.

Most of Chicago before the Civil War followed the prevailing mode, judging from contemporary prints and from the Henry B. Clarke house at 4526 S. Wabash Avenue, which survived the Great Fire. Records show that the first Chicago courthouse, built in 1830, had a Doric portico above a basement story of brick.

In the settlements along the Mississippi are found building types brought up from New Orleans. Typical of these is the Pierre Menard house near Kaskaskia. It is low and broad, of one story with the attic lighted by dormers and the roof sweeping out over a columned porch the entire length of the house. The New Orleans influence persisted and cast-iron porches and balconies were found in Cairo, Galena, Alton, and Shawneetown.

In 1893 the World's Columbian Exposition in Chicago generated a tremendous influence on regional architecture. It elevated the classical mode for formal structures to new heights and thereby displaced the movement toward the heavy granite blocks of the Romanesque, and obscured the budding development of a truly native style. Daniel H. Burnham, Chief of Construction, called a conference of architects East and West, and distributed the task of building the Fair among them. From the East came McKim, Mead & White, Richard M. Hunt, Peabody & Stearns, and Charles W. Atwood, the last responsible for the Palace of the Fine Arts that today, in reconstructed form, houses the Museum of Science and Industry. Burnham's partner, John Root, started the task with him, but died before the Fair opened. Solon H. Beman, Henry Ives Cobb, Louis H. Sullivan, and Dankmar Adler were among the Chicago architects enrolled. When Burnham decided to follow the classical mode in the Fair he did so over the protests of Sullivan, Adler, Frank Lloyd Wright and their associates, who saw the Fair as an opportunity to break with imitation of architecture of the past, "The damage wrought by the World's Fair will last for half a century, if not longer," said Sullivan. It proved, however, only a setback, for the conditions of building in the coming era made their own rules.

The main exhibition halls of the Fair followed Graeco-Roman designs. The long stretches of columns, pilasters and arches, in blazing white, produced an awe-inspiring effect. The Romans never had achieved such magnitude. The capacity of the great halls of exhibits was exceptional: the Manufacturers' Building covered nearly 32 acres; its roof was supported by trusses with a span of 382 ft., 212 ft. high, and whole houses could be placed inside. While the basic design was formal and columnar, there were variations by individual architects, but they blended harmoniously into the general scheme.

Only one building departed radically from the official pattern: the big Transportation Building, which had been assigned to Sullivan. It did not break the skyline, but its golden door of recessive arches set in a square frame entranced all viewers. Beyond a few Saracenic kiosks near the door, the building was unornamented, making up in glowing colors for its plain facade.

Sullivan's chief contribution to architecture lay in his all embracing philosophy of design. To reduce it to the formula "form follows function" is to overlook the emotional and spiritual qualities that he ascribed to architecture. He wanted a living, democratic, American way of building, based on the laws of nature, and disregarding the forms of the past. His tall buildings before and after the Fair embody these principles. First came the Wainwright building in St. Louis, then the Schiller Theatre, later Garrick, and the Stock Exchange in Chicago, all strongly vertical in feeling. The Carson, Pirie Scott store he treated in a horizontal pattern, with widely spaced windows.

In the spring of 1887 a young man less than 18 years old arrived from the farmlands of Wisconsin to seek a job in an architect's office. He was Frank Lloyd Wright, who was to leave his mark indelibly on Chicago and the world. He found a job at $8 a week and then landed another at $25 in the office of Louis H. Sullivan, who wanted a man to work on drawings for the new Auditorium. It was a moment of destiny; the meeting of the man and the hour.

Dankmar Adler and Louis H. Sullivan were about to acquire prestige by building the famous Auditorium, which they designed in 1887 and completed in 1892. This huge structure, fronting on Michigan Avenue, Congress Street and Wabash Avenue, combined a great theater with a hotel. Its chief contribution to architecture was the solution of certain technical problems. One was providing a foundation for the tremendous weight of the building before the days of caissons that go down to bedrock. The architects devised a wide platform of steel rails and concrete, and supported the extra weight of the tower separately from that of the adjacent walls. In the interior Adler produced what is considered an acoustically perfect theater, while Sullivan gave it rich plastic and mural decorations, which may be seen today in all their splendor. The windows followed the new trends for width, but the exterior showed a Romanesque influence.

Frank Lloyd Wright first made his reputation in the residential field. Departing radically from previous styles, his houses had lowpitched or flat roofs with widely projecting eaves and windows arranged in bands. By these devices Wright sought to make his houses appear to grow out of the prairie. Immediately the public spoke of his prairie style, and welcomed it as a change from adaptions of foreign styles. But there was a principle underlying Wright's designs which proved to be more important than the more obvious external appearance. He objected to the current practice of regarding rooms as separate cubicles to be assembled into a house. His plans became more open; rooms had less definite limits; the outdoor and indoor spaces flowed into each other in a more intimate way.

Wright experimented widely with new ideas in construction. Some he adapted from engineering practice for residential use, and some he himself developed. Many since have come into general use. Two examples are hollow walls of precast patterned concrete blocks, reinforced horizontally and vertically; and his method of supporting floors by the cantilever rather than the wall-to-wall principle.

Frank Lloyd Wright argued ceaselessly against the uses of foreign styles by architects. He said: "The practices behind even our best efforts are foreign. They belong to 'the Renaissance,' the setting sun of art all Europe mistook for dawn. This sudden thing, the Renaissance, has had the upper hand of art, has betrayed the artist. Let us be done with it forever."

Wright's suburban dwellings are visible in Oak Park, River Forest, Wilmette and Libertyville, and tours from Chicago include Oak Park.

Even during the Greek Revival period the Gothic style was often used for church buildings such as the Second Presbyterian Church in Chicago by James Renwick and Bishop Chase's Jubilee College near Peoria. But later it was developed into what was called castellated Gothic, exemplified by the Chicago Water Tower and the Potter Palmer mansion of Cobb and Frost.

In the period of tremendous expansion following the Civil War and especially after the Great Fire in Chicago there evolved a striving for grandiose formality, expressing itself in distorted imitations of styles then popular in Europe. Industrialists with newly amassed fortunes outdid each other in tasteless displays of extravagance. Today this work is labeled Victorian, but in reality it falls into two main classes: the neo-Gothic and one similar to that used in France under Napoleon III. Hallmark of the latter was the mansard roof. This florid version of the late French Renaissance was especially popular for public buildings; the State Capitol at Springfield dates from this period, as do many county courthouses with their heavy brackets and cast-iron domes.

In the 1880s the influence of the Romanesque Revival was added to the prevailing styles, and gradually became the most important. Henry Hobson Richardson, the originator of the movement, designed in a rugged and powerful manner, as may be seen in his one surviving example in Chicago, the Glessner House at 1800 Prairie Avenue. One of his pupils, John Root, almost caught the essence of his master's spirit in the Chicago Club at Michigan Ave. and Van Buren St., but the great host of his imitators missed the spirit and merely copied the form. Crudely picturesque rockfaced facades with low arches and Romanesque carving testify to the popularity of the style, and when tall buildings came they sometimes borrowed from the Romanesque.

While the Romanesque was at its height the revolutionary story of the skyscraper began to unfold one of the most exciting chapters in the history of building. The skyscraper has come to be accepted as America's outstanding contribution to architecture, and it was in Chicago that the technique of the tall building was developed in the two decades after the Great Fire of 1871.

Directly after that disaster fireproofing became a public issue, leading to stricter building regulations and fire laws. In 1872 George H. Johnson built the first fireproof floor of hollow-tile arches between wrought-iron beams in the Kendall building. The cast-iron interior columns to which the beams were bolted were regarded as fireproof because they were incombustible, but experience showed they would yield in the heat of a fire with disastrous results. Columns subsequently were also fireproofed with hollow tile.

The Montauk Block, built in 1882 by Burnham and Root, was the first all-fireproof building and embodied new developments in foundation design as well. This was a serious problem because of the insecure bed of clay underlying Chicago. In a striking innovation Root embedded a crisscross of steel rails in concrete to make a rigid support distributing the load, and this system was used until the development of the caissons in 1893 by Adler and Sullivan in the Stock Exchange building, which remained a part of the Chicago scene until 1972.

The most accomplished exponents of the Gothic style were Cram, Goodhue, and Ferguson, who built the Fourth Presbyterian Church in Chicago. Gradually Goodhue developed a more personal and highly distinctive version of that style, which reached a high point in the Rockefeller Chapel at the University of Chicago. This was followed to some extent by James Gamble Rogers in the Chicago campus of Northwestern University.

In 1922 a Gothic design by Raymond Hood and John Mead Howells of New York won first prize in the world-wide competition of the *Chicago Tribune* for its new building. Here a solution of height and tradition was indicated; the shaft of the building was frankly vertical and the Gothic detail and crown retained the note of traditionalism. The surprise was the second-prize design, the "building that was never built." The work of Eliel Saarinen of Finland, it followed no style but took Sullivan's creed and stated it boldly. It discarded the cornice, stripped ornament away, and frankly exposed its structural plan, relying solely on set-back masses and strong vertical lines. The basic elements in the design were soon widely imitated, and the Gothic and Classic styles were completely discarded thereafter for skyscrapers.

The most conspicuous adaptation of the Gothic style is seen in the original quadrangles of the University of Chicago, begun in 1892, an effort by William Rainey Harper and his associates to convey scholastic reminders of Oxford and Cambridge to the Illinois prairie. The university has gradually moved into modern times and among its recent architects have been Mies van der Rohe and Eero Saarinen.

The basis of skyscraper construction is the underlying steel frame—the bones that carry walls and floors, and have the name of skeleton construction. At the beginning of this period cast-iron columns inside the building carried part of the floor loads, but the walls carried the rest. For low buildings this was practical, until the soaring prices of Chicago real estate made tall buildings an economic necessity and the development of elevators made them a possibility. But in order to carry the weight of the additional upper stories the walls had to be so massive that they took too much space from the ground floor. This can be seen in the 16-story Monadnock Building by Burnham and Root, the last example of this style of construction, where the ground floor walls are

6 feet thick. Its design was admirably simple; ornamentation was renounced and a sharp flare at the roof replaced the traditional cornice.

The first step toward solving problems of height was the building of cast-iron columns into the walls to carry the ends of the floor beams. But in 1885 a more daring and satisfactory solution was achieved by William LeBaron Jenney in the 10-story Home Insurance building. There the outside columns of the two street-front walls and court carried not only the floor loads, but also the wall panels from floor to floor. In the Tacoma Building of 1887 Holabird & Roche found it convenient to fill in the upper wall panels first. With the development of the Bessemer and open-hearth processes, rolled steel gradually displaced wrought and cast-iron, though the latter persisted until 1904. Hydraulic elevators replaced the counter-balance types and local dynamos were sometimes installed to augment the supply of electricity.

Culminating this period was the 22-story Masonic Temple, later renamed the Capitol Building, designed by Burnham & Root in 1892. Highest building in the world at that time, the visitors to the World's Fair the following year gasped at the awe-inspiring height.

Next in importance to the steel frame in skyscraper construction is the Chicago window. This came about by making use of the space between steel piers, either for bays or horizontal windows. Usually there are one wide fixed window in the center and two movable panels at the sides. These bays may be seen on many of the early buildings, but their dimensions vary. The Reliance Building is one of the early examples of a structure of steel and glass bays and it stands conspicuously at 32 N. State St. It was designed in 1890 by John Root and originally consisted of only four stories. The present first story was placed under that structure four years later and the whole was reworked into the present 14-story building with terra cotta trim by D. H. Burnham. A better expression of the Chicago window is to be seen at Louis H. Sullivan's Schlesinger & Mayer store, later Carson, Pirie, Scott & Co. of 1899-1904, and the Sears, Roebuck & Co. retail store, built for Levi Z. Leiter by William Le Baron Jenney in 1891.

An effort to add to the major quasi-public buildings in Chicago was made by Samuel Insull in 1928-29 when he financed a building for the Chicago Opera at 20 Wacker Drive. This was to be the end of opera at the Auditorium, on the ground that the new property would have enough income to finance the opera. The great Auditorium was saved, after hard going, by its adaptation to the uses of a university, and now its theater is fully recognized as a major element in the great advantages of Chicago.

Another building of this decade made more of an architectural impression. This was the Palmolive Bldg., completed in 1929 from a design by Holabird & Root, who adapted the principle of setbacks to the skyscraper. This is now the Playboy Bldg.

The depression of the 1930s put a stop to skyscraper building, but it saw another great Chicago fair, the Century of Progress Exposition of 1933-34. The need for economy dictated a light temporary form of construction and prevented lavishness in design. Intense colors were used instead, which produced an impressive effect until they weathered to pastel shades.

In 1938 there arrived in Chicogo a German architect, Ludwig Mies van der Rohe, whose ideas and initiative were responsible for innovations in the building of skyscrapers. An improvisor with a firm knowledge of materials, he extended the functionalism of the earlier period to new levels and became the most influential architect of his time. In Berlin as early as 1920 he designed the tall steel building entirely sheathed in glass—the curtain wall now used freely in high-rise buildings. He became responsible for some of the milestones of modern building in Chicago, not only those, like the Promonitory Apartments and Crown Hall of Illinois Tech, that are wholly his own, but also the Federal Center, in which he had a hand, the Lake Point Towers, which grew out of a Berlin plan and the numerous other buildings throughout America that architects call Miesian, because they profited by his enterprise.

Mies—as everyone called him—in 1938 became director of architecture in the School of Architecture and Planning of Armour Institute, then quartered in the Art Institute. Two years later Armour merged with Lewis Institute to form Illinois Institute of Technology. When it cleared 120 acres of the worst slums in Chicago, west of Michigan Ave. between 30th and 35th Sts., Mies had an opportunity to design at least twenty new buildings. The result was a triumph in steel and glass, showing an economy of materials, wide interiors free from columns, adjustable partitions to create rooms, roofs suspended from girders and other technical devices. The most arresting structure is Crown Hall, quarters of the School of Architects, Planning & Design, an oblong structure of which Mies said: "I think this is the clearest structure we have done." The roof is suspended from four plate girders spanning 120 ft. and 60 ft. apart. The upper level is 220 by 120 ft. by 19½ ft. high, and is used by the architectural school, a huge room in which Mies once taught and where Myron Goldsmith lectures now. The lower level is used by the Institute of Design, which Laszlo Moholy-Nagy of the Bauhaus had established in the Art Institute in 1937.

There were other notable accomplishments among the new buildings: Alumni Memorial Hall, Perlstein Hall, for chemistry; the Commons, the Electrical and Physics Building, the Institute of Gas Technology, and St. Saviour Chapel, in which Mies went back to brick. His designs may be studied in many other Chicago buildings, especially in high-rise apartments where the curtain wall has been adapted successfully, as at 860 and 880 Lake Shore Drive, and 900 and 910 Esplanade. The breath-taking Lake Point Towers, a huge bronze-tinted structure in cloverleaf form with rounded corners, is reportedly based on a plan Mies once proposed to the city of Berlin, not carried out by him here. There is another collegiate building that Mies designed late in life; the Administration Building of the School of Social Service at the University of Chicago (*see the University*).

Mies van der Rohe did not live to see the Federal Center rise, but the first of three buildings, the United States Courthouse and Federal Office Building was completed in the 1960s. This structure, characteristic of Mies' planning, is a tall rectangle of steel and glass rising 30 stories on the east side of Dearborn St., Jackson to Adams. Opposite, from Dearborn to Clark, where the cruciform United States Postoffice stood for many years, is the space for another Federal office tower, 45 stories tall, and a lower building for the U. S. Postoffice. Continuing architects of the Federal Center are C. F. Murphy Associates, Schmidt, Garden & Erikson, and A. Epstein & Sons.

While Mies van der Rohe and Eliel Saarinen are often mentioned as precursors of the new architecture, groups of professionals who work under the firm names of Skidmore, Owings & Merrill, C. F. Murphy Associates, and half a dozen more, are responsible for Chicago's Second Period. The ideas of the originators are freely acknowledged, but most of their designs, such as Mies' curtain wall, have been absorbed into current practice. Lever House of New York, for instance, the first use of the curtain wall in a commercial structure in America, built by Skidmore, is known as Miesian design, although Mies was not associated with it and there is some indebtedness to Le Corbusier.

Louis Skidmore and Nathaniel Owings became partners in 1936. Skidmore had been engaged as designer of the Century of Progress exposition of 1933. They made John O. Merrill, an engineer, a limited partner in 1939. From then on their commissions have been spectacular and the firm has grown to include numbers of highly efficient professionals and large staffs. They built Oak Ridge, Tenn., for the Government, and the U. S. Air Force Academy at Colorado Springs. With Chicago as their central office, they erected important buildings from New York to San Francisco, and Brussels to Istanbul.

They helped change the face of Chicago. For by the early 1950s big money became available for massive building for the first time in twenty years. The skyscrapers they built embodied the newest techniques and materials, but the designs were not duplicated. It is said in the profession that their success is based on an ability to meet the needs and wishes of the client and still produce an individual design. Their first important Chicago building was the Inland Steel, completed in 1958, a 19-story tower of glass and stainless steel, with a 25-story service tower rising beside it. The firm became responsible for office structures of extraordinary size and height, including the Brunswick Bldg., the Hartford Fire Insurance Co. Bldg., the Harris Trust Co. Bldg., and the Equitable Bldg. Finally they obtained commissions to construct the tallest buildings in the world, the John Hancock Center and the Sears Tower.

In 1969 the John Hancock Center on North Michigan Avenue became the most spectacular object on the Chicago skyline. As seen from the Lake a tall black rhomboid rose above the foliage and towers. Close up it was seen to expose not only the steel columns that were now customary in Chicago construction, but immense braces that tied the house together. Its utility as an investment was conceded, but there have been many reservations about its aesthetic and social values.

The Sears Tower became the tallest in the world at 1,450 feet in 1973. The architectural project was to build on Wacker Drive, in a congested area of Downtown, an office building of 110 stories. It meant the concentration on a narrow spot of more than 30,000 persons, adding to the means of transportation at rush hours and crowding the dining and sanitary facilities of the city. At the time of building one of the architects remarked that with the technical knowledge now at hand it would have been possible to build a tower twice as tall.

The most arresting structure inside the Loop is the First National Bank Building, a demonstration of a wide base from which the steel supports slant inward on two wide fronts. It is 850 ft. tall and rises 60 stories. To erect this building a square block of business houses had to be cleared and a wide plaza had to be provided. The architects were C. F. Murphy Associates, working with the Perkins & Will Partnership. One block north is the new Civic Center, a 31-story office and court building set similarly in the middle of a square block a house of glass and ionized steel, on which C. F. Murphy & Associates worked with Skidmore, Owings & Merrill.

Another example of the freedom to build that makes Chicago an architectural testing ground is Marina City, two identical circular towers for apartments on the north bank of the Chicago River, famous for their scalloped balconies. Here Myron Goldsmith of Skidmore, Owings & Merrill, who had studied and worked with Mies van der Rohe and with Pier Luigi Nervi in Rome, was able to apply his ideas for the use of prestressed concrete and cylindrical cores. In close proximity is the 45-story skyscraper of International Business Machines (IBM), which stands out as a perfect example of the glass curtain facade, the legacy of Mies van der Rohe, here given an auspicious rendering by C. F. Murphy Associates.

The opportunity to design an entire college campus, which came to Mies van der Rohe, also came to Skidmore, Owings & Merrill and several other achitects, when the University of Illinois decided to build at Chicago Circle. The result is possibly the fullest demonstration of the theory that what counts in a college is what goes on inside, not outside the buildings. This latest application of functionalism to architecture makes no claims to mystical significance. The buildings seem more related to factories than to the tradition of academic architecture, which grew out of the ecclesiastical.

There are many other new buildings on Illinois campuses, for the opulent years that brought the rush to build new skyscrapers also opened the purses of the State, the Federal Government, and philanthropic foundations. When the State Legislature authorized the two-year community college many had to construct entirely new quarters. All through Illinois there were major additions to universities, such as the new library on the James Roscoe Miller campus of Northwestern University and the Regenstein Graduate Research Library at the University of

Chicago. New dormitories arose throughout Illinois and began to assume a standardized form; built of concrete and steel, they made generous use of window space, and resembled high-rise apartments more often than collegiate residences.

The frame taverns that once served livestock drovers on Illinois' roads have been succeeded in the course of a century and a half by motels that offer resort facilities. The original clusters of cabins needed no planning, but modern motel chains make use of the newest technical devices for controlling temperature, operating kitchens, and servicing cars. With demands for roomy living quarters in the suburbs of central cities a whole new phase of domestic architecture has developed, from narrow, one-story cottage-garage ranch house types, to terraces of two-story attached houses that have minor variations on the exterior. In larger undertakings in the cities, such as the Carl Sandburg houses in Chicago, the demand for variety is satisfied by placing low townhouses beside high-rise apartment structures. After the supermarkets had demonstrated the advantages of combining individual grocery and variety stores, the mall offered the biggest challenge for economic functional construction that architects had faced in twenty years. Those most successful in design and operation, like the Woodfield Mall at Schaumburg, base their growth on the motor car, good roads and the proximity of well-heeled neighborhoods.

Interest in architectural change has been concentrated on tall towers and residences, but innovations apply as well to industrial plants. The movement of light industry from congested cities to open country has enabled builders to use light and air to better advantage. Long one-story buildings with wide glass panels, standing on landscaped grounds, have become familiar sights outside of Illinois' central cities. In many instances trusses are used to free rooms from interior columns. A new type, infrequently used thus far, is the dome. At Wood River the Union Tank Car Company has a dome that encloses 110,000 sq. ft., is 120 ft. high and 380 ft. in diameter. Using no pillars, it is constructed of hundreds of hexagonal steel panels welded together. At Urbana the University of Illinois has Assembly Hall, the largest edge-supported dome in the world, 40 ft. in diameter, 125 ft. above the floor, used for concerts, opera, ballet, ice shows, basketball and many other activities. Scenery and lights for stage productions are suspended from an electrically controlled grid and up to 16,000 spectators can be seated.

The movement to restore buildings that have some historical or architectural significance has reached a high point in Illinois. The finest example is the rebuilding of the Old State Capitol in Springfield with the use of all original materials that could be salvaged. It is both a museum and a modern office center (*See Springfield*). Wellbuilt mansions of the 19th century, such as the David Davis house in Bloomington and the Rendleman house in Cairo, have been restored and refurnished with original objects as examples of gracious living in other times. In every county historical societies have discovered that the past is prologue.

A number of architectural landmarks have given way to the wrecker in recent years, to be replaced by larger, more profitable structures. One was the Wholesale Building of Marshall Field & Co., which stood like a great stone fort on Wells St., an example of the Romanesque of H. H. Richardson. Although architects lamented its disappearance, few persons knew that it represented a vanished style in American building. The purpose for which it was used—a repository of garments and household articles—hardly justified its massive walls. Another liability was the Garrick Theatre and Office Building on West Randolph St., designed by Louis H. Sullivan and including a proscenium of multiple golden arches that was a forerunner of Sullivan's golden door at the World's Fair in 1893. Attached was a 17-story office tower. The house had been built in 1892 as the Schiller Theatre, honoring the German poet Friedrich Schiller and intended for German repertory. It failed to pay. Renamed the Garrick it housed Broadway musicals, and finally movies. They were numerous protests by newspapers and cultural organizations when it fell, but the ground rent was too valuable for its maintenance. The third loss to architectural history was Sullivan & Adler's Chicago Stock Exchange Building, at LaSalle and W. Washington Sts., demolished in 1972. This well-built structure could have withstood the ravages of many more years, but, here, too, the site had become too valuable for the structure upon it.

Protests against demolition did not save these buildings, but they prompted cultivation of knowledge about Chicago's unique landmarks. The Commission on Chicago Historical and Architectural Landmarks was established in 1962 and is engaged in identifying and publicizing houses and areas. It has adopted a uniform plaque and arranged for ceremonies of installation, to make Chicagoans better acquainted with their notable past. The first landmarks so designated were Charnley House, the Rookery, the gate of the Union Stock Yards, and South Pullman. Also nominated are the Reliance, McClurg, and Monadnock Buildings and the Albert Madlener House. The Mayor's Commission for the Preservation of Chicago's Historic Architecture is another official recognition of local treasures. Tours to the works of famous architects, including the houses designed by Frank Lloyd Wright in Oak Park and River Forest, are now scheduled events. The Chicago School of Architecture Foundation conducts several. A loop tour meets at the Randolph St. entrance of the Chicago Library on Tuesday, Thursday, and Saturday at 10 a.m. and Sunday at 2 p.m., April to October, for a $1 fee. Other information can be had at the Foundation in the Glessner House, 1800 S. Prairie Ave., which is open Tuesday, Thursday, and Saturday, 10-5, Sunday, 1-5.

A plan to save buildings of architectural distinction on sites that have increased greatly in value has been proposed by John J. Costonis of the University of Illinois in *Space Adrift: Landmark Preservation and the Marketplace*. The plan "involves selling the landmark's unused development potential to builders for use on non-landmark sites, thus shifting preservation costs from the city and the landmark owner to the downtown development process itself."

Of the Making of Books

ILLINOIS is one of the great printing and publishing centers of the United States. While the metropolis, by its command of a large work force and many shipping facilities, remains a magnet for big employers, publishers have found out that there are advantages in establishing branches, and often headquarters, in suburbs of adjoining counties. These are preferred by many employees because of walk-to-work advantages in uncongested areas, where living in detached dwellings is possible. Deliveries by trucks reach a five-state area. In the six-county metropolitan area of Chicago publishing houses and book depots have been established in Evanston, Glenview, Homewood, Itasca, Lake Bluff, Naperville, Niles Center, Northfield, River Forest, Skokie, Westchester and Wilmette.

The issue of scholarly works occupies a large segment of publishing in Illinois. The funding of special research and projects by foundations and philanthropies, and at times by the Federal Government, has made possible the printing and distribution of many fine works that otherwise might have remained in manuscript or multigraphed form on the shelves of departmental libraries. Mention of many books so issued is not possible here. There are six university presses in Illinois—at the University of Chicago, the University of Illinois in Urbana, Loyola University in Chicago, Northern Illinois University in De Kalb, Northwestern University in Evanston, and the University of Southern Illinois in Carbondale. The Moody Press is a large undertaking for the religious printings of Dwight L. Moody Institute, and there are intermittent publications from specialized organizations, such as the American Library Association, the World Book Encyclopedia and other projects of Field Enterprises Educational Corp.; Marquis-Who's Who, Inc., the Encyclopedia Britannica, Comptons, and others of national scope.

It can be accepted as a truism that the first books to reach the land that is now Illinois were in French and were carried in the baggage of Father Jacques Marquette in the 17th century. For no priest would have travelled without his breviary. There also was the journal kept by Louis Jolliet, but this was in manuscript and destined to be lost in the waters of the St. Lawrence River, though Jolliet would incorporate his Illinois experiences in a later report. Other books of religious content were brought to Cahokia and Kaskaskia, and it is logical to assume that when Boisbriant arrived to build Fort de Chartres he was fully equipped with French works on military engineering. George Rogers Clark, however, wrote in English, and his report of his famous occupation of Kaskaskia and Vincennes in 1778-79 is Americana.

Henry R. Schoolcraft was an explorer and government official who wrote voluminously about Illinois, Chicago, and the Northwest; he first entered the Chicago River in 1820 with one of the expeditions of Lewis Cass, Governor of Michigan Territory. Cass travelled extensively in the socalled mackinaw boats that employed twelve rowers, and in the bow of his own boat he had a number of books, possibly the first informal "library" in Illinois.

Printing began almost as soon as Illinois became a territory and acquired politicians. Matthew Duncan came from Kentucky and in 1818 started the *Illinois Herald,* later called the *Intelligencer.* The next year he printed the first book, *Laws of the Territory of Illinois,* later known as *Pope's Digest* because it was prepared by Nathaniel Pope, secretary, acting governor, and territorial delegate to the U. S. Congress. One of the earliest writers to describe Illinois enthusiastically was Morris Birbeck, who wrote *Letters from Illinois* in 1818 to help push land sales in Edwards County. As the westward migration grew, New England churchmen came with their bibles and tracts about moral philosophy to found congregations and academies. In 1831 James Hall started the *Illinois Monthly Magazine* in Vandalia. In 1844 Kiler Kent Jones began *The Gem of the Prairie* in Chicago. News has been disseminated since 1835, when the *Illinois Bounty Land Register* regularly published reports about acquisition of land.

One book, written on the banks of the Chicago River, is an important milestone in the literary history of Illinois. It is Juliette Kinzie's *Wau-Bun, the "Early Days" in the Northwest.* Wau-Bun was an Ojibway word meaning early day or dawn; it was fashionable at the time to use an Indian word in a title. As Juliette Magill the author had come to Chicago when her uncle, Alexander Wolcott, of the Connecticut Wolcotts, was Indian agent at Fort Dearborn. Wolcott had married John Kinzie's daughter Ellen, said to have been the first white child born in Chicago. Kinzie's son John Harris Kinzie met Juliette here and married her. In 1844 Juliette published an account of the Fort Dearborn massacre, based on the memories of her mother-in-law, Mrs. John Kinzie. In 1856 she made this the base of *Wau-Bun,* which remains as a complete picture of the pioneer households on the Chicago River.

II

In 1871 Francis Fisher Browne founded the *Lakeside Monthly,* a literary periodical that lasted until 1874. In 1880 he founded the *Dial,* a rallying point for authors for more than 30 years. During his lifetime Browne was a leader of opinion, whose defense of John P. Altgeld was an example of independence and courage. William Morton Payne and Hobart C. Chatfield-Taylor were also leaders of opinion.

Of all the writers taking part in the literary turmoil of the 1890s

Hamlin Garland was the most conspicuous. Wisconsin born, educated in Iowa country schools, Garland had gone to Boston and returned at the time of the World's Fair to find Chicago swarming with literary activity. He decided this was the place to stay and soon became intimate with aspiring young men, including Brand Whitlock, George Ade, Melville Stone, and Lorado Taft. Eugene Field, already famous for his column of Sharps and Flats in *The Daily News* was the celebrity of the hour, whose house was crowded with upstarts and admirers. Field presided at the Amen Corner in McClurg's big bookstore, wrote ironic quips and drew tears from readers of his sentimental poems about children. Garland discovered an author of continental qualities in Henry Blake Fuller, but was out of sympathy with his romantic sauntering in Europe, as disclosed in *The Chevalier of Pensieri-Vani*. For Garland was a messenger for the movement led by William Dean Howells of getting away from Victorian smugness and viewing the richness of American life without illusions, what the period called "veritism." Garland, whose *Main-Traveled Roads* and other stories about farmland had this bucolic aim, wrote in reminiscence: "I went about saying that an aspiring use of local color was of more value than a derivative romance no matter now exquisite. 'We must have fiction as new in design as our skyscrapers,' I repeated, and then quite unexpectedly Fuller took me at my word and published a novel which had the definition of a steel tower wherein all of the characters were connected in one way or another with the newest of our architectural monstrosities" (*The Cliff Dwellers*). When scholars and authors formed The Cliff Dwellers club on the two upper floors of Orchestra Hall, Fuller's wellknown reticence kept him from joining. Garland gave high praise to Fuller's *With the Procession,* which was "cosmopolitan in its technique," a remarkable evocation of Chicago social ways in the 1890s. There is Chicago's artistic life in *Under the Skylights,* in which Fuller shrewdly with ironic humor portrayed the vibrant studio life of the time.

The short career of William Vaughn Moody flowered around the turn of the century. He lectured on English literature at the University of Chicago and won attention for his *Ode in a Time of Hesitation,* in which he expressed strong opposition to the popular Spanish-American War of 1898. He showed promise as a dramatist (*See Theater*) but his early death stilled all hopes. His widow, a woman of great generosity, built a successful career as a caterer, sponsored lectures by poets at Le Petit Gourmet restaurant and offered authors from abroad the shelter of her brick mansion on East 29th St.

An author's view of human affairs is largely subjective and individual, but he does not live in a vacuum and can hardly avoid being affected by the dominant ideas and issues of his time. In the early years of this century muckraking journalists turned a strong light on political and industrial abuses, and this was part of the climate that influenced Frank Norris, Upton Sinclair, Theodore Dreiser, and Robert Herrick. Norris returned to Chicago from his adopted California to complete his trilogy of wheat by incorporating the Leiter financial crash in *The Pit,* but his place in the naturalistic tradition rests on *McTeague*. Upton Sinclair, beginning a career of social crusading, made a national issue out of meat processing at the Chicago Stockyards in *The Jungle* and inspired reform legislation. Robert Herrick, Harvard-trained writer on the University of Chicago faculty, satirized success in *The Memoirs of An American Citizen* and placed the blame for the Haymarket riot on a sick society. Theodore Dreiser came to Chicago from Warsaw, Indiana, in 1887, a 16-year-old lad who needed a job; he washed dishes in a Greek restaurant, worked in a hardware house, and stored up the impressions he used later to write *Sister Carrie* and *Jennie Gerhardt*. In 1892 he had a reporter's job and picked up items at the Democratic National Convention that nominated Cleveland. The newspapers were full of Charles Yerkes' financial shenanigans and Cowperwood of *The Financier* was one result.

An event that helped create an audience for new forms in poetic expression was the establishment in 1912 of *Poetry, a Magazine of Verse,* by Harriet Monroe. Miss Monroe became a personality when she wrote the ode for the opening of the Auditorium in 1887 and a dedicatory ode for the World's Columbian Exposition in 1893, a work with all the earmarks of a formal Victorian address. Twenty years later Miss Monroe was an exponent of expression in poetry—hospitable to free verse, imagism, vorticism, or whatever; giving space to Ezra Pound's iconoclastic epistles from Europe, printing early T. S. Eliot, attracting a new audience for poetry. Associated editorially with her was Alice Corbin Henderson, with whom she collaborated in *The New Poetry; An Anthology of Twentieth Century's Verse,* which, often revised, became a guide to poets and public alike. Another ally of many years was the poet Eunice Tietjens. Miss Monroe asked her friends to support her magazine and they willingly helped; she maintained her policy of the open door, and kept the magazine to its original format, as it is to this day. She died while on a literary tour in South America in 1936. Her autobiography, *A Poet's Life; Seventy Years in a Changing World,* published in 1938, has many pages devoted to the literary activities of her time.

Early in its career the magazine established several annual prizes for poets. The Helen Haire Levinson prize is Poetry's highest honor. Among recipients of the Levinson prize, first awarded in 1914, were these poets of Illinois: Carl Sandburg, Vachel Lindsay, Edgar Lee Masters, Cloyd Head, Lew Sarett, Margery Allen Seiffert, Mark Turbyfill, Maurice Lesemann. Lew Sarett was a member of the faculty of Northwestern University for many years, following an earlier connection with the University of Illinois. His poems deal with nature and Indian life. Glenn Ward Dresbach, a native of Lanark and long a resident of Chicago, did his best work in the poetic recording of the experience of nature. *Poetry* was edited by Morton Dauen Zabel after the death of Harriet Monroe and later by George Dillon, whose poems, *The Flowering Stone,* won the Pulitzer Award. Daryl Hine is now editor.

Carl Sandburg's career in poetry opened with *Chicago Poems* in

Poetry. The famous lines about the city of broad shoulders have given Chicago a permanent slogan, even if it is no longer hog butcher for the world. In his poetry Carl expressed his identification with the prairie, which represented the continuity of life; in *Smoke and Steel* he projected his dreams in an industrial setting. His preoccupation with Lincoln, which was to make him a folk hero, began when he was a boy in Galesburg, recalling the Lincoln-Douglas debate. When Sandburg became immersed in the material, the hard, cynical attitude of a militant socialist faded before the compassion of the humanitarian. The Sandburg Lincoln (*The Prairie Years; The War Years*) is a monument to the American spirit, proof of which is the naming of numerous schools in the Middle West for Sandburg. As the years went on Sandburg's best expression was in prose, but *The People, Yes* is both poetry and folk lore. *See also Galesburg, in Tour 13.*

Elder Olson, poet, critic, and professor of English, is known for *The Poetry of Dylan Thomas,* which he issued in 1954. He contributes to *Poetry* and in 1963 published *Collected Poems. The Theory of Comedy* appeared in 1968. He has won both the Witter Bynner and the Eunice Tietjens awards.

Karl Shapiro, who, as poet, editor and educator was long active in the Chicago area, has departed permanently for California; he is professor of English at the Davis campus of the university. He won the Pulitzer prize for poetry in 1945 for *V-Letter and Other Poems,* and in 1950-56 edited *Poetry.* Then for 10 years he was professor of English at the University of Illinois at the Circle, but after a few years California lured him. He has published books of poetry and criticism, including *In Defense of Ignorance* and *Poems of a Jew.*

John Frederick Nims not only has won numerous prizes and citations for his poetry but has worked actively in the cause on the editorial board of *Poetry,* first in the 1940's and as visiting editor, 1960-61. He was on the faculty at the University of Illinois, 1961-65, and then went to the University of Chicago. He has written, among other work, *The Iron Pastoral, A Frontier in Kentucky,* and *Of Flesh and Bone.*

Heartland: Poets of the Middle West, edited by Lucien Stryk, was published by the Northern Illinois University Press of DeKalb in 1967.

III

Illinois fiction before 1900 was conventional and addicted to the happy ending, but the vigorous polemics by Shaw, Wells, Belloc, Chesterton and other British writers found a ready response among younger Americans. Stone & Kimball in Chicago printed British essays in *The Chapbook;* novels by Dostoievsky, appearing in translations from the French by Constance Garnett, opened a new world of philosophical fiction, and Tolstoyan ideas fitted so well the new mood of social responsibility that Jane Addams had a fresco of Tolstoy at the plow placed in Hull House. In the century's first decade a new wind was blowing through the lofty corridors of the *Chicago Post* in West Washington

Street, where first Francis Hackett, famous for *King Henry VIII,* and afterward Floyd Dell and George Cram Cook put together the weekly *Literary Review.* Dell came from Barry, Illinois; attended school in Davenport, Iowa, and worked on the Rock Island section of the *Daily Times* there; he met and married Margery Currey, whose father, J. Seymour Currey, was author of the five-volume *Chicago, its History and its Builders.* In Davenport Dell consorted with George Cram Cook and Susan Glaspell, who had won a national prize for a short story, as well as Arthur Davison Ficke, budding Harvard poet. Cook joined Dell in Chicago; he and Miss Glaspell were married and wrote plays for the Provincetown Theatre, and Miss Glaspell wrote a moving biography of Cook, *The Road to the Temple.* A biography, *Susan Glaspell,* by Arthur E. Waterman, appeared in 1966. Dell, like Sandburg, weighed socialism as a healing medicine for an imperfect economy. Before he left Chicago to edit *Masses* in New York he had written his dissection of adolescence in *Moon Calf*—vaguely autobiographical; had tackled marriage in *The Briary Bush;* started *Love in the Machine Age* and other books prompted by the social issues of the day. Dell and Margery Currey lived in that East 57th St., Chicago, oasis of stores that once served the World's Fair. In and out of their "salon" walked Anderson, Dreiser, Ficke, Maxwell Bodenheim, Lucian Cary, Llewellyn Jones, others of the coterie. Here came Lawrence Langner, a Welsh-born patent-lawyer who was establishing an office in Chicago and returned to New York to found the Theatre Guild. He describes his Chicago days in *The Magic Curtain.* Also present was Margaret Anderson, who solicited a consensus on a name for a little review, and *The Little Review* it was. This was the first Chicago magazine to make an issue of revolt against conventional content and expression and profited by the advice of Ezra Pound, Harriet Monroe's early helper. When Pound enabled Miss Anderson to publish parts of James Joyce's *Ulysses* and get sued for it her place in literary history was assured. She tells about her Chicago beginnings in *My Thirty Years War.*

Sherwood Anderson, Masters, and Sandburg were the major prose writers of that remarkable period, 1912-1930, sometimes called the Chicago Renaissance, which Anderson in retrospect described as "a robin's egg renaissance." The most original work of the period was his *Winesburg, Ohio* (1919), in which he reflected on the chilled hopes of commonplace lives. His stark, unembellished storytelling made a strong impression on young writers, and the smiling picture of America preferred by William Dean Howells disappeared from their writings. Anderson had a reflective mind; he meditated a lot about theories of the unconscious that had seeped into America. He had an obsession about the use of words that makes *The Triumph of the Egg, Death in the Woods,* and a dozen other stories such fine prose. Like Hemingway Anderson talked style with Gertrude Stein, but as his was already fixed she fortunately did not influence him. Anderson called himself a storyteller, and his memoir, *A Story Teller's Story,* describes his Chicago days.

Edgar Lee Masters has left an indelible mark on Illinois literature. Not only will *The Spoon River Anthology* always be cited as a mirror of rural life in Illinois but his *Illinois Poems* and other nostalgic verses revive the legends of the past. Masters was a lawyer who lived in Chicago 1892-1923, and was a partner of Clarence Darrow, 1903-1911. He had lived in Lewistown and his family had farms near Petersburg, where he is buried. His critical nature made him skeptical of hero worship and especially of the idealization of Abraham Lincoln, whom he considered inferior to Stephen A. Douglas. But despite Masters' cynicism a warm, sympathetic strain comes into his poetry and his tales of boyhood. *Across Spoon River* is autobiography and there are intimate glimpses of personalities of the Spoon River country in his last book, *The Sangamon* of the *Rivers of America* series. After Masters had moved to New York he wrote *The Tale of Chicago,* which is partly an analysis slanted by his political and economic views. *See Petersburg in Tour 21.*

Among Masters' later writings was a biography of Vachel Lindsay, the Springfield poet, which he used as an excuse to berate the public indifference to poetry, which he had experienced himself. But Lindsay did not suffer the ostracism that Masters described; he was rather a man of extreme sensitivity who felt slighted despite the acclaim that greeted his rendering of *The Congo* and other poems. Always to be remembered in Illinois is his moving tribute to John Peter Altgeld as the "eagle forgotten," and his *Abraham Lincoln Walks at Midnight.* Lindsay lectured at Mrs. William Vaughn Moody's Le Petit Gourmet in Chicago, and at one time was poet in residence at a southern girls' college, but unlike Robert Frost at Amherst he could not stand the routine. He could not make a living; unfortunately he matured before generous grants-in-aid were made to poets.

Midwestern literary history of the last 100 years has been pretty thoroughly recorded by this time, to some extent in period studies, but more often in recollections and autobiographies. The major authors of the first third of the 20th century and their works are frequent subjects of doctoral theses in Illinois colleges. There has been stronger interest in Ernest Hemingway than in any other midwestern author, but studies of Sherwood Anderson appear from time to time, one of the latest being *Tar: A Midwest Childhood,* with a critical introduction by Ray Lewis White of Illinois State University, one of the books in the series, *The Major Fiction of Sherwood Anderson,* of which White is editor. Two biographies of Carl Sandburg appeared in the 1960s—Harry Golden's *Carl Sandburg,* and North Callahan's *Carl Sandburg, Lincoln of Our Literature.* A recent study of Chicago's literary history is Bernard Duffey's *The Chicago Renaissance in American Letters,* which restores the contribution of writers of the 1890s to the record. A more anecdotal account is *Chicago Renaissance: the Literary Life in the Midwest, 1900-1930,* by Dale Kramer, which tells much about Floyd Dell, the *Literary Review* of the *Chicago Evening Post,* and the 57th St. colony.

IV

Authors who have achieved recognition quite properly dominate the historical records, because their work is visible and their careers are public. But their accomplishments do not embrace the whole literary ferment of their time. The issues that agitate the young and unrecognized generations often differ from those current in literary clubs and coteries. The turbulence of submerged forces in literature can only be detected in little magazines, writings that circulate on multigraphed sheets, and confessions by those active in what we now call counter-culture, underground, or revolution. Thus a useful supplement to the histories by Duffey and Kramer and the personal slants by Ben Hecht, is Kenneth Rexroth's ineptly entitled *An Autobiographical Novel,* which is not a novel at all but an invaluable account of what animated the underground in Chicago during the Depression, including an incomparably eloquent appraisal of the splintered radical politics of the time.

If the Twenties can be identified as the period of Anderson and Sandburg, the Thirties bear the indelible marks of James T. Farrell, or rather his creation, Studs Lonigan. Farrell was born in Chicago and attended the university; he lived in the area of Washington Park when it had an enclave of Irish who went to Father Gilmartin's church. When *Young Lonigan, A Boyhood in Chicago Streets,* appeared in 1932 few realized that it marked a new chapter in naturalism, but many were enthusiastic and some were affronted. The capers of Studs Lonigan and his associates were a frank disclosure of adolescent behavior, which was hardly comforting. The impact was due, of course, to Farrell's forthright prose that pulled no punches. It became a model for the enthusiastic young. In novels and books of comment Farrell has written since, he has disclosed himself as a combative and controversial debater, often reaching into his own reflections and experiences (*A World I Never Made, My Days of Anger, Childhood is Not Forever*) but the Lonigan story remains fundamental in his repertory. Farrell is not a graceful writer, but subtlety has no place in his forthright storytelling; he also has emphatic views on art, the Irish theater, social topics, and his alertness has not been dulled with the years. In 1973 he published his 44th book, *Judith,* a volume of short stories.

The fine record for strength and originality that distinguishes Chicago writing in the 20th century is upheld by Saul Bellow, novelist and college professor, whose *Herzog* (1964) is generally considered an excellent portrait of a sensitive individual trying to overcome the handicaps of his own personality in an unstable world. Bellow's writing brilliance has been recognized by numerous awards ever since his first novel, *The Dangling Man,* was published in 1944. Born in Quebec Province, Canada in 1915, he was brought up in Chicago and attended the University of Chicago in 1933-35, then obtained a degree of B.S. from Northwestern in 1937. He has taught English at the University of Minnesota and Bard College; has been a fellow in writing at Yale and Princeton, and is now a professor of English and Letters in the Committee on Social

Thought at the University of Chicago. He has twice won the National Book Award. He also has written *The Victim,* (1947), *The Adventures of Augie March,* (1953), *Seize the Day* (1956), *Henderson, the Rain King* (1959), *Mosby's Memoirs* (1968), *Mr. Sammler's Planet* (1972), and a play, *The Last Analysis.*

Bellow dedicated Herzog to "Pat Covici, a great editor, and, better yet, a generous friend." Pascal Covici, late editor for Viking Press, had a bookshop-publishing enterprise with William McGee on West Washington St. near LaSalle, which was frequented by the writers of the Twenties. The partners printed the *Chicago Literary Times,* in which Ben Hecht and Maxwell Bodenheim spiced the Chicago scene with pepper and salt. Covici-McGee published Henry Justin Smith's *Deadlines* and Hecht's *Thousand and One Afternoons in Chicago.*

Thornton Wilder, author of *Our Town, The Skin of our Teeth* and many other successful novels and plays, and weighted down with a record number of medals and honorary degrees, was a member of the English Faculty at Chicago from 1934 to 1936. In 1955 the English faculty acquired a Harvard ph.d., Richard G. Stern, who soon proved himself an author of what critics called "subtle, sophisticated fiction" and "tremendous charm"; using striking titles such as *Teeth, Dying and Other Matters* (1964) and *Stitch* (1965). In 1971 he published *Some Home Truths (from Abroad).* His most recent novel, *Other Men's Daughters,* deals with the infatuation of a middle-aged man for a young girl, a fashionable topic in a new frame.

Nelson Algren has been publishing fiction since 1935, and although his short stories have appeared in popular magazines he has a strong social slant and makes no concession to commercial patterns. He won a national audience with *The Man with the Golden Arm* (1949) and has written *A Walk on the Wild Side, Never Come Morning,* and other stories, and non-fiction, of which *Chicago, City on the Make* (1951), is an example. A collection of his writings, 1947-72, *The Last Carousel,* was published in 1973.

Harry Mark Petrakis attended the University of Illinois and lives just outside Chicago in the sand dune country of Chesterton, Indiana. He began writing novels with *Lion at My Heart* in 1959 and has won golden opinions with *Pericles on 31st Street, The Odyssey of Kostas Valakis, The Waves of Night,* and especially *A Dream of Kings.*

Ernest Hemingway was born in Oak Park but passed little more than his adolescence in Illinois and began his writing career abroad. When he received the Nobel Prize in 1954 he had exerted a strong individual influence on style in fiction. The Oak Park Public Library preserves a full collection of his works. Oak Park has been the home of a number of Illinois authors (*see Oak Park*). Its galaxy for years included Dr. William E. Barton, biographer of Lincoln, and his son, Bruce Barton, whose *The Man Nobody Knows* was long a best-seller. Frank Lloyd Wright's writings are elucidations of his theories of architecture, as in *Autobiography;* Frederick Gutheim, who was consultant

Agriculture

CORN AND SOYA BLENDED MEAL PRODUCED AT NORTHERN
REGIONAL RESEARCH LABORATORY USDA, PEORIA

FAYETTE COUNTY. PLOWING UNDER WINTER COVER CROP TO STOP EROSION

OGLE COUNTY. BAILING ALFALFA BY FARM MACHINERY

BUREAU COUNTY CONTOUR PLOWING, TISKILWA WATERSHED

BROMEGRASS WATERWAY INSIDE SOYBEAN FARM,
NEAR ROCHELLE

PIATT COUNTY. HARVESTING CORN ON PARALLEL TERRACES
THAT REDUCE SOIL EROSION

WOODFORD COUNTY FARM POND. AN EXAMPLE OF WATER MANAGEMENT BY THE U. S. SOIL CONSERVATION SERVICE, DEPARTMENT OF AGRICULTURE. A POND 10 FT. DEEP WAS DUG OUT TO HOLD 500,000 GALLONS AND SERVE FIFTY ACRES. IT IS FED BY FIELD TILE AT LEFT, DISCHARGED BY TILE AT RIGHT, HAS JET PUMPS AND FILTER AND PROVIDES WATER FOR STOCK, AND PROTECTION FROM FIRE

PIKE COUNTY FARM, WITH PLOWING COMPLETED ON TERRACED LAND

RANDOLPH COUNTY LAND SHOWING CONSERVATION METHODS

URBANA RESEARCHERS STUDY SOYBEAN PLANTING IN ROWS OF
7 IN. AND 30 IN.

DEWITT COUNTY, WELDON SPRINGS STATE PARK

U. S. REGIONAL SOYBEAN LABORATORY, URBANA, WITH SCIENTIST AT WORK

on architecture for the original *American Guide Series,* published a selection in *Frank Lloyd Wright on Architecture.*

Archibald MacLeish is another famous author whose Illinois associations have been limited; born in Glencoe, all his activities from prep-school days on have been in the East. His capabilities have won him high honors for poetry and prose, for administration as Assistant Secretary of State and Librarian of Congress, and in diplomatic posts. Among contemporary authors he is one of the few with a strong nationalistic bent and a constructive feeling for the future of his country.

Illinois is the birthplace of a number of important writers who made national reputations outside the State, including John Dos Passos, Allan Nevins, and Carl and Mark van Doren. Wayne Andrews, a native of Kenilworth, has done most of his literary work in the East, including historical editing for the house of Scribner, but when his interest turned to architecture he found material in Chicago. He has written *Architecture, Ambition and America,* 1955; *Architecture in America,* 1960; and *Architecture in Chicago and Mid-America,* 1968, and previously had published *Battle for Chicago* in 1946. He is now professor of art at Wayne State University.

Sam Ross worked with Nelson Algren and Saul Bellow when John T. Frederick had charge of the *Illinois Guide* and has written *He Ran All the Way, Someday,* and *The Sidewalks are Free.*

Mackinlay Kantor, who was born in Webster City, Iowa, and had Midwestern newspaper experience in his early years, lived in Chicago in 1925-26 and soaked up enough atmosphere to use the city in two novels, *Diversey,* 1928, and *The El Goes South,* 1929. Subsequently he embarked on his long association in fiction, prose, and poems with the Civil War, which came to a peak in 1956 in his strongest story, *Andersonville,* a Pulitzer prize winner.

When John W. Allen retired from teaching in 1956 he continued to practice his hobby of collecting information about the folkways of Southern Illinois. Much of what he found makes *Legends and Folklore of Southern Illinois* indispensable to anyone who loves the State. It was published by Southern Illinois University and reprinted in a special edition by the Illinois State Historical Society in 1964. The story of Allen's career, described by Irving Dilliard, shows what a variety of adventure and experience can come to a scholar who was born in a log cabin as late as 1887. After retirement Allen continued writing a weekly column about his favorite hobby, which the university distributed to newspapers.

An Illinois author whose first novel won the National Book Award in 1951 and became a national best-seller is James Jones, whose *From Here to Eternity* was one of the first outspoken stories about army low life. The novel also brought Lowney Handy, (Mrs. Harry E.), to public notice for coaching Jones and several other aspiring authors at her home in Sullivan, Illinois. Jones was born in Robinson, Illinois, served in the US Army, winning the Purple Heart, and briefly attended New York University. He has since written novels on a variety of subjects, entitled *Some Came Running, The Pistol, The Thin Red Line, Go to the Widow-maker, The Ice-Cream Headache,* and *The Merry Month of May.* Jones lives in Paris, France, but recently became writer-in-residence at a Florida college.

Mark Costello, who teaches in Urbana, is the author of *The Murphy Stories,* dealing with a marriage breaking up, which have been published in the *Chicago Review* and other periodicals.

Albert Halper lives in New York State but his heart is in his native Chicago and he has drawn upon it for his novels of mercantilism, such as *The Chute. This is Chicago* is an anthology to which he has added reminiscent footnotes. In 1967 he published *Chicago Crime Book;* in 1970, *Goodbye to Union Square.*

V

A recurrent theme in modern writing, the fight of the individual to maintain his integrity against social and economic pressures that inhibit his spirit, comes out sharply in the work of black poets, novelists, and journalists. Whereas the white writer feels hostility toward the acquisitive aims of modern life, the black has the added resentment against inequality and discrimination. If there is a major trend in today's literature it is the effort of the black writers to reject the critical and stylistic influence of the whites and write as blacks for blacks. In 1968 a symposium conducted by *Black World* (Chicago) concluded that "the function of black art is to liberate black people all over the world." Repeatedly black commentators assert: "Black art should be functional, not decorative."

To anyone who experienced the literary tensions of the depression years this has a familiar ring. Radical critics argued that the main function of writing was political and declared authors who ignored the class struggle were wasting their time in ivory towers. The emphasis on proletarian writing by non-proletarians had some educational value, but writing has continued to follow a multitude of inspirations, most of them intensely personal.

Earlier writers who knew the Black Belt used the English they learned in the schools to record frank descriptions of the talk and movement of black folk. Richard Wright's strong convictions in *Native Son* and *Black Boy* were no less authentic because expressed in sound English prose. He lived on the South Side, had a job as a sorter in the U.S. Postoffice and worked on the Illinois Guide of the Federal Writers Project before moving to New York and Paris. Another Chicago writer of good prose was Willard Motley, who wrote *Knock on Any Door,* and whose promise was cut short by his early death. Frank Yerby, author of numerous popular novels, studied briefly at the University of Chicago.

One of the younger generation who finds suitable themes for his stories in the black community is Cyrus Colter, whose *The Black Umbrella* is a collection of such stories. He also has written *The River of Eros.* He was the subject of a profile in *Chicago* for September-October, 1972.

Gwendolyn Brooks, who has been officially named poet laureate of Illinois, was born in Topeka but has lived all her life in Chicago. One of her poems appeared in *American Childhood* when she was only 13. She graduated from Wilson Junior College, went into newspaper and magazine work and became active in the South Side Community Art Center. She won the Poetry Workshop Award for three successive years at the Midwestern Writers' Conference at Northwestern University. The Gwendolyn Brooks Cultural Center has been established at Western Illinois University at Macomb. In 1971 black writers and poets joined in publishing *To Gwen With Love.*

Miss Brooks writes in her autobiography, *Report from Part One* (1972), how, after writing for years in the style of white people she realized the importance of becoming involved in the black revolution of the arts. "Today I am conscious of the fact that my people are black people; it is to them that I appeal for understanding . . . I know that the black emphasis must be not against white, but for black."

Miss Brooks' book of poems, *A Street in Bronzeville,* was welcomed in 1945; *Annie Allen* won the Pulitzer prize for poetry in 1950. She published a novel, *Maud Martha,* in 1953. Her more recent poetry includes *The Bean Eaters,* 1960, and *In the Mecca,* 1968. She has interested herself in aspiring writers and annually sponsors the Gwendolyn Brooks Literary Awards, $250 each for poetry and fiction.

Another militant poet and lecturer is Marl Evans, who won the poetry prize of the Black Academy of Arts and Letters for her collection of poems, *I Am a Black Woman.* She is visiting professor of Afro-American Literature at Northwestern University and commutes to Evanston from her home in Indianapolis. She also lectures before Chicago audiences.

Many slim quarterlies and monthlies have been published in the last decade to make a public for new writers. Don L. Lee is a poet and an encourager of poets; he established the Third World Press at 7850 S. Ellis Ave., Chicago, and writes critical comment on black literature. He recently edited *Dynamic Voices, Poets of the 1960s.*

A biography widely admired is *Black Troubadour: Langston Hughes,* by Charlemae Rollins, former children's librarian, who also wrote *Christmas Gif', Famous Negro Entertainers of the Stage, Screen and Television* and *They Showed the Way,* about 40 American Negro poets.

A scholarly study, *Black Poets of the United States From Paul Lawrence Dunbar to Langston Hughes,* by Jean Wagner, issued by the University of Illinois Press, was published originally in Paris. It contains chapters on McKay, Toomer, Cullen, Johnson, Hughes, and Brown.

Margaret Walker was at the threshold of a teaching career when she obtained her baccalaureate degree at Northwestern University in 1935. Richard Wright alerted her to an editorial job on the *Illinois*

Guide of the Federal Writers. She was already writing poetry and in 1942 received the Yale Award for Younger Poets for *For My People*. She went on to get higher degrees and a fellowship at Yale and in 1966 published a novel, *Jubilee*. After teaching English in several southern colleges she became associated with the State College at Jackson, Miss.

A career dealing with literature in relation to religion has been pursued by Nathan Alexander Scott, Jr., professor of theology and literature at the University of Chicago, author of *The Climate of Faith in Modern Literature,* and *Modern Literature and the Religious Frontier.* He has published studies of Camus, Hemingway, Beckett, Niebuhr, and existentialism; such provocative books as *Discomposure: Alienation and Reconciliation in Modern Literature, Four Ways of Modern Poetry,* and *Man in the Modern Theatre.* In practically every year of the 1960-70 decade Dr. Alexander contributed a study of literary and religious relationships.

Arna Bontemps had a long and productive writing career in the course of his 70 years, during which he issued about a dozen books dealing with Negro accomplishments and aspirations. He is claimed by Louisiana as one of its representative authors, was educated in California, taught and wrote in Harlem, collaborated on plays with Countee Cullen and Langston Hughes, earned a degree from the Library School of the University of Chicago, became a librarian at Fisk, professor of English at University of Illinois at Chicago Circle, and a curator at Yale. His novel, *Drums of Dusk,* written in Chicago, was about the Haiti revolt against the French; he wrote biographies of Frederick Douglass, W. C. Handy, and George Washington Carver, and about his main interest in *The Story of the Negro, The Book of Negro Folklore,* and *One Hundred Years of Negro Freedom.* As late as 1969 he wrote *Any Place But Here* and *Great Slave Narratives.* He wrote *The Cavalcade of the American Negro* for the Diamond Jubilee Exposition of 1940.

In several books Bontemps collaborated with Jack Conroy, who has retired to his birthplace, Moberly, Mo., after a long career as Chicago author and editor. Conroy in 1933 wrote *The Disinherited,* one of the best records of the rootless worker in the industrial system. With Bontemps he wrote *They Seek a City* about Negro migration, in 1935, and issued it in revised form as *Any Place But Here* in 1966; it won a Midland Authors award. Conroy and Bontemps also wrote *The Fast Sooner Hound* and *Sam Patch, The High, Wide and Handsome Jumper,* characteristic of Conroy's aptitude for humor in folk tales. He served on the *Illinois Guide* and years later wrote *Midland Humor; A Harvest of Fun and Folklore.* Conroy encouraged young radical poets when editor of *The Rebel Post, The Anvil,* and *The New Anvil,* whose work has been collected in *The Anvil Anthology,* and wrote reviews for the *Chicago Defender* and the *Chicago Globe,* but his longest service was in editing encyclopedias and reference books.

A Chicago author who pioneered with biographies of illustrious blacks, written from personal contact, was Margaret Saunders Holt, who wrote, under the name of Rackham Holt, *George Washington*

Carver, an American Biography (1943, rev. 1963) and *Mary McLeod Bethune* (1964).

Prof. Charles Allen, in discussing the fortunes of little magazines for *American Libraries,* found that during the 1960s "black magazines assumed prominence." There were at least 30, usually designed for black readers and contributors; they emphasized liberation, nationalism, and black strength. Said Allen: "Some were Muslim, some were Panther, some were existentialist independent. Most found a smattering of Swahili a desirable emblem of grace. Most feared genocide and were emphatic about survival, indeed favored a black population explosion." And the little magazines, in general, represented social protest, condemned the Vietnam war, violation of civil liberties, exploitation of resources and "myriad forms of natural and spiritual pollution." Sometimes there was a sharp reaction from conservative opinion. Prof. Allen mentions that Karl Shapiro encountered censorship at both *Poetry* and *Prairie Schooner,* and that when the student-edited *Chicago Review* exasperated the university authorities with too much Beat it was suppressed. One of its editors, Paul Carroll, retorted by printing *Big Table.* Carroll has written *Irish Stories and Plays* and edited *The Edward Dahlberg Reader.*

VI

A distinguished career in American historical writing has been built by Daniel J. Boorstin who was associated with the University of Chicago 1944-1969 and more recently was director of the National Museum of History and Technology in Washington. Among his many occupations has been lecturing on American history abroad for the U. S. Dept. of State. He has edited the *Chicago History of American Civilization* (23 vols.) written a trilogy, *The Americans,* including *The Colonial Experience* (Bancroft Award, 1959), *The National Experience* (Francis Parkman Prize, 1966), and *The Democratic Experience* (1973). Also *The Decline of Radicalism* (1968) and *The Sociology of the Absurd* (1970), and in 1970 completed his two-volume *Landmark History of the American People.* Boorstin has been admitted to the bar and is a member of the American Revolution Bicentennial Commission.

Harry Barnard's latest biography is *The Forging of an American Jew; the Life and Time of Judge Julian W. Mack.* He also has written biographies of John Peter Altgeld and Rutherford B. Hayes. Virgil J. Vogel, who teaches history at Mayfair College, Chicago, is the author of *This Country Was Ours; A Documentary History of the American Indian,* and writes about Illinois history.

A writing team of marked eminence is composed of Dr. and Mrs. George Wells Beadle; the husband's distinguished career in biology won the Nobel Prize in 1958; with his wife, Muriel M. B. Beadle he wrote *The Language of Life* in 1966. Muriel Beadle's amusing survey of living at Oxford University in *These Ruins Are Inhabited* introduced her to her Chicago audience in 1961; her writing career started as copywriter for Carson, Pirie; she has done fashion articles and lectured on education. *A Child's Mind* appeared in 1970. Her most recent book is *Where Has All the Ivy Gone?*

Chicago became a force in the popular dissemination of classic literature after Robert Maynard Hutchins became president of the University of Chicago in 1929. With Mortimer J. Adler, professor of the philosophy of law and a wellknown Thomist, he launched the Great Books reading program. Adler became editor of *The Great Books of the Western World.* With the help of reading classes that continue today the books gained a wide circulation in nonacademic circles. Adler wrote studies of education and capitalism with Milton Mayer, including *The Revolution in Education.* Mayer, who for a number of years served on the university faculty as professor on the Committee on Social Thought, also was a director of the Great Books Foundation. He lectured in numerous universities abroad and in 1969 published *The Art of the Impossible, a Study of the Czech Resistance.*

Associated with these men was William Benton (1900-1973), who developed the *Encyclopedia Britannica* as a great Chicago enterprise. The 15th edition of this work, issued in 1974, demonstrated its development as a "reference system" and a compendium of information, for it appeared in three parts and 30 volumes, 10 volumes of reference, 19 of knowledge in depth, and a single volume presented as "an outline of the whole of human knowledge." Benton also had acted as vice president and assistant chancellor of the University of Chicago.

The years leading to the centennial of the Civil War and the sesquicentennial of the State of Illinois (1968) were marked by intensified research into Illinois history and biography, notably in the career of Abraham Lincoln. The most prolific writer in this field was Allan Nevins, who also inspired others to creative effort. The extent of Nevins' interest was immense; the series that includes *The Ordeal of the Union, The War for the Union,* and *The Emergence of Lincoln* draws on the range of Lincoln scholarship. This period also saw publication of the fine studies of Lincoln by James G. Randall, late of the Urbana faculty, books that Nevins called remarkable for their accuracy, keen analysis and new material. Randall was ably seconded in research by his wife, Ruth Painter Randall, best known for her biography of Mary Lincoln and for *I, Ruth; the Biography of a Marriage.* Benjamin P. Thomas told the Lincoln story with distinction in one volume, and also wrote *Lincoln's New Salem.*

Illinois continues to produce historians of the first rank. The faculties of colleges and universities are especially strong in history and have done effective research on the past in Illinois. Donald F. Tingley, president of the Illinois State Historical Society (1972) recently edited *Essays in Illinois History in Honor of Glenn Huron Seymour.* The newest book about Illinois is *Illinois, A History of the Prairie State,* by Robert P. Howard, with an introduction by Paul M. Angle. Howard's book profits by his intimate knowledge of political machines and leaders, especially in the days of Deneen, Thompson, Lowden, Harrison, Small, and Stevenson.

The new Illinois Constitution and its predecessors are the subjects of *Studies in Illinois Constitution Making,* edited by Joseph F. Pisciotte and published by the University of Illinois Press. They include *To Judge With Justice, the History and Politics of Judicial Reform,* by Rubin G. Cohn, and *Lobbying at the Illinois Constitutional Convention,* by Ian D. Burman. Cohn is a professor of law at Urbana and Burman is on the faculty of Principia College.

William H. McNeill, professor of history at the University of Chicago, moves with ease across epochs and eras and won the National Book Award in 1963 for *The Rise of the West: A History of the Human Community.* He published two books of similar scope in 1967: *A World History* and *The Contemporary World.*

As historian and administrator Paul M. Angle has been active in making Illinois history and Lincoln lore more widely known. He has been historian of the Illinois State Historical Library, secretary of the Illinois State Historical Society, and director of the Chicago Historical Society. He has written *"Here Have I Lived"; A History of Lincoln's Springfield,* and *Mary Lincoln, Wife and Widow,* with Carl Sandburg. *Created Equal? The Complete Lincoln-Douglas Debates* is authoritative on this subject. In addition to other books about Lincoln and his period Angle wrote *Bloody Williamson* about the Illinois county that has had a violent history.

Lerone Bennett, Jr., editor of *Ebony,* has written poetry but his major writings deal with Negro history. He has published *Before the Mayflower: A History of the Negro in America, 1619-1964,* and *Black Power, USA.* His biography of Martin Luther King, Jr., *What Manner of Man,* first appeared in 1964, before Dr. King's death.

A major project in historical research has produced *The Papers of Ulysses S. Grant,* which is being published with the cooperation of the National Historical Publications Commission by the Southern Illinois University Press. The editor is John Y. Simon, a native of Illinois and a member of the history faculty of Ohio State University, who established his study in the Morris Library in Carbondale. The initiative for publication came from Ralph G. Newman and the Grant Association of which he was president, and which included Allan Nevins, John Hope Franklin, William K. Alderfer, Bruce Catton, and Esmond B. Long. Long, vice chairman, has been Catton's principal Civil War researcher. Volume I of the *Papers* deals with 1837-61 and has prefaces by Nevins and Catton; Vol. II covers April-September, 1861, with preface by T. Harry Williams; Vol. III, Oct. 1, 1861-Jan. 7, 1862, covers 14 weeks after Donelson; Vol. IV, Jan. 4-Mar. 31, 1862, goes up to Shiloh; Vol. V covers Shiloh to Vicksburg. Rodger D. Bridges and Thomas G. Alexander have helped Prof. Simon edit IV and V.

John Hope Franklin, specialist in American Negro history, became head of the department of history at the University of Chicago in 1967, and has lectured in many universities here and abroad. Among his books are *Reconstruction After the Civil War, Land of the Free,* and *From Slavery to Freedom: A History of the American Negro,* which has had several editions. He is editor of the series of *Negro American Biographies and Autobiographies* of the University of Chicago Press, which includes *Crusade for Justice* by Ida B. Wells, edited by Alfreda M. Duster, director of community relations in Chicago.

A literary history called *Proletarian Writers of the Thirties* was written by David Madden and published by the Southern Illinois University Press in 1967. Sidney Lens has written *Radicalism in America.*

International politics has been the special field of Hans Morgenthau who began an important career in Europe and after holding many scholastic posts in the United States became professor of political science and modern history at the University of Chicago in 1961. His recent studies have illuminated the position of the United States in foreign affairs, especially *A New Foreign Policy for the United States,* in 1969. Among his numerous books are *In Defense of the National Interest, Politics Among Nations,* and *Politics in the Twentieth Century,* a three-volume work published in 1969.

Arthur Weinberg has been an active member of the American Civil Liberties Union and is responsible for giving Clarence Darrow a fitting memorial in Chicago. He was a leader in the Chicago Darrow Centennial Observance in 1957 and has been associated with the Clarence Darrow Community Center. He published *Attorney for the Damned* in 1957 and *Some Dissenting Views* in 1967, and he and his wife Lila wrote *Verdicts Out of Court* in 1968.

Martin Emil Marty, historian and theologian, has been associate dean of the Divinity School of the University of Chicago, associate editor of the *Christian Century,* and has served as Lutheran pastor in River Forest and Elk Grove Village. In 1970 he won the National Book Award for *Righteous Empire.* Among his publications are *The Hidden Discipline, The Modern Schism,* and *Second Chance for American Protestants.*

VII

Chicago newspapers have proved a stepping stone for many of their witty and ambitious staff writers. Eugene Field gained a big following for his column. Finley Peter Dunne, in the *Times-Herald,* had his Mr. Dooley comment on affairs in a Bridgeport vernacular to the delight of a nation, and George Ade, collaborating with the cartoonist John T. McCutcheon, produced *Stories of the Streets and of the Town,* sidetracked schoolbook English in *Fables in Slang,* and wrote catchy lyrics for musical comedy. Even without television, BLT (Bert Leston Taylor) set the tone of the day's tabletalk by his *Chicago Tribune* column, which, a generation later, was piloted by John T. McCutcheon, Jr. Ring W. Lardner, who came from Niles, Michigan, obtained some of his first pay checks and a lot of baseball reporting experience from the *Tribune.*

George E. Morgenstern has had experience writing for the editorial pages of Chicago newspapers since 1925; he was editor of the editorial page of the *Chicago Tribune* when he withdrew in 1971. He has written *Pearl Harbor; the Story of the Secret War,* and *Pearl Harbor Fifteen Years After,* and his reflections on war led to *Perpetual War for Perpetual Peace.*

Fanny Butcher led the book reviewing of the *Chicago Tribune* for years and as literary editor had personal contacts with the principal authors here and abroad. Her autobiography *Many Lives, One Love,* recalls the lively literary life of Chicago in recent decades. Of interest is her description of associations of authors, such as the Chicago PEN, which, formed in 1932 with John Galsworthy's blessing, was disavowed five years later by the American Center of New York, which emphasized the international aims of the organization. The Chicago group included such established writers as Mary Hastings Bradley, Edith Franklin Wyatt, Donald Culross Peattie, Mignon G. Eberhart, Paul Scott Mowrer, and Tiffany Blake. Still going strong is the Society of Midland Authors, founded in 1915, which enrolls authors from the Midwest, and has had in its membership Hamlin Garland, Hobart C. Chatfield-Taylor, Zona Gale, Arthur Davison Ficke, Louis Bromfield, and the McCutcheons, John T., cartoonist, and George Barr, whose *Graustark* was a midwestern version of the romantic *genre* sparked by *The Prisoner of Zenda.*

Lloyd Wendt and Herman Kogan have collaborated in lively accounts of Chicago personalities and phenomena; their shelf of books will prove invaluable to future social research. Both men have top places in the newspaper profession. Jointly they have written *Lords of the Levee, Give the Lady What She Wants,* an account of Marshall Field & Co.; *Bet a Million, Big Bill of Chicago,* and *Chicago, A Pictorial History.* They also write books separately. Kogan's recent book is *A Continuing Marvel: The Story of the Museum of Science and Industry.* Kogan started as high school reporter and copy boy for the *Chicago Daily News* and the *Chicago Evening Post,* and after college and service in the U. S. Marine Corps during World War II, and employment with Encyclopedia Britannica, Inc., he became associated with Field Enterprises. In the course of 30 years he has held various editorial posts, including that of book and drama critic for the *Sun-Times,* originator and editor of *Panorama* for the *Daily News,* originator of Newscope for the Field television station; editor of *Book Week* of the *Sun-Times,* and editor of *Showcase.* His accomplishments have been recognized by three Emmy awards and a number of literary prizes.

Lloyd Wendt's career runs parallel with that of Kogan; a native of South Dakota, he had midwestern newspaper experience before he reached editorial posts with the *Chicago Tribune.* He became editor of the *Tribune's* associated newspaper, *Chicago's American,* in 1961, and of its successor, *Chicago Today,* in 1969. He also served in World War II and is a lieutenant commander in the Naval Reserve. After the war he wrote *Gunners Get Glory.*

The history of Chicago is packed with so many fantastic episodes and personalities that it well merits the title, *Fabulous Chicago,* given it by Emmett Dedmon in his 1953 book. The appeal of this work is perennial. Dedman has written several books: *Duty to Live,* 1946, and *Great Enterprise,* 1957, as well as a history of the Chicago Club, but his career as a top newspaper executive in the Field organization outshines all other activities. He is a trustee of the University of Chicago. He served with distinction in the Air Force during World War II. As a journalist he visited China in 1972 and published his impressions in *China Journal.*

Jack McPhaul dug up many newsroom experiences for *Deadlines and Monkeyshines.* Ben Hecht's years as a reporter provide bits in his autobiography *Child of the Century;* he also drew on them for *Gaily, Gaily* and numerous short stories.

Hoke Norris also has had extensive newspaper experience and during 1958-68 was literary editor of the *Chicago Sun-Times.* He is now director of public information of the Chicago Public Library. Besides numerous short stories and articles he has published two novels, *All the Kingdoms of Earth* (1956) and *It's Not Far But I Don't Know the Way* (1968).

James Weber Linn, who taught English composition to numerous budding authors at the University of Chicago and himself took a turn at writing editorials for the Hearst papers, wrote two biographies: *Jane Addams,* and *James Keeley, Newspaperman.* Keeley, one of the aggressive general managers of the *Tribune* who when alienated later tried to scare it with the *Chicago Herald,* once remarked ruefully that it was he who gave the *Tribune* its slogan, "The World's Greatest Newspaper."

Tom Fitzgerald, columnist for the *Chicago Sun-Times,* who won a Pulitzer prize in 1972 for reporting, is the author of *Fitz: All Together Now.* Mayor Daley has come under the appraising eye of Mike Royko, author of *Boss: Richard J. Daley of Chicago.*

Another author who has made the newspaper a springboard for a host of cultural activities is Van Allen Bradley, who had been literary editor of the *Chicago Daily News* and was writing its editorials when he retired in 1971. By that time he also had been associated with the Chicago Public Library, the Arts Council, and the theater, and become president of the Heritage Book Shop. His syndicated column on rare books prompted him to issue *Gold in Your Attic* in 1958; this has been followed by *More Gold in Your Attic,* 1961, and *New Gold in Your Attic,* 1968.

The Peatties deserve a place in the Illinois galaxy, both Roderick Peattie, the father, and Donald Culross Peattie, the son who wrote about Illinois in *A Prairie Grove,* and his wife Louise Redfield Peattie. And especially Mrs. Elia Peattie, long an outspoken book reviewer for the *Chicago Tribune,* memorable for her famous comment on Fannie Ward's *Three Weeks:* "This is twentyone days too much!" That was the last despairing cry of Victorian Chicago, for Mrs. Peattie was to be succeeded by Burton Rascoe, anti-puritan champion of naturalism, and Fanny Butcher, interpreter of the concise journalism of Rebecca West and the unsparing search for perfection of Willa Cather.

Medical journalism has been distinguished by the long and electrifying career of Morris Fishbein, editor of the *Medical World News* and for 36 years until 1949 editor of the *Journal* of the American Medical Assn. In 1969 he published an autobiography, *Morris Fishbein, M.D.,* which is also a chronicle of creative activities in Chicago.

John Drury was an able journalist whose research extended to old houses. He wrote *Historic Midwest Houses, Old Chicago Houses,* and *Old Illinois Houses; also Midwest Heritage.* His book, *Dining in Chicago,* has a foreword by Carl Sandburg. Among Drury's last undertakings was a monumental series of books about Illinois counties, which he produced for Loree Company, and which will be standard for years to come. His heart was in writing poetry.

VIII

Henry Justin Smith was the *Daily News* managing editor who gave assignments to Carl Sandburg, Ben Hecht, and the rest of the Wells St. galaxy. Smith wrote *Deadlines* and *Joslyn* about newspaper life; *The Captain of the Mayflower* was his essay into colonial history; he produced *Chicago, A Portrait,* and with Lloyd Lewis, *Chicago, the History of its Reputation.*

Lloyd Lewis was able to fill any editorial job, and eventually succeeded Smith; but he gave up that post to write a life of Ulysses S. Grant, completing only the first volume, *Captain Sam Grant.* It was carried forward by Bruce Catton. Lewis' heart was in Civil War reminiscence; *Myths After Lincoln* introduced Lincoln to many new readers; *Sherman, Fighting Prophet,* was both biography and history.

John Gunther was an energetic genius who worked for Smith but could not persuade Smith to send him abroad; he managed to get across on his own and by doing stints for the London and Paris offices got back on the *Daily News* payroll, finally landing the Vienna post when the Hitler *Anschluss* was brewing. By writing *Inside Europe* in 1936 at a publisher's invitation Gunther found a new channel for his curiosity and drive; more than 30 books came from his typewriter including *Chicago Revisited* in 1968. Gunther was a tireless worker and made elaborate preparations when starting a new project; he sent hundreds of queries to people who might be able to give him suggestions. His manuscripts and editions are at the University of Chicago.

At one point Gunther succeeded Paul Scott Mowrer in the Paris Bureau. Mowrer had worked for Smith and made a brilliant reputation reporting World War I; his brother Edgar Ansel Mowrer also served as correspondent for the *Daily News.* The Mowrers were born in Bloomington. Paul reported politics and war on several fronts, becoming an officer of the Legion of Honor, and writing *Balkanized Europe,* and *Hours of France,* a book of poems; also *The House of Europe* about his career. He eventually took charge of the editorial page of his newspaper during the Knight regime and published *Complete Poems* in 1968. He was poet laureate of New Hampshire when he died. Associated with these men was Raymond Swing, also foreign correspondent and later a distinguished newscaster, who wrote an autobiography, *Good Evening.*

Contemporary with Gunther and as ubiquitous in international reporting was Robert J. Casey, who served the *Daily News* from 1920 to 1947, covered every theater of war on land and sea, and published about forty books. The difference between the two authors was that Casey's work was straight reporting whereas Gunther's was also analytical and reflective. A native of South Dakota and alumnus *sans* degree of Armour Tech, Casey's first war experience was in the U. S. Field Artillery in World War I, when he rose from private to captain. Thereafter he reported fighting from the battle of London to Baghdad, the Far East, and the Pacific Ocean. In between wars he wrote about far places (*Easter Island*) and near ones (*The Black Hills*), sized up industry (*Lackawanna*) and saluted his hq (*Chicago Medium Rare*). With a touch of Irish wit he called his biography of Gutzon Borglum *Give the Man Room.* When he took on the artillery he called it *Cannoneers Have Hairy Ears* and published it anonymously.

Meyer Levin is one of the most competent novelists ever to come out of a newsroom. His strong identification with Jewish life and hopes gives authenticity to such books as *The Stronghold, My Father's House, Haggadah,* and *The Story of the Synagogue.* Levin achieved a solid popular success with *Compulsion,* which, prompted by the Leopold-Loeb tragedy, demonstrated his creative capacities. In *The Obsession* (1974) he described frustrating experiences with a play on Anne Frank.

Leonard Dubkin found an avenue for his research and writing that was neither crowded nor topical. His specialty was natural history. Among his last books were *White Lady* and *My Secret Place.*

Among other authors who worked for Henry Justin Smith were Robert Hardy Andrews, author of *A Corner of Chicago;* Ben Hecht, Harry Hansen, Charles H. Huff, Sterling North, Henry B. Sell, and Vincent Starrett. Starrett's long career as journalist, book collector, and discoverer of hidden talent, began on the *Chicago Daily News,* which sent him to Mexico to join General Fred Funston's expedition. He haunted bookshops and interpreted authors like Arthur Machen (*Buried Caesars*) but his hobby, the career of Sherlock Holmes, practically became his profession. He wrote *The Private Life of Sherlock Holmes* and became an authority on the mystery novel. His book comment appeared in the book section of the *Chicago Tribune.* His autobiography, *Born in a Bookshop,* tells much about Chicago's literary life, and *The Last Bookman,* compiled and published by Peter Ruber, adds piquant episodes to the Starrett saga. Henry Sell started his spectacular career of editor-promoter as book editor of the *Daily News;* his story is told in *A Talent for Living,* by Janet Leckie. Harry Hansen wrote *The Chicago* for the *Rivers of America* series and other books and this essay. Another of Smith's alumni was Charles H. Huff, who, under the name of Drexel Drake, wrote a series of books about the Falcon and invented the Falcon radio programs. Sterling North, another former book editor of the *Daily News* won awards with *Rascal,* the story of a pet raccoon, and other stories.

The many-sided aspects of Chicago life fill numerous books of fact and fiction. Arthur Meeker wrote feelingly about his city in *Prairie Avenue* and *To Chicago, with Love,* and Margaret Ayer Barnes won honors for her nostalgic *Years of Grace.* Finis Farr, who described a remarkable Chicago celebrity in *Black Champion: The Life and Times of Jack Johnson,* also wrote a biography of Frank Lloyd Wright. He is one of the latest authors to trace Chicago's fortunes in *Chicago: A Personal History of America's Most American City.* One of the warmest books ever written about a man's love for books and people is *The Seven Stairs,* in which Stuart Brent tells about his experiences with bookselling and broadcasting in Chicago.

Edna Ferber's imagination was strongly stimulated by her stay in Chicago, to which she came after newspaper experiences in her native Michigan and Wisconsin. She not only used the city for settings and personalities, but expressed her enthusiasm for its dynamic character. Her forte was portraying women in dramatic moments, and one of her most memorable was the hope-filled mother in the truck farm area of southern Chicagoland, in *So Big,* which won a Pulitzer prize. Her plays, written with George Kaufman, were the hits of their seasons; *Show Boat* lives on, chiefly because of Jerome Kern's melodic score, but Miss Ferber's revival of this romantic period in the theater was fortuitous.

Literary criticism and comment have acquired a wide range through the medium of television, as shown by Robert Cromie, former associate editor of *Book World,* of which Clarus Backes is editor. Cromie's interviews with authors on Book Beat have wide distribution via the National Educational Television network and have won a Peabody Award; he also maintains Cromie Circle for WGN-TV. From reporter he became war correspondent and then specialist in sports, notably golf. He first wrote *The Great Chicago Fire* in 1950 and returned to the subject with Herman Kogan in *The Great Fire* in 1971, its centenary. He has published *Dillinger, a Short and Violent Life,* an anthology of poetry, *Where Steel Winds Blow,* and *Chicago in Color* with Archie Lieberman, photographer.

Studs (Louis) Terkel has a place all his own in communications, for he is the principal commentator on jazz and folklore, and as organizer of programs reaches a large Illinois audience. Stuart Brent calls him "impresario of the wellsprings of culture." He holds both a bachelor's and a law degree, and has been in charge of folk festivals at Newport and the University of Chicago, and of the Ravinia Music Festival. Terkel adopted the testimonial method of narrative when producing *Hard Times, An Oral History of the Great Depression.* His *Giants of Jazz* is much consulted; he also has written *Division Street America, The Republican Establishment* and *Working,* a book of experiences related by many people. William H. (Bill) Mauldin's pencil, busy at the Sun-Times, knows little rest; his most recent publications are *I've Decided I Want My Seat Back* (1965), and *The Brass Ring* (1972).

And while guidebooks about Chicago blossom seasonally, there is one recent work that deserves a gilt-edged citation, *Chicago, An Extraordinary Guide,* by Jory Graham, which is exactly what the title says. Jory has also written *Instant Chicago: How to Cope,* and her column, Jory Graham's City, appears regularly in the *Sun-Times.*

Authors of new books are interviewed regularly in Chicago on both radio and television right through the week. Irv Kupcinet, who started his newspaper career by writing about sports on the *Chicago Times,* has been writing a column since 1943 and in 1960 established Kup's Show, which has a large following on television Channel 5. His column now appears in the *Sun-Times* and 90 other newspapers and his show in 13 other cities. Authors also appear on the Kennedy & Company Show on Channel 7 and the Lee Phillips Show on Channel 2.

Special awards were given authors in contests held by the Illinois Sesquicentennial Commission, which wound up a year's observance of the State's "Sesqui" at Springfield on Dec. 2, 1968. John B. Wolf, professor of history at the University of Illinois, Chicago Circle, received $1,500 for nonfiction for *Louis XIV;* David P. Etter of Geneseo shared the $1,500 award for poetry with Ralph Pomeroy of New York; Mrs. Anna Karkut, editor of the *Lockport Herald,* won $400 for distinguished newspaper work, and Mrs. Sol Yockley won $400 for the best magazine article, "The Village That George Pullman Built," in the *Chicago Tribune Magazine.* Citations went to the *Rockford Morning Star and Register Republic,* the Paddock Newspapers of Arlington Heights, the Talman Savings & Loan Assn. of Chicago and Scott Craig of NBC.

The citation of Paddock Circle Newspapers brings into focus a phenomenon of Illinois publishing: the proliferation of suburban newspapers and their growth from weekly, biweekly, and triweekly issues into dailies. Paddock has nine daily newspapers each named *Herald,* (Arlington Heights, Buffalo Grove, Des Plaines, Elk Grove, Mt. Prospect, Palatine, Rolling Meadows, Hoffman Estates-Schaumburg, and Wheeling). It has eight weeklies, including those at Mundelein and Waukegan. Many suburban weeklies are members of groups, such as the Economist, Peacock, and Crescent Newspapers and the Lerner chains. Field Enterprises in 1966 established *Arlington Day* and *Prospect Day,* but finding them unprofitable sold them to Paddock.

The Stage: Plays and Operas

I

DURING THE PIONEER PERIOD Chicago became the center of the theater in Illinois. In 1837, the year the city was incorporated, the first actors who came to Chicago were kept from performing because they could not afford to buy a license. Before long, however, two managers purchased a license, improvised a theater in the dining room of the Sauganash Hotel, and staged Kotzebue's *The Stranger.*

"In the year of 1838," wrote Jefferson in his autobiography, "the new town of Chicago had just turned from an Indian village into a thriving little place, and my uncle had written to my father urging him to join in the management of the new theater which was then being built there." The Jefferson family traveled part of the journey through the Erie Canal on a packet-boat. It was called the *Pioneer,* and it was most appropriate, for the Jeffersons were among the first players to migrate to the West.

In 1847 John Rice, later mayor of Chicago, opened the first Chicago Theatre on the second floor of a building near Dearborn and Randolph Sts. Here appeared both dramatic actors, in Shakespeare and current plays, and comedians with monologues and songs. Stars of these days and for several decades later, such as Edwin Forrest, Junius Brutus Booth and Edwin Booth, Charles Kean, and Charlotte Cushman, often traveled with a few supporting actors and filled their casts with local amateurs, who would be prompted from the wings, a practice called winging. Rice's theater burned down and he erected his second Chicago Theatre.

John H. McVicker, a popular actor, built the third theater in Chicago in 1857, at a cost of $85,000, and named it after himself. The name and location persist today. Crosby's Opera House, famed throughout the Midwest, was built in 1865 at a cost of $600,000. Other well-known theaters were Wood's Museum, North's Amphitheater, Aiken's, the Academy of Music, the Globe, and the Dearborn. In 1871 the Great Fire destroyed 14 showhouses.

In the lore of theaters Crosby's Opera House is famous. It served the public only six years, but it made its mark. It was, from all accounts, one of the finest theaters of its time. It was designed by W. W. Boyington in an Italianate style for Uranus H. Crosby, a distiller, and stood on the north side of Washington Street, nearer State than Dearborn. It had a tall arched entrance and a mansard roof and its ground floor was occupied by music houses. The auditorium seated 2,500 and was illuminated by hundreds of gas lamps. It was formally opened on April 20, 1861, with a performance of *Il Trovatore* by the Maurice Grau Opera Company.

The most notorious episode in Chicago theater history took place in January, 1897, when Crosby auctioned off his opera house in a lottery that made a national sensation. He offered 210,000 chances at $5 a ticket. The drawing was spectacular; 25,000 unsold tickets remained the property of Crosby. The winning ticket was said to have been held by a veteran named Lee who lived in Prairie du Rocher. Few persons ever saw him and his army record was never found. Lee was said to have resold the opera house to Crosby for $200,000. The *Chicago Tribune* figured that even if Crosby paid that sum he had cleared $650,000. Evidently Chicago became too hot for Crosby, for he turned the house over to his brother Albert and moved east. Four years later the house was destroyed in the Great Fire.

Between 1871 and 1894 dozens of theaters rose in Chicago, which sheltered stock companies, touring companies doing one-night stands, and stars of national repute. Sam T. Jack's became widely known for burlesque that appealed especially to farmhands that came with shipments of livestock. The floating theaters, with melodrama and variety programs on show boats, stopped at Shawneetown and Metropolis on the Ohio, Rock Island, Moline, Quincy, Alton and Cairo on the Mississippi, and Peoria, Pekin, Morris, Marseilles, Ottawa, LaSalle and Beardstown on the Illinois.

During and after the Civil War theatergoers began to patronize minstrels as entertainers. The social significance of minstrelsy did not engage the theatergoers of the time; they hugely enjoyed black-face comedians who told jokes in what was supposed to be a Negro vernacular, saw romantic sketches based on plantation life and applauded the songs of Stephen Foster. Christy's minstrels were among the earliest, and Dan Emmett, an Ohio actor who wrote *Dixie,* was a minstrel. Lew Dockstader, Barlow, Primrose and West had long careers in this musical form. Minstrel performances lasted until the turn of the century, and even after they became outmoded black-face was used by comedians down to the days of Eddie Cantor. Today the social consciousness of the Negro prohibits the use of such humorous sketches except by the black comedians themselves.

In the final quarter of the 19th century, when social topics began to vitalize the theaters of London and Paris, the American stage was deep in an emotional orgy. Clara Morris and Mary Anderson made audiences weep with their portrayal of hapless women. Augustin Daly, New York producer of topical drama as well as Shakespeare, sent John Drew and Ada Rehan annually to Chicago on tour.

At the turn of the century Richard Mansfield held an enviable position as a tragedian; Minnie Maddern married Harrison Grey Fiske, an independent producer, and became prominent as Mrs. Fiske; Clyde Fitch developed a career as a playwright of drawing-room dramas, and Sarah Bernhardt toured the country in repertory. These performers played to intelligent audiences at the Powers and the Grand in Chicago, but there were always dramas of violence, and a score of popular actors who appeared in melodrama and folk situations. William Gillette's art in *Sherlock Holmes* started the vogue of detectives as heroes and Kyrle Bellow gave social prestige to thieves in *Raffles,* while David Belasco became famous for reproducing every item of bric-a-brac in his materialistic settings for emotional plays, of which Charles Klein's *The Music Master* made a fortune for himself and David Warfield.

These performances were not limited to Chicago. The "road" at the turn of the century offered a vast variety of grave and gay plays to middle-sized towns, to Bloomington, Decatur, Freeport, Peoria, Rockford, Rock Island, and numerous other "opera houses" that did not see opera but could offer Robert B. Mantell, John Drew, Mrs. Leslie Carter, James B. Herne, David Warfield, James K. Hackett, the Barrymores—any number of stars who endured midnight trains, cold theaters, second-rate lodging and irregular meals to make a living, before the movies brought them the rewards of mass attendance.

In the pre-war days of the new century several changes took place in the theater. Vaudeville flourished, and the Majestic in Chicago kept pace with the Palace in New York. The Road died, and theaters in many cities closed their doors, while stars shifted to vaudeville. There was, however, a portent of things to come. At the end of every vaudeville program came a motion picture, silent except for the tinkling of a piano, which reflected the mood. In the midst of the war a great comedian, Charlie Chaplin, drew thousands of homebodies into the theater. An entirely new audience became the mainstay of a form of entertainment that reached every corner of Illinois; eventually the rural drive-in had the same fare as the gaudy palace of Balaban & Katz in the Loop.

In theatrical history Chicago is the place where the Little Theater movement originated, and Maurice Browne, a British lecturer who arrived around 1910, is usually considered the pioneer. This circumstance calls for a bit of explanation. Browne did not invent the little theater movement, for dedicated groups had been producing plays and playlets for years, but he came at the time when writing and producing plays for art and not for commercial gain became a fighting issue, and by his energetic propaganda inspired others. The Little Theater in the Studebaker Building had only 100 seats but it sufficed as a foundation. Browne produced plays by Bernard Shaw, Strindberg, Schnitzler, and the classic Greeks, and toured as far as the Pacific Coast with his little company. After World War I Browne had a big success as producer of *Journey's End,* and later he collaborated with Robert Nichols on *Wings Over Europe,* which forecast the devastation likely to be wrecked by the airplane of the future.

While the Little Theater was stimulating interest in a whole new repertory of plays of ideas, a group called the Hull House Players was producing plays of social import. On one occasion. Theodore Roosevelt attended their performance of Galsworthy's *Justice* and commended social issues in the theater so strongly that his remarks were carried by the Associated Press.

The agitation among amateurs did not keep the regular playgoer from enjoying himself in the commercial theater. A syndicate of New York producers, including Charles Frohman, Marc Klaw, Abraham Erlanger, and Al Hayman had tried to control theaters and dictate terms to actors and playwrights. David Belasco and Harrison Grey Fiske opposed them, and soon the young Shuberts, who built theaters and mounted productions, became as great a power in the theatrical marketplace. The Chicago public, eager for entertainment, patronized old favorites and novelties. Revues proved especially popular and developed many new comedians. The *Follies,* rich in pulchritude and opulently caparisoned, came annually, shepherded by a Chicagoan named Florenz Ziegfield, Jr., whose father had founded the Chicago Musical College and who himself had managed Sandow, the strong man of Europe, at the 1893 World's Fair. Similarly came George White's *Scandals* and Earl Carroll's *Vanities,* and from England *Charlot's Revue* introduced Beatrice Lillie, Gertrude Lawrence, Jack Buchanan, and Donald Meek. New York may have been the producing center, but Chicago welcomed as friends Fannie Brice, W. C. Fields, Al Jolson, Bert Lahr, Ed Wynn, and Eddie Cantor, and contributed to their success. The musicals of Victor Herbert and the D'Oyly Carte productions of Gilbert and Sullivan found a ready audience. The witty comedies of George S. Kaufman came frequently; sometimes he collaborated with Edna Ferber, whose *Show Boat* gave Jerome Kern a vehicle for a memorable musical and added *Old Man River* to the repertory of popular songs, first sung here by Paul Robeson. Robert E. Sherwood wrote *Young Lincoln of Illinois,* which has annual presentation at New Salem State Park. Noel Coward added a touch of sophistication to the playbills. And E. H. Sothern and Julia Marlowe toured Illinois annually and exhibited their fine diction in Shakespeare's plays.

There was always a ready welcome in Chicago for playwrights of promise. One of these was Edward Sheldon, whose first play, *Salvation Nell,* was enthusiastically commended by Mrs. Fiske. Sheldon, a fine craftsman, did not follow through with social themes but scored a big success with *Romance,* a nostalgic vehicle for Doris Keane. This opened in the Princess Theatre, which, with the LaSalle on West Madison, was a producing base for Mort H. Singer. Although the LaSalle had fewer than 800 seats it became famous for its long-run musicals starring Cecil Lean and Florence Holbrook, with Joe E. Howard as composer and demonstrator of popular songs. Today the LaSalle has been displaced by a religious chapel. Another reaching for literary honors was William Vaugh Moody, member of the English faculty at the University of Chicago and highly esteemed poet, who wrote *The Great Divide,* in which New England sophistication was pitted against Southwestern peasant brutality, but whose promise was cut short by his early death.

About this time the Chicago Theater Company was formed to produce a repertory of original plays. It was inspired by the acclaim that greeted the Irish Players from the Abbey Theater in Dublin, who exploited folk legends collected by J. M. Sygne, Lady Gregory, and William Butler Yeats. The honest portrayal of simple people in homely situations drawn from Ireland's tragic past pleased the American intellectuals. Dublin audiences had differed over the use of native material; some considered the vernacular degrading and familiar behavior irreverent of religion. When, for instance, Sara Allgood referred in a play to a chemise a new rising was narrowly averted. When the Abbey Players under W. G. Fay produced Sygne's *Playboy of the Western World,* there were brawls in Dublin, which were repeated several years later in New York. Certain interested persons hoped for similar outbursts in Chicago but the audiences there remained unmoved. Although the Irish Players opposed the conventional theater Fay and his troupe were sent to Chicago by none other than Charles Frohman, a member of the hated syndicate, who had no interest in the revolt of the young but merely wanted an amusing curtain-riser to bolster his main investment, a moribund French comedy. Lady Gregory had a play produced by the Chicago Theater Company, which closed after one season for want of suitable acting material.

In Chicago the new movement in the theatre was not isolated from the other arts; the young hopefuls who talked and theorized about plays and acting included poets, novelists, and newspapermen. George Cram Cook was Floyd Dell's associate on the *Chicago Post* before he wrote for the Provincetown Players and married Susan Glaspell, also a playwright; Charles MacArthur was a reporter for the Hearst papers in Chicago before he wrote *The Front Page* and other plays with Ben Hecht. Ben had his first comedy produced at the LaSalle Opera House with Leo Ditrichstein as the star. Lawrence Langner, a Welsh-born patent lawyer, came to Chicago to open an office and became infected with talk about playwriting at Margery Currey's hospitable salon on East 57th St. at Jackson Park; then went to New York to organize the Washington Square Players and the Theatre Guild and send Chicago *Oklahoma!* and Lunt and Fontanne.

Standard playhouses in Chicago are the Blackstone, on Balbo Drive; the Civic Theatre, 20 N. Wacker Dr., in the Civic Opera Building; McVicker's, 25 West Madison St.; the Shubert, 25 West Monroe, originally the Majestic; and the Studebaker, 418 S. Michigan Ave. The Auditorium, on Congress Drive, is used for ballets and musicals. Kenneth Sawyer Goodman Memorial Theatre at the Art Institute produces both original plays and repertory and goes on tour. The Arie Crown Theatre in McCormick Place is used intermittently. Fifty years ago there were 29 theaters in the Loop.

The inspiration of the Hull House Players continues in the 1970s. Today the Hull House Association is an amateur acting group that performs modern and avant-garde plays to small audiences and encourages original work. The organizer and sparkplug of the movement is William Robert Sickinger, who started in 1963. He endeavors to build support by subscription and by touring the colleges. The Hull

House Theatre at Jane Addams Center, 3212 North Broadway, has performances on Friday, Saturday, and Sunday, and seats 140. The Hull House Parkway Theatre, 500 East 67th St., in a predominantly black neighborhood, often has plays of ethnic interest, and has developed a Children's Theatre. The Hull House Playwrights Center, 222 W. North Ave., gives young playwrights an opportunity to talk shop and see their work performed. The Hull House Leo Lerner Theatre, 4520 N. Beacon St., puts on plays with music.

All major colleges have theaters and courses in playwriting, acting and stage management, and give a number of performances seasonally, with the townspeople becoming part of the audience. In the case of organizations that play repertory, professionals are often cast in the leading roles.

An impressive example of the important place the theater holds in the colleges is the Krannert Center for the Performing Arts at the University of Illinois in Urbana. Here are four indoor theaters and one outdoor amphitheatre including the Festival, seating 979; the Playhouse, 678; the Studio, 150. The Great Hall, seating 2,092, is primarily for concerts. The Center has facilities for rehearsing, building scenery, and making costumes. It produces five plays during the school year and a number during the summer. Studio presents six experimental plays. Krannert drew an attendance of 126,000 in its first year, 1969, and 140,800 the next.

The Court Theatre, at the University of Chicago, performs in Hutchinson Court, University Ave. and 57th St., July to September. Leon Mandell Assembly Hall has been used for plays for many years. Harper Theatre, 530 S. Harper Ave., attracts a college audience. At Northwestern University, Evanston, training for the theater is part of the curriculum of the School of Speech. The Northwestern Drama Festival presents three plays in rotation during its summer season and the University Theatre gives a group of plays during the college year.

For many decades patrons of the theater have profited by perceptive and intelligent criticism in the press. Percy Hammond, Burns Mantle, Ashton Stevens, and James O'Donnell Bennett established their reputations in Chicago. Claudia Cassidy, theater and music critic of the *Chicago Tribune* from 1942 to 1965 and now critic at large, continues to give her views in a weekly radio report.

Anyone consulting a city guide must conclude that Chicago and environs are a veritable testing ground of theaters. Some of the houses in the suburbs are quite substantial but many are small and limit performances to a few nights a week. A number concentrate on experimental plays, and there are several in which improvisation is cultivated. The Ivanhoe Theatre, 3000 N. Clark St., is a theater-in-the-square; the Oak Park-River Forest Civic Theatre has the audience seated close to the stage, and in a number of houses the stage is an arena. The Old Town Players, 1718 N. Park St., act in a remodeled church with a stage reaching into the seating zone. The Lincoln Players perform in the Boathouse at Lincoln Park and the Theater on the Lake uses the open Fullerton Pavilion on summer evenings.

There is another fashion in entertainment that has had its best response in the metropolitan area: the combination of playgoing with dining. The restaurant theater, or theater-restaurant, has found acceptance, chiefly in the suburbs. Music and dining (or drinking) have gone together successfully for a century—even Theodore Thomas presided over Strauss waltzes while his audience drank beer in the Exposition Hall. But plays demand more concentration, and most of the theater-restaurants separate them from food. For instance, the Forum, in Summit, in presenting a Broadway musical with an auspicious cast, announces that box lunches will be available an hour before show time. *The Fiddler on the Roof,* booked "indefinitely" at the Candlelight Dinner Playhouse, also in Summit, allocated one and one-half hours for dining before the curtain. The Drury Lane in Evergreen Park offered dinner-theater price combinations. The Second City, 1616 N. Wells St., had a dinner-show combination whereby diners were served in That Steak Joynt in Piper's Alley. Whether the playgoer received more enjoyment before or after dining was not on the record.

OPERA

The history of opera in Illinois is concentrated in Chicago, although smaller travelling companies sang operas and operettas in Peoria, Rock Island, Springfield and a dozen other towns during the last century. These were usually one-night stands, although longer engagements were to be found in St. Louis, Milwaukee and Indianapolis, easily accessible to Illinois followers of opera. Touring was dependent on the condition of the railroads. There are many anecdotes of theatrical troupes arriving hours late because of derailments and washouts, losing their wardrobe trunks and acting in borrowed costumes, for the show must go on.

Chicago had its first opportunity to hear opera sung on July 29, 1850, when four artists sang Bellini's *La Sonambula* at John H. Rice's Chicago Theatre. Years later it was to be sung by Lilli Lehmann, Rosa Raisa, and that incomparable coloratura, Amelita Galli-Curci. On the second night of the opera the theater burned down, and three years elapsed before a second group of Italian singers arrived to present *Norma* and *Lucia di Lammermoor* in Rice's rebuilt theater.

In the interval Chicago experienced a musical event portentous in retrospect, nothing less than the first appearance in the city of Adelina Patti, then 10 years old, who was to become the most famous and highest-paid lyric soprano of the late 19th century. She sang in the hall of the Tremont House, at Dearborn and Lake Sts., sharing the evening with Ole Bull, the violin virtuoso. She was to return many times and in 1889 sang at the dedication of the great new Auditorium.

Orchestral music paralleled the growth of opera in Chicago. From 1859 until 1905 the name of Theodore Thomas was synonymous with orchestral development in the Middle West. Thomas toured the region in 1859 with the operatic company of Karl Formes, famous German basso. On October 9, 1871, the young violinist led his own symphony orchestra in a concert at the Crosby Opera House, playing one of Beethoven's overtures to *Fidelio,* a scherzo from a Schumann symphony, and music by Chopin, Gounod, Schubert, and Wagner. Later that night the Chicago Fire forced the musicians of the Thomas Orchestra to flee from a North Side hotel. In 1891 Thomas formed the Chicago Orchestra. With nearly 8,500 Chicagoans contributing to a popular subscription fund, the present Orchestra Hall was erected on Michigan Avenue in 1904, but Thomas lived only long enough to direct three concerts there. He was succeeded in 1905 by Frederick Stock, who led the orchestra for 37 seasons, until his death in 1942.

In the 1840s and 1850s families of strolling singers and musicians were extremely popular throughout the State, and monopolized the musical entertainment field. The Sable melodist, the Negro minstrels, the Algerines, the Antoni, the Newhall, and the Peak families were welcomed warmly wherever they performed. In 1853 the Swiss Bell Ringers appeared before an overflow crowd of 800 persons at the Springfield courthouse. The trend toward musical self-expression also thrived at Alton, where "Professor" Van Meter conducted a music course attended by 500 pupils, 150 of whom appeared in graduation recitals. By the end of the period, bands and choral societies had been organized in many Illinois towns. Grierson's Band at Jacksonville gained wide attention for its unique method of playing by notation instead of by ear. The number of music lovers increased so rapidly that in 1852 a two-day statewide convention was held at Springfield. A *Sängerbund* was organized in Belleville in 1865, followed by a Philharmonic Society in 1867.

Between 1840 and 1850 American music was further stimulated by the arrival of immigrants from Europe. Early music in Illinois had a distinctly German flavor. Hans Balatka, once a choral conductor in Vienna, was appointed to lead the newly organized Philharmonic Orchestra at Chicago in 1860. His first program included the Second Symphony of Beethoven and a chorus from *Tannhäuser,* the first Wagnerian music to be played in the region. The Germania Orchestra of New York was one of the first large orchestras to tour Illinois. Among visiting artists at this time were Richard Hoffman, Gottschalk, and Rubenstein.

Choruses, instrumental groups, and recitals by artists were almost entirely suspended during the Civil War. Only minstrels singing war songs were popular. After Lee's surrender and peace, Chicago, Jacksonville, Peoria, Rock Island, Alton, Cairo, and many other places were again visisted by musicians. German violinists, who played for dances, filled out a meager living by giving lessons to the young at a standardized rate of 50¢ an hour.

Soon conservatories were created to meet a definite need: the Chicago Conservatory of music in 1866; the Illinois Conservatory of Music at Jacksonville in 1871; the Department of Music at Northwestern

University, with Peter Christian Lutkin at its head, in 1873; the Knox Conservatory of Music at Galesburg in 1883; and the Chicago Musical College, founded in 1887 by Dr. Florenz Ziegfeld. The Chicago Musical College is now a component part of Roosevelt University.

The development of music in the public schools was at first slow and difficult. With no folk songs in general circulation the early settlers from the East had only the hymns they had learned in the churches. Sometimes veterans remembered the patriotic jingles and ballads they had heard in camp; *The Girl I Left Behind Me* was a staple of every fife and drum corps. After S. F. Smith wrote *America* to the tune of *God Save the King* and *Heil Dir im Siegeskranz*, every schoolchild sang it. In the final half of the 19th century many schools used manuals that included such popular songs as *Columbia, the Gem of the Ocean, Hail Columbia*, and even the difficult *Star Spangled Banner*, which did not become the national anthem until 1931.

With the flood of immigration beginning in the 1870's a new influence for singing arrived in Illinois. People from North and Central Europe were bursting with song, and male singing societies were quickly formed by Bohemians, Germans, Austrians, including the Tyrolese; Poles and Swedes. The *Sängerfest* became general throughout the Middle West and was active as long as the original immigrants remained.

By 1885 nine Illinois towns boasted of large singing societies. A few years later Jacksonville had an excellent chorus; the Peoria Oratorio Society performed with 75 voices. The Northwestern University musical groups were giving well-attended recitals.

By 1908 26 conservatories, colleges and universities throughout the State, offered courses in music. The State university pioneered by crediting music toward a degree. The course of study prepared in 1915 by the committee of county superintendents' section of the Illinois State Teachers' Association included an outline for music in elementary grades.

School orchestras are as numerous today in the small towns as in the cities. Music festivals have become legion, beginning with competition in each town, then narrowing to a number of towns vying for honors in a district meet, and finally centering in a State contest.

In the decades between 1870 and 1900 Chicago audiences became thoroughly familiar with standard works and the great voices of the operatic stage. In *Opera in Chicago* Ronald L. Davis lists six major organizations that had regular seasons before the city began to support a home-based company. He calls Emma Abbott Chicago's "first real operatic discovery," since she came from Peoria as a girl in the early 1860s and sang at the Sherman House, returning in 1879 as a mature singer. In the 1880s Col. James Mapleson came with Adelina Patti as his star, and Henry Abbott brought Christine Nilsson and Marcela Sembrich. Walter Damrosch stepped into his father's shoes as director of their German Opera Company and brought *Tannhäuser* and other Wagnerian works.

Patti won all hearts. In the 1890s she appeared with the Abbey and Grau company as Juliet, Lucia, Violetta, Amina, Rosina and in other roles. It was truly the golden age of opera, for Nordica sang Aida, Tomagno Otello, Lilli Lehmann Elisabeth, and present also to delight their hearers were Emma Eames, Nellie Melba, Jean de Reszke and his brother Eduard de Reszke, Johanna Gadski and Calvé. Henry W. Savage bought the Castle Square Opera Company and presented all the standard operas in English at popular prices, getting such a response that, according to Davis, he was able to give the city a season of several months a year for nearly a decade. Savage could present *Lohengrin* and *The Mikado* on alternate evenings, both to crowded houses.

Not all the personalities of the operatic world had a warm welcome in Chicago. Pietro Mascagni made no impression; his visit to the United States came under poor auspices and his own bearing was ungracious. But when Heinrich Conried brought the Metropolitan Opera Company in 1905 he gained tremendous approval by introducing Enrico Caruso in *Lucia,* and the famous sextet. He also presented the first *Parsifal* with an air of religious dedication, defying the family of Richard Wagner, which had expected to restrict performances to Bayreuth and failed to get an injunction in New York. The Metropolitan came to Chicago for six seasons, and in 1909 Arturo Toscanini appeared for the first time, conducting *Aida* for Emmy Destinn's debut.

Out-of-town opera companies had done fairly well in Chicago. By 1909 local pride demanded a complete home-grown operation and Harold F. McCormick, Charles G. Dawes and John C. Shaffer rallied 47 other tycoons to subscribe to a guarantee fund of $250,000 to support the Chicago Grand Opera Company. Members of the board of the Metropolitan Opera Assn. joined the Chicago board. When Oscar Hammerstein sold his Manhattan Opera Company to the Metropolitan, the latter provided Chicago with much of Hammerstein's equipment, as well as artists. These included Cleofonte Campanini, who became musical director, and Mary Garden, soprano who had electrified New York. Andreas Dippel of the Metropolitan became general manager. The Chicago company, which made an agreement to perform one month annually in Philadelphia, opened November 3, 1910, with that staple of Italian opera, *Aida.*

Mary Garden, born in Scotland, lived her girlhood years in Chicago. When she was about 19 a patron of the arts, Mrs. David Mayer, financed her musical education in Paris, where Mary made her debut in *Louise* at 23. In Chicago, as in New York, Mary Garden became the sensation of the hour for her performances in *Salome* and *Thais.* Her Dance of the Seven Veils in *Salome,* in the course of which she kissed the severed head of John the Baptist, became the talk of the town and brought a famous quip from the Chief of Police: "Miss Garden wallowed around like a cat in a bed of catnip." The opera had two performances but the management cancelled a third, and the debate over morality in the arts went on at a feverish rate in a city where puritanism was dying hard.

The company also produced Puccini's *The Girl of the Golden West,* with Carolina White, an American soprano, and cast Melba in

La Boheme, Geraldine Farrar in *Madame Butterfly,* Tetrazzini in *Lucia di Lammermoor,* Jenny Dufau in *Lakmé,* Maggie Teyte in *The Marriage of Figaro,* and Mary Garden in *Pelleas and Melisande, The Jongleur of Notre Dame,* and *Carmen.* There were notable novelties: Wolf-Ferrari's *The Jewels of the Madonna* and *The Secret of Suzanne,* and an original work by Victor Herbert, *Natoma,* the story of a lovesick Indian maid for an American naval officer. In interviews, Herbert expressed his conviction that the time had come for Americans to write operas, but despite his conviction, original operas by Cadman, Walter Damrosch, Reginald de Koven, Arthur Nevin and Deems Taylor failed to hold the interest of producers and audience and were rarely repeated. Only short works by Menotti, such as *The Old Maid and the Thief,* were heard more often and were found adaptable for television.

THE ARRIVAL OF GALLI-CURCI

On the afternoon of Saturday, November 18, 1916, Campanini presented a new artist in a performance that changed the fortunes of the Auditorium. Amelita Galli-Curci opened her Chicago career by singing Juliet in Verdi's *Romeo and Juliet.* The coloratura was not unknown abroad; she had begun singing in Italy in 1906, had sung in two performances with Caruso in Buenos Aires in 1912, and in Madrid and St. Petersburg before coming to Chicago. Campanini had given her an audition in New York and on the urging of friends had agreed to give her a two-performance contract at $300 each. Better terms had been given her by the Victor Talking Machine Company of Camden, N. J. Thus Campanini seems to have taken her for granted, which accounts for the lack of promotion and the choice of a Saturday matinee for Galli-Curci's debut in Chicago. The performance was an explosion. The enthusiasm of the audience was indescribable; even the critics lost their bearings. Herman DeVries drew on superlatives: Never in 30 years had he heard "such matchless, flawless beauty of tone, so satiny a timbre, such delicately lovely phrasing, such God-given talent and feeling for the true *bel-canto."* Campanini also caught the fever and during the first rehearsal rushed to the singer's dressing room to raise her pay to $1,000 per performance. During the season Galli-Curci sang 15 times in five operas; *Rigoletto, Lucia, Romeo and Juliet, La Traviata* and *The Barber of Seville.* Her ability to fill the Auditorium resulted in a new contract at $1,500 a performance during ten weeks in Chicago and six weeks on tour, and a special arrangement for concerts.

In January, 1918, the Chicago company played its customary season in New York, where the enthusiasm was repeated and Galli-Curci as Dinorah drew 61 curtain calls. She gave innumerable concerts and in 1920 her prestige was so great that she was able to sign contracts with both Chicago and the Metropolitan.

Dippel was a German tenor and would have promoted German opera, but the preference for Italian and French works was so strong that no German opera was offered until 1911. Then the company produced *Die Walküre* with Fremstad and Nordica alternating and Schumann-Heink; *Tristan und Isolde* with Fremstad and Dalmores;

Lohengrin with Carolina White and Dalmores, and *Hansel und Gretel* with Schumann-Heink. When Dippel resigned in 1914 McCormick bought the shares of the eastern investors and made Cleofonte Campanini director with blanket authority. Campanini strengthened the cast by adding Rosa Raisa, Lucien Muratore, Cyrena van Gordon, Florence Macbeth and Frances Alda. His first year ended with a deficit of $250,000, which led to the hurried departure of some of the backers, including John H. Shaffer, publisher of the *Chicago Post.*

Thereupon the Chicago Grand Opera Company went into receivership and Harold McCormick bought the remaining assets. But his dedication was real and his cash had not yet run out, so in 1915 he formed the Chicago Opera Assn. Charles G. Dawes was still with him as vice president and so was McCormick's wife, Edith Rockefeller McCormick, daughter of John D. Rockefeller, who had spending money of her own. Among the new backers was Samuel Insull.

Cleofonte Campanini died of pneumonia in December, 1919, and the board appointed Gino Marinuzzi artistic director and Herbert Johnson, executive director. The addition of Tito Schipa, tenor, to the cast was widely approved. The performance of Charles Marshall as Otello caused another outburst of enthusiasm, but this casting did not sit well with the Italian members of the cast. This and other altercations caused Marinuzzi to resign. The board, at the insistence of the McCormicks, named Mary Garden artistic and business director, to the great surprise of the opera company and the public. Garden had returned to the cast to sing in *Aphrodite, Faust* and *Monna Vanna.* She now named Giorgio Polacco principal conductor and added Edith Mason, Polacco's wife, Claire Dux, Lina Cavalieri and Marguerite D'Alvarez to the roster. German opera was sung for the first time in English, a concession to the still lingering resentment caused by the world war. A novelty was *The Love for Three Oranges* by Serge Prokofiev, sung in French. The opera, with neither melodic line nor conventional plotting, confused and disappointed critics and public. It was given twice, with the composer conducting.

Mary Garden's management had been expensive, as expected; the deficit of the company in 1921 reached $1,100,000, which the McCormicks made up. In April, 1922, Mary Garden resigned, and the McCormicks dropped out, by previous agreement. The Association ended and a new corporation, the Chicago Civic Opera was formed, with Samuel Insull president and Charles G. Dawes vice president. The new backing was a fund of $500,000, made up by 500 guarantors who pledged $1,000 a year for five years.

Broadcasting of opera over radio began in Chicago over station KYW on Jan. 1, 1922, with *Rigoletto.* It was heard throughout Illinois but encountered static.

In his first year Insull had his first brush with the artistic temperament. Galli-Curci had agreed to open her season as Lakmé but changed to Dinorah. Polacco, whose plans were well advanced, refused to make the change. Galli-Curci appealed to Insull, who backed up Polacco.

Galli-Curci honored her contract, but served notice that this would be her last season with the company. Her departure brought much criticism of Insull's stand, for she was both a financial and an artistic asset to the opera.

Samuel Insull, who thus entered the field of opera by a side door, was at the height of his influence as a utilities magnate. Born in England, he came to the United States as a young man and obtained employment as secretary to Thomas A. Edison in New York. So well did he apprehend utilities management that in 1892, when he was 32, he was sent to Chicago to become president of the Chicago Edison Co. He became a naturalized American citizen in 1896. He won the confidence of business leaders and borrowed $250,000 from Marshall Field for his own purposes. He bought the Commonwealth Electric Co., a politically motivated corporation, and built up the Commonwealth Edison Co. He bought control of smaller utility companies, combined some, and developed holding companies. This brought him control of the Middle West Utilities Co., the Public Service Co. of Northern Illinois, and the Peoples Gas Light & Coke. He started rural electrification in Lake County, where he had his farm. During World War II he headed the Council of Defense for Illinois. Since utilities needed public franchises Insull cultivated the goodwill of office-holders by contributing to their campaign expenses.

Insull's control of the Chicago Civic Opera extended from November, 1922, to January, 1934, when the company, faced with another huge deficit in the midst of the Depression, closed. During those ten years the Chicago public heard many fine artists and saw superb productions, including some new work in order to keep abreast of the changing forms of musical expression. Among its highlights were the Boris Godunov of Chaliapin; *Königskinder* of Humperdinck and Strauss' *Der Rosenkavalier* with Kipnis; *La Juive* by Halevy and *Judith* by Honneger; Cadman's *A Witch of Salem* in English; and a new *Camille* by an American, Hamilton Forrest. Newcomers among the artists were Gladys Swarthout, a Chicago soprano, and Lotte Lehmann. Harling introduced jazz elements into the score of *A Light From St. Agnes* to the dismay of many. Mary Garden sang in Alfano's *Resurrection* and left the company—and opera.

The big event of Insull's regime was the building of the new home for the opera at 20 N. Wacker Drive, abutting on the Chicago River at Madison St. Insull had considered the Auditorium a liability and formed a separate corporation, with Stanley Field as vice president, to swing the new enterprise. He engaged the architects Graham, Probst, Anderson & White, who had designed the Merchandise Mart and the Union Station. The new building had a central section 42 stories and 550 ft. tall, flanked by two smaller office structures, each 21 stories tall. The main auditorium was 12 stories high and had no pillars; it seated 3,517 and had a foyer 119 ft. long and 39 ft. high. The stage was 120 ft. wide, 75 ft. deep, and had overhead space for the settings of ten operas. There was a smaller theater with 878 seats. Seen from the riverside the structure was nicknamed Insull's Armchair.

In April, 1932, Insull's utilities empire went into receivership. The great financial structure could not meet its obligations. Hungry investors who had gladly ridden on Insull's coattails when he was prospering now condemned him and sued him. Polacco, Edith Mason, Rosa Raisa, and Cesare Formichi, who had entrusted their earnings to Insull, lost them. Insull left for Europe, but was eventually brought back to face embezzlement charges. He was acquitted, but he was practically a pauper, and died soon after, his operatic dream unfulfilled.

While the censensus was that Insull had overreached himself, rational commentators agreed that never before had Chicago heard such a wealth of opera. There had been 88 performances in the 1931-32 season. There was none at the Civic Opera the next year. But on December 26, 1933, a new group ventured to recapture the audience in 27 performances, with Maria Jeritza and Lauritz Melchior as newcomers and Puccini's *Turandot* as the novelty. There were fewer performances, and salaries were pared, but Chicago could again hear opera. There were new voices, too; Kirsten Flagstad, Grace Moore, Lily Pons, Ezio Pinza, James Melton, Gigli; Licia Albanese, Bidu Sayou, Richard Crooks. A procession of conductors of the best orchestras in the country appeared at the podium. But the Chicago Opera Company expired in 1946, from malnutrition. Outsiders tried to start a new company at the Civic but failed. The New York City Opera Company came for three weeks in 1948, and then the great opera house went dark for seven seasons.

Despite all handicaps, the dream of grand opera created in Chicago persisted. By February, 1954, a new group, full of enthusiasm and energy, presented two sample performances of *Don Giovanni* and won enough support to launch three weeks of performances in October. The driving force of the organization, first called the Lyric Theatre, in 1956 the Lyric Opera, was Carol Fox, a woman of great energy and resourcefulness, who lined up backers and put Chicago society solidly behind the enterprise. She was general manager, Nicola Rescigno was musical director, and Lawrence Kelly business manager. The combination lasted two seasons; then Rescigno and Kelly withdrew to organize the Dallas Civic Opera.

Once again Chicago opera captured the attention of the musical world. Maria Calles, an artist with a glorious voice and an unpredictable temperament, opened the first regular season in *Norma,* with Nicola Rossi-Lemini as Orovesco. After two seasons she departed and Renata Tebaldi charmed the crowds. The roster grew, the seasons lengthened, and Miss Fox applied her lend-lease plan, whereby she was able to obtain use of stage settings from the opera houses of New York, San Francisco, London and Rome. The classic bills included *The Puritans, Masked Ball, Fidelio, Mefistofele, Flying Dutchman, Prince Igor;* among the novelties were *Il Ballo Delle Ingrate* by Monteverdi, *Lord Byron's Love Letter* by De Banfield and Tennessee Williams, *Jenufa* by Janacek in English; *The Harvest* by Giannini. The ballets were brilliant, with Vera Zorina, Alicia Markova, and Maria Tallchief.

A parade of the finest artists of the generation sang on the Lyric stage. Artists included Walter Berry, Inge Borgh, Jussi Bjoerling, Boris Christoff, Regina Crespin, Eileen Farrell, Tito Gobbi, Dorothy Kirsten,

Eva Likova, Robert Merrill, Anna Moffo, Mario del Monaco, Birgit Nilsson, Leontyne Price, Eleanor Steber, Gioletta Simionata, Brian Sullivan, Joan Sutherland, Elisabeth Schwartzkopf, Giuseppe di Stefano, Renata Tebaldi, Richard Tucker, Robert Weede, and William Wildermann. Among the noted conductors were Tullio Serafin, Dimitri Mitropoulos, George Solti, Leo Kopp, Arthur Rodzinski, Josef Krips, Peter Maag, and Pierre Dervaux.

An incident of great encouragement to the Lyric Opera was the action of the Italian Government, when it presented a gift of $16,000. By 1963 the drive for an endowment had netted $1,100,024, for which the A. Montgomery Ward Foundation made an incentive grant of $100,000.

The Lyric Opera Co. cooperates with the Metropolitan Opera National Council in the holding of auditions for young singers, usually in March. The auditions for the Northern District are usually held at the Center Theatre of De Paul University, 25 E. Jackson Blvd. The finals for the Central Region are held at the Opera House, 20 N. Wacker Dr., and free tickets may be obtained by applying at the Education Dept. of the Lyric Opera.

AND THEN RAVINIA

There were always musical programs in Illinois in the summer. Sometimes they were associated with chautauquas, which were extremely popular in the Nineties and around the turn of the century, and often they were festivals in which church choirs and high school choruses took part. On the North Shore Walter Damrosch in 1906 conducted a symphony in a wooded spot called Ravinia Park; it was located in the southern section of Highland Park and the enterprise of a Chicago business man named Louis Eckstein. Because he loved music Eckstein raised money for building a pavilion, and soon he had Frederick Stock and the Chicago Symphony Orchestra supply summer programs. Then he turned to hiring opera stars, and Ravinia acquired a commendable reputation for wonderful music under unequalled conditions, that brought people by train, interurban and motor cars. There they heard Lucrezia Bori, Claudia Muzio, Martinelli, Rethberg, Edward Johnson, Elizabeth Schwartzkopf; then excerpts from operas, and finally operas themselves. Ravinia Park had its problems, too, mostly the inevitable deficits, which Eckstein helped make up, but it has survived, and today, with symphonies, famous conductors, vocalists and musicians, jazz and rock and even plays, it is a center of music of distinction in northeastern Illinois.

JAZZ, ROCK AND OTHER TEMPOS

Ragtime was going strong throughout Illinois when the century changed its numerals. Syncopation was coming out of every bar that had an upright piano and a shirt-sleeved player. These performers were mainly white; their function was to "rag" any melody of the hour and even the classics. Syncopation, however, was natural to black musicians, and once the cornet players of New Orleans had mastered ragtime they subjected it to the most amazing improvisations. They had originated the blues, and now they evolved something called jazz, a style that had no literature and never sounded alike twice.

The blues and jazz came up the Mississippi and jazz began to electrify the blacks in South Side bars and whites at Dreamland and the Friars Inn. A procession of five-peace bands—trumpet, clarinet, bass viol, piano and drums—passed through the Chicago dance halls with their nervous, rhythmic beat. Joe "King" Oliver pioneered at Lincoln Gardens when he hired Louis Armstrong as second trumpet; Oliver also played at Kelly's Stables and led a band at the Plantation. Armstrong worked for Erskine Tate when he hit high C at the Sunset across the street. The New Orleans Rhythm Kings, with Jelly Roll Morton at the piano, professed to have the true gospel; the legend is that when they performed at the Friars Inn they inspired Bix Beiderbeck and other musicians to new heights of frenzy.

Practically all jazz bandmen of reputation grew up or learned their trade in Chicago: Louis Armstrong, Benny and Harry Goodman, Hoagy Carmichael, Gene Krupa, Sidney Bechet, Freddie Keppard, Louis Panico, Eddie Condon, Ben Pollack, Jess Stacy, Rapolla and Teagarden. Benny Goodman was still in knee pants when he worked at Electric Park in Waukegan and on the lake boat that carried picnic parties between Navy Pier and Michigan City, Indiana. Gene Krupa had his first experiences with the Austin High Gang. He recalled: "Great drummers like Baby Dodds, Davey Tough, George Wettling, Zutty Singleton, and Tubby Hall were all around, playing at clubs like the Sunset, or Grand Terrace, or Kelly's Stables."

This kind of jazz was welcomed at college proms and in dance halls patronized by the young; people of middle age were affronted by the blare of trombones and the thump of drums, and preferred the more soothing tempos of Rudy Vallee and Bing Crosby; Bing had sung in Chicago with the Orleans Rhythm group in the early 1920s, but his forte was balladry and he became the nation's top crooner. Paul Whiteman exploited George Gershwin's brand of blues and injected jazz rhythms into classical arias, which proved more popular with his public than plain jazz.

In the middle 1920s two new media opened to jazzmen. Record companies began to hire them to play jazz, and the radio opened the way to an entirely new audience. The early jazzmen played by instinct and had no transcribed music; in fact, most of them could not read. Since they rarely duplicated their improvisations they now had to memorize their tunes for the records. Here, too, was a new opening for the vocalists; Bessie Smith and Billie Holliday built reputations that reverberate down the years.

Historically, all true jazz after New Orleans came out of the night spots on the South Side. Commentators testify that only the black musicians performed with the complete dedication, or abandon, that gave jazz and all its successors the real impact. Moreover jazz is credited with having been an early agency of integration. Although a great many white bandmen seem to have had a sharper sense for bargaining, none ever played successfully without black musicians. After jazz came swing; after swing the guitar displaced the clarinet and the saxophone as a leading instrument, and the instrumentalists who continued to need frenzy to prove they were alive turned to gyrations of the torso and electrical amplification to command attention. In the 1970-80 decade records are the road to riches; albums of platters cut by the numerous vocalists and combos are rushed to the market, where they are immediately snapped up by their adolescent following. The unending beat of the drum that was once the signature of a primitive society is the pulsebeat of the newest aspiring generation.

Rock and roll, hard rock, and all the variations of jazz and pop played by nationally known name bands can be heard in many concert and dance halls in Chicago, including the Arie Crown Theatre at McCormick Place, where the Temptations hold forth and the Auditorium Theatre, where the Beach Boys check in. At other places throughout Cook County and environs large groups meet regularly for square dancing and folk festivals, with couples approaching middle-age joining practice classes sponsored by churches, community centers, and colleges. Classic and modern ballet, such as that staged by the Bolshoi and Joffrey, can be seen annually at the Auditorium Theatre and Ravinia Park. Folk dance programs are organized by the Folk Dance Leadership Council of Chicago, which includes the University of Chicago Folk Dancers, and dances at International House. Folk sessions are also held at Northwestern Illinois University Gym, Stevenson Park Field House in Oak Park, the Central YMCA, Jewish Community Centers, the American Youth Hostel. Folk dance clubs have been formed by the staffs at Argonne National Laboratory and the National Accelerator Laboratory. In Evanston the Recreation Department of the City sponsors the Evanston Squares. Folk festivals are held at First Chicago Center in the heart of the Loop in summer.

Part II

ILLINOIS

Cities and Towns

Alton

Air Services: Alton connects with all transcontinental lines at St. Louis Metropolitan Airport, 17 *m.* south. Helicopter and private planes use Civic Memorial Airport, 2.5 *m* east of East Alton.

Bus Lines: Jacksonville Trailways, Continental Trailways; station at 208 East Broadway.

Highways: Alton is on US 67 and Illinois 100, 111, and 140. Illinois 143 has jct. with Interstate 70. Illinois 3 connects with Granite City, jct. with Interstate 270. US 6 from Springfield runs about 18 *m.* east of Alton. There is a free bridge across the Mississippi River to West Alton, Mo.

Information and Accommodations: Greater Alton Assn. of Commerce, 112 East Broadway. *Alton Evening Telegraph,* 111 E. Broadway. Three major hotels, various motels; 4 hospitals; 111 churches of 26 denominations.

Recreation: Golf at 2 municipal courses, one private course, and Lockhaven Country Club. Tennis at municipal courts in Rock Springs Park, Lockhaven Country Club. Swimming at Y.M.C.A., Y.W.C.A., Summersport Swimming Club, Lockhaven Country Club.

Civic Events: Alton Civic Orchestra, Community Concert Assn., Little Theatre, college programs. Spectator sports by teams of Southern Illinois University (Alton Branch), Western Military Academy, others. Boat racing.

ALTON (488 alt., 39,700 pop. 1970; 43,047, 1960) is the northernmost industrial city in that crowded Madison County area (250,934 pop. 1970) that stretches along the Mississippi River through the city of Wood River and Granite City for about 24 *m.* to St. Louis. Alton, 279 *m.* from Chicago, lies on the last of the high bluffs overlooking the vast alluvial plain known as the American Bottom, where history has been made since the days when the French flag flew over it. The city lies below the confluence of the Illinois and the Mississippi Rivers, and above that of the Missouri and the Mississippi.

The U. S. Census for Alton does not reflect the population of its metropolitan area, which is near 70,000. Contiguous are the city of Wood River, 13,186 pop. 1970, and the village of East Alton, 7,309 pop. 1970. Two miles north on US 67 is Godfrey, unincorporated, with 1,223. Across the Mississippi is West Alton, Mo. The contiguous places are mainly industrial.

Alton has a normal work force of 25,000 and great diversity in manufacturing. It has large plants of the Owens Illinois Glass Co., Laclede Steel Co., engaged in specialty steel and brass; Alton Box Board Co., Peavey Flour Mills, the American Smelting & Refining

Co., and Olin Mathiessen Chemical Corp. The city has the aldermanic-mayoral form of government.

Residential Alton lies chiefly on the bluffs. Here the expression "going downtown" has literal meaning, for the streets that run to the river drop abruptly on a steep grade from immediately above the business district. The central section, with its unusually wide streets and Victorian houses, retains the spaciousness of the nineteenth century. Many of the older houses, built during steamboat days, are surmounted with lookout platforms that vary from a mere fenced-in rectangle to elaborate circular and octagonal cupolas. About 100 years ago steamboats vied with each other on the stretch between St. Louis and Alton, where a rich load of freight usually awaited the first steamer to dock. The lookout stations were an architectural outgrowth of this racing mania. Eventually they became ornamental rather than functional.

Although the site of Alton had been passed by Marquette and Jolliet on their voyage down the Mississippi in 1673, the first known settler, Jean Baptiste Cardinal, did not come to the vicinity until 110 years later. By the beginning of the nineteenth century an Indian trading post had been established. The site was obviously suitable for a permanent settlement, for above it the bluffs closed in on the river and for miles there was no sufficient setback for a boat landing. The confluence of the Mississippi and Missouri Rivers nearby marked the spot as a focal point for river traffic. Between 1816 and 1818 three towns were founded in the area now included in the Alton city limits. One of these, now the downtown business district, was planned by Col. Rufus Easton and named Alton for one of his sons. Proving the most satisfactory for river trade, his town eventually absorbed the other two. Alton was incorporated as a city in 1837.

The first period of prosperity came with steamboat transportation, and for a time it teamed with white steamboats and Alton rivaled St. Louis as a river port.

Alton felt many repercussions from the slavery dispute; here, in 1837, Elijah Lovejoy, noted Abolitionist editor, was murdered while protecting his press from the onslaught of a pro-slavery mob.

Alton was again the focus of the slavery question in 1858, when the last of the debates between Abraham Lincoln and Stephen A. Douglas was held here. Alton knew Lincoln because of the seriocomic Lincoln-Shields duel of 1842. Mary Todd, whom Lincoln later married, had lampooned State Auditor of Accounts James Shields in a Springfield paper; Lincoln assumed responsibility for the article and was challenged by Shields. Lincoln chose broadswords, and Alton as the dueling ground. With a crowd of the curious they rowed to a sandbar in the river. The lanky Abe practiced swings and told stories while the seconds conferred at great length, but the duel did not take place. Shields finally accepted a formal statement that although Lincoln "did not think . . . that said article could produce such an effect," he had not intended "injuring the personal or private character or standing of Mr. Shields."

The decline of steamboating was offset by the rise of industrial plants, notably that of the Owen-Illinois Company, which grew from a one-building concern to one of the nation's leading corporations. Alton proved an excellent location for railroad shipment. In the days of railroad building the name of Alton was used in the names of several roads. The St. Louis, Alton & Chicago became the Chicago & Alton and had a prosperous history; it was taken over later by the Gulf, Mobile & Western, now the Illinois Central Gulf. The Terre Haute & Alton became part of the New York Central, now the Penn Central.

POINTS OF INTEREST

McADAMS HIGHWAY is a scenic highway that makes an unusual impression on every visitor to Alton. This is actually a section of the Great River Road that the States have been building from Minnesota to Louisiana and the Gulf of Mexico. The Highway runs from Alton to Grafton, 23 miles. The view along the river is unique among water scenery and has been frequently photographed. On one side is the wide expanse of the Mississippi called Alton Lake; on the other are the Alton Bluffs. The highway was named for the late John D. McAdams, for many years business manager of the Alton Evening Telegraph. The scenic highway was his dream and was about 30 years in the making. McAdams was a vital force in the community, one of the most public-spirited citizens Alton ever had. Along with many civic improvements he worked tirelessly for the first paved highway, the bridges over the Mississippi and Missouri rivers that connect Alton and St. Louis, and the establishment of Pere Marquette State Park at Grafton, 30 miles upstream from Alton. He was also an authority on Indian lore. Of all the projects he headed the river road and Pere Marquette Park were his proudest accomplishments.

The LEWIS AND CLARK BRIDGE across the Mississippi commemorates the arrival of President Jefferson's expedition in 1804 at the site of Hartford, below Alton, where the men wintered before crossing the river.

One of the most remarkable Indian pictographs in history was that of the PIASA BIRD that Pere Marquette and Louis Jolliet saw painted on a bluff as they moved down the Mississippi River. It was destroyed when a road was built there in 1870, and reproduced with funds raised by private subscription. This suffered a similar fate. The latest reproduction dates from 1961. It may be viewed from the McAdam Highway, and from the river. In his journal Marquette thus described the painting:

> "As we were descending the river we saw high rocks with hideous monsters painted on them, and upon which the bravest Indians dare not look. They are as large as a calf, with head and horns like a goat; their eyes red; beard like a tiger; and a face like a man's. Their tails are so long that they pass over their heads and between their fore legs, under their belly, and ending like a fish's tail. They are painted red, green, and black."

The next account follows Marquette's description closely, but mentions only one bird. The Alton *Evening Telegraph* of September 28, 1836, gave what was perhaps the first published account of the story of the Piasa bird. In this version, the popularly accepted one, the Piasa bird lived in a cave in the bluffs, and came winging down the river to carry off any Indians it encountered. Chief Quatoga of the Illinois prayed to the Great Manitou for some means of delivering his people from this scourge and was told that the arrows of Quatoga's tribe alone could kill the monster. Accordingly, the chief exposed himself on the bluff and hid 20 of his warriors in the bushes behind him. When the bird swooped down on him, the warriors shot it with poisoned arrows, and it fell screaming into the river. The writer of the newspaper story reported that he had observed the supposed cave of the Piasa, and found it ample to house such a monster.

The CONFEDERATE SOLDIERS CEMETERY, Rozier and State Sts., North Alton, contains a monument commemorating more than 1,600 Confederate soldiers who died in a prison camp in Alton. This camp was established in the Illinois State Prison, first state prison in the State, which stood at Broadway and Williams Sts. Situated too near the river, undrained and ungraded, it aroused the insistent criticism of Dorothea Dix, pioneer in prison reform. With the outbreak of the Civil War it became a military detention camp. Overcrowding and lack of sanitation culminated in a smallpox epidemic in 1863, which raged uncontrolled for weeks for want of doctors. Prisoners died at the rate of six to ten a day. At the demand of citizens all stricken prisoners were transported to an uninhabited island in the Mississippi, where a deserted dwelling was converted into a hospital. There is no evidence that any of the victims ever returned alive, and although no record of deaths was kept, it has been estimated that several thousand prisoners died and were buried on the island during 1863-64.

The ALTON LOCK AND DAM on the Mississippi River are best viewed from observation platforms erected in Riverside Park in downtown Alton. This is No. 26 of a series of great dams in the Mississippi built to provide a 9 ft. channel. The rebuilding of the dam was specified in the 1973 Waterways appropriation bill of the U. S. Congress, which allocated $100,000 for planning and $1,400,000 for construction by the Corps of Engineers, USA. The water behind the dam is Alton Lake, a most popular boating area.

The ELIJAH LOVEJOY MONUMENT, at the north end of Monument Ave., stands at the entrance to Alton City Cemetery. Visible from the greater part of Alton, it was erected in 1897 by the State of Illinois and by the city in memory of the anti-slavery editor. A slim granite column, 93 feet high, supports a 17-foot bronze figure of *Victory,* flanked with two shorter columns, each bearing an eagle with outstretched wings.

Elijah Lovejoy came from Princeton Theological Seminary to St. Louis in 1833 to edit the *St. Louis Observer,* a religious periodical. In April, 1836, a mob burned a mulatto at the stake and a judge named Lawless condoned the crime by saying that while such action by an individual would be punishable action by the people was not. Lovejoy, whose principal activity had been fighting sin, reacted violently and denounced mob and authorities in such vehement fashion that he immediately was subjected to threats and abuse. In July, 1836, he went to Alton to edit an anti-slavery paper on a press friends were buying for him. When the press arrived and was standing on the waterfront it was broken up and thrown into the river, presumably by thugs from St. Louis. Alton opinion was divided on slavery and there were many anti-Abolition views but there had been no violent confrontations. Lovejoy's backers bought him another press, and in a public meeting he defied any who would try to suppress him, saying: "As long as I am an American citizen, and as long as American blood runs in these veins, I shall hold myself at liberty to speak, to write, and to publish whatever I please on any subject, being amenable to the laws of my counrty for the same."

Lovejoy's *Alton Observer* opposed slavery in such violent language that he lost support among moderates and some declared he had violated a promise not to publish an Abolitionist journal. After he had received numerous threats his press was destroyed Aug. 21, 1837. The *Alton Evening Telegraph* condemned the act as an outrage. A third press was destroyed on Sept. 21. Although Lovejoy's supporters were growing fewer there were still enough to pay for another press, which arrived on Nov. 6. It was placed in a warehouse and 14 armed friends stood guard. When a mob started to attack someone fired and one of the mob was mortally wounded. When Lovejoy came out of the warehouse he was shot down and killed. "I can die at my post" he had said, "but I cannot retreat." Members of the mob were indicted and tried, but acquitted. Lovejoy's name became a rallying cry for the anti-slavery movement in Illinois.

The frame of Lovejoy's press may be seen in the lobby of the *Alton Evening Telegraph,* 111 E. Broadway. The Sigma Delta Chi journalistic fraternity has placed a plaque in Riverside Park near the site of Lovejoy's death.

The site of the LINCOLN-DOUGLAS DEBATE, Broadway at the foot of Market St., is designated by a plaque suitably inscribed. Here, on October 15, 1858, Stephen A. Douglas and Abraham Lincoln met in their campaign for election to the United States Senate. From a platform erected on the east side of the old City Hall they addressed a crowd estimated at 5,000 to 10,000 people. Douglas, his voice worn with continual public speaking, maintained, as in previous debates, that each state should decide the slavery question for itself, and told the audience that Lincoln believed that a Negro was as good as a white. Lincoln restated his belief that a house divided against itself could not stand, that the states must be all slave or all free, and his conviction that the house should cease to be divided.

SOUTHERN ILLINOIS UNIVERSITY, which has its main campus in Carbondale and another in Edwardsville, has struck roots of its educational tree in Alton. It uses the former facilities of Shurtleff College, at Seminary St. and College Ave., for part of its enrollment of 33,000 students. The presence of Southern is a happy reminder to Alton citizens that the long educational tradition of Shurtleff is not entirely lost. After 126 years of operation Shurtleff closed its doors in June, 1957.

Shurtleff College could trace its beginnings back to the work of Baptist missionaries. According to the records now in the Illinois State Historical Library John Mason Peck was a missionary who came to St. Louis in 1817 to start a seminary to train ministers and teachers.

In 1827 he opened the Rock Springs Seminary near O'Fallon, Illinois, which the Baptists moved to Upper Alton in 1832 and called Alton Seminary. A charter for Alton College in 1835 prohibited the teaching of theology, so the college and seminary were operated by separate boards but with the same president. In 1836 Dr. Benjamin Shurtleff of Boston gave $10,000 toward the college endowment and its name was changed to Shurtleff College in recognition. In 1841 the seminary became a department of the college. The Administration Hall burned down in 1939, with the loss of valuable records. The college continued until 1956, when it was leased and then sold to Southern Illinois University. It had a campus of 35 acres when it closed.

The JENNIE D. HAYNER MEMORIAL LIBRARY, 401 State St., has about 70,000 books and a circulation of more than 215,000 annually. It is part of the Lewis & Clark Library System, in which 24 libraries cooperate.

To the northeast of the city, near the ALTON STATE HOSPITAL on the Fosterburg Road, is a marker commemorating the Wood River Massacre of 1814.

Aurora

Air Services: Aurora Municipal Airport, 7 *m.* west on State 30, provides air taxis, chartered planes, instrument approach landing facilities and UNICOM. No scheduled airlines. Runways, 3,600 ft. Restricted to daylight unless by special arrangement. Chicago O'Hare International Airport, largest in the Midwest, is less than 40 *m.* northeast of Aurora via expressways.

Buses: Burlington Transportation Co., Bluebird Coach Lines, Continental Trailways, Greyhound Lines, Joliet-Aurora. Union Bus Station, 94 N. Broadway.

Highways: Aurora has easy access to the great expressways that lead into Chicago. East-West Tollway, North Aurora, (State 190) connects with Interstate 294 for O'Hare Airport and with Interstate 90 (Eisenhower Expressway) for Chicago Loop. State 65 connects with US 34 (Ogden Avenue) into Chicago. State 31 runs down the west bank of the Fox River and State 25 down the east bank.

Railroads: Chicago, Burlington & Quincy (passenger); Chicago & North Western; Elgin, Joliet & Eastern.

Information: Aurora Chamber of Commerce, 40 W. Downer Place; Chicago Motor Club, 217 Main St.; the *Aurora Beacon-News* (evening) and *Aurora Star* (weekly).

Recreation: Aurora has the advantage of two park organizations. The City Park Department operates 4 major parks, including Phillips, at Parker and Hill Aves., and Lincoln, on N. Russell Ave. There are swimming pools, an 18-hole golf course, tennis courts, other facilities. There are 3 baseball leagues for boys, 8-12. The Stephen-Adamson Sealmasters play softball on Sealmaster Field. Bowling alleys are both public and private. There is a drag strip south of Aurora where car owners register and race. The Fox Valley Park District operates 18 major parks and 7 playgrounds, with riverside and nature trail programs along the Fox River. The District sponsors a variety of clubs for achers, radio amateurs, model cars, plays, square dancing, coin and stamp collectors, senior citizens and many others.

Cultural Activities include the Civic Music Assn., Aurora Drama Guild, Fox Valley Symphony Orchestra and the Aurora Art League. Aurora has 81 churches.

AURORA, in Kane County (638 alt., 74,182 pop. 1970; 63,715, 1960, inc. 16.4%) is an industrial and residential city 38 *m.* west of Chicago in the valley of the Fox River, which bisects it. Beginning with small factories using water power, the place began to attract larger industries after the coming of the first railroad in 1848; moreover it became a farm products distributing center for the valley. The expansion of Chicago has not changed the essential character of Aurora, which was settled in the same decade. Today more than 200 manufacturing concerns are located in the city and its environs, employing more than 21,000.

Aurora has a commission form of government with a mayor and four commissioners, elected for four-year terms. It profits by the City Park Department, which operates four major parks, and the Fox Valley Park District, which has 18 parks and 9 playgrounds in the area. Its public buildings were placed on Stolp's Island, in the middle of the business district, because of political rivalries on the opposite banks, which were known as East Aurora and West Aurora and not incorporated as a unit until 1857. Streets long bore different names on opposite banks and some were not made uniform until January, 1965. The island makes Aurora a city of bridges.

Large manufacturers were attracted to Aurora early because freight haulage on its railroad lines bypassed the congestion in Chicago. Besides the Burlington, the Chicago & North Western Railway and the Elgin, Joliet & Eastern Railway, commonly called the Outer Belt Line, were the chief carriers. Changes in methods of transportation have not affected the prosperity of the manufacturers. Aurora expects to attract a fair share of the 2,000 employees of the National Accelerator Laboratory, a federal research facility, which is to be in full operation in 1975 at the former site of Weston, 7 m. away.

The largest employer is the Caterpillar Tractor Co., which has 4,500 at work making construction machinery. Western Electric employs about 3,300 in making telephonic equipment, and the Barber-Greene Co. nearly 1,500 in producing belt conveyors, rock crushers, loaders, and paving apparatus. Others employing more than 1,000 each are All-Steel Equipment, Inc., the Austin-Western Division of Baldwin-Lima-Hamilton Corp., and Stephens-Adamson Manufacturing Co., a division of Borg-Warner.

East of the city line is a 4,200-acre development called Fox Valley East, which is being built by the Urban Investment & Development Co., a subsidiary of Aetna Life & Casualty Co., and Homart Development Co., a subsidiary of Sears, Roebuck & Co. The main unit is the Fox Valley Center, a shopping center approximately the size of the Woodfield Mall, which has stores of Marshall Field, Sears, and other Chicago retailers. The center is located at East New York St. and Illinois 59 and within a short distance from Naperville, North of Fox Valley East near East-West Tollway is an 800-acre project known as Country Lakes, which is expected to have 6,000 new housing units. A third development in this general area is West Valley, east of Elburn. The investments reflect an increased westward movement of people from Cook County.

When the first settler, Joseph McCarty of Elmira, New York, came to this region in 1834, he found a large Potawatomi village on the river. "It was not a wild, desolate, unpopulated region," he wrote, "for we had plenty of neighbors in the red men. The village and vicinity contained from 200 to 500 Indians, and we had many visits from them. Quite a commercial trade sprang up, especially swapping bread and tobacco for fish, of which we soon found they had much the larger supply. We could give but one slice of bread for a fish weighing from three to five pounds."

After beginning work on his cabin, McCarty took a short jaunt eastward to look over the little village of Chicago. Deciding the place was "more promising for the raising of bullfrogs than humans" he returned to his cabin. With his brother Samuel he built a dam on the Fox river and erected a mill. When the mill was finished in 1835 more than a dozen pioneers joined in the celebration. Platted in 1836, the settlement had 30 families and a postoffice within a year. Early settlers wanted to name the town Waubonsie, after an Indian chief, but when they learned the name was already in use they compromised on Aurora, said to have been suggested by a settler from Aurora, N. Y.

Aurora historians assert that the first application of the name Republican to a political party took place at a meeting of 207 delegates from the Second Congressional District in a small Aurora church in 1854, where the principles of the party were formulated. Many historians give priority to Ripon, Wisc., but it is also undisputed that the movement was fairly general.

In 1881 Aurora became the first town in Illinois to adopt the novel system of lighting the streets with electric arc lights hung on high steel towers. Aurora replaced its gas lamps by 16 200-candle-power electric lamps, which cast a glow like moonlight over the area.

POINTS OF INTEREST

AURORA COLLEGE is a four-year liberal arts college, which gives baccalaureate degrees in the arts, science, and theology. It was founded by the Advent Christian Church in Mendota in 1893 and moved to Aurora in 1912. It is located on Gladstone Ave. and Kenilworth Pl. A new library and a science building have been added in recent years. Enrollment is around 1,400, including evening classes, and there is a faculty of 110.

COMMUNITY COLLEGE is a two-year junior college that gives the degree of associate in the arts and vocational courses and prepares students for continuing their education in senior colleges.

AURORA HISTORICAL MUSEUM, Oak Ave. at Cedar St., was a gift to the Aurora Historical Society from the daughters of W. A. Tanner, early settler. Built in 1856 the 17-room house contains pioneer furnishings brought by boat from Buffalo to Chicago and then hauled to Aurora. Of special distinction is a grandfather's clock 9 ft. tall and 3 ft. wide, made by William Blanford. A carriage house, built in 1856, contains a stage coach and vehicles of the past.

The AURORA PUBLIC LIBRARY, 1 Benton St., has more than 140,000 volumes and circulates more than 650,000. It serves the local schools by bookmobile.

PHILLIPS PARK, at Parker and Hill Avenues, on US 30, is the best equipped of the four parks operated by the City Park Department. It comprises sunken gardens, a municipal zoo, a children's zoo of domesticated animals, a miniature railroad, two swimming pools, bowling alleys and movie theaters. The Fox Valley Park District has developed 18 miles of river frontage for recreation. The city also has been reclaiming parts of the waterfront.

The MEMORIAL BRIDGE is one of the notable structures spanning the Fox River. It is located just beyond the end of Stolp Island. It was designed by Emory P. Seidel, Chicago sculptor, and dedicated on Armistice Day, 1931. US 30 runs across the bridge.

PIONEER PARK, a reproduction of a rural Illinois farm village of the period 1880-1910, is located one mile west of the city limits on Galena Blvd., intersection of Barnes Road and US 30. Visitors are given a preliminary lecture on rural customs by a teacher in a schoolhouse; there are assembled a country store, blacksmith shop, mill, barn with animals, carriages, barber shop, and a museum. It interests children and school groups and is open April to mid-October. Adults 50c; school children 25c.

Bloomington and Normal

Air Services: Bloomington-Normal Airport. Ozark Air Lines, 6 flights daily, Chicago and St. Louis.

Buses: Greyhound Bus Lines, Central Trailways, Illinois Coach Co., 523 N. East St.

Highways: Interstate 55 combined with US 66 most of the way provide the direct route from Chicago and on to Springfield and East St. Louis. Interstate 74 is the northwest-southeast route from Galesburg and Peoria to Urbana. US 51 is a north-south route through the center of the State. Illinois 9 is east-west.

Railroads: Penn Central, Illinois Central, Gulf, Norfolk & Western.

Information: Assn. of Commerce & Industry of McLean County. The *Daily Pantagraph,* inc. Sunday; *The Normalite,* weekly. Radio and television, principal networks.

Accommodations: Three hotels, 11 motels. Three hospitals; associated with the Mennonite Hospital is a School of Nursing and the Mennonite-Gailey Eye Clinic, which has an eye-bank.

Religious and Educational: There are 64 churches of 38 denominations. Bloomington has 11 elementary schools, a junior high school and a high school that easily accommodates more than 2,000 pupils. Normal has 9 elementary schools, a junior high school, and a high school. The Normal Community High School is a four-year institution. There also are Lutheran and Roman Catholic parochial schools, including the Central Catholic High School. Illinois State University operates the University High School, Fairchild Hall of Special Education and Metcalf Grade School.

Recreation: Golf, Highland Park, 18 holes; Illinois State University, 18 holes. Picnics, Miller Park, Forest Park. Tennis, Miller Park. Swimming, YMCA, YWCA, Miller Park.

Special Events: American Passion Play, Scottish Rite Temple, Palm Sunday and 10 consecutive Sundays; concerts and lectures at the universities; band concerts, Miller Park. Consult newspaper.

BLOOMINGTON, seat of McLean County, and NORMAL, are contiguous cities with a total population of more than 66,000 in the heart of the central Illinois corn belt, 40 *m.* southeast of Peoria, 129 *m.* southwest of Chicago, and 158 *m.* northeast of St. Louis. The two share the same Main Street (US 51) and have similar municipal facilities, and although Bloomington exceeds Normal in industrial and political employment, the two work together for mutual welfare.

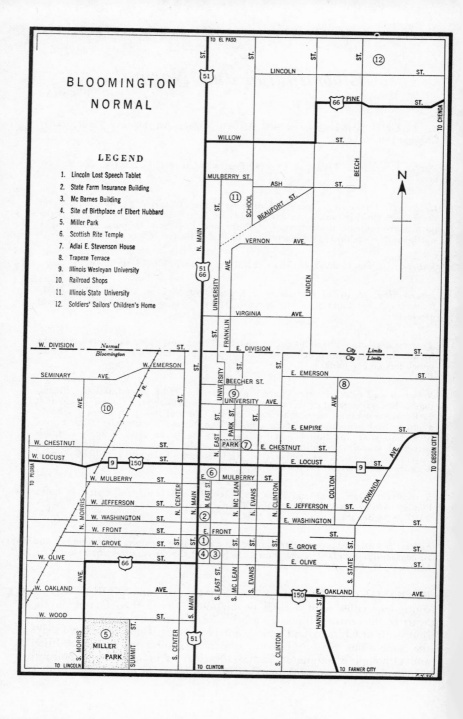

BLOOMINGTON
NORMAL

LEGEND

1. Lincoln Lost Speech Tablet
2. State Farm Insurance Building
3. Mc Barnes Building
4. Site of Birthplace of Elbert Hubbard
5. Miller Park
6. Scottish Rite Temple
7. Adlai E. Stevenson House
8. Trapeze Terrace
9. Illinois Wesleyan University
10. Railroad Shops
11. Illinois State University
12. Soldiers' Sailors' Children's Home

Bloomington, 830 alt., had 39,992 pop. 1970, an increase of 10.3% over the 36,271 returned by the Census of 1960. Normal had 26,396 pop. 1970, just short of doubling the 13,357 pop., 1960. The Standard Metropolitan Statistical Area had 104,389 in 1970, and 110,100 in 1972, an increase of 5,700.

Bloomington has a city council-manager type of government; Normal has a city council and mayor. Bloomington had 12,700 households with 66% home ownership in 1970; Normal had 7,500, with 77.5% home ownership. The tax rate in Bloomington is 4.50 per $100 assessed valuation; in Normal $4.07 per $100. Both cities get their fresh water from Lake Bloomington, 10 m. north of Normal.

McLean County, largest in the State, is an area of high production of corn, oats, wheat and other grains and livestock, and is an example of complete mechanization of agriculture. Most of its settlements have fewer than 1,000 people. The largest are LEROY, 2,430, pop. 1970, 2,088, 1960; LEXINGTON, 1,615 pop. 1970; CHENOA, 1,523 pop. 1970; HEYWORTH, 1,441 pop. 1970, and GRIDLEY, 1,007 pop. 1970. Others are Danvers, Downs, Colfax, Ellsworth, Hudson, McLean, Towanda and Carlock. The population of McLean County in 1970 was 104,389, an increase of 24.5% over the 83,877 figure of 1960.

The Census of 1970 reported that of Bloomington's population 36,096 were native-born Americans of American parentage, and only 3,252 were of foreign stock and 595 were foreign-born. Of the foreign stock the largest group, 1,276, was German, and there were 470 persons of Spanish language. Normal, with 26,406 pop., had 24,740 native Americans born of American parents, 1,424 born of foreign parentage and 242 foreign born. Bloomington had 38,308 whites and 1,574 blacks (3.9%). Normal had 25,795 whites and 442 blacks (1.7%).

There was little unemployment. In 1970 the male civilian work force in Bloomington was 10,146, unemployed 389 (3.8%); Normal had 5,963 males employed, 175 unemployed (2.9%). Women employed in Bloomington numbered 7,793; Normal, 5,262. Of the total employed in Bloomington, 4,207 were in clerical work, 3,312 of them women. There were 3,889 employees in wholesale and retail trade, 3,255 in manufacturing. In Normal, 2,823 were in clerical work, 1,851 in trade, 1,150 in manufacturing. Bloomington had 2,068 in education, Normal, 3857.

What makes one city prosper helps the other. In recent years Bloomington has profited by the addition of the General Purpose Control Dept. of General Electric Co.; the downstate headquarters of the Illinois Agricultural Assn., with its affiliated insurance companies; the Farm Bureau Serum Assn., the Auditing Assn. and others. The General Telephone Co. of Illinois makes Bloomington its State headquarters and has division offices in Normal. The State Farm Mutual Insurance Co. large insurer of motor cars, has its home office here. Industries with large employment are the Paul F. Beich Candy Co., Firestone Tire &

Rubber Co., Ralston Purina Co., Funk Brothers Seed Co. and Eureka William Co., a division of National Union Electric Corp.

Worth special mention is that each city has a major university— Bloomington has Illinois Wesleyan University, and Normal has Illinois State University and both are located along Main Street, within walking distance of each other. They annually add more than 15,000 to the population of the two cities.

The settlement of this locality is attributed to the familiarity of traders with Indian trails that crossed a wooded area originally called Keg Grove because Indians discovered a cache of liquor here. Later it was known as Blooming Grove, possibly for a profusion of flowers. Settlers of British stock named Hendrix, Dawson and Orendorff came as early as 1822. In 1830 James Allin entered claim to a quarter section on the north side of Blooming Grove. In December, 1830, Fayette County was divided and McLean County established. Allin offered part of his land for a courthouse; this was accepted and the town of Bloomington laid out adjoining Blooming Grove. It was incorporated as a city in 1850.

Bloomington was a small farm village until the 1850 decade, when the Illinois Central Railroad and the Chicago & Mississippi, later the Alton, arrived. The Alton established its repair shops there and for years employed up to 1,500 on an area of 124 acres. Access to all the great lines crossing the State made Bloomington a fine distributing point for industries.

The Bloomington Pantagraph has been publishing since 1846.

In 1856 the first Republican State convention met in Majors Hall and heard Abraham Lincoln on May 29 denounce the Nebraska bill and declare, "We say to our southern brethren, 'We won't go out of the Union, and you shan't!' ". This is known as his Lost Speech. It is commemorated on a tablet at the southwest corner of East and Front Sts. The original hall, built in 1852, was taken down in 1959.

POINTS OF INTEREST

Two notable 19th century houses are carefully preserved to recall the pre-eminence of two political families in Bloomington. One is CLOVER LAWN, the mansion of David Davis, friend of Abraham Lincoln and manager of his campaigns. The other is the Adlai E. Stevenson House.

David Davis came to Bloomington as a young man with "two-bits" in his pocket. An uncle put him through Kenyon College and he later married a wealthy Massachusetts woman. He served a term in the General Assembly, initiated court reform, and became judge of the Eighth Judicial Circuit at $1,000 a year. In this court Lincoln and Ward Hill Lamon practiced law and Davis became a strong supporter of Lincoln.

Judge David Davis was one of the most effective workers for the Lincoln nomination at both the State and National Republican conventions. He knew how to bargain and compromise. Lincoln complained that his backers had gambled on him; he said: "The bought and sold me a hundred times; I cannot begin to fill the pledges in my name." But he did not repudiate them, nor did he turn against Davis. He made Davis an associate justice of the U. S. Supreme Court. After fifteen years there Davis resigned to become senator from Illinois. Once he was nominated for President by the National Labor Reform Party, an organization of no great political power. He thanked the party, saying: "The chief magistracy of the Republic should neither be sought nor declined by any American citizen." He was known as a man of independence and common sense, as well as a shrewd manipulator of real estate that made him a millionaire. Although Judge Davis weighed more than 300 pounds most of his adult life he lived 71 years.

Davis built Clover Lawn in 1870. The house is an example of domestic Victorian Gothic, with the entrance hall brought forward from the facade in a tower-like projection that has a palladian window on the second floor and dormers and an iron grill on top. There is also an ornamental railing around the low roof. The rooms have ceilings that are 13 ft. 6 in. high and are trimmed with black walnut and retain the period furniture. The house was made a State shrine in 1959 and opened to the public by the Illinois State Historical Society in 1961. Major restorations in 1970 disclosed the original decorations on wall panels in hall and anteroom, a geometric blue pattern on a gray background, believed to go back 100 years.

The ADLAI E. STEVENSON HOUSE, 901 N. McLean St., is a two-and-a-half story dwelling in Tudor style. Adlai Ewing Stevenson (1835-1914) was the first of the Stevensons to live in Bloomington. He was born in Kentucky and came to Bloomington in 1852 to practice law on the Illinois circuits. He served two years in Congress before his election as a Democrat in 1893 as Vice President of the United States on Grover Cleveland's ticket. In 1900 he was nominated for the same office with William Jennings Bryan and defeated. He returned to resume his law practice. He was the grandfather of Adlai Ewing Stevenson II (1900-1965) whose career as governor of Illinois gave him national renown and made him the logical candidate of the Democratic Party for President in 1952 and 1956. During his boyhood he lived at 1316 E. Washington St.

Adlai E. Stevenson is Bloomington's most famous son. He died from a heart attack in London July 14, 1965, 50 yards from the American Embassy, while Ambassador of the United States to the United Nations. He was named for his grandfather, attended Princeton, Harvard Law School, and Northwestern, and was admitted to the Illinois bar in 1926. President Franklin D. Roosevelt named him special counsel to the Agricultural Adjustment Administration, 1933-34, and later he was legal assistant to Secretary of the Navy Frank Knox, special assistant to Secretaries of State Stettinius and Byrnes and representative at the UN conference in San Francisco. President Truman appointed him senior advisor to the US delegation to the UN at London and Geneva, 1946-47. Upon returning to Chicago he was nominated by the Democrats for Governor of Illinois and elected in 1948 by a majority of 572,000, largest in the State's history. He served from 1949 to 1953. Stevenson's accomplishmests in office caused him to be nominated for President in 1952. He had to oppose the national fame of General Eisenhower, to whom he lost then and in 1956. In 1952 Stevenson polled 27,000,000 votes against 34,000,000 for Eisenhower, and 40 vs. 443 electoral votes: in 1956 he had 26,000,000 votes against 35,000,000 and 73 vs. 457 electoral votes. He was a strong contender for the nomination at the convention that picked John F. Kennedy.

Services were held for Stevenson at the National Cathedral in Washington July 14, 1965, and his body lay in state at the Capitol in Springfield until interment in the family plot in Evergreen Memorial Cemetery in Bloomington. Services in the Unitarian Church were attended by President Johnson, Vice President Humphrey, Chief Justice Earl Warren, Associate Justice Arthur Goldberg, Governor Otto Kerner and many other dignitaries.

Historical markers in the same city block commemorate the home of Vice President Adlai E. Stevenson (1835-1914) at 901 North McLean St., and Governor Joseph A. Fifer (1840-1938), at 909 North McLean St. Fifer was Governor of Illinois 1889-1893. Another Governor from Bloomington was John M. Hamilton (1847-1905).

The site of the birthplace of Elbert Hubbard at the southeast corner of Grove and S. Main Sts. is marked by a tablet. Hubbard was a topical essayist and typophile, who established the Roycroft Shops, printers, at East Aurora, N. Y., and published *The Philistine,* a magazine that affected antique typography. He became famous for *A Message to Garcia,* an inspirational essay on self-reliance that was circulated in thousands of copies by a railroad official. He was lost in the sinking of the Cunard liner *Lusitania* by a German submarine in 1915.

STATE FARM INSURANCE COMPANIES is the corporate name of a large organization that began in Bloomington and for many years had its home office in a 12-store building at 112 E. Washington St. It provides car and home-owners insurance, as well as life policies. It also has its Illinois Regional Office in Bloomington. In 1971 it announced eventual removal to a 39-acre tract on the east edge of Bloomington, where eight buildings were to be erected, including a 12-store tower, two four-story office buildings and a four-story service building. State Farm employs more than 3,300 in the Bloomington-Normal area.

The SCOTTISH RITE TEMPLE, 110 Mulberry St., built in the Italian Renaissance style, is headquarters for the Scottish Rite Order in central Illinois. Here, on one of the largest stages in the Middle West, are given performances of The *American Passion Play* every Sunday from Palm Sunday to June 1. Carefully following the Biblical account, and lavishly staged, it is attended by large crowds annually.

The first Pullman car is reported to have been built in the shops of the Chicago & Alton Railroad, later used by the Gulf, Mobile & Ohio, now a part of Illinois Central Gulf.

The two cities are well provided with libraries, for in addition to those that serve the two universities Bloomington has the WITHERS PUBLIC LIBRARY, and Normal the NORMAL PUBLIC LIBRARY. Withers has approx. 95,000 volumes and circulates around

350,000 and Normal has more than 27,000 and circulates over 100,000. The Reference Room on the second floor at Withers is often used for displays of art by the Bloomington-Normal Art Assn. and the Illinois Midstate Educational Center. Both libraries are members of the Corn Belt Library System, which has its headquarters at 412 Eldorado Road, Bloomington, and comprises 21 libraries, which cooperate to put their facilities at the convenience of the reader. Inter-library loans are arranged without a fee and self-improvement is stimulated. Bookmobiles deliver books to villages in an area of 2,800 sq. m., where 163,000 people live. A fountain deigned by Lorado Taft stands east of the Withers Public Library.

Hospital facilities in Bloomington and Normal have made this a health center for central Illinois. There are three major hospitals with more than 600 beds. ST. JOSEPH'S HOSPITAL in Bloomington, founded in 1880 by the Sisters of the Third Order of St. Francis in Peoria, completed a new 153-bed facility in 1968 at its new location on US 66, raising its capacity to 200 beds. It operates a cobalt therapy unit. BROKAW HOSPITAL, a general 265-bed hospital in Normal, has the only electro-encephalogram laboratory in the community, as well as the Short-Term Psychiatric Unit. Associated with MENNONITE HOSPITAL in Bloomington is the Gailey Eye Clinic, which keeps an eye bank. It has a School of Nursing. All three hospitals sponsor the Bloomington-Normal School of X-Ray Technology, which gives a 2-year course.

ILLINOIS STATE UNIVERSITY is the title since 1964 of the big Normal institution founded in 1857 as the first State normal school. A state convention of teachers at Bloomington in 1853 agitated for the school, and in 1856 the State legislature agreed to support it if local communities would guarantee its construction. In a lively contest McLean County people, led by Jesse Fell, won over Batavia and Peoria with a bid of $143,725, underwritten by a guarantee drafted by Abraham Lincoln and signed by 85 individuals.

The university had a 56-acre site in North Bloomington when the area north of the Bloomington line was incorporated as Normal in 1865. To train teachers was its primary function until the present century, when it expanded as a liberal arts college. It has now become one of the largest colleges in the State. Although located in 40 major buildings in the heart of the Normal business area, Illinois State owns more than 650 acres. It still maintains a comprehensive program for teachers, including courses from kindergarten to college and for the handicapped, mentally retarded, and blind. There is also provision for adults who seek further study. In the 1972-73 school year Illinois State enrolled 17,169 students and had a faculty of 908.

The historic Old Main lost its cupola and third story in May, 1946. More than half of the present buildings was erected during the 1960-70 decade. Fell Hall, the pioneer residence for women built in 1918, is an old landmark beside the towering dormitories of recent construction. Watterson Towers rises 28 stories and has suite-style quarters in houses of five stories each, sheltering about 2,000 of the 7,000 students who live in halls. The Adlai E. Stevenson Hall for the Humanities, named for the Governor, houses the departments of English, foreign languages, and mathematics. The Stevenson Memorial Room contains documents and memorabilia of his career. Among new facilities are additions to the Milner Library of 1940, which has more than 375,000 vols.; Hovey Hall, the administration building; Turner Hall, for business and the practical arts; the Horton Physical Education Bldg. Horton Field House seats 8,700 for basketball contests. Hancock Stadium holds 20,000 when the Redbirds play on their own Astro Turf field.

ILLINOIS WESLEYAN UNIVERSITY occupies 30 acres in the residential area on the north side of Bloomington. It dates from 1850, when members of the Illinois Methodist Episcopal Conference proposed it and first classes were held in the basement of the Methodist Church. Listed among the early trustees were such prominent persons as Judge David Davis and Peter Cartwright, the pioneer preacher. Encountering financial difficulties, the school suspended operations between 1855 and 1857, when it was reopened with a new president, the Rev. Oliver Munsell. An intensive drive for funds soon put the university on a sound basis, and it has since operated continuously. In 1930 it absorbed Hedding College, another Methodist Episcopal institution, which had long functioned at Abingdon, Illinois.

The university is composed of the College of Liberal Arts, with Divisions of Business and Economics, the Humanities, Natural Science, and Social Science; the College of Fine Arts, with the School of Art, the School of Drama, and the School of Music. The university also maintains the Brokaw Collegiate School of Nursing, in association with Brokaw Hospital. Although Methodist in government, it makes no religious conditions for admission, and chapel attendance is voluntary.

A program for independent study, intended to give greater opportunity for individual advancement according to ability has been an innovation of recent years. In 1972 the university erolled 1,641 students and had a faculty of 130.

There are 33 buildings on the campus; of these 11 were built in the 1960 decade. The Memorial Center and a new field house are recent additions, and new dormitories for students and apartments for the faculty have been erected. Buck Memorial Library has approx. 90,000 volumes.

Many of the activities of the university are shared by Bloomington residents. The School of Music gives programs of symphonic music in Presser Hall. The Fred Young Field House is the scene of athletic competitions. The School of Drama presents plays in McPherson Theatre, which has an indoor and an outdoor stage.

EVERGREEN MEMORIAL CEMETERY on Main St. in Bloomington is visited annually by thousands of people who come to the grave of Adlai E. Stevenson, II. Also buried here are the remains of Adlai Ewing Stevenson (1835-1914), Vice President of the United States, 1892-1896, grandfather of the Governor.

Cairo

Air Services: Municipal Airport, 3 *m.* nnw. Runways, 3,600 and 2,600 ft.

Highways: US 51 is the principal highway from the north, having combined with Illinois 3, the Great River Road, at Future City, and Illinois 37 1 *m.* from Mound City. Direct route from Chicago is US 45 to Effingham, then Illinois 37 south. Interstate 57 is being built chiefly parallel with US 45 and Ill. 37; will bypass the city of Cairo but with junction about 1 *m.* north to cross the Mississippi River. US 51 is routed along Sycamore St. and Washington Ave. to a junction with US 60 and 62 and crosses the Ohio River bridge to Kentucky (free), whereas US 60 and 62 proceed south to Charleston, Missouri and a continuation of Int. 57 and Int. 55. There is an Illinois State Police station at the intersection of US 51 and US 62.

Bus Service: Greyhound Lines, Gulf Transport Lines, Trailways, Connor Lines. Station, 1006 Commercial Ave.

Railroads: Passenger service on Illinois Central Gulf, North Cairo, to Chicago, New Orleans. Freight, Illinois Central Gulf, Missouri Pacific, Penn-Central.

Information and Accommodations: One hotel, seven motels, in business district. Cairo Chamber of Commerce. Cairo *Citizen* (evening), 711 Washington Ave. Three television stations.

Recreation: Golf, Egyptian Country Club, north on US 51 (daily fee). Goose hunting in season at Horseshoe Lake State Conservation Area, also fishing. Fort Defiance State Park, south edge of Cairo on US 51 and Cairo Point. The excursion steamer *Avalon* observes a summer schedule.

CAIRO (315 alt., 6,277 pop. 1970; 9,348, 1960, dec. 32.9%) *pronounced Kay-roh,* county seat of Alexander County, is the southernmost city in Illinois, located on a peninsula just above the confluence of the Ohio and Mississippi Rivers. It is 374 *m.* by land from Chicago; 148 *m.* from St. Louis; 213 *m.* from Springfield. Its present status in the economy is as a distributor of farm products and lumber, and processor of cottonseed oil and feed. Its historic reputation rests on its importance as the principal shipping point for Illinois troops during the Civil War and the site of extensive marine ways and wharves up to Mound City on the Ohio, which made it a great naval outfitting base. After the war it flourished for several decades as a steamboat center, loading lumber and farm products of a wide Illinois and Kentucky terrain for shipment to river ports. With the shift of steamboating to barge traffic it also became the terminal of highways with easy access to Ohio and Missouri over one railroad and two highway bridges. In recent decades it has become a receation center and has exploited its nearness to wildfowl areas, representing the city in publicity material as "the goose capital of the world."

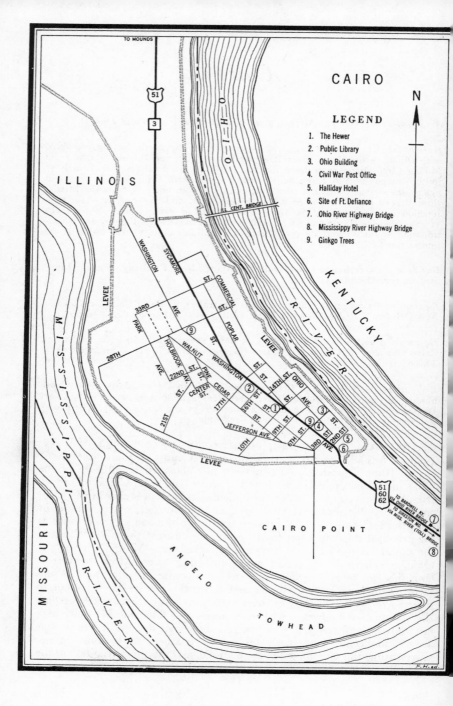

Cairo is protected from the ravages of floods by a huge levee that rises like the ramparts of a walled town. Its revetted slope is scoured clean by the river and has modern barges moored along its mile length. The street fronting the levee is lined with parking lots. Directly west of the Ohio River levee is Commercial Avenue, its southern end solid with business houses, with Victorian upper stories and modernized first-floor fronts. Between the business district at the south and industries at the north is a residential area with spacious lawns planted with mulberry, sycamore, magnolia and cottonwood trees.

Lumber processing remains important, and the industry produces building lumber, hardwood flooring, and chipwood. It has cypress cooling towers and a paper pulp mill. A division of Textron employing 900 makes urethane foam for the automobile and furniture industry. The river barges tow grain, oil, coal, and motor cars, taking advantage of lower freight rates for water transport. Grain elevators have a capacity of 7,000,000 bu.

Cairo owes its name to John G. Comegya, a St. Louis merchant who obtained from the Territorial Legislature an act incorporating the city and the bank of Cairo. He assumed the site resembled that of Cairo, Egypt. His investment failed but the name persisted and the region is popularly called Egypt.

In 1837 the State Legislature incorporated the Cairo City & Canal Company with Darius B. Holbrook, a Boston Yankee, as president. Holbrook hired several hundred workmen to build a levee, shops and houses. The settlement was widely advertised in England, where the bonds of the company found eager purchasers through the London firm of John Wright & Company. This latter failed on Nov. 23, 1840, and the population of Cairo dropped from 1,000 to less than 100 in two years. Those who remained conducted shops and taverns for steamboat travelers. Charles Dickens visited Cairo on April 9, 1842; he damned Cairo vigorously in *American Notes* (1842), using it as the prototype of the nightmare City of Eden in *Martin Chuzzlewit* (1843).

The Cairo City & Canal Company was reorganized as the Cairo City Property Trust in 1846. Plans were laid to make Cairo the main depot of a trade route running south to the Gulf by water and north to the Great Lakes by rail. This meant building a railroad financed by a Federal land grant. Congress gave Illinois more than 2,000,000 acres of public land in September, 1850. The Illinois Central Railroad Company, beneficiary of the grant, was incorporated in 1851, and four years later a track between Cairo and Chicago was opened to traffic.

Cairo took root at once and prospered; its population had increased to 1,756 by 1857, the year it became a city. Each succeeding month increased the volume of products transported along the north-south route. This route was destroyed by the Civil War. When gunboats drove the packets from the lower Mississippi, the corn and pork of southwestern Illinois began to move in increasing amounts to Chicago.

In pre-Civil War days Cairo was a regular port of call for circus troups, menageries, and theatrical companies. The Spalding & Roberts

Show used to stop there in the 1850s aboard the *Floating Palace,* a keel-bottomed barge 35 ft. wide, 200 ft. long, weighing 275 tons, and capable of holding 3,500 spectators, not counting those who paid to stand at the windows outside. Its superstructure blazed with red and gold paint. It was propelled by the steamer *Jack Raymond,* which had rooms for concerts and dance programs. Van Amburgh's menagerie of 150 caged animals, including a giraffe 17 ft. tall, was exhibited at Cairo on the *Floating Palace.* Every form of entertainment was offered on show boats—minstrels, melodrama, tightrope walkers, ballad singers, ventriloquists, and collections of stuffed birds, but most popular entertainment was by dancers, called *danseuses.* Sometimes such steamboats carried a steam calliope, the music of which was not always appreciated. One editor wrote: *"Pop Goes the Weasel* was excruciatingly executed. Either the whistles were out of tune or the organist was." *From the Journal of the Illinois State Historical Society.*

The safety of Cairo was much on the minds of military officers in Washington and Springfield when the Civil War broke out. It was feared that General Gideon J. Pillow, a noisy Tennessee Confederate, was planning an attack. Governor Richard Yates immediately sent several regiments of infantry and one of artillery to Cairo and by April 24, 1861, there were 2,000 men and 10 pieces on the peninsula. June 8, there were 6,000 there and at Villa Ridge. The Cairo camp was called Camp Union until May 5, when it was officially named Camp Defiance. The levee was 15 to 20 ft. above the campground, which was a huge mud pond after rains and full of mosquitoes. Benjamin M. Prentiss of Quincy, colonel of the 1st Brigade, Illinois Volunteers, and later general, was commander of the camp. A battery at the extreme point of the peninsula was called Fort Prentiss. Other camps were on the Big Muddy, where special squadrons guarded the 80 ft. high bridge of the Illinois Central. In September, 1861, General John C. Fremont, commander of the Department, ordered Ulysses S. Grant to take command causing threats of resignation from Prentiss, who claimed seniority in rank. Prentiss was transferred.

Grant massed men and gunboats for an offensive in February, 1862, that resulted in the capture of Fort Henry, February 6, and Fort Donelson, February 16. Fourteen thousand Confederates were transported to Cairo to be sent to northern prisons. When Vicksburg fell 30,000 Confederates passed through Cairo.

By the end of the war Cairo had an estimated population of 8,000. In 1867 more than 3,700 steamboats docked at the city. Later, when the railroad was supreme, Cairo offset the loss in part by developing plants to process cottonseed oil and mill lumber. In the last quarter of the century seven railroads served the city.

In February of 1937 the Ohio River swelled to record heights, inundating Paducah, Louisville, Cincinnati, and scores of smaller communities. As the huge crest moved downstream to the Mississippi, newsreel cameramen and newspaper correspondents rushed to Cairo to report the expected catastrophe. Women and children were evacuated, and a three-foot bulwark of timber and sandbags was built on top of the levee. The water rose swiftly to within four inches of the untested bulwark, wavered there for several hours, and then began slowly to recede. Of all the cities on the lower Ohio, Cairo alone withstood the flood. Since then channels have been deepened, dams have been built, and spring floods are now controlled.

Cairo has had a substantial percentage of black citizens and their numbers have increased with the movement of farm labor into industry. They maintain churches, retail business, and restaurants. In the 1960's blacks comprised an estimated 38% to 40% of the population, and the number has increased annually. For purposes of integration new schools were built in three major areas, but dissatisfaction over alleged discrimination in civic affairs led to rioting and burning of buildings. In 1969 the buildings housing the Tri-County Health Department and the Tuberculosis Sanitarium were burned in a dispute over an adjacent housing project, and the Department moved into the nurses' home of St. Mary's Hospital. The State Department of Public Health reported that health services have been available to everyone regardless of race or color, "and the clinic loads of the department heavily reflect and represent the black communities in Alexander County, as well as Pulaski and Union Counties." In February, 1973, the United States Civil Rights Commission criticized the city authorities for the slight representation of blacks on the police force and other civic bodies and said many white students had withdrawn from the public schools to attend a newly organized academy. The Commission reported that the schools had a low tax base, inadequate supplemental financing by the State, and an unwillingness to accept Federal funds. The County Housing Authority, it said, was separate and segregated.

POINTS OF INTEREST

The MUSEUM OF THE MISSISSIPPI is located in the Rendleman House at the southwest corner of Washington Ave. and 28th St., which was donated to the Illinois State Historical Library in 1957 by Mr. and Mrs. Frederick J. Grieve. This, one of the finest mansions of a wealthy family in southern Illinois, is a two-story brick house with a mansard roof, built in 1865 by Captain William Parker Halliday, a native of Ohio who came to Cairo before the Civil War and with four brothers formed Halliday Bros., controlling a bank and Cairo utilities, and owning, among other investments, the Ohio River front from Cairo to Mound City. The house was acquired in 1901 by Dr. John J. Rendleman, father of Mrs. Grieve. As Adelaide Rondell she had a Broadway and Hollywood stage career.

The house has an exemplary Victorian interior. It has an oval central stairway that rises 38 ft. 4 in. to the roof. There are five fireplaces trimmed with ceramic tile. A miniature theater on the third floor, 35 ft. long and 15 ft. wide, seats 40. One of the large gilt-framed mirrors is a relic of a river steamboat. The grounds have 28 varieties of trees, carefully selected by Dr. Rendleman, and numerous flowering shrubs and roses. Ginko trees were introduced by Capitain Halliday, who first saw them at Grant's Tomb in New York City.

Two other historic houses stand on corners opposite the Rendleman House, the Magnolia Mansion and The Magnolias. In the latter Mayor George Parsons entertained President Theodore Roosevelt in 1907.

MAGNOLIA MANOR, 2700 Washington Ave., a Victorian mansion built in 1869, is the seat of the Cairo Historical Society. It has iron lace trimming and authentic period furniture.

MAUD HOUSE, 703 Walnut St., was the home of the author Maud Rittenhouse Mayne. It was restored by the Cairo Historical Society during the Illinois Sesquicentennial of 1968.

HALLIDAY PARK, on Washington Ave., was named for Capt. William Parker Halliday, Cairo tycoon who built the Rendleman House and developed Cairo utilities. In the park stands *The Hewer,* a heroic bronze statue by George Grey Barnard, which was presented to the city in 1906 by Miss Mary H. Halliday, the Captain's daughter. It had been exhibited at the Louisiana Purchase Exposition in St. Louis in 1904. The widely known HALLIDAY HOTEL, General Grant's temporary home in 1861, was destroyed by fire in 1943.

The CAIRO PUBLIC LIBRARY, 1609 Washington Ave., erected in 1883, underwent a thorough updating in 1962. In 1971 it had 32,757 books and a circulation of nearly 70,000. It is a member of the Shawnee Library System, which has 34 member libraries and its hq at Carterville. There is a museum of Indian artifacts and Civil War relics on the second floor. A plaque honoring Mary J. Safford, Cairo's Angel, for her services at camps and hospitals, was placed by the Egyptian Chapter, DAR.

FORT DEFIANCE STATE PARK, which includes CAIRO POINT, the southernmost extension of the peninsula, occupies 38.1 acres at the confluence of the Ohio and Mississippi Rivers. It was dedicated July 3, 1960, by Illinois Governor William G. Stratton, who also turned a spadeful of earth on the site of the park Memorial Building. This is a concrete structure in the form of the prow of a ship, with the first floor open and consisting entirely of pillars and the second floor devoted to offices and rest rooms. There is an observation platform on the roof. The open first floor is a reminder of the numerous floods that have swept across parts of the peninsula.

BRIDGES TO KENTUCKY AND MISSOURI. The Ohio River Bridge, left from the south end of Washington Ave. carries US 51, US 60, and US 62 to Kentucky. It was opened in 1938, is 6,229 ft. long with approaches, and cost $3,000,000 (*free*). The Mississippi River Highway Bridge, right from the south end of Washington Ave., carries US 60 and US 62 to Missouri. It is a cantilever bridge, 3,720 ft. long, opened in 1929 (*toll*).

~~~~~~

Champaign and Urbana

Airline: Willard Airport of the University of Illinois, 6 *m.* south on US 45.

Buses: Greyhound, Swallow, Illini, Union Bus Depot, 118 S. Walnut, Champaign; Greyhound, Swallow, 109 N. Broadway, Urbana.

Highways: Interstate 74 from Danville and the east to Bloomington, connects with Interstate 57 west of Champaign; US 45 from Chicago to southwest, connects with US 40 to East St. Louis; US 150 from Danville, goes northwest to Bloomington, route to Lake of the Woods; State 10 west to Lincoln.

Railroads: Illinois Central Gulf, 116 N. Chestnut St.; Norfolk & Western, (Wabash) 304 N. Randolph St. Illinois Traction System, Champaign.

Information: Champaign Chamber of Commerce, 109 W. University, Champaign; Urbana Association of Commerce, 202 Busey Bank Bldg., Urbana. *Champaign-Urbana News Gazette, Champaign-Urbana Courier, Daily Illini,* University. Of 5 radio stations, one is owned by the *News Gazette,* one by the University, one by University students. Of 4 television stations, one is owned by the University.

Recreation: Champaign has 23 parks, Urbana 10. Golf, 6 courses: Champaign Country Club, Urbana Country Club, two University of Illinois courses open to the public; Lake of the Woods, Lincolnshire Fields. Swimming: At the 2 Country Clubs, Crystal Lake Park, and Windsor Swim Club, Urbana; Centennial Park, Indian Acres Swim Club, Champaign; Lake of the Woods. There are 2 roller skating rinks, 1 ice rink, 4 bowling alleys.

Special Events: For cultural and sports events, including football games at Memorial Stadium, consult newspapers and Daily Calendar of the University of Illinois.

Visits to the University of Illinois: Information about addresses of students and faculty, hotel accommodations, events on campus, tickets, see Main Desk, Illinois Union, east of Wright St., near Green. For tours, with guides, write in advance or phone Campus Tour Office, R. 420 Illini Union, (333-3668).

CHAMPAIGN (743 alt., 56,532 pop. 1970; 49,583, 1960, inc. 14%), and URBANA (32,800 pop. 1970; 27,264 1960, inc. 20%). Situated in the middle of the richest corn and soybean producing farmlands is this closely meshed community of two contiguous cities that gain their distinction and much of their prosperity from the presence of the main campus of the University of Illinois, which makes its address Urbana-Champaign because most of its plant is in Urbana.

Urbana is the seat of Champaign County, which had 163,281 pop. in 1970, up 23% from 132,436. The only other village of more than a small population is Rantoul, with 25,562. (The census noted that Allerton village, with 327 people, was divided between Champaign and

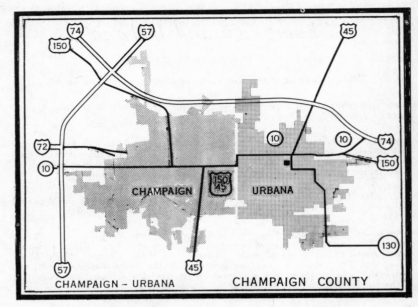

CHAMPAIGN – URBANA   CHAMPAIGN COUNTY

Illinois Dept. of Transportation

Vermilion Counties, with 6 individuals in Champaign, a decrease from 8 in 1960, or 25%.) In 1833, when Champaign County was formed, Urbana was named the county seat.

Without rivalry the two cities maintain two forms of government. Champaign has the council-manager system, Urbana the older alder-manic and mayoral system. They maintain separate police departments, Champaign with 58 men, Urbana with 30, to which the university adds 51 and the County adds 22 and a sheriff. The fire departments are also separate—56 men in Champaign, 26 in Urbana, 39 in the university. While most of their employed people are in trade and services, a fair-sized segment is in light industry, which has been finding helpful the research facilities and technical personnel of the university. Although the college population activates a large portion of business life, the community serves its own large retail trading area, and the two chambers of commerce reach out for conventions to fill the slack, citing the opportunities for relaxation, the merits of the hotels and motels, the good eating from steaks to pizzas, as well as golfing, swimming, and outdoor activity that ought to tempt visitors. The community is able to utilize some of the facilities of the university; the University Assembly Hall can be used as a convention center, and Robert Allerton House, 26 *m.* southwest, is opened by the university to the nonacademic public. While the farms pour their products into the markets, the industries produce a mixed variety of goods: electronic component parts, drop forgings, alloy castings, road machinery, deepfreeze units, air conditioners, athletic equipment, dairy products, soybean oil, salad dressing, margarine.

Settled in 1822 by Willard Tompkins, Urbana is 30 years older than Champaign. In 1854 the Illinois Central Railroad, first line of any importance in the State, was pushing south with its rails. At Urbana the engineers laid out three possible routes, two through the city and one about two miles west. To Urbana's dismay, the last route was chosen. What prompted this choice lies buried in legends, which hint at covert real estate deals.

Urbana, faced with the choice of moving to the depot or attempting to maintain its existence without a railroad, chose the latter. Almost immediately a town referring to itself as West Urbana sprang up around the depot, but farmers avoided confusion by calling the two towns the Depot and Old Town. In a bill for incorporation as a city in 1855, Urbana included a clause authorizing the annexation of the new town. Indignant Depot residents succesfully fought the bill and in 1860 incorporated under the name of Champaign. The cleavage thus established has been maintained since. Today the two municipalities are separated only by Wright Street, which both find most useful.

Champaign boomed as a trade center and soon passed Urbana in population. The rich prairies, opened for cultivation by the railroads, poured their bumper crops into the railroad town. Upstart and flushed with prosperity, Champaign attempted to wrest the county seat from Urbana, which, realizing that the courthouse was its chief asset, met the assult with successful vigor.

The University of Illinois

Official address: Urbana. Individual offices use name of city in which they are located.

Office of Public Information: Davenport, House, Champaign.

University symbol, an Indian. *Colors:* Orange and blue. *Motto:* Learning and labor.

The university gives the following description of its physical plant:

> The Urbana-Champaign campus is the oldest and largest campus of the University of Illinois. Seventeen colleges and schools offer undergraduate study, professional courses and advanced work. Here also are institutes, bureaus, experiment stations and headquarters for extension and other statewide services. The campus comprises 703 acres with 2,794 acres of agricultural experiment fields in the county and a total of 3,483 acres in Illinois. Nearby are timber reservations of 510 acres, 1,171-acre airport, 1,768-acre Allerton Park, Hott Memorial Center, 4-H Camp, 331-acre antenna research site, 15-acre Corps of Engineers Research Laboratory site, 476-acre radio telescope site, 82-acre optical telescope site and 41-acre radio direction finding and meteor radar site. The campus has 175 major buildings including residence halls. The plant centering here is valued at $464,868,855. The spring, 1974, enrollment was 32,392; the faculty numbered 3,347.

The UNIVERSITY OF ILLINOIS grew out of the Illinois Industrial College, chartered in 1867 and opened on March 2, 1868.

This was one of the 68 institutions formed under the Land Grant Act of 1862, signed by President Lincoln, by which public land was set aside in the states to support higher education of practical value. Bloomington, Chicago, Lincoln, and Jacksonville had bid for the university, but Urbana offered 970 acres, a building, county bonds, landscaping, and $50,000 in free freight on the Illinois Central Railroad, and no other town could match that.

Fifty students and three teachers were on hand for the opening, and at the end of the first year there were 77 students and ten teachers. The students put in two hours a day at manual labor, building sidewalks, roads, fences to keep the cows out, and classroom furniture.

The university is governed by a board of trustees of 11 members, nine of them elected for six-year terms by the voters of the State, and two *ex officio*—the Governor and the Superintendent of Public Instruction. The President of the university is the chief executive officer, and the Chancellor is the chief administrative officer.

The university at Urbana-Champaign is one unit of the system that includes the University at Chicago Circle and the Medical Center in Chicago, both of which have chancellors as administrative officers.

At the close of its fiscal year, June 30, 1973, the system reported income of $338,728,099, of which 49.9% came from State tax revenues, and expenditures of $337,571,042. For 1974 the State appropriated $183,431,544 from taxes.

Enrollment in the spring, 1973, at all units reached 54,684.

The COLLEGE OF AGRICULTURE was one of the first four units when the institution began in 1868, and has been of inestimable benefit to the farms of Illinois ever since. Its departments now take up every phase of farming and livestock raising, including dairying, food science, home economics, forestry, and horticulture. The Agricultural Experiment Station, active since 1888, publishes results of its studies. Cooperative Extension Service reaches each of the 102 counties and guides the 4-H Clubs, which now have 4,070 units and 77,400 youths and more than 13,000 adult leaders. The college has 2,600 acres of farms and fields, of which 1,850 acres adjoin the campus in Champaign County. Experimental areas are located in Crawford, Cumberland, DeKalb, Fayette, Franklin, Hancock, Hardin, Henderson, Henry, Lee, Logan and Will counties. An experimental research center is operated jointly with Southern Illinois University in Jackson County. A demonstration of good land use is given at the Dixon Springs Agricultural Center of 5,000 acres of land in the Shawnee National Forest area leased by the university.

Separately organized and conducted is the COLLEGE OF VETERINARY MEDICINE, which, besides teaching and research, provides diagnostic service and direct aid to the citizens of Illinois. In a recent typical year the veterinary medical clinics treated 8,824 small animals and 24,609 large animals.

The COLLEGE OF LIBERAL ARTS AND SCIENCES is the largest in the university. In addition to all the standard departments it has the School of Life Sciences and the Asian, Latin-American and

New and Old Landmarks

HISTORIC WATER TOWER AND WATER WORKS IN RELATION TO
JOHN HANCOCK CENTER, MICHIGAN AVENUE

MICHIGAN AVENUE FROM GROUNDS OF THE ART INSTITUTE OF
CHICAGO: THE PEOPLES' GAS BLDG., BORG-WARNER BLDG.,
ORCHESTRA HALL, AND THE RAILWAY EXCHANGE

MICHIGAN AVENUE, WEST FRONT, SOUTH FROM LAKE STREET

THE CHICAGO PUBLIC LIBRARY, MAIN BUILDING AT MICHIGAN AVE. AND E. RANDOLPH ST.

THE ART INSTITUTE OF CHICAGO. PRUDENTIAL BLDG. IN BACKGROUND

TIFFANY MOSAICS ON STAIRCASE, CHICAGO PUBLIC LIBRARY

TIFFANY MOSAICS AT TOP
OF MARBLE STAIRCASE,
CHICAGO PUBLIC LIBRARY

TWO SCULPTURES IN THE
LOOP. ABOVE, ONE OF TWO
BRONZE LIONS AT ART
INSTITUTE BY EDWARD
KEMYSS, 1893. BELOW,
METAL SCULPTURE AT
CIVIC CENTER BY PABLO
PICASSO, 1970

EQUITABLE CONCOURSE STAIRWAY TO LOWER LEVEL OF
MICHIGAN AVENUE

PIONEER COURT DURING THE HOLIDAYS. WRIGLEY BUILDING
AT RIGHT

NORTH LAKE SHORE DRIVE FROM LAKE POINT TOWER, SHOWING
HOLIDAY INN, FURNITURE MART, NORTHWESTERN CAMPUS,
JOHN HANCOCK CENTER

Russian and East European Centers. Among its special programs are African studies and the teaching of English as a second language. The COLLEGE OF ENGINEERING includes among its departments aeronautical, astronautical and nuclear engineering. The COLLEGE OF FINE AND APPLIED ARTS has urban and regional planning in its courses, also the School of Music, the Krannert Center for the Performing Arts and the five bands, which include symphonic and concert groups that have members from all colleges.

The university conducts several observatories Prairie Observatory near Oakland, 40 m. southeast of the campus, with two optical telescopes; two radio projects, Vermilion River Observatory, 5 m. southeast of Danville, and the Geophysical Observatory on the campus.

Museums and exhibits open to the public include the university's permanent art collections and special exhibits in Krannert Art Museum; the Natural History Museum in the Natural History Bldg.; literary and fine arts exhibits in the corridors of the Library, and World Heritage Museum, 484 Lincoln Hall.

One of the newest buildings on campus is ASSEMBLY HALL, a structure notable for its edge-supported dome, 400 ft. in diameter, rising 128 ft. at its peak. Built in 1863 at a cost of $8,350,000, the hall has 16,000 permanent seats that can be partitioned off in sections, and is used for large affairs, cultural and entertainment, including plays, for which scenery and lights are suspended from a grid at the center.

The LIBRARY is one of the glories of the University of Illinois. It contains more books and materials than any state university library, and is third in size among American universities, exceeded only by Harvard and Yale, and fifth among all American libraries. In a 1973 count the system had 8,237,020 items, including 5,660,351 vols. Of these totals the library at Urbana-Champaign had 6,883,527 books and several hundred thousand items of maps and photographs, and the same number of musical items. It receives more than 20,000 periodicals and newspapers, a tremendous fund of current scientific, cultural, and topical information. Among special collections are English literature of the 16th and 17th centuries, American humor and folklore, Abraham Lincoln and the Civil War, Latin-American Revolutionary records, original manuscripts of American history. The Undergraduate Library is located opposite the Main Library on Gregory Drive.

In April, 1892, trustees of the University of Illinois invited Woodrow Wilson, professor at Princeton University, to become Regent (President) of the University of Illinois. They offered him $6,000 a year salary, expenses while traveling on college business, a business manager and a secretary, but no house. Wilson considered the university still largely agricultural in policy, and decided against the offer because, there being no endowment, he would have to solicit the legislature periodically for funds, would not have time for writing, and told his wife: "I am not at all in sympathy with coeducation." Irving Dilliard commented in the *Journal* of the Illinois State Historical Society: "If Woodrow Wilson had taken the other fork of the road and come out to Illinois, what would history have held for him? Would he have risen in the politics of the Midwest just as he rose in the politics of the East?"

Illinois started a School of Journalism in 1927, which became the College of Communications in 1968. It has expanded to include advertising, journalism, radio and television, and also has the Institute of Communications Research and the Division of University Broadcasting. Station WILL operates noncommercial programs daily and Sunday, as do its FM and TV programs. A student radio station, WPGU, is conducted by the Illini Publishing Co.

WILLARD AIRPORT of the University of Illinois occupies 1,300 acres 6 m. southwest of the campus on US 45. It is a completely functioning airport operated by the Institute of Aviation, which offers three two-year courses in training and research. The field, opened in 1945, has scheduled commercial service by Ozark Airlines. The institute has a fleet of 40 aircraft and the Staff Air Transportation Service. It has courses for professional pilot, aircraft maintenance, and aviation electronics and pilot training leading to Federal aviation administration certificates and ratings. In 1968 the institute established an Aviation Research Laboratory devoted to human engineering and improved training methods and aids.

The financing of the University of Illinois System, including the main plant at Urbana-Champaign, the new university at Chicago Circle, and the Medical Center at Chicago, is a huge undertaking, for this system is one of the major industries of Illinois. The report for fiscal 1971 showed $324,710,791 was needed to balance expenditures. The State General Assembly appropriated more than $169,000,000 or 52%, the U. S. Government granted $9,000,000, gifts and grants brought $52,000,000, and student fees $15,500,000. The system uses 218 major buildings and 499 others at the three campuses and is erecting new ones.

OTHER POINTS OF INTEREST

The CHAMPAIGN CITY BUILDING, Neil St. and University Ave., was finished in 1937. Its design, an adaptation of the widely publicized City Building in Los Angeles, departs sharply from the classic and neo-classic forms prevalent throughout the Midwest. The lower portion is two stories in height, severely simple in treatment, and at the west end a six-story tower rises in a receding shaft to an octagonal, five-stepped crown.

The CHAMPAIGN COUNTY COURT HOUSE, corner Main St. and Broadway, was dedicated in 1901, the fourth courthouse to stand on this site. A memorial at the north entrance attests the fact that Lincoln traveled this way as he rode the Eighth Judicial Circuit. In the third building, one spring day in 1853, Lincoln argued a railroad case as attorney for the Illinois Central Railroad, receiving $25 for successfully prosecuting a condemnation suit. In the fall of 1854, no longer an obscure lawyer, he spoke again in the old building, assailing Senator Stephen Douglas and the Nebraska Bill.

PUBLIC LIBRARIES of standard size function in both Champaign and Urbana, despite the presence of one of the greatest collections of books in the country in the various libraries of the University of Illinois. This indicates the high proportion of library users in the population. The CHAMPAIGN PUBLIC LIBRARY, 306 W. Church St., was erected in 1894 and improved in 1971. In 1972 it reported a stock of 84,982 books and 334,054 "transactions," meaning use of all services. It maintains a branch library at Douglass Center. The URBANA PUBLIC LIBRARY, 201 S. Race St., reported 83,352 books and 218,917 transactions. Its building was erected in 1918 and improved in 1970. Both libraries are members of the Lincoln Trail Library System.

MORROW PLOTS is an area in the heart of the camputes marking the first field for agricultural experiment at any American college. The area was first planted in 1876 and has been used for study of soil management ever since.

An everlasting light burns at the LINCOLN MEMORIAL in the heart of the business district, lighted in 1964 as the two cities' commemoration of the greatness of Abraham Lincoln. The monument is a tall megalith with a bronze medallion.

LINCOLN SQUARE is the great indoor shopping center in downtown Urbana that covers six acres, opened in September, 1964, after 21 acres had been cleared for renewal. The center maintains a temperature of 72°. Allied with Lincoln Square are restaurant and hotel facilities for large and small groups.

THE COUNTRY FAIR is West Champlain's shopping center, with numerous shops and wide space for parking. It comprises a mall where special activities can be staged.

WASHINGTON SCHOOL PROJECT is a cooperative effort of city and University of Illinois in education begun in 1968. It is a part of Champaign Community School District No. 4 and has a volunteer teaching staff and enrollment, uses a computerized teaching system, and has a special project in elementary school mathematics and science.

CRYSTAL LAKE PARK, W. Park and Lake Sts., Urbana's largest park, contains wooded sections, a spring-fed lake used for boating in summer and skating in winter, a swimming pool, and an amusement hall. Within the park traces of the old Kickapoo Trail can still be seen.

WEST SIDE PARK, corner Church and Elm Sts., is the oldest of Champaign's parks. At its center is the bronze statue, *Prayer for Rain,* executed by Edward Kemeys, sculptor of the Chicago Art Institute's noted lions. The statue depicts an Indian brave praying for rain, while a panther and a deer join him in attitudes of supplication.

CARLE PARK, Iowa St. and Carle Ave. in Urbana, about 10 acres in extent, is distinguished by Lorado Taft's statue of heroic size, portraying Lincoln as a young lawyer on the old Eighth Judicial Circuit.

CHICAGO

Air Services: Chicago O'Hare International Airport, John F. Kennedy Expressway, for regional, continental, and overseas lines, with direct flights to Europe, Asia, South America. Helicopters, garage, hotel. Bus service to and from Loop and North Michigan Ave. hotels.

The O'Hare Airport Express Bus runs between the airport and Jefferson Park Terminal of the CTA. Passengers come by rapid transit, bus, or motor cars here get direct service to O'Hare 24 hours a day, 7 days a week. The bus covers the distance in 15 minutes on the Kennedy Expressway.

Chicago Midway Airport, 5600 S. Cicero Ave. Adlai E. Stevenson Expressway to Cicero Ave., then south. CTA buses. Domestic airlines especially.

Merrill C. Meigs Field, on Northerly Island, East 15th St. and the Lake. Commuter planes, private aircraft.

Buses: Greyhound Bus Terminal, Clark and Randolph Sts. Continental Trailways, 20 East Randolph St. Continental Air Transport Co. (hotels-airports).

Highways: Chicago is the hub of a huge network of highways that reach every part of Illinois. Expressways are parts of the Interstate system. Practically all except farm roads are concrete and blacktop, legibly marked with symbols for Interstate, US, and Illinois roads, with special markers for roads of historic or scenic significance. Chicago expressway and tollway system includes: Adlai E. Stevenson Expy., I-55: Northwest Tollway I-80, Edens Expy., I-94 and US 41, John F. Kennedy Expy., I-94 and Illinois 194, Dwight D. Eisenhower Expy., I-90, Dan Ryan Expy., I-90 and I-94, Calumet Expy., I-94, Illinois 394, Kingery Expy., I-94, US 6, Tri-State Tollway, I-94, I-80, I-294, Edens Expy., spur, I-94, East-West Tollway, Illinois 56, 190, Chicago Skyway (toll), I-90. Maps available at gas stations. Official highway map available from Dept. of Transportation, State of Illinois, 2300 s. 31st St., Springfield, 62706, or Office of Secretary of State, State Capitol, Springfield, 62706.

Railroads: Chicago & North Western, 500 W Madison St., across the Chicago River. Commuter service to north and northwest suburbs. Illinois Central Gulf, stations along the Lake Front, from Randolph St. and Van Buren. Chicago South Shore & South Bend, same stations. Rock Island Lines. LaSalle St. Station, 139 W. Van Buren St. Commuter service south and southwest. Amtrak, Union Station, 210 S. Canal St; also commuter trains of Burlington Northern, Illinois Central Gulf, formerly Gulf, Mobile & Ohio; Milwaukee, Penn-Central, Santa Fe.

Information: The Chicago Convention & Tourism Bureau, 322 S. Michigan Ave., is the principal source of information about conventions, sports events, entertainment, and dates. It has available folders, including *Discover the Great Indoors, Host City to the Nation,* and *Year 'Round Calendar of Chicago Events.* The Chicago Association of Commerce & Industry, 130 S. Michigan Ave., publishes a bi-monthly, *Chicago Headline Events,* a magazine of business, *Commerce,* and industrial reports. The Chicago Visitor Information Booth is in the lobby of the Civic Center, Clark & Randolph Sts., Monday through Friday, 9-5. The State Street Council operates an Information Booth for visitors at the northeast corner of State and Madison Sts. Mayor's Office of Inquiry and Information in City Hall.

Churches: Annunciation Greek Orthodox, 1017 N. LaSalle St. Chicago Loop Orthodox Synagogue, 16 S. Clark St. Christ the King Lutheran Ch., 24 W. Jackson Blvd. First Methodist-Chicago Temple, 77 West Washington St. St. Chrysostom's Ch., 1424 N. Dearborn St. Old St. Mary's Chapel, 23 E. Van Buren St. St. Peter's Catholic Ch., 110 W. Madison St. Cathedral of the Holy Name, Superior and N. State Sts. Temple Sholem, Reform, 3480 Lake Shore Drive. Seventeenth Church of Christ Scientist, 55 E. Wacker Dr.

Guides: Folders describing dining, entertainment and tours may be picked up at hotels and newsstands. The City of Chicago issues comprehensive reports on municipal activities, which may be consulted at the Municipal Reference Library, City Hall. The *Chicago Guide,* a monthly magazine published by Station WFMT has comprehensive lists of restaurants, performances, sports, night attractions, and summarizes movies. *Chicagoland's Community Guide,* (Law Bulletin Publishing Co.) is an annual report on living in the suburbs. The Forest Preserve of Cook County comprises 63,000 acres of forest, meadows, and waters for picnics, games, fishing, bicycling, horseback riding, hiking. The Commissioners publish trail maps and historical notes in folders for the various divisions; address Forest Preserve General Headquarters, 536 N. Harlem Ave., River Forest, Ill. Chicago has 8 of the 31 television transmitters in Illinois and 23 radio stations. Evanston has three radio stations.

TYPICAL ANNUAL EVENTS OF GENERAL INTEREST

January. Professional hockey at Chicago Stadium; basketball, same; Northwestern Univ. basketball, McGraw Hall, Central Ave., Evanston; Loyola Univ. Gymnasium, 6525 N. Sheridan Rd.; De Paul Univ. Alumni Hall, 1011 Belden.

February. Azalea and camellia show, Garfield Park Conservatory. Chinese New Year celebrations, Wentworth Ave. and Cermak Road. Sportsmen's Vacation & Boat Show, also Hot Rod Car show, both at International Amphitheatre. Chicago Auto Show, McCormick Place, continues into March. Harness Racing, Sportsman's Park, Cicero, through April.

March. Annual Medinah Shrine circus at the Medinah Temple. World Flower and Garden Show at McCormick Place. St. Patrick's Day Parade on State Street, with thousands of marchers, 50 floats and bands.

April. Easter flower show at Garfield and Lincoln Park conservatories. Arbor Day ceremonies at Grant Park and Madison. Final weeks of harness racing at Sportsmen's Park, 3301 S. Laramie St., Cicero. Opening of Major League baseball season, Chicago Cubs at Wrigley Field, Chicago White Sox at Sox Park. International Kennel Club dog show.

May. Buckingham Memorial Fountain begins daily schedule in Grant Park, including colors at 9 p.m. Greek Independence Day parade, State St. Armed Forces Day parade, State St. Memorial Day Parade, military and patriotic civilian units. Annual lilac festival in Lombard.

June. Chicago Park District beaches open. Annual Street Art Fair, West 57th St. and Kimbark Ave. Old Town Art Fair, 1800 N. Lincoln Park West. Park West Annual Antiques Fair, 600 W. Fullerton Ave. Midsummer Festival of the Swedish Community Berwyn and Clark Sts. Boy Scouts of America, parade. Grant Park Bank Shell concerts begin, Mon., Fri., Sat., 8 p.m., Sun. 7 p.m.

July. Independence Day exercises at Soldier Field, auspices American Legion, Military units, salute of the flags, fireworks in the evening. Annual Chicago to Mackinac Yacht Race from Chicago harbor at Monroe St. All Star Football at Soldier Field, college graduates vs. NFL champions, sponsored by Chicago Tribune Charities.

August. Gold Coast Art Fair, Ruth St. sponsored by Gold Coast Assn. and *Near North News.* Bud Billiken Day at Washington Park, with parade on

Martin Luther King, Jr. Drive. Ginza holiday by the Japanese community, near 1763 N. Park Ave. Chicago Lakefront Festival, with Venetian Night, a week of illuminated yachts, procession of boats in the Chicago River, and Downtown parade.

September. Mexican Independence Day Parade on State St. Van Steuben Day Parade on State St., featuring Revolutionary War memorials and German heritage. Start of Pro-football season, Soldier Field.

October. Columbus Day Parade on State St., with 62 professional and high school bands, marchers celebrating Italo-American backgrounds, and parochial school contingents. Ringling Bros. Barnum & Bailey Circus, International Amphitheatre. Chinese Independence Day Parade at Community Center. Pro hockey season opens at Chicago Stadium. Pro basketball season opens at Chicago Stadium.

November. Holiday Folk Fair at Navy Pier by Chicago ethnic groups. Chrysanthemum show at Garfield and Lincoln Park Conservatories. Miracle of Books Fair at Chicago Museum of Science & Industry, featuring books for children. International Live Stock Exhibition and Rodeo at International Amphitheatre. Veterans Day Parade by patriotic organizations, veterans, and military contingents.

December. Christmas Parade on Michigan Ave. Christmas Tree Lighting ceremony on Civic Center Plaza, with choristers. Nutcracker ballet suite performed at Arie Crown Theatre, McCormick Place. Christmas Around the World featured at Museum of Science & Industry. High School Championship Football Game at Soldier Field between teams of parochial and public schools. Christmas flower shows at Garfield and Lincoln Park Conservatories.

Chicago I

MUNICIPAL INFORMATION AND HISTORY

CHICAGO, second largest city in the United States, has within its environs the greatest concentration of financial, industrial, and mercantile power in the midcontinent. Like an enchanted city of legend its towers and antennae rise for 954 square miles along the yellow sands of Lake Michigan. Focal point of a tributary area that includes six counties in Illinois and two in Indiana, it is located at the southwestern end of the lake and is a port on the seaway that connects the Atlantic Ocean with the Gulf of Mexico.

POPULATION. The Bureau of the Census first published the preliminary count of the Census of 1970 and then issued corrected data; by 1972 it issued its final count: Chicago, 3,369,357, a loss of 181,047 from the 1960 total of 3,550,404; Cook County, including Chicago, final count, 5,493,766, a rise of 364,041 from the 1960 total. The Standard Metropolitan Statistical Area, which had 6,977,611 counted in 1970, had 7,084,700 in 1972, making the Chicago SMSA the second largest in the country.

The Census figures, however, do not disclose the billions of dollars going into new construction. The largest mail-order house in the country picked the Loop for the tallest building in the world. A bank bulldozed a 300-room hotel to erect a 60-story skyscraper. At the end of one of Chicago's farflung expressways almost 100,000 people daily step on and off airplanes in a pasture now filling up with hotels and office buildings. And in its front yard the city has struck gold—83 acres of freight yards turning into a metropolis.

Behind this glowing facade are accomplishments just as important though less visible. Barriers fallen from ghettoes, and open housing giving access to miles of integrated apartments. New colleges without entrance bars. Suburbs blossoming with luxury shops, theater-restaurants, libraries and playfields. New towns where habitations are tailored to suit incomes. And jobs where applicants are hired without reference to color or sex.

It's all there—a world of achievement. All except an industry that made Chicago famous. Meatpacking has moved on.

As the city plans for its crosstown expressway, for tearing down the elevated railroad structure, for dredging islands out of the lake, it gives small heed to its turbulent past. It has seen gangsters rub out gangsters. It has watched rioting youths throw rocks through office windows. It has had blocks of slum areas burned down and firemen shot at by snipers. But on balance its police have had the last word. Chicago's official concern is with keeping order, even if it hurts.

Chicago is multiracial and polyglot. It has the second largest population of blacks, of whom practically all are native-born and a vast number came up from the South. Non-whites number 1,102,620. It has large blocs of Jews, Poles, and Italians. Puerto Ricans and Mexicans are rushing into the central city faster than the Nordics rush out. Asians, including Japanese, find Chicago a second paradise. It has thousands of school children who have to be taught to speak English. Its telephone books use two languages and where signs once read *Hier wird Deutsch Gesprochen,* they now read *Se Habla Espagnol.*

THE GOVERNMENT OF CHICAGO

Chicago is governed by the Mayor and the City Council, of which the Mayor is the presiding officer. The primary election for the nomination of Mayor is held every fourth year on the last Tuesday in February. This is also the date for the election of 50 aldermen, one from each ward, which is nonpartisan, the names appearing on a separate ballot without a party name or circle. The election for Mayor and other municipal officers is held on the first Tuesday in April following the February primary. If no candidate for alderman receives a majority of the vote cast in the February election the two leading candidates have a run-off election on the first Tuesday of April following. There are 3,670 precincts for voting. Both the municipal officers and aldermen are elected for terms of four years. The salary of the Mayor is $35,000 a year.

The City Council is a true cross-section of the citizens of Chicago. The names of the aldermen reflect their varied ethnic and national backgrounds. There are still present a Burke, a Kelley, a Hines, and a Shannon to recall the solid Irish memberships of decades ago, but also a Vrodolyak, a Potempa, a Marzullo, and a Cohen to represent later stocks. The first black alderman to sit in the City Council was Oscar De Priest, in 1915. In 1928 he became the first black Representative in Congress from Illinois. In 1973 there were 11 blacks in the City Council, one a woman.

A similar ethnic variety is noted in the Chicago Board of Education of 11 members, which in 1973 had three blacks and one "person of Spanish language", and of which the vice president, Mrs. Carey B. Preston, was black. The Mayor appoints the board, with the approval of the City Council.

The City of Chicago operates on a budget of more than $1 billion. In 1973 the overall Executive Budget totaled $1,917,704,966 in estimated resources from which appropriations were made. After deducting Inter-Fund appropriations of $21,833,186, the net resources available were $995,871,780. The city allocated $557,668,773 to operations.

The City Government receives 38 cents out of every property tax dollar, the remaining 62 cents going to the support of six other separate bodies providing essential services. The Board of Education gets 39¢; the Chicago Junior College, 3¢; the Forest Preserve, 1¢; the Sanitary District, 4¢; Cook County, 7¢, and the Chicago Park District, 8¢.

The STATE OF THE ECONOMY

The healthy state of the economy of Chicago and its contributing area—comprising six counties in Illinois and two in northwestern Indiana—is shown by the commitments for expansion in the 1970s. The largest investment has been in heavy industry—in steel, pig iron, primary and secondary smelting of nonferrous metals, castings, and allied manufactures, such as the new slab casting mill of Inland Steel Co. in East Chicago. Second largest investment has been in chemicals and allied products, among them a big venture by Sherwin-Williams Co., already the largest paint-chemical complex; Chlorex at Bedford Park, and Economics Laboratory, Inc., soap products, in Joliet. Third largest activity is petroleum refining, including a plant of Humble Oil (Exxon) in Elk Grove Village, and additions to the American Oil plant in Naperville. Fourth largest investment has been in electrical machinery. The increase of motor car travel continues to tempt innkeepers, especially the chains; Hyatt House chooses sites on East Wacker Drive, near O'Hare, and in Oak Brook; Ramada Inn goes into Elgin; Holiday Inn opens in Mundelein and other suburban locations. The open area near O'Hare International Airport attracts office buildings and hotels.

Chicago remains the greatest railroad center in the country. Despite the decline in passenger traffic freight haulage demonstrates the tremendous importance of Chicago as an industrial terminal. The Chicago area has 28 railroads, of which 15 are major trunk lines; every day 47,700 freight cars in 1,400 trains move through or leave the terminal district, defined as an area of 1,750 sq. mi. stretching from Gary, Ind., to Des Plaines. According to figures quoted by Alan S. Boyd, president of the Illinois Central Gulf Ry. in Commerce, every third railroad carload in the country originates, moves through, or terminates in the Chicago area. Every 24 hours railroads interchange 18,000 cars at 150 different locations. There are more than 100 yards for sorting out trains and exchanging trailers and containers between trucks and trains. In 1973 a railroad terminal information system was established by cooperation among the railroads to relieve congestion, speed up transit, and remove time-consuming duplication and inefficiency.

The confidence of the financial community in the strength of the Chicago metropolitan areas is shown by the tremendous investment annually of more than three-quarters of a billion dollars in new commercial office buildings and plants. While the central city ordinarily takes the major share of the outlay, by 1970 municipal and suburban construction costs were almost even: $391,085,000 in the city and $397,763,000 in the suburbs, a total of $788,843,000.

Within recent years the largest amount of new housing in the suburbs (cottages and apartments) has been recorded at Schaumburg, which alternates with Bolingbrook for first place, followed in order by Wheeling, Elk Grove Village, Woodridge, Hanover Park, and Tinley Park. There is a continuing migration to Elgin and Aurora.

Trends in the suburbs indicate that while one-family houses will continue to be built at a good rate, financed by the large deposits in savings-and-loan banks, condominiums will increase to overcome the heavy costs of apartment house operation. Conversion of rental units to condominiums is a marked trend in built-up areas.

Chicago entered the 1970-1980 decade with an over-supply of offices and a problem in abandoned property. The Chicago Real Estate Board reported that real estate taxation rose 96 percent between 1960 and 1971 and was responsible for the abandonment of run-down property by owners unable to meet the cost of repairs, thus making necessary demolition by the city.

POPULATION PATTERNS

Chicago is the great polyglot center of the Midwest. Its earliest settlers came via the Erie Canal and the National Road, many of them attracted by land sales. Most of the early settlers were native-born. Thereafter Chicago received large accretions of foreign immigrants. In the 1840s and 1850s the Irish made up nearly 39 percent of the foreign born. They came in the days of the great potato famines, dug the canals, laid the rails, and took over the political machinery. They were strongly nationalist-minded and immediately began to agitate for the freedom of Ireland from British rule. There was a strong Fenian element in Chicago and funds to aid Irish independence were continually being raised. The Irish settled in the southwest wards; many political leaders and police captains came out of Bridgeport, where Mayor Richard J. Daley had his home.

Next to the Irish the immigrants from England and Scotland were the largest foreign group, but they were soon outnumbered by the

Germans, who claimed the near North Side as their own. In 1860 the Germans had 20 percent of the city's population. Although they came from different political divisions, including large groups from Bohemia, they were clannish, and supported daily and weekly newspapers. Persecution in Europe drove large numbers out of Poland and Russia; Czechs and Slovaks found work in the steel mills and on the truck farms of southeast Chicago. Persecution also forced Jews out of Russia; many thousands passed through the immigrant center of the old Union Station, followed by Italians and Balkanese. The Greeks came because they needed work; many found Chicago a good place for small shopkeeping on South Halsted St.

Prof. Bessie Louise Pierce in her *A History of Chicago* writes that only 323 Negroes were living in Chicago in 1850; and they were only one percent of the total population in 1870. Migrations from the South brought huge numbers to the northern cities, especially Chicago. Since World War II Chicago has received such large additions of Mexicans and Puerto Ricans that the schools have had to install courses in the English language for Spanish-speaking children.

The Mexicans who came to Chicago were largely day laborers who found it difficult to get permanent jobs with adequate pay. Colonies grew in the Hull House district, the Stockyards area and South Chicago. Eventually they started a newspaper, *Mexico*. The municipality organized the Mexican Health Center in 1930, especially to fight tuberculosis. With no political pull the Mexicans for a long time had difficulty getting advantages obtained by other minorities.

In the Standard Metropolitan Statistical Area that has Chicago as its central city, the Census counted 363,838 persons of Spanish language, of whom 327,168 were in the Illinois part, and 36,671 in the Indiana part. With 169,310 under 16 years of age and 175,019 at 21 or over, there were only 8,187 aged 65 or over, giving a median age of 19.9. Men and women were fairly well balanced: 180,547 males, 179,292 females.

The comparative youthfulness of Puerto Ricans or persons of Spanish language in Chicago itself was also recorded by the Census. Of 247,343 persons counted inside Chicago, 112,380 were under 18 and 120,583 were 21 and over. Only 5,463 were 65 and over. This gave a median age of 20.3.

Cook County had 286,882 residents speaking the Spanish language in 1970; of this number 101,578 males and 33,724 females were employed. Of the men 37,990 were operatives except for transport: 24,160 were employed on durable goods and 9,568 were in services. Of the females, 14,086 were operatives, 13,047 were in manufacturing and 10,016 were in clerical occupations.

Cook County in 1970 had a labor force of 1,422,379, or 79.7% of its male population. The 46,716 unemployed were 3.3% of the total. The 364,578 not in the labor force were enrolled in schools or institutions. There were 142,738 aged 65 or over. Of the female labor force of 928,237, 888,673 were employed.

Veterans of military service living in Chicago in 1970 and the wars they fought in were: World War I, 27,266; World War II, 208,949; Korean 70,238; Vietnam, 66,658. Veterans of both World War II and Korean, 7,212. Noncombatant services, 52,040.

Chicago's population began slipping downward after the World War II, in spite of the numbers of blacks who were lured from the farms of the South by jobs in metropolitan factories. The city's net loss of 183,447 between 1960 and 1970 was in residents only, for the daily working population increased. Families moved to the suburbs for a variety of reasons. Considering the length of time this migration had been going on it was clear that the principal impetus was the desire to get out of the crowded city into the open countryside. This was stimulated by developers, who found there were ready buyers when they platted farmland for town lots, built single-family dwellings in quantity and staked out supermarkets. Here were freedom from traffic jams, unpolluted air, and easy access to schools, church, library and markets. Many Chicagoans feared the rise in street crimes and drug addiction, and large numbers resented busing school children out of their neighborhoods to achieve racial balance. Many whites left for the suburbs, but open housing also enabled blacks to get out of ghettoes and public policy made provision for them. Shops followed people; State Street and Michigan Avenue stores opened branches in outlying villages; suburban shopping centers multiplied and several became showplaces of more than local renown.

The ability to finance and build a complete community has been demonstrated effectively in the environs of Chicago. Park Forest was established thus in the 1940s, and Oak Brook was a spectacular accomplishment in the 1960s. By 1970 the farmlands beyond Park Forest suddenly became a village called Park Forest South, with habitations for thousands of newcomers, developed under Title VII of the Urban Growth and New Community Development Act.

Light industries also have been moving out of Chicago into the environs. The reason is economic: as the planners have said, premium land sells for $100,000 an acre in the city, whereas a plant can find acreage in the suburbs for $25,000 to $40,000 an acre.

FOREIGN LANGUAGE NEWSPAPERS

Foreign language newspapers printed in Chicago demonstrate the continuing interest of many residents in their European backgrounds. The number of weeklies and dailies in foreign languages has shrunk considerably in recent decades, but many others are still printed in states other than Illinois. In Chicago are Czech, German, Lithuanian, Polish, and Slovene daily newspapers. The Czechs issue the *Derni Hlastel,* a daily, and two weeklies, *Katolika* and *Narod.* The Danes have the *Danske Pioneer,* a biweekly. The Abendpost Company, founded in 1889, is the surviving firm of a large number of substantial German publishers of generations ago; it issues *Abendpost,* a daily, and *Sonn-*

tagspost, and prints the *Milwaukee Deutsche Zeitung.* The weekly *Eintracht* is published in Skokie. There are two Greek weeklies, the *Press,* and the *Star.* There are four daily newspapers in Polish, two with more than 25,000 readers each, one with 18,000, and one with 12,000. There is also *Polonia,* a weekly. A Hungarian weekly appears on Friday, and a Japanese paper, the Chicago *Shimpo* twice a week. There is also the *China Times.* There are two dailies in Lithuanian with 28,000 and 29,000 readers, and another daily, and two weeklies, one of which, the *Sandara* is the organ of the Lithuanian National League of America. The *Sloboda* is the organ of the Serbian National Defense Council. *Prosveta* is a daily printed in Slovene. There are two Croatian weeklies, one in Slovak, two in Ukrainian, and the *Svenska Amerikanerer Tribunen* in Swedish. The Jewish Daily Forward, a daily, is written in Yiddish, which is read by a large segment of the 285,000 Jews accredited to Chicago. Seven publications written in English are devoted to the interests of the American Indian. A black Islamic organ, *Mahommet Speaks,* founded in 1961, reports a weekly circulation of 600,000.

CRIME IN CHICAGO

Like all great centers of population Chicago has a continuing crime problem, but takes satisfaction in the evidence that its crime rates are going down. When the Federal Bureau of Investigation published the figures for crimes committed during January-June, 1973, in the country's 23 largest cities, Chicago ranked 8th in homicide (12.9 per 100,000 pop.); 7th in robbery (375.3); 15th in rape (22.9) and 14th in larceny (1271.1). While the city continues to enlarge the responsibilities of its police, it cannot guarantee safeguards against violent crimes that arise from inflamed passions and individual resentments. Chicago people have suffered from outrageous acts by lunatics, such as the mass killing of nurses in a dormitory by one deranged man, and frequent rapes and muggings in peaceful neighborhoods.

When the Chicago Association of Commerce & Industry asked its members to name priorities for action on municipal problems the members ranked crime prevention as the most important. The Association advocates a commercial-industrial security guard training program for 2,080 guards a year and workshops on the nature of crime and consumer fraud.

In April, 1973, Chicago opened the first court to deal entirely with shoplifting. This is a division of the Circuit Court, formed at the request of merchants associations and civic bodies. A special police detail works on areas of greatest loss, spotting professionals who rob systematically. More insidious, however, is the infiltration of organized crime into legitimate business, now more subtle than in the mob-ridden days of the 1920s, yet difficult to apprehend because of the intimidation of witnesses. Chicagoans speak of the Syndicate as a sinister force that may be far away or close at hand. That racketeers control policy games and loan-sharking long has been accepted as a fact of life, but that other sinister devices of extortion are also thriving is a continuing challenge to officials and business leaders. One of the most useful agencies in combating illegalities is the U. S. Bureau of Internal Revenue, which keeps close watch on unreported income.

CONVENTION CENTER

Chicago is the great convention center of the nation. All around the year thousands of people throng into Chicago by land, water, and air, to take part in professional conventions, attend trade shows, meet in conferences, or report to headquarters. In a typical year of the 1970s, 7,000,000 visitors came to Chicago, and, as a report says, "injected almost $840,000,000 into Chicago's economy." In a year about 1,600,000 persons attend conventions, each spending an average of $189 during 3.2 days, generating revenues of $270,000,000. For the production of trade shows about $130,000,000 is spent annually. An army of employees of the various services moves this great American activity.

The principal agent for the city in this undertaking is the Chicago Convention and Tourism Bureau, Inc., 332 S. Michigan Ave. It was formed Jan. 1, 1971, by a merger of the Tourism Council of Greater Chicago and the Chicago Convention Bureau, Inc. It is a nonprofit organization that gets two-thirds of its income from a tax of 1 percent imposed by the State on hotel rooms. The remainder comes from dues of member firms. The Bureau operates on a budget of $1,100,000.

Providing for conventions is a highly technical job. Large conventions, which need up to 10,000 hotel rooms and the largest exhibition and meeting halls, make reservations four to six years in advance. While the College Baseball Coaches expect only 500 people, the Home Furnishings Market has an average attendance of 40,000, the Sportsmen's and Vacation Show at the International Amphitheatre draws 350,000 and the Chicago Auto Show at McCormick Place tops all with 900,000. The three major exposition centers can provide 1,500,000 sq. ft. There are 35,000 hotel bedrooms available and more coming. Hotels also have exhibit space and the largest hotel, the Conrad Hilton, has 67,000 sq. ft. available for exposition.

ANOTHER ATTRACTION IS DINING

The tall office buildings are supposed to be the biggest attractions for tourists, but many of the 7,000,000 that annually visit Chicago find dining the most satisfying adventure. And proof that this sprawling compound of peoples is still not a uniform culture is the international character of the cuisine. The restaurants of Chicago are not merely eating places; they are outposts of almost as many national kitchens as there are nations on the globe. A gastronomic tour provides evidence that Chicago is a vast assemblage of international chefs ready to cook their specialties and add a dash of currie powder, chili, paprika, garlic, and Heinz' catsup.

There is American food, of course, which is found at the ubiquitous lunch counters and coffee shops, where griddle cakes, hamburgers, scrambled eggs and bacon, and apple pie are at home. On the North and Northwest Sides, and a short distance south, are great numbers of bistros, nooks, taverns, *stuben,* dining rooms and restaurants. Here can be found Austrian wiener schnitzle, Hungarian goulash, Balkanese shish-ka-bab, French onion soup, Mexican chili con carne, Polish beef stroganov, German *sauerbraten,* Chinese chow mein. And amid all are restaurants with steaks and chops, whitefish from the Great Lakes, clams and lobsters from the sea, oases that experienced diners locate monthly in *The Chicago Guide* and in Jory Graham's *Chicago: An Extraordinary Guide.*

HISTORY

In September, 1673, there were seven Frenchmen here, but only for a day—Louis Jolliet, Father Jacques Marquette and five canoe-men—first white men known to have been at the site of Chicago. Returning to Mackinac after exploring the Mississippi as a possible route to the Pacific, they had ascended the Illinois and Des Plaines Rivers, portaged across a short swampy tract in the southwest section of the present city, and paddled down the South Branch and the Chicago River into Lake Michigan. They had failed of their original quest, but they had discovered something quite as important—the Chicago portage, a principal key to the continent—and they immediately appreciated the value of their find. Jolliet envisaged a canal penetrating the heart of the immense expanse of New France, reporting that it would be necessary to dig through only "half a league of prairie," to provide a continuous water route between the Great Lakes and the Mississippi Valley.

No Indian settlement appears to have been made here until 1696 when Father Pinet, a Jesuit, established the Mission of the Guardian Angel and came periodically during the next four years to minister to the Miami, recent arrivals. The stream was known to the Indians as the Checagou, signifying anything big or strong, but as the river was ever a small and sluggish stream, the strength was believed to refer to the pungent wild garlic that grew along its banks.

La Salle's schemes to colonize the Illinois Valley failed; hostile Indians closed the Chicago portage for long periods. When possession of the entire region passed to the British in 1763, there remained no permanent marks of the 90 years of French rule. Twenty years later the country became part of the United States, but actual control was exercised by the British and their Indian allies until Jay's Treaty was signed in 1794. The next year, by the Treaty of Greenville, the Indians ceded, among other territories, "a piece of Land Six Miles Square at the mouth of the Chickago River," recognized by the military authorities as a strategic point, but no attempt was made to occupy it for almost a decade.

In 1803, Capt. John Whistler arrived with six soldiers of the 1st U. S. Infantry from Detroit to inspect the spot where he was to erect "stockade works aided by blockhouses." At 19, he had served with Burgoyne and had been taken prisoner at Saratoga. After the Revolution he enlisted in General Anthony Wayne's army and fought Indians in Ohio. He was now 45. He went back to Detroit to get his family and the garrison for the fort. His family, including his son Lieut. William Whistler, who was to command the fort 30 years later, came by ship to the mouth of the St. Joseph River and thence was rowed across the lake, while 69 officers and men marched from Detroit and through the Indiana sand dunes to the Chicago River. At a narrow bend of the river, which curved sharply south before entering the lake, Whistler built the fort, named for Henry Dearborn, Secretary of War in Jefferson's administration.

Opposite the fort on the north bank of the river stood four cabins, three occupied by Frenchmen and their Indian wives; the fourth, a large cabin of squared logs surrounded by numerous outbuildings, was vacant. It had been built in the 1780s by Jean Baptiste Point du Sable, who, according to the researches of Milo Milton Quaife, was the son of a Frenchman and a Negro woman, and in 1788 had married an Indian woman named Catherine at the French mission in Cahokia. In 1800 Point du Sable sold his trading post on the Chicago to Jean la Lime for 6,000 livres and went on to Peoria and St. Charles, Mo. Dr. Quaife, who found Du Sable's bill of sale in the archives of Wayne County, Detroit, proved he was a trader of substance; he sold his house, 22 by 40 ft., two barns, a horse mill, a bake house, a poultry house, a workshop, a dairy, and a smokehouse; 30 head of cattle, 2 mules, 2 calves, 28 hogs, 11 copper kettles and an assortment of tools. That was the earliest real estate transaction on the Chicago River. John Kinzie, whose name became indelible in Chicago's history, witnessed the bill of sale.

Just why the trading post was sold to Jean la Lime is not of record. It is known that John Kinzie came to Chicago in 1804 and took over the trading post, and La Lime became an interpreter for the troops at Fort Dearborn. The houses on the North bank were inhabited by Kinzie, La Lime, Antoine Ouilmette and Pierre Le Mai. In the spring of 1812 Kinzie and La Lime had a violent quarrel; La Lime shot Kinzie in the neck and Kinzie stabbed La Lime fatally. La Lime was buried near the present Cass St., and in 1891 bones thought to be his were uncovered at the southwest corner of Cass and Illinois Sts. They were "presented" to the Chicago Historical Society by Joseph Kirkland, the author.

Chicago's first economic development came through the fur trade. Before the war of 1812 the British from Canada dominated the trade and kept Indians hostile to American agents. John Jacob Astor eased his way in with the American Fur Co., and hired John Kinzie to barter with the Indians. Kinzie was given territory extending from the Chicago River to the Fox River valley; another trader was assigned the Illinois River. The U. S. Government tried to regulate the trade by establishing factories—agencies—buying furs from Indians and selling them goods at cost, and prohibiting the use of liquor in trading. But the American Fur Co. disregarded regulations and sold liquor freely, and ruined the Government's trade, compelling it eventually to close its factories. Senator Thomas Hart Benton, a friend of the American Fur Co. in public office, finished them off. The Chicago agent had $13,000 in goods; a forced sale brought only $1,250. Numerous traders could not compete with the American Fur Co., which broke them and then hired them as its agents. This was the experience of Gurdon S. Hubbard. Kinzie was at times their agent, and at other times a Government sub-agent. Jean Beaubien was sent to Chicago to ruin a competitor. The relations of the agents at Chicago with their managers was often acrimonious. Some seasons were profitable; others bad for lack of game. Hubbard, one of the men who profited most, moved to Danville in 1826 to sell goods to white settlers instead of Indians, but it took several years to get the company to give him the needed support.

Kinzie was directly responsible for the removal of Captain Whistler from command of Fort Dearborn in 1810. Whistler had tried to stop the giving of liquor to the Indians but was overruled. Kinzie had friends higher up.

THE FORT DEARBORN MASSACRE

There also were Indian hazards. On April 6, 1812, a band of Potawatomi killed two men on the Lee farm near the present Racine Avenue on the upper Chicago. The War of 1812 aroused uneasy fears, especially after the news came that the British and their Indian allies had easily captured Mackinac at the head of Lake Michigan in July, 1812. General William Hull, commander of the American forces in the Northwest, reported to the Secretary of War that he was ordering the evacuation of Fort Dearborn, "provided it can be effected with a greater prospect of safety than to remain," but this conditional proviso was omitted in the order sent to Capt. Nathan Heald, Whistler's successor at the fort.

The proposal to evacuate was argued for eight days; Capt. Heald determined to obey the order to leave, but Kinzie and the traders tried to make him stay. General Hull ordered Capt. William Wells and 32 Miami Indians to help the evacuation. All dry goods was disposed of and liquor was poured into the river.

Black Partridge, a friendly Potawatomi, argued against removal, saying that he had been warned of trouble by "linden birds," but on the morning of August 15, 1812, the fort was evacuated, and the group, numbering approximately 100, started south along the beach on their way to Fort Wayne, led by Captain Wells. The nondescript column had not marched two miles when a large band of Indians fell upon the party, killing more than half—all of the dozen militiamen, 24 of the 55 regulars, two women, and 12 children. With the exception of the Kinzies, to whom the Indians were friendly, all survivors were taken and held captive until freed by ransom or death. The next day, the Potawatomi set fire to the fort. Four years elapsed before the fort was rebuilt.

Chicago might have become the metropolis of Wisconsin but for action taken by Congress in the days when territorial boundaries were still fluid. The Ordinance of 1787 provided that when a state was to be made from Illinois Territory, the northern boundary should be a line extending from the southern tip of Lake Michigan to the Mississippi River. Nathaniel Pope, who had been territorial secretary, acting governor and member of the U. S. Congress as Territorial Representative in 1816, on Jan. 23, 1818, introduced a bill moving the boundary 10 miles north. When the bill reached the floor of the House he offered an amendment placing the boundary 41 miles farther, to 42°, 30' north latitude, in order to include the Chicago River in a possible future waterway to the Mississippi.

The present wealthy area of Chicagoland was part of the 8,000 *sq. m.* added by Pope's moving the boundary to include Chicago.

Chicago remained a settlement of squatters, showing vigorous signs of life only when the State Canal Commissioners surveyed and started the sale of blocks on both sides of the river as the terminal site of the projected Illinois-Michigan Canal. The date of the filing of the survey plat, Aug. 4, 1830, is the first in Chicago's corporate history. The following year Chicago was designated as the seat of Cook County.

Chicago was the site of several councils with Indian chiefs during these early decades, and every time the Indians came they lost some of their lands. They received, however, heaps of silver dollars and bought gallons of firewater. In 1821 Lewis Cass, Governor of Michigan Territory, met with 3,000 Indians on the north bank of the Chicago. He managed to get the Potawatomi and Ottawas to agree to move out of the territory by paying them annuities and extra funds for blacksmiths and teachers, at the same time giving grants of land to half-breeds and traders. Henry R. Schoolcraft, explorer and Government agent, came with Cass and wrote later that there was "a village of ten or twelve dwellings and 60 people with a garrison on the south shore of Chicago creek, 400 or 500 yards from its entrance to the lake." He crossed the Chicago Portage to the Des Plaines River, commented on the "summer climate of delightful serenity," and predicted that once Indian titles were extinguished it would prove an attractive field for the immigrant.

On August 5, 1833, Chicago was incorporated as a town with a population of less than 200. Only 13 voted; 12 for, 1 against. On March 4, 1837, a charter incorporating the city was issued at Vandalia courthouse and William B. Ogden, who hailed from New York state, was chosen first mayor. The fort, in ruins from 1812 to 1816, had been partially rebuilt. When the Winnebagoes proved unruly along the Rock River in 1828 two companies of the 5th U. S. Infantry were sent to reoccupy Fort Dearborn. One of the first lieutenants was David Hunter, who married a daughter of John Kinzie and at Chicago met 2nd Lieut. Jefferson Davis. Thirty years later General Hunter was to order freed all slaves in his southern jurisdiction, in opposition to President Jefferson Davis of the Confederacy, only to be overruled by President Lincoln, who had been a volunteer in the Black Hawk War.

After the Black Hawk War President Andrew Jackson called a council for the Indian tribes in Michigan and Illinois at Chicago beginning Sept. 10, 1833, at which Governor Porter of Michigan was to offer terms. The council was the rowdiest ever held in Chicago. The Indians brought their families and set up camp. The settlers built temporary shanties and stocked garments, saddles, liquor, and tobacco. The Indians were painted up, and according to Charles J. Latrobe, an English traveler, the meeting brought together a lot of horse dealers, horse stealers, rogues, creditors, peddlers, and grog sellers. The Indians, after 14 days of procrastination, gave up 4,000,000 acres of land they were supposed to own for 5,000,000 acres west of the Mississippi and $1,000,000 annually for vocational schools. The first payment was $90,000 in goods and $56,000 in silver half dollars. The latter payment was especially prized. Says one historian: "The government's agents went among the Indians and threw half dollars on the blankets spread out before them. Some Indians had as many as 400 half dollars tossed into their blankets. The braves went on a drinking orgy. They quarrelled and drew their knives; they mounted their ponies and dashed madly over the prairie; finally they tumbled into the dust in a drunken stupor. The white men were not satisfied with getting the half dollars; they even whisked away the Indians' blankets." There was one more parade—in August 1935, when about 1,000 Indians returned for their last installments.

Land speculation reached fever heat in 1836 when lots along the route of the Illinois & Michigan Canal were sold to raise money to pay for it. In 1837 Chicago was incorporated as a city and the country suffered from a financial panic, but this did not deter energetic building of stores, offices, and houses in Chicago.

Chicago was already on the way to become a great market before any canal or railroad reached the town. Lake Michigan schooners carried grain and lumber. Cattle and hogs were driven in on the hoof, and farm products arrived in big prairie schooners pulled by three to five yokes of oxen. The drivers fought swamps, underbrush, and stumps of trees on crude roads and camped overnight in the open, until roadside taverns were built. To overcome bogs corduroy roads—tree trunks placed sidewise and held together by wooden strips—were laid down, and when these deteriorated traffic was more hazardous than ever.

The remedy was to ship by water; canalize the Illinois and the Des Plaines and lift barges by means of locks into the Chicago River. In 1835 the State authorized a public loan of $500,000 for a canal, and in June the first section was begun at Summit, a ditch 60 ft. wide at the top, 36 ft. at the bottom, and 6 ft. deep. The canal reached almost as far as Ashland Ave. and the South Fork of the South Branch of the Chicago River; here locks were built to move the barges into the river. In took 12 years to complete the canal, and when it opened in 1848 it was only one year ahead of the locomotive whistle that was to sound its doom.

The canal carried farm products from central Illinois to Chicago and planks, building material and machines from Chicago to interior towns. It also carried millstones, for every village was grinding its own corn. Also provided were excursions on packets, which had cabins 50 ft. long, 9 ft. wide, and 7 ft. high. The tariff was $14 per 100 miles, but it took 22 hours to cover that distance, approximately from Chicago to LaSalle.

Plans to build railroads had been sprouting since the 1830s; the first to name Chicago in its title was the Chicago & Vincennes, chartered in 1834 but not built for years. Two years later the Galena & Chicago Union was chartered but its trains did not run out of Chicago until 1848. By 1850 Chicago had a railroad running as far as Aurora and Elgin and during the rest of the decade other lines entered Chicago. By merging of smaller lines the major systems of the great railroad era began to expand.

Lake Michigan, interposing its 307 miles of deep water between East and West, focused to a point the railroad lines between the entire Northwest and the East. Chicago became the greatest railroad center in the world. For many years interchange of cargo between waterway and railway boomed both forms of transportation. In 1869 the 13,730 arrivals at the Chicago Harbor exceeded the combined number of vessels entered at the ports of New York, Philadelphia, Baltimore, Charleston, Mobile, and San Francisco.

Chicago's population increased six-fold between 1840 and 1850, rising from 4,470 to more than 28,000, and during the next decade vaulted to almost 100,000. By 1856 the city embraced 18 square miles, and was trying desperately to pull itself out of the mud. Its streets had been little better than swamps, a terror to horses and pedestrians and a serious menace to health, for the slops of the city were poured into these "noisome quagmires." A few streets had been paved with planking as early as 1849, and five years later the city had 27 miles of such pavement. The planks deteriorated and in 1855, Chicago decided to raise the level of its streets 12 feet. Sand was dredged from the river, providing fill not only for the streets but for the low ground between them. The new streets were huge ramps that ran level with second-story windows until people either packed up their houses or converted their original ground floors into cellars. In 1859 a mile of track for horse cars was laid on State Street, which soon replaced Lake Street as the business artery.

The panic of 1857 struck the city a staggering blow. One-tenth of its 1,350 business houses closed; many thousands were thrown out of work. In the midst of this distress Chicago built the Wigwam, a huge wooden shed, to accommodate the Republican National Convention, at which Lincoln was nominated for the presidency. Then came the Civil War to provide such stimulation of business as the city had never known. To feed great armies in the field, farmers broke new ground and grain shipments from Chicago more than doubled in two years. In 1864 the mile-square Union Stock Yards were built. The McCormick and other factories were humming making reapers, steel plows, agricultural implements of all kinds, harness, wagons, and a miscellany of wood and metal products.

In 1864 George Pullman built his first sleeping car, *The Pioneer,* marking the birth of another great local industry. Business transacted through the banks swelled to such a volume that the Chicago Clearing House was established in 1865. By 1870 Chicago's population numbered 300,000, a three-fold increase within a decade. Race tracks, gambling saloons, and bawdy houses multiplied. Lavish marble mansions went up along Michigan Avenue to 12th Street. Theaters, hotels, shops, and business buildings crowded into what is now the Loop. Coal yards, warehouses, flour mills, factories, foundries, and distilleries lined the river banks and the lake front. Scattered through the city were 170 churches.

In 1867, after years of violent protest that the entire community was being poisoned by "filthy slush, miscalled water" taken from the lake into which the city poured its sewage, a sanitary water system was installed and immediately reduced the appallingly high death rate. The flow of Garlic Creek was reversed in 1871, and some of its foul waters were carried down the Illinois into the Mississippi, but not in sufficient quantity, so that sewage continued to pour into the river and the lake.

Public high schools and evening schools, industrial and professional schools, including one of the first art schools in the country, two colleges, three theological seminaries, the Chicago Historical Society, and the Academy of Sciences were established in this period. In 1869 a ring of unimproved parks with boulevard connections surrounded the city.

A large part of Chicago consisted of frame buildings in 1871. After months of severe drought fire broke out west of the River during the first week in October. It destroyed four blocks and had been overcome with difficulty when a new blaze started on the evening of Sunday, October 8, behind the cottage of Patrick O'Leary on DeKoven St. A powerful wind swept flames to the north and northeast and hurled brands in advance of the roaring columns of fire, which destroyed practically everything north of Van Buren Street in Downtown and the Near North Side. So intense were the flames that hot blasts were felt in Holland, Michigan, 100 miles across the lake. Tapering to a point near the lake at Fullerton Avenue, the fire stopped after consuming 17,450 buildings in 27 hours. At least 250 persons perished. Homes of one-third the population, about 1,600 stores, 60 manufacturing establishments and 28 hotels, railroad structures, government and other public buildings and bridges, became three and one-third square miles of ashes and debris. Thousands had lost homes and possessions.

It has become customary to say Chicago was wiped out by the Great Fire and an occasional frame house is identified as a solitary survivor, but recent research contradicts this view. Herman Kogan, author with Robert Cromie of *The Great Fire, Chicago 1871,* in an address declared that much that was vital to Chicago was not destroyed. The fire had not reached three-fourths of the grain elevators, 80 percent of the lumberyards, some 600 factories, rolling mills, and machine shops, the rail connections of 18 trunk lines, 20 miles of Lake Michigan dockage, and that great processing center of Midwest livestock, the Union Stock Yards. Despite the destruction of the business center many vital services remained unimpaired.

The embers were scarcely cool before rebuilding began. Generous contributions of money and supplies came from the entire country and from Europe. Thousands of temporary structures provided for immediate needs while more than 100,000 artisans were reconstructing the city under stricter construction codes. Extensions of credit and payment of about half of the $88,634,022 insurance on the $192,000,000 loss helped rebuild the business district. Many buildings, particularly hotels and depots, were replaced by far costlier structures. Fashion took over Michigan Avenue south of 12th Street, and Prairie Avenue, and brought in granite and brownstone. Chicago dumped its debris within the lake breakwater, forming subsoil for a future park. Local manufactures doubled between 1870 and 1873; Chicago banks, alone of those in the larger cities, continued steadily to pay out current funds during the acute financial panic of 1873.

Nationwide labor unrest, became particularly acute. The division between wealth and poverty drew Chicago into the forefront of "radical" cities. In 1877, led by Albert R. Parsons, workers in the factories and on railroads struck for increased wages and the 8-hour day. Federal troops broke the strike, but without removing the causes of discontent. Industrial warfare over wages and hours drew increasingly bitter. When a police company tried to break up a meeting of agitators at the Haymarket May 4, 1886, a bomb thrown into their ranks killed 7. Although no evidence was produced that they had thrown the bomb, Parsons and three other labor leaders were hanged for the crime. *See article on Labor and Employment.*

Large strikes broke out in the depression years that followed 1893, notably that which began in the local Pullman shops and spread to the railroads; once more Federal troops broke the strike. *See Pullman City.*

Meantime, as one result of the Haymarket tragedy, the Civic Federation was founded by Lyman C. Gage, a banker, to provide free and open discussion of controversial questions. In 1889 Jane Addams opened Hull House settlement in the worst slum district on the West Side. By 1890 Chicago had more than 1,000,000 people, having added 200,000 the previous year by annexation of several surrounding municipalities. The Newberry Library, and the Public Library, had been founded, and in 1892 the University of Chicago began with the most auspicious program in educational history. Theodore Thomas had organized the Chicago Orchestral Association and had been presenting popular concerts that brought the city renown as a musical center. William Le Baron Jenney, Daniel H. Burnham, John W. Root, William Holabird, and other architects were constructing large new buildings on steel frames and evolving a new architectural form.

Commerce, manufacture, labor, and new cultural developments united to bring the city one of its great triumphs, the World's Columbian Exposition of 1893, the celebration of the 400th anniversary of the discovery of America. Jackson Park was developed out of swamp land on the South Side and here were built the great white buildings of the fair in accordance with a master plan drawn by Daniel H. Burnham. But the times were still hard, soup kitchens were established in the cities, and mortgage-burdened farmers were turning Populist. At Chicago in 1896 William Jennings Bryan, standing for monetary reform, overwhelmed the Democratic convention with a famous peroration: "You shall not press upon the brow of labor this crown of thorns; you shall not crucify mankind on a cross of gold." He won the presidential nomination but lost the office in a bitter campaign to William McKinley.

In 1900 the Sanitary and Ship Canal was opened, a wide channel 28 miles long, 20 feet deep. The Drainage Canal, as popularly known, served a triple purpose; it entirely reversed the polluting flow of the Chicago River, served as a link in the Lakes-to-Gulf Waterway, and by a generating plant built at Lockport, provided electricity to light the city's streets and parks.

A disaster that took more lives than the Great Fire occurred at the Iroquois Theatre, on West Randolph between State and Dearborn Sts. on Dec. 30, 1903. During a matinee performance of *Mr. Bluebeard,* a musical with Eddie Foy as star, the stage curtain caught fire from an electric floodlight, the stage set went up in flames and a draft from the opened stage door swept the fire over the audience. Many persons were suffocated in a rush for gallery exits, which were locked. A total of 596 persons died. An asbestos or iron curtain was installed thereafter in every American theater.

During World War I Chicago contributed 27,300 men to the Armed Services, 32.5 percent of the State's total. When thousands of workers were drawn from the plants an estimated 65,000 blacks came to Illinois from the farm areas of the South to fill the demand for labor. A tragic racial clash between whites and blacks on the South Side during the last week of July, 1919, resulted in the death of 14 whites and 22 blacks, and injuries to 537. It started at the E. 31st St. Beach when a Negro boy swam into an area used by whites and apparently was killed by a rock thrown by a white. The ensuing riot spread to the black area to the west and had to be stopped by troops. The incident uncovered tense hostility by whites against the spread of black population.

Chicago was a wide-open town for most of its history. During the 1890s a large vice district of saloons and dives became established south of the Loop as far as 22nd St. Agitation to curtail and eventually abolish it began after evangelists and reformers publicized its connection with official corruption. The Anti-Saloon League and the National Prohibition Party used Chicago as a prime example of civic degradation. In Chicago, however, many citizens recalled the place of wine and beer in decent European living and resented any curtailment of the right to drink. They supported the United Societies for Local Self-Government, led by Anton J. Cermak, an alderman of Bohemian nativity who had risen from work in the coal mines. But when Carter H. Harrison entered his fifth term as Mayor he abruptly closed the vice district and ended the franchise of the Washington Park Race Track, where the American Derby was run annually amid an orgy of betting and ostentatious display. This lost Harrison much support in the Democratic Party, but no future official dared revoke his order.

The dark side of Chicago's reputation, which portrays it as a citadel of corruption and lawlessness, grew to frightening proportions during the years when the 18th Amendment to the U. S. Constitution and the implementing Volsted Act (1917-1933) deprived the public of legal liquor. This coincided with the corrupt administration of Mayor William Hale Thompson 1915-23 and 1927-31, who in his first terms took an anti-war stand and opposed American participation in the League of Nations.

The Unione Siciliana and the extortionists known loosely as the Black Hand had been victimizing their compatriots for years before prohibition gave them a new field for illicit operations. The big profits in beer-running and cooking alcohol started bloody feuds among rival gangs, who eliminated competitors by shotgun. John Torrio, Dion O'Banion, "Bugs" Moran, Jim Colosimo, and Alphonse Capone became more powerful than the law, corrupted policemen and judges, and dealt in millions of dollars. During four years when Thompson was out of office Capone transferred his activities to Cicero, suborned its municipal government and filled the town with speakeasies, gambling bars and brothels. Later he turned the two upper floors of the Lexington Hotel, S. Michigan Ave. and 22nd St., into a fortress, where he ruled protected by bodyguards.

One spectacular event of this period was the "rubbing out" of bootlegger O'Banion, who operated a flower shop opposite the Holy Angels Cathedral. When rivals gunned him down inside his shop both friends and enemies competed to give him an impressive funeral. It was led by an open car in which sat a life-size effigy of O'Banion, followed by 26 cars filled with flowers, including pieces for which top gangsters had paid as high as $10,000. Another indelible incident was the St. Valentine's Day Massacre, 1929, when four men in police outfits surprised seven men, six of them belonging to Moran's gang, in a North Side garage, stood them up against the wall, and killed them with machine guns.

For a number of years the authorities were unable to get gangsters convicted for criminal acts. The prohibition of liquor brought about corruption among high officials and toleration of illegal activities by a large segment of the public. Murders committed by gangsters could not be proved in court because of intimidation of witnesses and juries. Eventually the Federal Government found the Internal Revenue Service an effective tool for tracing incomes based on illegal gains. With Dwight H. Green as special prosecutor Al Capone was convicted in 1932 of failing to pay $215,830 in five years' income tax and was sentenced by Federal Judge James H. Wilkerson to 11 years in prison. He served seven years at Alcatraz Federal Prison and was released when suffering from an advanced stage of syphilis, from which he died.

After repeal of the 18th Amendment civic authorities regained their power and the underworld turned to infiltration of legitimate business, which continues to be a major problem.

During the early 1920's Chicago experienced a business boom and the massive speculation that went with it, but the stock market crash of Oct. 28, 1929, knocked down the financial pyramids built by Samuel Insull and other utility barons. Building operations, which had poured millions into pay checks, ceased for ten years; unemployment spread; teachers and city employees waited long periods for their pay.

William Hale Thompson ran again for mayor in 1927, ousting William E. Dever, Democrat, who had served four years. Thompson had organized strong support among black voters. In 1931 he ran again on the Republican ticket but was beaten by Anton J. Cermak, who had entered ward politics and become a member of the State Legislature.

In 1932 both the Republican and the Democratic National conventions were held in Chicago. President Herbert Hoover was renominated by the Republicans and Franklin D. Roosevelt by the Democrats. The massive unemployment defeated Hoover and the promise of repeal of prohibition helped elect Roosevelt. Illinois voted 1,432,756 for Hoover, 1,882,304 for Roosevelt. Mayor Anton J. Cermak did not support Roosevelt for the nomination but after the election went to Miami to cultivate Roosevelt. While standing on the running board of Roosevelt's car Cermak was fatally hit by a bullet ostensibly intended for Roosevelt. In some Chicago quarters it was believed that Cermak, who had tangled with the crime syndicate, had been marked for assassination.

Henry Horner, judge of the Probate Court of Cook County, was elected Governor on the Democratic ticket in 1932, running ahead of Roosevelt. He was the first Jew to become Governor of Illinois. Horner had the State Assembly vote a 2% sales tax in order to meet the cost of relief payments, and in turn suspended the State property tax. In 1935 he had the sales tax increased by 1%. He was elected to a second term in 1936, when he campaigned for permanent registration of voters against the Chicago Democratic machine. Horner died October 5, 1940, and was succeeded for two months by John H. Stelle, Democrat, but Dwight H. Green, Republican, won the November election and served two terms, 1941-49.

In 1934 John Dillinger, ruthless bank robber who had been hiding out in Chicago, was "fingered" to the FBI by a woman companion and shot to death in an alley beside the Biograph Theatre, 2433 North Lincoln Ave., which he had been attending. A saloon next door exploited the robber's visits there as Dillinger's Last Stop.

In the midst of a world-wide depression Chicago saluted its organization as a city in its Century of Progress Exposition, which opened in 1933 on the newly-made Northerly Island and ran for two years. Since many expected funds were not forthcoming the builders of the fair under

Louis Skidmore's direction, used great ingenuity in applying color schemes to the plain, geometric buildings that represented money-saving techniques. The mechanical feature of the fair was a sky ride between two towers called Amos and Andy, after the most popular radio comedians.

Chicago was recovering slowly from the depression when it was confronted with preparations for national defense and another World War. Hundreds of thousands of Illinois citizens served in the armies and in the factories. Steel mills that had been running half-time changed to three shifts and converted closed plants; the United States Government poured millions into factories for making armament, military airplanes, armored vehicles, and even parts of submarines; the latter were transferred from Lake Michigan ports to the Gulf of Mexico via the Chicago River and the Illinois Waterway.

In 1946 the first subway was opened. It extended 4.9 miles under State St. The Federal Government contributed $23,000,000 for its construction. Excavation, chiefly in sandy soil, produced some difficulties for old buildings. The Great Northern Hotel, built for the World's Fair of 1893 before the use of caissons, was taken down because new foundations would prove too costly. The Monadnock, across Jackson Blvd. from the hotel, was not disturbed.

The consolidation of municipal transportation was effected by Chicago in 1947. It required enactment of the Chicago Transit Authority by agreement of State and city. CTA included the elevated lines of the Rapid Transit Co., surface transportation by street car and buses, and the buses of the Chicago Motor Coach Co. The CTA was to be operated by a board of seven, four named by the Mayor of Chicago and three by the Governor.

CTA serves 34 suburbs in the Cook County area. On a typical weekday CTA carries approx. 1,200,000 passengers of whom about 400,000 originate on the six rapid transit lines, the rest on buses. About 750,000 transfer slips are issued each weekday. The CTA operates 135 bus routes on more than 2,000 miles of city and suburban streets and about 90 miles of rapid transit over subway, surface, and elevated rights-of-way.

In 1973 the State Legislature enacted the REGIONAL TRANSIT AUTHORITY, which under date of July 1, 1974, after approval by popular vote on Mar. 20, 1974, took over the CTA and the six-county Metropolitan area. It has a nine-member board, four appointed by the mayor of Chicago, two from suburban Cook County, and two from the five other counties appointed by the president of the County Board, and the ninth a transportation engineer as chairman of RTA. Financing of $171,000,000 includes $80,000,000 from the State general revenues fund, $5,000,000 from Chicago and Cook County, $10,000,000 from parking fees, $60,000,000 from a 5% gasoline tax, and $16,000,000 from license plate fees.

The heaviest rainfall, 7 inches in 24 hours, fell on Chicago Oct. 10, 1954. The Chicago River rose so high that the Union Station was flooded and the paper stock of the *Chicago Daily News* was ruined. Damages were estimated at millions of dollars. The locks at Lake Michigan were opened and the flow of the river was reversed for the first time since 1900.

MUNICIPAL HOUSEKEEPING

The Chicago Plan. The strongest influence for an orderly development of the city is the COMPREHENSIVE PLAN OF CHICAGO, announced in 1966 on the basis of policies determined two years before. It is a guide for the Chicago Plan Commission and the Department of Development and Planning, which makes specific recommendations for improving neighborhoods, and deals with housing, job training, transportation, use of land, employment, health care, civic services, and whatever else is needed in a dynamic, expanding municipality. The Comprehensive Plan is the current outgrowth of the original Chicago Plan, which made its first impact on the mentality of Chicago when Daniel Hudson Burnham, who had been chief of construction at the World's Fair of 1893, first publicized it.

> For ten years Burnham argued that Chicago should follow a logical plan for a great lake front park, outer drives, connected parkways, forest preserves, widened highways leading to a monumental civic center at Congress and Halsted Sts., entailing a relocation of railroad terminals and rebuilding of bridges and river banks. In 1906 the Commercial Club and the Merchants Club agreed to stake him with $50,000 to complete his design and later added $25,000: Burnham worked for nothing with Edward H. Bennett, Jules Guerin, Fernand Janin and staff and in June, 1908, presented the Chicago Plan to the business men. It won the enthusiastic support of Mayor Fred Busse, who appointed 328 business leaders to the Chicago Plan Commission, of which Charles H. Wacker became chairman and Walter D. Moody managing director. Wacker's choice was a great gain; he was wealthy, and at 50 devoted his efforts solely to improving the physical aspects of Chicago. With Moody he published a series of projections, as well as *Wacker's Manual of the Plan of Chicago* for the public schools, in which children were told that Chicago's destiny was to become the greatest city in the world, larger, more beautiful, and more prosperous than any, if it followed the Chicago Plan. There is every reason to believe that attention to this subject in the schools gave many young people a feeling of identity with the city.

Rapid Transit and Crosstown Expressway. A great public enterprise that will change the face of Chicago is the CENTRAL AREA RAPID TRANSIT PROJECT, now in the planning stage, which has been started by a Federal grant of $5,800,000. This involves new subways that will expedite travel to an enlarged central business area, and makes possible the elimination of the Elevated Railroad Loop. The El contributed greatly to the mercantile wellbeing of Chicago by concentrating the principal retail stores in a compact area, with speedy access from the environs. It is now an anachronism, darkening the streets and adding to the roar of traffic. Owners of adjacent property have estimated the El reduces their values by one-third. Although much of the disadvantage is overcome in offices that rise skyward, the street-level gains after its removal will be immense. The Project will link all means of transportation at interchanges, so that commuters by rail can transfer to bus lines and subways, in what the engineers call "corridors of high accessibility." Progress of the work will depend on available Federal aid. Cost was estimated at $750,000,000 in 1973.

A second major project in transportation is the CROSSTOWN EXPRESSWAY, a link in communications that has aroused considerable opposition because of the valuable property that must be destroyed for its construction. Cost is estimated at $1 billion at the inflated prices for materials and wages, 90 percent to come from the Federal Highway Trust Fund. It is expected to give employment to 6,300 men for 10 years. The Dept. of Public Works reports that some right-of-way already has been acquired and that it conducts community meetings to explain the project to the affected neighborhoods.

Housing is a subject of immediate concern in Chicago, where huge efforts have been made to sweep away slums and rundown buildings and provide adequate and substantial shelter for many low-income families. The Department of Urban Renewal has the principal responsibility for construction with public funds on renewal sites, following the studies of the Department of Development and Planning, which has divided the city into 16 areas of 6 to 26 sq. mi. each and each containing 150,000 to 250,000 people.

Chicago began bulldozing slum areas and getting its urban renewal program started in 1947, two years before the Federal Housing Act made possible a two for one dollar matching arrangement with the Government. The latter paid two-thirds of what it cost the city to acquire and clear the site and what the purchaser paid. In 1947 the State had enacted a law that gave the city power of eminent domain to clear slums for private development. The city knocked out acres of broken down housing in the Near South Side along State St. where the bulk of black workers made their homes. This clearing meant provision had to be made for relocation of the dispossessed, for it took years to complete new housing to take the place of the slums. When Richard J. Daley took office as Mayor in 1955 he made urban renewal one of his chief objectives, but action was impeded at times when Chicago voters turned down bonds for urban renewal because of fear of increased taxes. But the need was imperative and renewal went on—in the Hyde Park-Kenwood area, in Woodlawn, in the Harrison-Halsted district, and elsewhere. As the cost mounted the city recognized the need of conserving what could be saved and made rehabilitation an important part of the program.

Annually enough industrial plants, dwellings, schools, and public buildings are constructed to make a medium-sized, self-contained city. In the 1970-80 decade, capital improvement in one year amounted to $2 billion; new construction and alterations, half a billion. The Department of Urban Renewal provides houses and apartments for families of low and moderate incomes, elderly couples and single individuals. All new construction is integrated. Among such developments is Lake Grove Village, sponsored by two South Side churches; Jackson Park

Terrace by The Woodlawn Organization (TWO), and Martin Luther King, Jr., Plaza, at Madison and Kedzie. There is extensive renewal activity in the Lincoln Park area, at Larrabee Court, West Park Place, Walpole Point, and other locations. One of the developments guided by the Dept. of Urban Renewal is the Place du Sable commercial-residential complex, occupying a six block site east of the Kennedy Expressway between Washington, Monroe and Clinton Sts. This bi-level center cost $350,000,000.

Model Cities-Chicago Committee on Urban Opportunity. In August, 1971, the Model Cities program was united with the Committee on Urban Opportunity, the city's anti-poverty agency, for the express purpose of improving living conditions and services for minority people. The Model Cities had operated demonstration programs in four areas— Woodlawn, Uptown, Grand Boulevard-North Kenwood-Oakland, and Lawndale. The combined project is financed at $115,700,000 annually, of which the city provides $3,900,000, other agencies give $14,400,000 and the rest comes from the Federal Government, when not curtailed or withheld by executive order. The program comprises medical, educational, crime prevention, employment, transportation, child care, family help and many other services. The agency operates 12 Urban Progress Centers that concentrate on the needs of their neighborhoods. The emphasis on equal opportunity provides that employers give an advantage to minority people, that in bidding for city work the awards go to the lowest bidder agreeing to hire the largest number of neighborhood residents and trainees.

Human Relations. Physical changes are visible in all sections of Chicago, but the eye does not see the fundamental changes in the welfare of the tenants. Chicago has a Fair Housing ordinance that guarantees open housing and freedom from discrimination because of color, age, or income. Complaints on abuses are filed with the Commission on Human Relations, which provides conciliation conferences and public hearings of grievances. The ordinance covers many direct and indirect abuses, as, for instance "for sale" signs displayed in windows by aggrieved owners who object to open housing. The commission orders their removal or gets a court citation.

This commission also investigates complaints relating to civil rights in areas other than housing. These include discrimination in public accommodations, health facilities, educational facilities, and places of employment. Every city contract contains a clause prohibiting discrimination and every firm doing business with the city signs it. Any business house that denies equal opportunity in employment is dropped from the city's eligibility lists.

Protection of Human Resources. The Reach-Out program is a summer activity of the Department of Human Resources that has the participation of as many as 270,000 children in athletics, field trips, art contests, plays and programs. Through this department the civic authorities concentrate on efforts to channel the energy of youngsters, help the youthful offender, aid drug addicts, and overcome racial tensions in neighborhoods. It is equipped to give special help to Spanish-speaking citizens.

The *Boys Clubs of Chicago* supports numerous programs to channel the active energies of Chicago's youth and improve their physical welfare. Administrative headquarters are at 304 W. Randolph St., and more than 20 branches direct the work throughout the city. The Head Start and Work Training Programs are part of their responsibilities. The Dr. Martin Luther King, Jr., branch at 2950 W. Washington Blvd. is hq for four separate projects, including the clinics named for Henry Horner, governor of Illinois 1933-1940. Associated are the Valentine Boys Clubs and the Valentine Girls Clubs.

The Neighborhood Swimming Pool Program designed and carried out by the Dept. of Public Works since 1968 annually adds new pools. These are constructed on land adjacent to police and fire stations. Pools are 40 to 65 ft. long and receive 30,000 gallons of filtered water every two hours. Firemen and policemen voluntarily serve as life guards and swimming instructors during their free hours.

Help for Veterans and Disabled. The City of Chicago in 1969 joined numerous unofficial agencies in the urgent task of finding jobs for returning veterans. It created the Mayor's Jobs for Vietnam Veterans program, joining the Illinois State Employment Service and the Chicago Committee on Urban Opportunity. As elsewhere it has been easier to place veterans with skills and talents than those unskilled. Outstanding applicants with some preparation in biology were sent to the Environmental Studies Center at Goodland, Florida, for a 48-week training course in water management. When veterans agreed to continue their education the city made an effort to get part-time work for them. It has been successful in placing handicapped and disabled veterans. The Mayor's Office of Manpower, formed in 1970, is the prime sponsor for the $2,000,000 Model Cities manpower development program. It organized Just Jobs, Inc., a nonprofit day-labor agency that located $150,000 available in wages in one year. Two-thirds of those hired come from minority groups and some come off welfare rolls. One project funded by the U.S. Conference of Mayors assists veterans to qualify for college or vocational training.

Aid for the Elderly. There are about 400 self-help clubs of senior citizens in Chicago and numerous other agencies conducted by churches, lodges, public and private organizations. The city is guided by recommendations of the White House Conference on Aging and the Older Americans Act of 1971, and took part in preparing the Urban Elderly Coalition with other major cities. The nutrition program for senior citizens is activated at 30 sites. About 6,000 senior citizens annually get help with their personal problems. A Federal grant provides aid to the elderly who serve as foster parents. Elderly artisans are encouraged to engage in handicrafts and their work is presented at Carson, Pirie. Model Cities funds recently enabled outreach activities for the elderly to be begun in Woodlawn and Uptown, and the Senior Central Friendship Van carries a trained staff to the neighborhood centers. The Chicago

Transit Authority provides reduced fares for the elderly, effective for 24 hours.

Drug Addiction and Other Menaces to Health. The Board of Health is the principal agency for coordinating means of fighting drug addiction and a variety of other dangers. Direct care and counseling are provided. The Board has enrolled a corps of young workers who use personal counseling and follow-up methods. A Federal grant of $400,000 for detecting hazardous levels of lead paint in dwellings was applied in cooperation with inspectors from the Department of Buildings, who use electrical devices to locate lead in painted woodwork. The Board manages a number of health centers where tests are made for cancers, heart disease, diabetes, tuberculosis, and venereal disease. It requires that all blood used for transfusions be tested for hepatitis. A State law requires all blood for transfusions to be donated voluntarily and not used from paid donors.

Campaign Against Air Pollution. Chicago has been fighting air pollution for years by ordinances regulating fuels, inspections, legal actions and fines. In 1962 it established a telemonitoring system of great usefulness. The low sulfur content ordinance adopted in 1970 had immediate effect, cutting sulfur dioxide in the air from 360,000 tons to 140,000 by 1971, and showing further decrease in subsequent years. Coal-burning furnaces are regularly being converted to oil and gas, and all new buildings are equipped for oil, gas, and electric heating. The Board of Education required the removal of all coal-burning furnaces from the city's schools by 1974. Phosphates in detergents are barred by law, which is enforced by cooperation of retail stores. Experiments are proceeding continuously to find effective means of controlling the discharge of carbon monoxide and hydrocarbons by motor car exhausts.

Methods of Controlling Noise. Studies are proceeding in the best methods to control noise. The number of decibells allowable before traffic and construction noise becomes hurtful is a subject of inspection and regulation. There are 29 major traffic centers in Chicago. Infractions are controlled by fines and in one of the biggest of recent cases $5,950 was assessed against a railroad for excessive noise in piggy-back operations.

SOCIAL PROTESTS AND READJUSTMENTS

In the great social readjustment of the 1950-1970 years Chicago fared no better than other American cities that had become the objective of a vast movement of nonwhite laborers from the South and Southwest to the North. The pressure on housing accentuated the hardships of areas not reached by urban renewal programs. The 1954 decision of the U. S. Supreme Court ordering desegregation of schools, and the subsequent act of the Illinois State Assembly of 1963, sharpened an issue that had created dissension for a long time. Opposition to the draft and general disapproval of the Vietnam war caused much disaffection among young Americans. Campus unrest, sparked by violent demonstrations in California, showed students a way to confront authorities when they considered them unfriendly to liberal, and even radical, issues. Blame was showered on municipal authorities for moving too slowly to remedy poor housing and inadequate schooling, and on the police of Chicago for reacting too forcibly against unlicensed protest marches, disorders and rioting.

In June, 1965, crowds of blacks and whites marched on City Hall and the Board of Education, and staged sitdowns in public offices. A school boycott was stopped June 8 by court injunction against its leaders. By June 15, 530 demonstrators had been arrested as a deterrent to action, so that grievances could be considered more calmly. To expedite changes the Rev. Martin Luther King, Jr., and his Southern Christian Leadership Conference conducted a civil rights campaign July 24-26, 1965. He led 18 rallies in black neighborhoods and addressed numerous meetings of whites, including 15,000 persons in the wealthy suburb of Winnetka. On July 26 he led a march to the City Hall and conferred with Mayor Richard S. Daley on ending racial discrimination in housing and the public services.

In midsummer of 1966 Martin Luther King, Jr., addressed the largest civil rights rally of all on July 10 at Soldier Field, in his campaign to make Chicago an "open city." Estimates of attendance ran from 30,000 to 45,000. The meeting was arranged by the Coordinating Council of Committee Organizations (CCCO). For three nights, July 12-15, street clashes broke out on the South Side when police shut off water from fire hydrants that boys had opened to fight the heat. Two blacks were killed and scores of police and civilians were wounded. The police made 372 arrests.

On July 29 to 31 King spoke on the Southwest Side under auspices of the Southern Christian Leadership Conference. Ruffians who tried to break up his meeting by throwing bottles were driven off by the police. In the Gage Park area a gang of 300 white persons overturned motor cars owned by blacks. More violence erupted on August 5 when King led a march of 600 through the Gage Park section, where tense racial feelings abounded. A hostile crowd of 4,000 whites gathered, but 960 police officers, including 100 trained for riot control, kept the situation in hand and no violence occurred. On August 6 King left Chicago with a promise to return when he could be free from further harassment.

VIOLENCE AFTER KING'S DEATH

The murder of King in Memphis on April 4, 1968, sent a wave of anger through Chicago and started an explosion of violence that included window smashing and burning of shops and dwellings. For about a week demonstrations expressed intense feelings of sympathy for the leader who, more than any others, had preached nonviolence. King was born in Atlanta, Ga., and was 39 years old; he led the nonviolent civil rights movement with great effectiveness, wrote *Stride Toward Freedom* and *Why We Can't Wait,* and received the Nobel Peace Prize in 1964.

About 3,000 rioters, white and black, were arrested. Lieut. Governor Samuel H. Shapiro, Acting Governor after May 19, 1968, sent Chicago 6,000 troops of the National Guard commanded by Brig. General Richard T. Dunn, and then added 1,570 more. He also asked

President Johnson for Federal help when fires continued and firemen were being shot at by snipers. The Chicago Conference on Relations and Race, and the Chicago Commission on Human Relations, worked to provide temporary quarters for families whose homes had been destroyed. The Negro Bar Assn. of Cook County protested the presence of troops. The curfew was lifted April 10 and the troops moved out April 12.

The Chicago authorities reported 162 buildings destroyed by fire April 5-7. The American Insurance Assn. on May 15 estimated the April riots had caused $13,000,000 worth of damage.

Students of Northwestern University in Evanston occupied the Administration Building May 3, 1968. White students occupied the office of the vice president of the University in Scott Hall in an anti-war demonstration of the Students for a Democratic Society (SDS). At the University of Illinois at Chicago Circle seven organizations were suspended for sponsoring a talk by a Communist.

Violent demonstrations took place in Chicago during the convention of the Democratic Party, Aug. 26-29, 1968, at which Sen. Hubert H. Humphrey was nominated for President and Sen. Edward Muskie for Vice President. Several thousand men and women who wanted the convention to take a stand against continuing fighting in Vietnam, and favoring various social reforms, attempted to march from Grant Park to the International Amphitheatre. Included were non-resident agitators. They were turned back by the Chicago police and members of the Illinois National Guard, and in the ensuing melee 100 persons were injured, included 25 police officers, and 175 others were arrested. The Rev. Ralph D. Abernathy, riding in a mule-drawn wagon to dramatize the poverty of small farmers, was refused a permit to address the Democratic convention. A crowd estimated at 2,000 to 2,500 clashed with the police in front of the Conrad Hilton hotel. The police were accused of rough-handling and using clubs and tear gas. Wisconsin delegates led a protest against the severity of the police. The authorities admitted the police were at fault, but never before had officers been subjected to such torrents of abuse and obscenity, most of it from adolescents.

When about 3,000 youths, many from other states, camped in Lincoln Park on Aug. 27, 1968, the city ordered a curfew at 11 p.m. When the campers refused to leave the police drove them out with tear gas. Here 60 were injured and 140 arrested. In the course of the week 600 persons were arrested for parading without a permit, obstructing traffic, disregarding police orders, and rioting.

On September 28, 1968, one month after the the Democratic convention, 10,000 anti-war protesters marched down Michigan Ave. They were members of the Chicago Peace Council, the Citizens for a Free Chicago, and the United Patriots International.

On Oct. 8 to 11, 1969, members of the SDS met in Chicago to demonstrate against the trial of the "Chicago Seven," who were charged with crossing state lines to incite riots during the 1968 convention of the Democratic Party. Governor Richard B. Ogilvie ordered 2,500 members of the National Guard to Chicago for four days. During a rally of demonstrators in Lincoln Park Oct. 8 three persons were injured and 80 arrested. A militant section of SDS, known as the Weatherman group, which advocated "bring the war home," and others calling themselves members of a Revolutionary Youth Movement, were accused of throwing rocks and breaking store and office windows. In a row on Oct. 11, 20 police officers and numerous demonstrators sustained injuries.

The trial of the Chicago Seven before Federal Judge Julius J. Hoffman in 1970 was marked by continuous disorder. Two were acquitted and five convicted of crossing state lines to incite riot, and Hoffman cited 175 instances of contempt against the defendants and their two lawyers. The U. S. Court of Appeals reversed the decision and ordered a new trial for contempt. On Dec. 4 the judge found two ringleaders and two lawyers guilty of contempt but considered time already served in jail and the improper conduct of Judge Hoffman in the original trial as mitigating circumstances and did not impose jail sentences.

UNIVERSITY HARASSED BY STUDENTS

The University of Chicago was spared student demonstrations until Jan. 23, 1969, when a student "committee of 85" demanded the rehiring of an assistant professor to positions "jointly in Sociology and Human Development" and that the "principle of equal student control over hiring and rehiring of faculty" be accepted by the university. If this were not done by a specific time the committee threatened "to take militant action." When these demands were not met students seized the office and files of the Dean of the Division of Social Sciences, and on Jan. 30 seized the Administration Building and ocupied it for 16 days impeding the routine work. The university refused to call in local police but appointed members of its faculty to supervise disciplinary action. For about six weeks dissident students engaged in various forms of harassment, disrupting classes, storming the President's house, and invading the Quadrangle (faculty) Club. The university offered to rehire the dismissed professor for one year in Human Development but not in Sociology, and this was refused. The disciplinary committee considered all cases individually, expelled 42 students and suspended 81 for varying periods. The upheaval cost the university $250,000 in work adjustments and damages. During the action a segment of SDS demanded that "more than 50 percent of the next entering class be working class students, with full scholarships, living allowances, and 'no-flunk' status."

Accusations of brutality have been made periodically against police officers for using clubs and tear gas. All complaints of excessive use of force are now investigated by the internal affairs division of the Police Department and then reviewed by the Commission on Human Relations. The Department conducts "conciliatory hearings" on complaints. Spanish-speaking members of the department in 13 district stations are assigned to improve relations between the police and Spanish-speaking citizens. The Chicago department has 13,172 officers and 1,677 civilian employees. More than 80 villages, towns and neighborhoods in the environs have their own police.

CHICAGO PUBLIC SCHOOLS

More than 572,000 students were enrolled in the Chicago Public Schools at the start of the 1970-80 decade, a rise of approximately 55 percent in the elementary section and of 48 percent in the high school section. A table published by the Board of Education in *Facts and Figures* shows that in the course of 15 years, from 1952-53 to 1970-71, the total enrollment increased as much as 8.4 and 10.5 percent in the middle 1960s, dropping to no increase in elementary schools in 1971 and to minus 1.3 percent in the high schools. By 1964-65 enrollment was 566,873 and average daily attendance 485,917. In 1970-71 enrollment was 596,375 and average daily attendance 504,616.

When the Chicago Board of Education made public its annual survey of enrollment in the fall, 1973, it verified the tendency of earlier years toward greater racial segregation in elementary and high schools. Black students totaled 57.6 percent, up from 56.9 percent in 1972, even though out of 544,971 students enrolled, the number of blacks had dropped 3,886, largely because black families were taking advantage of open housing and moving into suburbs. White students in Chicago schools were 29.5 percent, down from 31 percent of 1972, a total of 12,297 whites having withdrawn from Chicago schools, as against 15,169 who dropped out in 1972. Spanish-speaking students increased slightly, and are now 11.7 percent up from 11.1 percent in 1972.

The number of all-black elementary schools had increased to 144 from 128, and out of 537 elementary schools, 250 were 90 percent black, 104 were 90 percent white. Of the 70 high schools, 28 were 90 or more percent black, and 12 were all black; 11 were more than 90 percent white, but there were no all white high schools. The change in enrollment showed the direction of movement of the population. Large gains in black students were noted in Roseland on the southern edge of Chicago and in the Ashland Ave. area south of 63d St. When white families left certain sections and blacks moved in, integration that had been achieved by forced busing broke down as students sought their neighborhood school. Only two cities exceeded Chicago in having schools that are 80 to 100 percent nonwhite—Gary, Indiana, and Compton, California. The Chicago Teachers Union voted for racial integration in the faculties by 5,566 for, 1,631 against.

The civil rights and desegregation decisions of the U.S. Supreme Court called for major readjustments in the Illinois and especially Chicago public school systems. The Chicago school authorities, alerted by street demonstrations and boycotts, introduced new studies to meet the needs of black and Spanish-speaking minorities. High school students may now select courses in Afro-American history, which deal with the black experience from pre-colonial days in Africa to today. Latin-American history, with special attention to Puerto Rican and

Mexican subjects, has had the benefit of consultation with members of both communities. Greater attention is being given to anthropology and economics in high school, and experiments are being made in the upper grades of the elementary schools with courses on man's relation to the economy. Courses also deal with the responsibilities of 18-year-olds under the 26th amendment to the Constitution.

The city makes a special effort to tell school children what the municipal services are for and how they operate. It has 25 firemen and 47 police officers giving full time to instruction, and extends the Friend Officer program to parochial and private schools.

Desegregation has had the expected repercussions in Chicago, as elsewhere. Picketing and boycotting were still going on for various reasons in 1973, when one faction at the Gage High School was demanding a change in the color ratio of classes.

An Illinois Federal Court ruled that the State has no constitutional duty to attempt to equalize public education in all areas, and the U. S. Supreme Court refused to review the decision. By this action it indicated in effect that it was not unconstitutional for a well-to-do district to spend more on its schools than one less favored.

The Chicago schools recognize the importance of reading. Every teacher in Chicago receives a copy of *Teacher's Reader,* a book on teaching reading from kindergarten into 12th grade. Reading techniques and ideas contributed by teachers, were compiled and distributed as *Reading Ideas* to every teacher. Another guide for high schools is *Every Teacher A Teacher of Reading.*

Teaching the English language is another important objective in Chicago, where the Spanish-speaking population has multiplied with the migrations from Puerto Rico. Several guides and handbooks for teaching English to children who do not speak English have been compiled; in 1972 the program served more than 60,000 children. Chicago public schools exchange teachers with Puerto Rico and Mexico.

Opportunities in music for high school students have been enlarged by adding the Jazz Band Festival to activities. The schools for more than 46 years have presented the High School Band Festival, the High School Choral Festival, the Instrumental Solo Festival, and the Instrumental Ensemble Festival. The All-City High School Band, Chorus, and Orchestra has its culminating event of the year in a concert at Orchestra Hall.

The Driver Education Program enrolls up to 50,000 for classroom instruction and more than 32,000 for practical instruction. A driving center for handicapped students is an addition to the program.

The school board has introduced a program of education about drugs into courses from kindergarten through high school. Pre-kindergarten programs enroll three-year-olds and four-year-olds, served by the Head Start staffs. Pre-school children from the Indian community are served at the American Indian Center, 1630 West Wilson Ave.

When the Model Cities program established seven community-centered schools in black and Spanish-speaking areas it gave teachers and parents a voice in how the schools should be run and what the children are taught. It served hot breakfasts and lunches to the children, and opened the schools on evenings to classes for adults.

High cost of maintenance, increased tuition fees, and inflation have caused difficulties for parochial school systems of Chicago and environs. The Roman Catholic Archdiocese of Chicago has had to close a number of its elementary schools. In the fall, 1972, it reported that the number of schools in the archdiocese had dropped in ten years from 535 to 486. Enrollment in the 408 elementary schools was 184,295, down from 196,921 of the year before. In 78 city and suburban high schools enrollment slipped slightly from 66,793 to 65,018. Total enrollment in elementary and high schools was 249,313, down from 364,628 nine years earlier. The Archdiocese takes in a much larger terrain than the Chicago school system.

The Illinois General Assembly had enacted several laws giving aid in various forms to parochial schools, independent of religious instruction, which had to be re-examined in view of decisions of the U. S. Supreme Court based on the First Amendment.

CITY COLLEGES OF CHICAGO

The seven CITY COLLEGES of CHICAGO, which provide junior college courses with emphasis on vocational training and community service, are an outgrowth of the original City College that until July 1, 1966, was under the jurisdiction of the Chicago Board of Education. At that time it became part of the Illinois Public Junior College System organized under the Junior College Act of 1965, which has opened opportunities for acquiring skills and vocational training to thousands of young people who do not continue into senior and professional schools.

Chicago City Colleges acquired an independent board of trustees and reorganized the program toward practical ends with the help of the State. The curriculum added courses in data processing, environmental control, health and medicine, electronics, automotive technology, and skills needed by industry, government, and public and private institutions. Institutes were formed for training child care workers, teachers' aides, social service aides, and police trainees, supplementing the work of the Police Academy.

LOOP COLLEGE, one of the seven City Colleges of Chicago, occupies several floors in a 17-story building at 64 East Lake St. Plans have been drawn for a new tall building to be erected half a block away at an estimated cost of $30,000,000. This school serves students who desire training in various types of office skills, including accounting, banking, advertising, data processing, merchandising, hotel management, secretarial work, drafting, environmental control technology and highway engineering. Students qualify for positions in city, county and state offices. The college has been independent of the city school board since July 1, 1966. It attracts more than 9,000 students. Chicago residents pay no tuition, only a small registration charge. Illinois residents who live outside of Chicago pay $37.50 per credit hour of instruction, while students who live outside the State pay $50 a credit hour, or $150 for a three-hour credit course.

One of the new colleges is MALCOMB X COLLEGE, 190 West Van Buren St., successor to the former Crane College. It is enrolling many blacks from this area. In April, 1971, the college entered its new building, a block long, three stories tall and two stories below ground, which cost $21,000,000. First National Bank donated $10,000 for its library. It has approx. 4,000 students. The other colleges are:

SOUTHWEST COLLEGE, 7500 S. Pulaski Road, near the Ford City Shopping Center, emphasizes aviation technology, business education and office skills. It enrolls about 5,000 and has a library of 25,000 vols.

KENNEDY-KING COLLEGE, stresses technology, business education and service programs, such as child care. It enrolls around 5,000 and has room for an ultimate 15,000 students. It is named for John F. Kennedy and Martin Luther King, Jr. Its new headquarters opened for classes in September, 1972. Its complex is an innovation in school structures; from one angle it appears like a group of square blocks, with long, horizontal rooflines. It is built over Wentworth Ave. and cost $31,500,000. A new theater seating 450 was opened in this college in February, 1973, and plays presented by the company of the Drama Guild included *Allegro, She Stoops to Conquer,* and *Compulsion.*

OLIVE-HARVEY COLLEGE, 10001 South Woodlawn Ave., has technology and business education as its favored programs. It uses 9 buildings on an interim campus that cost $2,200,000, and plans to erect a new plant on this site. It enrolls about 4,500 from black areas.

MAYFAIR COLLEGE (Amundsen-Mayfair) 4626 N. Knox Ave., is occupied chiefly with providing students training for entering a senior college. This function will be superceded when the new North-east Side College, which is planned for a site at Wilson and Racine Aves., replaces Mayfair.

WILBUR WRIGHT COLLEGE, 3400 N. Austin Ave., enrolls about 7,500. Like Mayfair College it draws students from nearby suburbs, who must pay $37.50 per credit hour for semester instruction. Out-of-state residents must pay $50 a credit hour. Residents of Chicago pay a small registration fee but tuition is free.

Chancellor Oscar E. Shabat said: "Each college is going to be different. A school in the poor ghetto must be different from one in a middle class, white community.

"We're not going to drop students who are having problems, but redirect them into areas where they can go at their own rate. The more we give people a chance, the more truly are we a community college."

Chicago II

THE CITY BY STREETS AND SECTIONS

The Loop and Environs

The Loop is the heart of mercantile Chicago and also known as downtown. It has Lake St. on the north, Van Buren St. on the south, Wabash Ave. on the east and Wells St. on the West. Its name is said to have been applied in 1897, when the Elevated Lines were linked and ran around the area, but another tradition says the loop was originated by the street car lines. It is the most highly concentrated area of offices and stores in any American metropolis, with a huge daily turnover of goods, and most of its residents are transients in the hotels.

The name of the Loop has such important business connotations that real estate and building agencies have been trying to apply it beyond the historically designated area. Thus the Loop becomes the Central Loop; the area immediately west across the Chicago River is the West Loop; the new building area of Illinois Center is the East Loop.

The Loop poses the toughest transportation problem for the municipality because it is congested with traffic that nobody wants to see curtailed because it means business. In 1910 the Loop received 20,000 street cars and 130,000 horse-drawn vehicles daily; today it has 300,000 workers and 450,000 shoppers, making 750,000 a day, with the addition of 490,000 motor vehicles. As one of the city's transportation engineers reported: "These vehicles have congested the streets, polluted the air with noise and exhaust fumes, and driven the pedestrians to ever-shrinking sidewalks." The City Government is actively promoting plans to improve transportation. The first section of a subway was built in 1948 and carried one line of the Elevated into State St. Removal of the Elevated Lines from the Loop and expanding the subway system has been set for 1980. Official and independent bodies are studying truck movements, motor car parking, foot travel, and traffic volume, among them the Departments of Public Works, Streets and Sanitation, Development & Planning; the Central Area Transit Study, and the Regional Transportation Study.

MARSHALL FIELD & COMPANY is a name synonymous with Chicago the world over. This great retail store occupies a block bounded by State, Washington and Randolph Sts., and Wabash Ave., and has its Men's Store at the northeast quarter of Washington St. and Wabash Ave. Its reputation is based upon the completeness of its stock along the lines of quality, and the care taken in its presentation. The State St. store is the core of a large investment in retail merchandising which includes the Chicago Stores Division of 14 locations; the Frederick & Nelson Division of four in Washington state; the nine Halle's Stores in Ohio, and the Crescent group of three in Spokane, Wash.

Marshall Field, the founder, born in 1834 near Conway, Mass., began his business career in Chicago in 1856 as a dry goods clerk. In 1865 he and Levi Z. Leiter bought an interest in Potter Palmer's

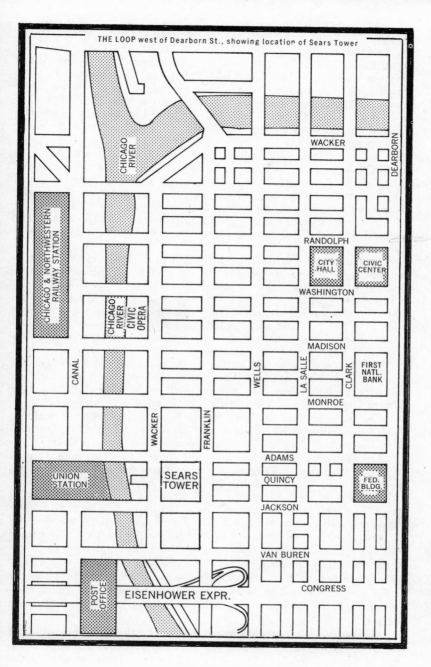

THE LOOP west of Dearborn St., showing location of Sears Tower

dry goods store, and in 1868 bought out Palmer and called the store Field, Leiter & Co. In 1881 Field bought Leiter's interest and named the store Marshall Field & Co. Field, Palmer and Leiter seized the great opportunities that opened up in Chicago real estate and profited handsomely. Field became known as the merchant prince of Chicago. He died in 1906, and his descendants have remained closely associated with Chicago enterprises, the most conspicuous of which is the Field newspaper operation.

The sound financial position of Marshall Field & Co. has been one of Chicago's prime assets. In a period when many stores encountered sliding profits Marshall Field reached record levels. Its net income of $21,457,000 in fiscal 1972 was a new high and 12% above 1971. Income before taxes was $41,563,000, a record amount. The Chicago suburban units showed the strong buying power of outlying areas. The larger units in this division were open Sundays for the first time on a year-round basis in 1972.

The expansion of Marshall Field & Co. is closely associated with the building of new urban centers. In 1973 Marshall Field, through its subsidiary Mafco, Inc. joined a subsidiary of Aetna Life & Casualty Co. in erecting WATER TOWER PLACE, on North Michigan Ave., a $130,000,000 urban center, in which the store reserved the first seven floors of a 12-story base above which rises a 62-story tower for a hotel and 260 apartments. The company also contracted for department stores in Fox Valley East, a new community east of Aurora, and Orland Park, joint ventures in association with Sears, Roebuck & Co. and Aetna Life & Casualty Co. The Marshall Field store was the first unit of Hawthorn Center, a shopping mall in New Century Town, a planned community in Vernon Hills, 30 m. north of Chicago.

On the west side of State St. at No. 32 the Reliance Building stands out conspicuously. It is one of the early examples of steel and glass construction developed in Chicago. *See Houses and Towers.*

On the north side of Randolph St. about 150 ft. west of State is the site of the Iroquois Theatre, where on December 30, 1903, occurred one of the most horrible disasters in theater history. While a matinee performance of *Mr. Bluebeard,* with Eddie Foy, was playing to a crowded house, the stage curtain caught fire, probably from an incompletely enclosed electric arc floodlight. The elaborate stage sets went up in flames, and a draft from the opened stage door swept a gale of fire over the audience. In a few minutes the locked gallery exits were further barred by piles of trampled bodies. When the flames were finally curbed, 596 persons were dead or dying—more than twice the toll of the Great Fire of 1871. The investigation disclosed lack of adequate precautions and led to drastic reforms in safety devices, such as the iron curtain.

An outdoor information booth at the northeast corner of State and Madison Sts. is operated by the State Street Council for the assistance of visitors. It provides guides and maps, and answers inquiries.

It was opened in 1958. *Monday through Saturday, 10-6, mid-June to September.*

The CARSON, PIRIE, SCOTT & CO. store at the southeast corner of State and Madison Sts. is one of the most famous commercial structures in the western world. It has become so because it is an admirable example of Louis H. Sullivan's ideas of construction for a special purpose, and it demonstrates the merits of the enlarged horizontal window that became one characteristic of Chicago architecture. In 1899 Sullivan began the first unit for the firm of Schlesinger & Mayer, a store only three bays wide, nine stories tall, between State and Wabash on Madison. By 1904 Schlesinger & Mayer were ready for expansion and had Sullivan build an addition, three bays wide on Madison, turn the corner and continue seven bays wide on State St. The rounded entrance seemed an invitation to the world to enter, and the long, horizotal windows in State St. added to the effect of open house. Sullivan, despite his conviction that a structure should be influenced by its purpose, was partial to elaborate metal scrollwork, which he applied at the second story level and to the entrance. He worked the initials of S. & M. into the decoration, and they remained there years after Carson, Pirie, Scott & Co. bought the store. In 1906 Daniel H. Burnham & Co. extended the facade on State St., and as late as 1960 Holabird & Root added another addition, both architects adhering to Sullivan's design, without the metal embellishment.

The great store at 1 South State St. is the core of a huge merchandising operation that has branches in approx. 14 towns and cities in the Metropolitan area of Chicago, as well as in Peoria, Danville, Decatur, Galesburg, Joliet, Kankakee, Kewanee, Moline, Ottawa, Quincy, and Urbana.

The magic of an address, State and Madison, is shared also by WIEBOLDT, a department store at the northeast corner, one of the busiest mercantile locations in Chicago for many years. Wieboldt Stores, Inc., started outside the Loop and as it grew moved in to join the giants. It has established branches in Chicago suburbs.

At 29 S. Wabash Avenue is the main office of the bookstore chain of Kroch's & Brentano's, Inc., which has the world's largest bookstore, in sales area and volume of sales, at this address. There were 15 stores in the chain in 1973, concentrated in the Chicago suburban area, but reaching out as far as the Mall at Cherryvale, Rockford. Adolph Kroch, chairman of the board, came fresh from the University of Vienna in 1902 and in 1907 opened a small bookstore on the south side of Monroe Street, between Michigan and Wabash Avenues. This 20 by 60 ft. shop became quickly known among discriminating customers for Kroch's remarkable ability to fit the reader to the book, and a stock of timeliness and vitality. As Kroch said, in an address at the University of Chicago, later published in book form, "bookselling is not merely a business to sell books but a serious responsibility for molding the minds of a nation." The Kroch store prospered at several Michigan Avenue locations; in 1933 Kroch bought the Chicago store of Brentano's and during the next three years reestablished Brentano's of New York on a sound financial basis. After his son, Carl A. Kroch, graduated from Cornell University he joined his father's organization, and when Adolph Kroch retired in 1947 to live in California Carl became president of Kroch's & Brentano's, Inc. His father's views and policies have been published in *The Practice of Book Selection,* reprinted as *A Great Bookstore in Action* (1940), and *Bookstores Can Be Saved* (1952). The chain has sales in excess of $15,000,000 annually. Among the outlying branches are stores in Evanston, Evergreen, Oak Brook, Old Orchard and River Oaks.

The PALMER HOUSE is a name famous in hotel history, and the great hotel of 2250 rooms that stands today at the southeast corner of State and Monroe Sts., and extending over to Wabash Ave., occupies the original site. Potter Palmer (1826-1902) was as big a mercantile tycoon as Marshall Field and Levi Z. Leiter, and bought State St. frontage before the Civil War as an investmnet of promise. In 1870 he built the first Palmer House, and it had hardly opened when the Great Fire of 1871 destroyed it. Palmer rebuilt it, and the second House was designed by J. M. van Osdel in the French Renaissance style of the Court House and a dozen other Van Osdel structures. The House had luxurious appointments that gave it a special reputation throughout the wheatlands of the Middle West. It had elevators and running water, and added electric globes to its chandeliers when Edison's lamp came in. The first thing any traveling man usually mentioned about the Palmer House was the barber shop with silver dollars cemented in the floor. By 1925 it was outmoded and replaced by the present hotel from designs by Holabird & Roche. It is a unit of the Hilton system.

Shops occupy the State St. facade of the Palmer House. At the northwest corner of State and Adams Sts. MONTGOMERY WARD & CO. operates a large department store in quarters originally built for The Fair. At the northeast corner of State St. and Jackson Boulevard is the clothing house of Henry C. Lytton & Co., long established in Chicago. South of Jackson on the east side is the huge department store of GOLDBLATT BROS. At the southwest corner of State and Jackson stands the 12-story Rothschild Building, long associated with merchandising men's clothing. Some of its upper floors accommodate extra classrooms of the JOHN MARSHALL LAW SCHOOL, which occupies the building at 315 S. Plymouth Court, once the home of the City Club. Organized in 1899, the school has only had two deans up to 1973. It operates three sessions a day and enrolls more than 1,600.

The retail area goes beyond the confines of the Loop. On the east side of State St. from Van Buren to Congress stands the retail store of SEARS, ROEBUCK & CO., occupying another historic building. It is an early example of steel skeleton construction, having been designed by the innovator, William LeBaron Jenney, in 1891 for Levi Z. Leiter, who began his dry goods experience with Marshall Field in 1865. In architectural records it is known as Leiter II. It is impressive for the fine uniformity of its unadorned eight-story facade of white marble, with large windows occupying the space between steel piers.

The First National Bank

The FIRST NATIONAL BANK BUILDING is one of the architectural phenomena of Chicago. It rises like a great gray colossus in the heart of the Loop and with its Plaza occupies a whole block from Madison to Monroe and from Dearborn to Clark Sts. With its eight exterior columns curving upward from a broad base it carries the eye of the spectator easily up its 850 ft. and 60 stories. At the south its Plaza extends to Monroe St.; at the west across Clark St. rises TWO FIRST NATIONAL PLAZA, a 30-story office building of 1972, 10 stories of which are occupied by the bank's offices. The bank itself was completed in 1969 and obliterated a dozen familiar structures, including the large Morrison Hotel. Architects were C. F. Murphy Associates and the Perkins & Will Partnership.

The slanting facades are explained as made necessary by the need of the bank to have the widest possible floor at street level, in order to accommodate commercial banking, savings, installments and loans, since the Illinois laws do not permit branch banking. The bank occupies about 20 floors and leases the remaining upper floors to tenants. To resist wind pressure loads are transmitted to the exterior columns and interior columns are omitted at the 18th floor. Long span steel girders transmit floor loads to hollow steel plate exterior columns and to rolled steel interior columns. Structural bays are 40 ft. wide. Tenant floor elevators are located at the extreme ends of the building, outside the main structure. Bank elevators are within the banking space.

The First National Bank of Chicago ranks tenth among the great commercial banks of the United States. On Dec. 31, 1973, it reported total assets of $15,558,497,000, and loans of $9,362,991,000.

The FIRST NATIONAL BANK PLAZA, on Monroe between Dearborn and Clark Sts., provides a landscaped setting that accentuates the monumental character of the 60-story bank building towering above it. The central area of the Plaza has a large square fountain, which projects square curtains of water. This is made possible by perforated water tubes connected to form the sides of a square. As the water falls back into the pool it flows uniformly over the walls.

The open terrace of the bank is the site of a "mosaic wall", designed by Marc Chagall and installed under his supervision. It was donated by Mr. and Mrs. William Wood Prince in memory of Frederick Henry Prince, railroad financier and investor who was active at the turn of the century. The Chagall work is described as part sculpture, part mural and part architecture, and is 70 ft. long, 14 ft. high, and 10 ft. wide. Mrs. Katherine Kuh, art critic and consultant for the bank's art collection, said the mosaic "will give off an iridescent glow" and that Chagall's vision "is peculiarly adapted to a medium where broken surfaces constantly react to shifting light."

The underground levels have shops and two floors are used by the bank. They connect with the Two First National Bldg. on the west side of Clark St. Part of the Plaza area has the First Chicago Center, an auditorium with 500 seats for meetings and films. Opposite the Plaza on the northeast corner of Dearborn and Monroe Sts. stands the new CONSUMER CREDIT BLDG.

Noontime Events are a summer diversion at First National Plaza. Here strollers may hear the Cavaliers, drum and bugle corps, Harry Brandon's orchestra, Harvey Levy and his ragtime sing-along band, the Dixie Wildcats jazz combo, watch Dick Wolf demonstrate physical fitness or see an art exhibit. This is but a brief hint of what goes on there all the time.

TWO FIRST NATIONAL PLAZA, the 30-story office building erected in 1972 by the First National Bank on Clark St. overlooks the three-level plaza south of the main bank. The building has a facade of dark brown finished steel and bronzed glass; its 10 lower floors are occupied by offices of the bank and its 17 upper floors are used by tenants. An underground pedestrian mall connects the office building with the bank building and plaza, and gives underground access to all contiguous subways. It was designed by C. F. Murphy Associates and the Perkins & Will Partnership.

The Civic Center, West Washington Street

The CHICAGO CIVIC CENTER, opened in 1965, is a massive rectangle of steel and glass that rises 31 stories, or 660 ft. on the north half of the block bounded by Dearborn, Clark, Randolph and Washington Sts. Designed by C. F. Murphy Associates, Skidmore, Owings & Merrill, and Loebl, Schlossman & Bennett, its steel has a pleasing patina of bronze and its huge windows on the lobby floor give an effect of openness. This is enhanced by the CIVIC PLAZA at the south, which enables the office buildings round about to get a full supply of light and air. The Center has an information desk, a restaurant called the Gavel Club, and a cafeteria. It connects with an underground passage of shops leading to State St.

An ETERNAL FLAME to commemorate the war dead of Chicago was lighted in the Plaza in 1972. The area is decorated with a fountain and flag-staffs. It can accommodate parades and rallies, and is sometimes used by demonstrators with placards in a variety of causes. Early in December a huge pine tree, constructed from several trees, richly adorned and brilliantly lighted, marks the Christmas holidays.

Directly on Washington St. stands a 50-ft. abstract sculpture in metal, dark-brown in color, made from a design by Pablo Picasso, Spanish-born artist, who died in Paris in 1973. A small model of the piece was given by Picasso at the urging of William E. Hartmann, Chicago architect. It is now in the Art Institute. The United States Steel Corporation worked the metal into its present form. The cost of manufacture and installation is reported to have been $300,000, which was borne by several local foundations. Although unveiled with official fanfare the sculpture, which has no relation to its site, or the city's history, mostly arouses curiosity as an example of an irrational period in art.

Beside the sculpture stands a small replica with the legend of its donation in braille, supposed to be helpful to the sightless.

Several other buildings are seen to advantage because of the open space of the Civic Center. The BRUNSWICK BUILDING, opposite the Civic Center on West Washington St. rises 37 stories and 475 ft., and was designed in 1964 by Skidmore, Owings & Merrill. West of it rises the 21-story office building and church of the CHICAGO TEMPLE, which gained international attention when erected in 1923 because it was a church adapted to a tall office building. The architects were Holabird & Roche. The building rises 21 stories and 400 ft. and houses the First Methodist Church, which dates its organization back to 1831. Above the office floors rises an ornate Gothic tower, surmounted by a sharp spire and a cross, which are illuminated at night.

The location of the Civic Center was dictated by the proximity of the massive CITY HALL-COUNTY BUILDING, across Clark St. from the Center, and bounded by Clark, LaSalle, Washington and Randolph Sts. Built in 1907-1911 and designed by Holabird & Roche, it fills the block up to the sidewalk line. This sturdy structure in a neo-classic mode has tall Corinthian columns as decoration on four sides and is divided between public offices of the City and Cook County.

The first City Hall was located in the Saloon Building, southwest corner of Clark and Lake. Its name was the popular pronunciation of *salon,* French for hall. In 1848 the city's offices were moved to the Market Building, in the middle of State St., fronting on Randolph, where the first floor was occupied by vendor's stalls. In 1851 the city began erection of a City Hall on the block bounded by Washington, Randolph, Clark and LaSalle Sts., a lot that had been reserved for city and county at the incorporation of the town in 1833. It was completed in 1853 and cost $110,000. It was built of brick faced with Lockport marble, three stories tall, with two domes and a cupola. Here the body of Abraham Lincoln lay in state. The hall was used from 1853 until destroyed in the Great Fire of 1871. A temporary hall was placed at the southeast corner of Adams and LaSalle Sts., where the tank of the old reservoir still stood, and this was called The Rookery because of the many pigeons that flocked there. This lasted until 1885 when a new City Hall was erected on the west half of the Washington St. site and connected with the east half, taken by the County Building. The identical buildings had a French Renaissance design by J. M. van Osdel, with blocks of Bedford stone and columns of polished marble, placed for decoration rather than support. The walls rested on wide foundations and thick walls of brick. In 26 years the city's business completely outgrew these quarters and in 1911 the city and county occupied the present City-County Building.

The MUNICIPAL REFERENCE LIBRARY in the City Hall provides an important statistical and general information service to official Chicago and to some extent to the public.

There was a hotel at the northwest corner of Clark and Randolph Sts. since the year Chicago incorporated as a city—1837, and after 1849 it was known as the SHERMAN HOUSE. Now the big 1,400-room hotel is closed and the New York owner, Milton Gilbert, has begun development of the site, from Clark to LaSalle on Randolph, for the

Mid-America Fashion Center, which includes an exhibition area for the garment industry, at Clark St., a new hotel extending from LaSalle St., and a large garage. The new hotel, 28 stories and 503 rooms, may be operated by one of the national chains.

Another LaSalle St. development is the erection of LA SALLE PLAZA at the southeast corner of LaSalle and Lake Sts., in the block where the new Hotel Sherman is located. It is 38 stories tall and has a net area of 800,000 sq. ft. West from LaSalle on Randolph, corner Wells, is the modern, long-established Bismarck Hotel.

Opposite the City and County Building at the southwest corner of Washington and LaSalle Sts. there stood until the spring of 1972 an office structure that carried above its entrance the words: CHICAGO STOCK EXCHANGE BUILDING. This name was merely a relic of other days, for metal tablets beside its doors designated this as the 30 North LaSalle Building. Before it was brought down to be replaced by another tall office structure it was a survivor of the era of Adler & Sullivan, who designed it in 1893. It was a milestone in the march of Chicago architecture, for in order to secure the south wall on a solid foundation the builders sank caissons to bedrock for the first time. Although its bays for windows were similar to other designs, it impressed observers by its great arched entrance, two stories tall. The stone carried two medallions, one the date of construction, 1893, the other a relief of the dwelling of P. F. W. Peck, which occupied this site in 1837. The building had a large trading room on the second floor, reached by stairs opposite the front entrance..

The destruction of the building brought much criticism from persons and organizations interested in preserving monuments of distinction, but the cost of preservation proved too great. During demolition Richard Nickel, architectural historian, was killed April 13, 1972, by a falling wall while trying to get photographs of the building.

In 1973 the Tishman Realty & Construction Co., builders of Gateway Center, began the erection of a 42-story office building on this historic site, to have 1,000,000 sq. ft. of space available in 1974.

The STATE OF ILLINOIS BLDG., 160 N. LaSalle St., has the Chicago offices of many of the State officials and departments which have headquarters in Springfield. Here are offices of the Governor, Lieutenant Governor, Attorney General, Auditor of Public Accounts, Assistant Secretary of State, Treasurer and directors of Departments of Conservation, Children & Family Services, Corrections, Insurance, Public Health, Revenue and Labor. Other State agencies are located as follows: Superintendent of Public Education, 188 W. Randolph St.; Agriculture, 300 W. Washington Blvd.; Public Aid, 209 W. Jackson Blvd. The Dept. of Law Enforcement has its suburban office at 2775 Algonquin Road, Rolling Meadows.

In the Financial District

LaSalle Street, down to the Board of Trade Building at Jackson Blvd., has the largest concentration of banks and brokerage houses, and has seen many new buildings arising in its environs.

At the northwest corner of LaSalle and Madison stands the LaSalle Hotel, a popular luncheon spot for bankers. It was erected soon after the turn of the century and has survived one disastrous fire.

The NORTHERN TRUST CO., 50 S. LaSalle St., was built in 1906 as a four-story bank building by Frost & Granger, architects. Two stories were added in 1930 by Holabird & Root, and more were added in 1965 by C. F. Murphy Associates.

The HARRIS BANK BLDG., 115 S. LaSalle St., rises 38 stories and has a net area of 625 sq. ft. It was erected by the Harris Trust & Savings Bank for occupancy in 1975.

The ROOKERY, 209 S. LaSalle St., corner of Adams, is one of the real pioneers of skyscraper construction, a building that marks the transition from solid walls to steel frames. It has stood on this site since 1886, when it was designed by Burnham & Root; in 1905 Frank Lloyd Wright remodeled the court on the ground floor. Its architectural significance is best described by the citation of the Landmarks Commission, which marked it "in recognition of its pioneering plan in providing shops and offices around a graceful and semi-private square and further development of the skeleton structural frame using cast iron columns, wrought iron spandrel beams, and steel beams to support party walls and interior floors." The Rookery stands across Adams St. from the site of the first skeleton steel and iron building in Chicago, the Home Insurance Building, designed by William LeBaron Jenney in 1884, and removed in 1931 to make room for the FIELD BUILDING, home of the LaSalle National Bank and offices of other corporations. The latter was built in 1934 from designs by Graham, Anderson, Probst, & White.

The site of the Rookery has historic connotations. Before the Great Fire of 1871 it had a municipal reservoir, with a huge iron tank. The fire destroyed the building but the tank offered temporary shelter, and here were stored the first books collected for the Chicago Public Library. A temporary structure built around the tank was used as the City Hall from 1872 to 1884. During that time many pigeons were attracted to the place by oats scattered by the horses tethered there. It became known as The Rookery and when replaced by the present building retained the name.

THE CONTINENTAL ILLINOIS NATIONAL BANK & TRUST CO., 231 S. LaSalle St., is the largest bank in Illinois, and ninth largest in the U. S. On Dec. 31, 1973, it reported assets of $16,870,180,000, and loans of $9,994,098,000.

The CHICAGO BOARD OF TRADE BUILDING, Jackson Blvd. and LaSalle St., 44 stories tall, has a most dramatic location. Typifying the Board of Trade's importance in Chicago's economy, it stands as a climax to LaSalle Street, at the apparent end of its long gorge. Designed by Holabird and Root and completed in 1930, the building towers in huge set-back masses to a statue of Ceres, goddess of grain, a 31-foot aluminum figure by John Storrs. Ornament throughout the building contains symbols of the harvest.

Extensive reconstruction and modernization of the building was completed by 1973. Heating, ventilating and air-conditioning was replaced by an all-electric energy system. Especially noteworthy was the introduction of 22 computer-controlled elevators.

Organized in 1848, the Board of Trade is the largest grain exchange in the world. Its biggest trading by quality and value in recent years has been soy beans and soybean oil, with corn, wheat, and silver following in that order. Value of the transactions in one year reached as high as $322 billion. It has opened bidding in stud lumber (2 × 4).

On the trading floor of the Exchange Hall (*visitor's gallery on the 5th floor open 9:30-1:15 Mon.-Fri.*), are the grain pits, bordered with batteries of telephone and telegraph instruments, and the small sections for trading in cotton, provisions, and stocks. Quotation boards cover three walls; at the north side of the hall nine tall windows open on LaSalle Street. The tables at the windows contain samples of cash grain, each bag representing a carload on hand and available for immediate delivery. Trading in futures constitutes the principal function of the Exchange. Shouting, gesticulating traders crowd the grain pits, as messengers scurry back and forth between the wire desks and the pits. Trading usually opens briskly and closes in a brief frenzy. The gong that marks these periods was used for many years in the old Board of Trade, the scene of Frank Norris' *The Pit*. A free pamphlet explains the intricate system governing the apparent bedlam. Also available is a movie about the grain market shown at intervals from 9:45 a.m. to 1 p.m. An observatory on the top floor gives a view of Chicago's topless towers (*small fee*).

The Chicago Board Options Exchange was established in March, 1973, the first central market for security options, known generally as puts and calls.

The MIDWEST STOCK EXCHANGE, 120 S. LaSalle St., is reported to have the largest exchange of securities outside of New York. Recorded transcriptions explain trading activity via telephones. There is a visitors' gallery. *Open Monday-Friday, 9-2:30.*

The CHICAGO MERCANTILE EXCHANGE entered its new building at 444 W. Jackson Blvd. November 27, 1972. It had cost $6,000,000 and housed its International Monetary Market, which in 1972 had trades worth an estimated $19.8 billion. The "Merc" was organized more than 50 years ago and its trading in commodity futures continues to accelerate at a swift pace. About 500,000 futures traders are active on the exchange, which expects the number to rise to 1,000,000 by 1980.

The MONADNOCK BUILDING, rising like a huge pylon at the southwest corner of Jackson Blvd. and Dearborn St., is a famous pioneer structure in modern architecture. Actually it is a monument to older ways of building, for it is a solid pile of masonry with brick walls 15 feet wide at the base. Its lines are as pleasing now as in 1892 when John Root designed the building. Not only is it devoid of ornament, but all the angles are rounded in a manner that would be called streamlined today. This is especially noticeable in the flaring base, the lower parts of the soaring bay windows, and the subtle swelling at the top that replaces the usual heavy cornice of the period.

The Federal Center

For many years the Federal Government had its courts and main postoffice concentrated in an oddly-shaped building bounded by Dearborn, Clark and Monroe Sts. and Jackson Blvd. This had the shape of four large wings, one fronting on each of the four streets and joined at the center, which was surmounted by an octagonal dome. Henry Ives Cobb designed it in 1905 and it stood until the late 1960's, when the building was displaced by the new FEDERAL CENTER, where the Government aims to concentrate its principal agencies. The new UNITED STATES COURTHOUSE AND OFFICE BUILDING, 219 S. Dearborn St. is the first of three units at the Center. A huge flat facade of glass and steel, it rises 27 stories and has the characteristics of the office buildings designed by Mies van der Rohe; other architects involved are Schmidt, Garden & Erikson, C. F. Murphy Associates, and A. Epstein & Sons. A metal sculpture by Calder was ordered by the U. S. Government. Plans call for a large plaza, a Federal office building of 40 stories, and a postoffice at the Center.

In the original Courthouse the central rotunda, embellished with marble pillars of various hues, was known for decorations that reached to the ceiling of the dome. It housed the United States District Court in which some famous trials were held. During the incumbency of Judge Kenesaw M. Landis the Standard Oil Co. was fined $29,000,000 for infraction of Federal laws; later it saw the trial and conviction of racketeer leader Alphone Capone for income tax evasion.

The MARQUETTE BUILDING, 140 S. Dearborn St., is notable for its decorations representing early historic figures and events. It has bronze reliefs over the entrance depicting Father Marquette's journey, and bronze medallion portraits of other explorers and of several Indian chiefs in the rotunda, the work of Hermon A. MacNeil. Martin Roche designed the mosaics around the mezzanine balcony to illustrate scenes from the journeys of discovery of Jolliet and others in this region.

THE CHICAGO METROPOLITAN COUNCIL of the NAACP (National Assn. for the Advancement of Colored People) has its main offices at 407 S. Dearborn St. and other offices at 53 W. Jackson Blvd. and 1631 S. Central Park Ave. This influential organization, which works tirelessly to maintain the civil rights of the Negro, entered the 1970 decade with 1,751 branches in American cities and 461,957 members. Its aim is racial integration and it opposes militant methods and programs for black nationalism in the United States. It was founded in New York on the 100th anniversary of Abraham Lincoln's birthday by W. E. B. DuBois and other black leaders with the strong support of whites led by Jane Addams of Chicago, John Dewey, William Dean Howells, and Lincoln Steffens. National headquarters are at 1790 Broadway, New York, N. Y.

The LOOP SYNAGOGUE, 16 S. Clark St., was erected in 1963 from designs by Loebl, Schlossman & Bennett. The impressive stained glass is by Abraham Rattner.

ST. PETER'S ROMAN CATHOLIC CHURCH, 110 W. Madison St., in the heart of the Loop, is served by the Franciscan Fathers.

The Downtown Center of the University of Chicago, 65 E. South Water St., which had classes for adults, ceased operations June 30, 1974, for reasons of economy. The Graduate School of Business continues to have classes for part-time students at 190 E. Delaware St., where it enrolls 1,200.

The INLAND STEEL BUILDING, 30 West Monroe St., at the corner of Dearborn, impresses by a design that accentuates its linear character. Its main supporting columns are placed on the outside of the frame, thus providing more space inside. Beside this 19-story structure of steel and glass stands a narrow, windowless building, taller than the first, which contains the elevators, stairs, and air conditioning system. The building has been widely praised as embodying many of the new factors of skyscraper construction and providing another example of the resourcefulness of Chicago architecture. It was designed by Skidmore, Owings & Merrill.

The CNA CENTER, a huge 45-story office building at the northeast corner of Wabash Ave. and East Van Buren St., was erected 1972-73 as headquarters for the manifold activities of CNA Financial Corp., a holding company formed in 1968 for the Continental Casualty Assurance Co. and the Continental Casualty Co., corporations with assets of more than $3 billion. The main CNA office for a number of years was at 310 S. Michigan Ave., which was made available for leasing. CNA owns the block bounded by Michigan Ave., Jackson Blvd., Wabash Ave. and Van Buren St. About 6,000 employees were transferred to the new building from Michigan Ave., as well as from other quarters in the upper floors of the Findlay Bldg., 318 S. Michigan Ave., and the Continental Center.

CONTINENTAL CENTER, 55 East Jackson Blvd., was designed by C. F. Murphy Associates in 1961-62. It has no interior columns; the outer spacing between columns is 42 ft. A flat black paint is used on the outer steel covering.

MID-CONTINENTAL PLAZA is another huge tower of recent construction that helps make the Loop the most concentrated office area in the country. This 50-story behemoth of steel and glass occupies the east side of Wabash Avenue between Monroe and Adams Sts. The first three floors are occupied by shops, restaurants, and the First Pacific Bank of Chicago. Then 39 floors are occupied as offices for various firms. Nine floors are given over to parking for 800 motor cars, available around the clock.

WACKER

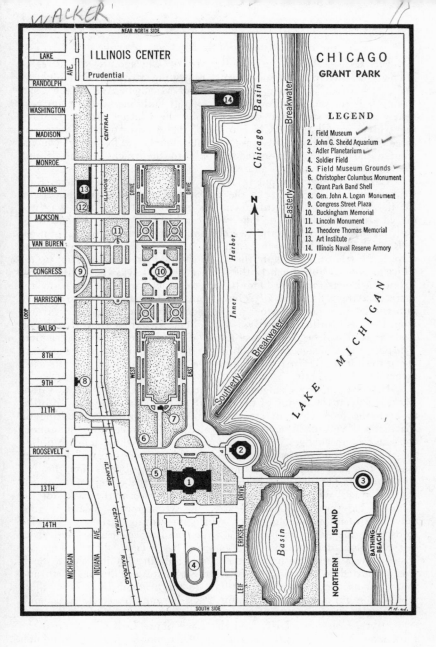

ILLINOIS CENTER
Prudential

NEAR NORTH SIDE

CHICAGO
GRANT PARK

LEGEND

1. Field Museum
2. John G. Shedd Aquarium
3. Adler Planetarium
4. Soldier Field
5. Field Museum Grounds
6. Christopher Columbus Monument
7. Grant Park Band Shell
8. Gen. John A. Logan Monument
9. Congress Street Plaza
10. Buckingham Memorial
11. Lincoln Monument
12. Theodore Thomas Memorial
13. Art Institute
14. Illinois Naval Reserve Armory

LAKE
RANDOLPH
WASHINGTON
MADISON
MONROE
ADAMS
JACKSON
VAN BUREN
CONGRESS
HARRISON
BALBO
8TH
9TH
11TH
ROOSEVELT
13TH
14TH

LOOP

CENTRAL

ILLINOIS

DRIVE

WEST

EAST

DRIVE

MICHIGAN

INDIANA AVE.

ILLINOIS CENTRAL RAILROAD

LEIF ERIKSEN DRIVE

Chicago Basin

Breakwater

Easterly Breakwater

N

Inner Harbor

Southerly Breakwater

LAKE MICHIGAN

Basin

NORTHERN ISLAND

BATHING BEACH

NEAR NORTH SIDE

SOUTH SIDE

F. H. ed.

Grant Park and South Michigan Avenue

GRANT PARK, the Front Yard of Chicago, is 303 acres of lawns, trees, drives, and monuments extending from E. Randolph St. to E. 14th Blvd., and from the east side of Michigan Ave. to the Lake. Facing it is the most impressive array of tall buildings in the country—nearly a mile of stone and steel including the Chicago Public Library, the University Club, the Chicago Club, the Auditorium Building, and three of the largest and most famous hotels. This park evolved from a barren area that extended only to the tracks of the Illinois Central Railroad 100 years ago.

Lake Park was laid out in 1844. When the Illinois Central Railroad reached Chicago in 1852 the city was prompt to grant concessions for its entry to the heart of town. As elsewhere the right-of-way was placed along the rim of the lake, where a base for the tracks had to be built on piles driven into the swampy soil. The railroad placed stations at Randolph, Van Buren, and 12th Sts., giving easy access to commuting trains. North of Randolph the road shunted freight cars up to the Chicago River. Subsequently the surface of what was then called Lake Front Park was raised by landfill, and the tracks were 20 ft. below the surface. After 1871 tons of refuse from the Great Fire were dumped into the lake east of Monroe St. Decades later the material excavated from the Loop utility tunnel was brought here. After 1960 the Illinois Central Railroad began to lease its air rights for building construction. The City of Chicago in 1965 brought suit to stop the railroad from doing so, but the United States Supreme Court confirmed the railroad's ownership of air rights.

In 1901 the city changed the name of Lake Front Park to Grant Park, chiefly at the urging of the G. A. R. Civil War veterans. In order to keep the park clear of structures, owners of property fronting on Michigan Ave. made a compact to demand practically unanimous consent to any changes. A. Montgomery Ward, whose office building for years was one of the show places of the avenue, became the watch dog of the park and kept it unspoiled. About 50 years ago the Art Institute was permitted to build extensions on the eastern side of the railroad tracks with the roof level with the surface of the park, for the Kenneth Sawyer Goodman Theatre. A. Montgomery Ward is gone now, as also is his famous tower, which no visiting farmer ever failed to ascend; the park has become a wide, landscaped terrain, and strict interpretation of the no-building compact has been modified. The Art Institute was already using another Loop building for its school. So it was permitted to expand, and two large two-story additions north and south, facing the Avenue, were added to the original 1892 unit; there is agitation for more space. Grant Park beyond the tracks was landscaped; groves of trees were planted, tennis courts were laid out, and two drives, Columbus Drive and the Lake Shore Drive, now cross the Park from North to South. Columbus Drive moves across E. Randolph St. as one of the new highways in Illinois Center to E. Wacker Drive. A project on the drawing boards carries it across the River on a new bridge. The pier that extends into Lake Michigan off the north end of Grant Park at Randolph St. serves the Illinois Naval Reserve Armory. Along the shoreline of the park is Chicago Harbor, lying inside two breakwaters. A light stands at the harbor mouth; inside a large fleet of sloops and motor cruisers lies at anchor. In the park near the shore is the building of the Columbia Yacht Club. This is the starting-point of the annual Chicago to Mackinac Yacht Race, usually held on a July weekend. Nearly 200 sloops of all classes have been known to start this 313-mile race; some make it in 28 hours, some take longer, and high winds and fog are possible hazards.

The PRUDENTIAL BUILDING stands like a great rampart on Randolph Street facing the northern edge of Grant Park, all 41 stories and 601 feet of it, carrying on its roof line the name of the great insurance company that owns it. This space always has been the most effective location for a huge signboard, and now there is nothing to interfere as the name blazes forth at night visible for miles. The building was the first to make use of the air rights of the Illinois Central Railroad, and the first tall office structure built in 20 years after 1934. It was completed in 1935 and credited with unlocking the funds for capital investment in office buildings and starting the building boom that is changing the face of Chicago. It also changed the scale of rentals. Before the Prudential Chicago office space topped at $4.50 a sq. ft.; the Prudential had to charge $6.50 and for the top three floors $7 a sq. ft. When this rental succeeded other investors were persuaded to remain in the central area. In 1968 it built an addition.

Its restaurants are popular with businessmen and the Mid-American Club meets for luncheon on the 39th floor. The Top of the Rock has a restaurant and cocktail lounge and recalls the owner's famous trade mark.

East Randolph Street, from Michigan Ave. to the outer Drive, marks the southern line of the fabulous real estate development called ILLINOIS CENTER. For more than 100 years the 83 acres in this area were devoted to loading and switching yards of the Illinois Central, and when it discontinued their use it was in the possession of a fortune in real estate. Building has just begun; no one at this time can forecast how many great structures will rise on this terrain.

STANDARD OIL PLAZA is located at 200 East Randolph Drive and the new skyscraper rises 82 stories to Prudential's 41, practically twice as tall. This is the investment of Standard Oil Co. of Indiana. The building is 275 ft. square at the base and its fine, perpendicular lines of steel give it the appearance of a lofty column. It has a net area of 2,250,000 sq. ft. and at 1,136 ft. ranks as the second tallest building in Chicago. When the final 2-ton steel beam, 45 ft. long and 30 in. thick, was raised to the 80th story by the hard-hats, it carried the autograph of Mayor Richard Daley.

On North Michigan Ave. between Randolph St. and the River are several noteworthy addresses. National Cash Register erected a seven-story building at 223 N. Michigan Ave. in 1956. Although 1 Illinois

Center, the IC INDUSTRIES BLDG., has its main entrance on E. Wacker Dr., 2 Illinois Center, has its main door at 233 N. Michigan. Both buildings are 30 stories tall and have 948,000 sq. ft. of net area.

One of the new buildings planned for Illinois Center Plaza will be the 36-story office building begun for Blue Cross-Blue Shield, which leased 400,000 sq. ft. for 25 years at $80,000,000.

THE CHICAGO PUBLIC LIBRARY

The heart of the vast reading and reference system that is called the CHICAGO PUBLIC LIBRARY occupies a long, narrow, and comparatively low building that stretches from Randolph to Washington Sts. on Michigan Ave. Designed by Shepley, Rutan & Coolidge and opened in 1897, it is an example of modified French Renaissance style used for formal public buildings at that time, adapted to the need for wide window space. Its principal architectural distinction is the extraordinary interior decoration by Louis Tiffany of favrile glass mosaics and marble on stairs, walls and domed ceiling, which have no counterpart anywhere. The building has entrances on porches at both Randolph and Washington Sts., but 78 E. Washington is the principal door for the Library. The Randolph St. opening leads to offices of the Library and the G. A. R. Memorial Hall, a museum of Civil War relics.

The Library occupies a historic site, for this land belonged to the Fort Dearborn Reservation, on part of which Jean Baptiste Beaubien built a house in 1817; lated this segment became Dearborn Park, and Lincoln spoke there. There were small collections of books in Chicago before 1870, notably at the Young Men's Assn., which called itself the Chicago Library Assn. in 1868, and the Chicago Historical Society, the Academy of Sciences and the Academy of Design, but there was no public library before the Great Fire of 1871. After the fire Thomas Hughes, member of Parliament and author of *Tom Brown's School Days*, led a movement in London to send a collection of books to Chicago. First 7,000 copies and in 1872 an additional 5,000 were sent, donated by Queen Victoria, Darwin, Huxley, Carlyle, Disraeli, Tennyson, Browning, Ruskin, and British authors of similar stature. At that time the fire had destroyed a building at a corner of Adams and LaSalle Sts. and left standing in isolation a huge iron tank that had served as a water reservoir. Shelves were built inside the tank and it became the seat of the first collection of the Chicago Public Library. An act to give support to public libraries was passed by the State Legislature March 7, 1872, and on Jan. 1, 1873 the library was opened. It occupied various quarters until the erection of the present main building in 1897.

The traditional concept of a library as a repository of books available to those who wish to consult them has yielded long since to the library as a dynamic force that projects its great store of wisdom and practical knowledge into every part of its community. The activities of the Chicago Public Library are no measure of its influence, but they show the extent of its reach. When the Library observed the centennial of its founding in 1972 it was circulating more than 9,000,000 books and 476,143 periodicals, films, phonograph records and other cultural materials; it had 70 branch libraries in all parts of the city, four reading and study centers in housing developments, and 30 traveling branch stops by bookmobile. It was operating on a budget of approx. $16,000,000, of which tax receipts provided nearly $12,000,000 and State and Federal funds more than $2,000,000. In 1971 it paid out $10,190,160 in salaries and $1,185,697 for books, a proportion observed in many other great libraries, and it collected $302,139 in fines assessed against readers who kept books beyond the permissible time.

In any summary of library work the digits are continually changing. Branch libraries are being opened in rented quarters; established branches are moving into new structures. There is always opportunity for architectural variation. The Blackstone branch at East 49th and Lake Park Ave. is a classical gem; the new West Belmont branch, with 40,000 books, has both exterior and interior walls of red and brown pressed face-brick. Another reading-and-study center goes into the Cabrini-Green housing development. Similarly the services find new uses. A grant from the Model Cities program paid for bussing 15 classes from each of 10 schools (9,000 pupils) to neighborhood libraries for one hour a week. A Federal grant provides special services to Spanish-speaking residents, and when the Board of Education starts bilingual centers the Library provides materials. When the Museum of Science and Industry has a Children's Book Festival, the Library sends 3,000 volumes.

A Federal grant for $90,000 was presented to the Hall Branch Library to strengthen the Vivian G. Harsh collection of Afro-American history.

Observance of the centennial of the Library in 1972 comprised lectures, musical programs, and exhibits. Queen Elizabeth II of England sent an autographed copy of *Buckingham Palace*, to recall the donation of books by British notables led by Queen Victoria in 1872, after the Great Fire. The Encyclopedia Britannica organization presented a copy of the first edition of the work, dated 1768. The National Endowment for the Humanities granted $22,000 for a lecture series on The City in Its Historical and Philosophical Context. The Friends of the Chicago Public Library sponsored a chamber music series by the Chicago Symphony String Quartet. A number of programs of musical, artistic and literary character were presented with the cooperation of ethnic organizations.

With the opening of a new Information Center the Central Library has augmented its ability to give a quick response to the numerous inquiries for information that come from students, schools, business houses, and organizations. Both the *Chicago Tribune* and the *Chicago Sun-Times* and *Daily News* have closed their information services and thus have increased the demands on the Information Center of the Public Library.

The Board of the Chicago Public Library in 1971 established the first Regional Library Center in Chicago at W. 95th and Halsted Sts., with large collections of books and materials of black interest. The Library also arranged for the publication of the *Chicago Afro-American Analytic Catalog: an Index to Materials on the Afro-American in Principal Libraries of Chicago,* comprising the contents of 75,000 cards.

The main building of the Chicago Public Library long has been inadequate for the tasks it performs. The Chicago Plan Commission has approved the appropriation by the City of $8,000,000 to rehabilitate and modernize the structure. Changes needed were spelled out by a commission appointed by Mayor Richard J. Daley earlier in 1972. This also endorsed erection of the proposed research center in the heart of downtown Chicago, which is to contain 500,000 sq. ft. of space. This will be part of a new development now in the planning stage. When realized, the main building will be retained as a popular library and cultural center.

The North entrance to the Library opens into a lobby with a marble staircase that leads to the rotunda on the second floor and the GRAND ARMY MEMORIAL HALL, provided for when the Library was built. The space was leased for fifty years to the Illinois section of the G. A. R. (Grand Army of the Republic) and in 1948 reverted to the custody of the Library. It is generally known as the Civil War Museum, which contains portraits, letters, documents, and other memorabilia of the war of 1861-65, cared for by veterans until all survivors had passed away. To be seen are Civil War drums, zouave and infantry uniforms, a saddle used by General Grant; flags of the Union and of the Confederacy; a bronze bust of Lincoln, and numerous portraits.

The last Civil War veteran of Illinois was Louis Fablinger, onetime commander of the Illinois Department of the GAR, who died Mar. 14, 1950, aged 103. The last Civil War veteran of Chicago was Capt. Thomas Ambrose, who died Nov. 9, 1949.

South on Michigan Ave., East Side

In 1873 the huge wooden INTERSTATE EXPOSITION BUILDING was erected in the park opposite Adams St., and opened with an industrial and farm exhibition. It was designed by W. W. Boyington, the popular architect after the Great Fire, and had a number of high gables and cupolas. In 1877 a musician named Theodore Thomas introduced Wagnerian music in a hall filled with beer tables. Until 1890 Thomas gave concerts on summer evenings.

Exposition Hall was the site of two spectacular national conventions of the Republican Party, in 1880 and 1884. At both the fanatical support of James G. Blaine by a strong wing of the party was responsible for the enthusiasm. Blaine (1830-1893), Maine senator, had been a founder of the new Republican Party in 1856, and had supported Lincoln. In 1880 the Stalwarts, conservatives, backed General U. S. Grant for a third term. Blaine had been speaker of the House of Representatives 1869-75, and had a large following. He was known as the Plumed Knight because of his Masonic affiliations. Intensely bitter opposition to Blaine was led by Roscoe Conkling. After hectic sessions the convention compromised on James A. Garfield, and when he was elected Blaine became secretary of state. In 1884 the Republicans again met in Exposition Hall and when Blaine was nominated for President pandemonium broke loose. John A. Logan was named for vice president. Religious bias entered the campaigning and Blaine was defeated by Grover Cleveland, Democrat. In 1888 Blaine supported Benjamin Harrison for President and after Harrison's election became his secretary of state.

In 1885 N. K. Fairbank and Ferdinand Peck sponsored an opera Festival. The stage was 120 ft. wide, 80 ft. deep, with a 60 ft. proscenium. Dankmar Adler had a hand in the arrangements. In 1892 the hall was torn down and the Hall of Congresses was erected in its place for use during the World's Columbian Exposition, later to become the Art Institute.

THE ART INSTITUTE OF CHICAGO

The ART INSTITUTE OF CHICAGO, one of the great cultural influences of the Middle West, stands on the east side of Michigan Ave., facing Adams St., spreading the inspiration of art in the heart of a commercial metropolis. Beginning as a school of instruction, it has became a museum showing the finest works of the master painters.

The Institute was incorporated in 1879 as the Chicago Academy of Fine Arts, an outgrowth of the Chicago Academy of Design, founded in 1866. It received its present name in 1882 and a few years later won international attention when its wealthy backers disclosed the size of their wallets by buying the Demidoff collection of 15 old Dutch masters. The promoters of the World's Fair of 1893, instead of building a temporary structure to house the Hall of Congresses, cooperated financially with the trustees of the Institute to erect the present main unit, into which the Institute moved.

By agreement with the Chicago Park District no other buildings were to be erected in Grant Park. This restricted expansion of the Institute until 1925, when it was enabled to build Gunsaulus Hall over the tracks of the Illinois Central and the Charles L. Hutchinson wing beyond it. This included the Kenneth Sawyer Goodman Theatre below ground level with an entrance on Columbus Drive in the park. In 1956 the Institute was authorized to build two extensions facing Michigan Avenue, the Bertram F. Ferguson wing for offices at the north and the Sterling Morton wing for new galleries at the south. This necessitated a new location for Lorado Taft's Fountain, *Spirit of the Great Lakes,* which stood at the middle of the south terrace. This was moved to the facade of the Sterling Morton wing. Five female figures representing the Great Lakes hold shells from which the water spills successively.

The main unit of the Institute, an adaptation of Italian Renaissance by Shepley, Rutan & Coolidge, has an approach of wide stone steps flanked by two bronze lions designed by Edward Kemeys. These lions, as well as bison and elk, were designed by Kemeys for bridges for the World's Fair of 1893 in Jackson Park.

The entrance hall, on the first floor, is devoted to modern sculpture, and is flanked by galleries of Egyptian and classical arts. The north half of the floor contains Fullerton Hall, the center of the extensive lecture activities, and the print galleries. In these galleries exhibits are frequently arranged from the Institute's collection of European and American prints; the important International print exhibitions are also held here. The Ryerson and Burnham Libraries, open to the public, are located on the main floor at either side of the grand staircase.

In the chronologically arranged galleries on the second floor are works by masters of almost every great school of painting from the 13th century to the present. The Institute is richest in French paintings of the late 19th and early 20th centuries. Many of the exhibits were gifts from Chicagoans. Earliest of these was the Henry Field collection, 41 canvasses of the Barbizon school, including Breton's *Song of the Lark.* Other notable collections include French Impressionists; British and Dutch paintings; Monets and Renoirs, primitives, and 18th and 19th century works; Post-Impressionists; Innesses; 19th century paintings, and American canvasses. El Greco's *Assumption of the Virgin,* Rembrandt's *Young Girl at an Open Half-Door,* Seurat's *Sunday on the Island of Grand Jatte,* Constable's *Stoke-by-Nayland,* Manet's *Jesus Mocked,* and Renoir's *Two Little Circus Girls,* are among the most famous paintings.

Some of the decorative arts collections are found in lower Gunsaulus Hall. Here the galleries are bright with English and Continental glass, pewter, American pottery, porcelain, wallpaper, and printed cottons.

The Alexander McKinlock, Jr. Memorial Court, in the center of the Hutchinson Wing, surrounds Carl Milles' *Triton Fountain.* The south half of the wing, together with the Allerton Wing, is given over mostly to European period rooms, furniture and rugs, metal and wood work, and textiles.

The north half houses the Oriental collection. The ceremonial bronze vessels are among the oldest existing works of Chinese art; other treasures are rare Cambodian sculptures, fine ceramics of various dynasties, and Mohammedan art objects. The history of Japanese prints is illustrated in the Buckingham collection.

The Henry Crown Gallery has a balcony railing of historic interest. It is made up of stair panels designed by Louis H. Sullivan for Carson, Pirie, Scott & Co. When the interior of the store was remodeled the panels were donated to the Art Institute.

The KENNETH SAWYER GOODMAN THEATRE in the Art Institute has been called "one of the busiest theatre centers in the country." It was designed by Howard Van Doren Shaw. Although it has only 784 seats and stage sets have to be installed sidewise, the theatre in a typical year gives approx. 800 performances by its performing components: the Resident Company, the Touring Company, the Children's Theatre and the Studio Theatre & Workshop. The Resident Company has 15 actors and three stage managers, and the Touring Company visits community and college theaters in Illinois, Indiana, and

Wisconsin. The playbill annually includes premieres, such as *The Night Thoreau Spent in Jail,* and *Assassination, 1865,* and repertory, including *Lady Audrey's Secret* and *Twelfth Night.* The Goodman is one of 44 resident theatres in the United States.

The Art Institute has plans, prepared by Skidmore, Owings & Merrill, to enlarge its physical plant by building several additions. These include galleries over the tracks of the Illinois Central Gulf north and south of Gunsaulus Hall, a new auditorium to replace Fullerton Hall, which was opened in 1898, and a building to house the School of the Art Institute. It also expects to mount a campaign for funds of approximately $50,000,000.

The SCHOOL OF THE ART INSTITUTE uses the facilities of the museum building in Grant Park and studios at 218 S. Wabash Ave. The School was founded as the Chicago Academy of Design in 1866, 16 years before the museum was organized. It gives the degree of bachelor of fine arts after a four-year course, and master of fine arts after two years of graduate work in design, crafts, films, painting, photography, printmaking, and sculpture. Provision is also made for those seeking a teaching career. Some of the liberal arts requirements may be filled by courses at the University of Chicago. There are also the Young Artists Studios, classes for children and high school students. Student tuition is $1,200 a year; room and board are $1,000 to $1,500. Incidental fees and supplies, including $300 at the University of Chicago, may run $500 to $800 additional.

The School has arranged with two South Side galleries to have students teach community art programs in black neighborhoods and explain opportunities for registration in the School. An arrangement also has been made with the Central YMCA College whereby students of the college may enroll for a degree of associate in art by including courses in the School of the Institute, and students of the latter may take academic courses at the college. Financial aid for Illinois students has been pushed up to $721,000 by the Illinois State Scholarship Commission, but cuts in Federal aid have curtailed scholarship help for out-of-state, foreign and graduate students.

Innovations at the School include affiliation with the Goodman School of Drama and Theatre Workshop, a kinetic art workshop, glass blowing, and the establishment of a gallery for exhibiting work of students and faculty called Wabash Transit.

The Institute annually receives numerous donations of works of art which enhance its collections in all categories. It arranges exhibitions, has a steady schedule of lectures by authorities, and cooperates with other museums to extend exhibitions to their communities. The Institute is handicapped by lack of exhibit space and need for more funds. However fine the exhibitions, they frequently show a deficit. In 1970-71 year the museum had 1,430,923 visitors; school attendance was 172,595, and the Goodman Theatre attracted 176,814. The programs of the Department of Museum Education included 1,990 lectures and an attendance of 186,897, an all-time high. During the year the Institute adopted a voluntary admissions policy, suggesting that nonmembers pay $1 for adults and 50¢ for children. The total collected in this way for six months was $185,000. *The museum is open daily 10-5 except Thursday, the free day, 10-8:30, and Sunday 1-6. It closes only on Christmas Day.*

South Michigan Ave., West Side

The CHURCH FEDERATION OF GREATER CHICAGO occupies the Lakeview Bldg., 116 S. Michigan Ave., which it purchased in 1962. It is the largest broadly-based ecumenical agency in the Chicago area, supporting programs to give aid to the needy, encourage business enterprises by minorities, provide legal aid clinics, extend the Christian ministry to migrant farm workers and Indians and has a counseling and job placement program for conscientious objectors. The Federation works with developers of new towns to provide interfaith services such as a day care center, pastoral visiting, community forums, arrangements for hospital needs, and ministry for youth. A conspicuous example was cooperation between churches when Park Forest South was begun as a planned community under the Federal Housing Act of 1970. Similarly the Federation organized a Protestant ministry for the employees of O'Hare Airport, with services, pastoral calls, communion breakfasts, and film showings. When a building at 2433 S. State St. was donated to the Federation it decided to make "an experiment in black capitalism," and let all goods and services be run by blacks.

The Chicago Institute of Pastoral Care is a division formed by the Federation in 1966; it offers personal, marital, and group counseling, regardless of religious affiliation. The Federation sponsors Chicago's Passion Play, formerly the Black Passion Play, and produces more than 200 television and 260 radio programs annually, including Everyman (WMAQ), Heritage of Faith and Chicago Church Hour (WGN) and Different Drums (WBBM).

The Church Federation works with an annual budget of about $300,000, which it derives from congregations, foundations, labor groups, and income from its office building. Donations are tax exempt.

The west side of Michigan Avenue has a variety of architectural styles. The PEOPLES GAS LIGHT & COKE COMPANY building at 122 S. Michigan Ave., is both a modern office structure of steel and windows and a throwback architecturally to the period when huge columns were considered imposing. The tall columns of polished granite that rise on Jackson Blvd. and the Avenue do not support any part of the building, only themselves. They have made show windows difficult. The Home Planning Bureau of the company shows new appliances and gives tips on housekeeping, Monday through Friday.

This side of the Avenue is also the place for hotels and clubs. The Chicago Athletic Club and the Illinois Athletic Club built tall structures that contain ball courts and gymnasia. At Monroe Street the tall, narrow University Club of Chicago rises in collegiate Gothic like a reminiscence of scholastic days; inside its dark wood trim conveys a monastic atmosphere. At the southwest corner of Van Buren Street stands the Chicago Club, rated as the most exclusive men's club, erected in the last decade of the 19th century by the tycoons of the time. Its style in solid brownstone blocks was designed by John Root along the lines of Richardson's Romanesque.

At 130 S. Michigan Ave. is the headquarters of the CHICAGO ASSOCIATION OF COMMERCE AND INDUSTRY, including the editorial offices of its official publication, *Commerce*. This is the city's largest research organization in the fields of trade and industry.

At 200 S. Michigan Ave. the Borg-Warner Corporation in 1958 erected its 22-story office building, occupying the corner of Adams St., north of Orchestra Hall, for many years the site of the Pullman Building, a familiar brownstone landmark.

Chicago Symphony Orchestra

ORCHESTRA HALL, 216 S. Michigan Ave., is the home of the Chicago Symphony Orchestra, the most influential and accomplished orchestral organization in Mid-America. This brick and limestone building in a subdued French Renaissance style, was designed by Daniel H. Burnham and completed in 1904 at a cost of $1,000,000. The hall seats 2,546 and is considered acoustically perfect. Approximately one-half of the cost was underwritten by the music-loving public as an expression of its regard for Theodore Thomas, founder and first conductor, whose name was originally attached to the orchestra. Thomas enjoyed the hall only one season. After his death in 1905 he was succeeded by the first violinist, Frederick Stock, who conducted for 37 seasons until his death in 1942, and built an extraordinary musical achievement. Among the musical directors who succeeded him were Fritz Reiner, Rafael Kubelik, and Jean Martinson. Georg Solti took the post in 1969. The regular season comprises concerts on Thursday evenings, Friday afternoons, and Saturday evenings. The orchestra also observes a June Festival and gives a series of concerts at Ravinia Park in August. When operas in concert form appear on the program the orchestra is augmented by the Chicago Symphony Chorus. This is the country's highest paid orchestra with a minimum of $380 a week.

An annual event at Orchestra Hall is the All-City High School Band, Chorus, and Orchestra Festival concert in June. The all-city groups were organized in 1963. They choose more than 400 high school students through city-wide auditions. Rehearsals are held throughout the year, and the whole organization and separate units have opportunities to perform on numerous occasions.

Orchestra Hall is the hub of an influential cultural enterprise. It is the headquarters also of the Symphony String Quartet, which gives recitals in the second floor foyer; the Chicago Symphony Chorus, and the Chicago Civic Orchestra, an organization for musicians in training for the Symphony Orchestra.

On the east side of Michigan Avenue is the Theodore Thomas Memorial, a half-draped figure in bronze symbolizing music. Behind it is granite seat with a bas relief of an orchestra grouped around a profile of the conductor. The bronze was designed by Albin Polacek in 1924.

The FINE ARTS BUILDING, 410 S. Michigan Ave., was built in 1884 and therefore is one of the oldest structures on the avenue. Solon S. Beman designed it. It contains the STUDEBAKER THEATER, as fine a stage of conventional proportions as any of those built later. Older Chicagoans recall that here were produced the musicals of Victor Herbert and Reginald de Koven; here Fritzi Scheff introduced her famous "Kiss Me Again" song and George Ade's comedies, *The College Widow* and others, found popular approval. The former Fine Arts Theater, holding about 100, is now called the World Playhouse.

In an imposing architectural setting is the Seated Lincoln, across Columbus Drive at the pedestrian extension of Van Buren St. One of the last of Augustus Saint-Gaudens' statues, it was completed in 1907, but was not placed until 1926.

At the east end of Congress Parkway stands the BUCKINGHAM MEMORIAL FOUNTAIN. Dedicated in 1927, the pink Georgia marble fountain was the gift of Miss Kate Buckingham in memory of her brother, Clarence Buckingham, a former trustee of the Art Institute. The main pool, 300 feet in diameter, contains four pairs of sea horses, facing the four states bordering Lake Michigan. For creating these fine figures, N. Marcel Loyau won the *Prix National*. In the center of the pool three concentric basins rise to a height of 25 feet, and from their outer rims spouts a series of diminishing water domes. A central column of water rises almost 100 feet above the apex of the highest dome. At night, hidden lights play colors on the spray. During displays the fountain shoots 15,500 gallons of water per minute from its 134 jets. It is twice the size of the Latona Fountain at Versailles, which in a measure inspired its design. The architects were Bennett, Parsons, & Frost, with Clarance Farrier and J. H. Lambert associates.

Adjoining the Buckingham Fountain is an area devoted to roses, where approximately 8,000 plants of 250 varieties, and countless numbers of blooms in season, are tended by Garfield Park Conservatory.

The Auditorium Building and Roosevelt University

The AUDITORIUM BUILDING, firmly anchored on Michigan Avenue at Congress Parkway, is a famous architectural landmark. Designed by Dankmar Adler and Louis H. Sullivan, it originally had three sections: a hotel fronting on Michigan Avenue, a great auditorium and stage for grand opera with its main entrance on Congress St., and a section for studios and offices, with the entrance on Wabash Avenue. In 1946 it became the seat of Roosevelt University.

The great hall was used in an incomplete state by the Republican Party's national convention that nominated Benjamin Harrison in the summer of 1888. It was formally opened December 9, 1889, and was the home of the Chicago Grand Opera Company, and the annual season of the Metropolitan Opera Company of New York, until 1929, when this function was displaced by the Civic Opera House, 20 North Wacker

Drive, built by Samuel Insull to enable its rental income to overcome the annual deficits of the opera. The great depression wrecked Insull's investments, and the removal wrecked the Auditorium, which went bankrupt in the late 1930's. During the war years it was the hq of the United Service Organization; in 1946 it was acquired by the newly organized Roosevelt University.

This is the best known of Louis Sullivan's buildings. Begun in 1887 and completed three years later, it is of masonry construction. Although Sullivan denied that he was influenced by H. H. Richardson, the Romanesque style is evident in the exterior, and Sullivan's partner, Dankmar Adler, admitted that alterations in the original plans were inspired in part by the Auditorium directors' admiration for Richardson's newly completed Marshall Field Wholesale Building, since demolished. The Auditorium is an excellent example of Sullivan's ambivalent theory of design. The massive and rather simple exterior illustrates his tenet that form should follow function, but throughout the interior examples of his intricate and graceful surface decorations abound. There are plaster reliefs in foliage designs; ornamentation is especially rich in the great series of arches in the auditorium proper.

Both the structural plans of the building and the complex acoustical design were drawn by Dankmar Adler. His solution of the construction problem posed by the massive tower was particularly ingenious. The foundation of the building is not on bedrock but on platforms of steel and concrete. Adler feared that the imposition of the heavy tower might cause uneven settling that would crack the masonry. By loading pig iron and bricks equal to the weight of the finished tower on the lower floors, he obtained an even settling before the masons had finished the body of the building and begun to erect the tower.

On the opening night, Dec. 9, 1889, 5,000 of Chicago's elite crowded into the Auditorium to hear Adeline Patti sing, in the presence of President Harrison and Governor Fifer of Illinois. At the inaugural ball of the World's Columbian Exposition, Oct. 1, 1892, Bertha Honore Palmer (Mrs. Potter Palmer), president of the Board of Lady Managers of the Exposition, led the festivities. She led them, as often later, in a great display of diamonds and pearls, which members of other wealthy families tried to match.

The return of the Auditorium Building to its rightful place as a monument to the greatness of Chicago is a romance of the modern age. This house was planned to be culturally useful and practical. On Feb. 16, 1923, the Chicago Opera Assn., lessees, sued the owners of the land to get the right to demolish the Auditorium and replace it with a 19-story office building. After two years of litigation Federal Judge James H. Wilkerson dismissed the suit on the ground that the building was a civic enterprise when built and the proposed replacement was solely a financial device. He was overruled by the Circuit Court of Appeals. The litigation was carried to the U. S. Supreme Court, which upheld Wilkerson and saved the Auditorium.

During these proceedings, which lasted five years, the Auditorium Theater was intermittently use by the Chicago opera and large-scale performances like Max Reinhardt's *The Miracle*. Samuel Insull, president of the opera association, in 1929 moved the organization to the Civic Opera House he had built at 20 Wacker Drive. The Auditorium was adjudged insolvent and a receiver was appointed. The building was rented for various purposes; during World War II the orchestra floor was used for bowling alleys by the Armed Services.

ROOSEVELT UNIVERSITY, originally College, was dedicated Nov. 15, 1945, by Mrs. Eleanor Roosevelt in the presence of city officials, leaders in social education, and sponsors. Its president and organizer was Edward J. Sparling and it had a most spectacular start. Dr. Sparling was president of Central Y. M. C. A. College when a controversy developed with its board over the proportion of black and white students in its enrollment. Dr. Sparling, rejecting any course that implied racial discrimination, resigned and a majority of the faculty left with him. Determined that Chicago should have a college where the doors were open to everyone without regard for color, creed, or sex, he hired a vacant building and announced formation of Roosevelt College, with a curriculum that promised full opportunity to study all the liberal issues of the day.

Followers of Franklin D. Roosevelt rallied at once to Sparling's support; they included Marian Anderson, Francis Biddle, Pearl S. Buck, Agnes DeMille, William O. Douglas, David Dubinsky, Murray D. Lincoln, Gunnar Myrdal, Vijaya Lakshmi Pandit, Frances Perkins, Jacob S. Potofsky, Walter Reuther, Irving Salomon, Adlai E. Stevenson, and James P. Warburg. The Julius Rosenwald Foundation pledged its support. Leaders of liberal causes were enheartened; conservatives feared the new college would be radical, socialist, and racially unbalanced.

In 1947 Dr. Sparling had sufficient backing to make a bid for the great Auditorium Building, which was only sporadically used. Its acquisition added greatly to the prestige as well as facilities of Roosevelt. Contrary to the fears of some educators that the college would be politically motivated or have low standards of admission Roosevelt developed a balanced curriculum. For admission it accepted students from the upper half of high school graduates if they had satisfactorily passed School and College Ability Tests, as well as tests provided by Roosevelt. By carefully screening applicants for evidence of ability to stay four years Roosevelt avoids possible dropouts. Both teachers and students may share in the policies of the school.

The university comprises the College of Arts and Sciences, the Walter E. Heller College of Business Administration, the Chicago Musical College, the College of Continuing Education, the College of Education, the Graduate Division, and the Labor Education Division. One of its degrees is bachelor of general studies, which includes courses often grouped under bachelor of arts.

In the College of Arts and Sciences special mention may be made of the American, African, Afro-American, Black, and Jewish Studies. For the latter, Roosevelt cooperates with the Spertus College of Judaica in a joint program. The Labor Education Division provides studies for union officers and members in such projects as collective bargaining, union administration, labor legislation, history, and others of like pertinence, moving into the social and political sciences. The College of Business Administration, in addition to providing fundamental studies in management stresses social responsibility and offers a cooperative program whereby the student in his junior and senior years may alternate periods of instruction with industrial employment, alternating four periods in school with three periods of employment.

The Murray-Green Library, on the tenth floor, was once the ballroom of the former Auditorium Hotel. It is open to the public for reference use. There were 216,000 vols. in 1972 and about 10,000 were being added annually; also 1,000 periodicals were received. The library has all forms of micro materials and earphone equipment for tapes and records.

In the meantime the theater was not used. In June, 1958, the Civic Opera was in financial trouble and there was talk of returning opera to the Auditorium. President Sparling saw an opportunity to help both the city and the university, and persuaded his board of trustees to offer the theater to the city as a civic enterprise, tax free and with no profit motive. They formed the Auditorium Theater Council, to raise funds and restore the hall. Mayor Richard J. Daley became honorary chairman, Harold W. Norman chairman, and Mrs. John V. Spachner co-chairman and principal fund raiser. Harry M. Weese, architect who had restored the Newberry Library, took on the restoration. By 1964 the work of uncovering the richness of the great hall, in which 4,200 listeners can hear perfectly every note of symphonic music or opera, was under way.

In 1970 the university opened the Herman Crown Center and Residence Hall, 14 floors adjoining the Auditorium Building on Wabash Ave. and providing 175 rooms for the possible accommodation of 350 students, with dining hall, lounge, and typing facilities, men occupying the lower floors, women the upper. To expand further the university built an 11-story addition inside the light well of the main building, an aperture long since superseded by modern ventilation and lighting.

In the 1972-73 school year Roosevelt enrolled 6,536 and had a faculty of 250. The forecast in some quarters that it would be predominantly black was unwarranted. Here, as elsewhere, the students registered according to their means, and racial discrimination was unknown.

Tours of university and theatre are available by reservation, students $1, visitors, $2.

The PICK-CONGRESS HOTEL, 520 South Michigan Ave., is considered a perfect example of the multiple bay window facade once favored by Chicago architects. Its first section was built in 1893 to supplement the accommodations of the Auditorium Hotel during the Columbian Exposition and was called the Annex. Under that name it became the rendezvous of Chicago society. Clinton J. Warren designed it. It had two additions, in 1902 and 1907, with Holabird & Roche as architects, and became the Congress. Its corridor became famous as

Peacock Alley. Its present title follows the hotel custom of identifying the operator or owner.

At the eastern end of Congress Parkway is a formal entrance to Grant Park, marked by stone pylons, bronze eagles by Frederick C. Hibbard, and two immense symbolic Indians on horses by Ivan Mestrovic.

Opposite the end of 9th St. on the east side of Michigan Ave. the equestrian statue of Major General John A. Logan stands on a mound sometimes referred to as the only hill in Chicago. The artist was Augustus St. Gaudens. Logan (1826-86) commanded the 31st Illinois Volunteer Infantry in the Civil War. His father was an early associate of Abraham Lincoln. As grand commander of the Grand Army of the Republic (G.A.R.) Logan instituted the first Memorial Day exercises.

Another Michigan Avenue office building has become an educational campus by the opening of the SPERTUS COLLEGE OF JUDAICA in the former IBM headquarters at 618 S. Michigan Ave. Long known as the College of Jewish Studies at 72 East 11th St., it now bears the name of the father of Maurice and Herman Spertus, brothers who long have been benefactors and board members. The Maurice Spertus Museum of Judaica was opened at the college in 1968, with more than 3,000 items of historic and ceremonial interest on display. Spertus is a liberal arts college of Judaica and Hebraica, which has cooperative teaching arrangements with the University of Chicago, the University of Illinois, and other leading institutions of this area.

The BLACKSTONE HOTEL, 636 S. Michigan Ave., at Balboa Drive, has been famous since it was built in 1910. It is a tall, narrow structure in the French mode of red brick, white quoins, and green mansard roof, and stands across the Drive from the Conrad Hilton. It was designed by Benjamin Marshall, who received the gold medal of the American Institute of Architects for this work. Until September, 1973, it was known as the Sheraton-Blackstone and owned by the Sheraton Corp. of America, a subsidiary of the ITT. Then it was bought for $5,000,000 by Mark Friedman, making the ninth hotel in the Chicago area built or acquired by him. This is the fifth time the hotel has changed owners. It was named after a prominent Chicago family that once lived on this site. It calls itself the Hotel of the Presidents and lists 11 Presidents, from Theodore Roosevelt to Richard Nixon, who have stayed there. It has an air of luxury with a decor of red and gold in the lobby and French white and gold in the upper corridors. Friedman has restored the original name and is using the Blackstone family crest on all services. West of the hotel on Balboa Dr. is the BLACKSTONE THEATRE, which Marshall & Fox built in 1911.

The CONRAD HILTON, 720 S. Michigan Ave., faces Grant Park for the length of a block between Balboa Drive and 8th St., and with nearly 3,000 rooms is usually considered the world's largest hotel. It is also a community in itself, with its ground floor filled with restaurants, shops, airline offices and agencies of various services. Its lobby is filled daily with milling groups of ticketed men and women who come to attend national and regional conventions of organizations that hold formal sessions in its large halls. It was designed by Holabird & Roche and completed in 1927 as the Stevens.

The CHICAGO WOMAN'S CLUB BUILDING, 72 E. 11th St., was designed by Holabird and Root and completed in 1928. Graceful ornament in a sophisticated modern style embellishes the building. Notable features of the interior are the little theater, and the Tudor Gallery, used for one-man shows by Chicago artists.

Field Museum of Natural History

Facing Roosevelt Road, overlooking the entire length of Grant Park, is the broad facade of the FIELD MUSEUM OF NATURAL HISTORY. The museum houses a vast and constantly growing collection of exhibits of anthropology, zoology, botany, and geology. More than 13,000,000 specimens, gathered by expeditions, exchange, purchase, and gifts, form the backbone of the Museum's interrelated functions—research, education, and exhibition. Founded in 1893 after the Columbian Exposition, it was endowed by a number of prominent citizens, led by Marshall Field, I. To his initial gift of $1,000,000 he added more than $400,000 during his life, and at his death in 1906 bequeathed $8,000,000. Until 1921, when the present building was opened, the museum was housed in the Palace of Fine Arts in Jackson Park. Nucleus collections were exhibits transferred from the exposition, purchases, and private gifts, notably an anthropological collection by Edward E. Ayer.

Special exhibits augment the regular collections. The Foundation for Illinois Archaeology was responsible for the one called A New Spirit in Search of the Past; Archaeology and Ecology in Lower Illinois River Valley; new discoveries at the Koster site. An exhibit was based on plates of John James Audubon's Elephant Folio. An Anniversary Exhibit, celebrated the 75 years of the museum's existence.

The massive white Georgia marble building was designed by Daniel H. Burnham, and completed after his death by Graham, Anderson, Probst, and White. Its architecture is pure Greek Ionic, with some of its details following the Erechtheum in Athens. A great flight of steps leads to the majestic pedimented portico, two rows of columns in depth. This is flanked by long wings, four stories high, that are decorated with Ionic colonnades ending in transverse halls.

The main hall, known as Stanley Field Hall, rises unbroken to the roof. The heart of the museum, it contains exhibits drawn from the divisions of the museum.

The North and South doors lead to the first floor. There is a ground floor where, besides such services as cafeteria, wardrobe and lounge, there are exhibits of Melanesian, Polynesian, Micronesian, African and Madagascar cultures, ancient Egyptians, Romans, and Stone Age men.

The Egyptian collection includes reproductions of the Rosetta stone and papyri, but most of the articles are originals, including a funeral barge 3,800 years old. One of the rare items is the body of a woman preserved in sand for more than 6,000 years. It antedates the period when bodies were mummified. The hall devoted to Stone Age relics contains dioramas of prehistoric scenes, with life-size figures. Adjacent to each diorama are authentic artifacts, and animal and human remains of the period, including the Cap Blanc skeleton.

The first floor has seven halls devoted to Indians of the Americas, offering a remarkable comprehensive display of the artifacts and habiliments of a vast population that once covered the continent. Here, too, are mammals of the world. In the middle of the west wing a staircase leads to the James Simpson Theatre and Lecture Hall.

The first floor of the west wing has the Department of Zoology's habitat animal groups. The sculptural methods of taxidermy, principally devised by Carl Akeley, account for the life-like appearance of the specimens. Hall 22, which includes some of Akeley's best work, contains all major African species of mammals. Several series of habitat groups, include groups of American mammals and birds. In the Hall of Domestic Mammals, west of the main stairway, is an unusual exhibit of quarter-sized statues, modeled by Herbert Haseltine from prize-winning livestock.

The H. N. Higinbotham Hall of gems and jewels, west of the main stairway on the second floor, contains examples of almost every known gem, including the famous Sun God opal and the De Vrees engraved diamond. Most of the other exhibits on this floor are devoted to China and Tibet, with a fine jade collection in Hall 30.

Botany occupies the second floor of the east wing. The Hall of Plant Life offers a view of the entire range from the lowest orders, such as bacteria and fungi, up through the flowering plants. Two halls are devoted to general economic botany—food products, palms, and plant raw materials. Nearby are halls showing varieties of wood from all over the world. Many of the botanical exhibits, skillfully processed in wax, glass, and celluloid in the museum's laboratory, cannot be distinguished from natural specimens.

Geology occupies the second floor of the west wing. Crystals, meteorites, and a systematic display of minerals are in Hall 35; the meteorites, with specimens from more than two-thirds of the known meteorite falls, includes one weighing 3,336 pounds. In the Ernest R. Graham Hall of Historical Geology is traced the development of life from earliest times to the present. A huge skeleton of a dinosaur of the species *Apatosaurus*, surrounded by other fossil reptiles, as well as mammals and birds, forms one of the exhibits. A series of murals by Charles R. Knight around the hall depicts various prehistoric animals as they probably appeared in life. There are also several life-size three-dimensional restorations by the sculptor Frederick Blaschke. Exhibits in Hall 34 illustrate geologic processes. Relief maps in the corridor represent the Chicago area in various stages following the glacial period.

Specimens and models in Hall 36 illustrate the occurrence, processing, and utilization of petroleum, coal, clay, and various ores.

Field Museum is open daily at 9, except Christmas Day and New Year's. Adults $1; families with children, $2.50; children, students, senior citizens, 35¢. Friday free. Free daily to teachers, military personnel, children under 6.

John G. Shedd Aquarium

At the east end of Field Museum a pedestrian subway leads under Lief Eriksen Drive to the JOHN G. SHEDD AQUARIUM. The Aquarium was endowed in 1924 with a gift of more than $3,000,000 by John G. Shedd, a Marshall Field executive. The displays of live fish and aquatic animals attracted 4,700,000 visitors in 1931, the first year after the aquarium was completed.

The many-sided white Georgia marble building, of simple Doric design, is effectively set in a terrace at the water's edge. The architects, Graham, Anderson, Probst, and White, used marine symbols throughout the decorations. Outside, this is seen in the wave-like cresting and the trident of Neptune on the pyramidal roof. Inside, a marble wainscoting has markings that give a wave effect and the clock in the foyer, which substitutes aquatic figures for numerals, is typical of the imaginative use of water symbols. In the center of the rotunda is a rockery with a swamp pool, in which carp wind in and out among tree stumps that serve as resting places for turtles and frogs.

Six main galleries radiate from the rotunda. The symbols that identify the majority of the exhibits are coded with the comprehensive guidebook; the numbers indicate the family and species of the fish; the colored oblong denotes the kind of water from which it was taken. Special attention is given to reproducing the appearance and conditions found in the natural habitats of the specimens.

As many of the fish cannot live long in captivity, there is constant fluctuation in the number of kinds of fish exhibited, but there are always many varieties of gorgeously colored and curiously shaped specimens from the warmer waters. American game fish, and the odd rays, eels, sharks, lungfish, and sea horses. Such invertebrates as shrimps, star fish, and sea anemones, are usually represented. Here is the octopus, a spineless eight-armed, primeval creature with relatives dating back 400 million years. This softbodied animal squirts a thick black fluid at enemies, then changes color and darts to safety.

Swimming in slow, undulating motions is characteristic of the South American arowana. His bony tongue is equipped with spikes for holding food, while two barbels on the jaw touch the water surface to "sense" food.

Crustaceans are also a part of the Aquarium's collection. The blue crab has five pairs of legs with paddles on the rear pair to allow him to swim in any direction. A native of the east coast of the United States, the crab is usually caught with traps or nets and is prized as a gourmet food.

The Coral Reef is a jewel from the sea studded with 1,000 colorful Caribbean fish. A dazzling array of over 75 species of fish set against a background of corals, sea fans, sponges and sea whips. This exhibit demonstrates the inter-relationship of varied life forms on a reef.

Delicate French angelfish and damselfish find protection within the branching coral. Schools of chubs, grunts and spadefish cruise the open water of the reef, avoiding the silvery barracuda. Lurking in the corals are ominous green moray eels. Triggerfish, Nassau groupers, striped burrfish, tarpon, porkfish and snappers are also members of the family. Every day of the week a diver enters the Reef and hand feeds the lively community.

Adler Planetarium and Astronomical Museum

Southeast of the Aquarium over a causeway is Northerly Island, officially a separate park; on its northeast corner stands the ADLER PLANETARIUM AND ASTRONOMICAL MUSEUM. The approach to the building is along a broad esplanade, which has a series of twelve cascading pools in the center. On the bottom of each pool is the zodiacal symbol of one of the twelve months. The building, designed by Ernest Grunsfeld, Jr., follows no historical style but achieves a monumental effect by its mass and its plain surfaces of rich rainbow granite. It is in the form of a regular dodecagon, topped with a circular dome of green copper. Bronze plaques of the twelve signs of the zodiac by Alfonso Iannelli are inset at the exterior corners. The gift of Max Adler, Chicago merchant-executive, the Planetarium was dedicated in 1930, the first in the western hemisphere. It is operated by the commissioners of the Park District. When the Planetarium needed more space for its activities it built a new extension underground at a cost of $3,500,000. C. F. Murphy Associates were the architects.

In the Sky Theatre on the Upper Level are reproduced the intricate phenomena of the heavens. Chairs arranged in concentric circles provide a comfortable view. The projection instrument, a highly complex machine weighing more than two tons was made by Carl Zeiss Company of West Germany. More than 100 lenses stud its exterior and cast images of all visible heavenly bodies on a linen screen shaped in the form of a dome. The motor-driven projector, moving on its various axes, enable the lecturer to show four types of apparent celestial motion: the change of latitude; the diurnal motion; the interlocked motion of the sun, moon and planets; and the processional cycle. Thus the heavens can be viewed as they appear from any spot on earth, at any time. The day, year, and even the processional cycle can be shortened to seconds by means of controls on the lecturer's desk. For sheer drama and realism the demonstrations are superb. The 500th birthday anniversary of Nicholas Copernicus was observed in 1973 when the Planetarium reviewed the changes in knowledge of the solar system from his time to the present.

The Lower Level of the building has a lecture hall and the Hall of Telescopes. The line of astronomical observations from Ptolemy and Galileo to a modern neutrino telescope located deep in a gold mine can be seen here. Highlights include one of the telescopes used by Sir William Herschel, discoverer of Uranus; the original tube of the 18½-inch Dearborn refractor, and working models of the 200-inch Hale telescope and the 140-foot Green Bank radio telescope. The new fields of radio, infrared, ultraviolet, X-ray, cosmic ray, and gravity wave astronomy are represented.

The sun and other stars are featured in a new exhibit area where the visitor may view types of solar telescopes, a solar eclipse, and surface features and the "lifetime" of the sun. On clear days during the summer months the Planetarium's solar telescope projects a one-foot image of the sun. Additional exhibits show the size, brightness, distance, motion, surface temperature, and chemical make-up of various stars.

The Planetarium owns a world-famous collection of antique astronomical, navigational, mathematical, and engineering instruments dating from 1131 A.D. to the present. Planetaria, astrolabes, sundials, nocturnals, timekeeping devices, and surveying instruments are displayed.

The underground Astro-Science Center contains the Universe Theatre, classrooms, a library, a bookstore, and a vast space-age exhibition arcade including a Lunar Lander, Rover, and Surveyor.

Adler Planetarium has classes for adults and youths. Astronomy and navigation are taught. College credit is given for some of the courses. Making a telescope mirror is taught on an individual basis. The school year is from September 1 through June 15 and elementary and high school groups make reservations for the Sky shows. The Planetarium is open from 9:30 to 4:30 except on Tuesday and Friday when it is open to 9:30 p.m. Admission to the exhibits is free; to the Sky Theatre 75¢ for adults, 35¢ for ages 6-17.

The BAND SHELL is located facing south north of Roosevelt Road and equidistant between the East and West segments of Lake Shore Drive in Grant Park. Concerts are given on Wednesday, Friday, Saturday, and Sunday evenings for 8 weeks beginning late in June.

At a corner of West Drive and Roosevelt Road stands a statue of Christopher Columbus by Carlo Brioschi, presented by citizens of Italian ancestry.

Grant Park also serves the public below the street level in ten underground garages with space for 10,000 motor cars. The first, opened in September, 1954, has two levels and was financed by a bond issue for $8,300,000. The second was opened in 1965. Escalators on the west side of Michigan Ave. give drivers access. Most of the later garages have been built between E. 14th Blvd. and McCormick Place, providing parking space for the latter area.

SOUTH SIDE

South Lake Shore Drive

When the South Lake Shore Drive reaches Roosevelt Road it faces the Greek facade of the Field Mueum of Natural History and turns right, while its eastern lane passes the John G. Shedd Aquarium and as Achsam Bond Drive, named for the wife of Shadrach Bond, the State's first governor, reaches Adler Planetarium and the entrance to Northerly Island, on which are located Merrill C. Meigs Field and Roosevelt Road Beach.

BURNHAM PARK begins at 14th Blvd. and the Lake and extends south to 56th St. where Jackson Park begins. The second largest of the Chicago Parks, it realizes Daniel H. Burnham's plan for the recovery of the lake front from the right-of-way of the Illinois Central

Railroad by building east of the tracks a strip of beaches and greenery one-eighth of a mile wide and five miles long, a total of 598 acres. At the beginning of the park is the Administration Building of the Chicago Park District, completed in 1939.

South of 14th Blvd. is SOLDIER FIELD, the great amphitheater built 1922-28 at a cost of $8,200,000. It is 890 ft. long and 30 ft. wide, and can accommodate 100,000 spectators. It has been the scene of major civic and other events, including the 28th Eucharistic Congress in 1926 and the second Dempsey-Tunney fight in 1927. East and south of Soldier Field is space for parking nearly 6,000 motor cars.

East of Burnham Park is the BURNHAM PARK YACHT HARBOR, formed by NORTHERLY ISLAND, a peninsula extending south from Achsan Bond Drive to a point opposite McCormick Place. This is 91 acres of made land that served in 1933-34 as the principal site of the Century of Progress Exposition. The small park at the north has the 12th St. beach. The island is wholly used by the MERRILL C. MEIGS FIELD, the third of the city's airports.

Near the south end of Soldier Field where the parking area begins is Waldron Drive, which, if continued across the railroad tracks would come to the spot where E. 18th St. turns south and becomes Prairie Ave. This is the general site of the FORT DEARBORN MASSACRE of August 15, 1812, and here for many years stood a bronze monument commemorating an episode in the slaughter. The memorial since has been removed to the Chicago Historical Society in Lincoln Park. At 1801 Prairie Ave. is the W. W. KIMBALL MANSION, built in 1887 and designed by Solon S. Beman after a 16th century chateau in Brittany. Kimball became wealthy as a manufacturer of pianos but died six months after building his chateau. It was lived in many years by his surviving family, which gave recitals on its pipe organ.

The GLESSNER HOUSE, 1800 Prairie Ave., seat of the Chicago School of Architecture Foundation, survives from the days when this area was the fashionable dwelling place of Chicago's wealthy families, including those of Marshall Field, George M. Pullman, Phillip D. Armour, and T. O. Blackstone. It was designed in 1888 by Henry H. Richardson, Boston architect of the Romanesque style, and is the only remaining example of his work in Chicago.

Its builder, John J. Glessner, was a vice president of the International Harvester Co. who paid $75,000 for a house of 35 rooms, built of solid granite in Richardson's best fortress style. The house stands flush on the corner of East 18th St. and Prairie Ave., whereas all the other Prairie Ave. houses of Chicago's wealthy merchants were set back. Glessner's garden was in the back and is now being restored. When Glessner died in 1932 he willed his house to the Chicago Chapter of the American Institute of Architects. The architects found the house too expensive to keep; it went to the Illinois Institute of Technology, which sold it in 1958 to the Graphic Arts Technical Foundation. This in turn sold it in 1966 to the Chicago School of Architecture Foundation for $35,000, largely through the efforts of Philip Johnson, early associate of Mies van der Rohe. Others have rallied to restore and rehabilitate the house and by 1973 $200,000 had been expended out of a needed $350,000 for this purpose.

Open Tues., Thurs., Saturday, 10-5; Sunday 1-5. (admission fee). The Foundation also conducts bus tours of historic buildings of the Chicago school, including those of Frank Lloyd Wright.

McCormick Place

McCORMICK PLACE, East 23d St. and the Lake Front, completed in 1970, is the second great convention and exposition structure erected on this site. It commemorates Robert R. McCormick (1880-1955) editor and publisher of the *Chicago Tribune.* The first building was destroyed by fire January 16, 1967. The new one, designed by C. F. Murphy Associates, is modified from the original. It takes the form of two buildings with a mall between them, the whole under one roof covering 19 acres. The largest of exposition areas, it has three exhibition halls on three levels, with 700,000 sq. ft. for exhibits and a similar area for conferences and meeting rooms. There are nine public eating facilities that can serve 2,000 regularly and there are facilities for handling banquets for 20,000 at one sitting. Its garage has room for 2,000 vehicles and the parking area outside can hold 9,000. In the south section is the ARIE CROWN THEATRE, seating 5,000. One of the largest of annual events is the Motor Car show in February. The Lake Shore Drive passes in front of the Place.

McCORMICK INN is a new 650-room hotel erected adjacent to McCormick Place to accommodate exhibitors and others who flock to the expositions. It uses a five-acre tract and the building stands above the right-of-way of the Illinois Central Railroad. Construction cost $30,000,000. It is a unit in the Aristocrat Inns of America. When caissons were sunk in 1970 the owners asked about 100 countries to send containers of their earth, to be placed in the caissons to continue an ancient European custom by which a traveler leaving his own country carried a bit of native soil with him. The hotel has three restaurants, health exercise and swimming facilities, and inside parking for 1,000 cars.

On the mainland at 22nd St. and the Lake is the LAKESIDE PRESS, home office of R. R. Donnelley & Sons Co., the largest commercial printing house. It traces its beginnings to 1884 and its present corporate title to 1892. It has four plants and 2,330,000 sq. ft. in use in Chicago and five plants in other states, and employs more than 12,000. Its output is greatly diversified; it prints telephone directories for about 1,000 municipalities, parts of the editions of mail-order catalogues for Sears, Roebuck & Co., and J. C. Penney Co.; the bulk of editions of the *Farm Journal, Fortune, National Geographic, New Yorker, Time,* and *Sports Illustrated;* textbooks and financial reports. The Lakeside Series of historical works long has been in high repute. Donnelley was the printer of *Look* and *Life,* and when these publications closed down, *Life* after 36 years of weekly issues, Donnelley is said to have lost 8% of its printing volume and released 800 employees. (*Commerce*).

The Donnelley Memorial Library and the Central Reference Library are located at the Press. The former has 10,000 volumes, including examples of the graphic arts from many lands.

Chicago is one of the great printing capitals of the world. Besides Donnelley it has a dozen other houses of national reputation, including the W. F. Hall Printing Co., 4600 West Diversey Ave., which calls itself the greatest printing plant for paperback books, catalogues and magazines; Cuneo Press, 2242 S. Grove St.; Regensteiner Public Enterprises, 1224 W. Van Buren St., Gunthrop-Warren Printing Co., 123 N. Wacker Dr., and many others.

The STEPHEN A. DOUGLAS MONUMENT is located in a small park at the eastern end of 35th St., beyond Cottage Grove Ave., and bounded by the tracks of the Illinois Central Gulf Railroad. It is a formal classical column rising 100 ft. above the ground, at the top of which is a 12-ft. bronze statue of Douglas. It consists of a circular base, 52 ft. in diameter, from which steps rise to a tomb, 20 ft. square, inside of which is a marble sarcophagus containing the body of Douglas. At four corners of the tomb are seated figures representing Illinois, Justice, History, and Eloquence. A pedestal and column rise 65 ft. above the tomb. The monument was designed by Leonard W. Volk, famous as the sculptor of Lincoln.

Efforts to raise a monument began a few months after Douglas' death in 1861. Because of his great popularity the promoters expected contributions of $1 each from individuals would cover the cost, but the response was so slight that the State Assembly had to be asked for funds. In the next few years the Douglas acreage was sold to satisfy a debt of nearly $84,000. A camp for Confederate prisoners was built on part of it west of the present Cottage Grove Ave. and named Camp Douglas. In 1864 Leonard W. Volk's design was accepted.

The 2⅕ acres now constituting the park in which the monument stands were part of prairie land bought by Douglas in 1849. The land began south of 31st St. In 1856 Douglas gave 10 acres to the original Chicago University, of which he was the first president. Near the southeastern part of the tract that he called Cottage Grove he erected a one-story frame house that cost $1,200. Douglas died in Tremont House, on Lake St. in Chicago, on June 3, 1861, after four weeks of illness. He was at the height of his fame, for as a leader of the Democratic Party he had repudiated the secession acts of the Southern Democrats, and called on everyone to support the Union. He had sat on the platform during Lincoln's inauguration as President, and by this act indicated his determination to oppose disunion. His funeral was made the occasion of a great public demonstration. Veterans, Masonic lodges, firemen's organizations, patriotic societies took part in a procession that extended for two miles from the City Hall. A Roman Catholic bishop and Masonic officials led the ceremonies. He was buried on his grounds until the monument was completed.

The biggest public demonstration came at the laying of the corner-stone on September 6, 1866, when about 100,000 attended. President Andrew Johnson and Secretaries Seward and Welles were present, also Generals Grant, Rawlins, Meade, Custer, Steelman and Rousseau, and Admirals Farragut and Radford. General John A. Dix made the oration. Another less pretentious ceremony was held on June 3, 1868, when the casket was placed in the tomb and the public was permitted to view the features of Douglas through a glass top.

The monument was not considered finished until Aug. 18, 1891. By that time it had cost $96,350, most of it contributed by the State. In 1954 the monument was thoroughly renovated and repaired. It is maintained by the State Division of Parks and Memorials and is illuminated by floodlights.

During the Civil War CAMP DOUGLAS, a prison for Confederate soldiers, was established on 42 acres of land sliced from the estate of Stephen A. Douglas west of Cottage Grove Ave. and south of the present 31st St. It extended west to the present Martin Luther King Drive and south to 36th St. Barracks were built and until February, 1862, 25,000 U. S. recruits were trained there. The main gate was near 32nd St. on Cottage Grove and was guarded by six soldiers with fixed bayonets. There was a tall tower for observation opposite the gate and a 14-ft. high fence three miles long.

Confederate prisoners began to come Mar. 1, 1862, when 7,850 captured at Fort Donelson arrived. The numbers varied but in December, 1864, they had moved up to 12,082. The quarters were also used for temporary accommodation of Union soldiers paroled by Confederates and on the way to noncombatant duties. Disease and death took a large toll; over 3,100 prisoners died. In February, 1863, temperatures reached 40° below zero. The authorities kept up a running fight against insanitation, vermin, lack of heat, cheating by food suppliers, and attempts to escape. Since the soil was sandy, tunnelling under the big fence was not difficult, but escaping prisoners were often caught. Attempts of a Copperhead group to lead an uprising known as the Northwest Conspiracy were thwarted by the informers who had infiltrated their ranks. (Data compressed from *Journal* of the Illinois State Historical Society, Spring, 1960).

HARPER SQUARE, a high-rise apartment development, of 606 units, rises at 47th St. and Lake Park Ave., at the northern boundary of the Hyde Park-Kenwood Conservation Area.

HARPER COURT is a group of three low buildings on a sunken court at E. 52nd St. and Harper Ave. in an urban renewal area opened for storekeepers and tenants on July 29, 1965. It is supported by the Harper Court Foundation, a community enterprise headed by Muriel Beadle (Mrs. George W. Beadle) and comprising members of the faculty and alumni of the University of Chicago. There are 27 units occupied, among others, by a bookseller, a candlemaker, a pet shop, a fabrics shop, a fret shop (guitars), three galleries and a restaurant. The sponsors hoped the Court would become a sort of literary-art colony reminiscent of the one that grew informally in old one-story stores at E. 57th St. and Stony Island Ave. in the 1910-20 period. The 57th St. oasis, built for the World's Fair of 1893 and razed in recent years, became famous for Margerv Currey's "salon," where gathered Floyd Dell, Sherwood Anderson, Theodore Dreiser, Arthur D. Ficke, Edgar Lee Masters, Ben Hecht, Maurice Browne, Margaret Anderson, and some of the free spirits of the university. The fret shop of Harper Court had been among the last few denizens of 57th St.

JACKSON PARK

JACKSON PARK was an area of more than 500 acres of scrub oaks, swampy soil and underbrush when Chicago officially outbid New York, St. Louis and Washington, D. C. for the World's Columbian Fair and Exposition, to commemorate the discovery of America by Columbus in 1492. Chicago business leaders raised $5 million and sold another $5 million worth of stock, while the U. S. Government appropriated $1,500,000. With Daniel H. Burnham as Chief of Construction, top architects from Chicago and the East converted the park into a fairyland of Graeco-Roman pillars, domes and vast halls holding extraordinary examples of art and industry from all over the world. The White City electrified the Middle West; it stirred the pride and ambition of Chicago and built a reputation that lingers on.

Today this most beautiful of parks contains few relics of those great days of '93. Buildings had been built of a plaster composition called staff, of no permanent value, but the fair administration decided to retain one building—the sprawling Palace of Art now the Museum of Science and Industry, described above. Other relics of the Fair are the brick shelter at the northeast point of the park, the rebuilt convent of La Rabida, and the restored Japanese house on Wooded Island, which was damaged by vandals during World War II. The Statue of the Republic stands on the approximate location where the original stood during the Fair.

The World's Fair was a great eye-opener for Americans and Europeans. It was held during the last phase of the horse-and-buggy age, when communications were extremely restricted and travel was only by rail and steamship. The internal combustion engine was about to change American life, for the first American automobile, by the Duryea brothers, was to have its first successful demonstration in September, 1893—though not at the Fair. (The first exhibit was at the Omaha Fair, 1898). There was an International Conference on Aerial Navigation that foreshadowed the practical airplane, but Kitty Hawk was still ten years away. However, the future was knocking at the gates—especially when the steam power needed at the Fair was raised by oil heat, piped all the way from Whiting, Indiana, to a 600-ft. bank of furnaces.

The most powerful engine to run the dynamos was the Allis quadruple expansion and condensing unit of 3,000 hp. Edison's incandescent globes burned on all cornices and pinnacles, but they needed frequent replacement. Exciting to visitors was the long distance telephone, even though it required cranking to ring a bell and an exasperating repetition of "Speak louder, please!"

The MUSEUM OF SCIENCE AND INDUSTRY, E. 57th St. and South Lake Shore Dr., in Jackson Park, is considered the most comprehensive exhibition of mechanical accomplishments ever gathered for display. Thus it becomes an auxiliary of general education and culture, appealing to young and old, who account for 5,000,000 annual visitors. It occupies a building of pure Greek elements that was erected in plaster as the Palace of Fine Arts of the World's Columbian Exposition of 1893, and reproduced in stone in 1926-33.

After the Field Museum of Natural History had vacated the art palace in Jackson Park no further use for it was in view, and as it was obviously deteriorating, the proposal to demolish it gained support in the South Park District. About this time an unforeseen incident led to its preservation. Julius Rosenwald, head of Sears, Roebuck & Co., known for his social philanthropy, recently had visited the Deutsches Museum in Munich and become enthusiastic over its technological and scientific exhibits. He proposed a similar museum for Chicago and in 1926 donated $3,000,000 to that end. The need for large quarters suggested the possible use of the crumbling art palace. When this was agreed on the South Park board allocated a $5,000,000 bond issue for reconstruction. The structure was stripped of its plaster cover and given a coat of stone; its walls and floors were strengthened with steel beams and in 1933 the replica of classical architecture opened as a museum of the technological age. Another $3,000,000 was expended to complete it and eventually Rosenwald's contribution exceeded $7,000,000.

The full-size exhibits include the German submarine U-505, the Empire Express locomotive that achieved 112½ mph in 1893, the Santa Fe 340-ton locomotive, the first Zephyr streamliner of the Burlington Ry. 1934-60, and a reproduction of a Southern Illinois coal mine in full operation. There are sections of airplanes, a steel mill, a blacksmith shop, an apothecary's shop, a modern kitchen, the makings of a newspaper, and exemplifications of the human heart, the human anatomy, sound and music, light, photography, natural gas energy, and communicative devices, such as the picturephone, which transmits a picture of a phone user. Colleen Moore's Doll House is favored by small children. Besides 14 acres of permanent exhibits the museum has frequent seasonal features and displays by the U. S. Atomic Energy Commission, the National Aeronautics & Space Administration and foreign governments. *Admission is free, except to the Coal Mine, adults 45c, children, 25c; U-505, same; nickelodeon, 5c. Open daily except on Christmas Day. Summer: 9:30-5:30, Monday through Saturday; 10-6, Sunday and holidays. Winter: 9:30-4, Monday through Saturday; 10-6, Sunday and holidays. Parking free.*

LA RABIDA CHILDREN'S HOSPITAL AND RESEARCH CENTER stands on a spur of land in Jackson Park overlooking the lake at the easternmost end of 65th St. The nucleus was a temporary wooden building erected for the World's Fair of 1893 and meant to represent the convent of La Rabida in Spain, where Columbus found shelter. The original building was retained until it burned down; then

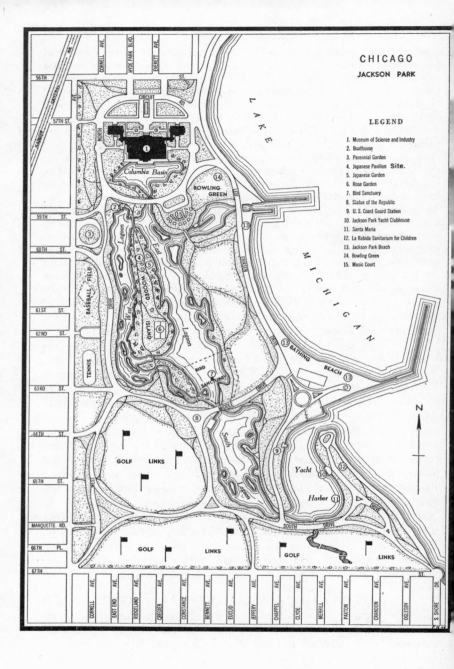

CHICAGO
JACKSON PARK

LEGEND

1. Museum of Science and Industry
2. Boathouse
3. Perennial Garden
4. Japanese Pavilion Site.
5. Japanese Garden
6. Rose Garden
7. Bird Sanctuary
8. Statue of the Republic
9. U. S. Coast Guard Station
10. Jackson Park Yacht Clubhouse
11. Santa Maria
12. La Rabida Sanitarium for Children
13. Jackson Park Beach
14. Bowling Green
15. Music Court

was reproduced with much embellishment and fully equipped for its present humanitarian services. It has about 600 admissions annually and a staff of 195. The research part includes the Lawrence Mercer Pick Memorial Library of 2,000 vols.

The MIDWAY PLAISANCE is a mile-long strip of trees and highways separated by a central sunken area of lawn, which extends from Jackson Park at 59th St. to Washington Park at Cottage Grove Ave. During the World's Fair of 1893 this strip was given over to amusements and informal theaters, displays, and exhibits, such as Blarney Castle, Kilauea volcano, Hagenbeck's trained animals, and Eskimo, German and other foreign villages, which set the pattern for subsequent expositions. The Streets of Cairo became notorious, but a sensation was caused by the original Ferris Wheel, designed by George W. Ferris, an Illinois engineer, and built by a Pittsburgh bridge-building firm. The great wheel was 250 ft. tall, 30 ft. wide, and 320 ft. in circumference. It carried 36 large cabins, each holding 40 passengers. In operation the cars moved up as they were being loaded; when all were full the wheel made one complete revolution, then resumed the process of reloading. It stood near the end of University Ave., opposite Foster Hall of the University.

At the eastern end of the Midway stands the equestian effigy of the Knight of Blanik, legendary hero of the Czech people, erected in 1949 to commemorate Thomas G. Masaryk, first president of the Republic of Czechoslovakia, by Chicago citizens of Czech descent.

Stony Island Avenue is the west boundary of Jackson Park. On the east side a short distance south of 63rd St. stood the Cold Storage Refrigeration plant, a Fair exhibit. It burned down in the fall of 1893 and firemen, caught in a tower as the flames spread below them, died there.

On the north side of 63rd St., about 75 ft. west of Stony Island Ave. stood the COLISEUM, where the Democratic Party convention of 1896 nominated William Jennings Bryan for President after he had rocked the delegates with his "cross of gold" speech.

The southern end of Jackson Park has a golf course, tennis courts, and yacht harbors along the lake. The Lake Shore Drive ends in the Coast Guard Drive, and the U. S. Coast Guard Station is located at the Yacht Harbor. Here are the Southern Shore Yacht Club, the Jackson Park Yacht Club, and the East 67th St. beach. South of the Park the South Shore Drive runs west of the South Shore Country Club and its private beach. At East 75th St. and the Drive is Rainbow Park and at E. 79th St. the South District Filtration Plant extends along the lake.

The PROMONTORY APARTMENTS building, 5530 South Shore Dr., built in 1949, is interesting architecturally because of the participation of Mies van der Rohe in the design. Others were Pace Associates and Holsman, Holsman & Klekamp. Its columns are stepped back at the sixth, eleventh, and 16th stories. There are panels of light-colored brick and aluminum window frames.

The University of Chicago

Address and telephone: The University of Chicago, 5801 Ellis Ave., Chicago, Illinois, 60637. Area code 312, 753-1234.

How to get there: By Illinois Central Railroad to 57th St. or 59th St. stations. By Bus No. 4 from Wabash Ave. in the Loop to 55th St. Also Bus No. 55, E. 55th St.; Bus No. 59, E. 61st St.; Bus No. 28, Lake Park and Stony Island Ave. By car, Lake Shore Dr. to Midway, then west.

Parking: Both sides of Midway and other city streets. Pay parking all day behind Center for Continuing Education, 60th St. between Kimbark and Kenwood Aves. Metered parking Ellis Ave. 57th to 59th Sts.

Information: Administration Bldg., 5801 Ellis Ave., 753-2381. Has student addresses. Conference information, Center for Continuing Education, 753-3184.

Meals: Hutchinson Commons, cafeteria; International House, cafeteria; Woodward Commons, cafeteria; Center for Continuing Education, dining room and cafeteria.

Hospitals and clinics: 950 E. 59th St., Chicago, Illinois, 60637. Phone 947-1000.

Campus tours: Saturdays at 10 a.m. from Ida Noyes Hall, 1212 East 59th St. Group tours on other days by reservation, phone 753-4429.

The best way to approach the University of Chicago is from the Illinois Central stop at East 57th St. and west on the long green mall that extends from Jackson Park to Washington Park—the original Midway Plaisance. As the visitor proceeds past the long gray stone buildings and the belfry of the imposing chapel, he arrives at a remarkable reminiscence of the turrets and gables of Oxford and Cambridge, the physical realization of a dream of a young Yale professor named William Rainey Harper. These neo-Gothic quadrangles are the core of the university, which opened under his presidency on October 1, 1892, and expanded from the liberal arts to the physical and social sciences, built a great school of medicine with accompanying hospitals, pioneered in atomic and social research, and finally covered 163 acres, 125 buildings and had more than 1,000 scholars teaching the young.

The University of Chicago is a private, nondenominational, coeducational institution of higher learning and research. It comprises the College for Undergraduates; four major Divisions, of Biological Sciences, Physical Sciences, Social Sciences, and the Humanities, and seven professional Graduate Schools, of Business, Divinity, Education, Law, Library Science, Medicine, and Social Science Administration. The Laboratory Schools, started by John Dewey, serve children from nursery school through high school; extension education, started by William Rainey Harper, is available at the Center for Continuing Education and the Delaware Pl. Center; advanced scholarship and research are pursued by such institutions as the Oriental Institute, dealing with the historic cultures of the Near East; the Enrico Fermi Institute for Nuclear Studies, and the Franklin McLean Memorial Research Institute, formerly the Argonne Cancer Research Hospital; in addition there are numerous institutes for the study of contemporary life and thought.

The President of the university is Edward H. Levi, former dean of the Law School, who assumed office on Nov. 14, 1968.

The determination to build a strong university in Chicago to carry on the work dropped by the original university years before long had been an objective of the American Baptist Education Society and a number of Chicago civic leaders who interested John D. Rockefeller in financing it. Their choice to lead the organization was a brilliant young Hebraic scholar at Yale, William Rainey Harper, who earlier had taught at Blue Island Theological College and whose administrative ability was little short of genius. He gathered a distinguished faculty of eminent scholars by offering them higher salaries than any university was paying and giving them freedom to carry on original research. The original faculty included eight college presidents and scores of younger scholars who became famous, among them Albert A. Michelson, the first American to win the Nobel Prize in science.

The university follows a policy of equal opportunity in employment and its staff has a substantial percentage of women and members of minorities, which remains fairly stable. In June 1973, the university employed 55.3% women and 38% minority people.

The first self-sustaining chain reaction of nuclear energy, an event that vitally influenced the fortunes of mankind, took place at 3:25 p.m. on December 2, 1942, in a room improvised under the concrete bleachers at the east side of Ellis Ave. near East 57th St. It took place in the presence of Enrico Fermi (1901-1954) and 41 other scientists. The event was first recorded on a plaque attached to a fence at this place, but exactly 25 years later the university sponsored a three-day program of scientific addresses and unveiled a memorial, a three-ton block of bronze designed by Henry Moore, British sculptor.

The bronze is 12 ft. tall and rests on a base of polished black granite 9 ft. 6 in. in diameter. Nearby is a slab of granite with four plaques explaining why this spot is a National Historic Landmark.

The monument was first conceived as a marquette, a sketch in clay, then became a wooden armature of pointed sticks of the dimensions of the marquette. A full size mockup was then made in bone plaster in the artist's studio in England. This was shipped to West Berlin for casting in bronze. The result was shipped to Chicago on the SS Trans Ontario. As with all contemporary sculpture the import is left to the spectator's imagination, but this time the sculptor has disclosed what he was thinking when he conceived Nuclear Energy. He sees it as related to the mushroom cloud of an atomic explosion, to the shape of the human skull, and to a hint of church architecture.

Opposite this spot stands the Enrico Fermi Institute for Nuclear Studies, a center for studying cosmic rays, elementary particle physics, meteorites, cosmogany and allied subjects. Associated are a number of related buildings: the High Energy Physics Building, built 1967; the Accelerator Building; the Institute for Computer Research, and the Laboratory for Astrophysics and Space Research, built 1964, by Skidmore, Owings & Merrill. The Laboratory has two floors above ground and two below; the subbasement is a concrete shielded laboratory for measuring radioactivity in selected objects. It cost $1,750,000, with $100,000 for instruments. The Laboratory has operated a number of spacecraft instruments called the Interplanetary Monitoring Platform (IMF) for the study of cosmic ray energy.

From its start, the university has exerted a profound influence on higher education. President Harper created the four-quarter academic year, thus establishing the first university summer school. Other innovations include the junior college concept, equal educational opportunities for women at all levels of instruction, extension courses and programs in the liberal arts, and a full-time faculty for the medical education program.

Most of the university's buildings are arranged around classic tree-shaded quadrangles. The neo-Gothic style, expressed in Indiana limestone, was used with great fidelity until the functional trend in design began to emphasize elimination of elements not consistent with the building's purpose. Gradually plainer facades began to be introduced, led by the Administration Building, which closed a gap next to Cobb Lecture Hall, the first classroom structure. In recent decades contemporary masters in architecture, such as Eero Saarinen, Ludwig Mies van der Rohe, and Bertram G. Goodhue, have expressed themselves freely in new construction.

One great monument closed the Gothic cycle long after contemporary design had been officially approved. This is the ROCKEFELLER MEMORIAL CHAPEL, facing the Midway in isolation at Woodlawn Avenue, a spacious church in restrained English Gothic, with a 207-ft. tower of solid masonary standing sentinel-like beside the hall, traditional in its strength, but with its edges smoothed down from the sharpness of the militant years. Designed by Bertram G. Goodhue, it is the only building that bears the name of the family that has given the university its strongest support. The building was dedicated Oct. 28, 1928, and was the University Chapel until 1937, when it was named in memory of John D. Rockefeller. John D. Rockefeller, Jr. gave $1,000,000 toward its endowment. The tower holds the Laura Spellman Rockefeller Carillon, a set of 72 bells weighing from 10½ to 18 tons, dedicated Thanksgiving Day, 1932.

The most impressive adaptation of the Gothic past is the Mitchell Tower complex at 57th St. and University Ave. The Tower is a replica of Magdalen Tower of Oxford, without the finials. It has a formal portal that leads to a long monastic corridor; to the right of the entry is Hutchinson Hall, a noble Oxonian room for dining popularly called the Commons, with portraits of Rockefeller, Harper and other worthies. To the left is the Reynolds Club for students; at the end of the corridor are the doors to Leon Mandell Assembly Hall, the original chapel, used also for symphonic concerts and plays. The inside grass-lined court carries the visitor into the enchantment of the 17th century; it is walled in by the Tower complex and by Ryerson Physical Laboratory, one of the oldest buildings, and Bernard A. Eckhart Hall, also for physics, one of the newest. This sunken court is the site of the Court Theatre and the annual University Sing, and has been used for convocations.

The original Ferris Wheel, invented by George W. Ferris of Illinois was elevating awed farm hands to the skies above the original quadrangle during the university's first year. A generation later, in 1912, the William Rainey Harper Memorial Library closed the aperture between the Quadrangles and the Midway, near which the Ferris Wheel stood. The library was still designed in neo-Gothic by Shepley, Rutan & Coolidge; it had space for 1,250,000 volumes, and did not begin to bulge until 50 years later. At right angles to it the same architects in 1903 had built another Oxonian reminiscence, for which President Theodore Roosevelt laid the cornerstone; it housed the Law School until that school moved across the Midway, and now shelters the Graduate School of Business without any anachronistic qualms.

A reorganization of facilities to bring undergraduate classrooms and administration together has been made by establishing the COLLEGE CENTER, with the former William Rainey Harper Memorial Library as the principal unit, to which is added Wieboldt Hall. The College is the undergraduate section of the university, where the general education leading to baccalaureate degrees takes place. The undergraduates normally number 2,200. When Harper was built 50 years ago it was intended to be the principal library and thus honor the memory of the man who had the idea of the university. Most of the books have now been moved to the Joseph Regenstein Library, but a collection of 60,000 of especial pertinence to the undergraduate courses remains on open shelves in Harper. The new College Center was hailed October 24, 25, and 26, 1973, with a series of events including a convocation, rededication, parade, reception, and dinner. The development of the Center included renovation of Harper, Wieboldt, Business East, and part of Classics, at a cost of $2,600,000, of which the Kresge Foundation gave a matching grant of $1,000,000. The three-semester year now costs $3,000.

The spot where the first controlled chain reaction of atomic energy took place has been designated a National Historic Landmark by the U. S. Department of the Interior. It is one of four such landmarks at the university; the others are Room 405 of the George Herbert Jones Laboratory, Ellis Ave. & E. 58th St., where Glenn T. Seaborg and associates first isolated plutonium, an element synthesized from uranium; the Robie House, 5757 S. Woodlawn, designed 1909 by Frank Lloyd Wright, and the Midway Studios of Lorado Taft, sculptor. In 1973 fire damaged Jones Laboratory but did not reach the historic room.

A vital segment of the university is the Medical Center of four square blocks comprising hospitals and clinics, extending from Cottage Grove Ave. to Ellis Ave. This complex includes the Albert Merritt Billings Hospital, the Wyler Children's Hospital, the Chicago Lying-in Hospital, the Bobs Roberts Memorial Hospital, the Goldblatt Pavilion and the Peck Pavilion.

The medical school was named the Pritzker School of Medicine in June, 1968; it accepts only 90 students each year. It is affiliated with Michael Reese Hospital and the Cook County Medical Center. The Argonne Cancer Research Hospital was renamed the Franklin McLean

Memorial Research Institute in honor of the first chairman of the university's Dept. of Medicine.

A recent count disclosed that the Center served more than 16,000 in-patients and 170,000 out-patients each year, with 200 physicians and surgeons and 300 interns allocated to practice, care, teaching, and research backed by a staff of 2,000. More than 3,000 babies are born here annually, and about 70,000 emergency cases are served.

Monumental in proportions is the new JOSEPH REGENSTEIN LIBRARY, 1100 East 57th St., near Ellis Ave., a graduate research library in the social sciences and the humanities. Opened in September, 1970, it stands on the original football field, donated by Marshall Field and called by his name until changed to Stagg Field, to commemorate the services of Amos Alonzo Stagg, athletic director and coach, who originated the forward pass. The library, built of reinforced concrete with the exterior walls of Indiana limestone heavily scored vertically, is 7 stories tall and extends 344 ft. on East 57th St. and 411 ft. north and south.

Regenstein was planned to hold 3,525,000 volumes and seat 2,897 students at tables in carrels or in the stacks. It cost $20,750,000, of which the Joseph and Helen Regenstein Foundation gave $10,000,000 and the Higher Education Facilities Act of 1963 gave $8,410,772. Joseph Regenstein (1889-1957), a Chicago industrialist, was an innovator in paper, plastics, and chemicals.

The university has more than 3,000,000 volumes in the Regenstein and nine other libraries and receives more than 36,800 periodicals and collateral items annually. There are more than 3,200,000 manuscript and archival items. Of early printings 226 were executed before 1501 A. D. The papers of Enrico Fermi and other atomic scientists, the files of Harriet Monroe's *Poetry*, William E. Barton's Lincolniana, and the papers of Stephen A. Douglas are among its rarities.

In 1972 the cost of operating the university libraries was $4,346,284, of which $1,062,121 was spent for books and periodicals and $2,557,413 for salaries and wages.

The LAW QUADRANGLE, 1121 E. 60th St., is one of the accomplishments of twentieth century academic architecture. This $4,100,000 complex, completed in 1959, was designed by Eero Saarinen and Associates. It adjoins BURTON-JUDSON COURT, 1005 E. 60th St., a large residence hall. The Law Quadrangle units, from west to east, include a two-level administration building, the law library, a law seminar and classroom building, and a circular, two-level auditorium and courtroom building. Architect Saarinen wrote that the problem in design he faced "was to relate the pseudo-Gothic architecture of the residence halls on the west with the architecture of the American Bar Center on the east by creating a group of buildings that would embrace the whole. That is how the central emphasis came to be placed on the library-office building and a spacious court and pool before it." The reflecting pool is 90 by 120 feet. A three-ton monumental bronze sculpture by Antoine Pevsner, which stands 10½ feet high, is mounted on a granite base rising from the pool.

The Administration Building of the SCHOOL OF SOCIAL SERVICE, southwest corner of Ellis Ave. and East 6oth St., was designed by Ludwig Mies van der Rohe and erected in 1964 as a two-level office and classroom building. Notable is the 120-ft. entrance lobby, which is 40 ft. wide and has a 19 ft. ceiling, and can accommodate 800 for meetings. Black and cream are the dominant colors; groups of lounge chairs have steel frames and black upholstery designed by the architect. Courses on social work date back to 1901, and the school was one of the first to offer graduate-level social work training. It publishes the *Social Service Review* and enrolls more than 350. Since 1969 it has housed the Center for the Study of Welfare Policy.

One of the original quadrangles that had remained incomplete since the founding of the university was closed when the ALBERT PICK HALL FOR INTERNATIONAL STUDIES was dedicated June 14, 1971. This closed the gap between Beecher Hall and Walker at the southwest corner of University Ave. and East 58th St., directly across the avenue from the Oriental Institute. The six-story rectangular Pick Hall is faced with limestone slabs and has columns supporting the overhanging three stories on the east and north elevations. A striking effect is produced by vertical elongated window bays of tinted glass and dark metal, and although the architects strove to attain "a sympathetic integration of style" with the adjoining structures of the Harper period, Pick Hall reflects the trends of its decade. The interior walls are concrete blocks and the corridors have dark brown tile or carpeted floors. The hall shelters the Center for International Studies, the Department of Geography and Political Science, the Committees on African Studies, Slavic Area, New National and allied subjects. Architects were Ralph Rapson & Associates, of Minneapolis and Burnham & Hammond of Chicago, with J. Lee Jones of Homewood associate.

The ADLAI STEVENSON INSTITUTE OF INTERNATIONAL AFFAIRS, an activity of the university that is self-explanatory, in 1967 took up headquarters in the ROBIE HOUSE at 5757 Woodlawn Ave., a block east of the Quadrangles on 58th St. This house is famous in architectural literature because it is the prime example of Frank Lloyd Wright's prairie design. Placed on a narrow lot it extends for a block along 58th St., with a long low overhanging roof and a brick wall in front carrying out the longitudinal effect. It was designed for a dwelling in 1909. It changed hands several times but its security was assured when William Zeckendorf, real estate investor, bought it and presented it to the university. A fund for restoration was raised and Skidmore, Owings & Merrill retained to supervise the work. It has been designated a National Historic Site.

The ORIENTAL INSTITUTE, a research organization long famous for its archaeological discoveries in the Near East, has its building at University Ave. and East 58th St. This also houses its Museum, filled with authentic relics of ancient cultures. The building was designed by the Goodhue Associates and erected in 1931.

The objects in the Museum were all unearthed by expeditions of the Institute in the Tigris-Euphrates Basin and the Nile Valley. In recent years the Institute has worked assiduously to recover ancient materials from the site of the High Assuan Dam in Egypt. A most spectacular exhibit is a 40-ton stone figure of an Assyrian winged bull with a human head found in the ruins of the palace of King Sargon II (724-705 B. C.) near Nineveh. A colossal red quartzite statue of King Tutankamon came from Thebes and is dated 1350 B. C. The head of a huge stone bull came from the Hundred-Column Hall built by Xerxes at Persepolis. There are ivories from Meggido, cylinder seals from Mesopotamia, gold articles from Hittite sites, even Dead Sea Scroll fragments and a scroll jar. *Open Tues. through Sunday, 10-5; closed Monday, free.*

One of the newest buildings at the university is the DAVID AND ALFRED SMART GALLERY, at the northwest corner of East 56th St. and Greenwood Ave. This is part of the Cochrane-Woods Art Center, erected with a gift of $1,000,000 from the Smart Family Foundation in honor of the late founders of *Esquire.* The Gallery was designed by Edward Larrabee Barnes and contains 7,000 sq. ft. of exhibition space for permanent collections and traveling exhibits, and administrative offices. A sculpture garden will separate the Gallery from a new classroom and lecture hall building, and the two will constitute the Cochrane-Woods Art Center. The Center is made complete by a $1,000,000 gift from the Woods Charitable Fund, and honors the family of the late Frank Henry Woods and his wife Nelle Cochrane Woods, who endowed the fund in 1941. Three other structures have been proposed for the Center: a theater, an art library, and a music building.

The CHICAGO THEOLOGICAL SEMINARY is located in a group of monumental buildings on the north side of 58th St. between University and Woodlawn Avenues, adjoining the campus of the University of Chicago. Its distinguished feature is the Victor Fremont Lawson Tower, 162 ft. tall, which commemorates the publisher of the *Chicago Daily News,* who left a legacy of millions to the Seminary when he died in 1925. The tower contains the principal offices of the Seminary, which was founded in 1855 by the New England Congregationalists and is now associated with the United Church of Christ. The Seminary offers courses leading to the degrees of bachelor of divinity, master of theology, master of arts in the sociology of religion, and in religious education. It enrolls up to 200 graduate students and has 15 fulltime professors and six clinical instructors.

Founded by strong opponents of slavery the Seminary has kept a close relationship with social conditions and trains its students to go "where the action is" and "gain knowledge by critical reflection on experience." In recent years it has cooperated with the Association of Chicago Theological Schools in the Black Theological Education Project, of which Prof. Archie Hargraves of CTS is chairman.

At a corner of University Ave. and 58th St. is Graham Taylor Hall, named for the man who first established a department of Christian theology. The Graham Taylor Chapel has stained glass windows based on patterns at Chartres. The Thorndike Hilton Memorial Chapel, 1150 East 58th St., also has windows with Scriptural connotations and is frequently used for weddings. Notable are the Clarence Sidney Funk Cloisters that connect units of the Seminary, one of them the Henry M. Hooker Hall, which houses the Charles Goodrich Hammond Library, of more than 70,000 vols. Documents of the westward missionary movement include 200,000 letters of pioneer church-builders to the American Home Missionary Society. The men's dormitory is the Ozora Stearns Davis Hall, 1164 East 58th St. while McGiffert House, across Woodlawn Ave. has the Hales Student Center and apartments for married students. Faculty families occupy eight adjoining homes in the Seminary Faculty Quadrangle in Dorchester Ave. Visitors are welcome and circulars describing the Cloisters and windows in some of the buildings are available at the business office.

The LUTHERAN SCHOOL OF THEOLOGY, 1100 E. 55th St., was opened there in 1960. The library contains 102,500 vols., including the archives of the Lutheran Church in America.

The CUMMINGS LIFE SCIENCE CENTER, located on E. 58th St., between Ellis and Drexel Avenues, was dedicated October 19, 1973, in ceremonies that included addresses by two Nobel Prize winners and other scientists of national repute. The Center, 11 stories tall and the second-tallest structure on the campus, houses 40 laboratories, research and administrative facilities for the Departments of Biochemistry, Biophysics, Theoretical Biology and Microbiology. Nathan Cummings, Chicago industrialist, is the principal donor of the Center, which cost $12,000,000.

The UNIVERSITY OF CHICAGO PRESS has published more than 5,000 scholarly books, among them *The Collected Papers of Enrico Fermi, Systematic Theology* by Paul Tillich, *The Papers of James Madison, The Selected Papers of Adlai Stevenson,* and Edgar J. Goodspeed's *The New Testament, An American Translation.* It issues more than 30 learned journals, on subjects from elementary schooling to astrophysics. A recent publication, *The Serengeti Lion,* by George B. Schaller, won a National Book Award.

A number of theological schools have found locations near the university advantageous. They include the Disciples (Christian) Divinity House of the University of Chicago, 1156 East 57th St.; Meadville-Lombard (Unitarian and Universalist) Theological School, 5701 South Woodlawn Ave.; Chicago Theological (United Church of Christ) Seminary, 5757 South University Ave.; Lutheran School of Theology, 1100 East 55th St.; Catholic Theological Union, 5401 South Cornell Ave.; Bellarmine School of Theology of Loyola (Jesuit), 5430 South University Ave.

The American Bar Center, 1155 East 60th St., is also the seat of the American Bar Assn. and eight national legal organizations, including the American Bar Foundation.

South on Cottage Grove Avenue

The CENTER FOR RESEARCH LIBRARIES, 5721 Cottage Grove Ave., organized in 1949, provides material for cooperating libraries. It has more than 2,500,000 volumes and compiles collections on film, such as African subjects and historical items.

The CONFEDERATE MOUND CEMETERY is the name sometimes applied to a section of Oakwoods Cemetery, East 67th St. and Cottage Grove Ave., because thousands of Confederate soldiers lie buried here under a mound on which stands a memorial pillar. On the 40-ft. shaft of Georgia granite is the bronze statue of a Confederate soldier in an attitude of mourning. The names, companies, and regiments of 4,275 buried here are inscribed on bronze plates at the base of the monument. Most of the soldiers came from the battles around Chattanooga and were prisoners of war at Camp Douglas, E. 31st St. and Cottage Grove Ave. Many had been wounded. The memorial was dedicated in 1895 by President Grover Cleveland in the presence of surviving Civil War generals and high Government officials.

CHICAGO STATE UNIVERSITY is the name, since July 1, 1971, of the long established Chicago State College, which began its usefulness as the Cook County Normal School in 1867, and after subsequent identifications as a teachers' college under several names, became a member of the State of Illinois system of Higher Education in 1965. It offers undergraduate and graduate programs in the liberal arts and teacher education. It enrolls approx. 5,700 and has a faculty of 326.

Located up to 1972 at 6800 Stewart Ave., the university has been developing its new campus on a 160-acre area, 140 acres of which were used as the Burnside Yards of the Illinois Central Railroad and were bought for $7,700,000. The location is at 95th St. and Martin Luther King, Jr. Drive. Calumet Expressway is south and Cottage Grove Ave. east. The State Legislature appropriated $34,404,550 for the first phase of construction, which included two academic, administrative, science, physical education buildings and utilities plant, and the Emily and Paul Douglas Library. The Library was planned to be the focal point of the campus. It has more than 160,000 vols. and 10,000 reels of microfilm, with large sections devoted to textbooks and children's reading.

The Student Government is an elective body that has representatives on the University Senate and the committee of the Senate. A Student Code of Conduct and the Procedures for Hearing Board review outline student responsibilities and rights. Camp Workshop twice a year provide students with leadership training experience and is planned by a student committee.

Of recent organization is the Black Cultural Center, which provides seminars, workshops, exhibits, African studies, and meetings with black artists, writers, and political leaders.

In September, 1967, Chicago State established its West Center at 500 North Pulaski Road at the urging of community leaders. The center has classrooms, student and faculty lounges, a library and a cafeteria. The university also cooperates with St. Francis Xavier College, 103d St. and Central Park South, in providing teachers for extension courses and other programs where needed.

Pullman

The town of PULLMAN, centering around 111th St. and Cottage Grove Ave., extends east to Lake Calumet Expressway (Int. 94). It is the result of a pioneer experiment in town planning, and its still beautiful old houses and public buildings give evidence of the proprietary Utopia that briefly flourished here. It is now a part of Chicago.

> In 1881 George M. Pullman, inventor and manufacturer of the Pullman sleeping car, hired a group of experts, including the architect Solon S. Beman, to build a model settlement within the municipality of Hyde Park for the employees of his immense new manufacturing plant. This gigantic enterprise attracted world-wide attention as an "extension of the broadest philanthropy of the working man, based on business principles." During the hard times of the early 1890s Pullman reduced wages, but not rents. This led in 1894 to a strike supported by the recently-organized American Railway Union, led by Eugene V. Debs. Pullman cars were boycotted and violence resulted between workers and strikebreakers in Chicago. President Cleveland sent U.S. troops to move the mails. Governor John P. Altgelt protested that he did not call for troops. Debs defied a court injunction and was sentenced to jail. Pullman broke the strike. Shortly afterward the Illinois Supreme Court ruled that the Pullman Company was exceeding its charter in leasing houses to its workers, and thereafter the cottages and apartments passed into the hands of private owners.

Rows of staunchly built brick cottages, simple in design extend south to 115th St. Some are well kept, with garden plots bright with zinnias and balsam.

At Cottage Grove Ave. and 111th St. stands the Florence Hotel. Completely Victorian in the furnishings of its public rooms, it has been carefully restored in its period with modern services added. The hotel faces Pullman Park Plaza, the center of which contains a circular flower bed with markers that describe the history of the community. The park has been reshaped and landscaped by the Dept. of Public Works in cooperation with the Pullman Park Civic Organization. A small stand of ginko trees derives from the first planting of the species here.

The Greenstone Church at 112th St. and Champlain Ave., has serpentine green walls, building material popular at the time Pullman was founded.

MORGAN PARK ACADEMY, 2153 West 111th St. is a college preparatory school with a history going back to 1873, when the Mount Vernon Military and Classical Academy was established here. Within a year it became the Morgan Park Military Academy and remained thus until 1892 when it became affiliated with the new University of Chicago and dropped the term military. In 1919, however, it once more was the Morgan Park Military Academy; in 1958 it was demilitarized and in 1960 became a coeducational day school. It has a 20-acre campus and added two new buildings, Barker Hall and Beverly Art Center, in 1968 and 1969. The Academy has courses of instruction from pre-first grade to grade 12, starts French in the pre-first grade; has a liberal arts program at all levels and laboratory sciences in the college preparatory courses, and competitive athletic teams. Tuition is from $600 to $1,750 annually with all except the pre-first grade including a noon meal.

South of the Loop on Wabash

OLD ST. MARY'S ROMAN CATHOLIC CHURCH, 911 S. Wabash Ave., officially designated a Chicago historical landmark on its 100th anniversary, July 18, 1965, is the city's oldest house of worship, for it escaped the Great Fire. It was designed by Gourdon P. Randall, a Bostonian architect who located in Chicago, for the Plymouth Congregational Church, and cost nearly $100,000. It was dedicated in the fall of 1867, but by 1872, after the Fire had laid Chicago low, the members of the congregation, who either lived or had taken new quarters about a mile and a half south, were anxious to leave 9th St. and move farther south. Since most of the city's churches had been destroyed they were easily able to sell the Plymouth Church to the Rt. Rev. Thomas Foley, Roman Catholic Bishop of Chicago, who bought it for $112,000 for St. Mary's parish, which had lost its church. The Congregationalists erected a new church at S. Michigan Ave. and 36th St. St. Mary's parish had been founded in 1833. In 1903 the Society of Missionary Priests of St. Paul, the Paulist Fathers, took charge of St. Mary's Church.

An important event in Chicago history was the meeting held in the church in January, 1872, led by Mayor Joseph Medill, editor of the *Chicago Tribune,* for the purpose of organizing the Chicago Public Library after the Great Fire. The books of the library, including some sent by Queen Victoria, had been assembled in the unused water tank at the City Hall.

The CHICAGO COLISEUM, 1513 S. Wabash Ave., was the first great amphitheater with a roof supported by 12 huge steel arches. It has a complicated history of architectural adaptations. Its low facade of stone battlements was built in 1890 to enclose an open space on which stood the veritable Libby Prison of Civil War time, removed from Richmond, Va. brick by brick, and reassembled here with all its timbers and graffiti. The exhibit drew spectators during the World's Columbian Exposition in 1893, but a few years later, when attendance dwindled, the promoters sold the prison to an Indiana farmer, who removed it and used it for a barn. Money was then raised for a Coliseum. The battlemented wall was retained and above it were placed large bays modeled on adaptations from Roman baths, also seen in railroad stations. One of the steel beams fell while being lifted into place, killing 11 steel workers. The hall was completed in 1900 and was found suitable for political conventions, including the Republican conventions that named Theodore Roosevelt for President in 1904, William Howard Taft in 1908, and 1912, Warren G. Harding in 1920 and Calvin Coolidge in 1924. For many years it was the site of the annual automobile shows, and the seamy side of Chicago was on exhibition early in the century in the First Ward balls at which the grand march was led by the two aldermen of the ward, John Coughlin (Bathhouse John) and Michael Kenna

(Hinky Dink). *See Fabulous Chicago, by Emmett Dedmon.* Because of its name the Coliseum is sometimes mistaken for the Coliseum of 1896, at which Jennings Bryan made his famous Cross of Gold speech and received his first Democratic nomination for President. That Coliseum stood on 63rd St. one block west of Stony Island Ave.

South on Michigan Avenue

The JOHNSON PUBLISHING COMPANY BUILDING, 820 South Michigan Ave., head office of the most successful black publishing enterprise in the world, is an 11-story structure of steel, concrete, marble and glass designed by John Moutoussamy, a black architect, and cost more than $7,000,000. The company, which publishes five widely-circulated magazines about black interests and has a book division, was founded in 1942 by John H. Johnson with $500 loaned by his mother, and is owned by Johnson and his family. It has an integrated staff of 300.

The Johnson magazines are *Ebony,* which circulates 1,250,000 and has an annual advertising revenue of $10,000,000; *Jet,* with 500,000 "a black-oriented weekly news magazine"; *Black Stars,* 200,000 circulation, which covers the news and personalities of the black entertainment world; *Black World,* 100,000 copies, which deals with black activities in literature, history and the arts, and is directed toward young black adults involved in the black liberation movement, and *Ebony, Jr.,* first issued in May, 1963, and intended to interest black boys and girls and acquaint them with their heritage, which started with 200,000 and quickly moved up to a press run of 400,000. *Negro Digest,* first of the magazines launched by Johnson in 1942, later became *Black World.*

In 1963 the Johnson Publishing Co. began issuing hard-cover books through its book division, dealing with biographies, poetry, history, religion, sports, and civil rights. Its initial publication was *Before the Mayflower,* by Lerone Bennett, Jr., senior editor of Ebony. Other successful titles have been the six-volume *Ebony Classics,* the *Ebony Book of Black Achievement,* the *Ebony Pictorial History of Black America, The Challenge of Blackness,* by Lerone Bennett, Jr., and *The Integrated Cookbook,* by Mary Jackson and Lelia Wishart.

The history of the Johnson enterprises is a success story of large dimensions which has given much confidence to black Americans. Johnson was working for the Supreme Liberty Life Insurance Co. when he started his first venture; later he became head of the company that had hired him. He believed black readers would respond to reports of black achievements, and that if he gave them what they wanted on this subject he would succeed. The result is rather solidly based on the business acumen of the founder, whose energy and imagination won in a field where others had failed. In December, 1972, national editors meeting in New York voted Johnson Publisher of the Year.

The decorations and equipment of the Johnson Building have been carefully chosen with relation to their use. The marble is Italian travertine and the walls in the lobby are bronze panels overlaid with an African wood called Mozambique. There is a collection of paintings and sculpture by black Americans and Africans. Electronic devices are used for processing and computing, and picturephones are in use throughout the building. Editorial offices are on the seventh and eighth floors. Executive offices are on the ninth floor. The tenth floor is given over to lounge and dining areas for employees. The president's private executive offices are on the eleventh floor.

CHICAGO TECHNICAL COLLEGE, 2000 S. Michigan Ave., founded 1904, is a private college for men offering two-year and four-year courses, industry oriented, specializing in technological fields. Architectural, civil and electrical engineering, tool and die design are some of the courses. It has the quarter plan and a summer session of 12 weeks, also evening courses. Tuition fees are $825 and off-campus room and board are estimated to cost $1,600. There is a faculty of 31 and enrollment is around 1,200.

The CHICAGO DAILY DEFENDER, 2400 S. Michigan Ave., was founded in 1905 as a weekly for Robert Sengstacke Abbott, in order to fight editorially for the civil rights of Negroes and publish news and opinion for the black people of Chicago. It became a daily in 1956 and is now published and edited by John H. Sengstacke, the founder's nephew. The editors keep a close watch on civil rights in the Chicago area, and issues affecting the welfare of blacks, in the General Assembly and nationally. The Defender takes a strong stand for equal educational opportunity and supports busing as a means to achieve the democratic objectives of school desegregation.

West to State Street

The ROBERT HILLIARD CENTER, 2030 S. State St., was erected in 1967 by the Chicago Housing Authority. The architects were Bertrand Goldberg Associates, and they applied some of their methods of concrete construction used in Marinea City. Of the four buildings, two are 15-story cylindrical towers with 350 apartments for senior citizens, and two 22-story semicircular buildings with 350 apartments. There are also a community building, an open-air theater, and playgrounds.

Chinatown

CHINATOWN extends for a number of blocks from the corner of Wentworth Ave. and Cermak Road (W. 22nd St.), where the headquarters of the On Leong Tong, the principal business mens association, occupies a brick building with curved rooflines on its corner towers. This area is the social and commercial center of Chicago's Chinese, many of whom are second and third generation Americans. While the district still has numerous two and three story brick buildings more than 50 years old, it also has modern apartment houses and has profited from recent rehabilitation of houses by local redevelopment.

Chinese who suffered from the hostility shown them on the West Coast filtered into Chicago after 1876 and settled near S. Clark and Van Buren Sts. Landlords exploited them, and around 1905 the most affluent Chinese bought property in the environs of Wentworth Ave. and W. 22nd St. As their numbers increased groceries, shops, and eating places multiplied.

Merchants formed associations for mutual help and protection. About 2,500 to 3,000 Chinese live in Chinatown, while possibly 2,500 more live on N. Clark St. and others, active in business and education, are not identified with any group. Because Bret Harte and other writers described the Chinese of the Old West as furtive and "peculiar" many Americans gained the impression that they were a dangerous element, whereas the Chinese in Chicago were primarily interested in a quiet home life and schooling for their children. Barkers in downtown Chicago still promote tours to Chinatown with hints of fearsome adventures but actually lead their customers to curio shops and restaurants.

Today's Chinatown is a well-kept area. There are two well-attended churches: the Chinese Christian Union Church, Wentworth Ave. and W. 23rd St., and the St. Therese Catholic Mission on Alexander St. The Catholic parochial school identifies itself by large crimson panels with gilt lettering. The On Leong Tong building is often called the City Hall, and may be visited. Adjoining the reception hall is the shrine room, with portraits of George Washington and Sun Yat Sen, father of the Chinese Republic. Teakwood chairs along the walls have backs of striped marble, selected to suggest seascapes, landscapes, and fantastic creatures of Chinese folklore. An elaborate memorial shrine is dedicated to Quan-Kung, a teacher of the third century who emphasized honest dealings in business. Here joss sticks are burned, and a perpetual oil light glimmers on ceremonial objects and ornaments symbolizing virtues of the good life. In the building are meeting halls and a classroom for the instruction of Chinese youth in the language and customs of China.

Jade and soapstone ornaments, incense, back scratchers, and all manner of charms and baubles are found in dim little shops, and in the Ling Long Museum, 2238 Wentworth Ave., which contains dioramas depicting the history and customs of China. Many food markets display a curious assortment of preserved foods from China and Chinese vegetables. Barbecued pork loins hang near boxes of succulent lotus roots; bright bitter-greens with yellow blossoms and fat bitter-melons nestle in window trays beside baskets of butter fish; flaky birds' nests, "thousand year" eggs, shark fins, and beetles rest in jars and tins on store shelves.

Chinatown observes a number of festivals. New Year's Day has elastic dates; it usually comes in late January or early February. Independence Day, October 10, celebrates the establishment of the Chinese Republic after the fall of the Manchu dynasty; this calls for a big parade that starts at the Chinese Community Center, 250 W. 22nd St., and includes a dragon and fireworks.

Chinatown was improved in appearance in the 1960-70 decade when a group of businessmen formed the Chinatown Redevelopment Assn. to provide new housing. They built town houses and aided the rehabilitation of commercial enterprises. Their initiative was followed by other investors and brought about improved earnings.

The Chinatown Branch of the Chicago Public Library was opened in April, 1972. The National Library of Taiwan presented it with a collection of 225 books in Chinese.

The ABRAHAM LINCOLN CENTER, 700 Oakwood Blvd., occupies a massive, foursquare brick building designed by Frank Lloyd Wright. Founded in 1905 by Jenkin Lloyd Jones to foster international, inter-religious, and inter-racial fellowship, the institution has progressed in helping young and old with educational and cultural programs.

Martin Luther King, Jr. Drive

The MARTIN LUTHER KING, JR. DRIVE, formerly the South Park Way, starts at the eastern end of Cermak Road (E. 22nd St.) and extends south to the entrance of Washington Park at E. 51st St. and beyond. It passes through the area sometimes called Bronzeville, which has the largest concentration of black residents. Part of the area has been the subject of considerable urban renewal. At E. 25th St. the Stevenson Expressway, Int. 55, crosses the Drive to connect with the Lake Shore Drive. At E. 25 to 26th Sts. is the new Mercy Hospital; below 26th St. the Drive passes a large section of new construction, including Michael Reese Hospital, the Dunbar Vocational High School, Prairie Shores, Lake Meadows and other highrise apartment groups.

MERCY HOSPITAL AND MEDICAL CENTER, E. 26th St. and the Drive is a completely modern plant. Its most conspicuous building is a 14-story structure of concrete and glass designed by C. F. Murphy Associates and completed in 1968. It is topped by what appears to be a very wide cornice but actually this is the effect created by the treatment of the 14th floor, which fans out and has penthouses for utilitarian uses on its roof.

An annual report in the 1970s said the hospital had 517 beds, 13,596 admissions, 1,899 births, and a staff of 1,550. It had an occupancy rate of 83.9%.

Across 26th St. from the hospital between the Drive and Prairie Ave., are the PRAIRIE COURTS, a middle-income housing project erected in 1954 and designed by Keck & Keck.

PRAIRIE SHORES, five huge high-rise apartment structures with 1,860 units lined up from E. 28th to E. 30th St. at right angles to King Drive provide a remarkable spectacle, which must be breath-taking to anyone who recalls the former state of the terrain. The 20-story structures of steel and glass were initiated by Michael Reese Hospital. They were designed by Loebl, Schlossman & Bennett and built in 1958-62. There is about one third occupancy by blacks.

MICHAEL REESE HOSPITAL AND MEDICAL CENTER, stretching along Ellis Ave. from E. 29th to E. 32nd St., has modern buildings and equipment constructed since 1952. Its research facilities have been greatly expanded. In a typical year it had 866 beds available and large clinical services, 22,543 admissions, 3,423 births and a staff of 3,499.

DUNBAR VOCATIONAL HIGH SCHOOL, located on the west side of King Drive from 29th to 31st St., was built in 1960 and designed by Holabird & Root. Adjoining it is Dunbar Park.

LAKE MEADOWS, a section of 10 21-story apartment buildings on 101 acres located along Martin Luther King, Jr. Drive from E. 31st, to E. 35th St., is an impressive example of urban renewal. Here about 100 acres of small stores and houses were replaced by this completely interracial complex, which provides for all the basic needs of its tenants. Designed by Skidmore, Owings & Merrill, it was built from 1956 to 1960 and financed by the New York Life Insurance Co.

There are 2,015 residential units in three types of buildings: five 12-story buildings with 595; four 21-story buildings with 1,280, and one 13-story building with 140 apartments. They are built with reinforced concrete columns and flat slab floors. The one and two-story high buildings contain shops, department store and bank and have steel framing and metal roof decks. The one-story school building has prefabricated concrete units for the roof deck. The steel framing of the bank is painted white and wall panels of gray tinted glass rise from ground level to roof. The club building has a white tile roof with a skylight; the upper floor has a glass wall and a surrounding balcony. The shopping center begins at the northeast corner of E. 35th St. and the Drive.

Opened in 1955 it had three levels of rentals. The low-income units became 90 percent black; the moderate-income units, completed in 1960, became 60 percent black, and the higher rental units, opened later, 80 percent white.

Another accomplishment of the Dept. of Urban Renewal is SOUTH COMMONS, E. 29th St. to E. 30th St., Indiana Ave. to Michigan Ave. It was designed by Gordon & Levin Associates in 1968 for an interracial community for middle income residents, with high-rise and lower apartment buildings and town houses. There are 1,613 apartments and town houses for rent and sale, a three-building shopping center, and a community center, part of which is leased to the Chicago Board of Education for a community elementary school.

The VICTORY MONUMENT, 35th St. and the Drive, the work of Leonard Crunelle, was dedicated in 1927 to the memory of soldiers of the Eighth Infantry of the Illinois National Guard who died in France. Around the central shaft stand three heroic figures in bronze symbolizing the tragedy and the glory of war. The bronze statue of a Negro doughboy surmounts the monument.

Illinois Institute of Technology

ILLINOIS INSTITUTE OF TECHNOLOGY occupies a campus of architectural distinction 27 city blocks or 120 acres between 30th and 35th Sts., Michigan Ave. and the Dan Ryan Expressway, 3 *m.* south of the Loop. Its low buildings, demonstrating the possibilities of glass and steel, are based on a master plan developed by Ludwig Mies van der Rohe, for 20 years director of its Department of Architecture. The Institute appeared on the roster of Chicago universities in 1940, when the Armour Institute of Technology, founded in 1892, and Lewis Institute, founded in 1896, merged under the new name.

Phillip D. Armour, meat packer, heard Frank W. Gunsaulus, a dynamic preacher, plead in a sermon for a technical school in Chicago for poor boys, and offered to underwrite one if Gunsaulus would head it.

The Institute of Design, founded in 1937, was the first school to be added, and on Sept. 1, 1969, the Chicago-Kent College of Law, which had been training lawyers since 1888, joined IIT. A corporation at Crystal Lake donated a campus of 107 acres and six buildings for additional facilities in research.

The Institute is a privately endowed, coeducational organization that offers courses in engineering, the physical and biological sciences, the social sciences and humanities, business management, design, architecture, city and regional planning, and the law. The School of Architecture and Planning was started in 1892 by Armour and the Art Institute of Chicago, and in 1938 acquired Ludwig Mies van der Rohe as director of architecture and Ludwig Hilberseimer as director of planning. The Institute of Design was originally the New Bauhaus, founded by Laszio Moholy-Nagy, of the Bauhaus faculty in Germany, and renamed in Chicago in 1937. The Pritzker Environmental Studies Center was formed in 1970.

Not least of the independent units that have joined IIT is the JOHN CRERAR LIBRARY, a scientific library that for years occupied 10 floors at 86 East Randolph St. This extraordinary aggregation of books on medicine, physiology, histology, historical medicine, constitutional law and aeronautics, has 1,120,000 vols., 13,400 current periodicals, and a budget of $1,125,000. It was founded in 1894 by a bequest from a Chicago railway magnate. The staff also administers the JAMES S. KEMPER LIBRARY.

CROWN HALL, designed by Mies van der Rohe for the architectural school, is a low building notable for its wide use of glass and the lightness of its framework. He also designed the CHAPEL, the ALUMNI MEMORIAL BUILDING, and a number of others. The HAROLD LEONARD STUART SCHOOL OF MANAGEMENT AND FINANCE, donated by an alumnus of Lewis Institute, entered its new building in 1971, sharing it with the Department of Computer Science, which uses a Univac 1108 Model 2 computer. All students take one or more courses in this department as part of the basic General Education.

The new gymnasium, ARTHUR KEATING HALL, is described as the first ever constructed of glass and steel. The GROVER M. HERMANN HALL is the student union. There are dormitories for men and women, and chapters of national fraternities have individual quarters in halls of the Institute.

The Evening Division has 300 courses available and enrolls more than 4,000 students in part-time work. The Institute enrolled 5,316 full-time students in the spring, 1973, term and had a faculty of 378. Student expenses for the 1971-72 year were $3,700 for campus residents and $3,400 for nonresidents. The totals in 1969-70 were $1,959 and $2,925.

Affiliated with IIT is the Armour Research Institute, occupying a 20-story tower and serving Government and industry by applied research; it has a staff of 1,500 and expends approx. $20,000,000 annually.

On June 28, 1956, it placed in operation a nuclear reactor to be used in studying industrial uses of atomic energy. The Institute of the Gas Industry has two buildings, a staff of 220, and operating income of approx. $7,600,000. Here also is the Research Center of the Association of American Railroads.

The ROBERT TAYLOR HOMES are 28 residential buildings that extend from East 39th to East 35th St. on State St., south of the campus of the Illinois Institute of Technology. They constitute one of the first low-income housing projects developed with municipal and Federal aid and cost around $70,000,000.

The SUPREME LIFE INSURANCE COMPANY OF AMERICA, a prosperous insurance organization owned by black citizens, has its head office at 3501 South King Drive.

The DU SABLE MUSEUM OF AFRICAN AMERICAN HISTORY, 3806 South Michigan Ave. is dedicated to making known the heritage and achievements of black Americans by exhibits, lectures, classes for children, teachers' training programs, and publications. The museum aims "to inspire black people and especially the youth to purposeful lives of achievement by acquainting them with the contributions of great Afro-Americans of the past and the worthwhile contributions of great black Americans of the present." The museum was started in October, 1961, in the apartment of Charles and Margaret Burroughs. First called the Ebony Museum of Negro History and Art it eventually was named to recall Jean Baptiste Point Du Sable, who established a trading post and raised a family on the north bank of the Chicago River near its mouth after the American Revolution. Du Sable was the son of a French father and a black woman, and the records show that he had a substantial establishment when he sold his place in 1800.

The museum has been building a valuable library of books, periodicals, manuscripts, and pictures. It conducts a correspondence course in Afro-American history, publishes the annual Heritage calendar, and prints its own publications. Its press has issued such books as *Poetry of Prison—Poems by Black Prisoners; Black Power in Old Alabama,* a biography of James T. Rapier; *My Name is Arnold,* by Essie Branch, and folk tales and poetry. The museum is supported by admission fees and contributions.

The CHICAGO URBAN LEAGUE has its headquarters in a greystone mansion at 4500 S. Michigan Ave. where it directs its extensive activities in aid of the social and economic condition of minority citizens. Organized in 1916 and governed by an interracial board, the League "acts to change the very systems and institutions that consign tens of thousands of Chicagoans to lives of degradation and despair." The League helps blacks to increase their skills, continue their schooling, get adequate housing, develop small business, and get legal help when needed. Its Survival Line is a 24-hour phone service for reporting crimes, injustices, and infractions of civil rights. Its Apprenticeship Training Program aims to place competent blacks in the building trades. In 1972 the New Chicago Plan was announced as a contract between the Urban League and the U. S. Dept. of Labor, "which makes the League the sole administrator of a Government sponsored project to put at least 10,000 black building trades craftsmen into the unions in four years and provide them with jobs." This rests on an agreement of 17 unions of the Chicago and Cook County Buildings Trades Council with the U. S. Dept. of Labor to accept specified numbers of minority workers as journeymen or advanced apprentices, and of employers agreeing to employ the men on equal terms with old members. A grant of $1,750,000 was to be made available by the Government for implementation. The League also maintains "action offices" at 2400 W. Madison Ave., and 1336 N. Sedgwick St.

The HENRY B. CLARKE HOUSE, 4526 S. Wabash Ave., often called the Widow Clarke House, is a frame dwelling with a square cupola, called the oldest extant building in Chicago. Its core is said to have been built in 1836 at the far-out site at Michigan Ave. and 16th St., where the Great Fire of 1871 did not reach it. In 1872 it was moved to its present location without its front porch. The cupola, with two windows on each side, was not part of the original Clarke house. It is now a community center.

PROVIDENT HOSPITAL is located at King Drive and E. 51st St., where Washington Park begins. East 51st becomes Hyde Park Blvd. Provident was established in 1891 by Dr. Daniel Hale Williams, who reportedly performed successful surgery on an injured heart. Williams abolished racial discrimination in admissions and labored to expand medical training to blacks.

At Greenwood Ave. is TEMPLE ISAIAH ISRAEL, designed by Alfred Alschuler for a reform Jewish congregation. Built of tawny brick of interesting texture and pattern and trimmed with limestone, the octagonal auditorium is roofed with gold-tiled dome, behind which rises a slender minaret. The whole effect is early Byzantine. Interior and exterior ornamentations were based on photographs of fragments of a second century synagogue unearthed at Tiberias.

CHICAGO OSTEOPATHIC COLLEGE AND HOSPITAL, E. 52nd St. at Ellis Ave. was founded in 1903. The college enrolled 332 in the 1972 year and had a faculty of 75. It is conducting a 15-year expansion program that will cost $30,000,000 and provide a new housing and community center and outpatient clinic. It has bought a site at 54th St. between Ellis and Ingleside Aves. from the Department of Urban Renewal for 90 apartments for faculty and students. The new clinic-teaching facility was designed for the north side of 53rd St. at Ellis Ave., east of the present building. Cost of the new clinic is placed at $12,300,000, with two-thirds from Federal and State sources.

Washington Park

WASHINGTON PARK, north from 51st St. to 60th St., and east from Martin Luther King, Jr. Drive to Cottage Grove Ave., is the largest inland park in Chicago, embracing 371 acres. In the 1880s and 1890s gay parties rode through in carriages and tallyhos to attend the races at the Washington Park Racing Course, a block south of the park, long since cut up into lots for houses. Today a large segment of Chicago's black population adjoins and uses the park. Large crowds of spectators and participants are attracted to the archery ranges, football, baseball, and cricket fields, tennis and roque courts, bridle paths, casting pools, and bowling greens. Pathways wind around the landscaped lagoons in the south half of the park.

The statue of GEORGE WASHINGTON, on the Drive at 51st St., sculptured by Daniel Chester French and Edward C. Potter, pictures Washington taking command of the American Army at Cambridge. The statue is a replica of one presented to the government of France by the Daughters of the American Revolution.

Behind the Refectory at 56th St. and the Drive are swimming pools, built by the Works Progress Administration.

Washington Park is the scene annually in August of an outpouring of black children on Bud Billiken Day, an event started in 1925 by Robert S. Abbott, founder of the *Chicago Defender*. A parade with gaily costumed bands precedes the big picnic in the park.

The Fountain of Time, Midway Plaisance at Cottage Grove Avenue, masterpiece of Lorado Taft, illustrates in sculpture lines from Austin Dobson's poem:

"Time goes, you say? Ah, no!
Alas, Time stays, we go."

The figures of people in various stages and stations of life appear to move from the surging waters at the right to the engulfing waves at the left—a procession of mankind from birth to death crossing a bridge along the border of a quiet pool, under the brooding gaze of Father Time.

Washington Park ends here and its highways cross Cottage Grove Ave. to the Midway Plaisance, a landscaped boulevard that leads to Jackson Park, about one mile east. North and south of the Midway are buildings of the University of Chicago.

South of the Midway is WOODLAWN, a community that became part of Chicago in 1889. Its principal business artery is East 63d St., which extends east to Stony Island Ave., the boundary of Jackson Park. In former years Woodlawn was a typical middle-income residential area, in which hotels and rooming houses accommodated many visitors to the World's Fair of 1893. On the north side of 63rd St. about 100 ft. east of Stony Island Ave. stood the COLISEUM, a large hall of World's Fair origin, where the Democratic National Convention met in July, 1896. The big issue was reform of the monetary system by replacing with silver the basic gold standard, which was believed to restrict the flow of money. At the debate on the resolutions William Jennings Bryan, Representative in Congress from Nebraska, made his famous "Cross of Gold" speech, which swung the convention to endorse silver and led to Bryan's first nomination for the Presidency and split the party.

The proponents of silver argued that it would place more money in circulation and help the farmer meet his mortgage payments. The banks and industries fought this issue. The so-called Gold Democrats, led by Grover Cleveland, refused to endorse Bryan. Governor John P. Altgeld of Illinois stood for silver and voted the Illinois delegation for Bryan on the fifth ballot. A splinter group of Democrats named another ticket with Senator John M. Palmer for President and Simon B. Buckner, former Confederate general, for vice president. The Republicans endorsed the gold standard and nominated Sen. William B. McKinley of Ohio for President. Sen. Mark Hanna of Ohio ran a campaign full of threats and promises, and had industries line up all their employees for McKinley. Bryan, also endorsed by the Populist Party, lost; McKinley had 271 electoral votes, Bryan, 176. Altgeld, who ran for Governor, lost to John R. Tanner.

Near at hand, on Stony Island Ave. is the Hyde Park High School. In the first decade of the 20th century an elaborate amusement park, called The White City, with roller coasters, slides, and shows, was built at the west end of 63rd St. and provided entertainment for the area for half a century.

After World War II Woodlawn had a gradual influx of Negroes, who met with barriers to expansion. Demonstrations for better living conditions took place and there were clashes with the conservative element before the city of Chicago was able to enforce open housing. Much of Woodlawn was run down and business on 63rd St. had deteriorated. The Dept. of Urban Renewal gave special attention to Woodlawn and The Woodlawn Organization (TWO) supported rehabilitation by private builders. TWO enlisted the cooperation of the University of Chicago in providing a site south of 60th St. for a 12-story building surrounded by 25 town houses of four stories, providing both low and moderate income and middle income facilities.

Whatever problems of housing developed in Woodlawn, many of its residents did not consider it a blighted area. In June, 1959, a substantial crowd observed its centennial with addresses, programs, and a pageant at the Woodlawn Regional Library, the James Wadsworth School, and the First Presbyterian Church. The first settler, Wadsworth, had lived at Woodlawn Ave. and 63rd St. Numerous residents recalled the impact of the World's Fair of 1893 on their families.

NEAR THE CHICAGO RIVER
Wacker Drive, East and West

WACKER DRIVE, comparable only to Michigan Avenue for its architectural power, is realizing its full possibilities in the 1970-80 decade, 50 years after it was begun by the Chicago Plan Commission and its chairman, Charles H. Wacker. In the early 1920s terrain west of State St. was given over chiefly to loading docks of South Water St. commission houses, which turned their backs on the river. East of Michigan Avenue were a few mooring docks for lake steamers opposite a soap factory; the rest was railroad yards. By 1926 Wacker Drive emerged as a wide double-deck boulevard running along the south bank west of Michigan Ave., the top level for passenger motor cars and pedestrians, the lower level for heavy vehicles, the surface embellished with stone embankments, and bascule bridges taking the place of the rusted iron girders of the old swing bridges.

Wacker Drive east of Michigan Avenue remained on the drawing boards, but by 1970 the plans were dusted off and surveyors began setting up their instruments. What brought about the change was implicit in the economic readjustment of American industry. The Illinois Central Railroad Company, losing profits from railroading, suddenly discovered that it had huge assets in the neglected freight and switching yards covering 83 acres in the front yard of Chicago. Corporate reconstruction produced a new conglomerate in IC Industries, of which the railroad became a subsidiary, but the most hopeful offspring was the Realty Division, formed to develop its air rights for office and residential use. One consequence of this development was the realization of Wacker Drive, East, which connects with Columbus Drive and extends to the Outer Drive. A new bridge to carry Columbus Drive across the Chicago has been proposed by engineers but remains in the planning stage. The Regency Hyatt Hotel Corporation was among the first enterprises to stake out a site on Wacker Dr. for the Chicago unit of the chain, a 1,000-room structure. Another enterprise is the Blue Cross-Blue Shield 30-story office building.

East of Outer Drive East in Illinois Center is a new complex called Harbor Point, of which the first building is a 54-story apartment house devoted to condominiums. It contains 742 units. One, two, and three beedroom condominiums were priced from $31,900 to $127,000.

The spot where Chicago began is the Michigan Avenue approach to the bridge over the Chicago River, for here, on a sandy hill that rose only about eight feet above the water level stood Fort Dearborn. Actually, the first habitation was on the north bank, where Jean Baptiste Point du Sable, son of a Frenchman and a black woman, developed a substantial trading post in the 1790s. The river, however, was not the clear, canalized stream that today mirrors tall office buildings but a sluggish drain for a swampy area that found its way around the fort hill and gradually entered Lake Michigan as far south as Madison Street.

Today a steady flow of vehicles moves north and south across the historic terrain where Captain John Whistler, USA, and 69 officers and men laid out Fort Dearborn in April, 1803. And the river flows in a straight line from Lake Michigan, drawing water that is carefully controlled in amount so that the level of the lake may be maintained.

The 333 N. MICHIGAN AVE. BUILDING commands the northern approach to downtown Michigan Avenue. Designed by Holabird and Root, its slender mass, seen edgewise from the bridge, rises to 435 feet. On the top floors the Tavern Club, a business men's organization, commands striking views over the area where Chicago began.

At the southwest corner of Michigan Avenue and Wacker Drive stands a 21-story building that seems monumental because it includes a reminder of Greek and Roman designs. It has a concave facade with a formal entrance resembling a Roman triumphal arch, while at the top of the building is an adaptation of the Athenian Choragic Monument. Alfred S. Alschular designed it in calm disregard of the strong drift to contemporary styles. For many years it was known as the London Guarantee and Accident Building; now it is the STONE CONTAINER BUILDING.

From Michigan Avenue Wacker Drive runs southwest before it turns west at Wabash. This creates a small triangle of open space that has been named HEALD SQUARE. Captain Nathan Heald was the commanding officer at Fort Dearborn on August 15, 1812, and carried out the order of his superior, General William Hull, to evacuate the fort. When the soldiers and civilians from the fort reached the vicinity of East 18th Street and the lake 63 men, women and children were murdered by the hostile Indians.

In the center of the Square stands a marble pedestal with three bronze figures of the American Revolution: George Washington in long campaign cloak flanked by his financial backers, Haym Salomon and Robert Morris.

South of the Square at 71 East Wacker is the broad front of EXECUTIVE HOUSE, a 40-story hotel erected in 1960 from designs by Milton M. Schwartz and Associates, which proclaims its name with a huge sign on its roof. On its top story is the 71 Club, a place for continental dining daily except Sundays, 6 p.m. to midnight. Adjoining it on the east is the 42-story LINCOLN TOWER, formerly called Mather Tower, tall and thin, its leanness augmented by the Gothic lines of its upper stories.

At the Wabash Ave. corner stands a semi-circular, domed structure in sharp contrast to its tall neighbors—the SEVENTEENTH CHURCH OF CHRIST, SCIENTIST, erected 1968 and designed by Harry Weese and Associates. Its facing of travertine marble makes it conspicuous. At the southwest corner of Wabash stands another tall structure that was called the Jewelers Building when erected in 1926, but is now the NORTH AMERICAN LIFE INSURANCE BUILDING. It has a central tower and four smaller ones at its corners.

Opposite Wacker Drive on the north bank of the Chicago River stands the block-long, seven-story newspaper plant that carries across its facade the names: CHICAGO SUN-TIMES and CHICAGO DAILY NEWS. It extends from the plaza of the Wrigley Building to Wabash Avenue and occupies one of the most conspicuous sites in Chicago. The two newspapers are published by Field Enterprises, Inc.; chairman of the board is Marshall Field, fifth of the name and great-great-grandson of the merchant prince who laid the foundations of the Field fortune. He succeeded as publisher on the death of his father, Marshall Field, IV, in September, 1965. Marshall Field III established the *Chicago Sun* as a standard-size morning newspaper in 1941 and issued it from the plant of the *Chicago Daily News* on West Madison

St. In 1947 he bought the tabloid *Chicago Times,* founded by S. E. Thomason, and published at that time at 211 W. Wacker Dr., built in 1928 for the *Chicago Post* and sold to the *Times* in 1932. Field combined it with the *Sun* as the *Sun-Times,* a morning tabloid. In 1959 Marshall Field IV added the *Chicago Daily News* to his group and built the present plant for the combined newspapers. Both have large circulations: the *Sun-Times* with more than 542,000 weekdays and 735,000 on Sundays; the *News* with approx. 445,000 weekdays. Victor F. Lawson and Melville E. Stone became publishers of the *Daily News* in 1876. Stone retired to become general manager of the Associated Press, and Lawson built a circulation that stood well above 300,000 during his lifetime. At his death in 1925 he willed part of it in trust to a theological seminary, but the institution was persuaded to let a group of investors take over, with Walter A. Strong as president and publisher. On Strong's death in 1931 Frank Knox, former general manager of Hearst Newspapers, became publisher; he was succeeded in 1944 by John S. Knight, who sold the newspaper to Field.

The Chicago Sun-Times took a new step in printing on Jan. 25, 1972, when it printed its edition on recycled newsprint. Thereafter nearly half of the editions of the Sun-Times and the Chicago Daily News were printed on recycled paper. The paper was produced by the plant of Field Enterprises in Alsip, a Cook County suburb on Cicero Ave. Old newspapers must undergo a special de-inking process invented by Richard B. Scudder of Newark, N. J. The Field plant produces more than 260 tons of newsprint daily and serves about 30 newspapers. According to the American Paper Institute for every ton recycled 17 trees can be saved.

Tours of the Sun-Times and Daily News plant by reservation, phone 321-2032, or write, 401 N. Wabash. No children under 9.

Across Wabash Ave. from the plant of the Field newspapers is the open space called IBM PLAZA, on which fronts the wide facade of the Midwestern headquarters of IBM, the International Business Machines Corporation. It is bounded on the west by State St. and on the north by Kinzie St. and is an all-electric tower type of office building, 670 ft. above the river's bank. The last design by Mies van der Rohe, it was completed by C. F. Murphy Associates. The exterior facade has 45 stories of bronze-finished aluminum and tinted, double-glazed floor-to-ceiling windows. The heating, ventilation and air-conditioning system is controlled by a computer, which is so sensitive to subtle weather changes that it is said a cloud shadow can affect temperature adjustments. An information control console in the lobby dominates every elevator and registers any variation, such as fire and smoke, in all parts of the huge structure. The Midwestern headquarters serves a 13-state area and houses the company's divisions devoted to data processing, office products, field engineering, information records, real estate and construction.

A self-parking motor car garage has been built adjacent to the IBM Building, designed by Schipporeit, Inc., architects.

South of the river, se. corner of State, is the 41-story UNITED OF AMERICA BLDG., appropriately No. 1 East Wacker Drive, because State St. is the central line for street enumeration. The building, faced with marble, was constructed in 1964 and designed by Shaw, Metz & Associates. There is a restaurant in the top story.

At this point there is a fine opportunity for neck-stretching in order to view one of the architectural phenomena of our time—MARINA CITY, two towers, 588 ft. and 61 stories tall, that rise on the north bank between State and Dearborn Sts. The eye-filling scalloped balconies are the widest parts of triangular apartments that taper inside the structure to the cylindrical cores that carry the loads. The first 18 stories are devoted to shops and garages. Each building contains all the facilities needed for domestic life; no tenant need go outdoors for supplies, services, dining or banking. There are also a television studio and a theater. The towers were erected in 1964 and 1967, designed by Bertrand Goldberg Associates. The open rooftop observatory is available 10-5 weekdays and Sunday, 12-5, May to October. At times a model apartment is open for inspection. The MARINA CITY OFFICE BLDG., 16 stories, was erected at 300 N. State St. in 1964.

On the north bank of the river between Clark and LaSalle Sts. stands the block-long CENTRAL OFFICE BLDG. of the City of Chicago, an eight-story brick structure with a square clock tower and a walk along the waterfront. It was designed by George C. Nimmons for Reid, Murdoch & Co. in 1913.

A well-proportioned street level bridge now crosses the Chicago River at Clark St. The ancient rust-covered drawbridge of girders and cross-ties, which operated on a turntable, was removed when Wacker Drive was built. The crumbling brick commission houses that backed up to the wooden dock are gone too, and the area bears no resemblance to the way it appeared on the morning of July 24, 1915. But below the southwest entrance to the bridge is still the spot where the steamboat *Eastland* turned on its side and drowned 812 young men, women, and children.

> The *Eastland* was a three-deck passenger vessel of 1,900 gross tons, one of four vessels that had been leased to carry employees of the Hawthorn plant of the Western Electric Co. to picnic grounds across Lake Michigan. It was expected to hold 2,500 people. Its average draft was 14 ft. When about to cast off at 7:24 a.m. the ship began to list to port and in a few minutes settled slowly, leaving half of the starboard hull exposed. In the ensuing panic crowds clambered on the hull and threshed about in the water; most of the lost were cut off on the submerged decks. The blame for the catastrophe was never convincingly established.

This precise spot has more pleasant connotations as the dock where the Christmas Tree Ship came for many years. Beginning in December, 1887, Herman and August Schuenemann sailed a schooner loaded with spruce trees down from Manistique, Michigan, tied up at the Clark St. bridge and sold the trees they had cut in the woods behind Manistique and Thompson, Michigan. They made a modest profit for six week's work and decided to return every year.

In December, 1968, August had just set sail with a load of trees when a storm arose and he and his ship were lost. Herman determined to carry on alone. In 1899 he was back with a new schooner, the *Rouse Simmons*. He continued to come every year until 1912, when Herman and a crew of 17 started for Chicago and "sailed into the silence that covers all the fine ships that have fallen victim to the gales of Lake Michigan." On Dec. 13 a bottle picked up on the beach at Sheboygan, Wisconsin, contained a farewell note from Capt. Schuenemann, in which he said that two men had been lost, the trees had been washed overboard, and the boat was leaking badly. "Everybody goodbye. I guess we are all through."

The chronicle of the Christmas Tree Ship does not end there. The Captain's widow obtained another schooner, and with the help of her three daughters, brought the trees to the Clark St. Bridge in 1913 and in 22 subsequent years after the *Rouse Simmons* went down. The Schuenemanns had supplied the Chicago market with Christmas trees for 47 years and created an imperishable legend.

The *Balled of the Christmas Tree Ship* has been written by Vincent Starrett. The story of this Chicago saga is summarized from *The Chicago,* of the *Rivers of America* series.

The possibilities of "landscaping" Wacker Drive were demonstrated when the Chicago Plan Commission in 1971 approved an ordinance creating a riverside park on the south bank of the Chicago River between Clark and LaSalle Sts. Today a narrow strip of trees and shrubs embellishes the lower level and an overhang with benches invites a halt on the top. Decorative posts with four white globes each provide uniform lighting.

The MERCHANDISE MART, the second largest commercial building in the world, stands opposite Wacker Drive on the north bank of the Chicago River, near its confluence with the North Branch, a structure not only remarkable for its immense size, but also for the multiplicity of wholesale displays by manufacturers of interior furnishings, ready-to-wear garments, and accessory lines. The building is 18 stories tall and has a tower seven stories taller, a total of 380 ft.; covering two blocks, its floor area is equal to 97 acres. Displays are attractively presented in 900 separate showrooms, and while approx. 500,000 buyers come anually from every part of the country and abroad to replenish their retail stock and study the trends, thousands of visitors go on tours throughout the building.

The Merchandise Mart was begun by Marshall Field & Co. and completed in 1930 as a wholesale market at a cost of $30,000,000. Architects were Graham, Anderson, Probst & White. It was later bought by Joseph P. Kennedy and placed in trust as an investment for his family. The National Broadcasting Co. has its studios of WMAQ and WMAQ-TV on the 19th and 20th floors. The Mart conducts 22 seasonal markets during the year, the largest of which are the International Home Furnishings Markets in January and June. All through the year there are special activities, such as those of the Quaker Test Kitchens of the Quaker Oats Co. on the second floor, which are given daily except holidays, 10-3.

STYLE EXHIBITORS CENTER was announced December 20, 1972, by Thomas V. King, general manager of the Merchandise Mart, and Stephen E. Smith, representative of the Kennedy family. It was planned for the north section of Wolf Point, site of a tavern in the pioneer days of Chicago, as the headquarters of Style Exhibitors, Inc., an organization of 900 traveling salesmen, who present women's and children's apparel and accessories to the grade. The group was formed in 1915 and had its main office at 222 West Adams St. Its first president, I. Jerome Harris, generally called Duke, was to have his name applied to the exhibition hall. The building, 27 stories tall, was planned as the center for the apparel industry of the country. The plans called for a 500-room hotel on floors 16 through 22 and a 5-floor penthouse. Skidmore, Owings & Merrill are the architects.

MONTGOMERY WARD & CO., one of the great corporations that make Chicago the mail-order capital of the world, has its headquarters and principal warehouses in a complex of structures centering on Chicago Ave., along the North Branch of the Chicago River. The most visible of the structures are three facing the river, one 500 ft. long, and two each one block long. This is the core of the mail-order house that has sales of more than $2.5 billion annually. With Container Corp. of America it constitutes Marcor, Inc., and with other subsidiaries had sales of more than $3.3 billion and net earnings of $72,672,000 in 1972.

Montgomery Ward & Co. began a long-range construction program with the erection of its new Corporate Office Building on the block bounded by West Chicago Ave., Superior, Larrabee and Kingsbury Sts. The building is 27 stories, 381 ft. tall, 234 ft. long, built of travertine marble, glass and anodized aluminum, and was designed by Minoru Yamasaki. It was the first Chicago building designed by Yamasaki, architect of the World Trade Center in New York. It has the principal offices of Montgomery Ward and Marcor, Inc., hitherto in the Administration Bldg., which has been retained for the merchandising division. Adjacent to the new building is a landscaped area facing Chicago Ave. The company also has built a five-level parking structure suitable for 800 cars and has plans for additional buildings and for landscaping an area bordering the Chicago River.

In 1972 100 years had passed since A. Montgomery Ward and George R. Thorne started their first mail-order house in a 12 by 14 room at 825 N. Clark St., with an investment of $1,600. Ward had toiled at all sorts of clerking and selling and Thorne had lost all but his house in the Chicago Fire. They combined to sell dry goods and household articles at low prices and cooperated with the National Grange, the farmers' organization founded in 1867. The partnership became a corporation in 1889 and the five Thorne sons began to join. Ward sold most of his interest to Thorne and both Ward and Thorne gave up their salaries and agreed to serve without pay. In 1899 they built the 25-story office tower on Michigan Ave., which became a great attraction for out-of-towners, for its 394 ft., including a gilded nymph, made it the world's tallest for a time. It was here that A. Montgomery Ward, gazing out of his windows, became the "watchdog of the Lake Front," fighting the city and private interests for 20 years to keep buildings out of Grant Park. In 1908 Ward left Michigan Ave. for the Chicago River location, where the first building of reinforced concrete was 500 ft. long and had 2,000,000 sq. ft. of space.

Today the far-flung mail-order business employs 104,100. In 1972 it had 465 retail stores, 644 catalogue stores, and many sales agencies. The figures have changed many times, depending on economic conditions and policies. In 1957 Ward acquired The Fair department store chain; the main store on State St. and four suburban branches were converted into Montgomery Ward stores in 1963. This policy of developing "clusters" of stores in metropolitan markets has resulted in increased sales. Ward sends out more than 45,000,000 catalogues annually. It conducts the Commercial Trades Institute as a vocational home study school. Ward uses computer control of inventory and has a network of 11 computing centers, with a central information processing unit in Chicago.

When the Chicago River turns south opposite the Merchandise Mart Wacker Drive follows it and becomes South Wacker Drive at Madison Ave. The northeast corner of Lake St. and the Drive is the site of the famous REPUBLICAN WIGWAM of 1860, where Abraham Lincoln was nominated for President. The Wigwam was a temporary frame structure two stories tall, which extended 100 ft. on Lake St. and 180 ft. on what was then Market St., and because of these proportions seats were placed along the Market St. side facing the platform at the east. The platform stood in front of the brick wall of an adjoining building, which constituted the fourth wall of the Wigwam. The hall cost nearly $7,000 and the builders were $2,000 short, and had to pass the hat.

> The convention took place May 16, 17, and 18, 1860 and the principal contenders were Lincoln, William H. Seward of New York, Simon Cameron of Pennsylvania, and Salmon P. Chase of Ohio. Anti-slavery sentiment dominated. The routine was similar to that of many conventions to come. There was ruction over seating southern delegates; there were efforts of favorite sons to hold their delegates until they could drive a bargain for jobs; there were sectional jealousies, with a fear of the dominance of New York. The delegates fought over the wording of resolutions. There were charges of bribery and corruption. The Lincoln managers packed the hall with sympathizers by issuing unofficial admission cards and their men yelled at every opportunity. Lincoln was nominated on the third ballot of the third day; after the Lincoln managers had won over delegates by making unauthorized promises of jobs. The nomination was resolved when Ohio changed four votes from Chase to Lincoln. There followed "a wild, insane, unearthly shout" and sympathizers outside began firing a cannon.

After the convention the Wigwam was used for a benefit concert to help victims of the great tornado that swept from Lee Center, Illinois, to the Mississippi River and into Iowa. But the hall proved unprofitable and was soon dismantled.

This corner played a part in the life of early Chicago long before the Wigwam stood there. Mark Beaubien, whose brother John was a sub-agent for the American Fur Co., brought his family from Detroit in 1826 and built a cabin at the bend of the river, now the southwest corner of Lake St. and Wacker Dr., and operated a ferry there. He also had a license to build a tavern and a few years later erected a substantial two-story frame house at the southeast corner, where the Wigwam was placed 30 years later. He called it the Sauganash (Indian for Britisher) after the nickname of Billy Caldwell, a half-breed Potawatomi chief. When the Indian tribes were induced to leave the State by the Federal Government at Chicago in 1833 they staged a wierd and fearsome dance in war paint, and it was at the Sauganash that they made a special demonstration for the women who watched from its windows, a wild riot that John Dean Caton compared to a carnival of doomed spirits in hell. The tavern burned down in 1851, but Beaubien had sold it years before.

At 20 N. Wacker Dr. stands the impressive home of the CHICAGO LYRIC OPERA COMPANY, originally the Civic Opera House built by Samuel Insull as his last great enterprise. The building, designed by Graham, Anderson, Probst & White, has a central unit 555 ft. tall that contains the opera auditorium seating 3,500 and the smaller Chicago Civic Theatre, flanked by two lower wings occupied by offices, which in Insull's plan were to provide income to defray the expenses of grand opera. The structure was completed early in 1929, before Insull had reason to expect the financial catastrophe that ruined him. The stage rises 13 stories and the facade on the river side suggests a huge throne, known locally as Insull's armchair. *For the story of the Lyric Opera Company see The Stage: Plays and Operas.*

The building was bought by James S. Kempner and named the KEMPNER INSURANCE BUILDING. In November, 1972, Kempner Insurance Co. opened its new international headquarters building in Long Grove, Illinois.

The ILLINOIS STATE CHAMBER OF COMMERCE has its offices at 20 N. Wacker Dr. Here, too, is the regional office of the Boys' Clubs of America.

HARTFORD PLAZA, at the southwest corner of S. Wacker Dr. and W. Monroe St. is the site of the Hartford Fire Insurance Co. building, erected in 1961. This 21-story structure, faced with gray granite, exemplifies an interesting variation in the architectural designs of Skidmore, Owings & Merrill. Instead of presenting a flat facade of windows and columns the windows are set back from the concrete frame. The Hartford Co. found the building so useful that it commissioned a duplicate in 1968, which rises to the south on Wacker Dr.

Across the street from Hartford Plaza, at the southeast corner of W. Monroe St., the U. S. GYPSUM BUILDING provides an unexpected variation in the rectangular vistas of city blocks. It has been built at an angle of 45 degrees to the street, so that it becomes diamond-shaped. Nineteen stories tall, its columns of white marble rise to the roof and end in sharply pointed finials, four to a side and one at each of the four corners, which accentuate its height.

The tall NORTHERN BUILDING of the Northern Trust

Company, 125 S. Wacker Dr., rises 31 stories at Adams St. and has a net area of 450,000 sq. ft.

Sears Tower

One block south on Wacker Drive, at Jackson Blvd., stands SEARS TOWER, the tallest office building ever raised by man.

It occupies approximately three acres bounded by Adams and Franklin Sts., Jackson Blvd. and Wacker Drive. It rises 110 stories and 1,454 ft. above ground, and has an area of 4,500,000 gross sq. ft., equal to 101 acres of floor space, exceeded only by the Pentagon in Washington, D. C. It is supported by 114 rock caissons, drilled 100 ft. to bedrock. It was designed by Bruce Graham and Dr. Fazlur Kahn of Skidmore, Owings & Merrill, and built by Diesel Construction, a division of Carl A. Morse, Inc.

The structural steel frame was fabricated in sections by the American Bridge Division of the United States Steel Corp. and bolted into place. From the Plaza through the 49th floor, the basic structure consists of nine 75 by 75 ft. column-free squares, creating a 225 by 225 ft. square at the base. At the 50th floor the northwest and southeast squares stop, creating the first setback through the 65th floor. From the 66th floor the northeast and southeast squares stop, and the tower rises to the 89th floor in a cruciform floor arrangement. The north, east, and south squares stop at the 90th floor. From the 90th to the 109th floor the building becomes a rectangular upper tower.

The tower was erected by four 40-ton, stiff-leg, climbing derricks. Each had a support platform, a 65-ft. tower, a derrick, and a 105-ft. boom, with the hoisting power supplied from a three-drum hoist.

The Tower is covered with black aluminum and has bronze-tinted glass. Lobby floors and core walls are surfaced with travertine marble and lobby columns are finished in a plastic laminate. Exterior doors and hardware are stainless steel. The outer plaza is surfaced with granite. There are three full levels below Franklin St. and a concourse level between Franklin St. and Wacker Dr. The area has shops, restaurants, and a parking garage for 150 cars. The American Room, two-thirds of an acre in size, is a cafeteria that can seat 1,700 at one time. It is decorated in national colors to stir the patriotic impulses and appeal to State pride at the same time.

The Tower was intended to shelter all the office personnel that had been occupying space in various parts of Chicago, up to 17,000 employees. While Sears, Roebuck occupies more than half of the Tower, provision was made for tenants, with completely independent facilities. Escalators reach the first three floors. The 102 elevators include 14 double-deck cabs. Two express elevators take passengers to the observation deck on the 103rd floor. The facilities are electrically operated throughout. A utility transmission station below ground has four transformers of 50,000 kilowatts each to produce power.

Sears Tower is headquarters for the largest mail-order enterprise in the world. Until the fall of 1973 the main office of Sears, Roebuck & Co. was located at its plant at Homan Ave. and Arthington St., where the 17 buildings occupying 54 acres long had proved inadequate for its needs. The first building was erected there in 1906. All West Side facilities here are still in use, primarily by the Chicago catalogue order plant.

The business was originated in 1886 by Richard W. Sears, railroad station agent at North Redwood, Minnesota. When a shipment of watches was refused by a local house Sears requested permission to sell the watches by mail to station agents along the railroad. The venture succeeded. Sears started a mail-order business and in 1887 moved to Chicago, renting space at 51 N. Dearborn St. The mail-order business prospered. A. C. Roebuck, Sears' partner, sold his interest to Julius Rosenwald, who had a genius for merchandising. Under Rosenwald the firm expanded across the continent. Rosenwald became known for his many philanthropies, which included aid to the underprivileged, Negro education, and various social causes. He founded the Museum of Science and Industry.

Sears, Roebuck & Co. is known for the remarkable efficiency of its whole system, and its strong position in the American economy. It has net sales of more than $10 billion, and net income of more than $621,-000,000, and pursues continuing programs of expansion. It operates 837 retail stores, of which 289 are complete department stores, has 12 catalog merchandise distribution centers, and has been building an eastern headquarters in suburban Philadelphia. It owns Allstate Insurance Companies, Allstate Enterprises, Inc., and Homart Development Co., operator of shopping centers and residential and office buildings.

North of the River Along the Lake Front

The bridge that carries the Outer Drive across the Chicago River is a double link bascule bridge, the largest of its kind. It is 331 ft. across and is made up of two leaves that rise upward from controls in twin towers located at both ends. The channel below it is 220 ft. wide, and the lower deck of the bridge is 22 ft. above the water, so that small cruisers move in safety below it. The two leaves of the roadway rise to a height of 132 ft. when open, as four 110-horse power motors operate the counter-balance. Each of the north and south roadways has four traffic lanes.

The bascule principle was first applied to bridges across the Chicago River in 1902. The word bascule is derived from the French see-saw. The trunnion bascle has fixed shafts on which the bridge resolves as on an axis.

When constructed in 1937 the bridge was said to have cost $11,-000,000, and engineers hesitate to guess what it would cost today. The Chicago Park District paid 70 percent of the cost by bond issues; the Public Works Administration of the Department of the Interior paid 30 percent. President Franklin D. Roosevelt dedicated the bridge on October 5, 1937, making the argument that aggressors among nations should be quarantined, a position sharply criticized by conservative Americans who wanted the country kept out of foreign entanglements.

East of the bridge, and separating the river from the outer basin of Chicago harbor, are the Controlling Works that regulate the amount of water Chicago takes from Lake Michigan. Four sluice gates, 10 ft. square, set in the basin walls on each side of the River, regulate the intake from the lake. On the landward side of each of the eight gates are tide gates that close automatically when the river begins rising higher than the lake. The navigation lock is 80 ft. wide, 600 ft. long and 24 ft. deep, and has long guide walls. Here pass not only the freight vessels that bring supplies into Chicago but those that are about to make the long journey on the Illinois Waterway to the Mississippi River, including those en route from the Atlantic to the Gulf.

The NAVY PIER, at the foot of Grand Ave., is a major unit of the Port of Chicago and provides dockage for ocean-going vessels that travel via the St. Lawrence Seaway. It extends five-eighths of a mile into the lake and is almost a city block wide (292 ft.). It can berth six ships alongside in a 29-ft. channel, with cranes, rails, and warehousing available. It can also provide terminal facilities for smaller boats. The pier was built in 1916 by the City of Chicago and has served the purposes of military instruction in two world wars. During World War II it had schools for training in radar, engine maintenance, and logistics.

In 1946 the University of Illinois made its first effort to provide undergraduate instruction in the heart of Chicago. It established a two-year program of college and pre-professional studies in the Navy Pier on Oct. 21, 1946, with an enrollment of 3,800 students. It cost nearly $1,000.000 to convert the pier to classrooms, kitchens and dining rooms, and routine facilities. This division operated there for 18 years and four months and had reached an enrollment of 5,200 when the students were transfered to the new commuter campus, the University of Illinois at Chicago Circle in February, 1964.

To the north of the Navy Pier extends a man-made area of 61 acres of extreme usefulness to the citizens of a large part of Chicago, who take it for granted. It is the CENTRAL DISTRICT WATER FILTRATION PLANT, where water conveyed in tunnels from far out in the lake is processed with chemicals and made potable. Approximately 960,000,000 gallons of clean water are sent daily into the city's water supply. On the facade of the building of the plant are lines of *A Hymn to Water* by Milton Horn.

This area, which is connected with the lake front at Ohio St., includes 10 acres devoted to OLIVER MEMORIAL PARK, which commemorates the heroic act of Pfc. Milton Lee Oliver III, a 19-year-old Negro who in 1966 threw himself on top of a grenade on a Vietnam battlefield and thereby lost his life but saved those of his comrades. He was awarded the Medal of Honor. The park, attractively landscaped with shrubs and trees has five large fountains with jets that throw water to 50-ft. heights.

LAKE POINT TOWER, 505 N. Lake Shore Drive, built in 1968, near the foot of the Navy Pier, has added another architectural phenomenon to Chicago's skyline, the world's tallest apartment house. What from the air must seem a clover leaf is this triangular house of 900 apartments, 645 ft. and 70 stories tall, a huge bronze mass of reinforced concrete and glass with rounded corners. It was one of the conceits of Mies van der Rohe, who proposed this design to the city of Berlin in 1921. Students of his have developed it with the financial resources of Chicago investors. Architects were Schipporeit-Heinrich and Graham, Anderson, Probst & White.

A century ago the large bulge of land south of Oak St. and east of Michigan Ave. did not exist. In 1886 a small craft, manned by Captain George Wellington Streeter, grounded on a shoal off the foot of Superior St. Unable to float the boat Capt. Streeter remained living on it. The shoal gradually filled in and Capt. Streeter's boat stood on solid ground connected with the mainland. The Captain served notice on city and State that this was newly-made land and laid claim to 168 acres as the District of Lake Michigan. He built a shack and when the city ordered him off he resisted. It became known locally as Streeterville and the Captain provided the newspapers with amusing interviews. After a number of disturbances at the shack Mayor Thompson ordered the Captain evicted for selling liquor and the land cleared.

Conspicuous at East Ontario St. and the North Lake Shore Drive is the Holiday Inn, with Chicago's only revolving restaurant, the Pinnacle, on its 33d floor.

The AMERICAN FURNITURE MART (*open to wholesale trade only*), 666 Lake Shore Dr., reflects the current merchandising custom of using centralized wholesale markets. The largest building in the world at the time of construction in 1924, it is the most massive structure on the lake front. Gothic entrances and ornamentation, as well as a blue campanile tower, added in 1927, mitigate the heaviness of this block of pressed brick. Housing the national showrooms of the country's leading manufacturers of home furnishings, it. provides a convenient year-round market for buyers, and semi-annually makes Chicago the greatest wholesale furniture market in the United States. The building was designed by Henry Raeder and Associates, N. Max Dunning and George C. Nimmons.

Facing the lake at Superior St. are the tall towers of the McGAW MEDICAL CENTER of NORTHWESTERN UNIVERSITY. Here on 14 acres are located the Medical School, the Dental School, the School of Law, the Graduate School of Management, and the Evening Divisions. Closely associated are three major hospitals: the VETERANS ADMINISTRATION RESEARCH HOSPITAL, 333 E. Huron St., the PASSAVANT MEMORIAL HOSPITAL facing the university buildings at 303 E. Superior St., and the CHICAGO WESLEY MEMORIAL HOSPITAL opposite the university on Fairbanks St.

The SEARLE REHABILITATION RESEARCH CENTER has been established by the Rehabilitation Institute of Chicago in its new 18-story building at Huron St. and McClurg Court. This is associated

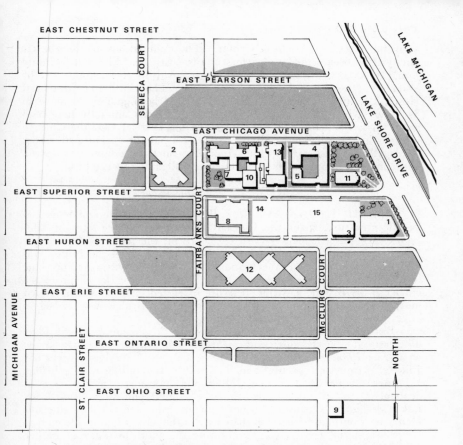

CHICAGO CAMPUS OF NORTHWESTERN UNIVERSITY

1. Abbott Hall.
2. Chicago Wesley Memorial Hospital.
3. Heating plant.
4. Levy Mayer Hall (Law).
5. McCormick Hall (Law).
6. Montgomery Ward Memorial Bldg.
7. Morton Medical Research.

8. Passavant Memorial Hospital.
9. Rehabilitation Institute, McClurg Court and E. Ohio St. Also 15.
10. Searle Medical Bldg.
11. Thorne Hall.
12. Veterans Admin. Research Hospital.
13. Wieboldt Hall.
14. Women's Hospital.

with the McGaw Medical Center. The foundations of the Searle family have been strong supporters of the Institute. The new building cost $20,000,000. Plans call for the removal to this campus of the Women's Hospital and Maternity Center. The Children's Memorial Hospital at Belden Ave. and Halsted St. has been invited to move to McGaw. More than 160,000 patients are treated annually here, and about 90,000 patients visit the clinics. In the 1970-71 year the Chicago Campus had a fulltime faculty of 265 and a parttime faculty of 1,164, principally on the staff of the Medical School, of whom 971 served without pay. About 1,800 students are enrolled at this campus.

North of the Chicago River

The MICHIGAN AVENUE BRIDGE, a massive double-decked bascule structure, spans the Chicago River between the sites of Chicago's earliest settlements—Fort Dearborn on the south bank, and the first houses, four log cabins, on the north bank. Until the bridge was built in 1920 Michigan Avenue north of the River was a narrow lane lined with old-fashioned mansions. Motor cars crossed the River on the old Rush St. Bridge, a swing structure of rusted girders, which carried most of the heavy traffic until the Outer Drive Bridge was opened in 1937.

Bas reliefs adorn the four pylons of the Michigan Avenue bridge. The east pylon at the north end celebrates *The Discoverers;* that on the west *The Pioneers*. Both are by J. E. Fraser. The Discoverers are Jolliet, Marquette, LaSalle, and Tonti. On the railing of the bridge a bronze plaque declares that Jolliet and Marquette passed here in September, 1673. They came from the Illinois and were headed for Lake Michigan. Opposite a bronze plaque says Sieur de la Salle and Henry de Tonti passed here on their way to the Mississippi in December, 1681. Memorial services commemorating the 300th birthday of Father Marquette were held here in May, 1937. At the south end of the bridge are two bas reliefs by Henry Hering: *Defense*, commemorating the Fort Dearborn massacre of 1812, and *Regeneration*, marking the Great Fire of 1871, after which the citizens built a new and greater city, "imbued with the indomitable spirit and energy by which they have ever been guided."

> Sightseeing motor launches are available at dockside at Wacker Drive and the Bridge, and at the north side of the River. At times such boats are also moored at West Wacker Dr. and N. State St. A launch regularly ferries commuters from the bridge to a landing at West Madison St. near the Chicago & North Western station.

The Equitable Building on North Michigan

The 38-story glass and steel building of the EQUITABLE LIFE ASSURANCE SOCIETY, erected 1965 on the north bank of the river east of Michigan Avenue faces the PLAZA OF THE PIONEERS, a landscaped area of 90,000 sq. ft. The building was designed by Skidmore, Owings & Merrill, with Alfred Shaw associated architect. Below the avenue level small shops and a restaurant border on the river and the lower level of the avenue, which admits vehicles to the bridge. For many years before the avenue was properly developed this was the site of a soap factory.

The Equitable Building stands on part on the site where Cyrus Hall McCormick built the reapers that helped make Illinois a great agricultural State. McCormick had improved on an invention made by his father in Rockbridge County, Virginia, and when he was ready to manufacture it he decided Illinois offered the best market, and water provided the best avenue for transport. He was 38 when he came to Chicago in 1847 with a sample reaper that had been built for him in Brockport, N. Y. With his brothers Leander and William he located his factory on the north bank of the Chicago and in 1848 built 700 reapers.

The INTERNATIONAL HARVESTER COMPANY, which is the successor to the McCormick enterprises, has its home office in the Equitable Building. The company is one of the biggest employers in the Chicago area. In Chicago it has four manufacturing plants, a research center covering 10 acres, and a printing plant covering four acres. The Tractor Works, 2600 W. 34th Blvd. makes crawler tractors; the West Pullman Works makes carburetors, bearings and parts; the Wisconsin Steel Works, 2800 East 106th St., makes carbon and steel alloys, coke chemicals and pig iron; the Melrose Park Works, at Melrose on US20, makes diesel engines, earth-moving machines, rubber-tired construction equipment. The steel mill in South Chicago covers 247 acres. There are Illinois plants in Libertyville, Canton, East Moline, and Rock Island, and a field test facility in Sheridan, Ill.

Products of the International Harvester Co. and animated displays may be seen at 401 N. Michigan Ave. Monday through Friday, 8:30-4:45.

PIONEER COURT is a tree-lined plaza that extends in front of the building of the Equitable Life Assurance Society of America from the river to the Tribune Tower. North of center is a fountain with a rim of travertine marble on which the names of 25 famous Chicago pioneers have been set in letters of bronze. They are:

JANE ADDAMS. She founded the Hull House Settlement in an immigrant district and worked for better living conditions and civic liberties.

PHILIP D. ARMOUR. Came in 1875 and built the great Armour packing house. Developed new methods and byproducts, refrigerated transportation, and Armour Institute of Technology.

DANIEL H. BURNHAM. Architect of the World's Fair of 1893 and designer of the Chicago Plan, on which great changes in landscaping, roads, parks, are based.

JOHN CRERAR. Gave a legacy of $4,000,000, to establish a great library of the physical, natural, and medical sciences.

STEPHEN A. DOUGLAS. Senator, lawyer, pioneer counsel for the Illinois Central Ry., worked to hold Democratic party in the Union, donated land to first University of Chicago.

RICHARD T. CRANE. Maker of brass and copper fittings, invented devices for elevators, started first manual training school, worked for reforms.

JULIUS ROSENWALD. Built up Sears, Roebuck & Co. after 1895; started profit sharing, pension plans; supported Tuskegee Institute and Negro welfare; also Museum of Science & Industry.

MARSHALL FIELD. Came in 1856, worked in a mercantile firm and became a partner in 1860. Formed Marshall Field & Co., 1881. Made large donations to the University of Chicago and the Natural History Museum.

WILLIAM RAINEY HARPER. First president and organizer of University of Chicago, 1891, had confidence of John D. Rockefeller, who donated millions.

GEORGE M. PULLMAN came in 1850, designed railway sleeping cars from two passenger coaches in 1858. Formed Pullman Palace Car Co., maker of sleeping cars, built town of Pullman to accommodate workers in his plant.

CARTER HENRY HARRISON came in 1855, invested in real estate. Served in U.S. Congress and was elected mayor of Chicago five times, 1879-1887, and 1893. After close of World's Fair of 1893 he was shot and killed by a frustrated office-seeker.

WILLIAM LEBARON JENNEY developed steel construction for office buildings starting in 1883. Called pioneer of the skyscraper. Served as army engineer on staff of General U. S. Grant.

JOHN WENTWORTH, political leader and editor, known as Long John because he was 7 ft. tall, was an incorporator of Chicago, mayor, representative in Congress, helped found the Republican party in Illinois.

GURDON SALTONSTALL HUBBARD, fur trader and after 1827 owner of Illinois interests of American Fur Co. Organized Board of Trade, built first hotel, water system, was banker and ship owner.

JOSEPH MEDILL came to Chicago in 1855 at age 32, acquired one-third interest in the *Press & Tribune*; had *Tribune* give solid support to Abraham Lincoln and helped nominate him.

CYRUS H. McCORMICK, inventor of the reaper, located his factory in Chicago in 1847 and by continuing improvement of the reaper and other farm implements helped make Illinois dominant in agriculture.

WALTER LOOMIS NEWBERRY came in 1833 and made a fortune in land. He supported literary and cultural movements, formed a library assn. and left $2,000,000 for a free public library.

CHARLES H. WACKER, chairman of the Chicago Plan Commission, 1909-26, carried forward the original plan, led in extending the Forest Preserve, parkways, Union Station, Wacker Dr.

WILLIAM BUTLER OGDEN, came in 1835, helped develop streets and bridges, railroads, utilities, was president of C. & N. W. Ry., first president of Ruth Medical College.

A. MONTGOMERY WARD, store clerk in Michigan town came in 1862 and built mail order business by selling goods from factory to consumer. With tall tower building on Michigan Ave. he became leader in conserving Grant Park as an open space.

POTTER PALMER, dry goods merchant, came in 1850's, built the original Palmer House and a second one after the Great Fire, developed State St. as major business avenue.

JOHN WHISTLER, Captain, USA, arrived in 1803 to lay out Fort Dearborn, commanded until 1810. His son William commanded there during the Black Hawk War and his son George became a great engineer. George was the father of James A. McNeill Whistler, the painter.

JOHN KINZIE, fur trader, came in 1804 to run trading post, helped conciliate Indians.

JEAN BAPTISTE POINT DU SABLE, West Indian Negro, was first settler of Chicago and had a substantial trading post on north bank of Chicago River, which he left in 1796.

The Wrigley Building

The WRIGLEY BUILDING at the northwest plaza of the Michigan Ave. Bridge, was the first tall building to take advantage of this superb location. Its builder, W. W. Wrigley, had gained a great commercial success with chewing gum, which he made nationally popular by effective outdoor advertising. The building itself became a showplace, for its facade was covered with white terra cotta, which blazed forth at night under floodlighting. Its tower carries four dials. The head of the corporation, Philip K. Wrigley, is owner of the Chicago Cubs baseball team, which plays in Wrigley Field. An addition to the main building has similar white tile. The building was designed by Graham, Anderson, Probst and White and is an adaptation of French Renaissance.

The next building north of the Wrigley Building on the west side of Michigan Ave. is the APOLLO SAVINGS & LOAN BUILDING, erected in 1964. Between this and the Wrigley Bldg. is an open space, the PLAZA OF THE AMERICAS, usually gay with flags of countries of the western hemisphere. Here a day in April is annually observed as Pan American Day, when consuls and other representatives of North, South, and Central America exchange felicitations.

At 425 N. Michigan Ave. is the editorial office of the Encyclopedia Britannica. Its library of 30,000 vols. is combined with the library of F. E. Compton & Co. Tuesday Publications is at 625 N. Michigan.

In February, 1974, ground was broken at 444 N. Michigan Ave. for the Educational Facilities Center, which planned a 34-story building for the Learning Environment and Operating Facilities that had been located at 223 N. Michigan. The organization conducts educational workshops, in-service training programs, and a teachers' resource laboratory, and allocated space in the new building for exhibits by 40 publishers of school materials, books and systems. The Center expected a monthly flow of 8,000 teachers through its new headquarters.

The original Michigan Square Building, 640 N. Michigan Ave., became known as the Diana Court Building, and was cited for its attractive court, which contained a statue of Diana by Carl Milles. It was occupied for a number of years by Time-Life. A new TIME BUILDING at Grand Ave. and Fairbanks, was designed by Harry Weese and Associates.

The imposing TRIBUNE TOWER, 435 N. Michigan Ave., rises north of Pioneer Court, conspicuous among the steel-and-glass skyscrapers in the area by its Gothic crown of small buttresses and pinnacles. It houses the principal executive offices of the *Chicago Tribune,* while a six-story wing at the east, faced with white marble, has the editorial rooms and the mechanical plant.

Flanked by built-in stone fragments from celebrated buildings, the richly carved entrance arch is three stories high; light enters the lobby through a pierced stone screen of fanciful design. Entwined in foliage are figures from Æsop's fables and facetious representations of the architects—a howling dog for John Mead Howells, a figure of Robin Hood for Raymond M. Hood—whose design won the $50,000 award in the world-wide competition held by the *Tribune* in 1921 for "the most beautiful and distinctive office building in the world." The second prize was won by the Finnish architect, Eliel Saarinen, whose design foreshadowed vertical setbacks and has had an extensive influence on skyscraper architecture. One design was submitted by Walter Gropius of Weimar, Germany, of the Bauhaus group. The Tribune Tower is 462 ft. tall and has 36 stories.

On the travertine walls of the lobby are quotations on the freedom of the press, a mural depicting man's struggle for freedom of speech, letters written by Abraham Lincoln to Joseph Medill, editor of the *Tribune,* and several weather recording devices.

The *Chicago Tribune,* occupying a large part of the building, was established in 1847. Oldest and most widely circulated newspaper in Chicago, it is one of the most profitable publishing enterprises in the world. Col. Robert R. McCormick, grandson of Joseph Medill, became editor and publisher in 1925 when his cousin, Capt. Joseph M. Patterson, took charge of the *New York Daily News,* which has the largest circulation in the country. Col. McCormick died in 1955, and was succeeded as publisher by Chester M. Campbell, 1955-1960; J. Howard Wood (1960-1969) and Harold Grumhaus (1969—). In 1972 Clayton Kirkpatrick was editor, Harold Hutchings executive editor, and Maxwell McCrohon managing editor.

Adjoining the Tribune on the north is the editorial office of *Chicago Today.*

William Randolph Hearst started the *Chicago Evening American* on July 4, 1900, on W. Madison St. near Wells, with a loud fanfare. He appealed for public attention with his press in the window, biting anti-Republican cartoons, comic strips, and huge headlines. It was an evening newspaper, competing with the *Daily News,* and *Evening Post,* and the *Daily Journal.* Hearst added a morning-and-Sunday newspaper, the *Chicago Examiner,* which later acquired the *Chicago Herald,* and became the *Herald-Examiner.* During the depression several newspapers died and when the Hearst investments became liabilities the Chicago Tribune Co. bought the *American* and eventually changed its name to *Chicago's American.* In 1969 it changed the name to *Chicago Today* and made it a tabloid. In 1972 the paper stopped publication of the Saturday and Sunday issues. On Sept. 15, 1974, it closed entirely.

North Michigan Avenue and its environs have special allurement for visitors and all in search of the fashionable chic. The shops of national renown—Tiffany, Bonwit Teller, Saks Fifth Avenue, Gucci, Neiman-Marcus—with Marshall Field & Co. putting down a seven-story anchor in Water Tower Place—are luxurious. Here, too, are the centers for decorative art and the shops where jewelry of exquisite design, and paintings, engravings, books, prints, and objects of art are on display. This, too, is the area of fine restaurants, some high in the sky, others just around the corner. West of Michigan Avenue is Rush Street, agleam with neon lights, packed with bars and restaurants of every price level, exuding the thump of drums and the endless balladry of night spots. The area from the Chicago River to North Avenue is attractive to hotels. In 1973 there were 11,064 rooms available and more than 3,000 under construction.

The SHERATON CHICAGO HOTEL is north of the Chicago Tribune Buildings. This 42-story tower, capped by a Moorish dome and minaret, was designed originally by Walter W. Alschlager as the Medinah Athletic Club and completed in 1928 at a cost of $10,000,000.

East Ontario Street

East Ontario St. and the 600 block on N. Michigan Ave. are favored by art galleries, both for public exhibition and commercial display. At 119 E. Ontario the long-established ARTS CLUB is a rendezvous for connoisseurs and amateurs. It gives a multiplicity of exhibitions, one-man shows, recitals, lectures, and films through the year.

The Arts Club was founded in 1916 and includes among its membership representatives of the seven arts. Fanny Butcher, in her autobiography, *Many Lives, One Love,* describes its leadership: "We have given Chicago the first look at many of the outstanding writers of the last half century . . . Chicago has seen there for the first time the work of most of the painters and sculptors of their day; from the first major American shows of Toulouse-Lautrec, Marcel Duchamp, Georges Braque, Marc Chagall, Paul Klee, Salvador Dali, Raoul Dufy, as well as the very latest electronic sculptors' devices. Among the musicians and conductors, Paul Hindemith made his first solo performance. . . . Schoenberg's *Kammersymphonie* had its first Chicago performance under the baton of Frederick Stock, with Schoenberg beaming on everyone, and Igor Stravinsky and Serge Prokofiev met Arts Club members before they met larger audiences. . . Its present rooms were designed by Mies van der Rohe and its permanent art collection includes the famous Brancusi Golden Bird, Miros, Dufys, and a Braque Tapestry."

The MUSEUM OF CONTEMPORARY ART, 237 East Ontario St., was opened in November, 1967, and has created astonishment and strong feelings ever since. *Avant-garde* is not an adequate name for its exhibits; its choice of bizarre and irrational contrivances leaves the advance far behind. A good place to observe the last vestiges of a dying order or the first intimations of a new one.

At 100 East Ontario St. is the KUNGSHOLM RESTAURANT, where people go not only to dine but to listen to grand opera, sung in a miniature theater by 13-inch puppets. In the course of decades the Kungsholm has perfected the performances to such an extent that it has acquired a national reputation. The theatre has an authentic decor and the voices are those of master artists on records. There are evening performances at 8 every night except Monday; also some afternoon programs.

At 333 East Ontario St. is the McCLURG COURT CENTER, two highrise apartment buildings with lower attached facilities that include a bank, shops, Henrici's, a theater, tennis and handball courts, and a children's playground.

The AMERICAN COLLEGE OF SURGEONS, 40 E. Erie St., is the national headquarters of a fellowship of surgeons. The gray stone building, formerly the mansion of S. M. Nickerson, a banker, was completed in 1883; the great entrance hall is entirely of marble; carved alabaster openwork graces the stair-rail. An enclosed passageway leads to the JOHN B. MURPHY MEMORIAL, 50 E. Erie St., an auditorium dedicated to the memory of one of the great surgeons of the early twentieth century. From the street the colonnaded façade appears to be wedged between the adjoining buildings. Panels in the imposing bronze entrance doors picture epoch-making discoveries in the history of medicine.

The SURGICAL MUSEUM AND HALL OF FAME of the International College of Surgeons, 1524 N. Lake Shore Drive, has exhibits demonstrating the advance of surgery from the days of primitive healing. *Open daily, 10-4, free.*

American Library Association

At 50 East Huron St. the AMERICAN LIBRARY ASSOCIA-TION guides and watches over the farflung activities of the public libraries of the United States. It occupies a modern building completed in 1963, which took the place of the venerable Victorian mansion of the McCormick family, where the ALA had functioned since 1946 with many discomforts. In 1951 the organization had 19,701 members and operated on a budget of $191,129; in 1971 it had 30,592 members and a budget of $2,262,971, and its officials had placed it in the forefront of the fight for social and intellectual liberties and extended the educational services of libraries into many new fields. The occupancy of a new, efficient headquarters saved the ALA for Chicago; an attempt had been made to establish a public relations office in Washington, D. C., but the fear of its becoming a bureaucratic lobby kept control in Chicago.

The ALA became a force for leadership when the Federal Government voted the Library Services Act of 1956, followed by the National Defense Education Act of 1958, the Elementary and Secondary Education Act of 1965, the Higher Education Facilities Act of 1963, and the Higher Education Act of 1965. The ALA embraced the opportunity and libraries expanded all over the country; they constructed new buildings, started branches and equipped bookmobiles. They applied the principles of the Library Bill of Rights. In 1961 the bill was amended to condemn racial discrimination and restrictions on reading; the ALA fought unfair employment practices, defended libraries harassed by censors, and extended book services to the handicapped and the deprived. It cooperated with the National Book Committee and helped dramatize National Book Week. In 1969 it established the Freedom to Read Foundation "to defend the principles of free speech and press and to support librarians and libraries who suffer legal injustices because of their support of these principles." At its Dallas Conference the ALA established a staff committee on mediation, arbitration, and inquiry, to deal with tenure, status, due process, and fair employment practices.

Although not the official head of the public libraries of the country, the ALA has made itself their guardian and mentor, watching over their welfare. It has been effective in starting new libraries, enlisting many new readers, and improving the status of librarians. Through conferences, divisions, councils, round tables, committees, affiliates, and publications it has made the public library a vital force in thousands of communities. It reaches all forms of library activities and originates new ones. It watches national agencies and state legislatures for protective laws and grants; aids the development of courses in library science; collects evidence of injustice to librarians and harassment of libraries; fights discrimination in jobs and book selections, supports civil liberties and the First Amendment; devises ways of supplying information; publishes materials for library use, and crosses international boundaries to help endangered libraries. In sum, ALA is Big Brother to the whole profession. It also distributes about thirty awards, medals, and scholarships, including the Newbery for text and the Caldecott for illustration of distinguished children's books, and the Clarence Day, Melvil Dewey, Grolier and Lippincott awards.

In addition to grants from the Federal Government ALA has had substantial sums from the Ford, Rockefeller and other foundations to support education for librarianship, international relations, research and experimentation, adult education and advances in library service. Between 1951 and 1972 private foundations gave the ALA $14,993,371. Librarians from all over the country attend the annual conferences of the ALA; at Chicago in 1972 there was a registration of 9,700, the majority professional librarians. ALA publishes a monthly organ, *American Libraries,* and the *Book List.*

The WESTBURY HOTEL, East Huron and St. Clair Sts., a new luxury unit of Knott Hotel Corp., presents a variation in the use of external steel columns that enclose the glass panels. The structure is 40 stories tall; the first seven floors are devoted to parking, the next six to offices, which have a separate lobby at 150 E. Huron St. The hotel has accommodations for conventions and conferences and an open-air swimming pool on the roof.

ST. JAMES CHURCH, Wabash Ave. at Huron St., was rebuilt around parts of the tower and rough stone walls that withstood the flames of 1871. The Episcopal Parish of St. James, established in 1834, built the original Gothic structure in 1857. At the north end of the church is the Chapel of St. Andrew, a beautiful bit of Gothic architecture, designed in 1913 by Bertram Goodhue; the chapel commemorates James L. Houghteling, founder of the Brotherhood of St. Andrew.

West of Michigan Avenue on Superior

The CATHEDRAL OF THE HOLY NAME, Superior and State Sts., a Victorian Gothic structure of limestone, dominates six diocesan and parish buildings. Containing the cathedral of the archbishop of the diocese, it is the center of Roman Catholic worship in metropolitan Chicago. At the Sunday noon high mass the Cardinal's cathedral choristers sing; the Cardinal himself celebrates the Pontifical high masses. The music of the cathedral is in authentic liturgical form.

According to the *Official Catholic Directory for 1973* (P. J. Kenedy & Sons) the Chicago diocese is the largest in Illinois with 2,489,320 communicants in Cook and Lake Counties. Enrollment at the six colleges and universities of the diocese was 27,377. Catholic students in all schools, parochial and public, were 425,077. The 24 hospitals conducted by the church had 8,552 beds and 1,195,303 patients annually, of whom 929,606 were outpatients.

There is one other diocesan organization in Chicago, the St. Nicholas-Ukrainian, which had 20,812 communicants and 2,228 students.

LEWIS TOWERS, 820 N. Michigan Ave., a 17-story building, is a component part of Loyola University of Chicago, which has its principal campus at 6525 Sheridan Road (*see Loyola University*) and its Medical Center at Maywood. Courses in business administration and lectures for adult classes are scheduled at Lewis. The Julia Deal Lewis Library has been expanded to use five floors, with provision for classrooms and offices. The Lewis Towers Art Galleries are open Monday through Friday, 9-9, Saturday, 9-4, free.

The WATER TOWER, rising 186 ft. above North Michigan Ave. at Chicago Ave., is dwarfed into what seems a decorated toy by the huge John Hancock Center a block up the Avenue. This pale yellow structure of limestone was designed by W. W. Boyington and built in 1869 to contain a standpipe 150 ft. tall and 3 ft. in diameter, which absorbed the pulsations caused by pumps in the Water Works, thus steadying the flow in the city's mains. The tower survived the Great Fire of 1871 and was preserved from destruction when Michigan Ave. was widened in 1928. The WATER WORKS that it served stands across the Avenue. It also was erected in 1867 and is the oldest of the stations that pumped water from Lake Michigan. The first station was built at Lake St. and Michigan Ave. in 1842 and pumped water through hollowed cedar logs. The first plant owned by the municipality was built on Chicago Avenue in 1854. The Chicago Fire burned out the 1867 plant but left the walls, which were used in reconstruction of the present building.

The centennial of the Water Tower and the Works was properly celebrated in 1967 by the Avenue's business association.

The tank-like structures in the lake, about two miles offshore north of Chicago Avenue, are two of the six cribs, or intakes, where approximately a billion gallons of water per day enter tunnels under the bed of the lake and flow to the pumping stations for distribution through the mains. The system was designed in 1864.

WATER TOWER PLACE, bounded by Pearson, Seneca and Chestnut Sts. at 845 N. Michigan Ave., 74 stories tall, is surpassed in loftiness in this area only by its neighbor, the John Hancock Center. This $130,000,000 commercial and residential enterprise is the investment of Mafco, Inc., a subsidiary of Marshall Field & Co., and the

Urban Investment & Development Co., a subsidiary of Aetna Life & Casualty Co. The complex includes a seven-story center for fashionable shops reserved by Marshall Field & Co., the new RITZ-CARLTON HOTEL starting at the 12th floor and using up to and including the 32nd floor, and private apartments filling the next 40 floors. There are four underground levels for parking 600 cars. The hotel is owned by Cabot, Cabot & Forbes Co., owners of the Ritz-Carlton in Boston, who considered Chicago a prime site for a luxurious inn that would appeal to the international trade. The lobby floor reached by elevators from Preston St. was planned with 18-ft. ceilings, glass-enclosed public rooms, a 350 ft. promenade, Greenhouse and Japanese garden, covering three acres over the roof of the 12th floor extension adjoining the tower. A formal dining room, restaurant, cafe, and English grill, swimming pool, sauna and exercise facilities are part of the design. Completion of the whole project was set for 1975.

The American Dental Assn. Building, 211 E. Chicago Ave., is 23 stories tall and was completed in 1965.

John Hancock Center

In Chicago it's Big John, the JOHN HANCOCK CENTER, which carries its 1,105 ft. skyward at 875 North Michigan Ave., between Chestnut St. and Delaware Place, dwarfing all the little 40 to 60 story buildings near the famous Water Tower. It is a combination of shops, offices, apartments, restaurants and garages, and was erected in 1969 by the John Hancock Mutual Life Insurance Co. It was built by Skidmore, Owings & Merrill from designs by Bruce Graham and Dr. Fazlur Kahn, who also designed Sears Tower.

Its height of 100 stories changed the Chicago skyline and for a time made it the tallest building in Chicago and hence of the West. That distinction was lost in 1972 when the new Standard Oil of Indiana building at 200 East Randolph St. "topped out" at 1,126 ft. Before a year had passed Sears Tower surpassed all man-made heights with 1,454 ft.

The John Hancock Center has several striking elements in its structure: one, its walls taper upward, and another, diagonal braces appear to hold the steel columns together. There is a set of braces for every 18 floors. They interfere to some extent with window space. Although they seem an innovation, they actually are a return to the old method of bracing barns and frame buildings. They also steady the structure against wind pressure. Although other methods might have been used and disguised, they brought about a saving of 27,000 tons of steel, and a reputation for honest disclosure of materials.

From the 45th to the 92nd floor is an area allotted to 703 apartments, originally leased at annual rentals. Within three years of operation the owners decided that more was to be gained by operating the apartments as condominiums, and in the spring of 1973 offered them to the tenants. The owners explained that many individual tenants had requested the change. The owners made a number of alterations to benefit resident-owners. They installed a restaurant for owner use on the 44th floor, as well as a commissary, a swimming pool, exercise rooms, a party room, and a lobby with a view over the city. The units are priced from $18,900 to $103,500, and the annual assessment for operating expenses is estimated at about 3% of the initial sales price.

The Center has a public restaurant on the 95th floor, with remarkable views. It also offers an observation platform for a look into four states, *9 a.m. to 12 midnight; adults, $1.25, children, 75¢, family of four or more, $3.50.*

On the same block with the Center is a small brick building, painted gray, occupied by the CASINO CLUB, a long-established organization wealthy enough to ignore any offers for its property.

The FOURTH PRESBYTERIAN CHURCH, Michigan Ave. and Delaware Pl., designed by Ralph Adams Cram in 1912, is a fine example of English Gothic in beautifully carved Bedford stone. The parish house adjoining was designed by Howard V. Shaw in 1925. The fourth side of the rectangle is an arcade through which passers-by glimpse the cloister garth and fountain. The church is a massive edifice with pinnacled gables, slender spire, and generous buttresses. The stained-glass windows were designed and executed by Charles Connick.

The Elizabeth Arden Corporation built its headquarters, a three-story building at 717 N. Michigan Ave., in 1965.

The CONTINENTAL PLAZA HOTEL, 909 North Michigan Ave., opened in 1964, with 16 stories, has added a new 27-story section facing East Delaware which gives the hotel a total of 747 rooms. Cost was approximately $20 million. The hotel is owned by Western International Hotels, a subsidiary of UAL, Inc., parent company of United Air Lines.

At 18 East Chestnut St. is the ABRAHAM LINCOLN BOOK-SHOP of Ralph Newman, specialist in Americana, notably the careers of Lincoln and Ulysses S. Grant. Newman and Daniel Weinberg have a department devoted to the Presidents of the United States and their contemporaries. Many activities associated with the centennial of the Civil War and the sesquicentennial of Illinois were inspired here. Newman, president of the board of the Chicago Public Library and former president of the Illinois State Historical Society, has initiated numerous historical enterprises.

The QUIGLEY PREPARATORY SEMINARY, training youths for the Roman Catholic priesthood, has expanded into two locations. The North Seminary, 103 E. Chestnut St., enrolls 395 students and has 26 in faculty in a typical year; the South Seminary, 7140 S. Western Ave., has 768 students and 46 in faculty. The North unit, with the Chapel of St. James reminiscent of the renowned Sainte Chapelle of Paris, is considered a notable adaptation of ecclesiastical Gothic architecture.

The Playboy Enterprises, Inc.

The PLAYBOY BUILDING, 919 N. Michigan Ave., opposite the Drake Hotel on Walton is the headquarters of the Playboy enterprises founded in 1953 by Hugh M. Hefner. It has 37 stories, was the first tall building in Chicago to use a setback design, and was planned by Holabird & Root as the Palmolive Building in 1929. Atop its roof is the Lindbergh Beacon of 2 billion candlepower, which rotated freely until the John Hancock Center rose to intercept its beam. A shield was built to protect the Hancock from its intense light. When the energy crisis came in 1974 the beacon was dimmed, as were the floodlights of the Wrigley Building. The Playboy building is connected by a promenade with Playboy Towers, a 300-room hotel, and the Playboy Club. Basic in the corporate structure is the magazine *Playboy,* first issued in December, 1953 (featuring Marilyn Monroe), which circulates more than 6,500,000 copies and ranks 12th in size among American magazines. It accounted for $83,000,000 income out of a corporate total of $159,450,000 and earnings of $18,782,000 in 1972. Its profitable condition, when hotels and other subsidiaries reported losses, may have influenced the decision to launch *Oui,* a second girlie magazine intended to compete with imitations of *Playboy.*

Playboy Enterprises also owns elaborate resort hotels at Lake Geneva, Wisc., Great Gorge, N. J., Miami Beach, and in Jamaica; has collaborated with Warner Communications and Universal Pictures in producing movies (*That Championship Season, The Naked Ape,* and *Third Girl from the Left*); has a book publishing division and a music and record issuing company and leases its trade mark to various products. Its second most profitable venture is said to be the investment in casinos in London, Manchester, Portsmouth and other places in England, including the established Clermont Club in Berkeley Square, where no Bunnies appear. The career of Hugh M. Hefner, a former subscription promotion copywriter on Esquire, began with an investment of $600 cash and the idea that men would welcome leisure-time reading and dining amid a display of pulchritude that did not threaten involvement. By starting a new version of look-but-don't touch he called the turn of the new permissiveness. Hefner's mansion at 1340 N. State Parkway became a showplace. He now lives part of the year on the Pacific Coast. At age 47 (1973) Hefner owned about 7,000,000 shares of the 9,407,000 shares of Playboy Enterprises, Inc.

The DRAKE HOTEL, 140 E. Walton St. at Michigan Ave. was one of the first major hotels to open on North Michigan Avenue. It is directly opposite the Playboy Building and has the Lake Shore Drive on its front. It is known for the Camellia House and the Cape Cod Room.

West on Oak St. near LaSalle an urban renewal project has made possible the construction of two large residential towers in what was once a run-down neighborhood. Twin towers 53 stories tall rise toward the sky in an improvement for which the U. S. Dept. of Housing &

Urban Development approved $40,000,000. The whole renewal area covers 90 acres bounded by N. LaSalle St., Chicago Ave., Division and Sedgwick Sts.

NEWBERRY PLAZA, N. State and Oak Sts., which reached its height of 554 ft. in February, 1973, is an apartment building of 624 units that dominates the Rush St. entertainment area. Its cost was placed at $18,000,000.

American Medical Association

The AMERICAN MEDICAL ASSOCIATION, 535 North Dearborn St., corner of Grand Ave. This is the headquarters of the largest organization of physicians in the country, which records the progress of medical research, works for health legislation, and keeps abreast of scientific information throughout the world. Its *Journal of the American Medical Assn.* publishes the results of medical research. The Archive has 100,000 items and the Library 55,000 volumes relating to its interests. There is a large collection of documents and materials on the subject of quackery—illegal and spurious projects and remedies. The AMA dates from 1847, the Archive-Library from 1868. It was consulted by Sinclair Lewis while writing *Arrowsmith,* his novel about a physician.

The Newberry Library

The NEWBERRY LIBRARY, on West Walton St., between Clark and Dearborn, is a library of rarities specializing in the humanities and acknowledged of first rank in the nation. It was established in 1887 by the trustees of the estate of Walter Loomis Newberry, who allocated about $2,150,000 for the purpose after the death of Mrs. Loomis. Walter Loomis, who had died at sea in 1868, was a native of Connecticut who had settled in Chicago in 1833 and by sagacious real estate deals, banking, and railroad administration acquired wealth and served as president of the Board of Education and Acting Mayor. The library's quarters, a five-story Romanesque building of granite designed by Henry Ives Cobb, stands on the site of the house of William Ogden, the only in this part of the North Side that survived the Great Fire.

The library was occupied in 1893 with William Frederick Poole as first librarian. Poole was a man of great energy and fine taste, who acquired the first outstanding collections, the library of early Italian music, history and theory of Pio Resse, a Florentine, including the first edition of the first opera, Jacopo Peri's *Euridici,* and another collection of 2,500 volumes including incunabula, Shakespeare folios, and rare bindings. Poole also laid the basis of a general reference library, which today makes the Newberry a gathering place for scholars. In recent years the library has confined itself to Western Europe and the Americas, covering the Middle Ages to the end of the Napoleonic era, to the revolutionary period in Latin America, and to World War I in North America.

An unusual benefactor of the library was Edward E. Ayer, a Chicago man who made a success of selling railroad ties. Alerted by Prescott's *Conquest of Mexico,* he began gathering books on Indian-

Transportation and Commerce

GOVERNMENT LOCK NO. 19 AT KEOKUK ON THE MISSISSIPPI,
OPPOSITE HAMILTON, ILLINOIS

STEAMBOAT QUINCY OF DIAMOND JO LINE BEFORE JOINING
STRECKFUS LINE IN 1911

TOWBOAT *TRUAX* WITH BARGES OF COAL APPROACHING LOCK
15 AT ROCK ISLAND

EARLY PHOTOGRAPH (C. 1850) OF U. S. MAIL STEAMBOAT
NOMINEE AT GALENA DOCK; PIGS OF LEAD IN FOREGROUND

EXCURSION STEAMBOAT PASSING UNDER HIGHWAY BRIDGE AT
EAST DUBUQUE, ILLINOIS, DURING HIGH WATER ON MISSISSIPPI

SANTA FE RAILROAD BRIDGE ACROSS ILLINOIS RIVER NEAR
CHILLICOTHE

OLD RAILROAD BRIDGE FROM FORT MADISON, IOWA,
TO HANCOCK COUNTY, ILLINOIS

CATERPILLAR TRACTOR COMPANY, GENERAL OFFICES, PEORIA

QUAD CITIES NUCLEAR POWER PLANT, COMMONWEALTH EDISON CO., CORDOVA

DEARBORN STATION RAILROAD TERMINAL, CHICAGO

TYPICAL BRICK AND RED SANDSTONE RAILROAD STATION; SANTA FE AT GALESBURG, 1887-1962

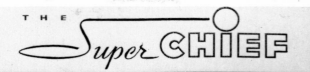

FIRST EASTBOUND RUN, MAY 15th, 1936

ᐧBREAKFASTᐧ

FRUITS AND PRESERVES

Orange, one 15	Sliced Orange 20	Apple, one 10

Orange Marmalade 25 · Apricot Jam 25

Preserved Figs 30; with Cream 35 · Preserved Strawberries 25

CEREALS

Shredded Wheat Biscuits with Milk 20; with Cream 30

Rolled Oats with Milk 20; with Cream 30

STEAKS, CHOPS, ETC.

Small Sirloin a la Minute 1.25 · Sirloin for one 1.60 · Sirloin for two 2.75

Lamb Chop (1) 45 · Lamb Chop, Extra Thick (1) 80 (to order——20 minutes)

Broiled Chicken, half 85 · Fried Chicken, half 85

Calf's Liver and Bacon 70 · Veal Cutlet, Plain or Breaded 65

POTATOES

French Fried 20 · Hashed Browned or Lyonnaise 20 · Au Gratin 25

BACON, HAM, ETC.

Bacon 65; half portion 40 · Ham 70; half portion 40

Bacon and Eggs 70 · Ham and Eggs 70

EGGS

Boiled or Fried Eggs 30 · Scrambled Eggs 30

Shirred Eggs 30 · Poached Eggs on Toast 45

Plain Omelette (3 Eggs) 50 · Spanish or Mushroom Omelette 65

BREAD, ETC.

Hot Rolls 10 · Corn Muffins 10 · Raisin or Whole Wheat Bread Toast 15

Dry or Buttered Toast 15 · Melba Toast 15 · Milk Toast 30

Wheat Cakes with Maple Syrup 30

COFFEE, TEA, ETC.

Coffee, per pot 25 · Kaffee Hag Coffee, per pot 25

Cocoa or Chocolate, Whipped Cream, per pot 20

Tea—Ceylon, Young Hyson, English Breakfast, Orange-Pekoe, per pot 20

Milk, per bottle 15 · Malted Milk 20 · Postum, per pot 15

An extra charge of twenty-five cents each will be made for all meals served outside of Dining Car

Guests will please call for checks before paying and compare amounts charged

SANTA FE DINING CAR SERVICE
Fred Harvey

BREAKFAST MENU ON THE FIRST EASTBOUND RUN OF THE
SUPERCHIEF, LOS ANGELES TO CHICAGO, MAY 15, 1936. TRAIN
DEPARTED FROM CHICAGO ON TUESDAY, LOS ANGELES ON
FRIDAY.

MAYOR RICHARD J. DALEY RECEIVES SKETCH OF NEW APPAREL MART. LEFT TO RIGHT: THOMAS V. KING, MANAGER OF MERCHANDISE MART, W. O. OLLMAN, CONSULTANT TO THE KENNEDY FAMILY (OWNER), AND MAYOR DALEY.

MERCHANDISE MART ON THE CHICAGO RIVER, WORLD'S LARGEST WHOLESALE BUYING CENTER.

white relations and donated 17,000 items to the library, as well as endowment, which has helped the expansion of the collection to 84,000 volumes. Everett D. Graff, a steel executive who became president of the Art Institute and the Newberry Library formed a remarkable collection of Western Americana, comprising items related to Lewis and Clark, the Mormon march across the Plains, and the Gold Rush of '49, while John M. Wing initiated a collection on printing. In 1964 Lawrence W. Towner, director-librarian, purchased the "great gathering of great books" of Louis H. Silver, including Shakespeare quartos, Caxton printings, and first editions of the *Divine Comedy, Don Quixote* and *Alice in Wonderland*. The library also has acquired the books of Stone & Kimball, with many manuscripts, and has the papers of Sherwood Anderson Floyd Dell, and other Midwestern writers, as well as the archives of the Chicago Daily News, the Illinois Central Railroad, the Burlington Railroad and the Pullman Company.

Among the many activities of the library are seminars in the humanities held twice each year, a Renaissance conference each spring, lectures, and publications. In cooperation with Northwestern University Newberry Library is issuing the *Writings of Herman Melville,* in 15 volumes. Another project is an *Atlas of Early American History.* The Library's cartographic resources have been brought together into the Hermon Dunlap Smith Center for the History of Cartography, which sponsors research and publication on the subject.

The library holds periodic exhibitions of its rare books, prints, maps, and manuscripts. It has 1,250,000 books and pamphlets, and around 4,000,000 manuscripts. *Open 9 to 9, Monday-Friday; 9 to 5, Saturday; Special Collections open until 5 p.m. daily.*

Astor Street

Astor is a short street of six blocks extending from Division St. to North Ave., one block west of Lake Shore Drive in Chicago's fabled Gold Coast. Its one-family houses, closely packed together, recall the days when this area was favored by social and industrial leaders. Highrise apartments have displaced the houses of wealthy Chicagoans on the Drive and threaten the exclusiveness of Astor Street. The Commission on Historical and Architectural Landmarks, the Landmarks Preservation Council, the Near North Preservation Group, and the North State, Astor & Lake Shore Drive Assn. are agitating municipal protection for the street, hoping to keep its landmarks from demolition.

The architecture expresses the eclecticism of the 1890s and later. Well known architects built houses for well known people. Two already have been cited for special acclaim: the CHARNLEY HOUSE, 1365 Astor St., and the ALBERT MADLENER HOUSE, 4 West Burton Place, at Astor. The Charnley House is a three-story and high-basement brick residence built in 1892 by Adler & Sullivan, but Ira J. Bach says it is ascribed to Frank Lloyd Wright because Wright was the draftsman for these architects at the time, and the house retains some elements of his style. An extension has been added at the rear. The Madlener House is a substantial brick building with white marble trim designed in 1902 by Richard E. Schmidt, which has been named an architectural landmark. It is occupied by the Graham Foundation for Advanced Studies in the Fine Arts. The interior was remodeled in 1963. It may be visited Monday through Friday 9-5 by reservation.

While some of the original houses have been maintained intact, others have been changed into apartments, and still others have been displaced. The Joseph P. Bowen house, 1430 Astor now replaced by Astor Villa, a tall condominium, was the home of Louise de Koven Bowen, associate in social betterment of Jane Addams, who often came there; here Theodore Roosevelt was tendered a dinner in 1912. At 1435 Astor David Jones was host to Woodrow Wilson before the latter's first nomination. Adlai Stevenson and his family lived at 1434 in the 1930s.

A large Italianate mansion at the northwest corner of Astor and Burton Place is known as the Cyrus McCormick II House, although McCormick actually lived in it only five years. It was built by Stanford White in 1892 for Mrs. Robert Patterson, daughter of Joseph Medill and wife of the editor of the *Chicago Tribune*; their children were "Cissy" Patterson and Joseph Medill Patterson. After McCormick became the owner he had David Adler add numerous rooms. It was bought in 1950 by the Bateman School, a private institution with elementary and high school curricula.

Several new buildings have been erected in Astor St. in recent years. The newest residence was built at 1524 Astor by Charles Haffner III in 1966 on a lot 20 ft. wide and 110 ft. deep. The Astor Tower Hotel at the northwest corner of Goethe and Astor was erected in 1963; it contains Maxim's restaurant. It was designed by Bertrand Goldberg, architect of Marina City, who lives in an old house in Astor St. Astor Terrace is a new condominium building at 1450 Astor.

William McCormick Blair occupies a house in Astor, and Joseph T. Ryerson, Gustavus F. Swift, Jr., and George W. Meeker once lived there. Astor St. also has been the home of writers, including Harriet Monroe and Dorothy Aldis; Fanny Butcher (Mrs. Richard Drummond Bokum) still lives there.

At the north end looms the large brick Archepiscopal Palace, home of the Roman Catholic Cardinal, a house of 19 chimneys, which really fronts on North State Parkway. At 1340 North State Parkway is the Playboy Mansion, owned by Hugh M. Hefner, once the residence of Dr. George Isham. At North State Parkway and Goethe St. are two famous luxury hotels, Ambassador East, with the Pump Room, and Ambassador West, both connected by a tunnel.

Site of Potter Palmer Mansion

A famous landmark at the turn of the century was the POTTER PALMER MANSION, a huge turreted residence of sandstone and gray granite, that stood on Lake Shore Drive between Banks and Schiller Sts. Palmer built it in 1885. After his death in 1902 his wife, Bertha Honore Palmer, social leader, continued to make it a center for receptions and concerts. The Palmers had a fine art gallery, specializing in early French impressionist paintings, which they donated to the Art Institute. As the Palmer and Field generation passed on, dwellings became more conservative. After Mrs. Palmer died the mansion was owned for a time by Victor Bendix, then replaced in 1950 by a high-rise apartment building, which has luxurious suites.

Old Town

OLD TOWN is the latest Chicago area to cultivate an informal bohemianism. Unlike its predecessors of Tooker Alley, Jackson Park, and the more class-conscious Petit Gourmet, Old Town is not a small group of poets and artists, but a neighborhood of oldfashioned brick buildings packed with snack bars, restaurants, curio shops, ice cream stands, and bars, calling forth large groups of aficianados and crowds of the curious on weekend nights. Proceed up North Wells St. to Division and prepare to plunge into a murky, feverish atmosphere, where electrified rock splinters the night air. With Wells as the principal thoroughfare the attractions spill over on sidestreets—Goethe, Burton, Eugenie, and North Ave. and one block east to LaSalle.

One of the attractions of Old Town is the Royal London Wax Museum, 1419 N. Wells St., which offers settings all the way from DaVinci's Last Supper to the traditional Chamber of Horrors. The notorious leaders of Chicago's gangland are among the 150 wax figures.

At 1608 North Wells St. is gaslit Piper's Alley, which was established for decades before Old Town began to develop as a tourist attraction. This is a brick building erected by Henry Piper, a baker. After the Great Fire destroyed the frame dwellings built by early German immigrants more substantial houses of brick and stone continued this as a popular residential area for Germans who arrived later. After fifty years of use these buildings were rehabilitated. Most of them had Victorian angles and curves, bays and oriel windows, and Harry Weese, architect, gave them substantial facade-liftings.

Second City, 1616 N. Wells St., has established a sound reputation for good acting and original satirical sketches. There are no performances on Monday; on some weekday evenings there are two or more shows; on Sunday there is one at 9. Shows may be combined with dinner in Piper's Alley.

Another "special" spot is NEW TOWN, on Broadway between Diversey and Belmont, for dining and relaxation.

For contrast, a walk beyond LaSalle St. leads to an old landmark —the MOODY BIBLE INSTITUTE, and a new one—CARL SANDBURG VILLAGE. The Administrative Building of Moody Institute is at 812 N. LaSalle St., a 12-story Gothic structure of red brick and Bedford stone, completed in 1938. Here is the core of a farflung evangelistic movement that originated when Dwight L. Moody preached a fundamental Christian faith for the disheartened in missions and Ira Sankey played the organ and led in sacred songs. The Moody Church is located at N. Clark Ct. and North Ave.

CARL SANDBURG VILLAGE, extending from Division St. to North Ave., between Clark and LaSalle Sts. is a fine example of change by the Department of Urban Renewal, for before the 1960 decade this was an area of rundown shops and sagging houses. Now the high-rise apartment buildings tower like great monuments over smaller two-story townhouses, named for the poet-historian who was born in a blacksmith's cottage and lived to become a national hero of letters. Sandburg is quoted by friends as saying he hoped the enterprise would benefit the man of small income, but there is doubt this can be accomplished. The project cost $60,000,000 and comprises 2,692 dwelling units and shopping center. The area also contains the Chicago Latin School and a new St. Paul's Lutheran Church.

MEDINAH TEMPLE, 600 N. Wabash Ave., is the seat of the Nobles of the Mystic Shrine, the Masonic organization generally called the Shriners. The building has an auditorium seating 4,000. One of its popular activities is the annual circus, at which it raises funds for various aids to children.

Lincoln Park

Along the lakeshore between North and Hollywood Aves. and from Lake Michigan to Clark St., Lincoln Park West, and Sheridan Road stretches LINCOLN PARK, 1,185 acres of rolling woodlands, bridle paths, placid lagoons, yacht basins, playgrounds, golf courses, and gardens, dotted with monuments, museums and a Zoo. Originally a 120-acre city cemetery, the tract was designated as a park in 1864, and most of the graves were moved to outlying cemeteries. Adjacent lands were acquired, but the largest part of the park was created with sand from the lake.

At the south end of the park, commanding the Dearborn Parkway entrance, is the statue of ABRAHAM LINCOLN, by Augustus Saint Gaudens, unveiled October 22, 1887. Larger than life, it portrays Lincoln in a reflective attitude in the mood of the Gettysburg Address. The simple base and the spacious exedra are the work of Stanford White.

West of the statue is the CHICAGO HISTORICAL SOCIETY MUSEUM. Georgian in style the red brick building with limestone trim has two stories, a ground-level basement and a flat balustraded roof; a broad flight of steps sweeps down from the Doric portico. Opened in 1932, the museum is the fourth home of the society, founded in 1856 to collect and preserve materials pertaining to the history of the United States, particularly those relating to Chicago and the Northwest Territory. Two earlier buildings were destroyed by fire; the original draft of the Emancipation Proclamation was lost in the Great Fire of 1871. A new wing was completed in 1972.

A dozen period rooms tell the story of America from the days of Columbus; several reproduce famous old rooms. Objects range from anchors used by Columbus to messages sent out by carrier pigeon from the Lost Battalion in the Argonne Forest during World War I. The George Washington Collection includes several noteworthy paintings of Washington, the velvet suit he wore at his second inauguration, and other personal effects. There is a collection of gowns worn by the First

Ladies. In the Chicago rooms are women's costumes of various periods, illustrations of the Chicago Fire and other historic events.

The Pioneer Room contains a reproduction of the Lincoln log cabin. The Illinois Room has a mask of Stephen A. Douglas and some of his effects, a first edition of the Book of Mormon, and part of the Lovejoy press. Lincoln Hall, lined with portraits and sculptures of the martyred President, contains his blanket shawl, the table on which he signed the Emancipation Proclamation, and the clothes he wore at the time of his assassination. His deathbed is preserved in a room that reproduces the one in which he died. The Lincoln Parlor, a reproduction of the original in his Springfield house, has authentic furniture.

In the foyer of the ground floor is the dynamic Massacre Monument, by Carl Rohl-Smith, which stood originally in East 18th St., near the site of the event. The Carriage Room contains a Conestoga wagon and other early vehicles. On the ground floor is the Auditorium, where lectures on Chicago history are given.

The research library has about 140,000 volumes dealing chiefly with Chicago and the Northwest. It has special collections of the American Civil War, Abraham Lincoln, and American sports. About 3,000,000 documents are in the Manuscript Division. It has about 300,000 negatives, photographs, and prints. The society publishes *Chicago History*, biennially, and occasionally books of unusual interest.

The society has acquired a collection of prints of great rarity dealing with the American Revolution. Four engravings of the battle of Lexington, including the seizure of the North Bridge at Concord, made by Amos Doolittle of New Haven from drawings made soon after the engagement, were bid in by the society at the Sotheby Parke Bernet galleries in New York for $82,500. The society also acquired one of the rarest of Revolutionary engravings, the only known impression of the first state of Paul Revere's rendering of the Boston Massacre of March 5, 1770, which was in the collection of J. William Middendorf, 2nd, now ambassador to the Netherlands, which went for $30,000.

Special programs for school children are presented on Wednesdays and Saturdays during the school year, and Summer Fun programs are offered during the vacation period. Guided tours and gallery talks (by appointment), are offered throughout the year. A free booklet *Key to Education Department Services* is mailed upon request.

The Chicago Historical Society is located at North Ave. and Clark St. *Museum open Monday-Saturday 9:30-4:30. Library, Tues.-Sat., 9-5, closed Saturday & Monday. Sunday Films and concerts, 2:15 p.m., free to visitors with stubs for current admissions. Regular admission, family $1; adults, 50¢, children 6-17, 25¢, senior citizens, 25¢.*

Also near the Historical Museum is the GREEN VARDIMAN BLACK monument, a memorial to the socalled Father of Modern Denistry, by Frederick C. Hibbard (1918). Dr. Black was dean of the Northwestern University Dental College from 1897 to 1915 when he died, aged 79.

North of the Chicago Historical Society building shrubbery screens the COUCH TOMB, relic of the old cemetery. It escaped removal by

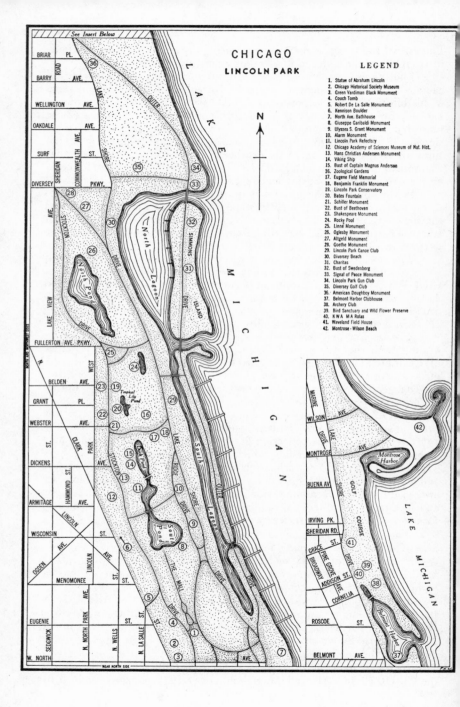

CHICAGO
LINCOLN PARK

LEGEND

1. Statue of Abraham Lincoln
2. Chicago Historical Society Museum
3. Green Vardiman Black Monument
4. Couch Tomb
5. Robert De La Salle Monument
6. Kennison Boulder
7. North Ave. Bathhouse
8. Giuseppe Garibaldi Monument
9. Ulysses S. Grant Monument
10. Alarm Monument
11. Lincoln Park Refectory
12. Chicago Academy of Sciences Museum of Nat. Hist.
13. Hans Christian Andersen Monument
14. Viking Ship
15. Bust of Captain Magnus Anderson
16. Zoological Gardens
17. Eugene Field Memorial
18. Benjamin Franklin Monument
19. Lincoln Park Conservatory
20. Bates Fountain
21. Schiller Monument
22. Bust of Beethoven
23. Shakespeare Monument
24. Rocky Pool
25. Linné Monument
26. Oglesby Monument
27. Altgeld Monument
28. Goethe Monument
29. Lincoln Park Canoe Club
30. Diversey Beach
31. Charitas
32. Bust of Swedenborg
33. Signal of Peace Monument
34. Lincoln Park Gun Club
35. Diversey Golf Club
36. American Doughboy Monument
37. Belmont Harbor Clubhouse
38. Archery Club
39. Bird Sanctuary and Wild Flower Preserve
40. K W A M A Rolas
41. Waveland Field House
42. Montrose - Wilson Beach

order of the Illinois Supreme Court, because the stone blocks, fastened with copper rivets, could not be taken apart without completely demolishing the mausoleum. Ira Couch, owner of the old Tremont House, several members of his family, and a stranger who died in the hotel, are interred here. ROBERT DE LA SALLE, by Count Jacque de la Laing (1889), faces the street that bears his name. The Kennison Boulder, at the foot of Wisconsin Street marks the approximate location of the only other known grave in the park. Here lies David Kennison (1736-1852), veteran of the Revolutionary War, and last survivor of the Boston Tea Party.

Lake Shore Drive, which throughout most of the length marks the former shore line of Lake Michigan, enters the park east of the Lincoln statue and the adjoining play fields. In 1938-39 sand was pumped in between North and Fullerton Avenues to form a beach a mile long. The North Avenue Bathhouse stands in the southeast corner of the park.

North of the Lincoln statue, the Mall runs through the heart of the old park. It divides into paths to skirt the South Pond and continues north to the Zoo. At the southeast corner of the pond is GUISEPPE GARIBALDI, a memorial (1901) by Victor Gherardi. Between Ridge and Lake Shore Drives, the ULYSSES S. GRANT monument, a heroic equestrian bronze, stands on a massive stone arch. The work of Louis Rebisso, it was erected by popular subscription and unveiled with elaborate ceremony on October 7, 1891. Northward, along Ridge Drive, is THE ALARM, a memorial to the Ottawa Indians, the work of John Boyle (1884). Lincoln Park Refectory, at the northwest corner of South Pond, contains a cafe and a rowboat concession.

West of the refectory, at Clark St. and Armitage Ave., is the CHICAGO ACADEMY OF SCIENCES MUSEUM OF NATURAL HISTORY, which portrays the natural history of the Chicago region. The ivy-mantled building, designed by Patton and Fisher in Italian Renaissance style, was made possible by a gift from Matthew Laflin. Governor John P. Altgeld laid the cornerstone in 1893. Collections include plants and animals of Chicago's dune and marsh regions, arranged with large tinted photographs of their habitats as backgrounds. Geological and paleontological specimens, systematic exhibits of flora and fauna—some once common but no longer found in the Chicago area—are labeled with cards bearing interpretative data. A section devoted to the Life of the World carries the interest farther afield.

The Academy of Sciences, founded in 1857, is one of the oldest scientific bodies in Chicago. The original collections were obtained by the first director, Robert Kennicott, on the Western Union survey for a telegraph-line route between Alaska and Russia in 1865. They were lost in the Great Fire. The Academy, supported by endowment memberships and the Chicago Park District, maintains the museum and a library, and engages in field studies and laboratory research. Talks and films on natural history, travel, and exploration are given in the lecture hall.

Eastward, across Stockton Drive, is HANS CHRISTIAN AN-DERSEN, a bronze by Johannes Gelert (1896) to the memory of the Danish author of fairy tales. The VIKING SHIP, northeast of the Andersen monument, is a reproduction of the vessels used by the Norse in crossing the North Atlantic 1,000 years ago. In this ship Captain Magnus Andersen and a crew of eleven crossed the Atlantic in 1893. The bust of Captain Magnus Andersen, at the prow of the ship, is the work of Carl Paulsen (1936).

Although the World's Fair of 1893 was formed to commemorate the discovery of America by Christopher Columbus, the Norwegian Government sent a replica of the ships sailed in 1,000 A. D. by the Vikings to the American continent. In 1893 there was no evidence other than the Icelandic Sagas that the Northmen actually had crossed the Atlantic. In 1960-63 remains of a settlement on the coast of Newfoundland were identified as Norse and by carbon dating placed at c. 900 A. D. by explorers of the National Geographic Society.

Flowers are admired, monuments are taken for granted, but the ZOO in Lincoln Park (Zoological Gardens, that is) is a must for every man, woman and child if the 4,000,000 annual visitors are any measure. Covering about 35 acres from Stockton Drive at Fullerton Parkway, the Zoo exhibits more than 2,600 birds and beasts in houses, pools, pits and stables. There are a Lion House (lions, tigers, jaguars, leopards); Reptile House, Small Mammal House, Children's House, and the Farm. Lions and elephants have had strong competition these days from the biggest gorilla in captivity, Sinbad, weight 550 lbs., and the chimpanzee tea party at 1:30 p.m. Then there are the sea lion splashing in his pool; birds of wonderful plumage but no music in their throats; modest little songsters with pure soprano; wild fowl. Among the most popular are the cows, lambkins and ponies, beloved by the young. *Open daily 9-5; children's zoo, 10-5, free.*

Near the center of the Zoo buildings is the EUGENE FIELD MEMORIAL, by Edward McCartan (1922). Depicted in bronze are the Dream Lady with two drowsy children, and inscribed on the granite base below are the poems of "Wynken, Blinken, and Nod" and the "Sugar Plum Tree in the Garden of Shut-Eye Town." End panels represent "The Fly Away Horse" and "Seein' Things." Northeastward is BENJAMIN FRANKLIN, by Richard Parks (1896).

The LINCOLN PARK CONSERVATORY. Stockton Drive at Fullerton Parkway, is a constant source of pleasure and satisfaction to the more than one million people who visit it winter and summer. It was begun in 1891-92 and today comprises four glass covered buildings, 18 propagating houses, and accessories, and covers three acres. At the entrance of the Palm House is a display of orchids. Here is the Fishtail palm of India and Malaya, which is tapped for its wine and can yield 3 gallons of juice a day. The 50-ft. Fiddleleaf rubber tree has leaves 12 to 15 in. long. Among other specimens the tapioca plant, the fig tree, and the banana stir interest for their usefulness, the Fifi island fan palm and the silver palm for their decorative qualities.

The Conservatory has a great variety of ferns, of which the Cycades are related to the oldest known plants. The Birdnest fern and the Staghorn fern get their names from their shapes. Of interest also is the yellow-flowered vanilla, from Colombia, which must be hand-pollinated to bear vanilla beans. From the fernery stone steps lead into the Tropical House, where the atmosphere is always kept humid. Here is the Grandleaf seagrape, with leaves 3 ft. across. Grouped together are a number of economic plants: the coffee tree, the coconut palm, the olive tree, the eucalyptus, kapok, and dwarf banana.

Four major shows are held annually, concurrently with those in Garfield Park Conservatory. They are the Chrysanthemum Show in November; the Christmas Show; the Azalea and Camellia Show in February-March, and the Easter Show. Plants with bright-colored foliage are shown in the summer. Three large gardens are landscaped out-of-doors. The Main Garden has eight formal beds, with the Bates Fountain, by St. Gaudens and Frederick MacMonnies, in the center and the statue of the poet Friedrich Schiller at one end. The Grandmother's Garden has many of the popular perennials. The Rock Garden displays about 3,000 annuals and 4,000 perennials and is a never-ending succession of blooms. *Open 9-5; major shows, 9-9; free.*

Across the Drive are a bust of BEETHOVEN, the work of Johannes Gelert (1897) and a SHAKESPEARE monument, by William Ordway Partridge (1894). Northeast of the Conservatory is a pool around which grow native wild flowers, hawthorns and willows. Overlooking the Conservatory from the north is an impressive bronze memorial to the Swedish botanist, Karl Von Linne (Linnaeus), by C. Dyfverman (1891), with four allegorical figures surrounding the pedestal.

North Pond lies across the parkway from the monument. On a wooded eminence the OGLESBY monument, dedicated to the memory of Richard James Oglesby, three times governor of Illinois (1865, 1872, 1885), the work of Leonard Crunelle (1919). To the north is the ALTGELD monument, by Gutzon Borglum (1915), a memorial to John Peter Altgeld, governor 1892-96.

Eastward in this section of the park are the North and South Lagoons, between Lake Shore and Outer Drives. On South Lagoon is the Lincoln Park Canoe Club (private); on North Lagoon is Diversey Beach. On Simmons Island, east of North Lagoon is CHARITAS, a statue by Ida McClelland Stout (1922), symbolizing the humanitarian work of the Chicago Daily News Fresh Air Sanitarium, which for years occupied the adjoining building. At the north end of the island is a bust of SWEDENBORG by Adolph Jonsson (1924).

Across the bridge is the PEACE SIGNAL, a mounted Indian with upraised arm, by Cyrus Dallin (1894). On the lake shore is the Lincoln Park Gun Club. Northward stretches the Diversey Golf Course (9-hole); at its northwestern end, on Lake Shore Drive, is the AMERICAN DOUGHBOY, by E. M. Viquesney (1927).

On Belmont Harbor, a 53-acre basin is the Belmont Harbor Clubhouse, the two-story houseboat of the Chicago Yacht Club. The harbor-master's office and slips for power boats line the east bank. This harbor is the starting point for the Chicago and Mackinac race, the longest fresh-water course in the world. North of the harbor, beyond the range of the Archery Club is a Bird Sanctuary and Wild Flower Preserve; facing Addison St. is a Haidan Indian totem pole from the Queen Charlotte Islands. Beyond is the Waveland Field House, with the Wolford chimes.

North of Montrose Avenue is a large peninsula, from the end of which is a fine view of the entire Chicago skyline, and Montrose Harbor for pleasure craft; on the north side spreads the Montrose-Wilson Beach. To the north the drives through the park turn westward on Foster Avenue to Sheridan Road.

North and Northwest Sides

Coursing southeasterly into Chicago, the North branch of the Chicago River divides the section north of North Avenue into the North Side and the larger Northwest Side. Up to the 1890s this section was made up of farmlands, truck gardens, hamlets and villages, subdivisions, and suburban towns. Settlements grew along the railroads and the former plankroads now followed in general by Clark Street and Milwaukee Avenue.

Great highways traverse the North and Northwest Sides and lead to the populated suburbs in Cook, Lake, Du Page, and McHenry Counties. These include the John B. Kennedy Expressway, which connects with Edens Expressway; Northwest Tollway, Tri-State Tollway, US 14, US 41, and their connections.

DE PAUL UNIVERSITY, an institution of learning that enrolls approximately 10,000 students annually, many of them in the heart of the Loop, has two campuses: Lincoln Park Campus, 2322 N. Seminary Ave., and the Frank J. Lewis Center, 25 E. Jackson Blvd., a 17-story office building on a corner of Wabash Ave., once the office of the Kimball Piano Co. The Lincoln campus has the Arthur J. Schmitt Academic Center, a five-story structure with library, classrooms and administrative offices; the University Church of St. Vincent de Paul; Alumni Hall, which contains a gymnasium and can seat 5,240 for formal exercises and athletic contests; the Hall of Science, the Liberal Arts Bldg., and the University Center, which provides a dining room seating 600, a lounge, a room for religious services, and student organization offices. The Main Residence Hall, 2312 N. Clifton, completed in 1970, accommodates 322.

The university offers an educational program in the following colleges: De Paul College, College of Commerce, College of the Liberal Arts and Sciences (with a division for evening classes) ; College of Law; the schools of Education, Music, and the Graduate School. The curriculum is closely related to the spiritual and vocational needs of the individual in modern society and makes provision for such subjects as minority interests, city planning, financial management, and nuclear developments. In the Department of History it studies Afro-American

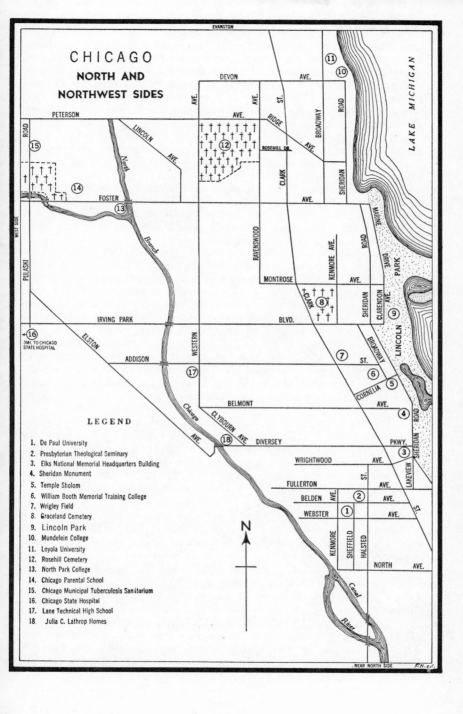

CHICAGO
NORTH AND
NORTHWEST SIDES

LAKE MICHIGAN

EVANSTON

DEVON AVE.
PETERSON AVE.
LINCOLN AVE.
RIDGE AVE.
ROSEHILL DR.
BROADWAY
SHERIDAN
ROAD
FOSTER AVE.
CLARK AVE.
RAVENSWOOD
KENMORE AVE.
MONTROSE AVE.
MARINE DRIVE
LINCOLN PARK
CLARENDON AVE.
SHERIDAN
IRVING PARK BLVD.
BROADWAY
WESTERN
ELSTON
ADDISON
CORNELIA ST.
BELMONT AVE.
SHERIDAN ROAD
Chicago
CLYBOURN AVE. DIVERSEY PKWY.
WRIGHTWOOD AVE.
LAKEVIEW
FULLERTON AVE. ST.
BELDEN AVE.
WEBSTER AVE.
KENMORE AVE.
SHEFFIELD
HALSTED
NORTH AVE.
North Branch
PULASKI ROAD
WEST SIDE
3MI. TO CHICAGO STATE HOSPITAL
Canal
River

LEGEND

1. De Paul University
2. Presbyterian Theological Seminary
3. Elks National Memorial Headquarters Building
4. Sheridan Monument
5. Temple Sholom
6. William Booth Memorial Training College
7. Wrigley Field
8. Graceland Cemetery
9. Lincoln Park
10. Mundelein College
11. Loyola University
12. Rosehill Cemetery
13. North Park College
14. Chicago Parental School
15. Chicago Municipal Tuberculosis Sanitarium
16. Chicago State Hospital
17. Lane Technical High School
18. Julia C. Lathrop Homes

N

NEAR NORTH SIDE

experience, black religionists, the Harlem renaissance, and immigrants and minorities. The Ibero-American Studies Program embraces Latin American origins, influences, and relation to the United States, and the Program of Jewish Studies includes courses in history, thought, philosophy, and theology. The College of Law, one of Illinois' foremost law schools, according to the university has among its alumni 21 percent of all practicing attorneys in the Chicago area.

The libraries have more than 250,000 volumes and subscribe to 1,600 periodicals. The Robert R. McCormick Memorial Library and the Law Library are located at Lewis Center, which also has the Center Theatre.

De Paul University was founded in 1898 as St. Vincent's College by the Fathers of the Congregation of the Mission. In the 1972 year it enrolled 9,194 students and had a faculty of 504. The full-time undergraduate pays $1,900 for tuition, fees and books, and bears individually the cost of meals and commuting.

McCORMICK THEOLOGICAL SEMINARY, 800 West Belden Ave., is directed by the General Assembly of the United Presbyterian Church, U. S. A., but its aim is to prepare students for the Christian ministry without denominational restrictions and to avoid isolation from world affairs. Study and living are inseparable, says the seminary. The original college was founded in Hanover, Indiana, in 1829 and moved to Chicago in 1859. It uses the quarter system and offers courses leading to the degrees of master of divinity, church and community, Christian education, theology, and science of theology. McCormick students may combine their studies with courses in social work at the University of Chicago, the University of Illinois, and Loyola University, and there are also some affiliated courses leading to a degree in library science.

The Seminary has been adding new facilities to its 18-acre campus. The James G. K. McClure Memorial Chapel was dedicated in October, 1963, at the same time with the new McGaw Memorial Library. The library houses 206,000 vols., 59,000 in microtext. The Stone Academic-Administration Bldg. was completed in 1969. McCormick faculty members and students have been associated with Biblical explorations in Palestine and other sites in the Near East.

The Chicago Institute of Pastoral Care was formed in 1966 as an ecumenical effort for counseling and education. The Graduate Fellow program in pastoral counseling is provided by McCormick Theological, Seabury-Western, and Chicago Theological Seminaries.

The TEMPLE OF ENLIGHTENMENT, usually called the Midwest Buddhist Temple, dedicated in November, 1971, on Menomonee Ave. near Lincoln Park, was erected on a site cleared by the Urban Renewal Project in this area. It cost $500,000.

The ELKS NATIONAL MEMORIAL HEADQUARTERS BUILDING, Lakeview Ave. at Diversey Parkway, a shrine to the Elks who served in the World Wars, was designed by Egerton Swartwout. It consists of a domed rotunda surrounded by a Roman

Doric colonnade above a high base; narrow wings connect the rotunda with end pavilions and house the national offices. The symbols of the order, a pair of reclining elk, by Laura Gardin Fraser, flank the entrance stairway. The frieze under the colonnade illustrates the theme, *The Triumphs of Peace Endure, The Triumphs of War Perish*. The frieze and Patriotism and Fraternity, symbolic groups by Adolph Weinman, fill niches in the ends of the wings.

The marble Memorial Hall is decorated with murals by Eugene Savage, inspired mainly by the Beatitudes, and with statues by James E. Fraser and panels by Edwin Blashfield. Peace is the theme of the panels, also by Savage, in the Grand Reception Room.

The SHERIDAN monument, Sheridan Road, Belmont Ave., and Lake Shore Drive, a bronze designed by Gutzon Borglum, represents Gen. Philip Sheridan mounted on his favorite horse, Rienzi. Sheridan was commander of the northern Illinois military area after the Civil War and both the scenic North Shore road and Fort Sheridan perpetuate his name.

TEMPLE SHOLOM, Lake Shore Drive at Cornelia Ave., a modern Romanesque structure of Lannon stone designed by Coolidge and Hodgdon, with Loebl, Schlossman, and Donnuth as associate architects, was built in 1930 for the North Chicago Hebrew Congregation, a reformed Jewish congregation organized in 1867. The temple has a seating capacity of 1,500, which can be doubled on holidays by moving a huge sliding partition separating it from the Frankenstein Memorial Center.

WRIGLEY FIELD, at Addison and North Clark St., is the home of the Chicago Cubs of the National Baseball League. It is owned by P. K. Wrigley, whose father became financially interested in the team in 1916. The field is also used by the Chicago Bears of the National Football League. It is reached on Clark St. bus No. 22 of the CTA.

A new statue of Abraham Lincoln was unveiled in Chicago on October 20, 1956, by Governor William G. Stratton of Illinois. Mayor Richard J. Daley and Clyde C. Walton, State Historian, took part in the exercises. The statue stands in Lincoln Square at the intersection of Lincoln, Lawrence, and Western Avenues on the Northwest Side. It is an 8 ft. bronze on a 4½ ft. base and represents Lincoln the lawyer as he appeared in Chicago courts. The sculptor was Avard Fairbank of the University of Utah, who also designed the Lincoln statue at New Salem State Park in 1954. It was proposed by Alderman John J. Hoellen of the 47th Ward and approved by the General Assembly, which appropriated $35,000. The Lincoln Chamber of Commerce awarded the design.

Loyola University

LOYOLA UNIVERSITY OF CHICAGO is the title adopted in 1968 by the Roman Catholic institution that has played a large role in the city's culture and learning since it was established by the Society of Jesus in 1870. It has two major locations in the city, the Lake Shore Campus of 25 wooded acres at 6525 Sheridan Road, and the 17-story

Lewis Towers at 820 N. Michigan Ave. Of its 15,815 students (1973), the largest number is enrolled in the College of Arts and Sciences on Sheridan Road. There are four other segments, the Loyola University Medical Center at Maywood; the Bellarmine School of Theology on University Ave., which trains Jesuit seminarians; Niles College, the seminary of the Catholic Archdiocese of Chicago at Niles, formerly the college department of St. Mary's of the Lake Seminary, and the Loyola Center of the Liberal Arts in Rome, Italy.

In the 1970 school year Loyola University completed its Centennial building program of $70,000,000. The principal accession was the university's Medical Center at Maywood, which includes the Stritch School of Medicine, the School of Dentistry, the School of Nursing, and the Foster G. McGraw Hospital. McGraw, founder and chairman of the American Hospital Supply Co., resident in Evanston, made an unrestricted gift of $7,000,000 to the university during its Centennial drive, the largest ever received by the university.

At the Lake Shore Campus recent construction includes Damen Hall, a 10-story classroom and laboratory building, an addition to the Elizabeth M. Cudahy Memorial Library, which has tripled its size, and the Mertz Hall complex, with a 19-story residence hall named for the Rev. James J. Mertz, S. J., former chairman of the department of classical languages; the Centennial Forum, student center, and the Kathleen Mullady Memorial Theatre.

At Lewis Towers the Julia Deal Lewis Library uses five floors. Other parts of the university at 820 N. Michigan Ave. include:

The School of Law, 41 E. Pearson St., was established in 1909. One of every 11 attorneys in Chicago is said to be a Loyola man and graduates serve with many of the city's largest law firms as judges and special government prosecutors.

The School of Nursing, 6525 N. Sheridan Rd., founded in 1935, offers an integrated program in the liberal arts and professional nursing, which leads to a bachelor of science degree of nursing. A graduate program prepares teachers and clinical specialists in nursing and leads to a master of science degree in nursing.

The School of Dentistry, in Maywood, founded in 1883 as the Chicago College of Dental Surgery, is the oldest dental school in Illinois. More than half of Chicago dentists are alumni of this school.

The Bellarmine School of Theology is located at 5430 University Ave. Niles College of Loyola Univ. is at 7135 N. Harlem Ave., Chicago. The Loyola University Press is located at 3441 N. Ashland Ave., Chicago. The University Guidance Center is at 1043 Loyola Ave. The university publishes *Mid-America,* a quarterly magazine.

The Graduate School, which offers a diversified program in the arts and sciences, including thirteen doctoral programs. Among its special divisions is the Center for Research in Urban Government, which gathers data about city government.

The School of Business Administration offers an undergraduate program, blending the humanities with business study. In 1966 the school established a Graduate Program in Business Administration, open to qualified students with bachelors' degrees in business or liberal arts.

University College, Loyola's late afternoon, evening and Saturday division, offers degree programs to part-time students. It is staffed by full-time professors who also teach in city schools.

The School of Education, founded in 1969, is the newest professional school of Loyola, although the Department of Education has contributed to the profession for more than 40 years. Featuring both undergraduate and graduate programs, the school has always worked closely with public and private schools. The first Ph. D. degree awarded, in 1928, was in education. By 1929 enrollment had increased to warrant the creation of a distinct Department of Education. In 1934 came the master of education degree and the doctor of education degree, in addition to the master of arts in education and the doctor of philosophy degrees.

The School of Social Work is the nation's oldest Catholic school of this category, having been organized in 1914. The Correspondence School Division also has its offices at 820 N. Michigan Ave.

Mundelein College

MUNDELEIN COLLEGE, 6363 Sheridan Road, a liberal arts college for women, was founded in 1934 by the Sisters of Charity of the Blessed Virgin Mary of the Roman Catholic Church and named for George, Cardinal Mundelein. It offers courses in teaching, including special, urban, and early childhood programs; pre-professional courses in medical technology, dietetics and physical therapy; women's studies and black studies; foreign study is elective. A student may designate her own topical majors. The Learning Resource Center has between 75,000 and 80,000 volumes. Mundelein enrolls more than 1,200 students and has a faculty of 94.

The BOOTH MEMORIAL HOSPITAL of the Salvation Army, 5040 N. Pulaski Road, is a complete maternity hospital, which serves unmarried mothers regardless of age, race, and creed, and does not withhold service because of inability to pay. Applying "friendship, care, understanding," the Salvation Army provides more than routine medical help. In a section called The Home it gives girls the comforts of rooms equipped for recreation, with television, games, sewing, materials for crafts and ceramics. The Chicago Board of Education provides junior and senior high school courses, so that a girl may continue her schooling with credits. There are daily devotions and a weekly chapel service, basically Christian and undenominational. If a girl wishes to continue working outside, she is free to go out daily. The Salvation Army provides counseling and advises a girl on making a sound plan for her baby; she may decide to keep it, or give it for adoption; in both cases the Army cooperates in her best interest. There are available 70 beds in the Home and 20 in the delivery section, and the girls stay an average of two months. In addition to medical care the hospital holds classes in pre-natal and child care, and has an out-patient clinic on

Saturday mornings. The operation of the hospital cost $616,000 in a recent typical year.

ROSEHILL CEMETERY, one of the older cemeteries of Chicago, has a castellated Gothic entrance at Ravenswood Ave. and Rosehill Dr., where the Chicago & North Western makes a stop. It occupies more than 330 acres.

NORTH PARK COLLEGE occupies a 25-acre campus in northwest Chicago with its principal office at 5125 North Spaulding Ave. It is a four-year liberal arts college sponsored by the Evangelical Covenant Church of America and emphasizes social responsibility and a Christian ethic in its courses. Its enrollment is around 1,400, with a faculty of 138, and it estimates the cost to a resident student for a year at $2,055 for tuition and fees and a total of $3,590. Recent additions to the campus are the Science-Learning Center, the Campus Memorial Center (the Student Union) and the Anna E. Anderson Residence Hall for Women. The College encourages off-campus activities such as working with neighborhood children and supporting community projects.

Wallgren Memorial Library occupies a building erected in 1958. It has approximately 80,000 vols., including bound volumes, and gets many periodicals. The Swedish Pioneer Historical Society has its library of Swedish Americana on the first floor. Also in the building is the Covenant Historical Library and Archives of the Evangelical Covenant Church.

There is a long-established Swedish community in this area and Swedish shops and restaurants are to be found in North Clark St. and environs.

NORTH PARK THEOLOGICAL SEMINARY shares the campus of North Park College. It is the graduate school of theology of the Evangelical Covenant Church and its aim is to train ministers. A student must have an A. B. degree to enroll and a degree from the Seminary is necessary for ordination in this church. The Seminary's Mellander Library of 38,000 vols. and 3,500 bound periodicals occupies the third floor of the Wallgren Memorial Library. Its Paul A. Westburg Memorial Collection contains the books of the late Prof. Harold R. Willoughby of the University of Chicago, which include copies of the Geneva Bible and the Erasmus Greek New Testament.

NORTHEASTERN ILLINOIS STATE COLLEGE, Bryn Mawr at St. Louis Ave., was opened in 1961 as Illinois Teachers College, Chicago North. In 1965 control passed from the Chicago Board of Education to the Board of Governors of State Colleges. It took its present name in 1967, at a time when its new plant was being constructed. The new buildings include general classroom, science, and library, and a services building. Its main subjects are in education and it has special courses for the disadvantaged. Its enrollment reaches nearly 6,000 and it has a faculty of 300.

The POLISH MUSEUM OF AMERICA, an outstanding display of memorabilia of the Polish people and Americans of Polish descent, occupies two floors at the Polish Roman Catholic Union of

America, 984 N. Milwaukee Ave. It is located where the most people of Polish origin and descent have congregated in Chicago, and is supported by the Union and donations. Organized in 1935, it was dedicated in 1937 and is the oldest ethnic museum in Chicago. Among its authentic collections is a remarkable exhibit of relics of Ignace Paderewski, among them the New York hotel suite in which he died, his Steinway with a Chopin composition on it, and the chair he used at concerts while touring. There are costumes worn by Helena Modjeska, and uniforms of officers who served in the Polish Army during the World Wars. Especially pertinent to the Polish story in America is the section devoted to Thaddeus Kosciuszko, who served in the American War of Independence and in his will asked Thomas Jefferson to use his personal property to help obtain liberty for slaves. *Open 1-4, Tuesday and Thursday.* Incorporated is a library of about 15,000 vols. and many Polish periodicals, dating from a lending library begun in 1915. *Open daily 1-4 and also Monday 6-8.*

The CHICAGO STATE HOSPITAL, 6500 Irving Park Blvd. and Narragansett Ave., also known as Dunning, is the city's major institution for the mentally ill. It was founded in 1869.

The CHICAGO MUNICIPAL TUBERCULOSIS SANITARIUM, 5601 N. Pulaski Road, has an important record of arresting early cases and treating thousands of patients successfully. It gained repute for its pioneering work in the field of home pneumothorax. It was opened in 1915. It is easily reached by car via the Kennedy Expressway and Edens Expressway to exit at Peterson Ave., thence east on Peterson to Pulaski. It is in the general area of the North Branch of the Chicago River and near LA BAGH WOODS, GOMPERS PARK, and EUGENE FIELD PARK. Adjoining its grounds are the BOHEMIAN NATIONAL CEMETERY, and the BETHEL and Ridglawn cemeteries.

North of Peterson Ave. (US 14) are the grounds of the GOOD COUNSEL HIGH SCHOOL and FELICIEN COLLEGE.

The CHICAGO PARENTAL SCHOOL, 3600 Foster Ave., trains boys and girls of school age committed to its charge for truancy by the Juvenile Court. Organized in 1902 and conducted by the Chicago Board of Education, the school attempts to provide normal home conditions by use of the cottage plan. Its red brick buildings are clustered on a 75-acre tract, partly landscaped, partly used as a farm.

Not all the architectural phenomena of Chicago is to be found in skyscrapers and parks; there is reason to admire modern technique in prosaic facilities. The Chicago NORTHWEST INCINERATOR is an object of pride for the Department of Streets and Sanitation. It is, as the Department of Works reports, "the largest of its kind in the western hemisphere." This incinerator handles 1,600 tons of refuse a day. It utilizes a magnetic metal separator and a bulk shredding metal salvage system. Tin cans are mechanically separated from the residue, the rest is ground up and burned. Electrostatic precipitators control pollution from stack emissions. The city collects more than 1,233,000 tons of refuse monthly.

O'Hare International Airport

At the end of the John F. Kennedy Expressway is the CHICAGO O'HARE INTERNATIONAL AIRPORT, for which see the article *By Air, Rail, Land and Water*. The informally designated O'HARE AREA, extending about 15 miles around the airport, is in the throes of a developer's boom. The immense movement of people, about 100,000 a day at the airport, has drawn hotels, motels, and branches of banks, insurance corporations and national manufacturers into the area and high-rise office buildings are piercing the horizon. The principal expansion is north and west into Park Ridge, Des Plaines, Elk Grove Village, Mount Prospect and Arlington Heights. (*See Tour 10*). The largest hotel is O'Hare International Tower, inside the airport area, but the most spectacular and largest outside is the Regency Hyatt House. There is a new Marriott hotel north of the Kennedy Expressway. O'Hare Lake Office Plaza in Des Plaines has been built adjoining a new 20-acre lake. Centex Industrial Park, west of the airport, has grown in 15 years from cornfields to a place with more than 750 industries, including branches of General Motors, Ampex, Goodyear, Chrysler, Ford, and Du Pont. There are industrial parks at Elk Grove Village and Bensenville. International Tower is a 10-story office center at Cumberland Ave. and the Expressway. O'Hare Plaza has executive offices of Jewel, Motorola, IGA, Aetna Insurance, Oscar Mayer, and a division of Continental Can Co. The leading aviation organization at O'Hare is United Air Lines, which built its own headquarters and employs more than 6,000 there.

The West Side

The West Side lies between the two branches of the Chicago River, but it is commonly limited on the north by North Avenue. Chicago has grown and flowered most conspicuously along the lake front, with the result that the West Side became an area useful for factories, warehouses, and workers' homes. Here have come thousands of immigrants year after year. Scandinavians and Germans and Irish, no longer found in the West Side in great number, had their roots here; still flourishing are the later arrivals, the great colonies of Poles and Jews, Italians and Czecho-Slovakians and in recent decades Spanish-speaking residents. Although the district is streaked with rail lines and gray manufacturing zones, there is a belt of fine parks and boulevards in the center from north to south, and farther west.

Since World War II the West Side has experienced great changes. Highrise apartment buildings have replaced the brownstones of 19th century living; developers have discovered that the lower costs of land per square foot west of the River offset some of the disadvantages of location. When the *Chicago Daily News* built its offices over railroad air rights at West Madison St. and the River, the West Side entered a new phase of construction, of which the Gateway Buildings are evidence. Urban Renewal programs have obliterated large areas of shabby housing, and huge sums have been poured into new college buildings and hospitals.

Across the West Madison St. Bridge to the West Bank

From the bridge the wide, white facade and terraces of the RIVER-SIDE PLAZA BUILDING at Madison St. and the river stand forth like a huge monument pierced with a multitude of windows. This structure, which is quite narrow on the Madison St. side, rose in 1929 at about the same time that the Civic Opera Building was being erected on the opposite bank. When Holabird & Root designed it for the Chicago Daily News Co. it was the first big skyscraper in Chicago using air rights over railroad tracks. Faced with Indiana limestone the building extends along the river from Madison to Washington St. Victor F. Lawson, owner of the *Chicago Daily News* from 1876 to 1925, had planned to build a modern newspaper plant when death overtook him in 1925; in 1929 Walter B. Strong completed the undertaking, but his early death resulted in a succession of new owners, including Col. Frank Knox, John S. Knight, and Marshall Field III. Field founded the *Chicago Sun* in 1941 and for a time published it at the *Daily News* plant. The offices of the Chicago & North Western Railway are located in Riverside Plaza Building today.

The next block west on Madison is occupied by the CHICAGO & NORTH WESTERN RAILWAY STATION, built in 1911 and designed along classical Roman lines by Frost & Granger. For more than 60 years it has accommodated multitudes of commuters who lived in the northern and western suburbs.

The WEST BANK of the Chicago River south of Madison Ave. has undergone a monumental job of landscaping by the imposition of limestone walls that support a pedestrian's walk lined with greenery. The completion of the high-rise office buildings of GATEWAY CEN-TER has transformed an area of shabby brick warehouses and stores into an unexpectedly attractive domain. The rehabilitation of the river is continuing. Gateway Center is an enterprise of three tall office buildings begun in 1965 by the Tishman Realty & Construction Co. The first building, 10 S. Riverside Plaza, built over the railroad tracks, is supported by 130 caissons sunk 80 ft. to bedrock, placed without interrupting train movements. It is 22 stories tall and has an area of 800,000 sq. ft. Gateway Center 2, at 120 S. Riverside Plaza, has similar dimensions. Gateway Center 3, at 222 S. Riverside Plaza, was built by Tishman in 1972 and at 35 stories is 13 stories taller than its two Gateway predecessors. Facing this building is MARLENNAN PLAZA, 35 stories, with a new area of 1,300,000 sq. ft.

The UNION STATION occupies a block on two sides of South Canal St. between Adams St. and Jackson Blvd. Built in 1925, it replaced a rambling brick structure built soon after the Great Fire that accommodated many hundreds of thousands of passengers who used the Milwaukee, the Burlington, and half a dozen other railroads that have lost their identities. The station was designed by Graham, Anderson,

Probst & White, who adapted the designs of Roman baths for the main waiting room and left bare the steel columns and girders in the concourse. It is used principally by commuters.

The GENERAL U. S. POST OFFICE, Van Buren St. from Canal St. to the river and extending to Harrison St., is the largest post office building in the world, a bulky Indiana limestone structure designed by Graham, Anderson, Probst, and White, and completed in 1934 at a cost of $21,500,000. The building is constructed over railroad tracks which permits the direct handling of one-third of the daily mail. Eisenhower Expressway passes through the building. Between 25,000 and 30,000 employees of the Postal Service work here. All are organized. In addition to the postal plant, the building houses the regional offices of several Federal departments. *Tours are available on weekdays; inquire at information desk in rotunda.*

The CHICAGO FIRE ACADEMY, 538 DeKoven St., near West 11th St., where instruction in fire fighting is given by the Chicago Fire Department, stands on the traditional site of the house and barn of Mrs. Patrick O'Leary, whose cow is said to have kicked over her lantern when she tried to milk it on October 9, 1871, and thus touched off the Great Fire. For more than 50 years thousands of tourists visited this site to gaze at a three-story dwelling that had an inscription about the fire chiseled into its stone facade. In front of the Academy stands a bronze representation of a huge flame by Egon Weiner. The Academy was built in 1960 and has on exhibition a hand-operated pumper of 1835.

CHICAGO COMMONS, the largest private social service organization in Illinois, was founded by Graham Taylor and is operated by the Chicago Commons Assn., 715 N. Walcott Ave. Long conducted as a single operation at this address, it has expanded since the 1960's by merging with several social agencies of long experience: the Mary McDowell Settlement, 4630 S. McDowell Ave., founded in 1894 as the University of Chicago Settlement and long conducted by Miss McDowell, who had been associated with Jane Addams at Hull House; also Camp Farr, a 40-acre McDowell facility at Chesterton, Ind.; the Olivet Community Center, 1441 N. Cleveland Ave.: Camp Reinberg, an independent year-around facility of 75 acres at Palatine; Robinson House, 1834 W. Washington St., and Emerson House, 645 N. Wood St. Chicago Commons also operates a camp on farmland at Buffalo, Mich.

UNION PARK, Ogden Ave. at Washington and Ashland Blvds., is a bit of green where apartment houses and churches were developed 100 years ago. There is a statue of Carter H. Harrison by Frederick C. Hibbard. Harrison, World's Fair mayor who was assassinated by a lunatic, lived on Ashland Blvd. Another statue commemorating the Haymarket Riot of 1886 near the site has encountered evil days. It is a bronze of a police officer with raised hand and the words *The Law is Common Sense,* quoted from Judge Joseph Gary's remarks at the sentencing of the labor agitators. The statue stood unchanged for more than fifty years. In the 1960s it was twice damaged by bombs and placed in storage.

The PRAIRIE FARMER, spokesman for the interests of farmers, has its editorial and business offices at 1230 W. Washington Blvd. It was founded in 1841 by John Stephen Wright as the *Union Agriculturist and Western Prairie Farmer*.

The University at Chicago Circle

The UNIVERSITY OF ILLINOIS AT CHICAGO CIRCLE was opened on February 22, 1965, on a campus of 118 acres in the southwest corner of the intersection of Dwight D. Eisenhower, John F. Kennedy, and Dan Ryan Expressways, completely replacing a rundown West Side area with more than 26 buildings of steel and concrete. The university began with 5,200 students, who had been attending an undergraduate division operating since 1946 in the Navy Pier at Grand Ave. and the Lake. In the fall of 1972 the university at the Circle had an attendance of 18,290, and a faculty of 1,170, thus demonstrating that it served a definite need as a commuter university in the heart of Chicago's densest population area.

With 40 acres to start with, the architects, Skidmore, Owings & Merrill and their designer Walter A. Netsch, Jr., took on the challenge of a project outlined by N. E. Parker, vice president and chairman of the building committee of the university. They began with certain objectives: lecture halls and classrooms for general academic use, not restricted to one field of study; ease of access by concentration of classrooms on two levels, with ramps and elevated walks serving the second level; buildings limited chiefly to four stories, served by stairs; all administrative offices in one place, and a single, easily reached library. There was no tradition to follow and no desire to impose extraneous decoration; the university was to develop from needs for use. Thus structures were not masked for unreal effects; the principal media, concrete and reinforced steel, were not disguised; plain concrete pillars stood where they performed their functions. Lighting and other utility systems were incorporated in the structure, not hidden in false ceilings; windows were permanent slits in the walls with glass that absorbed sunshine but did not exclude light and needed no shades. The university would be the latest exhibit in conforming structure to the needs of its users.

This preconceived plan was carried out. Aside from the 28-story University Hall that contains administrative and faculty offices, and a 13-story building for science and engineering staffs, buildings do not exceed four stories above ground. A 50-ft. wide elevated walkway connects the buildings at the second floor level above a similar walkway on the ground.

At the center of the campus is the Lecture Center, a concentration of four circular clusters. Three of the clusters have four 175-seat lecture halls each, while one has a single hall for 500, and three seminar rooms. Above each cluster is an exedra, a circular sitting place open to sun and air. The halls are on the lower level and above them is the great court

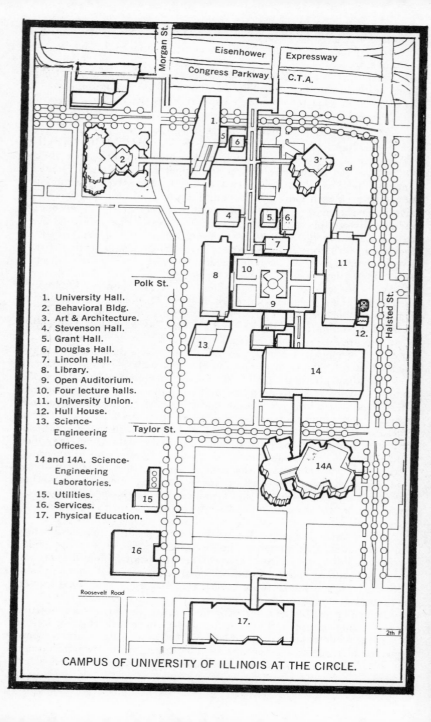

1. University Hall.
2. Behavioral Bldg.
3. Art & Architecture.
4. Stevenson Hall.
5. Grant Hall.
6. Douglas Hall.
7. Lincoln Hall.
8. Library.
9. Open Auditorium.
10. Four lecture halls.
11. University Union.
12. Hull House.
13. Science-Engineering Offices.
14 and 14A. Science-Engineering Laboratories.
15. Utilities.
16. Services.
17. Physical Education.

CAMPUS OF UNIVERSITY OF ILLINOIS AT THE CIRCLE.

of the campus. West of the court is the Library; east is the Student Union, joined to the lecture center at both levels.

The principal architects are Skidmore, Owings & Merrill. C. F. Murphy Associates is responsible for the Student Union, and Harry Weese & Associates for the Physical Education Bldg.

A variation in skyscraper architecture has been adopted in UNIVERSITY HALL, the administrative building. While the width remains uniform, for its 28 stories, the floors became longer toward the top. It is built of poured concrete with a central service core. From the ground level through the eighth story, the building is 150 ft. long; from the ninth through the 18th story, it is 160 ft. long; from the 18th to the 28th story it is 170 ft. long. In the first section the floors are cantilevered 5 ft. from the supporting columns at each end, thus adding 10 ft; in the second section they are cantilevered 10 ft. at each end. By limiting the number of elevators serving each section more space is made available for offices. The architects estimate that the usable space won by the cantilever design and the elevators is equivalent to six normal stories.

While University Hall seems more or less like a conventional highrise rectangle, there are buildings with geometrical patterns that differ startlingly from conventional college patterns. An observer, looking down from the narrow slits of windows on the 20th floor of University Hall was amazed to see below a group of roofs that looked like a batch of ginger cookies. This was the Behavioral Sciences Building.

As the library system of the University of Illinois is one of the best-equipped in the country, the main and departmental libraries at the Circle began their usefulness with 1,006,518 items.

HULL HOUSE, the original residence in which Jane Addams founded Hull House Settlement in 1889, stands on the University of Illinois campus at 800 S. Halsted St., a National Historic Landmark. Built in 1856 by Charles J. Hull, a real estate dealer, it is an example of the domestic architecture of the pre-Civil War period, and is in strong contrast to the concrete structures of the University. Also preserved is its separate dining hall. When demolition was threatened in 1961 restoration was achieved by donations of $350,000 from many individuals. When the settlement was founded this was an area settled by poor immigrants, which had a livery stable, an Irish saloon, a funeral home, a German bakery, and a Jewish junkshop. The settlement grew to 13 buildings. Nearly all had to be removed for the new university. *Hull House is open Mon.-Fri. 9-5; Saturday, 10-3; Sunday, noon-4. Campus tour office, phone 663-8686.*

The Department of Urban Renewal of the City of Chicago has been opening opportunities for developers to improve housing in the general area of the Circle and the Near West Side. Circle Court, west of the university campus, is a $5,000,000 commercial development on a five-acre site at the Eisenhower Expressway, Racine and Harrison Sts., housing 36 retail establishments, an office and bank building, and a theater. Another related development is the Campus Green on a site bounded by Ashland, Polk, Laflin and Taylor Sts., consisting of two 12-story apartment buildings and 46 town houses, the total costing $12,000,000.

The Great West Side Hospitals

The CHICAGO MEDICAL CENTER, together with the nearby Medical Center of the University of Illinois, constitutes the greatest concentration of hospitals and medical schools in the United States. There are other large medical groups, on the near North Side, at the Midway, and in the suburbs, but none has available an equal number of professionals of all phases of the art of healing, or as many buildings of recent construction, or as many available beds—estimated at more than 8,000, as this huge area.

The largest unit is the COOK COUNTY HOSPITAL complex, 1825 W. Harrison St. The Inpatient Section has 2,263 beds and more than 64,000 admissions in a typical year. It has 184 bassinets and more than 11,400 births annually. Personnel of the hospital is 5,316. There is a School of Nursing.

The PRESBYTERIAN-ST. LUKE'S HOSPITAL, 1753 W. Congress Parkway, is the next largest, with 828 beds and more than 24,000 admissions in one year. It has more than 3,000 births and a staff of 3,610. A School of Nursing is associated with the hospital, which is a unit in the RUSH-PRESBYTERIAN-ST. LUKE'S MEDICAL CENTER. This includes Rush Medical College, which has been a famous name in medical education since 1837, when Dr. Daniel Brainard founded it and named it for Dr. Benjamin Rush, a famous physician in 18th-century America. In 1923 Dr. Arthur Bevan of Rush faculty performed the first operation in which ethylene-oxygen was used as an anesthetic. Also included in this center are the Woman's Board, 1743 W. Harlan, the Outpatient Clinic, 1748 W. Harlan, the Pharmacy Professional Bldg., 1725 W. Harlan, the Mile Square Health Center, 2049 W. Washington, and the Poison Control Center.

The VETERANS ADMINISTRATION WEST SIDE HOSPITAL, 820 S. Damen Ave., has 545 beds, an annual admittance of more than 7,000, and year-around occupancy of 94%, with a staff of 1,169. The CHICAGO STATE TUBERCULOSIS SANITARIUM, is at 1919 West Taylor St. The ILLINOIS STATE PSYCHIATRIC INSTITUTE, 160 W. Taylor St. has around 866 admissions annually.

The UNIVERSITY OF ILLINOIS AT THE MEDICAL CENTER is the designation given the university's campus at the Center. Here the university concentrates four colleges, the Graduate College, a hospital, clinics and allied units in 14 major buildings on 14 acres. It has close working relations with Cook County Hospital, West Side Veterans Administration Hospital, and others in the area. The COLLEGE OF MEDICINE, 1853 W. Polk St., deals with basic medical science and clinical medicine. The GRADUATE COLLEGE, 1737 W. Polk St., places emphasis on the relationship between the basic medical sciences and their clinical uses. The SCHOOL OF

ASSOCIATED MEDICAL SCIENCES, 808 S. Wood St., gives professional courses toward a baccalaureate degree after preparatory studies in the arts and sciences at other units of the university. The UNIVERSITY HOSPITAL, 840 S. Wood St., has 600 beds and 36 outpatient clinics, and a complement of 600 physicians and a graduate training program with 46 interns and 342 residents. About 80 percent of the patients come from the Chicago metropolitan area. The COLLEGE OF DENTISTRY occupies a new building at 801 S. Paulina St. The COLLEGE OF NURSING, moved into a new 11-story building at 845 S. Damen Ave. in 1969. The COLLEGE OF PHARMACY, 833 S. Wood St. in 1972 was officially called "the only such institution in Illinois." It operates a greenhouse in the Morton Arboretum near Lisle. The SCHOOL OF PUBLIC HEALTH, 833 S. Wood St. which includes the Center for the Study of Patient Care and Community Health, opened in 1972 as "the first of its kind in Illinois." The INSTITUTION FOR TUBERCULOSIS RESEARCH, 1853 W. Polk St., produces the vaccine BCG and supplies it to more than 626 TB control projects.

The LIBRARY OF THE HEALTH SCIENCES, 1853 W. Polk St. is the newest library to provide service in Chicago. It is expanding beyond 200,000 volumes and receives 2,100 periodicals. It serves affiliated institutions as well as all units of the university.

Expansion of the Medical Center continues. In 1972 the value of the physical plant was placed at $111,175,267.

Directly related to the Medical Center is the DIVISION OF SERVICES FOR CRIPPLED CHILDREN, which has headquarters at 540 Illes Place, Springfield. This conducts around 300 clinics throughout the State annually. It is the official State agency for utilizing Federal grants-in-aid for the diagnosis, hospitalization, and after-care of children who are crippled or suffering from conditions that lead to crippling.

The CHICAGO MEDICAL SCHOOL, founded 1912 to train physicians, expanded its goals in 1967 by forming the UNIVERSITY OF HEALTH SCIENCES, which became bracketed with its official title to indicate incorporation of the health team concept. This involves training of personnel in health-related occupations. The School of Graduate and Post-Doctoral Studies opened in the fall of 1968 with 11 enrollments, and the School of Related Health Sciences in September, 1970. In 1968 all facilities were consolidated at 2020 West Ogden Ave., a modern 11-story structure built in 1961 as a research institute. In the fall of 1970 the School reported enrollment of 288, and a faculty of 650. It has a library of 38,000 vols., receives 1,000 periodicals annually, and has much scientific material on films and tapes.

MOUNT SINAI HOSPITAL MEDICAL CENTER, the primary medical teaching facility of CMS-UHS, is located at California Ave. and 15th St. About 100,000 people are served annually in its departments, including emergency and 40 specialty clinics. In 1970 it completed the Olin-Sang Pavilion, a 206-bed addition, increasing capacity to 525 beds.

The MAXWELL STREET MARKET, Chicago's traditional pushcart bazaar, is still drawing crowds of bargain-hunters on Sunday mornings, but it has spread considerably from its original location near Halsted and Maxwell Sts. It can be reached by the Dan Ryan Expressway or the Harrison St. bus, and it provides a remarkable spectacle of sidewalk merchandising. The market is a confusion of wagons, stalls, carts and cartons loaded with shirts, shoes, coats, umbrellas, faucets, motor car tools, and piles of oranges, potatoes, garden truck in season. The small stores that line the area also vie for the attention of the visitor. Bargaining is customary and shouting general. Grilled franks, hamburgers, sausages, sauerkraut, and cabbage soup are available and lend their odors to the environment. Originally settled by Jewish immigrants, the area now includes large blocks of Spanish-speaking people, Puerto Rican and Mexican, as well as the older Italian, Lithuanian, Polish, and Greek residents.

The SOUTH WATER WHOLESALE MARKET at West 14th St. and Blue Island Ave. is a complex of warehouses and produce stalls where huge trucks converge through the night delivering fresh meats and produce, and retailers arrive at dawn to pick up their supplies for the day. The name perpetuates the market that extended just south of the Chicago River north of Lake St. until Wacker Drive was built in the 1920s. Similar is the RANDOLPH STREET MARKET at West Randolph and Halsted, which, in addition of produce and supplies for groceries has a wholesale flower market.

The JENS JENSEN ELEMENTARY SCHOOL, 1924 Harrison St., at Sacramento Ave., is considered a notable example of modern architecture. In the design by Harry Weese Associates the hexagonal plan of the classroom floors forms the basic motif in the over-all pattern. Brick is the chief structural material. The school was named for the landscape artist who contributed greatly to Chicago parks.

West Side Parks

GARFIELD PARK, Central Park Ave. at Lake, has an immense CONSERVATORY covering 4½ acres. Erected in 1907, it has 8 exhibition halls for the display of more than 5,000 varieties of plants. At the entrance to the Palm House is a shadowy pool flanked by marble figures, *Pastoral* and *Idyl,* by Lorado Taft, and displays of orchids and other exotics. Opposite the pool lies a sunken garden of tropical ferns, with delicate fronds of tree-ferns and cycads arching over tufa rock formations and ponds. In the cool dry Cactus House are remarkable rarities, including the Senita or Old One and the Organ Pipe Cactus, which are no longer sent out of Arizona. Here also is the Saguaro or Giant Cactus, which grows the state flower of Arizona and is a staple of Indian diet. Others to be seen are the Century plant, Hemp plant, and Barrel Cactus. In the humid Aroid House tropical plants of brilliant foliage thrive, and the Economic House displays many useful plants prized for fruits, oils, fiber, spice or perfume; the Chewing Gum plant, Rose Apple, St. John's Bread, figs, lemons, olives, sugar cane, and similar species.

The Easter, Midsummer, Chrysanthemum, and Christmas Flower Shows fill the Show House and Horticulture Hall with thousands of blooms raised in adjoining propagating houses, and attract a large part of the 500,000 people who visit the conservatory each year.

The ADMINISTRATION BUILDING stands on a knoll between two lagoons south of the conservatory, a gold-domed Spanish Renaissance structure with a rotunda containing casts of classical statuary. Immediately south is the bronze monument of Lincoln, the Rail Splitter, by Charles J. Mulligan; a few yards west stands the bronze Robert Burns by W. Grant Stevens, a replica of the monument in Edinburgh, with bas-reliefs on the pedestal depicting scenes from Burns' poems. Formal flower gardens surround the tropical Water-Lily Pools, at Madison St.

Garfield Park is open daily 9-5; during major shows, 9-9. Washington Blvd. bus or Lake St. bus to Central Park Ave.; B train on Lake St. L to Homan Ave. Eisenhower Expressway to Independence Blvd. and north to Lake St.

COLUMBUS PARK, Jackson Blvd. at Central Ave., is a tract of 144 acres landscaped by Jens Jensen in his naturalistic style. The prairie motif is carried out in the long horizontal sweep of meadow threaded by running streams. Subtly adorned with sun-loving flowers, accented by thickets of hawthorn and other native trees and shrubs, the park is particularly charming in the autumn. Additional attractions are the waterfalls near the Refectory, and a 9-hole golf course.

HUMBOLDT PARK, Augusta Blvd. at Sacramento Ave., with its lagoons, islands, hills, and large variety of trees, is a 207-acre tract containing some of the most beautiful park landscapes in the city. Near Division Street is the Stable, a park maintenance building erected in 1896 from plans drawn by Emil H. Frommann and Ernst Jebsen. The building rambles near a stream and rustic bridge. In style it resembles a German hunting lodge, with a foundation of rock boulders, half-timbered walls of red brick, and a tile roof, romantically gabled. Little known, even to Chicagoans, the charming building is markedly appropriate in its park setting.

North of Division Street, bronze bison by Edward Kemeys flank the entrance to the ROSE GARDENS. Fountain figures by Leonard Crunelle rise from the four corners of the garden pool. Opposite the entrance is a statue of FRITZ REUTER, German poet, by Frederick Engelmann. HOME, a modest little sculpture of a miner and his child, at the east end of the park, is by Charles J. Mulligan. A statue of Alexander von Humboldt, German naturalist, by Felix Gorling, stands in the center of the park. Westward, near the Refectory Building, is the Leif Eriksen Monument by Sigvald Asbjornsen. The equestrian statue of Thaddeus Kosciusko, Polish hero of the American Revolution, by Casimir Chodinski, at the north entrance, is the center of the Polish Constitution Day celebration on the Sunday nearest May 3, when thousands of neighboring Poles parade to the park.

The CHICAGO STADIUM, Madison St. at Honore St., an indoor amphitheater seating more than 25,000, was erected in 1928 as a center for sports, circuses, and conventions. Here Franklin D. Roosevelt was nominated for President in 1932, 1940, and 1944.

The White Sox Ball Park, 324 West 35th St., is the home of the Chicago team of the American Baseball League. It is reached on the Elevated to the 35th St. Station, thence west on Bus 35 of the C. T. A.

The INTERNATIONAL AMPHITHEATRE, S. Halsted and W. 43d Sts., is another great covered exhibition complex. Built for livestock expositions, and seat of the annual International Livestock Exhibition in November, it is also used for political and professional conventions, sports events, rallies for special causes, rodeos, and horse shows. To compete with McCormick Place the Amphitheatre was air conditioned and otherwise improved at a cost of $1,500,000.

Among the events booked annually in International Amphitheatre is Black Expo, a five-day business and cultural exposition managed by the Operation Push (People United to Save Humanity), at which in a typical year more than 500 companies, most of them formed and managed by blacks, display their products. Attendance in 1972 was reported to reach 700,000. One of the features was the play *Don't Bother Me, I Can't Cope.*

The Amphitheatre adjoins the Stock Yards Inn, 4178 S. Halsted St., where the Sirloin Room is a prized meeting place for gourmets. The Live Stock National Bank Building, 4150 S. Halsted St., is a reproduction of Independence Hall of Philadelphia.

Union Stock Yards

Nearby is the stone gate that marks the main entrance to the UNION STOCK YARDS, for a century the greatest meat processing center in the world.

The Union Stock Yards closed its livestock market July 30, 1972, because the supply was steadily decreasing. What *Commerce* calls "the last vestige of a once great Chicago meat industry" is the Chicago-Joliet Livestock Marketing Center (*see Joliet*). In 1971 the Center had gross revenue of $200,000,000 and handled 42,000 cattle and 6,500 hogs daily. The packing industry has moved its plants close to the source of supply and eliminated the long haul of animals across the states of the Midwest to Chicago.

When the industry was at its peak in Chicago approximately 12,000,000 animals were shipped annually on railroads that connected directly with the Yards. Livestock was the chief source of cash income for the Midwestern farmer and the Yards handled about one-fifth of all American sales. About three-fourths of the animals were slaughtered here and the other fourth was shipped to eastern plants or sent to feed lots.

Slaughter houses were established early in Chicago's history, but there were no centralized stock yards until John B. Sherman opened the Bull's Head Stock Yards at Madison Street and Ashland Avenue in 1848, from which the several packing plants along the Chicago River and its branches drew their supplies. In 1856 Sherman replaced the Bull's Head with yards along the Illinois Central Railroad at 29th Street, and in 1865 organized the Union Stock Yard and Transit Company and opened the present yards. Within a few years, Philip D. Armour, Gustavus F. Swift, Nelson Morris, and others built their plants adjacent to the Yards. The rapid growth of the packing industry was stimulated by the development of the refrigerator car in the 1870's and by the utilization of by-products after 1885. But the poor working conditions in the plants and the unsanitary methods of waste disposal took their toll in human misery. Upton Sinclair's novel of protest, *The Jungle,* caused a public reaction; the report of an investigating committee, appointed by President Theodore Roosevelt in 1906, led to effective reform legislation.

The centenary of the Union Stock Yards was suitably observed on Feb. 15, 1965, 100 years from the day this, the bestknown industry of Chicago, received its charter from the State Legislature. Mayor Richard J. Daley cut a golden ribbon at the big stone gate at S. Halsted and W. 41 St. in the presence of officials and business leaders, and was presented with a 1,100 lb. steer by the president of the yard organization, in recognition of the Mayor's early employment as a bookkeeper for a firm of commission merchants, and his long residence in the area.

At West 43rd St. and Langley Ave., in the heart of a busy black neighborhood artists belonging to the Organization of Black American Culture in 1967 cooperated in painting expressions of Negro pride on the brick wall of a building, known as the WALL OF RESPECT. A legend says: "This wall was created to honor our black heroes and Beautify our Country."

The Third Baptist Church of Chicago, a large Negro congregation, is located at 938 W. 69th St. It is the home of the Dorie Miller Memorial Foundation.

FORD CITY, near Cicero Ave. and W. 77th St. is strategically located where Burbank begins. It is one of the swiftest growing mercantile developments in the Chicago area. It has more than 145 stores including branches of national chains, and is adding new ones every season. One of its attractions is the Peacock Alley Mall. Contests, musical programs, fashion shows, and flower exhibits are promoted and clubs are encouraged, including a Senior Citizens Club with 1,000 members.

The CARTER G. WOODSON Regional Library Center was established by the board of the Chicago Public Library at 95th and Halsted Sts. in 1971. Named for a black historian the center comprises a basic collection of books, periodicals, documents, tapes, records, and films of direct interest to the black population. It has reference value for high school and college students. The Vivian G. Harsh Collection of Afro-American History and Literature, long at the Hall Branch at 4801 S. Michigan Ave., was allocated to the new center. It has 7,000 titles, 350,000 manuscripts on microfilm, and 200 rolls of microfilm on the history of the black worker from the President's Committee on Fair Employment Practices.

The JANE ADDAMS HOUSES, 1002 S. Lytle St., are a group of fireproof buildings erected in 1937 by the Public Works Administration. Built of brick in austere, well-arranged groups, the 52 houses of 4 and 5 rooms, and 975 apartments of 2 to 5 rooms provide low-cost modern housing. More than three-fifths of the total ground area is devoted to lawns, gardens, and playgrounds. There are 20 recreation and social rooms, and a shower yard ornamented with sculptured animals.

DOUGLAS PARK, Roosevelt Road at Sacramento Ave., a 182-acre retreat for the large Jewish and Bohemian population of the adajcent neighborhoods, has lily ponds and flower gardens, a lake for boating, an open-air natatorium, athletic fields, and an outdoor gymnasium. Near West Douglas Park Drive and Ogden Avenue stands a heroic bronze statue of Karel Havlicek, 19th century liberal writer, sculptured by Josef Strachovsky.

The JEWISH COMMUNITY CENTER, 3003 W. Touhy Ave., is a social, educational and recreational center in the Lawndale area. It comprises what was formerly the Jewish People's Institute in Douglas Blvd., which has appeared in stories by Albert Halper, Louis Zara, and Meyer Levin. The activities include lectures, courses, physical and intellectual exercises, and it has a well-stocked reference library. The Hebrew Theological College, formerly at 3448 Douglas Blvd., has moved to new buildings in Skokie.

The COOK COUNTY CRIMINAL COURTHOUSE, California Ave. and 26th St., includes the Criminal Court Building, the Cook County Jail Building, and a number of cell blocks. Designed by Eric E. Hall in rectangular neo-classic pattern, the Indiana limestone group was completed in 1929 at a cost of $7,500,000. Inmates of the jail are persons awaiting trial, transfer, or execution, and prisoners whose sentences for any single charge do not exceed one year. Visiting groups must make reservations.

The HOUSE OF CORRECTION, immediately south of the Court House, is the municipal prison established in 1871 to supplant the old Bridewell. Around the castellated Gothic buildings are flower beds and a small vegetable garden tended by inmates. Shops in which prisoners work and other facilities can be visited upon application to the Superintendent.

The MARQUETTE MEMORIAL, Damen Ave. Bridge on the South Branch of the Chicago River, marks the site of Pere Jacques Marquette's dreary sojourn during the winter of 1674-75. E. P. Seidel modeled the bronze relief from a sketch by Thomas A. O'Shaughnessy.

LOUIS PASTEUR, French scientist, is commemorated in a small park of the Chicago Park District at 4334 W. 58th St.

MARQUETTE PARK, Marquette Road (West 67th St.) and California Ave., second largest inland park in Chicago, contains 322 acres, extensively improved by the Works Progress Administration. Recreation facilities include a nine-holf golf course. At the entrance on California Avenue stands a red granite monument of striking modern design by the sculptor Raoul Josset, commemorating Captain Steponas Darius and Lieutenant Stasys Girenas, and their attempted flight from New York to Kaunas, Lithuania, July 17, 1933. In the form of a faceted irregular pyramid suggesting the broken wing of an airplane, the front face bears a bronze globe with the figures of ten airplanes tracing the route of the flyers, who crashed to their deaths just short of their goal.

The VOLUNTEERS OF AMERICA is a social welfare organization with a strong religious base and a semi-military discipline. Its Chicago headquarters are at 6746 S. Jeffrey Ave. and 306 W. Devon. The organization was founded in New York Nov. 6, 1896, by Generals Ballington Booth and Maud Booth and is commanded by General John F. MacMahon. It has programs to alleviate the hardships of many low income and handicapped groups, providing health camps, daycare centers, hospices for working girls, maternity homes, home for the aged, help for released prisoners, treatment for drug addicts and alcoholics. Since 1969 the VOA has developed an $80,000,000 housing program for 120,000 low and moderate income individuals and families. It has a staff of more than 5,200 and 728 mission chapels and program centers.

Danville

Air Services: Allegheny Airlines, 4 flights daily to Chicago and Indianapolis. Charter flights. Vermilion County Airport, 420 acres, n. on Illinois 1 to first concrete road to right, then east for 2 *m.*

Buses: Two cross-country lines.

Highways: Illinois 1, n-s. Illinois 150 e-w. and Interstate 74, e. to Indianapolis. US 136 combines with Illinois 1.

Railroads: Three freight lines.

Information and Accommodations: Danville Chamber of Commerce, 103½ N. Vermilion St. *Commercial News,* daily and Sunday, 17 W. North St. Seven hotels with 630 rooms; 9 motels with 331 units; 6 mobile homes parks. Three hospitals, including Veterans Admin., 2,125 beds; 4 nursing homes, 428 beds.

Schools and Churches: Public, 18 elementary, 3 junior high, 1 high school. Parochial (Roman Catholic), 3 elementary, 1 high. Danville Junior College, Lake View School of Nursing & Medical Technology, Midwest Bible College. Churches, 90, of 24 denominations.

Parks and Recreation: Danville has 10 city parks, 300 acres, a Community Center with Olympic-size swimming pool; tennis courts, lighted baseball diamonds, supervised programs for children year around; 2 outdoor public pools, 2 auto racing tracks, 2 roller skating rinks, football, baseball, basketball, softball, leagues for men, women and children; 1 public 18-hole golf course, 2 private; archery, bowling, 56 lanes; 3 indoor, 3 outdoor theaters. The DANVILLE BALL PARK, Highland Blvd. off Ill. 1, home of Danville Warriors of Midwest Baseball League. Public and private beaches are located along Vermilion Lake.

Culture and Entertainment: Danville supports a symphony orchestra, Danville Art League, Danville Light Opera Co., Danville Musical Cycle, Oratorio Society, Red Mask Players, Vermilion County Museum Society and Vermilion County Audubon Society.

DANVILLE, 132 *m.* (611 alt., 42,570 pop. 1970; 41,856, 1960, inc. 1.7%) seat of Vermilion County, is only 5 *m.* west of the Indiana line and reached from Chicago on Illinois 1, the highway farthest east in the State. It also connects with Interstate 74, an expressway that parallels US 150 to Champaign-Urbana, Bloomington, and Peoria to the Quad Cities. An industrial city with a work force of more than 12,000, it produces a variety of machine tools, castings, farm machinery, fabricated metal components, welding machines, air conditioning equipment, air compressors, as well as animal feeds, meat packing, and food processing.

Among its principal industrial plants are divisions of Continental

Can Co., E. P. Du Pont de Nemours, and Quaker Oats. It is in the coal strip-mining area, which has a mine noted for its modern equipment. Danville was the first Illinois city to develop a Downtown Mall in its business district. It started with two city blocks, planting trees and shrubs, installing fountains, and providing a series of flower, art, and car shows.

Danville profits from its nearness to outdoor recreation areas. Public and private beaches are located along Vermilion Lake, which supplies the city with water. Kickapoo State Park, north on Logan Ave. to W. Williams, and west on Williams for about 4 miles, has been developed from 1,539 acres of land abandoned after strip-mining. There are hundreds of little ponds stocked with fish. Forest Glen Preserve of 1,800 acres is a few miles south toward Georgetown. North of Kickapoo State Park water stored up behind Middlework Dam will be known as Lake Kennekuk.

Danville occupies the site of an Indian village visited by Col. George Croghan, a trader, in June, 1765. The Vermilion River, Croghan noted, "is so called from a fine red earth found here by the Indians, with which they paint themselves." Croghan made no mention of salines a few miles west of the village, which the Indians had tapped by means of shallow wells. The first white man to learn of the salines was Joseph Barron, interpreter of Indian dialects for Gen. William H. Harrison. Barron is said to have inspected the salines in 1801, but, as the region was inhabited by the Kickapoo, he made no attempt to claim them.

In the summer of 1819 the Kickapoo ceded a large area, including what is now Vermilion County, to the Federal government. Barron immediately went to the salines with three white companions and tested the brine for its salt content; satisfied with his find, he returned to Fort Harrison. Truman Blackman, one of Barron's party, hastily organized a secret expedition and returned to the salines in October 1819. There he left two of his men, sent two others back to Fort Harrison for equipment, while he continued on to Vandalia where, contrary to an agreement with his fellow claim-jumpers, he sought full title to the salines.

The complaints of Barron and the duped partners of Blackman created a legal snarl that was not untangled until 1824, when Maj. John W. Vance (1782-1857) obtained a lease on the salines. He imported 80 iron kettles from Louisville, Kentucky, employed nine workers, and began making salt. When Vermilion County was organized in 1826, the Salt Works—grown to a settlement of a tavern and 12 cabins—was selected as the county seat. The county's citizens disapproved of the site, however, and in 1827 Guy W. Smith and Dan Beckwith (1795-1835), a trader at the Salt Works, offered to donate 100 acres for a new county seat a few miles to the east. Their offer was accepted. Beckwith, in his capacity as county surveyor, platted a new site, which was named Danville in his honor. Forty-two lots were sold in the new town on April 10, 1827.

Foremost resident of the new county seat was Gurdon S. Hubbard, who established a trading post in 1828 (changed to a "white goods store" in 1831), and led an unsuccessful movement to develop a trade outlet on the Vermilion River. He sent a flatboat loaded with corn, pork, and flour from Danville to New Orleans in 1831. In November 1833, Hubbard sold his store and pack train of 50 horses, bundled his possessions into four Conestoga wagons, and drove across the prairie to Chicago. A month later in a letter to his brother-in-law, Dr. William Fithian of Danville, he wrote: "So far I have no regret for having moved to a smaller town."

Ward Hill Lamon, a Virginian, settled at Danville in 1847. In the following year he met Abraham Lincoln, then making his first round of the Eighth Judicial Circuit. The two men became friends; in 1852 they formed a law partnership which lasted five years. In Danville, as in other towns on the circuit, Lincoln had a reputation as a wit and a story-teller. Here he is said to have amused fellow lawyers by wielding a lath to demonstrate the cuts he intended to use in his duel with Shields (*see Alton*).

POINTS OF INTEREST

DANVILLE JUNIOR COLLEGE, a State-supported coeducational institution, was opened in 1949. It stresses vocational and technical courses. In the fall, 1970, it reported 1,500 enrolled for the full curriculum; it also has part-time and adult classes, and a faculty of 140. To its original plant of seven buildings acquired from the Veterans Administration it has added buildings for physical education, horticulture, and food services.

The VETERANS ADMINISTRATION HOSPITAL, 1900 E. Main St., was established by the U. S. Government in 1897 and has 95 buildings on 535 acres. Neuro-psychiatric treatment has been its primary function since 1934. It has 1,680 beds and employs 1,150 persons.

The DANVILLE PUBLIC LIBRARY has its headquarters at 307 N. Vermilion St. The original building, erected in 1903, was considerably modernized in 1958. The library has more than 127,000 volumes and a circulation of 427,206. It is one of the three central libraries of the Lincoln Trail Library System, an organization of 34 cooperating libraries.

The VICTORY MONUMENT, W. Main and Gilbert Sts. was designed by Lorado Taft, and dedicated in 1922 to the men of Vermilion County who died in World War I. A short distance south is the MEMORIAL BRIDGE, a reinforced concrete structure, built across the Vermilion River in 1922.

The VERMILION COUNTY MUSEUM occupies the historic FITHIAN HOUSE, 116 N. Gilbert St. It is a two-story brick structure, built in 1830 for Dr. William Fithian. On September 21, 1858, a large crowd met Lincoln at the railroad depot and escorted him to Dr. Fithian's home. Lincoln expressed his thanks in a brief speech from the balcony at the south side of the house, as attested by a LINCOLN

MEMORIAL BOULDER on the lawn. The house is now filled with memorabilia of Lincoln, Fithian and Joseph Gurney Cannon (1836-1926), Representative in Congress from Illinois, who resided in Danville the latter half of his life. "Uncle Joe," as he was familiarly known, came from North Carolina and in 1861 succeeded Ward Hill Lamon as district state's attorney. In 1873 he was elected to the House of Representatives. Except for two defeats caused by the Populist and Progressive uprisings, he served continuously until 1923. Between 1901 and 1911 he was Speaker of the House. He was a standpat Republican.

The BARNUM BUILDING, in which Abraham Lincoln and Ward Hill Lamon maintained a law office, stood on the northwest corner of Redden Square, which was named for Col. Curtis Redden, a resident who was killed in World War I. The American National Bank Building, southeast corner of Redden Square is on the site of Gurdon S. Hubbard's Trading Post, operated by Hubbard between 1826 and 1833.

The Grier-Lincoln Hotel, 103 W. Main St., is on the site of the McCormick Hotel, in which Lincoln and his circuit-riding colleagues lodged on their visits to Danville. Here Lincoln was tried before an "orgmathorial court" of fellow lawyers on the charge that his fees were too low. Found guilty, Lincoln paid his fine with a gallon of whisky.

Decatur

Airline: Ozark Airlines, 20 flights daily with connections at Chicago, St. Louis, Indianapolis. Decatur Municipal Airport, 5.35 *m.* east of Post Office.

Buses: 6 intercity lines, 40 trips daily, Union Bus Depot, 214 Main St.

Highways: US 51, north-south, and US 36, east-west, intersect at Decatur. State 121, northwest-southwest, passes through city, has junctions with State 47, 48, crosses Lake Decatur with US 36. New east-west highway, State 135, connecting Champaign, Decatur, Springfield, will have access roads to Interstate 55, 57, 74, approx. 45 *m.* away. Chicago is 175 *m.,* northeast; St. Louis, 120 *m.,* southwest; Indianapolis, 150 *m.,* southeast.

Railroads: Norfolk & Western (Wabash), 700 E. Cerro Gordo St.; Baltimore & Ohio, Pennsylvania, Illinois Central; Illinois Terminal.

Information: Association of Commerce, 158 W. Prairie St. *Decatur Herald* (morning) and *Review* (evening), with combined Sunday issue.

Administration: Council-Manager government; Mayor and 6 councilmen are elected; city manager heads all departments. Separately elected are the Board of Education, Macon County officials; Sanitary District Board of 3 is appointed by County Court.

Recreation and Cultural Events: Decatur has 28 public parks of 1,545 acres, including Hess, Torrence, Fairview, Lincoln, Johns Hill, Mueller, Forest and Nelson, latter with Municipal Beach on Lake Decatur. Three golf courses, 24 playgrounds, 9 community centers, public and private swimming pools, riding clubs, shooting range. Macon County Fair is held in the fall. Decatur Commodores baseball team competes in the Midwest League. Concerts and lectures originate in Millikin University; there are a Fine Arts Series and Community Concerts.

DECATUR (682 alt. 90,397 pop., 1970; 78,004, 1960; inc. 15.9%) seat of Macon County, is an important industrial and railroad city in central Illinois, 117 *m.* east of Springfield and 175 *m.* southwest of Chicago. It is located on Lake Decatur, artificially created by a dam on the Sangamon River. In the heart of a productive farming area it has developed a profitable industry in soybean processing and is generally known as the Soybean Capital. With a labor force of approx. 50,000 employed in more than 150 industries, it makes metal products—fire escapes, doors, joists, rails—builds tools and dies, water supply systems, patterns; repairs railroad equipment: engages in meat packing and presents a nationally-known line of grocery items. Sounds of heavy and light industry are varied by the hum of printing presses, and the cheers emanating from the playing fields of Millikin University.

Certainly Decatur is a prairie town. It rests on a long swell of the

Illinois grass land, which rises gently from the Sangamon River, carries the business district on its crest, and drops again to the prairie level north of the Wabash tracts. Prairie grasses and flowers push against the doorsteps of the outermost houses, and each spring brighten the vacant lots. The swell imparts to the streets a sense of affinity with the land; the blocks of low weathered buildings seem a part of the prairie, in no way foreign to it. This is also apparent in the long, horizontal lines of the dwellings that are visible in the rapidly expanding outlying areas of Decatur. More than 5,500 new homes, valued at more than $40,000,000, were erected in a recent 5-year period. Households have increased by more than 20 per cent and 78 per cent of the dwellings are occupied by their owners.

The Decatur area was first settled by Leonard Stevens, who in 1822 built a house 3 miles northwest of the present city near a stream that bears his name. Macon County was formed in 1829 and named for Nathaniel Macon, who served 33 years as Representative and Senator in Washington. In July, 1829, Decatur was laid out on a 20-acre tract by Benjamin Austin and became the county seat. It was named for Stephen Decatur, naval hero. By 1834 Decatur had seven dwellings, two stores, a courthouse and a jail. A dam had been built across the Sangamon River and a grist mill and a sawmill started. A city charter was granted in 1855. The nucleus of the Great Western Mill at Cerro Gordo and Water Sts. dates from 1856. It grew into the largest grain mill in central Illinois.

Abraham Lincoln was closely associated with Decatur and it commemorates his career and marks the sites of his activities. Four days after his 21st birthday he left Spencer County, Indiana, with his father Thomas Lincoln and family to take up farming in Macon County at the urging of his cousin, John Hanks. The Lincolns passed through Decatur, stopping near the southwest corner of the present Lincoln Square. They settled on the Sangamon River nearly 8 m. from Decatur off US 36, in what is now the Lincoln Trail Homestead State Park. Here Abe split rails to fence off 10 acres. In 1831 the Lincolns moved to Coles County. Lincoln came back to Decatur as a young lawyer traveling the Eighth Judicial Circuit, and in 1856 he attended an antislavery meeting here.

From 600 in 1850 the population of Decatur rose to 3,839 in 1860 and more than doubled in the next two decades. Outstanding among the men who developed local commerce and industry was James Millikin, who established the Millikin Bank and helped to endow Millikin University.

The first post of the Grand Army of the Republic (GAR) was founded in Decatur April 6, 1866, by Dr. Benjamin F. Stephenson and 12 other veterans. The two first national commanders were Major General Stephen C. Hurlburt and Major General John A. Logan. The last Illinois member of the GAR was Lewis Fablinger of Downers Grove, who died in March, 1950.

In 1874 the city's economy was broadened when coal veins under the city were tapped, and with the opening of the new century the population had passed 20,000. In 1903 the university was opened, with President Theodore Roosevelt making the principal address at the dedication. Four years later the processing of corn products began here and has expanded continuously. In 1923, realizing that an inadequate water supply would soon restrict industrial growth, Decatur replaced its original dam with the present one, which impounds Lake Decatur, an area of 2,600 acres, now a favorite recreation spot.

World War II brought about a huge expansion in Decatur's industrial and commercial life, including the construction of a large military engine plant by the Caterpillar Tractor Co. and a U. S. Government plant that worked on part of the atomic bomb.

Its largest manufacturers are the A. E. Staley Co., corn and soybean processing; Caterpillar Tractor Co., motor graders; Borg-Warner Corp., condensers, carburetors, etc.; the Mueller Co., estab. 1857, water and gas distribution and service products; General Electric Co., sterophonic appliances; Pittsburgh Plate Glass Co., Firestone Tire & Rubber Co., and Warner Castings.

POINTS OF INTEREST

MILLIKIN UNIVERSITY, located in the 110 block on W. Main St., has won a distinguished name in scholastic circles since it opened in 1902. It offers undergraduate and graduate courses in the College of Arts and Sciences and the School of Music. The third component is the School of Business and Industrial Management, which is important to the industries of the city. In the fall, 1970, Millikin enrolled 1,716 and had a faculty of 141.

The university was named for James Millikin, Decatur business pioneer, whose initial gift of $200,000 and a tract of land encouraged the founding. Citizens raised $100,000 and the Illinois-Indiana-Iowa Presbyterian Synod gave a like amount. The three buildings of the original group of Elizabethan design are connected by corridors. Liberal Arts Hall opens on the west into West Hall and on the east into East Hall. At the western edge of the campus are the School of Music and Scoville Science Hall. The Orville B. Gorin Library has been building up its collections of books and periodicals and is moving toward 100,000 vols. Important buildings are the University Center, the Mueller Industrial Laboratory, and the Gymnasium. Of striking monumental design is the Kirkland Fine Arts Center. Dormitories are located at the eastern side of the campus and include new halls for men and women.

The DECATUR PUBLIC LIBRARY shares with the Lincoln Library in Springfield the headquarters of the Rolling Prairie Library System, a cooperative alignment of 28 libraries in eleven counties. Bookmobiles emanating from most of these libraries create a network of services that reach an extraordinary number of readers. The Decatur Library reports that more than 30,000 readers drew nearly 500,000 books and accessories in one year. Of the volumes here and at Millikin University 226,000 are classified as technical.

The WIGWAM, convention hall in which the State Republican

party met and on May 9, 1860 endorsed Abraham Lincoln for the Republican nomination for President, stood at 200 East Main St. and is suitably marked. It was here that John Hanks, cousin of Abe, carried into the hall two fence rails with the placard saying they were "from a lot of 3,000 made in 1830 by Thos. Hanks and Abe Lincoln." Thus Lincoln became the rail-splitter candidate. The convention passed a resolution reading:

> That Abraham Lincoln is the choice of the Republican part of Illinois for the Presidency, and the delegates from this State are instructed to use all honorable means to secure his nomination by the Chicago Convention, and to vote as a unit for him.

Three statues of Lincoln have been erected in Decatur. One, Lincoln as a young man, commemorates a political speech in Lincoln Square. Lincoln at 21 stands on the campus of Millikin University. Lincoln as a lawyer stands in front of the Macon County Building.

The RICHARD J. OGLESBY HOUSE (*private*) at 421 West William St., is a four-square, two-story dwelling built in the 1870's by another of Decatur's famous sons. Oglesby came to Decatur as a farm boy in 1836. He worked at odd jobs, attended school sporadically, and went to Springfield to study law. He became a State Senator, a United States Senator, three times Governor of Illinois and a major general in the Civil War. He was closely associated with the political campaigns of Lincoln. Oglesby was the first to mention Lincoln's name at the Wigwam convention. His house is excellently preserved.

The MACON COUNTY MUSEUM is the newest of such institutions in Decatur. It occupies the fifth floor of the Macon County Building. *Open daily except Saturday and Sunday.* The DECATUR CIVIC ART INSTITUTE is located in the dwelling built by James Millikin in 1863 at a corner of W. Main St. at Pine St. The two-and-a-half-story structure of red brick is set in a wide expanse of lawn. The interior of the building is finished entirely in walnut, and original furnishings of the Millikin home are still in use. Three rooms and the hallway on the first floor are used for exhibiting visiting collections of etchings, lithographs, and paintings. Commodore Stephen Decatur, for whom the city was named, is the subject of a statue on the grounds of the Millikin home.

The first MACON COUNTY COURTHOUSE, begun in 1829 when Decatur became the county seat, has been rebuilt in Fairview Park, McClelland and West Eldorado Sts. The original was standing when Thomas Lincoln and his family, including his big boy Abe, passed through Decatur to a farm 8 miles southwest on the Sangamon River. John Hanks, cousin of Abe's mother, received $9.87 for "chinking and daubing" the structure. It is two stories tall and constructed of notched, new logs, chinked with concrete. It was already too small in 1839, when the county built a new courthouse. The original survived somewhat precariously as a schoolhouse, church, and Boy Scout shelter. The Macon County Lincoln Memorial Assn. reconstructed it, using forty logs retrieved from a pre-Civil War barn near Ramsey. Fairview Park comprises 180 acres.

LAKE DECATUR on the Sangamon River has a 12-mile shore-line drive. To contain the lake Decatur organized a stock company and in 1922 built a new dam that produced a lake covering 2,600 acres, 13 *m.* long and half a mile wide. In 1956 the reservoir was enlarged by 5-ft. bascule gates on top of the dam to furnish storage capacity of 9.21 billion gallons. In the 1960's construction began on a new dam to impound Lake Oakley, with 11,000 acre-ft. of water.

A corporation that has been a big employer of labor through the years is the A. M. STALEY MANUFACTURING CO., N. 22 and E. Eldorado Sts., which occupies more than 380 acres. Its administration building is 14 stories tall and surmounted by a gold-crowned dome. With production of 100 carloads a day, the plant normally employs 3,200, making corn syrups, corn sugar, gluten feed, corn oil, soy bean meal, flour, oil and sauce, and a variety of chemicals, including lecithin and inositol.

The founding of the Grand Army of the Republic (GAR) in Decatur is commemorated by a statue in Central Park and a marker at S. Park St. On the second floor of the Union printing shop the national organization of Union veterans of the Civil War was founded April 6, 1866.

East St. Louis

Highways: East St. Louis is the focus for half a dozen of the State's heavily traveled highways, which also lead directly to St. Louis across four multilane bridges over the Mississippi. The principal north-south route, part of the Great River Route, is Illinois 3. There is a junction with Interstate 70 and 270 above Granite City. Int. 55 and 70 combine with US 40 and 66 to form the main highway into East St. Louis. From the southeast come US 50 and US 450 combined with Illinois 15.

Airports: Southwest Civic Memorial Airport, three miles south on Illinois 3. Serves as extension of St. Louis-Lambert Municipal Airport for private aircraft only.

Bus Stations: Continental Trailways Bus Depot, 505 Missouri Ave., East St. Louis, serves Continental Trailways, Gulf Transport Co., Jacksonville Trailways, Vandalia Bus Line, Inc., Peoria-Rockford Bus Co. Bi-State Transit System serves the East St. Louis-St. Louis area.

Railroad Stations: Relay Depot, 41 Missouri Ave., for Baltimore & Ohio Railroad, Louisville & Nashville Railroad, Penn-Central Railroad. More frequent service on most lines at Union Station, 18th and Market Streets, St. Louis. Passenger service largely restricted.

Steamboat Landing: Foot of Eads Bridge in St. Louis for local excursion lines.

Information and Accommodations: Metro-East Journal, 425 Missouri Ave., eve. and Sunday. Greater East St. Louis Chamber of Commerce, 234 Collinsville Ave. Holiday Inn and more than 12 motels.

Hospitals: Christian Welfare Hospital, 1509 Illinois Ave. 279 beds. St. Mary's Hospital, much new construction since 1963; first burn center in southern Illinois, 335 beds. 129 N. 8th St.

Recreation and Entertainment: 12 city parks, 7 playgrounds, 1,336 acres. Jones Park swimming pool can accommodate 1,000 persons at one time. Baseball, tennis, fishing in lagoon, games, ice skating. Catholic Youth Organization has annual All-Sports Jamboree in Jones Park Lagoon. Lincoln Park, Bluff Park. Golf in Frank Holten State Park.

Horse Racing: Mid-July through mid-October meet at Fairmont Jockey Club, 4 miles north of city on US 40, pari-mutuel betting; April to November meetings at Cahokia Downs, US 460, pari-mutuel betting.

Environs: Short drives to old Cahokia, with relics of French origins, Illinois 3. Cahokia Mounds State Park, 224 acres, 80 large mounds of Indian origin, includes nation's largest, Monk Mound. Our Lady of the Snows shrine with outdoor altar, 15 altars along Rosary Court, Angelus bells set in reflecting pool. Take Illinois 13 or US 460 change at junction to Ill. 163. Across the Mississippi the city of St. Louis with full metropolitan cultural facilities, museums, galleries, symphonic orchestra, theaters, colleges.

EAST ST. LOUIS (418 alt., 69,986 pop. 1970; 81,712, 1960, dec. 14.3%) is an important part of the huge industrial complex of South-western Illinois, which fills St. Clair County, a contiguous segment of Madison County, and is only separated from the millions of the St. Louis area by the Mississippi River. The census figures for city and the two counties disclose that there has been a movement from the city to its environs, for St. Clair County in 1970 had 285,186 people, an increase of 8.6% over the 244,689 of 1960, and Madison County had 250,204, an increase of 11.7% over the 244,689 of 1960. It is reported that the movement of population out of East St. Louis is even greater than the figure given by the U. S. Census, for it is offset by a movement into the city. Much of this is attributed to the migration of black workers from southern farms to cities along the river.

Changes also have taken place in transportation and manufacturing. Although the railroads have curtailed their passenger services, East St. Louis remains a major loading depot for freight produced by its numerous industries. Some adjustments have taken place in industry; for instance, National City, a separately incorporated area of packing plants, has lost plants by decentralization, but still remains a major employer. The trucking business continues to flourish, and the city profits by the fine roads, which include Interstate 55 and 70, and five United States highways. Many major manufacturers of the United States have been represented in East St. Louis and National City; Hunter Packing, a division of John Morrell & Co.; Swift & Co., Royal Packing Co., Chas. Pfizer & Co., Obear-Nester Glass Co., Agrico Chemical Co., Agway, Inc., Certainteed, Mobil Chemical (Socony), Sterling Steel Castings, Cerro Copper & Brass, American Zinc Co., many others. The W. G. Krummrich plant of the Montsanto Co., located just across the line at Saugus, covers 230 acres and at peak periods employs up to 2,050 and has an annual payroll of approx. $12,000,000. Hunter Packing paid $8,000,000 annually when in full operation. Southwestern Bell Telephone Co. is a major employer. Sears, Roebuck & Co. and Holiday Inns are among recent important additions to the city's economy.

National City became important in the meatpacking industry in 1893 when Armour & Co., Swift & Co. and several other firms built branch plants here. In 1902 they took part in organizing the National Packing Co., which extended its control to other cities. At this time agitation against the socalled beef trust filled the newspapers and there was much demand for Federal regulation of combines. Reform of packinghouse methods was effected in 1906 when Congress passed a meat inspection law as the result of public indignation sparked by publication of Upton Sinclair's novel, *The Jungle*. Federal suits against the big packers for actions in restraint of trade led to the breakup of the National Packing Co.

The concentration of railroad freight terminals in the Metropolitan area gives employment to about 6,000 in East St. Louis and an annual payroll of $43,000,000. Automatic switching aids efficient marshalling.

The Southwest Regional Port District routes barge, rail and truck service through Fox Terminal, and is empowered to issue bonds for construction and rehabilitation of industrial and cultural buildings and develop industrial parks.

East St. Louis owes its origin to Cahokia, the historic village several miles south of the city, where the French established an Indian mission in 1699. Cahokia became the chief trading center on the Illinois frontier in the 18th century, and then declined quickly as the result of floods and the commercial rivalry of St. Louis. Although an attempt at settlement opposite St. Louis had been made in 1770 by Richard "English" McCarty, the first permanent foothold was gained by Capt. James Piggott some 25 years later when he established a ferry service across the Mississippi. In 1816 McKnight and Brady, St. Louis land operators, auctioned lots in Illinoistown, near the ferry station.

Aided by the westward flow of pioneers and the rise of steamboat commerce, Illinoistown's permanence was further secured through an early development of natural resources. Coal deposits in the nearby bluffs were mined in 1837 by a company organized by ex-Governor John Reynolds. The coal was taken to the river in cars drawn by horses along wooden rails. The first steam railroad from the East was the Ohio & Mississippi, in July, 1855, followed in a decade by 10 other lines. All terminated at Illinoistown, connected with St. Louis by the Wiggins Company ferries, which had replaced Capt. Piggott's crude *pirogues*. Freight handling became Illinoistown's chief task.

Although the plat of Illinoistown was recorded in 1818, the town was not incorporated until January, 1859. Several months later a town named East St. Louis was platted northeast of Illinoistown. In 1861 the State legislature presented a new charter to Illinoistown, proposing that its corporate limits be extended and its name changed to East St. Louis. The charter was approved in a bitterly contested referendum, and Illinoistown, in growing larger, lost the name it had borne for almost half a century.

In 1874 East St. Louis became the beneficiary of a famous piece of engineering, the Eads Bridge to St. Louis. James Buchanan Eads (1830-1887) architect and engineer, was also responsible for the deepening of the channel of the Mississippi River at its mouth, which he effected by a series of jetties. His plans for the bridge at St. Louis were opposed by the ferries, which had a heavy stake in transporting freight across the river. When the Illinois legislature gave Eads a charter to construct a bridge from East St. Louis over Bloody Island to the western bank the Missouri opposition was overcome. But the ferries, far from being closed down, found their transport still needed by railroads. Continuous rail pasage was limited to certain roads, and the majority of companies, rather than pay heavy tolls for each box car sent over the bridge, used ferries or wagon vans. The construction of the Municipal Bridge in 1917 afforded cross-river passage to all railroads, but by that time warehouses and miles of track had been built at the East St. Louis riverfront. Today railroads still break carload lots into bulk at East St. Louis and transport the goods to St. Louis by motor trucks. Ferry boats are no longer used.

Because of its low site on the flood plain, East St. Louis has been constantly threatened by the Mississippi. The severest flood on record was that of 1844 when the American Bottom was so completely in-undated that a steamboat was able to load a cargo of coal at the bluffs east of the present city. To ward off possible disaster, John B. Bowman, many times mayor, proposed in 1870 that the streets be elevated above the 1844 high-water mark. This was accomplished after 1875.

During the last decades of the 19th century, East St. Louis declined as a river town and gradually assumed its present industrial condition. Then, on May 27, 1896, a tornado demolished the business district, killing more than 100 people. Buildings were splintered, fires raged unchecked, and the entire east approach of the Eads Bridge was ripped away. With the aid of a $90,000 relief fund contributed by neighboring communities, East St. Louis entered the new century with the scars of this calamity effaced.

In June 1903, despite frantic efforts of levee workers, the swollen Mississippi poured into East St. Louis, flooding one-fourth of the city. Eight thousand refugees were housed in St. Louis but no lives were lost. Public demand for protection resulted in the formation of the East Side Levee & Sanitary District in 1907.

Racial disturbances broke out in East St. Louis on May 28 and July 2, 1917, after many months of tension caused chiefly by the hiring of Negro workers to replace whites in the plants. The pressure to rush completion of war orders also induced employers to hire extra blacks coming up from the South. On May 28 a resentful white mob of 3,000 roamed the streets harassing Negroes. On July 2 white mobs invaded Negro homes near the downtown Broadway area, terrifying women and children, pulling houses apart and burning them. Blacks fleeing the town found the Eads Bridge closed but managed to cross to St. Louis on the Municipal Free Bridge. Forty-eight persons were killed—39 blacks and 9 whites, among the latter two detectives, and 240 houses were destroyed. Appeals to President Woodrow Wilson to intervene brought no response. Senator William Y. Sherman carried the com-plaints to Congress. Indictments of 144, including 5 police officers, were fruitless. (See *Race Riot at East St. Louis, July 2, 1917* by Elliot M. Rudwick).

The black population of East St. Louis, which stood at approx. 50 percent of the whole a decade or two ago, is now estimated to be 70 percent. In 1971 it elected a black mayor. State Street, its four-mile length lined with shops, restaurants, service stations, and automobile repair shops, is the main artery linking the downtown business district with the residential suburbs stretching into the bluffs at the easterly extremity of the city. Urban renewal campaigns have cleared some of the rundown areas but although the administration works energetically to remove blighted housing, much remains to be done.

POINTS OF INTEREST

NATIONAL STOCK YARDS, often called the Hog Capital of the Nation, cover 640 acres in a separately organized village called NATIONAL CITY, which has its own administrative, fire and police services (124 pop. 1970). Main entrance is at First St. and St. Clair Ave. (Illinois 3). Here more than 4,000 pens were originally available to receive, care and display for sale livestock shipped from an area of 150 miles around East St. Louis. In rush periods transactions often reach $1,000,000 a day. The Stock Yards was founded in 1873.

Swift & Co., Circle Packing Co., Hunter Packing Co., and Royal Packing Co. built large plants here, but much packing has been curtailed. There are public storage warehouses, cold and dry. Three large agrichemical producers and three major fertilizer plants add to the economic importance of East St. Louis. The East St. Louis Junction Railroad, owned by the St. Louis National Stock Yard Co., operates freight service for the area.

JONES PARK, a 130-acre tract centered at 25th St. and Lynch Ave., has a brick pavilion, picnic grounds, 17 athletic fields, 15 tennis courts, a playground area, a swimming pool and a lagoon for boating and fishing. Argonne Drive, the flower lined main thoroughfare in Jones Park is one of the beauty spots in the city, as is the park's lighted Lily Pond.

FRANK HOLTEN STATE PARK, 43rd Street and Lake Drive, comprises 1,325 acres of former swampland, known as Grand Marais. The site was originally developed by the East St. Louis Park Board. The large lake in the park is a haven for sailing enthusiasts. The park also contains an 18-hole golf course, a driving range, 9 miles of bridle trails, tennis courts, athletic fields and pleasure boating facilities. The park restaurant offers a beautiful view of the lake. The park was named for Frank Holton, State Representative from St. Clair County for 48 years.

CAHOKIA DOWNS, East St. Louis racetrack located on Highway 460, is the home of a former turf classic, the annual St. Louis Derby. The Derby, the richest event in local area racing, attracts many of the Midwest's top three year-olds to compete in the mile and one-sixteenth event. The clubhouse facilities are available to fans throughout the racing season.

EAST ST. LOUIS PUBLIC LIBRARY, 405 N. 9th St., was erected 1925 and modernized in 1963. It stocks more than 115,000 books and circulates approx. 160,000. It is a member of the Kaskaskia Library System, which has its hq in Belleville.

MacARTHUR BRIDGE has its approach at 10th St. and Piggott Ave. and is one of the largest double-deck steel span bridges known. Its overall length is about two miles; the main span is 668 ft. long. The bridge shares vehicle traffic with three other spans between East St. Louis and St. Louis. Owned by the city of St. Louis, the bridge was completed in 1917 at a cost of $6,000,000 (free).

POPLAR STREET BRIDGE was built by the State. This inter-city span carries all Federal and Interstate highways from East St. Louis to Poplar Street in St. Louis, at the foot of the Gateway Arch (*free*). The East St. Louis approach to the six-lane bridge has aroused wide architectural interest. The approach, sometimes termed the "spaghetti factory," consists of a series of stacked overpasses.

MARTIN LUTHER KING, JR. BRIDGE, the farthest upriver bridge in East St. Louis, carries traffic from highways US 40, US 50-66 direct to Interstate 70 on the Missouri bank in the heart of St. Louis.

EADS BRIDGE, named for its builder, James B. Eads, spans the Mississippi between Washington Ave., St. Louis, and Broadway, East St. Louis. Completed in 1874 after five years' work, the Eads Bridge was one of the engineering marvels of its day. It marked the first use of steel in a truss bridge and embodied the longest fixed-end metal arch. In building the piers on bedrock under the river, Eads was the first engineer in America to employ the compressed-air caisson. The central arch is 520 ft. long, the two others are 18 ft. shorter. The upper deck is used by vehicles and pedestrians; the lower deck—screened by diagonals—carries railroad traffic.

BLOODY ISLAND is bounded by Front St., Spring Ave., Trendley Ave., and the approach to the Eads Bridge. This area, now occupied by freight terminals and warehouses, was formerly an island in the Mississippi. The island, a sandbar in the early 19th century, soon grew to be a mile in length and 500 yards wide. Its dense willows and cotton-woods made it a favorite arena for illegal boxing bouts, cock fights, and duels. The most tragic combat was that between Maj. Thomas Biddle and Spencer Pettis, member of the 21st Congress. Armed with pistols and stationed but five feet apart, the men killed each other here on August 25, 1831.

As Bloody Island continued to enlarge, the Mississippi was diverted from the Missouri shore and the St. Louis harbor became dangerously shallow. Urged by alarmed St. Louisans, Congress appropriated funds in 1836 for the construction of diversion dikes. Under the supervision of Lieut. Robert E. Lee U. S. Corps of Engineers, a dike was built between the upstream tip of the island and the Illinois shore; another was built from the downstream end of the island. The current was consequently deflected toward the Missouri side, St. Louis harbor rapidly deepened, and the space between Bloody Island and the mainland filled with silt.

Elgin

Air Services: Elgin Airport is located 1½ *m.* north of the city limits at the intersection of Northwest Tollway and Illinois 31. It has shuttle service to other airports. O'Hare International Airport is 23.3 *m.* east on Northwest Tollway.

Highways: Northwest Tollway (Int. 90) ; Evanston-Elgin Road, Illinois 58; Irving Park Road, Illinois 19; Lake St., US 20; North-South roads, Illinois 25, Illinois 31.

Transportation. Northland Greyhound Bus Lines; United Motor Coach Co.; Intercity Bus & Truck Lines. Union Bus Station, 222 Dundee Ave. Commuter service to Chicago on the Milwaukee Ry., West Chicago St. station. Freight service on Milwaukee, Chicago & North Western. Elgin, Joliet & Eastern.

Information: Elgin Assn. of Commerce, 310 East Chicago St. Elgin Economic Development Commission, Tower Bldg. *Elgin Daily Courier-News.*

Hospitals. St. Joseph, 277 Jefferson Ave.; Sherman, 934 Center St. Elgin State, 750 S. State St.

Other Activities. Elgin has 53 Protestant churches, 4 Roman Catholic, 1 Jewish Temple. It has 17 parks of 3330 acres. The Tyler Creek Forest Preserve is 1½ *m.* north on Illinois 31.

Special Events: The Elgin Civic Symphony and Community Theatre are sponsored by Elgin Community College and have a winter season. The Hiawatha Pageant is held in June at Camp Big Timber, Boy Scouts, 3 *m.* northwest.

ELGIN (720 alt., 55,691 pop. 1970; 49,447, 1960; inc. 12.6%) is one of three equidistant cities on the western periphery of Chicago that have had independent industrial and community development for more than a century. The other two are Aurora and Joliet. Located on both banks of the Fox River, 38 *m.* west of Chicago, Elgin is easily accessible from the metropolis by numerous highways, including the highspeed Northwest Tollway (Int. 90), which have made the Fox River Valley highly desirable as a home for commuters.

Known internationally for many decades as the home of the Elgin watch, the city today is a center of diversified industry that includes manufacture of tools, oil seals and gaskets, electrical appliances, street sweepers, pharmaceuticals, dairy products, pottery, and Sunday school publications. It profits by shipping facilities that bypass the congested terminals of Chicago, and by the proximity of O'Hare International Airport. Long a semi-rural town, it finds no disadvantages in its trend toward suburban status, for its factories prosper and its retail markets are self-sufficient for the community.

Contiguous to Elgin on the South is SOUTH ELGIN, (4,289

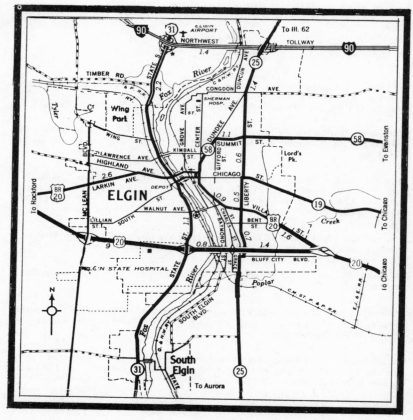

Elgin Economic Development Commission

pop. 1970; 2,624, 1960) an incorporated village on the Fox River, with Illinois 31 routed through it. South of South Elgin on the river and served by Illinois 25 is VALLEY VIEW. All of these places are profiting by the movement of Chicago residents into the Fox Valley.

With the announcement that Elgin has a new heart, the city administration in 1968 dedicated its new CIVIC CENTER after clearing 25 acres in midtown and investing $12,000,000 in new facilities. Modern structures that are chiefly steel, concrete and glass, include the Municipal Building, the Hemmens Community Center, the United States Post Office, the Appellate Court of the Second Illinois Judicial District, and the Gail Borden Public Library. There is space for parking 450 motor cars. A council-manager government was adopted by referendum in 1954.

The Black Hawk War was over when the first settlers, James and Hezekiah Gifford, came from New York in 1835. An Indian ferried them over the Fox River, but by the following year northern Illinois was cleared of the red men, and the Giffords built up their little settlement without interference.

Elgin's industry from the first was bound to the river. Samuel Kimball and James Gifford co-operated in 1837 in damming the river, building a sawmill on one side and a gristmill on the other. Hezekiah ran a tavern for stagecoach passengers, who noted with astonishment that he ran it according to a temperance plan then gaining strength in the East.

In 1838 B. W. Raymond purchased a portion of Gifford's tract, and although he lived in Chicago and served as its third mayor, he interested himself in the development of Elgin. Throughout the forties he invested in several local enterprises, and by 1846 Elgin was able to incorporate as a village. In 1850 Raymond, by pledging much of his property, had the Chicago and Galena Railroad routed into Elgin. For two years the village was the terminus of that road, and the great stream of west-bound pioneers here transferred to covered wagons. In 1854 Elgin was incorporated as a city.

Elgin began to ship milk to Chicago in 1852, and soon processed a growing surplus into cheese and butter. The city's importance as a dairying center was greatly enhanced by Gail Borden. During his youth he had observed the difficulty encountered by Western travelers in transporting food and began experimenting with condensed foods. Following a stormy trans-Atlantic voyage, during which the ship's cows refused to give milk, he concentrated on condensed milk, and soon had a successful plant running in Elgin. By 1875 it was using the milk from a thousand cows.

Elgin was named after a favorite Scottish hymn tune of James T. Gifford, who was an inventor and a strong Abolitionist. John M. Murphy invented the first practical motorized street sweeper. The population of Elgin doubled between 1880 and 1890 when many Germans and Scandinavians settled here. The Chicago, Aurora & Elgin was its principal railway for years, but in 1957 it could no longer compete with automobiles.

Among the industries now flourishing are tool makers and makers of metal parts. Woodruff & Edwards, castings, employing 335, dates back to 1867. Chicago Rawhide Manufacturing Co., maker of oil seals, is the largest employer, 1,600. Illinois Tool Works, Inc., maker of washers, screws, and similar products, employs 1,150. Elgin Machine Works, Inc., making automotive parts, has been here since 1919. Similarly Elgin Packaging Machinery was established in 1897. The Precision Diamond Tool Co. makes abrasives. One house over 100 years old is Haeger Potteries, Inc., which began making pottery in 1871. The dairy industry is still represented, but the specialty here of the Borden Company, founded in 1895, is ice cream. The Ludwig Milk Co. was formed in 1911. Manufacturers of plastics and pharmaceuticals are of recent origin; the Union Carbide Co. located here in 1963 to make plastic bottles.

The David C. Cook Publishing Co., Grove and Lincoln Aves., makes a specialty of serving Sunday School organizations with books periodicals, and supplies, and stocks numerous other mail-order items. It started its plant in 1890 and employs 280 persons. The Brethren Press is a denominational printing organization, employing 125.

The watch industry that made Elgin famous is represented principally by the Waltham Watch Co., which came in 1961, and makes jewelled watches.

For many decades Elgin was notable for two industries—dairying and watchmaking. At the center of a thriving dairy economy it became the chief distributing point for dairy products. But its international fame was based on the remarkable development of the Elgin National Watch Company, which was founded in 1864 as the National Watch Company by John C. Adams, a Chicago watchmaker, and Benjamin W. Raymond. Their first watch was finished in 1867 in Elgin and sold for $117. The firm made a specialty of accurate timekeeping. In 1873 it produced the first stem-winder and by 1881 was making 2,000 watches per day. The demand for Elgin-made watches was so strong, especially from railroad men, that the firm name became Elgin National Watch Co. in 1874. Its factory, a six-story building with a square tower, dominated the area.

The Elgin watch became widely known through the Elgin Almanac, and by advertising, such as reiteration of the fact that for four days during and after the Chicago fire of Oct. 8, 1871, a large stock of watch movements and one small mouse in a masonry vault remained unharmed. During World War I the U. S. Army had Elgin train over 350 men to make precise repairs for military watches. The firm endowed a Watchmakers College at Elgin and equipped an observatory by which to check time. During World War II Elgin made numerous watches and instruments for military use, including sapphire bearings for aiming guns.

When nearly 100 years old the watch company found radical changes necessary. It had experienced increased competition from Swiss manufacturers, who were able to undersell the American product. The main plant in Elgin was outmoded and working conditions had changed. The company built new plants in Neuchatel, Switzerland; Blaney, South Carolina, which it renamed Elgin; Alabama, California, the Virgin Islands, Toronto, Chicago, and New York. The corporation is now called Elgin National Industries, Inc., with headquarters in New York.

There are still units of the company in Elgin, but its products have become widely diversified. Since 1960 it has bought a number of corporations and now produces all kinds of decorator clocks, novelty timepieces, precious stones, wedding bands, transistor radios and lubricants. The Elgin plant with tower, for nearly a century a conspicuous landmark, has been torn down, the college closed.

The Elgin Watch Company Observatory was established to aid in the study of astronomical time. It has since been turned over to the

Public School System, which serves parts of three counties, seven townships and all of six municipalities: Elgin, South Elgin, Bartlett, Wayne, Streamwood, and Hanover Park.

POINTS OF INTEREST

The GAIL BORDEN PUBLIC LIBRARY, stocks more than 100,000 volumes and many periodicals, audio-visual materials, and documents, circulating more than 300,000 books annually. It is a member of the North Suburban Library System of 31 libraries. Its quarters were greatly improved in 1968.

ELGIN ACADEMY, Park and College Sts., one of the oldest preparatory schools in Illinois, was chartered in 1839, but did not open until 1856. Located on the highest ground in the city, it is popularly known as the School on the Hill. It is coeducational with both boarding and day students. The main building, a three-story Greek Revival structure, was built in 1855. Boys are housed in Sears Hall. The girls' dormitory is of modern architecture, with four classrooms on the lower level.

The LAURA DAVIDSON SEARS ACADEMY OF FINE ARTS, *open 1-4 daily,* is an adjunct of Elgin Academy. Most of its exhibits came from the late Judge Nathaniel Sears, donor of the building. Among 250 canvases are a Gilbert Stuart equestrian portrait of Washington, and one by Charles Willson Peale of Washington as a British colonel, made about 1770. There also are works by Samuel Morse, Copley, Homer, and Whistler. Rosa Bonheur's An Old Buffalo was painted when Buffalo Bill's Wild West Show performed in France.

JUDSON COLLEGE, 1151 N. State St., is a coeducational liberal arts college located on 65 acres on the west bank of the Fox River, with Tyler Creek running through the campus. It is Baptist-affiliated and has adopted the Apostles Creed as a guide to the Christian faith that it affirms. It dates back to the Northern Baptist Theological Seminary founded in Chicago in 1913. In 1961 it moved to Elgin and in 1963 opened as Judson College, granting the bachelor of arts degree. It has 12 buildings of a Colonial brick style, of which two are residences for single students and two for married students. The Administration Bldg. and the Fine Arts Bldg. occupy the center of the campus. The Dining Hall includes the rustic campus commons called the Eyrie, where students and faculty meet informally. There are a Grecian Amphitheatre, and an athletic field extending to the Fox River. The Benjamin P. Browne Library has more than 30,000 volumes and receives nearly 300 periodicals. It has special collections in journalism and Baptist history. Students have a voice in college affairs through the Student Senate. Judson offers a teacher education program in cooperation with North Park College, Chicago. It enrolls approx. 400 annually.

ELGIN COMMUNITY COLLEGE, organized in 1949, uses newly constructed quarters on a campus of 100 acres in the southwestern part of Elgin. It offers two-year courses in the liberal arts and science that enable a student to continue studies in a four-year college. It has both day and evening classes and in 1971-72 reported an attendance of 2,385 and a faculty of 164. All students come from the city and environs; there are no dormitories.

ELGIN STATE HOSPITAL occupies 1,000 acres bordering South State St. at the southern city limits. The three-story main building opened in 1872 for 300 patients; today the hospital has 32 buildings, consisting of 83 wards, and approx. 5,500 patients in residence. The institution has been decentralized into eight units. All concepts of modern therapy are utilized, including team approach, milieu therapy, group therapy, family therapy services, and treatment for the alcoholic. Patients are hospitalized for the shortest period and then referred to community-based facilities.

LORD'S PARK, 110 acres, at Park Ave., was given to the city in 1892. Poplar Creek, which winds through the park, has been dammed to produce lagoons on three levels, willow-shaded and connected by splashing little falls. The Zoo, containing monkeys, black bears, coyotes, deer, raccoons, and snakes, was built into the side of a bluff, so that the animals may be viewed from above as well as from cage level. There is also a Children's Zoo. The Audubon Museum of Natural Science contains a varied collection of mounted animals and historical relics of the Fox Valley.

WING PARK, 121 acres, has facilities for golf, tennis, baseball, swimming and all other outdoor recreation, with floodlighted fields for night events. A Band Shell was presented to the city in 1962.

TROUT PARK, 56 acres on the Fox River in northern Elgin, once a private estate, is a botanical oasis where much vegetation has been kept in its natural state.

Evanston

Highways: Evanston is the first city bordering on Lake Michigan north of Chicago, and its streets are contiguous. The dividing line is Howard St., except for small area north to the Calvary Cemetery, where Eastlake Terrace overlooks Lake Michigan and Rogers Ave. Park and Beach. The western line of Evanston is along McCormick Blvd. and the North Channel of the Chicago River, west of which is the city of Skokie. Important roads to Evanston are Sheridan Road along the lake; Clark St., which becomes Chicago Ave.; Ridge Road, which is connected with the Lake Shore Drive by Hollywood Ave.; Western Ave., which becomes Asbury, and California, which becomes Dodge. Evanston has quick access to Edens Expressway through Skokie, thence going south to John F. Kennedy Expressway and the Chicago Loop.

Airport: Evanston is within 20 minutes driving time of O'Hare International Airport, by going west on Dempster St. to the junction with Tri-State Tollway, Int. 294, and thence south to O'Hare.

Transportation: The Chicago Elevated, CTA, has eight stations in Evanston for Rapid Transit lines. Chicago & North Western Ry. runs commuter trains from the Davis St. station to Chicago in 20 min. Evanston Bus Co. carries passengers inside city and to adjoining suburbs.

Information: Evanston Chamber of Commerce, 828 Davis St. Evanston Public Library, 1703 Orrington Ave.

Government: The city is governed by a Council-Manager system, with a mayor and 18 aldermen elected for terms of four years, who set policies that are carried out by the city manager, whose office is at 1501 Oak St. There are 14 departments, with the principal ones located as follows: Community Services, 828 Davis St.; Health Dept., 1806 Maple St.; Traffic Engineer, 1501 Oak St.; Parks & Forestry, 1801 Maple St.

Other Important Institutions or Activities: Convalescent Center, 1300 Oak St. Art Center, 2603 Sheridan Road. Children's Home, 826 Ridge Ave. Day Nursery, 1835 Grant St. Historical Society, 225 Greenwood Ave. Cradle Society, 2049 Ridge Ave.

Sports: Dyche Stadium, of Northwestern University, where football games are held, is 1¾ miles west of Sheridan Road on Central St., north of the campus. Here also are the Coon Student Sports Center, Wells Field and McGraw Memorial Hall.

EVANSTON (601 alt., 79,808 pop. 1970; 79,283, 1960) the first of the residential cities north of Chicago to develop along the Lake Michigan shore, begins north of Chicago's Howard St. and is constricted inside a municipal area that has Skokie (68,627 pop.) on the west and Wilmette (32,134 pop.) on the north. Despite its compactness in 8.2 *sq. m.* Evanston produces an impression of open spaces and verdant groves by its wide, tree-lined streets, park-like lawns and detached scholastic buildings. With few smokestacks to darken its skies, Evanston thrives as a cultural oasis, the main seat of Northwestern University, and a retail sales center for branches of Chicago's fashionable stores. Its conservative government, strongly backed by its churches and a well-to-do middle class, accounts for its freedom from the political and social turbulence that has affected some other Chicago suburbs.

There are more than 60 churches in Evanston, of Christian and Jewish faiths, and their architecture offers a study in periods, for some have the tall New England spires of the 19th century and others follow contemporary styles. At Linden Ave. and the Wilmette line is the impressive Baha'i House of Worship of seven portals, one for each of the world's great religions. When the second World Council of Churches was held in Evanston President Eisenhower addressed an assemblage of 20,000 in Deering Meadow. The Garrett Biblical Institute is located here.

Pioneer travelers from Chicago to Milwaukee followed the Green Bay Road that Congress in 1832 had designated a mail route for four-horse teams, and that ran on the ridge above Lake Michigan. Ten miles north of the Cook County Courthouse Ed Mulford in 1836 built his Ten-mile Tavern and presided as the local justice of the peace. Isaac Burroughs came from Ohio and in 1848 opened his Buckeye Tavern a short distance farther north. As early as 1843 the settlers started a school in a log cabin.

By 1850 there were around 400 people and the majority of 93 entitled to vote formed the township of Ridgeville, which included the area known as Grosse Point, near which Father Marquette and Louis Jolliet stopped in September, 1673, and land as far south as Rogers Park.

In 1851 a group of Methodist leaders in Chicago decided to establish "a university of the highest order to excellence" and obtained a State charter for a North Western University. The organizers were Dr. John Evans, Orrington Lunt, and Grant Goodrich. When they asked Clark T. Hinman, president of Wesleyan Academy in Albion, Mich., to head the school he counselled buying a farm, reserving part for the college and selling or leasing the rest as town lots to obtain funds. The founders bought for $25,000 a Lake Shore farm of 379 acres that Dr. J. H. Foster had acquired for $473.75 some years before. Philo Judson, business agent for the college, drew the plat of a town, called it Evanston after Dr. Evans, and named the streets after their associates.

The college trustees built their first hall, a three-story frame structure, in use today, and opened it to the first ten students in 1855. Coincidentally they obtained an amendment to their charter prohibiting the sale of liquor within four miles of the campus. Thus Evanston became the logical site for the headquarters of the Woman's Christian Temperance Union. It remained "dry" for 116 years, or until the fall of 1971.

The change in Evanston's civic customs by lifting of the ban against the sale of liquor did not cause any undue exhilaration. A reporter in

November, 1972, found a short list of "refined places" and "dignified bars" and wrote, in the *Chicago Tribune:* "The very first nightclub in a town that has never authorized any joint gamier than a coffeehouse is a sedate corner of a balcony in the Orrington Hotel, . . . They call this unhectic nook the Living Room." A male entertainer sang "a nice variety of songs, none of them on the violent or protest side."

The Methodists were strong anti-slavery men and supported the aims of the new Republican Party. Chancellor Jenks of the university outwitted Federal officers for possession of a girl slave and set her free. Evanston incorporated as a town in 1863, annexed North Evanston in 1874 and South Evanston in 1892 and became a city with mayor and aldermen in March, 1892, and adopted the council and city manager system in 1952. Part of the old Ridgeville Township was absorbed by Chicago and the rest, as Evanston Township, was merged with the city in 1903. In 1903 also the business houses organized an association that grew into the present Chamber of Commerce.

Faced with the prospect of irresponsible growth Evanston in 1921 adopted the first zoning ordinance in Illinois. The post-war building boom saw the erection of major hotels, the North Shore, Orrington, Library Plaza, Evanshire, Ridgeview, Georgian, and Homestead. Fountain Square, where a small iron fountain had been formally greeted on July 4, 1876, amid mud-filled streets, became the center of shops and offices and a modern Honor Fountain. Chicago retail houses, such as Marshall Field & Co., established branches on a metropolitan scale. With a big stake in educational and religious establishments, and a wealthy residential section, the city administration fought destructive changes, protected the natural beauty of lawns, parks, and shoreline, and enforced traffic regulations in a manner that brought national citations for the safety of its streets.

To many organizations of national scope Evanston has become the ideal location for headquarters. The shaded streets free from traffic congestion, the unpolluted air, and the proximity to Chicago's metropolitan advantages, have led business, professional, and religious agencies to open offices here. A diversified industrial concern, Calumet & Hecla, Inc., built its corporate offices in Evanston. General Finance Corp., which has 350 offices and more than 2,000 employees around the country, built its hq on Central St. Others are the American Hospital Supply Corp., Assn. of American Medical Colleges, Assn. of Rehabilitation Centers, Inc., Assn. of School Business Officials, College Entrance Examination Board, National Intern Matching Program, National Merit Scholarship Corp., National School Boards Assn., Rotary International, Textile Bag Manufacturers Assn., Clayton Mark & Co., Old Equity Life Insurance Co., Washington National Insurance Co., Sigma Alpha Epsilon, Sigma Chi Fraternity, Sigma Delta Tau Fraternity, Acacia Fraternity, American Academy of Pediatrics, even the National Foundation of Funeral Services. The Methodists, who founded Northwestern University and built the First Methodist Church in 1856, chose Evanston for five major agencies of the United Methodist Church.

After 80 years in Chicago, the National College of Education built its new plant in Evanston.

Evanston is an outstanding example of civic alertness. Religion had a major part in the founding of Northwestern University, and church membership of residents always has been large. There is strong support for the schools and much participation in neighborhood groups, garden club activities, and local history. The 19th century mood was strongly conservative; the college outlawed liquor, and the WCTU found the city an ideal base for national propaganda for temperance. The city's Planning and Conservation Department watches over urban wellbeing. The Plan Commission regularly publishes a summary of municipal objectives for general guidance. It stresses participation in civic affairs, limitation of population density and maintenance of a balance between built-up areas and open spaces.

Typical of the care exercised to insure adequate facilities for education is the EVANSTOWNSHIP HIGH SCHOOL, which occupies a campus of 67 acres. Rather than build high schools on other locations the Board of Education arranged for expanding the plant by creating four semi-independent schools, each intended for a maximum of 1,500 students. The school is known for its innovations and for the record for scholarship of its graduates. It was the first high school to introduce closed circuit television; it has used team teaching with success, and it has a strong foreign language department, giving French, Spanish, German, Italian, Russian, Chinese, and Japanese.

The Children's Theatre of Evanston has become a popular civic institution by careful management. It is also known as Theatre 65 after the school district in which it originates. The Association for the Children's Theatre annually raises a fund of $50,000 for maintenance.

NORTHWESTERN UNIVERSITY

NORTHWESTERN UNIVERSITY occupies more than 150 buildings on 170 acres that run for about a mile along the shore of Lake Michigan. The area includes 84 acres of the James Roscoe Miller campus, added by extending the land into the lake. On the older land is the core of the university, where it began in 1851. Here are located the College of Arts and Sciences, the Graduate School, the Technological Institute, and the Schools of Education, Journalism, Music, and Speech. The university has expanded since to its Chicago campus, on the near North Side, where its Medical Center, School of Law, Graduate School of Management and several other facilities are located. (*q.v.*).

The buildings on the Evanston campus reflect the response of the architects and builders to the fashions of their times, from the first frame building of 1855, still in use, to the most modern concepts of functional steel and stone in the new University Library. Of late the university has been building new structures as part of a campaign called First Plan for the Seventies, a program of expansion that was to cost $180,000,000, and included more courses for undergraduates, larger graduate enrollment, and stronger financial support for the faculty.

Northwestern University enrolled 15,571 students in the 1972-73 school year and had a faculty of 2,375. Undergraduate enrollment in Evanston is held at 6,500. The university is coeducational, and although begun by Methodists, its chapel service is nondenominational Protestant. There are separate student centers for Jewish, Roman Catholic, and Protestant groups.

During the 1960-70 decade the university constructed new facilities that have attracted the interest of architects nationally. A most impressive example of the use of modern materials in a functional style is the UNIVERSITY LIBRARY on the James Roscoe Miller campus. The structure is described as a complex of three units, called towers, which have direct connection with the Charles Deering Library, built in 1932 in neo-Gothic style by James Gamble Rogers. The new library has approx. 1,300,000 volumes and cost $12,000,000. One of its segments is the Core Library of 50,000 noncirculating books "representing the whole spectrum of knowledge." The Map Library contains 110,000 maps. The main library has three departments of special subjects: the Curriculum Library, with teaching aids; the Africana collection, and the Chinese and Japanese collection. Besides the University Library there are seven other libraries in Evanston and four in Chicago, giving Northwestern a total of approx. 2,000,000 vols., 21,000 series of periodicals, and average additions of 95,000 vols. annually.

The TECHNOLOGICAL INSTITUTE occupies the largest building on the campus, erected 1942, the gift of Walter P. Murphy, builder of railroad equipment, who built, equipped, and endowed it to make it second to none in education and research in engineering and the engineering sciences. The building has 600,000 sq. ft. of floor space and besides the Institute houses Chemistry and Physics departments, the Materials Research Center, the Computer Sciences Center and allied schools. Its main auditorium seats 800. The cooperative education program enables a student to have 18 months of industrial employment in addition to the work required for a bachelor's degree. *A conducted tour of the Institute is available Saturdays at 11 a.m.*

CHARLES DEERING LIBRARY, completed in 1932, is an adaptation by James Gamble Rogers of the cathedral style of King's College at Cambridge, and is executed in white limestone and marble. An interesting and unusual detail of its Gothic design is the omission of gables over the three exquisitely molded and carved arches of the porch, its dominating architectural feature. The entrance doors open into a broad, low-roofed hall, with groined arches decorated in mosaic of delicate colors. Two stairways mount to the second floor, where stained glass, the lofty ceiling, and the fine Gothic carvings of the reading room give a grave and ecclesiastical air. The new three-towered library to the east was constructed in 1965-67.

At the east end of the Womens Quadrangles is SCOTT HALL, the student social center, erected in honor of Walter Dill Scott, president of the University from 1920 to 1939. Across Sheridan Road to the south are the ALICE S. MILLER CHAPEL and the Jeanne Vail Meditation Chapel, which together wtih Parkes Hall form the university's new religious center.

The three-winged REBECCA CROWN MEMORIAL CENTER is the University's administration building, built in 1965. At Sherman Avenue and University Place is the MUSIC ADMINISTRATION BUILDING. Peter Christian Lutkin, former dean of the music school, is memorialized in the beautiful LUTKIN HALL, an auditorium and recital hall for the School of Music.

Just north of Willard Place is GARRETT BIBLICAL INSTITUTE, a school of divinity maintained by the Methodist Episcopal denomination, cooperating without affiliation with the University. The building is an example of the perpendicular Gothic style of the Tudor period, finished in beautiful detail. On the first floor is the Bennett Museum of Christian Archeology, with reproductions of objects of early Christian and pre-Christian eras, vases, amphoras chalices, and a large group of reliquary panels. To the west of the building is HOWES CHAPEL. North is the entrance to the SHAKESPEARE GARDENS. Landscaped by Jens Jensen, it was planned like one at Stratford-on-Avon to display flowers and herbs mentioned in Shakespeare's plays. Across from the gardens is Seabury Western Theological Seminary, offering training for the Episcopalian priesthood and not affiliated with the university.

At the north end of the campus is PATTEN GYMNASIUM, and westward, at Central St. and Asbury Ave., is DYCHE STADIUM, where the football games are held. North of the Stadium is McGraw Memorial Hall, built in 1952, seating 11,000, where convocations and athletic events are held. Additional athletic facilities are in ANDERSON HALL and COOM SPORTS CENTER, built in 1963.

At the farthest northeast corner of the James Roscoe Miller campus, which the university built out into the lake, stand the twin towers of the LINDHEIMER ASTRONOMICAL RESEARCH CENTER, dedicated in May, 1967. They were erected with funds provided by the three heirs of Benjamin F. Lindheimer, executive director of the Arlington Park and Washington Park race tracks, to which were added matching grants from the National Science Foundation. The major instrument is a 40-in. reflecting telescope equipped with image orthicon (television camera tube) devices, computerized photometers, spectroscopes, donated by the A. Montgomery Ward Foundation. Another instrument is a 16-in. reflecting telescope, contributed by Hans D. Isenberg of Wilmette. Open Saturday, 2-4.

DEARBORN OBSERVATORY, 2131 Sheridan Road, located in the middle of the campus near Garrett Theological Institute, has a 18½ inch refracting telescope through which visitors may gaze at the stars on Friday evenings.

In tune with the times the university has provided for black students. Those who wish to study the history and development of African peoples may elect courses in various departments in addition to their regular academic programs. These courses are given in the departments of anthropology, art, English, history, linguistics, political science, and sociology. The courses in languages include Hausa, Amharic, Swahili, and Twi. *The Black Ghetto as an Urban Spatial Form* is studied under geography. *The African novel in English* and *Studies in Contemporary African Literature* are courses in the literary section. Africa House, 1813 Hinman Ave., is the center of the Program of African Studies, which sponsors lectures, films, musical performances, and faculty-student discussions.

While costs cannot be computed exactly, the university recently estimated the cost of undergraduate instruction at $780 to $800 a quarter or $2,170 to $2,400 for the academic year. Residence on campus costs $475 for a space in a double occupancy room, or $515 for a single room; board is around $588, but varies.

OTHER POINTS OF INTEREST

NATIONAL COLLEGE OF EDUCATION, established in 1886 in Chicago, located in Evanston in 1926 and has its main campus in the area between Isabella St., Evanston, and Maple Ave., Wilmette, extending west from the main building, Harrison Hall, at 2840 Sheridan Road. It is the oldest independent college for elementary teachers and provides preparation for teaching nursery and kindergarten through eighth grade in its undergraduate and graduate schools. Most important to its curriculum is the demonstration Children's School for children of average and superior ability. It also has a Guidance Center for children with learning difficulties. Until a few years ago it offered only degrees of bachelor of education and master of education; recently it expanded its liberal arts courses toward a bachelor of arts degree. With a $4,000,000 building program it added a new building enlarging its teaching facilities, and including a working library, a children's library, a gymnasium and larger food services. Another addition was a new residence hall. In the 1971-72 year the college enrolled 2,605 students and had a faculty of 149.

KENDALL COLLEGE, newest of Evanston's institutions of learning, is a private, coeducational, two-year liberal arts college, with its campus two blocks from Lake Michigan bounded by Sheridan Ave., Lincoln St., Orrington Ave. and Colfax St. It was founded in 1934 and is a member of the National Association of Schools and Colleges of the United Methodist Church. Students receive the degree of associate in the arts and are enabled to transfer to four-year colleges. Kendall stresses flexibility and says that in addition to traditional courses it offers latitude for independent revaluations, and names the modular math program, with a laboratory method of individual instruction; participation in community services, and seminars on personal identity and the human potential. Part-time study is offered in summer and evening classes and the Woman's Center enables women over 25 to enroll as special students. The buildings are designed for modern fenestration and compactness and include Wesley Hall for administrative offices and library; Firing Hall, for men; Penny Jane and Terra Hall for women; a major Academic Building, the Refectory and the Auditorium. Tuition is placed at $1,950, rooms for men, $550; for women, $600; food service, $685. In 1972 Kendall College enrolled 747 and had a faculty of 73.

The WOMAN'S CHRISTIAN TEMPERANCE UNION, with national and international hq. at 1730 Chicago Ave., probably did more in the late 19th century to make the name of Evanston known around the world than any other agency. Here are the national offices of the Union, the Bureau of Narcotics Education, the Publication Office, and the Frances E. Willard Library for Alcoholic Research. With about 250,000 active members the organization continues to fight to restrict the use of alcohol. It grew powerful with the inspiring leadership of Frances E. Willard, its president from 1879 to 1898 and a crusader for temperance, who organized the World WCTU. Miss Willard came to Evanston with her family from Janesville, Wisc., soon after Northwestern was opened. In the following 40 years she became Evanston's most famous citizen, serving as dean of women and professor of esthetics at the university. Among her writings is her appreciation of Evanston in *The Classic Town*.

On the grounds stands REST COTTAGE, Miss Willard's lifetime home, which became a National Historic Landmark in 1965. It consists of a many-gabled Victorian cottage built in 1865 and an addition used by Miss Willard's brother.

The sitting room of the Willard family has been dedicated to Miss Anna Gordon, Miss Willard's lifelong companion and later world WCTU president. The room contains, in addition to several pieces of Willard furniture, a cup and saucer of John Wesley and a pair of earrings worn by Susannah Wesley.

The Willard parlor is at the left of the entrance. Archaic and prim, it appears much as it did in the days of the family's occupancy. Here are portraits of Miss Willard, her parents, her brother, and her sister Mary, whose biography Miss Willard wrote in *Nineteen Beautiful Years*. In the dining room stands the bicycle which Miss Willard learned to ride when she had passed 50. A banjo clock, dated and signed by Simon Willard, 18th century clock-maker of Boston and an ancestor of Miss Willard's, hangs on the wall.

Miss Willard's study has her ink-spotted desk, and her bookshelves, filled with annotated books and faded family photographs. Nearby is the rocker where she held a tablet on her lap while writing her books and speeches. The grandfather's clock was also made by Simon Willard. On the wall is framed a piece of cloth used by Queen Victoria, as a child, for a doll's wrap. One of the documents preserved in the house is the Polyglot Petition, signed by 8,000,000 people from 51 nations petitioning governments to abolish alcohol and the opium traffic.

EVANSTON HOSPITAL, 2650 Ridge Ave., founded in 1891, has expanded into a medical complex covering nine acres, with the most modern facilities for treatment and research. Today it has available 522 beds and 45 bassinets. The medical staff numbers 294, which includes 26 physicians with emeritus standing. In 1968 Evanston Hospital completed the Frank Auditorium Building, which contains extensive educational facilities. Among programs and services instituted at the hospital that are evidence of continuing progress in numerous fields are the Child and Adolescent Medical Center for ambulatory patients; the Outpatient Adult and Child Psychology Program, the intensive care for coronary units, the practical nursing program, and long-range planning. It also has been given a State designation as a trauma center.

ST. FRANCIS HOSPITAL was opened in 1901 by the Sisters of Saint Francis. It has a staff of 250 physicians and surgeons working in 25 departmental classifications. The hospital has special equipment for radiology. One of its important facilities is the Adult and Child Guidance Center, an outpatient service for the diagnosis and treatment of children and adults with emotional and mental problems.

COMMUNITY HOSPITAL, which opened an entirely new plant in 1950, owes its origin to two doctors who in 1915 opened a sanitarium in their home for the care of Negro patients. Since that time Community Hospital has developed into a general nonracial institution with the most modern facilities and a staff of 80 physicians and surgeons.

THE CRADLE, 2039 Ridge Ave., is a nonsectarian adoption home that was established in 1923 to find homes for infants and has been conducted most successfully ever since. It is supported by funds raised by its Auxiliaries and by private donations.

The EVANSTON PUBLIC LIBRARY is one of the major agencies for book distribution and reading encouragement in the Chicago metropolitan area. With the facilities of its fine modern main building, its branch libraries in North Evanston and South Evanston, and its expanded bookmobile service, it circulates more than 600,000 adult and juvenile books annually in a city where the academic world has huge resources of its own. On January 1, 1971, the Public Library had a stock of 245,215 volumes. It adds about 20,000 new adult and children's books annually, subscribes to numerous periodicals, and has a large collection of recordings and of 16-mm sound films for public use. There are special programs for children, study courses, art displays and exhibits, and a slide service.

One of the special projects carried out by the library during 1970-71 was collection of historical data and materials relating to the black community of Evanston. This was done by several means: one, oral interviews with older citizens recorded on tape, which "show Evanston's past through the eyes of the people who have lived it." Other methods: collection of family trees to help discover migration patterns, occupational mobility, and educational habits; abstracting Evanston newspapers, 1861-1960, which disclosed business, crime, culture, and humor; letters and documents. The project microfilmed the *Evanston Newsette*, a black newspaper published in Evanston from the 1930's to 1950, and located the *Afro-American Budget*, published in Evanston in the late 19th century.

The Library is a member of the North Suburban Library System, a State-funded cooperative library system of 31 libraries located from Evanston north to Zion and west to Elgin. This helped finding books through the interlibrary loan, provided reciprocal borrowing, which gives a cardholder of any library in the system access to all member libraries; made copies of magazine articles; gave access to the film depot at Hinsdale, and a central reference system. An indication of the services the library performs for its community is its installation of annual reports for the top 200 corporations listed in *Fortune* and of telephone directories, which include most of the major cities of the country and all state capitals.

The WILLIAM C. LEVERE MEMORIAL TEMPLE, 1856 Sheridan Road, is the national headquarters of the Sigma Alpha Epsilon college fraternity. It is a two-story structure in modified ecclesiastical Gothic with a tower above the entrance, and contains offices, a library, and a chapel. The Peace Window in the chapel has a figure of Christ in the center panel and side panels portraying a Union and a Confederate soldier. The fraternity was founded in 1856 at the University of Alabama and in 1971 had 144,921 initiates and 176 active chapters, ranking first in membership but not in chapters. The Temple is named for a member of the Northwestern Univ. chapter distinguished for exceptional services to the fraternity.

SIGMA CHI, national college fraternity, moved into new quarters for its national offices at 1714 Hinman in 1964 when the city needed its ground for a park. It first came to Evanston in 1950. Founded in 1855, Sigma Chi in 1971 reported the second largest membership among college fraternities, with 126,000 initiates and 156 active chapters.

HARPER & ROW, New York book publishing firm, has its El-Hi Division at 2500 Crawford Ave. in a modern, extended two-story structure where all the facilities for editing, storing, and distributing elementary and high school textbooks are concentrated. These specialized educational materials were published for many years in Evanston by Row, Petersen & Co., which was merged in 1962 with Harper & Bros., under the combined name of Harper & Row.

The GROSS POINT LIGHTHOUSE does much to heighten the New England atmosphere of Evanston. Built in 1860, it was the indirect result of the wreck of the *Lady Elgin*, in which nearly 300 persons lost their lives in the lake off North Evanston. The LIGHT-HOUSE NATURE CENTER has a museum and laboratory at 2535 Sheridan Road. *Tours Friday 3-5, Saturday and Sunday, 2-5.*

Father Jacques Marquette and his Indian companions landed in 1673 in the natural harbor formed by the 25-foot bluff later called Gross Point. Marquette's diary has an account of the incident and a sketch of his fleet of ten canoes drawn up on the sands. In pioneer days, as lake traffic increased, Gross Point assumed some importance as a port, and a village grew up around it, settled by those who followed the inland seas. For some time a faint maritime atmosphere clung to the community.

Colleges and Libraries

UNIVERSITY HALL, UNIVERSITY OF ILLINOIS AT CHICAGO CIRCLE,
SHOWING ENLARGEMENT OF UPPER FLOORS, BEHAVIORAL
SCIENCES BUILDING

THE CONCRETE AMPHITHEATER BETWEEN CLASSROOM UNITS AT
UNIVERSITY OF ILLINOIS AT CHICAGO CIRCLE

ELEVATED WALK AT TAFT HALL, UNIVERSITY OF ILLINOIS AT
CHICAGO CIRCLE

JOSEPH REGENSTEIN LIBRARY, UNIVERSITY OF CHICAGO, FROM THE EAST

JOSEPH REGENSTEIN LIBRARY, UNIVERSITY OF CHICAGO, SOUTH FACADE

NUCLEAR ENERGY, SCULPTURE BY HENRY MOORE, IN FRONT OF
WEST FACADE OF REGENSTEIN LIBRARY, ON SITE WHERE
CONTROLLED NUCLEAR CHAIN REACTION WAS ACHIEVED

LAW SCHOOL, UNIVERSITY OF CHICAGO, BY EARO SAARINEN,
WITH PEVSNER SCULPTURE

LAW SCHOOL LIBRARY, UNIVERSITY OF CHICAGO

MORRIS LIBRARY, SOUTHERN ILLINOIS UNIVERSITY, CARBONDALE

HOME ECONOMICS BUILDING, SOUTHERN ILLINOIS UNIVERSITY, CARBONDALE

OLD MAIN, KNOX COLLEGE, GALESBURG, SITE OF LINCOLN-
DOUGLAS DEBATE

FIRST BUILDING AT
NORTHWESTERN UNIVER-
SITY, NOW SCHOOL OF
EDUCATION

ROCKFORD PUBLIC LIBRARY, ROCKFORD

HOWARD COLMAN LIBRARY, ROCKFORD COLLEGE

The CHARLES GATES DAWES HOUSE, headquarters of the Evanston Historical Society, was the residence of the man who was the Vice President of the United States during President Calvin Coolidge's second administration, who willed it to Northwestern University for purposes of historical research. The large French Provincial villa has 28 rooms, two rounded end towers and a gabled roof with dormers. The large grounds extend to the Lake and are used for an annual art fair. The first floor has two rooms, 80 by 30 ft., which contain Dawes family portraits and books by Evanston and Chicago authors. The society has files of early Evanston newspapers, old maps, flags and uniforms, and paintings of the Chicago Fire and the sinking of the *Lady Elgin*. One of the objects is a torch carried in parades during Lincoln's first campaign for the presidency. An item of interest to Evanston is the agreement with Cornelia Wheadon to open the first public school on June 1, 1846. Dawes (1865-1951), had an active and at times spectacular career as banker and politician. He was a descendant of William Dawes, Jr., who rode out of Boston to alarm the countryside on the evening that Paul Revere crossed to Charlestown on the same errand.

Galena

Highways: US 20, from Rockford and Freeport, combined with US 84, from Savanna. US 84 turns north 3 *m.* west of Galena; US 20 proceeds to East Dubuque, and Iowa and Wisconsin connections. From Chicago Northwest Tollway (Int. 94) to Rockford.

Air Services: Nearest airports, Freeport and Savanna.

Railroad: Illinois Central, freight service.

Bus: Greyhound Lines.

Information: Galena Gazette & Advertiser, 222 S. Main St. Convention Bureau, DeSoto Hotel. Grant Birthday Committee, DeSoto House. Greater Galena Restaurant & Lodging Assn. for hotels, motels & restaurants. Galena Historical Society, for tours.

Recreation: Three parks, swimming pool, outdoor roller skating rink, daily fee golf course, bowling alley. Duck and deer huting in season, game and pan fishing. Excursion trips on Mississippi River boat. Winter ski area, Chestnut Hills, 9 *m.* Drives in Illinois and Wisconsin, to Crystal Lake Cave, Dubuque, Ia.; Grotto at Dockeyville, Nelson Dewey Home and Park, Cassville, Wisc.; Apple River Canyon State Park.

Special Events: Annual Grant Fete Boy Scout Pilgrimage, last Saturday in April; Girl Scout Day, last Saturday in May; Historic Homes Tour, sponsored by Guild of First Presbyterian Church, last weekend in September. Violet Show at Community Hall, write Ladies Aid, Westminster United Presbyterian Church. Market Days on Market Square, write Jo Daviess County Home Bureau, Elizabeth, Ill.

GALENA (603 alt., 3,930 pop. 1970; 4,410, 1960, dec. 10.7%) seat of Jo Daviess County (21,766 pop. 1970; 21,821, 1960), in the northwestern corner of Illinois, is located on the Galena River approx. 14 *m.* east of the Mississippi River at East Dubuque, with which it is connected by US 20. It is also served by Illinois 84, which joins US 20 3 *m.* north of Galena. The city is built on terraces eroded by the river and streets are on different levels, with steep climbs and stairs between. Its unusual prosperity from lead mining in pre-Civil War days brought about a building era that filled the city with mansions embellished with porticos and cupolas, which have been restored and today make Galena a museum of authentic Americana. Filled with memorabilia of General U. S. Grant and his associates, Galena has become a tourist objective of large proportions. Thus the community finds it an asset to advertise itself as "the town that time forgot."

Galena is the best example in Illinois of a settlement that began with an essential resource, had a big trade boom in its early decades and

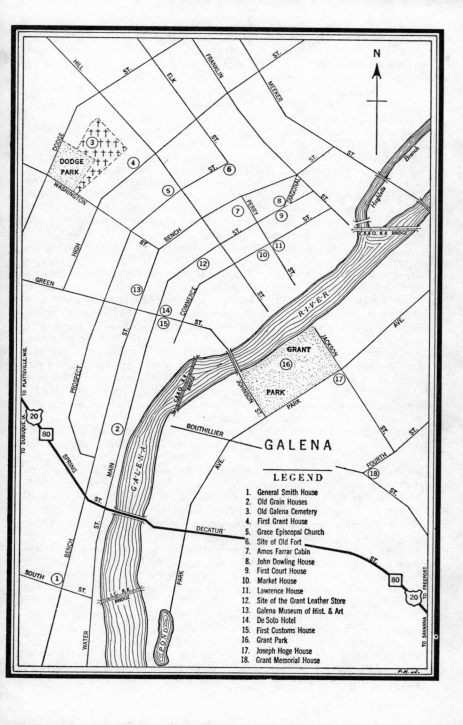

GALENA

LEGEND

1. General Smith House
2. Old Grain Houses
3. Old Galena Cemetery
4. First Grant House
5. Grace Episcopal Church
6. Site of Old Fort
7. Amos Farrar Cabin
8. John Dowling House
9. First Court House
10. Market House
11. Lawrence House
12. Site of the Grant Leather Store
13. Galena Museum of Hist. & Art
14. De Soto Hotel
15. First Customs House
16. Grant Park
17. Joseph Hoge House
18. Grant Memorial House

then froze as it stood when its products and commerce eroded. Its name defines a sulphite of lead called galena; its beginning was as a shipping center for lead mines operated by the French in an area that included parts of Wisconsin and Iowa. Here also the Indians traded in furs and the American Fur Company established one of its earliest outposts.

The Indians had found lead but the only use they had for it was as a medium of exchange with the whites. The French became aware of it quite early from the reports of Marquette and Jolliet and in 1699 Le Sueur and Iberville went north to investigate. Le Sueur is credited with finding the Galena River in August, 1700, calling it the River of Mines, and it is so named on a map published in Paris in 1703 by Delisle, geographer of the French Academy of Sciences. But to traders it soon became Fever River. In the next decade or two Phillippe Francois de Renault is said to have explored the mines with 200 miners and some slaves, brought from San Domingo.

Julien Dubuque was a successful operator of lead mines on the west bank of the Mississippi River. William J. Petersen records in *Steamboating on the Upper Mississippi* that when Dubuque died in 1810 the Fox Indians were melting 400,000 lbs. of mineral annually at Fever River. Congress had taken the mines under government protection in 1807 and required leasing of mine sites. Henry M. Shreve took a barge of lead out of Fever River in 1810. In 1816 George Davenport moved a flatboat loaded with lead to St. Louis. In 1826 the postoffice was established, the first in northern Illinois, and the town was laid out. Dr. Horatio Newhall in 1827 described the scene. He said any person could get a permit to mine 200 sq. yds. or half a mile square if he gave bond for $5,000 to the Government, employed 20 laborers, and paid the Government 10 percent of his gains. He sold lead at $17.50 per 1,000 lbs. at the furnaces. Newhall had a public smelter for which he gave bond for $30,000 to pay the Government one-tenth of all lead manufactured. He also had a goods store in Galena and never sold for less than a 50 percent advance. In 1827, he said, there were 115 houses and stores in Galena and there was no spot in America of the same size that had one-fourth of the capital and where so much business was done. In 1826 5,740,000 lbs. of lead had been smelted. "There are but comparatively few females. Hence, every female unmarried who lands on these shores is immediately married. Little girls, 13 and 14 years old, are often married here." In 1832 the *Miners Journal* reported that laborers received $15 to $20 per month and board. Zinc, found with lead, was considered worthless. In the vernacular of the day downstate men were called Suckers, miners from the west were called Pukes, and Wisconsin men living in pits were called Badgers.

Charles Fenno Hoffman, friend of Washington Irving, who made a trip through the Middle West in the winter of 1833-34, saw Galena as "one of the busiest places in the Union. The value of goods imported into this place last season amounted to $150,000; the export of lead amounted to 7,000,000 lbs. at $4.50 per cwt. There were 96 departures and 97 arrivals of steamboats during the last season." He thought this was doing very well for a frontier town, built indifferently of frame and log houses, thrown confusedly together on the side of a hill.

There were three churches and two temperance societies. Education was promoted and "most persons sleep with unbarred doors in safety." In one year 102 steamboats and 73 keel boats arrived and lead production had increased to 13,343,150 lbs.

The early 1830s saw the exploitation of agriculture and granaries were built along the river. These granaries ingeniously solved the elevator problem, for wagons unloaded from streets level with the top stories into shutes that carried the grain to the water's edge.

The lead in the surface veins was finally exhausted; the mines could no longer be operated at a profit. Galena's advantage as a market center vanished with the completion of the railroad in 1855, for the road diverted traffic from the river and picked up freight at the small farm villages. The river silted up and the heavily-laden cargo boats could no longer navigate the channel. The gold rush to California in 1849 drew off the more adventurous of the mining population, and the town turned slowly to general processing of farm products. The country as a whole lost funds for investment in the panic of 1857, and Galena, which had survived an earlier panic untouched, became a backwater.

In the tense days before the Civil War Galena was divided in its political faith. A large proportion of its citizenry being of Southern origin, it had been definitely a slave-holding community until the adoption of the State Constitution of 1848 put a ban on slavery. President Lincoln's appeal for troops after the fall of Fort Sumter brought a local controversy over political issues, but those who favored the Union prevailed, and two companies were formed to support the President.

Ulysses S. Grant, who had been a captain in the U. S. Army during the Mexican War, came upstream from St. Louis with his wife and four children on the steamer *Itasca* in the spring of 1860, to work in his father's leather goods store. He found a dwelling at 121 High St. In April, 1861, he attended a mass meeting at the Jo Daviess Court House, 312 N. Bench St., to support the President's call for troops. He declined the captaincy of one of the Galena companies but agreed to act as drillmaster, and drilled recruits on the grounds of the home of Representative E. B. Washburne, who used his influence to advance Grant's fortunes. Grant accompanied the troops to Springfield and six weeks later was commissioned colonel of the 21st Illinois Volunteer Regiment. In August, 1861, he was made brigadier general and in September took charge of the military post of southern Illinois at Cairo.

In order to fill gaps in the military structure General Grant called on experienced men he had known in Galena. As a result of his efforts and those of others Galena has eight Union generals in its gallery. John A. Rawlins, city attorney and a Democrat, joined Grant as a captain and became Chief of Staff. President Grant made him Secretary of War. The RAWLINS HOUSE stands at 517 Hill St. William

Rowley, clerk of the Circuit Court, became a brigadier general and Provost Marshal, and county judge after the war. The ROWLEY HOUSE stands next to that of Rawlins at 515 Hill St. Augustus L. Chetlain, captain of the first Galena regiment, became a brigadier general.

John Eugene Smith, a jeweler who had been county treasurer, organized Washburne's Lead Mine Regiment. He became a major general and served until 1881. The GENERAL SMITH HOME, 807 S. Bench St., was designed by Henry J. Stouffer with a portico of four Ionic columns and is a showplace of Galena. Jasper Maltby, who invented a telescopic sight for rifles, became a brigadier general. John C. Smith became a brigadier general and later was elected Lieutenant Governor. John Duer is considered a brigadier general by Galena, but the military records are not clear on his rank. Galena also claims Brig. General Ely S. Parker as one of its own. Parker, a Seneca Indian who had studied law and civil engineering, came to Galena in 1858 to supervise building of the U. S. Custom House, now the Post Office. Grant needed him on his staff, and he was a member of the group of officers assembled in the McLean house at Appomattox when General R. E. Lee came to surrender. It was recorded that when Parker was introduced Lee drew back, ostensibly taking Parker for a Negro.

Galena is a veritable museum of American domestic architecture of the first half of the 19th century. Many of its dwellings, picturesquely located on the sides of hills, are filled with period furniture and have been lived in continuously. Along the terraces of Bench, Prospect, and High Sts. are Greek Revival mansions of brick, and on the byways tiny Greek temples with Doric and Ionic columns stand among Cape Cod cottages. New Orleans galleries, with iron grilles from French foundries; dwellings with Pennsylvania gable ends, and two-story galleries of the Carolinas, are all here. By the time Victorian Gothic and carpenters' scrolls swept the State Galena did little building. The churches recall New England, except for Grace Episcopal, which is early English Gothic, built of rough gray stone hewn from the hollow in the bluff in which the church stands. The elegance of the DeSoto House was famous, but most business houses occupied one and two-story brick buildings.

Galena is not all museum. During the winter it tries to become a ski resort, at least for those who find the nearby Chestnut Hill a satisfying experience. Illinois lacks hills that make good ski runs and the sites favored by enthusiasts are mostly in Wisconsin.

POINTS OF INTEREST

The GENERAL GRANT MEMORIAL HOME, on Bouthillier St., is a two-story brick house, with wide, bracketed eaves and a heavy porch painted white. It was presented to Grant at the end of the Civil War by the citizens of Galena, who gave him a tumultous welcome on August 18, 1865. Grant lived in the house until 1867, when he was named Secretary of War by President Andrew Johnson and moved to

Washington, D. C. He returned to Galena in the fall, 1879, after he had served two terms as President and made a two-year tour of the world. He lived in this house until midsummer of 1881, when he moved to New York, N. Y. He died in 1885 at the age of 63. His son, Frederick Dent Grant, deeded the house to the City of Galena in 1904. In 1932 title was transferred to the State of Illinois. It is now administered by the Division of Parks and Memorials. The house contains furniture of the Grant family and china and a silver service used in the White House. The parlor is furnished in mid-Victorian patterns, with walnut settee and chairs upholstered with horse hair, a marble-topped table, two what-nots, and Rogers groups. *Open daily, 9-5.*

The first Galena observance of the Civil War Centennial took place April 29, 1961, sponsored by the U. S. Grant Council, BSA, the Galena Woman's Club, and the National War Centennial Commission, with participation of 3,005 Boy Scouts and Explorers. General U. S. Grant, III, chairman of the Commission, presided at a dinner in the Grant Memorial Home, which was lighted by kerosene lamps and candles.

The FIRST GRANT HOME, a two-story brick cottage at 121 High St., was occupied in 1860 by Grant, his wife, and four small children. Grant left here when he returned to the U. S. Army in 1861.

The site of the J. R. GRANT LEATHER STORE, 120 S. Main St., is marked by a plaque placed by the DAR. U. S. Grant came here in the spring of 1860 to work for his father. A replica of a leather goods store of the period has been reconstructed at 211 S. Main St. by the Galena Historical Society. *Open 9-5, April 27 to November 1. Donation.*

The DESOTO HOUSE, Main and Green Sts. exceeded the appointments of all Illinois hotels except those of Chicago when it opened in 1855. It flourished in the steamboat period, when Galena's lead mines were in full production; when mining declined the prosperity of town and hotel declined also. In the *Journal* of the Illinois State Historical Society, summer, 1971, Donald F. Tingley described Ralph Waldo Emerson's visit during his Illinois lecture tour of 1856:

> Emerson stayed at the DeSoto House, which from descriptions almost rivaled the Tremont of Chicago in elegance. The DeSoto had opened less than a year before. It had cost $85,000, was five stories high, and had 100 ft. of frontage on Main St. The dining hall could seat 300. Descriptions of the hotel mention its sliding doors, velvet carpets, rosewood furniture, marble top tables, gilt mirrors, and satin damask curtains. There was running water for the baths, and the kitchen boasted of ovens that could cook meat for 500 persons. Like the Tremont, the DeSoto had speaking tubes to each room. In spite of his comfortable accommodations in the booming town, Emerson's visit to Galena was unfortunate. He was the victim of the 'cruel kindness' of a Mr. McMasters who insisted that he go out to see the lead mines. Emerson thought that the sleigh ride would be much shorter than it was, and although he was interested in the history of the mines he caught a cold and was barely able to speak the next day. . . He spoke in the hall of the DeSoto House.

On July 23, 1856 Abraham Lincoln addressed a crowd from the iron balcony of the DeSoto House on behalf of the new Republican Party and the candidacy for President of John C. Fremont. He accused the Democrats of being soft on slavery and called them "an unarmed, undisciplined, unorganized minority." On the threat of the South that Fremont's election meant dissolution of the Union he retorted: "We won't dissolve the Union and you shan't."

Stephen A. Douglas spoke from the balcony on August 24, 1858. When Grant campaigned for the presidency in 1868 he made his headquarters in the DeSoto House. The prosperous days of Galena were already gone and the DeSoto House lost patronage. In 1875 it closed its upper two stories and in 1880 removed them; it also removed its iron balcony. Today it is a modernized hotel with 70 rooms.

The GALENA HISTORICAL MUSEUM and HISTORICAL CENTER, 211 S. Bench St., shares the building with the City Hall. This is a fine example of a brick mansion, which has large white cornices and eaves, entablatures over the windows, and a small railed balcony over the main entrance. The house is filled with memorabilia; Indian artifacts and costumes; pioneer farm implements; broadaxes used in clearing the wilderness; rifles and muzzle-loaders once owned by Dan Boone and Quantrell; Commodore Perry's flag from the USN *Lawrence*. Civil War flags; musical instruments, including Lafayette's clarinet, and a woolen shawl once used by Abraham Lincoln. A large painting by Thomas Nash, known as Peace in Union, depicts Grant greeting Lee in the McLean parlor at the surrender of Confederate arms. *Open 9-5, April 27-Nov. 1. Adults, 25¢, children, 10¢.*

Major Thomas Melvill, veteran of the War of 1812, and uncle of Herman Melville, author of *Moby Dick*, came to Galena in 1837 and lived in a house still standing at 1009 Third St. He was secretary of the Chamber of Commerce, 1838-40, and a land agent. Herman Melville visited him in 1840 and later wrote a poem, *Trophies of Peace; Illinois in 1840*, and presumably went from Galena to see the Falls of St. Anthony. He called Galena "the most picturesque and romantic place I ever beheld."

The UNITED STATES POST OFFICE, on Green St., was built in 1858 as a Custom House, to accommodate the large river traffic. It was built for the Government under the supervision of Ely S. Parker, an Indian, who had studied both law and civil engineering. He became a captain of engineers in 1863 and a brigadier general on Grant's staff. President Grant made him Commissioner of Indian Affairs.

GRACE EPISCOPAL CHURCH, Prospect St. near Hill St., was built in 1847 by C. W. Otis, a Buffalo, N. Y. architect. Its design is in the early English Gothic style. Later it was remodeled by William LeBaron Jenney, pioneer of the skyscraper, at which time the apse was enlarged and the original steeple removed. Simple lancet windows contain stained glass imported from Belgium. The furnishings are of local walnut, and members of the early congregation carved the altar, choir stalls, and lectern. The one-manual organ was brought from Philadelphia by sailing vessel to New Orleans in 1838 and relayed to Galena by steamboat.

The house of the priest of the church, the Rev. Paul Goddard, was described in 1973 as taking "advantage of the topography by sprouting lovely terraces and gardens. The house has a reversed floor plan with stone-walled living room downstairs and a kitchen and dining room upstairs." Another historic house is the Louis Felt house on Prospect St., now owned by the Genz family, which has black walnut trim, seven Italian marble fireplaces, hanging lamps of cranberry and amber glass and an enormous handcarved bed. The Telford house, 511 Park Ave., owned by James Richardson, has a portico with four tall pillars. The Winnie Cottle house, 206 Bouthillier St., now owned by George Dahlin, has Chippendale chairs and 18th century furnishings generally, with paintings by British masters. An authentic log cabin moved from the woods to Chetlain Lane by Walter Strandberg is now used as a guest house.

The site of the Old Fort, Prospect and Elk Sts., was marked by the DAR chapter in 1832. A brick house has been built around the original John Farrar Cabin, which sheltered women and children inside the stockade.

GRANT PARK, on the east bank, reached from the Post Office via the Johnson St. Bridge, contains a statute, Grant, Our Citizen, donated by Herman Kohlsaat, one-time Chicago newspaper publisher and native of Galena.

The OLD MARKET HOUSE, a State Memorial, stands at Commerce and Perry Sts., fully restored. This is a Greek Revival building erected by Henry J. Stouffer and opened June 27, 1846. It consists of a two-story brick center building, 42 ft. 4 in. by 28 ft. 4 in., surmounted by a square cupola, which contained offices and a meeting hall. On two frame wings each 24 ft. 3 in. by 22 ft. 4 in. were market stalls, one story high, with colonnades to shelter the customers. There were four porticos 7 ft. wide, 24 ft. 3 in. long. Stalls in the wings were rented at $25 a year; in the main section they were auctioned off, with a minimum base of $50 a year. In the early years a jail of two cells was in the cellar; during high water a prisoner was drowned in his cell and the jail was moved to the first floor. The city council used the second floor meeting room until 1936.

The WASHBURNE HOUSE, 908 Third St. was built in 1833, and enlarged and remodeled by E. B. Washburne in 1858. He served 10 years as Representative in Congress from Illinois and was ambassador to France during U. S. Grant's presidency. He was a friend of Grant, and it was in the library of this home that Grant received the news of his election in 1868.

The ILLINOIS CENTRAL RAILROAD DEPOT, foot of Bouthillier St. On April 25, 1861 the first volunteer company left for Springfield, escorted to the depot by the fire companies, the German Benevolent Society and citizens. On August 18, 1865, Grant returned to Galena, arriving at this station to be greeted by the assembled citizens. The Illinois Central reached Galena in 1854 and the depot was erected several years later.

The ORRIN SMITH HOUSE, Jackson St. and Park Avenue. Smith was one of the early riverboat captains. A religious man, Capt. Smith did not move his boat from midnight Saturday to midnight Sunday. If no clergyman was available he led service on board.

The UNION HOUSE, 403 Park Ave., a two-story log house (now shingled) was built in 1839 as a tavern, with accommodations for four boarders. A stairway led from the rear to the river below.

Joliet

Air Services: Daily scheduled limousine trips to Chicago Midway Airport and O'Hare International Airport from principal hotels. Joliet Municipal Airport, 178 acres, available for private planes.

Highways: Int. 80, the Tri-State Highway, passes through Joliet, east-west. Int. 55, the Adlai E. Stevenson Expressway from Chicago, combined with US 66, has a junction with US 52 west of Joliet city limits and conversely has a junction with Tri-State Tollway (Int. 294) for O'Hare. Joliet is served also by US 6, US 30, and Illinois 52, 53, and 121.

Bus Lines: Four major bus lines with transcontinental connections serve Joliet and Will County. The Joliet Mass Transit District has bus lines in the city. There are 79 motor freight lines.

Railroads: Joliet and Will County have a network of major railroads that move freight in this heavily industrialized area, including Illinois Central Gulf, Penn Central, Milwaukee, Rock Island, Santa Fe, and Elgin, Joliet & Eastern. Intercity rail passenger service is provided by Amtrak, using the Union Station, 50 E. Jefferson, where train information is available.

Waterway: The Illinois Waterway carries bulk shipments of commodities between the Great Lakes and the Gulf of Mexico, connecting ports on the Illinois River.

Information and Accommodations: Joliet Region Chamber of Commerce, 71 N. Ottawa St. *Joliet Herald News* (daily) ; *Farmers Weekly Review, Catholic News Register, Labor Record.* Four local radio stations and coverage from Chicago television stations. Three hotels, 11 motels.

Churches, Hospitals and Schools: More than 100 churches, 35 denominations. Largest denominations: Roman Catholic, Baptist, Lutheran, Methodist, Church of God, Presbyterian. Silver Cross Hospital, 450 beds, 36 bassinets, nondenominational, with schools of medical technology and radiologic technology. St. Joseph Hospital, served by the Franciscan Sisters of the Sacred Heart. New plant, 1964, 463 beds, 60 bassinets, schools of nursing, medical and radiological technology. Joliet has 24 elementary public schools and 19 parochial elementary schools. There are three public and three parochial high schools. *For colleges in Joliet and Will County see descriptive article.*

Recreation and Parks: The Park System of Joliet administers more than 1,490 acres equipped with all kinds of outdoor attractions, including sports programs, field houses, basketball courts, diamonds, tennis courts, fishing, boating, archery, etc. There is a ten-week supervised summer program. Golf courses, swimming pools, bridle paths are available. The Municipal Stadium seats 10,000 and has parking space for 5,000 cars. A swimming pool and covered ice-skating rink are adjacent. Joliet has its own bands, symphonic orchestra and plays, and easy access to similar cultural and sports events in Chicago and its suburbs.

JOLIET (541 alt., 78,887 pop. 1970; 66,780, 1960) county seat of Will County, is located on the Des Plaines River and the Illinois & Michigan Canal, a segment of the Great Lakes to Gulf Waterway. It is the hub of an expanding industrial area served by a multiplicity of Federal and State highways, freight-carrying railroads that fan out into the South, Midwest, and Southwest, and barge lines. The city (pronounced Joe-liet) covers approximately 20¼ sq. mi., and is the principal business outlet of Will County, an area of 845 sq. mi. In this region about 350 industries produce more than 1,800 products, including steel rods and tanks, wire, road-building machinery, packaging machinery, petrochemicals and wallpaper. A group of strong banks has assets of more than $300,000,000 and three savings and loan associations have more than $250,000,000. The livestock market is growing.

Will County, with a population of 247,825 in 1970 (191,617, 1960) had an increase of 30 percent during the decade. The movement of Joliet north in Troy Township is shown by its increase there from 297 people in 1960 to 9,895 in 1970. Du Page Township increased from 4,725 in 1960 to 20,037, a rise of 324%. Bolingbroke village, which did not report in the 1960 census, had 7,643 pop. in 1970.

More than one-fourth of the people in Will County live in rural areas but only 4.9% live on farms. Nearly three-quarters of the male labor force is made up of men 18 to 24 years old, and more than a quarter is over 65. Women 16 years old and over fill 40% of the female labor force, and 35.6% have husbands. Only 4.6% live below the poverty level and more than 28% earn $15,000 or more a year.

The new Will County Courthouse was dedicated Oct. 22, 1968.

Joliet has a council-manager form of government. In 1971, when it had a mayor and six councilmen, the voters adopted a revision of administration, effective April, 1975, enlarging the council to eight members, with five from specific districts and three at large. The mayor is elected every four years; the councilmen also serve four years but their terms are staggered.

Joliet is part of the oil-refining area of Will County, where much of the oil and gas needed in the Chicago industrial region is processed. The Mobil Oil plant at Joliet can handle 160,000 bbl. a day. Texaco, at Lockport, produces 72,000 bbl. a day and Union Oil at Lemont 140,000 bbl. a day.

The Joliet plant of the Caterpillar Tractor Co. and the latest generating plant of the Commonwealth Edison Co. are located on the limestone rock that underlies part of Will County and provides a natural foundation for heavy machinery. The reef extends along both sides of the waterway in Joliet and is from one to two and one-half miles wide.

The Joliet Works of the United States Steel Corporation produces wire rods, joint bars, bright, galvanized and aluminum-coated wire, nails and staples, woven and welded fence, welded fabric, baling and barbed wire.

The first settler here was Charles Reed, who came in 1831. The following year he, with numerous settlers in the vicinity, fled the region when the Black Hawk War broke out, but returned within the year. In 1834 a town was platted and the first sale of lots was held. At that time the town was known as Juliet, and a village farther north was called Romeo, now on the map as Romeoville. There was also a 60-foot hill called Mount Juliet—later Joliet Mound—which dominated the plain. When Harriet Martineau, the British traveler, was visiting the Kinzie family at the mouth of the Chicago River in the 1830's she drove out on the prairie to the Des Plaines River and climbed Mount Juliet, which she mentions in her book. The mount no longer exists; it was made of glacial deposits and builders quarried its gravel to build the city. But the lapse of a century did not obliterate memories of the landmark. On June 18, 1972, the Illinois State Historical Society placed a commemorative marker on the site.

When the town was incorporated in 1857 it adopted the name of Joliet, in reference to Father Marquette's companion on his voyage from the Des Plaines to the Chicago Portage in 1673. Historians usually spell the explorer's name Jolliet, on the basis of a signature. Residents pronounce the name of their city with a long o.

For ten years the fortunes of Joliet rose and fell as work went forward or languished on the Illinois & Michigan Canal (1836-48). The first boat arrived here April 11, 1848, and was met by bands, booming cannon, and oratory. With its new barge transportation, Joliet entered into its first industrial era, based on the large-scale shipping of limestone. In the fifties and sixties Joliet shipped blocks as far as New York, and its quarries provided the Middle West with material for such public structures as the Rock Island Arsenal, the Indiana State Prison, the Illinois State House and the Lincoln monument at Springfield.

The first railroad, the Rock Island, came here in 1852, followed by five other lines. Although the railroad eventually caused the decline of the canal it brought the new industry of steel manufacture, which was further attracted by the soft coal in the vicinity. The earliest mill manufactured spikes, track bolts, and other railroad items. Bessemer plants, rail and rod mills, blast furnaces followed, and then plants that made galvanized wire, barbed wire, nails, and other products for the growing agricultural west.

POINTS OF INTEREST

JOLIET JUNIOR COLLEGE, established in 1901, moved to its new location near the intersection of highways I-55 and I-80 in September, 1969. Here it occupied 17 temporary quarters during construction of permanent buildings on its new campus of 368 acres. The oldest public junior college in the United States, it became part of the Illinois Junior College system in February, 1967. Its area encompasses 12 high school districts in Grundy, Kendall, Will, LaSalle, and Kankakee Counties. It is a two-year educational institution, which gives two years of pre-professional and preparatory college training, occupational and technical courses, and continuing educational and community service programs. Its Evening College opened more than 90 college credit courses to part-time students, especially persons beyond high school age. This helped account for a four-fold rise in enrollment between 1960 and 1970. In 1972 it enrolled 4,431 and had a faculty of 269.

The COLLEGE OF ST. FRANCIS, a four-year Catholic college for women conducted by the Sisters of St. Francis of Mary Immaculate, was organized in 1925 as Assisi Junior College and became a senior college in 1930. It is an outgrowth of St. Francis Academy, a preparatory school for girls opened in 1869. It has a full liberal arts curriculum and special courses in law enforcement, library science, physical education, pre-dentistry, medicine and law, and secondary education. In the late 1960's St. Francis benefited from campus improvements. A new Library was completed in 1967, and Marian Hall, a dormitory, in 1966. Tower Hall has administrative offices and classrooms, and Albert Hall has laboratories. Enrollment is typically around 900, with a faculty of 76.

The ILLINOIS STATE PENITENTIARY has four major units in Joliet and environs. Two in the city are the Joliet Prison, established here in 1857, and the Adult Reception and Diagnostic Center. Outside are Stateville, 5 miles north of downtown Joliet on Illinois 53, the largest modern prison, with which is associated the Honor Farm, the whole covering 2,200 acres in Lockport Township. Stateville has approximately 3,400 adult male inmates and is considered a model of construction, especially with access to daylight. The complex comprises a complete hospital, chapel, dining room, grade, high school and vocational school facilities, college courses, and factories for making furniture, metals, soap, garments, textiles, shoes and canned goods. Flower gardens are maintained inside the walls. There are about 900 employees.

The RECEPTION AND DIAGNOSIS CENTER FOR BOYS of the Illinois Department of Corrections, Juvenile Division, is also located in Joliet. It receives all male juveniles over 18, who remain at the Center from four to five weeks. Here a youth will have consultation with a psychologist, caseworker, physician, dentist, Protestant or Catholic chaplain, and possibly a consulting psychiatrist. Some time may be devoted to educational diagnosis and tutoring. When this routine has been completed the youth is sent to the State institution best suited to his needs, which may be to work and school camps with minimum security to the Illinois Industrial School for Boys, with maximum security. A community placement is also a possible alternative. In 1970 2,678 youths passed through this center.

The BUREAU OF IDENTIFICATION of the State maintains all criminal records and its fingerprint file in Joliet. It has a main laboratory that provides scientific examination of evidence, polygraph examinations, and crime scene coverage for all law enforcement agencies in the State. The Bureau has statutory responsibility for the Fire Arm Owners Identification program, the collection and publication of crime statistics and copper purchase registration. The Bureau has another main laboratory in Springfield and cooperating laboratories elsewhere. The AMERICAN INSTITUTE OF LAUNDERING VOCATIONAL TRAINING SCHOOL, Chicago St. and Doris Ave., was established in 1930. It conducts research for members of a national laundry association, and maintains a separate training school that gives a 40-week course in modern laundering methods.

In OAKWOOD CEMETERY, 1919½ Cass St., is the Oakwood Mound, situated on a steep rise of 30 ft., a conical structure 8 ft. high, extending over an area 64 by 67 feet. Excavations conducted by the University of Chicago yielded skeletons, in addition to weapons, ornaments and implements. There is revealed a preponderance of women and child burials, and five instances where the mother and child were clasped in an embrace. The mound, dating back some 1,000 years, contained the scattered skeletal remains of over 300 persons. The confusion in placement and the lack of uniformity of the burials, which were characterized by both flexed and full length positions, indicate a great number of sudden deaths, and a hurried disposal of the bodies, which were probably gathered in a heap and covered with earth.

BIRD HAVEN is a 75-acre strip of land, reached by driving out Cass St., through Hobbs Parkway and the south drive of Pilcher Park. The dense natural growth of hawthorn, to which 300 evergreen species have been added, serves as natural protection of small birds from hawks and owls. The area includes a greenhouse with a desert room containing about 170 kinds of cactus, and a chrysanthemum show is given each fall.

PILCHER PARK ARBORETUM, 326 acres, from Maple to Gauger Road, was presented to Joliet by Robert Pilcher in 1922 with the stipulation that it should remain in its natural state. About 75 species of trees, including 9 kinds of oak, are native, as well as many shrubs, bushes, and almost innumerable wild flowers. A collection of imports started by John Higginbotham, original owner, includes southern magnolia, sweet gum, cypress, tulip-tree, white fringe, pecan, black birch, and hickories and black cherry trees. Higginbotham Woods, 238 acres, is adjoining. A five-acre picnic camp, across Hickory Creek, is connected with the main park by foot bridge. One-way motor lanes are supplemented by miles of narrow footpaths and bridle paths.

Five miles north of downtown Joliet on Broadway and its extension, Illinois 53, is LEWIS COLLEGE, located on 800 acres on the west bank of the Des Plaines River in Lockport. It is conducted by the Christian Brothers and Catholic laymen and was founded in 1930 as a technical high school for boys. It developed into a junior college and in 1950 became a four-year college of science and technology. In 1963 Lewis became a College of Liberal Arts and Sciences.

Most of its courses are for four-year terms with the baccalaureate degree, but there are several two-year courses, such as aviation maintenance. Pre-professional programs are given in law, dentistry, medicine and engineering. Aviation Maintenance management is a four-year course. The college has facilities for adults in the College of Continuing Education whereby employees of business and industry in the area may attend classes on evenings, Saturday and through the summer, working toward degrees.

In September, 1972, Lewis opened its College of Nursing, which offers four-year courses leading to the degree of bachelor of science, B. S. N. Here registered nurses may attend on a part-time basis working toward a degree.

In July, 1971, the Christian Brothers signed a lease with the Illinois Department of Corrections to establish a joint staff training and work release center on the campus. The department will utilize the staff center for orientation of new employees and in-service training for correctional officers and teachers. In the 1972-73 school year Lewis College enrolled 2,440 students and had a faculty of 104.

The CHICAGO-JOLIET LIVESTOCK MARKETING CENTER is a rapidly expanding market that has succeeded to the business formerly transacted at the Chicago Stock Yards. It has a newly built covered cattle house with a capacity of 8,000 head a day. In 1972 the Center had a gross revenue of $200,000,000 and handled 420,000 cattle and 6,500 hogs daily. The Center has rail and truck connections and limited air transport.

The Will County Forest Preserve District comprises 10 naturally-wooded areas totaling 1,054 acres. They are conveniently located throughout the county and have been improved with simple facilities such as shelters, fireplaces, picnic grounds and playing fields.

Many strip-mine sections of Will and Grundy Counties have been converted to recreational uses and have been developed by private recreation clubs. There are numerous lakes scattered throughout this mined land with a total water surface in excess of 1,000 acres. Some of these lakes have been stocked with fish; many acres have been seeded with grasses; other areas have been reforested with over 1,000,000 trees.

Nauvoo

Highways: Easiest drive from Chicago to Nauvoo is via Interstate 55 to Bloomington, thence west on Illinois 9 to the Mississippi River, where it joins Illinois 96 to Nauvoo. Via rail, if scheduled, to Fort Madison, Iowa, and Keokuk, Iowa, thence bus lines. Via airplane from Chicago to Burlington, Iowa, on Ozark Air Lines, thence south by bus.

Information and Accommodations: Nauvoo Restoration, Inc., centrally located in the Temple area, furnishes information, folders, and guide. The Reorganized Church of Jesus Christ of Latter-day Saints has an information office and guide opposite the Joseph Smith Homestead. There are two hotels and several motels. For timely information address Nauvoo Restoration, Inc. Box 215, Nauvoo, Illinois. For information concerning facilities at Nauvoo State Park address Division of Parks and Memorials, 100 State Office Bldg., Springfield, Illinois.

NAUVOO, a city in Hancock County, (620 alt., 1,047 pop. 1970; 1,039, 1960) is located on the east bank of the Mississippi River where it widens to form Lake Cooper, 10 *m.* s. of Fort Madison, Iowa, 12 *m.* ne. of Keokuk, Iowa, 58 *m.* n. of Quincy, Illinois, and about 225 *m.* sw. of Chicago. It is a growing tourist objective, important for its history and the restoration of a community of the 1840-50 decade.

Established in 1839 by Joseph Smith, founder and Prophet of the Church of Jesus Christ of Latter-day Saints, Nauvoo for many years has been a market for farm products, an area devoted to the cultivation of grapes and wine, and the manufacture of a variety of blue cheese. With the rise of touring it has been increasingly visited for its geographical beauty, and its designation as a National Historic Site has given impetus to restoration of the remains of its tragic Mormon period, 1839-45. The two Mormon organizations, the Church established in Utah by the Apostles who led the migration to the West, and the Reorganized Church of Jesus Christ of Latter-day Saints, which has its base in Independence, Mo., are engaged in restoring tangible evidence of the Mormon sojourn in Nauvoo.

Nauvoo was platted early in 1839 by Joseph Smith on 600 acres in Hancock County, partly included in earlier attempts to develop a river landing called Commerce. Smith sought a refuge for his followers, who had clashed so violently with Missouri settlers that Governor L. W. Boggs of Missouri had ordered that they be exterminated or driven out to save the public peace: "their outrages are beyond description." Smith had been put in jail there charged with treason and had been permitted to escape. Many of his followers had congregated in Quincy. They rallied to his call to build a substantial city at Nauvoo, a name he based on a Hebrew root, *nawa,* and interpreted as meaning a beautiful place. Bound together in a tightly disciplined religious community, the Saints contributed a percentage of their earnings and devoted a day's labor every week to the general welfare.

Smith began his career in an upstate New York farmhouse, where he announced in 1820 that the Angel of the Lord had directed him to golden plates buried in a hill at Palmyra, N. Y., from which he translated the *Book of Mormon*. In 1830 he had a church organization in Kirkland, Ohio, but trouble with non-Mormons (called Gentiles by the Mormons) led him to move to Missouri. Intensive missionary work brought thousands of converts, some of the elders (Apostles) proselytizing in Canada and England. The size of the population is often overstated; Mormon sources indicate that Nauvoo had 8,000 people in 1841, and the Illinois census gave it 11,050 in 1845, when it was the largest city in Illinois. The total number of Mormons in the Midwest at this time has been placed at 14,000.

In 1841 the Illinois General Assembly gave Nauvoo a charter with wide powers. It enabled the municipal court of Nauvoo to issue writs of habeas corpus, and the town to organize a militia, the Nauvoo Legion. Joseph Smith became lieutenant general on February 5, 1841. The Legion had horse and foot troops and its original strength was 1,490 men. In 1842 it had 26 companies and nearly 2,000 men. It had 13 major generals and on ceremonial days they made a great display of colorful uniforms.

The non-Mormons of Hancock County became most apprehensive at the military displays, the growing political power, and the sharp trading practices of the Nauvoo community. They accused the Mormons of ordering farm products and then refusing to pay for them. They asserted that when a Mormon was arrested outside of his town the Nauvoo court issued a writ of habeas corupus, after which he disappeared. The older faiths were shocked by Smith's claims to special revelations and by reports that he and several elders had taken plural wives. Smith was said to have begun this practice in 1841; in July, 1843, he announced this as a policy to the Nauvoo Council, but it was not openly acknowledged until 1852. Smith kept up demands for reparation for the confiscation of Mormon property in Missouri, and partly to build up political power he announced he would be a candidate for president of the United States on a Reform ticket, with Sidney Rigdon for vice president.

Dissension arose among the Saints over Smith's practices. In 1842 John C. Bennett, who was a major general and had been mayor of Nauvoo, fell out with Smith and published sensational charges, making the first printed accusations of polygamy. On June 7, 1844, two Canadian converts, William Law and his brother Wilson Law, backed by a number of others, published the *Nauvoo Expositor* to fight "tyranny and oppression." They denounced polygamy, accused Smith of seducing converts, and demanded repeal of the city charter. The paper had but one issue. The infuriated Nauvoo Council ordered the city marshal to "abate a nuisance" by destroying press and type. The Laws thereupon went to the County Court at Carthage and swore out warrants for the members of the Council, 18 in all, including Joseph Smith and his brother Hyrum, who was called the Patriarch.

The Smiths and two other officials agreed to answer the charges before the Circuit Court and a hearing was set for June 29. Other communities, fearful of the militancy of the Nauvoo Legion, armed and called on Governor Ford to intervene. As Carthage was full of hostility, the men were remanded to the County Jail for protection and were given the front room on the second floor. Squads of eight militiamen served in rotation at the jail. The Carthage company of the State Militia was ordered by Governor Ford to disband, but remained defiantly in camp.

At 6 p.m. on June 27 a mob of about 200, with faces painted red, appeared at the jail and threatened to hang the Smiths. They forced their way inside and when the Smiths kept their door shut fired through the panels, killing Hyrum and wounding Joseph and Bishop Taylor. Joseph dashed to a window and was in the act of climbing out when he was shot in the back, and as he fell out he was shot in the front and killed. *See also Carthage, Tour 7.*

After the murders violence against the Mormons did not abate. Brigham Young was elected lieutenant general of the Legion August 31, 1844, and certified by the Adjutant General of the State on September 23. In December the General Assembly revoked the Nauvoo charter. Governor Ford named a commission headed by Stephen A. Douglas to confer with the Mormons on their departure. On October 1, 1845, Brigham Young and other leaders agreed to take their people out in the following spring. Nauvoo turned to the making of wagons and the purchase of oxen for a long journey into the unsettled West. But the anti-Mormons continued so threatening that as early as February many of the faithful crossed the Mississippi, some on the ice.

By July, 1845, the majority of the Mormons had left Nauvoo. Some of those who remained continued to work on their Temple, the symbol of their religious aims, and thus irritated Hancock County men. In September an armed force of 700 came to rout out the Mormons. They met opposition and fought the socalled Battle of Nauvoo. On September 13 the defenders gave up. They were permitted to go peacefully, leaving behind a committee of five to dispose of property.

Not all members of the church accepted Brigham Young as a new leader or followed him 1,400 miles across the western plains to the Great Salt Lake. Nor were all the believers concentrated in Nauvoo. Stanley B. Kimball, professor of history at Southern Illinois University, in the *Journal of the Illinois State Historical Society* mentioned nine places in the State, including Springfield, that had "stakes," or ecclesiastical units consisting of several congregations, and 11 other places where Mormons continued to reside.

After the Mormons left Nauvoo the many vacant houses proved fortuitous for another cohesive band, the Icarians, who had come from France to Texas. Like many another group of the early 19th century trying communal living, the Icarians applied Christian teachings to daily living along lines elucidated by their leader, Etienne Cabet, a French jurist, author of *Voyage to Icaria*. They had a president, elected annually; a director for each division of labor, and workshops and labor units supervised by foremen elected monthly by the workers. Possession of money was restricted to the director of finance; shoes and clothing came out of a common fund. Children entered school at 7, lived in dormitories that they managed, and visited their parents only on Sunday. Such personal sacrifice and subordination to the common aim demanded a religious discipline that the Icarians did not have. Dissenters blamed Cabet, and after he was defeated for the presidency in 1856 the colony broke up. Cabet and some followers went to St. Louis, where he died; the rest left Nauvoo for a branch that had been established in 1853 at Corning, Iowa, which lasted for 20 years.

The Icarians contributed several important elements to the life of Illinois. They started vineyards and wine-making, which the Germans continued, and the making of cheese after the fashion of Roquefort. Thousands of gallons of wine and grape juice are pressed annually, and old wine cellars are still extant. Some of the grape crop is shipped out by truck. The ceremony of the wedding of wine and cheese, observed annually in Nauvoo State Park, stems from the Icarians. Two frame apartment houses on Mulholland St., built by the Icarians, lasted until March, 1951, when they were torn down. Until recent years one was occupied by Miss Rose Nicaise, daughter of Icarian immigrants of 1849.

POINTS OF INTEREST

No chapels were built in Nauvoo during the Mormon years. Religious services were held in a grove now occupied by St. Mary's Academy. Instructions and doctrines appeared in the numerous Mormon publications in the United States, chief of which was *Times and Seasons,* printed in Nauvoo 1839-46, the house of which still stands. The seat of the religion was the TEMPLE, erected on a high bluff and visible for miles.

Col. Thomas L. Kane, USA, wrote in 1846 that there was "a stately dome-shaped hill, which was covered by a noble marble edifice, whose high standing spire was radiant with white and gold." This was the Temple, an ambitious project that was to be the center of religious life, and to which every Mormon gave freely of his labor.

The corner stone of the Temple was laid April 6, 1841, and the house was dedicated April 30, 1846, amid a display of pageantry that included the military and a delegation of Indians from Iowa. The structure was a mixture of Romanesque, Egyptian and Greek; it measured 83 by 128 ft. and was topped by a tall, terraced spire, 157 ft. above the front entrance. On top of the spire was a gilded figure of the Angel Moroni. The Temple had 28 pilasters that helped support the walls, 9 on each side and 5 at each end. Each pilaster had a sun stone for a capital; this was 6 ft. 4 in. tall, 4 ft. 6 in. wide at its base, and 6 ft. wide at the top; it weighed 3,000 lbs. At the base of each pilaster was a moon stone, and above each capital around the cornice was a star stone. Sculptured sun stones can be seen in Nauvoo State Park, at the Nauvoo Hotel, and near the graves of Joseph and Hyrum Smith; there is one at the Historical Society in Quincy and another at the Smithsonian Institution in Washington.

The Temple was never completely finished. On Feb. 6, 1847, fire started by an overheated stove burned a 12-ft. hole in the roof. A week later the floor began to settle during a service and the communicants rushed out in panic. In September lightning struck the steeple. After nearly all Mormons had left Nauvoo an incendiary on Oct. 9, 1848, set the Temple on fire, destroying the interior. Later the Icarians bought the property and started reconstruction, but on May 25, 1850, a tornado knocked out the north wall and damaged the rest so severely that it had to be pulled down.

Some of the stones of the Temple were retrieved by the Icarians for the erection of a two-story Roman Catholic schoolhouse. In 1962 the foundations of the Temple were partly excavated by a research group from Southern Illinois University (Carbondale), exposing footings of walls and basement rooms.

On July 22, 1962, Nauvoo Restorations, Inc., was registered with the Secretary of State of Illinois as an agency of the Church of Jesus Christ of Latter-day Saints of Salt Lake City. It is active in restoration work. Its new VISITORS CENTER, erected on the 16-acre historic Mormon site was dedicated Sept. 4, 1971, in the presence of Elder Delbert L. Stapley of the Council of the Twelve Apostles of the Church of Latter-day Saints. The architect was Steven T. Baird, of Salt Lake City. In addition to services to visitors it has two theaters of 246 seats each, where a 25-minute color film on Nauvoo is shown.

The JOSEPH SMITH HOMESTEAD comprises the original log cabin, dating from 1823, into which Smith moved on coming to Nauvoo; a frame addition to the west and one at the rear. The house is furnished with objects once owned by the Smith family and is kept as a shrine by the Reorganized Church. On the river side of the house are the graves of Joseph Smith, his wife Emma Hale Smith Bideman, and his brother Hyrum. The bodies of Joseph and Hyrum were buried unmarked in a springhouse near the homestead and in more than half a century the location was forgotten. In 1928 a search was made and the remains were found, the bones of Hyrum being identified by a bullet hole in the skull. They were reinterred and the body of Smith's wife was placed beside them. She had remained behind at Nauvoo House and later married a non-Mormon named Bideman, with whom she conducted the hotel.

The foundation and basement of Joseph Smith's store are nearby. The store is to be rebuilt. A marker commemorates the founding here by Joseph Smith of the National Women's Relief Society on March 17, 1842.

The MANSION HOUSE, a two-story frame house with decorative pilasters, was Joseph Smith's home from August, 1843, until his death. It has been restored to its original condition by the Reorganized Church and contains Smith's desk and memorabilia.

The NAUVOO HOUSE was begun in 1831 when Smith declared

the Lord had commanded the erection of "a delightful habitation for man and a resting place for the weary traveler, that he may contemplate the glory of Zion." Bideman, Emma Smith's second husband, completed the building, which is 120 by 40 ft. It was to have another section of the same size facing Main Street.

The SIDNEY RIGDON HOUSE, a story-and-a-half frame dwelling, served as the first postoffice in Nauvoo. Rigdon was an early associate of Smith and was picked by Smith to run for vice president of the United States with him in a campaign that never materialized. After Smith's death he tried to get control of the organization but was expelled. He opened a church in Pittsburgh, which did not survive.

The BRIGHAM YOUNG HOUSE, a two-story red brick with stepped fire gables at each end has been restored recently. Young became second president of the Church and led the migration to Utah. Until his death in 1877 he was the strongest leader and administrator of the Church in Utah.

The WILFORD WOODRUFF HOUSE is a two-story brick with double chimneys at each end. Woodruff was a successful missionary abroad. He became fourth president and on Sept. 24, 1890, called on all Saints to obey the laws of the United States and abandon the practice of polygamy. The house, erected 1843-46, was restored and dedicated in May, 1970.

Many other houses built by Mormons are maintained in good condition and occupied, and the sites of others are marked. Among the best is the two-story brick with double end-chimneys built by HEBER C. KIMBALL. He ran a country store on the Commerce Road and Kimball's Landing bears his name. He was a native of Vermont and became an Apostle, a missionary to Great Britain, and a church official in Utah. The JONATHAN BROWNING HOME was built by a farmer who was also a gunsmith; his son, John M. Browning, learned gunsmithing in Ogden, Utah, and invented the Browning gun. The Browning blacksmith shop and gunshop have been rebuilt. The JOSEPH W. COOLIDGE HOME is a frame building used as both carpenter shop and home by its owner; after him a German named Johann Georg Kaufmann placed German inscriptions below the cornice reading: "This house is mine and yet not mine; whoever comes after me will be likewise. I have been here. Whoever reads this will also have been here."

Nauvoo now has a chapel of the Church of Jesus Christ of Latter-day Saints at Durphrey and Hibbard Sts. There is a Meeting House of the Reorganized Church, which also conducts an information office, with guides available. The Roman Catholic residents are served by the Church of Sts. Peter and Paul.

HOTEL NAUVOO was erected in part by J. J. Brendt, a Mormon, and completed by Adam Swartz, a German immigrant. In the hotel yard are fragments of a sun stone and a moon stone from the Temple.

NAUVOO STATE PARK, opened by the State in 1948, is

located on Route 96 south and east of the main part of Nauvoo. It is headquarters of the Nauvoo Historical Society and contains the best-preserved sun stone from the Temple. This stone was taken to Springfield in 1870 when plans were being made for the Capitol there. For six years it lay on the grounds of the old Capitol, then was removed to the new Capitol. From 1894 on it decorated a lily pond in the State Fair Grounds. In 1955 it was once more removed to Nauvoo State Park. The Rheinberger House is a cottage begun by a Mormon and enlarged by an Icarian. The Ritter wine press house and cellar are extant. In September the old French ceremony of the Wedding of the Wine and Cheese is enacted here. Grounds for camping are available.

Peoria

Air Services: Ozark Airlines, 44 flights daily, Greater Peoria Airport, 1900 S. Maxwell Road. Longest runway, 8,855 ft. Repair, fuel, and weather services. Airport Authority also operates Mt. Hawley Airport on Illinois 88 for private planes. Charter flights available. Tours, Mon.-Fri., 10-3, Apr. 15 to Nov.

Highways: Peoria is served by Int. 74, US 24, US 150, Ill. 8, 29, 88, 116. It is 116 *m.* ne. of St. Louis, 100 *m.* se. of Rock Island, 153 *m.* sw. of Chicago, 70 *m.* n. of Springfield.

Bus Lines: Union Bus Center, 225 S.W. Madison St. for Continental Trailways, Crown Transit Lines, Illini-Swallow Lines, Illinois Highway Transportation Co., Jacksonville Bus Lines, Peoria Charter Coach Co., and Peoria and Pekin Bus Co. Peoria City Lines provide bus service for the immediate Peoria area.

Railroads: Rock Island Lines, passenger service to Chicago, Station, Bond and Morton Sts. Freight service on five major lines and connections. Santa Fe passenger service from Chillicothe.

Barge Services: Peoria Barge Terminal and Kingston River Terminal, Illinois River; rail and truck handling facilities.

Information: Peoria *Journal Star,* War Memorial Drive. Peoria Travel Bureau, Inc., 443 Main St. Peoria Assn. of Commerce, First National Bank Bldg. Chicago Motor Club, 510 Main St. 8 radio and 4 television stations, major networks. WTPV, Channel 47, public noncommercial. *Peoria Today,* a quarterly magazine of information, by Walfred Co., Inc. in cooperation with the Peoria Assn. of Commerce.

Accommodations: Hotel Pere Marquette, convention and exhibit areas and ballroom seating 1,260 for banquets. Jefferson, Vonachen's Junction, Murphy's Holiday Inn, Howard Johnson, Peoria Sands, Ramada, Voyager Inn, other national chains. More than 1,700 hotel and motel rooms.

Churches: 162 churches, 56 denominations. St. Mary's Cathedral, Roman Catholic, 607 ne. Madison. St. Paul's Episcopal Cathedral, War Memorial Drive. Peoria Area Council of Churches, 1508 N. Sheridan. Catholic Chancery, 607 ne. Madison. Jewish Community Council, Citizens Bldg. Friendship House, 701 ne. Perry. Salvation Army, 331 ne. Adams. Dial-A-Devotion, 676-2174.

Recreation: Peoria has approx. 5,000 acres of wooded parks, drives and places set aside for games and picnics. The hot midsummer is ameliorated by scores of swimming pools; the Illinois River is used for boating and there is freshwater fishing in nearby lakes. Boat trips are scheduled on the steamer Julia Belle Swain, capacity 400. In addition to collegiate sports competition, there are golf and bowling events. The performing arts are cultivated and there are concerts by the Peoria Symphony Orchestra, the Peoria Civic Ballet, the Corn Stock Theatre, a theater-in-the-round in Bradley Park; the Peoria Players, and the Amateur Musical Club, which sponsors programs at Shrine Mosque and Lakeview Center, and supports the Philharmonic Chorale.

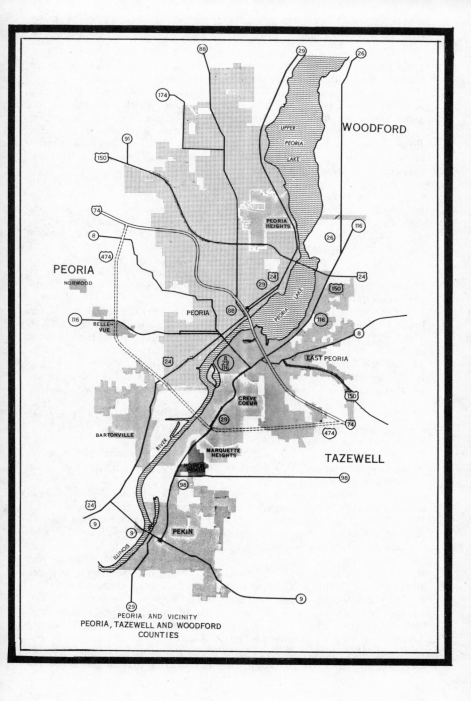

PEORIA AND VICINITY
PEORIA, TAZEWELL AND WOODFORD
COUNTIES

PEORIA, seat of Peoria County (608 alt., 126,963 pop. 1970; 103,162, 1960, inc. 23.1%) the third largest city in Illinois, lies on the northeast bank of the Illinois River in the rich north central farming country, 153 *m. sw.* of Chicago and 166 *m. ne.* of St. Louis. It is a manufacturing and distribution center for heavy machinery, of which its earth-moving apparatus is preeminent in the world's markets, and it has the largest distillery for spiritous liquors in the country. Its port is on Lake Peoria, a widened part of the Illinois River, 12 miles long and 3 miles broad, part of the Lakes-to-Gulf Waterway that has a channel from Chicago to the Mississippi River.

Peoria County grew in 10 years from 189,044 pop. to 195,318 (1970). In 1972 the Census Bureau estimated the county population at 200,000. The largest incorporated places besides Peoria are Bartonville (7,221 pop. 1970; 7,253, 1960): Chillicothe, (6,052, pop. 1970; 3,054, 1960); and Peoria Heights (7,943 pop. 1970; 7,064, 1960). Largest unincorporated areas are West Peoria, (6,873, 1970) and Elmwood (2,014 pop. 1970; 1,882, 1960).

The principal cross-State highway is Interstate 74, from Moline to Danville, and the best route from Chicago is west on Interstate 80 to Princeton, thence south on Illinois 29.

On the opposite, southeastern, bank of Lake Peoria and the River lies EAST PEORIA, an incorporated city of Tazewell County (18,445 pop. 1970; 12,310, 1960, inc. 49%), with interests identical with those of Peoria. It is reached by US 150 over the McClugage Bridge, by Int. 74 over the Murray & Baker Bridge, and by Illinois 29 over the Cedar St. Bridge. South of East Peoria are Creve Coeur, a village (6,440 pop. 1970; 6,684, 1960), and Marquette Heights (2,758 pop. 1970; 2,517, 1960).

Ten miles south on the Illinois River is Pekin, seat of Tazewell County, part of the Peoria industrial area (31,375 pop. 1970). *See article on Pekin.*

Tazewell County in 1970 had 118,549; in 1972 the Census estimate was 123,800. Woodford County in 1970 had 28,012; in 1972 the estimate was 28,700.

Peoria bears the name of one of the six Illinois Indian tribes, according to Virgil J. Vogel. Hennepin wrote that the Indians called Peoria Lake Pimitesui, which he thought meant a place with an abundance of fat beasts. Vogel commented that this merely meant fat and probably a wide place in the river, "which is what Peoria Lake is."

Peoria has well absorbed the immigrant workers who came in the 19th century, for the bulk of its citizens, 113,273, were American-born of American parents, according to the 1970 Census. Only 10,879 had foreign or mixed parentage, and only 2,844 were foreign-born. Of the 13,723 first generation Americans, born of foreign stock, 3,409 had German parents, 1,647 Irish, 812 Canadian, 675 Italian, 262 Mexican. There were only 17 persons of Puerto Rican birth or parentage.

According to the Bureau of the Census Peoria is part of the SMSA (Standard Metropolitan Statistical Area) that includes Peoria,

Tazewell, and Woodford Counties and the main cities of Peoria and Pekin. The 1970 Census for this SMSA reported 341,974 pop., of which 325,934 were white and 14,927 black (4.4%). Peoria, 126,963 total pop. had 111,731 white, 14,550 black (11.5%). It had 60,285 males and 66,078 females. It had a labor force of 50,337; of this 31,167 males had civilian employment, 1,060 were unemployed (3.3%); 19,140 females were employed, and 983 were unemployed (4.9%). Of those employed the largest group, 14,949, was in industry, while wholesale and retail trade used 11,095.

The manufacturing area spreads out over three counties. The largest employers are makers of earth-moving machinery, including Caterpillar Tractor Co., LeTourneau-Westinghouse, and Hyster Corp. Keystone Steel & Wire is the principal fabricator in steel. For more than 100 years Peoria has been a distiller of spiritous liquors, made possible by its location in the center of the corn belt, with plenty of clear water and coal. Meat processing is another profitable industry. Among many Peoria products are animal and poultry foods, brick and tile, cutting parts for harvesters, furnaces, washing machines, wire rope and wash dresses. Among the national corporations represented are Continental Can, Corn Products Co., B. F. Goodrich Chemical, Libby, McNeil & Libby, National Aluminum, Olin Matthiesen, Pabst Brewing Co., Quaker Oats, Sealtest Foods, and Standard Brands.

Until 1960 Peoria was a huge railroad center, exceeded in the State only by Chicago. Fourteen railroads moved the products of the area and two, the Rock Island and the Santa Fe, had a thriving passenger business. The development of air travel and portal-to-portal trucking curtailed the business of the rails and by 1970 only the Rock Island Lines had a station in town and a daily train to Chicago and one returning. The Santa Fe main line stopped at Chillicothe, about 10 *m*. north on Illinois 29. For about fifty years the big Union Station had more than 200 trains arriving and departing daily on 12 railroads. A huge dome-like train shed covered the tracks, where the Burlington, Chicago & North Western, Illinois Central, and Alton came. The Peoria & Eastern was the sole survivor; finally it made Pekin its terminal. On October 14, 1967, it ended its run. The train shed was demolished and the station became a warehouse.

Today motor freight is carried by 145 lines; 8 motor bus lines run on schedules to every part of the continent; 5 barge lines provide freight transport by water. Shipments have been shifted from rails to other means without loss of business.

The first white men to reach this site were Father Jacques Marquette, S. J. and the explorer Louis Jolliet, who passed through Lake Peoria in the fall of 1673, returning from their trip down the Mississippi. In his *Recite* Marquette mentions meeting the Indians "of Peourea," but this encounter did not occur here. The expedition erected no buildings, but the teachings of Marquette and his promise of the French king's protection against the Iroquois warriors from the north established mutual confidence. Marquette did not return, but in 1680 Robert

Cavelier, Sieur de La Salle, with Henri de Tonti, Père Louis Hennepin, a group of Recollect friars and artisans, about 33 men in all, descended the Illinois River to Lake Peoria. At the outlet of the lake, on the left bank of the river, they erected Fort Crève Coeur, "the refuge of the broken heart," probably named to commemorate the French capture of Fort Crève Coeur in the Netherlands. Within three months it was plundered and abandoned by its forces during La Salle's absence. A granite shaft marks the general area.

In 1691 Fort St. Louis, upstream from Peoria on Starved Rock, was abandoned, and the post moved to Lake Peoria, where it was usually referred to as Fort Pimiteoui (Ind., fat lake). On the settlement that grew up about it, Peoria bases its claim to being the oldest city in Illinois against the claim of Cahokia, founded in 1699.

In 1763 the British wrested control of the area from the French, but the treaty that concluded the French and Indian War exerted little influence here. Although the settlement was virtually abandoned during the Revolutionary War, the French returned to a new village on the right bank of the river, and continued their trading well into the American period. The village at Peoria Lake was visited by two military expeditions during the Revolutionary War. The first, a group of George Rogers Clark's men, destroyed the Indian village here. In 1781 a company of Spaniards, French, and Indians came up the Illinois river to Peoria Lake, and from here crossed by land to the British post of St. Joseph, in Michigan, which they captured without a battle.

The new village to which the French returned was variously referred to as Au Pé, Le Pé, Opa, and Au Pay, and as early as 1790 there is reference to it as Piorias—the "s" was not pronounced—but it is not known when that name became common usage.

During the War of 1812 a military blunder by the American forces resulted in the partial destruction of Au Pé. Alarmed at the depredations of the Indians, Governor Ninian Edwards led troops up from Edwardsville and destroyed the village of Black Partridge, unaware that the chief was trying to recover Americans kidnapped at the Fort Dearborn massacre. Shortly afterward, another part of the same force, under Capt. Thomas Craig of Shawneetown, destroyed a large part of the French village and carried off its inhabitants. Subsequently the friendliness—or at least the neutrality—of the French was proved, and they were released.

On the site of Au Pé late in 1813 the Americans erected Fort Clark, and about it grew up the nucleus of modern Peoria, although the name of Fort Clark clung to it for more than 10 years. In 1819 the first American civilians arrived, a party of seven, forerunners of the swarm of land-seekers soon to follow. In 1825 Peoria County was created, and the community of Fort Clark, with the French-Indian name of Peoria officially restored, was designated county seat. From here, for a period of six years, jurisdiction was exercised over one-fourth of Illinois, including the stripling village of Chicago.

When the first steamboat came up the Illinois about 1828, it found a sizeable cluster of cabins at the lake. In 1835, when Peoria was

incorporated as a town, it had a population of more than 500. A decade
later it had grown to 2,000, and by 1845 had adopted a city charter.

In 1854 the village was the scene of a highly important event in
the career of Lincoln. On October 16, after Stephen Douglas had
spoken all afternoon, Lincoln rose and requested that the crowd return
after supper to hear his rebuttal. That evening he delivered a longer
version of a speech he had given 12 days earlier at Springfield. Concerning the speech, Albert Beveridge says, in his *Abraham Lincoln, 1809-
1858*: "Thus did Lincoln, for the first time in his life, publicly and in
forthright words denounce slavery, and assert that it was incompatible
with American institutions." The speech was not one of the Lincoln-
Douglas debates, which it antedated by four years.

POINTS OF INTEREST

The PEORIA COUNTY COURTHOUSE, completed in 1963
at a cost of $4,500,000, has helped modernize the central core of Peoria.
A modern office building on a landscaped plaza, it was part of a major
urban renewal project called Progress Center, which inspired reconstruction of banks and office buildings without recourse to Federal aid. This
Courthouse replaced one with a domed clocktower that had stood there
since 1876. This also is the site of Abraham Lincoln's Peoria speech of
1854 denouncing slavery. The familiar Soldiers and Sailors Monument
now stands near the Adams St. entrance of the Courthouse. It was
designed by Fritz Triebel and dedicated October 6, 1899, in the
presence of President William McKinley.

Dominant on the Plaza stands the imposing world headquarters of
the CATERPILLAR TRACTOR Co., which is principally responsible for
Peoria becoming the earth-moving capital. Four huge wings in cruci-
form, six stories tall, use the major part of two city blocks. Facing it on
Hamilton St. is the Security Savings Bldg.; opposite on Main St. is the
Citizens Office Bldg. Facing the Courthouse on Jefferson St. are the
First National Bank Bldg., originally known as the Alliance Life Bldg.,
the First Federal Savings, and other Savings Center buildings.

The CATERPILLAR TRACTOR CO. moved into its new headquarters in Progress Center in 1967. It is the largest employer in Illi-
nois and with sales of $1.5 billion (1968) one of the nation's 50 major
industries. It is a monument to the development of earth-moving
machinery that has become essential for highway and urban purposes.
It was formed in 1925 by the merger of two tractor manufacturers from
Stockton and San Leandro, California. Holt Manufacturing Co. of
Stockton came to East Peoria in 1909 to serve the Midwestern market.
Holt had built the crawler tractor in 1904 and C. L. Best of San
Leandro had developed the tracklayer crawler tractor in 1913. The
Allies used the Holt tractor in World War I and it inspired Lt. Col.
E. D. Swinton to design the military tank.

The Holt-Best combination adopted the Holt trademark, Caterpillar,
for its products. Later in the decade the Russell Road Grader Mfg. Co. of
Minneapolis was acquired. In 1931 Caterpillar offered the first crawler
tractors powered by diesel engines. During World War II the company

developed a special diesel engine for the M4 tank. The East Peoria plant turned out M4 tank transmissions and final drive assemblies, as well as 155 mm. howitzer carriages, shells, and bomb parts. The Federal government asked for full-time production of tractors and motor graders. Army officers called the tractor-bulldozer essential for winning beachheads.

When the war ended Caterpillar had two plants, one at East Peoria and another at San Leondro, Calif. Demands for its products became so big that the company began a period of expansion. It doubled the floor space at the East Peoria plant, which produces track-type tractors, loaders and pipe-layers, engines and powershift transmissions. The Joliet plant began production in 1951 and has been tripled since. The Decatur plant began production in 1955 and has been enlarged four times its original size. It makes wheel tractors, motor graders, and off-highway trucks. The Aurora plant began in 1958 and was doubled in 1967. The Industrial Engine plant was begun in Mossville in 1959, and a huge Technical Center was opened there in 1961. Today it occupies five laboratory and research buildings. In 1967, the year Caterpillar moved into its new offices in Peoria, the electric melting foundry was opened in Mapleton. There are other plants outside of Illinois and in foreign countries. By 1968 the company employed 49,500 in the United States and 61,000 worldwide.

HIRAM WALKER & SONS, INC., at the foot of Edmund St., is a subsidiary of the original distilling firm of Hiram Walker in Walkerville, Ont., Canada that has grown larger than its parent. It incorporated in the United States after repeal of prohibition. The plant produces 125,000 gallons or 800,000 bottles of 100-proof whiskey daily, consuming 25,000 bushels or 16 carloads of grain every 24 hours. The lecture tour explains the process of manufacture from the arrival of the grain to the labelling of the bottles. *Tours Monday through Friday, 10-2, minors under 12 not admitted.*

KEYSTONE STEEL & WIRE COMPANY, one of the pioneer industries of Peoria, is a division of Keystone Consolidated Industries, Inc., which has its headquarters at 411 Hamilton Blvd., and supervises 27 plants making steel, wire, fencing, and other durable products. The Keystone plant, 700 S. Adams St., occupies 913 acres. It was founded by Peter Sommer in 1889 as the Keystone Fence Co., and supplied fence to great areas of farmland in Illinois and the Midwest. As its products multiplied it kept close contacts with farm customers and those sold to farm markets still account for a large part of the company's output. Keystone manufactures its own steel from scrap and pig iron. The steel mills use the open hearth process. The wire mills have facilities for cleaning, drawing, annealing, galvanizing, bundling, and shipping products. The plant has approx. 3,500 employees. *Tours by appointment for groups of 10 to 25, minimum age 12.*

The PEORIA PUBLIC LIBRARY reached another milestone when it entered its new main building, the Downtown Library at 107 Northeast Monroe St., in March, 1968. This modern, three-story structure houses more than 400,000 volumes accumulated since 1881. On its lower level it has an auditorium seating 270 and the film services; on its intermediate level is the hq of the Illinois Valley Library System.

DETWEILLER PARK, largest of the parks—756 acres—offers a variety of drives, trails, and picnic sites in a natural setting. The

DETWEILLER MARINA on Lake Peoria has facilities for boat launching, dock service and storage.

GRAND VIEW DRIVE is a part of the Peoria Park System that uses 211 acres on the crown of a high bluff overlooking the valley of the Illinois River. The area is much prized for dwellings. It overlooks Peoria Lake, an arm of the river, 3 miles wide and 12 miles long.

The MARQUETTE-JOLLIET CROSS, a four-ton cross of New Hampshire granite, stands near the entrance of St. Mary's Roman Catholic Cathedral. It was erected by Bishop Joseph H. Schlarman and dedicated on December 14, 1947. An inscription on the front base reads: "This cross recalls to the passer-by the heroic journey of Father Marquette and Louis Jolliet and their brave companions, who camped on the banks of Lake Peoria August, 1673. On the other side of the base is a tribute to the sons of the Peoria diocese who fell in World War II.

The NORTHERN RESEARCH AND DEVELOPMENT LABORATORY of the Agricutural Research Division of the U. S. Department of Agriculture, 1815 N. University, is important to the welfare of farming in the Midwest. Here scientists develop new strains and uses of wheat, corn, grain sorghum, soybeans, flax and other native crops. *Open Monday through Friday, 8-4:30.*

The McCUTCHEON ANIMAL PARK was established in 1970 in the environs of Peoria by the Chicago Zoological Society after the Forest Park Foundation donated 440 acres and $100,000 for the purpose. The park is named for the first president of the society, John T. McCutcheon, and will be used as a breeding farm for exotic and native hoofed animals. Facilities for spectators are included.

GLEN OAK PARK, one of the most popular of Peoria's many parks, occupies 106 acres on the Bluffs, bounded by Springdale Road, Abingdon St., Prospect Road, and Springdale Cemetery. It has facilities for tennis, baseball, softball, archery, baitcasting, and skating. Here is Peoria's Zoo, clean and modern, with collections of tropical birds, reptiles, monkeys, apes and a chimpanzee; small animals, and lions, tigers, and leopards. Behind the Zoo is the Animal Fair, where small animals may be petted and fed by children. At the Perry Ave. entrance of the park stands a statue of Robert Ingersoll, once a Peoria lawyer, by Fritz Triebel. Boulder Monument, erected by the Boulder County Old Settlers Assn., commemorates early residents. There is also an Alaskan totem pole, with a tablet of interpretation.

LAKEVIEW CENTER FOR THE ARTS AND SCIENCES, 1125 W. Lake Ave., is a recently constructed cultural complex that has enlisted the artistic interests of Peoria most successfully. Art and natural science exhibits, ballet, plays, concerts, lectures, a museum and a planetarium draw around 30,000 persons a month to the Center. *Open Tuesday through Saturday, 9-5; Sunday, 1:30-6; Saturday and Wednesday evenings, 7-9; closed Mondays.* The PLANETARIUM changes its sky shows monthly and has performances *Wednesday, 4-7:30; Saturday, 2:30, 4, 7; Sunday, 1:30, 3, 4:30.*

EXPOSITION GARDENS, on Northmoor Road, is the site of the annual Heart of Illinois Fair in the fall. It also has the Museum of Central Illinois Agriculture, a permanent exhibit of a farm house, barn, and general store, with farm tools and furnishings of the last century. *Open first Sunday of every month 2-5, March to November.*

FOREST PARK, 5809 Forest Park Drive, is the Forest Wildlife and Nature Center, 500 acres largely left in their natural woodland state and with five miles of trails. There is a museum with displays of flora and fauna and an area is set aside for picnics. *Tuesday through Saturday, 2-5, Sunday, 1-5, closed Monday.*

BRADLEY UNIVERSITY, 1501 W. Bradley Ave., a privately endowed, nonsectarian institution, occupies an area of 18 city blocks in the bluff district of Peoria. It was endowed in 1897 by Mrs. Lydia Moss Bradley and opened Oct. 4, 1897, as a four-year academy offering an additional two years of college work. It was affiliated with the University of Chicago and the principal buildings adopted the collegiate Gothic style of the original Chicago campus. It absorbed Peoria Musical College in 1920, discontinued the academy in 1922 and adopted a four-year college curriculum. It was known for some years as Bradley Polytechnic Institute.

Its excellent facilities for technical training were of advantage to the United States Army during the World Wars. At one time it had the only School of Horology for the teaching of watch-making; this has since been closed. The original Bradley Hall was destroyed by fire in 1963 and rebuilt; numerous other buildings erected since 1946 have adopted contemporary architecture. In 1946 it added the master's degree and became Bradley University. It has five colleges and five schools and in the 1972 enrolled 5,206 and had a faculty of 404.

Bradley University has colleges of Business Administration, Engineering & Technology, Liberal Arts & Sciences, Education, and the Evening College. It has schools of Art, International Studies, Journalism, Music, and Speech & Hearing Sciences. It also has a Department of Computer Science and formal training in computer operations is available to all full-time students and faculty. Nursing has a four-year program integrated with liberal arts. The Evening College offers opportunities for continuing education, on a credit and non-credit basis. There is an Air Force Reserve Officers Training Corps (ROTC). Two semesters a year cost the student $950 each; there is also a summer session. There are five residence halls for women, with room and board at $410 to $565 per semester, and three residence halls for freshman men, at $430 to $565 per semester.

The CULLOM-DAVIS LIBRARY of the University has been the recipient of a number of donations by collectors of Lincoln material. It esteems the Lincolniana given by Martin Luther Houser, and the Lincoln Collection of Judge Claude U. Stone; in all there are 1,800 different Lincoln items, listed in a guide published in 1962. There are also the Charles A. Bennett Collection of 1,141 books and 6,692 pamphlets on industrial education; the Eugene Baldwin private library, the John S. Stevens Memorial Library, and the John Herman Dougherty collection.

The PEORIA SCHOOL OF MEDICINE opened in September, 1971, at 1400 Main St., with 20 students. It has a three-year clinical program. It is a unit of the University of Illinois and directly affiliated with its Chicago Medical Center. It was called the first medical school in Illinois outside the Chicago area.

Peoria is the headquarters of the DIOCESE OF PEORIA of the Roman Catholic Church, which covers a wide area in this part of Illinois, with a membership of 222,608 according to the 1973 Official Directory. It had 55,434 students in its school system and administered 16 hospitals.

Of the Peoria suburbs PEORIA HEIGHTS (7,943 pop. 1970) is located at a strategic point dominating Upper Peoria Lake. Although surrounded by Peoria on the west bank it includes areas in Tazewell and Woodford Counties on the east bank. It is notable for its Observation Tower, a tall structure with three decks, served by a glass-enclosed elevator, providing remarkable views over the lakes and countryside. Peoria Heights has 2,000 acres of park and woodland. One block south of the Tower is Kiddie Park, which has a sandbox containing 100 tons of washed sand, ready for the youngest generation. Although the Peoria Heights Public Library was built only in 1963, it was "improved" in 1968. It has more than 25,000 books and is a member of the Illinois Valley Library System.

Quincy

Air Services: Baldwin Field, 10.5 *m.* east of Quincy, has 21 daily flights on Ozark Airlines connecting Chicago, St. Louis, Des Moines, and Kansas City, and one cargo flight to and from Chicago. Private plane facilities.

Bus Lines: Continental Trailways. Kirksville Bus Co. Jacksonville Bus Lines. Union Bus Depot.

Railroads: Burlington Northern (C. B. & Q.) 4 passenger trains daily connecting with Chicago and Kansas City at West Quincy Station. Freight on Burlington and Norfolk & Western (formerly Wabash).

Highways: US 24 to Peoria and eastward connects with the principal routes to Chicago. Illinois 96 and Illinois 57 share the Great River Road. Illinois 104 connects with US 67.

Water Services: Quincy Municipal Barge Terminal ships steel, coal, grains, salt, oil, LP gas tanks, sand, rock, and fertilizer.

Information: Quincy Chamber of Commerce. Industrial Assn. of Quincy. *Quincy Herald-Whig,* daily and Sunday. WGEM-TV and WGEM-FM, affiliated with national networks.

Accommodations and Services: Churches, 64 in Quincy, 95 in Adams County. Five hotels. Blessing Hospital, 365 beds, 25 bassinets; St. Mary's Hospital, 318 beds, 25 bassinets; Illinois Soldiers & Sailors Home, 491 beds; 11 nursing homes.

Recreation: Quincy has 900 acres of city parks with outdoor facilities. Swimming at Indian Mounds Park, Sheridan Swim pools, Quinsippi Island beach. Westview Municipal Golf, 27 holes; 3 country clubs, gun club.

QUINCY, 132.8 *m.* (602 alt., 45,288 pop. 1970; 43,793, 1960; inc. 3.4%) seat of Adams County, begins at the Mississippi River, hurdles steep bluffs, and levels out on the uplands. Both city and county were named for John Quincy Adams, President of the United States at the time of their founding. An important outlet for farm products and agricultural equipment for more than a century, Quincy was a prosperous port in the days of steamboating and an Illinois gateway for the C. B. & Q., which still provides some passenger service at West Quincy, Mo., and shares freight business with the Norfolk & Western. Baldwin Airport, 2½ *m.* east of the city, has 21 passenger flights daily to and from Chicago, St. Louis, Des Moines, and Kansas City, and one cargo flight on Ozark Air Lines.

Quincy is at a junction of a number of fine highways. Illinois 96, which runs on high bluffs is part of the Great River Road. as also is Illinois 57 below the city. Illinois 104 connects with US 67 at Jacksonville, which is 34 *m.* to Springfield on US 54. US 24 crosses the Mississippi on the Quincy Memorial Bridge (*free*). Lock and Dam 21 is located just below the city.

Quincy has a mayor and aldermanic form of government and has built modern quarters for its city and county offices. Its work force was more than 11,000 in the 1960 decade and dipped slightly in the early 1970's. The city has one liberal arts college and a number of technical and vocational schools, a well-equipped public school system and parochial schools of three denominations.

MoorMan Manufacturing Co., maker of livestock feeds and feeding equipment, has its main office in Quincy and divisions and warehouses in 16 other states. It usually employs 1,200; its plant and laboratories occupy 33 acres. Quincy Soybean Co., a subsidiary of MoorMan, processes soybeans into oil and meal, ships by barge, rail and truck and operates seven country elevators in Illinois and Missouri. Gardner-Denver Co., maker of mining and construction equipment, started in Quincy in 1859 as a maker of fly-ball governors to control the speed of steam-powered machines. Its sales are international and in a typical year reach more than $149,000,000. Motorola, Inc., usually has 1,500 engaged in producing radio, television, and phonograph materials. Electric Wheel Co., a division of Firestone Tire & Rubber Co. makes products for farm vehicles and employs up to 1,200. The Quincy Compression Division of Colt Industries has manufactured unit type industrial compressors since 1920. The Packaging Corp. of America doubled its paperboard output by opening a new mill in 1965. A number of plants making mixtures for fertilizer and feed products testifies to Quincy's agricultural patronage. Some industries are operated by descendants of the founders; the Huck Manufacturing Co., maker of store fixtures, has the third generation in charge, and the fourth manages the Knapheide Manufacturing Co., maker of grain and livestock truck bodies.

The site of Quincy was passed by Pere Marquette and Louis Jolliet during their exploration of the Mississippi River in 1673. An Indian village had stood there for many generations. The locality was part of a large segment of territory in western Illinois set aside by Congress as bounty land for veterans of the War of 1812.

John Wood (1798-1880) and Willard Keyes, two young Easterners, established claims on the site of Quincy in 1822. Their cabins, along with those of several other pioneers, comprised a tiny settlement called The Bluffs. John Wood became a power in State politics and in 1860, as Lieutenant Governor, filled the unexpired term of Gov. William H. Bissell, who died in office. It was at Woods' petition that the State legislature created Adams County in 1825, and empowered commissioners to select a site for the county seat at the center of the area. Willard Keyes thereupon led the commissioners to this spot, and under his guidance the delegation scrambled through "bogs, quicksands, and quagmires," to Keyes' cabin. There they were persuaded to designate The Bluffs as the seat of Adams County. Quincy was platted later in the same year. It was incorporated as a town in 1834 and as a city in 1840.

Despite an epidemic of Asiatic cholera in 1832, Quincy grew rapidly. Across the river from the slave state of Missouri, the village was in the border region where clashes between pro-slavery and anti-slavery groups foreshadowed the Civil War. Pioneer abolitionist of Quincy was the Rev. Asa B. Turner of Templeton, Mass., brother of Jonathan Turner, then a teacher at Illinois College, Jacksonville. Under the Rev. Mr. Turner's direction, the first church in Quincy, called the Lord's Barn, was completed in 1831.

Dr. David Nelson, Presbyterian minister, having narrowly escaped assassination by a Missouri slave-owner, sought refuge in Turner's home. An abolitionist society organized shortly after Nelson's arrival was attributed to the two ministers. An open meeting, scheduled to be held in the Lord's Barn, prompted pro-slavery partisans to rally to "help clean out the abolitionists." When they gathered before the Lord's barn and pelted the structure with stones, the forewarned audience seized clubs, hatchets, and muskets and led by deacons of the church, routed their opponents.

In 1835 residents of Columbia began to demand that their village be declared county seat because of its position at the true center of Adams County. An election to settle the question was held in 1841; Columbia won by 91 votes. Although Stephen A. Douglas, then circuit judge, issued a mandamus ordering immediate recognition of the voters' decision, the county commissioners at Quincy delayed action. Residents of Quincy, convinced that the supporters of Columbia had stuffed the ballot boxes, appealed to the Supreme Court of Illinois. While their case was pending, the State legislature looped off ten eastern townships from Adams County and created the new county of Marquette. When the Columbians learned that their village now occupied a borderline position in Marquette County identical to that of Quincy in Adams County, they refused to organize a local government. The legislature enlarged the new county in 1847 and changed its name to Highland, but the inhabitants obstructed all attempts to form a government. At last the legislature reunited the territory with Adams County.

Orville H. Browning of Quincy was a political associate of Abraham Lincoln in the Illinois Whig-Republican campaigns with a strong conservative bent. He was a member of the State legislature in Vandalia in 1836 and held several other offices, while Lincoln was a member of the house, 1834-42. Both men were circuit lawyers and both supported Henry Clay. Browning opposed Douglas on the Kansas-Nebraska bill and joined the new Republican Party. Preceding the convention of 1860 he proposed the candidacy of Edward Bates of St. Louis to Lincoln and other party leaders but as a delegate to that convention he was instructed to vote for Lincoln. He appealed for harmony and as a moderate criticized the "fence rails and Old Abe" tactics. As a member of the board of Knox College Browning was instrumental in getting Lincoln an honorary degree. He was appointed to fill the unexpired term as senator of Stephen A. Douglas in June, 1861 and lost the seat to the radical faction in 1863. He urged President Lincoln to appoint Bates secretary of state and put himself on the U. S. Supreme Court bench, but despite their intimacy Lincoln did not follow his advice.

During the 19th century Quincy became the second largest city in Illinois. Some 20,000 hogs were shipped by steamboat to St. Louis in 1847; in later years annual hog shipments rose to 70,000. Quincy factories produced plows, shoes, stoves, wagons, carriages, organs, corn-planters, and steam engines. These plants, together with tobacco works, flour mills, tanneries, saw mills, and breweries, employed 8,000 men. Goods exported during the 1850's annually averaged $15,000,000 in value. Steamboat landings for the 10 months that the Mississippi was open to navigation in 1853 averaged five a day.

Quincy was displaced as second city in Illinois by industrial communities that boomed in the post-Civil War decades. Its commerce declined with the decrease of steamboat traffic, but with the proliferation of railroads in western Illinois it became a busy center for freight. The principal railways were the Wabash and the Chicago, Burlington & Quincy, and although the latter was exploited as the Burlington Route it was known locally and in the territory that it served as "the Q". In 1898 the road built a Quincy station that caused comment because it had a tall tower locally called the minaret. The station has since been closed. The Wabash was merged in 1964 with the Norfolk & Western, which uses 20 miles of C. B. & Q. track to connect with its main line freight service. The Burlington crosses the Mississippi on a high-level bridge of recent construction that cost $8,000,000. A new passenger station was built in 1964 at West Quincy, Mo. Four trains run daily between Chicago and Quincy, and Kansas City and Quincy.

Barge line tonnage of commodities moved through Lock and Dam No. 21 at Quincy in 1972 was 22,956,367, according to the Rock Island District, Corps of Engineers, USA.

Newspapers have been published regularly in Quincy since 1835, when the *Illinois Bounty Land Register* was first issued. This became the *Quincy Herald*. In 1838 the *Quincy Whig* appeared as the organ of the political party to which Abraham Lincoln adhered before the Republican Party was founded. Both newspapers carried on until 1926, an unusual record of competitive publishing. That year they were consolidated as the *Quincy Herald-Whig,* which is isused today from a fine modern plant where the presses may be viewed by visitors.

Every style of ecclesiastical architecture has been built in Quincy since the earliest permanent religious structure rose in 1834. That was the First Union Congregational Church, which now has a large brick edifice with two low towers. The First Presbyterian Church recalls the ornate period of Victorian Gothic; the Salem Evangelical United Church of Christ, also in neo-Gothic, has a sharp, highly decorative central spire. Modern designs are used in the Trinity Church of Christ, the Calvary Baptist, the Union Methodist, the St. James Lutheran, and St. Peter's Catholic Church.

The medical services available in Quincy include two hospitals (457 beds), five clinics, a mental health center, a tuberculosis sanitarium, 13 nursing homes and homes for the aged. ST. MARY'S HOSPITAL added a new building in 1962. BLESSING HOSPITAL, founded 1875, conducts a three-year School of Nursing.

POINTS OF INTEREST

WASHINGTON PARK, in the heart of town, was the scene of the fifth debate between Abraham Lincoln and Stephen A. Douglas on Oct. 13, 1858. A large plaque in bronze by Lorado Taft depicts Lincoln standing to make his speech, with Douglas seated beside him surrounded by listeners.

The statue of Governor John Wood on the west side of Washington Park is signed C. G. Volk, 1883. Cornelius G. Volk was the older brother of Leonard Wells Volk, who made the life mask and bust of Lincoln. The Volks were related to Stephen A. Douglas through their wives.

The MANSION OF GOVERNOR WOOD is the hq of the Historical Society of Quincy and Adams County. It was built in 1835 by John Wood and is a 12-room frame house with four ionic pillars and a gallery at one end. The society, founded in 1896, acquired it in 1907 and installed a museum of regional history. Among its objects are the desk of John Quincy Adams, a capstone from the Mormon Temple at Nauvoo, keys from the temple, two crystal chandeliers, a pilot wheel, bell cord and anchor from Mississippi River steamboats, furniture and documents. *Open Tuesday through Sunday, 2-5.*

Quincy is served by a number of technical and vocational schools. GEM CITY COLLEGE, founded in 1870 and teaching secretarial, accounting and business administration, in 1961 bought the School of Horology from Bradley University. QUINCY TECHNICAL SCHOOLS train students in Diesel and automotive mechanics, airconditioning, drafting, electronics, and allied vocations. The CHADDOCK SCHOOL for boys is conducted by the Methodist Church.

The QUINCY ART CENTER, 1515 Jersey St., occupies a remodeled carriage house that has a recital hall and offices of the Quincy Society of Fine Arts. Organizations that are members of the society include the Quincy Symphony Orchestra, the Community Little Theater, the Progressive Playhouse, the Civic Music Assn., the Quincy Art Club, which sponsors monthly loan exhibits; the Quincy Conservatory of Music, the Junior Theater, and other groups of similar interests.

QUINCY COLLEGE, in the northeast residential section of Quincy, is a four-year coeducational liberal arts college conducted by the Franciscan Fathers, who incorporated it in 1873 as St. Francis Solanus College and in 1917 changed its name to Quincy College and Seminary. It opened its classes to women in 1932 and in 1940 adopted its present organization. It offers the baccalaureate degree in the arts and science, and in professional fields gives the degree for accounting, management, education, physical education, medical technology and music education. There are two semesters and a summer session. In the

1971-72 year Quincy College had a faculty of 119 and enrolled 1,991 students.

During the 1960-70 decade Quincy College added a number of new buildings in the contemporary mode. These included Centennial Hall, Gardner Hall, Padua Hall (for men), and the Quincy College Center. In 1967 came the new QUINCY COLLEGE LIBRARY, a collection of more than 160,000 books. It subscribes to more than 1,000 periodicals and can accomodate 600 students in individual carrels. Among special collections are the Fraborese Library of Spanish-American subjects in 4,000 vols.; the St. Bonaventura Library of early Christian and medieval materials; the Quincyana collection of local history, and a rare book section of 4,000 vols., including 31 incunabula.

QUINCY COLLEGE MEMORIAL GYMNASIUM, site of basketball contests and the physical education program, commemorates students and alumni who died in the military service, and Mart Heinen, former athletic director, and his three companions who perished in the Hotel LaSalle fire in Chicago while on business for the college. The administrative offices and chapel are located in Saint Frances Hall. The Quincy College Center, with facilities for food and recreation, was added in 1969.

Student expenses for tuition, room and board for the academic year of two semesters are estimated at $2,500.

OUR LADY OF ANGELS FRANCISCAN SEMINARY was established in 1964 as an independent division with access to the curriculum of the college. After four years here candidates for the priesthood continue four years of theological studies.

The FREE PUBLIC LIBRARY of Quincy, 4th and Maine Sts., was opened in 1889 and remodeled in 1929. With more than 112,000 books in its collection it circulates more than 250,000 annually. It is the headquarters library of the Great River Road Library System, which was approved by the State in 1966. The system enbraces the libraries of eight counties. Funds allotted to the system average $138,000 a year, and its income is based on the State formula of 50c per person and $15 a sq. m. The system effects centralized ordering and processing through the Keosippi Library Development of Keokuk, Iowa.

QUINSIPPI ISLAND is a most popular recreation center of 130 acres, with numerous attractions. It has a narrow-guage steam railroad, a log cabin village, an excursion boat, the *Quinsippi Queen,* a marina, and nature trails. An aerial cable car operates hourly between the city and the island. More than 900 acres are devoted to parks in Quincy, including the Westview Municipal Golf Course of 27 holes.

ERROKE INDIAN MOUNDS AND MUSEUM, in Indian Mounds Park, has a large collection of Indian artifacts discovered in the burial mounds of the late Woodland Indians, dating back 1,200 years. Some of the Indian skeletons are shown *in situ.* Members of an Explorer Scout Post supervise the museum and act as guides for tours, describing archaeological discoveries. *Daily, 9 a.m.-8 p.m.*

RIVERVIEW PARK, first of the northern chain of parks, is entered from Chestnut St. and Second St. A great panorama of the Mississippi River enfolds to the viewer on the bluff where stands a statue of George Rogers Clark designed by Charles J. Mulligan, when director of sculpture at the Art Institute of Chicago. The prospect includes the bridges, the U. S. Naval Reserve Training Center, Quincy Bay, and the Sid Simpson State Park.

In WOODLAND CEMETERY, S. 5th St., is the grave of JOHN WOOD, marked by a monument. SOLDIERS MONUMENT, a white marble shaft dedicated to Adams County men killed in the Civil War, surmounts an Indian mound in the cemetery.

BALDWIN PARK, 30th and Main Sts., an amusement spot and site of the annual Adams County Fair, was the home of Maj. Thomas B. Baldwin, a pioneer balloonist and aeronautical experimenter for the U. S. Government. Major Baldwin thrilled residents of Quincy in 1887 by making a parachute jump from 4,000 ft. Baldwin Airport is named for him.

The ILLINOIS SOLDIERS AND SAILORS HOME, at the north end of 12th St., was established in 1887 for veterans of American wars and their dependents. The 200-acre grounds along wooded bluffs above the Mississippi contain an artificial lake and beautiful sunken gardens.

SILOAM SPRINGS STATE PARK, 3,025 acres, 25 m. east of Quincy, a recreation area, has medicinal springs known to the Indians. In the 1880's a resort village was built here to exploit the springs.

The VILLA KATHRINE, 532 S. Third St., known as The Castle, is a house in Moorish style erected as a dwelling by an engaged couple and never lived in because the fiance died before the marriage. It is now a community house owned by the Quincy Park District.

Rockford

Air Services: Ozark Air Lines, daily scheduled flights; commuting service to O'Hare, Chicago. Hangers leased for private planes. Greater Rockford Airport at jct. of Illinois 2 and US 20. Also two private fields.

Bus Lines: Greyhound Bus Lines, Interstate Transit Co., Peoria-Rockford Bus Lines. Station, 623 E. Jefferson St. Three daily nonstop roundtrip bus trips between Rockford and O'Hare, 1 hr. 20 min. one way. Private cars, using Northwest Tollway, Int. 90, 1 hr. 5 min.

Highways: Principal east-west route is US 20, Chicago-Rockford-East Dubuque, entering city on Branch Route 20. Fastest route between Chicago and Rockford is Interstate 90, Northwest Tollway, connecting with State St. on Branch Route 20 and Main Road (Main St.) on US 20. Direct north-south route is US 51 from Janesville, Wisc. to Bloomington, Decatur, Southern Illinois. Illinois 2 from Beloit is Black Hawk Trail through Rock River valley to Moline.

Railroads: Illinois Central, Chicago & North Western, Burlington, Milwaukee.

Information and Accommodations: Rockford Morning Star, Rockford Register-Republic; 4 weeklies. Rockford Chamber of Commerce, 634 E. State St. Chicago Motor Club, 522 N. Main St. More than 2,000 rooms in 40-odd hotels and motels. Special cuisine in Sweden House, Hoffman House. More than 130 churches, 30 denominations; Rockford is seat of Roman Catholic Diocese for Northern Illinois. There are 4 radio stations and 2 television stations.

Recreation: There are 87 units of land totaling 2,366 acres supervised by the Rockford Park District. These include two 18-hole golf courses, and one 9-hole course, 30 tennis courts, 7 wading pools, 6 football fields, a ski-lift, 2 toboggan chutes, 2 outdoor swimming pools, 8 baseball diamonds, 60 softball diamonds, and 2 lighted outdoor basketball courts. The Board of Education operates 25 gymnasiums, 9 indoor swimming pools, a football and track stadium. On the southwest edge of Rockford is Gayle Park, where the Junior Pony League plays during the summer, and the Illinois Junior Pony League championships are played at the end of the season.

There are 3 private golf courses: Rockford Country Club, Forest Hills Country Club. All have outdoor swimming pools, as do the University Club, Jewish Community Center, Spring Brook Swim Club, Tullock Woods Community pool, and the new Surf Club.

Hospitals and Health Care: Four hospitals, 896 beds, 113 bassinets, St. Anthony's Swedish American, Municipal Tuberculosis Sanitarium, Rockford Memorial. Singer Zone Center, a State mental hospital. Senior Citizens Activity Center.

Cultural Activities: Rockford Symphony Orchestra, winter months. Junior Symphony Orchestra, summer concerts in Sinissippi Park. Mendelssohn Club, Community Concert Assn., WREX Theater Assn., Svea Soner Society, Rockford Men Singers, Barber Shop Quartet. Dramatic offerings fall and winter by Center Players, Fine Arts Guild, Community Players. Principal auditorium, National Guard Armory, seats 5,300; one theater seats 800.

Annual Events include Home Show, Hobby & Antique Show, Mexican Festival, Kiwanis Club Pancake Day, Lions Club Rose Day, Greenwich Village Fair, 4-H Fair, Fly-in at Greater Rockford Airport (7 day air festival).

ROCKFORD (690 to 860 ft. alt., 147,370 pop. 1970; 126,706, 1960. inc. 16.3%) seat of Winnebago County, is the second largest city in Illinois. It is bisected by the Rock River, 17 *m.* south of the Wisconsin line, 84 *m.* west of Chicago and 92 *m.* east of East Dubuque and the Mississippi River. It has access to Interstate 90, toll expressway to Chicago, and is on the north-south US 51. Favored by its location in the panoramic Rock River Valley, it has remained a desirable residential city despite the spread of huge industrial plants from its southern areas. Originally successful as a distributing center for livestock and farm products, it became a manufacturer of farm implements and then grew into the largest maker of machine tools in the country. By 1970 14 large organizations were making machine tools; 24 others were making special types of machinery; 18 were making precision screw machine parts; among more than 500 plants operations included designing and making dies, gages, jigs and fixtures; internal, external and surface grinding machines, and plastic molds; fabricating steel, casting precision tools, making experimental models and prototypes, weldings. As a producer of screw products, foundry materials, automobile and airplane accessories and air-conditioning appliances, Rockford gained high rank among the nation's industries, while its furniture, made by Swedish craftsmen who started coming in 1852, became famous for its quality.

Rockford was named for the shallow rock-bottomed ford used by the Chicago-Galena stagecoach line before any settlement existed here. Winnebago County bears an Indian tribal name meaning fish-eater. The County (246,623 pop. 1970; 209,765, 1960, inc. 17.6%) has as its next largest community the unincorporated North Park in Harlem Township, (15,679 pop. 1970). Near Rockford are the city of Love's Park (12,394 pop. 1970, 9,086, 1960); Ken Rock, uninc. (5,945 pop. 1970) and West End, uninc. (7,554 pop. 1970). Rockford has an aldermanic form of government, with a mayor, twenty aldermen, and other major officials elected for four-year terms.

Rockford can testify that many of its small machine shops grew to national stature without deserting their place of origin. This is attributed to two factors—stability of the work force, and ability to raise capital at home, both considered characteristic of the stolid Scandinavian character. Thus Amerock Corp., which began in 1929 with 10 employees, now has up to 1,600; Barber-Colman, with 40 employees in 1903, now uses up to 4,000; National Lock Co., with 8 men in 1903, employs up to 3,000; Atwood Vacuum Machine Co., starting in 1909 with 2, employs 1,400; Sundstrand Corp., with 8 in 1905, employs 3,600. Most of these corporations favor the low, well-lighted plants that blend into the landscape.

Typical of Rockford industrial growth is the career of Ingersoll Milling Machine Co., which started in 1891 with 19 employees and now has approx. 1,500 in Rockford, and many others in foreign subsidiaries.

Ingersoll gave a new definition to the term machine tool. Ingersoll's main work is to build machines to order. In 1965 it formed Ingersoll, Inc. (Advanced Manufacturing Strategies) and sent salesmen abroad to study the market for automation and design tools that Rockford could produce on order. The size and weight of a gigantic tool does not inhibit Ingersoll; for example, a machine for milling parts for turbine generators may rise to a height of three stories and cost even more than it weighs. Ingersoll now has control of two machine-tool companies in West Germany and a partnership with the largest machine-tool maker in Great Britain.

There are many names of Swedish derivation in Rockford, but most of the citizens are several generations removed from the 19th century immigrants. The Census of 1970 reported Rockford had 118,406 American citizens born of American parents, 21,563 Americans with some mixed parentage, and 7,279 foreign born. Of the foreign stock, 9,146 Swedish, 2,322 German, 1,813 Polish, and 5,604 Italian beginnings, the last were the most recent arrivals.

The Census of 1970 also reported that 61,161 were employed, of whom 23,755 were women. Of the total, 26,170 were employed in industry and 11,878 in wholesale and retail trade 10,955 in clerical work (8,727 women) and 8,801 in professional-technical occupations. Out of the male labor force of 38,682 only 1,276 or 3.3% were unemployed.

Founded in 1834 by Germanicus Kent and Thatcher Blake of Galena, Rockford was settled mainly by New Englanders. Kent dammed a tributary of the Rock River, and erected a sawmill to cut the virgin timber that was to become homes for the settlers. Kent and Blake were followed in 1835 by Daniel Haight, who founded a small rival settlement across the river. The two communities incorporated as the town of Rockford in 1839.

Winnebago County was organized in 1836, and Rockford chosen as the seat in 1839 after a spirited contest with other settlements. Early comers thought the Rock River navigable, but because of rapids and shallow water between Rockford and Rock Island, only two steamers ever docked here.

The first years of the 1850's marked the beginning of Rockford's industrialization. Four major events started this: the Chicago & Galena Union Railroad reached the town; the Rockford Water Power Company was founded; the wooden dam across the bed of the old ford was replaced by a permanent one, and an L-shaped millrace greatly increased space for factories and warehouses. Also important to Rockford's progress was the arrival in 1853 of John H. Manny. Inventor of a combination reaper and mower, Manny joined the local firm of Clark & Utter and turned out 150 machines the first year. The following year the machine was considerably improved by a new method of tempering knife sections in oil. Producing 1,100 reapers and mowers in 1854, the Rockford plant became competition for Cyrus H. McCormick, the Chicago reaper maker. When McCormick sued Manny for $400,000 for infringement of patent rights on the reaper in the US District Court in

Chicago, Manny, who already had retained Edwin M. Stanton as counsel, also retained Abraham Lincoln with a retainer of $500. The suit was changed to Cincinati and Lincoln was informed he would not be needed. When the original Manny Company was absorbed by the J. I. Case Company in 1928, it was capitalized at $50,000,000.

Other firms manufactured plows, pumps, cultivators, and horse-power threshing machines. After the Civil War industries became more diversified. In 1870 John Nelson and W. W. Burson founded Rockford's hosiery business. Important inventions in the trade, including the first fully automatic machine, were installed here.

Swedish settlement dates from 1852, the year the Chicago & Galena Union Railroad was completed to Rockford. The story goes that the Swedes bought tickets to the end of the line, which happened to be Rockford. Following their native craft and working on a cooperative basis, they established Rockford's furniture industry. The depression of 1893 wiped out the co-operatives, but the industry was re-established with private capital, and continues to thrive.

POINTS OF INTEREST

For more than 100 years ROCKFORD COLLEGE operated in the ivy-covered brick buildings of a traditional campus in the heart of town; then, in 1964, it moved to a completely new plant of contemporary style on the eastern outskirts. Founded in 1847 as Rockford Seminary for women, it was extended to a college in 1892 and admitted men in 1950. The new campus of 304 acres has an entrance at 5050 East State St. (US 20). The original buildings dating from 1852 were sold in 1967.

Rockford has two regular semesters, fall and spring; an 8-week Summer Session, and Evening Sessions with courses leading to degrees. It has advantages for students wishing to teach, and its degree of Master of Arts in Teaching is available to successful teachers and graduates. The honor system prevails and students sit on the Student Judicial Board, which considers violations and appeals. Enrollments are kept low and balanced between men and women; in the fall, 1970, Rockford had 1,600 students and a faculty of 108. Tuition is $1,900; room and board are $1,100 approximately.

The campus is rolling and the Howard Colman Library stands on the tallest elevation as symbolic of its importance; taller buildings are placed in valleys so as not to dominate it. The library has room for 210,000 vols., has seats for 540, 270 at individual carrels. There are a rare book room, music rooms, a room for typing, etc., and the Frank E. Maynard Foreign Language Laboratory, equipped with electronic devices.

Fisher Memorial Chapel is unique in its equipment, which can serve the ritualistic requirements of Jewish, Roman Catholic, and Protestant groups. It seats 200 and can accommodate a 60-voice choir.

The whole college community may dine, visit, play games, and relax in the Blanche Walker Burpee Center. An addition built in 1970 provides quarters for student publications, student government, television viewing and record playing.

The new Science Building contains, among its many facilities, a greenhouse and nuclear storage space. The Seaver Physical Education Building is fully equipped with a basketball court, swimming pool for classes, quarters for classes in dance, gymnastics and other exercise.

The new class and lecture halls reflect the results of experience in building. Henry Scarborough Hall, a 2-level seminar center has each room with a seminar table seating up to 15 and the professor on a lower level. Built-in desks on a raised level around the area can serve up to 35 students. Severson Auditorium is in this building. Clark Arts Center has the Maddox Theatre, seating 570 and capable of providing four different stages via hydraulic lift. The smaller Cheek Experimental Theatre is used for student productions. Other quarters are for music and dance, sculpture, ceremics and applied arts. There is also an art gallery.

The Residence Halls follow several patterns in which groups of buildings are connected by corridors with a living center for general social life. The Kent-Johnson Complex has 7 halls, each accomodating 43 students, and special facilities, such as country kitchen, group study room and common living room on each floor. The Cummings Complex has 4 halls, each for 42, and a living center. The 7-story hall for 210 women completed in 1969 is located in a maple woods at the far end of the campus drive.

Among the honors and awards given by Rockford College is the Jane Addams Medal for a distinguished career. It commemorates the work of Miss Addams, founder of Hull House Settlement, Chicago, who was an alumna of Rockford.

ROCK VALLEY JUNIOR COLLEGE won an immediate welcome when it opened its courses to students in 1965, although without permanent quarters. It was the response of Winnebago County to the invitation of the State Board to participate in the establishment of two-year community colleges in Illinois. By fall 1970, Rock Valley was enrolling 2,898 students and had a faculty of 104. Like other junior colleges it filled a gap for students who could afford only a two-year program; others found it a convenient stepping-stone to the four-year college.

THE ROCKFORD SCHOOL OF MEDICINE opened at 1601 Parkview Ave., in the fall of 1972 with a three-year clinical curriculum. It is a unit of the University of Illinois and directly affiliated with its Chicago Medical Center.

Two privately operated institutions for vocational training are the ROCKFORD SCHOOL OF BUSINESS and its subsidiary, the ROCKFORD SCHOOL OF ENGINEERING. The former gives the degree of associate in arts in finance, accounting, sales management, production management, and secretarial courses, and teaches use of business machines. It has dormitories for men and women on Park Ave. and N. Church St. In 1961 it opened the Rockford School of Engineering to give courses in production management, motion and time study, slide rule, drafting, electronics and automation, for 200 students.

Public education in Rockford is notable for its buildings of recent construction and special facilities. Guilford High School, in the northeast section, and Auburn High in the northwest, are examples of modern school construction. The public school system has 4 senior high schools, 5 junior high schools, night schools with classes in secondary and vocational subjects for adults, and summer school. Public health services include correction of defects as well as preventive methods; there are programs for the handicapped and metally retarded. Atwood Park, south of Rockford and one-half mile east of New Milford, is administered by the Board of Education for its Outdoor Education Center, with lodging for 60 persons. During the school year day and week-long classes relating studies to nature are held here.

The ROCKFORD PUBLIC LIBRARY, 215 N. Wyman St., established in 1872 and occupying since 1903 a building donated by Andrew Carnegie, has operated in a completely modernized main building since 1969, when the Carnegie Library was remodeled and enlarged. It has five branches and a bookmobile that serves the environs. It has available more than 275,000 vols. and an average annual circulation of 1,110,326. There are also more than 10,000 discs, 1,700 filmstrips, 8,000 color slides and about 1,200 films. Its influence in the promotion of libraries and reading is tremendous, for it is the headquarters of the Northern Illinois Library System, a cooperative of 56 libraries in a 12-county area, covering more than 5,000 *sq. m.* and serving more than 700,000 people.

The ERLANDER HOME MUSEUM, 404 S. Third St., is owned and maintained by the Swedish Historical Society of Rockford. It is a two-story, 14-room brick house that was built by a Swedish immigrant family named Erlander in 1871, and exemplifies the taste and prosperity of the last decades of the 19th century. Mary Erlander, last survivor of the family, lived in the house for 80 years until August 1, 1951. When opened to the public April 6, 1952, it was dedicated by the Prime Minister of Sweden, Tege Erlander.

Its furnishings are largely of Rockford make, including examples of the furniture that set the Rockford style, dating back to 1853 and 1856. The library contains many old books, some brought here by Swedish immigrants. There are also more than 1,500 artifacts of regional origin. *Open Sunday afternoons and to groups by appointment.*

The FEDERAL BUILDING, S. Main and Green Sts., completed in 1933, is a three-story structure of white limestone and granite, adorned with Corinthian columns. The floors of the main and outer lobbies are of Tennessee marble; walls of the main lobby of St. Genevieve rose marble. The first floor is occupied by the U. S. Post Office, U. S. Army, the U. S. Navy and other official bodies.

The TINKER SWISS COTTAGE, 311 Kent St., was built by Robert Tinker in 1865, following a sojourn in Switzerland. Reached by a suspension bridge across Kent Creek, the 26-room cottage contains curios collected by Tinker in Europe and the South Seas, as well as many early American pieces from the Manny home. The hexagonal library, with its carved spiral stairway, is patterned after that in Sir Walter Scott's house, Abbottsford. Given to Rockford by its owner, the house is open to the public.

The BURPEE ART GALLERY (10-5 *weekdays;* 2-5 *Sundays; free*), 737 N. Main St., headquarters of the Rockford Art Association, provides a meeting place for handicraft, literary, and little theatre groups. Surrounded on three sides by a broad veranda and surmounted by a cupola, the Victorian house has been adapted to its present use from the home of John Nelson, local hosiery mill executive. Its exhibits include a small collection of paintings and it provides rooms for traveling exhibitions.

The ROCKFORD NEWS TOWER, 98 E. State St., consists of a two-story main section, surmounted by a six-story tower. On the river level are the news and press rooms of the Rockford *Morning Star* and the Rockford *Register-Republic.*

BEATTIE PARK, bounded by Park Ave., N. Main St., Mound Ave., and the river, contains Turtle Mound, of the rare effigy type, two small round mounds, and an oblong one. In accordance with the donor's wishes none has been excavated. Turtle Mound is an unexplained misnomer, as the mound has the form of a lizard. The sprawling 150-ft. figure stands 6 ft. high, despite erosion, and is surpassed in size only by the great serpentine mound in Ohio.

The BURPEE NATURAL HISTORY MUSEUM, in the Rockford Park District Bldg., 813 N. Main St., has collections of artifacts from excavations and other discoveries in the Woodland Indian culture.

ROCK CUT STATE PARK, north of Rockford and located between US 51 and Int. 90, is combined with Pierce Lake as a recreation area.

Rock Island, Moline, East Moline
with Davenport, Iowa, the Quad Cities

Air Services: United Air Lines and Ozark Air Lines, daily scheduled flights at Quad-City Airport, 4 *m.* south of Moline, on US 6, US 150, Int. 74. More than 32 flights daily, 250,000 passengers annually. Moline Seaplane Base, 3.5 *m.* south of Moline, operated by Flying Country Club, Inc. Rock River surface runway, 5,000 x 400 ft.

Highways: US 6 is a direct multilane route from Chicago to Moline and thence across the Mississippi River to Iowa. Interstate 80 parallels US 6 and bypasses its cities; west of Geneseo it turns north and is routed across the Mississippi from Rapids City, Ill. to Le Claire, Iowa. Its traffic is taken up by Interstate 74, which crosses the Rock River to Moline near the Quad-City Airport, thence crosses the Mississippi to Bettendorf, Iowa, on the Iowa & Illinois Memorial Bridge. Illinois 92, combined with Illinois 2, comes down the Black Hawk Trail to Silvis, East Moline, Moline and Rock Island, then goes south. Illinois 84, the Great River Road, comes down the east bank of the Mississippi. Illinois 150 comes from the south to Moline. US 67, from central Illinois, crosses the Rock River near Milan to Rock Island, crosses the Mississippi on the Centennial Bridge to Davenport, Iowa, proceeds west as US 61. US 150 from Bloomington, Peoria, Galesburg, crosses the Rock River east of the Airport and joins Int. 74 in Moline and across the Memorial Bridge. Int. 280, a continuation of Int. 74, remains on the south side of the Rock River and is expected to cross the Mississippi to Iowa on a new bridge.

Buses: Black Hawk Motor Transit Co. and Burlington Trailways, Rock Island; Greyhound Bus Lines, Crown Transit, and Scenic Stage Lines, Moline and East Moline.

Railroads: Rock Island, Burlington, Milwaukee, D. R. I. & W.

Information and Accommodations: Rock Island *Argus,* evening, 1724 Fourth Ave., Rock Island. Moline *Dispatch,* evening, 1720 Fifth Ave., Moline. *Davenport Times-Democrat,* Davenport, Iowa. Rock Island Chamber of Commerce, 1910 Third Ave. Moline Chamber of Commerce, 622 19th St. Chicago Motor Club, 1908 Third Ave., Rock Island. East Moline and Silvis Chamber of Commerce, East Moline. The Quad-City Development Group, Rock Island.

ROCK ISLAND, MOLINE and EAST MOLINE are three industrial cities in northwestern Illinois that contribute approximately 120,000 people to a two-state concentration of more than 360,000 population, known as the QUAD CITIES. The fourth and largest unit of the group is DAVENPORT, Iowa, which occupies the northern bank of the Mississippi River at the only place where the river flows from east to west. It accounts for nearly 100,000 population.

The U. S. Census for 1970 reported that Rock Island, seat of Rock Island County, had 50,166 pop., as compared with 51,863 in 1960. Moline had 46,237, up 8.3% from 42,705 in 1960. East Moline had

20,832 up 24.5% from 16,732 in 1960. The return for Rock Island County was 166,734 up 10.4% from 150,991 in 1960. Davenport reported 98,469 pop. in 1970, up from 88,981 in 1960. The two central counties, Rock Island in Illinois and Scott in Iowa have 900 *sq. m.*

The great influence of this conglomerate extends far beyond its municipalities. Adjoining East Moline is SILVIS, 5,907 pop. 1970; 3,973, 1960, with manufacturing plants and workers' homes. On the Iowa side BETTENDORF, 22,126 pop. 1970; 11,534, 1960, an industrial city connected with Moline by the Iowa and Illinois Memorial Bridge, contributes heavily to the economy of the group and is sometimes included in the term Quint Cities.

The U. S. Census of 1970 located one of the largest metropolitan statistical areas of Illinois in the Quad Cities. It reached its total of 362,638 population by including Davenport and Scott County, Iowa, which accounted for 142,687 of the total.

Rock Island had 43,603 persons of native American parentage, 5,482 American-born who had one parent who was either foreign-born or foreign-American born, and 1,153 foreign-born. Moline had 37,000 American-born, 7,312 of mixed parentage, and 1,993 foreign-born. Davenport had 87,169 native Americans, 9,256 of mixed parentage, and 2,056 foreign-born. Moline had the most Swedish stock, 2,405, Davenport the most German, 4,511. The largest number of blacks lived in Rock Island, 10.2% of that city's total population, whereas Moline had

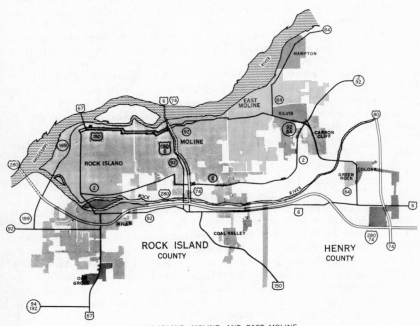

ROCK ISLAND, MOLINE, AND EAST MOLINE

Illinois Dept. of Transportation

1% and Davenport 4.2%. Few persons of Puerto Rican origin had reached the Quad Cities: Davenport had 55, Moline 22, and Rock Island 8.

Rock Island, Moline and East Moline constitute the hub of farm implement manufacturing in the United States. When John Deere produced the plow that broke the hard black soil of Illinois he also made Moline the capital of a huge industry that has expanded across the country and into foreign parts. Today the Administrative Center of the John Deere Corp. controls a great organization from Moline, while the International Harvester Company has two of its largest plants in Rock Island and East Moline. The Farmall Works in Rock Island covers 72 acres and employs an average of 4,400. It was here that International Harvester produced its 4-millionth Farmall all-purpose tractor. The East Moline Works has 156 acres on the banks of the Mississippi River, employs up to 3,000 and produces combines, corn pickers, beet harvesters, forage harvesters, mowers and much other equipment. Both plants may be visited Monday through Friday, 7:30-4.

Another element of growth is the U. S. Government Arsenal on the island of Rock Island, which lies in the Mississippi River across the front yard of the two cities, and the normal employment of 4,000 to 6,000 works in its military equipment shops.

The Port of Rock Island is a large and prosperous river shipping center. The Inland Waterways Corporation of the Government started the Federal Barge Line in 1927. Rock Island was considered the logical site for the terminal of the Quad Cities by the Corporation. Clinton had an opportunity to become a terminal but voted down the bond issue. Rock Island voters accepted it three to one and completed the terminal in 1931 at a cost of $380,000. This was well before the completion of the 9-ft. channel, made possible by the construction of 26 locks and dams on the Upper Mississippi, of which No. 15 is located at Rock Island. A floating wharf barge, 230 ft. long and 40 ft. wide, was installed at the terminal. It was built in Jeffersonville, Indiana, and towed to Rock Island. Towboats of 1,000 to 5,000 hp haul oil, coal, grain and manufactured goods. Oil companies also have their own tankers.

Barge line tonnage of commodities moved through Lock and Dam No. 15 at Rock Island in 1972 was 17,978,089, according to the Rock Island District, Corps of Engineers, USA. Traffic in the Rock Island District was reported by the Corps of Engineers to have reached 25,484,821 tons in 1972, the record, and increasing.

The Government disposed of the Federal Barge Line in 1953 to avoid competition with private shipping lines. It is now a subsidiary of Pott Industries, Inc., which has one of its principal offices in Davenport and reports large returns from barge operations.

The business and industrial areas of Rock Island and Moline lie on the flat plain that borders the Mississippi; behind it rise bluffs occupied by dwellings. Several miles to the south limestone cliffs stop abruptly at the Rock River, which flows west to meet the Mississippi below Rock Island. The Hennepin Canal, officially the Illinois &

Mississippi Canal, joins the Rock River in this area but is no longer used commercially. The flat fields south of the Rock River were the last seat of the Sauk and Fox Indians before they were forcibly pushed out of Illinois by the white settlers in 1832.

HISTORY

The first settlement on the south bank of the Mississippi was called Farnhamsburg, then Stephenson. George Davenport started a ferry there in 1825. In 1835 it was platted and on October 21, 1837, was incorporated as a town. The name lasted less than four years for on February 27, 1841, it received a charter as a city and was named Rock Island and seat of Rock Island County.

Moline had settlers as early as 1829 and when a man named Stephens came from St. Louis with 20 slaves a warrant was issued for his arrest and he hurried south. The narrow channel produced water power; in 1837 the Illinois legislature authorized a dam in the south channel and another to Benham's Island above the island of Rock Island. John W. Spence and David B. Sears built a sawmill, planing and shingle mill, sash and blind factory; in 1844 Sears introduced six runs of French burr stones for milling grain. The place was known as Milltown; in 1843 it was platted as Moline, a corruption of *moulin* (mill); in 1848 it was incorporated as a town and in 1872 became a city. East Moline began as an overflow of workers from the Moline plants; it was organized in 1902-03 and as a city has a faster rate of growth than Moline.

Spoken every day in the marts of trade, Rock Island is the name of a railroad, a county and a municipal unit of the Quad Cities, but the origin of the name is a limestone island owned by the United States Government and referred to as the site of Rock Island Arsenal. This has 946 acres, is 2½ miles long and ¾ of a mile wide, and is separated from Moline and a segment of Rock Island (city) by a shallow slough that is not navigable. On May 10, 1816, Colonel William Lawrence arrived with a detachment of the United States Army to establish a fort on the western end of the island, where it commanded a broad sweep of river and hills. This outpost in Indian country—land used by the Sauk and Fox, Winnebago and Potawatomi tribes—was named Fort Armstrong, honoring John Armstrong, secretary of war under President Madison.

Major Stephen H. Long, U. S. Corps of Engineers, best known for his expedition to the Rocky Mountains, where he discovered Long's Peak, stopped at the new Fort Armstrong in 1817. He described it as 300 ft. long, with two-story blockhouses 21 to 26 ft square, at three corners. The sides of the fort were the rear walls of barracks and storage buildings, with space between the buildings closed by walls of stone about 8 ft. high, supporting a breastwork of timber 5 ft. high. On the two open sides stood two buildings 64 ft. long and 16 ft. wide, with four rooms each for officer's quarters. In the corner between the buildings was a two-story structure with wings and piazzas on both sides, for the commanding officer and offices. Outside the fort were a smithy, sutler's and contractor's stores, and a stable.

Traders and settlers moved in around Fort Armstrong in the 1820s, and land speculators appeared along the river. George Davenport and Russell Farnham acquired land on the site of Rock Island and ran a trader's store at the stockade. An act of the General Assembly in 1831 established the County of Rock Island from Jo Daviess County, incorporating the island in it. In 1831 the Sauk and Fox Indians, who lived along the Rock River, were raiding other tribes and the settlers petitioned for protection. General Edward P. Gaines was ordered up from Jefferson Barracks, St. Louis, with six companies of Regulars, and Captain B. F. Bike organized 58 men as the Rock River Rangers. When Governor Reynolds called for volunteers 1,600 farmers responded at Beardstown on June 10, 1831. They were provisioned by Fort Armstrong, which used the steamboat *Virginia*. Brig. General Joseph Duncan camped with 1,000 horses on the river bank where the city now stands and when the boat arrived with blasts of steam the horses stampeded. The show of force impressed the Indians and on June 30, 1831. Black Hawk agreed to remain west of the Misssissippi with his people, and the farmers went back to their plowing and the militia went home.

In April, 1832, Black Hawk recrossed the Mississippi with his warriors and the alarm of the settlers began anew. The Indians went to the village of The Prophet, a chief named White Cloud, who was warning the Indians that the whites were out to destroy them. Governor Reynolds once more called for volunteers, and the Federal Government alerted the Army. General Henry Atkinson was ordered to take command at Fort Armstrong and Captain Phillip Kearny was sent to order Black Hawk to observe his treaty and return to Iowa. Three hundred mounted volunteers gathered at Beardstown, among them Abraham Lincoln.

Black Hawk stood his ground and the resulting war was the shortest and cruelest in American history. The army chased the Indians into Wisconsin and routed them at Bad Axe on the Mississippi. When the Indians tried to swim to safety through a group of islands the steamboat *Warrior*, loaded with riflemen, churned the waters among them and the soldiers picked them off. More than 600 are supposed to have died in the flight. Years later farmers of the area conducted a dance hall called Battle Assembly on one of the islands.

In 1834 Dr. John Emerson came from St. Louis to Fort Armstrong to be post surgeon and brought with him a Negro slave named Dred Scott. In 1836 Dr. Emerson moved to Fort Snelling in Wisconsin Territory and took Scott with him. Some years later Scott returned to St. Louis and anti-slavery agitators made him plaintiff in several court actions, asserting that his stay on free soil in Illinois had made him a free man. The suit reached the U. S. Supreme Court, which, under the leadership of Chief Justice of the United States Roger B. Taney, rendered a decision that Dred Scott had remained a slave while on free soil. This sharpened a vital issue and was denounced by Abraham Lincoln in his debates with Stephen A. Douglas in 1858.

The Chicago & Rock Island Railroad reached Rock Island in 1854. In 1855 it completed a railroad bridge from the Government island to Davenport, on the Iowa bank of the Mississippi, the first of its kind. On April 22, 1856, Rock Island gave a civic welcome to the first train that crossed the bridge. On April 22, 1956, Rock Island observed the centennial of that event. The bridge had been denounced as an invention of the devil by steamboat interests. Two weeks after the celebration May 6, 1856, the steamer *Effie Afton* struck the bridge and burned. The steamboat owners sued the Rock Island railroad for damages. Abraham Lincoln was counsel for the railroad and argued in court in Chicago that the steamboat's starboard wheel had gone dead before the crash. The jury was deadlocked and the steamboat owner dropped the suit.

In the middle of the 19th century, especially from 1850 to 1890, Rock Island was the most active river port in Illinois. The use of the river for transportation began with the shipment of lead to St. Louis from the mines of the Fever River area around Galena, which filled the Upper Mississippi with steamboats. When the sawmills were cutting up the forests of the north, huge rafts were floating down to Rock Island, where the mills of Weyerhauser, Denkman and other pioneer lumbermen were making planks, beams, shingles, sash and doors to meet the demands for housing in the Midwest.

The arrival of the Chicago & Rock Island Railroad on February 22, 1854, made Rock Island the terminal for great waves of immigrants seeking farm land.

The first comers, from New England and the eastern states, were looking for homesteads. After the Franco-Prussian War of 1870-71 waves of German immigrants came this way. Another result of this improved transportation was the rail and steamboat excursion. Hardly had the first train reached the Mississippi when eastern promotors proclaimed the delight of western travel.

In *Steamboating on the Upper Mississippi* William J. Petersen has described "the Grand Excursion of 1854." This included many well knowns, and some soon to become known. Millard Fillmore, former President, was in the group; also Edward Bates, a future member of Lincoln's cabinet, and Samuel J. Tilden, who was to win the popular vote for President in 1876 and lose the election. Also present were John A. Dix, Elbridge Gerry, George Bancroft, Thurlow Weed, Charles A. Dana, Samuel Bowles, and Catherine Sedgwick. The party boarded two Rock Island trains at Chicago at 8 a.m. and after stops for speechmaking reached Rock Island at 4 p.m. Five steamboats were ready to carry the travelers to the Falls of St. Anthony, but two others had to be added. Petersen says there were welcoming speeches at Rock Island and Davenport, to which Fillmore responded. When the steamboats cast off bells rang, whistles blew, and Fort Armstrong shot off fireworks.

The U. S. Army had evacuated Fort Armstrong in 1836. It remained as a storehouse for army supplies. During 1837-38 it had the office of Joseph M. Street, Sauk & Fox agent. In 1840-45 it was used as a Government armory. On Oct. 7, 1855 it was maliciously set on fire and all but two blockhouses burned down. All this time there had been agitation to continue it as a Government post but Congress did not appropriate the money needed. However, the Government had been clearing its title to the island by buying up claims and cleaning out squatters. Therefore, when the Civil War came and places had to be found to accommodate Confederate prisoners, the War Department chose this island. In July, 1863, it built a stockade and wooden shelters, and from then through 1865 12,215 Confederate prisoners were confined there. Many came from the battles around Lookout Mountain. A total of 1,960 died, 500 from smallpox.

In 1864 the Government erected the first permanent building for the Rock Island Arsenal, a monumental stone structure with a tall clock tower at the west end of the island. Its clock has four faces, each 12ft. in diameter. The minute hands are 6 ft. long and the hour hands 5 ft. The faces and hands are carved from wood. The pendulum is 30 ft. long. This is now the headquarters of the Army Weapons Command and the Rock Island District of the U. S. Army Corps of Engineers.

In the center of the island the Government erected eight four-story stone buildings and in 1865 began making equipment for the United States Army. It became the largest employer in the area, using 4,000 to 6,000 in normal times and expanding during wartime to as much as 15,000 employees. There are now 200 buildings and the functions include production and servicing of military tools and weapons; research and production of artillery weapons and components; basic research on rubber, corrosion, gaskets, greases and packaging; tank overhaul, and training of 5,000 management engineering students annually.

On the island is the John M. Browning Memorial Museum, with exhibits of ancient and modern weapons. *Open 11-4, Wednesday through Sunday.* There is also the monument to General T. J. Rodman, first commandant of the Arsenal. There are two cemeteries, Confederate and U. S. Army. On the north bank is the restored house of Colonel George Davenport. The Arsenal is open to the public and a tour guide with maps may be obtained at the entrance gates.

POINTS OF INTEREST

AUGUSTANA COLLEGE is located on nearly 100 acres of the rolling hills of Rock Island, where the classical dome of its Old Main facing Seventh Ave., has been a conspicuous landmark for more than 75 years. Augustana College & Theological Seminary was founded in Chicago before the Civil War, moved to Paxton, Ill., in 1863, and to Rock Island in 1875. The seminary became a separate institution in 1948 and moved to the Chicago area in 1967. Since 1962 the college has been associated with the Lutheran Church in America. In 1973 it enrolled 2,174 students and had a faculty of 138.

Augustana offers courses leading to baccalaureate degrees in the arts, music, music education and medical technology. There are pre-professional studies in Christian ministry, dentistry, engineering, law, medicine, nursing, physiotherapy, pharmacy and veterinary medicine. Students can attend semesters on the United Nations and the U. S. Government, and summer programs in Germany, France, and Spain. Tuition and board and room in a residence hall total $975 for a quarter of 12 weeks.

The campus has been embellished in recent years with buildings of architectural distinction. Centennial Hall seats nearly 2,000 and its Croswell Memorial Pipe Organ is noted among such instruments. The Augustana Art Gallery is located here. The John Deere Planetarium, completed in 1969, has a Spitz A-3-P projector, while the Carl Gamble Observatory has a 6-in. Zeiss refracting telescope with a deck accommodating 40 persons. Founders Hall is dominated by Ascension Chapel. New Science Hall contains the Fryxell Geology Museum and a library with 35,000 maps of diversified scientific subjects. The new, modern Physical Education Center is a 1971 addition to athletic facilities and adjoins Ericson Field, where the Vikings compete in intercollegiate contests.

Some of Augustana's richest treasures are contained in the Denkmann Memorial Library, which was rededicated on October 17, 1969, after the remodeling and expanding of the original structure of 1911. Today it has more than 155,000 volumes and room for 240,000, while its seating capacity is 500. Special collections include 4,000 volumes about revolutionary Europe of 1789-1848, donated by King Charles XV of Sweden; the Spencer collection of first editions of English and American literature, and the John Hauberg collection of the history of the Upper Mississippi Valley and especially of the Sauk and Fox Indians. There is also a collection of black literature.

BLACK HAWK JUNIOR COLLEGE is one of the new 2-year colleges that have been organized in recent decades with the help of the State. It was authorized in 1946 and in 1969 moved to a new campus on John Deere Road, Moline, and began erecting study halls of modern collegiate design. In 1970 it reported attendance of 2,550 students; by 1973 it enrolled 3,458 and had a faculty of 210.

The QUAD CITIES GRADUATE CENTER was opened in the fall, 1969. It is a consortium of nine colleges and universities in Illinois and Iowa, which offers a master's degree in education, engineering, and business administration.

PUBLIC LIBRARIES offer extensive facilities for reading, research, audio-visual viewing, and inter-library loans. The public libraries of Rock Island, Moline, and East Moline, are members of the River Bend Library System, which uses Moline as its headquarters library, although its executive offices are in Coal Valley. Rock Island and Moline have approximately the same number of volumes and a similar circulation; Rock Island in 1972 had more than 130,000 volumes and a circulation of 313,000; Moline had 123,000 and a circulation of more than 314,000. East Moline, with 37,693 volumes, gets a circulation of 141,288. These libraries obtain 16mm films through the Quad-City

Scott County Film Cooperative. The Moline Public Library was founded in 1873 and opened its Carnegie building in 1904; in 1965 its interior was completely modernized.

Residents of the Quad Cities also have access to the libraries of Davenport, which include the Davenport Public Library, which has more than 200,000 books and an annual circulation of around 600,000; the Davenport Public Museum, with 50,000 books of historic interest; the Grant Law Library in the Scott County Court House, with 12,000 vols., and the libraries of Marycrest College, Scott Community College, St. Ambrose College, Palmer Junior College and the art reference library of the Davenport Municipal Art Gallery.

The DAVENPORT HOUSE is the restored house built by Colonel George Davenport in 1833 on the north bank of Rock Island when he had a trading post at Fort Armstrong. One of the earliest settlers, he built his first house in 1816. He laid claim to a quarter section of the island and farmed it, offering the United States Government $1.25 an acre, but it took him 10 years with the help of Senator Stephen A. Douglas to get title to the property. It was held by the Davenport family until 1867, when the Government liquidated all claims on the island and paid $40,740 for it.

The house is a two-story frame structure with rooms balanced on two sides of the central hall. It was neglected for nearly 100 years before its historical significance was prized and the ruin had to be substantially rebuilt. It was in the original house that Colonel Davenport was murdered on July 4, 1845.

Davenport was a fur trader, army supplier, and land speculator of considerable enterprise, who came to the island in 1816, the year Colonel William Lawrence arrived with U.S. troops to build Fort Armstrong. With his partner Farnham Davenport bought land, and in 1825 operated the first ferry. During the Black Hawk war he helped supply the troops and Governor Reynolds named him colonel in the Illinois Quartermaster's Department. When General Winfield Scott made the final treaty with the Sauk and Fox Indians across the river in Iowa on September 21, 1833, the Indians were forced to pay $40,000 to Davenport and his associate, Farnham, for goods bought, and Antoine LeClaire, French-Canadian interpreter, received a section of land opposite the fort in Iowa, which he platted and named Davenport.

Colonel Davenport's family had left to attend a patriotic celebration on the afternoon of July 4, 1845, leaving him alone in the house. Seven brigands came by boat and demanded $20,000 in gold he was said to have in his safe. When the safe yielded only $700 they bludgeoned him and left. A stroller heard his moans and brought help but the Colonel died that evening. There had been a rash of such crimes on the frontier and the criminals were known as Banditti of the Prairie. William Bonney, a detective, tracked them down and three of them were publicly hanged. The site of the hanging on 14th St. between 3rd and 4th Aves. in Rock Island is marked.

BLACK HAWK STATE PARK, 205 acres, is located about 4 m. south of Rock Island on the Rock River. Nearby the Sauk and Fox tribes had the largest Indian village in Illinois prior to the Black Hawk War of 1832. Every inch of the soil has historic connotations and Indian artifacts are often found. In front of an impressive Lodge constructed of native stone is a stone statue of Black Hawk. Part of the Lodge is occupied by the HAUBERG INDIAN MUSEUM. Although the settlers forced the Indians out of this area a Sauk and Fox Pow Wow is staged annually during the Labor Day weekend in September, during which Indians demonstrate their mode of life.

DEERE & COMPANY ADMINISTRATIVE CENTER, John Deere Road, Moline, is an architectural achievement by Eero Saarinen, combining an office building, an exhibit building, and an auditorium seating 387. The main entrance to the Center is through the Product Display Building, which offers a complete exposition of farm and other implements made by the company, historical documents, photographs and old advertisements, as well as memorabilia of rural America. The three-dimensional display, Reflections of an Era, organized by Alexander Girard, gives a survey of the tremendous changes that took place in farming and agricultural machinery from the time when John Deere made his first plow in Grand Detour until now, when the world headquarters of Deere & Company demonstrates the far flung influence of American invention and industry. *Tours Monday to Friday, starting at 10:30 a.m. and 1:30 p.m.*

BUTTERWORTH CENTER, Moline, is used for cultural activities related to art, literature, drama, and related subjects the year around. It is located in Hillcrest, the former home of Mrs. William Butterworth, granddaughter of John Deere, who established a trust in memory of her husband and gave this home to the trust.

The ROCK ISLAND COUNTY HISTORICAL SOCIETY MUSEUM of historical memorabilia is located in a 15-room mansion at 822 Eleventh Ave., Moline, once the home of Willard Velie, widely known fifty years ago as maker of the Velie motor car and later of airplanes. In 1914 Velie built one of the big mansions favored by successful manufacturers on the bluffs overlooking Rock River—VILLA VELIE, an Italian-style house of 46 rooms, now occupied by the Plantation Restaurant.

ROCK ISLAND COUNTY COURTHOUSE between 2nd and 3rd Aves. and 14th and 15th Sts., Rock Island, occupies the original site designated for a courthouse in 1835. The present building, dedicated March 31, 1897, was once surmounted by a tall tower; in 1960 the tower was removed and the building remodeled, with a subsequent gain in efficiency.

HAUBERG CIVIC CENTER, 1300 24th St. and 14th Ave., Rock Island, is located in the former home of John H. Hauberg and Susan Denkmann Hauberg, members of the family that participated in founding the Weyerhauser & Denkmann lumber company in Rock Island. Of special interest is the garden maintained by the Men's Rose and Garden Club.

John Henry Hauberg (1869-1955) often called one of the most useful citizens of Rock Island County, was an industrialist and historian, the grandson of German pioneers who began farming in Rock Island County in 1848. When a young man he worked in lumber camps and on a ranch, and won degrees from Valparaiso University in 1897 and from the Law School of the University of Michigan in 1900. He practiced law in Moline and Rock Island, became active in starting Sunday schools and boys' camps, and fought gambling and official corruption. In 1911 he was married to Christine Denkmann and became associated with the management of the Weyerhauser & Denkmann lumber interests, serving on the boards of banks, sash and door works, planing mills, and coal companies in a number of states. He wrote frequently on history of the Black Hawk country. He was president of the Rock Island County Historical Society, equipped the museum erected by the Civilian Conservation Corps at Black Hawk State Park, and founded the annual Indian pow-pow there. He became a director of the Illinois State Historical Society in 1918 and filled several offices until he was elected president in 1941-42. He and Mrs. Hauberg supported YMCA and YWCA activities, including Camp Hauberg for boys near Port Byron and the Archie Allen Camp. He was a member of the Illinois National Guard, the Illinois Red Cross board, the board of Augustana College, and of the Tri-City Symphony Orchestra, and once was president of the Illinois Anti-Saloon League.

The MODERN WOODMEN OF AMERICA has its national headquarters at 230 16th St., Rock Island. This legal-reserve insurance company began its career in Fulton, Whiteside County, in 1884. At that time it was a fraternal insurance company that paid death benefits by dues and assessments of members. As the average age of members became older and deaths increased, new members could not be recruited in sufficient numbers, and assessments on survivors finally became excessive and organizations either changed to legal reserve or closed down. The Illinois State Historical Society has placed a historical marker at the site of the original office of MWA in Fulton.

The GOVERNMENT BRIDGE spans the Mississippi River between Illinois and Iowa and begins at the northwest end of the Arsenal island and extends to Davenport, Iowa. It carries the heaviest traffic in the Quad-City area with pedestrians and vehicles using the lower level and the Rock Island Railway main line the upper. After crossing the tip of the island traffic reaches the city of Rock Island on a viaduct over Sylvan Slough. The first bridge across the Mississippi, made of wood, was opened April 21, 1856, and part of the pier and a marker are located a short distance east. The bridge was built by the railroad company despite opposition from steamboat companies.

CENTENNIAL BRIDGE spans the Mississippi River from 15th St. and 2nd Ave. in Rock Island to Davenport, Iowa. It has a box girder, tiered arch construction. It carries US 67 and connections.

The ROLLER GATE DAM, socalled, is Lock and Dam No. 15 in the series of engineering feats built in 1934 to provide a 9-ft. channel down the Mississippi River. It extends to Davenport below the Government Bridge and consists of 11 metal gates, each weighing 220 tons, that roll back and permit the water to flow underneath them.

The QUAD CITIES NUCLEAR GENERATING STATION, largest in the Midwest, is located on the Illinois bank of the Mississippi River 20 m. north of Moline. It is the principal source of power in the area and throughout the ten-state interconnected Mid-Continent Area Power Planners (MAPP) System. It is a joint product of the Iowa-Illinois Gas & Electric Co. and the Commonwealth Edison Co. of Chicago. It has two generating units, each of 809,000-kilowatt capacity, and cost $160,000,000.

Springfield

Air Services: Ozark Airlines, 25-30 passenger flights, 18 freight, daily; private planes, charter, instruction, at Capital Airport, 1,300 acres, 3.8 *m.* northwest on Walnut St., Illinois 29. Hq. of Illinois Dept. of Aeronautics, Illinois Air National Guard, U.S. Army Air Reserve, U.S. Weather Bureau, Federal Aviation Agency.

Highways: Chicago to Springfield, 193 *m.* fastest route is US 66 combined with Int. 55, which bypasses cities. US 36, east-west, from Decatur also joins Int. 55 and the south bypass. BR 66 goes to center of Springfield, as do Illinois 29, Illinois 54, Illinois 97.

Buses: Southern Greyhound Lines, Eastern Greyhound Lines, Crown Transit Lines, Peoria-Rockford Line, Jacksonville Bus Line, Northeast Missouri Bus Line. Union Bus Station, 2-8 N. Sixth St.

Railroads: Illinois Central Gulf, Norfolk & Western, Chicago & North Western. Some passenger trains on Illinois Central Gulf, others freight.

Information: Illinois State Journal, daily mornings; *Illinois State Register,* daily, evenings. *Springfield Sun,* Fridays. Springfield Assn. of Commerce & Industry, 325 E. Adams St. Greater Springfield Chamber of Commerce, Myers Bldg. Map and guide to city and Lake Springfield by City Water, Light & Power Dept. The Historical and Tourist Development Committee of the Central Area Development Assn., First National Bank Bldg., provides a map and description for *A Walking Tour of Historic Springfield.*

Churches and Schools: 123 churches, all major denominations. The Public School system enrolls about one-third of the public school total in 3 high, 11 elementary schools, 1 area vocational training center. The Roman Catholic parochial school system enrolls about one-third of the public school total in 3 high, 11 elementary schools. The Lutheran Church has 4 elementary schools. There is one elementary school of the Christian Church. Two junior colleges, 1 university.

Recreation and Events: The Park District and Playground & Recreation Commission operate 2 18-hole and 2 9-hole golf courses. There are 3 country clubs for golf; numerous tennis courts, swimming pools, bowling centers, ice-skating rink. The annual Illinois State Fair is held late in August and early in September and has exhibits, of farm products, livestock, horse shows, and harness races. Located on Peoria Road and Branch US 66, north of Sangamon Ave.

Also Springfield Municipal Opera, 3 weeks; Springfield Symphony Orchestra; Springfield Theatre Guild, sponsoring children's plays; Clayville Theatre, plays; annual Beaux Arts ball.

SPRINGFIELD (598 alt., 91,753 pop. 1970; 83,271, 1960, inc. 10.2%) capital of Illinois, seat of Sangamon County, is the executive, legislative, and judicial center of the State. It is the site of the home and tomb of Abraham Lincoln, 16th President of the United States, and has a greater concentration of original and restored places associated with a President's career than any other city in the country.

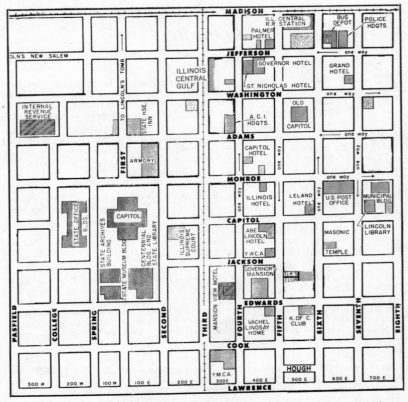

Courtesy Springfield Association of Commerce and Industry

Springfield SMSA had 171,020 pop. in 1970. In 1972 the Bureau of the Census estimated its metropolitan population at 174,600. Springfield is easy of access by highways, railroads, and airplanes and almost centrally located. It is 34 *m.* from Jacksonville, 62 *m* from Bloomington, 70 *m.* from Peoria, 85 *m.* from Champaign, 94 *m.* from East St. Louis, 156 *m.* from Rock Island, 167 *m.* from Quincy, 192 *m.* from Rockford, 193 *m.* from Chicago, and 213 *m.* from Cairo.

Originally the distributing center for farm products of Central Illinois, it attracted most of the major railroads that entered the State. After it became the capital it acquired a growing bloc of public employees, and although it has an expanding number of industries, its largest work force is employed in the offices of the State. Its other major source of income is tourism, for annually hundreds of thousands of visitors, mainly from the Midwest, come to attend conventions and inspect the Lincoln memorabilia, and more than 1,000,000 spectators annually arrive at the Illinois State Fair.

Springfield's strong financial position is supported by its place as the center of State operations and of prosperous agricultural counties. The latter advantage has made it the hq of numerous insurance companies and savings and loan associations. The Springfield Marine Bank has been operting since 1851. The First National Bank has an 80-ft. long mural about Springfield that makes it a showplace; the Illinois National Bank provides a landscaped Bank Park. The principal insurance companies include Franklin Life, Illinois National, Inland National, New York Life, Acme Life, Standard Mutual, Capital Security, and the Horace Mann Educators, which has a new building designed by Minoru Tamasaki. The Illinois Bell Telephone Co. has its downstate area hq here, and numerous Federal bureaus divide their Illinois offices between Springfield and Chicago.

Sangamon is a name of a river, a township, a county, a lake and a village; it is also applied to a great many civilian enterprises, including a university. In the Sanganois Conservation Area is the confluence of the Sangamon and Illinois Rivers. Virgil J. Vogel (*Journal, Illinois State Historical Society*) cites mention of the Saguimont by French writers in 1721 and 1755.

Elisha Kelly came from North Carolina to the future area of Springfield in 1818 and was so impressed with the land that he persuaded his father and four brothers to settle there. Sangamon County was organized in 1821 and when a temporary county seat was placed near a spring on one of the Kelly's fields on April 10, 1821, it was called Springfield. It defeated the efforts of Sangamon Town, 7 *m*. northwest, to become the permanent county seat. The *Sangamo Journal* was begun in Springfield in 1831. In the following spring the steamboat *Talisman* made its way up the Sangamon River from St. Louis but was grounded by low water. New settlers poured in and on Feb. 25, 1837, the capital of Illinois was moved from Vandalia to Springfield, largely by the efforts of Abraham Lincoln and fellow legislators. It was incorporated as a city in 1840.

Industrial expansion has been helped by the opening of an industrial park of 200 acres with easy access to principal highways and railroads. Among the largest employers are Allis-Chalmers Manufacturing Co., maker of crawler tractors and road building machinery, which has been located here since 1929; Barker-Lubin Co., mill work; John W. Hobbs Division of Stewart-Warner Corp., motor car and aircraft accessories; Pillsbury Co., baking ingredients; Weaver Division of Walter Kidde Co., automotive equipment; Sangamo Electric Co., Certified Equipment & Manufacturing Co. and Scherf Steel.

Light and power facilities are owned by the City and operated by its City Water, Light & Power Department. It has invested large funds to enlarge its electric generating capacity and water purification. The City bought a private water works in 1869 and used water from the Sangamon River. In 1912 it changed to wellwater, and to this ascribed a drop in the death rate of from 70 to 8 per 1,000 population. In 1924 it adopted chlorination. It began generating electricity in 1916. In

1935 the water and electric plants were moved to Lake Springfield, built in part with Federal aid. The Municipal Electric Plant added new facilities in 1964 and has a generating capacity of 146,000 kilowats per hour. The water purification plant can treat 40,000,000 gallons per day. The Census of 1970 reported that Springfield had 80,531 citizens who were American born of American parents; 9,034 were Americans born of foreign or mixed parentage, and 2,188 were foreign born. The largest foreign stock represented was German, 2,475, and Italian, 1,096. Of the male civilian work force of 21,887 only 743, or 3.4%, were unemployed. The largest number of workers were in government, 11,397, of whom local government employed 2,850.

OFFICIAL SPRINGFIELD

To the thousands of Illinoisans who visit Springfield the CAPITOL is the most important object in town. This is true partly because it is the seat of government, and partly because the ornate dome and cupola, the columns and pediments, symbolize the greatness of the State. The building may be completely outmoded for modern usage, but to many citizens it has the prestige of authority, and they love it.

The Capitol is post-Lincoln. Abraham's voice rang out in the Old Capitol, which, in its restored form, is the newer building. The present Capitol was started March 11, 1868; its cornerstone was laid October 7, 1868; and the architect was Alfred H. Piquenard, who also designed the Iowa capitol. The administration moved in during 1876. It was built in the years after the Civil War when immense new energies were released and the people's ambitions were soaring. The states were erecting state and county buildings inspired by St. Peter's, Rome, and the Palace of Versailles. The Capitol of Illinois was supposed to cost $3,000,000 and true to custom actually cost $4,500,000. It is located on a nine-acre plot and in the form of a Latin cross. The dome rests on a circular foundation 92½ ft. in diameter, set on solid rock. The building measures 379 ft. by 268 ft.; its height to the top of the dome is 361 ft. The top of the flagstaff is 405 ft. above ground. There is a red beacon for the guidance of pilots.

Varicolored marble was popular when the Capitol was erected and there are many examples of its use here. The grand staircase is built of solid marble. The columns in the third story of the rotunda are of Missouri red granite with bases of blue granite and Tuckahoe marble. Wainscoting of the corridors has imported and domestic marble, including white Italian, green Alpine, Lisbon, Glens Falls, Tennessee, and Concord varieties. Murals have scenes from Illinois history. At the first landing on the grand stairway is a large painting of George Rogers Clark making a treaty with the Indians in 1778 after the capture of Fort Gage. The Lincoln-Douglas debates are commemorated in a plaster panel and a painting, and there are separate paintings of Lincoln and Douglas in the House. George Washington is represented in paintings that hang behind the Speaker's desk in both Senate and House. *Official guides are available.*

Metropolis

COMMERCE ON THE CHICAGO. STREET BRIDGES OPEN FOR STEAM-SHIP. WASHINGTON STATUE AND WACKER DRIVE, LEFT; MARINA CITY AND MERCHANDISE MART, RIGHT.

DANISH STEAMSHIP MOVES UP CHICAGO RIVER. ON THE LEFT BANK: NORTH AMERICAN LIFE INSURANCE BLDG., UNITED OF AMERICA BLDG. ON THE RIGHT BANK: CHICAGO SUN-TIMES, CHICAGO DAILY NEWS BLDG.

BURNHAM PARK YACHT HARBOR AND FACADE OF SOLDIER FIELD

NEW HIGHRISE APARTMENT HOUSES ON THE LAKE FRONT

LOOKING NORTH ON STATE STREET FROM THE MARSHALL FIELD CORNER. ONE SECTION OF MARINA CITY IN THE MIDDLE DISTANCE.

THE HEART OF CHICAGO FROM THE SOUTHWEST SIDE OF THE LOO

FTER CONSTRUCTION IN 1973 OF SEARS TOWER,
HE WORLD'S TALLEST BUILDING, RISING 1450 FT. ON S. WACKER DR.

NEW MODULAR HOUSING, CITY OF CHICAGO, SOUTH SIDE

TYPICAL TWO AND FOUR FAMILY HOUSES, CHICAGO WEST SIDE

BYWAY IN OLD TOWN ON A SUNNY AFTERNOON

DEMONSTRATION BY SOCIAL WELFARE UNIONS, WOODLAWN

TOWERS ON NORTH MICHIGAN AVENUE: THE SHERATON CHI-
CAGO HOTEL, THE CHICAGO TRIBUNE, AND THE WEST FACADE
OF THE WRIGLEY BUILDING ANNEX

FIRST NATIONAL BANK OF
CHICAGO, SOUTH FACADE,
PLAZA, AND NO. 2 FIRST
NATIONAL PLAZA BLDG.
SKETCH BY ARCHITECT.

Statues at the Capitol. In the center of the ground floor stands a bronze figure of a woman representing Illinois welcoming the world to the Columbia Exposition of 1893. It stood in the Woman's Building there. In the niches above the second floor rotunda are statues of Lincoln, Douglas, Governor John Wood, Speaker of the House David E. Shanahan, and State Senator Richard J. Barr. On pedestals near the base of the inner dome are bronze casts of eight men distinguished in military and civil history, namely Ninian Edwards, Shadrach Bond, Edward Coles, governors; Justice Sidney Breeze, Sen. Lyman Trumbull, President Grant, General Logan and Representative Morrison.

Five distinguished sons of Illinois are represented by statues on the grounds of the Capitol. Lincoln stands in front of a granite slab on which is engraved his farewell to Springfield. The statue was dedicated Oct. 5, 1918, the 100th anniversary of the first session of the General Assembly. The sculpture, by Andrew O'Connor, was unveiled by Lord Charnwood, British biographer of Lincoln. On the same day the statue of Stephen A. Douglas by Gilbert P. Riswold was dedicated. The statue of Pierre Menard, president of the first three Territorial Assemblies and first Lieutenant Governor, 1818-1822, was dedicated June 10, 1888. The artist was John H. Mahoney and the statue was the gift of the son of a business associate of Menard. Pierre Menard lived in Kaskaskia 1791-1845.

Another statue, by Leonard Cruelle, is that of John McAuley Palmer, 13th Governor of Illinois, Civil War major general, U. S. Senator, and candidate for the presidency of the Democrats who supported a gold standard ticket against W. J. Bryan in 1896. The statue was dedicated Oct. 16, 1923, on the same day that a statue of Richard Yates was unveiled. Yates was Civil War Governor and U. S. Senator. The statue is by Albin Polacek.

On October 16, 1964, the COAL MINER, a 7-ft. bronze statue, was added to the Capitol lawn. The figure in workman's togs was modeled by Michael F. Widman, an official of the United Mine Workers of America, and honored the 9,000 miners killed during worktime in 130 years of mining. John Szaton of Tinley Park was the sculptor and the legislature appropriated $15,000 for the work.

Directly west of the Capitol on Spring St. stands the ILLINOIS STATE OFFICE BUILDING. Completed in 1956, it exemplifies the functional trend of its time as truly as the Capitol reflects the ornate Victorianism of the 1870's. It is built in the form of the letter H, with a center portion eight stories tall, and two wings of seven stories. Its dimensions are 381 by 252 ft., its floor space is approximately 10 acres, and it cost $11,500,000 to build. It is connected with the Capitol by a tunnel, as are some other buildings. Today it houses 20 important departments and about 2,100 employees. Governor William G. Stratton placed the cornerstone, a 100-lb. slab of black granite, on April 27, 1955. Sealed behind it is a 150-lb. box of documents.

The CENTENNIAL BUILDING, facing the south side of the Capitol, is socalled because it commemorates the 100th anniversary of

Illinois as a State. The cornerstone was laid October 5, 1918 and the building was completed in 1923 at a cost of $3,000,000. It was constructed of limestone and the north facade rises four stories, with 12 Corinthian columns supporting a frieze inscribed with the names of distinguished Illinoisans. In five years after completion the State needed more office space and added an Annex, 210 ft. at the south along Second St. at a cost of $700,000. This has six floors and no columns. In 1965 the building was enlarged once more and converted into a square structure at a cost of $6,500,000. The most important offices here are the departments of the office of Secretary of State and the Illinois State Library.

Memorial Hall, inside the two main entrances, is the first objective of all visitors. In it are displayed the regimental colors of Illinois regiments. Makanto stone is used for walls and floor, and the ceiling is decorated in gold leaf.

The original part of the Centennial Building stands on the site of the house of Ninian Edwards, in which Lincoln and Mary Todd were married. A replica of the house and its furnishings now stands at 406 S. Eighth St.

The ILLINOIS STATE MUSEUM, at Spring and Edwards Sts., occupies the southwest corner of the square that holds the Capitol and other official buildings. Established in 1877, it has occupied since 1963 a modern structure of New Bedford limestone that offers fine areas for exhibits and expansion. It is a general museum of natural history and art, and sponsors exhibits, educational services, and research. The first floor front is trimmed with black opalescent granite and the porch floor has multicolored slate.

The first floor is notable for its Hall of Developing Life, which shows mushrooms, sponges, fish, amphibia, reptiles, etc., and the small habitat groups of badger, mink, coyote, raccoon, rabbit, squirrel, fox and other little animals. The second floor has Man's Venture in Culture, showing the changes in costumes and living conditions through the ages, and The Story of Illinois, in dioramas depicting special situations of the past. The museum also exhibits firearms, clocks, glass, furniture, paintings, prints, and sculpture. The Library on the third floor is open to the public. The Thorne Deuel Auditorium is in the basement. The museum issues a number of publications, of which *The Living Museum* is a free monthly, available also in braille. The museum supports lecture and film programs. *The museum, free, is open weekdays, 8:30-5, Sundays, 2-5; from June 1 through Labor Day, 9:30-6, Sundays, 2-6; closed New Year's Day, Easter, Independence Day, Thanksgiving Day, and Christmas.*

The ARCHIVES BUILDING stands west of the Centennial Building and has the Archives-Records Management Division of the office of the Secretary of State. The cornerstone was laid March 30, 1936, and the building was opened in January, 1938. It cost $820,000. Its modified classical style is similar to that of the Centennial Building, except that it has pilasters instead of pillars on its facade. To support the great weight of steel cabinets filled with records the foundations go down 35 ft. to bedrock. The building is connected with the Capitol and the Centennial Building by tunnels. The public has access to the lobby, museum, reference room, and public catalogue. The museum is decorated in empire, with white panelled wainscot and Williamsburgh blue wall; the reference room is panelled to the ceiling in knotty pine of Georgian design, and the catalogue room has an ivory ceiling trimmed with gold and red, and ivory walls.

The SUPREME COURT BUILDING, at the southeast corner of Second St. and Capitol Ave., was dedicated in 1908 and cost $500,000. It shelters the State's two highest courts, the Supreme Court and the Appellate Court, which use two formal courtrooms, finished in dark mahogany, on the second floor. Here also is the State Law Library. The offices the Clerks of the two courts, and of the Attorney General, are on the first floor. The third floor has living quarters for the justices of the Supreme Court.

The STATE ARMORY AND OFFICE BUILDING on Monroe St. faces the north side of the Capitol. Its large auditorium and drill hall seats 6,000. Numerous state offices associated with law enforcement are grouped here, including the Parole and Pardons Board, the Adjutant General, the Accounting Division, and the General Services Printing and Purchasing Sections. The State hq of the Illinois National Guard is located here.

The GOVERNOR'S MANSION completed its first century in 1955 and recently underwent complete modernization. It is located in a landscaped square bounded by Jackson, Edwards, Fourth and Fifth Sts., and was first occupied in November, 1855, by Governor Joel A. Matteson. It is a two and one-half story brick house that now has a flat roof with a balustrade where originally it had an "observatory." The building cost was $45,794.31 and furnishings cost $6,437.36, both exceeding the original appropriation of the State Assembly. The architect was John Murray van Osdel, who had come to Chicago from the East at the invitation of William B. Ogden, Chicago's first mayor, and had built Ogden's residence, which survived the great Chicago fire of 1871. Van Osdel also designed the Cook County Court House, the Palmer House, and the Tremont House, which were burned, and the John Wood house in Quincy, now an exhibit. During the Chicago fire Van Osdel buried his architectural blueprints, recovering them later.

The Old State Capitol

The OLD STATE CAPITOL, occupying the historic square bounded by Fifth, Sixth, Washington and Adams Sts., is a remarkable architectural achievement. It is actually a new structure dedicated as a Lincoln Historic Shrine on December 3, 1968, but all its outer walls and the eight Doric entrance columns of dolomite are the originals erected during 1837-1841, and the whole outer appearance is that of the building occupied as the State Capitol from 1841 to 1876, and as the Sangamon County Courthouse after that. As the building began to show the ravages of time and usage, patriotic groups, including the Lincoln Memorial Commission and the Abraham Lincoln Association, agitated for its preservation. In August, 1961, during Governor Otto Kerner's term, the State bought the building from Sangamon County and voted for its reconstruction.

Earl W. Henderson, Jr., was named architect. He saw that little could be saved of the worn interior, the roof and the cupola, and decided for complete dismantling and rebuilding. The sandstone exterior was taken down, block by block, properly labelled, and stored on the State Fair grounds. The site was dug out so that two new floors could be placed underground, and the rest of the square was excavated to permit construction of a two-level garage for 450 motor cars below a landscaped street level. A new frame was erected and then all the stone walls were replaced. Inside everything was rebuilt to conform to the original layout of offices and legislative chambers that had known the presence of Lincoln. The underground floors, 35 ft. below the surface, were allocated to the Illinois State Historical Library and the Illinois State Historical Society.

The Sangamon County Courthouse had undergone some changes in appearance since Lincoln's day. When the State decided in 1867 to build a new capitol, it sold this building to Sangamon County for $200,000 and a tract of land. The capitol then became the Courthouse. Twenty years later the County began to study ways of enlarging the building and during 1899-1901 remodelled it. By an extraordinary engineering effort the rebuilders raised the whole structure 11 feet on jacks and beams and inserted a new floor. They also built a new roof and a new cupola. Thus by 1901 there were already great changes from the house Lincoln knew.

Abraham Lincoln was 28 and serving his second term as Representative in the lower house at Vandalia in February, 1837, when as one of the Long Nine from Sangamon County, who collectively were 54 ft. tall, he helped get a vote moving the capital to Springfield. This was considered a more central location, although a town of only 1,100, with muddy streets where hogs ran wild. In less than two weeks the State Assembly accepted the public square of 2½ acres from Springfield and ordered a State House. Lincoln moved from New Salem the next month. John F. Rague, Springfield architect, was authorized to erect a formal Greek Revival building, 123 ft. long, 89 ft. wide, and 44 ft. high. It was not completed for 3½ years and cost $260,000. During most of Lincoln's term the House had to use the Second Presbyterian Church. Lincoln's term ended March 1, 1841. He was frequently in the capitol on political and legal business, and was a Representative in Congress during the Mexican War. On June 16, 1858, the Republican State convention here endorsed him for United States Senator and in the evening he accepted the nomination with his first House Divided speech, in which he declared: "I believe this government cannot endure, permanently, half slave and half free." During the 1860 presidential campaign Lincoln made his headquarters in the office of the Governor, an interim appointee who passed most of his time in Quincy. Lincoln's secretary, John G. Nicolay, slept in the capitol. Senator Stephen A. Douglas, supporting Lincoln, addressed a joint session of the legislature here on April 25, 1861, a few days before his death. Ulysses S. Grant served several months as military assistant to Governor Richard Yates, who named him colonel of volunteers. Lincoln's body lay in state in the Hall of Representatives May 3-4, 1965, before burial in Oak Ridge Cemetery.

After being elected President Lincoln made use of Governor John Wood's rooms in the Old Capitol to meet friends and office seekers, from Nov. 6 to Dec. 29, 1860. A large wooden chain of 45 links, which had been whittled out of a log, and sent to Lincoln, hung on the wall. A reproduction of the original now hangs in the governor's room.

The marble statue of Stephen A. Douglas in the second floor rotunda was made by Leonard W. Volk at the request of Governor Joel Matteson in 1858-59. It is life size, only 5 ft. 4 in., and explains why Douglas was called the Little Giant. When the Matteson house burned in 1873 the statue was saved with the loss of one finger.

Three major libraries are located in Springfield. They include the ILLINOIS STATE LIBRARY in the Centennial Building, which is directed by the secretary of state as State Librarian. It is at the head of the library systems, serves the needs of officials, allocates funds, and develops ways to extend library services throughout the State. In 1972 it had 555,027 volumes, 690,720 Federal documents, and 70,000 State documents. Plans for a separate building are in the making. *See Education, Public Schools and Libraries.*

The ILLINOIS STATE HISTORICAL LIBRARY is one of the most distinguished historical libraries in the country. It has new quarters in the Old Capitol Building, and is administered by the State Historian, under direction of a board of three trustees appointed by the governor. It has the finest collection of Lincoln letters, papers, and documents, as well as more than 140,000 volumes, and nearly 3,000,000 manuscripts dealing with Illinois from the earliest times.

An example of the work done by the Library to make documents accessible is the microfilming of the papers of Pierre Menard (1766-1844) Kaskaskia pioneer and first lieutenant governor of the State. There were 4,700 separate items which, with 75 bound ledgers, filled 28 reels of microfilm. A descriptive guide includes a five-generation Menard genealogy. A Federal grant of $15,125 was called for. *See also Education, Public Schools and Libraries.*

One of the most prized treasures of the library is a copy of Lincoln's Gettysburg Address in his own hand. Lincoln wrote five copies of the address at different times. The third copy was prepared for Edward Everett for sale at the New York Sanitary Fair and is here with the manuscript of Everett's address at Gettysburg November 19, 1863. In 1944 Lincoln's address came up for sale and was bought for the State for $60,000, raised by five-cent contributions from school children with the help of $10,000 from Marshall Field III.

An exceptionally fine collection of Lincolniana, compiled by the late Oliver R. Barrett of Chicago and Kenilworth, was bought for the State in February, 1952, at auction at the Parke-Bernet galleries in New York. A committee headed by Newton C. Farr of Chicago bid in items of the collection for $70,000 and presented it at the Illinois State Historical Society on April 22, 1952. Governor Adlai E. Stevenson accepted the gift for the State. The collection comprises 37 letters in Lincoln's hand, 28 documents, 87 letters and papers of Lincoln's Coles County relatives, and 170 newspapers of the period. The most valuable item is a group of 14 letters from Lincoln to Joshua F. Speed, 10 of which deal with their love affairs and marriages, which cost the donors $35,000. Some of the letters have been published in *Lincoln Collector,* by Carl Sandburg (Harcourt, Brace, 1949), who had access to the Barrett collection when writing his Lincoln biography. At auction the collection brought $273,633.

No state keeps its citizens better informed of historical personalities and events than Illinois. Many houses associated with incidents of political and cultural significance of the last 150 years are still standing and bear markers describing their occupants and the historical events associated with them. This work has been strongly promoted by the Illinois State Historical Society. A program of cast aluminum markers was conceived by Paul M. Angle, State Historian, in 1934. He chose sites along the highways and prepared inscriptions. Two styles were used; cast aluminum and plywood panel. The Bureau of Maintenance of the Illinois Division of Highways looked after them. After 1950 the markers bore the line: "Erected by the Illinois State Historical Society", and an effort was made to place them on the exact site of events. In 1960, when Clyde C. Walton was State Historian, the society decided to use large plywood markers for historical events, buildings and persons, and a supervisor was appointed jointly by the society and the Division of Highways.

The Springfield Public Library, 306 S. Seventh St., is known as the Lincoln Library. It was built in 1904 and recently had a stock of 263,503 books and transactions of 885,429. The library has receipts of $790,188, $695,653 from an annual tax levy, and in 1972 had expenditures of $667,109. It has four branches in Springfield and is one of the two headquarters libraries of the Rolling Prairie Library System, of which the other is in Decatur.

LINCOLN LAND

ABRAHAM LINCOLN'S HOME, northeast corner of 8th and Jackson Sts., is a National Historic Site by virtue of an Act of Congress signed by President Richard M. Nixon in the Old State Capitol on August 18, 1971. The act also provided for the restoration of a four-block area around the house to its state during Lincoln's time, and gave jurisdiction to the National Park Service. This, the only house that Lincoln ever owned, was intimately associated with his domestic life, for he and his family lived here from 1844 until his departure for his inauguration as President on February 7, 1861, with the exception of his stay in Washington while Representative in Congress. The house when bought was a 1½ story frame cottage built in 1839 for the Rev. Charles Dresser, the Episcopalian rector who had performed the marriage ceremony for Lincoln and Mary Todd, and from whom Lincoln bought the property for $1,500 on May 2, 1844. It stood on a small eminence, but had neither the brick wall nor the picket fence that

Lincoln added in 1850. In 1857 Lincoln raised the roof and placed a second story under it at a cost of $1,300.

The Lincoln family moved here from the Globe Tavern where Robert was born and where they were paying $4 a week. During the first part of Lincoln's term in Congress in 1847 he rented the house to Cornelius Ludlum for $90 a year. Mrs. Lincoln and the two little boys, Robert and Edward, spent part of the time in Washington and part at her father's home in Lexington, Kentucky. Three of their sons were born in this house: Edward Baker (Eddie, 1846-1850); William Wallace (Willie 1850-1862); and Thomas (Tad 1853-1871) Edward died here.

Lincoln received formal notice of his nomination in the north parlor, after which members of the committee were introduced to Mrs. Lincoln in the sitting room. On Feb. 6, 1961, the Lincolns held open house. Lincoln received the guests as they entered and then they met Mrs. Lincoln in the parlor. She was described as "dressed plainly but richly with beautiful full train, white moire, antique silk, small lace collar, and a string of pearls." They next day the Lincolns took rooms in the Chenery House, where they remained until their departure for Washington on February 11.

Lincoln retained ownership of the house and rented it to Lucien Tilton, head of the Great Western Railroad, for $300 a year. Tilton lived there until 1869. He bought some of the furniture and took it with him to Chicago, where it was lost in the Chicago fire of 1871. From 1869 to 1880 the house was occupied by George H. Harlow, private secretary to Governor Richard J. Oglesby, city editor of the *Illinois State Journal,* and Secretary of State for two terms. Dr. Gustav Wendlandt, editor of a German language newspaper, lived there for three years. In 1883 Osborn H. Oldroyd rented the house and installed his collection of Lincoln and Civil War relics. He persuaded Robert Lincoln to give the property to the State of Illinois and this was done July 29, 1887, when it became the first State Memorial. Oldroyd remained as custodian until 1893, when he moved his collection to Washington. He sold it to the Federal Government and it is now shown in the Ford Theatre building.

The house remained open to the public. A few pieces of furniture owned by the Lincolns were recovered and others of the period were added. There were Lincoln's rocking chair, a cupboard used as bookshelves, Mrs. Lincoln's sewing chair, and a photograph taken in 1860 for the campaign. The deterioration of the house prompted a thorough restoration in 1950-52 by the Division of Parks and Memorials of the State Department of Conservation. Richard S. Hagen, historical consultant for the Department, was placed in charge, in cooperation with Virginia Stuart Brown, custodian from 1925 to 1953, and the Lincoln Home Commission appointed by the Governor.

The restoration disclosed the materials used in the house. The frame is of oak. The original floors were of weathered oak; the sills, joists, and interior woodwork of walnut and laths of split hickory and pine. There were no wooden pegs. An addition and a porch at the rear, built for the custodian, were removed. The house had been painted white, but scraping disclosed that the original color was a light Quaker brown and this was restored. Some of the original wallpaper in Lincoln's bedroom was uncovered and is now protected under glass; for the rest the pattern has been reproduced. The original staircase is extant. Railings were placed in the rooms to guide the visitors.

The restorers brought the carriage house and woodshed back to their original appearance. As the privy had been removed a duplicate was found in Oakland, Illinois, at the house of Lincoln's friend, Dr. Hiram G. Rutherford, and moved to Springfield. The house, carefully refurbished by the National Society of the Colonial Dames of America, was reopened to the public Feb. 12, 1955. About 500,000 persons visit it annually. *Open 9-5 daily, except Thanksgiving Day, Christmas, and New Year's Day.*

On August 18, 1971, President Richard M. Nixon visited the Illinois State Historical Society and the Illinois State Historical Library in the Old State Capitol and signed the Act of Congress creating a National Historical Site of the Abraham Lincoln Home and a four-block area around it under jurisdiction of the National Park Service. The President signed the act in the chamber of the House of Representatives in the presence of Governor Richard B. Ogilvie, Representative Paul Findley, Mayor William Telford of Springfield, Clyde C. Walton, former Illinois State Historian, and other officials and guests. The President used a desk that once stood in a back room of the dry goods store of Lincoln's brother-in-law, G. M. Smith, on the Square, which Lincoln used in the weeks between his election in November, 1860, and his departure for Washington on Feb. 11, 1861. At this desk Lincoln wrote a draft of his first inaugural address.

The LINCOLN LAW OFFICES start at 109 N. Fifth St. When Lincoln came from New Salem in April, 1837, he joined John T. Stuart in a law partnership in the front room on the second floor. The circuit court of Sangamon County occupied the first floor and the Lincoln office was sometimes used as a jury room. In 1841 Lincoln moved across the street to 106 N. Fifth St. and joined Stephen T. Logan. A short time later they moved to the Tinsley Bldg., southwest corner Sixth and Adams Sts. Several years later Logan left and Lincoln formed a new partnership with William H. Herndon. In 1856 Lincoln & Herndon moved to a second floor rear room at 105 S. Fifth St., in a house where Lincoln had roomed in 1837 with Joshua F. Speed above Speed's store.

The C. M. SMITH STORE was located at 524-528 E. Adams St. Clark M. Smith opened a grocery and dry goods store here in 1852. He was married to Ann Maria Todd, youngest sister of Mrs. Lincoln. The Lincolns traded here. In January, 1861, Lincoln found it difficult to do any work at his office because of many callers so Smith offered him a back room on the third floor. Here Lincoln drafted his first inaugural address on the desk now owned by the Illinois State Historical Library at the Old State Capitol.

The site of the GLOBE TAVERN is 315 E. Adams St. Lincoln and Mary Todd came here on their wedding night, Nov. 4, 1842. They left here soon after Robert was born Aug. 1, 1843. The Globe was torn down in 1893. In the fall, 1843, the Lincolns moved to a one-story cottage at 214 S. Fourth St. Next spring, 1844, they moved into their own house at Eighth and Jackson Sts.

The FIRST PRESBYTERIAN CHURCH stood at 302 E. Washington St. when Mary Todd Lincoln joined it on April 13, 1854. The Lincoln pew is preserved in the present church at northwest corner of 7th and Capitol Ave.

The ABRAHAM LINCOLN MUSEUM, 421 South 8th St., across the street from the Lincoln Home, occupies a brick dwelling once owned by Lincoln's law partner, John Todd Stuart. It is said to be the only house in the area except Lincoln's that stands on its original site. The museum offers the story of Lincoln's life in dioramas and among its Lincoln memorabilia is a life-sized wax figure of which face and hands were reconstructed from molds made before Lincoln left Springfield.

The NINIAN EDWARDS HOUSE, five doors north of Lincoln's Home on 8th St., is a complete reproduction of the original house in which Lincoln and Mary Todd, younger sister of Mrs. Edwards, were married November 4, 1842. The original house was taken down when the State Office Building was erected on the site. Some of the furnishings, including the horsehair sofa, are authentic. Mrs. Lincoln died in the original house in 1882 and lay in state there. The Lincoln life story is told here in 28 dioramas by Arthur G. Sieving.

THE LINCOLN DEPOT, 10th and Monroe Sts., was the Great Western Depot when Abraham Lincoln said farewell to his fellow-citizens of Springfield there on February 11, 1861, upon leaving for Washington, never to return alive. The depot later became the Wabash Freight Depot, and had a second story added. Except for that change it appears today as it did when Lincoln departed. The interior has been restored. It became a Lincoln shrine on May 3, 1965. The Division of Parks & Memorials of the Dept. of Conservation, thus describes Lincoln's Farewell:

> The *Illinois State Journal* of February 12, 1861, reported "despite bad weather . . . hundreds of his fellow citizens, without distinction of party had assembled . . . to bid him God-speed." After silently shaking hands with many of his well-wishers, the President-elect and party boarded the train. Shortly before 8 o'clock, "On the platform of the rear car Lincoln bared his head to the rain, faced his friends, and stood silently struggling with his feelings . . . then slowly, solemnly spoke . . ."
>
> "My Friends: No one, not in my situation, can appreciate my feelings of sadness at this parting. To this place, and the kindness of these people, I owe everything. Here I have lived a quarter of a century, and have passed from a young to an old man. Here my children have been born, and one is buried. I now leave, not knowing when, or whether ever, I may return, and a task before me greater than that which rested upon Washington.

Without the assistance of that Divine Being, who ever attended him, I cannot succeed. With that assistance I cannot fail. Trusting in him, who can go with me, and remain with you and be everywhere for good, let us confidently hope that all will yet be well. To his care commending you, as I hope in your prayers you will commend me, I bid you an affectionate farewell."

The original draft of the above version is in the Robert Todd Lincoln Collection in the Library of Congress. The *State Journal* version is on a plaque in the Lincoln Tomb.

After the train pulled away Lincoln wrote down a few sentences of his Farewell and it was then completed by John G. Nicolay, his private secretary.

The LINCOLN TOMB, at the end of Monument Ave. in Oak Ridge Cemetery, shares with the Lincoln Home the distinction of being the most visited historical site in Springfield. It contains the bodies of Abraham Lincoln, his wife, Mary Todd Lincoln, and three of their four children—Edward, William and Thomas; the fourth and eldest, Robert, rests at Arlington National Cemetery.

The son of Robert Todd Lincoln, Abraham, called Jack by his family, died March 5, 1870 aged 16½ years, and was buried in the Lincoln Tomb. His body remained there until May 25, 1930, when it was placed beside that of his father in Arlington National Cemetery.

The body of President Lincoln reached Oak Ridge cemetery on May 4, 1865, after it had been viewed by many thousands of people in the principal cities en route from Washington to Springfield via New York and Chicago. It was placed in a temporary vault while citizens of Springfield formed the National Lincoln Monument Assn. to raise funds for a suitable memorial. Larkin C. Mead, Jr., of Brattleboro, Vermont, designed it and construction began in 1869. The original cost was $180,000. The monument was dedicated on October 15, 1874. In 1875 the sponsoring association turned the tomb over to the State. There was reconstruction in 1901 and interior remodelling in 1931. President Hoover rededicated the structure on June 17, 1931.

The monument, of marble, stands on a landscaped and partly wooded area of 12.4 acres and on the ground floor contains a foyer with statuettes and the burial chamber with cenotaph. Two outside staircases lead to the balustrated roof, from which rises the 117-ft. obelisk. In front of the shaft is a 10-ft. tall bronze statue of Lincoln, and at four corners are heroic bronze groups representing Infantry, Cavalry, Navy, and Artillery. In front of the entrance on the ground floor a bronze of Lincoln's head by Gutzon Borglum stands on a tall pedestal. In the foyer is a small bronze replica of the statue by Daniel Chester French in the Lincoln Memorial at Washington, and in niches are 4-ft. statuettes representing phases of Lincoln's career: *Lincoln the Ranger,* by Fred M. Torrey; *Lincoln the Soldier,* by Leonard Crunelle; *Lincoln the Circuit Rider,* by Torrey; *Lincoln the President,* by Augustus St. Gaudens; *Lincoln the Debater,* by Crunelle; *Seated Lincoln,* by Adolph A. Weinman; *Lincoln Thinking,* by French, and *Lincoln the Lawyer,* by Lorado Taft. On four bronze tablets are inscribed the Gettysburg

Address, the Springfield Farewell, part of the Second Inaugural, and a biographical statement.

Halfway around the passage, directly opposite the entrance rotunda, is the burial chamber, a semi-circular room of St. Genevieve Golden View marble, with black pilasters and frieze. The Cenotaph bears a marker of Red Arkansas fossil granite, with the inscription, Abraham Lincoln 1809-1865. Beyond is a bronze grill admitting light; above the grill are inscribed, in black marble, the words of Stanton: "Now he belongs to the ages."

Around it are four flags representing Lincoln family settlement: Massachusetts, New Jersey, Pennsylvania, and Virginia, and three flags of Kentucky, Indiana, and Illinois, where Lincoln lived, as well as the national colors and the President's flag.

The body of Lincoln reposes in a cement vault 30 inches north of the Cenotaph and 10 ft. below the surface of the floor. It was placed there on Sept. 26, 1901, after it had been moved several times when changes were made in the tomb.

In the south wall are vaults containing the bodies of Mrs. Lincoln and the children. The entrance and exit to the chamber have bronze grills which reveal the cornstalk motif, typical of Illinois and the prairie states that nurtured Lincoln.

Eleven years after Lincoln's death a fantastic attempt was made to steal his body. Ben Boyd, engraver for Big Jim Kenealy's gang of counterfeiters, had been caught and sentenced to Joliet for 10 years. Unable to replace Boyd, the gang decided to steal Lincoln's body, bury it in the Indiana dunes, and then secretly inform Boyd. Boyd was to force the Governor to "ransom" the body by paying $200,000 and granting him a pardon. The Secret Service learned of the plot and decided to catch the ghouls actually desecrating the tomb. The attempt was made on the night of Nov. 7, 1876, and was permitted to progress to the point where the gang had removed the casket from its stone covering. Then one of the service men accidentally discharged his gun; in the confusion the officers began shooting at each other, and the gang escaped. Two of them, John Hughes and Terence Mullen, were later caught and given the maximum sentence for grave-robbing—one year in the penitentiary. Kenealy was subsequently sentenced for counterfeiting.

OTHER POINTS OF INTEREST

WASHINGTON PARK, 150 acres, largest of the parks devoted to general recreation inside the city limits, is located in the west central part of the city and notable for its flower gardens and the THOMAS REES MEMORIAL CARILLON that decorate a hilltop. The ROSE GARDEN contains more than 3,000 plants that bloom profusely throughout the spring and summer; the DAHLIA Garden of more than 1,000 plants and the CHRYSANTHEMUM GARDEN of 5,000 plants embellish the hill during succeeding months. On the highest point of elevation in Springfield stands the 132-ft. tall tower that holds 66 cast-bronze bells, all of which can be played manually by means of a keyboard and 32 of which can be played by an electric mechanism or a roll player. The bells were cast in the ancient foundry of Petit & Fritsen, Ltd., in The Netherlands; the smallest bell weighs 22 lbs., the largest 7½ tons. The tower, of reinforced white concrete, brick and steel contains a marble memorial room, a study and practice clavier, and three observation decks. The carillon commemorates Thomas Rees, publisher of the *Illinois State Register,* 1881-1933, and one-time senator in the Illinois General Assembly. He became interested in carillon music while traveling in Holland and Belgium and bequeathed a trust fund of $200,000 to the Springfield Park District for the tower carillon, which was dedicated in June, 1962. An International Carillon Festival is held annually in June. *Concerts from June 1 to October 1 on Sundays, 4-5 p.m. and Wednesdays, 8-9 p.m.; during rest of year on Saturday and Sunday afternoons, 4-5.*

Washington Park is located on West Fayette Ave. and South Mac-Arthur Blvd. *Tours are available weekdays, May 30-Sept. 1, and on Sunday afternoons.*

The VACHEL LINDSAY HOME, 603 South Fifth St., where the poet was born, lived, and died, is filled with his books, papers, and furnishings, carefully maintained by the Vachel Lindsay Assn. The house has Lincoln connotations, for it was built about 1850 by C. M. Smith, the dry goods merchant who married Mrs. Lincoln's sister. It was the site of the last reception for the Lincolns before they left for Washington. Dr. V. T. Lindsay bought the property in 1878. Nicholas Vachel Lindsay was born Nov. 10, 1879, and died Dec. 5, 1931. He attended the Springfield schools, Hiram College, the Art Institute of Chicago, and the Chase School of Art in New York. He combined the writing of poetry with recitations and became famous for such poems as "The Congo." "The Callyope," and "General William Booth Enters Into Heaven." He wrote "Abraham Lincoln Walks at Midnight" and other poems about Springfield. A bust of Lindsay stands at a bridge named for him.

The FREEMAN-HUGHES HOUSE, 704 West Monroe St., has the distinction of having had no association with Lincoln. The owners, Dr. and Mrs. Floyd Barringer, present it for its comprehensive records of Springfield life in the 19th century. The house was built in 1878 by Clarkson W. Freeman and passed to his nephew, Arthur Freeman Hughes. Hughes and his wife were great collectors, and they specialized in Springfield memorabilia—furniture, city directories, playbills, costumes, china, household utensils. *Open daily 1-5 until Sept. 1, when it is closed for the winter; fee.*

The ABRAHAM LINCOLN MEMORIAL GARDEN, on the northeast shore of Lake Springfield, 9 m. from the Old State Capitol, consists of 60 acres of woodland trails and open spaces laid out in 1936 by Jens Jensen, landscape architect. The Garden Club of Illinois originated the project, now supported by the Abraham Lincoln Memorial Garden Foundation and by proceeds from annual tours of the Hazelwood estate of Mrs. Charles R. Walgreen north of Dixon. Maintenance of the Memorial Garden is by the city of Springfield and Boy

Scouts and Girl Scouts help in plantings. There are 13 foot bridges including the 80-ft. Walgreen Bridge, which uses approaches built more than a century ago for a railroad that was never completed. State Garden clubs have contributed benches for the trails; each bench has a Lincoln quotation carved in oak planks.

SANGAMON STATE UNIVERSITY is a newly organized upper-level institution that started classes in temporary buildings with 816 students in September, 1970. It is located on a new campus of almost 1,000 acres developed near Lake Springfield for this and its neighbor, LINCOLN LAND COMMUNITY COLLEGE. The area is about six miles southeast of the city on West Lake Shore Drive and Interstate 55.

Sangamon is strongly slanted to education in public affairs, administration of public offices, and business management. In 1973 it added health administration. It is especially attuned to the needs of students who expect to enter the public service or are already employed by the State. It gives the degrees of B. A. and M. A. in biological science, economics, history, literature, mathematics, political studies, psychology, sociology, and anthropology. As an upper-level institution it uses the College Level Examination Program, which enables a student who passes the tests to enter Sangamon as a junior. Counseling is continuous, enabling a student to fit a program to his needs. The university has introduced the Public Affairs Colloquia, a seminar that focuses on public issues. Four special programs deal with communication in a technical society, environments and people, justice and the social order, and work, culture and society.

In order to give State employees access to courses the university opened a Downtown Center in the old Leland Hotel building, now called the Capital Campus. The State's Environmental Protection Agency took advantage of this move to enroll up to 25 of the EPA staff in a two-year program leading to a master's degree in public administration. These students were reimbursed for the fees from the State's in-service training program. The university accepts junior college transfer students for completion of a four-year course.

The other educational institution is LINCOLN LAND COMMUNITY COLLEGE, organized in 1967 under the State junior college program and opened in the fall, 1968. It began with 10 temporary structures at 3865 South Sixth St., Frontage Road, just off US 66 and south of the area where the Sangamon State University is located. The college offers two-year programs leading to degrees of associate in arts and associate in science, which are preparatory for higher degrees in four-year colleges, and associate in applied science, for practical courses. The college teaches accounting, busines management, agricultural mechanics, data processing, electronics, farm management, secretarial work and similar vocational courses, and admits high school graduates as well as non-graduates who have taken the General Education Development Tests.

The oldest junior college in Springfield is called SPRINGFIELD

COLLEGE IN ILLINOIS, a coeducational institution conducted by the Ursuline Order. It was founded in 1929 and offers courses in the liberal arts and sciences, teacher training, music, art, and business. In the 1972 school year it reported enrollment of 380 and a faculty of 55. SACRED HEART ACADEMY, Lincoln Ave. at Monroe, was founded in 1895 by the Dominican Sisters as a Roman Catholic high school for girls. ST. JOSEPH'S URSULINE ACADEMY, 1400 N. Fifth St., is a high school for girls.

CONCORDIA THEOLOGICAL SEMINARY, a training school for the Lutheran ministry, established here in 1874, offers a six-year course with a high school education prerequisite.

The DIVISION OF SERVICES TO CRIPPLED CHILDREN, 540 Illes Park Place, is under the administration of the Medical Center of the University of Illinois in Chicago. As the official agency for utilizing Federal Grants in aid for the diagnosis, hospitalization, and after-care of children who are crippled or suffering from conditions that lead to crippling, it conducts about 300 clinics throughout the State annually.

Springfield has two major hospitals, ST. JOHN'S, with 750 beds, conducted by the Roman Catholic Church, and MEMORIAL, with 600 beds. Special funds have enabled them to enlarge plant and special services. An air ambulance is provided at Capital Airport. Appropriations by the State Assembly have been allocated to an enlargement of facilities of the MEDICAL CENTER for the training of medical students from Southern Illinois University of Carbondale, who also will have access to the two hospitals.

LINDBERGH FIELD, 3½ m. west of Springfield, was the city's first airport, in use until 1929. A marker placed there in 1968 explains that the field of 35 acres was chosen with the aid of Charles Lindbergh, chief pilot of the Robertson Aircraft Corp. of St. Louis, who flew the mail on the St. Louis-Chicago route until he began planning for his solo trans-Atlantic flight of May 20-21, 1927. The field was named for him on Aug. 15, 1927.

A new LINCOLN TRAIL for the Boy Scouts of America was opened in May, 1962, as an improvement on the customary route of 21 miles between Springfield and New Salem. The old trail follows Illinois 97 and 125. The new one runs east of it along country roads and the Sangamon River. More than 3,000 Scouts follow the trail annually to help qualify for a Lincoln badge.

CLAYVILLE INN, 12 m. west of Springfield, a roadside dining place that exhibits and demonstrates folkways, was revived in the 1960s after various vicissitudes. The original two-story brick building was built in the 1820s by Moses Broadwell, a veteran of the American Revolution who came from Ohio in 1819. Peter Cartright saw it in 1825 and at one time lived in the village, as did Mentor Graham, Lincoln's teacher, whose class Lincoln is said to have visited in later life. The inn was partially destroyed by fire in 1834, rebuilt, and named for Henry Clay in 1842. It was the first stage stop on the Springfield Beardstown Road.

Tour 1

CHICAGO SOUTH TO THE WABASH RIVER RECREATION AREA AND SHAWNEE NATIONAL FOREST

Suburban Chicago—Blue Island—Chicago Heights—East Chicago Heights — Momence — Hoopeston — Danville — Paris — Marshall — Lawrenceville — Mount Carmel — Carmi — Shawneetown — Shawnee National Forest—Cave-in-Rock.
Illinois 1.

ILLINOIS 1 is the easternmost highway in Illinois and runs close to the Indiana border from Chicago to the Ohio River. After passing through the industrial areas of South Chicago it gives access to the hunting and fishing areas of the Wabash River Valley in both Illinois and Indiana, and to the huge SHAWNEE NATIONAL FOREST. It runs in a fairly direct line to White County. After by-passing Norris City by one mile it has a junction with US 45 and turns sharply southeast to its terminal at Cave-in-Rock on the Ohio River, after junctions with State roads into the Forest.

To continue on to Paducah, Kentucky, drivers take Illinois 146 from the junction with Illinois 1, 2 *m.* from Cave-in-Rock to the junction with US 45. Paducah is 372 *m.* from Chicago.

CHICAGO, 0 *m.* From the Loop the Dan Ryan Expressway, Interstate 94, leads to the Halsted St. exit to Illinois I at about 100th St. Between Chicago and Chicago Heights a succession of suburbs established during the early 20th century stand in marked contrast to the subdivisions and newer suburbs built since World War II. South of Crete, Illinois I traverses farmland settled in the first half of the 19th century. The trade centers arising from the cornfields owe their founding either to the Hubbard Trail, the Chicago-Vincennes State Road, or the Chicago & Eastern Railroad, built between Chicago and Danville in 1871. The highway approximates the Hubbard Trail, which was marked off in the 1820's by the wagon wheels of the fur trader Gurdon E. Hubbard (1802-1886). The Chicago-Vincennes State Road was routed along the Hubbard Trail in 1833-1834.

South on Halsted St. to the city limits at 123d St. and the first suburb on Illinois 1: CALUMET PARK, 15.7 *m.* (605 alt., 10,069 pop. 1970; 8,448, 1960, inc. 19%). This village, largely residential, extends down to the Little Calumet River and the Control Lock of the Calumet Sag Channel. Int. 57 runs south through Calumet Park, Blue Island, Dixmoor, and Posen.

Right from Calumet Park on 127th St. and Int. 57 to BLUE ISLAND, 2.1 *m.* (605 alt., 22,958 pop. 1970; 19,618, 1960, inc. 176%). This village, incorporated 1872, is located on a glacial ridge. The earliest farmers settled here in 1835; in later decades German immigrants predominated, and in the 20th century Italians came. The name is attributed to the position of the village on slightly higher ground above the surrounding marshland, from which dense woods were often shrouded in a blue haze. Blue Island is an industrial center, with factories turning out forgings, electrical equipment, chemicals, paper, plastics, and processing food. Blue Island is on the main line of the Rock Island Railway and has its commuter service, and also South Suburban Safeway bus lines. Its newspapers are the *Blue Island Star*, a weekly, and the *Sun-Standard*, semi-weekly.

Adjoining Blue Island on the west is ROBBINS (9,641 pop. 1970; 7,511, 1960, inc. 28%), which is intersected by Tri-State Tollway, Int. 294. The village, incorporated in 1917, was named for Eugene S. Robbins, who developed the site. It is largely residential, its people working in nearby towns. It began as a community of Negroes who moved up from the South and wanted homes with garden plots. It is still largely a black suburb.

Also west of Blue Island and north of Robbins is the larger terrain of ALSIP (11,141 pop. 1970; 3,770, 1960, inc. 195%). The Tri-State Tollway runs through the suburb and has a junction with Illinois 50, Cicero Ave. The village has five large industrial parks and a number of large truck terminals, and has direct service by the Baltimore & Ohio Chicago Terminal and Indiana Harbor Belt Line railroads.

Between Blue Island and Alsip is the little village of MERRION-ETTE PARK (2,303 pop. 1970; 2,354, 1960, loss 2.2%), subdivided by J. E. Merrion and incorporated in 1947.

CRESTWOOD (5,543 pop. 1970; 1,213, 1960, inc. 357%) adjoins both Alsip and Robbins and is the home of many who are employed in those suburbs. The Calumet Sag Channel passes along the limits of Alsip and Crestwood, and the Crestwood Airport is on the east bank of the Channel.

Return to Halsted St., Illinois 1, for RIVERDALE (597 alt., 15,806 pop. 1970; 12,008, 1960, inc. 31.6%), east of Blue Island and south of Chicago's 130th St., which began at a ferry operated across the Little Calumet River, 1836-1842, by George Dolton and J. C. Mathews. Its fields were farmed originally by German and Dutch immigrants. The Little Calumet River, deepened to provide a link between Lake Calumet and the Calumet-Sag Channel flows through Riverdale.

Before settlement, the Little Calumet flowed westward from its source in La Porte County, Indiana, and entered Lake Michigan near Riverdale. When the lake receded the river made a hairpin turn at Blue Island and flowed eastward to an outlet north of Miller, Ind. When a channel, called the Calumet River, was dug from near Hegewisch to an outlet at Calumet Harbor, South Chicago, the lower part of the river, called Grand Calumet River, was reversed and provided outlets for Lake Calumet and Wolf Lake. The Calumet-Sag Channel was built 1911-1922 by the Sanitary District of Chicago to take the flow of Little Calumet, Grand Calumet and the sewage emptied into them, to the Chicago Sanitary & Ship Canal in the Des Plaines

River valley. It is also a route for traffic from the industrial area and part of the Illinois Deep Waterway System.

Riverdale had a work force of 4,767 in 1970.

DOLTON (25,937 pop. 1970; 18,746, 1960, inc. 38%) is directly east of Riverdale and south of the Chicago line. It is separated from the suburb of Calumet City by the Calumet Expressway, Int. 94, and like its neighbors is crossed by railroad lines, including Chicago & Eastern Illinois, Baltimore & Ohio, and the Indiana Harbor Belt Line. It bears the name of the four Dolton brothers, of whom George, the ferryman of the area, became postmaster of Dolton.

CALUMET CITY, 8.7 m. (585 alt. 32,956 pop. 1970; 25,000, 1960, inc. 31%) a village in Cook County is contiguous with Hammond, Indiana, where many of its people work. US 6 turns west here for Joliet. North of Calumet City is the village of BURNHAM (3,634, 1970; 2,478, 1960, inc. 46%), which has the BURNHAM WOODS FOREST PRESERVE and the POWDER HORN LAKE (fishing). The latter was excavated to provide fill for the Calumet Skyway. The surrounding sandy area has growths of prickly pear. The Burnham Wood Golf Course has 18 holes.

Adjoining Riverdale on the west is DIXMOOR (4,735 pop. 1970; 3,076, 1960, inc. 53%), which has commutation service on the Rock Island main line. Its neighbor, POSEN, on Western Ave. (5,498 pop, 1970; 4,517, 1960, inc. 21%) was populated in the 1890's chiefly by Poles, who bought 12,000 lots sold them by 75 energetic Polish salesmen. When Harvey in 1901 tried to extend prohibition of liquor to the village it promptly incorporated and remained open.

HARVEY, 19 m. (602 alt., 34,636 pop. 1970; 29,071, 1960, +19.1%), in Cook County, is a manufacturing and merchandising city developed since Turlington W. Harvey, Chicago lumberman, bought a piece of open prairie here in 1889. It has nonstop driving to Chicago via Illinois 1 and Int. 94 and access to Int. 80; Illinois Central suburban service, and B. & O. and Grand Trunk Western freight lines. Industrial products include diesels, alloys, cold rolled steel forgings; it also has petrochemical laboratories. THORNTON JUNIOR COLLEGE, (municipal) founded 1929, occupies a new plant; it enrolls more than 3,500 with a faculty of 124, and has courses for adult education as well. The Harvey Public Library has more than 26,000 books and special facilities. The *Harvey Tribune* appears semi-weekly, the *News Bee* weekly. The South Suburban Chamber of Commerce & Industry is at 15328 Center Ave.

The City Hall of Harvey, dating from the 1890 decade, has been sold by the City Council to the Harvey Area Historical Society, which also took responsibility to restore the firehouse and jail of that time. The Thornton Township Museum was placed at 154 East 154th St., Harvey. Ingalls Memorial Hospital (334 beds) is in Harvey. At 159th St. Illinois 1 has a junction with US 6.

PHOENIX, 19.8 m. (605 alt., 3,596 pop. 1970; 4,203, 1960, dec. 14.4%), a Cook County village, adjoins Harvey on the east and is largely residential. At 20.5 m. is a junction with US 6, east-west. The

Tri-State Highway, Int. 80, has a junction with Illinois 1, 2 *m*. south. East of Phoenix is SOUTH HOLLAND. *See Tour 14.*

EAST HAZELCREST (1,885 pop. 1970; 1,437, 1960, in. 27%) is a small village that starts at 171st St., where Harvey leaves off. The Tri-State Tollway runs through it. It has a nursing home of 200 beds. Adjoining it on the west is the larger HAZEL CREST (10,320 pop. 1970; 6,205, 1960, inc. 66%) incorporated as a village in 1912 and 23 miles south of the Loop. It has some light industry at an industrial park and is zoned for apartment buildings. The Illinois Central Railroad provides commutation and the South Suburban Safeway buses run direct to the Loop. South Suburban Hospital has 250 beds. Tri-State Tollway turns northwest in Hazel Crest, while Int. 80 proceeds due west to Joliet and across the State.

South and east of HAZEL CREST is HOMEWOOD, 23.3 *m*. (659 alt., 18,871 pop. 1970; 13,371, 1960, inc. 41%) where the WASHINGTON PARK RACE TRACK is easy of access from Illinois 1. Some of Chicago's most popular country clubs are located in these southwest suburbs and Homewood especially has swimming and fishing in man-made pools. The Illinois Central Railroad and the South Suburban Safeway bus lines provide service to the Loop. The Chicago Military Academy is located here. The Homewood Public Library has a collection of nearly 50,000 books and a circulation of 155,000.

Homewood was originally named Hartford for James Hart, who platted the site in 1852.

On a 250-acre campus is the GLENWOOD SCHOOL FOR BOYS, 23.8 *m*., established in 1887 for normal boys from broken homes. The institution is privately endowed and maintained by tuition fees and contributions. The 240 boys, enrolled through private application or social agency referral, receive education in grades 2 through 12. They live in residence halls with house parents for 11 months each year, spending the remaining month at the Glenwood Boys Camp in Northern Wisconsin.

East of Homewood on US 1 is THORNTON (3,714 pop. 1970; 2,895, 1960, inc. 28%). East is a large terrain of woods, creeks, and several good-sized lakes, including Thornton Woods, Brownell Woods, Jorgenson Woods, and North Creek Meadow, a fine recreation area reached via the Tri-State Tollway and the Calumet Expressway (Int. 94). At the Indiana border is Lansing, (25,805 pop. 1970; 18,098, 1960, inc. 42%). This is one of the older settlements in the Calumet area, tracing its history back to the arrival of two Lansing brothers in 1864. It is served by the Penn Central, Int. 80, Int. 94, and Illinois 83.

CHICAGO HEIGHTS, 27.5 *m*. (640-710 alt., 40,900 pop. 1970; 34,331, 1960, inc. 19.1%) a city in Cook County, 8 *m*. south of the limits of Chicago, is built on the Valparaiso Moraine, which was deposited by the Wisconsin glacier. Although augmenting the industrial activity of the area with a work force of approx. 40,000, the city has attractive parks and wooded residential areas and is adjacent to 1,350 acres of the Forest Preserve.. It is governed by a mayor and four commissioners and is served by 9 freight railroads and two bus lines, the Greyhound and the South Suburban Safety lines. Among the large steel makers represented here are Allied Products, Corp., Keystone Steel & Wire, Mid West Forging & Manufacturing Co. and Triem Steel & Processing, Inc.

The site was a meeting point for travelers from east and south. Here the Hubbard Trail from Vincennes to Fort Dearborn crossed the Sauk Trail, along which Indians traveled between their hunting grounds and the fur post and garrison at Detroit. The Sauk Trail became the westward artery for trappers, soldiers, settlers, and the mail. Covered wagons traversed it to the Plains; the forty-niners followed it to California; New Englanders hurried over it to settle Kansas and Negro slaves used it to escape from Missouri to Indiana.

The settlement at the junction of the trails became known as Thorn Grove in the 1830's. German settlers renamed it Bloom in 1849, honoring Robert Bluhm, a German patriot executed at Vienna in 1848. The present name and industrial character of Chicago Heights date from 1890 when the Chicago Heights Land Association induced manufacturers to establish plants here, bringing with them hundreds of workmen and their families. Chicago Heights was incorporated in 1892 and was once the most important of the steel-making communities of the Chicago district. But when the blast furnaces were moved to newer facilities on Lake Michigan, local production was reduced to steel fabrication. Chemical plants also were early migrants to the town.

The plant of United States Steel at Chicago Heights belongs to the USS Agri-Chemicals Division, which manufactures chemical fertilizers that are marketed, along with pesticides, to farming areas everywhere through company-owned farm and ranch service centers and individual dealers.

Industrial plants and millworkers' houses occupy the east side of the city; the west side consists of the more spacious residences of plant officials and Chicago commuters. Glass, metal products, and chemicals are among the chief manufactures.

PRAIRIE STATE JUNIOR COLLEGE, 197th and Halsted Sts., was opened in 1958 and enrolls nearly 3,000 students annually. It has a faculty of 135.

A Downtown Redevelopment Program has modernized the business section in recent years. The city has seven parks with fieldhouses and eight public playgrounds. The Harold Colbert Jones Memorial Community Center has a professional staff and a migrant health clinic. The Chicago Heights Free Public Library has more than 52,000 vols. and an annual circulation of around 108,000. It is a member of the Suburban Library System, in which 54 libraries cooperate.

More than a dozen golf and country clubs, public and private, are concentrated in this general area, among them Calumet, Cherry Hills, Chicago Heights, Flossmoor, Glenwoodie, Idlewild, Lincolnshire, Longwood, Olympia Fields, Prestwick, Ravisloe, Shady Lawn and Urban Hills.

EAST CHICAGO HEIGHTS (5,000 pop. 1970; 3,270, 1960, inc. 52.9%) adjoins Chicago Heights on the east and has developed from the movement of suburbia into what was once farm land. The Calumet Expressway (Interstate 94 and Illinois 394) runs east of the village line while US 30, the Lincoln Highway, intersects it. Continuing south on Int. 94 the highway reaches SAUK VILLAGE, (7,479 pop. 1970; 4,687, 1960, inc. 59.6%) another village in the expanding suburban area of Cook County.

SOUTH CHICAGO HEIGHTS, 29.7 m. on Illinois 1 (4,923 pop. 1970; 4,043, 1960; inc. 21.8%) in Cook County has the homes of many of the employees of industries in the area, mostly descendants of Polish, German, and Italian immigrants. The Sauk Trail runs through the suburb and the Sauk Trail Forest Preserve lies west of it.

STEGER, 30 m. (8,401 pop. 1970; 6,432, 1960, inc. 26%) is bisected by the line separating Cook and Will Counties. Originally called Columbia Heights by a real estate promoter, it became Steger in 1897 because the principal industry was the piano factory of John V. Steger. The decline of the piano, caused by the rise of radio, closed the factory and started the Steger Furniture Co. to make radio and television cabinets in the same premises.

CRETE, 31.2 m. (720 alt., 4,650 pop. 1970; 3,463, 1960; inc. 34.4%) a village in Will County, was first settled by Willard Wood who operated a tavern on the Hubbard Trail in the 1836-40 period sold lots to settlers and named the place Crete. The Lincoln Field Race Track started racing east of the village in 1926 and more recently has become known as Balmoral Park and offers harness racing in September and other cards during the year.

PARK FOREST (30,638 pop. 1970; 29,993, 1960) is west of Chicago Heights in Cook and Will Counties. It is a prime example of how a planned community can come quickly into existence when there is a big demand for housing. After World War II Chicago had a great many families, including numerous newly-weds, looking for new dwellings. Park Forest was incorporated as a village in 1949 when most of its terrain was covered with cornfields. When one-family houses began to be produced on a large scale new migration flooded into the place. It became known as a young folks' village. Houses were made for middle-income people; when their buying power became evident 70 large stores came to surround Park Forest Plaza, including Marshall Field & Co., Goldblatt, Bramson, Sears, Lytton, Ace Hardware, and Jewell-Osco. Townhouses and cooperatives were kept in a reasonable rental range. In 1972 the village had 14 churches and 20 parks with full equipment for sports and games. It has 78 acres allotted to an industrial park. The Townsend High School serves the area.

PARK FOREST SOUTH, in Will County contiguous to Park Forest and west of Steger and Crete, had its first census in 1970: 1,748. It was laid out by Park Forest South Developers, Inc., the main investors of which are Nathan and Lewis Manilow, in partnership with Mid-America Improvement Corp., a subsidiary of Illinois Central

Industries, and United States Gypsum Urban Development Co., a subsidiary of U. S. Gypsum. The extensive plans include a large residential community with independent educational and shopping facilities.

A program of interfaith cooperation was sponsored in Park Forest South in 1971 by the Church Federation of Greater Chicago before any church had begun services there. Working together were ministers, priests, and rabbis, to accomplish a day care center, social agencies, community forums, pastoral counseling, and welcomes for newcomers.

GOVERNORS STATE UNIVERSITY opened its doors in September, 1971, in temporary quarters on Central Avenue between Richton Park and Monee. It has in reserve 753 acres of a new campus east of Governors Highway and Cicero Ave. in Park Forest South, where the permanent buildings for a completely functioning university are being erected. It was established July 17, 1969, to serve junior-community college transfer students enrolling to complete a four-year course toward baccalaureate and master degrees. Governors began operations with a nontraditional grading system, by which a student chooses his objectives after conference with his professor and is not judged A-B-C-D- on a scale of 100 points but given credit on his showing in a conference with the faculty or by writing a paper. Only 2 percent of U. S. colleges had adopted this method of valuation by 1972, but more than half had introduced variations in the older method, such as permitting a pass/fail system for one course only, according to the American Assn. of College Registrars & Admissions Officers. The university is under the jurisdiction of the Board of Governors of State Colleges and Universities. It has four colleges: Environmental and Applied Science, Cultural Studies, Humane Letters, and Commercial and Public Service. In 1973-74 it had 1,511 students, 100 faculty.

RICHTON PARK (2,558 pop. 1970; 933, 1960, inc. 174%). MONEE, (940 pop. 1970; 646, 1960, inc. 45%) are also within a few minutes drive of Int. 57.

Return to Illinois 1:

In the late 1820's droves of hogs owned by Gurdon S. Hubbard roamed the prairie between Crete and Danville. At intervals Hubbard and a crew of what might be termed "pigboys" rounded up the half-wild animals and drove them to Chicago where they were slaughtered.

BEECHER, 38.2 m. (723 alt., 1,770 pop. 1970; 1,367, 1960) a village in Will County, was named for Henry Ward Beecher (1813-87), noted divine and leader of anti-slavery forces, and provides retail facilities for the surrounding area. The village was platted in 1870 as a shipping point on the Chicago & Eastern Illinois Railway.

South of Beecher Illinois 1 crosses an agricultural district of orchards, truck farms, and cornfields, already being crowded by suburban housing.

ST. JUDE'S SEMINARY, 50.3 m., is a two-story brick structure of neo-Romanesque design, built in 1938. The loggia contains a heroic marble statue of St. Jude. The institution is maintained by the Claretian

Missionaries, a Roman Catholic order, as a preparatory seminary for young men.

At GRANT PARK, 45 m. (801 pop. 1970; 757, 1960) Illinois 1 has a junction with Illinois 17, which comes from the Indiana line and combines with Illinois 1 for 7 m. to Momence, after which it goes west to Kankakee. At Kankakee are junctions with US 45, US 52, and Illinois 49. Illinois 17 is another highway that runs straight west across Illinois farmlands. It passes through Dwight (*see Tour 17*), a junction with US 66 (Bloomington, Springfield, East St. Louis). West of Dwight, 12 m., a parallel route, Illinois 18, splits off from Illinois 17, then goes west 9 m. to Streator in LaSalle County, crosses the Illinois River and terminates at Henry, and a junction with Illinois 29 (south to Peoria). Illinois 17 continues west and terminates at NEW BOSTON on the Mississippi River, in Mercer County 15 m. west of Aledo.

Continue south on Illinois 1:

MOMENCE, 52.7 m. (626 alt., 2,836 pop. 1970; 2,949, 1960, dec. 3.8%), a village in Kankakee County on the Kankakee River, was platted in 1844 by Dr. Hiram Todd and named for Momence, half-breed husband of Jeneir, daughter of a Potawatomi chief. Momence was an important point on the Hubbard Trail and the Chicago-Vincennes Road. As many as 200 wagons and pack trains camped here overnight. A flour mill was built on the island in the river in 1844. Today Momence produces pet food, textiles, steel and concrete products, and custom-built truck bodies.

The Kankakee crossing often presented serious problems to pioneer travelers. Gurdon S. Hubbard was unable to ford the stream in November, 1830, because of floating ice. "My wagon," he relates, "was one of those heavy, large-box vehicles called a Pennsylvania wagon, the box of which we chinked with snow, over which we poured water, which soon froze and made it water tight. Into this we put our harness, blankets, and utensils, and using it for a boat passed safely over, the horses being made to swim. . . ."

For his memorable ride between Chicago and Danville in 1827, Hubbard has been likened to Paul Revere. Informed that the warring Winnebago might attack Chicago, Hubbard volunteered to get help. He left Chicago in the afternoon and arrived at Danville the next day. There he raised a force of 50 men who returned with him. The attack did not occur; later the Winnebago signed a truce.

The area immediately south of Momence is one of the nation's largest producers of gladiolus flowers and bulbs, and a three-day Gladiolus Festival is held annually in Momence, usually the second week in August.

ST. ANNE, 65 m. (678 alt., 1,271 pop. 1970; 1,378, 1960) a village in Kankakee County, was founded by Father Charles Chiniquy, who, suspended from his pastorate in Bourbonnais, came here in 1852, accompanied by most of his French-Canadian parishioners. Father Chiniquy was excommunicated in 1856, and many of his congregation joined the Presbyterian Church; the log church he had built became a mission. The inhabitants of St. Anne are still largely of French-Canadian stock. French names predominate and the French language is spoken to some extent, as it is throughout this section.

St. Anne's Roman Catholic Church, one block east of the highway, was built in 1872 to replace Father Chiniquy's log church, and was restored after a fire in 1893. A stone structure of Gothic design, topped with a bell tower, the church contains a shrine to St. Anne, established in 1888 to provide parishioners with a counterpart of the shrine at Beaupré, Canada. St. Anne's Day, July 26, brings hundreds of visitors to venerate the relic of *la bonne Sainte Anne*.

MARTINTON, 73 *m*. (627 alt., 278 pop. 1970), in Iroquois County, named for Porter Martin, a settlor from Vermont, was platted in 1871 as a shipping point on the Chicago & Eastern Illinois Railway.

At 75 *m*. is the junction with US 52 (*see Tour 15*), and at 80.7 *m*. is the junction with US 24 (*see Tour 16*), which unites with State 1 for 2.7 miles.

WATSEKA, 82 *m*. (634 alt., 5,294 pop. 1970; 5,219, 1960, inc. 1.8%) seat of Iroquois County, is located on the upper part of the Iroquois River at a junction with US 24 (west to Peoria, Quincy). It is in the heart of a high-income farm country with a remarkably stable population—Iroquois County reported 33,532 in 1970, 33,562 in 1960—where the average farm unit is valued at $900,000, the soybean crop is the largest in the State, and there are large herds of beef and dairy cattle and flocks of sheep. Much of this income supports the enterprise of Watseka, which in recent years has built modern facilities for government and retailing.

A distinctive contrast in architecture is provided by the new Iroquois County Courthouse, and the older one built in 1866. The new building, a modern quadrilateral structure with a flat roof, was built in 1965 with the legacy of more than $1,500,000 willed by Mrs. Kathryn Clifton, who ordered farm land sold and the courthouse built without the use of public funds. The Old Courthouse, which cost $28,000 in 1866 and had the period embellishments of a mansard roof and a cupola, is now the Iroquois County Historical Museum. It has 15 rooms devoted to Indian artifacts, pioneer furnishings, paintings, a one-room school, a chapel, a courtroom and the old jail. *Open daily 1-5 Sept. through May; 9-5 weekdays and 1-5 Sundays rest of year.*

A plaque on a boulder names Gurdon S. Hubbard, the fur trader, as the first settler, building a log cabin in 1821. He married Watch-e-kee, niece of a Potawatomi chief, but after two years gave her to his partner, Le Vasseur. "Our separation was by mutual agreement . . . because I was about to abandon the Indian trade," explained Hubbard later. On Feb. 12, 1833, Hubbard was a representative of Vermilion County in the legislature and moved the organization of Iroquois County, approved in 1835. In 1835 Micajah Stanley settled here and in 1859 laid out a village known as South Middleport. In August, 1863, this was recorded as a village and in September named Watseka. In 1865 Watseka became the county seat and in 1867 a city.

Watseka is served by the Chicago & Eastern Illinois Ry. and the Toledo, Peoria & Western, which runs through the city. Its principal industries are T. & D. Metal Products, Electronic Components Corp., and UARCO, Inc. It has 13 churches, a branch of the Eastern Illinois Mental Health Clinic, and the new Iroquois Hospital, 210 beds, completed in 1970. The Watseka Public Library, modernized in 1961, is a member of the Lincoln Trail Library System. Shagback Airport is located northeast of the city. Watseka is hq for Nimz Transportation, Inc., which specializes in air freight in eastern Illinois communities. The Watseka Chamber of Commerce is at 102 S. Fourth St. The *Iroquois County Daily Times* is a six-day newspaper and the *Watseka Republican* is published weekly.

MILFORD, 96.5 *m.* (666 alt., 1,656 pop. 1970; 1,699, 1960), a rural center in Iroquois County, was platted in 1836 by William Pickerel, proprietor of a mill near the ford where the Hubbard Trail crossed Sugar Creek, and was incorporated as a village in 1874.

At 107.7 *m.* is a junction with Illinois 9.

Left on Illinois 9 is HOOPESTON, 0.5 *m.* (717 alt., 6,461 pop. 1970; 6,606, 1960) a canning center in Vermilion County. Following the construction of the Chicago & Eastern Illinois Railway in 1871, which here intersected the Lafayette, Bloomington & Muncie Railroad (later the Nickel Plate), three land companies platted townsites on the Hoope farm. By January, 1872, there were 70 buildings and 245 inhabitants. Residents of the boom town were so confident of its rise to metropolitan stature that the first copy of the local paper, North Vermilion *Chronicle,* Jan. 11, 1872, was auctioned off for $32.50. Besides its canneries (corn and beans) and factories making cans and canning machinery, Hoopeston has grain elevators and machine shops. Grain, hay, and livestock are shipped in large quantities.

Near the entrance to 30-acre McFerren Park (*swimming, small zoo, and picnic grounds*), 107.8 *m.,* a bronze plaque marks the Hubbard Trail.

ROSSVILLE, 113.4 *m.* (700 alt., 1,420 pop. 1970; 1,470, 1960), entered on a street flanked with fine trees and large houses, was named for Jacob Ross, an early settler. Platted in 1857 at the junction of the Chicago-Vincennes and the Attica-Bloomington roads, the site had previously been known as Henpeck. On the lawn of the Take-A-Rest Masonic Home, a two-story brick house with a mansard roof, is a marker designating the course of the Hubbard Trail.

At 118.7 *m.* is a junction with Illinois 119.

Left on Illinois 119 to ALVIN, 3 *m.* (663 alt., 318 pop.), a grain elevator village platted in 1876; L. from the north of Alvin on a graveled road to an Old Mill, 4.2 *m.,* built in 1838. The weatherbeaten frame structure contains much of its original machinery, including stone burrs imported from France; the mill was operated until the early 1930's.

Southward the route traverses the eastern Illinois coal mining region; the terrain is broken by river valleys and the broad ridges of the Bloomington Moraine (*see Tour 4*).

In a small grove, 126.5 *m.,* is a Roadside Picnic Park, the first to be established on a principal route by the Illinois State Planning Commission (1936).

Lake Vermilion (*boating, fishing, swimming*), 129 *m.,* impounded by a dam across the North Fork of the Vermilion River, is eight miles long and nearly a mile wide. Although an artificial lake, it has the appearance of a natural body of water, with summer cottages along its heavily wooded banks. At the northern end of the lake is 233-acre Harrison Park, a gift of the late John H. Harrison of Danville.

DANVILLE, 132 *m.* (42,570 pop. 1970; 41,856, 1960, inc. 1.7%) is a junction of the north and south forks of the Vermilion River. It is the county seat of Vermilion County and has a junction with US 150 and Interstate 74. *See article on Danville.*

KICKAPOO STATE PARK, 6 *m.* west of Danville on US 150 (Main St.) is a park of 1,578 acres developed from a wasteland made by strip-mining. The State acquired the first segment in 1939 after Clinton C. Tilton, a retired newspaperman, raised $15,000 in Danville, Champaign, Urbana, and other towns. In the park is the grave of John Cox, Indian fighter after the Revolutionary War and scout in the Black Hawk War, who settled on the Middle Fork River in 1829. The park is near the site of the pioneer salt springs, and an iron evaporating kettle found here is kept in a small memorial off US 150, 0.5 *m.* west of the park entrance.

BELGIUM, 137 *m.* (670 alt., 578 pop. 1970) incorporated as a village in 1909, was named for the homeland of its predominant group. Prior to the exhaustion of local coal seams in early 1930's, mining was the chief industry here and in the adjoining WESTVILLE, 138 *m.* (671 alt., 3,655 pop. 1970; 3,499, 1960), which was platted in 1873 by W. P. and E. A. West. Both communities now send their workers to Danville.

GEORGETOWN, 142.5 *m* (676 alt., 3,984 pop. 1970, 3,544, 1960), in Vermilion County, laid out in 1827, has a town square and maple-shaded streets. Among the first settlers were Quakers who emigrated from Tennessee and North Carolina because of their anti-slavery sympathies. Coal mining was the chief occupation until the 1940's.

OLIVET, 144.5 *m.,* consists of Olivet College, a coeducational Bible school and college maintained by the Church of the Nazarene. The student body, numbering 1,700 in 1970-71, is housed in three-story brick structures on a 14-acre campus.

At 145.5 *m.* is a junction with a graveled road. Right on this road is VERMILION GROVE, 0.4 *m.,* site of the first Quaker settlement in Illinois (1820).

RIDGE FARM, 147.5 *m.* (694 alt., 1,015 pop. 1970; 894, 1960), was platted in 1853 and incorporated as a village in 1874.

Left from Ridge Farm on Main Street to a junction with a blacktop road, 2 *m.*; R. to the HARRISON PURCHASE MARKER, 2.3 *m.,* a boulder placed by the Women's Club of Ridge Farm in 1927. At this site in 1809 Gen. William Henry Harrison (1773-1841) negotiated a treaty whereby the United States obtained more than 1,000,000 acres from the Indians in return for $4,000.

CHRISMAN, 154.6 m. (645 alt., 1,265 pop. 1970; 1,221, 1960) in Edgar County, was platted in 1872 by Mathias Chrisman when his farm on the Vincennes Trace was crossed by two pioneer railroads. One mile south Illinois 1 has a junction with US 36 (west to Decatur, Springfield).

The highway passes Twin Lakes, 166.7 m., and 100-acre Twin Lakes Park (cabins, picnic grounds, swimming, fishing, boating).

PARIS, 168 m. (739 alt., 3,984 pop. 1970; 3,544, 1960), seat of Edgar County, was platted in 1853 and named after Paris, Kentucky. Here, while attending the county fair, Lincoln's kinsman, Dennis Hanks (see Tour 21) was run down and killed by a team of horses. Lincoln addressed an enthusiastic Paris audience in 1856 on behalf of presidential candidate John C. Fremont (1813-90). Two years later, returning as a candidate for the United States Senate. Lincoln spoke from 3 to 5 on the afternoon of September 17; that evening Owen Lovejoy, brother of the martyred Elijah Lovejoy (see Alton), denounced slavery from the same platform. Throughout the Civil War, Edgar County was beset with Copperheads, disaffected Northerners. In February, 1864, they had minor clashes with Union troops, who dispersed them.

Paris is at a junction of Illinois 16, (west to Charleston, Mattoon) and Illinois 133 west. US 150 from Terre Haute, Ind., joins Illinois 1 at Paris and proceeds with it 36 m. north to Danville. Paris has diversified industries, making buses, trucks, aircraft and automobile parts, and food machinery.

The CARNEGIE PUBLIC LIBRARY, built in 1904, has a collection of about 25,000 books and circulates around 95,000. It is a member of the Lincoln Trail Library System.

Southward the highway traverses farming country. The old expression "everything's lovely and the goose hangs high" is claimed by old residents to have originated in the robust pioneer sport of "goose pulling," once popular in this region. A live goose, its neck stripped of feathers and greased, was suspended from a tree barely within reach of a man on horseback. Contestants, mounted bareback, galloped down a gauntlet of shouting spectators who spurred on the horses with hearty thwacks. The rider who succeeded in tearing off the goose's neck was declared the winner and awarded the remainder of the fowl.

Section b. Marshall to Cave-in-Rock. The Valley of the Wabash

MARSHALL, 183 m. (606 alt., 3,468 pop. 1970; 3,270, 1960, inc. 6%) seat of Clark County, is located 9 m. west of the Indiana line and 16 m. west of Terre Haute. It is at a junction with Illinois 1, which follows the old road from Chicago to Shawneetown and at this point is part of the Lincoln Heritage Trail. When the survey for the National Road was completed Governor Joseph Duncan and William B. Archer selected a spot between the State line and Vandalia for a town and Archer named it for the Chief Justice of the United States. Marshall is a city of homes on well-shaded streets; shops, and light industries. In 1902-1920 it had a limited boom from oil found in the vicinity. The Marshall Public Library has a circulation of approx. 15,000 books annually and is a member of the Lincoln Trail Library System.

The LINCOLN TRAIL STATE PARK, 186 *m*., is an area of 932 acres for recreation with a man-made lake stocked for fishing. It commemorates the passage in 1830 of the Lincoln family, when Abraham was 21 years old.

As Illinois 1 proceeds south in a straight line it comes closer to the Wabash River and its fishing areas. Parallel with it is a line of the Penn-Central Railroad. A number of hamlets of nominal population lie along the Lincoln Heritage Trail; they include Ernst, Hatton, Walnut Prairie, West Union, and West York.

HUTSONVILLE, 1 *m*. east of Illinois 1 on the Wabash River (544 pop. 1970; 583, 1960), has a free bridge connecting with an Indiana highway that has junctions with US 41 and US 150, combined, which goes north to Terre Haute and south to Vincennes, Ind.

At GORDON, a Crawford County village of nominal population Illinois 1 has a junction with Illinois 33. The ILLINOIS TRAIL COLLEGE is at Gordon. Illinois 33 has come north from opposite Vincennes along the Wabash River, now several miles east of Illinois 1. This is the Lincoln Heritage Trail along which the Lincolns moved into Illinois in 1830. *See Tour 21.*

PALESTINE, 4 *m*. east of Gordon on Illinois 33 (1,640 pop. 1970; 1,564, 1960) was a village in Crawford County where the Lincolns stopped.

ROBINSON, 3 *m*. west of Gordon on Illinois 33 (7,178 pop. 1970; 7,226, 1960) is the seat of Crawford County. It profited from the production of oil in the area and had a spurt in population before 1960, but with the decrease in oil its population has become static, and that of Crawford County has lost 4.5%, from 20,751 in 1960 to 19,824 in 1970. The city nas named for U. S. Senator John M. Robinson of Carmi and became the county seat in 1843. It has light industries, including electronics. Robinson Municipal Airport is located 5 *m*. east, hence 2 *m*. east of Gordon and Illinois 1. The Robinson Carnegie Library, built 1906, had approx. 30,000 vols. and a circulation of 258,484 in 1970, a large turnover for its size. It is a member of the Cumberland Trail Library System.

Continue west on Illinois 33 for 22 *m*. to a junction with Illinois 130, north-south; thence south on Illinois 130 to NEWTON (3,024 pop. 1970; 2,901, 1960, inc. 4.2%) seat of Jasper County. This is in the area of the Embarras River oil fields. After many of the wells had been shut down as unproductive a new lessee, the Union Oil Co. of California, which had acquired considerable acreage from the Pure Oil Co., on Dec. 17, 1965, opened a new flow of 538 bbl. a day at a depth of 2,940 ft. in a sealed well. Another flow of about 1,500 bbl. a day was located a short distance away.

Newton is only 22 *m.* southeast of Effingham, where Illinois 33 has a junction with expressways to East St. Louis and Cairo.

LAWRENCEVILLE, 202 *m.* (5,862 pop., 1970; 5,492, 1960, inc. 6.8%) seat of Lawrence County, is at a junction with US 50, which comes from Vincennes, Indiana, and moves across Illinois to East St. Louis. Rock Hills State Park, near Sumner, 12 *m.* west, is a recreation area covering 948.4 acres. *See Tour 20.*

ST. FRANCISVILLE (997 pop. 1970; 1,040, 1960) a city in Lawrence County, is located on the Wabash River 2 *m.* east of Illinois 1. There is a ferry to Indiana.

ALLENDALE, 216 *m.* (425 pop. 1970; 465, 1960) a village, is on the main highway 14 *m.* south of Lawrenceville.

MOUNT CARMEL, 226 *m.* (465 alt. 8,096 pop. 1970; 8,594, 1960) a city and seat of Wabash County, is located where the highway again comes close to the river's bank and is only 1 *m.* from the confluence of the White River and the Wabash. Available are a ferry and a free bridge to Indiana on Illinois 15, and Penn Central and Southern Railroad lines. The town was laid out in 1818 by the Rev. Thomas S. Hinde of Ohio, with the project of establishing a "moral, temperate, and industrious village." In 1900 the mussels of the river were found useful for making pearl buttons and the industry continues. Occasionally pearls were found in mussel shells. The city makes chemicals useful to the oil industry of the Wabash Valley. In 1970 the Mount Carmel Public Library reported a collection of 26,635 books and a circulation of 65,222 annually. It is a member of the Cumberland Trail Library System. The WABASH VALLEY COMMUNITY COLLEGE was opened in 1960 and in 1971 enrolled 650 students with a faculty of 35.

Mount Carmel is the birthplace of Robert Ridgway (1850-1929), noted ornithologist, whose studies of birds in eastern Illinois first awoke naturalists to the rich resources in this area. His pioneering books included *The Ornithology of Illinois* and *The Birds of North and Middle America.* He was the first to publish studies of the relation of bird colors to geographical distribution. His principal work took place in Olney. *See Tour 20.*

KEENSBURG, 233 *m.* (242 pop. 1970; 263, 1960) a village in Wabash County, is 3 *m.* west of BEALL WOODS NATURE PRESERVE AND CONSERVATION AREA, a section of 636 acres open for camping, picnics, and studies of bird life and trees. It is described by the State as having the finest stand of virgin timber in Illinois. Descriptions of the flora to be seen in the lower part of the Wabash Valley show an extraordinary richness. While the trees in the northern part are closer to northern species and the southern part has many southern varieties, the two are mixed in most parts of this and the Shawnee National Forest farther south. Here are found the beech, hard maple, and oaks of the north and the cypress, pecan, catalpa, tupelo gum, and water locust of the south. The buckeye, honey locust, black locust and sycamore thrive. "By candlelight the sycamores are gleaming" wrote Paul Dresser in his famous song, *On the Banks of the Wabash*, and in this valley sycamores have been found at a height of 175 ft. with a girth of 30 to 40 ft., while pecans and white ash have their first branches 90 ft. above the ground and sassafras is sometimes 80 ft. tall.

GRAYVILLE, 241 *m.* (2,035 pop. 1970; 2,280, 1960) a city on the Wabash River that straddles the boundary between Edwards and White Counties, has a ferry and is on the projected route of Interstate 64. The first oil well in this region was discovered 3 *m.* east in 1902 and oil accounts for most of the city's economy.

CROSSVILLE, 249 *m.* (860 pop. 1970; 874, 1960) a village in White County, is at a junction with US 460, which comes from Evansville, Ind., and moves across Illinois in a northwesterly direction, combines with Illinois 15 at Mount Vernon and reaches the Mississippi at East St. Louis. East from Crossville on US 460 to the Wabash River, 8 *m.*, and over toll bridge to NEW HARMONY, on the Indiana bank, site of two historic socio-religious and economic reform settlements of the early 19th century. The New Harmony Memorial Commission of the State of Indiana has restored buildings and marked sites in this quiet rural town where men once dedicated themselves to the eradication of social inequality.

George Rapp broke with the Lutheran church to preach a form of primitive Christianity in his native Württenberg and in 1805 acquired 5,000 acres of Government land in Butler County, Pennsylvania, to start a communal settlement. About 600 supported him, recognized him as their spiritual leader with full authority over them, shared all property and in a year adopted celibacy for men and women. Finding Pennsylvania difficult, in 1814 he bought nearly 25,000 acres of Government land in the Wabash Valley and started a settlement called Harmonie. Under Rapp's strict discipline his followers, about 1,000 German immigrants, cleared land, drained swamps, planted crops, raised sheep, cultivated grapes, and built a church, a granary that could serve as a fort, a communal house, and a tavern. After 10 years, during which Rapp bought another 14,000 acres, dissension split the colony. Rapp finally returned to Pennsylvania with the core of his band and sent an agent to London to offer the settlement for sale.

There a successful textile mill owner named Robert Owen, who had been applying reforms to factory labor, determined to make a new start free from the inequalities of British industrialism. He bought Rapp's settlement for the equivalent of $182,000, brought workers over, and called it New Harmony. He had extended education to the very young and encouraged self-governing workshops, forerunners of trades unions. He introduced communal ownership of property and representative government. British scientists and educators visited New Harmony and William MacLure, a distinguished scientist, came to apply the Pestalozzi system of education, in which the natural bent of the child is emphasized. He organized the Workingmen's Institute. But Owen was no more successful than Rapp in averting dissension. In 1828 he ended his experiment and returned to England. New Harmony, however, continued. Until 1856 it was the seat of the U. S. Geological Survey. Robert Dale Owen, the founder's eldest son, became an eminent Indiana legislator who supported rights for women. Another son, David Dale Owen, was a notable geologist.

CARMI, 257 *m.* (399 alt., 6,033 pop. 1970; 6,152, 1960) was platted in 1816 as the seat of White County. It is on the Little Wabash

River and the eastern terminal of US 460. It is a distribution point for farm products and oil and has freight service by the Penn Central and the Louisville & Nashville. The Ratcliff Inn, 216 E. Main St., where Abraham Lincoln stopped in 1840, has been restored as the headquarters of the White County Historical Society, and has Town Board records, antiques, letters of U. S. Senator John M. Robinson and pioneers. Furnishings of Senator Robinson's home are preserved in the Robinson-Stewart House, 110 S. Main Cross St., as well as household wares from other places. A cottage built in 1814 was once the home of Robinson. He served as senator 1830-41 and had been appointed associate justice of the Illinois Supreme Court just before his death in 1843.

Leonard White, who had been justice of the peace and judge of the court of common pleas in Gallatin County, in 1816 joined Lowry Hay in starting a water mill at Carmi. Hay laid out the town in 1816 and opened his house to the first county court, and the White County courthouse was built on land he donated. He became county surveyor and justice of the peace. Hay and White were members of a committee that arranged for the first bridge across the Little Wabash River at Carmi.

From Carmi Illinois 1 proceeds 13 *m.* southwest to a junction with US 45 1 *m.* east of NORRIS CITY (1,316 pop. 1970). Here Illinois 1 turns sharply southeast toward the SHAWNEE NATIONAL FOREST, while US 45 continues as the main highway to Massac County on the Ohio River and Paducah, Kentucky. Between this point and Cave-in-Rock Illinois 1 crosses the eastern tip of the Illinois Ozarks, a narrow range of hills that runs east and west across the State. The southern end of the route moves into the thickly wooded areas of the Shawnee National Forest and the flood plain of the Ohio River.

SHAWNEE NATIONAL FOREST came under the control of the Forest Service of the U. S. Dept. of Agriculture in 1933. By 1970 the Federal Government had acquired 242,215 acres and was adding several thousand annually. The forest has more than 500 camp and picnic sites, where visitors may camp for two weeks. More than 1,000,000 people come annually to hunt, fish, and camp. There are now more than 20,000 deer and 3,500 wild turkeys, and waters are stocked with bass, bluegill, catfish, and crappie. State game laws apply. The Illinois Dept. of Conservation joins the Service in building water holes and areas for wildlife.

The Forest Service promotes multiple use: timber, water, forage, wildlife, recreation. In 1970 it sold 7,845,000 board feet and gave 25% of receipts, $34,959, for county use. It developed the first ecological area in LaRue-Pine Hills; built the Lake of Egypt, 2,300 acres, jointly with Southern Illinois Power of Marion; restored the Iron Furnace that was charcoal-fired from 1839 to 1883. *For information, reservations, address Shawnee National Forest, Harrisburg, Ill. 62946.*

At 17.9 *m.* there is a junction with Illinois 13. East on Illinois 13 4 *m.* to EQUALITY, (732 pop. 1970; 665, 1960) a village in Gallatin County, in an area where salt was the principal product for years. Here is a memorial to Michael K. Lawler, Civil War General, who organized a regiment that fought at Fort Donelson and other Kentucky and Tennessee sites. He commanded with distinction at Vicksburg.

Equality and Half Moon Lick were centers of salt mining in the 19th century. Salt Spring was located at the south bank of the Saline River, 3 miles east of Equality; Salt Lake was 4 miles west of Salt Spring. Old Spring was developed in 1803 and Gallatin Springs in 1814. Slaves were once employed at the mines. Most operations had ended by 1873.

SHAWNEETOWN, 4 m. east of the junction on Illinois 13 (1,742 pop. 1970; 1,280, 1960) seat of Gallatin County, one of the newest cities in the State, stands on hilly land about 450 alt., 3 m. west of OLD SHAWNEETOWN, (350 alt., 342 pop. 1970; 433, 1960) a village on the Ohio River since pioneer days. Shawneetown has the Courthouse, several banks and business houses, half a dozen industries and numerous dwellings, chiefly belonging to residents of the old town who moved here after the Ohio River flood of 1937 had devastated it. That flood was so disastrous that many people, who had helped preserve their architectural relics of the Federal period, declared "This is the end!" With the help of State and Government building funds they moved to a site laid out as long ago as 1810. A Federal Housing Project added new dwellings to the city.

The sesquicentennial anniversary of Shawneetown was observed on July 1-4, 1960. In connection with it the Illinois State Historical Society held sessions in the Gallatin County Courthouse. A time capsule was placed in Shawneetown.

The Shawneetown Bridge across the Ohio (Illinois 13) was opened June 1, 1956. It replaced a ferry operated 146 years, 110 of them by one family.

Settled early in the 19th century, the original Shawneetown soon became the seat of Gallatin County and the land office for a vast territory; as such, it was one of the most important financial centers in the new country. Shawneetown's income was augmented materially by the nearby salines, from which salt was carted into the town and there transferred to keelboats for shipment to the East and South.

The Bank of Illinois, first bank in Illinois Territory, was established by John Marshall of Shawneetown when the Territorial Legislature authorized it December 28, 1816. The Shawneetown State Bank came after Illinois was a State. The banks were authorized to issue currency.

The town bore the yearly invasions of the Ohio unprotected until the unusually severe flood of 1884, after which it constructed a comprehensive levee system. But in 1898, and again in 1913, Shawneetown was under water. In 1932 the levee was raised 5 feet above the 1913 high-water mark, a margin of safety that seemed to be ample for any emergency.

But Shawneetown had not envisioned anything like the 1937 flood. By January 24 water was only a few inches from the levee top. Meteorologists predicted a further rise. Small groups of people huddled on street corners, terrified, waiting; the telephone service ceased; hemmed in by the ever-swelling Ohio, Shawneetown flashed a desperate cry for help over an amateur's short-wave radio. Responding to the call, a river packet and several motorboats evacuated the townspeople just as the waters began to trickle over the levee. A roaring crashing avalanche soon inundated the cuplike townsite. At its height the flood topped the levee by 6 feet and covered three-fourths of Gallatin County, between Shawneetown and Harrisburg, some 25 miles distant. Route 13 was under 8 to 14 ft. of water; motorboats navigated the entire distance to rescue marooned families.

The 1937 flood marked the end of Shawneetown's "pertinacious adhesion" to the riverbank, for there was no longer reason to remain. Gone were the packets and keelboats. Gone was the steady traffic of settlers, goods, and singing rivermen. With the aid of the State the RFC and the WPA, a project for moving the town to the hills 4 *m.* away was begun and completed in the early 1940's. The historic site became OLD SHAWNEETOWN STATE MEMORIAL.

The remains of the old town presented a scene of devastation. Old stores and boarding houses, with broken windows and sagging roofs, leaned precariously against one another. But some diehards persisted in occupying the usable shelters. Several commercial enterprises continued to use the port for barges carrying coal and farm products brought by truck from interior Illinois. Some funds became available; the old levee was repaired and a new bridge carrying Illinois 13 to Kentucky opened in 1956, after the ferry ended 146 years of operation. Historical groups supported the organization of the terrain as a State park. Efforts are continuing to save some of the most conspicuous historic structures. The most impressive is the First National Bank Building of 1839, which has a Greek portico with five ionic pillars and a flight of stone steps. In 1971 the Gallatin, Saline, Pope & Hardin County Bankers Federation presented the Gallatin Historical Assn. with a donation to spur restoration, which was expected to cost $100,000. Most of the other familiar landmarks have disappeared.

The balconied, two-storied, brick Rawlings Hotel was constructed on the site of a old tavern bearing the same name. Here in 1825 a splendid fete honored Lafayette, who walked from the boat landing to the hotel on a gayly colored path of calico. At the height of the feasting and drinking, it is said, an old and tattered French soldier appeared at the door of the reception room. He made no effort to intrude but stood eyeing the celebration wistfully. Suddenly Lafayette recognized the man in the doorway as one of his bodyguard during the Revolution. The general rushed across the room, embraced the soldier, and led him to a place of honor at the table. The old hotel burned down in February, 1937.

Another legendary structure was the Posey Building, erected as a residence by a son of Gen. Thomas Posey, officer under Washington during the Revolution. The two-storied wing in the rear had an outside stairway leading to the second floor. Robert G. Ingersoll's first law office was at the top of the stairway. Gen. Thomas Posey is buried in Westwood Cemetery, north of town.

The Old Slave House, 18.7 *m.*, topping a hill, sits back from the highway almost obscured by trees. The Southern Colonial house was built in 1834 by John Cranshaw, an Englishman. Local opinion is divided as to the building's original use. Some believe that it was a prison for captured runaway slaves who were resold in the South. Cranshaw it is said, gave elaborate parties on the lower floors with profits he gained from the slave trade. The first floor has spacious drawing rooms; the second floor has five large bedrooms. But under the eaves on the third floor are tiny cells, each less than the height of a man, equipped with two narrow wooden bunks. Chain anchors are imbedded in the floors of these cells, and the door frames appear to have been cross-hatched with bars.

At the southern end of a bridge across the Saline River, 20.5 *m.*, is a plaque indicating the road to Nigger Spring.

Right on this road to Nigger Spring, 0.7 *m.*, encased below ground and flush with the surface in a lining of old timbers. This spring is almost the last vestige of what was once one of the most important industries in Illinois. Here brine slowly oozes to the surface in a slimy pool, giving off an unpleasant, pungent, sulphurous odor. Indians made salt here long before the coming of the white man; it was the discovery of their workings that led to the development of a great salt industry. Scattered in surrounding fields are shards of pottery used by the Indians in evaporating the brine. White men introduced iron kettles to facilitate this process. To aid in the development of the industry, the State legislature set aside more than 180,000 acres of woodland as a fuel supply, and the Constitution of 1818 exempted from the antislavery clause "the tract reserved by the salt works near Shawneetown." The salines reached their greatest productivity during the first half of the 19th century, when output more than 500 bushels of salt a day. Production gradually declined when other sources of salt were discovered, and by 1875 the springs had been abandoned.

At 29.5 *m.* is a junction with a graveled road. Right on this road to High Knob Tower, 10 *m.* This 60-foot tower, perched on the highest point of a knob of rock, affords a view of an area perhaps 50 miles in diameter.

At 30.5 *m.* is the junction with a graveled road. Right on this road to Potts Hill Spring and the site of Potts Tavern. The tavern, razed in 1938, was a balconied, two-storied, frame structure. Numerous gruesome legends center around the nearby spring and the tavern; in one of its rooms 100-year-old bloodstains were still visible at the time of its demolition. Billy Potts operated this charnel house in collusion with a gang of renegades at Ford's Ferry, 15 miles to the east. The gang used to direct travelers to the tavern, where Potts murdered them for their money. Potts Tavern was the legendary scene of a story that occurs in the folk tales of many races. Potts' son, it is said, committed such a flagrant and brutal murder that he had to flee the country. Some 15 years later he returned, wealthy from crime, heavier and fully bearded. Young Potts was amused that his father did not recognize him; he made the mistake of displaying his wealth and was promptly killed by his father, who learned his identity the following day when the gang at Ford's Ferry, to whom the son had made himself known, came to the tavern.

CAVE-IN-ROCK, 39 *m.* (340 alt., 503 pop. 1970; 495, 1960) is a village on the Ohio River, at the eastern edge of which is CAVE-IN-ROCK STATE PARK (64.5 acres), named for a natural cave in the river bluff. The yawning cavern opening, midway between the summit of the bluff and the normal water line, was long a landmark for Ohio

River boatmen. The arch is 55 ft. wide at the base and about 20 ft. high; the cave tunnels about 200 ft. into the bluff, with a small chamber branching right from the rear.

The front and interior of the cave are etched with a mosaic of names and initials of picnickers, but the most interesting words ever daubed on its smooth limestone walls were long ago effaced. In 1797 Samuel Mason, an officer of the Continental Army and the black sheep of a distinguished Virginia family, came to frontier Illinois. Converting the den into a wilderness caravansary, he fashioned a great sign above its entrance, announcing it as a "Liquor Vault and House of Entertainment." Snaring victims with these lures, Mason plundered travelers and flatboat crews. When Mason's life became threatened, he abandoned the cave and left the territory. His hide-away was soon appropriated by a long line of scoundrels, thieves, and counterfeiters. Among these were the notorious badmen, Duff, Sturdevant, Philip Alston, Big Harpe, and Little Harpe. Vigilante bands finally routed the outlaws from Cave-in-Rock. Unused for more than a century, the cave and the surrounding tract were acquired by the State in 1929 and developed into the present park.

At 37 *m.*, 2 *m.* before reaching Cave-in-Rock, Illinois 146 leaves Illinois 1 and proceeds along the river valley 9 *m.*

ELIZABETHTOWN, 12 *m.* (436 pop. 1970; 524, 1960, dec. 16.8%) a village on the Ohio River in Hardin County, is the only county seat that never had a railroad. It was named by James McFarland for his wife. He arrived in 1806 and in 1812 built a house on the rocky point and operated a ferry to Kentucky. On Aug. 8, 1882, the village began an annual celebration of Emancipation Day; more recently it changed the name to Hardin County Homecoming. Rose Hotel, originally McFarland's Tavern, is called the oldest continuously operated hotel in Illinois by John M. Allen in *Legends and Lore of Southern Illinois*. Built of brick in 1912 it was bought by Sarah Rose in 1884. She managed it for 55 years and was succeeded by her daughter.

About 3 *m.* south of Elizabethtown a small road, Illinois 34, runs 3 *m.* to the Ohio River and ROSICLARE (1,421 pop. 1970; 1,700, 1960) long a port from which miners shipped flourspar. The mines are operated intermittently. The mineral is chiefly useful to the steel industry. An explosion on April 12, 1971, took seven lives.

More than half the flourspar produced in the United States comes from mines in Hardin and Pope Counties. The mines are located near the Ohio River and ship their product by barge, truck, and rail.

The highway follows the bend of the Ohio River to GOLCONDA, 28 *m.* (922 pop. 1970; 864, 1960) an incorporated city in Pope County. Its first ferry began in 1797, the last closed in 1957. At Golconda the Cherokee Indians entered Illinois in 1839 to cross the State to Jonesboro on their forlorn march west when they were forced out of their southern lands. Here Illinois 146 turns west and follows approximately the route taken by the Indians to the Mississippi River. Below Golconda are Lock and Dam No. 51.

At 10 *m.* west of Golconda is the Dixon Springs junction with Illinois 145 (north-south) and DIXON SPRINGS STATE PARK, 399 acres, a former Ozark Mountain resort with fantastic formations that resulted when a huge block of rock dropped 200 ft. along a fault line. Nearby are the LAKE GLENDALE RECREATION AREA and the Dixon Springs Experimental Station of the University of Illinois.

Illinois 145 proceeds south 15 *m.* to a junction with US 45 and FORT MASSAC STATE PARK (*See Tour 3*). It goes on to Brookport on the Ohio River and crosses on a toll bridge to Paducah, Kentucky (*See Tour 3*).

~~~~~~

Tour 2

THREE PARALLEL HIGHWAYS TO NORTH SHORE SUBURBS

I   Sheridan Road. From Chicago to the Wisconsin Line. Evanston— Wilmette—Kenilworth—Winnetka—Glencoe—Highland Park— Highwood—Fort Sheridan—Lake Forest—Lake Bluff—North Chicago—Waukegan—Zion—Winthrop Harbor

II   Edens Expressway (Int. 94) and US 41 Lincolnwood—Skokie—Morton Grove—Wilmette—Glenview— Northfield—Northbrook—Deerfield—Highland Park—Lake Forest—North Chicago—Park City—Gurnee—Wadsworth

III   Tri-State Tollway (Int. 294, 94) Illinois 21, US 45 Wheeling—Deerfield—Riverwoods—Lincolnshire—Half Day— Prairie View—Vernon Hills—Indian Creek—Diamond Lake— Mundelein—Mettawa—Libertyville—Green Oaks

Excellent concrete and blacktop highways serve the huge suburban population that moves in a steady stream of motor vehicles between Chicago and the Wisconsin border. Although the great majority spends its daylight hours in the city, it does not figure in the city's census. Nearly all the towns and villages above Devon Avenue are incorporated individually, and even Cook County can include residents only up to the Lake County line, which begins at Highland Park.

Settlements along the Lake Shore have been the objectives of the well-to-do for more than a century, but a large segment of the terrain farther west remained unexploited farmland until after World War II. The three parallel highways described here run either along the shores of the Lake or just a few miles inland. Sheridan Road is known for its scenic qualities. US 41, routed part of the way with Edens Expressway, Int. 94, grew out of pioneer roads that followed the ridges farther west. In Lake County Int. 94 is the latest of the roads carrying Chicago commuters and vacationists north.

Section I. Sheridan Road, from Chicago to the Wisconsin Line, about 53 to 57 m.

Sheridan Road can be entered from Broadway north of Lincoln Park. Although moving through residential areas and sometimes through wooded districts, it rarely loses sight of Lake Michigan. It passes through a succession of suburbs in which 80 percent of the residents own their homes and where high-rise apartment buildings are comparatively few, although condominiums are coming in.

When Sheridan Road crosses Howard St. to Evanston it is 13 miles from the Chicago Loop.

EVANSTON (79,808 pop. 1970). *See article on Evanston.* The North Shore Channel runs between Evanston and Skokie, the city to the west. Skokie is easily reached from Sheridan Road via Dempster St. *See Skokie, Section II.*

On the way from Evanston to Wilmette Sheridan Road approaches the North Shore Channel, created by the Chicago Sanitary District to draw water from Lake Michigan to augment the flow of the North Branch of the Chicago River in a dry season. The pumping station is directly below the Sheridan Road bridge. Here the sloops of the Sheridan Shore Yacht Club often create a lively spectacle as they slip their moorings for a race, especially on weekends. To the right of the highway at Linden Ave. appears the graceful white dome of the Baha'i House of Worship, visible for a distance of several miles on the North Shore. On the north bank of the inlet is a station of the U. S. Coast Guard.

The exact title of the Baha'i temple is The Dawning Place of the Mention of God. The building was designed by Louis J. Bourgeois to conform with the traditions of the sect and combines different styles to achieve a harmonious whole. A nine-sided structure, it rests on nine caissons of steel and concrete; the nine sides of the clerestory and dome are staggered on the nonagonal base. Glass in metal frames is used extensively on all surfaces. The steel, concrete, and glass skeleton is concealed and framed by molded shells of architectural concrete, white on the exterior, faintly pinkish on the interior. The design of the ornamentation is geometric, although the symbols of the world's religions are on the pylons, the outer arches, and over the doorways. Fine, intricate tracery characterizes the exterior, while bolder, simpler designs are used in the interior.

From the auditorium, beneath the 191-foot dome, nine bays open to the gardens through huge windows. The 1,200 seats in the auditorium face east to the lake, the dawn, and to Israel, the Holy Land of Baha'is as well as Jews, Christians, and Moslems. The temple is the center of the national administration of the American Baha'i community. Staff homes, offices, a publishing trust building, and the Baha'i Home for the Aged foreshadow a larger complex of buildings in the national center.

This is the sole North American house of worship of a faith founded in 1863 by the Persian religious leader, Baha'u'llah (1817-92). The Baha'i faith correlates the major religions under the tenet that God has periodically revealed, through such prophets as Buddha, Zoroaster, Moses, Jesus, and Mohammed, as much of the truth as man has been capable of assimilating at any one time. Members of the faith believe that Baha'u'llah (The Glory of God) was the latest of the prophets, or "manifestations." The unity of all peoples and religions is sought through one religion and a world federal system of democracies with universal education, equality of the sexes, dependence upon a united science and religion, and a universal auxiliary language. A full life of service is advocated. There is no clergy; all believers are obligated to participate in the wide functions of the faith. Contributions are accepted in secret from members only. Government of the Baha'i communities is by elected assemblies. The faith came to America in the early 1900s, and was given strong impetus through the visit of Baha'u'llah's son, Abdul'l-Baha (1844-1921), who laid the cornerstone of the temple in 1912. Actual construction was begun in 1930 and was finished in 1951. The gardens were completed in 1952.

WILMETTE, 15.3 m. (614 alt., 32,134 pop. 1970; 28,268, 1960, inc. 13.7%) is a tree-shaded residential village with older houses of large acreage near Lake Michigan and newer sections running to 5 m. west. The Chicago & North Western provides commuting service and the CTA lines reach the southern limits of Wilmette at Linden Ave. Edens Expressway runs through the western areas of Wilmette. Several high-rise apartment and condominium buildings have been erected on Sheridan Road foreshadowing similar developments, but there is strong support behind single-family units and property values are high. Wilmette was named for Antoine Ouilmette, whose Indian wife received 1,280 acres of land under a Government treaty with the Indians in 1829.

The Wilmette Historical Museum, 825 Green Bay Road, has among its exhibits more than 1,000 photographs of a local historical nature, and among documents the Treaty of Prairie du Chien.

On Charter Day, Sept. 19, 1954, the Wilmette Historical Commission dedicated a plaque on the site of the log cabin of Antoine Ouilmette at the foot of Linden Ave. On the same day in 1955 it placed a marker on the Green Bay Trail. The Lake Shore chapter of the Daughters of American Colonists on May 15, 1955, placed a plaque at Sheridan Road and Canterbury Court, site of the North Ridge Meeting House and the first school.

A small area near the lake overlooked in the plat of Wilmette became known as No Man's Land. Not amenable to the ordinances of Wilmette and Kenilworth it became a popular place for buying fireworks that could not be obtained in the cities. When finally it was made a part of Wilmette it became a profitable shopping center called Plaza del Lago, using a Spanish decor.

A tragic steamboat disaster took place when the *Lady Elgin* sank in Lake Michigan near the Evanston-Wilmette line on the night of Sept. 7-8, 1860, with a loss of 293 lives. The passengers, mostly of Irish extraction, who lived in Milwaukee's third Ward, were returning from a political rally in Chicago. The ship was struck amidships during a storm by the lumber schooner *Augusta*. The upper deck cover was chopped loose and used as a raft, but those who clung to it were lost in the surf off Winnetka. A student of Garrett Biblical Institute of Evanston, Edward Spencer, helped 17 persons to the shore before he collapsed from exhaustion. A memorial service for the dead was held annually in St. John's Cathedral, Milwaukee. The *Lady Elgin* was built in 1851, was 300 ft. long and weighed 1,000 tons. It had been named for the wife of a governor of Canada.

West of Wilmette on Wilmette Ave. (Glenview Road) to Glenview. *See Section II.*

KENILWORTH, 17 *m.* (615 alt., 2,980 pop. 1970; 2,959, 1960) a village in Cook County, extends from Wilmette to the Indian Hill section of Winnetka. It was named after Walter Scott's novel, as were some of the streets, when it was incorporated in 1896. Edens Expressway combines with US 41 at the western border, beyond which lies the village of Northfield.

Kenilworth acquired a new village hall in 1972 when the Kenilworth Historical Society Building was erected at the northeast corner of Richmond Road and Kenilworth Ave. The building was financed from proceeds of a $500,000 trust fund established by Harold L. Stuart, late Chicago investment banker, and houses the historical society, the village hall, the police department, and the park district, which donated the land. The building is a two-level limestone structure.

In the cloistered yard of the Church of the Holy Comforter (Episcopal) 333 Warwick Rd., is the grave of Eugene Field, poet, who died in 1895. His remains were brought here from Graceland Cemetery, Chicago, in 1925. Mrs. Field, who survived him by more than 40 years, was buried beside him in 1936.

West of Kenilworth and Winnetka is Northfield. *See Section II.*

The NEW TRIER TOWNSHIP HIGH SCHOOL, at the southern line of Winnetka, adjoining Kenilworth, is considered one of the foremost secondary schools in the Chicago environs.

WINNETKA, 18 *m.* (651 alt., 14,131 pop. 1970, revised to 13,998 in 1973), a village contiguous to Kenilworth, incorporated in 1869, is frequently mentioned in surveys as representative of the best elements of middle-class America. Large estates fronting on Sheridan Road have riparian rights and private beaches on the Lake, and many of the dwellings inland have large acreage. The Village Hall, an attractive two-story structure, has a white tower containing a clock and a cupola, facing a landscaped mall. The newest sections are the Indian Hill area at the south and the part going west to the Skokie Lagoons; an older area is the Hubbard Woods section to the north.

The Winnetka schools led the experimental movement in 1919 under the direction of Carleton Washburne, superintendent. Washburne's method was the individualization of instruction, with the self-education of children in a controlled environment as the ultimate ideal. Winnetka-prepared instructional material and textbooks are designed to allow the student to progress at his own speed, under the general supervision of his teacher. Group and creative experiences in self-government also are emphasized within the framework of the educational program. Since 1962 closed-circuit television instruction and a Learning Center for students who wish to pursue supplementary research have been part of the program.

The North Shore Country Day School is a private non-profit school for children from kindergarten through high school. Since its founding in 1919 on the campus at 310 Green Bay Road, it has become one of the leading preparatory schools in the country.

The Hadley School for the Blind has headquarters at 700 Elm St. Founded in 1922 by William A. Hadley and Dr. E. V. L. Brown, it offers extension courses by correspondence to the blind free of charge. It is supported by donations and community chest funds.

On Tower Road is the Water Tower (1893) of the community-owned and operated water plant. The plant, at the base of the steep bluff on which the tower stands, is integrated with the municipal electric plant, resulting in numerous economies in operation.

The CHEWAB SKOKIE, a recreation ground administered by the Forest Preserve District of Cook County, consists of seven lagoons with a flood plain of 400 acres, held within dikes by a main control dam at Willow Road. Three low dams maintain a water level close to the ground surface thus preserving marsh vegetation. There are 190 acres available for fishing. Trails have been developed for use by hikers, bicyclists, and horseback riders. At Willow Road trails cross the dam and run along the west side of the lagoons to Tower Road. A foot trail runs east of the lagoons to Tower Road.

The first segment of the Green Bay Trail, a highway for cyclists and hikers, starts at Ash St. in Winnetka and runs north to Highland Park on the abandoned right of way of the North Shore Electric Line. Eventually the trail is to include most of the old road from Wilmette north.

GLENCOE, 22 m. (73 alt., 10,542 pop. 1970; 10,472, 1960) a village in Cook County, was first settled about 1836 and incorporated in 1869. The name is a combination of glen and Coe, the maiden name of the wife of Walter S. Gurnee, one of the founders. The GURNEE HOUSE, a three-story brick structure with porches and gables, stands opposite the Chicago & North Western station. Glencoe is known for its progressive public schools. Like other North Shore suburbs it carefully guards its lake front against trespassers.

A building of note is the Temple of North Shore Congregation Israel at 1185 Sheridan Road, designed by Minoru Yamasaki and built in 1963. It includes quarters for offices, classroom, and social work.

Glencoe has many facilities for comfortable living and recreation. It is near the Forest Preserves and the Skokie Lagoons, has numerous parks for public use and a Community Golf Club of 126 acres owned by Glencoe and the Forest Preserve Commission, open for a fee. Transportation facilities are similar to those of other North Shore villages, with commutation on the Chicago & North Western and easy access to Edens Expressway, Int. 94, which follows the line that separates Glencoe from Northbrook. *See Section II.*

HIGHLAND PARK, 26 *m.* (691 alt., 32,263 pop. 1970; 25,532, 1960, inc. 26.4%) is one of the larger suburbs not given over entirely to industry. It covers considerable territory, having for its southern segment, just across the Cook County-Lake County line, the attractive residential sections of RAVINIA and the famous musical center at RAVINIA PARK. Just south of the line Int. 94 leaves US 41 and turns west, becoming the Tri-State Tollway, which has been moving up as Int. 294 from the Indiana line past the O'Hare International Airport.

RAVINIA was the last section of Highland Park to be developed for dwellings. Composed almost entirely of ravines, it provided builders with an unusual opportunity to adapt houses to an irregular terrain. Instead of levelling the hills they fitted the structures to the contours and obtained effects that have been widely praised and imitated. The place is a commuters' stop on the Chicago & North Western.

RAVINIA PARK, contiguous on the north, is a wooded section of 30 acres famous for the Ravinia Festival of symphonic music in midsummer. Originally an amusement park, it was taken over in 1910 by North Shore residents who promoted a series of symphony concerts each summer. After 1916 the burden of sponsorship was assumed by Louis Eckstein, Chicago mail-order executive, who changed the programs from symphony to grand opera. Audiences were large, but the policy of maintaining popular prices while presenting top-rank opera stars resulted in a deficit each year. Eckstein met the deficits, which often exceeded $100,000, but in 1931 the burden became too great and the programs were discontinued. Five years later the park was reopened with a series of more modestly budgeted symphony concerts. Since then the symphonic program again has become the mainstay of the programs. Today the Festival is the musical event that keeps northeastern Illinois a cultural capital. Amid the salubrity of a wooded area Ravinia during the summer months provides an extraordinary program of symphonic music, string quartets, piano and violin soloists, ballet, folk songs and jazz. Under its big pavilion and in the Murray Theatre the public hears the Chicago Symphony Orchestra with James Levine conducting, Arthur Fiedler and the Boston Pops, the Original Benny Goodman Quartet, the Preservation Hall Jazz Band, and the New York Chamber Soloists, and views the programs of the Joffrey Ballet. Typical bills have comprised the *Missa Solemnis* of Beethoven, Mahler's Third Symphony, Bellini's *Norma,* the Bartok First Piano Concerto, and dances from Michael Tippett's opera, *The Midsummer Marriage.* Soloists have included Maureen Forester, Leon Fleisher, James Starker, John Browning, John Denver, Roberta Peters. In the course of Ravinia's half century all the great vocal artists of opera and the concert stage have sung at Ravinia and refreshed themselves in its invigorating air.

Highland Park stands on the site of two Potawatomi villages. White settlement began with the construction of the Green Bay House (1834), a tavern on the Chicago-Milwaukee post road, now Waukegan Road. The name Port Clinton was used in 1850, during the city's brief career as a lake port. The railroad company named its station Highland Park in 1854, and the town was incorporated under that name in 1867. It was laid out to take full advantage of the natural beauty of its lake shore, bluffs, woods, and ravines. Homes of modified Colonial designs are features of the older residential neighborhoods.

Like other suburbs on Sheridan Road Highland Park has the commuting service of the Chicago & North Western Railroad. It also has North Suburban Transit. Highland Park Hospital (256 beds) is the apex of a number of medical services.

A timber cabin built by Francis Stupey in 1847 is located in Laurel Park near the City Hall and maintained by the Highland Park Historical Society. *Open Sundays, 2-4, closed January through March.*

The Jean Butz James Museum of the Highland Park Historical Society, 326 Central Ave., occupies a Victorian brick house more than a century old. Two rooms are furnished in 1880 style; rotating summer displays include a children's playroom. *Open Sundays, 2-4.*

HIGHWOOD is a small residential area on Sheridan Road surrounded by Highland Park and Fort Sheridan (4,975 pop. 1970; 4,400, 1960). The first camp of US Army contingents called to Chicago by the anarchist scare and Haymarket riot of 1886 was located here. The next year the camp was made permanent at the request of Chicago business men and named Fort Sheridan for General Philip H. Sheridan, Chief of Staff, USA. Highwood retained its identity and was incorporated as a city, and became an oasis for the famished.

FORT SHERIDAN, 27 *m.,* United States Army post, consists of about 725 acres of wooded bluffs rising in places to 100 feet above Lake Michigan. The post contains the Headquarters of the Fifth U. S. Army and of the Fifth Region, U. S. Air Defense Command, which operates the anti-aircraft missile bases around midwestern industrial centers and is the chief administrative and logistics support center for National Guard and Army Reserve units in the 13-state Fifth Army area. Established in 1886, Fort Sheridan was an army camp during the Spanish-American War and became an officers' training center during World War I. During World War II it was a reception center, anti-aircraft training base, and separation center.

LAKE FOREST, 30 *m.* (713 alt., 15,642 pop. 1970; 10,689,

1960; inc. 46.4%) a city in Lake County, is considered one of the wealthiest of Chicago's North Shore suburbs. Magnificent estates, many surrounded by high iron fences, border both sides of the highway. Large groves of timber outline landscaped lawns; statues, formal gardens, pavilions, and stone benches are placed with an eye to beauty and functional use; occasionally a tennis court or swimming pool is visible from the road. The architecture of the costly homes ranges from French Renaissance to the ranch-house style of today.

Lake Forest was first settled in 1835. Deerpath Avenue, once an actual deer and buffalo path leading to the lake, made a convenient portage track to the Des Plaines River and was a thoroughfare for trappers, traders, and explorers in early days. Green Bay Road, west of the North Western tracks, was once an Indian trail to the Green Bay region. In 1856, two years after the railroad came Chicago businessmen bought 1,300 acres and planned the town. David Hotchkiss, a St. Louis landscape architect, laid it out, making use of the beauty of the deep ravines and wooded bluffs. The winding streets through which Sheridan Road twists are part of his handiwork. The conformity of the railroad station and its adjuncts to a uniform design was one of the first efforts of this kind in the country.

LAKE FOREST COLLEGE occupies a wooded campus of 107 acres divided into three areas by ravines, where the buildings are set among winding roads, including Sheridan Road. The college was chartered under Presbyterian auspices in 1857 and opened in 1861; it called itself a university from 1865 to 1965, when, contrary to the prevailing practice, it became a college. It offers the liberal arts and sciences, is open to all religious faiths, and has no social or economic restrictions, offering financial help and scholarships to offset the annual fees of $3,920. It has courses in Black Studies and study terms in Madrid, West Berlin, Florence and Athens. It enrolls approx. 1,239 and has a faculty of 108.

In recent years Lake Forest has amplified its physical plant of fine old Gothic and traditional designs with contemporary scholastic architecture. Donnelley Library (1964), of glass and brick, has 110,000 volumes and room for 250,000, and 600 seats. The Leverton Collection of the drama, the Hamill Library of fine editions, and the Stuart Collection of Scottish literature are important. The Freeman Library (1962) a circular building of glass, steel and wood, has a collection of natural sciences and mathematics, and is part of the Ernest A. Johnson Memorial Science Center (1962), which includes the Robert R. McCormick Auditorium. Many of the older buildings exemplify the architecture of earlier periods. Durand Institute (1891) is a brownstone in Romanesque; Holt Memorial Chapel (1899) has a graceful tower and Gothic vaulted hall; Holt House, acquired in 1965, is a Victorian dwelling more than 100 years old.

The college was developed in three stages. The first unit was Lake Forest Academy, for boys, one of the earliest preparatory boarding schools in the Middle West. The second unit, for girls, Ferry Hall,

541 N. Mayflower Rd., was opened in 1869. The college provided higher education for graduates of the two lower schools. In 1925 the Academy and Ferry Hall became separate institutions. In 1948 the Academy moved to its present location, a 200-acre campus, the former estate of J. Ogden Armour, Chicago meat packer, five miles west of Lake Forest.

Across Sheridan Road stands the Presbyterian Church, organized in 1859. The limestone used in the construction of the present building, erected in 1871, was salvaged after the Chicago fire from the Second Presbyterian Church in that city. The Public Library, 360 Deerpath Ave., of pink Holland brick and white stone, is surmounted by a large glass dome that serves as an effective skylight. The library has more than 60,000 volumes and circulates more than 128,000 annually. It is a member of the North Suburban Library System, a cooperative group of 30 libraries on the North Shore including Waukegan, Winnetka, and Wilmette.

At the intersection of Sheridan and Westleigh Rds. is the entrance to the grounds of Sacred Heart Academy and Barat College. The preparatory school and liberal arts college operate in connection with a convent, vicariate headquarters for the order. The red stone main building, all but hidden from the road by trees, dates from 1904. Barat, opened in 1919, had 512 students and a faculty of 82 in 1972.

LAKE BLUFF, 34 *m.* (683 alt., 5,008 pop. 1970; 3,494, 1960) is located on bluffs that sometimes rise 130 ft. above the lake shore, and like its neighbors it profits from ravines that make picturesque sites for dwellings. After 1874 it was a Methodist campmeeting ground for annual convocations. A tabernacle on the campgrounds was the scene of an important State WCTU convention in 1881, and of a conference of the national Prohibition Party in 1885, a period when there were strong movements to control the liquor traffic. The grounds and buildings were disposed of in 1898.

West of Lake Bluff on Illinois 176 to junction with US 41 (Skokie Highway) and Int. 94 (Tri-State Tollway) to Libertyville (*see Section III*).

NORTH CHICAGO, 36 *m.* (673 alt., 47,275 pop. 1970; 22,938, 1960. inc. 106.1%) a city in Lake County, constitutes with Waukegan a continuous industrial area with 60-odd diversified industries making more than 200 commodities. In North Chicago, Illinois 42 follows the main business street, along which are located the more important shops and restaurants and the City Hall. Along the lake shore east of the business district is Foss Park, a 34-acre municipal recreational tract. This stretch of wooded bluffs and sandy beach has picnic sites, playgrounds, tennis and horse-shoe courts, baseball diamonds, and supervised swimming.

Abbott Laboratories has been the largest employer here and at its new location, Abbott Park, six miles southwest, averaging 4,700.

Fansteel, Inc. which employs more than 2,700, produces refractory metals and alloys, including aerospace components; electronic metal and components; tools for mining and drilling. Other industries include Goodyear Tire & Rubber Co., Reliance Universal, Inc. Stone Container Corp., United Educators, Inc., publishers of encyclopedias; North Chicago Refiners & Smelters. The *North Chicago Tribune* is published weekly.

In 1937, 63 sit-down strikers were driven from the Fansteel plant with tear gas. Two years later, in March, 1939, the U. S. Supreme Court, by reversing an order of the National Labor Relations Board that the strikers be rehired, ruled, in effect, that sit-down strikes are illegal.

The GREAT LAKES NAVAL TRAINING CENTER, the only major naval unit in the Middle West, is one of the few permanent naval training bases in the United States. The station dedicated by President Taft in 1911, was designed to accommodate 1,500 but during World War I was expanded to receive and train 50,000 men. Closed for some time after the war, it was reopened in 1935 to train naval recruits for assignment to ships or trade schools. Before and after World War II, Great Lakes underwent tremendous expansion. In the latter part of the war it became an important separation center. The 1,600 acres now contain the Naval Training Center, headquarters of the Commandant of the Ninth Naval District, Electronics Supply Office, United States Naval Hospital, and Fleet Home Town News Center. Training is the primary function. More than 60,000 recruits receive their basic naval training each year, as do 20,000 students attending the 27 advanced technical schools.

The station is in a wooded area, an excellent setting for the Colonial style of its permanent buildings. The North Western Railway connects the base with Chicago. Armed Forces Day (third Saturday in May) is Great Lakes' chief "show off" day.

Guided tours for organized groups on Friday, Saturday, Sunday and holidays upon written request; graduation reviews open to the public each Friday at 1:30 P.M., except during Christmas holidays.

Near Green Bay Road (Illinois 13) is DOWNEY VETERANS ADMINISTRATION HOSPITAL, operated by the U. S. Veterans Administration, with bed capacity of 2,487. It is equipped to care for veterans requiring medical, surgical, and mental treatment.

ARDEN SHORE HOME FOR BOYS, a home for gifted boys from broken or unstable homes, was founded in 1899 as a year-around recuperative center for poor boys from Chicago and as a summer camp for mothers and children. In the late 1940's the camp programs were discontinued and the institution acquired its present purpose. The Home can accommodate 48 boys from sixth through eleventh grades, who are referred by welfare agencies. It is supported by donations.

PARK CITY (2,855 pop. 1970; 1,408, 1960, inc. 102%, adjoins North Chicago and Waukegan on the west and has a junction with Illinois 120, the Belvidere Road.

WAUKEGAN

Air: Waukegan Memorial Airport, 5 *m.* northwest, executive and charter planes.

Highways: Illinois 42 (Sheridan Road); US 41, Skokie Highway, connects with Edens Expressway; Tri-State Tollway, 2 *m.* west on Grand Ave., Illinois 132; Illinois 120, Belvidere Road, Western connections; Illinois 43, old Waukegan Road south.

Buses: Greyhound Bus Lines, Waukegan-North Chicago Transit.

Railroads: Chicago & North Western, passenger and freight; Chicago, Milwaukee, St. Paul & Pacific, freight and some passenger; Elgin, Joliet & Eastern, freight.

Information: Waukegan *News Sun,* daily; Waukegan-North Chicago Chamber of Commerce, 228 N. Genesee St.

Accommodations: More than 15 hotels and motels, including Holiday Inn (2) and Sheraton chain. Victory Hospital, 380 beds; St. Therese Hospital, 420 beds; Lake County General Hospital.

WAUKEGAN, 41 *m.* (669 alt., 65,269 pop. 1970; 55,719, 1960, inc. 17%) seat of Lake County, and the Illinois metropolis nearest the Wisconsin line, is an active port on Lake Michigan, a busy retailing center, and shares a large industrial section with North Chicago, contiguous on the south.

Waukegan was incorporated as a city in 1859. It has a mayor and 16 aldermen, and a City Hall of recent construction that is a model for civic buildings. Similarly the Lake County Courthouse, entirely of contemporary design, represents the prosperous character of the region. More than 18,000 are regularly employed and the work force shows little variation. Of the major corporations Abbott Laboratories, pharmaceuticals and chemicals, employs 5,100, and Johnson Motors Division of the Outboard Marine Corp. has 3,600 at work, whereas the plant of the Outboard Marine Corp. that makes the Johnson and Evinrude outboard motors, stern drive engines, and snowmobiles employs 550. Among others are Johns Manville Products Corp., 1,760; American Hospital Supply Corp., 1,300; the Waukegan Works and Cyclone Fence Dept. of U. S. Steel Corp., employs 1,200 and produces bright and metallic coated carbon, alloy, and stainless wire; strand, chain link fencing, chain link and flat wire belting, and fine cords. Also Cherry Electrical Products Corp. and Chicago Rubber Co. Waukegan workers are employed also in North Chicago (Fansteel, Inc. and Goodyear) and GURNEE (2,736 pop. 1970; 1,831, 1960, inc. 49%) which adjoins Waukegan on the west.

Waukegan Harbor is the first port of call in Illinois on the St. Lawrence Seaway. The port is open and two large steamships can be moored at one time and docked without tugs.

A stockade built by the French and used as a trading post around 1675, was called the Petite Fort, or Little Fort, and this name continued to be applied to the later settlement. When the French withdrew around 1760 the Potawatomie continued to occupy the area. In 1836 the Indians were forced out by treaty and Thomas Jenkins of Chicago ran a general store. In 1841 Little Fort obtained a postoffice and was named the county seat. In 1844 it had 150 people, in 1845 there were 452. By 1846 it was doing enough shipping to be designated a U. S.

Port of Entry. It shipped furs, hides, pork, oats, wheat, and timber, and imported salt, household goods, and tools.

On Feb. 12, 1849, effective April 13, 1849, the place was incorporated as a village called Waukegan, which was near the Potawatomi way of saying trading post. John H. Kinzie and Solomon Juneau had considered Waukegance, little trading post; by eliminating the last two letters they removed the "little".

In 1855 the Chicago & Milwaukee Railroad connected Waukegan with those important terminals, and as the Chicago & North Western it has played a part in Waukegan's growth ever since.

Waukegan had the Lake County Anti-Slavery Society as early as 1845, and sent its sons to the Civil War. Orion Howe, a 14-year-old drummer boy, was awarded the Medal of Honor for valor at Vicksburg.

On April 2, 1860, Abraham Lincoln made a campaign speech in Dickinson Hall in Waukegan. After he began to speak a fire alarm went off outside. A member of the audience declared it was probably a device by Democrats to break up the meeting. Lincoln continued to speak until the audience showed much uneasiness. Thereupon he stopped and said: "Well, gentlemen, as there really seems to be a fire, let us all go and help to put it out." This was said to be his only unfinished speech.

The steamship *Sea Bird* of the Goodrich Line burned off the shore of Waukegan in 1868 with a loss of 73 lives.

Waukegan is important as a medical center, with Victory Memorial Hospital (344 beds), St. Therese Hospital (348 beds) and the Lake County Tuberculosis Sanitarium.

DUNES PARK is a stop on Sheridan Road for the recreation area of ILLINOIS BEACH STATE PARK, 1,651 acres of duneland, which extend for 3½ miles along Lake Michigan. Here are groves of low-growing oaks and varieties of pines; cactus, juniper, and barberry clinging to the windblown sandhills, interspersed with marshes where wildflowers show their brilliant colors and, to quote the State, "Wolffa Columbiana, the smallest flowering plant in the world, floating just below the park's marsh water." Old Indian trails and new ones make the park popular with hikers. Most of the park remains in its natural state, but there are a lodge with a year-around swimming pool, separate areas for tent and trailer campers, ample picnic grounds, and life guards continually on duty.

Sheridan Road moves west of the Beach Park and has a junction with Wadsworth Road, which leads west to two Lake County villages that are reached also by US 41 and the Tri-State Tollway, Int. 94. The Tollway provides a high-speed expressway for this area, connecting with Edens Expressway to the Loop and Int. 294 to O'Hare International Airport.

OLD MILL CREEK is the site of the Mill Creek Hunt Club, and much of its terrain is hunting and fishing territory, for the U. S. Census found only 164 residents in 1970, and 149 in 1960. The other village,

WADSWORTH, in similar terrain, had 756 residents in 1970 and was not counted in 1960.

ZION, 49 *m.*, in Lake County (633 alt., 17,268 pop. 1970; 11,941, 1960) is a growing city originally planned by a Scottish religious zealot and owned and dominated by his church. A little over 30 years ago it deviated from its religious base and adopted private ownership and free enterprise. Today it is governed by a mayor and four commissioners, and among its civic departments are a shade tree commission and a citizens' advisory commission on human relations.

John Alexander Dowie (1848-1907) was a Scottish fundamentalist preacher who won a large following and organized the Christian Catholic Apostolic Church in 1896. On Dec. 31, 1899, he announced acquisition of acreage in Lake County on which he would build the city of Zion, with the object of establishing "the rule of God in every department of the government." He announced that "where God rules, man prospers." As thousands of his followers flocked to the area frame buildings were hurriedly erected to accommodate them, including a lace factory, for the operation of which Dowie brought skilled workers from Nottingham, England. Dowie's sermons denouncing the evils of his time made good copy for the Chicago newspapers, and when he declared he was another Elijah many followers left him. He died while combatting bitter dissension in his ranks.

For more than 30 years after Dowie's death Wilbur Glenn Voliva was overseer of the Church. A fundamentalist, he seriously contended that the earth was flat. He strictly enforced laws initiated by Dowie, which made the Church owner of all industrial and commercial establishments, and prohibited theaters, drug stores and pharmacies, and offices or residences of practicing physicians and surgeons. Also prohibited was the sale and use of liquor, tobacco, playing cards, oysters and clams, rabbit meat, and pork—whence Zion beef bacon. The city alternated between prosperity and bankruptcy, and in 1939 Voliva lost political control. In a reorganization real estate was allotted to individual owners and the managed economy was drastically modified. Today Zion differs little from neighboring communities. Physicians and surgeons are on duty at the 114-bed hospital. Fourteen churches of different denominations flourish, although the largest is still the Christian Catholic Church. It sponsors the annual PASSION PLAY, which is performed Sundays, Easter through June.

Zion was chosen by the Commonwealth Edison Co. as the site for the Zion Nuclear Generating Station. It was designed by Westinghouse and Sargent & Lundy, to be built in two units. The City Hall has been remodelled, the Public Library placed in Shiloh Park, and there is a modern Post Office on Shiloh Blvd. The Lake County Water District has built new intakes and treatment plants at the Lake shore, and the Zion Park District has developed a boat launching project. Zion Industries manufactures the popular Zion fig bars, employing 325. The Richard Abel Co. publishes books for scholarly use; there are printing services and among other products fittings for the dairy industry. The *Zion-Benton News* is the city's weekly newspaper.

ELIJAH HOSPICE, on Sheridan Road, built in 1904 as a 350-

room divine healing home, is now a nursing home and residence for the elderly. On 27th Street is the block-long building that housed Dowie's lace mill. In the bankruptcy of 1906, the mill was purchased by Marshall Field & Company of Chicago, which continued making lace there for about 50 years before transferring the equipment to its textile plants in the South. The building now is occupied by Warwick Electronics Corp., a division of Whirlpool Corp., which manufactures television sets for Sears, Roebuck & Co. and employs approx. 1,200.

WINTHROP HARBOR, 51 *m.* (alt. 598, 4,794 pop. 1970; 3,848, 1960, inc. 24%) is the last village in Lake County on the way to Wisconsin. US 42 crosses the line 8 *m.* south of Kenosha, Wisc. This line is also the northern limit of Winthrop Harbor, which grew out of the acquisition in 1892 of 2,700 acres of dairy farmland by the Winthrop Harbor & Dock Company, which planned to build an industrial town. The plan failed and dairying remained the principal business until the land was developed for dwellings of commuters.

On the south edge of Winthrop Harbor an area on the Lake has been set aside for CAMP LOGAN, a training ground for the Illinois National Guard, with a station on the Chicago & North Western Railroad.

The Spring Bluff Forest Preserve begins at Main St. and extends north to the Wisconsin line. At the west of the Preserve is the Chicago & North Western right-of-way and Illinois 42, which becomes Wisconsin 32.

Section II. The Edens Expressway, Int. 94, and US 41, parallel with Sheridan Road.

The Edens Expressway leaves the John F. Kennedy Expressway at Wilson Ave. to move into the northern suburbs about one mile or less west of Sheridan Road. Just beyond the Dundee Road Intersection (Illinois 68) it moves west to a junction with Tri-State Tollway, which then proceeds north as Int. 94 (*see Section III*).

The Edens Expressway was named for Col. William Grant Edens, a life-long worker for good roads who served for 37 years as president of the Illinois Highway Improvement Assn. A plaque honoring him was placed at the overpass on Cicero Ave., north of Foster Ave., in October, 1949. Col. Edens, then nearly 86, was present at the dedication, at which Richard J. Finnegan, editor of the *Chicago Sun-Times,* made the principal address.

US 41 leaves Chicago at Devon Ave. for the suburb of Lincolnwood, joins Cicero Ave. at the Skokie line and merges with Int. 94 at the Kenilworth-Northfield line. When the Expressway ends at Deerfield Road in Highland Park US 41 follows Skokie Highway until it merges with the Tri-State Tollway at Russell Road one mile from the Wisconsin border. Thus it serves the western sections of some of the suburbs on the Lake Michigan shore reached by Sheridan Road.

LINCOLNWOOD, 12 *m.* (12,929 pop. 1970; 11,744, 1960,

inc. 10%) is one of those desirable residential areas adjacent to Chicago. Actually it is an extension of Chicago beyond Devon Ave., which was incorporated separately in 1911 by thrifty Luxemburg Germans before the Chicago fathers were aware that its 3¼ sq. mi. were available. It started as a stop on the North Shore branch of the Chicago & North Western Railway.

The Village of Skokie

SKOKIE, 16 m. (68,322 pop. 1970; 59,364, 1960) located north of Lincolnwood and west of Evanston, is a phenomenon of the post-war period, profiting by the migration from Chicago during the same years that Des Plaines, Arlington Heights and Northbrook had a similar expansion. It is separated from Evanston by the North Shore Channel and McCormick Blvd. The quickest drive to and from Chicago is via Edens Expressway, which has an entrance at Dempster St. and the quickest ride is via the CTA. The North Western commutation trains stop in Evanston and the Milwaukee in Morton Grove. United Motor Coach has direct service to Chicago and there is daily motor car service to O'Hare Airport.

Most of the terrain was a marsh with scrub oaks and truck farms forty years ago, on part of which was located the village of Niles Center, incorporated in 1888, now absorbed inside the 10 sq. mi. that since 1940 has become the prosperous village of Skokie. When its population passed that of Oak Park in 1962 it could claim the distinction of being "the world's largest village." Although many of its buildings are less than 20 years old it has a bank that advertises occupation of the same location since 1907, when its postoffice was Niles Center.

Skokie has the largest number of Russian-born citizens in the northern suburbs of Chicago. Its foreign stock (foreign-born or Americans of foreign or mixed parentage) in 1970 was 9,110 Russian, 4,902 Polish, 2,780 German, and 1,212 Italian. The Russian stock is largely Jewish. Skokie is one of the few suburbs with Jewish parochial schools; Jewish houses of worship are the most numerous (10), with Roman Catholic and Lutheran next; these also have their own schools. The Public School system has three Niles Township high schools, Niles East, West and North.

The largest mercantile operation in Skokie is the OLD ORCHARD SHOPPING CENTER, which has a concentration of luxury shops and large branch stores of Marshall Field & Co., Saks Fifth Avenue, and other chains. An example of recent business expansion is the CONCOURSE, a complex occupying 18 acres at Golf Road and Skokie Blvd., which has 12-story towers, for offices, 580-room Hilton hotel, and parking for 2,300 motor cars. Light industry in Skokie employs about 22,000, and the largest employer is Rand, McNally & Co., publishers, printers, and mapmakers.

New office buildings include the Old Orchard Office Bldg., 6 stories; the Kenroy Office Plaza, 7 stories; the six-story addition to the Westmoreland Bldg.; and the Fairway Bldg., 4 stories.

The Skokie Valley Community Hospital has 153 beds.

The SKOKIE PUBLIC LIBRARY, 5215 Oakton St., is one of the youngest and most active libraries on the North Shore. It was opened in 1959 and in 1972 reported "transactions"—use of books and materials—of 493,412, with a stock of 213,859 books, 838 periodicals, and 37,551 registered borrowers, more than half of the population. Operating expenses, $589,479, were comfortably below income. It is a member of the North Suburban Library System, which has its hq in the Evanston Public Library.

Higher education is represented by the HEBREW THEOLOGICAL COLLEGE, which calls itself the Jewish University of America. It occupies three modern buildings on a 16-acre campus at 7135 N. Carpenter Road. Its courses are planned to give the student a thorough education in the classical literature of the Jewish people and in the precepts of his faith. The college gives the degrees of bachelor of arts, bachelor of science, and bachelor of Hebrew literature. The Rabbinic Seminary Dept. has a six-year sequence of intensive studies leading to ordination. There is also a Teachers Training Program leading to a Teachers Certificate and a degree, and an evening program of advanced Hebrew courses for college girls. Graduate studies in Biblical and Talmudic research are open only to ordained rabbis or graduate students of equivalent background and lead to degrees of master and doctor of Hebrew literature. The college has an annual budget of approx. $800,000 and a one-year scholarship, with room and board, is placed at $2,400.

The Skokie Park District has provided nearly 200 acres of playgrounds and wooded areas in widely scattered locations for neighborhood use. The North Branch Division of the Cook County Forest Preserve District begins at Foster Ave. and Edens Expressway. Beyond it are the Skokie Lagoons, which, while not directly related to the village, are easy of access and a remarkable recreation asset for the contiguous North Shore villages. Control of seasonal flooding in what is known as the Chewab Skokie was accomplished by the construction of seven lagoons with a flood plain of 400 acres, held within dikes by a main control dam at Willow Road. They provide many new picnic spots and 190 acres of fishing waters.

The SKOKIE SWIFT RAPID TRANSIT LINE began as an experiment of the Chicago Transit Authority to develop and test a high-speed, two-station shuttle line on a five-mile section of an abandoned interurban railway. The service paid its way and was continued as a regular run serving 8,000 rides each weekday, with parking facilities and buses at the Skokie terminal at Dempsey St.

MORTON GROVE, 16.5 m. (26,369 pop. 1970; 20,533, 1960, inc. 28%) is directly west of Skokie and separated from it by the Edens Expressway. This completes the crowded population area that appears like an extension of Evanston. This village, incorporated in 1895, had a slow growth until after 1950 when dwellings multiplied so rapidly that nearly all available lots were taken. The village has the advantages of good roads and wooded recreation areas. With Edens Expressway on the east and Waukegan its western line, the North Branch of the Chicago River with woods and open areas of the Forest Preserve is in the middle. The Milwaukee Railroad cuts through the village on Lehigh Avenue. It was named for Levi P. Morton, railroad official and vice president of the United States, in Benjamin Harrison's administration, 1889-1893. (*See also Tour 10*).

Edens Expressway ends in Highland Park and US 41, which has been identical with it, proceeds north on the Skokie Highway. The Waukegan Road, Illinois 43, runs west of US 41 through Morton Grove, Glenview, Northfield, Northbrook and Deerfield.

North of Deerfield is the village of BANNOCKBURN (585 pop. 1970; 466, 1960) site of Trinity Evangelical Divinity School. West of Deerfield and west of the Tri-State Tollway is another area that has become desirable to developers: RIVERWOODS. In 1960, 96 people lived in this sprawling terrain; in 1970 the Census counted 1,517, a rise of 536.5%. Similarly its neighbor on the north, LINCOLN-SHIRE, also was favored by developers; it increased in population from 555 in 1960 to 2,531 in 1970, a rise of 356%.

Tri-State Tollway moves north through sparsely settled country to METTAWA (285, pop. 1970; 126, 1960, inc. 126.2%) and GREEN OAKS (656 pop. 1970; 198, 1960, inc. 232.6%), both of which have their principal shopping centers in Libertyville.

In the midst of residential areas that run well over 100,000 population sits the little village of GOLF, surrounded by Glenview at the northern border of Morton Grove, with a count of 474 people in 1970, which, up from 409 in 1960, is actually a rise of 15.9%. Golf is well named, for golf is the principal recreation of these northern suburbs.

GLENVIEW, 20 *m.* (24,880 pop. 1970; 18,132, 1960, inc. 27%) is a prosperous village on the North Branch of the Chicago River, directly west of Wilmette. It is older than most of its neighbors and was incorporated in 1899. Commuters use the Milwaukee Railroad and motor cars use the Edens Expressway. The Glenview Park Golf Club is located on the Skokie Lagoons and there are numerous other golf courses in the western part of the village. Scott, Foresman & Co., publisher, opened its main office here in 1966, using a new building at 1900 E. Lake Ave. designed by Perkins & Will. In the northern part of Glenview is the seat of the United States Naval and Marine Air Training Commands, a field of 1,300 acres, part of which was once a flying field of the Curtiss Wright Corp. The Waukegan Road runs through Glenview.

Both US 41 and Int. 94 (Edens Expressway) are easily accessible from Chestnut St. in Glenview and merge as they enter Northfield.

NORTHFIELD (5,010 pop. 1970; 4,005, 1960, inc. 25%) a village west of Kenilworth, incorporated in 1926, is served by the Edens Expressway. It is located in an area of golf clubs and recreation opportunities. The increased population of these North Shore suburbs caused the building here of New Trier Township East High School. The St.

Louise de Marillac Catholic High School for girls is located in North-field.

A. C. Neilsen Co., research organization known for its ratings of television programs, has moved its headquarters into a new building on a 77-acre site near the intersection of Willow Road and the Expressway in Northfield. The three-story building has 200,000 sq. ft. of office space.

Directly west of Glencoe is NORTHBROOK (27,297 pop. 1970; 11,635, 1960; inc. 134.6%) a rapidly growing suburb separated from Glencoe by the Edens Expressway (Int. 94 and US 41). For many years this locality was a milkstop for dairy farms called Schermerville after a German owner. The Milwaukee Railroad came in 1871 but growth was slow. In 1901 the place was incorporated as a village and in 1925 the 525 residents adopted the name of Northbrook; they were in Northfield Township and the North Branch of the Chicago River ran through it. Schermer Road is still in use. The big boom in popula-tion came after 1950 with the extension of the big expressways. North-brook has bus service from the Glenview Bus Co. and boards the Chicago & North Western at Winnetka. Dundee Road runs through the village. It has some light industries and is adding 5-story office buildings. North-brook Plaza is a well-developed shopping center. Northbrook has an extensive recreation program and profits also by its nearness to the Skokie Division of the Forest Preserve District of Cook County, which has trails running through the Sunset Ridge Woods, the Chipilly Woods, and the Somme Woods, the latter two on Dundee Road. There is also boating in the Chewab Skokie east of the Edens Expressway.

After turning west Int. 94 runs along the southern border of Deerfield 4.4 m. to a junction with the Tri-State Tollway, which has come up from the Indiana line as Int. 294, passing O'Hare Interna-tional Airport.

DEERFIELD, 27 m. (18,949 pop. 1970; 11,786, 1960, inc. 60%), just north of the Cook County line and west of Highland Park, is another of the Lake County villages that owes its rapid growth to the migration of Chicago residents to the North Shore suburbs. It has the use of Tri-State Tollway (Int. 94) and Illinois 43 and another access to Edens Expressway via Deerfield Road in Highland Park. It was incorporated as a village in 1903. Deerfield has a number of light industries, especially Sara Lee Kitchens, 500 Waukegan Rd., where Sara Lee products are baked. *Tours Monday through Friday, by prior reservation.*

Sec. III. Alternative Route from Chicago to Lake County Suburbs. Tri-State Tollway, Int. 294 and 94; US 45

Tri-State Tollway enters Illinois from Hammond, Indiana, moves west of the South Chicago industrial area and as far west of Downtown Chicago as O'Hare International Airport, thence goes north to Wiscon-sin. In Cook County it is marked Int. 294; in Lake County it joins Int. 94 for its route north. At the Wisconsin line it merges with US 41 and moves on to Milwaukee.

US 45 is the great north-south highway that proceeds down the length of Illinois from Wisconsin to the Ohio River at Paducah. It bypasses the Loop and is one of the feeders of O'Hare International Airport. Its northern segment goes north of the Des Plaines River Road, and has a junction with Milwaukee Avenue, Illinois 21, at the Palatine Road.

Before reaching the Palatine Road where Illinois 21 comes up the Milwaukee Road to merge with US 45, the two roads create a triangle occupied by the RIVER TRAIL NATURE CENTER of the Forest Preserve District of Cook County, which extends up from Euclid Ave. Here is a protected wilderness, with trails for hiking, ponds and the Des Plaines River for fishing, bridle paths and Indian sites. Here is the PORTAGE GROVE, where a rock on the river bank is designated as the site of a landing of Father Jacques Marquette on his trip from the Illinois River and the Des Plaines to Lake Michigan.

The WHEELING PAL WAUKEE AIRPORT is located north of the intersection of Palatine Road and US 45. It handles about 700 planes a day and can park 300 planes.

Continuing on US 45:

WHEELING, 2.6 m., 27 m. from the Loop (640 alt., 14,746 pop. 1970; 7,169, 1960, inc. 105.7%) has been known as a Cook County village since its incorporation in 1894, but it remained little more than a collection of frame dwellings and a few taverns until after World War II, when the migration northward began. When the first edition of this *Guide* was published it counted a population of only 670. Farmers from the 1830's on found it a useful crossroads, and the road between Chicago and Milwaukee made it a stagecoach stop for relays of horses. The old road is now Illinois 21.

Wheeling has an elective mayor, a board of trustees, and a village manager. The Des Plaines River flows parallel with US 45 and the Tri-State Tollway touches its eastern limits, where new housing is filling gaps in the landscape toward Northbrook. Condominiums and town houses are rising and units are reserved for senior citizens. Shopping centers operate in all sections of the village. Parks completely equipped for sports and recreation are maintained by the Park District. The proximity to major highways and two airports has made the industrial center desirable for light industry. Industrial employment in 1970 was 3,511 and principal employers were Illinois Lock Co., Olin Mathieson, Tower Packaging Co., Cockle Ventilator Co., Lurch Food Products Co., Nationwide Business Forms, Martin Metals Co., and others.

The Community Presbyterian Church, built in 1865, has been bought by the Wheeling Historical Society, in cooperation with the Park District, and moved to Chamber of Commerce Park. It has been restored and turned into a community center and historical headquarters.

The Wheeling Public Library has more than 36,000 books and circulates almost 130,000 books and other materials. Its building was improved in 1970. It is a member of the North Suburban Library System.

Contiguous to Wheeling on the west is BUFFALO GROVE, (11,799 pop. 1970; 1,492, 1960, inc. 690.8%) a village in both Cook and Lake Counties. The Dundee Road, Illinois 68, is its principal east-west highway. It is also north of Arlington Heights. It is a prime example of the big migration into suburbia, which created a boom for town lots in the Wheeling-Arlington Heights meadowlands. A church built in 1847 on Buffalo Grove Road is about the only memento of the crossroads hamlet that now has modern dwellings and shops, the Ranch Mart Plaza and the Buffalo Grove Mall. It has no industries and its municipal services are the same as those used by adjoining Wheeling, including North Western commuting, United Motor Coach, Tri-State Tollway and Edens Expressway.

Illinois 83, the old Elmhurst Road, which comes north from the Calumet Sag Channel through Des Plaines and Mount Prospect, has a junction with the Dundee Road in Wheeling and proceeds northwest through Buffalo Grove to LONG GROVE (1,196 pop. 1970; 640, 1960), 4 m. from Wheeling, and another place favored by Chicago firms for suburban headquarters, recently made international headquarters by Kemper Insurance Co. Contiguous on the west is KILDEER (643 pop. 1970, 172, 1960, inc. 271%) with more land than people, stretching out to LAKE ZURICH (*see Tour 9*).

Return to US 45 from Wheeling.

US 45 proceeds north from Wheeling west of Deerfield and River-woods through Lincolnshire to HALF DAY, an early crossroads settlement where Adlai E. Stevenson voted when his country place in Lake County was his legal residence. Half Day is supposed to be a translation of the name of Aptakisic, a Potawatomi chief; the village of Aptakisic is on a dirt road 3 m.sw. In Half Day US 45 has a junction with Illinois 22, an east-west road from Highland Park to Prairie View, Lake Zurich and Fox River Grove. When US 45 leaves Milwaukee Ave. at Half Day to turn northwest, the Milwaukee Road becomes Illinois 21 and a direct route to Libertyville.

VERNON HILLS, 4.2 m. northwest of Half Day on US 45, is a Lake County village that had 123 inhabitants in 1960 and by growing to 1,056 by 1970 achieved an increase of 758%. This may have turned the attention of developers to the place, but it is more likely that the proximity of Long Grove, Mundelein, and Libertyville and the prospects of the whole well-to-do region started the investment in NEW CEN-TURY TOWN, a planned community north of Illinois 60, where the principal attraction was to be Hawthorn Center, an enclosed mall shopping area with a Marshall Field & Co. store as one of the important units. Marshall Field has reserved 250,000 sq. ft. for its store, beauty salon and restaurant. Hawthorn Center is a joint venture of Mafco, Inc., a Field subsidiary, and the Urban Investment & Development Co., a subsidiary of Aetna Life & Casualty Co. Sears, Roebuck will be associated with the builders in developing New Century Town.

Adjoining Vernon Hills and contiguous to the extreme southeast corner of Mundelein is INDIAN CREEK with 270 inhabitants.

US 45 has a junction with Illinois 83 (north-south) and turns sharply north into MUNDELEIN (16,128 pop., 1970; 10,526, 1960, inc. 53.2%), 37 m. north of the Loop. It was named after the former Archbishop of the Chicago Diocese and Cardinal of the Roman Catholic Church. Mundelein is well built up, and new areas are being developed on the outskirts. One is DIAMOND LAKE, an unincorporated place near the lake of that name, which had its first census count, 1,343, in 1970. In 1920 Cardinal Mundelein moved the St. Mary of the Lake Seminary from Chicago to this location and sponsored the erection of new buildings in the brick and stone Georgian style of a New England village.

On 1,200 wooded acres bordering Lake St. Mary in the northern quarter of the town is ST. MARY OF THE LAKE SEMINARY, one of the most elaborate and carefully planned Roman Catholic theological seminaries. The average enrollment is 300. Ranged on the beautifully landscaped grounds, site of the final session of the International Eucharistic Congress in 1926, are brick and stone Colonial structures, designed by Joseph McCarty of Chicago. At the center of the group is the CHAPEL, its refined Colonial lines modeled after those of a frame Protestant meetinghouse at Lyme, Connecticut, that Cardinal Mundelein admired as a boy. The interior is decorated in Renaissance style. Above the altar is a picture of the Holy Family by Francisco Zurbaran (1598-1662). The chapel was the gift of Edward Hines, Chicago lumberman, whose son, Edward Hines, Jr., killed in the first World War, is entombed in a small chapel nearby.

South of the chapel are a Lourdes Grotto and Stations of the Cross. Beyond, St. Augustine's Bridge affords a good view of vast flower beds, one of which depicts the Cardinal's coat-of-arms. The Feehan Memorial Library, nearby, contains valuable incunabula. Among the seminary's collection of autographs are those of several saints, and of signers of the Constitution and Declaration of Independence. Other important items are a numismatic collection and a series of medals struck by the popes. Adjoining the seminary grounds on the east is the Benedictine Convent of Perpetual Adoration (*open to public 8-5 daily; services at 4:15*), in the chapel of which nuns kneel in constant prayer.

The Fremont Township Public Library circulates about 63,000 books and other materials annually. Its building, erected 1910, was improved 1964. It is a member of the North Suburban Library System.

Illinois 176, which crosses both Mundelein and Libertyville on Maple St. is a most useful east-west artery, connecting with Skokie Highway (US 41) which leads to Edens Expressway; Tri-State Tollway (Int. 74); Rand Road, which joins Kennedy Expressway; and Northwest Highway.

East and north of Mundelein and contiguous with its streets is Libertyville.

LIBERTYVILLE, 35 m. from the Loop (698 alt., 11,684 pop.

1970; 8,560, 1960, inc. 36%) highly favored for many years by wealthy Chicago business men for large estates, was known as Independence Grove until given its present name when the postoffice was established in 1837. Densely wooded at one time and with Butler Lake and part of St. Mary's Lake in its environs, it was reached by the Milwaukee Road, now Illinois 21, which is joined partway by US 45. Tri-State Tollway, Int. 94, is within 1½ m. of its limits, which are 6 m. west of Sheridan Road on Maple Ave., Illinois 176. The town is 15 miles south of Wisconsin. The Des Plaines River flows along its eastern line. Libertyville and Mundelein have contiguous areas. One of the early purchasers of land was Daniel Webster (1782-1852).

Libertyville is a busy shopping center and has a number of heavy industries of which the largest employer is the Frank Hough Division of the International Harvester Co., acquired in 1952, which builds rubber-tired tractors and other construction equipment. Another is International Minerals & Chemical Co. Condell Memorial Hospital is located here. Adler Memorial Park, formerly the estate of David Adler, Chicago architect, has an art center and is the largest park.

The Cook Memorial Library, founded in 1889 and improved in 1968, has a stock of approx. 50,000 books and 198,104 transactions a year. It is a member of the North Suburban Library System.

Illinois 176, a route to the recreation area of western Illinois, runs along Maple Ave. in Mundelein and Libertyville and proceeds east to Sheridan Road in Lake Bluff. Samuel Insull developed his estate, Hawthorne Farm on 4,445 acres south of Libertyville from 1903 to 1929. In 1921 he built a fine mansion and landscaped 101 acres of gardens, walks and shrubbery around it. He raised pure-bred Swiss cattle and Suffolk Punch draft horses.

Illinois 21 moves north from Libertyville to junctions with Tri-State Tollway and US 41, which combine to Milwaukee, Wis. US 45 moves north through the Chain o' Lakes country to Milwaukee. Milwaukee is 93 m. from Chicago. *See Tour 9.*

Tour 3

CHICAGO TO CAIRO AND PADUCAH

I   Kankakee — Champaign — Mattoon — Charleston — Effingham —Salem—Mount Vernon—Benton—Mound City—Cairo.

II   Effingham — Flora — Fairfield — Norris City — Harrisburg — Metropolis—Fort Massac State Park—Paducah Interstate 57, US 45

Chicago to Cairo, 373 m. Chicago to Paducah, 372 m.

THE PRESENT TOUR has two sections. One is a speedway from Chicago to Cairo, and the other from Chicago to Paducah, Kentucky. Both have the advantages of Interstate 57; the Cairo tour all the way, and the Paducah tour as far as Effingham, or 298 miles. Parallel with Int. 57 are US 45 and Illinois 37 on the Cairo route, and US 45 all the way on the Paducah route. Exits from the expressway enable the driver to connect with bypassed towns by means of the parallel routes.

Section a. Chicago to Kankakee, 58 m.

The Dan Ryan Expressway, Int. 90 and 94, continues south from the Eisenhower Expressway and the John F. Kennedy Expressway at Taylor St. to 95th St., where Int. 94 turns east as the Calumet Expressway, and its western segment becomes Int. 57. This moves south parallel with Illinois 50, which comes down Cicero Ave.

At 31 m. Int. 57 has a junction with Illinois 30, the direct highway to Joliet. Here is MATTESON (4,741 pop. 1970; 3,125, 1960, inc. 47%). It was settled in 1855 during the term of Governor Joel A. Matteson. The Allis Chalmers Corp. is the principal employer, Matteson Public Library has 35,000 transactions a year and is a member of the Suburban Library System.

After crossing into Will County Int. 57 and Illinois 50, the Governor's Highway, run parallel.

PEOTONE, 42 m. (2,345 pop. 1970; 1,788, 1960) was settled in the 1850s when the Illinois Central came this way.

MANTENO, 48 m. (2,864 pop. 1970; 2,225, 1960, inc. 28%) in Kankakee County, incorporated in 1878, has the name of a Potawotomi daughter of the French trader, Francois Bourbonnais. In the allocation of land to Indians by the Treaty of 1832 a section at this site was given to Manteno. The Manteno State Hospital for the Mentally Ill is located 2 m. east of the village.

On approaching the area of the city of Kankakee the north-south highways undergo several changes. After Manteno and before reaching Bradley Int. 57 crosses Illinois 50 and moves southeast of Bradley, bypassing the larger part of Kankakee. US 45 and US 52 combined, coming southwest of Int. 57, pass through the suburbs of Bourbonnais and Bradley, to enter the city of Kankakee.

BOURBONNAIS (5,909 pop. 1970; 3,336, 1960, inc. 77%) the most northern of the Kankakee suburbs, has been attracting new residents who work in Bradley and Kankakee. It is the oldest settlement in this area, going back to the first traders who used this road. It was named for François Bourbonnais, a coureur de bois. Noel La Vasseur (1799-1879), fur-trader and partner of Gurdon Hubbard (see Tour 1), is credited with founding the settlement. He established a trading post here in 1832, and was responsible for the immigration of French-Canadians to the region in the forties. "From Bourbonnais," wrote an early historian, "went people who established every other French town in Kankakee and Iroquois Counties. Kankakee in a large measure, St. Anne, L'Erable, St. Mary, Papineau all acknowledge Bourbonnais as the mother." Its older inhabitants still speak French in their homes.

OLIVET NAZARENE COLLEGE, founded 1907 by the Church of the Nazarene, is a four-year liberal arts college occupying a campus of 150 acres. It gives masters degrees in religion and elementary education; 50 percent of its graduates enter teaching and 20 percent enter the ministry. In 1973 it enrolled 1,670 and had a faculty of 88.

BRADLEY (9,881 pop. 1970; 8,082, 1960) was laid out in 1902 as North Kankakee, and three years later was named Bradley when David Bradley started a farm implement factory here. The factory is no longer here, but other industries have come, including Kroehler Manufacturing Co., fine furniture, employing 660; Jones & McKnight Construction Co., steel bars, employing 240; Chicago Bridge & Iron Co., Crown Cork & Seal, and Roper Co., Bradley Division, maker of garden tools and employing 548.

KANKAKEE, 58 m. (631 alt., 30,944 pop. 1970; 27,666, 1960, inc. 11%) a city, is the seat of Kankakee county. It is 18 m. west of the Indiana line. Kankakee County (97,250 pop. 1970) is especially favored by sportsmen for hunting and fishing in the Kankakee River bottoms, which for centuries have been part of the wildlife flyway. The county embraces Aroma Park, Bonfield, Bourbonnais, Bradley, Buckingham, Cabery, Chebanse, Essex, Grant Park, Herscher, Irwin, Manteno, Momence, Reddick, and St. Anne.

Kankakee is an industrial and mercantile city that fabricates castings, tools, steel for buildings and roads, and processes foods. Its principal employers are Roper Corp., cooking appliances (1,340 employees); General Foods Corp., dog food (1,200) Armstrong Cork Co. (320) and General Mills (285).

Since 1963 the Kankakee Development Corp. has been rebuilding the core of the city, removing obsolete buildings, arranging offstreet parking, and opening trading mills and plazas such as Dearborn Park, where the First Trust & Savings Bank, the city's oldest bank, has erected a modern office building. The city is also known for its response to the public need for parks and recreation; by the 1970's the Kankakee Valley Park District was supervising 25 parks of 605 acres, offering every facility for games, competitive sports, and picnics. There is a small zoo in Bird Park. Important is the Small Memorial Park, 20 acres at 8th St. and Calista Ave., named for former Governor Len Small, which contains the Small Mansion that he gave to the city, and the Civic Auditorium. The Centennial Room at the Park is used by clubs such as those devoted to art, stamps, coins, and photography. Several of the parks have supervised winter programs for young people.

KANKAKEE COMMUNITY COLLEGE is the newest addition to general public education, with two-year courses. It opened in temporary quarters in the fall of 1968, inviting students of all ages. In adult education it offers classes ranging from antiques to welding, basic education to Japanese, cake decorating to horseshoeing, chemistry to psychology—whatever the community is most interested in. In 1971-72 it enrolled 1,185 and had a faculty of 64.

The city has two excellent general hospitals, Riverside, 350 N. Wall St., which opened in January, 1964, and St. Mary's, Fifth Ave. and Court St., which added two wings in 1959 and 1962, and serves up to 12,000 patients annually. Riverside cooperates with Olivet Nazarene College and Kankakee Community College in providing programs on nursing leading to degrees of registered and practical nurse.

Known for its high standards is the KANKAKEE STATE HOSPITAL FOR MENTAL HEALTH, operating since 1878 at Jeffery St. and the River. In 1969 it added a special section for treating mental retardation, with approx. 500 patients. It has academic education for adolescents and courses in family living, literacy and similar topics for adults; there is an alcoholic unit with medical-surgical treatment, and psychotherapy for individuals and groups. The 400 acres of hospital grounds have been leased to the Kankakee Valley Park District for development. The hospital has tours for visitors and provides speakers for lectures to community groups. For details of admittance procedures for patients address the Medical Records Librarian at the hospital.

The Kankakee Public Library, 304 S. Indiana Ave., occupies a building with Corinthian columns that was erected in 1899 and extensively improved in 1971. It has a collection of more than 75,000 books and an annual circulation of more than 170,000. It is a member of the Bur Oak Library System.

Minority groups make up about one-fourth of the population. During the 1960s there were racial disturbances of varying degrees and in 1971 a major racial conflict at Westview High School was reported. In January, 1970, the U. S. Dept. of Health, Education, & Welfare had warned that District III must desegregate its schools or face a Federal compliance order. The district reorganized and reported that it had achieved a racially balanced system after making a 20 percent increase in transporting pupils. The faculty also was desegregated and black teachers were recruited. This compliance opened the door to Federal funds and the district received about $300,000 in Federal aid. This fund helps a program for disadvantaged pupils and plans for a rural school with a school council partly from the community.

Section b. Kankakee to Mattoon

Between Kankakee, 0 *m.* and Mattoon are large fields of corn, the great food product of central Illinois. Hedgerows separate the fields, oak groves shade the farmsteads, but no hill breaks the prairie, and only a few tributaries of the Wabash cut their willow-marked courses across its surface. This is the great cash-grain region, where every phase of cultivation is mechanized, farmhouses are fully equipped with electrical appliances, and radio and television keep the family informed.

Fertile, unbreached black loam, developed from the thick, flat deposits of the Wisconsin ice sheet; a long, hot growing season, and properly distributed rainfall, provide ideal conditions for raising corn. Second in importance to corn is oats, which fits well in crop rotation, enabling the farmer to spread his work. In this area corn is a cash commodity, stored not on the individual farms but in elevators in the towns along the route.

Int. 57 bypasses Kankakee, while US 45 passes through it. Int. 57 then follows the old route that touches the villages of upper Iroquois County, but after Ashkum these are reached by US 45 while Int. 57 runs about one mile west.

CHEBANSE (Ind. little duck), 11 *m.* (1,185 pop. 1970; 995, 1960, inc. 19%), a German community dependent chiefly on agriculture, is divided by the county line; part of its residents live in Iroquois County, part in Kankakee County.

DANFORTH, 24 *m.* (404 pop. 1970; 396, 1960), a village of trim white and green houses, is named for A. H. and George Danforth, who in the late 1850s purchased 27,000 acres of swampland and induced 30 families to emigrate from the Netherlands and settle here. The Dutch built windmills and dug ditches, drained the land, and established farms. Danforth was platted in 1872.

At 27 *m.* is the northern junction with US 24 (*see Tour* 16); for two miles US 24 and US 45 are united.

GILMAN, 28 *m.* (1,786 pop. 1970; 1,704, 1960) is the birthplace of James Robert Mann (1856-1922), Illinois Representative who sponsored the Mann Act.

On the northern limits of Onarga, 31.5 *m.*, is a junction with a graveled road. Right on this road to Larch Farm, 0.3 *m.*, the former home of the detective, Allan Pinkerton (*see Tour* 11). Completed in 1873, the one-story building with watch tower was once a show place of Iroquois County. Pinkerton developed the farm along original lines. It was enclosed by a hedge of osage-orange trees inside of which were planted seven rows of larch trees, placed four ft. apart. The Illinois Central Railroad intersected the land from north to south and its right-of-way was similarly treated. More than 85,000 larch trees and, 1,000 evergreens were said to have been planted; also numerous shade trees of other varieties and 2,000 apple trees. The greenhouse contained 2,000 varieties of flowers. Corn and oats were the principal crops. In 1880 Pinkerton was said to have employed 10 men regularly, doubling this number in the spring.

ONARGA, 32 *m.* (657 alt., 1,436 pop. 1970. 1,397, 1960) a village in Iroquois County, is at an intersection with US 24 and Illinois 54, a direct route to Springfield. There are several light industries, including woodwork and furniture, and a nursery for fruit and shade trees. Onarga was the home of Benjamin Hardy, composer of *Darling Nellie Gray*.

PAXTON, 50 *m.* (4,373 pop. 1970; 4,370, 1960) seat of Ford County, was settled in the 1850's by Swedish immigrants and was the second site of Augustana College from 1863 until 1875. South of Paxton thousands of acres are planted in soy beans, of which Illinois produces more than any other state. An important element in the economy of the corn belt, soy beans rotate well with corn and serve to fix nitrogen in the soil.

Paxton is at a junction with the east-west Illinois 9. About 15 *m.* west on Route 9 GIBSON CITY (3,454 pop. 1970; 3,453, 1960) has the distinction of having lost only one resident in a decade, according to the U. S. Census report. In the heart of the soybean area the city processes and ships soybeans. It is at a junction with Illinois 47, north-south, and US 54, northeast-southwest.

RANTOUL, 61 *m.* (25,562 pop. 1970; 22,116, 1960, inc. 15.6%) in Champaign County, became a stop on the Illinois Central railroad when its tracks came this way in 1854. It was named for Robert Rantoul, a director of the road and remained a farm village until the U. S. Army established a training base here for the Air Force when the United States entered World War I. Its population is made up chiefly of personnel of the air base, Chanute Field. The Rantoul Public Library, opened 1961, was enlarged in 1960. It is a member of the Lincoln Trail Library System.

CHANUTE FIELD, at the southeastern limits of Rantoul, became an Air Force base for training pilots, gunners, mechanics and other specialists in the spring of 1917, after the United States entered World War I. According to the *Illinois Fact Book and Historical Almanac* the U. S. Signal Corps, which had been training military pilots at Ashburn Field, Cicero Ave. near 79th St., Chicago, moved to Chanute in July, 1916. Flight training began at Chanute in July, 1917. By 1918 Chanute sent 10 squadrons into combat abroad. From 1921 Chanute was the air technical training center and by the end of World War II had educated more than 200,000 air technicians.

Octave Chanute (1832-1910) is associated in aviation history with the success of Orville and Wilbur Wright, to whom he contributed information that proved useful to their successful biplane flight. Born in Paris and brought to the United States as a child, Chanute became a civil engineer, chief engineer of the Chicago & Alton Ry., and a leading theorist on aviation. He had an office in Chicago, experimented with gliders on the Indiana dunes, and wrote and spoke freely on the theory and technics of aviation.

From Rantoul US 45 proceeds 16 *m.* south to URBANA (32,800 pop. 1970), whereas Int. 57 moves several miles west to bypass CHAMPAIGN (56,532 pop. 1970). Both US 45 and Int. 57 have junctions with Int. 74, coming from Danville and proceeding west to Bloomington, Peoria, Galesburg and the Quad Cities.

From Champaign Illinois 10 runs 9 *m.* west to a junction with

Illinois 47, which has come down the State in a straight line from Lake Geneva, Wisc., west of the Fox River Valley. Illinois 47 is the chief route between Champaign and Decatur, and about halfway is MONTI-CELLO (4,130 pop. 1970; 3,219, 1960, inc. 28%) seat of Piatt County, known for its rich soil. Monticello was founded on July 4, 1837, and named for Thomas Jefferson's home in Virginia. It is a distributing center for farm products.

About 5 *m.* south of Monticello on the Sangamon River and 26 *m.* southwest of Urbana-Champaign is ROBERT ALLERTON PARK, a wooded country domain of 1,500 acres, once the estate of Robert H. Allerton, who gave it to the University of Illinois shortly before his death in 1964. His whole donation was 4,500 acres of farmland, which is operated by the College of Agriculture and produces income for the university. Allerton was the son of Samuel Allerton, Chicago banker. A memorial 4-H camp has been developed inside the park. The mansion, Allerton House, is used by the Division of University Extension for conferences.

Hott Memorial Center, a magnificent large residence in Monticello, was given to the university in 1960 by Maxwell R. Hott and is used by Division of University Extension in conjunction with Allerton House for short courses and conferences.

About 8 *m.* south of Monticello on Illinois 105 to BEMENT, (1,638 pop. 1970; 1,558, 1960) where a cottage in which Abraham Lincoln and Stephen A. Douglas met on July 29, 1858, is a State Memorial. Douglas came here at Lincoln's invitation to arrange for debates on the issues of 1858, now famous as the Lincoln-Douglas Debates. The cottage was presented to the State by Mr. and Mrs. Francis E. Bryant on July 29, 1947.

Piatt County is small (15,509 pop. 1970; 14,960, 1960, inc. 3%). Besides Bement, Cerro Gordo, named for a battle of the Mexican War, has 1,368 pop. All other places are small farm villages and most of them lost people in the 1960-1970 decade.

Tour 3 returns to US 45.

TOLONO, 87.3 *m.* (736 alt., 2,027 pop. 1970; 1,539, 1960) in Champaign County, bears a name coined by J. B. Calhoun of the Illinois Central Railroad. It was platted at the intersection of the Illinois Central and the Great Western (later Norfolk & Western) in 1856. A marker at the Union Station tells that Lincoln spoke from the rear of his train on Feb. 11, 1861, en route to Washington, his last remarks in Illinois.

PESOTUM, 92.5 *m.* (720 alt., 536 pop. 1970; 468, 1960) is a farm village on the Illinois Central Gulf Railroad.

TUSCOLA (Ind. a level plain), 101.5 *m.* (633 alt., 3,917 pop. 1970; 3,875, 1960), seat of Douglas County, began its existence as a stop on the Illinois Central Railroad for shipping farm products in 1855. It was platted in 1857 and made the county seat in 1859. Joseph G. Cannon, "Uncle Joe," Speaker of the U. S. House of Representatives and a standpat Republican leader, practiced law here 1861-72 and became state's attorney. Located in the broom corn country, the town made brooms. In 1952 it acquired an interest in big industry when the United States Industrial Chemicals Co. located a huge petrochemical plant five miles west of Tuscola. It employs 1,200 to 1,500 men and receives gas by pipe line from the South Oklahoma, Kansas and Texas fields.

At 102 *m.* is a junction with US 36 (*see Tour* 18).

ARCOLA, 110 *m.* (2,276 pop. 1970; 2,273, 1960) a city in Douglas County named for a town in Italy, was platted in 1855. The community is at the northern border of the broom corn belt, which extends south to Neoga. Used in the manufacture of brooms, the plant differs from grain corn in its finer leaf and brushy tassel. The species most common to Illinois are white Italian and Black Jap (or Spanish), which grow from 8 to 15 feet tall. Bordering the railroad tracks in Arcola are large red sheds where the "broom" is graded and shipped. Some of the product is used in a local broom factory. West of Arcola is a large Amish colony (*see Tour* 18).

Arcola is at a junction with Illinois 133, east-west.

MATTOON, 125 *m.* (725 alt., 19,681 pop. 1970; 19,088, 1960), an industrial city in Coles County, was established as a shipping center in the early 1850's when the Big Four Railroad laid its tracks through this section. The young community was named for William Mattoon, an official of the Illinois Central, who was instrumental in developing the town. Mattoon manufactures shoes, furniture, road-building machinery and Diesel engines, and does a considerable retail and wholesale business in grains, feed, and fertilizers.

In June 1861, Gen. Ulysses S. Grant mustered the Twenty-first Illinois Infantry into the State service at Mattoon. Grant's local military activities are narrated on a Bronze Tablet at the east side of the Illinois Central depot, Broadway and 18th St.

Mattoon is at a junction with the Lincoln Heritage Trail formerly the Lincoln National Memorial Highway (*see Tour* 21), and Illinois 16, which has a new multilane highway between Mattoon and Charleston, 11 *m.* east, site of one of the Lincoln-Douglas debates.

LAKE LAND COLLEGE is a new community college opened under the State Junior College Act in 1966. It has academic and occupational courses and by 1973 had 2,600 students and 130 in the faculty.

LAKE MATTOON is fed by the waters of the Little Wabash River, and serves both as water supply and a place for recreation.

Mattoon is 10 *m.* west of Charleston, seat of Eastern Illinois University and seat of Coles County. The county had a pop. of 47,815 in 1970, a gain of 11% over 42,860 in 1960. The county plants approximately 113,300 acres to corn, 77,000 to soybeans, 26,400 to wheat, 2,700 to oats, and 6,100 to hay.

Section c. Side Trip to Lake Shelbyville

Northwest of Mattoon on Illinois 121 to SULLIVAN (4,112 pop. 1970; 3,936, 1960, inc. 4%), seat of Moultrie County, located at a junction with north-south Illinois 32, 3 *m.* from the head of the huge reservoir, LAKE SHELBYVILLE, made by the Kaskaskia River. It was named for the occupation of Sullivan Island in Charleston, S. C., harbor by Col. William Moultrie during the American Revolution. Sullivan is on the Lincoln Heritage Trail. The County, 13,263 pop. 1970, was established in 1843. In 1965 Sullivan built a new Civic Center for its public offices. Its Little Theatre on the Square has performances from May to October with professional stars. The Illinois Masonic Home has cared for the aged since 1904. The Sullivan City Library has more than 13,000 books and circulates around 43,000. Among industries the branch of the Brown Shoe Co. of St. Louis employs 400. Here also are divisions of Kaiser Agricultural Chemicals and the Yardman of Illinois Leisure Group, gardening tools.

LAKE SHELBYVILLE, 3 m. west and south of Sullivan, is a reservoir of 11,100 acres fed by the Kaskaskia River, the West Okaw River, the Brush, Marrowbone, Opossum, Whittley, Wilborn, and other creeks, with a normal pool 20 m. long. The project was begun in 1963 by the Corps of Engineers, USA, and water was impounded beginning in 1970. A number of areas were opened for hunting, fishing and recreation in spring, 1971. The Findlay Bridge of the Chicago & Eastern Illinois, 3,200 ft. long, crosses the lake from FINDLAY in Shelby County (809 pop. 1970) to Sullivan. Near the head of the lake on Illinois 121 is BETHANY, in Moultrie County (1,235 pop. 1970; 1,118, 1960). East of the lake on Illinois 16 is WINDSOR, in Shelby County (1,126 pop. 1970; 1,021, 1960).

Lake Shelbyville floods so many irregular valleys among the hills of the Shelbyville Moraine that it has a shore line of 250 m. Two large State parks have been located here: Wolf Creek, formerly State Park East, and Eagle Creek, formerly State Park West. No hunting is permitted in recreation areas; at other places only shotguns are permitted. State regulations are enforced and wildlife is protected. More than 5,000,000 fingerlings of northern pike, walleye, and smallmouth bass are stocked by the Illinois Dept. of Conservation. Sport fish include large-mouthed bass, crappie, sunfish, and channel cat. Water skiing is permitted if kept beyond 300 ft. of the shoreline, and every boat must carry two persons.

SHELBYVILLE (4,597 pop. 1970; 4,821, 1960) seat of Shelby County is located at the foot of Lake Shelbyville, just beyond the dam and the Administration Building of the reservoir. It is at a junction of Illinois 16 and Illinois 128 and is served by the Chicago & Eastern Illinois Ry. and the Penn Central. It is 16 m. east of Pana and US 51. Abraham Lincoln's attendance at circuit court sessions is commemorated.

Tour 3 resumes from Mattoon on US 45.

Section d. Mattoon to Norris City

Between Mattoon, 0 m., and Norris City US 45 crosses a region of mixed farming, a prairie land that differs sharply from that of the cash-grain area to the north. The two regions are separated by the Shelbyville Moraine, a long ridge immediately south of Mattoon that marks the maximum advance of recent glaciation. The country south of the moraine, though once glaciated, has been exposed to erosion perhaps 40 times as long as that to the north. Numerous streams cross its surface, and leaching has robbed its soils of much of their fertility. Corn, conspicuous in the landscape, shares the fields with hay and winter wheat. Rougher lands are in pasture, and peach and apple orchards are common.

In the northern half of the region numerous valleys, steep sided and wooded, break the level of the prairie. In the south, where the glacial drift is very thin and topography is controlled by underlying bedrock, the surface is one of gently rolling slopes, broad valleys and rounded divides. The northern border of the Shelbyville Moraine is marked by a slight rise of land, 7 *m.*, and then a descent of nearly 100 ft. in a few miles. This terminal moraine extends from east of the Indiana line west to the center of Illinois, then north into Wisconsin.

NEOGA, 14 *m.* (1,270 pop. 1970; 1,145, 1960) in Cumberland County, is a farm products distributing center near the end of Lake Mattoon. It ships apples and peaches. It was given a station by the Illinois Central in 1855 and has been incorporated as a city.

EFFINGHAM, 28 *m.* (591 alt., 9,458 pop. 1970; 8,172, 1960, inc. 15.7%) seat of Effingham County, calls itself the Crossroads of America. It is the place where the two Tours, Chicago-Cairo and Chicago-Paducah, take separate routes. It profits as a distributing center by its access to good roads. It is located at an intersection of Illinois Central Gulf and Penn Central Railroads. US 45 has a junction with US 40, northeast of Terre Haute, southwest to St. Louis, Illinois 33 and 37. Interstate 70 and Int. 57 combine to bypass Effingham and thereby provide an excellent location for national-chain motels. Greyhound Lines and Continental Trailways also serve the city. The County Memorial Airport is 3 *m.* south on Illinois 37.

Incorporated in 1861, it received a large number of German immigrants, who also farmed in the county. It has a mayor and council form of government and recently allocated $2,300,000 for a new water supply from Lake Sara, 2,200 acres, and built a new National Guard Armory. It has 18 churches representing 14 denominations, and public and parochial high schools. St. Anthony's hospital has 140 beds and there are three nursing homes. In 1970 20 factories were employing 2,563 persons. One of the principal industries is the Norge Division of Fedders Corp., which makes combination washers and dryers, self-service dry cleaners and similar equipment and employs 1,600. The World Color Press employs 500 and the Peerless of America, refrigeration and air conditioning, also employs 500.

The town of Broughton was settled in 1854 with the arrival of the Illinois Central Railroad. Broughton changed to Effingham when it became the county seat in 1859. It was named for Lord Effingham, a British general who resigned rather than fight the colonists. Effingham grew as pioneers moved to the west along the Cumberland road.

The *Effingham Daily News* appears weekdays. The Helen Matthes Library, established 1955, was improved in 1966. It circulates more than 65,000 volumes and is a member of the Rolling Prairie Library System.

Section e. Effingham to Cairo

Effingham is the junction for a number of important highways. Drivers wishing to cross the Ohio River for Paducah here take US 45. Those following Interstate 57 to Cairo can bypass Effingham and continue south. Seven miles beyond Effingham a road leaves US 45 and becomes Illinois 37, which runs parallel with Int. 57.

The principal cities between Effingham and Cairo are Salem, Mount Vernon, Benton, West Frankfort, Marion. Both highways pass through the Rend Lake recreation area and the Crab Orchard wildlife and forest areas. Most of the villages are bypassed by Int. 57 but are accessible via interchanges.

MASON, 15 m. (415 pop. 1970; 332, 1960).

EDGEWOOD, 18 m. (495 pop. 1970; 515, 1960).

FARINA, 26 m. (634 pop. 1970; 692, 1960). Fayette County. Jct.

KINMUNDY, 30 m. (759 pop. 1970; 813, 1960). Marion County.

ALMA, 35 m. (369 pop. 1970; 358, 1960).

SALEM, 43 m. (544 alt., 6,187 pop. 1970; 6,165, 1960) seat of Marion County, was laid out in 1813 on the Vincennes-St. Louis stage route now followed by US 50. It was incorporated as a city in 1837. Salem profited by the oil boom that began after the first oil well in Clay County was brought in in February, 1937, and for a time it was a large supplier of oil field equipment. It has a number of light industries.

Salem was the birthplace of William Jennings Bryan (1860-1925), three times Democratic nominee for President, Secretary of State under Woodrow Wilson, and boss of the Democratic Party. He was also nominated by the Populist Party. His home at 408 S. Broadway is now a museum of personal effects, family furnishings, letters to his mother, and other memorabilia. He lived here until 19 years old, when he entered Illinois College at Jacksonville. There he fell in love with Mary Elizabeth Baird, a student in the Female Seminary. He opened a law office in Jacksonville in July, 1883, and they were married in 1884. Salem has a William Jennings Bryan Memorial Park and a statue of Bryan by Gutzon Borglum near the entrance.

West on US 50 20 m. to LAKE CARLYLE, recreation and fishing center. On the east bank is SOUTH SHORE STATE PARK; on the west is ELDON HAZLETT STATE PARK.

About 1 m. west of Salem is the junction of Int. 57 and US 50. South on Int. 57 7 m. to jct. with Illinois 181, thence west 10 m. to CENTRALIA (15,217 pop. 1970). See Tour 4.

MOUNT VERNON, 65 m. (15,580 pop. 1970; 15,566, 1960) seat of Jefferson County, entered by Illinois 37 but bypassed by Int. 57, which has junction with east-west Illinois 15. Also jct. with US 460, which goes west to East St. Louis. Mount Vernon was settled by Southerners and today is peopled largely by descendants of Southern families. The city retains its Southern charm and emphasis on family ties and traditions, despite its industrial development. Although the site of Mount Vernon was chosen as seat of newly formed Jefferson County in 1819, it grew very slowly; new residents came mostly from Kentucky and Tennessee. With the coming of the railroads the community began a period of industrial growth. It has profited from the county coal mines.

The Appellate Court Building, 1400 W. Main St., a gray brick and stone structure in the shape of a Maltese cross, was built in 1854. Of Greek Revival design, the entrance pavilion is adorned with fluted Ionic columns, and topped with a fine classic pediment. The arched portal is approached by a long double flight of cast-iron steps. The building originally housed the southern grand division of the Illinois Supreme Court. When the Supreme Court was centered in Springfield in 1897, the Mount Vernon building became headquarters of the Fourth District Appellate Court.

The Mount Vernon State Tuberculosis Sanitarium is located 5 *m.* north of the city. The Mount Vernon Game Farm is 8 *m.* south. At 10 *m.* south begins the northeast arm of REND LAKE, a huge reservoir filled by the Big Muddy River covering 25,000 acres and establishing a new recreation area. Int. 57 and Illinois 37 proceed along the eastern shore line for 22 *m.* to Benton. Villages along the east shore that have known little change in population are offering camp sites. In Jefferson County BONNIE had 314 pop. 1970; INA, credited with 333, is the site of the new REND LAKE COMMUNITY COLLEGE, opened in 1955, which enrolled 1,266 students in 1973, with a faculty of 80. NASON, a "city", had 186 pop. in 1970, down from 188 in 1960.

The Mount Vernon-Outland Airport is 2.5 *m.* northeast of the city. It is served by Ozark Airlines.

BENTON, 88 *m.* (6,833 pop. 1970; 7,023, 1960) seat of Franklin County, is at the northeastern end of the big coal field of southern Illinois. Its fortunes have risen and fallen with the state of the bituminous coal business. Illinois 37 passes through Benton where it has junctions with Illinois 14 from Carmi and Illinois 34 from Harrisburg; on the west Int. 57 has a junction with Illinois 14 at WEST CITY (637 pop. 1970; 814, 1960). Benton is directly south of the big dam that has created REND LAKE from the waters of the Big Muddy, a reservoir of 25,000 acres. Rend Lake State Park has been renamed WAYNE FITZERRELL STATE PARK.

Benton was made a county seat in 1839 and named for Thomas Hart Benton. In recent years it has acquired a new Federal Office Building and Postoffice, the Farmers' Administration Bldg. of the Illinois Dept. of Agriculture, a new Public Library, the Airport Administration Bldg. and the District Office Bldg. of the Rend Lake Conservancy. Its Library, opened in 1956, is a member of the Shawnee Library System.

WEST FRANKFORT, 95 *m.* (8,836 pop. 1970; 9,027, 1960, loss 2.1%) is another town of the southern coal region that depends on the market for soft coal. It has a junction with Illinois 149, which moves west to Zeigler, a city in Franklin County (1,940 pop. 1970; 2,133, 1960, loss 9%). West Frankfort Lake, a small reservoir, supplies water to the area. West Frankfort is 3 *m.* north of the Williamson County line. On Dec. 21, 1951, it was the scene of a disastrous mine explosion in which 119 miners died.

JOHNSTON CITY, 108 *m.* (3,928 pop. 1970; 3,891, 1960) first city in Williamson County in the heart of the coal region that has been the scene of violent action. About 4 *m.* west on a market road is HERRIN (9,623 pop. 1970; 9,427, 1960) a busy industrial city that is successfully exploiting its labor surplus. Coal was first mined in 1893. In 1898 Herrin was incorporated as a village, and in 1900 became a city. As coal production rose its population increased until about 1920, when it had over 10,000.

In subsequent years first strip mining and then the oil industry provided the strongest competition and deep shaft coal-mining declined, as it did throughout the country. Herrin in recent years had made an effort to attract industries to its labor pool and profiting from the presence of the Norge washing-machine division of Borg-Warner, employing up to 1,600; the motor accessories plant of Allen Industries, Inc., which employs up to 1,000; the Duro Containers plant, and others of like stature.

In June, 1922, Herrin experienced a hard blow to its fortunes when the socalled Herrin Massacre was precipitated by a labor dispute. The country was suffering from lockouts and strikes in the coal industry. An attempt was made by owners to operate a strip mine near Herrin with non-union labor, which representatives of the United Mine Workers of America tried to stop. On June 21 an armed clash occurred at the mine; two union men were killed and a third was mortally wounded. On June 22 the attack was resumed, but the strip mine workers soon surrendered and agreed to leave the county under a promise of safe conduct. On the way to Herrin the mine superintendent was taken aside and shot; the strikers' leader who had promised safe conduct was deposed; the workers were ordered to run for their lives under fire. Thirteen were killed immediately; later in the day seven others lost their lives. A special grand jury examined more than 300 witnesses and returned 214 indictments for murder and other charges. Local sentiment was such, however, that after several verdicts of acquittal, all remaining indictments were dismissed. A new courthouse replaces the one in which the miners were tried.

MARION, 115 *m.* (419 alt., 11,724 pop. 1970; 11,274, 1960) is the seat of Williamson County, a marketing center and gateway to the Crab Orchard National Wildlife Refuge. Illinois 37 passed through it, and Int. 57 has an interchange on its western edge with Illinois 13, east-west, which runs from Harrisburg on US 45 to Carbondale on US 51. It is the seat of a Veterans Administration Hospital. Williamson County (49,021 pop. 1970; 46,117, 1960) is governed by a three-man Board of Commissioners. The Board determines the budget and appoints, among others, the supervisor of assessments, the relief administrator, and the superintendent of highways. In the 1960s Marion replaced its Victorian courthouse with a modern rectangular, almost windowless, structure.

In the years preceding the Civil War, Marion was the home of Robert G. Ingersoll and John A. Logan. Here both young men were admitted to the bar. At the outbreak of the War, both men organized regiments of which they became colonels: Ingersoll, the 11th Illinois Cavalry; Logan, the 31st Illinois Infantry. Logan's first recruits were two veterans of the Mexican War, who volunteered for service during a speech delivered by Logan on Marion's public square. Logan's oratory was highly instrumental in winning southern Illinois to the Union cause.

The Carnegie Public Library at Marion reported a circulation of 186,224 volumes in 1970. It is a member of the Shawnee Library System.

Williamson County Airport is adjacent to Illinois 13 and 148 and has four-lane access to Int. 57. It has runways of 6,500 and 3,800 ft. and daily airline and charter service by Ozark Airlines.

Illinois 13 continues eastward to HARRISBURG, 40 m. (400 alt., 9,535 pop. 1970; 9,171, 1960) in Saline County, at a junction with US 45 (see Tour 3d).

Marion is in the heart of the southern Ozarks and is surrounded by forests, lakes, springs and vacation spots. The Shawnee National Forest extends from the Mississippi River to the Ohio, much of it primitive woodland capable of vast use for recreation. The wildlife areas are part of the Mississippi flyway and are visited annually by thousands of flocks of wildfowl and many species of migrating birds.

CRAB ORCHARD LAKE, west of Marion and east of Carbondale, was completed in 1938. It covers 7,000 acres and has a shoreline of 125 miles. LITTLE GRASSY LAKE is in the southwestern corner of Williamson County and covers 1,000 acres. DEVIL'S KITCHEN LAKE, west of Int. 57 on the border of Union County, was completed in 1958 and covers 800 acres.

These lakes are near the CRAB ORCHARD NATIONAL WILDLIFE REFUGE of 43,000 acres, a carefully administered refuge and recreation area of the U. S. Fish & Wildlife Service. More than 1,000,000 visitors come annually to hunt, fish, swim and camp here. Seasonal hunting and fishing are regulated, as are motor boating. Camping is available at Crab Orchard and Little Grassy Lakes, 15 days at one site, 30 days in all. Bass, crappie and bluegill abound; Canada geese live here in winter. State licenses apply.

About 12 m. south of Marion on Illinois 37 is the head of LAKE OF EGYPT in Shawnee National Forest.

About 9 m. southwest of Marion on Int. 57 is the UNITED STATES PENITENTIARY, the smallest of more than 30 correctional facilities administered by the Bureau of Prisons of the U. S. Dept. of Justice. It was opened as a Federal Prison Camp in 1963 and was designated a penitentiary in January, 1964. It accommodates approx. 525 men in one-man cell units. Every prisoner is able to pursue a personal program in privacy and security. Meals are served cafeteria style. The prison staff includes a Catholic and a Protestant chaplain and there is a chapel for services. If a prisoner has a good record on the job to which he has been assigned he may request transfer to a more satisfying job, and also become eligible for awards for merit. The regulations prescribe standards of personal appearance; mustaches and sideburns are permitted but a mustache must not hang over the upper lip or have hair over half an inch in length, and hair must be tapered and not extend over the back of the collar, while sideburns may not extend below the ear lobe, exceed one inch in length or have flaired ends. A prisoner may use the law library and read other books for improvement or enjoyment and participate in vocational training. Educational programs include elementary and high school work and anyone with a high school diploma may join a college program prepared by Southern Illinois University and John A. Logan College. Outdoor games, group counseling, and group activities are encouraged; the latter include Alcoholics Anonymous, Egyptian Jaycees, Black Culture, Historical Society, and Outstanding Young Educators. The Federal Prison Camp, conducted outside the fence, usually accommodates 92 men.

After Marion Illinois 37 continues straight south into Johnson and Pulaski Counties whereas Int. 57 swerves westward and then goes south into Union County before entering Pulaski. The highways are now tapering toward the apex where the Ohio River joins the Mississippi. Towns in Johnson County include GOREVILLE, (1,109 pop. 1970; 625, 1960); BUNCOMBE, (187 pop. 1970; 200, 1960) and CYPRESS (261 pop. 1970; 264, 1960). Both highways have junctions with Illinois 148, the east-west route followed by the Cherokee Indians from Golconda to Jonesboro. East 5 m. on Illinois 146 is Vienna (1,325 pop. 1970; 1,094, 1960) at a junction with US 45. Down along the Ohio River Illinois 37 reaches MOUND CITY (1,117 pop. 1970; 1,669, 1960).

On the river bank at the southern end of town are the MOUND CITY MARINE WAYS, highly important during the Civil War. Here were laid the keels of three of the famous Eads iron-clad gunboats, and here also the boats of the western fleet of the Union army were repaired. This fleet played an important part in the western campaign, giving valuable support to General Grant's troops on the Tennessee River and at Vicksburg. The ways consist of a series of inclines up which the boats are hoisted by huge chains attached to a steam winch.

PULASKI COUNTY MEMORIAL PARK was the scene in 1954 of a celebration of the centennial of the town bell. It was made in Cincinnati in 1853 and used on a southern plantation until Rear Adm. David D. Porter brought it to Mound City in 1864. It was used at the Marine Ways and is now in the park above a time capsule, to be opened in 2054 A. D.

Near the junction with US 51 is a U. S. NATIONAL MILI-

TARY CEMETERY, with graves of 5,686 soldiers of the Civil, Spanish, and World Wars. It was established here in 1864 because of its proximity to the Marine Hospital at Mound City.

At 153.5 m. is a junction with Illinois 3 (see Tour 8); between this point and Cairo, US 51 and Illinois 3 are one route.

CAIRO, 159 m. (318 alt., 6,277 pop. 1970). See Cairo.

US 51 crosses the Kentucky Line by bridge over the Ohio River, 5 m. north of Wickliffe, Kentucky (see Kentucky Guide of the American Guide Series).

II. Chicago to Paducah, Kentucky

The second route to the Ohio River with Paducah as its objective has been outlined for those who wish to proceed from Effingham on US 45, a major north-south highway. This leads to Metropolis on the Ohio River and Fort Massac in Massac County, and crosses the Ohio at Brookport.

However, the motorist who wishes to use the expressway as far as possible can proceed on Int. 57 from Effingham to Marion, where he can turn southeast on Illinois 168 and in 15 miles reach a junction with US 45 at New Burnside, and proceed thence to Metropolis. An extension of Int. 57 called Int. 24 has been under construction to turn southeast and reach the Ohio River and a new bridge near Fort Massac State Park.

Effingham County, given over largely to grain, had 24,608 pop. in 1970, 23,100 in 1960, inc. 6.5%.

At 32 m. from Effingham is the western junction with US 50 (see Tour 20), with which US 45 is united for 4 miles 1 m. from FLORA, 33 m. (5,283 pop. 1970; 5,331, 1960). The city, platted 1854 and incorporated 1857, was named for a daughter of one of the surveyors. The Baltimore & Ohio ran its main line to St. Louis through Flora in 1857, and a later north-south branch ran from Beardstown to Shawneetown. Fruit storage and seed were its first products; around 1900 oil was found near Clay City. Flora industries include a division of the Anaconda Wire & Cable Co., another of the International Shoe Co., making shoes for men and boys; other products are radio parts, automotive equipment, light fixtures, and pipe couplings.

Flora has a commission form of government, with a mayor. The city exerts a cultural influence because of its fine library facilities; its Carnegie Public Library dates back to 1870. Of special importance is the Cumberland Trail Library System, which in 1970 opened a spacious headquarters building here at a cost of $236,758, built to hold 100,000 vols. and serve the libraries of 14 cities with interlibrary services. Architects were Wilson, Hodge & Groth of Mt. Vernon. Associated in the system are the libraries of Albion, Altamount, Centralia, Fairfield, Flora, Mt. Carmel, Mt. Vernon, Newton, Olney, Robinson, St. Elmo, Salem, Vandalia, and West Salem. The Flora Airport is located 1 m. southeast of the city.

FAIRFIELD, 66 *m.* (451 alt., 5,897 pop. 1970; 6,362, 1960, dec. 7.3%) was incorporated Feb. 25, 1857. Its principal industries are Airtex Manufacturing Co., pumps, auto parts, employing more than 600, and Fairfield Garment Co., 250. It has freight service of Southern Ry. and Baltimore & Ohio, and a municipal airport connecting with Wayne County Airport, 27 *m.* west. Besides shipping farm products it handles oil, but although Wayne County is fourth in oil production in Illinois the output has been decreasing. A new Public Library building was erected in 1951; the library has around 20,000 vols. and circulates more than 33,000. The Wayne County Historical Society uses its rooms. William E. Borah was born about six miles northeast of Fairfield in 1865. General Lew Wallace is said to have worked on the manuscript of *Ben Hur* here in the 1870's while attending a law suit over land.

A marker records that Wayne County Republicans here were the first group to endorse Abraham Lincoln for President on March 31, 1860.

East from Fairfield on Illinois 15:

ALBION, 17 *m.* (447 alt., 1,721 pop. 1970; 2,025, 1960, dec. 11.6%) seat of Edwards County. Abraham Lincoln addressed a political rally at Albion on Oct. 20, 1840, which was commemorated Oct. 27, 1957, by the Edwards County Historical Society, which dedicated a brick and concrete memorial holding a cast aluminum tablet provided by the Illinois State Historical Society. It reads: "Abraham Lincoln spoke in the oak grove of General William Pickering north of here in the presidential campaign of 1840. He was stumping southern Illinois as a Whig elector for General William Henry Harrison in the Tippecanoe and Tyler Too campaign. In 1861 Lincoln appointed Pickering Governor of Washington Territory."

The Edwards County Historical Society conducts a library and a museum in the house in which Louis L. Emmerson, former Illinois Governor, was born.

Albion was founded in 1818 as the central settlement of the English colony organized by Morris Birkbeck and George Flower. Dissatisfied with economic conditions in England after the Napoleonic Wars, Flower and Birkbeck came to America to establish a colony that would provide better opportunities than those afforded the English working class. They traveled through Pennsylvania, Ohio, Indiana, and Illinois in search of a suitable site; they did not consider the region farther north because of the climate, and their hatred of slavery prevented them from settling farther south. Their final selection was the prairie between Bon Pas Creek and the Little Wabash River in Illinois. Wrote Flower:

"Bruised by the brushwood and exhausted by the extreme heat we almost despaired, when a small cabin and a low fence greeted our eyes. A few steps more, and a beautiful prairie suddenly opened to our view. At first, we only received the impressions of its general beauty. With longer gaze, all its distinctive features were revealed, lying in profound repose under the warm light of an afternoon's summer sun. Its indented and irregular outline of wood, its varied surface interspersed with clumps of oaks of centuries' growth, its tall grass, with seed stalks from six to ten feet high, like tall and slender weeds waving in a gentle breeze, the whole presenting a magnificence of park-scenery, complete from the hand of Nature. . . . From beneath the broken shade of the wood, with our arms raised above our brows, we gazed long and steadily, drinking in the beauties of the scene which had been so long the object of our search."

While Birkbeck completed the business of acquiring the land with their pooled funds, Flower returned to England where he sold his holdings. He organized and sent several parties of prospective colonists over from England and in March, 1818, returned to America with about 51 persons, as well as agricultural implements, seeds, and animals for breeding. New colonists continued to flock in—on foot, horseback, and in wagons. The English colonists did not take to pioneer hardships as readily as did so many of the American frontiersmen, but their suffering was mitigated by an intense desire for land ownership. The colony prospered, and by October, 1818, had grown to 200 colonists, all English.

The need of a central village to accommodate incoming colonists and to furnish supplies and services became increasingly apparent. One evening a group of men met with Flower in his cabin to plan the new town; there were no candles in the house, so in the dark "each one took his couch and carried on the discussion." Late in the night the site of the village was finally decided upon. "Now for a name," wrote Flower. "We were long at fault. At last we did what almost all emigrants do, pitched on a name that had its association with the land of our birth. Albion was then and there located, built, and peopled in imagination. We dropped off, one by one, to sleep, to confirm in dreams the wanderings of our wakeful fancies."

The comparative wealth and intelligence of Albion's leaders subsequently influenced the culture and politics of the surrounding country. Birkbeck's *Notes on a Journey* and *Letters from Illinois,* which were widely read in America and abroad, attracted many travelers and called attention both to the English settlements of Illinois and to the West as a whole.

According to the Edwards County Historical Society, Edgar Thompson, who received national attention for marrying a Fiji island princess, was a native of Albion. His father was Dr. Samuel Thompson, and his brother Ralph Thompson was founder and editor of the *Albion Pioneer,* 1868-73.

Albion Public Library had improved quarters in 1967. It circulates approx. 10,000 vols. and is a member of the Cumberland Trail Library System.

Left, north, from Albion 10 *m.* on Illinois 130 to a junction with a graveled road; R. on this road to WEST SALEM, 12.5 *m.* (506 alt., 979 pop. 1970; 956, 1960), settled by German Moravians from North Carolina in 1838. At the grave of Emma Pfeil in the now abandoned Moravian Cemetery is a marker said to be the State's smallest tombstone. It is 5⅞ by 10½ by 2 inches. The graves are in four groups, according to the choir system: married men, married women, boys and bachelors, girls and maiden women. To indicate the equality of all before God, interments were made by death dates rather than by families.

Return to US 45 at Fairfield.

ENFIELD, 109 *m.* (422 alt., 764 pop. 1970; 796, 1960) in White County, was settled in 1813. It is located at a junction with east-west US 460, and is 8 *m.* west of Carmi on US 1. The village observes an annual homecoming day the first Saturday of October. William E. Borah, Senator from Idaho, attended school here. Borah lived in southern Illinois from 1865 to 1883. His grandfather, John Borah, came from Kentucky in 1820 to a farm in Jasper Township, Wayne County. In 1822 he helped establish the Cumberland Presbyterian Church at Tom's Prairie and the first school. William E. Borah attended school at Tom's Prairie and in 1881-82 at Southern Illinois Academy, later college, at Enfield, 25 m. south of the Borah farm. In 1884 he went to Lyons, Kansas.

Left from Enfield on US 480 to CARMI, on Illinois 1, described in *Tour I*.

NORRIS CITY, 116 m. (1,319 pop. 1970; 1,243, 1960) is located in White County 1 m. west of Illinois 1, at an intersection of the Penn Central and the Baltimore & Ohio. It was named for William Norris, a pioneer settler.

Between Norris City and the Kentucky Line, US 45 is a highway of transition. The landscape becomes increasingly rolling until the first unmistakable hills, the State's lone mountain range, the Illinois Ozarks, appear on the horizon. As the landscape changes, so do the people. Homesteaded by infiltration from the Ohio River, earliest avenue of entry, southern Illinois saw the first homogeneous settlement of any considerable size. Here, more than anywhere else in the State, the people are aware of their historical background; here family ties, often amounting to clannishness, give the region a solidarity rarely encountered in the north. While a Chicagoan is commonly a stranger to his apartment neighbor, most residents of southern Illinois know several people in any town within a hundred miles.

The early history of Illinois is peppered with the names of the southern towns: Kaskaskia, Cairo, Cahokia, Vandalia, Shawneetown. But with the opening of the Erie Canal and the transfer of the State capital to Springfield, the tide of commerce and politics swept northward until 80 per cent of the population was massed in the northern half of the State.

ELDORADO, 13 m. (3,876 pop. 1970; 3,573, 1960) in Saline County, is a trading center and outlet for coal in the years when mining was more productive. It has light industries and freight service on three railroads.

MUDDY, 18 m. a village that had a 14% rise in population by growing from 95 in 1960 to 109 in 1970, was formerly a lively recreation outlet for miners.

HARRISBURG, 20 m. (9,535 pop. 1970; 9,171, 1960) seat of Saline County, is the center of the coal mining in the area. In 1970 it shipped 2,394,825 tons on the Penn Central and Illinois Central lines. Of its six mines, three are underground and three are strip mines, production from underground mines exceed strip by 1,500,000 tons against 900,000, but strip is increasing. Four mines are owned by the Sahara Coal Co.

SOUTHEASTERN ILLINOIS COLLEGE, a community college under the new State law, provides vocational education and two-year terms with the degree of associate. It is located about 5 *m.* east of Harrisburg on Illinois 13.

Williams Hill (1,065 alt.), highest elevation in southern Illinois, is visible at 21.3 *m.* On clear days the 100-foot steel lookout tower at its summit is discernible against the blue sky. Womble Mountain, north of Williams Hill, is smaller but clearly visible between two gaps in this ridge of the Illinois Ozarks.

CARRIER MILLS, 27 *m.* (392 alt., 2,140 pop.), is a mining town named for William H. Carrier, who established a sawmill here in 1870. Known locally as Cat Skin or Cat Hide, the community faces the Ozarks, two ridges of which lie in the distant blue haze. There is strip mining near the town.

The highway passes under the Edgewood freight cut-off, 32.5 *m.* of the Illinois Central System. South of the subway the line tunnels through the Ozarks at three points, with a total tunnel length of 10,424 feet.

STONEFORT, 35.5 *m.*, originally two miles southeast of its present site, moved in 1872, when the Big Four Railroad was built through this section. The name is derived from the ruins of an old Stone Fort. In the Illinois Ozarks there are seven of these prehistoric structures, each consisting of an area on a cliff or bluff, barricaded on its accessible side by a loose stone wall. The walls here were originally 4 feet thick and 8 feet high, with one opening, but the stones now lie scattered about or have been carried away. The function of the structure is conjectural: a prehistoric fort, or a pound in which buffaloes were trapped and easily slain by being stampeded over the cliff.

The Johnson County line, 35.5 *m.*, approximates the northern edge of the Ozark Ridge. This uplifted and folded belt of sandstone and conglomerates, in places 700 feet above the surrounding country and more than 1,000 feet above sea level, is a continuation of the Ozarks of Missouri. From the Mississippi to the Ohio, the belt is 70 miles long and from 15 to 40 miles wide.

NEW BURNSIDE, 38 *m.* (560 alt., 249 pop. 1970; 227, 1960), a village in Johnson County, founded in 1872 when the Big Four Railroad was built, was named for the railroad president, Maj. Gen. Ambrose E. Burnside. Fruit raising in the region is now so important that the U. S. Weather Bureau maintains a reporting station in the village.

South of Burnside the highway climbs into the fruit section of the Ozark Ridge, which is blanketed from mid-April to mid-May with pink and white blossoms.

At 4 *m.* is a junction with the Eddyville Road.

Left on this graveled road to Trigg Tower, 1 *m.*, a forest lookout named for L. O. Trigg of Eldorado, who devoted years of voluntary service to the establishment of a national forest in the Illinois Ozarks.

At 8 *m.* a road branches downhill to Burden Falls, a narrow scarf of water tumbling into a jagged gorge.

Ahead on Eddyville Road is the Bell Smith Spring Recreation Area (*swimming, picnic facilities, hiking trails*), 1.06 *m.* Along Bay Creek and its tributaries, within a mile of each other, are Bell Smith Spring, a deep Swimming Hole, a semi-circular Grotto carved in limestone by a stream, and a Natural Bridge with a span of 150 feet and a center clearance of more than 20 feet. In gorges 25 to 75 feet deep are clear blue streams that flow through jungles of fern. After heavy rains, torrents 15 feet deep roar down the rocky canyons.

The Old Fort Massac-Kaskaskia Trail, 42 *m.,* as late as 1880 was plainly marked with mile signs carved or burned into the tree trunks. A short distance beyond the junction with the old trail, US 45 begins the southward descent of the Ozark Ridge. Cooper's Bluff, a high wooded cliff, is visible left.

VIENNA, 53 *m.* (1,225 pop. 1970; 1,094, 1960), is built around a public square in which stands the Johnson County Courthouse. The county was organized in 1812, and Vienna was selected as the county seat six years later.

South of Vienna, US 45 descends into a valley and winds through wooded hills. On the first night of his march from Fort Massac to Kaskaskia (June 20, 1778) George Rogers Clark camped at the western base of INDIAN POINT, a forested bluff visible at 59 *m.*

At 60 *m.* is a junction with Illinois 168.

Right on this road to KARNAK, 6.1 *m.* (641 pop. 1970; 667, 1960), largely a company-built logging and milling town. Oak, willow, black gum, sweet gum, and cypress are cut in the surrounding forests and hauled to Karnak to be milled.

Ahead on the improved road to a junction with Illinois 37, 9.3 *m.,* on Illinois 37 to NEW GRAND CHAIN, 12.2 *m.* (215 pop. 1970), named for a chain of rocks in the Ohio River, three miles distant. The town, once on the river banks at that point, was moved to its present site in 1872, with the coming of the Big Four Railroad. Immediately south of the village, a marker commemorates Va Bache Tannery and Fort (1702-04) and Cantonment Wilkinson-Ville (1787-1804). Of these sites—a short distance upstream and inaccessible—that of Cantonment Wilkinson-Ville has been definitely established, but many authorities place the site of Va Bache several miles north of what is now Cairo.

Va Bache Tannery and Fort was built in 1702 by a party of French and Indians led by Charles Juchereau de St. Denys, lieutenant general of the jurisdiction of Montreal. Outpost were established from which Juchereau's hunters shipped buffalo skins downstream to be tanned. At the Belle Garde outpost Father Jean Mermet, Jesuit chaplain of the expedition, founded the mission of Assumption. In the summer of 1703 an epidemic caused the death of half of those at Va Bache, including Juchereau. The tannery was operated until the following year and then abandoned.

METROPOLIS, 75 *m.* (329 alt., 6,940 pop., 1970; 7,339, 1960) seat of Massac County, is the principal beneficiary of tourist travel to Fort Massac State Park on the Ohio River. The completion of Interstate 24, an offshoot of Interstate 57, makes Metropolis and the park easy to reach. Although the city has had a drop of 5.4% in population in ten years according to the latest U. S. Census, the General Chemical Division of the Allied Chemical Co. has built a $14,000,000 plant, and leather glove manufacture is expanding. The Missouri Portland Cement Co. moved into Metropolis in the 1960s.

Metropolis developed from two pioneer towns, Massac and Metropolis City. About 1796 a small settlement was established immediately west of Fort Massac, and 40 years later it was platted as the City of Massac. In 1839 William A. McBane and James H. G. Wilcox, dreaming of a metropolis that would be the City of the West, platted another town north of Massac and called it Metropolis City. McBane believed this to be the only feasible place, near the mouth of the Ohio River, to build a railroad bridge. In 1917, long after his death, the present bridge was completed. When Massac County was formed in 1843, Metropolis City was chosen as the seat, and two years later incorporated as a town. In 1892 the two communities united under the present name.

In January, 1972, enterprising publicists became aware that Metropolis was a name known to every reader of a popular comic strip as the home of Superman. To capitalize on this businessmen introduced the Superman of Metropolis Award. In short order Superman's figure appeared on the city's water tower and on welcoming billboards; the *Metropolis News* became the *Metropolis Planet,* and Superman souvenirs sparked a thriving business.

FORT MASSAC STATE PARK, 76 *m.,* 933 acres, is the oldest State park, dating from 1903. It is located on a promontory that commands a view of 24 miles of the Ohio River.

Fort Massac was an outpost established by the French in their effort to hold on to the vast Illinois area in the early 18th century. Its strategic position on the Ohio River was recognized as early as 1702 by Charles Juchereau de St. Denys, the military explorer, who was unable to get sufficient support. The French needed a dependable supply of food from the Illinois territory for Fort DuQuesne and other posts on the upper Ohio and suffered from raids by Cherokee tribes, who were in the pay of the British. From 1753 to 1758 convoys to Fort DuQuesne carried flour, corn, fats, bacon, salt, tobacco, and lead, traveling 1,250 miles upstream in three months. The French command ordered Capt. Aubrey to built a fort below the mouth of the Tennessee River, a focal point for Indian raiders. Aubrey completed the fort on the Illinois side of the Ohio in June, 1757, and it was called Ascension for the day in the religious calendar. Later it was named Fort Massaic for the French minister of the marine and colonies. It was built of upright logs banked with earth, originally 100 ft. square, mounted eight guns and could shelter 100 men. The land was cleared for 400 yards around it. Although Fort DuQuesne fell to the English in 1758, the French continued a trading post at Fort Massaic as allies of the Cherokees and Shawnees. In 1760 it was reinforced under Lieut. Rocheblave. When the English finally were able to enforce the peace agreement in 1763 the French gave up all holdings east of the Mississippi and transfered 15 men and one officer from Fort Massaic to Ste. Genevieve, Mo. But before the English could occupy the Illinois territory they had to defeat Pontiac and the Ottawas in 1763-64. They took possession of Fort Chartres on Oct. 10, 1765. Shortly thereafter the Cherokees burned the installations at Fort Massaic.

During the English occupation (1765-1778) the ruins were left untouched. In 1794, owing to trouble with Spain and the Indians, President Washington ordered General Anthony Wayne to refortify the site. Capt. Zebulon Pike was placed in command and here his son, Zebulon Montgomery Pike, subsequently the discoverer of Pike's Peak, served as a subaltern. The new fort was named Massac, a corruption of its previous name rather than, as persistent legends have it, a shortened form of massacre.

Fort Massac figured obscurely in the Spanish Conspiracy. From it were dispatched the troops that garrisoned Cantonment Wilkinson-Ville, ostensibly to protect Fort Massac from a downstream attack. Historians are agreed that Wilkinson, then in command of the United States Army, was implicated with Carondelet in the conspiracy to place Kentucky and possibly other contiguous parts of United States territory under the jurisdiction of Spain. The plan envisioned the capture of Fort Massac, but no attack was made. Wilkinson, it is said, revealed the conspiracy to his government.

After service in the War of 1812 the fort was abandoned. Although never important as a military post, it played a large part in the economic history of the region. At the end of the eighteenth century the Ohio River came into prominence as a trade medium, and Congress created several districts for the collection of duties on tonnage and merchandise. One of these was the district of Fort Massac, with the fort as port of entry. All boats carrying goods along the Ohio were compelled to stop at the fort where inventories of cargoes were made and taxes assessed. After 1807 the districts were rearranged; Illinois and the surrounding area were incorporated in the district of Mississippi.

As described by Gov. John Reynolds, who visited Fort Massac in 1855, the "outside walls were 135 feet square, and at each angle bastions were erected. The walls were palisaded with earth between the wood. A large well was sunk in the fortress, and the whole appeared to be strong and substantial in its day. . . . The site is one of the most beautiful on La Belle Riviere, and commands a view that is charming."

Dedicated as a State Park in 1908, the site retains only the scarcely discernible bastions and ditch. Four cannons mark its corners. At the center is a bronze statue of GEORGE ROGERS CLARK, by Leon Hermant, which commemorates Clark's crossing of the Ohio at this point on his way to Kaskaskia in 1778.

In addition to US 45, there is a shorter route to Fort Massac from Harrisburg via Illinois 145, which passes through Shawnee National Forest and has a junction near Dixon Springs with the east-west highway Illinois 146, the route taken across Illinois by the dispossessed Cherokees.

BROOKPORT, 84 *m.* (335 alt., 1,046 pop. 1970; 1,154, 1960), is an agricultural trading center on the north bank of the Ohio River. During the Ohio River flood of January, 1937, parts of Brookport were under 6 to 14 feet of water.

Right from Brookport on an improved road to Dam 52, 1.4 *m.,* built in 1926 as part of the Government system of dams to facilitate navigation on the Ohio River during low water. It is one of the largest movable wicket dams in use. When the river rises toward flood-stage, the 487 wickets, each 4 ft. wide, are laid down and the lock gates opened. Traffic then passes over the dam instead of through the lock.

US 45 crosses the Kentucky Line on a free bridge spanning the Ohio River to Paducah, Kentucky.

Tour 4

DOWN THE MIDDLE OF ILLINOIS FROM ROCKFORD TO CAIRO

South Beloit — Rockford — Rochelle — Mendota — Peru — La Salle — Oglesby — Streator — El Paso — Bloomington — Clinton — Vandalia — Centralia — Mount Vernon — Du Quoin — Carbondale — Cobden—Anna—Jonesboro—Mound City—Cairo

US 51. Interstate 90. 430 *m.*

US 51 closely follows the third principal meridian, established when the Northwest Territory was surveyed and divided into townships. Practically bisecting the State, the route connects the wooded dairy lands of the North with the bald cypress and orchard country that borders Cairo. Crossing the corn belt and mixed farming regions, traversing mining and industrial districts, passing through remnants of hard-wood forests and the Illinois Ozarks, US 51 offers a representative cross-section of the State.

Interstate 90 runs parallel with US 51 in Wisconsin and proceeds from Beloit south to a point east of Rockford, where it has a junction with US 20 (east-west). I-90 then proceeds southeasterly as a toll road to Chicago and enters Indiana at Whiting.

Section a. Wisconsin Line to Bloomington, 156 m.

In its northern section US 51 follows the valley of the Rock River for a short distance, crosses the rolling prairies and woodlands of a diversified farming country, and enters the Illinois River gorge at

La Salle, head of river navigation and terminus of the Illinois & Michigan Canal. It moves southward toward Bloomington and the rich corn fields and scattered coal beds of central Illinois.

US 51 and Int. 90 move north into Wisconsin to BELOIT, which is just across the line from South Beloit. Beloit is a city of 36,729 pop. (1970) and is easily reached from Chicago on Int. 90, the Northwest Tollway, which connects with the John F. Kennedy Expressway. An industrial and farm distributing center, Beloit also serves the north central counties of Illinois.

US 51 crosses the Wisconsin line from Beloit, Wisc. into SOUTH BELOIT, 1 *m.*, an incorporated city in Winnebago County (742 alt., 3,804 pop. 1970; 3,781, 1960). An industrial city, South Beloit shares the advantages of a large labor force that extends as far south as Rockford and north as Janesville, Wisc., drawing about 12,000 employees from this area. Its largest output is heavy machinery, in which up to 2,500 are employed at peak times; it also makes automotive and industrial brakes and clutches, concrete products, iron castings, grinding and abrasive machinery, papermaking machinery, disc grinders and woodworking machines. Freight carriers include the Milwaukee and Chicago & North Western railways and interstate trucking lines.

South Beloit grew up south of the Wisconsin line and thus was able to incorporate as a city separate from Beloit, Wisc., on Sept. 17, 1917. It has a mayor and four commissioners. Settlements in the Beloit-South Beloit area were made along Turtle Creek by traders. When Black Hawk and his band were being pursued by General Atkinson's army they crossed the Wisconsin-Illinois state line near the spot where Illinois 51 crosses Turtle Creek. The Indians had villages at the junction of Turtle Creek and the Rock River. The land south of the Wisconsin line was developed by the New England Emigrating Co., which built houses, mills, and the first bridge across Turtle Creek in South Beloit.

The South Beloit Public Library occupies a building erected in 1952. It circulates more than 62,000 books and materials. It is a member of the Northern Illinois Library System.

Illinois 2 starts at South Beloit for the Quad Cities.

Southward, US 51 winds through the sand and gravel plains and terraces of the beautiful Rock River valley. In the boulder-strewn bed of the powerful Rock many waterpower sites have been developed; a chain of manufacturing cities extends along its banks to Rock Island.

ROCKFORD, 17 *m.* (720 alt., 147,370 pop. 1970) *see Rockford.* Rockford is at the junction with Illinois 2 (*see Tour 4A*) and US 20 (*see Tour 11*).

ROCKFORD CITY AIRPORT, 24 *m.*, is located on part of the 4,000 acres of the former Camp Grant, training center for recruits during the two World Wars. In peacetime it was maintained by the State for the National Guard. The camp was closed Sept. 9, 1946. At the Kishwaukee Street entrance stand stone columns formerly those of Camp Grant. On the drive to the Terminal Building is a memorial consisting of a World War II anti-aircraft gun on a stone pedestal erected by the Veterans of Foreign Wars. Rockford Park District took over 312 acres for a park.

At 38 *m.,* is the junction with Illinois 64.

Right on Illinois 64 through the hamlet of KINGS to the junction with a blacktop road, 2.5 *m.*; R. on this road to WHITE ROCK CENTER CEMETERY, 3.7 *m.* In the middle of the cemetery, marked by a large granite boulder, is the grave of JOHN CAMPBELL, captain of the Regulators, a pioneer vigilante group. The inscription on the grave reads: "John Campbell, assassinated by prairie bandits in June 1841. His life was sacrificed for law and order." Campbell was killed by David and Taylor Driscoll, leaders of a bandit gang that for years made life and property insecure in DeKalb and Ogle Counties. The murder was the answer of the gang to a concerted action on the part of Campbell and other settlers to rid the region of the renegades. In retaliation the Regulators rounded up all Driscolls. The two leaders escaped, but John Driscoll and his sons, William and Pierce, were caught. Pierce, aged 13, was spared because of his youth; the others were shot.

Upton Swingly (1834-1919) was 10 years old at the time of the Campbell incident. Three years before his death he set down his reminiscences, which were published in the *Journal* of the Illinois State Historical Society. He wrote: "The Vigilance Committee went to the home of the Driscolls and arrested the father and one son, neither of whom had taken a direct part in the shooting. They were taken to Oregon . . . were tried, convicted and executed in one day, the execution taking place in a grove east of Daysville. They stood blindfolded on a mound and were shot by 12 men belonging to the committee. This determined action cleared the country of the robbers. At one time a hollow tree was found filled with 23 saddles."

ROCHELLE, 44 *m.* (793 alt., 8,594 pop. 1970; 7,008, 1960, inc. 22.6%) in Ogle County, is one of those pleasant northern Illinois towns that seem to have grown out of the soil. Attesting the fertility of these prairies are the magnificient maples that shade attractive houses and overhang colorful gardens. Extensive fields of peas, corn, pumpkins, and asparagus in the vicinity feed the local Del Monte cannery, and in the summer canning season Rochelle is crowded as additional hands are employed. Other industries produce farm equipment, furniture, yarn and printed materials.

The Flagg Township Library made extensive improvements in its facilities in 1964. It circulates up to 80,000 books. It is a member of the Northern Illinois Library System, which has 35 member libraries.

Two residents of Rochelle are remembered as composers of popular songs. Charles Butterfield wrote "When You and I Were Young, Maggie" and Francis Roe composed a Civil War song, "Just Before the Battle, Mother."

SPRING LAKE, off US 51, is an unusual combination of landscaped pool and beach, framed by a beautiful waterfall and rock terraces.

Rochelle is a junction with Illinois 38 (*see Tour 12A*).

At 56 *m.,* is a junction with US 30 (*see Tour 12*).

The highway ascends the northern slope of the Bloomington Moraine, one of the longest and largest glacial ridges known to geologists. The Bloomington, here merged with the Shelbyville Moraine, marks the farthest advance of the Wisconsin Glacier, last in the series of ice sheets that blanketed most of Illinois long ago. These irregular ridges, west of the highway between this point and Bloomington, were formed by the glacial debris that the huge ice sheet deposited as it melted at its outer edge.

MENDOTA, 74 *m.* a city in La Salle County (750 alt., 6,902 pop. 1970; 6,154, 1960) serves the needs of the surrounding agricultural area, and processes and markets its products. An important canning center, Mendota annually ships millions of cans of peas, corn and lima beans. Some area farms yield 120 bu. of corn to the acre. Industries make gluing and laminating machinery, cranes, hoists, farm equipment, women's sportswear.

Mendota is at the junction with US 34 and US 52 (*see Tour 15*); US 51 and US 52 are united for 6½ miles.

Mendota has rail passenger service on the Burlington Northern and freight service on three roads. It also has Continental Trailways and Peoria-Rockford Bus Line. Its senior citizens are accommodated in a new Federal project and the Mendota Lutheran Home.

Lake Mendota Park is getting a new dam and larger lake. The Tri-County Fair at Labor Day weekend has livestock exhibits, harness racing and carnival.

American domestic and civic life in the late 19th century is portrayed in the Time Was Village Museum, seven buildings showing utensils, furniture, contents of shops, and vehicles, developed by Kenneth B. Butler, 4 *m.* south on US 51. *Open May-October, children under 12 free.*

The National Sweet Corn Festival is a 3-day affair, at which the National Sweet Corn Queen is named.

South of Mendota the route enters the northern edge of the La Salle coal district. The first recorded discovery of coal in what is now the United States was made by Jolliet in 1673, when he and Father Marquette reached the Indian village, Kaskaskia, on the Illinois River, a few miles east of La Salle. Below an east-west line across the State at this point, the whole of Illinois—with the exception of the Ozark region and strips along the Mississippi and Ohio Rivers—is underlaid with coal deposits of varying thicknesses.

At 79 *m.,* is the southern junction with US 52. At Troy Grove 2 *m.* right is the Wild Bill Hickok State Memorial (*see Tour 15*).

At 86.9 *m.* US 51 divides, one branch entering Peru, the other skirting the city to La Salle.

PERU, 90 *m.* (959 alt., 11,772 pop. 1970; 10,460, 1960; inc. 12.5%) a city in La Salle County, has streets contiguous with La Salle, which adjoins it on the east. Both owe their early growth to the Illinois River, and both lie on its northern bank. Founded in 1835 Peru (Indian, plenty of everything) was made the terminus of the Illinois & Michigan Canal because it was at the head of navigation on the river. It lost the canal-to-river transshipping business to La Salle when that city built a steamboat and canal basin. However, both cities profited greatly from the flood of commerce that came down the river on barges and steamers. The twin communities began life on the river terraces, but their growth soon forced them up the slopes and out on the prairies. Water transportation forced the railroads (Illinois Central and Rock Island) to lower their rail rates in competition.

Peru's residential sections have been expanding. Big Ben Park is a new recreation area. Favorable results have been obtained by Hi-Society Youth Center, opened 1954, which has received awards for meritorious community service from the Illinois Youth Commission.

Cole Porter, composer of popular musicals, was born in Peru June 9, 1893 (d. 1964).

Many of Peru's original industries are still operating. They include W. H. Maze Co., 1854, making nails and glazer points; Star Union Products Co., 1845, beer and ice; American Nickeloid Co., 1898, metal sheets and coils; National Sheet Metal Co., 1901 and Westclox Division of General Time Corporation, which was founded in 1885. Westclox employs 2,900 and makes the Big Ben and Westclox time-keepers here.

The Illinois River Bridge, 1700 Water St., a wooden swing-type span turned by hand, is one of the oldest major bridges in the State, having been constructed in 1869. At that time its middle girder, 310 feet long, was considered a remarkable engineering achievement. At the base of the bridge is the South Shore Boat Club.

Peru is at the junction with US 6 (*see Tour 14*), which unites with US 51 for 2 miles.

LA SALLE, 92 *m*. (526 alt., 10,736 pop. 1970; 11,897, 1960) in Ogle County, was named for the French explorer who came down the Illinois River in 1679. The town stands on the site of Fort Horn, 1828, and attracted settlers in 1836, when work began on the Illinois & Michigan Canal. Its opening in 1848 was greeted with enthusiasm or apprehension by Midwestern cities, depending on their location. As the lock swung open to pass the first freight-laden boat, the transportation system of the whole region was changed. The rich central prairies of Illinois now poured their crops into Chicago rather than St. Louis; within four years Chicago was receiving almost four times as much corn as St. Louis. Far across Lake Michigan sawmills began to buzz in the wooded sections of Michigan, and lines of steamers moved across the lake and into the canal with lumber for booming prairie towns.

The new waterway pumped money and prosperity into La Salle for a decade. The decline of steamboating began here somewhat earlier than on the Mississippi. The competitive advantage of the railroads was increased by the comparative shallowness of the Illinois River, the irregularity of steamboat service, and the lack of co-ordination between river and canal vessels. By 1890 canal traffic had greatly diminished. In this crisis La Salle turned to mining nearby coal deposits, and the railroads influenced many enterprises to remain in the town.

Principal revenue source for La Salle is the Matthiessen & Hegeler Zinc Company, 1375 9th St., which employs 600 and was established in

1858 by two German immigrants who were attracted by the town's coal and water facilities, and proximity to Galena zinc ore. Smelter and sheet zinc and zinc wire, are the chief products, from which the most important by-product is sulphuric acid. Illinois Zinc Co. dates from 1870. Another major industry is the Electrical Utilities Co. LaSalle is the home of the Big Ben clocks.

The Hegeler Home, 1307 7th St., built in 1874 by Edward C. Hegeler, co-founder of the zinc company, is a large stone and concrete structure, with mansard roof and cupola. Hegeler Park commemorates the brothers.

Illinois Valley Community College, established 1924, serves the closely united La Salle-Peru-Oglesby community, especially by its evening classes. It enrolls 2,750 and has a faculty of 128. It offers two years in liberal arts and pre-professional courses. Also complete courses in electronics, data processing, secretarial and managerial subjects. It gives an associate degree in nursing. Its main building is in La Salle, its stadium in Peru.

La Salle is at the junction with US 6 (*see Tour 14*).

The highway crosses the old Illinois & Michigan Canal between Locks 14 and 15, only a short distance apart. In the basin at Peru boats were lowered into the Illinois River. Along the canal front are old pilings and antiquated warehouses, reminiscent of steamboat days. The canal and towpath have been improved, and are now a pleasant recreational area.

The viaduct across the canal merges into the SHIPPINGSPORT BRIDGE over the Illinois River. At its southern end is the site of FORT WILBOURN, where the 22nd army of Illinois Volunteers was mustered into service for the Black Hawk War. Here on June 16, 1832, Abraham Lincoln enlisted as a private in Jacob N. Early's company.

Although coal mining was once of major importance in this area, production has fallen off materially. The more profitable strip mines around Wilmington to the east and the thicker seams exploited by the Southern Illinois collieries have reduced activities here.

OGLESBY, 95 *m.* (465 alt., 4,175 pop. 1970; 4,215, 1960) in LaSalle County, named for Gov. Richard J. Oglesby, is one of the largest cement-producing centers in the State, utilizing the vast deposits of limestone and slate which outcrop in the Vermilion Valley nearby. Hence it was incorporated as Portland in 1902, but in 1913 the voters substituted Oglesby.

MATTHIESSEN STATE PARK, 174 acres, is located in the valley of the Vermilion east of Oglesby on Illinois 178, and shares the beauty of the limestone bluffs of the area.

At 97 *m.* is the junction with a hard surface road. Left from Oglesby on Illinois 71 to Mathiessen, Starved Rock and Buffalo Rock State Parks (*see Tour 14*).

Left on this road to the junction with a blacktop road, 1.8 *m.*; L. on this road along the top of the bluff overlooking the deep Vermilion

Valley to BAILEY FALLS, 2½ *m.,* where Bailey Creek tumbles into the Vermilion. Immense limestone blocks, loosened by rains and weather, have crashed down the steep slopes and now lie in the stream bed below the falls like houses left stranded by a flood. Lumbering has recently revived in this wilderness area; long ago there was a sawmill at the falls.

At 108 *m.* is the junction with Illinois 18.

Left on this paved road, past many barns with Gothic windows and steeple-like cupolas, to STREATOR, 14 *m.* (625 alt., 15,600 pop. 1970, 16,868, 1960), center of an important clay-producing area along the Vermilion River. Streator owes its highly industrial character to the great shale, clay and sand deposits which crowd up to its southern limits. Coal mining began here in 1872, and the importance of the enterprise is reflected in the fact that the city soon changed its name from Union-ville to Streator in honor of the coal company's president. Coal is no longer mined.

On the heels of coal came glass. A small bottle works was established in Streator in 1873. Beds of siliceous sand used in the manufacture of glass lay at the community's doorstep, and quantities of coal were available. Until the 20th century the delicate and involved task of converting sand into glass bottles was performed by glass-blowers. Many of these highly skilled craftsmen were itinerant workers, but they could command high wages. In time machines replaced these artisans, and the town's glass plants passed to the Owens Illinois and Thatcher glass corporations.

In Riverview Cemetery, at the western city limits, is the grave of George "Honey Boy" Evans, born in Streator in 1870. Evans first appeared in amateur theatricals, then clerked in a bookstore, and finally joined Haverly's Mastodon Minstrels at Chicago in 1892. Composer of songs and monologues, author of the immensely popular song, "The Good Old Summer Time," he was an outstanding black-face comedian of his day. In New York, Evans headed Cohan & Harris Minstrels, eventually took over the company, and toured with it until his death in 1915.

WENONA, 113 *m.* (696 alt., 1,080 pop. 1970; 1,005, 1960) is a marketing and shipping point for soy beans and corn, for this area lies on the western edge of the east-central Illinois grain region. The city is located in La Salle and Marshall Counties.

Soy beans are cultivated both for their seeds and for forage. Flour prepared from soy beans is a standard food for diabetes sufferers; soy is the basic ingredient for a popular sauce or liquid condiment used with fish and meat. Many fields of this cash crop border the highway south of Wenona, part of the huge crop of which Illinois produces more than any other state.

EL PASO, 137 *m.* (749 alt., 2,291 pop. 1970; 1,964, 1960) is a shipping center for grain and farm products of Woodford County. It was the birthplace of Bishop Fulton J. Sheen of Rochester and the place where Lester Pfister perfected a notable hybrid corn along lines devised by Henry Wallace, later U. S. Secretary of Agriculture and Vice President. Pfister, at great personal sacrifice by himself and his family, put in 10 years, from 1925 to 1935, experimenting with corn. He placed paper bags over tassels and ear shoots of corn and gathered uncounted number of seeds for hybridization. When his success was established he marketed his corn seed in large quantities in the middle western states.

El Paso is at the junction with US 24 (*see Tour 16*).

At 144 *m.* is a junction with a paved road. Left on this road to Lake Bloomington (*swimming, fishing, boating*), 3.6 *m.*, the source of Bloomington's water supply, and now a major recreational area; many attractive permanent and summer homes border its shores. Created by damming Money Creek, 700-acre Lake Bloomington, with a maximum depth of 40 feet, has a wooded margin of 1,400 acres. The Italian Renaissance Pumping Station, brick with red tile roof, is near the dam at the northern end of the lake. Just southwest of the station is a stone gateway in which is embedded a plate in memory of Silas Hubbard (1855-1900), a family doctor, whose kindness and philanthropy have become a legend. Inside the gate is the Stone-Hubbard Memorial, a stone bench constituting a dual memorial to Melville E. Stone (1848-1920), co-founder of the *Chicago Daily News,* later general manager of the Associated Press, and Elbert Hubbard (1856-1915), author and humanist. The beautiful Money Creek valley was the boyhood playground of both Stone and Hubbard.

At 147 *m.* is the junction with a blacktop road. Left on this road is HUDSON, 0.7 *m.* (768 alt., 802 pop. 1970; 493, 1960) in McLean County, where a group from New York, known as the Hudson Colony, settled in 1836. The original town lots were apportioned by lottery, each buyer paying $235 for four lots and 160 acres of land. The first house of the Hudson Colony, built by James T. Gildersleeve, is called Five Oaks and is the birthplace of Melville E. Stone. The gray frame, two-story Greek revival structure has a square wing and a small porch. The formality of its fine walnut interior is relieved by numerous stone fireplaces. Five Oaks received its name from a cluster of oak trees.

In Hudson is the site of the last village of the Potawatomi in this area. In 1831 white boys burned down the wigwams while the Indians were away hunting. The Indians made no attempt to retaliate but moved to Galesburg and thence west of the Mississippi.

BLOOMINGTON, 156 *m.* (799 alt., 39,992 pop. 1970) and NORMAL (790 alt., 26,396 pop. 1970) *See Bloomington* and *Normal.* Bloomington is at the junction with US 66 (*see Tour 17*).

Section b. Bloomington to Vandalia, 115 m.

Between Bloomington and Vandalia the highway winds among the great grain fields of east central Illinois, a region of rich black loam. The flat or gently rolling terrain, the result of glaciation, makes mechanized agriculture both possible and profitable.

South of Bloomington, 0 *m.*, US 51 again crosses the Bloomington Moraine. At this point the formation, a chain of low hills, follows an east-west line. West of the city the Bloomington Moraine merges with the Shelbyville Moraine and swings northward.

At 7 *m.* is the junction with a blacktop road. Left on this road is RANDOLPH, 0.2 *m.*, a small settlement. Among its first settlers was Gardner Randolph, who with his family, moved here in 1822 from North Carolina. Their first shelter was made by driving four poles into the ground and covering three sides with bush and bark. This shelter gave scant protection from the bitter cold and merciless blizzards of Illinois winters, but the family managed to survive. The site of the first Randolph home is marked by a red granite boulder.

At 0.8 *m.* is the junction with a graveled road, here to the junction with another graveled road, 1.4 *m.*; on this road to the Stewart house 1.7 *m.*, built in 1833, the oldest house in McLean County. The brick used in its construction was baked on the site, an early utilization of the excellent clay in the region.

HEYWORTH, 12 *m.* (747 alt., 1,441 pop. 1970; 1,196, 1960) in McLean County, was named for an Illinois Central railroad official. The site was once a camp ground of a Kickapoo tribe.

CLINTON, 24 *m.* (746 alt., 7,570 pop. 1970; 1,355, 1960) seat of De Witt County, reputedly was the first town to hear a famous Lincoln aphorism. Here, on July 27, 1858, Stephen A. Douglas falsely charged Lincoln during their campaign for the United States Senate with advocating political equality for Negroes. Lincoln was in the audience, and at the conclusion of Douglas's speech announced that he would speak that same evening at the courthouse. Today on the courthouse lawn, a life-size Lincoln statue by Van den Bergen, Belgian artist, marks the site of the speech and quotes Lincoln's remark that "you can fool all of the people part of the time and part of the people all of the time, but you cannot fool all the people all the time."

Clinton was on the circuit of the Eighth Judicial District, and was frequently visited by Lincoln. Here, while opposing Douglas in a railroad case, he first met George B. McClellan, then a civil engineer for the Illinois Central, later appointed by Lincoln to the command of the Army of the Potomac.

The Barnett Hotel, 738 N. Grant St., an old buff frame building, Greek Revival in design, was a stopping place much favored by Lincoln and other notables of the time. The building, now a private residence, has been moved from its original site, and the old bar rail, still a steadying influence, serves as the hand-rail on the stairway.

The Vespasian Warner Public Library, 120 W. Johnson St., was named for a former U. S. Representative and Commissioner of Pensions. It was modernized in 1969, stocks around 40,000 volumes and circulates more than 50,000. It is a member of the Rolling Prairie Library System.

The Homestead, 219 East Woodlawn, an 18-room mansion of late Victorian days, has been restored in the style of the 1890s and expanded with exhibits of farming and railroading. *Open daily except Monday, 1-5 in summer, weekends only in winter.*

Left from Clinton on US 54 to junction with Illinois 10, 2 *m.;* right on 10 to a blacktop road, 1 *m.;* right on road to WELDON SPRINGS STATE PARK. A lake of 28 acres was made by damming Salt Creek. From 1901 through 1920 the park had summer chautauquas, with an auditorium seating 4,500. President W. H. Taft, William J. Bryan, Robert LaFollette, Carry Nation, Eugene V. Debs, and Helen Keller, were among the personalities who appeared.

South of Clinton US 51 runs along the inner edge of the Shelbyville Moraine, which roughly divides Illinois into three agricultural sectors. To the north and east is the cash grain area, where corn is raised for the nearby Chicago market on soil formed by the most recent glacier, the Wisconsin. To the south and west are the older leached soils of the Illinois glacier. The western section, younger and heavily mantled with loess, also achieves a high yield of corn, which is fed to cattle and hogs or shipped to the more distant markets.

DECATUR, 46.9 *m.* (619 alt., 90,397 pop. 1970) (*see Decatur*).

Decatur is at the junction with US 36 (*see Tour 18*) and the Lincoln Heritage Trail (*see Tour 21*).

South of Decatur the highway traverses the Shelbyville Moraine. The large glacial ridge, which enters the State from Indiana along an east-west line, here swings abruptly northward to join the Bloomington Moraine, west of that city.

MACON, 57 *m.* (721 alt., 1,249 pop. 1970; 1,229, 1960) is the home of Eastern Star Sanitarium, an institution maintained by the Order of the Eastern Star of Illinois for its aged and infirm members.

MOWEAQUA, 63 *m.* (632 alt., 1,687 pop. 1970; 1,614, 1960) an agricultural and mining community, in Shelby County was the scene of a Christmas Eve mine disaster in 1932 that smothered the holiday spirits of the whole region. Fifty-four men working in a local mine were entombed and fatally burned by an explosion of gas. Scores of rescuers rushed from family celebrations to the mine and dug frantically in the bitter cold in a vain effort to save the men. A memorial marker in Moweaqua Park carries the names of the victims.

PANA, 82.1 *m.* (693 alt., 6,326 pop. 1970; 6,432, 1960), is marked by smokestacks rising from acres of tilted glass panes. Of the many enterprises that cluster around Illinois coal mines, Pana's rose-growing is perhaps the strangest and certainly the simplest in operation. Because the chief requisite of hot-house floriculture is steam heat supplied by coal, rose culture is particularly suited to mining regions. The flower firms cultivate acres of roses and ship millions of cut flowers annually. Local production of coal for domestic and industrial use is also important.

KITCHELL PARK, in the southern part of the city, has tennis courts, a swimming pool and picnic accommodations. In the park, visible from the highway, is a statue of Liberty, guarded on either side by a soldier and a sailor, erected by the citizens of Pana Township to their men who served in World War I.

Kitchell Park was donated to the city by Capt. and Mrs. John W. Kitchell, who were public benefactors. They commissioned Charles J. Mulligan, pupil of Lorado Taft, to design a statue of Abraham Lincoln for Rosemont Grove Cemetery. On a tall rock stands the bronze statue of Lincoln with right arm upraised in the act of delivering the Gettysburg Address, as Kitchell imagined it. When critics asserted Lincoln did not use gestures freely Kitchell replied he had seen Lincoln three times in this attitude. Kitchell served as a clerk of the State legislature while Lincoln used an office in the Old State Capitol prior to his inauguration. When Kitchell died in 1914 the *Pana Palladium* said "his charities were practically as innumerable as the stars of the heavens."

At 98 *m.* is a junction with a hardsurface road. Right to RAMSEY STATE PARK, 2 *m.* Originally fox and raccoon hunters met here to work their dogs in September. In 1947 the State bought 815 acres and built a 50-acre lake, now stocked with fish. In 1955 this became a State Park.

At 110 *m.* the ILLINOIS STATE PENAL FARM is bisected by the highway. Convicts who work the 1,531-acre tract and the additional 900 acres that are leased by the State have nicknamed the institution the Peanut Farm. The low buff-color buildings, with their cloistered walks, are more suggestive of a quiet place of learning than of a penal colony. In 1937 a hospital and six dormitories were added to the institution, increasing the prisoner-capacity from 700 to 1,400. Only petty offenders, such as those guilty of misdemeanors, are kept here; their sentences range from 60 days to a year.

VANDALIA

VANDALIA, 115 *m.* (512 alt., 5,160 pop. 1970; 5,537, 1960), seat of Fayette County, lies in the fertile Kaskaskia River Valley banked by one of the Illinoisan moraines. It was the second capital of Illinois, 1819-1839. Created in virgin wilderness and growing rapidly in its first few years, Vandalia played a large part in the early politics of the State.

The State legislature, meeting at Kaskaskia in 1819, decided to bolster its treasury by selling town lots. Accordingly a land grant was procured from the Federal government and a new State capital, 60 miles east of the Mississippi, was laid out. For the next 20 years Vandalia was the political center of Illinois, the forum of such frontier statesmen as John Reynolds, Ninian Edwards, Stephen A. Douglas, and Abraham Lincoln. But in 1837 the Long Nine, a group of 6-foot legislators under the leadership of Lincoln, organized a majority that obtained legislation removing the capital to Springfield two years later.

Modern Vandalia is a distributing center for farm products and is near new oil developments. It is 64 *m.* south of Decatur and 239 *m.* southwest of Chicago on US 40. It is also reached by Interstate 70, expressway to St. Louis. Among its industries are Crane Packing Co., Princess Peggy, Inc., Ralston-Purina, Van-Tran Electric, and Imco Container. A new Tourist Information Center and Chamber of Commerce Bldg. was completed in 1971. Vandalia Municipal Airport is 4 *m*. northwest of town.

The EVANS PUBLIC LIBRARY was opened in 1960; it has Lincoln memorabilia and circulates approx. 50,000 vols. It is a member of the Cumberland Trail Library System of 14 cooperating libraries.

Vandalia is much visited by tourists interested in Illinois history. It has placed markers at important sites, but most of the pioneer houses and taverns were lost before the Civil War. The core of the present Masonic Hall once served as a trading post and a shelter on the Underground Railroad. The First Presbyterian Church preserves a bell of 1830, said to be the State's oldest Protestant church bell. A monument at the grave of Colonel Lucien Greathouse recalls that he was killed while leading his regiment at the Battle of Atlanta and that General W. T. Sherman said "his example was worth 10,000 men."

The VANDALIA STATE HOUSE (*open daily 9-5*), erected in 1836, was the fourth capitol of Illinois. The first was a rented building in Kaskaskia. The second, in Vandalia, was a two-story log structure, destroyed by fire in 1823. The third, of brick, was razed to make room for the one now standing. This two-story, white brick building, of simple Greek Revival design, has been restored to its original appearance and is preserved as a State Memorial. The main entrance is protected by a porch with slender posts supporting the pediment; above the gabled roof is a cupola. The restoration included plans to furnish the whole building with furniture of Lincoln's period. Lincoln served as a member of the House from Sangamon County in this capitol, 1836-1839; on July 4, 1839, Springfield became the capital. Stephen A. Douglas was a member of the 1836-37 session and here Lincoln met him. On March 4, 1837, the city charter of Chicago, a village on Lake Michigan, was issued here. From 1839 to 1933 this building was the Fayette County Courthouse.

On a corner of the lawn stands the MADONNA OF THE TRAIL, a monument 18 ft. high, erected by the DAR in 1928 to mark the western terminus of the National Road, popularly known as the Cumberland Road. The pioneer woman holds an infant in her arms while a small boy clings to her skirts. *For an account of the National Road see Tour 19.*

The Kaskaskia River, which flows by Vandalia, is the chief source of CARLYLE LAKE, in the southern part of Fayette County. This lake covers 18,729 acres, has a shore line of 83 *m*. and is 15 *m*. long by 3½ wide. Carlyle Lake State Park is in Clinton County.

Section c. Vandalia to Cairo, 159 m.

South of Vandalia, 0 *m*., US 51 enters a country where coal becomes more and more important, reaching its culmination at Carbondale, which lies close to the most productive bituminous veins in the United States. South of Carbondale stretches the cross-State range of the Illinois Ozarks. Here the coal veins, so prevalent a few miles north, were stripped from the uplifted belt of hills by age-long processes of erosion. Fruit farms cover the hillsides for a 40-mile stretch and then the road drops abruptly from the hills into the lush delta region near Cairo, the lowest point in the State.

VERNON, 12 *m.* (505 alt., 203 pop. 1970; 235, 1960) in Marion County, in the Keiffer pear district, is a shipping point for peaches and pears.

PATOKA, 15.6 *m.* in Marion County (507 alt., 562 pop. 1970; 601, 1960) named for an Indian chief, drowsed for generations and then, in 1937, suddenly found itself the center of a feverish oil boom in which much of southern Illinois was leased by oil companies. The old oil fields to the south and east had been producing sluggishly for many years, but the new wells of Patoka gushed sufficiently to excite the landowners.

SANDOVAL, 26 *m.* (509 alt., 1,332 pop. 1970; 1,356, 1960), a small mining and farming community in Marion County, was a busy railroad terminal until the adoption of standard gauge tracks by the Baltimore & Ohio in 1871. At Sandoval freight had to be carried from the 6-foot tracks of the B. & O. to the narrower tracks of the Illinois Central. The transfer was made by an arrangement of parallel tracks along which freight cars were drawn by oxen, and the freight shifted from car to car by hand. On changing to standard gauge tracks the B. & O. had to reduce its entire line 15 inches between Cincinnati and St. Louis. To avoid interruption of schedules company officials determined to effect the change overnight. On July 21, 1871 an army of 1,000 track-layers was distributed at five-mile sections of the road and proceeded to sever the tracks and respike them closer together. At 8 A. M., July 22, 1871, the B. & O. became a standard gauge road and Sandoval ceased to be a freight terminal.

Sandoval is at a junction with US 50 (*see Tour 20*).

CENTRAL CITY, 30 *m.* (498 alt., 1,377 pop. 1970; 1,422, 1960), has grown but little since its incorporation in 1857, and retains its original German atmosphere. The Illinois Central Railroad located some of its shops here.

CENTRALIA, 32.9 *m.* (495 alt., 15,217 pop. 1970; 13,904, 1960, inc. 9.4%), in Marion and Clinton Counties, like Central City, received its name from the Illinois Central Railroad, which platted it in 1853 and located its shops there. For many years it was the principal employer. With Central City to the north and Wamac to the south Centralia is now part of a cohesive population that works for the welfare of the whole. Today its industries are diversified. Centralia profits by its easy access to the markets of populous southern Illinois long known as Little Egypt.

From its earliest days Centralia attracted a strong German immigration, which influenced its schools, where both English and German were taught; its churches, where many services were in German, and its musical activities. Today Centralia is known for its extensive school system, which is topped by KASKASKIA COLLEGE, the first Class I junior college organized under the Public Junior College Act of the State of Illinois. This college enrolls 1,500, has a faculty of 75, and grants the degree of associate in arts, applied science, and general education. Courses in pre-professional and liberal arts lead toward transfer into four-year schools; vocational-technical courses serve as a two-year introduction to business. There is also provision for adult education.

Today the largest industry in Centralia is Hollywood Brands, Inc., maker of millions of candy bars, employing 785. The Illinois Central Car Shops now employ 452. The same number is employed by the Siegler Heater Co. division of Lear Siegler, Inc., an organization that has heating and cooling plants in 24 states. North American Rockwell Co. here makes reinforced plastic products; Valley Steel Products Co. makes pipe casing and tubing; others make a variety of products from cartons to potato chips. Centralia, Central City, and Wamac work together to bring industries into a new 165-acre industrial park. The *Centralia Evening and Sunday Sentinel* has been published for more than a century.

It 1964 the WARREN G. MURRAY CHILDREN'S CENTER opened its gates to retarded children, with 14 buildings completed. Today 700 children live in the seven cottages and more than 700 employees operate the center.

It was at Centralia that the Illinois Central started the conversion of its wood-burning locomotives to coal. The first locomotive to burn Illinois coal successfully was converted in these shops, and by 1868 the use of coal had become general. Centralia's location in the heart of the southern Illinois fruit belt resulted in early attempts to produce refrigerated cars, and in 1868 the Thunderbolt Express, first temperature-controlled fruit train in America, began regular operation between Centralia and Chicago. Today the bulk of the fruit crop is shipped by trucks.

Fruit crops were formerly valued at more than $1,000,000 annually. Until some time after the Civil War, strawberries constituted the principal crop, followed by peaches and pears, but today grain is the chief crop.

An explosion of gas in a coal mine near Centralia on March 25, 1947, killed 111 men.

WAMAC, 34 *m.* (497 alt., 1,347 pop. 1970; 1,394, 1960) is a name coined from the first letters of the counties in which the town lies—Washington, Marion and Clinton. Incorporated as a city in 1913, Wamac for awhile enjoyed a boom as an oasis for surrounding dry towns.

IRVINGTON, 39 *m.* (530 alt., 489 pop. 1970; 387, 1960) in the 1890's was the strawberry capital of Egypt. Hundred-acre strawberry patches were common, and the Illinois Central ran non-stop trains to Chicago with the fruit. As the picking season approached, a horde of transients invaded Irvington to exchange their labor for food and drink. Strawberries are still a valuable crop, but many farms grow soybeans and corn instead. Some peaches are raised.

ASHLEY, 50 *m.* (559 alt., 655 pop. 1970; 662, 1960) was named for John Ashley, an early settler. The Hoben Candy Co. employs around 300.

Left from Ashley on Illinois 15 to MOUNT VERNON, 15 *m.* (15,980 pop. 1970), seat of Jefferson County. *See Tour 3.* Illinois 15 continues east to Fairfield and US 45.

TAMAROA, 66 *m.* (510 alt., 799 pop. 1970; 696, 1960), a village in Perry County was named for the Tamaroa Indian tribe that lived here.

At 66 *m.,* south of the village limits, is a junction with an improved road. Left on this road is a 60-acre tract of narcissus, daffodils, and peonies, known as Maple Lawn Gardens. During the blooming season, at its height about Easter, the flowers are shipped out by trucks. A private road system enables visitors to drive to the heart of the gardens.

Four miles south of Tamaroa US 51 has a junction with Illinois 154. West 8 *m.* on 154 to PINCKNEYVILLE, (3,377 pop. 1970; 3,085, 1960, inc. 9.5%) seat of Perry County and on a junction with Illinois 127, which is joined here by Illinois 13 from Belleville and East St. Louis. The city was named for Charles Cotesworth Pinckney, member from South Carolina of the Constitutional Convention of 1787. This center for bituminous coal was opened by the Illinois Central Railroad in 1856. Perry County had 19,757 people in 1970, 19,184 in 1960.

DU QUOIN, 76 *m.* in Perry County (461 alt., 6,691 pop. 1970; 6,558, 1960) was named for Jean Baptiste du Quoigne, an Indian of French extraction, chief of the Kaskaskia tribe. It is a vital link in the mining communities that make southern Illinois an important coal area. A number of strip mines are operated in the territory around Du Quoin. Although this is primarily a mining region, farms are profitable. Du Quoin is the home of the Hambletonian harness races, held during Perry County Fair in late August. It has a bottling plant and machine works.

West of Du Quoin 5 *m.* on Illinois 152 one of the largest strip mining operations in the county, uses an electric shovel that uncovers 70 cubic yards of earth at one dip. A few miles west on a farm road is PYRAMID STATE PARK.

DOWELL, 81 *m.* in Jackson County (400 alt., 423 pop. 1970; 453, 1960), was named for George Dowell, legal advisor of the Progressive Miners of America.

ELKVILLE, 83 *m.* in Jackson County (400 alt., 850 pop. 1970; 743, 1960), narrowly escaped total destruction when a fire swept through its business district, May 17, 1936.

DE SOTO, 91 *m.* (386 alt., 966 pop. 1970; 723, 1960), had 80 persons killed by a tornado in 1925, including 38 children trapped in a school.

Southern Illinois University at Carbondale

CARBONDALE, 97 *m.* (416 alt., 22,816 pop. 1970; 14,670, 1960; inc. 55.5%) in Jackson County, center of the Illinois coal fields, has become famous in recent decades as the core of an educational sys-

tem that is drawing thousands of students to its SOUTHERN ILLI-
NOIS UNIVERSITY. This State-supported institution, founded in
1869 as a normal college, enrolled 22,600 students in the 1971-72 year,
(not counted in Carbondale population figures), and more than 33,000
at all its campuses, including Edwardsville, Alton, and East St. Louis.
The total faculty reaches 2,684.

This was first called Southern Illinois Normal University and
made the training of teachers its principal task until 1943. The first
graduate courses were given in 1944; the name was changed to Southern
Illinois University in 1947; the Graduate School was established in
1948, and the first doctoral degree was conferred in 1959. From 1950
on the physical plant showed large expansion, and in the 1960-1970
decade the campus in Carbondale gained numerous new buildings. The
university envisions a medical school, a law school, and expanded international programs.

Although much at Southern Illinois is new, there is evidence of its
century of effort on the Old Campus. The first college building, dedicated July 1, 1874, remains as a ruin. After a fire in 1883 Old Main
was rebuilt. It was used for classrooms, offices and the University
Museum until June 8, 1969, when, the university tersely records, "it
was completely destroyed by arson." An offer of a $10,000 reward did
not uncover the perpetrator. ALTGELD HALL, dedicated to Governor
John P. Altgeld on December 22, 1896, once a science building, is now
used by the Department of Music. Anthony Hall, the first residence
hall for women, bears the name of Susan B. Anthony, woman's rights
agitator. It has been remodelled and the President has his offices
there now. Shyrock Auditorium, dating from 1918, has become a
cultural center.

The new buildings, with their functional lines and many windows,
emphasize the modern spirit of the university. The Delyte W. Morris
Library, named for its current President, reached its seventh floor in
1970. It holds more than 1,000,000 vols. in open stacks; rare books,
archives, manuscripts, record collections. Pulliam Hall is a laboratory
school for education, and is connected with Wham Education Bldg.
built 1964, which contains the Computing Center and Davis Auditorium. University Center, completed in 1961, has a modular ballroom
that can accommodate 900 couples, a 500-seat dining room and a 300-seat
auditorium. Sui Arena, of 1964, can seat 10,014; it has a revolving
circular stage, and half of the building is underground. Based on the
use of a low ring dome framed of steel with a diameter of 300 ft. Communications Bldg. has a broadcasting station for radio and television,
the University Theatre, seating 578, the Calipre Theatre for experimental use, and the departments of speech, journalism, and related
interests. The Technology Bldg., for many kinds of engineering, was
completed in 1966, and the Physical Sciences Bldg. was built during
1968-1970. Residence Halls make provision for library and dining
services, and the University Health Service, the 15th building in the

Small Group Housing Area, staffed by physicians and nurses, looks after the health of the students on a 24-hour basis.

The university makes provision for the comfort of visitors. It maintains a Tour Train, which moves through the campus, the city, and the outlying areas, with a guide. Its time table is available at the Information & Scheduling Center.

The Vocational-Technical Institute offers associate degree programs in art, business, and technology. It began in 1951, when the university leased a Federal ordnance plant 10 *m.* east of Carbondale. In 1965 the Government deeded the plant and 138 acres to the university. It is located at the northern edge of the Crab Orchard National Wildlife Refuge.

The Outdoor Laboratory at Little Grassy Lake consists of 3,542 owned acres, 190 leased acres, and 1,400 expansion acres available by an agreement with the U. S. Fish & Wildlife Service. It has an arboretum, a camp area for handicapped children, a hospital for totally retarded children, and similar specialized programs.

The SIU campus in Edwardsville was opened in 1965. *See Edwardsville.* The Alton Residence Center occupies a score of buildings, some temporary, on 40 acres originally the campus of Shurtleff College. The East St. Louis Residence Center was opened in 1957 in senior high school. The School of Medicine opened at Springfield Dec. 18, 1971.

In addition to the reading facilities available at the university, the Carbondale Public Library ably serves the city with more than 30,000 vols. and an annual circulation of more than 125,000. It is a member of the Shawnee Library System.

Carbondale industries include the Good Luck Glove Co., the Technical Tape Corp. and several others employing about 2,000. They have access to two airports: the Southern Illinois Airport, on Illinois 13, 3 *m.* north between Carbondale and Murphysboro, and Williamson County Airport, on Illinois 13 10 *m.* east on Illinois 13. The city is also served by Illinois Central Railroad, Greyhound Bus Lines, and Peoria and Rockford lines.

The first concerted effort to decorate the graves of veterans of the Civil War took place in Carbondale on April 5, 1867, when Major General John A. Logan, a native of nearby Marion, sponsored the decoration of graves in Woodlawn Cemetery by a group of 30 children, led by six adolescent girls. Jacob Cole, chaplain of the 31st Illinois Regiment, gave the prayer. A year later, on May 5, 1868, Logan as commander of the Grand Army of the Republic (GAR), issued his famous General Order No. 11, in which he asked that May 30 be set aside "for the purpose of strewing flowers or otherwise decorating the graves of comrades who died in defense of their country during the late rebellion, and whose bodies now lie in every city, village and hamlet churchyard in the land." He also said: "Let no ravages of time testify . . . to the coming generations, that we have forgotten as a people the cost of a free and undivided Republic."

Illinois 13, east-west, moves through Carbondale to MURPHYS-

BORO, 7 m. (10,013, pop. 1970; 8,673, 1960, inc. 15%) seat of Jackson County. Founded in 1843 it was virtually rebuilt after a destructive tornado in March, 1925. The tornado, crossing Illinois to Indiana from Missouri left a total of 659 dead on its route. Murphysboro has a number of light industries. It is the birthplace of John A. Logan; the site is marked opposite 310 S. 17th St. A bronze equestrian statue of General Logan by Leon Hermant is located at 2123 Spruce St.

South of Carbondale the highway enters the Illinois Ozarks, an uplifted and folded belt 15 to 40 miles wide and 70 miles long, extending from the Mississippi to the Ohio. A continuation of the Missouri Ozarks these hills in places rise as high as 700 feet above the surrounding country.

The Midland Hills Golf Course, 103 m., is entered by a gravel road leading through the heavily-wooded hills. In the center of the grounds is a private, spring-fed lake, surrounded by summer cottages. The 9-hole golf course is open to the public.

At 106 m. is a junction with a paved road. Left on this road 2.4 m. is the entrance to GIANT CITY STATE PARK (cabins and picnic facilities). Established as a State park in 1927, the 1,675 acres of hills, forest, and fantastic rock formations have a rich historical background. Here, during the Civil War, was a headquarters of the Knights of the Golden Circle, a secret organization that favored the Southern cause. Lying slightly south in the latitude of Richmond, Virginia, and settled largely by immigrants from Southern or border states, this locale harbored many southern sympathizers. The Knights of the Golden Circle stimulated resistance to the draft, circulated treasonable publications in the Union ranks, and carried on espionage for the South.

A short distance within the park is the OLD STONE FORT. It consists of a sandstone knoll, with steep, unscalable walls on three sides. Across the fourth side, the only approach to the top, is a 7-ft. wall of rough, unquarried stone. The fort is one of seven in the Illinois Ozarks and is believed to have been a buffalo trap of Indian make.

Near the center of the park is the section that gives it its name. Passages that are almost streetlike in their orderly arangement run between sundered blocks of standstone. On each side the standstone rises 30 or 40 feet, its weathered pockmarked surface resembling the walls of a medieval castle. High upon the face of one rock a visiting soldier chiseled "Albert S. Thompson, Fremont Bodyguard, Feb. 22, 1862, A. D." At the Park's highest point is a large Stone Lodge (lounge and dining room), built by the CCC rock gathered in the vicinity. There is a 2,400-ft. landing strip for airplanes. Reservations must be made for guest houses. The park is open from mid-March to mid-November. Address Managers, Giant City State Park, Makanda, Illinois.

At 111 m. is a junction with a paved road.

Right on this road to ALTO PASS, 3 m. (748 alt., 304 pop. 1970; 281, 1960) in Union County, the highest point in southern Illinois served by a railroad. BALD KNOB CROSS, 9 m., is a huge cross

110 ft. tall, with arms 63 ft. wide, built by donations of the Bald Knob Christian Foundation, of steel covered with marble and porcelainized panels. It is floodlighted at night. Easter Sunrise Services are held here. The Forest Service uses the 11th floor as a lookout.

COBDEN, 113 *m.* (594 alt., 1,114 pop. 1970; 918, 1960) a village in Union County and fruit shipping point on the Illinois Central, was named for an English director of the railroad. It has been claimed that the refrigerator car was an outgrowth of a strawberry refrigerator box invented by Parker, Earl of Cobden. Cobden is the birthplace of Agnes Ayres, motion picture actress, who starred with Rudolph Valentino in *The Sheik.*

ANNA, 119 *m.* (629 alt., 4,766 pop. 1970; 4,280, 1960), an important fruit shipping center in Union County, is the home of ANNA STATE HOSPITAL, an institution that provides psychiatric care for 2,000 patients from the 16 southernmost counties of Illinois. In recent years many new buildings have been erected. Although the Illinois Central Railroad was deterred by law from influencing land speculation, a division engineer bought part of a cornfield owned by Winstead Davie. When the surveyors for the railroad reached Union County in 1851 they obligingly located a station on Davie's farm. Davie platted a town and called it Anna after his wife. In 1853 it had four log structures, in 1855 it had 251 people. John Y. Simon, professor of history at Southern Illinois University, wrote in the Journal of the Illinois State Historical Society that Du Quoin, Carbondale, and Anna drew settlers from the north. "The first city ordinance made Anna a temperance town, and it became a haven for Republicanism as well, a heresy no less damnable in the eyes of the rest of Union County."

Right from Anna on Illinois 186 2 *m.* to JONESBORO (429 alt., 1,676 pop. 1970; 1,636, 1960), seat of Union County and famous in Illinois history as the site of the third Lincoln-Douglas Debate, Sept. 15, 1858. Laid out in 1816 and named for a physician who was an early settler, Jonesboro is the oldest town in the county. A marker in the town square commemorates the debate, which took place in the Fair Grounds on N. Main St. In the 9th Congressional District, Jonesboro was a Democratic stronghold and Lincoln could expect little sympathy for the Republican point of view. According to Prof. Simon, David L. Phillips of Anna, Republican candidate for Congress, met Lincoln at Centralia Sept. 14, 1858, and escorted him to Anna. With Lincoln were Horace White, secretary for the Republican State Committee and reporter for the *Chicago Press and Tribune,* and Robert R. Hitt, stenographer, both of whom went to the Union House in Jonesboro. After dinner Lincoln and Phillips went to the Union House, and sat on the porch and discussed the significance of Donati's comet. The Union House burned down in October, 1937.

There was no rousing welcome for Lincoln at Jonesboro. Even the Jonesboro band had gone to Cairo, to parade in honor of Douglas the day before the debate. Douglas was the guest at a political luncheon and spoke in the afternoon; in the evening he led the grand march at a ball in his honor. Next day he went to Anna in a special train to which was attached a flat car with a brass cannon, which fired salutes. A special train brought listeners from the State Fair at Centralia to the debate, but the crowd was smaller than at other meetings. When the Jonesboro band marched up the road to the Fair Grounds the leader observed a tall, solitary figure striding along and asked who he was. He was Lincoln. In Union County people hated Abolitionists and Douglas tried to pin the abolitionist label on Lincoln.

Left from Anna on Illinois 146 5 *m.* to junction with Interstate 57, which parallels US 51 to Cairo.

WETAUG, 132 *m.* (360 alt.) perpetuates the name of a tribe of Cherokee Indians who camped at a large spring in the vicinity while passing through the country on their historic march from Georgia to Oklahoma. The spring ceased to flow following an earthquake that shook southern Illinois in 1896. The grave of one of the chiefs of the tribe is on the grounds of a local residence.

PULASKI, 140 *m.* (471 pop. 1970; 415, 1960) is a Pulaski County village.

MOUNDS, 148 *m.* (1,718 pop. 1970; 1,835, 1960) is 2 *m.* from a junction with Int. 57 and Illinois 37. US 51 and Illinois 37 combined are joined by Illinois 3 at Future City.

CAIRO, 159 *m.* (6,277 pop. 1970) US 51 enters Cairo on Sycamore St., proceeds through the city to a junction with US 60 and 62 to cross the Ohio River to Kentucky. *See article on Cairo.*

~~~~~~

Tour 4 A

THE BLACK HAWK TRAIL AND THE ROCK RIVER VALLEY

Rockford—Byron—Oregon—Mount Morris—Grand Detour—Dixon

Illinois 2 ; 42 *m.*

ILLINOIS 2, the Black Hawk Trail, between Rockford and Dixon is a route of historical interest and scenic beauty. The road and the region, popularly known as the Black Hawk Country, are named for the chief of the Sauk and Fox, who, upon his exile from the State in 1833, said of this valley: "Rock River was a beautiful country. I loved my towns, my cornfields, and the home of my people. I fought for it. It is now yours. Keep it as we did."

Rock River flows across rich plains in a deep wooded valley. The highway winds with the river, and the hills sweep gradually from the banks and then converge again upon them. Where bluffs line both banks, river and road are narrowly pressed between sloping walls. Occasionally rock outcroppings jut above the river in bluff formation and innumerable islands, tree-covered and varying in length, stud the blue-gray water.

In several places where the hills open out to widen the valley floor are located communities with more than a century and a half of history. Byron is near Stillman Valley, where the volunteers had their first brush with the Indians during the Black Hawk War; Oregon is an educational community with literary memories; Grand Detour evokes memories of early American enterprise.

ROCKFORD, 0 m. (147,370 pop., 1970. *See Rockford*. In Rockford are junctions with US 51 (*see Tour 4*) and US 20 (*see Tour 11*). US 20 connects with Interstate 90, the Northwest Tollway.

Southeast of Rockford, Illinois 2 bends with the river, losing sight of it frequently. Several well-marked State picnic grounds (*tables and fireplaces*) are set in grassy places on the river bank.

At 4.6 m. is a junction with a paved road. Left, across the river, to Greater Rockford Airport.

ROCK RIVER FARMS, 12.3 m., border the road for 3 miles. The largest unit of this successful enterprise is noted for its herd of registered Holstein-Friesian cattle and is owned by R. B. McLaughlin and his wife. This is the home of Haven Hill Crescent Gewina Count, whose lifetime total of production was 208,000 lbs. milk, 8,400 fat. Her top record for one year, 365 days, was 38,878 lbs. of milk and 1,523 lbs. of fat. The progenitor of an immense family of milch cows, bred by insemination, Gewina raised the standards of the breed. Cows in the Rock River Farms often produce above the 1,000-lb. fat level. The Farms are considered a model for feeding, breeding, sanitation and longevity of stock.

Originally the 1,800-acre tract was developed by Medill McCormick, U. S. Senator Progressive Republican political leader, and an owner of the *Chicago Tribune*. His French provincial house and garden farm were sold in 1944 to Albert Martin of Chicago. The main dairy farm operation was sold to H. H. Slingerland in 1942. A 400-acre farm north of the house was sold to a Rockford investor. Land across the Rock River, east of the Farms, was donated to the Girl Scout organization for a camp. The McLaughlins own the Slingerland purchase.

Illinois 2 skirts the river side of BYRON (1,749 pop. 1970; 1,578, 1960) in Ogle County. The community, a market for surrounding farms, was founded in 1835 and named for the poet, Lord Byron, then at the height of his popularity in America. Settled largely by New Englanders, the community was vehemently anti-slavery; many of its members were active in abolitionist societies, and offered their houses and farms as stations on the Underground Railroad. The Soldiers Monument, Chestnut and 2nd Sts., erected in 1866, was the first memorial to Civil War soldiers in the State. A. G. Spalding was born in Byron in 1850.

Left from Byron on Illinois 72 to STILLMAN VALLEY, 4.7 m. (707 alt., 871 pop. 1970; 598, 1960), a village in Ogle County, site of the Battle of Stillman's Run on May 14, 1832. The creek, or run, was named for Major Isaiah Stillman, whose militia of 300 was routed by about 50 Sauk warriors led by Black Hawk. It is believed that 12 of the militia were killed; the others fled to Dixon. Graves of nine were located November 15, 1899, and in 1901 the Illinois General Assembly appropriated $5,000 for a monument that stands in a small military cemetery at the eastern edge of Stillman Valley. It has a 50-ft. granite plinth surrounded by the figure of a citizen soldier. The names of the dead are inscribed thereon. The dedication on June 11, 1902, was attended by William Copes of Atlanta, Ill., a veteran of the battle.

South of Byron are many beautiful stretches of country; the road levels off and is comparatively straight, with the hills a short distance from the highway.

The crossing of the LEAF RIVER, 19.7 m., marks another scenic variation in the highway, which curves through rolling hills before it returns to the river level. Briefly the valley widens, to narrow again as the road runs through sloping groves of trees.

A wide bend in the river at 21.7 ml. reveals a sweeping view of the bluffs, crowned by the STRONGHOLD, a modified medieval castle built by Walter Strong, once publisher of the *Chicago Daily News,* who did not live to enjoy it. It is now used as a conference and rest center by the United Presbyterian Church.

Downstream, at 23.7 m. and 24.8 m., are two fine views of the Black Hawk Monument. Rising majestically from the heavily wooded bluff across the river, the huge figure, with folded arms and a gaze fixed on the country beyond the placid river, is impressive even from a distance.

LEGION SHAFT (R), 25.1 m., a concrete block about four feet high, was erected in honor of Ogle County soldiers and sailors of World War I.

OREGON, 24 m. (701 alt., 3,539 pop. 1970; 3,732, 1960, dec. 7.2%) seat of Ogle County, is a center for distribution of farm products and some light industry. It is noted for its artistic associations dating back to the time when Margaret Fuller (1810-1850) critic and contemporary of the New England authors, visited the locality in 1843 and commended its natural beauty. Lincoln spoke here on Aug. 16, 1846, and this is commemorated on a boulder in the North 500 block. Lorado Taft contributed several pieces of sculpture when he passed his summers here; the Soldiers' Monument on the Courthouse lawn (1916); a small fountain "In Memory of Ruel and Maria Peabody, Pioneers," and the famous Black Hawk statue overlooking the Rock River Valley.

Left from Oregon on Illinois 64, across the Rock River, to the first road and left on this road to LOWDEN MEMORIAL STATE PARK, estab. 1945 to honor Frank O. Lowden, former Governor of Illinois, who died in 1943. Originally, 247 acres of woodland, in 1951

66 acres were transferred to Northern Illinois University of DeKalb for a campus in which to teach natural science and outdoor courses for teachers.

Inside the latter tract is the historic EAGLE'S NEST ART COLONY, at which artists, writers and educators from Chicago lived during the summers in cabins and houses since remodelled for classroom and dormitory use by the university. The site, of incomparable scenic beauty, had won the praise of Margaret Fuller, Countess d'Ossoli, who called the bluff Eagle's Nest. In the river below is MARGARET FULLER ISLAND, and at the riverside is Ganymede's Spring, with a marble table on which is inscribed the naming of the spring and the bluff by Miss Fuller on July 4, 1843.

The present park area was bought in 1898 by Wallace Heckman, distinguished Chicago attorney and business manager of the University of Chicago during its early development. On the bluff was a tall, gaunt cedar tree once the nesting place of eagles, which had inspired Margaret Fuller to write "Ganymede to His Eagle." Mr. and Mrs. Heckman invited friends to join them, asking that in turn they give two lectures annually in Oregon on art subjects. The colony became filled with such personalities as Lorado Taft and Nellie Walker, sculptors; Ralph Clarkson, Charles Francis Browne and Oliver Dennet Grover, painters; Hamlin Garland, Henry B. Fuller and Horace Spencer Fiske, writers; Irving K. and Allen B. Pond, architects; Harriet Monroe, poet and editor of *Poetry;* Clarence Dickinson, organist; James Spencer Dickerson, university secretary, and their friends.

On the edge of the bluff is the Black Hawk Monument, a 48-foot statue executed by Lorado Taft and presented by him to the State in 1911. The statue was intended by Taft to depict an idealization of the Indians who lived in this region, but popular fancy named it Black Hawk and that name is now generally accepted. Taft and his assistants worked an entire summer erecting the frame for the mold, covering it with burlap, and coating it with 10 tons of plaster of Paris. Into this mold they poured 265 tons of concrete. The head, attached later, was cast separately in the studio. Because the statue must withstand wind pressure, its foundation runs 30 feet deep into the bluff.

The Oregon Township Public Library reported more than 32,000 books and other materials on hand in 1972. It was built in 1907 and is a member of the Northern Illinois Library System. It has paintings contributed by artists of the Eagles Nest Colony in a gallery contributed by Mrs. Frank O. Lowden.

Outlaws of Ogle County known as part of the Banditti of the Prairie were run down by vigilantes calling themselves Regulators, as recorded on a historical marker near Oregon.

Ahead on Illinois 64 to the first paved road (R), 0.8 *m.;* R. on this road to the 4,600-acre SINNISSIPPI FARM (private) 4 *m.* The farm, once the property of Col. Frank O. Lowden, former Governor of Illinois, is noted for its Holstein cattle and soil conservation methods. The checkered fields are dotted with small stands of white pine. The word Sinnissippi, found frequently in this region, is a corruption of Sin-Sepo, Indian for Rock River.

Right from Oregon on Illinois 64 to MOUNT MORRIS, 6 *m.* (916 alt., 3,173 pop. 1970; 3,075, 1960) in Ogle County. It was settled in 1838 by colonists from Maryland, whose first act was the establishment of a school. From this vigorous interest in education grew the Rock River Methodist Seminary, established in 1840. In 1879 the seminary buildings were purchased by the Church of the Brethren, a a German Baptist sect, who founded Mount Morris College, an institution which functioned until 1931, when four of its five buildings were destroyed by fire. In 1932 the college merged with Manchester College, North Manchester, Indiana.

In 1855 the Illinois Central laid its rails through nearby Polo instead of Mount Morris and the young community, which had enjoyed a boom as the principal industrial and commercial center of the vicinity, settled down to a more gradual development. Among the industries established in this later period is the Kable Brothers Company, a printing enterpise which has grown from a one-room shop in 1898 to a modern 10-acre plant in which 37 presses print national publications and catalogues. The company employs as many as 1,300 workers and has an annual payroll of $9,500,000. It was bought by Western Publishing Co. in 1959. Kable Printing Co. is at 404 N. Wesley Ave.

Right on a road south of Oregon to WHITE PINES FOREST STATE PARK, 385 acres with lodge and cabins.

South of Oregon the route climbs into the wooded hills, and passes along the base of Devil's Backbone, 28.6 *m.,* the first of a series of fantastic rock formations along the route.

CASTLE ROCK, 31 *m.* rises between the highway and the river. An easy climb to the 150-foot summit offers a splendid view of the river and the surrounding hills and valley. BIG CUT, 31.7 *m.,* exposes the rock structure on both sides of the highway. South of the cut the hills open again, giving a rolling edge to the horizon.

GRAND DETOUR, 36 *m.* is an unincorporated village with a historic past, but identified by the U. S. Census as a township with 668 pop. 1970 (606, 1960). It is located at the Great Bend, as the pioneers knew it, or Grand De Tour, as the French traders had named it and lies on a horseshoe bend of the Rock River, fronting the water on two sides. Many of the buildings are almost a century old; shops are few; wells and cisterns supply water. In the 1930's Grand Detour was a flourishing art colony, where a number of artists from Chicago had homes.

Major Leonard Andrus of Vermont visited Grand Detour in 1834, returned in 1835 with other settlers, and in following years built a dam for water powers and erected saw and flour mills. He surveyed and built the road from Dixon to Grand Detour, extending it through Oregon to Rockford, and established various stage lines. In 1836 John Deere, also from Vermont, settled in the village and opened a blacksmith shop. The next year he made a steel plow to break the sticky Illinois prairie loam, which had so disheartened other pioneers using wooden and cast-iron plows. For his plow share Deere used a Sheffield steel saw blade from Major Andrus' mill; in 1841 Deere and Andrus became partners in Illinois' first successful plow manufactory. Grand Detour's industries began to decline after 1855 when a railroad was refused a right-of-way through the village. John Deere had withdrawn from the partnership with Andrus in 1847 to open a plow factory in Moline. In 1869, two years after Andrus' death, his factory was removed to Dixon.

Between the highway and the river is the MAJOR LEON ANDRUS MEMORIAL, designed by Avard Fairbanks of the Fine Arts Institute of the University of Michigan. The memorial bears a bronze plaque picturing Major Andrus in front of his plow factory as it appeared almost 100 years ago. A brief inscription on the monument, which marks the site of the factory, records the history of the enterprise.

The John Deere Foundation of Moline has been engaged in developing the John Deere Historic Site in Grand Detour as an educational attraction. This site now comprises several buildings: the home that John Deere built for his family; Deere's reconstructed blacksmith shop; an exhibition building constructed over the excavated area where the original blacksmith shop stood; a visitors' center and reception area. Displays in the exhibition building show various parts of Deere's original shop and illustrate how it operated. The blacksmith shop is furnished with tools of the trade, and from time to time a blacksmith works at the forge.

The National Park Service has designated the John Deere site as a National Historic Landmark. It is open daily 9-5. Guides are on hand and admission is free.

Among several old buildings in Grand Detour is St. Peter's Episcopal Church, completed in 1850, the second oldest church of that denomination in Illinois. Built of local limestone with a charming pinnacled belfry of wood, its most unusual feature is a series of triangular-headed windows lighting the nave. Although the entrance door and window above have pointed Gothic arches, the cornice and all the mouldings are based on Greek originals.

South of Grand Detour the highway crosses the Rock River and the lowland that lies within the Great Bend, and then swings away from the river, which is encountered again on the outskirts of Dixon, partly screened by factories along its bank. From the lowland the highway climbs abruptly to the higher ground of Dixon's business district.

DIXON, 42 m. (18,147 pop. 1970) is at the junction with US 30A, US 52, and Illinois 2 and 26. See Tour 12. Dixon to Rock Island on Illinois 2, 67 m. Dixon to Peoria via Princeton on Illinois 26 and Illinois 29, 90 m.

Tour 5

FROM WISCONSIN TO THE ILLINOIS RIVER

Warren — Prophetstown — Hooppole — Annanwan — Kewanee —
Elmwood — Farmington — Canton — Havana — Bath — Virginia
Illinois 78 ; 196 *m.*

Illinois 78 crosses a section of western Illinois from the sweeping
hills and valleys of Jo Daviess County to the pleasant level prairies that
border the Illinois River Valley. Industrial development is slight, and
the region is given over largely to diversified farming. The raising of
livestock, including blooded horses, and the cultivation of corn and small
grains are the primary activities of farmers.

Section a. *Wisconsin Line to Kewanee, 96 m.*

Along this northern section of the highway there are no large cities,
and traffic is usually light. Wild life is more plentiful than on heavily
traveled roads. Hawks, soaring from their fence posts, circle into the
air, screaming defiance; cottontail rabbits, suddenly alarmed, scurry
across the road to safety; quail feed nervously by the roadside, emitting
their plaintive calls; and groundhogs, less easily disturbed, munch clover
a few feet from the road.

Illinois 78, a continuation of Wisconsin 78, crosses the Wisconsin
Line, 0 *m.*, 6 miles south of Gratiot, Wisconsin.

WARREN, 1.7 *m.* (1,005 alt., 1,523 pop. 1970; 1,470, 1960), a
village in Jo Daviess County settled by Alexander Burnett in 1843,
developed at the junction of the Chicago-Galena Stagecoach Road and
the Old Sucker Trail, which ran from St. Louis to Wiota, Wisconsin.
Organized as the town of Courtland in 1850, the community changed its
name three years later to honor both its founder's son Warren, and the
Pennsylvania city from which he came. In that year it became a station
on the new railroad from Chicago to Galena. It was a rough and ready
pioneer community, and an early writer noted that "being situated
within a mile of the state line of Wisconsin, Warren is a great resort
for criminals who wish to get out of that state." The weather-worn
stone TISDEL HOTEL, built in 1851, serves as the Community Building,
with village headquarters.

Warren was the birthplace of William Langson Lathrop (1859-
1938), who as an unknown artist gained fame overnight when a
painting he had entered in a New York exhibit won the highest awards.
Lathrop moved East after this success, and spent the latter part of his
life in Pennsylvania. Other well-known residents were Paul Myron

Minebarger, lawyer, who became legal adviser to the Chinese Nationalist Government, and Abner Dalrymple, star of the old Chicago White Sox.

At the Fairgrounds on the eastern outskirts of Warren the annual fair of Jo Daviess County is held early in August.

At 5 m. is a junction with a blacktop road. Right on this road to APPLE RIVER CANYON STATE PARK, 3½ m., established in 1932. Limestone cliffs, wooded bluffs, a clear stream, wildflowers, songbirds, and small animals recommend it both to the casual visitor and the overnight camper. Striking rock formations, small caves, and gulches are indicated by arrows painted on a flat-topped rock on a small knoll near the river. The rock, at the far end of the playing field, marks the site of MILLVILLE, the sole reminder of a once prosperous milling and mining community. Its two mills, built in 1836 and 1838, were the heart of a busy village, frequently harassed by Indians. After 1854, when the Frink & Walker stage line through Millville was replaced by the railroad through Warren, most of Millville's families moved to the more promising community 8 miles away. A few pioneers remained until the disastrous floods of 1892 forced complete abandonment of the village. From the Apple River bluffs can be seen CHARLES MOUND, 1,241 ft., highest point in Illinois.

At 11 m. is the eastern junction with US 20, which is united with Illinois 78 as far as STOCKTON 13.1 m. *See Tour 11.*

South of Stockton the country becomes more rolling. The highway winds through valleys banked by some of the highest hills in the State, or follows ridgetops, which bring into view far-flung stretches of countryside.

MOUNT CARROLL, 33 m. (2,143 pop.) is at a junction with US 52 combined with Illinois 64 (east-west) and with Illinois 88. *See Tour 15.*

At UNIONVILLE, 51.1 m. is a junction with US 30, which Illinois 78 follows to MORRISON, 53.1 m. (4,387 pop.). *See Tour 12.*

South of the Rock River is Indian terrain, where Abraham Lincoln and Jefferson Davis served during the Black Hawk War.

PROPHETSTOWN, 65.6 m. (627 alt., 1,915 pop. 1970; 1,802, 1960), in Whiteside County, is at a terminal of Illinois 172 and occupies the site of the village of Chief White Cloud, called the Prophet, who warned the Indians of hostilities by the whites. On May 10, 1832, Federal-State troops under Major Stillman came in pursuit of Black Hawk and his band and destroyed the Prophet's village. The Illinois State Historical Society erected a commemorative marker here in 1934, calling the action "the first act of hostility in the Black Hawk War." White Cloud (1794-1841) was the son of a Sauk father and a Winnebago mother.

In former years Prophetstown had a unique annual event known as Rooster Booster Day, when the merchants displayed crates of roosters. This has been given up. Today the Boosters support an annual Kid's Day, usually in June, when children up to 12 years are invited to be entertained free by the town. There are rides, refreshments, prizes for window painting, performances, and a parade in costume with decorated vehicles. About 3,000 children take part.

PROPHETSTOWN STATE PARK, 53.5 acres, is highly popular as a playground and recreation area, with fishing and boating.

HOOPPOLE, 76 *m.* (618 alt., 227 pop. 1970; 227, 1960) a village in Henry County, received its name from the practice of coopers who cut hickory bands for their barrels in a nearby grove. A. A. Haff in 1880 dehorned his herd of Texas longhorns to keep them from injuring each other in the feeding pens, and was arrested and charged with cruelty to animals. He was acquitted when it was proved that the practice was neither cruel nor harmful. The practice has been generally adopted.

Illinois 78 crosses the Green River, 79 *m.*; settlers found this district extremely swampy, filled with high weeds, which afforded refuge for thousands of game birds. Many hunters made a living by shooting these birds, and a cold-storage company was established in Kewanee to pack them for shipment. Flocks of passenger pigeons were so huge that they darkened the light of the sun. Pioneers killed them in countless numbers, believing the flocks would never be reduced. But by the seventies the birds were dying out, and are now extinct.

The ILLINOIS AND MISSISSIPPI CANAL, 84 *m.* (*see Tour 22*), commonly known as the Hennepin Canal, is today utilized solely for fishing and drainage. The HENNEPIN CANAL PARKWAY STATE PARK, 6,331 acres, is open for limited use. One mile of public shore line on Lake Sinnissippi offers fishing and picnic places.

Just north of Annawan is a junction with Int. 80, which crosses Illinois in a straight line from Indiana to Iowa.

ANNAWAN, 85 *m.* (626 alt., 787 pop. 1970; 701, 1960) is at the junction with US 6 and Int. 80. *See Tour 14.* At 90 *m.* is a hard-surface road. Left to JOHNSON SAUK TRAIL PARK, 857 acres, a fine park built around a man-made lake stocked with game fish.

In the part of Henry County near Annawan, Atkinson, and Kewanee, Belgian soldiers play a game called *rolle bolle*. The game, played with heavy discs of wood, combines features of bowling and horseshoe pitching. So popular is the game that the Henry County Fair, held annually at Cambridge, features a Rolle Bolle Day.

KEWANEE, 96 *m.* (853 alt., 15,762 pop. 1970) is at the junction with US 34 and Illinois 81. *See Tour 13.*

Section b. Kewanee to Jacksonville, 114 m.

In its southern section Illinois 78 passes through some of the most productive farmland in the State, and roughly parallels Spoon River, which has its origin near Kewanee and empties into the Illinois River opposite Havana.

Between Kewanee, 0 *m.*, and 5.4 *m.* Illinois 78 and US 34 are united, after which Illinois 34 goes west to Galva. *See Tour 13.*

At 9 *m.* is the junction with Illinois 17, from the East.

Right on this road to Lake Calhoun, 4 *m.*, an artificial private lake set among thickly wooded hills. The highway is built across the dam, and the lake and grounds are visible from it. Many summer cottages encircle the lake, which is well stocked with fish; large picnic grounds with brick fireplaces are set in sylvan surroundings. Swimming and boating are particularly popular here, since there are no natural lakes in this part of the State.

The highway crosses SPOON RIVER, 19 *m.*, made famous by Edgar Lee Masters in his *Spoon River Anthology. See Tour 16.* Percy Grainger wrote a piano solo, "Spoon River," based on an old folk tune played by fiddlers in 1857 at dances in Stark County.

This region is highly productive; the soil, a rich black prairie loam, produces large crops of corn and small grains. Livestock breeding, including blooded horses, is a major source of income. Veins of coal lie near the surface at various points, and are strip-mined by gigantic mechanical shovels.

ELMWOOD, 33 *m.*, a city in Peoria County (626 alt., 2,014 pop. 1970; 1,882, 1960), was the birthplace of Lorado Taft (1860-1936). The sculptor's bronze statue, PIONEERS OF THE PRAIRIES, a memorial to his parents, is in Central Park. The heroic figures represent a young settler, with his wife and child, dog and gun; the statue stands on a large square base of polished granite. Speakers at the dedication ceremony in 1928 included Taft and Hamlin Garland, novelist.

For many years there was much mining activity between Elmwood and Canton and many of the mines located along the road were loading trucks. Today there is strip-mining.

FARMINGTON, 41 *m.* in Fulton County (742 alt., 2,959 pop. 1970; 2,831, 1960), a mining town, was laid out in 1834. In March 1856 a "whiskey war" was fought here, when a group of crusading women, after numerous unsuccessful attempts to stop the sale of liquor marched on the saloons, broke windows, smashed barrels and bottles with axes, and poured the contents into the streets.

Numerous wolves, which killed young stock and poultry, were a serious problem to the pioneers, who organized wolf-hunts on a large scale. Hunters formed a circle several miles in diameter, and gradually closed in toward the center, driving the wolves before them. In the hunt of 1842 almost 5,000 participated.

CANTON, 51 *m.* (655 alt., 14,217 pop. 1970; 13,588, 1960) is the largest city in Fulton County. It is at the junction with Illinois 9, which connects with US 24, and is served by the C. B. & Q. and T. P. & W. Rys. Among its manufacturers are a major plant of International Harvester Co., the Caterpillar Tractor Co., the Canton Manufacturing Co. (men's clothing), Ayrshire Colliers, and United Electric, Truax Traer, and Peabody mines. Its newspapers are *Canton Daily Ledger* and *Canton Community Sentinel,* a weekly. There is one airport.

In 1959 Canton opened SPOON RIVER COLLEGE, a community college with a two-year curriculum, which enrolls around 1,000 students and has a faculty of 75.

Canton was founded in 1825 by Isaac Swan, who came to Fulton County in 1824. Swan staked claims and offered one lot free to anyone who would build on it. He erected the first building, a log cabin, which was used as a temporary home for new arrivals who gave it the name of Swan's Catch-all. Swan named his town in the belief that it was antipodal to Canton, China.

The INTERNATIONAL HARVESTER COMPANY plant, E. Elm St. and 2nd Ave., employs from 1,500 to 2,000 men in the manufacture of more than 1,400 types of plows, harrows, discs, and other agricultural implements. Sprawling over an area of 19 acres, the plant has a production capacity of two implements a minute. Under the name of Maple & Parlin, the local enterprise began the production of steel moldboard plows in 1846. In 1852 William J. Orendorff supplanted Maple, and the P. & O. Plow Works, now one of the largest in the world, was created; in 1919 it became a part of the International Harvester Company. In 1969 the company celebrated its golden anniversary in Canton.

Frank F. Kolbe of Canton developed the gigantic Kolbe Wheel Excavator, 2,100 tons, at the United Electric's Canton mine. The largest excavator in use, it is operated by electricity for over-burden removal in open-pit mining. It is as tall as a 15-story building, 420 ft. long and can move 4,800 cubic yards per hour.

The original Parlin Library, donated in 1891 by William Parlin, manufacturer, was succeeded in 1958 by a limestone and granite building with all modern facilities donated by Charles D. and Elizabeth M. Ingersoll. It is now the Parlin-Ingersoll Library. The present capacity is 40,000 vols.

LAKE CANTON was completed in 1939 in a natural basin to supply water to the city. It has a surface area of 250 acres and a 13-mile shore line, and is a popular place for summer cottages, fishing, swimming and camping.

The hamlet of Maple Mills, 60 *m.*, was originally the saw-mill village of Slabtown, established in 1851 when timber was being cut for the Canton and Liverpool plank road.

At Little America, 62 *m.*, is a junction with US 24 which unites with Illinois 78 for 3 miles.

At 69 *m.* is a junction with a hard-surface road. Right on this road to DICKSON MOUNDS MUSEUM of the ILLINOIS INDIAN, 4 *m.*

This extraordinary vista into Indian burial customs before 1000 A. D. is esteemed by archaeologists. It is a State Memorial, part of the Illinois State Museum. It is described in detail under *Tour 16.*

Illinois 78 joins Illinois 136 in crossing the Illinois River.

HAVANA, 73 *m.* (451 alt., 4,376 pop. 1970; 4,363, 1960), seat of Mason County, is at the confluence of the Spoon and Illinois Rivers. Once this water route was a busy artery of commerce. John Eveland transported wheat and immigrants until 1824, when Maj. Ossian M. Ross (*see Tour 16*) initiated ferry service. Two years later Ross rented his ferry and trading rights to Samuel Mallory, and thereby inadvertently precipitated the only clash between pioneers and Indians in Mason County. Unaccustomed to dealing with the Indians, Mallory was forced to exchange whiskey for furs. Only the timely intervention of settlers saved Mallory in the excitement that ensued; 15 mounted men from Lewistown routed the Indians, who had consumed sufficient whiskey to threaten the destruction of the entire settlement.

Major Ross was the father of Havana. His home, known for years as Ross's Hotel, was used as a stopping place by settlers; the first session of the circuit court was held in this building. Ross also kept the first store and later built other houses, which he rented to settlers.

The arrival of the steamboat on the Illinois in 1828 marked the beginning of prosperity for many river towns, in which Havana shared, becoming the shipping point for the grain and produce of a large area. By 1836 some 35 steamboats were operating on the river; in that year Havana had 445 "sailings." Then came the railroad, causing a decline in river traffic, but water commerce has been developed since by barge lines carrying grain, coal, and other heavy freight.

Lincoln appears in Havana history for 26 years, as a returning soldier, surveyor, lawyer, and senatorial candidate. Lincoln's most memorable visit occurred in August, 1858, during the course of his senatorial campaign against Stephen A. Douglas. Arriving early in the afternoon of the 13th, while Douglas was still speaking, Lincoln listened to him and arranged to reply the following day. A marker in Rockwell Park commemorates the speech.

For many years Havana was the largest fresh-water fish market in the Middle West. Daily catches reached 100,000 lbs. and when the seines were hauled in at the end of the day crowds assembled at the river front. From 1906 to 1908 the Illinois River was second only to the Columbia River in freshwater commercial fishing. This activity was reduced by drainage and pollution. There is still fishing in small lakes and the Havana Fisheries Field Headquarters are on the west bank of the Illinois River today.

Havana has developed new industries, several of them making farm equipment. The city is a grain center and a large turkey and melon market.

Northeast of Havana on the River Road are a number of conservation areas supervised by the State. These include the Mason State Tree Nursery and the Mason State Forest. Along Chautauqua Lake is the CHAUTAUQUA LAKE NATIONAL WILDLIFE REFUGE, administered by the U. S. Fish and Wildlife Service. This is a station on the great migratory flyway, where huge flights of ducks and geese from the north feed on their way south. Among the fowl observed are mallards, blue bills, blue wing teal, red heads, wood ducks and snow geese. There are feeding and storm shelters and nests for wood ducks placed high in the branches of trees. The refuge has facilities for caring for wounded birds and for banding.

South of Havana the Illinois River has numerous pools and small lakes and after the confluence of the Sangamon River spreads out into Muscooten Bay. Anderson Lake covers 2,068 acres and is a State Conservation Area.

At Havana Illinois 78 has junctions with Illinois 97, which has come down via Galesburg and Lewistown, and proceeds southwest to Springfield, and Illinois 136, which has a junction with US 24 to Quincy.

MATANZA BEACH, 77 *m.*, is the heart of the summer colony district along the Illinois River.

BATH, 81 *m.* (462 alt., 472 pop. 1960), a village in Mason County, was surveyed November 1, 1836, by Abraham Lincoln, then Deputy Surveyor of Sangamon County. It was incorporated in 1870. A white pole in MARKET SQUARE, marks the starting point of his survey. A post office was established in 1842; B. H. Gatton, the first postmaster, received 43½¢ as his first three months salary. In 1843 Bath became the county seat but was supplanted by Havana in 1851. When Mayor Russell P. Kramer dedicated the new telephone building on June 1, 1964, he exchanged greetings with Councillor George Mayer, 736th mayor of Bath, England, for which the Illinois village was named.

The OLD RUGGLES HOUSE, one block left on State 78, two blocks beyond the square, was built by Gen. James M. Ruggles, friend and political ally of Lincoln. It is a large square building, with a cupola on the roof. From its porch Lincoln delivered a political speech on August 16, 1858, during his campaign for the senate. His friend Ruggles, a member of the Illinois General Assembly, although sick at the time, was so desirous of voting for Lincoln that he had himself carried to the Capitol on a stretcher.

The highway crosses the SANGAMON RIVER, 90 *m.* Bath annually plays host to the hunters and fishers who crowd into the area, especially on weekends. Many have cottages at Bath and Patterson Bay and North Matanzas Beach. The town's most prized celebration is the annual Fish Fry, started in 1936. Crowds come to eat the 1,800 lbs. of carp steak.

CHANDLERVILLE, 91 *m.* (464 alt., 762 pop. 1970; 718, 1960) was named for its founder, Dr. Charles Chandler, who is associated with an early Lincoln story. By an unwritten agreement early settlers left 80 acres on each side of a man's land free, so that the settler, as soon as he was able, could enter this additional land at $1.25 an acre. Violation of this rule was considered as reprehensible as stealing. A man whom Dr. Chandler had befriended insisted upon violating the code, at the expense of Chandler, with the remark: "To hell with the customs; I'm going to Springfield and enter the whole tract." Chandler, short of money, borrowed funds, and started on horseback for the land office. Ten miles from Springfield he overtook two young men, one of whom became so indignant on hearing Chandler's story that he offered the

doctor the use of his horse Chandler accepted and beat his riv
Springfield. A short time later he decided to have his land surveye
a neighbor recommended Abraham Lincoln, a young surveyor of Salem.
Chandler was pleased when, on sending for Lincoln, he recognized the
young man who had lent him his horse.

The Sanganois Conservation Area, 7,030 acres, is part of the fine
hunting and fishing area along the Illinois River between Havana and
Beardstown. It is reached west of Chandlerville.

VIRGINIA, 100 *m*. (593 alt., 1,814 pop. 1970; 1,668, 1960) seat
of Cass County, was platted in 1836 by Dr. Henry A. Hall, a former
surgeon in the British Navy, who came to the region by way of the Ohio,
Mississippi, and Illinois Rivers. The county is named for General
Lewis Cass (1782-1806) Secretary of War under President Jackson
and Secretary of State in President Buchanan's cabinet. Virginia was
incorporated as a village in 1842. In early days the county seat was
moved back and forth several times between Beardstown and Virginia,
but Virginia was finally allotted the seat in 1872, the year it became a
city.

Illinois 78 has a junction at Virginia with Illinois 125, which runs
southeast to Springfield. Illinois 78 continues south 16 *m*. to JACK-
SONVILLE. Here are junctions with US 67, US 36, and Illinois 104.
See Tour 7.

Tour 6

NORTHERN ILLINOIS SEGMENT OF THE GREAT RIVER ROAD

East Dubuque—Galena—Hanover—Savanna National Forest—Missis-
sippi Palisades State Park — Savanna — Thomson — Fulton — Albany
—Cordova—Port Byron—Rapids City—Hampton—Campbell's Island
—East Moline—Moline

Illinois 84, 75 *m*.

Dubuque, Iowa, on the Mississippi River, lies opposite the dividing
line between Wisconsin and Illinois. East Dubuque, Illinois, also on
the river, is below the Wisconsin line on US 61, which comes south from
Wisconsin and crosses the river into Iowa, and US 20, which comes
from Galena in Illinois. The Great River Road and the Hiawatha
Pioneer Trail may be followed along the banks of the Mississippi in
both Iowa and Illinois. In Illinois the Great River Road is chiefly on

US 84, which joins US 20 3 *m*. west of Galena, and combines with it for 12 *m*. after Galena, whence it moves south.

To the north lies a country of sweeping grandeur—graceful rolling woodlands, blue hills, broad deep valleys, and rushing streams. Winding through the valley of the beautiful Apple River toward the distant Mississippi bluffs, the highway skirts numerous rocky cliffs quarried for their road-building material.

HANOVER, 5 *m*. a village in Jo Daviess County (632 alt., 1,243 pop. 1970; 1,396, 1960) named in 1837 for Hanover, N. H., was settled around 1830. Originally a mining town it became a center for farm products when lead mining gave out. A dam across Apple River provided power for a grist mill. In 1864 a woolen mill was established.

At 11 *m*. is the junction with a concrete road.

Right on this road to the SAVANNA ARMY DEPOT (*official business only*), 1.8 *m*., in the SAVANNA NATIONAL FOREST, a 12,000-acre game and forest preserve along the Mississippi. Adjoining the depot is a proving ground where guns from the Rock Island Arsenal have been tested.

Low bluffs are seamed with shallow valleys and miniature ravines. The flood plain—damp, cool, green—presents a quiet picture of pastoral loveliness. Herds of dairy and beef cattle dot the low-lying meadows; the better drained fields are in corn, hay, or small grains. Dense forest mass up along the water's edge to obscure the broad river.

Highway and railroad are narrowly squeezed between bluff and river at the northern entrance, 14 *m*., to MISSISSIPPI PALISADES STATE PARK (*picnic, camping facilities*), a beautiful 1,368-acre park on the towering cliffs. Its sheer bluffs, fern-clad slopes, weather-worn crags and densely wooded areas bring to mind the Palisades of the Hudson. In summer the valleys and slopes are brightened with a mosaic of violets, bluebells, lobelias, bellworts, and wild geraniums. In this northern section is a magnificent stand of white birch. The deep ravines are filled with ferns, and rare plants interest botanists.

The main entrance, 17 *m*., leads to the custodian's lodge, a shelter house, picnic grounds, and a refreshment stand. Foot and bridle trails—some 15 miles in length—radiate from the valley and wind through the park. SUNSET TRAIL, near the entrance, SENTINEL TRAIL, and FERN VALLEY TRAIL are among the most popular. Below the summit of the bluffs the river sweeps far to the north and south, the force of its current opposed only by bayous and side-channels, islands and wooded marshlands. In the background above the river rise the imposing hills of Iowa.

Another entrance leads to a Lilliputian valley in which camp sites border a broad expanse of lawn and trees; tables, a fountain, and fireplaces have been built here in shady nooks. INDIAN HEAD, a promontory, rises from the shaded depth of woodland and surveys the river. According to an old legend, the rock face was carved by an Indian. Another natural formation, a pair of tall columns, spring from a huge rock base. Their general outlines are those of human figures and they are called Twin Sisters. Numerous Indian mounds have yielded relics; old Indian trails and stagecoach roads can still be traced.

The Southern Entrance, 18.4 m., opens into a tiny parking and picnic ground, backed by high bluffs. The trail to the south winds up a wooded, mossy ravine to a shelter on the cliff top, from which is a fine view of downstream of Savanna's waterfront. The northern trail to the shelter is longer and rougher. The view upstream from the cliff reveals an impressive profile of the bluffs, cutoff channels, wooded islands, meandering inlets, and a vast forested expanse of bottomland.

At the southern edge of the park, 18.9 m., is the junction with US 52 (see Tour 15), which unites with Illinois 84 for 2 miles through SAVANNA, 20 m. (592 alt., 4,942 pop.). See Tour 15.

Proceeding southward, Illinois 84 swings back several miles from the river and traverses a broad sandy terrace near the base of valley bluffs. The country with its short sear prairie grass suggests the arid high plains; the impression is heightened by the herds of white-faced Herefords that graze by the roadside, seeming as much at home as on the staked plains of Texas, from which many of them were brought to be fattened before being shipped to market. Near occasional cultivated fields stand fine white farmsteads, with large corncribs, clean barns and tile or concrete silos. Many farms along the railroad have their own chutes and pens for handling the large herds of yearlings and 2-year-olds, which are each year imported from the western range, fattened on pasture, grain, and silage, and sold in the markets.

The region around THOMSON, 31 m. (606 alt., 617 pop. 1970; 543, 1960) is a popular rendezvous for duck hunters; the marshy backwaters, bayous, and sluggish tributaries of the Mississippi are feeding grounds for the flocks of ducks and geese that twice annually follow the Mississippi Flyway between the Gulf of Mexico and northern Canada.

On the lawn of the new Community High School two milestones inscribed Pettit Mill, 1860, recall the early industry that created many an Illinois village.

Between Thomson and Fulton the landscape assumes an even more arid appearance, intensified by large areas of low sand dunes. The dry bluffs and terrace are not the result of a deficiency in rainfall, but are due to the sandy nature of the soil. Melons once were the principal crop in the area; general farming is now characteristic.

At 35 m. is the junction with a graveled road. Right on this road is Lock and Dam No. 13, 18 m., built by the Federal Government as a link in the 9-foot channel of the Upper Mississippi. The streamlined facilities are navy-trim in their bright coat of aluminum paint. Barge line tonnage of commodities moved through Lock and Dam No. 13 in 1972 was 15,329,270, according to the Rock Island District, Corps of Engineers, USA.

FULTON, 83 m. (598 alt., 3,630 pop. 1970; 3,387, 1960, inc. 7.2%) a city in Whiteside County, is at a junction with US 30; also is reached over a toll bridge by Iowa 136, which connects with nearby

Clinton, Iowa. The small village of East Clinton, Ill., is opposite Clinton.

ALBANY, 45 *m.* (596 alt., 942 pop. 1970; 637, 1960) a village in Whiteside County, is in a truck garden area where fertile farmland has been reclaimed by building dikes and draining river sloughs. Because of its location on high bluffs Albany escapes flood damage from the Mississippi River. Chemical plants are located in an industrial park south of the village.

CORDOVA, 54 *m.* (589 pop. 1970; 502, 1960) a village in Rock Island County that has been little more than a steamboat landing for a century, is expanding with new industry. It is the site of the QUAD-CITY NUCLEAR GENERATING STATION, a joint project of Iowa-Illinois and Commonwealth Edison Co. of Chicago. It has two generating units each of 809,000 kw. The 3M Company of St. Paul, Minn., has been erecting a new chemical plant of 11 industrial buildings on 375 acres including office building, warehouse, fire station and maintenance housing. The Cordova Industrial Park has attracted other large enterprises.

PORT BYRON, 59 *m.* (1,222 pop. 1970; 1,153, 1960) a village in Rock Island County, is popular with the residents of the nearby Quad-City metropolis for camp sites and recreation. In the early steamboat days it was a station for refueling wood-burning boats.

RAPIDS CITY, 63 *m.* (656 pop. 1970; 675, 1960), a village in Rock Island County, lies a short distance above Lock and Dam No. 14. This dam, like all others on the Mississippi from Alton to the Twin Cities, is designed to maintain a 9-foot channel throughout, to prevent floods on the upper reaches, and to regulate the volume of water in the great river below its confluence with the Missouri and the Ohio. The locks are opened to any craft, day or night, summer or winter, principally to long tows of barges carrying heavy cargoes of limestone, sand, potash, and petroleum products. Many of the boats are twin-screw powered by Diesel engines.

Interstate 80, expressway from Chicago, after bypassing Moline and East Moline has a junction with Illinois 84 at the south limits of Rapids City and crosses the Mississippi River to Iowa at a point south of Le Claire, Iowa.

HAMPTON, 65.5 *m.* (1,612 pop. 1970; 742, 1960), a stop during steamboat and stagecoach days. Hampton long retained the appearance of a mid-19th century village, but in recent decades it has replaced taverns and warehouses with modern shops and new housing. It also attracts vacation parties, because the ILLINIWEK FOREST PRE-SERVE of 160 acres is located entirely inside the village.

At 68 *m.* a side road leads to CAMPBELL'S ISLAND on the Mississippi, where 5 acres have been set aside as an Illinois State Memorial commemorating the battle of Campbell's Island. In 1812 a number of keel boats carrying 42 soldiers of the First U. S. Infantry and 66 rangers commanded by Captain John Campbell came upriver from St. Louis to intercept a force of Indians coming downstream in canoes from Prairie du Chien, led, it is said, by British officers. Campbell's force was surprised by the Indians and in the ensuing fight one American longboat was destroyed. No further action is reported. The boat was left for many years on the island. A shaft recording the battle has been erected by the Daughters of the American Revolution.

Illinois 84 continues to SILVIS and EAST MOLINE, then climbs the bluffs to the upland level, turns abruptly westward, and ends at the junction with US 6 in MOLINE, 75 *m. See Tour 14 and article on ROCK ISLAND and MOLINE.*

⪼⪻⪼⪻⪼⪻⪼⪻⪼⪻⪼⪻⪼⪻⪼⪻⪼⪻⪼⪻⪼⪻⪼⪻⪼⪻⪼⪻⪼⪻⪼⪻⪼⪻⪼⪻⪼⪻

Tour 7

DOWN WEST CENTRAL ILLINOIS FROM ROCK ISLAND TO EAST ST. LOUIS

Rock Island — Monmouth — Macomb — Carthage — Rushville — Beardstown — Jacksonville — Carrollton — Jerseyville — Godfrey — Alton—Hartford—Granite City—East St. Louis

US 67. Illinois 287. Illinois 3. 245 *m.*

US 67 is the principal north-south highway from Rock Island, a unit of the Quad Cities, to East St. Louis, part of the industrial complex dominated by St. Louis, Mo. The route runs south in a fairly straight line and crosses the Mississippi at Alton, while the road to East St. Louis becomes Illinois 3. After Jacksonville the original US 67 is now Illinois 287, and because this touches Carrollton and Jerseyville and places west it is described as an optional part of this Tour.

Section a. Iowa Line to Beardstown, 121 m.

This section of western Illinois is a fertile upland, crossed at regular intervals by forested valleys, which drain east or west into the great rivers that bound the region. In the small towns and old cities remain many relics of post-Civil War housing—plain brick houses close to the street, and gabled frame cottages exemplifying the carpenter's ingenuity.

ROCK ISLAND, 0.5 *m.* (50,166 pop.) and MOLINE (46,237 pop.) are at a junction with US 6. *See Rock Island and Moline.*

US 67 crosses the Rock River, 5 *m.*, and enters MILAN, 5.7 *m.* (4,873 pop. 1970; 3,065, 1960), in Rock Island County. The Mississippi bluffs, high above the water level, recede a mile or two from the river at Moline and Rock Island, but converge upon the Rock River at Milan. Their summits afford an excellent view of the low alluvial bottom land that borders both streams.

A marker, 6.4 *m.*, indicates that Abraham Lincoln, on May 8, 1832, while encamped approximately one mile west of this point, was mustered into the military service of the United States. A few days earlier he had been elected captain of a militia company from Sangamon County, which had assembled at Beardstown.

At the marker is a junction with an improved road. Right on this road to ANDALUSIA, 7.8 *m.* (950 pop. 1970; 560, 1960). Clark's Ferry, from Andalusia to Buffalo, Iowa, was a noted river crossing above St. Louis in the 1830s, and carried thousands of settlers to the Iowa territory. Early land speculators laid out a paper town at this site. Their elaborate maps, plats, and design showing a beautiful city with thriving steamboat wharves, were so convincing that the schemers sold thousands of dollars worth of town lots in the East. When the bubble burst, the city that was destined to be the "metropolis of the Middle West" became the peaceful village of Andalusia.

Today the community's sole industry is the manufacture of pearl buttons from clam shells found in the shallow sloughs and lagoons of the Mississippi. The clams are gathered in flatboats that drag behind them chains with dozens of four-pronged hooks. Open mussels close their shells instantly upon the hooks and are hauled into the boat; in shallow water the clams are gathered with rakes and forks. Button-making is a slow and tedious hand operation; each button is shaped singly by a rapidly revolving, water-cooled, cylindrical cutter, against which the shell is held. The size of the buttons is determined by the shape and thickness of the shell, which vary widely in different kinds of mussels.

South of Milan the highway climbs the Mississippi Bluffs to the upland level, a pleasantly varied region of broken prairie and woodland and deeply incised valleys. Numerous birds, among them the colorful cardinal and bluejay, hawks, owls, and an occasional eagle, inhabit this area. On the prairies are fine farms, with large corn cribs and silos, that specialize in hogs and dairy cattle. Sheep are pastured on the rougher lands.

VIOLA, 23.3 *m.* (797 alt., 946 pop. 1970; 812, 1960), is the center of local coal mining activities. Several mine shafts are visible from the highway in the vicinity of the village.

Right from Viola on Illinois 17 to ALEDO, 7.9 *m.* (738 alt., 3,325 pop. 1970; 3,080, 1960), seat of Mercer County. Because of the extensive trading area it serves, the business district of Aledo is unusually large and modern in appearance. Although the land here ranks among the most productive in the State, the first settlers bought it so cheaply that a single crop sometimes paid for an entire farm.

Aledo is at a junction with Illinois 94. The Essley-Noble Historical Museum, started by the late E. L. Essley and conducted by the Mercer County Historical Assn., was opened in October, 1959.

West on Illinois 17 15 *m.* to NEW BOSTON (706 pop. 1970;

726, 1960) on the Mississippi River opposite its confluence with the Iowa River. Once a steamboat landing, it was surveyed by A. Lincoln on Sept. 30, 1834. The original town site was 240 acres acquired from the Federal Government by John W. and William Denniston.

Between Viola and Monmouth, US 67 crosses numerous tributaries of the Mississippi that have carved their wooded valleys deep in the fertile upland. The first settlers came up these streams and homesteaded in the valleys. One man, it is said, housed his family in a hillside cave, dug a vertical passageway for a chimney. One evening, while the settler's daughter was entertaining a suitor before the fireplace, a venturesome calf that had been grazing on the hill above lost its footing and tumbled down the chimney.

MONMOUTH, 47 m. (762 alt., 11,022 pop. 1970; 10,312, 1960, inc. 6%), commemorates the Revolutionary War battle of Monmouth, New Jersey. Established in 1831 as the seat of Warren County, which honors the memory of Joseph Warren, major general of militia at Bunker Hill, Monmouth, in common with other prairie towns, was long handicapped by bad roads. Early roads were wagon ruts at best; at worst, an endless succession of mud holes. In wet weather flatboats on wheels, drawn by horses, were used to transport people and merchandise. When Lincoln visited Monmouth in 1858 the streets were in such condition from recent rains that he had to proceed on foot. Plans for the welcoming committee to meet him on the Oquawka road had to be cancelled. Not until 1891, when Dr. William Taylor was elected mayor on a platform of paving the streets, were conditions bettered. Two years later Monmouth Township set to work surfacing its roads, and Warren County shortly after led the way in hard road construction.

Setting the cultural pace of the community is Monmouth College, on E. Broadway between 7th and 9th Sts., a coeducational institution founded in 1853 by the United Presbyterian Church. The college buildings on the tree-shaded, 30-acre campus lend a pleasant quiet beauty to the civic scene. In 1972-73 the college enrolled 1,275 and had a faculty of 104.

The Birthplace of Wyatt Earp, famous western marshal, was commemorated September 5, 1956, when a plaque on a 15,000-lb. block of granite was placed at 406 S. Third St., during the Warren County Prime Beef Festival. The granite was brought from Minnesota and presented to the city of Monmouth by the Minneapolis & St. Louis Railroad. A direct descendant of the marshal, 8-year-old Wyatt Earp of Reynolds, was present.

The WARREN COUNTY LIBRARY, 60 West Side Square, was erected in 1907 and modernized in 1970. In 1971 it had approx. 100,000 books and a circulation of 225,000. It is hq of the Western Illinois Library System.

Monmouth is 15 m. west of Galesburg on US 34, which proceeds west to the Mississippi River and crosses to Burlington, Iowa, on a toll bridge.

South of Monmouth the country is flat and largely cropped. This is a region of beef cattle finishing. The white-faced Herefords shipped in from the western range and the Aberdeen-Angus raised locally are fattened on corn here. Attractive houses and corn cribs are conspicuous features of most farmsteads.

ROSEVILLE, 60 *m*. (736 alt., 1,111 pop. 1970; 1,065, 1960), a livestock shipping point on the Burlington Railroad was originally called Hat Grove, because a nearby clump of trees resembled a man's hat. In early days farm products of the region were hauled by wagon from Roseville to Oquawka and shipped by Mississippi River boats to southern markets. Today the community is the center of an important clover, oats, and soy bean producing area.

GOOD HOPE, 71.6 *m*. (714 alt., 447 pop. 1970; 394, 1960), a village in McDonough County, is spotted from afar by its grain elevator. Many communities in this district have had two or three names in succession, but Good Hope had three, and possibly four, at once. In 1866 J. E. Morris platted the village of Sheridan here on the proposed line of the railroad. The following year W. F. Blandin laid out a rival town bordering it on the west, and called his future metropolis Milan. In the meantime the local post office was already known as Good Hope. While the railroad issued tickets to Sheridan the mail was addressed to Good Hope. There is a junction here with east-west route Illinois 9.

MACOMB, 79.5 *m*. (702 alt., 19,643 pop. 1970; 12,135, 1960, inc. 61.6%) seat of McDonough County, in the heart of the western prairie, is 150 *m*. north of St. Louis and 230 *m*. southwest of Chicago. It is served by US 136, connecting with Inter. 55; US 67, connecting with Int. 80, and is on the Burlington Route main line. It has 692 acres of park and recreation land and Argyle Lake State Park a few miles west near US 136. Macombs' principal products are roller bearings, pottery and thermos ware.

Macomb has a mayor and city council. It was called Washington in 1830, later changed its name to honor Alexander Macomb, commanding General of the United States Army (1828-1841), who, according to a tablet in Chandler Park, "served his country during a period of more than forty years without stain or blemish upon his escutcheon." It was incorporated as a village in 1841, and as a city in 1856. That the settlers of western Illinois, many of whom came from New England, honored their early military leaders is shown in the name of McDonough County, which commemorates Commodore Thomas Macdonough, hero of the battle of Lake Champlain (1814).

Abraham Lincoln stopped at the Randolph House in Macomb during his campaign against Stephen A. Douglas. The McDonough County Courthouse, of red brick painted a cream color with foundation and trim of Sagetown limestone, was completed in 1872. An inscription on the cornerstone states that it was laid by the Grand Lodge A. F. & A. M., A. D. 1869, Aug. 14—A. L. 5869. The house is the third to occupy the site. The first, built in 1831 of logs, cost $69.50. The second, a two-story, square brick building was erected 1833-34 and used until 1869.

WESTERN ILLINOIS UNIVERSITY was established in 1899 as Western Illinois State Normal School when citizens of Macomb and vicinity donated 70 acres to the State. It opened September 23, 1902. After several changes of name it became Western Illinois University in 1957. It now has nearly 40 buildings on its campus of more than 750 acres, a farm of 90 acres, and a Life Sciences Station on the Mississippi River, 40 *m.* away. Education is still important in its curriculum but it has seven schools and one graduate school. Its architecture is eclectic, but recent construction has been of modern high-rise design. Among the new buildings at the university is the Katharine Thompson Hall, a 19-story building that cost $8,000,000 and has quarters for 615 men and 615 women. Another is a 13-story structure with accommodations for 824 students, and there is a housing complex of 233 units for married students.

WIU has a faculty of 618 and enrolls more than 10,000 students annually. It has instituted faculty and student representation in councils that recommend policies to the President. A program of Black Studies includes African and American black history, civil liberties, and social problems. Student expenses are estimated at $1,406 for a year of 36 weeks, including tuition, board and room. Varsity teams take part in 11 intercollegiate sports. A flight training program, leading to a pilot's license, is available to senior cadets in R. O. T. C.

Macomb opened a new Comprehensive High School and Vocational Training Center in September, 1969. The Macomb City Public Library, 235 S. Lafayette St. stocks around 35,000 books and circulates 65,000. It is a member of the Western Illinois Library System.

A commercial airport 3 *m.* north of the city provides two daily round trips to O'Hare International Airport, carrying 10 passengers.

The Midwest Horseshoeing School is described as one of three in the United States that "offers an advanced course in horseshoeing."

Side Trip to Carthage

An easy side trip from Macomb is west 37 *m.* on US 136 to CARTHAGE (3,350 pop. 1970; 3,325, 1960), seat of Hancock County and a distributing point for livestock and farm products. It has a number of industries producing feed, fertilizer, and cheese. Carthage is at a junction with Illinois 94 (north-south).

Incorporated in 1837 the community subsequently became an anti-Mormon stronghold. In the old jail Joseph Smith, founder of the Church of Jesus Christ of Latter-day Saints (Mormon), and his brother Hyrum were killed by a mob on June 27, 1844. Awaiting trial on charges of destroying an opposition press in Nauvoo, Joseph and Hyrum Smith had been lodged in jail to protect them from attack. To insure Smith's safety, Governor Ford had previously disbanded several companies of militia, gathered, against his orders, at Carthage with the avowed purpose of going to Nauvoo to search for alleged apparatus for making counterfeit money, but in reality "to strike a terror into the Mormon people by an exhibition of the force of the State." The governor assigned the Carthage Grays to guard the jail while he went to Nauvoo to acquaint the Mormons with the "excitement and hatred prevailing against them" and to warn against their use of "open or secret violence."

During his absence more than a hundred members of the disbanded militia companies, faces blackened to hide their identity, returned to Carthage, overpowered the non-resisting Carthage Grays, and stormed the jail. The Mormon leaders, accompanied by their friends, Willard Richards and John Taylor, later head of the Mormon Church (1877-1887), were lodged in an upper room. A volley fired from the stairway killed Hyrum Smith. For a brief moment the Prophet armed with a small "pepper box" gun, tried to hold off the attack. When his gun missed fire, he ran to the window to leap out, but as he was silhouetted there three musket balls struck him. With an agonized "Oh Lord, my God," he toppled from the window. The mob rushed out, ascertained that he was dead, and then hastily dispersed. Richards had not been harmed, but Taylor received several wounds. *See the article on Nauvoo.*

The OLD CARTHAGE JAIL, a sturdy two-story building of gray stone, has undergone several changes since that distant afternoon. The building was sold to a private family in 1870. More recently it was acquired by the Mormon Church and restored in a small park, which also has an information office. It is visited by about 30,000 tourists annually, many of them Mormons.

Following the departure of the Mormons from Illinois, Carthage went its prosaic way as a farm trade center. Abraham Lincoln in his senatorial campaign against Stephen A. Douglas visited the city on October 22, 1858, and addressed a crowd of 6,000. A stone marker south of the entrance to the courthouse on the public square indicates the site where Lincoln spoke.

Until 1964 Carthage was the seat of CARTHAGE COLLEGE, a four-year coeducational institution under Lutheran sponsorship. It had been established as Hillsboro College in Hillsboro, Illinois, in 1847 and moved to Carthage in 1870. In 1964 the campus was closed and the college merged with one already established at Kenosha, Wisc., which continued the name of Carthage College. It remains an Illinois college legally.

ROBERT MORRIS JUNIOR COLLEGE, opened in 1965, under the State program for junior colleges, moved into the buildings of Carthage College. It enrolled 509 students in 1971 and had a faculty of 25.

Ahead on US 136 is HAMILTON, 37 *m.* (515 alt., 2,764 pop. 1970; 2,228, 1960) a city in Hancock County and shipping point for the fruit and farming area. Hamilton has shared with Keokuk, Iowa, the advantages of river transportation and development. Lock and Dam No. 19, commonly known as Keokuk Dam, is clearly visible from the bridge 1.5 miles west of Hamilton, over which US 136 crosses the Mississippi, here the Iowa Line, to Keokuk, Iowa (*see Iowa Guide*).

One of the 26 locks and dams designed to improve navigation on the Upper Mississippi, the Keokuk development is at the foot of the Des Moines Rapids at a point where the river drops sharply over a limestone ledge. It was originally built in 1913 at a cost of $23,000,000. In 1952-57 the lock was enlarged to 1,220 ft. at a cost of $13,500,000. Today a towboat with 12 barges fits easily into Lock 19, thus completing in one operation what formerly took three to five. The Burlington Railroad bridge crosses at the foot of the lock; it is 403.1 ft. long and gives the boats a clearance of 153 ft. The power-house is on the Iowa shore, flanked by the lock and a seawall that protects nearby railroad tracks. Nearby are the only dry docks on the Upper Mississippi. The dam develops 200,000 horsepower, which is transmitted to municipalities in Iowa, Illinois, and Missouri by cables supported on tall steel towers. St. Louis, 144 miles south, is supplied with power under a 99-year contract. Dam and power plant are owned and operated by private enterprise; lock and dry dock are controlled by the Federal government.

Right (north) from Hamilton, Illinois 96, part of the Great River Road follows the Mississippi 12 miles to Nauvoo, along the shore of beautiful LAKE COOPER, formed by Keokuk Dam and named for Hugh L. Cooper, chief engineer of the dam's construction. The Missisippi, subdued by the downstream dam, provides a placid surface for boating, bathing, fishing and duck-hunting. Summer cottages are on the wooded bluffs of the Iowa shore and among the hills bordering the roadside. The Illinois shore throughout the 12-mile drive is a succession of hills where dense woods shade patches of fern and wildflowers. *See article on Nauvoo.*

Illinois 96 continues 9 miles east and north of Nauvoo, through a region of vineyards that have long supported the local production of wine, to NIOTA, a tiny cluster of dwellings at the Illinois end of the bridge (*toll*). Illinois 96 crosses the Mississippi River to Fort Madison, Iowa.

Return to US 67:

INDUSTRY, 88 *m.* (669 alt., 558 pop. 1970) in McDonough County, was first settled by William Carter, who built a log cabin here in 1826. The village, organized two decades later, reflects in its name the condition on which Johnson Dowin gave John M. Price an acre of ground—that he open a blacksmith shop on the plot.

At 107 *m.* US 67 has a junction with US 24. West of the junction is KING-WEINBERG STATE PARK, suitable for picknicking. Northeast of the junction is RUSHVILLE (3,300 pop. 1970; 2,819, 1960), the seat of Schuyler County. Founded in 1825 it was named for Dr. William Rush, the famous Philadelphia physician.

It is the trading center of an extensive grain and fruit-growing district. During the Black Hawk War, Abraham Lincoln and his troops camped near Rushville. While they waited to move on a wrestling match was arranged between Lincoln and one Dow Thompson. When Thompson threw Lincoln twice, the latter's friends claimed a foul, but Lincoln declared that the two falls were fair, and added admiringly that Thompson "was as strong as a grizzly bear."

A tablet in the center of the public square recalls that here "Abraham Lincoln addressed the people of Rushville October 20th, 1858. He also practiced law in the courthouse which formerly stood on this spot." When Stephen A. Douglas arrived in Rushville to speak in the same senatorial campaign of 1858, his supporters borrowed a cannon from Beardstown, hauled it to the public square, and loaded it with powder and wet scraps of leather. When the salute to Douglas was fired, the cannon was blown into bits but no one was hurt.

Another story involving cannon is told of early Rushville. In 1844, it is said, Governor Ford left Springfield with a company of militia, and camped overnight in the village square on the way to Nauvoo. Ford decided to amuse himself with pistol practice, and set up a target near the home of James Little. Little, furious at having his sleep disturbed, invoked the local ordinance against shooting firearms in the village, swore out a warrant, and had Governor Ford arrested. Ford paid a fine and left for Nauvoo. On his return to Springfield, he passed through Rushville in the middle of the night, and ordered his men to fire a howitzer in the village square. When the cannon went off the frightened residents tumbled out of their beds. By the time they approached the scene of the shooting the governor and his troops were leaving the village.

The present Schuyler County Courthouse, dating from 1881, is a two-story building of brick, topped with a square clock tower. The cornerstone is dated according to the Masonic calendar, June 24, A. L. 5881. The first county building was a log cabin on the north side of the square; in 1829 it was replaced by a plain unornamented brick building which served until the present courthouse was built.

On the western border of Rushville is Scripps Park, formerly the 80-acre farm of Edward Wyllis Scripps (1854-1926), founder of the Scripps-Howard chain of newspapers. The park was given to the city in 1922 by Mr. Scripps and his sisters, Virginia and Ellen Browning Scripps. The latter contributed the $100,000 Community House that marks the site of the Scripps' farmstead, the birthplace of E. W. Scripps. Also provided by Miss Scripps were a golf course, tennis courts, athletic field, and caretaker's house.

US 67 has been routed south of Rushville to Beardstown and thus bypasses the old road, which reaches the valley of the Illinois at FREDERICK, a village on Illinois 100 and then proceeds 4 m. south to Beardstown. Between Frederick and the toll bridge the highway parallels the river across the flood plain. From the bridge the seawall and natural levee that protect Beardstown are clearly visible.

BEARDSTOWN, 121 m. (444 alt., 6,222 pop. 1970; 6,294, 1960) is located on the floor of the Illinois River valley, near the foot of Muscooten Lake and south of one of the finest fishing and wild fowl hunting grounds in the State. It is at a junction of US 67 with Illinois 100 on the east bank of the river. In 1819 Thomas Beard, from Ohio, rode up with General Murray McConnel of Edwardsville, and finding an Indian village at the foot of a burial mound decided to locate there. He built a cabin at the river's edge and began trading. This was bounty land, extremely fertile, and it soon attracted settlers from the east. In 1829 the place was platted for town lots and named after Beard. The town had seven blocks along the river front, three blocks deep, with a public square in the center block.

This public square, where concerts are given on summer evenings by the municipal band, is opposite the historic City Hall, built in 1844 as the Courthouse of Cass County and used thus until 1872, when the seat was moved to Virginia. This is a severe, two-story, red brick structure, distinguished by a single classical cornice, a gable pediment, and striking but somewhat modified classic lintels above the windows.

The courtroom was the scene of Abraham Lincoln's famous defense of Duff Armstrong, son of Lincoln's friend Jack Armstrong, who was tried here for murder. This was the Almanac Case, in which Lincoln controverted the testimony of an eyewitness by referring to the position of the moon. Duff and James H. Norris were charged with the murder of James Preston Metzker during a fight on Aug. 29, 1857, at a temporary bar set up one mile from a camp meeting near Virgin's Grove in Mason County. Norris was tried in Mason County, convicted and sentenced to eight years in prison, Lincoln, appealed to by Hannah Armstrong, Jack's widow and Duff's mother, agreed to assist William Walker in Duff's defense and obtained a change of venue to Cass County. At the trial, May 6-7, 1858, in Beardstown, the prosecutors based their case upon the testimony of Charles Allen, who stated that he saw Duff hit Metzker with a "slungshot" from about 150 ft. away by the light of the moon, which was nearly overhead. Lincoln produced an almanac by which he ascertained that the moon had been about to set. He then made an emotional appeal to the jury on behalf of this son of his old friends. This appeal and a doctor's testimony that Metzker's skull fracture could have been caused by a fall from a horse caused the jury to acquit Duff Armstrong. On the basis of this evidence Norris' case was reopened and he was released.

A re-enactment of the trial took place during the observance of the Beardstown centennial in 1929. This was repeated May 5, 6, and 7, 1958, by the Beardstown Rotary Club.

The City Hall is maintained as it was originally. It contains a collection of guns and Indian arrowheads, owned by Rudy Black, dishes used by Nancy Beard, wife of the founder, and other antique objects. The police headquarters is on the first floor.

Beardstown was the place of assembly of volunteers for the Black Hawk War in April, 1832. Lincoln was chosen captain of the company from Sangamon County and installed April 22, 1832, at a spot near the river, now the Recreation Park at the north end of Wall St. A plaque on a rock commemorates this event. The volunteers were mustered into State service on April 28 and marched to Rock Island, where they were sworn into the Federal service. In their 30 days in uniform they marched to Dixon's Ferry and Ottawa, where they were disbanded without having seen any fighting.

The city formerly suffered from severe river floods. In 1922 the water rose 23 ft. and broke through the levees to inundate an area 18 miles wide. A concrete wall, 29 ft. high, was built thereafter and the spring floods were checked.

The lakes in the conservation areas of the Illinois north of Beardstown are as important to commercial fishing as to vacationists. The lakes have large-mouth bass, crappie, bluegill, sunfish, and catfish.

Beardstown has freight service on the Burlington-Northern and the

Baltimore & Ohio. US 67 crosses the Illinois River on a high bridge of recent construction.

At Beardstown US 67, which formerly continued southeast 13 *m.* to Virginia and then turned south 16 *m.* to Jacksonville, has been rerouted to continue south in combination with Illinois 100 to within 3 *m.* of MEREDOSIA (1,178 pop. 1970) in Morgan County (*see Tour 22*) and MEREDOSIA LAKE, an arm of the Illinois, thence turning east via CHAPIN (582 pop. 1970) to Jacksonville. The former route is now Illinois 125, which climbs to the upland level of the valley of Lost Creek. The hamlet of BLUFF SPRINGS is located at the base of the sandy bluffs. Illinois 125 moves through Virginia to Springfield. US 67 continues on its newer route to Jacksonville.

Section b. Jacksonville to Alton

JACKSONVILLE, 0 *m.* (613 alt., 20,583 pop. 1970; 21,690, 1960, dec. 5.2%) is the seat of Morgan County (36,148 pop. 1970), which is largely agricultural. South Jacksonville, an incorporated city, had 2,950 pop. 1970; 2,340, 1960. Jacksonville is located 35 *m.* west of Springfield, 85 *m.* northeast of St. Louis and 235 *m.* southwest of Chicago. It is a junction for US 36, 54, 67; Illinois 78, 104, and has freight service from three railroads, Burlington, Illinois Central Gulf, and Norfolk & Western. The Municipal Airport on US 67, 2.7 *m.* north of the city, has regular connections with Springfield.

Jacksonville has 13 national industries employing approx. 3,500 making clothing, plastics, foods, margarines, industrial resins, adhesives, and bookbindings. One specialty produces ferris wheels for carnivals. Bookbinding for school use by the Hertzberg New Method binderies (Perma Bound) supplements the strong educational concentration in Jacksonville. Here are located two senior colleges, ILLINOIS COLLEGE, founded in 1829, and MacMURRAY COLLEGE, founded 1849. There are three long-established State institutions: ILLINOIS SCHOOL FOR THE DEAF, 125 Webster Ave., founded 1843 with nearly 500 students; ILLINOIS BRAILLE AND SIGHTSAVING SCHOOL, 658 E. State St., 1847, with about 220, and the JACKSONVILLE STATE HOSPITAL for the mentally retarded, 1201 S. Main St., with room for approx. 3,000.

Jacksonville Public Library, 201 W. College Ave., has more than 60,000 books and circulates approx. 90,000. It is a member of the Great River Library System, which has headquarters in Quincy. Two daily newspapers, morning and evening, are published by the Journal Courier Co.

Jacksonville was founded in 1825 and named for Andrew Jackson. First settled by Southerners, Jacksonville attracted so many Yankees that by the 1830s it was more New England in character than any other community in the State. Lincoln was often in Jacksonville, and his lecture on Discoveries and Inventions, February 11, 1859, was received with "repeated and hearty bursts of applause." The lecture was sponsored by Phi Alpha Society of Illinois College, which had elected Lincoln an honorary member.

ILLINOIS COLLEGE has a campus of 63 acres in the western part of the city. Beecher Hall, built in 1829 and restored in 1950, was named for the first president, Edward Beecher, brother of Henry Ward Beecher. It is now the meeting place of two literary societies. Sturtevant Hall, with a square tower, was built in 1847 and remodeled in 1865. A number of fine buildings are of recent construction, including Rummelkamp Chapel (1962), Crispin Science Hall (1963), and the Student Center (1967).

The college is associated with the United Church of Christ (Congregational Christian) and the United Presbyterian Church of the U.·S. A. It became coeducational in 1903 when the Jacksonville Female Academy was merged with it.

The TANNER MEMORIAL LIBRARY has more than 60,000 vols. in open stacks and numerous other materials. It has a collection of Lincolniana and one of books on the Civil War established by the Civil War Round Table of Springfield as a memorial of Benjamin P. Thomas, historian and a former trustee of the college.

The college charges $1,200 per semester for tuition, board and room, or $2,400 for the school year. It enrolls 800 students and has a faculty of 53.

A famous graduate of Illinois College was William Jennings Bryan, who was born in Salem on March 9, 1860 and entered Illinois College in 1889, when 19. After graduating in 1881 he attended Union College of Law in Chicago for two years. At Jacksonville he met Mary Elizabeth Baird of Perry in Pike County, who was attending the Female Academy, and on July 4, 1880, they became engaged. Bryan wanted to earn at least $500 a year before marrying, therefore their marriage was put off four years until 1884. On July 4, 1883, he had opened a law office in Jacksonville. Mrs. Bryan also studied law. Four years later they moved to Nebraska, where Bryan began his extraordinary political career as leader of the grass roots wing of the Democratic Party, three time candidate for President, and Secretary of State in the administration of President Woodrow Wilson. A granite boulder marks the site at College and Webster Aves. where the Bryans lived.

Another graduate of Illinois College was William H. Herndon, Lincoln's law partner in Springfield. Stephen A. Douglas began the practice of law here in 1834. On an occasion when the Democrats were pessimistic about the prospects of their party Douglas made a rousing speech in Jacksonville, causing his associates to call him the Little Giant. Jacksonville was the home of three Illinois Governors: Joseph Duncan (1834-38), Richard Yates the elder (1861-65), and Richard Yates the younger (1901-05). In Duncan Park, 4 Duncan Place, the Georgian house built in 1835 by Governor Duncan, Daniel Webster, Martin Van Buren, and Abraham Lincoln were entertained; it is now a chapter house of the Daughters of the American Revolution. Oldest woman's club in the United States is the Ladies Education Society of Jacksonville, organized in 1833.

The MORGAN COUNTY COURT HOUSE, built 1868, has two unusual square towers with mansard tops. A marker tells that Stephen A. Douglas was states attorney here in 1835.

MACMURRAY COLLEGE, 425 E. State St., is a senior liberal arts college established by Methodists in 1846 as the Illinois Conference Female Academy. Its present name was adopted in 1930 to honor Senator James H. MacMurray, who made large donations, including more than $4,000,000 for buildings and endowment. In 1955 the trustees founded MacMurray College for Men as a coordinate institution. In February, 1969, the college became coeducational. It is non sectarian but Christian in purpose and gets part of its support from the Central Illinois Conference of The Methodist Church.

There are about 20 Georgian and contemporary style buildings on a campus of 60 acres. The Annie Merner Chapel dates from 1949. The Chemistry Building was erected in 1964 and the Campus Center in 1965. The Henry Pfeiffer Library contains more than 100,000 volumes and many periodicals and reference materials, and provides seats for 314 students. It has collections of Lincolniana and Pepsysana. The college enrolls nearly 1,000 students and has a faculty of 68. It has two semesters and the separate month of January, and charges $3,500 a year, divided between $2,250 for tuition and fees and $1,150 for room and board.

SOUTH JACKSONVILLE (2,950 pop. 1970; 2,340, 1960) developed from a farming community to an extension of Jacksonville and incorporated as a city in 1911. It has several light industries including a book bindery.

In a realignment of highways US 67 was routed in a straight line south from Jacksonville to Alton. The former route, which has a bulge westward, is now Illinois 267. The towns that follow are reached on Illinois 267.

ROODHOUSE, 19 m. (650 alt., 2,357 pop. 1970; 2,352, 1960), a railroad center, was laid out by John Roodhouse, a pioneer farmer, at the junction of two branch lines of the Alton.

WHITEHALL, 23 m. (585 alt., 2,979 pop. 1970; 3,012, 1960), founded in 1820, is the center of an important clay field, in use since 1824, when William Heath began the manufacture of redware. The field supplies a large pottery which manufactures sewer pipe, stoneware, and drain tile; a narrow-gauge railroad connects the pottery with the clay pits. In the center of town is Lorado Taft's memorial to Anne Louise Keller, a teacher who lost her life saving her pupils during a tornado that destroyed the Centerville School in 1927. Illinois Central Gulf and the Burlington railroads give freight service.

CARROLLTON, 33 m. (625 alt., 2,866 pop. 1970; 2,558, 1960), settled in 1818, the seat of Green County, honors the memory of her two statesmen; Thomas Carlin (1789-1852), founder of Carrollton and seventh governor of Illinois, and Henry T. Rainey (1860-1934), Speaker of the House in the Seventy-third Congress. A monument to Thomas Carlin is on the courthouse lawn. On the north edge of Carrollton, in Rainey Memorial Park, stands a bronz life-size statue of Henry T. Rainey. Executed by Frederick C. Hibbard, Chicago sculptor, the statue depicts Rainey gavel in hand, as he presided over the House of Representatives.

Indian artifacts found at the Koster farm near Eldred are preserved at the Lower Illinois Valley Archaeological Museum in the Geers Building at Carrollton. The Greene County Historical Museum on the west side of the Square has portraits of Henry T. Rainey and other pioneers among its collections.

Left, west, from Carrollton on Illinois 108 to WALNUT HALL, 1 *m.*, the estate of Henry T. Rainey. The spreading three-story brick house with imposing columns and solid black walnut woodwork throughout marks the entrance to a 485-acre model farm. Rainey was an enthusiastic farmer; during the years he practiced law in Carrollton and later he took an active part in the management of the farm. He also collected many unusual antiques, including engravings, rare editions of books, early American furniture and a Seth Thomas clock once the property of Thomas Jefferson. North of the house a campground borders an artificial lake.

Continue west from Carrollton on Illinois 107 7 *m.* to ELDRED (292 pop. 1970; 302, 1960), a village that has become a stop for the KOSTER ARCHAEOLOGICAL SITE, 6 *m.* south on a country road. Here in 1969 Dr. Stuart Streuver, urged by a farmer, opened a large pit that disclosed evidence by soil and artifacts that this had been inhabited by Indians from as long ago as 6,000 B. C. Investigating a cornfield owned by Theodore Koster, Dr. Struever found 15 horizons, or layers of separate settlements. With donated funds and the help of student scientists and high school boys he had opened a pit 120 ft. long, 30 to 77 ft. wide, and 34 ft. deep by summer, 1973. Three miles west is the Illinois River and on the west bank in Calhoun County is KAMPSVILLE (439 pop. 1970; 453, 1960) where Dr. Struever has installed a laboratory and a computer in an old store. The soil is put through screens, and bones, shells, and other Indian objects are cleaned and studied. The age of the artifacts is established by carbon dating. The digging has attracted thousands of tourists, some of whom stop at motels in Hardin and Carrollton. The site is open weekdays 9-5, Sundays 10-5, and a ferry and a bus run from Kampsville. At times lectures are given in St. Anselm's Hall there. Kampsville was partially inundated during the April, 1973, floods. The *Delta Queen* has made it a port of call for excursionists who wish to visit the diggings.

Return east on Illinois 108 to Carrollton and proceed south on Illinois 267 13 *m.* to:

JERSEYVILLE, 46 *m.* (652 alt., 7,446 pop. 1970; 7,420, 1960) is the seat of Jersey County and the home of many retired farmers. The town ships, in addition to local produce, much of the apple crop of Calhoun County, which is trucked in from Hardin.

Right from Jerseyville on Illinois 16 to HARDIN, 19 m. (440 alt., 1,035 pop. 1970; 1,040, 1960), on the Great River Road. It is the seat of Calhoun County and distributing center of a prosperous apple-growing region. The only county in Illinois not served by a railroad, Calhoun is a rolling, sparsely settled strip of upland squeezed between the Mississippi and Illinois Rivers.

An apple blossom festival is held here each spring, when the countryside is festooned with fragrant white flowers; participants in the festival travel a 15-mile route that pierces the region's finest orchards. In October an apple harvest celebration is climaxed by the crowning of an Apple Queen.

Hardin history contains several colorful anecdotes. Formed from a section of Pike County in 1825, Calhoun was so heavily wooded and its lumberjack population so unstable that a bill entitled An Act to Abolish Calhoun County narrowly escaped ratification by the State Assembly of 1836-37. John Shaw, otherwise known throughout the region as the Black Prince, controlled the political affairs of the county during its first decade of existence. Of heroic physique and compelling personality, the Black Prince, according to tradition, operated a country store, raised cattle, speculated in land, and rigged county elections. Shaw became county commissioner following a turbulent election marked by charges of poll-book tampering, deed-forging, and other flagrant irregularities. Deposed in a subsequent political encounter, the Black Prince finally fled the county.

South of Jerseyville the landscape becomes more rolling as the highway nears the Mississippi River.

At 4 m. is a junction with Illinois 109. Right on 109 is a junction with an improved road, 3.1 m.

Left 3 m. on this road to ELSAH (928 pop. 1970; 507, 1960) a village in Jersey County, isolated in a valley on the river. Here in 1847 came Addison Greene, to build a cabin and live by selling cordwood to steamboats. Other wood-choppers followed Greene, and eventually the settlement of Jersey Landing came into being. Attracted by the prospect of river commerce, Gen. James Semple, one-time senator from Illinois, acquired Jersey Landing in 1853, changed its name to Elsah, and developed the community by giving a lot to any settler who would build a stone house thereon. A distillery and two grist mills were established, and the village enjoyed brief prosperity as a shipping port for farm produce. When the locomotive superseded the steamboat Elsah died as a port.

In 1888 the isolated village was almost reconnected with the outer world. In that year the owners of Eads Bridge, the only bridge then to span the Mississippi at St. Louis, thwarted the entry of Jay Gould's railroad into that city. Gould's engineers thereupon mapped their route to Elsah, where a bridge was to carry the rails to Missouri. Elsah, aroused by the possibility of a new lease on life, was disappointed at the last minute, when, after grades and culverts had been completed. Gould made an eleventh-hour deal with the proprietors of Eads Bridge, and abandoned his Elsah enterprise.

Askew Creek, straddled by a stone bridge, trickles through the center of the village. Songbirds call across the tree-choked hollow. Iris, tulips, and hollyhocks border walks and roadway; rambler roses strew their color over fences and gates. Stone cottages front narrow streets.

East 1 *m.* from Elsah to PRINCIPIA COLLEGE, established by Christian Scientists. The college was founded in 1910 and moved to this site from St. Louis in 1935. Dormitories and classrooms of neo-Gothic and Tudor Gothic architecture are grouped to suggest the compactness of an English village. The Chapel, designed in the manner of the Georgian churches of Sir Christopher Wren, has a lofty spire, a white panelled interior, and box pews lined with red damask. The college confers a bachelor of arts degree in foreign languages, history and social science, English and aesthetics, and mathematics and natural science. In 1972 the college enrolled 787 and had a faculty of 71.

Ahead on Illinois 109 is GRAFTON, 7.5 *m.* (446 alt., 1,018 pop. 1970, 1,084, 1960), at the confluence of the Illinois and the Mississippi. Peck, in his *Gazetteer of Illinois,* summed up Grafton in 1834 as "a postoffice, one store, one tavern, and a number of families." The town at that time was owned by James Mason, who predicted that his village would become chief river port of Illinois. An incorporation was granted to Mason "for the purpose of converting into manufactured products, any article of the growth and production of this state, whether animal, vegetable, or fossil, and for the digging and exporting of stone." Peck optimistically observed, "It is expected that some of these branches of business will go forward." Forward they went, but tediously. In the post-Civil War years Grafton reached a fixed economic level which, though including a comfortable share of river commerce, was far below that hoped for by its founder. By the turn of the century the decline of the steamboat had forced Grafton to revert to fishing, boat-building, and "the digging and exporting of stone." Today, barge lines are carrying freight in increasing amounts.

West of Grafton Illinois 100 follows the bluff-bordered shore of the Illinois River. A Stone Cross, 9.7 *m.,* man-high and rough-hewn, marks the place where Marquette, Jolliet, and their companions entered Illinois in 1673, "dawn-heralds of religion, civil government, and consecrated labor."

PERE MARQUETTE STATE PARK, 14 *m.,* commemorates the explorer, who described the bluffs as "frightful for their height and length." Its area has been increased through the years to 6,017 acres and its rugged hills tower above the Illinois. From their summits the Illinois and Mississippi look like tiny streams threading their way across a meadow of uninterrupted green. At the entrance is the Park Lodge, its broad terrace commanding a sweeping view of the great valley. The main park road winds upward over successive hills to McAdams

Peak. Other roads, bridle paths, and hiking trails wind for miles through the park, connecting picnic grounds and hill-top stations.

South of Jerseyville continue on Illinois 267 through the farm villages of Delhi and New Delhi to GODFREY, 64 *m.* (242 pop. 1970; 97, 1960). Here 267 joins US 67, which has been routed due south from Jacksonville, passing through several farm villages, including ROCKBRIDGE, (256 pop. 1970, 253, 1960); MEDORA (505 pop. 1970, 447, 1960) and BRIGHTON (1,889 pop. 1970; 1,245, 1960).

Godfrey is the site of the former MONTICELLO COLLEGE, one of the first institutions west of the Alleghanies to offer advanced education to women. It was founded in 1835 and lasted until July 1, 1971, after 133 years of service. Godfrey was named for Benjamin Godfrey (1794-1862) a retired Cape Cod sea captain, who financed the first stone college building with $45,000 and thereafter continued as a benefactor of college and town, serving as college trustee for many years. The first principal of Monticello was Theron Baldwin, who had come west in 1834 with the Yale Band, "a group of Yale Seminary graduates dedicated to bringing culture to the prairie by building educational and religious institutions."

The Monticello College Foundation was formed in 1971 to administer the school's endowment funds. Records, comprising 37,500 items, were turned over to the Illinois State Historical Library; they included a letter by Lincoln of 1851, not previously known, and other historical papers of value.

When Monticello closed the gray stone buildings and wooded campus of 214 acres were bought by the board of trustees of the LEWIS AND CLARK COMMUNITY COLLEGE, which opened with 946 students. It offers a comprehensive junior college program, with courses in academic, vocational, adult education, and technical subjects. In 1972 it reported enrollment of 2,170 and a faculty of 139. Its historic chapel has been designated one of America's landmarks.

The Godfrey Mansion is a two-story gray limestone building housing a private collection of Indian artifacts and early Illinois farm implements.

ALTON, 66 *m.* (438 alt., 39,700 pop. 1970). *See Alton.*

US 67 moves through North Alton on Belle St., has a junction with Illinois 3 at the river's edge and proceeds across the Mississippi over the Lewis & Clark Bridge (*free*) on which it crosses the Missouri line. After 3.1 *m.* it passes close to the village of West Alton, Mo., and 3.4 *m.* farther on crosses the Missouri River, 22 *m.* north of St. Louis.

Illinois 3 now proceeds south along the east bank of the Mississippi River to East St. Louis.

Section c. *Alton to the Missouri Line, Illinois 3*

EAST ALTON, 4 *m.* (430 alt., 7,309 pop. 1970; 1,630, 1960) is one of the industrial towns of Wood River Township. Its largest plant, the Olin Works of the Olin Matthiesen Corp., originated here in 1893 from a start made by Franklin W. Olin, who manufactured black powder to be used in mining coal in the area. This plant covers 1,260 acres and employs approx. 7,000 in three divisions, one of which, the Winchester-Western, continues the small arms production of the former Western Cartridge Co. Another division deals with brass casting and milling.

East Alton has a village board and an elected mayor who presides. Its Municipal Bldg. was erected in 1960 and has a large lobby with a decorative fountain, around which the public offices are located. The East Alton Vital Services Bldg., opened in 1969, has offices of the police and fire departments and a courtroom.

The Airline Drive leads to the Civic Memorial Airport, 3 m. which is near the village of BETHALTO (7,074 pop. 1970; 3,235, 1960, inc. 118%). The airport has three runways and covers 1,000 acres. Bethalto opened its new Municipal Bldg. in December, 1963.

Wood River enters the Mississippi in East Alton. The Wood River Massacre, July 10, 1814, took place between the two forks of the Wood River.

WOOD RIVER, 5 m. (430 alt., 13,196 pop. 1970; 11,694, 1960, inc. 12%) is located east and south of the Wood River and East Alton, with which it is contiguous. It is part of the tightly concentrated industrial area in Wood River Township (40,479 pop. 1970) dominated by oil refineries. Settlement in the area took place as early as 1810 at a vanished village named Milton, 3 m. from the mouth of Wood River. On July 10, 1814, occurred the Wood River Massacre, when Indians descended upon settlers between the two forks of the river. Among those killed were members of the Moore family; despite this another Moore took title to land here the following August.

The city of Wood River owes its corporate existence to the Standard Oil Co., which located a refinery here in 1908. It is now the American Oil Co. and processes 90,000 bbl. a day. When Wood River became the home of its labor force a construction camp nearby called Benbow City irritated the townspeople by its rowdy behavior and led to hostilities. Two policemen from both places are said to have fought a duel at the town line, in which the Benbow officer was killed. Later the Standard Oil Co. bought the site of Benbow and cleared the ground.

The city of Wood River has a council and manager form of government. Its suburbs and adjoining contiguous areas are so closely connected that the Township becomes the subject of civic promotion. The principal industries are located just outside the city limits. They include the largest refinery of Shell Oil Company, in ROXANA (1,882 pop. 1970, 2,090, 1960) employing 2,300 and processing 250,000 bbl. a day, and the Clark Oil Refinery, bought from the Sinclair Oil Corp. in 1967. A striking spectacle is that of the white geodesic dome of the Union Tank Car Co., built of hexagonal steel panels 120 ft. tall and 380 ft. in diameter.

The city has a part in the East Alton-Wood River Community High School District. The Wood River Public Library, built in 1957, stocks more than 36,000 books and circulates approx. 100,000 vols. a year.

HARTFORD, 7 *m.* (425 alt., 2,243 pop. 1970; 2,353, 1960) in an industrial village in Madison County. Its modern city hall was built in 1967.

The LEWIS AND CLARK STATE MEMORIAL, 5.9 acres, overlooks the confluence of the Missouri and Mississippi Rivers and commemorates the starting of the expedition into the Northwest ordered by President Thomas Jefferson and led by Meriwether Lewis and William Clark, 1804-06. The men camped in this area during the winter of 1804, broke camp May 14, 1804, and left St. Charles, Mo., May 21, proceeding up the Missouri River. They reached the future site of Bismarck, N. D., in November. On November 15, 1805, they reached the Columbia River. After studying the topography, climate, and contacting Indian tribes who had never seen white men, they returned to St. Louis Sept. 23, 1806, with 49 men, one Indian woman with infant, four horses, and one dog. An Indian woman, Sacjawea, had acted as guide.

Historians who have examined the records of the Lewis and Clark Expedition and the topography of the Mississippi, Missouri, and Wood Rivers, have concluded that the site of the camp was first completely obliterated by the Mississippi and later restored, but is now on the Missouri bank, whereas in 1803-04 it was on the Illinois bank of the Mississippi River.

Hartford named a city playground and park for Clint Walker, star of the television serial, *Cheyenne,* who grew up in Hartford and came back to dedicate the park.

GRANITE CITY

GRANITE CITY, 18 *m.* (431 alt., 40,440 pop. 1970; 40,073, 1960) in Madison County, is a major steel and metal fabricating center that has developed a market independently of the huge manufacturing organizations of East St. Louis, Ill., and St. Louis, Mo. Its industrial, financial, and residential interests are associated with those of MADISON (7,042 pop. 1970) and VENICE (4,680 pop. 1970), constituting the Tri-Cities. Workers have spread into adjacent communities, notably PONTOON BEACH and MITCHELL, and unincorporated areas in Madison County.

Granite City gets its name from a 19th-century process for coating iron kitchen utensils with a smooth enamel made with ground granite. Although settled by pioneers from Virginia, Kentucky, and Tennessee as early as 1815, the site remained in corn and wheat until near the present century. William F. Niedringhaus, a St. Louis industrialist, bought 3,000 acres in 1891. On a sultry August afternoon, Niedringhaus, accompanied by his son, George, ferried across the Mississippi and from the eminence of a buggy selected a plant site for his National Enameling & Stamping Company. The plant, along with scores of two-family flats, was constructed in 1892. Shortly afterwards the Niedringhaus interests built a rolling-mill; in 1893 the American Steel Foundry was established and, in 1896, Granite City was incorporated. It has a mayor and city council form of government.

Granite City Steel Co., which dates its origin back to 1878, has been the major employer for decades, enlisting the efforts of up to 5,000. Its integrated plant occupies 550 acres and its production is concentrated in plates, sheets, and other flat rolled steel products, including galvanized and tin plate. The minimum thickness of a sheet of flat-rolled steel is .004 of an inch; the maximum is one-half inch. Iron ore comes from the Lake Superior region in Michigan, southern Minnesota, and Iron Mountain, Missouri. The company's two blast furnaces can produce more than 3,500 tons of pig iron a day. Seven open hearth furnaces can each make more than 30 tons of steel per hour. The plant is completely equipped with automatic machinery and among the numerous "workhorses" that move huge loads are 91 electric overheadtraveling cranes. There are 32 miles of railroad inside the plant over which operate nine diesel switch engines. The Granco Steel Products Co., a subsidiary, carries on research and testing of products useful to the construction industry and markets them through its sales organization.

Important to the economy of the area is the Granite City Army Depot, established 1942 and administered by the Supply & Maintenance Command of the U. S. Army since 1962. In its vast installations on 1,000 acres it stores and issues supplies to the U. S. Army, repairs and overhauls equipment, and supervises training and gives logistical support to the U. S. Army Reserve and the National Guard. Its annual expenditures exceed $10,000,000.

Granite City has access to trunk line railroads, which move heavy freight. It has ten parks of 143 acres, of which Wilson Park is fully equipped for recreation and sports, and has a Community Center that features Music Under the Stars. The Tri-City Speedway has stock car and midget racing and in the environs Horseshoe Lake is a popular resort. The Acre of Art is a spring art show fostered by the Tri-Cities Chamber of Commerce; the Masquers bring Broadway shows to town, and the Children's Theatre is a year-round undertaking.

The Granite City Public Library has upwards of 115,000 books and circulates around 350,000. It is a member of the Lewis & Clark Library System. The Public School system supports a comprehensive vocational training and apprenticeship program with evening classes for all ages.

Much of the employment in Granite City is in heavy industry. Granite City Steel Industries, Inc., employs up to 2,500; American Steel Foundries, maker of castings for diesel locomotives, about 1,500; A. O. Smith Corp., maker of pressed steel auto frames, 1,800; Laclede Steel Co. 500. Other industries include Union Starch & Refining Co., The Nestle Co., and National Lead Co. The *Granite City Press-Record* is published on Monday and Thursday.

TRI-CITY PORT, the principal shipping area of Granite City

and environs is located on the CHAIN OF ROCKS CANAL, a waterway 8.4 *m.* long, which extends from one mile south of the Missouri River to approximately 3,800 ft. upstream from the Merchants Bridge, adjacent to the Granite City Engineer Depot. It was built by private contractors under direction of the Corps of Engineers, USA, to provide navigation around the Chain of Rocks Reach of the Mississippi River, where ledges of rock produce a current that often has a velocity of 12 ft. per second. The canal is 300 ft. wide at the bottom, 550 ft. wide at the top and has an average depth of 32 ft. About 23,000,000 cu. yds. of excavated material was used to build levees.

LOCK AND DAM NO. 27 are near the lower end of the canal. The main lock is 1,200 ft. long and the longest in the Mississippi River system, permitting the passage of long tows without having to break them into sections. Lock walls are 92 ft. high and rest on bedrock. An auxiliary lock is 600 ft. long and 110 ft. wide. The maximum lift at low water is 21 ft. and time required for filling the main lock is 7½ minutes. The canal and locks were opened to river traffic on February 7, 1953.

A NEW HIGHWAY BRIDGE to carry the combined US 66 and Interstate 270 over the canal was completed in December, 1949, at a cost of $1,585,072. It begins 3 *m.* west of MITCHELL in Chouteau Township and connects with the CHAIN OF ROCKS BRIDGE that spans the Mississippi to Missouri. It has an overall length of 2,368 ft. and 17 spans, of which the span over the canal is 465 ft. long and gives a clearance of 42.5 ft. above high water.

MADISON, 29 *m.* (425 alt., 7,042 pop. 1970; 6,861, 1960, inc. 2.6%) in Madison County, is the second largest of the Tri-Cities. The Madison Land Syndicate was formed in 1887 by St. Louis industrialists who wished to evade the high cost of bringing coal into St. Louis over the Eads Bridge. The Merchants Bridge was built in 1890 and is owned by the city. The American Car & Foundry Co. located a plant here in 1891. Madison was incorporated as a village in 1891 and as a city in 1942. The Madison Public Library received a new addition in 1968. It circulates between 25,000 and 30,000 books and is a member of the Lewis and Clark Library System. Among the industries are Owens Illinois Co., making paper products, and Dow Chemical Co., making aluminum and magnesium extruded rolled products in one of the country's largest mills.

VENICE, 1 *m.* from Madison (4,680 pop. 1970; 5,360, 1960, dec. 13%) is the third of the Tri-Cities. It is connected with St. Louis by the McKinley Bridge, which it controls. In its early days it was often inundated. It was platted in 1841 and became a village in 1873. Its interests are industrial. The Public Library, augmented in 1965, stocks over 25,000 books. It is a member of the Lewis and Clark Library System.

BROOKLYN, 1 *m.* from Venice, (415 alt., 1,702 pop. 1970; 1,922, 1960, dec. 11%) is just over the county line in St. Clair County.

It was settled largely by Negroes. When incorporated in 1874 it was named Lovejoy, after the Abolitionist editor, Elijah Lovejoy.

ILLINOIS 3 passes through Granite City, Madison and Venice to East St. Louis Illinois 111 from Alton, designated part of the Great River Road, has a junction with Illinois 162 at Madison and then joins the combined US 40, and Interstate 55 and 70, to East St. Louis.

EAST ST. LOUIS, 26 m. (69,996 pop., 1970). Numerous Illinois highways lead to East St. Louis, where some continue across the bridges to St. Louis. These include Interstate 55 and 70, US 40, US 56, US 50, US 66, and Illinois 3, 13, 15, 111. *See East St. Louis.*

Tour 8

HISTORIC OUTPOSTS OF THE FRENCH EMPIRE

East St. Louis—Old Cahokia—Red Bud—The American Bottom—
Prairie du Rocher—Fort Chartres State Park—Old Kaskaskia—Chester
—Murphysboro—Illinois Ozarks—Cairo
Illinois 3, 150 m.

Illinois 3 is a segment of the Great River Road and roughly parallels the Mississippi River. Traversing the southern portion of the East St. Louis industrial area, the route crosses a region of rolling prairies and woodlands which saw the first extensive settlement in the State—the heart of the American Bottom, center of French colonization in the 18th century. Between Chester and Cairo the highway follows the Mississippi bottom lands, sometimes at the water's edge, generally inland at the base of the bluffs. In its southern half the route crosses the Illinois Ozarks, most rugged section of Illinois, and then drops to the lowest point in the State, the delta on which stands Cairo, once a busy port at the confluence of the Ohio and Mississippi Rivers.

EAST ST. LOUIS, 0 m. (413 alt., 69,996 pop. 1970) *see East St. Louis.*

In East St. Louis are junctions with US 40, 50, 66, 460; Interstate 55, 70; Illinois 13, 15.

The Cahokia Power Plant, 3.4 m. one of the largest in the Mississippi Valley, was the first designed expressly for the use of low-grade Illinois coal in pulverized form. Large mills reduce the coal to a powder that is blown by compressed air into the fireboxes beneath the immense boilers. Each of the six smokestacks is 265 feet high and 21 feet in diameter at the top. The plant devours coal at the rate of one ton every 30 seconds.

CAHOKIA, 3.9 *m.* (407 alt., 20,649 pop. 1970; 15,829, 1960; inc. 30%), the oldest town in Illinois, has almost been swallowed by the encroaching industrial area of East St. Louis. Cahokia still exhibits a few relics from days when it was the seat of government.

Originally a summer camp of the Tamaroa Indians, it was visited in 1698 by Fathers Jolliet de Montigny, Antoine Davion, and Jean François Buisson de St. Cosme. The missionaries were guided by Tonti, the explorer called Iron Hand by the Indians, who marveled at this artificial hand. By May, 1699, St. Cosme had completed a house and chapel here, the first church in Illinois. These founders of Cahokia were of the Seminary of Foreign Missions, and shortly were opposed by the Jesuits, who previously had conducted all the missionary work in the Mississippi Valley. To Cahokia came the Jesuit Fathers, Julien Binneteau, Pierre Pinet, and Joseph Limoges, who began erecting another building as evidence of the rights of their order. When relations between the two orders became strained, Father Montigny went to France to obtain a settlement at court. On June 7, 1701, it was decreed that the Seminary of Foreign Missions "shall dwell alone in . . . Tamaroa and that they shall receive in a friendly manner the Jesuit fathers when they shall pass there in going to attend the Illinois and Tamaroa at their fishing and hunting grounds, where the said Jesuit fathers may establish themselves . . . ." The Jesuits retained jurisdiction over all the Mississippi Valley save Cahokia.

Around the the little mission grew a sizable trading post. Trade flourished and great cargoes of flour, lumber, pork, lead, and pelts were shipped by keelboat down the Mississippi to New Orleans.

Although Cahokia passed in British hands in 1765 and into American in 1778, it remained almost wholly French in character until the end of the century. George Rogers Clark's troops came in 1778, but were removed in 1780 and for 10 years the settlements in the American Bottom functioned largely as autonomous city-states. Cahokia, having a strong religious element, governed itself with admirable discipline, in sharp contrast to nearby settlements. In 1786 Cahokians requested Congress to refrain from placing them under the jurisdiction of Kaskaskia where the citizens were guilty of "incapacity, spite, and partiality." When the county of St. Clair was set up in 1790, Cahokia, Kaskaskia, and Prairie du Rocher were made joint county seats.

But hard feelings persisted, and in 1795 Gov. Arthur St. Clair carved the county in two and created St. Clair and Randolph Counties, and named Cahokia and Kaskaskia as their respective seats. In 1809 the boundaries of these two counties were redrawn so that they included all of what is now the State of Illinois. Cahokia was county seat for a territory now included in the 80 northern counties.

But Cahokia's decline was already under way. British jurisdiction had broken the influence of the Catholic Church, and in 1809 Father Urbain Guillet found the church buildings so dilapidated and the

Cahokians so indifferent that he announced he would refuse to read the mass until they repaired the roof and windows of their church. Political decline followed; in 1814 the county seat was moved to Clinton Hill, later called Belleville. The economic rise of St. Louis and East St. Louis, and the annual floods of the Mississippi, hastened Cahokia's decline.

Today the old French town is recalled by the CHURCH OF THE HOLY FAMILY, which in 1949 was restored to its original appearance with the use of vertical logs for its walls. Completed in 1799, it was the second church on the site, and was blessed in September by Father Rivet, pastor of Vincennes. The original walnut logs, hand-hewn and set upright, in the Canadian palisade type of construction, had been covered with clapboard, but are now exposed. A small cupola houses the bell. In the spring, 1971, it was proclaimed a national historic landmark. This culminated a 23-year campaign for national recognition, in which the St. Clair County Historical Society took the leading part. The church was founded in 1699 and is the oldest ecclesiastical structure west of the Alleghanies.

Behind the church is the old CAHOKIA CEMETERY, where for more than a century Indians, French colonists and Negro slaves were interred.

The old CAHOKIA COURTHOUSE, a cabin built of vertical logs, stands on its original site after numerous removals. Built as a dwelling before 1790, it was sold to St. Clair County in 1793 and used by the court until the county seat was moved to Clinton Hill, the later Belleville, in 1814. It was sold for $225 and used for storage and as a saloon. In 1904 it was removed to the St. Louis World's Fair, and after that to Jackson Park in Chicago, where it stood until 1939. Then the State bought it and returned it to its original site. Obviously little is left of the first cabin except the logs.

Nicholas Jarrot (Jarreau), a Frenchman who settled in Cahokia in 1794 and prospered as fur trader, land speculator, and office holder, has been called the mill builder of his times. Donald Zochert, Chicago writer, wrote in the *Journal* of the Illinois State Historical Society (Summer, 1962) that Jarrot first set up a horse mill, and later built a succession of water mills on Indian Creek. In 1815 Jarrot built a mill dam on Indian Ford at Cahokia Creek, but the pond was inadequate and the mill had to be rebuilt. A German immigrant, Ferdinand Ernst, in 1819 reported that the water wheel of Jarrot's mill operated while lying in the water with the shaft projecting upward. Zochert comments that the wheel was obviously a primitive turbine.

A four-story frame water mill was built by William Robb on Cahokia Creek in 1813. Robb shipped goods to St. Louis and New Orleans.

The JARROT MANSION a large two-story brick house, Colonial in design, stands just to the east of the church. Built between 1799 and 1806, it is the oldest brick house in Illinois. Staunchly constructed, with walls 1½ ft. thick, it withstood the earthquake that rocked Cahokia in 1811. The use of the black header (bricks from the inside of the kiln laid to expose their ends) in every sixth row of bricks results in a horizontal banding of red and black in the south and east walls. The building once served as a Catholic school. Of Jarrot's hospitality, a visitor once wrote that so many balls were held here he "often wondered how the ladies are enabled to support themselves under this violent exercise." In 1807 another guest commented on gambling at the Jarrot Mansion: "Never did I see people embark with so much spirit and perservance to win each other's money—I have frequently known them to sit 30 hours at the same table without any other refreshment than a dish of coffee or a glass of claret."

DUPO, 8 m. (422 alt., 2,842 pop. 1970; 2,937, 1960), a village in St. Clair County, bears a name contracted from Prairie du Pont (Fr., meadow of the bridge), so called because of a small bridge constructed across a creek in this region by Cahokians more than a century ago. Near the outskirts of Dupo, oil was discovered in 1928 and the town enjoyed the excitement of a boom. Wells were sunk in front lawns; the population grew rapidly, and land speculation ran high. But it soon became evident that the resources of the field were limited, and the boom subsided. The chief occupation of the workers in Dupo has been working in the marshalling yards of the Missouri Pacific Railroad.

South of Dupo the highway gradually ascends from the bottom lands to reveal the Missouri bluffs.

The prim whitewashed brick cottages of COLUMBIA, 15 m., hug the highway and are evidence in their freshly scrubbed appearance of the predominantly German ancestry of the inhabitants. Numerous unpretentious doorways of Greek revival influence similar to those of old St. Louis contribute to the charm of quiet streets. Columbia was one of the major stops on the old Kaskaskia-Cahokia trail and was settled by veterans of George Roger Clark's campaigns. Quarrying of Keokuk limestone has been carried on here since 1840.

Between Columbia and Waterloo Illinois 3 dips and rises through gently rolling farmlands.

WATERLOO, 22 m. (717 alt., 4,546 pop. 1970; 3,730, 1960, inc. 21%), is the seat of Monroe County. On the old trail from Fort Chartres to Cahokia, it has grown up adjacent to the original settlement of Bellefontaine, which long ago lost its identity, although called the first wholly American community in the old Northwest, as distinct from French settlements. Until the passage of the stricter marriage laws in 1937, Waterloo had a reputation as the Gretna Green of the St. Louis area. Signs advertising the marriage parlors of justices of peace lined the highway for several miles outside the city limits, and competition among the justices was spirited.

In the hamlet of LEMENS, 25 m., is a junction with graveled road. Right on this road to RENAULT, 11 m., a hamlet, named for Phillipe Francois Renault, director-general of mining operations for John Law's Western Company, known to history as the Mississippi Bubble. Renault left France in 1719 with 200 miners to search for precious stones and metals in the Louisiana Territory. En route he stopped at Santo Domingo and bought 500 slaves, a number of which were brought to Illinois and taken as far as Galena. After an unsuccessful treasure hunt Renault returned to France in 1742, and his slaves were sold to French colonists in this region. Until the present century there were Negroes in the vicinity of Renault and Prairie du Rocher who clung to French customs and spoke a mixture of French and English.

RED BUD, 36 *m.*, (444 alt., 2,559 pop. 1970; 1,942, 1960, inc. 31%) a city in Randolph County, was named for the red-bud trees that once grew in profusion near the village site. The tableland south of the village is known as HORSE PRAIRIE. Ponies roamed the prairie until captured by incoming American settlers.

In RUMA, 42 *m.*, (154 pop. 1970) Illinois 3 has a junction with Illinois 155.

Right on Illinois 155 to PRAIRIE DU ROCHER, 7 *m.* (396 alt., 658 pop. 1970; 679, 1960) a village in Randolph County at the base of the bluffs. Prairie du Rocher was founded about 1722 as a result of John Law's Mississippi Bubble. Law, a Scotch promoter, organized a company to exploit the resources of the New World and obtained a charter that granted him the right to exploit the Louisiana Territory. The charter provided that 6,000 whites and 3,000 Negroes should be brought to the territory within 25 years. Law promised fabulous profits, and for several years the French indulged in mad speculation. The Bubble burst in 1720, resulting in financial ruin to thousands and damaging the French financial system. The colonists that Law sent into the Mississippi Valley, however, encouraged settlement in this area. French New Year's Eve festivities are still observed here. High-calcium limestone for special uses is quarried at Prairie du Rocher.

The MODOC ROCK SHELTER, an overhanging sandstone cliff in Randolph County between Modoc and Prairie du Rocher, has been provided with a descriptive marker by the Illinois State Museum and the Illinois State Historical Society. Archaeologists have found evidence that Indians camped below the bluff at 8000 B. C. and used the area for more than 6,000 years. The shelter was also used by white pioneers.

Four miles west from Prairie du Rocher to the terminus of Illinois 155 and FORT DE CHARTRES, famous outpost of France in the 18th century, which fell to the British and then to the United States. The remains of the fort, partially restored, are in the center of FORT CHARTRES STATE PARK, 19.6 acres. This spot, where the French attempted to consolidate their hold on the American wilderness, witnessed events of crucial importance to the political future of America.

In 1718 France sent Pierre Duque, Sieur de Boisbriant, to erect a fortress in Illinois country. Two years later the work was completed and named for the Duc de Chartres, son of the French regent. Warehouses soon sprang up about the fort, large tracks of land were cultivated; and a town grew up in the shadow of the fort. All roads lead to Fort de Chartres was a favorite saying of the day.

The first fort was built of timber and soon fell into disrepair. A dozen years after its completion it was abandoned for a new fort at a nearby site, but this too was soon dilapidated. In 1751 the French decided to erect a fortification that would be both permanent and impregnable. The foundation was laid in 1753; three years later the new Fort de Chartres was finished.

Its massive walls were 18 feet in height and enclosed four acres of ground. Each of the four bastions of masonry contained eight embrasures, 48 loopholes, and a sentry box. Within the walls were a storehouse, a guardhouse with a chapel and priests' rooms on the second floor, a government house, a coach house and pigeon loft, and two great rows of barracks. Set apart from the other buildings, to avoid the danger of an explosion, was the magazine. Fort de Chartres' soldiers fought on many battlefields of the French and Indian War. Washington surrendered to them at Fort Necessity, and later they aided the defeat of General Braddock.

The Treaty of Paris of 1763 ceded this area to the British, but it was not until 1765 that Louis St. Ange de Bellerive, commander of the fort surrendered it to Capt. Thomas Stirling. Many of the French left; those that remained saw the Mississippi encroach on the fort. One of the bastions was undermined by the river. Finally, it 1772, its situation became so serious that the British withdrew their garrison and destroyed what remained of the structures.

In 1915 the State of Illinois acquired the site of Fort de Chartres for use as a park. Underbrush was cleared away and the work of restoration begun. Today the foundations of Fort de Chartres, cleared of underbrush and repaired, sharply delineate the plan of the old fort. A park building, constructed on the foundation of the original supply house, contains a museum (*open 8-5 daily*) in which are preserved numerous relics unearthed on the site. The powder magazine has been restored; a guard house and chapel, an exact reproduction of the original structure, has been built. The well inside the fort wall, dug in 1754, is still in use.

Back on Illinois 3 to EVANSVILLE, 47 *m.* (838 pop. 1970) a Randolph County village on the Kaskaskia River, and ELLIS GROVE, 53 *m.* (277 pop. 1970) near the entrance of Kaskaskia State Park.

A marker off Illinois 3, about 3 *m.* sw. of Ellis Grove records the location of the house of Elias Kent Kane, Illinois first Secretary of State, 1818-1822, and U. S. Senator, on a bluff overlooking submerged old Kaskaskia.

At 55.5 *m.* is a junction with a hard-surfaced road. Right on this road 1.5 *m.* to the entrance to FORT KASKASKIA STATE PARK a 234-acre tract at the crest of the bluffs. The first fort was built here in 1733, more than 30 years after the first settlement. Rebuilt in 1736 with the aid of a special grant from the French crown, it was occupied until 1755, when the garrison was moved to Fort de Chartres. When the British took over after the Treaty of Paris, Kaskaskians destroyed their fort to prevent British occupation.

A turbulent period followed the removal of George Roger Clark's troops in 1780, when this territory was theoretically in the hands of the Americans but no local government had yet been set up. The ruins of the Kaskaskia fort were seized in 1784 by a renegade named John Dodge, who once had enjoyed the confidence of George Washington. For two years he ruled Kaskaskia like a tyrant, bullying the people, murdering the messengers they sent to bring aid. Describing Dodge's reign, Father Gibault wrote, "Breaking of limbs, murder by means of a dagger, sabre, or sword (for he who wills carries one) are common, and pistols and guns are but toys in this region. . . . The most solemn feasts and Sundays are days given up to dances and drunkenness . . . with girls suborned and ravished in the woods, and a thousand other disorders which you are able to infer from these." After Clark restored order, the fort was never again used. Its site and plan can be traced by the earthworks, all that remain of the old fort.

A stone's throw north is Garrison Hill Cemetery. The founders and residents of old Kaskaskia were buried in the lowlands near the confluence of the Kaskaskia and Mississippi. After the Mississippi threatened to wash away the old graveyard, the State removed approximately 3,800 boxes, some containing whole families, to the new graveyard.

Facing the river at the base of the bluffs is the PIERRE MENARD HOUSE, a State Memorial and a National Historic Landmark.

It is a one and one-half story structure, raised above a high basement with a wide gallery porch, low hip roof, and dormer windows. The design of the house recalls the minor plantation houses of Louisiana. Menard was the presiding officer of the Illinois Territorial Legislature and the first Lieutenant Governor of Illinois. Born in Quebec in 1766, he entered the fur trade at Vincennes in 1787 and came to Kaskaskia in 1789 to establish a store. His enterprises prospered and he became a rich man, admired and respected by both pioneers and Indians. Old documents show that in 1820, while sub-agent of the Indian department, Menard spent $13 to have a Delaware chief and his party ferried across the Mississippi, $19.50 to furnish supper and breakfast for 13 Indians and to feed their horses, and $23 to purchase 400 pounds of beef and have a coffin made for an Indian who had been accidentally killed.

The Menard House was completed in 1802, and by pioneer standards was lavishly conceived and maintained. The foundation is of stone blocks, which support hand-hewn timbers, several of which are more than a foot square. The original furnishings were sold by Menard's descendants, and the present pieces were replaced by the State only after their authenticity had been established. The drawing room where Lafayette was entertained in 1824 contains a mantelpiece imported from France. Behind the house is a detached Stone Kitchen, with a huge fireplace, a cavernous Dutch oven, and a sink carved from a solid block of stone. The Slave House nearby has been carefully restored. The Randolph County Historical Society led a movement to restore the Pierre Menard house and sponsored essay contests in the Sparta Twp. High School in support.

Down the slope from the Menard House, and under the waters of the Mississippi, lies the site of OLD KASKASKIA, the first capital of Illinois. Kaskaskia was founded as a Roman Catholic mission in 1703, four years after Cahokia. For a hundred years their histories ran roughly parallel, for the struggle for the Mississippi Valley affected each. The town was built around a square, on which stood the buildings of the Jesuits. On the narrow streets that branched from the square at right angles were log houses, usually a story and a half high, with pointed roofs of thatch or bark.

Wearied of brutal British rule that followed the Treaty of Paris, Kaskaskia yielded peacefully to George Rogers Clark on July 4, 1778. It declined gradually until 1809, when it revived on becoming the capital of Illinois Territory, acquiring also the regional land office. In 1818 Illinois became a state, with Kaskaskia as the capital, but two years later the seat of government was transferred to Vandalia (*see Tour 4*). Occasional floods hastened Kaskaskia's decline, and in 1881 and later the Mississippi broke through the low peninsula which separated it from the Kaskaskia River, changed its course and eventually destroyed the town.

Kaskaskia was the site of the first Masonic Lodge in Illinois, the Western Star, opened Dec. 14, 1805, by members originally from other places who obtained authority from the Grand Lodge of Pennsylvania. The first Mason known to have entered the Illinois country was George Rogers Clark, who captured Kaskaskia. In 1806 the lodge admitted to membership an affiliate from Maryland, Shadrach Bond, Jr., who became active in politics and in 1818 was elected first Governor of Illinois without opposition.

In 1816 the *Western Intelligencer* of Kaskaskia was the only newspaper in Illinois.

In the final decades of the 18th century Kaskaskia carried on a lively trade with frontier towns and young men of energy and ambition found it a good place to make a start. Governor John Reynolds in his *Pioneer History of Illinois* mentions among others John Edgar, a native of Belfast, who resigned a captaincy in the British Royal Navy in 1772 and helped the American cause during the Revolution. In 1784 he settled in Kaskaskia, bought French land claims, held judicial offices, and amassed a fortune in land. By 1798 he had received 2,240 acres from the U. S. Government for his part in the Revolution and also owned 39,700 acres in St. Clair County. In 1808 he had 130,499 acres in Randolph County. He owned several flour mills and a ferry. He was called the wealthiest man in the Northwest Territory. It is also recorded that when his wife died in 1822 she was 86 and he 89, and that he then took to wife a 15-year-old girl.

KASKASKIA, a village, was built after Old Kaskaskia was inundated by the Mississippi River. It is located on KASKASKIA ISLAND, the only part of Illinois now west of the Mississippi. The Census of 1970 found only 79 residents, down from 97 in 1960. The island is connected with St. Marys, Mo. by a bridge over the shallow old channel, and gets its mail by RFD from there. The island is protected from floods by a dirt levee. In order to get a clear legal title to the island the State of Illinois in 1965 brought suit against Missouri, which resulted in an agreement that won concurrence from the U. S. Supreme Court on Jan. 20, 1970. The agreement verified Illinois' title to Kaskaskia Island, 16,300 acres, and Beaver Island, and Missouri's title to Roth Island and the Cottonwoods, 1,200 acres. In the village is a State Memorial, a small brick building that shelters the bell of the

Church of the Immaculate Conception of Old Kaskaskia, called Liberty Bell of the West. It was rung by the villagers on July 4, 1778, when George Rogers Clark announced that France had joined the War of Independence. A church of later construction stands near.

On the outskirts of Chester appear the stacks and building of the MENARD STATE PENITENTIARY; the grounds and farm lands cover 1,600 acres. In 1971 the institution had 1,714 inmates.

CHESTER, 62 m. (381 alt., 5,310 pop. 1970; 4,460, 1960), seat of Randolph County, (31,379 pop. 1970; 29,988, 1960) was founded by a land company formed in 1819 in Cincinnati, Ohio, to establish a settlement as a commercial rival of Kaskaskia. In GREENWOOD CEMETERY a white granite monument erected by the State in 1883 marks the grave of Shadrach Bond, first Governor of Illinois.

The H. C. Cole Milling Co. is believed to be the oldest milling operation in Illinois still controlled by the original family. In 1839 Nathan Cole built a sawmill with a corn-grinding attachment on the banks of the Mississippi River. His enterprise developed with steamboat trade. The Cole FFFG was the first flour brand copyrighted in the Government Patent Office. In 1883 the Cole family built the first full-roller process mill. The fifth generation of Coles is active in the huge mill, still located on the river bank.

Left from Chester on Illinois 150 4 m. to an Old Covered Bridge that spans Mary's River downstream from the Highway Bridge. It was on the original plank road between Chester and Sparta, was built at a cost of $530 and opened in 1854. The span is 90 ft. long, 20 ft. wide, and 20 ft. high, and has stone approaches. In 1930 citizens moved to preserve it and gave it to the State, which has kept it in repair. Local legends say it was used by highwaymen for stagecoach holdups. Northeast of Chester on Illinois 150 is the Randolph County State Conservation Area, 1,001 acres.

The CHESTER TOLL BRIDGE across the Mississippi makes connections easy for the motorist from Illinois 3 and 150 to US 61 and Interstate 55 in Missouri. It was erected in 1942.

ROCKWOOD, 71 m. (377 alt.) had only 59 people when the census taker came around in 1970, a drop from 98 in 1960 or a decrease of 30 percent. It was known as a timber market before the Mississippi changed its channel and receded from the town's backyard. In addition to supplying steamers with wood for fuel, the villagers manufactured flatbottomed boats used in floating cargoes down the Mississippi.

On the southwest corner of the intersection with the Jacob Road, 81 m., an INDIAN MOUND is clearly visible from the highway. The mound, approximately 20 feet high and half an acre in extent, has not been excavated. Numerous mounds dot the valley throughout this section.

At 81.3 m. is the junction with a hard-surfaced road, marked by deep cuts on each side of it; that on the northeast corner has been cut through an Indian mound, showing a cross-section.

Left on this road is Footprint Rock, 0.5 m., encircled by a wooden railing. On the flat top of its huge bulk are impressions resembling those made by naked human feet; one resembles a very sharply outlined hand. Several of the clearest prints have been chiseled from the rock by vandals. The footprints are of adult size, with the exception of one set resembling those of a small child. These so-called prints were probably sculptured by Indians. Similar ones have been found in the vicinity under circumstances that render it highly improbable that they are of natural origin. One set of footprints, for instance, ascends a vertical wall; others have been found in various patterns, accompanied by circles and other geometric figures, indicating that the tracks had some symbolic significance.

At 85 *m.* is a junction with Illinois 149. Left on 149 to Scenic View, 1.4 *m.,* a graveled parking space at the top of the steep bluffs. On the horizon to the southeast the Illinois Ozarks rise abruptly, a great dark wall, thickly wooded to the summit. To the southwest the distant Missouri Ozarks loom faintly beyond the smooth Mississippi and the vast expanse of the bottomlands.

MURPHYSBORO, 8 *m.* (420 alt., 10,015 pop. 1970; 8,673, 1960; inc. 15%) seat of Jackson County, (55,008 pop. 1970; 42,151, 1960, inc. 30%), is in the apple-growing country and celebrates apples in an annual festival. Industries make aluminum windows and doors, shoes, clothing, and print labels on highspeed presses. The birthplace of Major General John A. Logan, Civil War leader, is marked and his bronze statue in front of the Township High School is part of a State Park honoring him. The Illinois Central Gulf Railroad serves the city. Northwest is Lake Murphysboro, a recreation area.

Several miles beyond is Crisenberry Dam, behind which Kinkaid Creek is filling Lake Kinkaid Reservoir, a new recreation area. The dam is 437 ft. above sea level and will impound 79,000 acre-ft. of water. Commercial use of recreational facilities is encouraged by the Conservancy District, which has charge of the project.

Ahead from Murphysboro on Illinois 13 is CARBONDALE, 16 *m.* (416 alt., 22,816 pop. 1970) at a junction with US 51 (*see Tour 4c*).

Proceeding south, Illinois 3 enters the Illinois Ozarks, which reach heights of more than 1,000 feet above sea level. Their heavily wooded slopes, slashed with deep dark ravines, change brilliantly with the seasons.

Illinois south of the Ozarks is an overlap between the North and South. Southern styles of architecture are common. The inhabitants speak with decidedly Southern accents. Such southern trees as the bald cypress and the tupelo gum grow in the swamplands, and the mistletoe is found on trees along the rivers. Azalea and southern short-leaf pine have been transplanted to these Ozark hills from the "piney woods" of the South and Southwest. Cotton is cultivated in occasional patches; orchards of peaches, apples, or pears are numerous. The southern black vulture is found here, as well as the turkey vulture of the North. In the lowlands the venomous water moccasin inhabits sluggish waters. The woods rattler is common. Numerous other plants and animals find either a northern or a southern limit to their range in this locality.

At 89 *m.* is a junction with a dirt road at the foot of Fountain Bluff, a freak formation, 6 square miles in area, which juts from the level flood plain like a huge loaf on a table top. The bluff takes its name from the many springs that flow from its surface.

At 1.5 *m.* a foot bridge spans a bog and leads up through a fissure. Here are a dam and a small swimming hole fed by springs. Above the dam are several paths leading to the upper levels. The geologic formations on all sides are of interest. Huge boulders of fused iron and sandstone line the way and shallow sandstone caves flank the paths at intervals. The summit can be reached from this point, but the climb is difficult.

At 91 *m.* is a junction with a graveled road. Right on this road to the Fountain Bluff Fire Tower, 2 *m.* The 60-foot tower (*inside stairway*) has a lookout platform, where, during dry weather, a ranger of the State Forest Service is constantly on duty. Fires noted through field glasses are reported by telephone to district headquarters. The summit of Fountain Bluff commands a far-flung view of the hills and the river, the fields, forests, and farms of the vast bottom lands.

At 94 *m.* is a junction with a graveled road. Right on this road to GRAND TOWER, 1 *m.* (367 alt., 664 pop. 1970; 847, 1960). In the Mississippi River, between the Missouri shore and the town, is Tower Rock, for which the town was named. During President Grant's administration the River was dredged and cleared of rocks hazardous to navigation, but Tower Rock was left standing because it might some day form a natural foundation for a bridge. Protected by the Federal government, the rock is called "the smallest national park in America." It is 60 feet high, and about an acre in extent. A popular picnic spot, the Tower Rock can be reached from Grand Tower by motorboat. Two iron towers north of Grand Tower carry pipes of natural gas across the Mississippi from Texas and Oklahoma. The tower on the Illinois bank is near the south side of a rocky hill called the Devil's Bake Oven.

WOLF LAKE, 103 *m.* borders the crossroads community of the same name, and offers the best fishing water along the route.

Left from Wolf Lake is a graveled road to the Pine Hill Skyline Drive, 0.6 *m.* The five-mile drive climbs steadily until it reaches the top of a range of the Ozarks and continues along the ridge. At 4.4 *m.* and at 5.2 *m.* are two Observation Points; the view from the first is the better; a jutting rock serves as the observation station. On the steep sides of the bluff below are numerous pines, rare in Illinois.

In the hamlet of WARE, 107 *m.*, is a junction with Illinois 146. This east-west route crosses the State from Golconda on the Ohio River, where the Cherokee Indians entered the State on their march to Oklahoma. Illinois 146 leads to Jonesboro and Anna (*see Tour 4*) and has a junction with Interstate 57, 5 *m.* east of Anna.

Left on Illinois 146 to the site of the CHEROKEE ENCAMP-

MENT of 1839, 3 *m.*, designated by a marker. On this spot, during the winter of 1839, 13,000 Cherokee Indians en route from Georgia to a new reservation in Oklahoma, and unable to cross the Mississippi because of ice floes, made their camp. Unaccustomed to the northern winter nearly 2,000 of the tribe died of cold and privation.

At 5 *m.* is the entrance to UNION STATE TREE NURSERY AND FOREST (*shelter house, picnic facilities*). A 7-mile circular drive through the forest reaches many beautiful spots. South of the picnic grounds, in the center of the forest is a Wild Turkey Farm, where the state raises stock for its forest preserves.

From Ware south along the Mississippi runs the Union County Conservation Area, 6,000 acres.

Right from Illinois 3 is THEBES (335 alt., 442 pop. 1970, 471, 1960), once the seat of Alexander County (12,015 pop. 1970; 16,061, 1960, dec. 25%). The old Alexander County Courthouse was built in 1846 of brick and stone in the general proportions of the Greek Revival, but in a starkly undecorated mode. Thebes, first known as Sparhawk's Landing, was laid out in 1844. It figures briefly in Edna Ferber's novel, *Show Boat*.

HORSESHOE LAKE, 133 *m.*, a State Conservation Area, is an extensive game preserve and feeding ground for migratory fowl. (Fishing permitted June 1-Sept. 30, from the lake shore only; no trot lines, set line, or motorboats.) The preserve of 7,901 acres includes a 2,000-acre lake, shaped like a great horseshoe, in the middle of which is a 1,400-acre island, which can be reached by the custodian's motorboat (*arrangements by telephone from Olive Branch*). The lake has been stocked with black bass and crappie. To protect fingerlings and fish eggs, the State annually traps turtles in the lake.

Between the middle of October and the end of March it is not uncommon to see 30,000 or 40,000 wild geese feeding at one time in the wheat fields of the preserve. Horseshoe Lake is at the approximate point of convergence of two of the three major flyways of the Canadian goose. Many ducks also feed at the preserve during the winter months, and the rare American egret and the great blue heron are frequently seen.

Although the principal function of the preserve is to supply a feeding ground for migratory fowl, many species of fur-bearing animals also inhabit the island: opposums, raccoons, mink, woodchucks, and skunks. Deer have been introduced but are seldom seen, except during the severe winter months, when they come to the edge of the wheat fields to feed.

Part of the island is planted in cereal crops, mainly wheat, to supply food for wild fowl, and 200 acres of virgin timber on the south end afford sanctuary for deer and small animals. The island, in the late spring especially, is brilliant with wild flowers.

At 145 *m.* is the northern junction with US 51 (*see Tour 4*), which unites with Illinois 3 at Future City and continues into Cairo.

CAIRO, 149 *m.* (318 alt., 6,277 pop. 1970) *See Cairo.*

Cairo has a junction with US 60, which crosses the Kentucky Line by bridge over the Ohio River 8 miles west of Wickliffe, Kentucky. Cairo is on Interstate 57 and the Illinois terminal of the Great River Road.

Tour 9

CHICAGO TO CHAIN O' LAKES RECREATION AREA

Chicago—Des Plaines—Lake Zurich—Wauconda—Volo—Lake Pistakee—Fox Lake—Grass Lake—Chain o' Lakes State Park—Channel Lake—Antioch—Lake Villa—Lindenhurst—Venetian Village—Round Lake Area—Grayslake.

US 12, Illinois 59, 132, 173, Interstate 94. Approx. 50 *m.*

US 12, Rand Road, is the principal highway for direct access to the highly popular recreational area in Lake and McHenry Counties, approx. 40 to 50 *m.* northwest of Chicago, directly south of the Wisconsin border. It leads to the greatest concentration of lakes and wooded areas in Illinois, the largest units of which are Grass Lake, Fox Lake, and Pistakee Lake. The Fox River flows into Grass Lake, west of which is the Chain o' Lakes State Park of 960 acres. US 12, which comes from Indiana, can best be reached from Grant Park by taking the Eisenhower Expressway straight west to its junction with US 12. Illinois 59, which comes up east of the Fox River Valley joins US 12 in Wauconda and leaves it at the town of Fox Lake, proceeding northeast as US 12 goes northwest.

Drivers heading for the eastern areas of the Chain o' Lakes can get a clear, fast road on Tri-State Tollway, Int. 274, which has junctions with east-west highways Illinois 137, 120, 132, and 173. Another excellent northern route is US 45 (*see Tour 3*).

Hunting and fishing are the principal sports activities in the Chain o' Lakes area. Swimming, boating, tenting are general; skiing and tobogganing are available in some areas in winter. When this region had been worked over by the glaciers there were left numerous depressions that became lakes of varying sizes, strongly wooded, among rolling moraines. The hills display the beautiful colors of spring and fall and the bright blanket of winter. Within recent decades permanent residents have multiplied, many of them driving to jobs in Waukegan and other North Shore towns. In spring and summer the population is augmented many times by cottagers and motor car tourists. While

State areas are free there is some exploitation of facilities on the smaller lakes and fees are asked for locations and supplies. Visitors should become familiar with the State hunting and fishing regulations.

The Fox River is the principal outlet of these lakes. The most southernly is Lake Pistakee. The river flows through McHenry, Kane, and Kendall Counties. It passes villages that are growing into towns, and towns that have developed large industrial areas because shipping facilities are better away from the congested traffic of Chicago. The work force values the advantages of suburban living. The cities have tree-lined streets, detached dwellings, standardized shopping centers, and easy access to forest preserves.

From Chicago Milwaukee Ave. connects directly with the cloverleaf at Des Plaines where US 14, has a junction with Tri-State Tollway and the Rand Road begins. Rand Road was named for Socrates Rand, pioneer land-holder along the Des Plaines River, who was largely responsible for the routing of the road. The path followed an Indian trail between what is now Chicago and Janesville, Wisconsin. The highway was the principal northwestern road in 1845, and was known as the United States Mail Route.

US 12, after leaving Des Plaines, passes along the northern limits of Mount Prospect and Arlington Heights, described in *Tour 10*. In sparsely settled areas are several small villages, DEER PARK (834 pop., 1970, 476, 1960) and KILDEER (643 pop. 1970, 173, 1960). This gives Kildeer an increase of 271 percent.

At 15 *m.* north of Des Plaines US 12 reaches LAKE ZURICH (873 alt., 4,082 pop. 1970; 3,452, 1960, inc. 18%). After a junction with Illinois 22, which runs west from Highland Park to Fox River Grove, US 12 moves west and north of the lake.

In 1836 Seth Paine, a Chicago merchant, purchased a lake-shore tract, erected a house, hired tenant farmers, and began a real estate development. His first step was to change the name of Cedar Lake to Lake Zurich, which he hoped would suggest the beauties of the Swiss resort. It was incorporated as a village in 1896. The early immigrants were Germans, who worked small farms. West of Lake Zurich are the Barringtons. *See Tour 10.* Return to US 12.

WAUCONDA, 20 *m.* (800 alt., 5,460 pop. 1970; 3,227, 1960), began with the house of Justus Bangs, built in 1836 on the shore of the lake that now bears his name. There years later a school was opened and a young man appointed teacher. He is said to have given the village its name—that of an Indian character in a story to which he had taken a fancy. An academy opened in 1856 functioned for a decade, and then rented its building to the district for use as a public school. The mainstay of economic life is the farm trade and there are several small industries. The village admits visitors to its beaches for a small fee and provides a regatta and an ice carnival. Illinois 175 is an east-west highway from Illinois 42; there is a junction with Illinois 59, which joins US 12.

At 25 *m.* is a junction with Illinois 120. Left on 20 to VOLO,

0.5 *m.*, a small hamlet known since 1877 as The Forks. The community is composed of the gray and yellow frame houses common in the lake country, but achieves a certain distinction by being set atop a low hill. Sharply contrasting with the rural hamlet aspect is ST. PETER'S CHURCH (Roman Catholic), of English Gothic design, which dominates the entire countryside. The handsome yellow brick building, modeled after Salisbury Cathedral in England, has a red slate roof and a bell tower. St. Peter's School, also of yellow brick, abuts the church on the east.

McHENRY, 5½ *m.* west on Illinois 120 (758 alt., 6,772 pop. 1970; 3,336, 1960, inc. 103%) a city in McHenry County, on the Fox River, is the western gateway to Chain-O-Lakes. The first settler was Dr. Christy C. Wheeler, who erected a log cabin in 1836, and became McHenry's first storekeeper and postmaster. Early prosperity came to the settlement with the erection of several hotels on the Chicago Pike, a much-used route in the early days. In 1844 the town lost the county offices to Woodstock, but a decade later gained the Chicago & North Western Railway, which brought the development of such small industries as butter and cheese and pickle manufacture. The community today comprises many permanent residents who commute to Waukegan and other North Shore towns. McHenry was at one time the county seat; it became a city in 1923.

Proceeding north again on US 12 combined with Illinois 59 the highway reaches FOX LAKE, 30 *m.*, (4,511 pop. 1970, 3,700, 1960, inc. 21%), which occupies the land between Fox Lake and Pistakee Lake. It is served by the Milwaukee Railroad. In summer and fall cottagers come by the hundreds and week-end trippers by the thousands to enjoy Fox, Grass, Duck, Red Head, and numerous smaller lakes. On the July 4 weekend all of Chicago seems to crowd beaches, bath houses, barbecue counters, dance floors, and picnic grounds.

PISTAKEE is bestknown as the name of a lake, but it is also the name of a village too inconsequential to be reported by the U. S. Census. It is the pioneers' interpretation of the Indian name for the Fox River, and was reported as *pisikue* by Father Marquette. The name signifies buffalo.

The overflow of visitors bridges the narrow straits that connect Nippersink and Pistakee Lakes and jams the facilities of CHAIN-O-LAKES STATE PARK (*parking lots, bathing beaches, fishing, and picnic groves free; moderate rentals for canoes, rowboats and bath-houses*). It was developed by the CCC on 1,541 acres of reclaimed land bordering the lakes. From Fox Lake motorboats take visitors through the Chain o' Lakes, past the Lotus Beds and down the Fox River as far as Fox River Grove.

West of the State Park in McHenry County is the SPRING GROVE FISH HATCHERY, operated by the State to stock the lakes.

At Fox Lake Illinois 59 leaves US 12 and goes northeast. At 2.6 *m.* is FOX LAKE HILLS, an unincorporated village with 1,869 pop. in 1970, its first census. Illinois 132, which joined Illinois 59 at Fox

Lake, turns east at 4 *m.* while Illinois 59 proceeds north to Antioch Lake.

ANTIOCH, (3,189 pop. 1970; 2,268, 1960, inc. 40.6%) a village in Lake County 54 *m.* from the Loop, only 3 *m.* from the Wisconsin border, is the farthest north village in the big lake country. Antioch is an old farm settlement that became a village in 1892. Near are Sequoit Creek and Antioch Lake. Ever since good roads made the Chain o' Lakes region easily accessible fishermen, riders, and golfers have thronged the village in summer. In recent years apartment houses for year-round living have proved profitable. Of the light industries Pickard China is nationally known. Antioch is on the Soo Line, 2 *m.* from the Milwaukee at Fox Lake, 15 *m.* west of Waukegan. There is an airport for small planes 2 *m.* southwest of the village.

Illinois 173, an east-west route, passes through Antioch. In going west it moves past the bottoms of Lake Catherine and Channel Lake and goes north of Lake Marie and the Chain o' Lakes State Park. At 11 *m.* west on Route 173 is RICHMOND, a village in McHenry County devoted to processing dairy products. (819 alt., 1,153 pop. 1970; 855, 1960, inc. 34%). It has a junction with US 12, which moves to Lake Geneva and other Wisconsin resorts.

At Antioch Illinois 59 has a junction with Illinois 83, another north-south highway. Proceeding south on 83 4.2 *m.* parallel with the Soo Line right of way, the route passes Loon Lake, Cedar Lake, and Deep Lake, and reaches LAKE VILLA, (758 alt., 1,090 pop. 1970; 903, 1960, inc. 20%). Here is the Allendale Farm School, a project in practical philanthropy. Founded in 1897 to help homeless boys to acquire a vocation while enjoying the advantages of country living. Another project, the Children's Home, is supported by the Christian Baptist organization.

At Lake Villa Illinois 83 has an intersection with Illinois 132, which runs east 10 *m.* to Gurnee and Waukegan. East on Route 132 2 *m.* to LINDENHURST (3,141 pop. 1970; 1,259, 1960, inc. 149%) on Hastings Lake, which before 1950 was grassy pasture-land. The area was platted and incorporated as a village in 1956. It is crossed by Hastings Creek, which feeds Hastings Lake, and the Grass Lake Road, which has a junction with US 45. Hastings Lake is the location of three major YMCA Camps.

South of Lindenhurst is VENETIAN VILLAGE (2,554 pop. 1970; 2,084, 1960, inc. 22%), another growing resort on Fourth Lake, lying between Illinois 83 and 132.

South of Lake Villa Illinois 83 reaches a group of villages clustered around ROUND LAKE, which became the focal point for real estate developments that found favorable acceptance. The original enterprise was the village of ROUND LAKE (1,531 pop. 1970; 997, 1960, inc. 53%). In 1899 a landowner, Amarias M. White, persuaded the Milwaukee Railroad to establish a depot at Round Lake instead of Hainesville by donating the necessary site. In 1901 he filed a subdivision and in 1908 brought about incorporation of the village and became its mayor. The first industry in 1901 was the Armour & Co.

ice house. The former boarding house for ice makers is now the Alpine Country Club. The next year George P. Renehan built a hotel on the east shore of the lake and the area began to attract vacationers and small-home owners. The first industry was the Forest Glen Creamery.

As Round Lake developed municipal services and built schools, churches, and some factories, other villages started up. In 1929 a Chicago real estate developer started ROUND LAKE BEACH (5,717 pop. 1970; 5,011, 1960, inc. 14%) east and north of the lake, which had the largest area. South of the lake he established ROUND LAKE PARK (3,148 pop. 1970; 2,565, 1960, inc. 22%). North of Round Lake Beach was a subdivision called Indian Hill; in the late 1950's is incorporated as ROUND LAKE HEIGHTS. The Census of 1960 did not find it, but in 1970 it counted 1,144 people there.

In the meantime the village of HAINESVILLE, which failed to get the Milwaukee depot, remained dormant. The Census of 1970 counted 142 residents, up 7.6% from 132 in 1960. However, promoters include it in the Round Lake Area and have hopes for it. The Industrial Development & Educational Assn. of the Area Chamber of Commerce has *Progress in Motion* for its slogan. Round Lake is 40 *m.* northwest of Chicago and 40 *m.* southwest of Milwaukee. Holiday Park, 3 *m.* west, is a fully equipped recreation ground. The Soo Line and the Milwaukee serve the area.

Contiguous is Gray's Lake and the village of GRAYSLAKE (4,907 pop. 1970; 3,762, 1960; inc. 30%), where the COLLEGE OF LAKE COUNTY is located. This village is only 3 *m.* from the outskirts of Libertyville, which can be reached by several routes from the Chicago Loop: Kennedy Expressway and Edens Expressway connecting with Tri-State Tollway at Deerfield; Illinois 21 from Elston Ave and the Milwaukee Road.

〰〰〰〰〰〰〰〰〰〰〰〰〰〰〰〰〰〰〰〰〰〰〰〰〰〰

Tour 10

ROUTE OF THE GREAT NORTHWEST MIGRATIONS

Morton Grove—Niles—Park Ridge—Des Plaines—Mount Prospect—Arlington Heights—Rolling Meadows—Palatine—Inverness—The Barringtons—The Fox River Valley—Crystal Lake—Woodstock—Harvard.

Northwest Highway, US 14

Elk Grove Village—Schaumburg—Hoffman Estates—Streamwood.

Northwest Tollway, Interstate 90.

Here are the routes that lead to what Chicagoans in the 20 years between 1950 and 1970 considered most desirable locations for suburban living. To an area roughly west and northwest of O'Hare International Airport newcomers moved in such numbers that villages reported an increase in population of from 50 to 800 percent. The land most coveted is part rolling and partly flat, chiefly in the general direction of Elgin. Except for depressions in the Barrington hills it does not have the many lakes that make desirable the great fishing and recreation spots in Lake County.

Villages and towns not directly on US 14 and the Northwest Tollway (Int. 90) are within easy driving distance from junctions. The Eisenhower Expressway is planned to continue east of Schaumburg, with a junction with US 14 at Rolling Meadows.

Section a. Chicago to Wisconsin line, US 14, 68 m.

US 14 is routed west from near the end of Lincoln Park on Peterson Ave. and after a junction with Eden Expressway (Int. 94) proceeds in a general northwestly direction. Mileage is figured from State and Madison Sts., Chicago, center of the Loop.

NILES, 16 *m.* (580-600 alt., 31,432 pop. 1970; 20,393, 1960; inc. 50%) is the first incorporated suburb beyond the Chicago line on the Northwest Highway. Its streets are contiguous with those of Skokie, Morton Grove, and Park Ridge. The North Branch of the Chicago River runs through the Forest Preserve in the southeastern part of Niles.

It is also served by Rand Road to Zurich (US 12) and Illinois 21, the old Milwaukee Road. Despite the increase in population Niles has retained its village organization, with a president and a board of six trustees. It has a board of commissioners that administers its 10 parks. Niles has 12 churches, five hospitals and two homes for the aged. It is hq. for the American Printers & Lithographers and the Chicago Medical Book Co., and has depots of several eastern publishers. The Niles Public Library District, 6960 Oakton street, has more than 56,000 volumes and circulates 187,000. It is a member of the North Suburban Library System, which has 30 member libraries with hq in Evanston.

Niles is hardly the place where a motorist expects to come upon the LEANING TOWER OF PISA, but there it is, on Touhy Ave., rising to a height of 96 ft., which, although one-half the size of the original, is impressive enough to call for a closer look. Robert A. Ilg built it in 1933, applying much engineering ingenuity to anchor it solidly while giving it a list of 7 ft. off the perpendicular. The tower is now owned by the YMCA.

MORTON GROVE 16.5 *m.* (26,369 pop. 1970; 20,533, 1960, inc. 28.4%) adjoins Niles on the East and is another of the Cook County settlements that has retained its village status despite its growth. Established 1874 and named for Levi P. Morton, an official of the Chicago, Milwaukee & St. Paul Railroad and later Vice President of the United States during Benjamin Harrison's administration, Evanston's Dempster St. extends through it from Skokie, and Edens Express-

way (Int. 94) runs north along the line of Skokie and Morton's Grove.
US 14 touches its southwest corner. The village has some light industries. The Morton Grove Public Library, which improved its building
in 1963, has more than 55,000 books and circulates approx. 180,000. It
is a member of the North Suburban Library System (*See also Tour 2*).
PARK RIDGE, 17 *m.* (658 alt., 42,466 pop. 1970; 32,659, 1960,
inc. 30%) contiguous to Chicago, south of Niles and directly north of
the John F. Kennedy Expressway and northeast of O'Hare International Airport, is one of the populous suburbs that is actually an extension of Chicago's tight population. It is located on a wooded moraine,
one of the highest points in Cook County, and benefits also from the
Des Plaines Division of the Forest Preserve, which follows the Des
Plaines River on the west of Park Ridge. The first man to exploit the
red clay found in the area was George Penny, who came in 1853 and
started a brickyard and lumber yard, and in the course of time produced
5,000,000 bricks annually. The first train came in 1856 and the community called itself Pennyville, but when Penny objected the name was
changed to Brickton. In 1871 numerous Chicago families moved in to
avoid the danger of another Chicago fire, and in 1873 the place was
incorporated as a village named Park Ridge. It became a city in 1910
with 2,009 residents.

Park Ridge has two of the highly-rated Maine Township High
Schools, East, which enrolls approx. 3,900 and has a staff of more than
225, and South, which has 3,300 students and 175 teachers. Maine
Twp. High School West is in Des Plaines. The Park Ridge Military
Academy for boys in the first eight grades enrolls 120. Park Ridge
School for Girls, founded 1877, provides a home and education for
dependent adolescent girls; it has seven cottages and a number of school
buildings on a 15 acre campus. There are a number of parochial secondary schools, a Montessori school, and the Lutheran General School
of Nursing. Park Ridge is especially well equipped with medical care.
The Lutheran General Hospital, opened in 1860, has 650 beds, extensive
laboratories and facilities for intensive care in many areas. Resurrection
Hospital, located on West Talcott Ave. in Chicago, is a large center
that serves contiguous suburban communities.

In January, 1958, the new Park Ridge Public Library building
replaced the original that dated from 1913. It has more than 75,000
books and a circulation of more than 325,000 books, periodicals, and
records.

Park Ridge has easy access to the John F. Kennedy Expressway at
the Cumberland and Canfield interchanges. It has commuter service
on the Chicago & North Western and also the United Motor Coach
line.

The southern boundary of Park Ridge is Higgins Ave., on the south
side of which is ROSEMONT and its big interchange of expressways
at the gate of O'Hare International Airport. Rosemont, which also is
just outside the Chicago line, had 978 residents in 1960 and 4,360 in
1970, thereby achieving the distinction of a rise of 345.8% in 10 years.

A new Holiday Inn of 520 rooms, costing $13,500,000 to build has located here.

Also south of the John F. Kennedy Expressway and crossed by Lawrence Ave. are NORRIDGE and HARWOOD HEIGHTS, villages platted since World War II in the open country not reached by the city of Chicago. Norridge (16,880 pop. 1970; 14,087, 1960, inc. 19%) is known as the site of a popular shopping area at the Harlem-Irving Plaza. The heights at Harwood are not breath-taking. There is a Kennedy cloverleaf at Cumberland Ave.

The Forest Preserve District of Cook County has saved and protected woods and open recreation country on both banks of the Des Plaines River. General Headquarters of the District are at Lake St. and Harlem Ave., Chicago. The Indian Boundary Division follows the river past the big interchange of Northwest Tollway and Tri-State Tollway.

The Forest Preserve along the Des Plaines is narrowest between Fullerton and Belmont Avenues. Between Grand Ave. and the right of way of the Milwaukee Railroad near the Franklin Park area is a wooded triangle that is a segment of the La Framboise Reserve. This was originally an area of 1 sq. mi. given to Claude La Framboise, a half-breed Potawatomi Indian, by the Treaty of Prairie du Chien on July 29, 1829. It adjoins the Indian boundary line of the cession of 1816. Claude and his brother Joseph enlisted in the Black Hawk War. Claude received a section of land on Thorn Creek by the Treaty of Tippecanoe of 1832. The Treaty of Chicago of 1833 gave $300 to each child of Claude and land to Joseph.

The widest part of the Preserve starts at Belmont Ave. and has Cumberland Ave. on the east and the Des Plaines River Road on the west. Part of this area has been designated the Seymour Simon Preserve. The locality has interesting associations with Potawatomi times. Here are Robinson Woods, North and South, and Che-che-pin-qua Woods, all named for Alexander Robinson, the settlers' name for Chechepinqua, a halfbreed Potawatomi Indian who received substantial acreage here under provisions of the treaty of Prairie du Chien in 1829. Instead of leaving for Iowa when his tribe was forced out in 1835 he remained living in these woods. He was a prized member of the Chicago Temperance Society and routed John Barleycorn dramatically by smashing a whisky bottle with a tomahawk. Unfortunately there were other bottles available. He retained his popularity with the settlers and when he died in 1872 was buried in the family graveyard on West Lawrence Ave.

DES PLAINES, 20 *m.* (643 alt., 57,239 pop. 1970; 34,886, 1960, inc. 64%) in Cook County directly north of O'Hare International Airport had 8,798 pop. when this *Guide* was published in 1939. In the late 1950s Chicago businessmen began to recognize the remarkable advantages of locating in Des Plaines and by 1960 the rush was on. All the major highways that led to O'Hare reached Des Plaines. The big cloverleaf at Rosemont adjoins Des Plaines; here the John F.

Kennedy Expressway has a junction with Northwest Tollway, Tri-State Tollway, US 12 and US 45; other highways run through the town. The Chamber of Commerce and Industry, recognizing the thousands of air passengers at O'Hare writes: "It is a green place from the air, a pleasant vision. It is at the edge of a region of oak-covered knolls. Vegetation is lush; it is one of the most verdant spots on earth." French explorers called the river, Riviere aux Plaines. By 1835 New Englanders settled here and the locality was called Rand, after Socrates Rand, a pioneer. In 1840 its mills cut timbers for the plank road to Chicago. In 1853 the Illinois & Wisconsin Railroad arrived. In 1869 it was called Des Plaines and in 1874 adopted a village board. In 1925 it annexed Riverview. It is governed by a mayor and a city council.

In the late 1960s builders invested large sums in office structures of moderate height that proved highly acceptable to Chicago agencies and professional people. The O'Hare Lake Office Plaza on Devon Ave. comprises 5 buildings 3 stories tall; O'Hare Office Center on Des Plaines Ave., 3 buildings of 2 stories and a lower level; O'Hare Northwest Office Park, 2 of 5 stories each; Touhy Office Plaza, 5 stories; Continental Office Plaza, 5 stories; Nall Office Bldg. on the River Road, 4 stories; Jefferson-Pearson Bldg., 640 Pearson St., 4 stories; O'Hare East Office Bldg., on Devon, 8 stories; Le-Ronde Office Bldg., on Lee St., 3 stories.

Des Plaines profits by the presence of the Cylinder Group, makers of hydraulic and pneumatic power cylinders, including Hannifin Press of the Parker-Hannifin Corp. It has a division of Matsushita Electric Corp. of America, and research sections of Nuclear-Chicago Corp., U. S. Gypsum Co., Xerox Corp., Universal Oil Products Co., Borg-Warner, General Molded Products, Illinois Tool Co., and the plant where General Telephone Directory Co. produces the *Yellow Pages*.

One of the first condominium office buildings in the suburban areas, known as Continental Office Plaza, has been erected at Touhy Ave. and River Road, Des Plaines. Pace Associates are the architects.

McDonald's, Inc., the hamburger chain, marked a special occasion in Des Plaines in 1972, when it established its 2,000th restaurant there. There is sentiment even in business, for the first McDonald's was opened in Des Plaines in 1955, and the 1,000th there in 1962. Before Jan. 1, 1963, McDonald's had sold 11 billion hamburgers and grossed $1 billion. It conducts Hamburger University in Elk Grove Village for the instruction of its licensees and managers. In 1971 McDonald's Corporation moved its main offices to an eight-story office complex in Oak Brook.

Des Plaines has 36 churches and well-equipped hospitals. The Des Plaines Public Library has more than 90,000 books and a circulation of 335,000. The library, erected in 1959, gained new facilities in 1970. It is one of the key units in the North Suburban Library System of 31 libraries. It has an exceptionally large collection of children's books and the Izaak Walton League Collection.

De Lourdes College, a Roman Catholic institution, is located near the Evanston-Elgin Road north of Des Plaines. In 1972 it had 168 students and 15 faculty members.

Lake Opeka is used for international winter sailing races and is the site of the National Skating Championship.

The Des Plaines Division of the Forest Preserve District of Cook County controls wooded and open areas between the Tri-State Tollway and the Des Plaines River Road, where the river winds erratically to the Lake County line. US 45, combined with Illinois 21, follows Milwaukee Ave. diagonally through the Preserve north of US 14. Here are lakes stocked for fishing, camp grounds, developed trails, foot paths, and picnic shelters. Included in the section are Camp Dan Beard and Camp Baden Powell of the Boy Scouts, and Camp Pine of the Girl Scouts. There are ramps for canoes and rowboats at dams. The Indian Portage to the North Branch of the Chicago River is marked. There is a camp ground used for many years by the Methodists for summer meetings. There is a spot where the Indians had charcoal pits and a chipping station, where chips may still be found. And there is a remnant of the original Illinois prairie.

MOUNT PROSPECT (34,995 pop. 1970; 18,406, 1960, inc. 85%) is located between Des Plaines and Arlington Heights, 22 *m.* from the Loop and served by US 14, US 12 (Rand Road) and Illinois 83, which has a junction with the Northwest Tollway. This village, incorporated 1917, occupies part of the farmland settled by Lutheran immigrants, whose descendants support four churches and one parochial school. Many are named Busse after the original settler, and this name recurs on streets and offices. Bestknown was Fred Busse, mayor of Chicago at the beginning of the century, who died in 1955 aged 91. Most of the hospital and school facilities are in adjoining towns, but the Randhurst Market Center, at the intersection of Rand Road and Elmhurst Road, opened 1962 has 12 acres of stores, shops, and eating places, mostly under roof. There are parks, a golf course, and several community houses available for recreation of all kinds.

The Mount Prospect Public Library, with more than 32,000 books, has about 320,000 transactions annually. The 1950 building was enlarged in 1969. It belongs to the North Suburban Library System.

ARLINGTON HEIGHTS, 24 *m.* (704 alt., 64,884 pop. 1970; 27,878, 1960; inc. 40.6%) was settled in 1836 by Asa Dunton and called Dunton when it became a station on the predecessor of the Chicago & North Western Ry. in 1854. When incorporated in 1887 as Arlington Heights it was still largely an area of small farms. In 1927 ARLINGTON PARK RACE TRACK was opened and started a rush of motor cars and special trains during the racing season, but the solid growth in the village did not come until after World War II, when there was a new movement of homeseekers to the suburbs from Chicago. The track has two of the largest purses in racing—the $100,000 American Derby, and the $100,000 American Classic.

Arlington Heights has a president and trustees, who employ a city manager. The residential advantages are protected by strict zoning regulations. There are 25 churches of 13 denominations; the Community Hospital with 225 beds, and the Museum of the Historical Society of Arlington Heights. The Memorial Library entered its new building in 1968. In 1971 it reported a stock of 114,521 books and a circulation of 680,129, indicating a high percentage of book readers in the community.

Arlington Heights has developed an audience for plays, lectures, and exhibits. Its mercantile interests are associated with the expanding O'Hare area, newest evidence of which is the Chicago O'Hare International Trade Center, at Arlington Heights Road and the Northwest Tollway, which aims to capture some of the convention business that has been coming to hotels near O'Hare International Airport. The Trade Center was planned for expositions and conferences, with 47 meeting rooms, parking places for 5,000 cars, and a hotel with 1,000 rooms.

The Arlington Heights Museum, 500 N. Vail St., occupies three buildings once the home of Frederick W. Mueller, and now restored to the decor of 1882. The house was once used as a factory for making carbonated beverages and the coach house has some of the original delivery wagons and accessories. The carpenter shop has early motorized fire engines and other antiques.

The Countryside Art Gallery, 407 N. Vail St., has a monthly change of exhibits, special programs, and art classes. *Open Tues.-Sunday, 1-5.*

ROLLING MEADOWS, 28 *m.* a city in Cook County (19,178 pop. 1970; 10,879, 1960, inc. 76.3%) was incorporated February 24, 1955, after Kimball Hill, a real estate developer, had laid out a city with provision for shops, schools, churches and parks, south of Arlington Park Race Track. Since 1960 the city has added Plum Grove Countryside and Plum Grove Village and started an industrial section south of the Northwest Highway. The city elects a mayor and 10 aldermen for four-year terms and supports a city manager. The Public Library, 3110 Martin Lane, has approx. 25,000 vols. and is a member of the North Suburban Library System. At Rolling Meadows there is a junction with Illinois 53, north-south.

Rolling Meadows, like its neighbors in this region, is favored for offices as well as dwellings. Three buildings of 10 stories each have been announced as Kenroy Towers of Rolling Meadows, 3555 Algonquin Road; two buildings of 150,000 sq. ft. each and a third of 300,000 sq. ft.

PALATINE, 30 *m.,* a village in Cook County (c. 700 alt., 25,904 pop. 1970; 11,504, 1960; inc. 125.2%) is in the center of a growing suburban township that includes sections of Arlington Heights, Hoffman Estates, Inverness, Schaumburg, Barrington and South Barrington, and the city of Rolling Meadows. Palatine was settled by New Englanders and had four houses when the Illinois & Wisconsin Railroad, now the Chicago & North Western, arrived in 1853. The name may derive from Germans. The village was incorporated March 19, 1866. In 1940 it had only 2,222; the big push northwest has come since World War II. There is a Village Manager, appointed by the elective Village Board. The Palatine Public Library has approx. 50,000 vols., many records and films and is tax supported. It circulates more than 190,000 vols. annually. It is a member of the North Suburban Library System.

The Township is run by elected officials who levy taxes for roads, bridges, general assistance and mental health services. In 1969-70 they expended $321,000. The Palatine Park District provides opportunities for recreation and levies its own taxes. Included are the Palatine Hills Golf Course and Recreation Area, 180 acres, Community and 5 other parks. The Palatine Rural Park District is a separate area. The Deer Grove Forest Preserve District, Quentin Rd. and Illinois 68, has 1,100 acres and year-around use. Its hq is at the County Bldg., Chicago.

The William Rainey Harper College is a two-year community college established in 1965 and already enrolling 6,000 students a year, with a faculty of 300. It was named for the first president of the University of Chicago.

The township of Palatine in Cook County is intersected by the Northwest Tollway, Interstate 90, to the south of which are suburban communities of HOFFMAN ESTATES and SCHAUMBURG. Hoffman Estates, a village, had 22,238 pop. in 1970, 8,296 in 1960, a 168 percent rise that illustrates the movement away from the metropolis. Schaumburg, which lies partly in DuPage County, had 18,730 pop. in 1970, and 986 in 1960, a rise of 799 percent. This shows how the open country between Chicago and Elgin is being built up. *See pages 573-574.*

INVERNESS, 32 *m.* a village in Cook County (1,647 pop. 1970) was incorporated on April 28, 1962. Its terrain had been devoted chiefly to farming. George Ela settled here in 1836. In 1848 Thomas Atkinson built a house of brick molded from a nearby clay pit. Arthur T. McIntosh platted the land in the 1930's. The village has a zoning and plan commission that supervises its development. At Inverness there is a junction with the Dundee Road, Illinois 68, east to Int. 94.

After Inverness the Northwest Highway passes Baker's Lake and enters BARRINGTON, 35 *m.* (824 alt., 7,701 pop. 1970; 5,434 1960, inc. 41%). Its main street is the dividing line between Cook and Lake Counties. This is the original Barrington, which attracted farmers from Great Barrington, Mass., who gave it the name. Early in the present century it brought Chicagoans who wanted large country estates. It has some light industries.

The Barrington Historical Society conducts a museum of local history at 111 West Station St. A blacksmith shop and farm tools are exhibited.

In Barrington there is a junction with north-south Illinois 59 and 63 combined. At 2.2 *m.* Illinois 63 proceeds northeast to Mundelein, Libertyville, and Lake Bluff; Illinois 59 continues north to NORTH BARRINGTON, in Lake County (1,411 pop. 1970; 262, 1960, inc. 400%). West of North Barrington is Barrington Lake, and contiguous on the west is the tiny village of LAKE BARRINGTON, which had a ten-year rise in population of 101 percent, rising from 172 in 1960 to 347 in 1970.

The Northwest Highway continues along the northern edge of BARRINGTON HILLS, 38 *m.* (2,712 pop. 1970; 1,726, 1960, inc. 57%), which comprises terrain in Cook, Kane, Lake, and McHenry Counties. South of Barrington Hills on Illinois 59 is SOUTH BARRINGTON, which has been losing population; in 1970 it had 348, down from 473 in 1960, despite its location on Northwest Tollway (Int. 90).

FOX RIVER GROVE, 43 *m.* (771 alt., 2,245, pop. 1970; 1,866, 1960, inc. 20%), stretches along the Fox River and is at a junction with Illinois 22, which comes straight west from Highland Park and the Edens Expressway (US 41). Here US 14 enters McHenry County and its numerous recreation and sports resorts. Fox River Grove had the first important ski lift, and the Norge Ski Club conducts tournaments and has annual jump contests in January, with bigger crowds of spectators every year. Overnight facilities have been increasing.

The Fox River is the dividing line between Fox River Grove and CARY (811 alt., 4,358 pop. 1970; 2,520, 1960, inc. 72%). Bordering the river at the southern edge of the village is the Cary Country Club. John D. Herz located his racing stable here several decades ago. Cary has a junction with Illinois 31 (south to Elgin and Aurora).

CARY, 44 *m.* (4,358 pop. 1970; 2,530, 1960, inc. 72.3%) a village in McHenry County, is a doorstep to the Chain-o-Lakes recreation area. It is served by the North Western commuting line and has numerous facilities for sports, fishing and riding. Otto Scheuering College of the Curtiss Breeding Service is located here.

CRYSTAL LAKE, 51 *m.* (875 alt., 14,541 pop. 1970; 8,314, 1960, inc. 74.9%) takes its name from the lake. It was incorporated as a city in 1914 and for a time was chiefly residential, but in recent years has welcomed industry and built some apartment houses. The high school offers courses in vocational training. McHenry Community College has been located here. The Illinois Institute of Technology is developing a new center for research and education on its new Crystal Lake campus of 103 acres and six buildings, which became available by donation. The Public Library has approx. 36,000 books and circulates 170,000.

South from Crystal Lake, 4 *m.* to LAKE IN THE HILLS (3,240 pop. 1970; 2,046, 1960) a village incorporated in 1952 at the Lake in the Hills, 62 acres, formed in 1923 when an outlet from Crystal Lake was dammed. Southeast of the village, where Illinois 31 meets the terminal of Illinois 62, is the village of ALGONQUIN, on the Fox River (3,515 pop. 1970; 2,014, 1960, inc. 74%).

WOODSTOCK, 57.3 *m.* (943 alt., 10,000 pop. 1970; 8,897, 1960, inc. 14%) began its civic life in 1844 as Centerville. It has been a distributor of dairy products and today has a large unit of the Borden Co., which bottles 1,000,000 lbs. of milk daily and makes cottage cheese and yogurt. It is the home of the Woodstock typewriter, which most recently has been manufactured by the R. C. Allen Business Machines Co. The largest employer is the Woodstock Die Casting Co., a division of Eltra Corp., which makes zinc and aluminum die castings and employs 1,350. The city cooperates with the McHenry County Planning Commission, which supervises planning for best use of residential, industrial and agricultural property. It also follows a comprehensive city plan. It has restored the historic Opera House and made it the center of cultural programs.

HARVARD, 62.5 *m*. (908 alt., 5,177 pop. 1970; 4,248, 1960, inc. 21.9%) is another dairy center on the Chicago & North Western that has been found attractive to Chicagoans who seek the recuperative air of the northern lake country. Just across the Wisconsin line are the favored communities on Lake Geneva, Lake Como, and Delavan Lake.

US 14 crosses the Wisconsin line, 68 *m*. at Big Foot, 3 *m*. south of Walworth, Wisc.

YERKES OBSERVATORY of the University of Chicago is located at Williams Bay on Lake Geneva. Drivers continue across the Wisconsin line to Walworth, Wisc., and turn right on Wisconsin 67 to Fontana and Williams Bay on the lake.

The observatory was built in 1897 with funds furnished by Charles T. Yerkes, street railway magnate, after suitable persuasion by William Rainey Harper and George Ellery Hale. Hale, famous astronomer, was 24 years old when he managed the purchase of two 40-inch refracting discs at a bargain because the original customer had defaulted. The discs had been exhibited at the World's Columbian Exposition in 1893.

The observatory in 1967 installed a new 41-inch reflector telescope especially efficient for inspectographic analysis of celestial bodies. It also uses an IBM computer and a 24-inch telescope for high precision polarization measurements; also a two-dome laboratory for independent experiments, combining a 7-inch Schmidt and a nebular spectrophotometer.

Section b. O'Hare Field to Elgin

The big migration into the cornfields and dairy pastures west of O'Hare International Airport from 1950 on corresponds to the historic relocation of whole populations. In this instance neither fire nor flood caused the transition but the eagerness of city dwellers to seize bargains in town lots in the open country and the financial enterprise of developers ready to support complete towns. Suburbs that have changed the face of Cook County are Elk Grove Village, Schaumburg, and Hoffman Estates.

ELK GROVE VILLAGE (21,907 pop. 1970; 6,608, 1960) is located 25 *m*. west of the Loop and west of O'Hare Field, from which it is separated by York Road and the right-of-way of the Chicago & North Western. It is south of the Northwest Tollway, which has an entrance on York Road, and south of Higgins Road (Illinois 72). Higgins Road has become the principal thoroughfare for new mercantile, office, and hotel-motel developments sustained by the movement to O'Hare Field.

Salt Creek flows through Elk Grove Village, coming down from the Ned Brown Forest Preserve and Busse Forest, which fill a large area between Elk Grove Village and the Northwest Tollway. The extension of the Eisenhower Expressway, Int. 90, also moves through the western part of the village.

Elk Grove Village was laid out with streets, housing, municipal facilities, shopping centers and an industrial park by the Centex Construction Company and incorporated in 1956. It has facilities for swimming and sports and one hospital, St. Alexius (257 beds), a lake and condominiums. A feature has been made of the cultivation of peonies and an annual Peony Pageant is publicized as unique in Peony Village. South of Elk Grove Village, crossed by the Irving Park Road (Illinois 19) are the growing suburbs of BENSENVILLE (12,954 pop. 1970; 6,608, 1960, inc. 271%) WOOD DALE (8,831, pop. 1970; 3,071, 1960, inc. 187%) and ITASCA (4,630 pop. 1970; 3,564, 1960, inc. 30%).

SCHAUMBURG, 30 m. (18,739 pop. 1970; 986, 1960, inc. 799.6%). South of the Northwest Tollway and north of the Du Page County line sprawls the "new" village of Schaumburg, incorporated in 1956 and expanding at a furious pace to cover what a few decades ago were wide acres owned by descendants of the original German immigrants, served by dirt roads leading to a single Lutheran church. The original farmers began to come from the principality of Schaumburg-Lippe after the Civil War and brought their Lutheran faith with them. Schaumburg still retains a Lutheran core, with four churches and one parochial school of this denomination. But according to the Census of 1970 only one-sixth of the Schaumburg population, 3,155, was of foreign birth or mixed parentage. Those with German backgrounds numbered 698, Polish, 482, Italian, 434, and Canadian, 274, and while 464 were of Spanish origin or descent only 8 persons were described as of Puerto Rican birth or parentage.

Schaumburg has become the site of a major enterprise in retailing— the WOODFIELD REGIONAL SHOPPING CENTER, which opened in the fall of 1971 and quickly became the sensation of the business world. This, the largest enclosed center, occupies 191 acres. It was started by A. Alfred Taubman of the Taubman Co., Southfield, Michigan, with 2 million sq. ft. of interior space, 215 shops and services, and three major department stores. More than 40,000 persons visited it on an average day in 1972 and weekends had 100,000. During December, 1972, more than 1 million shoppers were counted. Gross sales for the year exceeded $163 million. In 1972 the promoters began building an addition of 300,000 sq. ft. adjoining the grand court opposite Marshall Field & Co. *World* magazine, New York, said: "This maze of ramps, escalators, corners, pits, and protrusions, as architecturally adventurous as most centers are dull, contains an amphitheater, and stage, a 20,000 gallon fountain and waterfall, and an aquarium. In three subordinate court areas there are monumental sculptures of artists of established reputation; one by Robt. Engman has curved stainless steel arcs, weighing 3,500 lbs. held 24 ft. in air by steel cables. Schaumburg has no bond issues and no corporate, real estate, utility or district taxes. Another less imposing market is Weathersfield Common on Schaumburg Road.

Adjacent to Woodfield Mall is Woodfield Executive Plaza, at the intersection of Golf Road and Illinois 53, comprised of two 11-story towers on an area of six acres, completed in 1973. The buildings have parking facilities for 1,300 and cost $20,000,000. Perkins & Will, Inc., were the architects. Two other 11-story towers, to be known as Woodfield Mall Office Plaza, were announced. The first of three five-story office buildings, Walden Office Square, Algonquin and Meacham Rd., was ready in 1972. A five-story office building was leased by the Addressograph-Multigraph Corp. for two of its divisions.

The old Chicago-Elgin Road, Illinois 19, runs along the southern limits of Schaumburg. At the north the Evanston-Elgin Road, Illinois 58, runs between Schaumburg and HOFFMAN ESTATES, another fast-moving development (22,238 pop. 1970; 8,296, 1960, inc. 168%). Northwest Tollway, Int. 90, runs along its northern limits to Elgin and to the north are the Barringtons. There are Forest Preserves throughout this general area, adjoining Hoffman Estates and STREAMWOOD, which is west of Schaumburg (18,176 pop. 1970; 4,821, 1960; inc. 277%). A branch of Poplar Creek runs through Streamwood. South of Streamwood are two villages that straddle the Cook and Du Page County boundaries. HANOVER PARK (11,916 pop. 1970; 451, 1960) had an increase of 542.1% in the decade, while BARTLETT (3,501 pop. 1970; 1,540, 1960) rose 127.3%. Both villages are served by US 20, an extension of Lake St. *See also Tour 11.*

Directly west of Barrington Hills on the Fox River is the Kane County village of CARPENTERSVILLE (24,058 pop. 1970; 17,424, 1960, inc. 36%), which has experienced the large addition of residents because of the construction, since 1953, of a self-contained subdivision by the L. W. Bensinger interests called Meadowdale.

South of US 14 in Kane County and including most of Barrington Hills is DUNDEE TOWNSHIP. The Township had 34,575 pop. in 1970, up 40% from 24,683 in 1960. The old Dundee Road, Illinois 72, passes through Barrington Hills. South of Carpentersville is EAST DUNDEE, (2,920 pop. 1970; 2,221, 1960, inc. 31%). Adjoining is WEST DUNDEE (3,295 pop. 1970; 2,530, 1960, inc. 30%). Immediately west, and west of Illinois 31, is SLEEPY HOLLOW (1,729 pop., 1970; 341, 1960; inc. 455%). These villages are only a few miles north of the Elgin city limits.

ELGIN, 38-40 *m.* northwest of Chicago Loop, (55,691 pop., 1970) on the Fox River, with the bulk of its population in Kane County, is showing its greatest growth in its eastern areas in Cook County. Speed highways from Chicago: John F. Kennedy Expressway to O'Hare interchange, then Northwest Tollway to junction with Illinois 31; US 20, Ill. 19, Ill. 58. *See article on Elgin.*

Tour 11

CHICAGO TO DUBUQUE THROUGH THE WESTERN SUBURBS

Oak Park—River Forest—Forest Park—Elmwood Park—River Grove — Melrose Park — Maywood — Stone Park — Bellwood — Hillside — Northlake — Berkeley — Elmhurst — Addison — Bloomingdale — Hanover Park—Bartlett

Elgin — Dundee — Marengo — Belvidere — Rockford — Freeport — Stockton—East Dubuque

US 20. Eisenhower Expressway, Int. 90.
Chicago to Dubuque, 178 *m.*

Directly west of the Chicago Loop are located some of the most populous and attractive suburbs of Cook County. Most of them were laid out for residential purposes, with single-family dwellings dominating; independent local governments, schools, and municipal facilities. The older suburbs, by strict zoning, have managed to regulate types of buildings and light industries, but since World War II high costs of administration have led some of them to open industrial parks and invite larger plants.

With the building of the Dwight D. Eisenhower Expressway, Interstate 90, the highway system has provided a fast multilane route to the suburbs directly west of the Loop and into the affluent, rapidly growing villages west and northwest of O'Hare International Airport. The Eisenhower is a direct route into the desirable residential areas of Oak Park, Forest Park, Maywood, Oak Brook and Elmhurst. When it connects with north-south Illinois 53 north of Lake St., it provides a multilane highway up into the Schaumburg and Arlington Heights area, with the prospect of an alternate highway into Lake County.

The route of Eisenhower Expressway and connections is as follows: From Grant Park and Congress west through the U. S. Postoffice, west into Oak Park, junction at Harlem Ave., Illinois 34; Forest Park; Maywood, with Illinois 171, north-south; Bellwood-Hillside interchange on Mannheim Road with US 45, Illinois 12, 20, north-south; between Hillside and Elmhurst, interchange with Tri-State Tollway to O'Hare, East-West Tollway to Oak Brook; north in Elmhurst, junction with St. Charles Road, junction with Lake St., US 20 and North Ave., Illinois 64; northwest to Itasca and junction with Illinois 53, north-south, which becomes multilane; at Irving Park road, Illinois

19, direct connection east with O'Hare; through Elk Grove Village; junction with Higgings Road, Illinois 72, into Schaumburg; Rolling Meadows and junction with Northwest Tollway, Int. 90; junction with Northwest Highway, US 14; Arlington Heights and junction with Palatine Road. Terminal at Dundee Road, Illinois 68 (1973).

Beyond the Fox River Valley US 20 crosses northern Illinois to the Mississippi River, traversing a region rich in historical associations closely linked with its topography. In its eastern half the highway crosses the most recently glaciated part of the State, a rolling country of fields and woodlands, low morainic ridges and frequently marshy depressions. The irregular, poorly drained land, with extensive areas suitable only for pasture or woodland, coupled with its nearness to large urban markets, makes this northeastern section a most important dairy region.

Elgin and Rockford, manufacturing centers of national stature, lie in the broad valleys of the Fox and Rock Rivers—glacial outlet channels carved by the outpouring torrents of the Wisconsin ice sheet. Their industrial development stems from early utilization of local water power.

Section a. Chicago to Elgin, 38 m.

West on Washington Blvd. to Austin Ave., the city's boundary, or west on Eisenhower Expressway.

OAK PARK, 10.5 *m.* (630 alt., 62,511 pop. 1970; 61,511, 1960, inc. 2%) is a residential village that lies directly west of the Chicago Loop and is easily reached by a half-hour's drive on Washington Blvd. or Eisenhower Expressway. The village begins at Austin Blvd. Although Oak Park adjoins Chicago it has retained its individuality through careful administration and has the air of a prosperous middle-class citadel. It has numerous detached dwellings on tree-shaded lots, few light industries, and laws against the sale of liquor, which have kept the place free from night life. It enjoys a reputation for cultural achievement; it has 40 churches, several colleges and libraries, and was the home of Ernest Hemingway as boy and young man, and of Frank Lloyd Wright, whose earliest designs in architecture are on view here and in the adjoining River Forest.

Oak Park is bounded on the north by North Ave., along which runs Illinois 64, on the south by Roosevelt Road (Illinois 38), on the east by Austin Ave. and Chicago, and on the west by Harlem Ave. and Illinois 43. Lake St. goes northwest and becomes US 20 in Elmhurst; Washington Blvd. becomes Illinois 56 to Aurora. Both connect with the Tri-State Tollway for O'Hare International Airport. Oak Park commuters to Chicago use the Chicago & North Western Railroad, the Lake St. trains of the CTA, and the West Suburban Transit bus lines.

Oak Park has the council-manager form of government, with a president, a board of six trustees and a village clerk, elected on a nonpartisan slate. The board appoints the village manager, who is the chief executive of municipal affairs.

Oak Park was first settled in 1833 by Joseph Kettlestrings, who came with his wife in an ox-drawn covered wagon from Baltimore, Maryland. Their descendants, and those of other early settlers, hold prominent positions in the social and civic life of the community.

Almost since its inception Oak Park has been bone dry and well governed. For 50 years the village fathers fought for local option so that saloons might be legally barred. This the legislature was not empowered to grant until the passage of an enabling act in 1907. By that time local option was scarcely needed, so dry was Oak Park in sentiment and fact. Deeds to much of the land within the corporate limits and beyond contained anti-saloon clauses inserted by the original owners.

One of the citizens who fought to keep Oak Park free of saloons was Henry Warren Austin, who arrived in 1850 and owned much acreage in what are now Oak Park and Austin. He helped eliminate several saloons by buying and closing them. He was once nominated for President of the United States by the Prohibition Party. He served in the State Assembly, as did his son, Henry Warren Austin, a banker, who died in 1947. The latter donated to the village a four-acre tract called AUSTIN GARDEN, which contains two acres of primeval woods that are to be left unchanged in perpetuity. The rest of the land has the Austin family home and a meadow, also to be kept in their original condition.

The early architectural designs of Frank Lloyd Wright (1869-1959) are visible in 24 dwellings and one church in Oak Park and six dwellings in River Forest. Wright's first family home, 951 Chicago Ave., dates from 1891 and with his Studio is open weekdays except Monday, 10-5, for a fee of $1.25. Other houses are private and may be viewed only from the street.

The Unitarian-Universalist Church, originally Unity Temple, at Lake St. and Kenilworth Ave., was built in 1905 of concrete and has some of the horizontal planes that are visible in later designs by Wright. It was designated a National Historic Landmark in 1971. Restoration has been undertaken, and by summer, 1972, $100,000 had been expended. The Federal Government then made a grant of $37,500 under the National Historic Preservation Act. Admission is free.

The birthplace of Ernest Hemingway (1899-1961), 339 North Oak Park Ave. is not a shrine, nor is the house at 600 N. Kenilworth Ave. where he lived during his adolescence, but both are often subjects of inquiry at the Public Library. A bronze plaque commemorating the birth of Ernest Hemingway on July 21, 1899, was placed in the cement carriage walk at 339 N. Oak Park Ave. by Universal Pictures, when its film, *The Killers,* opened in Chicago. Ronald Reagan appeared in the film.

The OAK PARK PUBLIC LIBRARY, Lake St. at Grove Ave. is not only custodian of the cultural interests of the village but reaches out to children and adults with special services such as films, periodicals, exhibits of fine arts and crafts, adult education programs, storytelling for little folks, programs for grade school children and junior book discussion groups. It maintains branches in South Oak Park and North Oak Park. With a collection of more than 150,000 books it reaches a circulation of more than 450,000. Its Reciprocal Borrower's Card gives any cardholder access to the resources of the Suburban Library System of 56 libraries, which has its headquarters here. The system has a depository of more than 16,500 books, making the available total in Oak Park more than 166,500.

The main library, completed in 1964, displays on its terrace a sculpture of copper and brass entitled Unity and Growth, designed and executed by Carole Harrison. This 9 by 12 ft. piece was chosen in a competition supervised by the Village Art Fair, which awarded the sculptrees $6,000 for the work.

Oak Park authors have found a special friend in the library, which leads with collections of Ernest Hemingway and Frank Lloyd Wright, and gives recognition to the writings of nearly 100 other authors and journalists. Local authors are defined as persons born in Oak Park and River Forest, graduates of a local elementary or high school, and persons who have lived there at least a year or who have gained local prominence. Thus the library has the books of the Bartons—Dr. William E. Barton, who was a Lincoln biographer, and his son Bruce Barton; John Stewart Carter, Mignon G. Eberhart, Kenneth Fearing, Dr. James B. Herrick, Janet Lewis, George Morgenstern, James Park Sloan, Vincent Starrett, Anna Louise Strong and many others. The library has prepared a bibliography of the Frank Lloyd Wright collection and published *A Guide to the Architecture of Frank Lloyd Wright,* which describes his houses in Oak Park and River Forest ($1.15).

Oak Park Conservatory, East Ave. and Garfield St., has an agricultural display that offers close study of many unusual varieties of tropical plants, with guidance for visitors, especially Saturday and Sunday, 2-4.

RIVER FOREST (631 alt., 13,402 pop. 1970; 12,655, 1960, inc. 5.6%), 11 *m.* from the Loop, is contiguous to Oak Park on the west and shares its residential attractiveness. Lake St., later Illinois 20, moves through it, and Harlem Ave., the dividing line between the two suburbs, gives River Forest quick access to the Eisenhower Expressway. The two villages share the Oak Park-River Forest High School.

In 1836 came the first settlers-Ashbel Steele, his wife, two sons, and seven daughters. In a clearing on what is now Thatcher Avenue, Steele and his sons erected their house. The pioneer home became the center of neighborhood hospitality, and the small square piano, brought overland with much labor, lent a note of grace to frontier life. In 1833 a sawmill and gristmill were built on the east side of the river, north of what is now Lake Street. This mill, the only one for 40 miles around, finished some of the lumber that went into the building of early Chicago. Today rigorous zoning laws limit commerce and industry.

Early communication with Chicago was by means of the old Frink & Walker stagecoach. Drawn by four horses, it carried 10 passengers-9 inside and one on top with the driver. The fare was 50 cents for adults, and 25 cents for children. In 1849 the Galena & Chicago Union Railroad laid a single track of strap iron along the old stage route as far as Elmhurst. The rails were wooden riders sheathed in iron, the ties were small and widely spaced. Wood was used for fuel and stored in long sheds along the right-of-way, and the small boilers of the engines needed water tanks every few miles.

Associated with the railroad was Daniel Cunningham Thatcher. Formerly a Chicago business man, Thatcher retired to River Forest in 1854. Two years later he purchased a section of land near the Des Plaines River and built a house. The land is now known as Thatcher's Woods of the Cook County Forest Preserve. In 1859 and 1860 Frances Willard (1839-1898), Evanston temperance leader, boarded with the Thatcher family. At that time she was teaching in the lone River Forest school. In 1929 the village named one of its new schools for her.

In 1862 Thatcher persuaded the Chicago & North Western Railway to build a station on his property. The station was called Thatcher, and River Forest was known by that name until 1872, when the present name was adopted. On October 24, 1880, the community was organized as the village of River Forest. The village seal, bearing the motto, *Silva in Flumine* (Lat., forest on the river) attests its attractive site.

The old Thatcher House, 511 Edgewood Place, houses the Trailside Museum of Natural History. The collections, planned to show the phylogenic relationships of the several life forms, are composed of invertebrates, fish, amphibians, reptiles, birds and mammals. A geological exhibit comprises fossils from local quarries, cross-sections of underlying formations, and studies in rock structure. Assisting the curator is a junior staff of boys and girls who receive training in biology, geology, and museum methods. *Open daily except Thursday, 10-12; 1-5.*

ROSARY COLLEGE, Forest Ave. and Division St., a Roman Catholic liberal arts institution for women, was opened in River Forest in 1922. The board of trustees consists of five sisters of the order of St. Dominic. The Gothic buildings, of Bedford stone, designed by Ralph Adams Cram, show to the best possible advantage against the natural beauty of the wooded campus. Central Hall (1925) has a cloister walk extending its entire length; it contains the chapel, library, refectory, and social hall. Lewis Memorial Hall houses a little theater, exhibition gallery, and portrait studios. Collections include paintings, tapestries, and period furniture, contributed by Mrs. Edward Hines of Evanston.

Rosary College permits students to have their junior year in Fribourg, Switzerland. In 1934 the Rosary College Program of Education for Leisure, without fees, was begun.

CONCORDIA TEACHERS COLLEGE, Bonnie Brae and Division Sts., opened in 1913, is maintained by the Missouri Synod of the Evangelical Lutheran Church to train teachers for Lutheran elementary schools. Its library has 100,110 volumes.

The DOMINICAL HOUSE OF STUDIES, Division St. at

Harlem Ave., is a preparatory college fitting students for the priesthood. The AQUINAS INSTITUTE OF PHILOSOPHY, founded in 1929, has a library of 27,000 books.

Among the Frank Lloyd Wright houses in River Forest are the Winslow House (1893), on Auvergne Place, one of Wright's first buildings; and the Elizabeth Roberts House (1906), on Edgewood Place. Each house reveals Wright's desire to harmonize his buildings with the terrain, to recognize and accentuate the "natural beauty of the plain, its quiet level." The River Forest Tennis Club, 615 Lathrop Ave., and the Richard W. Bock Studio, 7820 Chicago Ave., both built in 1906, are other examples of Wright's work. These are private homes, not open to visitors.

The River Forest Women's Club (1913), 526 N. Ashland Ave., was the first women's clubhouse in the State.

River Forest Public Library was built in 1929 and enlarged in 1955. It stocks more than 30,000 books and has more than 100,000 transactions annually. It has much information about the Wright houses. It is a member of the Suburban Library System.

FOREST PARK (15,472 pop. 1970) is directly west of Oak Park and south of River Forest, and is crossed by the Eisenhower Expressway, Int. 90, which has connecting ramps at Harlem Ave. *See Tour 12A*.

West of Forest Park and River Forest, 1 *m.*, on the west bank of the Des Plaines River is MAYWOOD (30,036 pop. 1970) also reached by the Eisenhower Expressway. *See Tour 12A*.

ELMWOOD PARK, (26,160 pop. 1970; 23,866, 1960, inc. 9%) incorporated as a village in 1914, is directly north of River Forest on North Ave. (Illinois 64), which separates the two suburbs. The east boundary of both is Harlem Ave. (Illinois 43). Grand Ave., lined with shops, is the principal retail street; other streets radiate from a central circle around which are stores, offices, and the Village Hall. It has easy access to the Des Plaines Forest Preserve. There is commuting service on the Milwaukee Railroad and CTA buses.

RIVER GROVE, (11,465 pop. 1970; 8,464, 1960, inc. 35%) west of Elmwood Park, 15 *m.* west of the Loop on Grand Ave. and bisected by the Des Plaines River and its Forest Preserve, was incorporated as a village in 1888 but traces its settlement by German immigrants back to 1863. Its principal retailing business is on Grand Ave. and at Thatcher Woods Plaza. It is fully built up and investors are turning to apartment houses and condominiums. It gets commuting service from the Milwaukee Railroad, which runs along Grand Ave. West Towns and CTA buses connect with Chicago lines. River Grove has the Oak Park Country Club, and the Indian Boundary golf course is in the Forest Preserve. River Grove workers are employed by industries in Northlake and Franklin Park. In 1964 TRITON JUNIOR COLLEGE was established here and in less than eight years had nearly 10,000 students and a faculty of 548.

MELROSE PARK, 13 *m.* (22,706 pop. 1970; 22,291, 1960, inc. 1.9%) in Cook county north of Maywood and west of River Forest and the Des Plaines River, is an industrial suburb on Lake St. The Proviso marshalling yards of the Chicago & North Western fill a long stretch of rails westward from Melrose Park and into Berkeley. During World War II this became a center for heavy industry. Since then the International Harvester Co. has established a division here for making diesel engines, tractors, and road-building machinery. Westlake Hospital and Gottlieb Hospital are located here.

An attraction at Melrose Park is Amling's Flowerland, a large garden center with more than 40 greenhouses and landscaped areas with displays of blooms. *Open daily 8:30 to 8:30; Sunday until 6 p.m.*

A direct route from Chicago to Melrose Park and the Maywood Race Track is North Ave., Illinois 64. At the Mannheim Road on the west line of Melrose Park Lake St. joins US 20, which, combined with US 45, comes up from the south.

STONE PARK 14 *m.*, (4,451 pop. 1970; 3,038, 1960, inc. 46%) is a small Cook County village north of Melrose Park bounded by North Ave. (Illinois 64) and Lake St. (US 20).

FRANKLIN PARK, 15 *m.*, (20,497 pop. 1970; 18,322, 1960) incorporated in 1892, extends north of Melrose Park to O'Hare field. It is one of the most intensely industrialized of the western suburbs, having a number of plants employing 500 to 4,000, including Motorola, and is also a distributing center for factories in other suburbs. This is accounted for by the network of railroads, including marshalling yards of the Milwaukee, the North Western, the Indiana Harbor Belt Line, and their connections. A small part of Franklin Park north of Belmont Ave. borders on the Des Plaines River and the Indian Boundary Forest Preserve; across the river are the Indian Boundary Golf Course and the Seymour Simon Preserve.

NORTHLAKE, 16 *m.* (14,212 pop. 1970; 12,318, 1960, inc. 15%) is crossed at its southwest corner by US 20 (Lake St.), and Eisenhower Expressway. The Tri-State Tollway runs between Northlake and Elmhurst, with O'Hare International Airport about 5 min. north. A branch of the Chicago & North Western Ry. has been run from its Proviso yards near Melrose Park to the Airport, thus giving Northlake industries new access to the North Western system. Because this city grew up at the intersections of North Ave. and Lake St. it became known as North Lake; when it was incorporated in 1949 the two names were combined. It has a thriving industrial center in which the Automatic Electric Co. employs approx. 10,000 in making telephonic and electronic equipment. Here also are General Foods, Hunt-Wesson Foods, Kroger, and Scholle Chemical Corp. In 1972 a 16-story motel, Chicago's O'Hareport, fully equipped with facilities for conventions, was completed at a cost of $16,000,000. Northlake is served by West Towns and Greyhound bus lines; for train service to Chicago commuters board the Milwaukee in Franklin Park and the North Western in Elmhurst.

GTE Automatic Electric, a subsidiary of General Telephone & Electronics Corp., is the largest manufacturer in Northlake, with 10,000 employees, an annual payroll of $100,000,000, and sales of dial telephone equipment and other accessories valued at more than $620,000,000 annually. Its plant in Northlake occupies 44 acres. Founded by Almon B. Strowger, inventor of the automatic switchboard and the dial telephone, Automatic Electric became a subsidiary of General Telephone & Electronics in 1955 and moved to Northlake after many years at Van Buren and Morgan Sts., Chicago. In 1969 it shifted part of its manufacturing to Huntsville, Ala. It has warehouses and some other facilities in Elk Grove Village, Des Plaines, Elmhurst, and Melrose Park, and feeder plants in Waukesha, Wisc., and Geneva, Ill. A subsidiary is Lenkurt Electric, maker of multiplexing equipment, which permits transmission of as many as 24 voices on a pair of wires. The Northlake research laboratory of Automatic Electric has 1,100 specialists with their eyes on the future.

ELMHURST, 16.5 *m.* (681 alt., 50,547 pop. 1970; 36,991, 1960, inc. 36%) a city in Du Page County, has access to a network of expressways. Eisenhower (Int. 90) and Tri-State Tollway, Int. 294, run along its eastern limits; US 20, and Illinois 64 pass through it. Elmhurst was first known as Cottage Hill because of a cottage built by J. L. Hovey in 1843, which became a hotel for farmers driving to the Chicago market. The road became Cottage Hill Ave. and its rows of elms later suggested the name of Elmhurst. Wilder Park, west side of Cottage Hill Ave. and south of the Chicago & North Western Tracks, was originally the estate of Seth Wadham, who built a massive house there. It passed to Thomas E. Wilder, who transferred it to the city with the proviso that the estate be a public park and the house a public library. The Elmhurst Public Library was established there in 1869 and was completely rehabilitated in 1965. It has nearly 100,000 books and cited 323,559 transactions (use of all services) in 1972.

Carl Sandburg lived at 333 S. York St. when doing newspaper work in Chicago. Jens Christian Bay, author, and long curator of the John Crerar Library in Chicago was also a resident.

LIZZADRO MUSEUM OF LAPIDARY ART, 220 College Hill, Elmhurst, offers a large display of semi-precious stones and the gems made from them, as well as the methods used by professional gem cutters. Television shows supplement the exhibits Sunday at 3 p.m. *Open Tues.-Thurs. 10-5; Saturday, 10-5; Sunday, 1-5; closed Monday.*

ELMHURST COLLEGE, opposite Wilder Park, is a private, four-year liberal arts institution that gives the degree of bachelor of arts. Founded in 1871 by the efforts of two German Evangelical synods to prepare students for theological careers it developed into Elmhurst Academy and Junior College in 1919 and became a senior college in 1924. In 1930 it became coeducational. It is associated with the United Church of Christ and seeks to relate the Christian faith to the academic disciplines. A two-year Common Course taken by all students is intended to give an understanding of the issues of contemporary life. Since 1970 the college has been offering Afro-American Studies to help black students get a basic knowledge of black literature, history, religion, art and civic aims. Urban studies include opportunities for field work in Chicago. A student may work 15 hours a week for 16 weeks to help defray costs of a course in Europe.

Two buildings belong to the first decade: Kranz Hall, 1873, and Old Main, 1878. Among new buildings of recent construction are the A. C. Buehler Library, donated by the Buehler family of Barrington, Ill.; Niebuhr Hall, named for H. Richard Niebuhr, former president, and Reinhold Niebuhr, who graduated here; Science Center, 1966, and Stranger Hall, men's residence, 1968. Total costs for the school year, with board and room, is estimated at $3,000; non-resident, $1,900. In the 1972-73 year Elmhurst enrolled 2,731 students and had a faculty of 178.

US 20 has a junction with Eisenhower Expressway in northwest Elmhurst (*see Tour 12A*), and with Illinois 83 north-south.

Beyond Elmhurst US 20 turns into the areas of Cook and Du Page Counties that have proved especially profitable to developers of suburban residential property. The migration from Chicago has boosted values of farm land to heights undreamed of by the thrifty German immigrants who farmed here more than a century ago.

ADDISON, 20 *m.*, (24,482 pop. 1970; 6,741, 1960, inc. 263%) in Du Page County, is a sprawling area that has had a large expansion in recent years, especially along Lake St. It is located northwest of Villa Park and Elmhurst and north of Lombard. Salt Creek Forest Preserve runs along its eastern limits and Illinois 53 take a north-south route through it. Large apartment houses have been built and there is a new industrial park of 1,500 acres. The place has about 500 light industries. The Green Meadows Shopping Plaza and three other market centers serve the area.

North of Addison on Illinois 53 is ITASCA (4,638 pop. 1970; 3,564, 1960, inc. 30%), also reached by the Eisenhower Expressway. In addition to new residential areas it has developed an industrial park for light industry. It is on Illinois 19.

BLOOMINGDALE (2,964 pop. 1970; 1,262, 1960, inc. 135%) is an older settlement that formerly included the present ROSELLE, contiguous to the northwest, 27 *m.* from the Loop. The recent suburban development has reached to Roselle, which has the Irving Park Road, Illinois 19, and the Milwaukee commuter line running through it. (4,583 pop. 1970; 3,581, 1960, inc. 28%). Roselle was incorporated as a city in 1922. A community project of 156 acres called The Trails at Woodfield comprises detached houses, townhouses, recreational projects and a shopping center.

HANOVER PARK, 30 *m.* (11,916 pop. 1970; 451, 1960, inc. 542%) holds the record for growth on US 20. The hamlet of 451 people is practically lost in the development that expanded after it was incorporated in 1958. In its northeastern part Illinois 19 runs along the town lines of Hanover Park and Schaumburg. The area of Hanover Park is divided between Du Page and Cook Counties. Contiguous on the west are BARTLETT (3,501 pop. 1970; 1,540, 1960, inc. 127%), a village incorporated in 1891, and STREAMWOOD (18,176 pop. 1970; 4,821, 1960, inc. 277%). The latter is on Illinois 19.

West of Elgin, which marks the northeastern border of the Chicago urban area, the landscape is essentially rural. Crossroad communities serve nearby farms. Cities of consequence are Rockford, Freeport, and Galena. Between Elgin and Rockford US 20 crosses a rolling country of poorly drained fields, pastures, and woodlands, a region of intensive dairy farming.

Interstate 90 crosses the Fox River on the northern outskirts of Elgin and is a speed highway to within 2 m. of Rockford.

Westward on US 20 a service station marks what was once a stop on the Chicago-Galena stage road called Henpeck. It dates from a log cabin built in 1836 by Tenas Allen. During the Galena lead rush of the late 1830's and early 1840's as many as 50 men encamped here overnight. At the time of the Civil War, Henpeck had a post office, shops and more than 100 people. The country road that turns left follows the route of the old Galena Trail, also known as the Grant Trail.

The dominance of dairying throughout this region is everywhere apparent in herds of fine dairy cattle, large red barns, tall silos, and uniformly well-kept farmsteads. Croplands are largely in corn, with extensive areas in hay and pasture. In contrast to agricultural practices in central Illinois, where corn and other grains are harvested as cash crops, most of the corn in this region is cut before maturity for use as silage.

MARENGO, 77.4 m. (819 alt., 4,235 pop. 1970; 3,568, 1960, inc. 18%) in McHenry County, is noteworthy for its elm-arched roadway and the McGill Metal Products plant, 127 E. Prairie St., one of the world's largest manufacturers of mousetraps. Marengo is the birthplace of Egbert Van Alstyne, composer of "In the Shade of the Old Apple Tree." The name of the town commemorates one of Napoleon's famous victories. Here US 20 has a junction with Illinois 23, which runs straight south until it joins US 66 at Pontiac, and with Illinois 176, eastward. The Marengo Public Library, built 1930, circulates approx. 25,000 vols. and is a member of the Northern Illinois Library System.

East from Marengo on Illinois 176 to UNION (579 pop. 1970; 480, 1960), noted for the Illinois Railway Museum, an open-air exhibit of more than 80 locomotives of all types and periods, also coaches, interurbans, and street cars. Electric cars are operated daily in June, July and August; and on weekends in September and October. Steam locomotives are operated Sundays and holidays.

The crossroads community of GARDEN PRAIRIE, 83.3 m. and the site of Amesville, two miles west, bear witness to the competition between the old stagecoach lines and the early railroads. Garden Prairie came into being in 1849 when the Galena & Chicago Union Railroad built its station in the settlement rather than in Amesville, because of the refusal of one Ames, whose business came from the stagecoach trade, to allow its erection near his tavern. Part of the Ames Tavern (1835) is incorporated in a frame residence, 84.9 m.

BELVIDERE, 89 m. (778 alt., 14,061 pop. 1970; 11,223, 1960, inc. 25%), seat of Boone County, on the Kishwaukee River, was a city of small industries until 1965 when the Chrysler Corp. opened a large car assembly plant with provision for employing up to 3,000 workers.

Belvidere is strategically located on highways serving north central Illinois and southern Wisconsin, with easy access to Interstate 90, the direct route from Chicago, bypassing the cities of US 20 and Illinois 72. Another route from Wisconsin, Illinois 76, terminates at Belvidere.

The city dates from 1836 and was a stop on the Chicago-Galena stage route. One of the State's early industries, the National Sewing Machine Co., was formed here in 1879. A local legend perpetuates the story of Big Thunder, a Potawatomi chief whose body after death was exposed in a small stockade near the site of the present courthouse in the Indian fashion. In the course of time the chief's knife, tobacco pouch, and even clothing were filched by souvenir hunters, and eventually even his bones disappeared.

The IDA PUBLIC LIBRARY, 320 N. State St., built in 1913, was remodeled in 1969. Its collection of more than 20,000 vols. circulates approx. 65,000. It is a member of the Northern Illinois Library System, with hq in Rockford.

CHERRY VALLEY, 5½ m. west of Belvidere on US 20 (952 pop. 1970; 875, 1960) a Rockford suburb, is at a junction where Int. 90 turns north to bypass Rockford.

ROCKFORD, 95 m. (147,370 pop.) While the main route, US 20, bypasses Rockford a branch route from Belvidere moves to and through the city and rejoins US 20 two miles west of the city limits. *See article on Rockford.*

Section b. Rockford to Iowa Line, 93 m.

West of Rockford, 0 m., US 20 crosses first the rolling hill lands of the Pecatonica Valley, a region of old glacial drift, then the sharply dissected driftless area of Jo Daviess County, part of the remarkably beautiful region unaffected by glaciation that lies in southwestern Wisconsin and adjacent parts of Illinois and Iowa. Sharp profiles of ridges, mounds, and valleys, clearly etched patterns of fields and woodlands varying in color and tone as the hour of the day or season of the year indicate, are revealed in panoramas as the highway follows a ridge crest, or are hidden from view as the road dips and winds through forested valleys.

This westernmost section is the old lead mining country, one of the earliest developed parts of Illinois. The mineral veins lie just below the upland level, exposed in the countless tributary valleys of the Galena and Mississippi rivers. The region abounds in landmarks of the frontier; the highway often approximates the old Galena stage route. Indeed, US 20 throughout much of its course follows closely this pioneer road, broken more than a century ago by the lumbering oxcarts that carried east-bound lead from the nation's most productive mines to the young port of Chicago. Today richer fields have forced the mines from a competitive market, and little remains of the old days save the quiet little city of Galena and the enduring loveliness of the countryside.

An entrance 14.3 *m.*, leads to the Seward Forest Preserve developed as a small park. The road leads through and across a forested valley in which flows a small brook. Stone bridges and embankments, fireplaces and shelter house are in keeping with the wilderness aspect of the park. A children's playground is well equipped.

FREEPORT, 28 *m.* (781 alt., 27,736 pop. 1970; 26,628, 1960, inc. 4%), seat of Stephenson County, is a shipping center for field and dairy products of a large farming area, a growing industrial city and headquarters for major farm insurance agencies. It is a junction for Illinois 26, which continues north into Wisconsin, and Illinois 75, which joins other roads at East Beloit. It is served by the Illinois Central Railroad, two freight lines, the Milwaukee and the Chicago & North Western, as well as Greyhound Bus Lines, Scenic Stage Lines, and Badger Bus Line. The Freeport-Albertus Airport is located 3 *m.* southeast of the city.

Freeport in 1968 completed a notable change in the downtown business district by transforming two blocks into The Plaza, a mall that excludes all vehicles except fire trucks and provides shade trees, shrubs, pools and playgrounds, all paid by private funds. Work also was begun on the ten-year construction project of HIGHLAND COMMUNITY COLLEGE, of which the first buildings are the Natural Science unit and the Library. A local bond issue provides $4,200,000 and the Illinois Junior College Board makes up the rest of an estimated $10,700,000. The college opened its doors in 1962 and in 1971 had a faculty of 85 and enrolled 919 students.

Other completed projects that reflect the soundness of Freeport's economy is the new Carl Sandburg High School, which cost $2,000,000; a new building added to the Freeport Medical Clinic; the new 12-story bank and office building of the State Bank of Freeport, which covers one block and cost $2,750,000 and the 14-story apartment house of the Freeport Housing Authority. Civic plans include a new City and County Building, expected to cost $2,100,000.

Of industries that have developed in Freeport those making electrical equipment and tires account for the largest employment. Kelly Springfield Tire Co., which employs 1,200, opened a $10,000,000 plant in 1963 and tripled its capacity in eight years. Wages and salaries accounted for nearly $10,300,000 in 1969 and county and township taxes added more than $250,000 to the public's coffers. The *Journal-Standard* reported that the Freeport unit had grown at a much faster pace than the tire industry. Micro Switch, a division of Honeywell, switching devices and motors, employs up to 3,000; Burgess Battery Division of Gould, Inc., has 760; Newell Manufacturing Co., household supplies, 600. Tours of plants are available by appointment at W. T. Rawleigh Co. and Furst-McNess Co., both making proprietary products, and at Structo Division of King Seeley Thermos Co.

These major insurance agencies have offices here: Bankers Mutual Life, Crum & Forster Companies, Economy Fire & Casualty, General Casualty of Wisconsin, Security Insurance Group, and Western States.

Some of the early settlers at Freeport were miners returning from Galena; others were Pennsylvania Germans. In 1853 the first railroad, the Galena & Chicago Union, reached Freeport. On August 27, 1858, Freeport was the host of the second Lincoln-Douglas Debate, the site of which, at N. State Ave. and E. Douglas St., is marked by a memorial boulder with a plaque giving two quotations: Lincoln's "This government cannot endure permanently half slave and half free," and Douglas' "I am not for the dissolution of the Union under any circumstance."

One of the State's earliest monuments to the dead of the Civil War was erected on the Courthouse square in 1869. It is a tall stone shaft with a bronze statue of an infantryman at the top and four bronze figures at the base of a sailor, a soldier, cavalryman, and artilleryman. Names of all men enlisted from Stephenson County are recorded on a bronze plaque.

Of the three major parks Taylor Park has a bronze statue of LINCOLN THE DEBATER by Leonard Crunelle. The city has five neighborhood parks, 45 churches, two orphanages and six homes for senior citizens.

FREEPORT PUBLIC LIBRARY had more than 75,000 books in 1971 and a circulation of nearly 400,000. Its quarters were modernized in 1963. It has a branch in Henny and is a member of the Northern Illinois Library System of 30 libraries with headquarters in Rockford.

The Farm Museum of the Stephenson County Historical Society in Freeport exhibits, among other relics, a Manny reaper, similar to the early machines built in Freeport. The farm museum is built of gray concrete blocks and is located near the Historical Museum at 1440 South Carroll Ave.

From Freeport north on Illinois 26 to:

CEDARVILLE, 5.2 *m.* Left three blocks from the crest of the hill and right to the end of the road to the birthplace of Jane Addams. A marker placed on Illinois 26 by the Illinois State Historical Society reads:

JANE ADDAMS, 1860—1935. Humanitarian, Feminist, Social Worker, Reformer, Educator, Author, Publicist, Founder of Hull House, Pioneer Settlement Center, Chicago, 1889. President Women's International League for Peace and Freedom. Nobel Peace Prize, 1931.

Miss Addams was the daughter of John Hay Addams, who served in the Illinois State Legislature (1854-1870) and Sarah Weber Addams. Her first American ancestor spelled his name Adams but that man's son made it Addams. This led Lincoln to address Jane's father as "My dear double-d'ed Addams." He became a miller in Illinois in 1844 and raised a company for the Civil War. His wife died when Jane was 2 years old and he married Mrs. Anna H. Haldeman when Jane was 5. The Addams homestead, a substantial two-story brick house opposite the site of the mill, is owned by members of the family. Jane Addams attended Rockford College and became acquainted with the work of Toynbee Hall, the social settlement in London. On September 14, 1889, with her associate Ellen Gates Starr, she opened a settlement in Hull House, the former mansion of Charles J. Hull at Polk and Halsted streets, Chicago. From then on she devoted her life to social betterment, provided nursery schools for children, literacy classes for adults, encouraged handicrafts, worked to abolish sweatshops and helped to obtain legislation improving working hours and conditions.

The grave of Jane Addams is located in the family burial plot about 1,200 ft. west of the farmhouse.

At 40 *m.* is a junction with Illinois 73. North on this road 1.7 *m.* to LENA (964 alt., 1,691 pop. 1970; 1,552, 1960, inc. 9%). A dairy town in Stephenson County, it makes various brands of cheese.

At 43 *m.* is a junction with a graveled road. Left on this road 4.2 *m.* to the site of the Battlefield of Kellogg's Grove. The grove, developed as a small park on the crest of a low hill, commands a magnificent view of the surrounding countryside. A granite shaft, surmounted with cannon balls, marks the site of the battle, fought on June 25, 1832, between Black Hawk's forces and the militia commanded by Col. John Dement. Within the iron fence that surrounds the monument are 25 small bronze plates, commemorating the volunteers killed in the encounter.

A few miles farther north on a farm road is LAKE LE-AQUA-NA STATE PARK, 614.5 acres, described by the State as "an attractive family type park built around a fine fishing lake."

Immediately west of the junction the country becomes more rolling as the highway enters the deeply dissected, unglaciated region of Jo Daviess County, a land of far horizons, of ever-changing hills and valleys revealed in grand panoramas.

At 48.5 *m.* is the junction with Illinois 78, which unites with US 20 for 2 miles.

North on Illinois 78 6 *m.* to APPLE RIVER CANYON STATE PARK, 297 acres, for fishing and camping. *See also Tour 5.*

STOCKTON, 50 *m.* (1,000 alt., 1,930 pop. 1970; 1,800, 1960, inc. 7%) a village in Jo Daviess County, was named by Alanson Parker, an early settler, who envisaged the fertile prairie country as a stock raising center. In the latter decades of the 19th century this promise was realized. Then, with the development of cheap grazing land in the West and the centering of the stock yards in Chicago, farmers found it more profitable to fatten cattle for market than to raise them.

Before this, however, Stockton had had its great days of another kind. Its lead smelters were running full blast. Money was plentiful and soon spent. Today the mines of Jo Daviess County are closed and Stockton is content to look upon itself as an agricultural center.

Stockton is at the western junction with Illinois 78.

The crest of Terrapin Ridge, 60.8 *m.*, commands sweeping vistas to the north and east of the rolling farm lands and wooded hills, the deep, broad valleys and sharply silhouetted mounds of the Driftless Area.

ELIZABETH, 62 *m.* (790 alt., 707 pop. 1970; 729, 1960). On its eastern border a marker defines the site of APPLE RIVER FORT, established during the Black Hawk War. On June 24, 1832, the fort was attacked by 200 warriors, but successfully defended until relief arrived. Many such sites in this northwestern region mark skirmishes between the Indians and encroaching settlers.

At 65.5 *m.* is the junction with Illinois 84, the Great River Road.

From a ridge top a mile west is an excellent view of the Apple River Valley, and the rolling hills backed by the Sinsinawa Mounds of Wisconsin. In this vicinity the highway enters what was once known as Rattlesnake Woods, now a Roadside Park (*picnicking*). The good second-growth of oak throughout this region has stimulated small-scale logging operations. Sawdust heaps, piles of seasoning lumber and cord-wood, and occasional portable sawmills and crew shacks are contemporary manifestations of the great industry that swept these hills and valleys of their virgin forests. The summit of HORSESHOE MOUND (1,070 alt.), 76 *m.*, is the highest point on the route.

GALENA, 78 *m.* (603 alt., 3,930 pop. 1970) *see article on Galena.*

West of Galena back-country roads wind among the hills past log cabins, native stone huts, abandoned lead mines and furnaces, and Indian effigy mounds. In the fastness of the hills much corn whiskey—"Menominee dew"—was distilled during Prohibition.

Leaving the upland at 88 *m.*, the highway begins its long descent to the Mississippi bottoms, across which it winds its way along the base of the bluffs to EAST DUBUQUE, 92.5 *m.* (615 alt., 2,408 pop. 1970; 2,082, 1960, inc. 15%), which is located on high bluffs above the Mississippi River opposite Dubuque, sixth largest city in Iowa with a population of 62,309 (1970). In East Dubuque US 20 has a junction with a highway combining a group of roads from Wisconsin—US 61 and US 151 combined, and Wisconsin 35. A large number of people living in East Dubuque find employment in Dubuque. US 20 crosses the Iowa line, 93 *m.* on a free bridge.

Tour 12

LAKE MICHIGAN TO THE MISSISSIPPI RIVER
ON THE ORIGINAL LINCOLN HIGHWAY

Indiana Line—East Chicago Heights—Chicago Heights—Park Forest and Park Forest South—Olympia Fields—Matteson—Frankfort—New Lenox—Joliet—Plainfield—Aurora—Sugar Grove—Rock Falls—Sterling—Morrison—Fulton—Mississippi River (Clinton, Iowa)

US 30, 160 *m*.

US 30 is one of half dozen highways that provide short routes from Lake Michigan to the Mississippi River in the northern third of Illinois. Through junctions with north-south routes it has connections with the principal cities. US 30 is the original LINCOLN HIGHWAY, initiated in 1912 by Carl G. Fisher of Indianapolis, manufacturer of automobile bodies and accessories. Fisher led the agitation for the road and collected funds. In 1921 the US Congress voted aid to the states through which the highway passed. It started at Jersey City, N. J., and ran via Philadelphia, Gettysburg, Pittsburgh, Fort Wayne; then crossed Illinois and Iowa to Omaha, Cheyenne, Salt Lake City, Sacramento, and San Francisco. It covered more than 3,300 miles and cost $90,000,000 from 1914 to 1927. It then became US 30. The original title is still used in numerous places, but must not be taken for the Lincoln Heritage Trail, *Tour 21,* which follows the route taken by Abraham Lincoln after his entry into Illinois.

The landscape along the route is essentially rural in character. A long-settled agricultural region, the farm lands of northeastern Illinois are rich in legend and history, peaceful and prosperous in appearance.

Between the Fox and the Rock Rivers is the highly productive dairy and beef cattle country of northern Illinois. Corn, hay, wheat, and oats roll in long swells in the cool of spring breezes, ripen to waves of green and gold in the warmth of summer sun, or impart to the haze of early autumn their rich harvest colors. Fine beef and dairy cattle attest the wealth of the region. Sheep, hogs, and occasional flocks of goats feed in barnyards or woodland pastures.

Although much of the country crossed by US 30 was termed by Washington Irving the Grand Prairie, this northern section of Illinois is frequently forested and generally more rolling than flat. From the lake plain of the east the highway rises and falls over the hilly, forested moraines of Will and Kane Counties, then rolls gently onward across the old drift-covered upland of western Illinois, past the valley of the

Rock River, on to the gorge of the Mississippi, which it enters abruptly at Fulton.

Section a. Indiana Line to Aurora, 53 m.

US 30 enters Illinois from Dyer, Ind. The Old Sauk Trail, by which Indians and traders crossed Illinois to Indiana, joins US 30 at the Indiana line. Here also US 30 has a junction with Illinois 83, the Dyer-Glenwood Road, which gives access to Washington Park Race Track. North of US 30 between the Indiana line and Torrence Ave. are several Cook County villages where live many employees of the steel mills in South Chicago and Hammond, Ind.

LYNWOOD (1,042 pop. 1970; 255, 1960, inc. 308%) is another example of the movement of population into this area in the last 10 years.

LANSING (618 alt., 25,805 pop. 1970; 18,098, 1960, inc. 42%) directly north of Lynwood was settled on the Ridge Road by Dutch and German farmers in the 1860's. Wooded areas are found in the Gurdon S. Hubbard Forest Preserve and the Shabbona Woods Forest Preserve farther north.

At 5 m. US 30 has a junction with the Calumet Expressway, Illinois 394, which leads into Int. 94. South on the Expressway to SAUK VILLAGE (7,479 pop. 1970; 4,687, 1960, inc. 59.6%) a village dating back to the early immigrations but not incorporated until 1957.

EAST CHICAGO HEIGHTS (5,000 pop. 1970; 3,270, 1960, inc. 52%) directly west of Calumet Expressway on US 30, has freight service on the Penn Central and the Elgin, Joliet & Eastern, and easy access to roads serving Chicago Heights. (See Tour 1.) A subdivision platted to provide new housing for Negro families gave an incentive to growth and the village is approx. 95% Negro.

CHICAGO HEIGHTS, 6.7 m. (40,900 pop. 1970) see Tour 1. Here Illinois 1, Halsted St., crosses US 30, which continues west on a line between OLYMPIA FIELDS (3,418 pop. 1970; 1,503, 1960) a Cook County village where the 674-acre Olympia Fields Country Club was established in 1926. The club, distinguished for its four 18-hole golf courses, is often the scene of championship tournaments. This is the seat of Tolentine College, a major seminary of the Augustinian order, which averages 54 fathers and 62 scholastics.

Governor's Highway runs south through Olympia Fields, Matteson, and Richton Park, to join Illinois 50.

Also west of Chicago Heights is Park Forest, which is divided from Olympia Fields by US 30. Park Forest and Park Forest South, the fastest growing suburbs at the southern border of Cook County are described in detail under Tour 1.

Adjoining Olympia Fields is MATTESON, (4,741 pop. 1970; 3,225, 1960) a Cook County village settled by Germans from 1855 on and incorporated in 1889. It was named for Joel A. Matteson, Governor of Illinois in the days of settlement. It is at a junction with Illinois

50 (Cicero Ave.) which connects with US 54 south of RICHTON
PARK (2,556 pop. 1970; 933, 1960, inc. 174%). About 2 *m*. west of
Matteson US 30 has a junction with Illinois 43, (Harlem Ave.) and
crosses into Will County.

The highway crosses Hickory Creek at LINCOLN ESTATES,
16.7 *m*. and the creek roughly parallels US 30 into Joliet. All communities north or south of the highway trace their origin to the old Hickory
Creek settlement, which grew up in the 1820's along the winding miles
of this tributary of the Des Plaines River. Indian occupancy of the
section preceded the white man's coming by at least a hundred years.
The Indians favored hickory wood for making bows and arrows, and
stone arrowheads are yet found along the creek. Mounds and other
Indian remains exist throughout the region.

At 18 *m*. there is a junction with US 45 (96th Ave.) and the
village of FRANKFORT (2,325 pop. 1970; 1,135, 1960, inc. 104%),
on the edge of the Van Horn Woods, part of the Forest Preserve. Also
settled by Germans, Frankfort was named after Frankfurt-am-Main.

The so-called LINCOLN HOTEL, 21.8 *m*., is a red-brown brick
structure built in 1846 and reputedly visited by Lincoln when traveling
the old Sauk Trail. The bricks were molded by hand from mud and
grass, and set in mortar made of clay from the creek. About 200 yards
east of the building are excavations said to have been used as a hiding
place for runaway slaves.

NEW LENOX, 24.7 *m.,* is a Hickory Creek settlement of the
1820's. Its McIntosh Subdivision, on both sides of the highway, is a
community of small farms, poultry yards, and kitchen gardens. The
subdivision is the product of the "back to the land" movement.

At 26.9 *m*. is a junction with a graveled road at the east end of the
18-hole Cherry Hill Golf Course.

Right on this road, immediately over the steep railway embankment,
is GOUGARS, site of the first post office in Will County (1832) and
"downtown" for the entire Hickory Creek settlement.

Across Hickory Creek is the Gougars School House. The small
frame building marks the site of the Hickory Creek log schoolhouse
built in 1832. Nearby in Higinbotham Woods are earthworks tradi-
tionally known as the Old French Fort.

North of the schoolhouse the graveled road separates two units of
the Joliet park system. Left is the Public Greenhouse. The greenhouse,
bordered by formal flower gardens and trimly kept lawns, lies on a
slight rise of ground from which trails lead westward to other units of
the park system. The conservatory, which houses a variety of the more
common garden flowers, is distinguished by an unusually inclusive Cactus
Collection. Higinbotham Woods is a wild land preserve of 238 acres.
An earth road, opposite the greenhouse, passes a firetower. An inside
stairway leads to a platform at the top, which affords a sweeping view
of the surrounding forest area, the city of Joliet, and farm land for
miles around.

Immediately south of the greenhouse a hard-surfaced road follows

Hickory Creek westward for 2 miles through several units of the park system to a junction with US 30 on the outskirts of Joliet. Enroute are Bird Haven, Pilcher Park and Arboretum, Hobbs Parkway, and 60-acre Highland Park.

At 28 *m.* on US 30 is the entrance to the Joliet Park System, marked by Leonard Crunelle's statue of Robert Pilcher.

JOLIET, 31 *m.* (545 alt., 78,887 pop. 1970). *See Joliet.*

Joliet is the focus of numerous highways and US 30 has easy access to all of them. They include US 6, US 52 connecting with Int. 55 and US 66, Illinois 7, 53, and 171.

US 30 crosses diagonally through Joliet and CREST HILL, which starts at Theodore Street (7,460 pop. 1970; 5,887, 1960, inc. 26%).

The vast form of STATEVILLE STATE PRISON north of Crest Hill (*see Tour 17*) is distinctly visible at 33.5 *m.*, its light stone structure in sharp contrast with the green fields that surround it.

Between Joliet and Aurora lie the long-settled Plainfield farm lands, a prosperous agricultural region between the Des Plaines and Fox Rivers. Flat to gently rolling, the country is largely under cultivation; only occasional farm wood lots relieve the monotony of the unending cornfields.

An extensive water-filled gravel pit forms small Lake Renwick, 38.9 *m.*, which borders the roadside for a quarter-mile. The extent of the resource, one of the largest in Illinois, may be judged from the activities along the railroad on the far side of the lake, where whole trainloads of gravel are frequently made up.

PLAINFIELD, 40 *m.* (601 alt., 2,928 pop. 1970; 2,183, 1960), named for its prairie topography, originated as an Indian village, and was first known as a trading post, founded by the Frenchman Du Pazhe about 1790, later operated by Vetel Vermette for the American Fur Company. It is next recorded as a stop on the rounds of Jesse Walker, Methodist missionary to the Indians, who preached here in 1826. He died in 1835 and is buried in Plainfield Cemetery. Walker's son-in-law, Captain James Walker, built a cabin near the Indian village in 1829; the settlement that grew up around it was for some time known as Walker's Grove.

On Old Main Street, Illinois 126, right of the highway along the river are several examples of the Greek Revival style of architecture popular in the 1830's, among them the Halfway House, built in 1834 as a station on the Chicago-Ottawa State Road. The building served as postoffice on the first Chicago-St. Louis mail route. At that time the Joliet postmaster was obliged to come to Plainfield for the mail. Two decades later, however, following the completion of the Illinois & Michigan Canal (1848), Joliet quite eclipsed Plainfield.

On the western edge of Plainfield the route crosses the Du Page River, named for Du Pazhe, the trader. The stream, bordered by a magnificent growth of oak and maple, is dammed near the city. Downstream, just off the highway, is the Wood Homestead, girlhood home of Mrs. Thomas Alva Edison.

At 49 *m*. is a junction with US 34 (*see Tour 13*).

AURORA, 53 *m*. (74,182 pop. 1970) *See Aurora*.

Aurora is a junction with Illinois 31, which follows the Fox River northward past Mooseheart and Batavia to Geneva, 9 *m*., at a junction with Illinois 38 (*see Tour 12A*).

Section b.   Aurora to Iowa Line, 107 m.

West of Aurora, US 30 crosses a rolling, partly wooded region of dairy farms. Shortly beyond the city limits are several estates of prominent Chicagoans. Fitchome Farms, 3.6 *m*., affords an opportunity to inspect modern dairying methods. Long plate glass windows open on the milking parlor where twice daily a herd of Holsteins is mechanically milked.

For 30 miles the highway parallels the tracks of the Chicago, Burlington & Quincy Railroad. SUGAR GROVE, 7 *m*., is a Kane County farm village (1,230 pop. 1970; 326, 1960, inc. 277%). There is a junction with Illinois 47 (north-south).

WAUBONSEE COMMUNITY COLLEGE is located on a campus of 183 acres. In addition to teaching the humanities and science the college offers vocational courses and adult education.

WATERMAN, 24 *m*. a farm village (990 pop. 1970; 916, 1960).

SHABBONA, 30.5 *m*. (730 pop. 1970; 690, 1960) a village in DeKalb County, bears the name of the Ottawa chief who kept his tribe friendly with the white settlers. He made a wild ride across the prairies to persuade his tribe not to support Black Hawk in the Sauk and Fox uprising. He was married to Victoria Pothier, who escaped the Fort Dearborn massacre because she was in the Kinzie House, Chicago, at the time. He died in Morris, Ill., in 1859, aged 84.

Immediately west of Shabbona is a junction with a road. Left on this road to a junction with another road, 5.9 *m*., to the Rookery, 8.5 *m*., a grove of larches that serves as the summer home of a colony of black-crowned night herons. Known as "quawks" because of their bickering nature, they have migrated to the grove for years, usually coming about April. The birds are more than two feet in height, with a green or black crown and back, pearly gray wings and tail, and yellow legs and feet. When frightened the entire flock takes flight. The colony of several hundred flies 20 to 25 miles daily to feed in the swamps bordering the Illinois and Fox Rivers.

Shabbona Lake State Park was established in August, 1972. Its area is 675 acres.

At 40.5 *m*. is a junction with US 51. *See Tour 4*. At 54 *m*. is a junction with US 52, which goes 10 *m*. northwest to Dixon. *See Tour 12A and Tour 15*.

At 61 *m*. is a junction with Illinois 26, north to Dixon.

ROCK FALLS, 73 *m*. (646 alt., 10,287 pop. 1970; 10,281, 1960) in the Rock River Valley, is located on the south side of the river, while Sterling is on the north side. The two cities have separate governments but share many of their business and cultural enterprises. Rock Falls, platted in 1837, grew slowly until 1857, when a dam across the river brought it into association with Sterling. The Illinois & Mississippi Canal, 30 *m*. south, ran a feeder up to the Rock River here. Between the twin cities is Lawrence Park, used by both. For a number of years industries here have prospered as makers of builders' hardware.

Rock Falls has an aldermanic form of government with a mayor and 10 aldermen. The Burlington Railroad enters Rock Falls from the south. Greyhound Bus Lines serve the city.

Rock Falls Public Library has a circulation of more than 55,000 books. It is a member of the Northern Illinois Library System.

Whiteside County Airport is 3 *m*. south of Rock Falls on Illinois 88. Ozark Airlines has four flights daily.

At 4 *m*. west of Rock Falls US 30 has a junction with Illinois 2, which has passed through Sterling and follows the west bank of the Rock River.

STERLING, (645 alt., 16,113 pop. 1970; 15,688, 1960; inc. 2.7%) in Whiteside County, is an industrial city on the north bank of Rock River, which separates it from Rock Falls, on the south bank.

The earliest settlements were the villages of Chatham, 1835, and Harrisburgh (1836), which combined as Sterling to capture the county seat, but held it only briefly. The present Central Park occupies the square of Chatham, and Lincoln Park is the site of Harrisburgh. The Rock River broadens out to form Lake Sinnissippi and in the middle on an island is Lawrence Park, recreation center for Sterling and Rock Falls.

On July 18, 1858, Abraham Lincoln addressed a Republican rally at a spot now marked by a boulder with a plaque at the Central school. The grounds of three schools, elementary, junior high, and senior high, are contiguous. Lincoln spent the night at the house of William Manatan. The house of Robert L. Wilson, one of the Long Nine of the Vandalia legislature, is also extant.

Sterling is known nationally as a producer of builders' hardware and is promoted as the Hardware Capital. Principal manufacturers in this field are the National Manufacturing Co. and the Lawrence Bros. Manufacturing Co. The Northwestern Steel & Wire Co. is called one of the few completely integrated electric furnace steel makers in the country.

Sterling is governed by a mayor and four commissioners, each elected for four years. The city offices are in the Coliseum. Illinois 2, which comes down from South Beloit, Rockford, and Dixon, moves on the north bank of the Rock River through Sterling and has a junction with US 30 4 *m*. west of Rock Falls. Sterling is served by the Chicago & North Western and the Burlington railroads. Illinois 88, north-south, reaches both Sterling and Rock Falls.

The Public Library has approx. 40,000 volumes in circulation. The Whiteside Area Vocational Center, which has the cooperation of 12 high school districts, is located at Sterling High School. In 1966 SAUK

VALLEY JUNIOR COLLEGE was opened on a campus of 150 acres east of Sterling. It had completed a $10,000,000 building program by 1970. The *Sterling-Rock Falls Daily Gazette* circulates widely in Whiteside and Lee Counties.

US 30 continues west from Rock Falls.

MORRISON, 90 *m.* (670 alt., 4,387 pop. 1970; 4,159, 1960) seat of Whiteside County, is an old city on the Chicago & North Western Railway. The city and nearby Unionville were settlements before the railroad came. Because of prohibitive land prices in Unionville, the stage stop, the railroad was constructed through Morrison, which consequently progressed, while Unionville remained unincorporated.

In May 1874 James Sargent, inventor of the time lock, placed his invention in the door of the iron safe in the First National Bank of Morrison, where it gave satisfactory service for forty years. This was the first time-lock installation in the United States.

Morrison is a farm trade center in an area where Herefords, Shorthorns, and Angus cattle thrive. The Whiteside County Farm Bureau occupies a new brick building that houses the Extension Service and the Norrish Auditorium. Industries make furniture, electrical equipment, and ready-mix concrete, which is delivered over a wide area in trucks. Grain storage and feed mixing are active operations. Besides the C. & N. W. Morrison is served by Greyhound Lines and Ozark Airlines at Sterling Airport. The Institute of Drafting & Technology was established in 1891. There are two weeklies, *Whiteside County News* and *Whiteside Sentinel.* Reformed Churches are well established and the Resthaven Nursing Home is sponsored by the Holland Reformed.

A famous landmark is the Old Stone Mill, on Rock Creek at US 30 and Illinois 78. It was built in 1858 on a site that had been used by a sawmill since 1839, and operated until 1941. In 1943 the late Harvey L. Shawver bought it for preservation as a historic landmark.

The stone walls are 2 ft. thick, and the heavy beams in the walls and ceilings are of handhewed oak. The cement dam is 9 ft. high and 84 ft. long.

West of Morrison the highway winds through wooded hills cut by deep ravines as it approaches the Mississippi.

The Abbott Farm is right on the highway at 98 *m.* The region was early associated with the activities of a notorious band of counterfeiters, who centered their operations in the basement of the farm-house later purchased by the Abbotts and moved across the road. In the process of moving the building several bundles of bogus money and plates used in printing them were discovered. This led to the capture of Ben Boyd, master engraver of the gang, in his workshop in Fulton. The evidence readily convicted him and he was sent to Joliet prison. The gang thereupon plotted to steal the body of President Lincoln and to use it as a basis for negotiating the release of Boyd. (*See Lincoln's Tomb, Springfield*)

At 102 *m.* is a junction with Illinois 84, the Great River Road, on the outskirts of FULTON, 106.5 *m.* (597 alt., 3,630 pop. 1970; 3,367,

1960). The city in Whiteside County, which commemorates the inventor of the steamboat, owes its early growth to river commerce, but is today largely a residential community, the center of a prosperous agricultural area. Local greenhouses have acres of rich prairie soil under glass. Thousands of baskets of tomatoes and boxes of cucumbers are shipped annually.

US 30 crosses the Iowa Line, 107 *m.,* on a toll bridge of recent construction spanning the Mississippi to Clinton, Iowa (*see Iowa Guide*).

~~~~~~

Tour 12 A

CHICAGO TO DIXON VIA ROOSEVELT ROAD SUBURBS

Forest Park—Maywood—Broadview—Bellwood—Hillside—Westchester—Elmhurst—Villa Park—Lombard—Glen Ellyn—Wheaton—Winfield—West Chicago—Geneva—St. Charles—Batavia—National Accelerator Laboratory—De Kalb—Sycamore—Dixon
Dwight D. Eisenhower Expressway, Int. 90
Illinois 38

The Eisenhower Expressway and Roosevelt Road are two of the best highways for quick passage from Downtown Chicago to the Fox River Valley. Eisenhower Expressway has exits in Oak Park, Forest Park, Maywood, and from its junction with Mannheim Road (US 45) connects with westbound Illinois 38 and Roosevelt Road.

OAK PARK, 10.5 *m.,* is the first Chicago suburb reached by the Eisenhower Expressway, which has exits at Austin Blvd. and Harlem Ave. (Illinois 43). *See Tour 11 for article on Oak Park.*

FOREST PARK, 11 *m.* (620 alt., 15,472 pop. 1970; 14,452, 1960, inc. 7%) starts at Harlem Ave. and is west of Oak Park and south of River Forest on the Des Plaines River. It has some light industry, and an ordnance manufacturing plant of the U. S. Navy. In the last century this was one of the earliest areas where cemeteries were established outside the city limits of Chicago, the favored locations being along the banks of the Des Plaines. A block south of the castelated entrance to Waldheim Cemetery, in the 900 block on S. Des Plaines Ave., is a monument to four men who were hanged Nov. 11, 1887, after being adjudged guilty of the socalled Haymarket Riot in Chicago in May, 1886, where a bomb thrown into the ranks of police killed 8 and injured about 65. The bomb-thrower was never identified. (*See article on Labor*). For many years memorial exercises for the four, Engel, Fischer, Parsons, and Spies, were held annually at the graves.

Forest Home Cemetery, south of Waldheim and north of the highway, is on the site of a Potawatomi village and burial ground. Indian relics found by gravediggers are on display in the office of the cemetery. South of the highway are several congregational tracts of the Jewish Waldheim Cemetery. Showmen's Rest in Woodlawn Cemetery, left from Des Plaines Ave. on Cermak Road, is owned by the Showmen's League of America. Their first plot, marked by a group of five granite elephants, was purchased to bury 63 circus performers who were killed in a train wreck at Ivanhoe, Indiana, June 22, 1918.

When the Eisenhower Expressway was routed through Forest Park cemetery several thousand graves were removed to another section.

MAYWOOD, 12 *m.* (30,000 pop. 1970; 27,330, 1960, inc. 9%) in Cook County, is an industrial village west of the Des Plaines River and the suburbs of River Forest and Forest Park. It was settled principally by people of Italian descent. In recent decades its industries have attracted Negroes, who now constitute 22% of its population, according to the 1970 census. The Eisenhower Expressway is contributing to the growth of Maywood. An example is the erection of the Intercontinental Center at the First Ave. interchange, an office building of 14 stories with a net area of 207,000 sq. ft.

Illinois 38, Roosevelt Road, is partly on the line between Maywood and Broadview. South of the road at 9th Ave. are the buildings of the EDWARD R. HINES, JR., MEMORIAL HOSPITAL, a unit of the U. S. Veterans Administration with more than 100 buildings on 320 acres. The hospital's main endowment was given by Edward Hines, Chicago business man, and the original main building was erected on the foundations of the former grandstand of an automobile speedway, so that the place is sometimes referred to as Speedway. The hospital first served veterans of World War I and then opened its services to veterans of all wars, and is now helping men from the Vietnam War. It has more than 2,000 beds and covers all surgical and medical needs.

In 1970 the LOYOLA UNIVERSITY MEDICAL CENTER was established near the Edward Hines, Jr., Memorial Hospital of the U. S. Veterans Administration near Roosevelt Road in the southeastern corner of Maywood. The center comprises the Stritch School of Medicine, the School of Dentistry, the School of Nursing, and the Foster G. McGraw Hospital.

BROADVIEW, (9,307 pop. 1970; 8,588, 1960) is directly south of Maywood and east of Westchester. Cermak Road (W. 22nd St.) is its southern boundary. Its Village Hall is on Roosevelt Road. It was incorporated as a village in 1914 and attracted light industry, and became favored by the Seventh Day Adventist denomination, which supports a parochial school. The village area extends north to the Eisenhower Expressway at several places.

BELLWOOD, 13 *m.* (22,096 pop., 1970; 20,729, 1960, inc. 6.6%), directly west of Maywood on Washington Blvd. was platted in 1900 and occupies only 2.3 sq. mi. It has access to Eisenhower Parkway. Northwest of it is BERKELEY, (6,152 pop. 1970; 5,792, 1960, inc. 6.2%), which was incorporated as a village in 1924 and named for Berkeley Calif. North of Bellwood and Berkeley are the Proviso Yards of the Chicago & North Western Ry. South of both villages is Hillside.

HILLSIDE, 14 *m.* (22,096 pop. 1970; 20,729, 1960, inc. 6.6%), has become widely known for Hillside Plaza, a wellequipped shopping center easily reached by a wide radius of suburban dwellers because of its location near major highways. Associated with it are a movie theater, a large ice skating rink and bowling alleys. The area was settled by farmers as early as 1837 and the Immanuel Lutheran Church was built during the last century. The first industry in this area was a stone quarry, from which thousands of tons of limestone were removed to build Chicago churches and warehouses; the huge hole is located west of the Mannheim Road and near the interchange, where the Eisenhower Expressway connects with the combined US 12, US 20, and US 45 (north-south).

The village is located on a ridge and was incorporated in 1837. It has the offices of the S. & H. Corp. first to exploit trading stamps and now a diversified business and some light industries and has laid out a new industrial park. There are also junctions with East-West Tollway (Illinois 190) and Tri-State Tollway (Int. 294), which moves from Oak Brook along the east side of Elmhurst to O'Hare International Airport.

WESTCHESTER (20,003 pop. 1970; 18,092, 1960, inc. 10%) is a village incorporated in 1925 as one of the land enterprises of Samuel Insull. It is contiguous to Broadview on the east, extends up to Bellwood, and is both east and south of Hillside. It is another of the western suburbs that appears to have more people under than above ground, for large areas are devoted to cemeteries, but it also has the Fresh Meadow Golf Club. It is a gateway to the expanding Oak Brook and shares with Oak Brook and Elmhurst the advantages of the junctions with East-West Tollway, Tri-State Tollway, and Eisenhower Expressway, and Illinois 38. Its recent surge has brought it fully equipped parks, a public golf course in the Forest Preserve, shops on Roosevelt Road, and new apartment buildings. Its library circulates approx. 130,000 books a year.

Eisenhower Expressway begins to turn northwest in Hillside. It moves to the Du Page County line and proceeds north on the east boundary of Elmhurst, then northwest, passes Lake St. (US 20) and turns up toward Elk Grove Village. Illinois 38 moves straight west from Hillside, has a junction with Tri-State Tollway in Oak Brook and touches the southern limits of ELMHURST (50,547 pop. 1970) in Du Page County. *See Elmhurst, Tour 11 and Oak Brook, Tour 13.*

VILLA PARK, 19 *m.* (25,891 pop. 1970; 20,391, 1960, inc. 27%) a village in Du Page County was developed in 1914 as a Garden Village and received its name in 1917. Salt Creek flows between Villa

Park and Elmhurst and the village extends from North Ave. Illinois 64, on the north to Roosevelt Road, Illinois 38. It has Chicago & North Western commutation and West Town buses. Illinois 83 provides a direct 6 *m.* drive to the offices and stores of Oak Brook. The Lutherans have the largest number of churches, Catholics next.

LOMBARD, 21 *m.* (708 alt., 35,977 pop. 1970; 22,561, 1960, inc. 59%) directly west of Villa Park, is one of the oldest of the Du Page suburbs, having been platted in 1868 by Joseph Lombard and incorporated in 1869. Its terrain lies between Illinois 64 on the north and Illinois 38 on the south. The first settler was Winston Churchill, who built a log cabin and established a claim to an area now enclosed in the Winston Forest Preserve on St. Charles Road. Sheldon Peck came from Vermont in 1838 and opened the Peck House, which aided fugitive slaves north on the underground railroad. Lombard is esteemed by adjacent suburbs for its YORKTOWN CENTER, which has a large enclosed mall and branches of State St. stores. The Midwest College of Engineering and the National College of Chiropractic are located here. The town has commuter service on the North Western and West Towns buses.

Lombard is famous for its annual display of lilacs in bloom, most of which are concentrated in Lilacia Park, W. Maple St. and S. Park Ave., which contains more than 300 varieties of lilacs. The park is the former estate of Col. William Plum, who, in pursuit of a life-long hobby, collected lilacs from throughout the world. Plum bequeathed the estate to the city of Lombard, and upon his death in 1927 the gift was accepted and the Lombard Park District was organized. The Plum home, in accord with the bequest, houses the Helen W. Plum Memorial Library, which honors the memory of Colonel Plum's wife, Helen Williams, a descendant of Roger Williams. Jens Jensen, Chicago landscape architect, planned the beautiful arrangement of the park, which has since been developed by others. Tulips border winding paths, with lilac bushes set slightly back from them.

The Lombard Lilac League presents a pageant each May when the lilacs are in full bloom. Admission to the park is free, except during Festival Week, when there is usually a small charge.

The Helen W. Plum Memorial Library has a collection of approx. 50,000 volumes and a circulation of about 280,000. It is a member of the Du Page Library System of 22 libraries, with hq in Wheaton.

GLEN ELLYN, 23 *m.* (766 alt., 21,909 pop. 1970; 15,972, 1960; inc. 37%) a village in Du Page County, was called Babcock's Grove after the first settlers, the Babcock brothers, in 1833. It received its present name from Thomas Hill, who in 1885 chose Glen for a glen at the foot of Cooper Hill and Ellyn for his wife. The name became official in 1892. According to a historical marker Moses Stacy, veteran of the War of 1812, came in 1835 and built an inn, and the stop, about one mile north of the present business district, became known as Stacy's Corners. In 1849 the pioneer Galena & Chicago Union Ry. was constructed south of Stacy's Corners and the residents moved shops, houses, and church to the new location. The town was platted in 1851. But the true antiquity of Glen Ellyn was established when workmen in 1963 uncovered the well-preserved bones of a mastodon.

The Chicago & North Western Ry. provides commuter service to Chicago. Glen Ellyn has a Community Center, and its Public Library has more than 55,000 books and circulates approx. 260,000 a year. It is a member of the Du Page Library System. Lake Glen Ellyn in the northern part of the city is a small, picturesque recreation area, with a Yacht Club. There also are the Glen Oak Country Club and the Willowbrook Wild Life Haven.

The DU PAGE JUNIOR COLLEGE was opened in 1966 on the State plan of a two-year coeducational college with vocational courses. In the 1971-72 year it enrolled 7,200 students and had a faculty of 272.

WHEATON, 25 m. (753 alt., 31,138 pop. 1970; 24,312, 1960, inc. 28%), seat of Du Page County, a self-sufficient city in the Chicago suburban periphery, is renowned as a cultural center by virtue of Wheaton College, dating from 1860. Wheaton was settled in 1837 by Erastus Gary and Warren and Jesse Wheaton. In 1848 the Galena & Chicago Union Ry. reached Wheaton on a right of way contributed chiefly by Warren Wheaton. In that year the settlement opened its first school and in 1850 had its first shops. The town was platted in 1853 and incorporated in 1859.

Wheaton became a city in 1890, when it had 1,600 people. It adopted a mayor, council, and city manager form of government in 1961. On Saturday mornings from 10 to noon the Council invites citizens to a Coffee with Council meeting to discuss civic issues. The city has commissions for beautification, human relations, and pollution control, and a planning board. In January, 1965, the city purchased with a bond issue a Georgian brick building at 303 West Wesley St. for its City Hall.

On the organization of Du Page County in 1839 Naperville was named the county seat. Wheaton, more centrally located and on a railroad, agitated for the seat as early as 1857. Ten years later the voters of the county decided in Wheaton's favor, and a courthouse was built. Warren Wheaton gave the land, and he and his brother each subscribed $2,000 for the building. But Naperville refused to recognize the election as legal. Although the circuit court, after months of contention, upheld the vote, Naperville refused to give up the public records. Injunctions were served and counter proceedings instituted. Impatient of longer waiting, Wheaton resorted to direct action. One night in July, 1868, a band of men entered the Naperville courthouse and made off with a wagonload of public records. Save for several that were overlooked, and which subsequently disappeared, they are now in the safe keeping of the county clerk in the Wheaton COURTHOUSE, a large modern structure completed in 1938, which stands on the site of three earlier ones.

In 1852 a small group of Wesleyan Methodists knelt on the summit of a hill and dedicated the site to the freedom of human souls as well as bodies. In 1853 they established Illinois Institute. In 1860 it was named Wheaton College in recognition of land donated by Warren Wheaton, and gained interdenominational support under the leadership of Jonathan Blanchard, first president. It was fundamentalist in Christian teaching and the cornerstone of its Main Building carried the motto: *For Christ and His Kingdom.*

WHEATON COLLEGE is located on an attractive campus of 65 wooded acres. Blanchard Hall, its main building, is a four-story structure with a tower that was started in 1853. Notable among the buildings is Edman Memorial Chapel and Auditorium, which seats 2,600, and has a smaller chapel seating 100. Music is an important segment of the Division of Fine Arts and its McAlister Conservatory of Music Bldg. was erected in 1963. Conservatory students may practice on the organ of the Orlinda Childs Pierce Memorial Chapel, which seats 1,100. In 1971 the college completed the New Science Bldg. of laboratories and classrooms, a rooftop observatory with 12-in. refracting telescope; greenhouse, auditorium, and Mastodon reconstruction exhibit. This supplements the Breyer Chemistry Bldg. In computer science a PDP-12 computer is available for student use. Summer course in biology and geology may be taken at Black Hills Science Sta., Rapid City, S. D.

The Library in the Robert E. Nicholas Bldg. has more than 155,000 vols. and receives more than 800 periodicals. It profits also by membership in the Lebras union card catalogue of 75,000 titles available in seven west suburban liberal arts colleges.

Wheaton College aims "to integrate Biblical Christianity with scholarship and all related activities." It states it is "committed to the Biblical teaching that man was created by God not from previously existing forms of life and that all men are descended from Adam and Eve, first parents of the entire human race."

The college estimates that the approx. cost per quarter for tuition, board, room and incidentals is $1,135 or $3,405 a year.

The WHEATON PUBLIC LIBRARY, 225 N. Cross St., opposite Adams Park, occupies a building erected in 1963. It has more than 90,000 books and circulates more than 340,000 annually. It is the hq of the Du Page Library System.

The Du Page County Historical Museum, 102 East Wesley St. has well-equipped exhibits of a Victorian parlor, a children's playroom, a country store, a barber shop, a doctor's office and a barn; also a War Memorial Room, Pioneer's Hall, and Railroad Open House. *Monday, Wednesday, Friday, Saturday, 10-4, closed holidays.*

The Illinois Prairie Path has been developed along the former right of way of the Chicago, Aurora, & Elgin Railroad to Wheaton, where the trail runs southwest to Aurora and northwest toward Elgin. It is part of the National Trails System and is open for riding, hiking, bicycle riding and bird-watching.

WINFIELD, 59 *m.* (4,285 pop. 1970; 1,575, 1960, inc. 173%) a village in Du Page County, contiguous to Wheaton, was settled in

1849 and named for Major General Winfield Scott. It is located on the West Branch of the Du Page River and has commutation service on the Chicago & North Western. This is the site of the Du Page County Fair Grounds and of the Central Du Page County Hospital (113 beds).

Two miles south of Illinois 38 (Roosevelt Road) on Winfield Road is CANTIGNY, an elaborate museum of two World Wars on the estate of Col. Robert Rutherford McCormick, editor of the *Chicago Tribune,* who died in 1955. McCormick's suburban home is also located here on a 450-acre terrain, part of which was a farm originally bought by Joseph Medill, McCormick's grandfather and owner of the *Tribune,* who took a big part in securing the Republican nomination of Abraham Lincoln for President. For a number of years the *Tribune* conducted an experimental farm here.

Cantigny, the War Memorial Museum of the First Division, AEF, is a realistic reenactment of two major engagements, the assault on the German position at Cantigny on May 28, 1918, and the landing at Omaha Beach on D Day, June 6, 1944. A trench at Cantigny is reproduced and the din of artillery and machine-guns and flash of explosions provide a terrific spectacle. *Open daily 9-5, May through September; 10-4, Oct. through April. Closed Mondays, Thanksgiving, Christmas, New Year's Day. No tours June, July, August.*

The McCormick Mansion, begun by Medill and extended by Col. McCormick, includes his library and museum of weapons, and personal apartments. It is open Wednesday through Sunday, 1-4, closed Monday, Tuesday and above-named holidays. The granite tomb of Col. McCormick and his wife, designed by A. Rebori, stands near the Mansion.

WEST CHICAGO, 61 *m.* (10,111 pop. 1970; 6,854, 1960, inc. 47%) in Du Page County, was at one time known as Turner Junction after a railroad official and became a division point on the Galena & Chicago Union Railroad in 1849. It was incorporated as a city in 1906. The lines of the Chicago & North Western, Burlington Northern, and the Elgin Joliet & Eastern serve West Chicago and the C. & N. W. provides commuter service. West Chicago shares with Bavatia the proximity of the National Accelerator Laboratory of the Atomic Energy Commission, from which it is separated by Roosevelt Road, and provides part of the labor force. The East-West Tollway is 6 miles south on Illinois 59, which runs along the eastern limits of the city. The West Branch of the Du Page River runs through Timber Ridge and West Du Page Forest Preserves on the eastern boundary. The Du Page County Airport is located 3 miles northwest of the city. North of the city is the St. Andrews Golf Club and Pheasant Run, which includes golf, swimming, shops, a theater and a restaurant.

Du Page Horticultural School, in addition to its own program, conducts workshops at intervals for the establishment or improvement of classes in horticulture in elementary and secondary schools in Illinois.

GENEVA, 66 *m.* (720 alt., 9,115 pop. 1970; 7,646, 1960, inc.

19%) seat of Kane County is located on both banks of the Fox River about midway between Aurora and Elgin, with St. Charles at the north and Batavia at the south. Like other cities in Kane and Du Page counties it expects economic gains from the development of the NATIONAL ACCELERATOR LABORATORY, the large facility of the Atomic Energy Commission, which lies between Roosevelt Road, Illinois 38, at the north, Butterfield Road, Illinois 56, at the south, Batavia at the west and West Chicago at the north. *See Batavia*.

Geneva has a mayor and council type of government. It has commuting service on the Chicago & North Western Railroad and easy access to Du Page County air and helicopter services. Settlement began after veterans from the Black Hawk War told their eastern friends about the attractions of the Fox River Valley, although that had played no part in the hostilities.

Geneva has been expanding its industries and acquired several large plants in metals, electronics, and specialties, such as cabinets. Burgess Norton Manufacturing Co., maker of screw machine products and stampings, employs more than 900; the Portable Electric Tool Division of G. W. Murphy Industries employs 875; National Electronics, Inc., employs 500; Mutual Mill Sales Co. makes drive-in store fronts, and John T. Clarke Co. makes contraceptive diaphragms. The Houghton, Mifflin Co., Boston book publisher, has its midwestern hq in Geneva and the Dura Craft Book Bindery, Inc. binds, prebinds, and rebinds books. In 1919 Col. George Fabyn (1867-1936) expert in acoustics, founded the Riverbank Laboratories nearby for research and manufacturing tuning forks, sound meters and acoustical equipment. Col. Fabyan had served the U. S. Government during World War I as export on codes and ciphers. The Fabyan Forest Preserve, south of Geneva, honors his name.

The ILLINOIS STATE TRAINING SCHOOL FOR GIRLS is located east of the Fox River in Geneva. It provides academic, commercial and vocational instructions. The ILLINOIS STATE TRAINING SCHOOL FOR Boys, St. Charles Branch, is 3 *m.* west of Geneva on Illinois 38.

The Geneva Township Public Library, 27 S. Second St., has a circulation of more than 100,000 vols. a year. Its building, erected in 1908, was remodeled in 1969. It is a member of the Du Page Library System.

The Island Park is entered from the State St. Bridge. The Geneva Historical Society is open Saturday and Sunday, 2-4:30, closed Dec. 15 through March 15.

ST. CHARLES adjoins Geneva on the north (12,945 pop. 1970; 9,269, 1960, inc. 39%). Like Geneva it has the Fox River running down its middle and is served by two north-south highways, Illinois 25 on the east bank and Illinois 31 on the west bank. It also has Illinois 64 running through it and coming in a straight line from Chicago on North Ave. St. Charles is served by several bus lines to the Loop but for rail commuting it must depend on Geneva. The Du Page County Airport is east of St. Charles on Illinois 64.

St. Charles has a Municipal Center that shelters both the city administration and the Historical Society. A conspicuous landmark is the Hotel Baker, erected by Col. Edward J. Baker at a cost of $600,000. It stands on the site of the old mill that served the original settlement. St. Charles is the site of Community Hospital (115 beds) and Delnor Hospital (105 beds). St. Charles Public Library remodeled its building in 1964. It has a collection of more than 50,000 books and circulates approx. 140,000. It belongs to the Du Page Library System.

The city has numerous outlets for sports and recreation, including Potawatomi Park, supervised baseball and swimming, musical comedy in the summer, and boating and fishing on the Fox River.

BATAVIA, a city in Kane County, adjoins Geneva on the south (8,994 pop. 1970; 7,496, 1960, inc. 20%). Like its sister cities it is divided by the Fox River and Illinois 25 runs down its east bank and Illinois 31 its west bank. It is located west of the terrain of the National Accelerator Laboratory. With easy access to the facilities of Elgin and Aurora, and the shopping centers inbetween, Batavia does not lack for retail trade. As in Aurora, the post office, city hall, and other municipal service buildings are centrally located on an island. Two factories manufacture windmills.

Among the earliest sites chosen for settlement following the Black Hawk War (1832), Batavia, because of its triple advantage of water power, fertile soil, and surface limestone, began its industrial career in 1837 with a flour mill. By 1850 it had developed an extensive commerce in limestone, which gave it the nickname of Quarry City. Several fine old houses built of this local stone still stand along the highway. Among these are Lockwood Hall and the Snow House, at the southern edge of town, both in the Greek Revival style. Right on Union Avenue is BELLEVUE REST HOME, built in 1856 for the Batavia Institute, a private academy soon superseded by public schools and taken over in 1867 by Dr. R. J. Patterson, a specialist in mental and nervous disorders.

Bellevue Place Sanitarium in Batavia is the institution where Mary Todd Lincoln (Mrs. Abraham Lincoln) was confined from May 20, 1875, to September 10, 1875. Mrs. Lincoln was adjudged insane by a jury in Chicago after her son, Robert T. Lincoln, had been persuaded by physicians that her erratic conduct made this necessary. The death of her son Tad had accentuated her mental distress. In Chicago Mrs. Lincoln preferred to stay at the Grand Pacific Hotel instead of at her son's home, so Robert provided a woman companion, and a Pinkerton detective to protect her in the city. She would go on shopping tours with securities valued at $57,000 on her person, and at one time carried $1,000 in cash. When adjudged insane she attempted to buy laudanum but was frustrated by the druggist. At Bellevue Place Mrs. Lincoln was free to walk and ride. Through the interposition of friends she was permitted to go to the house of her sister, Elizabeth, Mrs. Ninian Edwards, in Springfield. In 1876 a Cook County court declared her restored to reason and capable of managing her estate. Subsequently she traveled extensively in Europe. She blamed Robert for her detention and was not reconciled to him until 14 months before her death in 1882.

Quarry Park, named from an old stone quarry that is now the swimming pool, has a wide recreational and sports program. Limestone from Batavia at one time was used on numerous Chicago buildings, including its famous Water Tower.

The eastern limits of Batavia are close to the western line of the NATIONAL ACCELERATOR LABORATORY (NAL), which occupies an area of 6,800 acres south of West Chicago, west of Illinois 59 and north of the Butterfield Road to North Aurora, Illinois 56. The terrain was donated by the State of Illinois and has 5,500 acres in Du Page County and 1,300 acres in Kane County. NAL is operated for the U. S. Atomic Energy Commission by the Universities Research Assn., Inc., of Washington, D. C., a consortium of 52 major universities, 51 in the United States and one in Canada. The purpose is explained by NAL as to further the understanding of elementary particles through the use of a 200-500 billion electron volt proton accelerator—the world's largest basic scientific research instrument."

The principal scientific instrument is described as a proton synchrotron of 200-500 BeV energy. The most prominent component is a ring of specially developed magnets one and one-quarter miles in diameter and about four miles in circumference. Acceleration to 200 BeV was achieved March 1, 1972, four months ahead of schedule. It also appears possible that the protons can be accelerated to an energy close to 500 BeV at reduced intensity not long after the synchrotron is brought into operation.

The proton-synchrotron is considered the highest energy instrument of its kind ever devised. It is composed of three phases: the linear accelerator, which serves as injector of the proton beam; the booster ring, which receives the beam and accelerates it, and the main ring, where the proton beam will move around the 4-mile circumference about 70,000 times in 1½ seconds. When the beam is removed and directed against other protons the results are expected to give new clues to the laws of matter and energy.

While NAL was being built the scientists established headquarters in the houses of the village of Weston, which has disappeared as a settlement. In the first half of 1972 NAL had 950 employees. By 1975 there were to be 1,500 scientists and supporting staff members. There is provision for visiting researchers and by 1975 350 will be accommodated at any given time.

The Central Laboratory on completion will have twin towers, 16 stories tall, standing back to back and connected with a sort of umbilical cord of passageways, both outside facades sloping back for a number of stories. Appropriations include $250,000,000 for construction, $60,000,-000 for apparatus, and $60,000,000 for annual operating expenses. NAL has a 340,000 kw. power station that gets power from the Commonwealth Edison Co. at a cost of $2,000,000 a year.

Robert Rathbun Wilson, professor in the field of high energy physics, came from Cornell University to become director of NAL.

The Information Office of NAL can be addressed at P. O. Box 500, Batavia, Illinois, 60510.

MOOSEHEART, 5 *m.* south of Batavia on Illinois 31, is a community founded by James J. Davis, former United States senator from Pennsylvania, and supported by the Loyal Order of Moose. The institution provides home, educational training through high school, and technical training in several trades for children of deceased members of the order. The grounds are open from 8 to 4. Visitors must be accompanied by a member.

Known as the City of Childhood, Mooseheart answers the description in almost a story-book sense. Here is a scientifically directed miniature society whose affairs are conducted by the child citizens, aided by adult advisers. The children live in small groups in cottages, each headed by a housemother. Living conditions approximate home life as nearly as possible, and although all children, because of admission limitations, are fatherless, Mooseheart provides jobs for many mothers, thus saving a further break in the family.

Boys have a choice of training in one or more of eleven trades or professions girls, in six. Each boy or girl receives full apprentice experience. When a new unit is to be built, the drafting class draws the plans and makes the blue prints, the concrete class produces structural materials, and the sheet metal class provides roofing and drain pipes. Other groups stand ready to paint, paper, or varnish; and the tin shop makes such utensils as dish pans and dust pans.

Apprentices in beauty culture and barbering gain experience here. Students in the sewing class see the suits and dresses they make actually worn by the members of the community. Girls manage the cafeteria, under a trained supervisor. Student typists and bookkeepers assist in the business office. Journalism classes co-operate with the print shop in producing local reading matter. Children with musical or artistic gifts are trained to earn an income in orchestra, band, or designing studios. At the age of 8 each child is taught to do his own shopping and to keep a check book. From junior high school his work is paid for and he must budget his accounts.

The international headquarters of the Moose fraternity is located in the brick building at the right as one enters Mooseheart from Illinois 31. Directly in front is the Campanile with its clock tower. This building is the central meeting place for students and visitors alike and student guides, souvenirs and refreshments may be obtained here.

Other outstanding buildings on the campus include the House of God, a unique children's cathedral; the modern high school building, the field house with a seating capacity of 3,500, the new Museum of Moose History, and the Baby Village.

Return to Illinois 38 west of Geneva. At 75 *m.* is a junction with Illinois 47.

Left on Illinois 47 is ELBURN, 0.8 *m.* (848 alt., 1,122 pop. 1970;

960, 1960, inc. 16%), a farming center that dates from 1854, when it was platted along the Galena & Chicago Union Railroad. Public sentiment in the vicinity, as in all of Kane County in the 1850's, was definitely abolitionist. Tradition has it that Lincoln, while visiting a cousin in Elburn in 1858, was greeted by a local organization calling itself the Lincoln True Hearts, which pledged him its active support in the senatorial contest. Northern Illinois was as strongly pro-Lincoln as southern Illinois was pro-Douglas.

At 2 *m.* on Illinois 47 is a junction with a graveled road.

Left on this road to Johnsons Mound, 4.9 *m.,* in a unit of the Kane County Forest Preserve. The mound, which rises noticeably above the low, rolling farm lands, is attractively developed as a county park. From the keeper's cottage at the entrance a road (*closed to automobiles*) circles the mound to its summit. Right on this road, a few hundred yards into the woods, is Shabbona Elm, standing in solitary grandeur in an opening of the forest. The tree has been identified by experts as approximately 325 years old. Portia Gilpin, in *Memoirs of a Giant Tree,* tells the stories this lofty water-elm might tell, could it speak. A bronze tablet in front of the tree, placed by the Fox River Valley Woodcraft Council, states that the tree was named "in honor of the Potawatomi chieftain of this region . . . on the 12th Sun of the Wild Rose Moon, 1922."

DE KALB, 91 *m.* (886 alt., 32,949 pop. 1970; 18,486, 1960, inc. 78%), the largest city in the county, transacts its county business in Sycamore, one-fourth its size. It has an aldermanic-manager form of government, distributes food and seed, and produces wire, electric motors, pianos, organs, and plastics. The city has 40 churches, a 110-bed hospital, 153 acres of parks and 12 playgrounds. It continues an old custom of weekly band concerts in the principal park during the summer. The De Kalb Public Library has approx. 60,000 books and circulates nearly 165,000 annually. It is a member of the Northern Illinois Library System of 30 libraries, which has its hq at the Rockford Public Library. Ellwood House is the city's historical museum.

De Kalb was named for Baron Johann De Kalb (1721-1780) who served in the American War of Independence. The city gained fame as the "wire capital of the world." In 1874 Joseph E. Glidden patented a barbed wire and Jacob Haish patented a barbed wire manufacturing process. A long litigation for infringement followed. Both men are generally credited with developing a usable barbed wire.

NORTHERN ILLINOIS UNIVERSITY is the name granted July 1, 1957, by the State Assembly to the De Kalb institution that opened its doors in September, 1899, as a normal school with a two-year course. Its principal function was to train teachers and it continued this work until July 1, 1955, when it was authorized to give baccalaureate degrees in the arts and sciences. Development into a full-scale college with a graduate school followed. With groups of new residence halls and classrooms erected in the 1960's, it enrolled 21,313 students in the 1971-72 school year with a faculty of 1,289, thus becoming an institution of first rank in the State.

NIU occupies 417 acres along the Kishwaukee River. It has six major divisions: College of Liberal Arts and Sciences, College of Fine and Applied Arts; College of Education, College of Business, the Graduate School and the College of Continuing Education. It has two semesters and a summer session of eight weeks. It provides accommodations for 7,600 students in six residence hall complexes. Fees per semester for in-state students are $243.50; for out-of-state students, $603.50. Room and board for two semesters run approx. to a little over $1,000 and total expenses for the school year are approx. $1,950 to $2,000.

The LeBaron stabile by Alexander Calder was installed on the campus of the university in May, 1968, in honor of its president, Dr. Rhoten A. Smith.

The university uses the LORADO TAFT FIELD CAMPUS, originally the Eagles Nest Camp, 35 m. west of De Kalb on the Rock River near Oregon, 140 acres, for outdoor courses of study (see Tour 4A).

At De Kalb is a junction with north-south Illinois 23. Right, north, on Illinois 20 to SYCAMORE, 6 m. (7,843 pop. 1970; 6,961, 1960, inc. 12%), seat of De Kalb County, 58 m. west of the Chicago Loop. A farm products distributing center Sycamore was incorporated in 1869. It is hq of the De Kalb Agricultural Assn. In recent years it has acquired some industries, including the Anaconda Wire & Cable Co., making fence wire. Sycamore has two weekly newspapers, the *Tribune* and the *True Republican;* the latter was first published in 1858, two years after start of the Republican party. North of Sycamore 7 m. on Illinois 23 is GENOA, (3,003 pop. 1970; 2,330, 1960, inc. 28%). *Pronounced Gen-oh-a.* Sycamore is reached direct from Chicago on US 64.

Right from De Kalb on 1st St. is COLTONVILLE, 3.2 m., identified by a rural schoolhouse at a junction with a graveled road. On the R. side of the road, immediately opposite the schoolhouse is a monument that marks the site of the first court held in De Kalb County. Nearby, slightly to the north, was an old Potawatomi Indian village.

MALTA, 97 m. (961 pop. 1970; 782, 1960) a farm village, became an educational landmark in 1697 when the State opened its KISHWAUKEE COMMUNITY COLLEGE there. In the 1973 year the college enrolled 1,800 students and had a faculty of 100.

ROCHELLE, 108.5 m. (793 alt., 8,594 pop. 1970) in Ogle County, is at a junction with US 51 (see Tour 4). West of Rochelle extensive fields of asparagus line the highway for two miles.

ASHTON, 118 m. (817 alt., 1,112 pop. 1970; 1,024, 1960), a thrifty German-American village, centers upon the Mills and Petrie Memorial, a community building named for the partial donors. The modern structure of stone and yellow brick, erected in 1936, houses a library, a stage, and a gymnasium that may be converted into an assembly hall, play room, or roller skating rink.

The Library was remodeled in 1970. It circulates between 15,000 and 20,000 vols. and is a member of the Northern Illinois Library System.

FRANKLIN GROVE, 123 m., is a farm village in Lee County of 968 pop., 1970, up from 773, 1960.

DIXON, 133 m., 659 alt., 18,147 pop. 1970; 19,568, 1960) seat of Lee County, is located on the Rock River, 100 m. west of Chicago and 66 m. northwest of Rock Island, at a junction with Illinois 2 from Rockford, Illinois 26 from Freeport, and US 52 from Savanna. It is served by the Chicago & North Western (passenger and freight) and Illinois Central Gulf (freight), Greyhound Bus Lines, and Peoria-Rockford Bus Line. The Municipal Airport, Charles R. Walgreen Field, named for the drugstore clerk who developed the Walgreen stores, has shuttle service to O'Hare Field, Chicago. The town was incorporated in 1843, the city in 1859; it has a mayor and four commissioners. A city with fine residential sections, it has 27 churches representing 13 denominations. The *Dixon Daily Telegraph* serves all of Lee County.

Dixon cherishes its historic past. Joseph Ogee, a French-Canadian trader, started a ferry and tavern in 1828 and sold it in 1830 to John Dixon for $550. During the Black Hawk war, 1832, volunteers were mustered in at Fort Dixon, on the banks of the Rock. In a park between the bridges on the site of the fort is a bronze statue of Abraham Lincoln as a captain of volunteers, by Leonard Crunelle, with a tablet and bas-relief commemorating John Dixon. The original Nacusha House, 215 Galena Ave., commemorates the visits of Abraham Lincoln and U. S. Grant in period rooms. There is a museum of pioneer relics in Loveland Community House, and an active Historical Society.

Heavy enlistment from Illinois farms and rural towns during the Civil War greatly depleted the supply of farm labor, and combined with the high prices of war times to stimulate further the invention and use of machinery. The Illinois State Agricultural Society, formed in 1853, noted in 1865: "As men were withdrawn from the farms, improved implements . . . were introduced to supply their places." In 1862 this society conducted an extensive field trial of new machines near Dixon, at which 22 different reapers and 13 mowers were demonstrated. Among the important Illinois manufacturers represented, in addition to McCormick, were John H. Manny of Rockford, H. H. Taylor of Freeport, George S. Curtis of Chicago, Thomas H. Medell of Ottawa. Barber, Hawley & Company of Pekin showed a heading machine called the Haines Harvester, and W. W. Burson of Rockford demonstrated a pioneer grain binder.

Dixon is the seat of SAUK VALLEY COLLEGE, a two-year community institution opened in 1965, which gives courses in business administration, health, industrial and engineering subjects. It enrolls more than 1,400 students and has a faculty of 88. DIXON STATE SCHOOL, founded in 1918 as a hospital and assumed by the State in 1931, treats about 4,000 mentally and physically handicapped persons and employs 2,500. The city raised more than $850,000 for its Family

YMCA in 1969. One of the new structures is the Lee County Enforcement Building.

Dixon Public Library has a collection of more than 65,000 books and a circulation of approx. 130,000 annually. Its building was extensively remodeled in 1970. It is a member of the Northern Illinois Library System.

~~~~~~

Tour 13

FROM CHICAGO TO BURLINGTON, IOWA, THROUGH NORTH CENTRAL FARMLANDS

Riverside—Brookfield—LaGrange—Oak Brook—Hinsdale—Downers Grove — Naperville — Mendota — Princeton — Kewanee — Galva —Galesburg—Monmouth—Gulfport—(Burlington).
US 34 Riverside to Iowa Line, 221 *m.*

This is one of the older highways out of Chicago to the Mississippi River, avoiding the larger north central cities but with connecting routes to all of them. There are opportunities to switch to Interstate highways at Princeton and Galesburg. This is a route to certain important objectives: the Brookfield Zoo, the restored Bishop Hill of the earliest Swedish immigration, and the scholarly precincts of Galesburg. While Mendota and Princeton are on US 34 they are described more in detail under *Tour 4* and *Tour 14*.

From the Loop this route runs southwest on US 66 (Ogden Ave.) through Cicero and Berwyn to Harlem Avenue between Riverside and Lyons. Here US 34 leaves US 66 and proceeds west, while US 66 turns south into Lyons.

RIVERSIDE, 0 *m.* (630 alt., 10,432 pop. 1970; 9,750, 1960, inc. 7%). This suburban village has been designated a National Historic Landmark by the U.S. Department of the Interior, which considered it a model of suburban planning, with streets and areas conforming to natural contours.

Occupying densely wooded park land, Riverside was one of the earliest residential communities in the United States to be laid out on a preconceived plan. The project originated in 1866 when the Riverside Improvement Company commissioned Olmsted and Vaux, New York landscape architects, who designed Central Park and later the Columbian Exposition grounds, to plan an ideal Chicago suburb. Noting the "low, flat, miry, and forlorn character" of what was then the Chicago suburban area, the architects selected the site of Riverside because of its forest, the Des Plaines River, and existing railroad facilities. Frederick Law Olmsted drew the plans, using the winding course of the river as a guide. The improvement company, estimating a net profit of $7,000,000, spent $1,500,000 to establish the village. Subsequent development has followed Olmsted's plan. The community resembles a park, its houses and shrubbery complementing the scenic beauty of the river. One third of Riverside is reserved as park land.

Riverside is in the northern section of the Chicago Portage crossed by the pioneers who used the Des Plaines-Chicago River route. It has been named a national historical landmark as a planned site where the natural elements have been preserved. Riverside commuters reach the Chicago Loop on the Burlington on a 25-minute schedule and have the added advantages of West Town Suburban Transit buses and a short drive to the Eisenhower Expressway. The village has access to about 800 acres of the Forest Preserve in its area. It shares the Riverside-Brookfield High School. An old water tower remains a conspicuous landmark.

Adjoining Riverside on the north is NORTH RIVERSIDE (8,097 pop. 1970; 7,686, 1960, inc. 1.4%), located between West 26th St. and Cermak Road. It has the same type of dwellings as Riverside.

US 34 moves along the south limits of Riverside to a junction with Illinois 171; north on this road into BROOKFIELD (20,284 pop. 1970; 20,424, 1960), a residential suburb laid out after 1893 by Samuel E. Gross and called Grossdale until 1905. It is about 12.5 m. from the Loop. It developed in three communities: Brookfield, Hollywood, and Congress Park, which are now stations on the Burlington for commuters. Brookfield Woods is part of the Forest Preserve.

Chicago Zoological Park, popularly called the BROOKFIELD ZOO, is located at First Ave. and 31st St. in Brookfield. The Zoo was opened July 1, 1934, on land donated by Edith Rockefeller McCormick, is owned by the Forest Preserve District of Cook County and operated by the Chicago Zoological Society. Much of the construction was guided by Stanley Field, and the original design, following a provincial Italian style, was drawn by Edwin H. Clark. The grounds are divided into quadrants by an east-west mall and a thoroughfare connecting the north and south gates; at their intersection is the Theodore Roosevelt Memorial Fountain.

The animals in the Zoo are displayed in surroundings natural to them and instructive to the spectators. An extraordinary installation is the Seven Seas Panorama, where the porpoise tank, 100 ft. long, 25 ft. wide and 18 ft. deep, is surrounded by seats for 900. Two other pools are for seals, sea lions, and porpoises. The Dall sheep on Arctic Island constitute the only herd in an American zoo. The Children's Zoo permits close observation and contact by youngsters. The Reptile House has a large collection of alligators, crocodiles, giant snakes, giant turtles, and other scaly varieties. Of birds there are many kinds, with four major exhibits in the Aquatic Bird House. There are Antelope Yards, a Giraffe House, a Mountain on which the Siberian ibex can cavort; a pachyderm building. Since 1968 the Brookfield, Salt Creek & Western

Railroad has puffed its 2¼ miles around the park, visiting herds of Plains animals in their natural surroundings.

Open every day, 10-5. free on Tuesday; other days, $1 for those 15 and older; children with adults free, unaccompanied children, 25c. Illinois school groups are admitted free upon advance reservation, including one supervisor for every five pupils. Children's Zoo, adults 25c, children, 15c. Porpoises perform 3 time daily in winter, 4 times daily in summer, 5 times on Sundays and holidays; adults, 75c, children 25c. Parking fees, 50c per motor car, $2 per bus.

LA GRANGE, 3.7 *m.* (16,773 pop. 1970; 15,265, 1960, inc. 9.7%) largest of the La Grange suburbs, has a village organization since 1879. High-rise apartment buildings are adding to its older substantial mansions, and there are some industries. The Burlington gives commutation. The Lyons Township High School has two large units and the La Grange Community Memorial hospital serves a wide area. There is a junction with US 45.

US 34 skirts the northern limits of WESTERN SPRINGS, 5.1 *m.* (668 alt., 12,147 pop. 1970; 10,838, 1960, inc. 12%). It is a Cook County village named for springs that have since gone dry. The village, however, has plenty of water from wells, one of them one-third of a mile deep. Spring Rock Park, Central Ave. and 47th St., was named for one of the springs; the former pool is now planted with flowers. The village was incorporated by Quakers in 1866. An interesting historical landmark is a brick watertower, once used as the village hall and currently a museum. Western Springs has the Lyons Township High School and the recently built Theatre of Western Springs, which presents legitimate plays and symphonic concerts and is patronized by a wide suburban area. Its public library circulates approx. 175,000 books a year. The community is served by the Burlington Railroad, and Tri-State Tollway, Int. 294, provides quick access to O'Hare International Airport, 15 *m.* north. There are numerous private golf clubs in this general area.

Replicas of period and commercial interiors are features of the exhibits of the Western Springs Historical Museum in Hillgrove Ave. They include an early grocery store, the showcase and wares of an early drug store, Victorian furnishings and fashions, and pioneer household objects. *Open Tuesday 2-4:30, Saturday, 10-2.*

North of US 34, which runs along the northern limits of La Grange and Western Springs, is LA GRANGE PARK (15,626 pop. 1970; 13,793, 1960, inc. 13.3%), served by the Burlington commuter line and West Towns and West Suburban Transit buses. US 45, north-south, passes through the village and Tri-State Tollway is at its western limits.

LA GRANGE HIGHLANDS, (6,920 pop. 1970, no census 1960) is a new unincorporated development.

West and north is the village of WESTCHESTER (20,033 pop. 1970; 18,092, 1960, inc. 10.7%) which has shown a remarkable growth as a residential site since World War II brought new industries to the environs. It had been founded by Samuel Insull in 1925 but scarcely had been offered to the public before the 1929 financial crash.

West of Westchester and La Grange Park with US 34 on its

southern line is the village of OAK BROOK (4,164 pop. 1970; 324, 1960, inc. 171%) a newly developed prestige community, which has the Tri-State Tollway on the east and the East-West Tollway on the north. A junction of these routes with the Eisenhower Expressway is directly north and provides an 18-minute trip to the Loop by motor car. This village was laid out on a farm of 3,600 acres in 1959 by Paul Butler, honorary chairman of the board of the J. W. Butler Paper Co., now a subsidiary of the Great Northern Nekoosa Corp. The first residential lots were sold in 1961. The place is the site of the INTERNATIONAL SPORTS CORE of 500 acres, which developed out of Butler's polo field. Almost immediately fashionable stores, corporate headquarters, and a complement of hotels moved into the development, as the word passed through the affluent Chicago business community that Oak Brook was destined to be the cream of the suburbs. Although the owner had intended it to be called Oak Brook, an error in registration papers caused it to be incorporated as Oakbrook, and 11 years passed before the title was officially separated into two words.

Paul Butler was the grandson of Julius Wales Butler who opened a paper mill in St. Charles in 1850, moved his offices to Chicago and flourished as the J. W. Butler Paper Co. after the Great Fire of 1871. Paul Butler, born in 1892, served as a lieutenant in the Army Air Service during World War I. His son Michael became one of the producers of "Hair." His daughter, Mrs. Jorie Butler Richardson, first woman member of the U. S. Polo Assn., today has charge of the International Sports Core, which has the Polo Club, with one indoor and three outdoor courts; two riding rings and an outdoor riding arena; two tournament polo fields; the National Horse Show field, and an airfield for light aircraft. There are also two golf courses, one reserved for the Western Open in 1974; a Polo Club, Saddle Club, and Bath and Tennis Club. These, with the hotel facilities already established, make Oak Brook the center for horse shows, golf tournaments, archery, swimming, and other sports.

Oak Brook's hotels and office buildings have assumed metropolitan proportions. The Oak Brook Sheraton has 350 rooms and 21 meeting rooms; the Hyatt House has 350 rooms; there are the Drake Oakbrook and Stouffer's Oakbrook Inn. Across 22nd St. in Oakbrook Terrace, is the Holiday Inn with 236 rooms. In 10 years Oak Brook Center attracted some of the finest stores of Chicago, and Lord & Taylor of New York established its first western branch there. The center occupies 110 acres.

General Motors Corp. moved 14 of its divisions and zone operations from the Chicago metropolitan area into one headquarters building in Oak Brook. McDonald's, with more than 2,600 outlets in 1973, built McDonald's Plaza, an eight-story building of 261,754 sq. ft. and reserved the three top stories for its national hq. Bunker Ramo, knit fabrics with 39 locations and 12,000 employees, made Oak Brook its top office. Two Executive Plaza buildings, 11 stories each, have a net area of 157,300 sq. ft.; International Office Center, three buildings of three stories each, has 600,000 sq. ft.; Oak Brook Professional Bldg., at the Center Mall, has eight stories, so has the Oak Brook Bank. Eight stories is the present restriction on height; there are also zoning regulations, limits on signs, etc. Every residence must have two acres. All possible sites in the village itself are said to have been sold, and developers are exploiting acreage in the environs.

OAKBROOK TERRACE (1,126 pop. 1970; 1,121, 1960) is located between Oak Brook and Villa Park on Roosevelt Road. It is incorporated as a city.

HINSDALE, 6.7 *m.* (691 alt., 15,918 pop. 1970; 12,859, 1960, inc. 23%) is a residential village on the Cook-Du Page county line located between 39th St. and 55th St. north and south, and the Tri-State Tollway and Illinois 82 east and west. Many of its workers commute to Chicago on the Burlington Railroad, which was built from Chicago to Aurora in 1864. The village was laid out in 1865 and incorporated in 1873. Its name is ascribed locally to H. W. Hinsdale, a Chicago merchant. On the north edge of Hinsdale is Fullersburg, settled in 1835 by Jacob Fuller with six sons and six daughters, and annexed to Hinsdale in 1923. Fullersburg Inn was a noted landmark on the Southwestern Plank Road. It was the birthplace of Loie Fuller (1862-1928), dancer.

Hinsdale has a village president, a board of six trustees, and an appointive village manager. The Hinsdale Community Caucus, organized in 1934, makes possible nominations for public office both by parties and by nonaligned individuals. The HINSDALE MEMORIAL BUILDING, 19 East Chicago Ave., houses the village administration and the Public Library. It was erected by public subscription in 1927 to commemorate Hinsdale's war dead. The Hinsdale Public Library has more than 38,000 books and a circulation of more than 215,000. It is a member of the Suburban Library System.

The Hinsdale Health Museum, 40 South Clay St., in the Medical Center, aims to disseminate information about the physiology of the human body. It has transparent figures that light up as recordings explain the functions of the organs. A film on how life begins is shown Saturdays and Sundays at 2 and 3 p.m. The museum was established in 1958 by the Kettering Family Foundation, owned by the family of Charles F. Kettering, former official of General Motors Corp. There are 50 volunteer guides and aids. *Weekdays 9-5, Sunday 1-5, closed holidays. Admission 50¢, $1.50 per family.*

The Hinsdale Sanitarium and Hospital, 120 N. Oak St., has 360 beds and 34 bassinets.

North of Glendale Ave. is the Fullersburg Forest Preserve. At the intersection of York Road and Spring Road stands a water-driven grist mill, the GRAUE MILL, built by Frederick Graue between 1848 and 1850 of native stone and oak and operated commercially until the 1920's. When its centennial approached a group of citizens formed a corporation to restore it and exhibit it as an example of a pioneer economy. Visitors watch the corn meal being stone-ground and may buy it. The mill, built of brick, has a farm museum on its upper floor, showing contents of a barn of 1860, merchandise of a country store, an early American kitchen, a victorian parlor and living room, and a child's room. *Open daily 11-6, May 1 to October 1; small fee.*

CLARENDON HILLS (6,750 pop. 1970; 5,885, 1960, inc. 16%), adjoins Hinsdale on the west and has US 34 on the north, 55th St. on the south, and Richmond Ave. on the west. Set in the rolling hills of Du Page County, it was once frequented by Indian tribes. In 1839 the U. S. Government was selling land here for $1.25 an acre. The Burlington (C. B. & Q.) came in 1864 and a former president of the road named the village. It was platted in 1870. Henry C. Middaugh had 270 acres north of the tracks and built a house at Norfolk and Chicago Aves. that is now a convent for nuns of the Notre Dame School. The village has 45 acres of parks and its swimming pool is a project of the Lions Club Community Service Corp. The Hinsdale Golf Club is located north of Chicago Ave.

Between Clarendon Hills and Downers Grove is the Du Page County village of WESTMONT (740 alt., 8,482 pop. 1970; 5,997, 1960, inc. 41%), also a commuting stop on the Burlington. South of Westmont on 63rd St. is the Illinois Pet Memorial Park, 2 acres, in which favorite dogs, cats, rabbits and other pets are buried.

DOWNERS GROVE, 11.2 *m.* (717 alt., 32,751 pop. 1970; 21,154, 1960, inc. 54.8%), in Cook County, was incorporated as a village in 1873. It traces its settlement back to 1833 when Pierce Downer came from Rutland, Vermont, and settled down at the crossing of two Potawatomi Indian trails, between what are now Oakwood and Linscott Aves., and Grant and Lincoln Sts. A bronze tablet on a granite boulder from the foundation of Downer's barn marks the spot of Downer's rest.

A favored residence for many persons employed in Chicago, Downers Grove has commutation service from three stations on the Burlington railroad, as well as buses, 400 individually owned shops, and five shopping areas. The village has a council-manager form of government, with a mayor and four councilmen, who name a village manager as administrative head.

Downers Grove has 27 churches of the major denominations. Its residents take part in numerous musical activities, including a season by the Community Concert Assn., and programs by the Oratorio Society, the Choral-Aires, the Sweet Adelines, and the Grove Players. Several Little Theaters are associated with the village's nine parks. Light industry engages an average of 4,500 employees, most of the plants being located in Ellsworth Industrial Park. The Medical Center is of recent construction.

GEORGE WILLIAMS COLLEGE, founded 1890 by the Young Men's Christian Assn., occupies 14 buildings on a 200-acre campus in Downers Grove. The college trains students for social service, community and youth projects. After years at 5315 Drexel Ave.

in Chicago it moved in 1964 to Downers Grove, where it has erected a library, classroom buildings, and dormitories.

Downers Grove Park District has 230 acres fully equipped for sports and recreational uses, 86 of them devoted to the Golf Club.

Downers Grove Public Library has a collection of more than 68,000 volumes and more than 25,000 registered borrowers. It is a member of the Suburban Library System of 58 libraries. The original Carnegie Library building, erected in 1915, is still in use, additions having been placed at two sides of it in 1956.

Right from Downer's Grove on Highland Ave., 1.7 *m.* is the burial ground of the Thrasher Family, now surrounded by the Yorktown Shopping Center. This goes back to pioneer days. The Allerton Ridge Cemetery, 1.8 *m.* on Highland Ave. has all markers laid even with the turf. A children's section is called the Eugene Field Memorial Plot, dedicated in 1928 by the Rev. Leland H. Danforth, who caused Field's body to be reinterred in an Episcopal church in Kenilworth, Ill. (*see Tour 2*).

LISLE, 14.7 *m.* (5,329 pop. 1970; 4,214, 1960) is located on the east branch of the Du Page River and has the East-West Tollway on its northern line. Its principal industry is a plant of the Western Electric Co., which employs up to 2,000. The Public Library circulates approx. 60,000 vols. This is the site of the Lisle Community High School.

Here US 34 has a junction with Illinois 53, north-south, the old Joliet road, which serves an area where pastures are turning into town lots. South of Lisle on the East Branch of the Du Page are WOOD-RIDGE and BOLINGBROOK. Woodridge was only one year old as an incorporated village when the Census of 1960 arrived and found only 542 inhabitants. In the following decade real estate developers became active and the Census of 1970 reported 11,028, an increase of 934.7%. It is a recreational area and location of the Woodridge Golf Club and the Maple Crest Golf Club. Just across its southern line in Will County is Bolingbrook (7,275 pop. 1970), for which see Tour 17.

North of Lisle on Illinois 53, 1 *m.* is the MORTON ARBO-RETUM. It was established in 1921 by Joy Morton (1855-1934), whose father, Julius S. Morton, a pioneer in reforestation, inaugurated Arbor Day. The Morton residence adjoins the Arboretum and the family burial ground is nearby. The Georgian Administration Building contains a bureau of horticultural information. Within the 1,425-acre tract are roads and lanes that give access to all trees and shrubs, which are placed in groups and properly tagged. The favorite visiting seasons are crabapple time in early May, lilac blooms in late May, iris displays in June, and petunias in early fall. Pedestrians are admitted free; there is a slight charge for motor cars.

ILLINOIS BENEDICTINE COLLEGE, a coeducational Catholic college of the liberal arts and sciences known until July 1, 1971, as St. Procopius College, occupies a campus of 100 acres on Maple Ave., west of Illinois 53, about 5 minutes from the East-West Tollway and 7 miles north of the Stevenson Expressway (Int. 55) both on Illinois 53.

Thus the college is midway between Lisle and Naperville. It was established in Chicago in 1890 by the Benedictine Fathers, largely for men of Czechoslovak descent and moved to its present location in 1900. It has since enrolled students of varying national backgrounds and opened its doors to women.

Benedictine Hall, the largest building, was built between 1901 and 1914, largely by hand by the monks. Among recent structures are the Lownik Library (1963), which has a 100-seat hall; Science Learning Center (1969), which includes the Hilary S. Judica biology museum; three residence halls for men, and one for women.

Besides the regular curriculum leading to the baccalaureate degree the student may choose from pre-dental, pre-engineering, pre-legal, pre-medical, pre-veterinary, and pre-pharmacy courses. The college offers evening and summer sessions to the community. The Institute for Management is a program of continuing education intended for middle managers, sponsored by Chicago area business houses. Both these courses are described in separate catalogues available on request. The college enrolled 1,022 students in the fall, 1972, and had a faculty of 75. It estimated student expenses as $882.50 for commuters, and added $212.50 to $237.50 for lodging and $350 for board, for residents.

The college cooperates with three organizations: St. Procopius Abbey, home of the Benedictine monks, a new monastery at 5601 College Road, adjacent to the college campus; Benet Academy, formerly St. Procopius Academy, 2200 Maple Ave., Lisle, north of the college, and St. Procopius High School for girls, 1625 S. Allport St., Chicago, affiliated with St. Procopius parish.

NAPERVILLE, 18.7 *m.* (693 alt., 23,885 pop. 1970; 12,933, 1960, inc. 84%) is the last large suburb out of Chicago on the Ogden Avenue highway (US 34) toward the more heavily industrialized Fox River Valley. Incorporated in 1857 as a city in Du Page County, it has been adding new sections of medium-priced homes and opened two new industrial parks. It is also near the National Accelerator Laboratory and the Standard Oil Research Laboratories, and expects a further rise in population when these are fully manned. The city lies on the West Branch of the Du Page River, which provides a beach for Centennial Park. The East-West Tollway extends along its northern line, and when US 34 turns sharply southwest Illinois 65 picks up the Ogden Ave. route and moves straight west to Aurora. Like the other places on US 34 Naperville has commutation service to Chicago on the Burlington Railroad and the buses of the West Suburban Transit Co.

Naperville is the home of the Kroehler Furniture Manufacturing Co., nationally known for its upholstered furniture, which was established in 1887 as the Naperville Lounge Factory. It also has the Du Page Boiler Works, the Du Page Precision Products, Inc., and electronic industries.

Shortly after the first settlers came here in 1831, the Black Hawk War forced them to flee to Fort Dearborn. Returning with a company of volunteers, they built a stockade known as Fort Payne in June, 1832.

The settlement profited from the caravans of covered wagons rolling west and by 1833 had 180 people.

The first settler in Du Page County was Bailey Hobson, who staked his claim in 1830, and established a grist mill. In 1832 came Joseph Naper, who built the first sawmill and platted the town site. Naperville became county seat in 1839, a distinction it retained until 1868 when Wheaton displaced it in an election. Naperville refused to yield the county records, whereupon a band of men from Wheaton raided the Naperville courthouse next year and removed the books.

NORTH CENTRAL COLLEGE, a coeducational institution under religious sponsorship, was founded in Plainfield in 1861 by the Evangelical Church. In 1870 the college was removed to Naperville. An elevation on the Fort Hill campus is the site of the original Fort Payne. In 1971 the college enrolled 836 students and had a faculty of 70. The Evangelical Theological Seminary is an associated institution.

The Nichols Library, built in 1897 and modernized in 1962, has a collection of nearly 50,000 books and circulates nearly 300,000. It is a member of the Du Page Library System.

Naperville has 26 churches and the Edwards Hospital (133 beds). It has eight parks and a community swimming pool. In Pioneer Park near the intersection of S. Washington St. and Goodrich Rd. are two millstones, once part of Bailey Hobson's mill, which stood on this site.

North on West Avenue across the East-West Tollway to the Warrenville Road, 2.9 m. to WARRENVILLE, an incorporated city (3,854 pop. 1970; no record, 1960), which was settled a few years after Naperville. It had a busy tannery, a grist mill, and the Warrenville Academy, which was removed to Rockford in 1854 to become the nucleus of Rockford College. The place declined when the Burlington railroad made Naperville a trade center.

US 34 moves southwest from Naperville into Kendall County, bypassing AURORA (*see article on Aurora*) and MONTGOMERY (3,278 pop. 1970; 2,122, 1960, inc. 54%). US 30, coming north from a junction with US 66 2.5 m. south of Plainfield, crosses the Fox River at Montgomery, which adjoins Aurora on the south. Industries spill over from Aurora, including divisions of Armour & Co. and Western Electric.

OSWEGO, (1,862 pop. 1970; 1,510, 1960) on the Fox River 8 m. southwest of Naperville, is at a junction with Illinois 71. Here US 34 crosses the Fox River. Six miles farther west US 34 has a junction with Illinois 47, north-south, north of YORKVILLE (2,049 pop. 1970; 1,560, 1960, inc. 30%) seat of Kendall County, and incorporated as a city. The Fox River flows through it and it is served by the Burlington Railroad. A State game farm is located at Yorkville.

Left on Illinois 47 to a junction with an unimproved road, 0.9 m. Right to a Fish Hatchery. About 1,000,000 fish are bred here annually. North of the hatchery is a 75-acre State Game Farm where silver, golden, mutant, Amherst, and ring-necked pheasants are bred.

PLANO, 41.5 m. (649 alt., 4,664 pop. 1970; 3,343, 1960, inc. 39%) a city in Kendall County, its skyline dominated by a water tower and grain elevators, is the trading center of a rich agricultural area. Kleng Peerson led a band of Norwegian Quakers to this region in 1835. Three years later one of the party, Ansten Nattestad, visiting Norway, stimulated further immigration to the district by circulating Ole Rynning's *True Account of America for the Instruction and Use of the Peasants and Common People*.

Left from southwestern Plano on a graveled road is MARAMECH HILL, 1.5 *m*. between the confluence of Big Rock and Little Rock creeks. The hill is believed by many to be the site of a dramatic siege during the wars between the French and the Fox Indians in the early part of the eighteenth century. In the late summer of 1730 a band of 300 Foxes with their families, bound for the Iroquois country, were surprised by a large force of French soldiers and their Indian allies. The Foxes entrenched their position and were besieged for more than three weeks. Under cover of a storm on the night of September 8, 1730, the Foxes slipped out of their "fort," but their departure was detected, and on the following day they were overtaken and ruthlessly slaughtered.

SANDWICH, 46.1 *m*. (657 alt., 5,026 pop. 1970; 3,842, 1960, inc. 31%) a city in De Kalb and Kendall Counties. It was named by Long John Wentworth, Chicago mayor, for his birthplace in Massachusetts.

At 59.2 *m*. is a junction with Illinois 23. Left on Illinois 23 to a junction with a graveled road, 3.1 *m*.; r. to a junction with another graveled road, 4.8 *m*.; l. is SHABBONA STATE PARK, 5.6 *m*. The 7-acre tract, bordering a tributary of the Fox River, commemorates the Potawatomi chief who befriended the settlers at the time of the Indian Creek Massacre. In 1832 Black Hawk urged Shabbona to unite his tribe with the Sauk in a war to drive all white inhabitants from the frontier. Shabbona refused and fled from the war council. In the night he mounted his pony and rode eastward to warn the settlers, although he knew few white men and did not speak or understand English. Sauk spies pursued him as he zigzagged his way over 200 miles of prairie and forest, spreading the alarm. His son, Pepys, traveled to the west on the same errand. Most of the settlers heeded the warning and escaped, but fifteen were caught and killed.

The Indian Creek Massacre took place on May 21, 1832 at the cabin of William Davis on Indian Creek north of Ottawa. The band, mostly Potawatomi, is believed to have included some of Black Hawk's men. They carried off two occupants of the cabin, Rachel and Sylvia Hall, and later gave them to the Winnebagoes, who returned them to their people. The first marker on the site was a stone erected in 1877. In 1906 a granite shaft was erected by the State of Illinois.

MENDOTA, 77.2 *m*. (750 alt., 6,902 pop. 1970) is at junctions with US 51 (*see Tour 4*) and US 52 (*see Tour 15*).

PRINCETON, 102 *m*. (719 alt., 6,959 pop. 1970), is at a junction with US 6 (*see Tour 14*).

Section b. Princeton to Iowa Line, 115 m.

West of Princeton, 0 *m.*, US 34 and US 6 are united for 16 miles (*see Tour 14*). At 27 *m.* is a junction with a graveled road. Right on this road to Francis Park, 40 acres donated to Kewanee by Fred Francis (1856-1926), who was born in a log cabin that stands in the park. A brilliant mathematician and inventor, he was a graduate of the University of Illinois and during 11 years with the Elgin Watch Co. patented several manufacturing processes. He built Francis House, preserved in the park, in which he installed air conditioning and automatic doors long before these came into general use.

KEWANEE, 30.5 *m.* (15,762 pop. 1970; 16,324, 1960, dec. 3%) an incorporated city in Henry County, became nationally known for its boilers and steam fittings, originally made here by one firm, and now produced by the Kewanee Boiler Co., a plant of the American-Standard Co., and the Walworth Manufacturing Co. Boss Gloves are another familiar Kewanee product. There is a plant here of the Hyster Co., maker of road-building trucks.

The older part of Kewanee, south of Division St., is still known as Wethersfield, although it has been part of the corporate city since 1924. In 1836 it was a new colony, the enterprise of the Connecticut Association, a group "having in view the establishment of a colony for promoting the cause of education and piety in the State of Illinois." The Roman Catholics had already established a number of thriving communities in Illinois. The members of the Connecticut Association deemed it their duty to foster Protestantism.

Wethersfield was accordingly founded and named for the parent community in Connecticut. Shares sold to New Englanders at $250 each gave title to 160 acres of prairie, 20 acres of woodland, and a town lot. In the summer of 1836 John Kilverton built the first log cabin. The first church, a plain structure of logs, was erected the same summer. Three years later the first school was opened; soon an academy was founded. The colony subsequently became a center of anti-slavery and Union sentiment.

In 1854 the Military Tract Railroad, later the C. B. & Q., was built one mile north of Wethersfield. A settlement, destined to become Kewanee, took root near the depot, and many colonists removed to the new community; with the establishment of industrial plants along the railroad, scores of European immigrants arrived. By 1857 Kewanee, its population exceeding 2,000, had far outstripped the older Wethersfield, now strictly residential.

The Kewanee Public Library, with a collection of more than 65,000 volumes, has a circulation of around 135,000. It is a member of the Illinois Valley Library System.

Kewanee is at a junction with Illinois 78, which connects with Inter. 80 and US 6, westbound to Moline, Rock Island, 11 *m.* north.

About 6 *m.* north, east of Illinois 78 is Johnson Sauk Trail State Park, 857 acres, a scenic park built around a man-made lake stocked with fish.

Illinois 78 unites with US 34 for 5.4 miles. At 35.2 *m.* is a junction with Illinois 91.

Left on this road to the hamlet of ELMIRA, 5.2 *m.*, known in early days as the Scotch Settlement, which celebrated its centennial in 1938 with pageants and Scottish ceremonials. The immigrant founders were six weeks on the ocean, many more on the cross-country journey, and reached Stark County only after innumerable hardships. These pious settlers became strong Abolitionists, and made the village an important station on the Underground Railroad. Escaped slaves were hidden by day in attics, barn lofts, or in the timber, then escorted on moonless nights to the next station north.

GALVA, 43 *m.* (849 alt., 3,061 pop. 1970; 3,060, 1960) a city in Henry County, has the distinction of having gained one inhabitant in ten years according to the U. S. Census. It was named for Gefle, a seaport in Sweden from which its settlers came, and established in 1854 by dissenters from the Swedish colony at Bishop Hill because of its economic restrictions. Galva shared in the recent centennial observances of Bishop Hill. The city has light industries, including farm equipment and electronics.

At 47 *m.* is a junction with a paved road. Right on this road 2.6 *m.* to BISHOP HILL (191 pop. 1970) a village at BISHOP HILL STATE MEMORIAL, 5 acres. The place was named for Biskopskulla, Sweden, birthplace of Erik Jansson. The 125th anniversary of the settlement of Bishop Hill by Swedish immigrants was observed in 1971. The Bishop Hill Heritage Assn. in August welcomed a delegation from the Swedish Museum of National Antiquities. Dr. Olaf Isaksson, curator of the Museum and author of *Bishop Hill, A Utopia on the Prairie,* had obtained grants for restoration of Bishop Hill from the King of Sweden and the American Scandinavian Foundation, and co-operated with the Illinois Department of Conservation and Illinois Arts Council in the restoration of paintings of the settlement by Olof Krans, primitive painter whose paintings also were exhibited at the Illinois State Museum in Springfield in 1971. The artist, originally Olof Olson, assumed the name Krans when he volunteered during the Civil War. The *Journal* of the Illinois State Historical Society said: "The Krans paintings are valuable historic documents because of their realistic portrayal of life in the colony. They have artistic value because Krans, though a primitive, was skilled in his handling of form, color, and composition."

Bishop Hill was settled in 1846 by a group of Swedish emigrants led by Erik Jansson, a religious farmer who broke with the established church of Sweden and preached that the Bible alone could properly be used in religious services. Jansson conducted public burnings of hymn-books and catechisms, and was frequently arrested by Swedish officials. He finally announced that "inasmuch as the inhabitants of my own country refuse to accept the truth," he and his followers would "turn to the heathen."

The small group crossed to America, came by way of canal and the Great Lakes to Illinois, and settled here in Henry County. They literally dug themselves in the first winter, hollowing out caves in a gorge near South Edwards

Creek. In the following spring they began the establishment of a communistic colony.

It prospered for a brief period. Families lived separately but worked together 18 hours a day. They ate in a common dining hall and received their clothing from the community storehouse. These hard working and progressive farmers readily adopted contemporary agricultural inventions. Flax, from which they made linen, and broomcorn, which they exported in large quantities, were the principal crops. In time Bishop Hill, with a population of 1,500, became the most important settlement between Peoria and Rock Island.

Dissension over policies and beliefs eventually disrupted the colony. John Root came from Sweden in 1848 and married Jansson's cousin, promising to let her stay in the colony. Unable to get her to leave with him, he kidnapped her. This started a feud with Jansson leading to lawsuits. When Jansson appeared at the Henry County Circuit Court at Cambridge in 1850, Root shot and killed him. Root was tried in Knoxville and given two years in prison for manslaughter. After one year in Alton State prison Root was pardoned by Governor Joel Matteson.

After Jansson's death his wife became administrator until forced to give up the office to Olaf Johnsen, business manager, at Galva. He in turn was attacked for financial mismanagement. Groups split from the colony and divided the communal property. The members joined Methodist and Seventh Day Adventist churches. Without a railroad Bishop Hill declined. The colony ended in 1861.

The STEEPLE BUILDING, northeast corner Main and Bishop, is a three-story brick and plaster structure, built in 1854 and now used as a museum. A classic portico dominates the facade. Pilastered pediments ornament the side walls and an octagonal cupola surmounts the hip roof. The bell, which still tolls the hour, and the clock in the cupola, were made by the colony blacksmith. The clock, running since 1859, has no minute hand; as a villager explained: "In Bishop Hill we don't watch the minutes. Even the hours don't need watching here." Here are exhibited a law office, a doctor's office, a store, a barber shop and collections of the Henry County Historical Society.

The OLD COLONY CHURCH, southwest corner Front and Bishop Hill Sts., a white two-story frame structure, was built in 1848 and is now used as the village meeting hall. Among the Janssonite memorabilia housed here are a spinning wheel, 93 oil paintings by Olof Krans, a lathe upon which the bedposts of the colony were fashioned, and a colorfully decorated bandwagon, designed for either wheels or runners. Krans, a blacksmith by trade, was a self-taught artist; most of his paintings are portraits of the founders, both men and women, but some depict early buildings, landscapes, and pioneer farming practices.

The ball park west of the church is the site of BIG BRICK, the four-story communal living quarters built in 1848-51. Men and women worked side by side in constructing the Big Brick. The basement was used as a kitchen and dining hall. In the 96 rooms of the upper stories families occupied suites or single chambers, according to their needs. The building was destroyed by fire in 1928.

Among other old buildings that remain are the School House (1860), west end of Main St.; the Colony Storehouse, a two-story brick building that now houses the post office; and the Colony Hospital, a two-story structure of brick and yellow plaster, west of Park Street. Several old colony houses, now private residences, border the park on the south. In the park is the Bishop Hill Memorial, a granite boulder dedicated to the memory of pioneers of the community "by surviving members and descendants, on the 50th anniversary of the founding of the colony, Sept. 23, 1896."

In the Bishop Hill Cemetery, E. Main Street, a white marble

monument marks the grave of Erik Jansson. Below a shallow depression
near the monument are the remains of 96 colonists who died during the
winter of 1846-47. The site of the dugouts in which the colonists lived
during the winter of 1846-47 is along the upper edge of the ravine that
extends northwest at the north end of Park Street.

Between Galva and Galesburg, a distance of 26 *m.* on US 34 are
several farm villages: ALTONA, which had 505 people in 1960 and
expanded 7% to 542 in 1970; ONEIDA, a city, which expanded from
672 in 1960 to 728 in 1970, actually 8%, and WATAGA, which held
570 people and neither added nor lost a single inhabitant between census
enumerations. Wataga advertises itself as "fastest growing little town
around."

US 34 has a junction northeast of Galesburg with Int. 74, an
expressway that crosses the State from Indiana and is routed parallel
with Illinois 150 to bypass cities and towns. Coming up from Peoria
Int. 74 turns sharply north at EAST GALESBURG (706 pop. 1970;
660, 1960, inc. 7%). Int. 74 then moves straight north to Moline and
crosses the Mississippi River to Iowa at Rapids City, Illinois.

GALESBURG

GALESBURG, 70 *m.* (788 alt., 36,290 pop. 1970; 37,243, 1960)
seat of Knox County and an outlet for farm products, has won national
renown for its historical and literary associations. It is the only site of
the Lincoln-Douglas debates that retains the original setting; it has Knox
College, with a list of famous alumni, and it is closely tied to the career
of Carl Sandburg, whose birthplace has been made a literary memorial of
him and Lincoln. It commemorates also the career of Mother Bickerdyke, Civil War nurse. Also honoring the historian-poet are the Sandburg Mall, the Sandburg National Bank, Carl Sandburg College, and
Carl Sandburg Learning Center.

The town was planned in Oneida, N. Y., in 1835 and the site
chosen after examination of land in Indiana and Illinois by George
Washington Gale, a Presbyterian minister, who circulated among his
parishioners in the Mohawk Valley a prospectus for a community he
contemplated founding on the frontier. Land was to be bought with a
joint fund, and the nucleus of the village was to be a manual labor
college for the training of ministers. Gale believed that settlement by
industrious farmers would raise land values, and the sale of farms would
produce a fund to endow the college.

Into Gale's plan some 50 families invested more than $20,000.
A committee purchased 20 square miles of land at $1.25 an acre. In
1836-37 the families came west, some overland, some by way of the
Erie Canal and the Great Lakes, a few along the Ohio and Mississippi
Rivers. On arrival they settled at a temporary town, Log City, at the
grove on Henderson Creek. From here they went to the selected site on
the prairie and built substantial houses, because there were to be no crude
log cabins in the new city. Many built sections of their houses at the

grove, where lumber was plentiful, and then hauled them with oxen to the new town.

The strict morality of the early settlers was combined with hard-headed practicality and versatility. Among them were the Ferrises, one of whom, Olmsted Ferris, experimented with popcorn and later introduced it into England. The Prince Consort, Albert, became interested and Ferris gave a "command performance" of corn-popping before Queen Victoria. Another Ferris invented the Ferris wheel, first exhibited at the Columbian Exposition in Chicago in 1893 and part of carnivals here and abroad ever since. The word ferris-wheel is now a common noun. Harvey Henry May in 1837 invented a steel self-scouring plow.

Archetype of all the moral New Englanders who settled here in the West was Jonathan Blanchard, early president of Knox College. In 1854 Galesburg obtained its first railroad by raising a $250,000 subsidy. On the second Sunday of the railroad's operation Blanchard, in black frock coat, strode out to the tracks and curtly commanded the locomotive engineer to put aside the engine and refrain from profaning the Sabbath. "You can go to hell and mind your own business," replied the engineer, "I'll take my train out as ordered." Galesburg became a division point on the "Q" as the Chicago, Burlington & Quincy was called—now the Burlington Northern, which established its shops here. The railroad helped increase the population; from 882 in 1850 it expanded to 4,000 in six years.

In 1857 a large number of Swedes from the Bishop Hill colony came to Galesburg. Galesburg's increased importance enabled it to wrest the county seat from Knoxville, causing the decline of the latter. During the Civil War the abolitionist sentiment of the New Englanders made Galesburg a strong anti-slavery town in the midst of communities that favored the South.

The early settlers were Presbyterian fundamentalists, who interpreted the Scriptures literally. Later comers from New England represented the drift to more liberal thinking. Among the latter were the Universalists. Irritated by the strictness of the Presbyterians, the Universalists in 1852 established their Illinois Liberal Institute. It had hardly been opened when its quarters burned down. A friendly supporter named Benjamin Lombard came to its aid and when a divinity school was added its title was changed to Lombard University. Young David Starr Jordan, later president of Stanford University, was one of its early instructors. Eventually its title was reduced to Lombard College. In 1930 it was taken over by Knox and its three buildings went to the city for school purposes.

KNOX COLLEGE was founded in 1837 by George Washington Gale and his associates, who wanted an institution in which to train men for the ministry. It was spoken of as Prairie College, but the fame of General Henry Knox, for whom Knox County was named, weighed heavily in choosing a name, and on February 15, 1837, it was chartered as Knox Manual Labor College, because Gale believed ministers ought to be able to work with their hands. This name was used until 1857, when the manual part was dropped. Knox opened its classes in 1841; in 1846 it graduated its first class of nine men, five of whom became preachers. The college had a joint board divided between Presbyterians and Congregationalists who were often at odds, but it was 1870 before Knox severed its tie to the churches.

In 1860 Knox gave Abraham Lincoln an honorary degree, his first. Knox had no racial bias, and Hiram Revels, a black alumnus, was seated in the U. S. Senate during Reconstruction, occupying the place once held by Jefferson Davis. Knox also favored education for women and formed its Female Collegiate Department in 1850, but did not grant degrees to women until 20 years later, and then only after six years of study, whereas men earned them in four. Today Knox permits qualified students to complete the course in less than four years by an advanced placement program and credit by examination.

The day cherished over all others at Knox College is October 7, 1858, when Lincoln and Stephen A. Douglas met before the Old Main for the fifth of their great debates. The building has been preserved and contains furniture of the Civil War period. The day has been relived many times and its centennial was properly observed with the presence of Carl Sandburg and other historians at exercises in front of the building.

Knox College now occupies a campus of 85 acres and has added a number of new buildings in recent years, including the Science-Mathematics Center, the Center for the Fine Arts, the Memorial Gymnasium, and Knox Center. The Seymour Library has been enlarged and has approx. 150,000 volumes. In 1973 Knox had a faculty of 104 and enrolled 1,349 students.

Two alumni of Knox who had influential careers in American journalism were Samuel S. McClure and John H. Finley. McClure was born in Ireland, came to the United States at the age of 9. He entered Knox Academy in 1874 and was graduated from the college in 1882, working at all sorts of odd jobs. He was married to a daughter of Prof. Alfred Hurd. As editor of *The Knox Student* he caused enough controversy to bring about the issue of *The Coup d'Etat*, of which Finley became editor years after McClure's departure. McClure invented the literary syndicate, acting as agent for Theodore Roosevelt, Robert Louis Stevenson, Ida Tarbell, Sarah Orne Jewett, and A. Conan Doyle. In 1893 with two other Knox alumni, John S. Phillips and Albert Brady, he founded *McClure's Magazine* and made many innovations. He sent Ida Tarbell to Kentucky to find records of the early years of Abraham Lincoln and his family. In 1897 he began publishing inquiries into municipal and political abuses, written by Lincoln Steffens, Mark Sullivan, Samuel Hopkins Adams, Ray Stannard Baker, William Allen White, Frank Norris, and Finley Peter Dunne. In literary history they are termed Muckrakers, but when Theodore Roosevelt used the term he applied it to their imitators. One of McClure's authors was Willa S. Cather, who "ghosted" his *Autobiography*.

John Huston Finley (1863-1940) came from a LaSalle County farm and entered Knox in 1883, dropped out to earn money, returned later to be graduated in 1887. Part-time he worked in a Galesburg printshop, learning typesetting. He took graduate work at Johns Hopkins and embarked on an educational career. In 1892, five years after graduating, Finley became president of Knox at 29. He was married to Martha Boyden, a classmate. He shook up Knox, started observance of Founders' Day and of the Lincoln-Douglas debate, and invited presidents and national celebrities. He was professor of politics at

Princeton, 1900-1902; president of the City College of New York, 1903-1913; Commissioner of Education of New York State, 1913-1921. In 1921 he joined the *New York Times* and in 1937 became editor-in-chief.

Eugene Field was enrolled at Knox by Prof. John W. Burgess, who had been made educational guardian of Eugene by the lad's father. Field had been dropped by Williams College because "his wit was such that the faculty could not cope with it, it made them ridiculous." Field became the most popular student at Knox. Burgess, who founded the School of Political Science at Columbia University, is thus described by Earnest Elmo Calkins. "Burgess lived at Hi Belden's Union Hotel. One day he stuffed a $1,000 bond and $500 in cash, his entire means, in his pocket and went for a walk. When he returned the hotel was on fire. He watched it burn to the ground." Calkins recalled Edgar Lee Masters, Otto Harbach, the librettist; Ralph Waldo Trine, and Don Marquis as Knox students. He grew up in Galesburg, attended Knox College and started his advertising career in Peoria. In 1937 he was the official historian of Galesburg and wrote *They Broke the Prairie*. George Fitch, who created the Old Siwash stories, attended school in Galesburg. Knox is usually identified with Old Siwash.

CARL SANDBURG COLLEGE, a two-year community college established by vote of the junior college district, began its vocational-technical courses in September, 1967, in a group of interim buildings, one mile north of Galesburg on US 150 and one mile west on South Lake Storey Road. In 1972 it had a faculty of 123 and an enrollment of 1,863 students. It is in process of developing permanent facilities with an investment of $8,000,000.

On October 1, 1967, the college board presented Mrs. Carl Sandburg with a plaque saying that "through his contributions in the fields of history and literature and his sensitivity to his fellow man, Carl Sandburg earned world-wide acclaim and brought honor to the country which he loved. . . . It is the desire of the board that through the comprehensive nature of its program and quality of its instruction, the college will become a permanent memorial to the ideals and achievements by which Carl Sandburg brought dignity to man and honor and recognition ot this area of his birth."

The college has an open admissions policy and uses the quarter system, with a summer session available. Its junior college district includes parts of Knox, Warren, Fulton, Henderson, Mercer, and Stark Counties. Its courses in applied science include administrative accounting, commercial pilot aviation, data processing, and machine tool, radiologic and electrical technology; there are also courses in nursing and public service occupations and one-year certificates for practical nursing, law enforcement and secretarial programs. Adult education is available and evening classes are provided. Credits may be transferred to senior colleges toward a higher degree. The first president is Eltis Henson.

Adults who wish to complete their basic education can enroll in the Carl Sandburg Learning Center, conducted in the Positive Attitudes Bldg., Main and Henderson Sts. The program, supported by the Superintendent of Public Instruction with State aid offers the equivalent of high school courses on an individualized basis. A day care section is provided for mothers who bring their children.

The CARL SANDBURG BIRTHPLACE, 331 East Third St., is a monument to greatness sprung from humble beginnings. In a tiny cottage behind a picket fence Carl Sandburg was born January 6, 1878, son of Swedish immigrants. His father worked as a blacksmith in the shops of the Burlington railroad. The Sandburgs moved out of the cottage when Carl was 3. His ashes have been placed in its backyard, now a park.

The cottage, only 20 feet square, had rough vertical siding and no plaster in the interior. In its present state it has been completely rehabilitated, a Lincoln room has been added, there are a new picket fence and a new wooden sidewalk, and a caretaker's house next door. The place has been supported by State aid and contributions from the public. It is the responsibility of the Illinois State Historical Association.

Carl was the second of seven children and named Charles August. He delivered newspapers, and after he completed the eighth grade in 1891 he acquired a milk route. This led him to cross the Knox campus every day, and when he passed Old Main he read the plaque that records the Lincoln-Douglas debate held there on October 7, 1858. When 15 he became a porter in the Union Hotel barbershop for $3 a week and tips. At 19 he took a look at western towns, doing odd jobs and picking up some of the ballads that he later sang before audiences and included in *The American Songbag*. In 1898 he joined Company C, 6th Infantry Regiment of Illinois Volunteers for the Spanish-American War, but only reached Puerto Rico. He returned to Galesburg and determined to get more schooling, so he entered Lombard College. He got a job as a "call man" with the Fire Department at $10 a month, and sold stereopticon slides. He began writing poetry and Prof. Phillip Green Wright published his poems in two pamphlets printed on his own press.

Sandburg sympathized with the workers and in 1907 became organizer for the Social Democratic party in Wisconsin. When Emil Seidel became socialist mayor of Milwaukee, Sandburg served as his secretary. At party headquarters he met Lillian Paula Steichen and they were married. She was a sister of Edward Steichen, art photographer. Sandburg had small pay from newswriting and contributed to Cochran's *Daybook,* a political commentary, in Chicago. In 1914 Harriet Monroe's *Poetry, A Magazine of Verse,* printed his "Chicago" and gave it a prize. Its realistic theme and free verse form expressed the dynamic energy of Chicago and its most famous lines were quoted endlessly:

> Hog butcher for the world,
> Toolmaker, stacker of wheat,
> Player with railroads and the nation's freight handler;
> Stormy, husky, brawling
> City of the Big Shoulders . . .

This opened Carl Sandburg's prolific writing career, in which every year brought proof of his wide-ranging interests and versatility. Then came books of poetry: *Chicago Poems, Cornhuskers, Smoke and Steel, Slabs of the Sunburnt West.* He wrote *Rootabaga Stories* and *Rootabaga Pigeons* for children; foreign correspondence for a syndicate and features for the *Chicago Daily News.* Always interested in Abraham Lincoln he started the long research that produced *Abraham Lincoln, the Prairie Years, and Abraham Lincoln, the War Years,* the great biography of a prairie President by a prairie poet. Many other books followed: *Good Morning, America; The People, Yes;* autobiography in *Always the Young Strangers.* In his 80th year he published more poems in *Honey and Salt.* He wrote a long novel about the spirit of America in *Remembrance Rock.* He wrote books about his associates: *Steichen, the Photographer,* and *Lincoln Collector,* about Oliver R. Barrett. He lectured widely and sang folk ballads to the accompaniment of his guitar.

Sandburg won two Pulitzer prizes and 34 honorary degrees. The United States Congress recognized his position as a national spokesman when it asked him to address a joint session on the 150th anniversary of Lincoln's birth. His interpretation of the humanity of Lincoln and his common touch made him a hero to the public schools. Elementary and high schools east and west bear his name. After living for a number of years in the environs of Chicago he established a home in Harbert, Michigan, and later moved to Flat Rock, N. C., where he died on July 22, 1967, at the age of 89, his literary fame having been achieved in his last fifty years.

The importance of Sandburg's Birthplace in American literary history was recognized by Adda Gentry George (Mrs. John E.) a retired teacher of English, who inspired the Carl Sandburg Association and agitated for the purchase of the cottage by voluntary contributions. The house, only 20 ft. square, was bought in 1946. Mrs. George saw to the restoration and guided the work for 19 years until her death in 1968, when nearly 95. Among pieces of furniture used by the Sandburg family are three chairs, a washstand, and two whatnots. There also are a family Bible and photographs of Carl's parents, August and Clara Sandburg. Some of the furniture was made by Swedish craftsmen at Bishop Hill. The bedroom has a trundle bed; the kitchen is without running water; there is a wood stove, of the kind that provided the only heat for the house.

In 1949 the Lincoln Room was added with State funds to commemorate Sandburg's biography of Lincoln. It contains his bust, a portrait of Lincoln by N. C. Wyeth; a complete set of works that Sandburg autographed for his publisher, Alfred Harcourt; first editions of all the books including the rare pamphlets of poetry printed by Prof. Phillip Green Wright in Galesburg, and the typewriter on which Carl wrote *The Prairie Years* and *Rootabaga Stories*.

The lot on which the house stands is 132 by 198 ft. in size and has been landscaped as a small park. In the center is a large red granite boulder that was uncovered during the construction of Interstate 74, now suitably inscribed Remembrance Rock, the title of Sandburg's novel. Carl asked that his ashes be buried there and this was done by Mrs. Sandburg and her eldest daughter Margaret on October 1, 1967.

Adjoining the Birthplace is a two-story frame dwelling called the Adda George House, where the caretaker lives.

On June 24, 1970, Governor Richard B. Ogilvie signed an act giving the Sandburg Birthplace to the Illinois State Historical Library. The act specifies that "the Library, in conjunction with the Illinois State Historical Society, shall establish, maintain and operate the property as a museum and historic site depicting and portraying the life and times of Carl Sandburg and his influence in disseminating an appreciation of the history of Abraham Lincoln." The State voted $35,000 to defray operating expenses for one year. Present at the ceremony were Lauren W. Goff, president of the Carl Sandburg Assn.; Martin Sandburg, the poet's nephew; Gunner Benson, president, Illinois Historical Assn., and William K. Alderfer, State Historian and director of the Illinois State Historical Society.

Governor Ogilvie was the principal speaker when an expository marker about Carl Sandburg was placed at the Birthplace on Aug. 5, 1972. Mr. Alderfer presented the marker to the community and other speakers were Mayor Robert Cabeen of Galesburg, John Keene of the State Historical Library, and Martin Sandburg.

The GALESBURG PUBLIC LIBRARY has a book stock of approx. 80,000 volumes and an annual circulation of nearly 215,000. It also has 9,664 bound periodicals, 840 reels of microfilm, and more than 1,000 recordings. In its special collections it has much on the early history of Illinois; also atlases, plat books, city, town, and county histories; and books about Abraham Lincoln. The Library serves two branches. The initial unit of the building was erected in 1961, and in 1967 it added a multi-tier stock area, a children's room, a film room, and a technical processing room. It is a member of the Western Illinois Library System.

The latest acquisition of the library is the Mother Bickerdyke Historical Collection. Mary Ann Bickerdyke left Galesburg for Cairo in 1861 to become a nurse of the Christian Commission. Her energy and resourcefulness soon made her indispensable. She provided dressings for the wounded, made soup for the soldiers, and traveled about on a mule accompanied by a Negro woman with supplies on another mule. Once she collected 200 cows and 1,000 hens and had them conveyed on flatboats to Memphis. General Grant gave her the use of President's Island for livestock. After the war she moved to Kansas and expedited pension claims for veterans. In 1968 Martin Litvin located descendants of Mrs. Bickerdyke and retrieved a big collection of documents for the Galesburg library. From this material Litvin edited *Sergeant Allen and Private Renick,* a memoir of the 11th Illinois Volunteer Cavalry and a three-year war diary, published by the Wagoner Printing Co. of Galesburg in 1971.

A statue of Mother Bickerdyke has been placed in Courthouse Park.

The only surviving dwelling of Log City, the pioneer settlement that preceded Galesburg, burned down on September 23, 1956. Known as the Lincolnshire Log Cabin, it had been built in 1832 by the Rev. Jacob Gunn, a veteran of the American Revolution. It was destroyed on the eve of its removal to a park.

In June, 1972, the city of Galesburg dedicated the Ray M. Brown Memorial Fountain in Standish Park, a gift of the Knox Fifty-year Club. The park was named for Prof. Myles Standish of the Knox faculty.

Galesburg Municipal Airport is located 1.5 *m*. west of the city. It is served by Ozark Airlines and MATS cargo airlines.

KNOXVILLE (2,930 pop. 1970; 2,560, 1960, inc. 14%) a city about 6 *m*. southeast of Galesburg on Illinois 97 was the county seat of Knox County until 1872, when the seat was moved to Galesburg. The historic courthouse of 1839 is carefully preserved and contains both offices and the Knox County Museum. The Historical Sites Commission and the Society of the Sons of the American Revolution (SAR) are active in furbishing notable relics, among which is the Old Jail, preserved as an exhibit. There are portraits of General Henry Knox and Stephen A. Douglas. Douglas was originally state's attorney and from June, 1841, to 1843, judge of the Circuit Court. His first decree, written in 1841 when 28, hangs on the wall of the museum. Autograph letters by General Henry Knox are owned by the museum, which has received memorabilia from Knox descendants. One of them, James Knox of Knoxville, was the first president of the Peoria & Oquawka Railroad.

The traditional Knox County Fair is held here usually in August with the customary carnival attractions—rides, sky wheel, exhibits of farm implements, and harness racing.

MONMOUTH, 87 *m.* (762 alt., 11,022 pop. 1970; 10,372, 1960, inc. 6.3%), is at a junction with US 67 (*see Tour 7*).

The highway enters Bogus Hollow, 104 *m.*, a wild ravine leading to the bottom lands of the Mississippi. The hollow is said to have been the rendezvous of a band of counterfeiters once notorious throughout this region. On the upland level that flanks the ravine are several Indian mounds of the Mississippi cultural group. Emerging from the ravine at the foot of the bluffs, the highway traverses a broad flood plain.

At 106 *m.* is a junction with Illinois 164. Right on 164 to GLADSTONE (344 pop. 1970; 356, 1960, dec. 3.4%) a village in Henderson County, platted in 1856, its houses clustered about a grain elevator. Early settlers were largely Irish, Swedish, and German immigrants. Limestone quarries along nearby Henderson Creek have yielded much of the stone used in the piers of bridges on the Upper Mississippi.

Left from Gladstone 2.5 *m.* on a graveled road just north of the railroad tracks is Lock and Dam No. 18, one of the 26 on the Upper Mississippi designed to assist in the control of floods on the lower river and to maintain a 9-foot channel between St. Louis and the Twin Cities.

Ahead on Illinois 164, roughly parallel to the highway bridges over Henderson Creek is a Covered Bridge, 3.4 *m.* The bridge is more than 100 years old, with massive oak beams held together with wooden pegs. The structure has been reconditioned by the State. Above the entrance is this warning: "Five dollars fine for leading or driving any beast faster than a walk, or driving more than thirty head of cattle, mules, or horses at a time on or across the bridge."

OQUAWKA, 62 *m.* (548 alt.) Henderson County seat, originated as a small trading post established in 1827 by Phelps brothers. Its name is derived from Ozaukee (Ind. yellow banks), by which the site was known to Indians who crossed the Mississippi at this point on northward hunting expeditions. Oquawka's principal industry is the manufacture of pearl button blanks from mussel shells. It is also the base of small scale lumbering operations.

The Henderson County Courthouse, one block north of Illinois 164 on 3rd Street, is a two-story tetrastyle structure of Classic Revival design. Overshadowing the portico is a open cupola, topped with a weathervane. The building was given to Henderson County by the Phelps brothers in 1842. First circuit court judge to preside here was Stephen A. Douglas, whose handwriting appears on the records (1841-43).

North of Oquawka along the Mississippi are several beaches and camp sites. Natural sand beaches afford good swimming; the adjoining woodlands support a variety of wild life.

East of Oquawka on Illinois 164, at the east end of the bridge across Henderson Creek, 8 m., a dirt road leads to RADMACHER MILL, 0.2 m., built in the 1830's. The mill, operated by the waterpower of Henderson Creek, grinds feed, flour, corn meal, and buckwheat. Its tightly fitted woodwork of bins, chutes, cleansers, and elevators is of California redwood; the huge mill stones are French burrs. The Covered Bridge opposite the mill was built in 1846, and is still in use.

GULFPORT, 114.5 m., (220 pop. 1970; 214, 1960) consists of cottages on the bottomland at the eastern approach to the Burlington Bridge. The village is all that remains of East Burlington, platted as a ferry port in 1855, but abandoned after completion of the bridge.

US 34 crosses the Iowa Line, 115 m., midway on the toll bridge spanning the Mississippi to Burlington, Iowa (see Iowa Guide).

Tour 14

CHICAGO TO ROCK ISLAND ON TWO PARALLEL HIGHWAYS

Indiana Line — Joliet — Channahon — Morris — Seneca — Ottawa —Starved Rock State Park—La Salle—Peru—Depue—Princeton— East Moline—Moline—Rock Island
US 6, 182 m. Interstate 80, 182 m.

Here is a direct east-west route across the upper half of the State from Indiana to Iowa, easy of access from Chicago, with the choice of two fine parallel highways. US 6 passes through all the major cities from Joliet to Rock Island, and Interstate 80 a parallel route, enables the motor car driver to bypass cities as needed and follow a speedway all the way.

Along most of the route runs the right-of-way of the Rock Island Railroad. After moving past the industrial area to Joliet the route follows the Illinois River to the town of Depue, where the river swings sharply south. The route then traverses prairie land given over to farming, with occasional industrial plants, and reaches the large industrial complex of Moline and Rock Island, which, with East Moline and Davenport, Iowa, constitutes the metropolitan area of more than 350,000 population known as the Quad Cities.

When this highway enters Illinois from Indiana, it is one of the major roads of the Midwest. It is a combination of the Tri-State Tollway, Int. 80, Int. 94, and US 6.

Conversely, several of these roads are leaving Illinois for Indiana. The Tri-State Tollway has come all the way from Wisconsin. Actually, it is also Int. 94 to the Cook County line, where the Tri-State Tollway becomes Int. 294 and Int. 94 becomes the Edens Expressway and the Dan Ryan Expressway. Chicago drivers wishing to take the highway west, start on Dan Ryan Expressway and join Int. 80 at the 171st street cloverleaf in South Holland.

In the meantime US 6 has left the combined highways at 171st St., moved north on the Calumet Expressway to 159th St., thence west to a junction with Wolf Road on 159th St., and then via Maple Road into Joliet.

Section a. Indiana Line to La Salle, 96 m.

US 6 crosses the Indiana Line, 0 *m.* from Hammond, Indiana. Contiguous with Hammond is CALUMET CITY, (32,956 pop. 1970; 25,000, 1960, inc. 31%), an incorporated city in Cook County.

The highway crosses the Little Calumet River into SOUTH HOLLAND, 4 *m.* (600 alt., 23,931 pop. 1970; 10,412, 1960, inc. 129%) a village in the heart of the truck farming region described by Edna Ferber in *So Big*. Three out of four of the mail boxes before the neat houses bear typical Dutch names, for the community settled in 1840 with a great influx of farmers from the Netherlands, has preserved its racial composition against the later influx of Poles and Italians to the industrial towns that adjoin South Holland. In recent years the village has had an influx of workers employed in adjacent industries.

The chief pursuit of the community for many years was the raising of onion sets from seed, stored until the following season, then planted by commercial growers to produce marketable vegetables of larger size and better quality than those raised directly from seed. On the rich black muck that was once lake bottom flat as a calm lagoon, seed is sown thickly in late March and April. Throughout the summer the young plants are carefully weeded then, in August, are harvested. During the winter they are stored in long low warehouses; early the following year they are sifted, cleansed, culled, and packed. The entire job, from planting to packing, is done by women of Italian and Polish descent from the nearby industrial centers. The South Hollanders do the marketing and buying, largely on a co-operative plan. At one time almost the entire onion set crop of America was produced in this vicinity. Other important centers have since entered the field. The seed, about 75,000 lbs. a year, is purchased from western states.

HARVEY, 6.1 *m* (608 alt., 34,636 pop. 1970; 29,071, 1960, inc. 19%) is at a junction with Illinois 1 (*see Tour 1*).

MARKHAM, 7.9 *m*. (593 alt., 15,987 pop. 1970; 11,704, 1960, inc. 36%) named after an official of the Illinois Central Railroad, was settled largely by German farmers who bought acreage here and in neighboring areas. Int. 57, splitting from the Dan Ryan Expressway near 96th St. crosses the Tri-State Tollway in Markham and has a junction with US 6; after crossing US 50 it joins a cloverleaf with Int. 294 and Int. 80; the latter will parallel US 6 across the State beyond Joliet. After Markham the road rises above the flat lake plain and winds over the rolling Valparaiso moraine, which extends almost to Joliet.

OAK FOREST, 10.5 *m*. (590 alt., 17,870 pop. 1970; 3,724, 1960, inc. 379%) is one of the fastest growing suburbs in the Chicago periphery. It is located 22 miles southwest of the Loop and has commuter service on the Rock Island Railway, South Suburban Safeway buses that connect with Chicago Transit and access to Int. 57 on 159th St. in Markham. The most important institution in town is the Oak Forest Hospital, a Cook County establishment devoted to rehabilitation, with 2,216 beds and up to 2,000 employees. It was founded in 1911 as an infirmary and tuberculosis hospital. Oak Forest has several busy shopping centers, including Oaks Plaza, Friendly Oaks Center, and Oak Creek Center. The Acorn Public Library District of Oak Forest circulates approx. 100,000 books a year. It is a member of the Suburban Library System, which has headquarters in the public libraries of Oak Park and Park Forest and uses the facilities of 57 libraries in this general area.

The ST. MIHIEL RESERVATION and YANKEE WOODS of the Forest Preserve are south of US 6 in Oak Forest, and the MIDLOTHIAN MEADOWS are northeast.

TINLEY PARK (12,382 pop. 1970; 6,392, 1960, inc. 93%) south of Oak Forest along US 6, has practically doubled its population in ten years. It owes its rise to the energetic exploitation of its fine site amid wooded areas, the building of many new detached dwellings, and the easy access to the Chicago Loop on Interstate and US highways and railroad. It extends from 159th St. to 185th St., from US 6 to Int. 80, with connections on Int. 57 and Int. 294, and Illinois 43, north-east, straight down the middle of the village. It was settled by Germans before the Civil War and was known as Bremen; this name is perpetuated in one of the new subdivisions, Bremen Towne. It was incorporated as a village in 1892. On the main line of the Rock Island, it has commutation to the Chicago Loop, 26 miles away, and South Suburban Safeway bus lines. Apartment buildings have been moving in and there is a new Tinley Park High School. The Tinley Park State Mental Health Center occupies large wooded acreage south of 183d St. At the intersection of Illinois 43 and Int. 80 is an airport for small planes and servicing.

At 17.7 *m*. beyond WESTHAVEN (470 pop.) is a junction with US 45 (north-south). North of US 6 is ORLAND PARK (6,391 pop. 1970; 2,592, 1960, inc. 146%) another prospering Cook County suburb, which has easy access to Tri-State Tollway, Stevenson Express-way, and Chicago Midway Airport. The Norfolk & Western offers commutation to Chicago. There is a recently built Carl Sandburg High School. With the Palos Hills nearby Orland Park sees itself as the Golf Center of the World.

North and northeast of Orland Park are the wooded hills of the Palos suburbs that are south of the Des Plaines River and west of the Tri-State Tollway.

Orland Park is at the southernmost point of the area of forested hills and ponds known as the Palos Hills. North of 143rd St. is McGinnis Slough. Proceeding north on US 45 into the hill country one comes to the Palos Division of the Forest Preserve District of Cook County, the largest and most diversified of the areas managed by the Commission. Its hills and valleys are the result of the invasion of the last glacier. The ponds and sloughs lie within potholes resulting from the melting of huge blocks of ice. Trees include oaks, sycamores, iron-woods, pawpaw; there are hawthornes and wild crabapples and many varieties of wild berries. Waterfowl and shore birds feed and rest in the sloughs. The Palos area lies southeast of the Des Plaines River and the old Illinois & Michigan Canal, and the Calumet Sag Channel runs through it.

PALOS PARK (3,297 pop. 1970; 2,160, 1960, inc. 52%) is the oldest of the communities, having been settled around 1900, incorporated in 1915. It is separated by the Calumet Sag Channel from PALOS HILLS (6,627 pop. 1970; 3,766, 1960, inc. 76%). Here is the MORAINE VALLEY COMMUNITY COLLEGE, which was opened in 1960 and reported an enrollment of 3,093 in the 1970-71 year, with a faculty of 160. It was incorporated in 1938 as a city. When some old foundation stones were uncovered they were attributed to a possible French fort, or a Father Jacques Marquette's winter quar-ters, but the latter have been located elsewhere.

Largest of the three Palos suburbs is PALOS HEIGHTS (9,915, 1970; 3,775, 1960, inc. 162%), located east of Palos Park on the Calumet Sag Channel. It was incorporated as a city in 1959 and is the site of Trinity College. The suburb has been strongly publicized for its advantages as a sylvan retreat.

At Orland Park US 6 has a junction with US 45 (north-south), which can be taken south 3.5 *m.* to a junction with Int. 80. US 6 pro-ceeds west 2 *m.* to a junction with Wolf Rd., which it follows to the Southwest Highway and thence west 13 *m.* to Joliet. *See article on Joliet.*

Int. 80, moving west in Will County, passes through NEW LENOX (2,855 pop. 1970; 1,750, 1960) to Joliet, 5 *m.* and along the southern edge of Joliet, through its suburb of ROCKDALE (2,085 pop. 1970; 1,272, 1960).

At the southern-limits of Joliet, on the west side of the river, the basin of the BRANDON ROAD DAM borders the road. The LOCKS, 35.7 *m.,* provide a 33-foot step for the traffic on the Lakes-to-

Gulf Waterway. Nearby is a lock of the old Illinois & Michigan Canal, its 100-ft. length and 20-ft. width in sharp contrast to the 600 x 110 ft. dimensions of the later installation. At this point, the canal channel has been absorbed by the Brandon Pool, which rises 15 ft. above parts of Joliet. Over the spillways of the 1,569-foot dam, connecting with the lock, glides a thick sheet of water. Facilities for utilization of the drop in developing hydroelectric power were installed by the State.

Before Channahon there comes a junction with US 66—Int. 55.

CHANNAHON, 44 m., (1,505 pop. 1970) is a village in Will County at the confluence of the Du Page and Des Plaines Rivers. Settled in 1832, Channahon shortly received impetus in its development from the Illinois & Michigan Canal. In its prosperous days there were six grain elevators within four miles of the town. Several steamboats with barges carried corn to Chicago depots, but most of the freight was carried in canal boats drawn by mules along the towpath. This port also shipped limestone from local quarries, which was used in many public buildings and churches of the time.

Left from Channahon, near its northern border, on a graveled road are the BRISCOE MOUNDS, 0.5 m., on the Briscoe farm. Two mounds— one 90 feet in diameter by 10 feet in height, the other half as large, both nearly round and sloping smoothly to the top—comprise this mound group, one of five in the Joliet area.

Bordering the highway bridge is one of the most attractive parts of the Illinois & Michigan Canal Parkways System, which extends the length of the canal, in a narrow belt. In Channahon Parkway State Park, 22 acres, are visible a system of spillways and wastegates, and two old canal locks. One lock drops water from the canal into the Du Page River, and the other drops it again into the canal channel on the other side of the river.

Left from the roadside park on the tree-arched towpath along the canal is McKINLEY WOODS, 3 m., a Will County Forest Preserve (*picnic facilities, shelters*).

Immediately across the river from the woods is the site of the FISHER MOUNDS. Comprising two large mounds, 60 ft. and 50 ft. in diameter, and 6 smaller ones, they were thoroughly excavated by a University of Chicago field party in 1929 and gave a rich yield. The Fisher Mounds revealed three successive civilizations and cultures, the last giving evidence of contact with white men. Several hundred fully articulated skeletons were discovered. These and the pottery, tools, and other artifacts are housed in the Museum of the Anthropology Department, University of Chicago.

Ahead on the towpath is a parking area, 4 m., commanding a view of the confluence of the Des Plaines and Kankakee Rivers, which here form the Illinois DRESDEN HEIGHTS LOCK AND DAM, 5.7 m., on the towpath, is the next below the Brandon Lock on the Illinois deep waterway system. The towpath ends at the lock, but connects, on the same side of the canal, with a graveled road leading to the AUX SABLE CREEK AQUEDUCT AND LOCK of the Illinois & Michigan Canal, 8.7 m. An iron aqueduct carries the canal across the creek, and a few yards beyond, Lock No. 8 drops the canal to a lower channel. The road crosses the canal, 8.8 *m.,* turns R., and leads back to the highway, 10.5 *m.,* 5.4 miles west of the park.

South of the Illinois River is the DRESDEN NUCLEAR POWER STATION of the Commonwealth Edison Co., one of the largest elements in the production of electrical energy for the industries of this part of Illinois. The station is a group of white rectangular buildings and one domed structure, with tapering stacks giving the whole the appearance of a mosque. Commonwealth Edison led the commercial development of boiling water reactors with Dresden I, which went into operation in 1960 with one generating unit of 200,000 kilowatts. Unit 2 began operation in 1970 and Unit 3 in 1971. The last two units have each an ultimate capacity of 809,000 kilowatts.

West of Channahon, US 6 roughly parallels the Illinois River for 60 miles. In the early days of the Illinois country the river was of tremendous importance, an avenue of exploration and later, of commerce. In 1673 Jolliet described the valley as "most beautiful and most easy to be settled. This river is wide and deep," he wrote; "it is stocked with brills and sturgeons. Game is there in abundance. There are prairies three, six, ten, and twenty leagues in length and three in width. . . . A settler would not be required to spend ten years cutting down and burning timber." Although the valley of the Illinois was not settled under the flag of France as he had hoped, its rapid development following the completion of the Illinois & Michigan Canal amply supported Jolliet's judgment.

MORRIS, 55 *m.* (504 alt., 8,144 pop. 1970; 7,953, 1960), on the north bank of the Illinois River, was platted in 1842 and named for Issac N. Morris, one of the Illinois and Michigan commissioners, who was instrumental in having the village selected as the seat of Grundy County. Completion of the canal (1848) hastened the development of the community. Its favorable location on the railroad and waterways has made Morris an important shipping point for the surrounding region and an important paper manufacturing center. Morris is 1 *m.* south of Int. 80.

Excavations in the business district have unearthed archeological material, indicating that the site was long occupied by Indian tribes. La Salle records a large Indian village in the vicinity. A fine collection of fossils gathered in the Mazon River fossil beds and some 5,000 Indian relics are exhibited in the Courthouse.

On the western edge of Morris is GEBHARD WOODS STATE PARK, on the north bank of the Illinois & Michigan Canal. The 29-acre woodland was donated by Fred Gebhard in 1932. The park adjoins the ILLINOIS & MICHIGAN CANAL STATE PARKWAY, a 100-mile strip of land along the waterway acquired by the State Division of Parks in 1935. The old towpaths are pleasure drives. South of the Illinois River is the W. G. STRATTON STATE PARK, 6.5 acres, named for a Governor of Illinois.

East from Morris, on a road along the canal, is Evergreen Cemetery, 1.5 *m.,* where a rough boulder marks the grave of SHABBONA (1775-1850), Chief of the Potawatomi, who, with his tribe, remained friendly to the settlers during the Black Hawk War.

SENECA, 67 *m.* (521 alt., 1,781 pop. 1970; 1,719, 1960) is a village in LaSalle County located on the base of 100-ft. bluffs. The chief industry is an explosives plant of E. I. DuPont de Nemours & Co.

Seneca was a quiet river town of 1,235 people until May, 1942, when a wartime industrial boom suddenly flooded it with laborers. The Chicago Bridge & Iron Co. obtained a Federal contract to build landing ship tanks (LST) in large quantity and decided to concentrate the work in Seneca. The village had remained rural and unprogressive. One policeman and one night watchman had sufficed to keep the streets safe; volunteer firemen operated a single booster pump; there was no movie theater to mislead the young, and sanitary conditions were primitive. In two years 6,000 people were living in Seneca and 10,000 were employed on war work, many driving in from nearby villages. School attendance rose to more than 1,000. When the war ended the boom subsided.

A study of Seneca called *The Social History of a War-Boom Community* has been made by Robert J. Havighurst and H. Gershon Morgan of the University of Chicago, which relates that during the war boom the initiative in government passed from the village council and the county supervisors to a series of Federal agencies with subsequent friction, which became most acute in the housing administration. The authors conclude that "Seneca did the war job well enough to deserve its Army-Navy award for excellence. The village played a passive, willing role, but it emerged from the boom relatively unchanged, with the familiar basic characteristics of a midwestern rural town."

The General Electric Co. chose the Seneca environs for a nuclear power plant. The first unit of the LaSalle County Nuclear Station, a boiling water reactor, was scheduled for 1975. A second unit was to be operative in 1976. The Commonwealth Edison Co. was designated operator.

MARSEILLES, 73.5 *m.* (506 alt., 4,320 pop. 1970; 4,347, 1960) an industrial city in LaSalle County lies athwart a stretch of rapids in the Illinois River. It made use of water power even in days when coal was cheap. Today a paperbox factory of the National Biscuit Co. is the principal industry.

Left from Marseilles on Main Street, across the Illinois River, is the 406-acre ILLINI STATE PARK (*picnic facilities, shelters*). The large island in the park, two and a half miles in length, was formed when a channel was cut for the deep waterway. Between Marseilles and the island is the MARSEILLES DAM, part of the system used for passing the Marseilles rapids. The MARSEILLES DOCK, at the west end of the island, drops traffic into the river below the rapids.

OTTAWA, 81 *m.* (489 alt., 18,716 pop. 1970; 19,408, 1960) is an industrial and distribution center, county seat of LaSalle County, at the confluence of the Fox and Illinois Rivers. It is served by US 6 and

Int. 80, and north-south Ill. 23, which has junction with US 66 at Pontiac. The Rock Island Lines and the Burlington-Northern Railroad give freight service. The Airport accommodates up to 400 flights a month.

LaSalle County population rose from 110,800 in 1960 to 111,409 in 1970. The county labor force is approx. 68,000 of which 52,000 are non-agricultural. A region rich in silica, it has a major plant of the Libbey-Owens-Ford Co., which in 1969 put into effect the float process of glassmaking for the first time in Illinois, in a new $19,000,000 plant. It employs 1,500 to 2,000. Other plants include the Henderson Division of Borg-Warner (automobile clutches); its Marbon Division (plastics); Ottawa Silica Co., Wedron Silica Co., and makers of tools, packaging and fabricated steels.

The first settler came in 1825. Ottawa, an Indian word meaning trade, became the county seat in 1831 and was incorporated in 1853. It has a mayor and commission form of government. William D. Boyce, a publisher, organized the Boy Scouts of America in 1911 and is remembered in the Boyce Memorial Trail. Ottawa has 28 churches and a number of public parks and swimming pools and supports the Indian Valley Symphony Society. The LaSalle County Courthouse, of Renaissance-Romanesque design, was erected in 1881. Washington Park, in midtown, is bounded by churches, the Rose Society, Reddick's Library, and the Appellate Court. In the park is a huge boulder marking the site of the first LINCOLN-DOUGLAS DEBATE, held August 21, 1858, before a large crowd that came by wagon, rail, and canal.

The Lincoln-Douglas Debates were high spots in the senatorial campaign of 1856, in which Lincoln ran for senator against the incumbent, Stephen A. Douglas. As chairman of the Committee on Territories of the Senate Douglas had sponsored the Kansas-Nebraska bill, which was to repeal the Missouri Compromise that stopped slavery north of the southern boundary of Missouri by letting new states decide by popular vote on whether or not to allow slavery. The anti-slavery people believed this would extend slavery. Abolitionists and Democrats joined the Republicans to get a majority in the Illinois legislature, in which Lincoln sat as a representative. Lincoln resigned in order to run for senator against Douglas, who was up for reelection.

Lincoln had opposed the Kansas-Nebraska bill in 1854. He recognized that the Constitution kept the North from interfering with slavery in the South and believed that if confined to the South slavery would gradually become extinct. Douglas believed the people in each state should vote on whether or not they wanted slavery (popular sovereignty). He was also against slavery but supported democratic methods and did not wish to endanger the Union. The Dred Scott decision of the U. S. Supreme Court in 1857 declared a slave did not become free by living in a free state. When Lincoln was nominated for senator by the Bloomington Republican convention he asserted in his House Divided speech that the nation could not survive half free and half slave.

Lincoln invited Douglas to share time with him. In the Bryant Cottage in Bement on Illinois 105, now an Illinois State Memorial, the men agreed to appear together in seven congressional districts from Aug. 21 to Oct. 15, 1858. They spoke at Ottawa, Freeport, Jonesboro, Charleston, Galesburg, Quincy, and Alton. In the voting, which instructed the legislature, Lincoln was defeated.

The Lincoln Sun Dial, on the lawn of the Ottawa Boat Club, at the bridge, designates the spot where Lincoln was mustered out of service at the close of his enlistment for the Black Hawk War.

REDDICK'S LIBRARY, facing Washington Park, was established in the mansion of William Reddick in 1885. It is fully modernized and stocks more than 60,000 books and circulates more than 122,000 annually. It is a member of the Starved Rock Library System, which has had its hq here since it was formed on July 1, 1967. The System includes 26 local public libraries in LaSalle and Putnam Counties and parts of Bureau, DeKalb, Marshall, and Lee Counties. The System makes possible the borrowing of books by member libraries from one another, as well as 16mm films, art prints, tape cassettes, photocopies and other materials.

The major part of Ottawa covers the terraces formed by the Illinois River. To the north rise the river bluffs, on which stand many imposing old homes. Overlooking the valley is the Caton House, a red brick structure with bays and dormered windows, built by John Dean Caton, former chief justice of the Illinois Supreme Court. Mrs. Arthur Caton, the judge's daughter-in-law, who later married Marshall Field, acquired the house and it became a summer social center. From the Fields, the house passed into the hands of Mrs. Albert J. Beveridge.

Nearby is The Oaks completed in 1860 for the Civil War General W. H. L. Wallace, who was killed at the Battle of Shiloh. The greystone house, with an overhanging gabled roof, and a Gothic window above the entrance, contains many original furnishings and relics, including a Boston piano, and a 33-star blood-stained flag from Shiloh. In a small plot in the grove of white oaks is the Grave of General Wallace.

Railroad buffs go to Ottawa to see the exhibit of steam locomotive Old 4978, with tender and caboose, south of the Ottawa Silico Bldg., on Boyce Memorial Drive. Nearby are huge sandpits associated with the silica industry.

Left from Ottawa on Illinois 71 to the East Entrance to STARVED ROCK STATE PARK (*hiking, boating, swimming, and fishing; picnicking, camping, lodge facilities*) 7 m. This oldest of Illinois State parks, a narrow strip for more than 4 miles between Ottawa and La Salle, contains in its more than 900 acre wildlands as varied as any in Illinois. Its principal natural and historical feature, Starved Rock, towers 140 feet above the river, commanding a scene of extraordinary beauty, the locale of French and Indian associations.

Within the park, which was opened in 1912, are almost 50 points of interest —canyons, caves, bluffs, and rocks—fancifully or historically named, all well marked and connected by 18 miles of trails. The two main trails parallel the river, one along the banks, the other on the bluffs. The many canyons are narrow gorges, carved deeply in the sandstone of the bluffs, of varying lengths, cool and shady, and overgrown with ferns, vines, and flowering plants. In wet seasons in some of the canyons water pours in tiny cascades over the rocky floors. Caves are shallow, high vaults carved in the base of the bluffs.

Within the eastern section of the park are a Sulphur Well and a Salt Well, two of the numerous mineral springs along the river in La Salle County. Here also are Skeleton Cave; Illinois, Kaskaskia, Ottawa, and Hennepin Canyons; Council Cave and Cave of the Winds; and Dimmick Hill. In the central section natural features include Hidden, Owl, La Salle, Horseshoe, Tonti, Lone Tree, and Wildcat Canyons, and the odd formations, Pulpit Rock and Witch's Kitchen. Rustic signs point the way to these several features.

The South Entrance, 11 *m.*, leads to the western third of the park. At the entrance is the Camp Ground. A lodge and a dozen cabins have been built of logs by the CCC. In this western section the bluffs recede from the river; on the broad terrace are the main parking area and the refreshment and food concessions. Here also are a Swimming Pool and a Pier from which park boats make an hour-and-a-half excursion on the river.

Starved Rock dominates the natural features of this section of the park, but associated with it are many lesser formations. Lovers Leap is a popular promontory overlooking the river; at its base is Starved Rock Lock and Dam and Lake Starved Rock. Nearby is Lost Lake and such fantastically eroded forms as Jacobs Ladder, the Devils Bathtub, and the Devils Nose.

Starved Rock rises from dense woodland that covers and obscures the Rock from the park side. Artificial and natural steps lead to the summit, which affords a commanding view of the river and of Buffalo Rock State Park (*see below*) across the Illinois. It was in September 1673 that Jolliet and Marquette, returning from their exploration of the Mississippi River, stopped at an encampment of Kaskaskia Indians across the river from Starved Rock. Marquette recorded in his journal that the village consisted of 74 cabins. Two years later, fulfilling his promise to the Indians, Marquette returned to establish a mission at the village.

After giving preliminary instructions to the chief and old men at the village, he called together a great council, which was held three days before Easter. Mats and bearskins covered the council ground, and four large pictures of the Virgin Mary were hung by pieces of taffeta from lines that had been stretched overhead. The father stood in the center and seated in a circle about him were the 500 chiefs and elders; in the background stood the young men, who numbered about 1,000 in all, and the women and children. Marquette gave the Indians ten presents, symbolic of the ten religious messages that he delivered, and concluded by saying mass. A second council was held two days later, after which the father made preparations for his return. The journey out to the village had been an exceedingly strenuous one, and Marquette's health was seriously impaired. Certain that he could not live much longer, he hastened on the return trip to Mackinac in order that he might die within its walls, but death overtook him on the way.

In 1679 La Salle and Tonti visited the same village, and were impressed with the strategic value of the Rock. Three years later they undertook the erection of a fort, Fort St. Louis du Rocher, on its summit. The fort was maintained by Tonti after La Salle's death in 1687, but was finally abandoned in 1702. French fur traders occupied the structure intermittently until 1721, when it was burned by the Indians. Today no relic of the fort remains. Only the strength of the Rock suggests the power that Louis XIV let slip through his hands when he turned a deaf ear to the plans of La Salle to colonize the Mississippi Valley.

On the summit of the Rock a Memorial Tablet records the legendary incident from which Starved Rock derives its name. During the early French Occupation of the region, Indians of Illinois Valley settled in large numbers along the river banks under the protection of the fort. Allied with their protectors, they fought against the other Indian tribes. After the French withdrew from the region the tribal wars became more bitter, culminating in the annihilation of a band of Illinois Indians (1769) on the summit of Starved Rock. Pontiac, Chief of the Ottawa, fleeing from the British, who had broken his tribe, was murdered at Cahokia by one of Illini among whom he had taken refuge. The remnants of the Ottawa, allied with the Potawatomi, thereupon waged war fiercely upon the Illinois, finally forcing one of the remnants of the tribe to seek shelter on the summit of the Rock. Here they were safe from attack, but not from hunger and thirst. Baskets lowered to the river to draw up water were seized by their enemies. In a desperate attempt to escape all but a few were slain. These lived to tell the tale that has given Starved Rock its name.

The episode is purely legendary, but it harmonizes so perfectly with the geography of the region that it has become part of the folklore of Illinois.

At 11.6 *m.* on Illinois 71 is a junction with Illinois 178.

Left on Illinois 178 is DEER PARK (*open May-Oct.; adm. 25¢; closed 1 hr. before sundown*), 1 *m.*, a 240-acre heavily wooded estate, with a deep gorge carved in the sandstone by a tributary of the Vermilion River. The canyon is one and a half miles in length. Under an arched bridge a waterfall drops 55 feet to a lower dell. Seepage of mineral waters has in places streaked the grotesquely carved walls with bright color. Tradition has it that the Indians used the park's canyons as enclosures for deer, which furnished the winter's meat supply. A herd of deer and a reproduction of a pioneer stockade and blockhouse attract visitors.

From the junction of Illinois 71 and Illinois 178 the route is continued north on Illinois 178 past the west entrance to Starved Rock State Park, 12.6 *m.* to the site of OLD UTICA, 13.2 *m.*, on the north bank of the Illinois River. Old Utica, failing to gain the terminus of the Illinois & Michigan Canal moved bag and baggage to its present site when the canal was opened (1848) a mile to the north.

NORTH UTICA, 14.2 *m.*, (974 pop. 1970; 1,014, 1960) serves Starved Rock visitors with postoffice and tourist accommodations, and operates a cement mill and associated industries.

Memorabilia of the Illinois & Michigan Canal are among the items in the collections of the La Salle County Historical Society in Utica. Exhibits include pioneer furnishings, Indian artifacts, Lincolniana, Victorian toys, and Zouave (Civil War) equipment.

At 15.5 *m.* is the end of Illinois 178 at a junction with US 6.

West of Ottawa US 6 leaves the valley to cross rolling farm lands. At 84.9 *m.* is a junction with a graveled road.

Left on this road is BUFFALO ROCK STATE PARK, 2.3 *m.*, which takes its name from a huge, tree-topped rock rising 100 feet from the north bank of the Illinois River. Erosion detached the rock from the valley bluffs, forming a channel which is now used as a passage for the Illinois and Michigan Canal and the Rock Island Lines. The rock served the French as an early military, trading, and missionary post, and later became a principal stronghold of the Illinois Indians in their losing fight against the encroachment of the northern tribes into the Illinois Valley. These, in turn, pressed by the white men, stayed on briefly. Today, picnic benches and shelters occupy the site of trading posts and forts, and shod feet tread the trails worn by mocassins and buffalo hoofs.

At 90.2 *m.* is a junction with Illinois 178, the western entrance to Starved Rock State Park.

LA SALLE, 96 *m.* (448 alt., 10,736 pop. 1970) is at junction with US 51 (*see Tour 4*).

Section b. La Salle to Iowa Line, 86 m.

Contiguous with La Salle, 0 *m.*, is PERU, 2 *m.* (459 alt., 11,772 pop. 1970), at a junction with US 51 (*see Tour 4*).

ST. BEDE COLLEGE AND ACADEMY, 3.9 *m.*, founded in

1889 by the Benedictine fathers, is the preparatory seminary of the Peoria Catholic diocese. The long red-brick, four-story building, half a mile from the highway, is surrounded by spacious grounds. A Natural History Museum on an upper floor contains a large collection of local and foreign specimens and Indian relics.

The highway passes through the northern fringe of SPRING VALLEY, 5.6 *m.* (465 alt., 5,605 pop. 1970; 5,371, 1960) in Bureau County, once the scene of extensive mining operations and a population of 7,916 (1913), now has manufacturing, including a plant of the Stewart-Warner Corp. The last mine closed in 1946.

At 7 *m.* is a junction with Illinois 89.

Right on Illinois 89, 7.1 *m.,* is CHERRY, (682 alt., 551 pop. 1970; 501, 1960) scene of the State's worst industrial disaster, a mine fire of November, 1909, in which gas and smoke took the lives of 259 men; only 21 were rescued after being entombed for eight days. In the cemetery at the south edge of the village stands a memorial to the victims of the Cherry Mine disaster; on November 13 of each year, services are held in their memory. The site of the mine, at the north end of Cherry, is marked by a huge pyramid, a pink and gray mine dump.

The mine disaster was commemorated and explained by the Illinois State Historical Society on a plywood marker placed at Princeton in the spring, 1971. It reads:

"Just north of town are remnants of the Cherry Coal Mine, where 259 men lost their lives in one of the worst mine disasters in United States history. The St. Paul Coal Co. began mining coal at Cherry in 1905 and by 1909 was mining 300,000 tons annually. The owner and sole customer was the Chicago, Milwaukee, and St. Paul Railroad. On Saturday, November 13, 1909, the mine caught fire. A load of hay intended for the mule stables at the bottom of the mine was apparently ignited by burning oil dripping from a kerosene torch. The fire spread rapidly. Several miners reached safety; others were trapped in the mine. Twentyone of the trapped men were later rescued. The remainder died in the mine. The dead included twelve rescuers. Public response to the need of the victims was great. Individuals and organizations from various communities donated time and money. Chicago and other towns sent fire-fighting men and equipment. More than $400,000 in relief funds was raised and the Cherry Relief Commission was organized to distribute the funds. Another $400,000 was added as a result of the settlement made with the railroad company."

At 10.7 *m.* is a junction with Illinois 29.

Left on this road is DEPUE, 1.5 *m.* (473 alt., 1,919 pop. 1970; 1,920, 1960), which functioned as a river port until the decline of the steamboat. In recent years industry has revived with the New Jersey Zinc Co.

LAKE DEPUE, a three-mile inlet of the river, served as a harbor in early river traffic days. The lake is the scene of the annual Labor Day water sports carnival of the Midwest Outboard Association. William Cullen Bryant, who visited his brother, John Howard, at nearby Princeton, is said to have received the inspiration of his poem "To a Water Fowl" from Lake Depue. An unusual change in the habits of wild life has taken place along the Illinois River. The advent of the mechanical corn picker has caused thousands of wild ducks of several varieties to winter in the valley. The corn picker leaves many kernels of grain on the fields, thus furnishing a winter food supply for the ducks.

At Depue the Illinois begins the Great Bend to the southwest and US 6 and Int. 80, continuing westward, no longer follow the river. Instead their route roughly parallels the Illinois & Mississippi Canal, which is laid out in an abandoned valley of the Illinois. The glaciers blocked this ancient course with deep drift and forced the river to carve the Great Bend and swing far southward before joining the Mississippi. The Canal, opened in 1907, was built at a cost of $7,000,000 and was expected to connect Rock Island, Moline, and Davenport, Iowa, with the towns along the Illinois & Michigan Canal to Chicago. But the Rock Island Railroad, following the same course, accomplished the same purpose more successfully, and the canal was scarcely opened before it fell into disuse. Today it finds greater use as a fishing stream than as a commercial waterway.

The route is across the western upland of the State, a region of glacial drift, partly wooded, partly prairie—a gently rolling countryside of villages and small towns, of corn and hogs, of sober industry and quiet beauty.

PRINCETON, 22 m. (719 alt., 6,958 pop. 1970; 6,250, 1960, inc. 11%) is the seat of Bureau County and a center of nursery, orchard, and farming activities. Laid out in 1833 by colonists from Northampton, Mass., Princeton's streets are arched by the great elms planted by its founders. Strongly abolitionist before the Civil War, it was the home of Owen Lovejoy, (1811-1864) abolitionist preacher and brother of Elijah P. Lovejoy, the abolitionist editor who was killed by a pro-slavery mob at Alton in 1837. At the east edge of town is the 14-room white frame Owen Lovejoy Homestead. Red brick chimneys rise from the gabled roof of the newly painted house, and contrast with the bright green shutters. It is now owned by Ed Finn and James English, Princeton business men.

A plaque was placed in front of the Lovejoy house by the Illinois State Historical Society. It became the home of Lovejoy in 1838, when he came to Princeton as pastor of the Hampshire Colony Church, the oldest Congregational church in Illinois, organized 1831. He was a Republican, member of the General Assembly, 1855-1857, and Representative in Congress for four terms 1857-1864. The Princeton house was a shelter for runaway slaves.

Owen Lovejoy was an uncompromising fighter for the abolition of slavery and one of the extremists in the young Republican Party who forced the party to adopt a stronger anti-slavery position. He represented the Third Congressional District in the House of Representatives and his stand was clearly stated when he said: "I hate slavery with a deathless and earnest hatred and would like to see it exterminated, as some time by some means it must be. But because I thus feel toward slavery, it does not follow that I shall seek its extermination in unjustifiable modes."

When Lovejoy campaigned for a second term in Congress in 1858, he and Lincoln were often associated. During the Lincoln-Douglas debates Lovejoy sometimes sat on the platform behind Lincoln, and he was always ready to make a stump speech against Douglas. This association made some Lincoln managers apprehensive; they thought they might lose some votes in southwestern Illinois, where people hated abolitionists. But Lovejoy was so strong in Princeton and adjoining counties that they needed him to the extent that they even suppressed attempts to divert votes from Lovejoy by naming competing candidates. Lovejoy announced when he was nominated: "I am for Lincoln, not because he is an old Whig, but because he is a true-hearted man and that, come what will, unterrified by power, unseduced by ambition, he will remain true to the great principles upon which the Republican Party is organized." Douglas insinuated that Lincoln had embraced the extremist views of "Parson" Lovejoy, but this Lincoln denied. Lovejoy won election in 1858; Lincoln lost the senatorial nomination to Douglas.

The Stephen G. Paddock house was host to Abraham Lincoln on July 4, 1856.

The Matson Public Library was built in 1913 and modernized in 1971. It circulates between 50,000 and 60,000 volumes and is a member of the Starved Rock Library System.

The Bureau County Historical Society is an active organization that maintains the Grace Clark Norris Museum, which has three floors of exhibits of artifacts and pioneer household objects.

The Cyrus Bryant House, 1110 S. Main St., was built of brick in 1844. Its wide black walnut wainscoting and other original features are little changed. In the front yard, a boulder marks the site of the log cabin that Cyrus and his brother John built when they preempted the land. The John Howard Bryant House, 1518 S. Main St., of the same period, is a brick structure, with a porch made of boulders. The Bryants were brothers of William Cullen Bryant. John was a poet in his own right, a representative in the State legislature, a founder of the Republican Party, and a friend of Abraham Lincoln. The Bryants arrived in 1832 and later were joined by their other brothers Austin and Arthur.

The Stevens House in Princeton was built by Justus Stevens, Princeton's first mayor, in 1849.

The Red Covered Bridge of Bureau County is located 3½ miles

north of Princeton. It is 50 ft. long, was built in 1863, and cost $3,148.57.

At Princeton is a junction with US 34 (*see Tour 13*), with which US 6 is united for 16 miles.

WYANET, 28.5 *m.*, (656 alt., 1,005 pop. 1970; 938, 1960) in Bureau County, is on the Illinois & Mississippi Canal. At the western edge of the village are the Wyant Fish Hatchery and Lock No. 21.

The highway crosses the Illinois & Mississippi Canal 30.5 *m.* The level terrain in this area facilitated the construction of the canal; little cutting or grading was necessary. Of this unbroken prairie a Scottish traveler wrote in 1835, "I recommend (it) to British sportsmen, as a country likely to afford them amusement and instruction. A person may cross the Atlantic with a brace of dogs in one of the best vessels, and travel to the prairies, and devote a year to the excursion, living in the best style the country affords, for the sum of £200 sterling. If he were economical in crossing the ocean and living with settlers, and serving himself while in Illinois, the expense would be under £120."

ANNAWAN, 47 *m.*, (626 alt., 787 pop. 1970; 701, 1960) a town in Henry County, center of a stock-farming and coal-mining region, is at a junction with Illinois 78.

Between Annawan and ATKINSON, 52.8 *m.* (1,053 pop. 1970; 944, 1960) a town in Henry County, the area has been worked over for strip mining. Much of the wasteland has been replanted by the State. The region was settled by Belgian immigration.

GENESEO, 60.8 *m.* (639 alt., 5,840 pop. 1970; 5,169, 1960) a city in Henry County, was settled in 1830 by people from Bergen and Geneseo, N. Y. The city distributes farm products and livestock. The highway uses the original business street. When the railroad arrived the commercial section was moved three blocks north. Right from Geneseo is the Geneseo State Fish Hatchery and a lock of the unused Illinois & Mississippi Canal.

The Division of Tourism of the Illinois Dept. of Business & Economic Development lists several attractions of agricultural interest near Geneseo. One is the Horseshoe Farm Museum and Ropp's Draft Horse Farm, where Belgian draft horses and Morgans are bred. This is the home of the longest draft horse hitch in the Midwest, driven in tandem teams with lines on all the horses. The museum has farm apparatus and furniture from the earliest settlements. *Open April 15-Nov. 1.*

Four miles east of Geneseo on US 6 is the Johnson 1910 Living Farm, with farmhouse 130 years old, farm machinery, picnic areas and hiking trails. *Open May 1-Nov. 1.*

West of Geneseo 9 *m.* Int. 80 turns north, bypassing the Quad Cities, crossing the Green and the Rock Rivers, and the Mississippi at Rapids City to proceed into Iowa. The multilane highway proceeds west to Moline, Rock Island, and Davenport (Iowa).

Also 9 *m.* west of Geneseo Int. 80 has a junction with Int. 74, an expressway that runs diagonally across the middle of the State. It proceeds south to Galesburg, then turns southeast to Peoria, crossing the Illinois River, thence to Bloomington, where it has a junction with Int. 55 from Chicago; thence to Champaign, and a junction with Int. 57 from Chicago, (route partially incomplete) and east to Danville and Indiana. The route bypasses all the cities except Peoria but has access highways.

ANDOVER, a farm village 10 m. south of Int. 80, increased 42% in population over 1960, although it went up only from 295 to 420. It was settled in 1835 by Dr. Thomas Baker with Swedish immigrants. Twelve years later it had a Swedish Lutheran Church and a Swedish Methodist Church.

On US 150, 6 m. south of US 6 in Henry County, is ORION (1,801 pop. 1970; 1,269, 1960, inc. 41%) a farm village on the Burlington. A historical marker commemorating the Illinois Military Tract was dedicated Aug. 20, 1972, in a rest area on the east side of US 150, 3 m. south of Orion. The marker was placed by the Illinois State Historical Society and the State Dept. of Transportation, and the principal speaker was Herman Muelder, professor of history at Knox College. The Military Tract of more than 5,000,000 acres was set aside for land bounties of 160 acres each to veterans of the War of 1812, and was located in an angle formed by the Illinois and Mississippi Rivers.

US 6 has a junction 11 m. west of Geneseo with Int. 80, which turns north to cross into Iowa at Rapids City. A few miles west of Int. 80 are GREEN ROCK (2,744 pop. 1970; 2,677, 1960) and COLONA (1,293 pop. 1970; 491, 1960). Int. 80 crosses the Rock River and 2 m. beyond has a jct. with Illinois 2, which moves west into CARBON CLIFF (1,369 pop. 1970; 1,268, 1960) and SILVIS (5,907 pop. 1970); 3,973, 1960, inc. 48%) and follows the John Deere Road in East Moline and Moline and the Black Hawk Road in Rock Island.

EAST MOLINE, 78.3 m. (576 alt., 20,832 pop. 1970; 16,732, 1960, inc. 24.5%) is an extension of Moline and was incorporated as a city in 1907. It has easy access to all the highways that serve the Quad Cities and adds to the industrial production and consumer needs of this metropolitan area. Before factories expanded from Moline into the pastures outside its limits, Moline, Rock Island and Davenport (Iowa) were known as the Tri-cities then East Moline grew and the group became the Quad Cities. In recent decades the industrial city of Bettendorf developed east of Davenport. It is included in the statistics of the metropolitan area, but the Quad City title remains unchanged. The Census of 1970 counted 22,128 in Bettendorf, nearly double the 11,534 population of 1960, and exceeding that of East Moline by 1,296.

East Moline State Hospital, overlooking the Mississippi River and Illinois 84, provides psychiatric care for alcoholics, the mentally ill, and mentally disturbed adults.

West of the hospital grounds, separated from the bank by a narrow channel is CAMPBELL'S ISLAND STATE PARK, site of an attack by Sauk Indians on keelboats carrying U.S. Army soldiers during the War of 1812. *See Tour 6.*

MOLINE, 82 *m.* (46,237 pop. 1970), and ROCK ISLAND, 85 *m.* (50,166 pop. 1970) *see article on Rock Island and Moline.*

∞∞∞∞∞∞∞∞∞∞∞∞∞∞∞∞∞∞∞∞∞∞∞∞∞∞∞∞∞∞∞∞∞∞

Tour 15

INDIANA TO JOLIET; JOLIET TO THE NORTHWEST COUNTIES OF ILLINOIS

(Kentland, Ind.) — Kankakee — Joliet — Mendota — Dixon — Polo — Lanark—Mount Carroll—Savanna—(Dubuque, Iowa) US 52.
Indiana to Iowa 218 *m.*

This route serves two purposes. As it crosses the Indiana line and proceeds to Joliet it reaches a number of villages in eastern Illinois not touched by other westbound routes. Then, from Joliet, it provides a direct westbound highway into some of the richest farmlands of northern Illinois. Anyone heading only for the northwest corner of Illinois from Chicago would take US 30 or Illinois 38 for Dixon and then change to US 52.

Section a. Indiana to Joliet

US 52 crosses the Indiana Line, 0 *m.,* 4.5 miles W. of Kentland, Indiana (*see Indiana Guide*). West of the Indiana Line US 52 and US 24 (*see Tour 18*) are united to SHELDON, 2.3 *m.* (685 alt., 1,455 pop. 1970; 1,137, 1960), which has grown from a switch established in 1860 by the Toledo, Peoria & Western Railroad and which was named for one of its directors. Latter came the Big Four Railroad now part of Penn-Central, and the town became an important shipping point for grain. It is in the area of soybean production. A 1,200,000-bushel terminal grain elevator and a small local one rise from the railside.

IROQUOIS, 6.5 *m.* (649 alt., 226 pop. 1970), on the north bank of the Iroquois river, is the successor to the pioneer towns of Concord and Montgomery, on the south bank, site of a Gurdon Hubbard trading post and first seat of Iroquois County; the two were long known as Bunkum. In 1871 the Big Four Railroad called its station Iroquois, and four years later Concord, which had survived Montgomery, incorporated under that name.

DONOVAN, 11 *m.* (343 pop. 1970), was settled by Swedish immigrants after the coming of the railroad. The settlement bears the name of the keeper of the Buckhorn Tavern, an inn that stood on the nearby Hubbard Trail.

At 17.8 *m*. is a junction with Illinois 1 (*see Tour 1*).

At 23.6 *m*. is a junction with a graveled road. Right on this road is L'ERABLE, 1 *m.,* a tiny hamlet settled by French-Canadians and named for the maples that were once numerous on the site. The tall white spire of the church dominates the community, which before the advent of the automobile was a thriving farm center. Descendants of the original settlers remain, and French is still spoken.

KANKAKEE, 42 *m*. (30,944 pop. 1970), is at a junction with US 45, US 54 and Int. 57.

BOURBONNAIS and BRADLEY are part of the Kankakee metropolitan area through which US 52 passes north. Bourbonnais has 5,909 pop., (1970) and Bradley has 9,881 pop. (1970). These are also on US 45. *See Tour 3.*

US 52, combined with US 45, goes north at the eastern edge of KANKAKEE RIVER STATE PARK, 2,421 acres of woods and waters on the site of a former Indian reservation. At 56 *m*. US 52 turns west 4 *m*. to WILTON CENTER, a hamlet, then north 5 *m*. to MANHATTAN (1,530 pop. 1970; 1,117, 1960, inc. 37%), a residential village on the Norfolk & Western and near a junction with the Milwaukee, in Will County. It was incorporated in 1886.

In Will County US 52 moves northwest through the center of JOLIET (*see article*). At its western line it has a junction with Int. 55 (north-south) which is combined with US 66. Practically adjoining is the village of SHOREWOOD (1,749 pop. 1970, 499, 1960) which has known an increase of 250%, largely people from Joliet who have established homes here.

From Shorewood US 52 moves west in a straight line across the farmlands of Kendall and LaSalle Counties. At 14 *m*. west of Shorewood is a junction with Illinois 47, north-south, 11 *m*. north of Morris (*Tour 14*). At 18 *m*. is LISBON, (261 pop.) a farm village. At 29 *m*. is a junction with Illinois 71 and the Fox River valley. Two miles south of US 52 on Illinois 71 is NORWAY, a tiny farm village with a marker on a boulder identifying this place as an Illinois State Memorial commemorating the first permanent Norwegian settlement in America. North of US 52 at SHERIDAN (724 pop. 1970) is the Sheridan Branch of the Illinois State Training School for Boys.

At 38 *m*. US 52 has a junction with Illinois 23, which joins it for 2 *m*.

TROY GROVE, 52 *m*. (281 pop. 1970; 271, 1960), is the birthplace and boyhood home of James Butler Hickok (1837-76), the Wild Bill of the West. At 18 he went to Leavenworth, Kansas, where he took part in frontier struggles. During the Civil War he served as a scout for the Union Army and later (1866-71) he was United States marshal at various places in the West. He toured the East with William F. Cody (Buffalo Bill), during 1872-73. The following year he went to Deadwood in the Black Hills of South Dakota, where, two years later, he was murdered by Jack McCall. The Wild Bill Hickok State Monument, one block from the highway, erected in 1929, commemorates the frontiersman.

At 132 m. is a junction with US 51 (see Tour 4), with which US 52 is united for 6.5 miles through MENDOTA, 137.5 m. (750 alt., 6,902 pop. 1970), which is at a junction with US 34 (see Tour 13).

SUBLETTE, 61 m. (361 pop. 1970; 306, 1960) is a farm village in Lee County.

In AMBOY, 70 m. (752 alt., 2,184 pop. 1970; 2,067, 1960, inc. 5.7%), the small-town grocery store out of which grew the mercantile firm of Carson Pirie Scott & Company was opened in 1854 by Samuel Carson and John T. Pirie, Scotch-Irish immigrants. Four years later their fellow-countryman, J. E. Scott, arrived at Amboy and the firm was established. By the close of the Civil War the company had branch stores in Mendota and Polo, and headquarters in Chicago. In 1934 the firm presented the city of Amboy with a drinking fountain, Main St. and the highway, to commemorate their first store.

The first newspaper in Lee Country was published in Amboy in 1854 by Augustus Noel Dickens, brother of Charles Dickens. The enterprise was short-lived. A Memorial Boulder on a lawn at 109 Main St. marks the site where Lincoln spoke briefly, August 26, 1858, on the night before his Freeport debate with Douglas.

At 72 m. is a junction with US 30, which proceeds west to Rock Falls. US 52 continues 10 m. northwest to DIXON, 82 m. (18,147 pop. 1970). US 52, combined with Illinois 26, proceeds northwest into Ogle County.

POLO, 95 m. (836 alt., 2,542 pop. 1970; 2,551, 1960) a livestock trading center, was named for Marco Polo.

Polo and Ogle County became the center of hemp raising and processing during World War II, after the Japanese had cut off shipments of Asiatic rope fiber to the United States. The Dept. of Agriculture ordered the Commodity Credit Corp. to supervise the production and processing of hemp in six Midwestern states, including Illinois. There were 11 mills in Illinois with the pilot plant at Polo. Hemp grew profusely in Ogle County, with stalks 12 to 14 ft. tall. Because of the shortage of labor German war prisoners were sent from Camp Grant at Rockford to help harvest the hemp. The farmers earned slightly less from hemp than from corn. Farmers in Illinois planted 36,000 acres and averaged 920 lbs. to the acre. Hemp averaged $93.19 per acre to farmers in Ogle County. By 1944 foreign shipments had been resumed. A proposal to process hemp for uses other than cordage failed and the Polo plant was closed in 1945. Its buildings are now used by a cooling equipment corporation.

A marker at the home of Zenas P. Aplington, state senator, records the visit of Lincoln on Aug. 15-17, 1856, when he was campaigning for John C. Fremont.

The Ogle County Historical Society has placed a marker on Eagle

Point Road, 1½ *m.* west of Polo, marking the spot where William Durley was killed by Indians, May 19, 1832.

Beyond Polo Illinois 26 leaves US 52 and proceeds north to Freeport. *See Tour 11.* At 4 *m.* north of Polo Illinois 26 has a junction with Illinois 64, which joins US 52 5 *m.* west and is combined with it.

LANARK, 116 *m.* (1,495 pop. 1970; 1,473, 1960) was laid out near a junction of two lines of the Milwaukee Railroad in 1861. It was the home of Glenn Ward Dresbach, Illinois poet.

MOUNT CARROLL, 124 *m.* (817 alt., 2,143 pop. 1970; 2,056, 1960) seat of Carroll County, is a distributing point for livestock and farm products on the Milwaukee Railroad. The combined US 52 and Illinois 64 have a junction here with Illinois 78 (north-south) and a new highway, Illinois 88, starts southeast here.

SHIMER COLLEGE, an oasis of culture in Mount Carroll since 1853, closed its doors December 31, 1973, because its board of trustees was unable to get sufficient funds for further operations. With steadily rising costs and a declining enrollment it was unable to meet the competition of the larger colleges. It was founded as Mount Carroll Academy, and after the Civil War was limited to female students. In 1896 it became the Frances Shimer Academy of the University of Chicago. It was intended to provide a channel for students to continue their education at the University of Chicago. It resumed a coeducational structure in 1950, and in 1958 became Shimer College and gave baccalaureate degrees. It became known for close cooperation between teacher and student, for accepting qualified students before they completed high school, and for advancing undergraduates on the basis of competence. It conducted classes in Oxford, England, and Chicago Center, 58th St. and Woodlawn Ave. The campus in Mount Carroll has several residence halls of recent construction and the Karyn Kupcinet Playhouse (1968). Its tuition was $2,160 for day students, and tuition, board and lodging for those living on campus reached $3,340. In 1973 it had an enrollment of 335 and a faculty of 34.

On closing the University of Chicago arranged to accept for admission the entire Shimer senior class and to make possible its graduation the following June. The university also accepted other qualified Shimer undergraduates and extended loans to those needing them. Basic tuition at Chicago is $2,475, with living expenses additional.

Right from Mount Carroll on a graveled road is Smith's Park, 2 *m.* In their wildland beauty the grounds are typical of much of Carroll County. Wooded ravines, steep-walled canyons, tall trees, winding streams, and the caves of an abandoned lead mine are features of the park.

After leaving Mount Carroll Illinois 88, on the way to Sterling, passes through several Carroll County towns, including CHADWICK, a village of 605 pop. that increased by only 3 since 1960, and MILL-EDGEVILLE (1,130 pop. 1970; 1,208, 1960). This village is located on Elkhorn Creek and produces cheese and fertilizer. It has freight service of the Burlington Railroad.

SAVANNA, 135 *m.* (592 alt., 4,942 pop. 1970; 4,950, 1960) in Carroll County on the east bank of the Mississippi River, was named for the grassy plains below the bluffs, which producers of livestock have found valuable as feed lots. In 1828 the town began as a farm settlement and river port. The land was fertile, the Indians were friendly and the place prospered. In 1838 John Smith came with his wife and eight children from Louisville, Kentucky, and started a brick kiln. The railroad arrived in 1850 and Savanna became a center for transshipment of livestock. It became one of the principal terminals of the Chicago, Milwaukee, St. Paul and Pacific. On the 50 miles of tracks in its yards 35,000 cars of perishable commodities were iced annually before the growth of motor truck lines reduced the intervals between deliveries. The city was also a terminal for the Burlington Route. The growing popularity of the Mississippi Palisades as a recreation area has given the highways a busy appearance during the summer months, but the movement of trade is indicated in the static population.

US 52 and Illinois 64 skirt the southern edge of the MISSISSIPPI PALISADES STATE PARK of 1,591 acres, which is filled with massive eroded limestone cliffs and opportunities for picnics, swimming and outdoor living. *See Tour 6.* The highway crosses the Iowa line on a toll bridge spanning the Mississippi River to Sabula, Iowa, and the two routes split and go separate ways in Iowa.

≈≈≈≈≈≈≈≈≈≈≈≈≈≈≈≈≈≈≈≈≈≈≈≈≈≈≈≈≈≈≈≈≈≈

Tour 16

ACROSS NORTH CENTRAL ILLINOIS TO QUINCY VIA PEORIA

Watseka — Chatsworth — Chenoa — El Paso — Eureka — Metamora — East Peoria — Morton — Pekin — Peoria — Lewistown — Astoria — Rushville — Mount Sterling — Quincy.
US 24. Indiana Line to Missouri Line, 249.8 *m.*

This route across the north central part of Illinois runs in a straight line from the Indiana border to Peoria, and then runs southwesterly more or less parallel with the Illinois River to within 9 miles of Beardstown; then more directly west to Quincy. It has junctions with all the major highways that fan out from Chicago—Illinois 1, US 45, US 66, and Interstate 55—and the north-south highways west of Peoria: Illinois 78, Illinois 97, Illinois 41, US 67, Illinois 94, and Illinois 96, the Great River Road.

A second direct line from the Indiana border to Quincy is US 138, which combines with Illinois 1 at Danville to go north 13 *m.*, then turns west through prairie country with only one sizable city, Rantoul, (25,562 pop.) until Havana on the Illinois River, thence across the river to a junction with US 24 and on that highway to Quincy.

Section a. Indiana Line to Peoria, 116 m.

US 24 crosses the Indiana line, 0 *m.*, 5 miles west of Kentland, Indiana. West of the Indiana line US 24 and US 52 are united for 2 *m.* to Sheldon, where US 52 turns north and eventually joins US 45 at Kankakee.

SHELDON, 2 *m.* (685 alt., 1,455 pop. 1970; 1,127, 1960, inc. 28%) in Iroquois County is a grain distributing center at a junction of the Penn Central and the Toledo, Peoria & Western railroads. *See Tour 15.*

At 9.7 *m.* is a junction with Illinois 1, which unites with US 24 for 2.7 *m.*

WATSEKA, 11.9 *m.* (634 alt., 5,294 pop. 1970; 5,219, 1960) seat of Iroquois County. *See Tour 1.*

CRESCENT CITY, 18 *m.* (597 pop. 1970, 409, 1960). At 19.2 is a junction with Illinois 49, north-south.

South on Illinois 49 to CISSNA PARK, 16 *m.* (684 alt., 773 pop. 1970; 603, 1960), the center of a community of the Apostolic Church, known in Illinois as New Amish. The founder of the church, Samuel Frolich, a deposed minister of the Reformed Church in Argau, Switzerland, enlisted converts for his new sect from among the Amish, and his followers continued proselyting among the Amish in America. Because of this close association in their early history, the customs and habits of the Apostolic Church members differ little from those of the Amish, and the error in calling them such is a technical one. Both men and women wear simple dark clothing. The men are bearded, but do not have mustaches. Simplicity of habit, dress, and home is practiced; and they keep themselves strictly aloof from non-member neighbors, avoid civil government, do not take oaths, and refuse to bear arms. This last prohibition caused them embarrassment at the time of the World War, but their appeal to President Wilson was successful. Farming is their chief occupation.

An expression of their religious severity, their large bare frame church is utterly devoid of ornament. The men and boys sit on one side of the hall, the women and girls on the other. The sermon is delivered by one of six men who sit on a raised platform; any of these who feel moved to speak may rise and deliver the sermon. Singing by the members is without accompaniment. Following the service, the congregation moves to a large dining hall in the building, where a simple lunch is served on plain tables; the families take turns in providing the Sunday communal meal. This custom is a survival of the time when meetings were held in the members' homes and the distances traveled were great.

At 25 *m.* US 24 is joined by US 45, north-south. The combined highways proceed 1 *m.* to GILMAN (1,786 pop. 1970; 1,704, 1960). At 26 *m.* US 24 turns west at a junction with Int. 57.

PIPER City, 36 *m.* (817 pop. 1970; 807, 1960) is at a junction with Illinois 115, north-south.

CHATSWORTH, 43 *m.* (1,255 pop., 1970; 1,830, 1960) in

Livingston County, has several small industries, including a manufactory of tile and brick. The town, platted in 1838, lives in railroad annals because of a fatal wreck, one-half mile north on the Toledo, Peoria & Western Railroad. At midnight on August 10, 1887, an excursion train of two locomotives and approx. 20 wooden coaches going from Peoria to Niagara Falls plunged through a burned trestle over a branch of Vermilion Creek. Of 500 passengers about 65 were killed and scores were injured. A marker was placed near the site in September, 1954, by the Illinois State Historical Society.

FORREST, 48.8 m. (688 alt., 1,219 pop. 1970; 1,220, 1960) a town in Livingston County, is at a junction with Illinois 47 and about halfway between Dwight, north, and Gibson City, south. It produces feed for stock and has a large chicken-raising enterprise conducted by the Honegger brothers, who raise white leghorns for breeders and ship millions of eggs. The place was settled in 1836 and owed its development to the railroads that opened up the area two decades later and to the arrival in the 1860's of German Amish immigrants. Men of this faith, soberly dressed and bearded, but with clean-shaven upper lips, and women in equally sombre attire, are frequently seen along the streets and in the communities along the highway between Forrest and Peoria. They may be Mennonites, Amish-Mennonites, or members of the Apostolic Church.

The first Amish in Illinois settled along the Illinois River above and below Peoria, in what are now Woodford, Tazewell, and Bureau Counties. They had emigrated in 1831 from Alsace and Lorraine, and in the next 20 years others came from the same provinces, and from Bavaria and Hesse-Darmstadt. A few traveled westward from Ohio; and in the 1850's a number of Pennsylvania Amish joined the colony in Illinois. These pioneer settlements were all made in the timbered sections along the Illinois and its tributaries. In the late 1850's an eastward movement began to more fertile prairie lands, and the original congregations were gradually transplanted to these new communities, many of which are on or near US 24.

The first Mennonites reached Illinois in 1833 from Virginia, and many from Ohio, Pennsylvania, and Bavaria continued to settle here until the late 1840's. Their movement was similar to that of the Amish, except that some colonies were established along the northwestern border of the State.

Doctrinal differences soon split the Mennonite Church, for the Amish insisted on rigid adherence to early precepts. Gradually even the Amish subdivided; the conservative group became known as the Old Order, or "hook and eye" Amish, because their clothing is fastened with hooks and eyes instead of buttons. Other Amish divisions, several named after their leaders who broke from the parent body, are more elastic in their social and religious customs, and co-operate to some extent with the several Mennonite branches. The principal centers of the Old Order Amish in Illinois are in Douglas and Moultrie Counties (*see Tour 3*).

FAIRBURY, 55.5 *m.,* (686 alt., 3,350 pop. 1970; 2,927, 1960) an incorporated city in Livingston County, has a coal mine in operation. Of the city's churches, two are Apostolic. MoorMan Manufacturing Co. of Quincy opened a feed distributing center here in 1970.

CHENOA, 66.5 *m.* (722 alt., 1,860 pop. 1970; 1,523, 1960) a city in McLean County is at a junction with US 66 (*see Tour 17*).

MEADOWS, 71 *m.,* was settled by Mennonites from Alsace and Lorraine; their church building is on the southern edge of the village. A large settlement of Amish farms is north of the community.

GRIDLEY, 75.1 *m.* (752 alt., 1,007 pop. 1970; 889, 1960), has a congregation of Egli Amish, a group formed in the 1860s around Henry Egli, an Amish minister in Indiana. Today this division works in close cooperation with the old church. The town is named for Asahel Gridley (1810-81), a native of New York, who came to Illinois in 1831 and embarked on a career that included banking, law, politics, and the militia.

EL PASO, 82.6 *m.* (749 alt., 2,291 pop. 1970; 1,964, 1960) seat of Woodford County, is at a junction with US 51 (*see Tour 4*).

EUREKA, 96.3 *m.* (738 alt., 3,028 pop. 1970; 2,538, 1960, inc. 19%) has developed around EUREKA COLLEGE, a coeducational school with a student body of 541 and faculty of 37 (1971). It occupies wooded acres in southeastern part of the city. The Disciples of Christ, followers of Alexander Campbell, founded a seminary here in 1848, which was expanded to an academy the following year and chartered as Eureka College in 1855; it was the first college in Illinois to admit men and women on an equal basis. In 1933 Eureka College inaugurated the Eureka Plan, which affords students part-time jobs to pay their tuition and board.

An established community since the 1830s and seat of Woodford County since 1896, Eureka is the trading center of a prosperous farm area, and absorbs the local crops of peas, corn, pumpkins, and tomatoes in its canning factory.

On the northern outskirts of Eureka is the Mennonite Home for the Aged, a three-story building of brown brick, with spacious porches, erected in 1922 and maintained by the Mennonite Conference. Aged members of the sect are supported by their church; non-members pay their maintenance, but are usually cared for after their funds have become exhausted.

Right from Eureka on Illinois 117 to a junction with Illinois 116 at 5 *m.*; left on 116 to METAMORA, 5 *m.* (813 alt., 2,176 pop. 1970; 1,808, 1960, inc. 20%), site of the Metamora Courthouse, a State Memorial. Here in the 1840's gathered lawyers and jurists who were to become renowned; among them, Abraham Lincoln, Stephen A. Douglas, Robert Ingersoll, and Adlai Stevenson. The courthouse, substantially the same today as when built in 1845, is a two-story brick and walnut timber structure of Greek Revival design; the bricks were burned in the village. Four fluted Doric columns support the pediment, and an octagonal cupola encircled with an iron railing overshadows the portico.

A hall, with offices on either side, runs the full length of the first floor. On the second floor is the old courtroom restored as nearly as possible to its original condition, in which are pioneer relics of the Woodford County Historical Society. Just south of Metamora, a marker in a locust grove designates a site where Lincoln spoke in 1858.

WASHINGTON, 104 m. (766 alt., 6,790 pop. 1970; 8,919, 1960, inc. 14%) is the home of workers who are employed chiefly in the plants of East Peoria and Peoria and is on the lines of the Santa Fe and Illinois Central Gulf Railways.

A network of highways approaches East Peoria and Peoria from all directions.

US 24 enters East Peoria near its northern limits and crosses the McClugage Bridge to Peoria, where it is joined by Illinois 29. The two routes proceed as far as Washington and Cedar Sts., Peoria, when Illinois 29 crosses to East Peoria on the Cedar St. Bridge and turns south.

US 150 comes up from Bloomington, proceeds north through East Peoria to the McClugage Bridge, crosses to the War Memorial Drive in Peoria and goes west to Galesburg and Moline.

Int. 74 runs parallel with US 150, bypassing towns. It crosses the Illinois River on the Murray & Baker Bridge to Peoria.

Illinois 116 enters East Peoria from the north, combines with US 150 in East Peoria, crosses the river to Peoria on the Cedar St. Bridge and runs straight west through farming country.

EAST PEORIA, 114 m. (478 alt., 18,455 pop. 1970; 12,310, 1960, inc. 49%) a city in Tazewell County, is located at the base of the bluffs on the flood plain of the Illinois River, and is an industrial and residential adjunct of Peoria. It is the site of one of the major plants of the Caterpillar Tractor Co., which employs from 18,000 to 20,000 during peak times, and has its head offices in Peoria (q.v.). East Peoria was incorporated as a village in 1889 and as a city in 1919; it extends along the east bank of Lake Peoria.

In 1909 the Holt Manufacturing Co. of Stockton, Calif., which had built the crawler-tractor since 1904, moved to East Peoria. Its tractors served in World War I and gave the idea of the military tank to the British inventor, Lt. Col. E. D. Swinton. In 1925 Caterpillar Tractor Co. was formed by the merger of Holt and C. L. Best, another California manufacturer. The East Peoria plant built military armament during World War II and since has been building tractors, loaders, pipe-layers, engines and other roadbuilding machines.

ILLINOIS CENTRAL COLLEGE, one of the newest of the two-year community colleges in the State, was authorized by a referendum of District 415 on May 25, 1966, to serve an area comprised of Peoria County and parts of Tazewell, Woodford, Marshall, and McLean Counties. Its 440-acre campus is located near the intersection of Illinois 116, US 24, and US 150 in East Peoria. When the college opened on Sept. 18, 1967, 2,500 students entered its first class. By the fall of 1972 it had a faculty of 367 and an enrollment of 7,968. To expedite the erection of permanent buildings the District in 1968 approved a bond issue of $9,500,000.

The Fond Du Lac Township Library was built in 1955 at 235 Everett St. It has a circulation of around 110,000 volumes and is a member of the Illinois Valley Library System.

Closely associated with industrial expansion in the Peoria-East Peoria area is the village of MORTON in Tazewell County, 9 m. from East Peoria on US 150 and with an access route to Int. 74 (10,419 pop. 1970; 5,325, 1960; inc. 95%). It has access to the freight services of the Santa Fe, Penn-Central, and Illinois Terminal Railroads and is also on Illinois 121. It is an assembly center of Caterpillar Tractor Co., which employs 1250 (950 men, 300 women). Farm equipment is handled by Allis Chalmers, Clay Equipment Corp., Meyer-Morton Co.; Libby, McNeill & Libby has a canning plant employing 225, and provides "pumpkin and corn to the world," and there is the Pioneer Hybrid Corn Co., shipping seed corn. The village was settled from 1830 to 1835 by people from the East; after 1860 came Swiss and South German immigrants. The village was incorporated in 1877.

South from East Peoria 5 m. on Illinois 29 is the village of CREVE COEUR (6,440 pop. 1970; 6,684, 1960) incorporated 1921, the residence chiefly of people employed in East Peoria. Although the area has prospered Creve Coeur had a loss in population of 3.7 percent between 1960 and 1970.

Bordering on the Illinois River south of the village is the CREVE COEUR STATE PARK, a wooded tract of 86.6 acres on limestone hills overlooking the river. This has been identified as the spot where LaSalle erected a temporary outpost, or fort, in 1680, and named it Creve Coeur (Broken Heart) after a fort in the Netherlands. The fort was completed in January, and in March LaSalle left for Quebec, leaving Henri Tonti in command and sending him word to explore Starved Rock for a permanent fort. (*See Tour 14*). After Tonti left the dissatisfied troops destroyed Fort Creve Coeur and went off into the wilderness with its store of ammunition and provisions. The fort, the second French outpost in this territory, was never rebuilt.

Right on US 150 to a junction with a graveled road, 9 m.; R. on this road to JUBILEE COLLEGE STATE MEMORIAL, 11.5 m., where stands the main building of a pioneer college founded by the Rt. Rev. Philander Chase (1775-1852), first Bishop of the American Protestant Episcopal Church in Illinois. The Chapel-Dormitory-Classroom is a sandstone structure with recessed portals and Gothic windows. The stone was quarried in a ravine near Kickapoo Creek and the lumber was shipped from St. Louis by way of the Illinois River. The cornerstone was laid April 3, 1839, "the day fine," as noted by Bishop Chase, "the sky serene, and just enough wind to remind us of the breath of God." The preparatory school of the college was opened in 1840. Jubilee College was chartered by the State in 1847.

Jubilee College, the second school established by Bishop Chase (as first Bishop of the American Protestant Episcopal Church in Ohio he had founded Kenyon College in 1824), continued to prosper for several years after the Bishop's death in 1852, then fell into financial difficulties, and was finally closed during the Civil War. Attempts to reopen the college immediately after the war and again in 1883 failed. The site was acquired by the State in 1934 and covers 976 acres. The one-time campus, shaded by spruce and oak, overlooks the peaceful valley of Kickapoo Creek. In Jubilee Churchyard, marked by a stone lectern, is the Grave of Bishop Chase.

Section b. Peoria to Missouri Line, 133.8 m.

Southwest of Peoria US 24 follows hilly terrain, offering beautiful views of the lowlands, and for about 35 miles the broad Illinois River is visible. The villages and towns passed are scarcely more than crossroad communities, with a general store; a post office, and a name; many of the latter suggest the chief industry of the region, coal mining.

BARTONVILLE, 5.3 m. (694 alt., 7,221 pop. 1970; 7,253, 1960) a suburb of Peoria, was formerly a mining center, but is now a site for plants with offices in Peoria, such as the Keystone Steel & Wire Co., Laidlaw Wire Corp. and Allied Mills. At the southern edge of Bartonville is the gateway to a road leading to the bluff on which are the buildings of the PEORIA STATE HOSPITAL, an institution for mental health.

ORCHARD MINES, 8.7 m., is at a junction with Illinois 9.

Illinois 9, which crosses the State in a fairly straight line from Hoopeston on the Indiana border to Fort Madison, Iowa, crosses the Illinois River at Pekin and joins US 24 at Orchard Mines and combines with it for 13 m. On the east bank of the Illinois River is Pekin.

PEKIN

Air Services: Pekin Municipal Airport, 6 m. ssw., 3,800 ft. runway; shop and hangar facilities. Greater Peoria Airport, 8 m. west, has daily flights by Ozark Air Lines.

Bus Lines: Highway Transportation Co., Peoria-Rockford, Jacksonville, Crown Transit, Illini Swallow lines; all Peoria connections.

Highways: Illinois 6, east-west. Illinois 29, north-south. Illinois 121 jct. with Illinois 9; Int. 74 jct. with Illinois 121.

Railroads: Illinois Central Gulf, Santa Fe, Chicago & Illinois Midland, Peoria & Pekin Union (freight). Rock Island passenger service at Peoria.

Marine Services: Upper Mississippi Towing Corp. Federal Barge Lines. Mississippi Valley Barge Co. Ohio River Co. Meckling Barge Co. Rose Barge Line. American Commercial Barge Line.

General Information: Pekin Memorial Hospital, 400 beds. 40 churches, 17 denominations. *Pekin Daily Times.* Pekin Chamber of Commerce, 319 Court St.

Recreation, sports: High school stadium seats 10,000. Mineral Springs Park, 92 acres, has golf course, lake, the Memorial Arena. Veterans Memorial Fairgrounds in Park, has annual exhibits and events.

PEKIN (479 alt., 31,375 pop. 1970; 28,146, 1960, inc. 11.5%)
seat of Tazewell County, is a major city in the Peoria Metropolitan
Area (SMSA) and a port on the Illinois Waterway. It has a substantial
industrial section of its own and ships grain and processed foods by land
and water. Its 32 plants produce starch, corn oil, malt, distilled liquors,
feeds, metal castings, structural iron, dairy and meat items. It has three
Cargill grain elevators with a capacity of 1,140,000 bu. Its largest
industries are Corn Products Co., employing 1,136 (1972); American
Distilling Co. (756), Standard Brands, Quaker Oats, and Pekin
Foundry. It has the home office of the Pekin Farmers Insurance Co. as
well as three savings and loan associations.

The Caterpillar Tractor Co. has located a large induction melting
foundry with 12 electric furnaces on the west bank of the Illinois River.

The Census of 1970 reported that Pekin had a civilian labor force
of 13,163, of whom 8,271 were males and 4,892 females; 4,872 were
engaged in manufacturing, 4,382 in clerical and office work, and 2,343
in wholesale and retail trade. The Metropolitan Area (SMSA) had a
population of 341,974, of whom 325,984 were white and 14,977 Negro
(4.4%). The Census reported 51 Negroes in Tazewell County and
none in Pekin.

The drift of population from the villages to Pekin is evident. North
Pekin village had 1,886 pop. 1970, down 6.9% from 1960; South Pekin
village had 955, 1970, down 5% from 1,007, 1960.

Pekin has a mayor and four commissioners. Both the city and the
county have their principal offices in modern buildings of recent construction. The trend toward plain functional buildings without embellishment is seen also in the youth center, Memorial Arena, in Mineral
Springs Park, and in the new St. Joseph's Roman Catholic Church.

According to local records Jonathan Tharp came up from what is
now Kingston Mines, 4 m. southwest on the west bank of the Illinois,
built a cabin on the east bank in 1824 and started farming on what is
now downtown Pekin. Members of his family followed and planned a
town. Traders along the river knew it as Town Site. In 1827 Tazewell
County was formed; in 1829 the Town Site was auctioned in Springfield.
It is said the first plat was made by a county surveyor who used a
knotted string in place of instruments, so that annoying variations in
lot lines turned up later. One of the first owners was Major Nathan
Cromwell, whose wife named the town Pekin and gave feminine names
to the streets, including Ann Eliza St. for herself; it is legendary that
she thought the town was opposite Pekin, China, but this is not
verifiable.

The first steamboat arrived in 1827. In 1829 William Clarke
started a ferry and Gideon Hawley opened a tavern, charging 12½¢ for
a night's lodging and the same for a half-pint of whiskey. The court
sat in the Snell schoolhouse and when the Black Hawk war erupted the
citizens attempted to fortify the schoolhouse and called it Fort Doolittle.
Capt. John G. Adams led a Pekin company in a battalion of Major
Isaiah Stillwell and took part in Stillman's Run; a rear-guard action took

the lives of Capt. Adams and eight other Pekin men. Pekin became a town in 1835. It won the county seat in 1849 after years of bitter battling with Tremont and was incorporated as a city on Aug. 20, 1849. The Scott Wagon Company and the Jonathan Haines Reaper factory were early successful enterprises.

When the Mexican War broke out in 1846 Pekin furnished men who were mustered in at Springfield as Company G of the 4th Illinois Volunteer Regiment. Attached to the division of General James Shield they took part in the battle of Cerro Gordo, where they were sent to the rear of the Mexican forces. According to the *Journal* of the Illinois State Historical Society, a squad under Sergeant John N. Gill came upon a disabled coach, from which a Mexican officer left in great haste on a horse unhitched from the carriage. The soldiers captured a roasted chicken, a bag of gold, and a wooden leg, which, it turned out, belonged to the Mexican commander General Santa Anna. Sergeant Gill took the wooden leg home as a souvenir. It was later presented to the State and is in the collections of the Adjutant General.

Pekin was the home of Senator Everett McKinley Dirksen and his labors are honored in the recently established DIRKSEN CONGRESSIONAL LEADERSHIP RESEARCH CENTER. A library was established with private funds in the 1840's, and the Pekin Public Library was built in 1902 and remodeled in 1956. It has approx. 50,000 books and circulates 160,000. It is a member of the Illinois Valley Library System.

Tour 16 now continues south from Peoria on US 24 to Quincy.

KINGSTON MINES, 13.9 *m* (502 alt., 380 pop. 1970; 375, 1960), is on the site of an ancient Indian village; from local gravel pits have come innumerable Indian skeletons and relics. Slag piles of active and inactive mines line the highway.

At 31.8 *m.* is a junction with a graveled road.

Left on this road is LIVERPOOL, 2.5 *m.* (218 pop. 1970; 184, 1960, inc. 18.5%). Once a river town of considerable importance, Liverpool served as a convenient depot at which to transfer goods bound for Canton, Lewistown, and other inland cities. Today it is a commercial fishing port, and the center of one of the State's finest hunting grounds, as is proved by numerous private hunting lodges in the vicinity.

At 32.3 *m.* is a junction with State 78 (*see Tour 5*), which joins US 24 for 3 miles.

At 37.3 *m.* is the junction with a graveled road.

Here is the DICKSON MOUNDS MUSEUM OF THE ILLINOIS INDIAN, occupying a building of recent construction, dedicated Feb. 7, 1972, in the presence of Governor Richard B. Ogilvie. Part of the building covers the excavated portion of one mound, where the skeletons of generations of Indians are exposed in their original positions and can be viewed from a high walkway, while a taped documentary describes the exhibit. It is possible to observe cultural changes of the Archaic, Woodland, and Mississippian periods. The auditorium, named for the archaeologist Fay-Cooper Cole, holds 200.

Due to the extraordinary care used by Dr. Don F. Dickson, member of the family that settled here in 1833, 234 Indian burials have been exposed and provide a remarkable source of information about the tribesmen who lived here prior to 1,000 A. D. The character of the soil helped preserve the skeletons, which appear in all kinds of positions in small groups, family groups, and singly. The excavated portion discloses at least five burial tiers, each of which supposedly correspond to the existing surface of the hill. Underlaid with earth, burials were placed upon preceding ones, until the mound reached a height of 50 ft. Tools, pottery, weapons, and ornaments found here may be viewed in the Museum. The project is part of the Illinois State Museum, which gets appropriations from the General Assembly to support continuing excavation. *Open daily, 8:30-5, except New Year's, Easter, Thanksgiving, Christmas. Free.*

LEWISTOWN, 39.3 *m.* (596 alt., 2,706 pop. 1970; 2,603, 1960) seat of Fulton County, is a farm center and profits also from the coal mining in Fulton County, which usually leads the State with more than 7,000,000 tons.

Lewistown was one of the first towns laid out in the Military Tract, a huge section between the Illinois and Mississippi Rivers set aside by the government for soldiers of the War of 1812. Maj. Ossian M. Ross, a veteran, came here in 1821, accompanied by his wife, three children, a blacksmith, a carpenter, and several other workmen; this group founded the present city of Lewistown, naming it for Ross' son.

By 1823 Ross had organized Fulton County, carving it from old Pike County, which then extended from the Illinois River to the Mississippi. In the same year he donated land for a frame courthouse and jail and built a small tavern. The tavern rates were two shillings for "victuals," three shillings per night for "horsekeeping," one shilling for lodging, and one shilling for a half pint of whiskey.

Until 1825 Fulton County embraced the entire northern part of Illinois, including Fort Dearborn (Chicago); residents of this large area journeyed to Lewistown to pay their taxes, and to secure marriage, tavern, and ferry licenses.

In addition to the "public squear," as an old document has it, the town founder donated a "burying yard," and sites for a meeting house, a schoolhouse, and a Masonic temple. Having thus dowered Lewistown, Ross, after a decade, established Havana (*see Tour 5*) on the Illinois River, where he spent his remaining days.

Lewistown is active in preserving relics of its pioneer past and identifying sites associated with the writings of Edgar Lee Masters (1869-1950), who passed part of his boyhood in Lewisburg and drew on sites in and around the city for *The Spoon River Anthology*, the book that made him famous. Masters meditated over the stones in Oak Hill Cemetery for his Spoon River epitaphs. The house in which Masters lived stands at the northeast corner of S. Main St. and Avenue D. On Main Street is the Hotel Spoon River, in operation since 1854. In 1968 the SPOON RIVER SCENIC DRIVE was laid out and marked. It comprises 65 miles of highways, dirt roads and trails, with

London Mills at its northern end and the Dickson Mounds at its southern. The Illinois Division of Tourism actively supports the Spoon River Scenic Drive and associates it with the tourist interest in the Dickson Mounds and the Lincoln country.

One of the recent restorations is the RASMUSSEN BLACK-SMITH SHOP MUSEUM on Main St. Nels Rasmussen came from Denmark about 1890 and his shop has occupied this site since 1893. It was operated by him and his sons until his son Don died in 1969. Tools used in the smithy and horseshoeing section demonstrate the changes in usage that came with the years. From forge and anvil the shop expanded to grinders, buffers, and drill presses; still on hand is the electric arc welder that saw use for 40 years. Wagons and buggies were fitted with new tires here and the apparatus for shrinking steel tires to fit the wooden spokes is exhibited. When the owner died the Lewistown Society for Historic Preservation raised $10,000 to preserve the shop. The museum is free, but donations and sales of souvenirs help its maintenance. Several times a year it stages live programs demonstrating forge operations and horseshoeing.

Lewistown has had four courthouses. The courtroom of most renown, built by Major Newton Walker in 1838, heard the arguments of Abraham Lincoln and Robert Ingersoll; Stephen A. Douglas presided as a judge in the 1840's. On a memorable night in 1895, Major Walker's 90th birthday, the courthouse was destroyed by an incendiary as the last act in a county-seat war between Lewistown and Canton; the incident provided material for several of Masters' poems. A new courthouse was built by popular subscription. The two central pillars, between which Lincoln stood while speaking in 1858 are known as the Lincoln Pillars and serve as a memorial to the soldier dead in the Protestant Cemetery.

Two of the ten denominations that have churches in Lewistown are objects of historic interest. They are the United Presbyterian Church and the Episcopalian Church of St. James. The latter, built during Civil War days, is a red brick structure with a shingle roof and 10-ft. buttresses, designed by Edwin Tuckerman Potter, a son of Bishop Alonzo Potter. Services are held there regularly.

In Proctor's Grove, in southwest Lewistown, Stephen A. Douglas addressed a crowd of 5,000 during the senatorial campaign of 1858, prior to the Lincoln-Douglas debates. Edgar Lee Masters made the event a subject of a poem in which he said:

> But Douglas!
> People out younder in Proctor's Grove
> A mile from the Court House steps
> Could hear him roar . . .

The Major Newton Walker House, 1127 N. Main St., built in 1833, is a commodious white brick structure, in which Abraham Lincoln was several times a guest.

Over a grave in Oak Hill Cemetery, on a gentle knoll north of town, stands a figure of a woman on a marble shaft. The inscription reads: William Cullen Bryant, Died March 24, 1875, Age 24 years.

Not Bryant the poet, but a young namesake is buried here. He was accidentally killed while duck hunting on Thompson's Lake in the vicinity; he is the Percy Bysshe Shelley in Masters' *Anthology*:

> At Thompson's Lake the trigger of my gun
> Caught in the side of the boat
> And a great hole was shot through my heart.
> Over me a fond father erected this marble shaft,
> On which stands the figure of a woman
> Carved by an Italian artist.

DUNCAN'S MILLS, 43.9 *m.* site of one of the first grist mills in this farming region, is at the spot where US 136 from Macomb joins US 24 for 3 *m.* after which US 136 turns east for Havana and runs in a straight route across the central farmlands of Illinois, with Rantoul and Danville the only cities of any size before it reaches Indiana.

Right from this site on Illinois 10 to a junction with a graveled road 7.5 *m.*; R. is BERNADOTTE, 10.5 *m.*, a pioneer village on the Spoon River, once an active community built around a flour mill but now practically abandoned. The old mill is in ruins. William Walters, first settler (1826), legend says, bought the town site from the Indians for 50 deerskins. Later, Walters and a band of whites drove the Indians across the Mississippi. Bernadotte had many thriving years; its one fishing and two packing plants prospered; it gained a substantial income from summer visitors; its future seemed assured until the railroads passed it by.

ASTORIA, 57.6 *m.* (662 alt., 1,281 pop. 1970; 1,206, 1960) is an amalgam of two earlier villages. The eastern part of the town was named Washington when it was laid out in 1836; in 1837 Vienna was platted just to the west. Later these twin villages were named for John Jacob Astor, who owned land in the vicinity. Astoria was a station on the old four-horse stagecoach line between Peoria and Quincy. William H. Scripps came in 1840 from Rushville and began a successful career as merchant and pork packer.

RUSHVILLE, 72.8 *m.*, (683 alt., 3,300 pop. 1970; 2,819, 1960) is a city in Schuyler County at a junction with US 67 (*see Tour 7*).

The highway crosses the La Moine River, 81.8 *m.*, to RIPLEY (701 alt., 159 pop. 1970), a village of small weathered farmhouses clinging to hillsides between which US 24 sharply turns. In the 1830's and 1840's the community enjoyed a period of prosperity, when its 18 potteries employed over 200 workers.

MOUNT STERLING, 90.6 *m.* (711 alt., 2,182 pop. 1970; 2,262, 1960), seat and largest city of Brown County, was settled in 1830 by Robert Curry, who built a house upon the highest elevation in the vicinity. He named the village that developed around him for the mound and the "sterling" quality of the soil. The community became the county seat in 1839.

CAMP POINT, 109.8 *m.* (738 alt., 1,143 pop. 1970; 1,092,

1960) a village in Adams County, was settled by Germans in the 1870's. Several institutions—a church, a bank, and a newspaper—date from the beginning of the settlement. Bailey Park, a 50-acre wooded tract, formerly the meeting place of annual chautauquas, is now a picnic ground.

COATSBURG, 115 m. (188 pop. 1970; 178, 1960) in Adams County, was surveyed by R. P. Coates in 1855. One of the first German Lutheran churches was opened here in 1862. When the courthouse in Quincy burned in 1875 Coatsburg vainly aspired to become the county seat because it was more centrally located.

At 127 m. US 24 has a junction with Illinois 96, the Great River Road. Left on Route 96 5 m. to URSA, 423 pop., which, although settled in 1825, made its first appearance on the U. S. Census list in 1970. A local historian wrote that this village grew "with abandon" for more than 125 years. "It had a town board that spent little time in planning anything for the future. It was in the heart of the rich Adams County farmland and as a small pleasant community grew with an informal organization." In 1963 it determined to incorporate as a town. A planned, progressive program was adopted. It included a new water distribution system, a housing development, and a new sewage system. It is served by the C. B. & Q. Railroad. In 1838 the Bear Creek Christian Church was organized and in 1840 changed its name to Ursa Christian Church. The Ursa Farmers Co-op, principal grain buyer, has a 140,000 bu. forage capacity at Ursa and more than 1,000,000 bu. capacity at the Meyer, Ill., barge terminal.

QUINCY, 132.8 m. (45,288 pop. 1970). *See article on Quincy.*

US 24 crosses the Missouri Line, 133.8 m., midway on the Quincy Memorial Bridge (*toll*) spanning the Mississippi, 7 miles east of Taylor, Missouri (*see Missouri Guide*).

Tour 17

CHICAGO TO ST. LOUIS SPEEDWAY VIA SPRINGFIELD

Chicago—Cicero—Berwyn—Lyons—Des Plaines River Valley—Connections with Joliet — Dwight — Pontiac — Bloomington-Normal — Lincoln—Springfield—Litchfield—Edwardsville—East St. Louis—St. Louis. US 66. Int. 55.

Chicago to St. Louis, 288 m.

US 66 is a direct route from Chicago to St. Louis. For years it was considered the best way to reach Springfield, and traffic was always heavy. Originally it went southwest by way of Joliet and through the congested East St. Louis area before crossing the Mississippi River. With the construction of the Interstate System with Federal funds it became possible to speed up the Springfield-St. Louis route by routing Int. 55 parallel with US 66 for bypassing cities. Thus Int. 55, the Adlai Stevenson Expressway, joins US 66 at the 71st St. junction in Burr Ridge and the combined highway bypasses Joliet. It is also possible to bypass Dwight, Pontiac, Bloomington, Springfield, and East St. Louis, or to visit those cities via US 66.

Section a. Chicago to Springfield, 186 m.

CHICAGO, 0 *m.* (598 alt., 3,366,957 pop. 1970). From the Loop area US 66 takes a southwesterly direction on Ogden Ave. At Cicero Ave. it enters the first suburb, the incorporated town of Cicero.

CICERO, 7 *m.* (610 alt., 67,058 pop. 1970; 69,130, 1960, dec. 3%). This industrial town has the largest concentration of diversified manufacturing in the Chicago area, if not in Illinois. Its northern limits are on Roosevelt Road and a corner of Oak Park is directly north, Berwyn is west, and Stickney is south. The Eisenhower Expressway runs a short distance north; commuters get quick transit on the Douglas Park Elevated, the Burlington Northern and bus lines. The largest employer is the great Hawthorne Works of the Western Electric Company.

Cicero had its first township election in 1857, when 9 out of 14 persons who voted were elected to office. The community grew with the arrival of homesteaders after the Civil War, and in 1869 Cicero was incorporated as a town. Its low, swampy areas were drained by approx. 50 miles of ditches.

Land speculators perceived that Chicago would advance westward, and in the last quarter of the 19th century boulevards were laid out along cornfields and elegantly named. Hetty Green, New York millionaire, and Portus Weare, wheat speculator, were early dealers in Cicero real estate. With a flair for promotion, Weare built a 20-room frame house, designated Ranch 47, which stood at the northeast corner of 52nd Avenue and 25th Street. Surrounding the ranch were rows of cabins copied from those in the Klondike. In the following decades Cicero was weakened by territorial losses and strengthened by industrial gains. Two sections of Cicero were annexed to Chicago in 1892, and in 1901 the contiguous communities of Berwyn and Oak Park seceded to establish separate municipalities. Cicero and its neighbors profited from a large Bohemian (Czech) immigration.

During the Prohibition years Cicero became a center for speakeasies, gambling parlors, and dives dominated by Al Capone, the Chicago purveyor of illegal beer and gangster overlord. Crowds from Chicago patronized the establishments, which could not have flourished without official tolerance. In 1931 the Federal Government managed to snare Capone on tax evasion, and in 1933 the end of Prohibition finished Cicero as an "oasis". It now has many of the amenities of suburban living, including competitive sports, college dramatics, and bowling. Its parks and playgrounds have facilities for tennis, baseball, and all other outdoor activities.

The educational facilities of Cicero are topped by the MORTON JUNIOR COLLEGE, which was established in 1924 and for the 1971-72 year enrolled 2,345 students and had a faculty of 188. The J. Sterling Morton High School (East) is at the head of public education and there are Roman Catholic and Protestant parochial schools.

The Cicero Public Library, erected in 1920, was extensively modernized in 1960. It has a collection of more than 55,000 books and circulates approx. 320,000.

Cermak Road, which follows the line of 22nd St. in Chicago, Cicero, and Berwyn, was named for Mayor Anton J. Cermak of Chicago, a politician of Bohemian descent, who was fatally shot Feb. 15, 1933, in Miami, Fla. when an anarchist attempted to assassinate President-elect Franklin D. Roosevelt, with whom he was riding. The bullet hit Cermak, who died March 6. The assassin, Joseph Zangara, was electrocuted March 20, 1933.

The HAWTHORNE WORKS of WESTERN ELECTRIC CO. is the major support of the economy in this area. In 1971 it had 19,172 employees. It was opened here in 1904 and now uses more than 6,000,000 sq. ft. of floor space. The plant produces, as summarized by the company, "cable, rod, wire, No. 1 and No. 2 electronic switching systems and associated apparatus, PBX switching systems, step-by-step and common systems equipment; power board equipment; Touch-Tone and Automatic Intercept Systems; molded products, permalloy powder cores, loading coils, relays, capacitors, B wire connectors, inductors, territe cores, tools, and thin-film circuits."

By Oct. 1, 1971, Western Electric had 126,372 employees in the manufacturing division and 72,102 in service locations; the grand total, including other offices, was 205,027. Western Electric has two additional plants in Illinois: one at Montgomery, which employs more than 2,600, and another at Lisle, with 1,895 employees. The Service Division for the Central Region is located at Rolling Meadows.

Tragedy darkened many homes in Cicero and Berwyn on July 24, 1915, when the excursion steamer *Eastland,* packed with 2,500 employees of the Hawthorne Works for their annual outing, turned over on its side, at the Clark St. bridge in Chicago, drowning 812.

Left from Ogden Ave. on Cicero Ave. 1.5 *m.* to Sportsman's Park, (half-mile track) and Hawthorne Race Track (one-mile track), on the line between Cicero and Stickney Sportsman's has a 25-day meeting starting in mid-April, and Hawthorne has 24 days beginning in mid-September. Early in September Sportsman's has harness racing.

BERWYN, 9.2 *m.* (612 alt., 52,502 pop. 1970; 54,224, 1960, dec. 3%), in Cook County, voted on Dec. 1, 1901 to become a village and incorporated as a city June 6, 1908. Its name is said to have been bestowed either by Wilbur J. Andrews, a developer from Berwyn, Penn., or by P. S. Eustis, railroad general passenger agent, to commemorate Berwyn Hills in Wales. It has a mayor and 8 aldermen elected for four-year terms, and a Park District managed by commissioners.

Berwyn is directly west of Cicero and its western line is Harlem Ave., the route of Illinois 43. It has Roosevelt Road and Oak Park to the north, Forest Park, North Riverside, and Riverside to the west, and Stickney to the south. It is the dormitory of the adjoining industrial areas of Cicero and Stickney, for unlike them it has discouraged industries and remained a retailing center and place of residence for those who are employed elsewhere. The ethnic base of the population is Czech and Cermak Road is its principal thoroughfare. The principal shopping center is at Cermak Plaza. It has the Morton High School (West) and the Mac Neal Memorial Hospital of 426 beds. It uses means of transportation identical with those of Cicero.

During the first two decades of the present century, Berwyn was a typical suburb in which harried commuters relaxed of an evening, weeded gardens, set hens, and mowed their lawns. A large part of the commuting population then worked in the Western Electric Company plant at Cicero, by reason of which the city was plunged into mourning on July 24, 1915, when the *Eastland,* chartered for a company excursion, rolled over in the Chicago River and drowned 812 persons. The majority came from Berwyn.

The Berwyn Public Library stocks more than 70,000 books and circulates more than 175,000 annually. It built its library in 1961 and enlarged it in 1971. The library has two branches. It is a member of the Suburban Library System.

The GAGE FARM, 225 acres, Harlem Ave. between Cermak Rd. and Riverside Dr. came into the possession of the City of Chicago in 1881 as part payment by David A. Gage for a loss of $507,700 during his term as city treasurer, 1869-73. Gage's daughter, Mrs. Clara Gage Clark, brought suit to obtain the difference between the city's judgment and the value of the farm years later, when it was worth more than $1,000,000. Federal Courts upheld the title of the City, the last in 1934. Until converted into a nursery the farm cost Chicago $99,500 in taxes paid annually to Berwyn.

The City of Chicago sold its interest in the Gage farm, 148.18 acres, in North Riverside and Berwyn in 1964 to a real estate firm for $2,177,500. The Missouri Synod of the Lutheran Church acquired 78.625 acres of this tract for church and school purposes in connection with its Concordia Teachers College of River Forest. Part of the farm became an addition to the Morton High School in Berwyn and 60 acres south of Cermak Ave. on Harlem Ave. were set aside for Nicholson Center of light industry.

West of Berwyn along Cermak Road, not served by US 66, is NORTH RIVERSIDE, a village in Cook County (8,097 pop. 1970; 7,989, 1960, inc. 1.4%). It is located on the Des Plaines River and touched by Salt Creek. The latter flows south into Brookfield (*see Tour 13*) and joins the Des Plaines in Riverside. The Riverside Golf Club is located in North Riverside.

US 66 has a junction with east-west US 34 at 10.3 *m*. (Harlem Ave.), where it also touches the limits of Riverside, Lyons and Stickney (*see Tour 13*).

STICKNEY, 10.8 *m*. (6,601 pop. 1970; 6,239, 1960, inc. 5.8%) a village in Cook County, lies on the southern limits of both Cicero and Berwyn, north of the Chicago Sanitary & Ship Canal and the Stevenson Parkway (Int. 55). This is the region of the CHICAGO PORTAGE, the land bridge between the Des Plaines and the Chicago Rivers, over which Marquette and Jolliet moved with their canoes and baggage from one river to the other in 1673, followed by thousands of voyageurs and trappers in the subsequent century. Stickney is an industrial city with a Czechoslovakian base and is the location of the big Sewage Treatment Plant of the Chicago Sanitary District, which converts sewage into activated sludge, sends some of it down the canal and packs some as fertilizer.

In the southwest corner of Mount Auburn Memorial Park, 41st St. at Oak Park Ave. is a Chinese burial ground, where traditional Chinese rites are practiced. Before the Chinese Revolution bodies of persons born in China often were sent back to be buried in the national soil. This custom is no longer followed.

LYONS, 11 *m*. (615 alt., 11,194 pop. 1970; 9,936, 1960, inc. 12%), a village in Cook County, traces its history back to 1673, the year Marquette and Jolliet laboriously dragged their packs and canoes across the portage, or carrying-place, between the Des Plaines River and the South Branch of the Chicago. Although the portage covered a much wider area, a spot in Niles has been set aside to commemorate the CHICAGO PORTAGE, thanks to the efforts of the Chicago Historical Society and the Forest Preserve Commissioners, and is now a National Historic Site. It is reached from Harlem Ave. (Illinois 42 A) and US 66, and lies south of 47th St. and the right-of-way of the Santa Fe Railroad. The driveway that leads to the memorial has stone walls, one of which bears the words The Chicago Portage, 1673. Three broad stone steps lead to several grassy squares at the end of which stands a granite boulder, on which the historians in 1938 placed a bronze tablet that described the site as "the earliest factor in determining Chicago's commercial supremacy."

The ordeal of crossing the Chicago Portage in the days of the fur trade has been described by Gurdon S. Hubbard, who, as agent for the American Fur Co. crossed it many times. In October, 1818, he had a dozen boat crews on the job. Four men propelled a boat with oars while six or eight walked beside it in the mud, tormented by bloodsuckers and mosquitoes. Some of the boats were equipped with rollers for use in dry weather. In the spring of 1819 the water was so high that Hubbard could use sails to cross the Portage. In 1824 he began using pack horses and taking the southern trail that now bears his name.

According to historians the portage route varied often. Marquette and Jolliet seem to have crossed near Riverside and followed the bank of Mud Lake to the Chicago River at the present Damen Ave. LaSalle located it at what is now Kedzie Ave. Sometimes the travelers swung far north to avoid the marshy area, sometimes south.

Lyons, incorporated as a village in 1888, calls itself the Gateway to the West. Because of its proximity to major plank roads out of Chicago it first attracted taverns and drovers' inns. In recent decades it had a busy night life.

South of Lyons US 66 runs diagonally through the terrain of McCook, a village that has title to more land than it needs, for in an area larger than that of Lyons its population in 1970 was 333, down 24% from 441 in 1960. To the east of McCook are the Des Plaines River, Summit, the Sanitary & Ship Canal, the Adlai Stevenson Expressway, and the right of way of the Santa Fe Railroad.

HODGKINS, 15 m. (2,270, 1970; 1,126, 1960, inc. 101%), a village in Cook County, incorporated 1896, has been a major producer of limestone for Chicago building operations for many decades. The quarries now cover approx. 500 acres. The Adlai Stevenson Expressway, Int. 55, has a jct. with US 45 at the LaGrange Road in Hodgkins.

COUNTRYSIDE, west of Hodgkins, was incorporated as a city in 1960 and had 2,888 pop. in 1970, its first appearance on the Federal census lists.

INDIAN HEAD PARK, (473 pop. 1970, 385, 1960) is a village where US 66 crosses the Tri-State Tollway.

BURR RIDGE, (1,637 pop. 1970; 299, 1960, inc. 447%). Here at 71st St. and the Du Page County line Int. 55 combines with US 66 on the old Joliet Road. At WILLOWBROOK (1,169 pop. 1970; 157, 1960, inc. 644%) it has a junction with Illinois 83 (north-south) and runs within a mile of DARIEN, which entered the Census list for the first time in 1970 and reported 8,077 pop. This area, north of the Des Plaines River, has benefited from the building of the Adlai Stevenson Expressway, here routed with US 66. The villages have been marked by considerable real estate development. Many employees of the Argonne National Laboratory have bought dwellings in this part of Du Page County. US 66 runs along the north border of the Laboratory to a jct. with Lemont Road, which leads across the Des Plaines River to the village of Lemont on the south bank.

ARGONNE NATIONAL LABORATORY is one of the major sites of the U. S. Atomic Energy Commission for the development of atomic energy for useful purposes. It is operated by the University of Chicago under terms of a tripartite contract that includes the AEC and the Argonne Universities Association, a group of 30 midwestern universities. The laboratory employs approx. 4,700 scientists and support personnel and occupies 3,700 acres. Its facilities include the Zero Gradient Synchroton, a 12.5 billion-volt atom smasher. *Tours may be arranged via Chicago phone 739-7711.*

BOLINGBROOK, the first village in Will County, was incorporated in 1965 with 7,275 pop. It is on the East Branch of the Du Page River and crossed by Illinois 53 (north-south). After the Joliet Road leaves US 66 it combines with Illinois 53 in a direct route to Joliet. US 66 (with Int. 55) now moves north of Romeoville and east of Plainfield to bypass Joliet.

SHOREWOOD, 40 m. (1,749 pop. 1970; 499, 1960, inc. 250%) practically a suburb of Joliet is at a jct. with Illinois 59 (north-south) and US 52 from Mendota, which reaches Joliet 1 m. east. On the outskirts is the Joliet Junior College, founded 1901. In the 1972 school year it had a faculty of 182 and enrolled 4,421 students.

Sec. b. Chicago Suburbs south of the Stevenson Expressway

The Adlai E. Stevenson Expressway, Interstate 55, leaves the Lake Shore Drive at 2500 South, moves southwest parallel to the Sanitary & Ship Canal, has an exit at Cicero Ave., at the southeast corner of Stickney, and passes through FOREST VIEW, a Cook County village that dropped 11% in population from 1,042 in 1960 to 927 in 1970.

CHICAGO MIDWAY AIRPORT is located between West 55th St. and West 63d St., and Cicero Ave. (Illinois 50) and Harlem Ave. Both Cicero Ave. and Harlem Ave. have junctions with Stevenson Expressway and Summit is directly west. The Belt Railway runs into the area and the Clearing Industrial District starts at W. 65th St. Midway dates from 1926 and is the second largest airport in Chicago, with 182,348 flights in 1970. (*See article, page 55*). It was handicapped by its inability to serve jumbo jets, but extensive improvements have been made by the City, which has agitated to have large carriers transfer to Midway some of their domestic flights serving a radius of 800 miles.

We continue south on Cicero Ave., Illinois 50.

BEDFORD PARK (585 pop. 1970; 737, 1960, dec. 20%) south of Midway Airport extends from 65th St. to 79th St., is given over largely to the Clearing Industrial District and is served by the Belt Railway of Chicago. Its western segment is located along the route of the old Illinois & Michigan canal and the Sanitary & Ship Canal just beyond and the rights-of-way of the Santa Fe and the G. M. & O., now part of Illinois Central.

BRIDGEVIEW (12,522 pop. 1970; 7,534, 1960, inc. 70%) occupies a long narrow strip of land from 67th St. to 103d St. and from Harlem Ave. to Roberts Road. An industrial village, most of its workers live in the adjoining suburbs. These are JUSTICE (9,473 pop. 1970; 2,803, 1960, inc. 238%) and HICKORY HILLS (13,176, 1970; 2,707, 1960, inc. 386%).

BURBANK (29,900 pop. 1970; earlier figures not available) is located directly south of Bedford Park between Cicero Ave. and Harlem Ave. and has Chicago at its eastern line and Bridgeview at its western. It has a number of large shopping centers that serve this and adjoining villages.

One of the swiftest growing mercantile developments on the West Side is FORD CITY, which begins at 7601 South Cicero Ave., which avenue is also the boundary between the city and Bedford Park and Burbank. Laid out with extreme regard for all ages and incomes, it had 145 stores by 1973, including most of the major chains. Notable was its Peacock Alley Mall. Contests, fashion shows, musical programs, and flower shows are promoted; clubs are encouraged, including a Senior Citizens organization with 1,000 members.

HOMETOWN (6,729 pop. 1970; 7,479, 1960, dec. 10%) is another village in this area that lost population in the 1960s. Some of this may be attributed to the destruction created by a tornado on April 21, 1967, when approx. 500 houses were damaged or wrecked. The village, in the northeast corner of Oak Lawn, between Cicero Ave. and Pulaski Road, was developed as a subdivision of Chicago by a builder beginning in 1949 and incorporated in 1953. The Southwest Highway (Illinois 7) and the Wabash Railroad pass diagonally through the suburb.

OAK LAWN, 60,305 pop., 1970; 27,471, 1960, inc. 119%) in Cook County, 14 m. from Grant Park, one of the largest of the suburbs in terrain is located west of Evergreen Park, east of Chicago Ridge, and northwest of Blue Island. Its principal streets are Cicero Ave. and 95th St., (US 12, 20) which connects with Dan Ryan Expressway (Int. 94) farther east. Illinois 7, Southwest Highway, runs through Homewood, Oak Lawn and Chicago Ridge and connects with Tri-State Tollway. Oak Lawn became a village in 1909 and the next year had 287 people. Its Administrative Center comprises the Village Hall, Center of Public Safety, and Public Library. It has Christ Community Hospital (615 beds). Oak Lawn is principally residential with more than 40 churches, and Catholic and Lutheran parochial schools. There are 20 parks of 162 acres in its Park District and it is within a short distance of the Palos Hills Forest Preserve. There is commuter service on the Norfolk & Western and Suburban Transit System.

The Oak Lawn Public Library, opened in 1955 and improved in 1963, with a collection of around 40,000 gets a circulation of 188,420 (1971).

EVERGREEN PARK (25,487 pop. 1970; 24,178, 1960, inc. 5%) a Cook County village incorporated in 1893 is the first of the residential suburbs 12 m. southwest of the Chicago Loop and has Western Ave. on the east, Crawford Ave. on the west, 87th St. on the north and 103d St. on the south. It is a residential suburb with several parks, the Evergreen Country Club and a number of golf courses. Its early settlement was largely by Dutch farmers, who had a school by 1875. The Evergreen Shopping Plaza at 95th St. and Western Ave. is widely patronized and there are two miles of stores on 95th St. Rock Island commutation trains can be boarded at Wood Ave. Here also is the Little Company of Mary Hospital (579 beds). The Public Library erected in 1958, has a collection of about 45,000 books and an annual circulation of more than 145,000. It is a member of the Suburban Library System of 29 libraries.

St. Francis Xavier College, 103d St. and Central Park Ave. south of Evergreen Park, is a 4-year liberal arts college for women of the Catholic Church, which began as a school for improving speech and hearing in 1848. In the 1972 school year it enrolled 1,051 and had a faculty of 105.

Section c.   Return to Combined US 66 and Int. 55 after Shorewood

After Shorewood the combined US 66-Int. 55 highway passes through the northwest segment of the coal-mining region that lies between Joliet and Kankakee. There is very little shaft mining now but strip mining still goes on in Grundy, Will and Kankakee Counties. Large areas have been reclaimed under the Reclamation Act that became law in 1962 and established new standards in 1968. In most cases peaks and ridges have been graded and the land has been seeded from an airplane with grass and legumes.

A few miles out of Shorewood are junctions with US 6 and Int. 80, which run west in parallel routes. The former route of US 66 is now served by Illinois 53, which runs parallel with the Illinois Central Gulf, formerly the Gulf, Mobile & Ohio Ry., between the limits of the Des Plaines Conservation area at the west, and the Joliet Army Ammunition Plant at the east.

On the present Illinois 53 are Elwood and Wilmington. EL-WOOD (794 pop. 1970) is east of the DES PLAINES CONSERVA-TION AREA of 4,252 acres, which has US 66 at the west. This is described by the State Department of Conservation as "the largest and most used pheasant hunting area." WILMINGTON (4,335 pop. 1970 4,210, 1960) 7 m. south of Elwood, has most of its work force employed at the JOLIET ARMY AMMUNITION PLANT, which was established here in 1941. In the 1840s Thomas Fox laid out the town of Winchester on this site. In 1854 another town proved prior rights to the name and Winchester became Wilmington. Fox improved his investment by building a grist, saw, and carding mill, around which the community developed. Coal diverted attention from agriculture for a short time during the 1860s. There has been rehabilitation of land eroded by strip mining.

ISLAND PARK, a 35-acre wooded island in the Kankakee River, is a popular picnic spot.

BRAIDWOOD, 22 m. (585 alt., 2,323 pop. 1970 1,944, 1960), at one time was the busiest coal mining center in Illinois. In 1865 settler William Henneberry, in sinking a well, struck a rich 3-foot vein of coal 70 feet down. The new field attracted many mining syndicates. By 1873 the community had grown to 3,000 and was incorporated as a city in 1880 the population numbered 9,000, and as many as six long coal trains pulled out of Braidwood daily. Miners lined up for three blocks at the pay window on pay day; 117 saloons, a large race track, and a music hall flourished. In the following decade more pits were closed than opened; as new fields were discovered in the vicinity, residents jacked up their houses and wheeled them to the new bonanzas. Mining was resumed in 1928.

During the boom days, with an influx of thousands of transient miners of every nationality, Braidwood served as a laboratory both for labor organization and the establishment of safety practices in mining. Impetus was given the movement by such tragic disasters as the flooding of the Diamond Mine (*see Tour 15*), which in 1883 took the lives of 74 men. Racial strife complicated the problems of labor, especially in 1877, when Negroes were imported by the operators to break a 9-month strike. Out of the Braidwood field have come such figures as John Mitchell, former president of the United Mine Workers of America; W. D. Ryan, Illinois arbitrator of mining disputes; Dan McGlaughlin, union leader and mining executive, and John H. Walker, State representative. Anton J. Cermak, Bohemian youth who later became mayor of Chicago, worked in the mines here until he was 17.

Braidwood is at the junction with US 52 (*see Tour 15*).

GODLEY, 24.5 *m.*, (242 pop. 1970; 97, 1960, inc. 149%), was once a booming coal town peopled by a thousand Scotch, Irish, and Welsh, the overflow of Braidwood's mining population. During the 1880s, 21 mines were in operation within a mile and a half of Godley; by 1906 all were closed. Bohemians have since settled in the village. Their pursuits are largely agricultural.

BRACEVILLE, 26.5 *m.* (583 alt., 668 pop. 1970) in Grundy County repeats the story of Godley—the census of 1890 reported a population ten times today's. Slag heaps in the vicinity are monuments of past activity.

GARDNER, 29.5 (590 alt., 1,212 pop. 1970; 1,041, 1960), is surrounded by slag piles, but beyond lie the farmlands that support the town as the center of a grain and stock-raising region. Grundy County mined only 288,938 tons of coal in 1970.

DWIGHT, 36 *m.* (641 alt., 3,841 pop. 1970; 3,086, 1960, inc. 24%) a village in Livingston County, was platted Jan. 30, 1854, when the Chicago & Mississippi Railroad, now the Illinois Central Gulf, came. The owner of the land, R. P. Morgan, named the settlement for Henry Dwight, Jr., of New York, a fellow engineer. Dwight is also served by the New York Central and Greyhound and Continental Bus Lines. Although Dwight is primarily a place that serves the needs of a large farming area it has profited recently by the branch operations of large corporations. R. R. Donnelley & Sons Co., printers with hq in Chicago, opened a $12,000,000 plant here in 1968.

The village is administered by a president and six trustees. The public school system has several buildings of recent construction. The Dwight Township High School, (1957) occupies 20 acres and the elementary school has 30 acres. The Dwight Public Library was built in 1926 and given new facilities in 1967. It is a member of the Corn Belt Library System.

In June, 1970, the new St. Patrick's Roman Catholic Church was dedicated at a corner of Mazon and Prairie Avenues. The dark brick structure is fan-shaped and pews for 750 are arranged in a semicircle. The roof is white and there is a white portico with extended laminated beams.

The William W. Fox Children's Center was opened in October, 1965, in the quarters formerly used by the Veterans Administration. It cares for approx. 250 mentally retarded children and has a staff of 300.

Dwight was known for many years as the seat of the Keeley Institute, where sufferers from acute alcoholism received what was called the Keeley Cure. Dr. Leslie Keeley, an Army surgeon during the Civil War, established the institution and announced: "Drunkenness is a disease and I can cure it." He was challenged by Joseph Medill, editor of the *Chicago Tribune,* who sent six alcoholics to Keeley for treatment. When they returned to Chicago Medill admitted "They went away sots, and returned—gentlemen." The Institute treated many thousands of patients before it closed in 1966.

The building occupied by the First National Bank has an interesting architectural history. It was designed by Frank Lloyd Wright, and in the course of years was altered to suit the needs of the bank. In recent years it has been restored to Wright's original plan.

Right from Dwight on Illinois 17 2 *m.* to Oakdale, the Illinois State Reformatory for Women. Completed in 1930, it is a small community in itself, occupying 160 acres, a third of which are wooded. Limestone buildings of the Normandy cottage type are arranged informally around a burr oak grove. Other structures include the Medium Security Building, where sick inmates are treated; a recreation center named in honor of Jane Addams; administration offices and a receiving cottage. The reformatory resulted from the concerted action of State clubwomen to secure an advanced penal institution for women in Illinois. It has a program of vocational education. In 1971 it had 102 enrolled.

PONTIAC, 57 *m.* (647 alt., 9,031 pop. 1970; 8,435, 1960, inc. 7%) in the heart of the rich farmlands of central Illinois, is the seat of Livingston County and a center of light industry and vocational training. It has a mayor and aldermen elected by popular vote. It is hq of the Livingston County Farm Bureau and the Livingston Area Vocational Center.

Pontiac was organized in 1837 and according to one tradition it was named for the chief of the Ottawa Indians by Jesse W. Fell, political associate of Abraham Lincoln. Another version holds it was named by settlers who came from Pontiac, Michigan, which actually was named for the chief. It is also the name of a village in St. Clair

County, located near the site where Chief Pontiac was slain by an Illinois Indian in 1768.

The County Courthouse is a notable example of late Victorian style modified by American elaborations, with a pillared portico and a large square tower with clock dials on four sides. In the courthouse Square a cairn of boulders bears a plaque describing Chief Pontiac. There is also a Soldiers and Sailors Monument that was erected after the Spanish-American War.

Pontiac has good freight service on the Illinois Central Gulf, the Norfolk & Western, and the Illinois Central. It has daily bus service by the Greyhound and Trailways lines. There is a municipal airport for small planes 1½ m. south. The Consumer Products Division of Motorola, Inc. employs approx. 400. Other major industries include the Storage Products Division of Interlake Steel Corp. and the Roof Manufacturing Co. The *Pontiac Daily Leader* has been publishing since 1879. Two presses specialize in business, industrial, and trade magazines. Morton Printing & Lithographing Co. employs 280 and the Johnson Press has 185.

Pontiac has 17 churches, several of them occupying buildings of striking contemporary design. The St. James Hospital (115 beds) organized in 1907, added new wings in 1969. It is conducted by the Sisters of the Third Order of St. Francis.

The Pontiac Branch of the Illinois State Penitentiary has been organized to provide vocational training and general education for the "improvables" among State offenders. In 1971 it had 1,068 enrolled.

The Pontiac Public Library was built in 1894 and considerably remodeled in 1952. It circulates more than 50,000 volumes and is a member of the Corn Belt Library System.

The Vermilion River figures prominently in recreational activities. The Pontiac Sportsmen's Club sponsors an annual canoe race. There are seven parks with supervised programs and contests. The Holiday Basketball Tournament has been conducted for more than 40 years and draws teams from many places. The Steam Threshermens' reunion and Horse Show is an annual feature at Labor Day weekend, with parades and threshing demonstrations.

CHENOA (Ind., white dove), 68 *m.* (722 alt., 1,860 pop. 1970; 1,523, 1960, inc. 22%), grew up at the junction of the Peoria & Oquawka and Chicago & Mississippi Railroads during the 1850's. Matthew T. Scott laid out the town in 1856. Chenoa is at a junction with US 24 (*see Tour 16*), and the Illinois Central Gulf and Toledo, Peoria & Western railroads.

LEXINGTON, 76 *m.* (746 alt., 1,615 pop. 1970; 1,244, 1960, inc. 29%) a city in McLean County, on the Illinois Central Gulf Ry., was named for historic Lexington, Mass. When settlers came to the townsite in 1828, they found villages of the Kickapoo and Delaware tribes about 3 miles south. Although alarms during the Black Hawk War caused fortifications to be erected hastily along the streams, the little band of settlers weathered the uneasy period without losing a single scalp. With the coming of the Chicago & Mississippi Railroad in 1854, the town became an outlet for farm products. The Lexington Public Library, built in 1914, was remodeled in 1970. It is a member of the Corn Belt Library System. In 1970 Lexington unexpectedly found itself front-page news when it was hit by a tornado.

TOWANDA (Ind., where we bury our dead), 84.7 *m*. (787 alt., 578 pop. 1970; 586, 1960), is in one of the first settled regions in this part of the State. In 1826 John Smith homesteaded at Smith's Grove, and a post office was established in W. D. Moore's house near the present village, long before Towanda was laid out in 1854 when the Chicago & Mississippi Railroad came through. Among the founders was Jesse W. Fell, leader of half a dozen similar pioneering efforts. Most of Towanda's inhabitants are retired farmers, and the surrounding area is noted for the quality of its grain and livestock.

BLOOMINGTON, 93.5 *m*. (830 alt., 39,992 pop. 1970) and NORMAL (790 alt., 26,396 pop. 1970). *See Bloomington and Normal.*

Bloomington is at a junction with US 51, north to Rockford and south to Decatur with US 150, northwest to Peoria and southeast to Champaign, and Int. 74, northwest to Peoria, Galesburg, Rock Island and Moline. Int. 55 permits bypassing Bloomington and Normal. Illinois 9, east-west, passes through Normal and Bloomington and can be followed to the Mississippi River and Fort Madison, Iowa (*via toll bridge*).

Section d.   Bloomington to Missouri Line, 154 m.

Between Bloomington, 0 *m*. and Springfield there are reminders of Abraham Lincoln at practically every mile post. Here the young lawyer rode the circuit, made friends and gained the political support that made him a leader in his party. South of Springfield are farmlands, coal fields, and conservation areas leading to East St. Louis and its surrounding industries.

This is the heart of the cornfields of central Illinois. US 66-Int. 55 bypass the little farm villages located between the two cities and only Lincoln gets special attention. MCLEAN, (820 pop. 1970) added only 62 persons in ten years.

ATLANTA, 21.5 *m*. (720 alt., 1,640 pop. 1970; 1,568, 1960), repeats the story of the town that moved to the railroad. In 1854 the 8-year-old village of Newcastle, over a mile from the newly laid tracks of the Chicago & Mississippi Railroad, moved bag and baggage to the site of Atlanta, then known simply as the station stop of Zenia. The railroad prospered, the town boomed, and in 1855 the present name was adopted. The Atlanta *Journal* records that at a Fourth of July rally four years later, the "Hon. A. Lincoln was present and made a few remarks in reply to Mr. Sylvester Strong, who then and there presented him with a walking cane."

The light industries here ship seeds and fertilizer and there are agencies for farm machinery. The Atlanta Public Library is a member of the Corn Belt Library System. Atlanta is a station on the Gulf, Mobile & Ohio, now the Illinois Central Gulf Ry.

LINCOLN, 32 *m.* (591 alt., 17,582 pop. 1970; 16,890, 1960; inc. 4.1%) seat of Logan County, is the only town named for Abraham Lincoln with his knowledge and consent. The original settlement was Postville, a short distance to the west; the coming of the railroad brought the change of site and name. In 1839 speculators Isaac and Joseph Loose of Franklin County, Pennsylvania, acquired title to a quarter section of land from the Federal government at a cost of $200. In 1853 Robert B. Latham, a promoter, bought the tract from them, for $1,350. Meanwhile, his colleague, Assemblyman Colby Knapp, persuaded the legislature to call a special election to determine whether the county seat should remain in Mount Pulaski or be removed to Latham's quarter section. Latham granted the Chicago & Mississippi Railroad a right-of-way through the townsite, and exchanged a two-thirds interest in his land for the financial backing of Virgil Hickox and John Gillett.

The three partners engaged the Springfield lawyer, Abraham Lincoln, to prepare documents that established joint ownership of the land and gave power of attorney to Latham. When they discussed a name for the town in Lincoln's Springfield office on Aug. 24, 1853, one of the men suggested calling it Lincoln. Lincoln said: "All right, boys, go ahead, but I think you are making a mistake. I never knew anything named Lincoln that amounted to much." After the townsite had been surveyed lots were offered for sale. Contracts drawn up by Lincoln provided for the release of the buyers if the county seat was not established there within one year. To be on the safe side Latham deeded to the county the sites for courthouse and jail, and areas now North and South Parks. In the election that followed the town was duly authorized the seat of Logan County.

Fourteen years before, when Abraham Lincoln was running for a seat in the Illinois Assembly, he promised voters to split Sangamon County into four counties, and when this was effected in 1839 he named one of the counties after his fellow representative, Dr. John Logan of Murphysboro, whose son John A. Logan, became a Civil War general.

The sale of town lots took place on Aug. 29, 1853, and netted $6,000. Someone suggested that the town be christened, whereupon Lincoln picked up a watermelon from a farm wagon, caught its juice in a tin cup and spilled it on the ground while naming the town. This is the subject of a statue by Eda Goodenough, now in the foyer of the Lincoln Savings & Loan Assn., which erected a modern bank building at Sangamon St. and Broadway in 1970. The artist used the Lincoln life mask and casts of hands and copied authentic garments. The gallery also has four busts, depicting Lincoln from youth to middle age.

Twelve sites identified with Lincoln and other historic events have been carefully marked by the town for the information of tourists. They are:
Postville Park, once the town square of Postville, first Logan County seat,

laid out in 1835 by Russell Post of Baltimore; here Lincoln and his associates played ball and pitched horseshores.

Postville Courthouse, a reproduction of the original, which was removed by Henry Ford to his museum of Americana at Dearborn, Michigan.

Deskins Tavern site, Lincoln, David Davis, and other lawyers met here during court sessions.

Stephen A. Douglas speech of Sept. 4, 1858, site. Lincoln, en route, stopped by to hear it.

Town Lot on the Square, location. It came into Lincoln's possession because he had endorsed a note that was not repaid.

Inn in Pulaski St. In 1876 counterfeiters here plotted to hold Lincoln's body for ransom to force release of an indispensable collaborator from jail. *See also Springfield.*

Watermelon juice marker. Here Lincoln named the town by spilling juice.

Lincoln House site. Opened 1854, Lincoln stayed here.

Logan County Courthouse. Successor to two earlier courthouses frequented by Lincoln.

Christian Church site. Used as temporary courtroom in 1857 after courthouse burned.

Robert B. Latham home site. Latham was a founder, whose house burned.

Lincoln College.

LINCOLN COLLEGE, Ottawa and Keokuk Sts., founded in 1865, was named for the President with his consent, the only college so named during his lifetime. It is a Presbyterian coeducational junior college that enrolls nearly 600. In the McKinstry Memorial Library the college has two museums of historic value. The Lincoln Collection, begun in 1942, was a legacy from Lawrence B. Stringer, County Judge. There are more than 2,000 books and items, including the original power of attorney for the town, a campaign poster carried in torch light parades, the table at which Lincoln studied in Mentor Graham's house, and his desk from the Assembly. The other museum, the Museum of the Presidents, has memorabilia from every President of the United States.

Lincoln attended the first sale of lots but made no purchase. Four years later, however, he acquired one as compensation for $400 that he, as endorser of a note given by James Primm to a New York bank, had been obliged to pay.

The LOGAN COUNTY COURTHOUSE, in the center of the city, stands on the site of two earlier buildings in which Lincoln practiced law in the years 1854-59. Previously, when Postville had been the county seat, Lincoln had included that court in his rounds of the Eighth Judicial Circuit. The POSTVILLE COURTHOUSE, off US 66 on 5th St., has been reproduced; the original was moved by Henry Ford to his museum at Dearborn, Michigan. On Broadway, adjoining the present depot, is the site of the Old Alton Depot, where the first Lincoln County volunteers entrained for the Civil War, April 19, 1861; where Stephen A. Douglas, enroute from Springfield to Chicago, spoke briefly for the Union cause, April 26, 1861; and where the Lincoln funeral train halted at sunrise, May 3, 1865.

At the southern edge of town stands the LINCOLN STATE SCHOOL, an institution for the mentally handicaped.

Brainerd Park, at the southwestern limits of Lincoln, was for years the site of an annual summer chautauqua.

MIDDLETOWN, (626 pop. 1970), in Logan County about 10 *m.* west of Lincoln, dedicated a historical marker when it celebrated its 125th anniversary Sept. 21, 1956. The marker relates that Abraham Lincoln was present when the village was surveyed and lots were sold in 1832.

On the bank of Salt Creek is the site of a Kickapoo Village, to which Mrs. James Gillham and her three children were brought from Kentucky by Indians in 1790, thus becoming the first white persons to set foot in Logan County.

South from Lincoln on Kickapoo Street are the Lincoln Lakes, 3 *m.*, a 114-acre body of water in old gravel pits. Annually restocked, the lakes are popular among fishermen. A sand beach, bathhouse, and pure water afford good swimming.

Southeast from Lincoln on Illinois 121 is MOUNT PULASKI, 10 *m.* (637 alt., 1,677 pop. 1870; 1,689, 1960), which in 1847 succeeded Postville as seat of Logan County. The MOUNT PULASKI COURTHOUSE, built in that year at a cost of $3,000, functioned as the seat of justice until 1853, when the town of Lincoln was chosen by popular vote. The building served various public purposes, and in 1936 was acquired by the State as a historical monument. It is a small structure, about 30 by 40 feet, of two stories; originally, the lower floor was devoted to county offices, and the upper to the court chamber. The Greek Revival building is of brick, and the unadorned walls support wooden pediments of free classical lines devoid of ornamentation. The interior of the courthouse has been restored to its original appearance.

US 66 crosses Salt Creek, 35 *m.,* in the vicinity of the Logan County Scully Lands, part of the vast properties of William Scully (1821-1906), who at one time was one of the greatest landholders in the United States. Scully, an Irish landowner, arrived at Philadelphia in 1851 with much money and a passion for land. With a horse and a spade the young Irishman rode through Western states, probing the soil, What land he liked, he bought. In 1853 he settled in Logan County, imported several Irish families, and engaged in farming on a vast scale.

After the Civil War, Scully inaugurated a system of tenantry and returned to Europe. This aroused a storm of criticism, leading to the passage of a State law in 1889 against alien ownership of land. Scully circumvented this by taking up residence in Washington, D. C., and becoming a citizen. His holdings assured, he returned to England where he was known as "the great American farmer," and there he resided until his death. Of the 200,000 acres he once owned, 50,000 acres were in Illinois.

ELKHART, officially ELK HART CITY, 43 *m.* (502 alt., 438 pop. 1970) a town in Logan County, is the home town and burial place of Richard J. Oglesby (1824-99), farmer, carpenter, ropemaker, lawyer, forty-niner, Mexican and Civil War soldier, three times Governor of Illinois, and United States Senator. Left from Elkhart to Elkhart Hill,

1 *m.* On the crest of the sharply rising moraine stands Oglehurst (*private*), a 30-room house built by Governor Oglesby in 1891. Here too lived his son, the late John G. Oglesby, one-time lieutenant-governor of Illinois. Nearby is the Oglesby Mausoleum, in Elkhart Cemetery.

At 54 *m.* Int. 55 leaves US 66 in order to bypass Springfield on the east. US 66 separates into two routes near Riverside Park.

SPRINGFIELD, 61.9 *m.* (91,753 pop. 1970). *See article on Springfield.*

US 66 and Branch US 66 pass north-south through the main part of Springfield and rejoin Int. 55 at the Adlai E. Stevenson Drive and pass across Lake Springfield on a bridge, 68.3 *m.*

Int. 55 has cloverleaf interchanges at Sangamon Ave., Clear Lake Ave., S. Grand Ave., East Lake Drive, and Hazel Dell Road.

LAKE SPRINGFIELD, one of the finest man-made recreational areas in Illinois, was actually built to provide a site for the municipal electric generating plant and water purification system. In 1930 a bond issue was voted to create a water reservoir. Spalding Dam was built to impound the waters of Sugar Creek and in 1935 the plants of the City Water, Light & Power Dept. were moved from the Sangamon River to a site near the dam at the head of the lake, which fills 4,270 acres of the 9,000 acres that have been reserved for utilities and recreation. The lake is normally 15 to 40 ft. deep, has 57 miles of shoreline and two public beaches, open daily from Memorial Day through Labor Day. It is stocked for fishing with crappie, black bass, cat, blue-gill, ring perch, white perch, and carp. The park authorities have made specific provision for all sorts of public activities—golf, yachting, boat and shore clubs, launching docks, camps, summer assemblies of religious bodies, and the Abraham Lincoln Memorial Garden. Summer homes are built on leased land along the lake. The electric plant has a capacity of 146,000 kwh and the water purification plant can handle 40,000,000 gallons per day.

Lake Park, on the east side of the lake, is a naturally wooded park with a good beach and beach house. The VACHEL LINDSAY MEMORIAL BRIDGE, a low graceful concrete span, connects the park with the west shore, across a narrows in the lake. At the far end of the bridge is a bust of the Springfield poet by Adrien Voisin.

At 84.5 *m.* is a junction with a gravel road. Right on this road is VIRDEN, 7.3 *m.* (674 alt., 3,504 pop. 1970; 3,309, 1960), a coal mining town, the scene of the Virden riot, October 12, 1898. Miners struck when the local company withdrew from the Illinois Coal Operators Association and refused to pay the rates established by that association and the miners' union. According to the Carlinville *Democrat,* the company imported 300 Southern Negroes and 75 armed guards. The miners opposed the efforts of the guards to bring the men into the mine. Ten miners and six guards were killed and about 30 wounded. Governor Tanner, who had sought arbitration of the strike, declared: "This shall not be tolerated in Illinois while I am governor." Warrants charging company officials with conspiracy to murder were drawn but never served.

Virden Day is observed by the town and surrounding communities each year at Mount Olive.

At 97 *m.* US 66 has a junction with Illinois 108. Right on Illinois 108 to CARLINVILLE, 13 *m.* (627 alt., 5,678 pop. 1970; 5,440, 1960, inc. 4.3%), widely known for its MACOUPIN COUNTY COURT-HOUSE (*open 8-5*). In February, 1867, the county commissioners ordered a $50,000 bond issue to erect new quarters for the county offices. The bonds bore 10 percent interest and were to be repaid within 10 years, but this sum scarcely laid the foundation. More and more bonds were issued, and taxes rose higher and higher, until a courthouse tax of 50¢ on each valuation in real, personal, and mixed property was levied. This the taxpayers bitterly fought, but without success. In January, 1870, the building was completed, at a total cost of $1,380,500, but not until July, 1910, was the last bond retired. Citizens of the country then staged a two-day celebration, which was attended by Governor Charles Deneen. Natural gas, recently discovered in the vicinity, was piped to the courthouse square, and as a climax to the celebration the last bond was burned by the Governor.

The limestone Courthouse consists of two rectangles, which cross at the center and are surmounted by a dome. The larger rectangle is 80 by 181 ft.; the dome rises 191 ft. above the street. The 40-ft. columns that support the roof of the portico, the detail of the cornice, and the decoration of the interior are Corinthian. Every door in the building is of iron; each of the elaborate outer doors weighs more than a ton. All interior trim is of iron or stone. The most impressive chamber is the Circuit Court Room under the dome; facing the rows of polished walnut seats stand the $1,500 judge's chair, mounted on a track behind the varicolored marble bench.

Carlinville has a mayor and 10 aldermen. Its industries include six major plants: the Prairie Farm Dairy, Inc., the Valley Steel Products Co., (tubing, sheets and plates); Schien Body & Equipment Co. truck beds and bodies; Prairie Grove Division of Advance Glove Co.; Ketring Products Division, Bonney Forge, Inc., oil and gas pipe fittings; Central Illinois Steel Co., flat steel products; Trenchit Corp., hydraulic ditching machines. In 1969 Monterey Coal Co., a subsidiary of Carter Oil Co., opened a new coal mine 5 *m.* south.

Lake Carlinville, on Illinois 4, supplies city water and is a recreation center. Fishing, boating and camping are available at Beaver Dam State Park, 737.3 acres, 5 *m.* southwest of Carlinville. The municipality built a public swimming pool in 1968.

The city has freight service on the Illinois Central Gulf and the Illinois Terminal railroads, and bus service by Greyhound Bus Lines.

The Carlinville Public Library circulates upwards of 36,000 volumes. The building, erected in 1914, was modernized in 1962. It is a member of the Lewis & Clark Library System. There are 13 churches, an area hospital, and two weekly newspapers: the *Carlinville Democrat* and the *Macoupin County Enquirer*. The American Hotel, on the Square, although modernized, is able to boast that Lincoln slept there.

BLACKBURN COLLEGE dates its existence from 1837, but that was actually only the time when a Presbyterian minister named Gideon Blackburn decided that if he could buy public land at $1.25 an acre and resell it at $2, he could use the profit to start a seminary. He obtained support to buy needed acres and got enough funds to acquire 80 acres on the northwest edge of Carlinville. The founders obtained a charter for Blackburn Theological Seminary in 1857; in 1858 they built part of University Hall and in 1859 used it for a primary school. College courses began in 1864. In 1869 the State Legislature authorized its designation as a university, but it still calls itself a college.

In 1914 two railroad cars were donated by the Pullman Co. and used as dormitories. After Old Main burned in 1927 the college obtained two parlor cars from Pullman and two coaches from Standard Oil Co. for temporary use.

The college is affiliated with the United Presbyterian Church, USA. In 1971-72 it enrolled 590 and had a faculty of 45. It is a coeducational college with a liberal arts program.

Since 1913 Blackburn has made its students work for their suppers. A student is expected to do manual labor 13 hours a week, from cooking food, washing dishes, serving as laundryman, bookstore clerk or secretary, to constructing buildings. The Lumpkin Library and the Alumni Hall of Biology were built by students. The authorities say this work program enables them to charge lower rates; for instance, $815 a semester for tuition, room and board.

During the 1960 decade Blackburn added new buildings and remodeled others, partly with Federal aid. The Clegg Chapel, which seats 300, was remodeled with funds provided by the First Presbyterian Church of Springfield. The Isabel Bothwell Conservatory of Music was completed in 1970. The Theresa M. Renner Art Center was built in 1969. The F. W. Olin Science Bldg. was opened in 1957. The Lumpkin Library, completed by 1970, has facilities for eventually housing 150,000 vols. It has 230 study stations, including 38 carrels.

In Carlinville, August 31, 1858, Lincoln addressed a scattered audience whose sympathies were largely with Douglas. Black Republicanism was not popular in southern Illinois. But 71 years later, during the celebration of the city's centennial, 1,500 people gathered at South Broad and 1st South Streets to unveil the LINCOLN MEMORIAL, a 7,000-pound boulder upon which is recorded in bronze the fact of Lincoln's address.

The Otwell Iris Fields, North Road at the city limits are a patchwork quilt of color every May, when the 25 acres of ordered beauty, bearing 300 varieties of irises, attract thousands of visitors. For years the Otwell Tree Planting Clubs, organized by Will Otwell, conducted a private reforestation program, annually planted more than 1,000,000 trees.

LITCHFIELD, 105 m. (683 alt., 7,190 pop. 1970; 7,330, 1960) in Montgomery County, is 1 m. east of US 66 in the center of what was once a highly productive coal mining region. Litchfield was incorporated in 1859; coal was discovered in 1869, and oil was found in the shafts in 1882. The oil was exhausted in little more than a decade, but mining continued in diminishing quantity until the 1940's. Litchfield was a busy shipping center with service on the Burlington, Norfolk & Western (formerly Wabash), and Illinois Central; a number of light industries have found the present freight service profitable. The Litchfield Carnegie Public Library, built in 1904, was greatly remodeled in 1970. It circulates approx. 50,000 vols. and is a member of the Lewis & Clark Library System.

Illinois 16, east-west, passes through Litchfield. Seven miles east on Route 16 is HILLSBORO, (4,267 pop. 1970; 4,252, 1960) seat of Montgomery County. Formerly a coal center, it is now a distributing point for farm and metal products. Industries include Eagle Picher Co. and the American Zinc Co. The Hillsboro Public Library was largely rebuilt in 1967. Illinois 16 crosses a fork of Shoal Creek between Litchfield and Hillsboro near the big dam that impounds its waters to create a reservoir of 1,700 acres called Lake Lourager. Eight miles west of Litchfield on Illinois 16 in Macoupin County are EAST GILLESPIE and GILLESPIE, also former coal-mining towns. The former, separately incorporated as a village, has only 187 pop. now, but Gillespie had 3,457 in 1970, a slight drop from 3,569 in 1960.

MOUNT OLIVE, 115.8 m. on US 66 (681 alt., 2,280 pop. 1970; 2,295, 1960) became widely known in labor circles as the home of Mother Jones (1830-1930), who was born Mary Harris in Cork, Ireland. Brought to America at the age of 5 she attended the local school and married, and until the death of her husband and four children in 1867 she kept house. Thereafter she became an untiring agitator for better working and living conditions in the mines. She organized protest marches, led a column of children into New York to demonstrate against child labor, and helped striking miners in the big fights in Illinois. She had expressed a wish to be buried in the Union Miners' Cemetery and this was done. In 1936 a granite shaft was erected "to the everlasting memory of Mary 'Mother' Jones, 'General' Alexander Bradley and the martyrs of the Virden riot of 1898."

Olive was the home of Alexander Bradley (1866-1918), English-born, a leading figure in the struggle for union organization and recognition. He gained the title of "General" in 1897, when he led an army of organizers into the southern Illinois fields and welded together the weak miners' locals. At this time, according to his autobiography, he was wined and dined by the mine operators at Tony Faust's in St. Louis and offered $600 to cease his activities. Instead, he bought a Prince Albert, a silk hat, and a silk umbrella, and returned to camp to scatter $5 bills among his followers, saying, "Here's shoes for you."

STAUNTON, (4,396 pop. 1970 4,228, 1960) another city in fields where coal is no longer mined, was formerly served by US 66, which has since been routed about 6 miles east. Staunton is on Illinois 4. In 1817 John Wood of Virginia built the first log cabin; the village was laid out in 1835 and incorporated as a city in 1859. It has freight service on the Norfolk & Western.

EDWARDSVILLE, 140.2 *m.* (554 alt., 11,070 pop. 1970; 9,996, 1960, inc. 10.7%) seat of Madison County, is 3.6 *m.* west of US 66-Int. 55 on Illinois 143 (the Marine Road), which continues through Edwardsville to Wood River and East Alton and joins Illinois 3 at East Alton. Illinois 143 passes Dunlap Lake outside of Edwardsville. The city on Caholia Creek has a network of roads with Illinois 157 and Illinois 159 (north-south) having junctions with major highways in the East St. Louis periphery.

Edwardsville was named for Ninian Edwards, governor of Illinois Territory (1809-18) and one of the first landowners in the vicinity. It was platted in 1813. In the same year, an Indian agency and a Government land office to record deeds given the militia of the War of 1812 were established here. Soon after Illinois became a State in 1818, a board of trustees was created by the legislature to supervise the affairs of the town, which did not incorporate until 1837. The community developed slowly until the fear was laid that the seat of Madison County was to be transferred to Alton. Eight governors of Illinois have made Edwardsville their home.

James Gillham visited the locality in 1794 in search of his wife and children, who had been taken captive from their Kentucky home by a band of Kickapoo. He learned from French traders that his family was being held for ransom in the Kickapoo village on Salt Creek, near the present site of Lincoln. With two Frenchmen as interpreters and an Irishman as intermediary, he effected their return. So impressed was Gillham with the beauty and fertility of the Edwardsville region that in 1800 he settled on the site. Several of his relatives from South Carolina followed, and the Gillhams became the most numerous family in the area.

Madison County has been growing by approx. 11%, according to the Census of 1970. The Census reported 250,934 people in the County, as compared with 224,689 in 1960. The County was formed on September 14, 1812, and named for President James Madison. Madison's association with the first government of Illinois Territory was commemorated with special services at Edwardsville on Sept. 11, 1955, when a plaque describing his career was unveiled at the Madison County Courthouse by the Madison County Bar Assn. It was accepted by Irving Dilliard of Collinsville, director at that time of the Madison County Historical Society and past president of the Illinois State Historical Society. The principal address was made by Irving Brant, authority on Madison and author of numerous studies of Madison and his great services to the American Constitution. Dilliard said: "To have heard from Irving Brant is almost to have heard from the Father of the Constitution himself." Madison was Secretary of State when Lewis and Clark set out for the Northwest from their camp on the Mississippi River. He was President when Illinois Territory was organized in 1809 and appointed Ninian Edwards first governor. This territory included parts of Wisconsin, Michigan and Minnesota. In 1812 the area was redefined and Governor Edwards named five counties, one of them for Madison. At the same time general suffrage was guaranteed to the people and election control by the freeholders was removed.

Among the first enterprises was coal mining. As early as 1850 strikes are recorded. On a single day in that year miners "sat down" three times in the pit of Henry Ritter, the pioneer operator. The first strike Ritter met by agreeing to pay a higher percentage. The second he met in like fashion. When news came of the third, he went to the shaft and announced that the hoist would be removed in 15 minutes; the strike ended.

The Land of Goshen Historical Society has placed markers at highway entrances to Edwardsville to announce that Edwardsville was home of four Illinois governors: Edward Coles, 1822-26; Ninian Edwards, 1826-30; Thomas Ford 1842-46; Charles S. Deneen 1903-1913.

The Madison County Historical Museum occupies a restored Federal brick house at 715 North Main St., built in 1836, and exhibits, among other objects, Indian and pioneer items and household articles.

Dominating Valley View Cemetery is a State Memorial, the EDWARD COLES MONUMENT, a tall shaft with a bust by Leon Hermant of Illinois' second governor (1822-26). The son of a Virginia planter, Coles once served as secretary to President Madison. In 1819 he came to Illinois by wagon and flatboat; on reaching the State he freed his slaves and gave each 160 acres of land. This section of Illinois contained many who defended slavery, and Coles' repudiation of slavery became a bitter issue in subsequent political campaigns.

The Edwardsville Free Public Library circulates more than 100,000 vols. annually. It occupies a building erected in 1905 that was extensively remodelled in 1965. It is a member of the Lewis & Clark Library System.

SOUTHERN ILLINOIS UNIVERSITY, which has its principal seat at Carbondale, has its newest and liveliest unit at Edwardsville. The parent institution already had established the Alton Residence Center in the buildings of the former Shurtleff College, and had begun the East St. Louis Residence Center. In 1958-59 a movement for a major segment of the university found support among citizens of Madison and St. Clair counties and in a short campaign they obtained title to 2,600 acres of rolling farmland and wooded valleys along the Mississippi River south of Edwardsville. This has become the Edwardsville campus. In the 1971-72 school year SIU reported an enrollment of 22,600 students at Carbondale, and with the addition of Edwardsville and the other two centers, reached approx. 33,000.

With excellent highways providing quick access to Edwardsville from a wide area in Illinois and Missouri, the institution is planned as a commuter college, while Carbondale remains residential. Illinois 157 and 159 have junctions with Interstate 55, 70, and 270. The university is following a master plan that enables it to add new buildings at a regular pace and plan for an eventual attendance of 18,000. By 1972 the campus had the Elijah P. Lovejoy Library, the Peck Classroom Bldg., the Communications Bldg., The Science Laboratory Bldg., the University Center, and the General Office Bldg. The Lovejoy Library contains upwards of 475,000 vols., 225,000 national and international governmental documents, 10,000 phonograph records, and many periodicals. The Lovejoy association is continued in books and pamphlets dealing with anti-slavery, abolition, and civil rights.

A General Studies Program, dealing with the elements of civilized life and thought, is basic before the student specializes. Other units are Divisions of Business, Education, Fine Arts, Humanities, Science and Technology, Social Sciences, and Nursing, and Aerospace Studies, a two-year Air Forct ROTC program. Masters degrees are given by the Graduate School. Tuition and fees for Illinois residents are normally $165.50 a quarter for out-of-state students, $446.50.

At 3 *m.* south of the intersection with Illinois 143, Int. 70 joins US 66-Int. 55 to proceed south. Int. 270 proceeds due west to bypass East St. Louis north of Granite City and cross the Mississippi River over the Chain-of-Rocks Bridge to a junction with US 67, which joins Int. 70 into St. Louis, Mo.

US 66 and Int. 55 are joined by US 40 into East St. Louis. Branch Route 40 enters Collinsville and proceeds independently of the combined highways into East St. Louis. *See Tour 19.*

Tour 18

INDIANA TO MISSOURI ACROSS ILLINOIS VIA SPRINGFIELD

(Rockville, Ind.) — Decatur — Springfield — Jacksonville — Pittsfield—(Hannibal, Mo.)
US 16. Indiana to Missouri, 225 *m.*

Here is a route that enables the motorist to cross from Indiana to Springfield in a straight line. US 36 is a good concrete highway but it is not an expressway. The only city of size on the way to Springfield is Decatur; beyond Springfield the only important one on the way to the Mississippi River is Jacksonville. No Interstate speed, but also, no traffic congestion.

US 36 extends almost directly east and west across central Illinois through one of the most fertile sections of the State. Between the Indiana line and Decatur the land is level, except where notched by streams. Many of the prosperous farms along the route have been reclaimed from swamps. The money crop of much of this region is broom corn, cultivated locally since 1865. The forty miles west of Decatur, a segment of the Lincoln Heritage Trail (*see Tour 21*), is rich in Lincolniana. In its western section the land becomes more rolling after the highway crosses the Illinois River and proceeds to the valley of the Mississippi.

Junctions with north-south highways are plentiful. The motorist has opportunities for turning into the principal Interstate routes that proceed to East St. Louis, Cairo, and the Ohio River.

US 36 crosses the Indiana Line, 0 *m.*, 8 miles west of Montezuma, Indiana (*see Indiana Guide*).

At 8 *m.* is a junction with Illinois 1 (*see Tour 1*).

NEWMAN, 24.2 *m.* (651 alt., 1,018 pop. 1970, 1,097, 1960, dec. 7%) a city in Douglas County, was founded in 1857 and named for B. Newman, son-in-law of the Methodist circuit-rider, Peter Cartwright. The village was industrially active during the 1890's, with two tile factories which supplied materials for draining nearby swamps; the factories closed when drainage operations ceased. Newman processes dairy products.

At 30.1 *m.* is a junction with a paved road. Right on this road is MURDOCK, 0.5 *m.*, platted in 1881 and named for John D. Murdock, who had built a grain elevator here three years earlier. Exploratory shafts sunk in 1929 revealed a 7-foot vein of coal under the community at a depth of 200 feet. The Pentecost Church served in Chicago as a dance hall at the Century of Progress Exposition; in 1936 the structure was moved to Murdock and dedicated as a religious tabernacle.

A Log Cabin, 35.2 *m.*, was built in 1830 by John Richmond, the first settler in what is now Douglas County. He emigrated from West Virginia in 1829.

At 35.4 *m.* is a junction with an oiled road. Right on this road is Patterson Springs, 0.1 *m.* (*fishing, swimming, and picnicking*).

At 39 *m.* there is a junction with Int. 57.

TUSCOLA, 41.3 *m.* (653 alt., 3,917 pop. 1970; 3,875, 1960, inc. 1%) seat of Douglas County, is at a junction with US 45 (*see Tour 3*). Tuscola was platted in 1856 when the main line of the Illinois Central came this way. It developed commercial interest when a booster pumping station was located four miles west on US 36, the object of which was to boost oil and natural gas on its way from Oklahoma and Kansas fields to important industrial centers. The station has expanded with the increased demand for gas and is now the center of a huge petrochemical plant of the U. S. Industrial Chemical Co. Tuscola was on the lines of the Baltimore & Ohio and the Chicago & Eastern Illinois.

The CARTWRIGHT CHURCH, 45.7 *m.*, a white frame structure, was named for Peter Cartwright, fighting Methodist preacher who came to Illinois from Kentucky in 1823. His reasons for moving were: "I had six children and felt that my holdings of 150 acres were insufficient. . . . In Kentucky, there was class discrimination shown in favor of the children reared without work as against those who were taught to work. There was the dangerous possibility that my four daughters might marry into slave families. Lastly, the new country needed preachers."

In the cemetery beside the church is the grave of DR. DAVID HANSON, an infantry captain killed in World War I while attempting to rescue a fellow officer. The Alumni Association of Northwestern University, from which Hanson was graduated, marked his grave with a 10-ton memorial boulder, on which the French government placed the Croix de Guerre.

From Tuscola US 36 proceeds in a straight line to Decatur, crossing the Kaskaskia River and passing through a number of farm villages with nominal population, parallel with the Baltimore & Ohio roadbed. These include ATWOOD, 49 m. (1,254 pop. 1970; 1,258, 1960), which is located in both Douglas and Piatt Counties. Left on a farm road 7.5 m. to ARTHUR (2,214 pop. 1970; 2,120, 1960, inc. 4%), located partly in Douglas and partly in Moultrie Counties. This is the trading center of an Amish colony. The village was platted in 1873 by surveyors of the Paris & Decatur Railroad. It has broom factories and a plant that makes burial vaults and storage tanks.

The Amish, a branch of the Mennonites (see Tour 16), settled near the site of Arthur in 1864. The colony now approximates 3,000. Modernism and mechanization have made no impression on it; native customs and manners have been rigidly preserved. Traditional crafts are handed down from father to son, mother to daughter. The men wear black, broad-brimmed felt hats and home-made suits, fastened with hooks and eyes. The women wear aprons, bonnets, tight-waisted blouses, and voluminous skirts. A horse and buggy, as evidenced by rows of hitching racks in Arthur, is the usual mode of conveyance. "Pennsylvania German" is spoken in the Amish homes.

Amish children attend public elementary schools, but receive the equivalent of high school training in private schools supported by the colony. Church services are held in members' houses, the wall partitions of which are generally constructed so that they can be hooked to the ceiling, thus providing space for the congregation. Frugal, industrious, and skilled in agriculture, the Amish are the most prosperous farmers in the region. When an aged couple is no longer capable of arduous work, they give their farm to their eldest son and retire to the Grandpa House, a small cottage near the main dwelling.

Another Piatt County village is HAMMOND (502 pop. 1970; 471, 1960). US 36 has a junction with Illinois 32. North on Illinois 32 6 m. to CERRO GORDO, in Piatt County, (368 pop., 1970; 1,067, 1960, dec. 28%). This was named for the battle of Cerro Gordo in the War with Mexico, 1847, when it was settled in 1855.

After crossing LAKE DECATUR US 36 enters DECATUR (90,397 pop. 1970). Decatur is at a junction with US 47-US 48 combined, from Champaign, where US 45 and Interstate 57 came from Chicago; US 51 from Bloomington, and Illinois 121, from Lincoln. See article on Decatur.

At 74 *m.* is a junction with the Lincoln Heritage Trail, which unites with US 36 for 44 miles (*see Tour 21*).

SPRINGFIELD, 118 *m.* (598 alt., 91,753 pop. 1970). Springfield is a hub of highways. US 36 proceeds directly into the heart of the city. It is also possible to bypass it. US 36 has a junction with Int. 55, which moves east and south of the city. US 54, which comes from Chicago by way of Kankakee, combines with US 36 at Springfield and continues west with it as far as 4 *m.* west of Pittsfield, where the two highways separate. Int. 55 follows the route of US 66.

BATES, 133 *m.,* with houses clustered about a white church and grain elevators, is at the west end of the Bates Experimental Road, built by the State Highway Department in 1921. The 2-mile stretch of highway had 63 kinds of paving material, periodically examined for comparative wear.

Between Bates and Jacksonville, US 36 passes through four agricultural centers, New Berlin, Alexander, Orleans, and Arnold, with nominal populations. The fertile countryside is a checkerboard of corn and wheat fields. A comfortable standard of living is shown by large and well-maintained farmhouses. The barns, an infallible barometer of agrarian economy, are frequently topped with cupolas, lightning rods, and weathervanes.

JACKSONVILLE, 154 *m.* (613 alt., 20,553 pop. 1970) is at a junction with US 67, to Rock Island, north, and Alton, south; also Illinois 78 and 104 (*see Tour 7*).

WINCHESTER, 171 *m.* (546 alt., 1,788 pop. 1970; 1,657, 1960, inc. 7%), seat of Scott County, had a grist mill as early as 1824, but was not platted until 1830 when, according the tradition, surveyors permitted a Kentuckian to name the townsite in exchange for a jug of whiskey.

The business district fronting the minute square consists of shops built in the late nineteenth century. In the square is the STEPHEN DOUGLAS MONUMENT, a life-size bronze of the Little Giant, who "taught his first school and began his legal career here in 1833-34." A nearby boulder marks the spot where Lincoln made his first speech on the Kansas-Nebraska issue. A building on Main Street just north of the public square occupies the site of the schoolhouse in which Stephen A. Douglas taught.

The SCOTT COUNTY COURTHOUSE, northeast corner of the square, a two-story brick and stone structure of Romanesque style designed by James Stuart, was built in 1885. A stone tablet on the courthouse lawn marks the site of the Aiken Tavern, in which Lincoln lodged in 1854.

West of Winchester the route traverses rolling hills along the valley of the Illinois River. The highway crosses the river on a lift bridge, ascends a winding road through outcrops of limestone, and emerges on agricultural uplands. At Detroit, 13 *m.,* (124 pop. 1970; 126, 1960) there is a junction with Illinois 100.

PITTSFIELD, 191 *m.* (725 alt., 4,244 pop. 1970; 4,089, 1960), seat of Pike County was founded by settlers from Pittsfield, Massachusetts. The site was purchased from the Government for $200. On May 5, 1833, eleven lots were sold and several others were reserved for public purposes. A courthouse and a Congregational church were subsequently built on the town square. Pork-packing became the chief local industry, the meat being packed in barrels made of white oak from the forests that flourished nearby. Cheese and dairy products are processed today.

Early Pittsfield was a genuine transplantation of New England culture. John Hay (1938-1905) private secretary to President Lincoln, ambassador to Great Britain (1897-98), Secretary of State under Presidents McKinley and Theodore Roosevelt, spent two years here as a student and spoke of the community as a center of "light and learning," especially during the circuit court season. In a single case involving $50, it is recorded, six of the eight participating lawyers later became United States Senators. Life as he saw it during his student days at Pittsfield, Hay portrayed in his Pike County Ballads. With John G. Nicolay, Hay collaborated in the ten-volume Abraham Lincoln: A History.

Dominating the Pittsfield skyline is the spire of PIKE COUNTY COURTHOUSE, a three-story structure of Indiana Limestone, designed by Henry Elliot and built in 1894. The Worthington House, 626 W. Washington St., built for a female academy was acquired in 1847 by Dr. Thomas Worthington, who entertained Abraham Lincoln, John Hay, and John G. Nicolay.

Abraham Lincoln was closely associated with Pittsfield. As early as 1839 he lost a case in the Pike County Circuit Court. During the 1856 presidential and congressional campaign he and U. S. Senator Lyman Trumbull addressed a Republican meeting here. His host, John G. Shastid, whom he had known in New Salem, acquainted him with John G. Nicolay, who was serving as printer's devil for the *Pike County Free Press*. Two years later Nicolay became Lincoln's private secretary.

Lincoln spoke in Winchester Sept. 28-29, 1858. After his address Winchester Republicans escorted him to Florence on the Illinois River, where Col. William Ross met him and drove him to his home in Pittsfield. Ross and Lincoln had both served in the Black Hawk War and in the Illinois General Assembly. On Sept. 30 Lincoln made an address in the Pittsfield Square, explaining how he differed with Douglas on the issues. Later he posed for two ambrotype photographs. One was eventually acquired by Oliver R. Barrett, collector of Lincolniana, who lived in Pittsfield when his father was a Methodist minister there. The photograph is now in the Library of Congress. (*Journal of the Illinois State Historical Society.*)

Pittsfield's EAST SCHOOL has been placed on the National Register of Historic Places by the National Park Service. The school was designed by John M. Van Osdel and erected during the Civil War. It was in use for 100 years and never has been altered. Van Osdel also designed the Executive Mansion at Springfield. The Pike County Historical Society uses the school as a museum and cultural center.

At 195 *m.*, or 4 *m.* west of Pittsfield, US 54 leaves US 36 and moves southwest toward the Mississippi River. It passes several small farm villages—New Hartford, Summer Hill, and Atlas, the latter a junction with Illinois 96, part of the Great River Road in Illinois. At Pike on the Mississippi River is the Champ Clark bridge (free) to Louisiana, Mo.

US 36 proceeds northwest.

BARRY, 206 *m.* (683 alt., 1,444 pop. 1970; 1,422, 1960), entered on a tree-arched street, is the trading center of a dairying, agricultural, and horticultural area, noted for its large shipments of fine apples.

West of Barry the highway traverses wooded hill country and then descends to the wide valley of Hadley Creek.

Old-fashioned tin awnings until recently projected from the facades of several shops in KINDERHOOK, 212 *m.* (471 alt., 281 pop. 1970; 276, 1960), a village built on a hillside. Once ubiquitous in Illinois towns, over-walk awnings of wood or tin have in recent years gone the way of cigar store Indians.

US 36 crosses the Missouri Line, 225 *m.*, on the Mark Twain Memorial Bridge (free), spanning the Mississippi to Hannibal, Mo. (*see Missouri Guide*).

~~~~~~

Tour 19

ACROSS ILLINOIS ON THE OLD NATIONAL ROAD

(Terre Haute, Ind.)—Marshall—Effingham—Vandalia—Greenville-Chain-of-Rocks Bridge—St. Louis, Mo. Diversion to Highland—Collinsville—East St. Louis; US 40, Int. 70, Int. 270, Branch US 40. Indiana line to Missouri line, 158 *m.*

In a straight diagonal across Illinois from the Indiana line to the Mississippi River US 40 follows the original route of the famous National Road as far as Vandalia, its terminus in 1837, and then proceeds the rest of the way on a highway built by the State.

The National Road was authorized by Congress March 29, 1806, and approved by President Thomas Jefferson, after years of dispute between Ohio settlers who demanded the road and southern legislators who feared it would drain their population. It started at Cumberland, Maryland, on the Potomac, and was generally known as the Cumberland Road. It was to be paid for by the sale of public lands, and actually started a huge rush to buy land along its route. In Illinois alone, sales of land from 1819 to 1837 reached more than $10,500,000.

Construction of the road was one of the momentous (and exasperating) achievements of American enterprise. A 66-ft. wide clearance had to be hacked and shovelled through a wilderness of oak, intertwined underbrush, over hills and gullies, across creeks and rivers. The 30-ft. roadway was surfaced with stone that had to be broken en route with hammers and cleared of tree stumps by horses and oxen, while labor camps had to be built and provisioned. Contract labor was often unreliable, but no slaves were ever employed on the great road.

The National Road, bore a never-ending load of traffic. Great freight wagons lumbered over its length, crammed to overflowing with manufactured goods for the frontier, and returned laden with raw materials for the Eastern seaboard. Travelers of every description ate, drank, sang, and cursed in its roadside taverns and stage houses. Andrew Jackson, William Henry Harrison, James Polk, Henry Clay, and John Marshall rubbed elbows and exchanged a passing word with teamsters, actors, settlers, and soldiers of fortune. The east-west mail was carried on the road; in 1837 it took about 94 hours to travel from Washington to St. Louis.

In Illinois, as elsewhere along the route, stagecoach stations often bloomed into villages. Later, as the railroads inched their way westward and the State maintained a steady growth, these mushroom communities either dissolved into ghost towns or expanded into thriving cities. Today, as deserted sites or as prosperous county seats, they appear at short intervals along the cross-country chain that is US 40.

When the Interstate system was planned, this was the logical route for an expressway from Indiana to Missouri. Interstate 70, lacking a segment or two, easily bypasses the cities, with junctions that give access to US 40, which passes through them. Both Int. 70 and US 40 have junctions with the principal north-south highways.

US 40 crosses the Indiana Line, 0 *m.,* 8 miles west of Terre Haute, Indiana (*see Indiana Guide*).

Entering Illinois, the route dips into four or five deep wide valleys which form a natural trench-work draining this productive region.

MARSHALL, 9.5 *m.* (606 alt., 3,468 pop. 1970; 3,270, 1960, inc. 6%), a city and seat of Clark County. It is located about 16 *m.* west of Terre Haute, Ind. The first log cabin was built here in 1835. When the survey for the National Road was completed Governor Joseph Duncan and William B. Archer chose a spot between the State line and Vandalia for a town and Archer named it for John Marshall, Chief Justice of the United States. At this point a road ran from Chicago to Shawneetown, which is now Illinois 1.

Marshall is at the junction with the Lincoln Heritage Trail (*see Tour 21*).

West of Marshall, US 40 crosses a Stone Arch Bridge built by Army engineers as part of the Cumberland Road. Each stone in this bondless type of bridge was shaped to exact proportions by hand, and clamped together with keys to prevent slipping. When this section of US 40 was realigned and resurfaced the bridge structure was also repaired. Today, traffic races across the same span that carried prairie schooners and stagecoaches many years ago.

CLARK CENTER, 14.4 *m.*, a tiny hamlet, dates from 1835. Its prospects were bright at its founding, but they were blighted in 1837, when Marshall was designated the county seat. Clark Center was a stagecoach stop on the Cumberland Road.

MARTINSVILLE, 20 *m.* (562 alt., 1,374 pop. 1970; 1,351, 1960), on the North Fork of the Embarras River, was platted in 1833 by Joseph Martin and became a trading center and stagecoach stop. Although incorporated as a city in Clark County it remained a farm village until 1904, when the discovery of oil and natural gas in this area gave it a share in the boom that followed. Storage tanks were built to make this a supply depot, and after the local oil ran out it stored oil from Texas and Oklahoma. The city has a few industries, including a maker of castings. A bronze plaque on a boulder at the high school grounds commemorates the centennial of Martinsville.

CASEY, 26 *m.* (648 alt., 2,994 pop. 1970; 2,890, 1960) in Clark County, incorporated as a city in 1871 when the Pennsylvania Railroad arrived. It shared in the oil boom and since has been attracting light industry.

GREENUP, 36 *m.* (554 alt., 1,618 pop. 1970; 1,477, 1960) near the Embarras River, is located at a junction with Illinois 130 (to Charleston) and Illinois 121 (to US 45 and Mattoon). Greenup was named for William C. Greenup, clerk of the Illinois Territorial Legislature, 1812-1815, who came to this site as the Government agent for the building of the National Road and obtained incorporation as a village in 1836.

West of Greenup US 40 slips down to the Embarras River bottoms and passes the Cumberland County Fairgrounds bordering the river, where exhibits of farm products and racing are held annually, usually in mid-August.

JEWETT, 41 *m.* (587 alt., 211 pop. 1970; 238, 1960) is a tiny village developed from the former town of Pleasantville, a stagecoach stop. WOODBURY, 44 *m.,* is a similar village with a small lake.

TEUTOPOLIS, 55 *m.* (602 alt., 1,249 pop. 1970; 1,130, 1960, inc. 9%) was founded as a German Catholic community in 1838 by a Cincinnati group which invested $16,000 collected from prospective German immigrants and bought 10,000 acres at this spot. The immigrants came down the Ohio River to Cincinnati, then went to St. Louis by water and overland to their new site on the National Road. They built a church and a windmill, and raised farm products that they sold at Marshall, 40 miles away. Some took up sheep raising. ST. JOSEPH'S SEMINARY, south of US 40, was established in 1860 by Franciscans. The community was known for its piety and the strict discipline that outlawed all frontier excesses.

EFFINGHAM, 59 *m.* (591 alt., 9,458 pop. 1970; 8,172, 1960,

inc. 15%) seat of Effingham County, is an important highway center for south central Illinois. Not only does Int. 70 run parallel with US 40 to St. Louis but Int. 57 comes down from Chicago parallel with US 45. There are also junctions with Illinois 33 and Illinois 37, which connect with other routes in this part of central Illinois. The city has freight service on the Illinois Central and Penn Central railroads, is served by Greyhound Bus Lines and Continental Trailways, and the County Memorial Airport, 3.6 m. south on Illinois 37. *See Effingham under Tour 3.*

A marker, 62.2 m., at a dirt road immediately south of the Pennsylvania Railroad bridge, indicates the site of EWINGTON, named for W. L. D. Ewing, Vandalia statesman, whose bill was responsible for inducing the legislature to create the county. Ewington was the first county seat.

A few hundred feet south of the marker are the last remains of this once important village. Here, in the age-worn Ewington Cemetery, are well-preserved headstones over the graves of early settlers, some of whom were soldiers in the American Revolution.

ALTAMONT, 71 m. (1,929 pop. 1970; 1,656, 1960, inc. 16%) was named for a rise of ground about a mile to the west. It was organized as a village in 1872 and is today a city at a junction of the Baltimore & Ohio and the Penn Central. Its principal manufactures as blue jeans.

ST. ELMO, 76.8 m. (618 alt., 1,676 pop. 1970; 1,503, 1960, inc. 11%) in Fayette County, was settled in 1830 by a group of Kentucky Catholics. It is in the center of an oil field that has produced moderately since the 1930's.

BROWNSTOWN, 85.8 m. (689 pop. 1970; 659, 1960) is a farm village in Fayette County.

VANDALIA, 90 m. (503 alt., 5,160 pop. 1970) on the Kaskaskia River, is at a junction with US 51 (north to Decatur, south to Centralia). *For description see Tour 4.*

Vandalia was the terminus of the National Road, generally known as the Cumberland Road because it began at Cumberland, Maryland, on the Potomac, voted by Congress and approved by President Jefferson. The covered wagons of settlers that had filled the road in Ohio in the 1820's were moving westward to Vandalia in the 1830's and often pushing on into southeastern Illinois. That road was nothing like the smooth concrete highway that the motorist uses today. Philip D. Jordan in *The National Road* (1948) quotes one traveler's view of what it looked like a few miles east of Vandalia. Parts of it ended in swamps and other sections were full of stumps. No effort was made to surface the road with crushed stone or gravel. Ruts in the center were leveled by a plow. Sometimes farmers "blocked the pike with fences, not caring that such antics forced travelers to detour through wet and spongy fields which sucked at wagon wheels and sapped the strength of horses." He described the newcomers:

"The early settlers, clad in buckskin and coonskin caps, were men and women from Tennessee and Kentucky, . . . They handled long rifles with ease and grace. They liked the taste of wild meat and could tree a coon with skill born of long experience. One pioneer knocked over 184 in a single season. Some settlers held that slavery was good, others felt it was a sin. As the years passed no topic in south central Illinois provoked more heat and less light than slavery, unless it was the road itself."

MULBERRY GROVE, 101 *m.* (559 alt., 697 pop.), ships molding sand from large deposits in nearby Hurricane Creek.

GREENVILLE, 110 *m.* (563 alt., 4,631 pop. 1970; 4,569, 1960), settled first in 1815 and today the seat of Bond County, is a hilly prosperous looking town with fine large houses. It has attracted a concern that manufactures steel balls for crushing concrete. The De Moulin Brothers & Company plant, manufactures such unusual articles as costumes and paraphernalia for lodge ceremonies, banners, and circus uniforms.

Greenville was the boyhood home of Robert G. Ingersoll (1833-99), Attorney-General of Illinois (1867-1869), orator and agnostic. In 1851 the Congregational Church called his father to its pulpit. Young Bob, then a devout studious youth of 18, remained here studying law for two years.

GREENVILLE COLLEGE, 315 E. College Ave., is an independent institution devoted to higher education for young men and women under Christian influence. In 1892 the Central Illinois Conference of the Free Methodist Church bought Almira College, which had been founded in 1855 as a Baptist school for women. In May, 1893, the new institution became Greenville College, no longer church-owned but operating in the Wesleyan tradition.

An enterprising educator, James P. Slade (1837-1908) personally bought Almira College in 1881 for $10,000. It is believed that he mortgaged his home to do so. Almira had only one brick building, now William T. Hogue Hall, the administrative center of Greenville College. After Slade sold Almira College in 1882 he became Supt. of Schools of East St. Louis, at $2,000 annual salary Supt. of Schools of St. Clair County at Belleville, and State Supt. of Public Instruction.

Greenville College offers degrees of bachelor of arts, bachelor of science in education, and bachelor of music education, and certain professional and pre-professional courses. By affiliation with the College of Engineering at the University of Illinois and New York University a student may obtain a bachelor of arts degree from Greenville and a bachelor of science in engineering in a five-year plan. In similar fashion pre-legal, pre-medical, pre-medical technology, and nursing courses are available, and there is a pre-seminary program for candidates for the ministry.

The oldest building on the campus is the William T. Hogue Hall, which once housed all of Almira College. It now contains the administrative offices. Marston Hall brings together the LaDue Memorial Chapel of 1906 and a new classroom building of 1961. The Ruby E. Dare Library, built in 1950, was enlarged by one-third in 1970 and has available 65,000 books, 390 periodicals and 1,000 recordings. In 1960 the college completed the H. J. Long Gymnasium, which seats 1,600; it is attached to the original Burritt Gymnasium of 1913, now used for individual instruction. The college has added many new facilities in biological, chemical, and physics laboratories. Residence halls accomodate 570 students. The cost of tuition, fees, board and lodging is estimated at between $2,234 and $2,408 a year. In the fall of 1971 Greenville College enrolled 769 students and had a faculty of 60.

Right from Greenville on Illinois 140 to 106-acre Greenville City Park, constructed largely by WPA labor. The park, which includes 25 acres of woods and a lake (*swimming, boating, fishing*), is the result of 40 years of campaigning and fund-collecting by the clubwomen of Greenville. The women planned either an opera house in Greenville or a pleasant recreational spot in the vicinity; they chose the latter when WPA assistance was offered for such a project.

Settled in 1838, POCAHONTAS, 119 *m*. (515 alt., 764 pop. 1970; 718, 1960) a village in Bond County, was one of the numerous stagecoach stops on the Cumberland Road. Today it derives part of its income from coal mines in the region.

HIGHLAND, 129 *m*. (545 alt., 5,981 pop. 1970; 4,943, 1960, inc. 26%) has many descendants of Swiss immigrants who came to this part of Illinois in the 1830 decade. First settlement is traced to families from Kentucky and North Carolina who came around 1804. Among them was Joseph Duncan, who became justice of the peace, an important office in which he served 40 years. In 1831 Dr. Caspar Koepfli of Sursee, Switzerland, inspired by the book of a German traveler in the Midwest, led a party of 15 compatriots to Illinois and approved the site of Highland, to which other Swiss immigrants soon followed.

The best-known of these early Swiss was the poet, Heinrich Bosshard, who lived in Highland from 1851 until his death in 1877. Here Bosshard composed *Sempacher Lied,* part of which was incorporated in the Swiss national anthem. In Lindenthal Park, east end of Lindenthal Avenue, is the Bosshard Monument, a granite memorial to the poet.

As a Swiss community, Highland early acquired a reputation for its dairy products. In 1884 John Mayenard brought from Switzerland a new process for preserving milk and established a factory here, which developed until the enterprise had eight branches, with total assets of many millions. After a strike here in 1920, the original factory was closed and the headquarters of the company were moved to St. Louis.

Among the varied industrial establishments of Highland is the Wicks Organ Company plant, 5th and Zschokke Sts. In 1914 this firm gained international attention by developing a direct electric action which greatly simplified the operation and maintenance of its organs.

Highland has a mayor and four aldermen, and a city manager. Int. 70 is two miles north. US 66, combined with Int. 55, is 14 miles west. The city has freight service of the Penn-Central. There are a number of makers of precision tools and electronic equipment, and the Dow,

Jones & Co. plant, printing the *Wall Street Journal* for southern Illinois, Missouri, and Kentucky, is located here. The *Highland News Leader* is its weekly newspaper. The Highland-Winet Airport is the site of large glider operations and hq of the St. Louis Soaring Club and glider school.

The Louis Latzer Memorial Library, erected in 1929 and remodelled in 1971, circulates more than 18,000 vols. and is a member of the Lewis and Clark Library System. Indoor sports center is the Weinheimer Memorial Bldg., which has a large auditorium-gymnasium, while the most popular outdoor recreation area is Silver Lake, the city's reservoir, which is 5 *m.* long and cost $1,000,000.

West of Highland, US 40 enters the major dairy region of the St. Louis area. Cows dot the hillsides black, white, and brown. Small modern farms, each with a gleaming white barn, appear along the highway.

In the vicinity of ST. JACOB, 134.8 *m.* (508 alt., 659 pop. 1970; 520, 1960), a dairy village, a fort was built during the Indian scares of 1812 to protect the pioneer families. Fort Chilton, was never attacked and was abandoned soon after the Indians had been overcome. No trace of the early stockade remains, but numerous stories about it have survived. One relates that Abraham Howard, commander of the fort, became so enraged at the audacity of a troublesome Indian in the neighborhood that he set out alone and chased him 90 miles through the wilderness. Howard returned days later with a scalp.

TROY, 141 *m.* (549 alt., 2,144 pop. 1970; 1,778, 1960, inc. 20%), in Madison County, is an outgrowth of three villages—Columbia, Mechanicsburg, and Brookside. The first, Columbia, was a tiny community huddled around a tavern and a grist mill built by John G. Jarvis about 1814. Five years later land speculators bought the property and renamed it Troy for the New York town. Mechanicsburg was platted in 1836, and merged with Troy in 1857. The union proved a happy one. Nearby coal fields continued their productivity; in 1888 a railroad connected the town with East St. Louis; in 1891 Brookside joined the fold, and in the following year Troy was incorporated as a city.

US 40 touches the southernmost edge of Troy, while Int. 70, from which US 40 is now separated, proceeds straight west about 2 *m.* north of Troy. The combined US 66 and Int. 55, coming down from Springfield, have a junction with Int. 70, which merges with them. The motorist who wishes to bypass East St. Louis now continues west on the highway that is designated Int. 270, to:

GLEN CARBON (1,897 pop. 1970; 1,241, 1960) a village of Madison County that grew up around coal mines, which shut down in 1931. Its working force is employed in industries of the area.

Int. 270 crosses the Missouri line on the Chain of Rocks Bridge, 158 *m.* West of where US 40 and Int. 70 started.

After leaving Troy, US 40 combines with US 66, Int. 55, and Int. 70 for East St. Louis. At 5 *m.* is MARYVILLE (809 pop. 1970; 675, 1960). Here Illinois 159, coming from Edwardsville, has a junction with the highways, and moves south through Collinsville on Vandalia Ave.

US Branch Route 40 leaves US 40 at Maryville, follows Vandalia Ave. and Main St. in Collinsville and turns west on the boundary line of Madison and St. Clair Counties.

COLLINSVILLE, 7.9 *m*. (473 alt., 17,773 pop. 1970; 14,217, 1960, inc. 25%) in both Madison and St. Clair Counties, was incorporated as a village in 1856 and as a city in 1872. Its first railroad came in 1869 and today it has freight service of the Penn Central. During the latter years of the last century it shipped a large quantity of the bituminous coal of the region, but mining has been greatly curtailed.

Collinsville was named for William Collins, one of five brothers from Litchfield, Connecticut, who established a settlement here in 1817. Pooling their interests, the Collins brothers, models of Yankee industry and jacks-of-all-trades, built a store, a blacksmith shop, a shoe shop, a wagon shop, a sawmill, a tannery, a distillery, and a small church, in which they took turns reading the services. The oldest brother, William, suffering a dearth of ideas for suitable sermons, wrote to the Rev. Lyman Beecher, his former pastor in Litchfield, asking for suggestions. The Rev. Mr. Beecher quickly forwarded six temperance tracts, the substance of which William passed on to his congregation.

After one of these sermons on abstemiousness, so it is said, his wife asked, "Doesn't it look peculiar to be preaching against strong drink on Sunday and then be making and selling whiskey on Monday?" William wrestled with his conscience and the following day wrecked the distillery, which caused his brothers to move away from the village. When William died a decade later, his widow had a townsite platted and sold lots, stipulating in each deed that whiskey was not to be made or sold on them; the courts later nullified this restriction.

The frame house built by the Collins family in 1821 was a well-known landmark for more than a century, but since has been removed. Another unique enterprise, a shop where cowbells were made by hand, started in 1880, also has yielded to the march of time.

Most marked in this area has been the decline of the miners' organizations with the closing of the coal mines. Five strong locals of the United Mine Workers, who dominated the labor market, built the Miners' Institute at Main and Clinton Sts. By assessing themselves one per cent of their earnings the total cost, $140,000, was paid by 1925. The miners have found employment elsewhere, but they still own the building, which is known as the BAC Miners' Theater and has the only stage in the city.

Bethel Baptist Church, 5 *m*. southeast of Collinsville, built 1840, was used to shelter fugitive slaves before the Civil War.

West of the city limits on US BR 40 is the FAIRMOUNT PARK JOCKEY CLUB, which has racing meets in spring and fall. On the south side of the highway is the EAST ST. LOUIS DOWNTOWN AIR PARK, 4.5 *m*. east of East St. Louis.

CAHOKIA MOUNDS STATE PARK, now enlarged to 590 acres, is a National Historic Landmark that protects the largest surviving aggregation of mounds built by Indian tribes that lived here from 800 to about 1500 A. D.

The Museum, a low brick building, exhibits axes, pipes, pottery, arrowheads, skulls, and miscellaneous artifacts unearthed in nearby mounds. North of the parking lot looms the bulk of MONKS MOUND, the largest in the United States, named for the Trappists who built a monastery at its base in 1809. In 1813 the monks, decimated by fever, returned to France. A truncated pyramid with four terraces, Monks Mound is 104 ft. wide and 1,000 ft. long.

From the time of the early French settlers, the origin of the bulbous hills in this region had prompted speculation. Superstitious pioneers refused to tempt the wrath of native gods by cultivating the land. Skeptics who boldly plowed the rich level fields were sometimes unnerved by turning up human bones. After intensive surveys of the mounds, the first in 1921, Professor W. K. Moorehead of the University of Illinois concluded that they were built between 1200 and 1500 A. D. by a people whose culture showed distinct Southern influences, much more advanced than that of other early American Indians. He found that the tumuli were the hub of a village that extended 7 or 8 miles along Cahokia and Canteen Creeks. At one time more than 300 lesser mounds spread out fan-like from Monks Mound, but the cultivation of farms and the coming of villages obliterated many. The best of these are now in the Cahokia Mounds State Park.

South of the museum are Temple Mound and Red Mound, the latter named for the red earthenware it contained. Nearby is a mound made of dark pliable soil; the others in the Cahokia group are of clay and gumbo. Many fragments taken from Round Top Mound, south of the museum, suggest that it was a site for the manufacture of pottery. Opposite Round Top is another mound of similar shape in which were found flint tools used to decorate pottery. Farther south is a broad shallow pit, occasionally filled by rains and known as Lake Cahokia. The mound builders probably dug much of the earth used in construction from this pit.

US Branch Route 40 skirts FAIRMOUNT CITY, 15 *m.* (420 alt., 2,769 pop. 1970; 2,688, 1960), an industrial suburb of East St. Louis. Fairmount City began life in 1910, fathered by a roundhouse of the Pennsylvania Railroad. It was first called Willow Town; its present name was adopted in 1914 when it was incorporated as a village. During a prolonged strike in 1918 at the local zinc works Mexican workers were imported. They became rooted here and members of their families continue to be employed in local plants.

EAST ST. LOUIS, 19 *m.* (69,996 pop. 1970) *See article on East St. Louis.*

Tour 20

THE OLD TRACE ACROSS ILLINOIS

(Vincennes, Ind.) Lawrenceville—Olney—Clay City—Flora—Salem—Carlyle—Lebanon—Scott Air Force Base—Belleville—Shrine of Our Lady of the Snows—East St. Louis.

US 50. Indiana to Missouri, 151 *m.*

US 50, in following the old Trace Road, marked out by Indians and buffalo, runs through rolling broken prairie west of Lawrenceville, across the lowlands of the Embarras and Little Wabash Rivers, and descends into the American Bottom to reach the Mississippi at East St. Louis.

The Trace Road connected Bear Grass, now Louisville, Kentucky, with Cahokia on the Mississippi, a few miles below East St. Louis. From 1805 to 1824 post riders on horseback carried the mail over the road. In 1824 a four-horse stage and mail route was established; in 1837, under an ambitious State improvement program, the road was graded. Bridges and culverts were hewn from white oak felled along the road, and between Vincennes and Lawrenceville miles of trestle-work were constructed. But too many expensive improvement schemes soon plunged the young State into bankruptcy, and the Trace Road was turned over to a private company, which completed the work, planking the treacherous swamp sections. Toll gates were set up and all travelers paid tribute to the company. Eventually the plank road decayed and the State first graveled the highway and then, with the advent of the automobile, paved it with concrete and eliminated many dangerous curves.

US 50 crosses the Indiana Line, 0 *m.*, on the LINCOLN MEMORIAL BRIDGE, spanning the Wabash River from Vincennes, Indiana. The bridge, erected jointly by Illinois and Indiana in 1931, marks the place where the Lincoln family crossed to Illinois in 1830. It commands an excellent view of the Wabash and of the George Rogers Clark Memorial on the Indiana bank.

At 0.5 *m.*, at the Illinois end of the bridge approach, is the junction with the Lincoln Heritage Trail (*see Tour 21*).

LAWRENCEVILLE, 8.8 *m.* (472 alt., 5,863 pop. 1970; 5,492, 1960), lies on the west bank of the Embarras River, so named by French explorers because of the difficulty of crossing the stream at flood time, when the river, joined with the Wabash, spread over lowlands to form a lake 7 or 8 miles wide. Lawrenceville, the seat of Lawrence

County since 1821 when both were organized, was named for Capt. James Lawrence, commander of the *Chesapeake* in the War of 1812, remembered for his dying exclamation: "Don't give up the ship."

Lawrenceville is in the heart of the Lawrence County oil fields, and oil refining is its principal industry. The first paraffin-free oil was produced here in 1924. Pipe lines convey oil to local refineries from fields in Illinois, Kentucky, and Oklahoma. In 1906 the first oil well in Lawrence County was brought in. Gushers were frequent, and the county enjoyed a boom. Lawrnce quickly became first among oil-producing counties of Illinois; production in the field enabled Illinois to rank third among the States in the output of crude oil in 1907 and for many years thereafter, but has now declined to a negligible amount.

The French were the first settlers in the Wabash River region, many entering Illinois from Vincennes, an old French settlement and the capital of Indiana Territory. Captain Toussaint Dubois, veteran of the American Revolution, settled about 1780 in this vicinity, where he built a house and planted the first orchard in the region. His holdings included 1,000 acres within the present city of Lawrenceville. Jessie K. Dubois, the captain's youngest son, was a friend of Abraham Lincoln, with whom he served in the legislature. He accompanied the President-elect to Washington for his first inauguration, and four years later was one of those who brought Lincoln's body home to Springfield and served as a pall bearer at his funeral.

A large granite boulder, in the yard of the Elks Club, 12th and Walnut Sts., marks the site of the first circuit court held in the county on June 4, 1821.

The Lawrence County Courthouse, of red brick and stone trim, was built in 1889. A bronze tablet on the wall of the north entrance honors 21 Revolutionary War soldiers buried in the county.

The first woman executed in Illinois, Elizabeth Reed, was tried, convicted, and hanged at Lawrenceville in 1845. She was convicted of poisoning her husband so that she might marry another.

Twin millstones, on the high school lawn, 8th and Walnut Sts., relics from the old Brown Mill on the Embarras River several miles downstream from Lawrenceville, show plainly the wear of many years.

Linco Tank Farm, 12 *m.*, contains oil storage tanks. A deep moat to prevent the spread of fire surrounds each of the 35,000-barrel tanks; steel pumps mark many oil wells. Local pipe lines connect with a nation-wide trunk system of pipe lines at Martinsville, some 40 miles to the north.

BRIDGEPORT, 13.1 *m.* (449 alt., 2,262 pop. 1970; 2,260, 1960), was the center of the early oil boom; the first producing sand was named Bridgeport. A large oil company maintains a pumping station and supply yards here. Otherwise, Bridgeport is a typical prairie town—a trading center, the home of retired farmers, a well-ordered community of schools, churches, and modest homes.

SUMNER, 18 *m.* (1,201 pop. 1970; 1,030, 1960), is an incorporated city in Lawrence County. Near it is Red Hills State Park, an area of 948 acres with swimming, boating, and camping available. This has the first park lake in Illinois built in part with Federal funds.

OLNEY, 31 *m.* (484 alt., 8,974 pop. 1970; 8,780, 1960), seat of Richland County, was named for John Olney, lawyer and lieutenant in the Civil War, the lifelong friend of Judge Aaron Shaw, who successfully campaigned to have the site chosen as county seat and named for Olney. A shipping and trading center, Olney has some light industry and food processing.

Olney is a city of fine old mansions, surrounded by lawns and large trees. During the early summer season the houses are covered with crimson ramblers. The Olney *Times* is said to have been the first newspaper to support Lincoln for the Presidency. The issue of November 1, 1858, bore a streamer reading: "For President in 1860, Abraham Lincoln of Illinois." William Beck, the owner, lived to see Lincoln elected, but died before the inauguration.

The Richland County Courthouse, a three-story, white stone building of Colonial design, with four fluted columns across the front, is surmounted with a clock steeple.

Larchmond, on the east side of Morgan St., south of Baird St., is a white, brick house of Colonial design, the former residence of Dr. Robert Ridgway, naturalist and one-time curator of the U.S. National Museum in Washington. The attractive grounds are open and contain many shrubs planted by Dr. Ridgway, founder of the Ornithologists Union, who died in 1929.

Olney publicizes itself as the Home of the White Squirrels. In 1902 a hunter captured a pair of albino squirrels and displayed them in a cage. A citizen ordered them released in the woods. Soon numbers of white squirrels appeared and the area became famous for this variety. The city adopted the white squirrel as an emblem and in 1925 made it unlawful to kill a squirrel with a car or take one out of town. Police and firemen wear the squirrel on a shoulder patch. In 1943 the State Legislature adopted a law prohibiting the taking of white squirrels.

Olney is administered by a mayor and four commissioners. The *Olney Daily Mail* is its newspaper. It has freight service on the Baltimore & Ohio and a branch of the Illinois Central, and access to the Olney-Noble Airport, 4.8 *m.* west of Olney. It has 25 churches, the Richland Memorial Hospital, and Weber Medical Clinic. In 1962 Olney Central College was established under the State junior college plan. It has a faculty of 60 and enrolls approx. 1,000.

Olney Carnegie Library was built in 1903 and remodelled in 1963. It has about 22,000 books and circulates approx. 62,000 annually. It is a member of the Cumberland Trail Library System.

NOBLE, 39 *m.* (719 pop. 1970; 761, 1960) is a farm village in Richland County. Illinois 50 crosses the Big Muddy and the Little Wabash Rivers to CLAY CITY, 44 *m.* (1,049 pop. 1970; 1,144, 1960, dec. 8.3%) a village in Clay County. It adjoins the site of Maysville, first county seat, which faded when the original railroad, the Ohio & Mississippi, later the Baltimore & Ohio, bypassed it. The Shawneetown-

Vandalia Road crossed the old Trace here. The first oil well in Clay County was brought in on Feb. 26, 1937, southeast of Clay City, and a mild boom followed. The city is a distributing point for fruit and a trading point for farm machinery and fertilizer.

FLORA, 54 *m.* (490 alt., 5,283 pop. 1970; 5,331, 1960) was incorporated in 1857, after the Baltimore & Ohio Railroad made it a station on its main line. It is bypassed by Illinois 50 and served by US 45. It is an area of fruit orchards and has profited also by the oil production in the Clay City field. Several large corporations have divisions here, notably Anaconda Wire & Cable and International Shoe Flora has excellent library facilities because of the hq of the Cumberland Trail Library System, erected here in 1970. *See FLORA, Tour 20.*

SALEM, 80 *m.* (6,187 pop. 1970) seat of Marion County, was laid out on the Vincennes-St. Louis stage route, now US 50, in 1813. It is in the center of the Clay County oil area. It has a junction with north-south Illinois 37 and west 1 *m.* is a junction with the Chicago-Cairo route, Int. 57. *See Tour 4.*

ODIN, 86 *m.* (527 alt., 1,263 pop. 1970; 1,242, 1960), a peaceful mining and farming center, was known in the 1860's as "the hell-hole of the Illinois Central" because of a form of piracy practiced by young hoodlums of the community. Concealing themselves along the railroad embankment until the train stopped, they would scramble on board and scuttle off with the passengers' luggage.

SANDOVAL, 90 *m.* (509 alt., 1,332 pop. 1970; 1,356, 1960), is at a junction with US 51, 6 *m.* north of Centralia. (*See Tour 4*). West of Sandoval the highway traverses prairie lands underlain by seams of coal and small oil pools.

The Carlyle State Fish Hatchery, 102.8 *m.,* distributes fingerlings throughout the State every year; graveled drives permit approach to the three large ponds, in which bass, bluegill, and catfish are hatched.

A Suspension Bridge, 102.8 *m.*, built in 1860, was once the principal means of crossing the Kaskaskia River on the St. Louis-Vincennes Trail. Its 35-foot towers supported a span 280 feet long.

CARLYLE, 103.7 *m.* (461 alt., 3,139 pop. 1970; 2,902, 1960, inc. 8%) seat of Clinton County. It is located near the foot of Lake Carlyle, a man-made lake covering 18,729 acres in Clinton and Fayette Counties, impounded from the waters of the Kaskaskia River and East Fork of the Kaskaskia, on the west bank of which is the new ELDON HAZLETT STATE PARK, open for fishing, boating, and other recreation. Here also is the SOUTH SHORE STATE PARK.

Carlyle is the site of John Hill's Fort, erected to protect settlers from Indian attacks. A local legend tells that a settler named Young was killed and buried near the fort. When the man's mother declared she had sewed $5,000 in his clothes attempts were made to find it, but without success.

In 1836, when Indian forays had ceased, a notice posted throughout the area proclaimed: "Whereas, the town of Carlyle has been troubled with divers nuisances such as hogs, dogs, etc., notice is hereby given that on Tuesday, the 10th of January next, there will be a meeting of the town of Carlyle at the schoolhouse for the purpose of incorporating the said town; all persons interested will please to attend."

BREESE, 112 *m.* (458 alt., 2,885 pop. 1970; 2,461, 1960) originally a coal mining center, incorporated as a city, was named in honor of Judge Sidney Breese (1800-1876), eminent Illinois jurist and one-time resident of the city. King Edward VII, then Prince of Wales, spent two days hunting near the village in 1860. While lost in the Santa Fe Bottoms south of Breese, the prince somewhat testily ordered a settler to lead him back to the village, so it is said. The man refused, and when the prince offered him money, declared he was "not for hire."

TRENTON, 121 *m.* (498 alt., 2,328 pop. 1970; 1,866, 1960), incorporated in 1865 as a city in Clinton County, grew with the development of the Illinois coal fields in 1876. Today it is a farming center bordering fertile Looking Glass Prairie, which Charles Dickens described in his *American Notes* as a "typical American prairie."

LEBANON, 128 *m.* (457 alt., 3,564 pop. 1970; 2,863, 1960, inc. 24%), a city in St. Clair County, is one of the oldest settlements in this part of southern Illinois, having been laid out first in 1814. It was incorporated Feb. 16, 1857. It is at a junction of US 50 and Illinois 4 (north-south).

The Mermaid Inn, 112 East St. Louis St., preserved by the Lebanon Historical Society, was built in 1830 on the old Vincennes-St. Louis highway by a retired sea captain. It had as guests Abraham Lincoln and Charles Dickens. In his *American Notes* Dickens declared that the Mermaid Inn "compared favorably with any village ale house of a homely kind in England."

McKENDREE COLLEGE was founded as Lebanon Seminary by a group of Methodist pioneers in 1828. In 1835, when Peter Cartwright was president of the board of trustees, the name was changed to McKendree College to honor Bishop William McKendree, who had presented the school with 480 acres of land in Shiloh Valley. It is the oldest college in the United States continually under Methodist support, and emphasizes a program of liberal arts with academic distinction. Students with six semesters of high school work may qualify for admission after taking the ATC test. The college has five divisions: Languages and Literature, Science and Mathematics; Social Science, including business and economics; Teacher Preparation, and Fine Arts. Students may elect pre-professional courses.

On the shaded campus the spire of the college chapel rises above mellowed brick buildings of older decades as well as over six major buildings of recent construction on the north campus: the library, Campus Center, a science hall, cafeteria, and dormitories. In 1972 the college enrolled 468 and had a faculty of 40. General tuition costs $1,450 a year; music tuition, $1,400, total cost for tuition and board and room in the dormitories is estimated at $2,946 to $3,065 a year. McKendree is a member of the Prairie College Conference and its teams make records in basketball, baseball, tennis, golf, and bowling. The

Stagecrafters and the Lewis & Clark History Club lead in student activities.

Immediately west of a State Picnic Ground, 130.8 *m.*, is the site of ROCK SPRING SEMINARY, founded in 1827 by John Mason Peck, religious author and educator. The seminary was removed in 1831 to Alton, where it later became Shurtleff College.

At 131.8 *m.* is a junction with Illinois 158.

Left on Illinois 158 4.3 *m.* to SCOTT AIR FORCE BASE, headquarters of the Military Airlift Command (MAC) and subordinate units: Aerospace Rescue and Recovery Service, Air Weather Service, Aerospace Audio-Visual Services, Aerospace Cartographic and Geodetic Service, 375th Aeromedical Airlift Wing, 89th Special Airlift Wing, 443d Military Airlift Wing (training) and 1400th Air Base Wing (administrative).

The Base was founded in 1917, covers 2,396.35 acres and has more than 800 buildings, many of them of recent construction, for all the older facilities are being replaced. Flyers were trained here during World War I. Between the wars the Base was used by Army lighter-than-air ships. From 1940 to 1957 it was training base for communications specialists. Today Scott has many other responsibilities, and there is continuous reorganization and augmentation. Belleville and the surrounding area profits by the Base, for in one fiscal year ending July 1, 1970, it expended $144,824,671, a share going to civilian employees who live in Belleville.

The Base was named for Corporal Frank S. Scott, the first enlisted man to die in an air crash, which occurred at the first aviation school at College Point, Md.

US 50 skirts the edge of O'FALLON, 134 *m.* (550 alt., 7,268 pop. 1970; 4,018, 1960, inc. 80%), named for the town site owner, developed in 1854 along what is now the Baltimore & Ohio Railroad. Farming, mining, and manufacturing have sustained the town at various periods. It is now essentially a residential community, many of its workers finding employment in Scott Air Force Base and East St. Louis.

At 138 *m.* is a junction with State 159.

BELLEVILLE, 6.5 *m.* south on Illinois 159 from US 50 (400-700 alt., 41,699 pop. 1970; 37,264, 1960, inc. 11.9%) is the seat and second largest city of St. Clair County, which had a total population of 285,176 in 1970, including East St. Louis. It is located on the eastern bluffs of the American Bottom, in the heart of a bituminous coal region, and is a busy unit of the big East St. Louis manufacturing area. Belleville produces boilers, batteries, boots and shoes, beer, castings, dies, enamelled ware, furnaces; also lighter goods such as paper boxes and women's garments. The Peabody Coal Co. has mines nearby. Belleville has a normal work force of 4,200 and annual wages at peak times of $30,000,000. The city has the advantages of the network of freight railroads centering at East St. Louis, truck lines and highways, especially US 460 combined with Illinois 15. It is also served by Greyhound and other bus lines.

Belleville was settled by American citizens of Cahokia and vicinity who were dissatisfied with the French administration. George Blair, who built the first house in 1806, donated a section of his farm for a town square. In 1814 the court was moved from Cahokia to Belleville. A town was laid out and immigration increased when Territorial Governor Ninian Edwards, a large landowner, placed advertisements in American newspapers offer inducements to settlers. Belleville was incorporated as a village in 1819. In 1828 coal was found underlying the area and many Germans arrived. In 1850 the place became a city. Belleville took on a German coloring and became known as a Dutch Town; German singing societies flourished—the *Liederkranz* was founded in 1873—but by 1970 90 percent of Belleville residents were American-born.

Belleville is governed by a nonpartisan mayor and elected aldermen. It has a daily newspaper, the *News Democrat*, and tunes in on the numerous radio and television stations of the southern Illinois-St. Louis region. There are 102 acres of parks, and two hospitals: St. Elizabeth's with 374 beds and Memorial with 108. The city is a banking center for the area. It has been erecting new public buildings and in January, 1971, dedicated a new St. Clair County Jail, costing $4,000,000 during three days of ceremonies. Then it allocated $7,500,000 for a new Courthouse.

The Belleville Junior College, a two-year coeducational State institution, was opened in 1946 and enrolls more than 4,000 students with a faculty of 273.

The Belleville Public Library, opened in 1916, was modernized in 1968. With nearly 90,000 volumes in its collection it has a circulation of more than 250,000. It is a member of the Kaskaskia Library System. The West Branch Library was dedicated after remodeling in April, 1971.

A tornado hit St. Clair County on March 5, 1938, leveling 50 houses and a grade school in Belleville, and killing 8 persons.

On US 460 on the outskirts of Belleville is the National Shrine of Our Lady of the Snows of the Roman Catholic Church, a place of pilgrimage. First located in St. Mary's Seminary, it has been served since 1958 by the Oblate Fathers of Mary Immaculate on high bluffs above the Mississippi Valley, where 200 acres are devoted to its cause. Here are the impressive Outdoor Altar and Amphitheater seating 6,000; the Chapel of Perpetual Adoration, the Christ the King Chapel, Our Lady of Guadalupe Chapel, the Rosary Court of 15 altars for private masses; the Way of the Cross, with recorded meditations at each station; the Annunciation Gardens with the Angelus Bells, set in a reflecting pool; the reproduction of the Grotto of Lourdes, the Visitors Center and the Pilgrim Inn. The season of pilgramage extends from May 1 through November 1 with five Masses daily and confessions before and after each.

The climax of the shrine's pilgrim program is reached on August 5, the final night of the annual Novena, when thousands of men, women and children take part in a candlelight procession in the amphitheatre. As many as 12,000 persons have attended these closing services.

EAST ST. LOUIS, 149 *m.* (69,996 pop. 1970) is at a junction of the combined US 40, US 66, Int. 55 and Int. 70, and Illinois 3. *See East St. Louis.*

US 50 crosses the Missouri line on the Martin Luther King, Jr. Bridge to St. Louis, Mo. *See Missouri Guide.*

~~~~~~

Tour 21

THE LINCOLN HERITAGE TRAIL

Wabash River—Palestine—Marshall—Charleston—Decatur—Mt. Pulaski-Springfield—New Salem State Park—Petersburg.

Indiana Line to Petersburg, 224 *m.*

This, the first section of the Lincoln Heritage Trail, is the original Lincoln National Memorial Highway and was so designated in the first edition of this *Guide.* The Highway was determined by a commission appointed to determine the much disputed path of the Lincoln family in moving from Indiana to Illinois in 1830. From the Indiana line to Decatur it closely follows the route of their migration and around Decatur identifies the sites where Thomas Lincoln farmed and whence Abraham left to make his own way. Then it extends west to Springfield, New Salem State Park, Petersburg, and other places rich in Lincoln associations.

In truth, all Illinois is filled with memorials of Lincoln's life there, for in his active career as lawyer and political leader he left very little of the State untouched. Through the enterprise of the Illinois State Historical Society markers have been placed on roads, dwellings, and public buildings associated with Lincoln. It is possible therefore to follow the Lincoln trail throughout the State. Anyone interested in seeking historic localities other than those designated here can get aid from the Division of Tourism, Department of Business and Economic Development, 222 South College Ave., Springfield, Illinois 62704.

Interest in the Lincoln story also has stimulated tourist travel to Lincoln beginnings in Kentucky and Indiana. These states also have placed markers and provided maps for tours. The Division of Tourism for Illinois, mentioned above, will send a folder of the Lincoln Heritage Trail in the three states. Additional information may be obtained from the Tourist Division, Indiana Department of Commerce, 334 State House, Indianapolis, Indiana 46204, and the Travel Division, Department of Public Information, Capitol Annex, Frankfort, Kentucky 40601.

The Lincoln Heritage Trail crosses the Indiana Line, 0 *m.*, on the LINCON MEMORIAL BRIDGE, a low graceful span erected in 1931, over the Wabash River from Vincennes, Indiana. At the bridge approach on the Illinois side, in a small roadside park (*camp sites, picnic facilities*), is the LINCOLN TRAIL MONUMENT. The work of Nellie Walker, Chicago sculptor, the monument depicts the Lincoln family entering Illinois.

At 0.5 *m.* is the junction with State 181, along which the Memorial Highway turns abruptly northward, following the route of the Lincoln family in its journey up the Wabash to Palestine. For 50 years it had been the main traveled route between Vincennes and Canada.

The Lincoln family, a closely-knit family group of thirteen, crossed the Indiana line into the new country of Illinois in March of 1830.

They included Abraham's father and stepmother, Sarah Bush Lincoln; her son, John D. Johnston; her two daughters and their husbands, Sarah E. (Mrs. Dennis Hanks) and Matilda (Mrs. Squire Hall) ; four Hanks children ; and the Halls' son. All of their belongings were loaded on three wagons, one drawn by two teams of horses and the others by two yoke of oxen each—Abraham drove one of the ox-drawn wagons.

Years later when someone asked Lincoln about his early life, he replied briefly that "it was the short and simple annals of the poor." He was seven years old when Thomas Lincoln moved the family from Hardin County, Kentucky to Spencer County, Indiana. The family came in the late fall, a difficult time to enter a new country, and had only a short season in which to cut logs for shelter before winter closed in on them. The winter was spent in a "half-faced camp," a rude three-sided shelter of logs open to the south, heated with an open fireplace. They lived on game, which was plentiful, drank melted snow, and slept on leaves and skins of wild animals. In the spring they built a cabin, cleared a plot of land, and planted a crop. During the summer, relatives from Kentucky joined them and life was less lonely. But in the second year "the milk-sick," a dread disease of the pioneers, struck the small community and in a few days Nancy Lincoln died. Her aunt and uncle died soon thereafter, and Dennis Hanks, a cousin, moved in with the Lincolns.

For a year the household struggled forlornly, and then Thomas Lincoln left for Kentucky and returned after a few weeks with a new wife, Sarah Johnston Lincoln, her three children, and a load of household goods. Sarah Lincoln, energetic, kindly, with a passion for cleanliness, swept out the corn husk beds, ordered a wooden floor for the cabin, and washed up her husband's children. Soon she won their confidence and affection.

Abraham Lincoln at an early age was strong and tall. He performed with ease the many tasks of a settler's life. He chopped wood, tended crops, fed the animals, threshed the grain, carried water, and even assisted his father in occasional jobs of carpentry and cabinet-making. School was a luxury; he attended only "by littles"—not more than a year throughout his life. But he learned to read, and before he left Indiana, he had read every book within reach. He read at meal times, before the fire at night, on fence rails during the noontime rest, on his way to the mill. Sarah Lincoln kept the other children from disturbing him, and smoothed over the impatient disapproval of his father. She inquired earnestly about the things he read, and he told her about them, explaining carefully and simply when she did not understand. Knowing always that a book was his for only a limited period, he committed long passages to memory or made notes on whatever paper was available. He made calculations on the hearth shovel, on the walls around the fireplace, on the hearth stone. He acquired extraordinary powers of concentration, and a habit of contemplation that distinguished him throughout his life.

Lonely as he was in his groping for knowledge, he was also deeply social. He frankly disliked isolated labor and found most satisfying work performed with other people. He enjoyed going to the mill, the conversations around the stove in the store, house-raisings, the life along the river. He talked with strangers and discussed politics, religion, law, and the slavery question with the men about Gentryville. He attended spelling-bees in the school house until—so the legend goes—he was ruled out because his side always won. He learned the bluff roistering ballads of the frontier and roared them tunelessly around the log-burning with his cousin, the "irrepressible" Dennis Hanks. His insatiable curiosity was ever concerned with people, events, problems, in the scene about him, and in the past. He knew the lore of his day and was a popular story teller, droll, witty, and Rabelaisian. At nineteen he made a trip to New Orleans in a flat boat.

On February 12, 1830, he was twenty-one years old and stood six feet four inches in his raw-hide moccasins. His legs were so long that his buckskin breeches scarcely covered half of them. He was sincerely loved and admired by most of the inhabitants of Spencer County, but he was restive. His sister, Sarah, had died in childbirth. His foster sisters were married, one of them to Dennis Hanks. Life in Spencer County was becoming constricted. The community was static; the land poor. In that year the "milk-sick" returned. The Lincolns, remembering Nancy Lincoln, and watching their cattle drop in their sheds, sold their farm and set out for the limitless plains and virgin soil of central Illinois.

RUSSELVILLE, 9.6 *m.*, a tiny river town of 174 people (1970), was the first community encountered by the Lincoln family in Illinois. Residents maintain that it was here, rather than at Vincennes, that the party crossed the Wabash.

Settlements in eastern and central Illinois in 1830 were few and scattered. The party often traveled for hours without seeing a person, a house, or an animal. The half-thawed ground softened to the great iron-bound wheels of the wagons, and the oxen strained at the yoke, the long whips of the drivers lashing over their backs. Young Lincoln had a small stock of peddler's goods—needles, thread, knives, and buttons, which he had bought from a storekeeper in Gentryville. These he sold to occasional settlers along the trail, observing the ways of the new people, eager with questions. There were no bridges over the streams, and often the men and beasts painfully broke a layer of ice formed on chilly nights. The March winds, unobstructed by hills, swept across the open prairies, harsh and biting. Fifteen miles was a "good piece" to make in a day.

PALESTINE, 25 m. (450 alt., 1,640 pop. 1970; 1,564, 1960) was a Crawford County village of some importance in 1830, although it consisted merely of five stores, two taverns, a steam saw and grist mill, and thirty families. Here was one of the six land offices in the State, to which settlers came from as far as Chicago to register their claims. Here at the time William H. Byford, later a distinguished surgeon and professor of gynecology at Rush Medical College, was learning the tailor's trade to support his widowed mother with whom he had that year migrated from Indiana.

The Lincoln family, it appears, was impressed with the town. One of the children always remembered it because it had a "holy name." A traveling juggler passed through on the same day as the Lincolns, and Abraham, watched with amusement and some wonder the performance of sleight-of-hand.

The Heritage Trail proceeds west from Palestine on Illinois 33 to a junction with Illinois 1, 29.8 m., on which it moves north. At 54 m. is LINCOLN TRAIL STATE PARK, a recreation area of 952 acres, with a man-made lake, boating, fishing, and camping.

MARSHALL, 57 m. (3,460 pop. 1970) is at a junction of Illinois 1 and US 40. See Tour 19.

Northwest from Marshall on a farm road (marked) crossing Int. 70 (from Terre Haute) through small villages; Clarksville, 65 m., and WESTFIELD, 76 m. (618 pop. 1970). Westfield College was opened as a coeducational seminary by the United Brethren in Christ in 1861 and became a college in 1865. It was closed in 1914 for lack of support. Its main building, used by the Westfield Township High School, burned down in 1917.

CHARLESTON, 85 m. (720 alt., 16,421 pop. 1970; 10,505, 1960, inc. 56.3%) is the seat of Coles County, home of Eastern Illinois University, with a basic trade in farm products, growing industries, and a rich legacy of Lincoln lore. It is located at the junction of Illinois 16 (east-west) and Illinois 130 (north-south); Interstate 70 connects with Illinois 130 16 m. south, and Interstate 57 with Illinois 16, 6 m. west, where the Coles County Memorial Airport is located. Ozark Airlines has numerous daily flights. The Penn Central and Norfolk & Western Railways serve Charleston. The Times-Courier is the city's daily news-paper.

Coles County was named for Governor Edward Coles. It has approx. 113,330 acres devoted to corn and 77,600 acres to soybeans, other major crops being wheat, oats, and hay, bringing an annual income of more than $14,688,000. Sales of livestock average more than $5,000,000 annually.

Charleston's first settlers came around 1826. It became the seat of Coles County in 1831, a village in 1835, and a city in 1865. Charleston was probably deep in mud the day in 1830 when the Lincolns passed through with nothing to distinguish them from other westward settlers. Twenty-eight years later Abraham Lincoln was to ride into Charleston again, a candidate for the United States Senate and a political adversary for whom Stephen A. Douglas had a shrewd respect. In 1858, in the full still heat of an early fall day, Lincoln drove into Charleston in a carriage. The roads were thickly laid with dust; the day was fair; the town bulged with visitors. Farmers and townspeople came from miles around in wagons, carriages, on horseback, on mules, on foot. There was a special train of seven cars from Indiana. An 80-foot banner overhanging the main street pictured the young pioneer driving a team of oxen on his first entry into Charleston. A parade was held to honor the occasion. In a wagon decorated with blue and white cloth, and festooned with leaves and flowers, clustered 31 girls wearing blue velvet caps, representing the states of the Union. Back of them a young woman rode a spirited horse and bore a banner, "Kansas—I will be free." The correspondent of the *New York Post* was shocked; "an unfortunate decoration for a young lady," he wired his editor.

The FOURTH LINCOLN-DOUGLAS DEBATE, between Abraham Lincoln and Stephen A. Douglas, took place at the eastern end of the present Coles County Fairgrounds on September 8, 1858. The debate was a big political event and created great excitement throughout the county. A crowd of 12,000 heard Lincoln answer the charge of Douglas that he advocated intermarriage with Negroes. As in other debates Douglas charged that Lincoln had voted against supplies for the army in Mexico. Lincoln turned to the back of the platform and seizing Orlando B. Ficklin, a former fellow Representative and a staunch Douglas man, pulled him to the front and made him testify that Douglas' charge was untrue.

Near the western end of the Fairgrounds is the grave of Dennis Hanks, marked by a tombstone that bears his claim that he taught Abraham Lincoln to read and write.

The COLES COUNTY COURTHOUSE, in the Public Square, stands on the site of one in which Lincoln appeared as a lawyer. The Square was the site of the fatal draft rioting of March 26, 1864. The tunnel, from Courthouse to jail, where prisoners were held, is extant.

EASTERN ILLINOIS UNIVERSITY has its main entrance on Lincoln Ave. (Illinois 16) and its campus between Fourth and Seventh Sts., where it occupies 35 buildings on 316 acres. It was founded by the State on May 22, 1863, as a normal school, became a college in 1921, and a university in 1957. It offers bachelor and master degrees and that of specialist in education, and in the 1972 school year enrolled 8,300 and had a faculty of 738.

The Robert G. Buzzard Elementary School has been operated by EIU as a laboratory for teachers. The Mary J. Booth Library, which has more than 300,000 vols., recently received a new addition, which gives it room for 600,000. Old Main, on Lincoln Ave., is sometimes called the Castle on the Rhine because of its German Gothic facade, but newer buildings favor the functional style. The university favors small classes and remains open the years around. It was one of the first in Illinois to offer Afro-American studies. Students have a student senate and representation on some faculty boards.

The Charleston Public School System has named elementary schools for Franklin, Jefferson, Lincoln, Mark Twain, and Carl Sandburg.

The Carnegie Public Library on Van Buren St. has more than 25,000 volumes, 900 recordings, and many periodicals. Its facilities include a room for lisetners, with many records available, and special group readings for children.

There are eight public parks in Charleston and two State parks in the environs, Lincoln Log Cabin State Park and Fox Ridge State Park. The latter on Illinois 130 8 *m.* south, is stocked for fishing. Fishing and swimming are available at Lake Charleston, on Illinois 130. This lake is expected to become part of the projected LINCOLN LAKE, which will impound waters of the Embrarras River and tributaries in Coles, Douglas, and Cumberland Counties. The dam will be located 6 *m.* south of Charleston and the lake will extend several miles north of it. The dam will be 2,400 ft. long and the lake will cover 4,310 acres, the fifth largest body of water in Illinois.

Among the industries in Charleston are Trailmobile, a division of Pullman, Inc., and Celetox Corp. There are 22 churches and 70 civic organizations or clubs, automobile racing groups. Banking is led by the Charleston National Bank, with assets of more than $31,700,000.

South on Fourth St. the Lincoln Heritage Trail runs past the house of Mrs. Matilda Moore, now preserved as a State Memorial. Lincoln came here as President-elect on January 31, 1861, to see his stepmother, Sarah Bush Lincoln, who was visiting her daughter, Mrs. Moore. Neighbors provided a basket dinner at noon in his honor. It was his last visit here.

The LINCOLN LOG CABIN STATE PARK, 94.5 *m.*, comprising 86 acres of the last Lincoln farm, is a memorial to Thomas Lincoln rather than to his son. The old pioneer never realized the hopes that impelled him toward Illinois. He was past 50 when he came—a thick-set man with a round face, dark eyes, and coarse black hair. Here Thomas Lincoln died in 1851. Sarah Lincoln lived here until her death in 1869.

In 1841 Abraham Lincoln purchased from his father the 120-acre farm on which his parents were living. After Thomas Lincoln's death ten years later, Lincoln sold 80 acres to his stepbrother, John D. Johnston, from whom his father had bought the land. A later owner cultivated the 40 acres that Lincoln had retained, and in 1888 obtained title to them by virtue of his undisputed occupation of the property for 20 years.

The reconstructed Thomas Lincoln Cabin stands in the park. The original cabin was shown at the World's Columbia Exposition in Chicago in 1893, and then disappeared. The reconstructed cabin, built by the State, stands on the old stone foundation. Like the original, it has two sections; the west room of the original was built by Thomas Lincoln in 1837 when he acquired the farm; the east half was a cabin purchased by him, moved to the site, and joined to the first section with clapboards. The root cellar to the east has been rebuilt on the brick floor of the original, and a grindstone and other crude implements have been replaced. Beside the kitchen door is a duplicate of the ox yoke that Thomas Lincoln always hung there. The 32-ft. well dug by Thomas Lincoln was restored in 1936; all but the top 4 ft. of the original stonework was retained.

The Lincoln Heritage Trail continues northwest from the State Park to SHILOH CEMETERY, 97.5 m., a small plot along the road containing the graves of Thomas Lincoln and his wife Sarah. The original sandstone shaft has been almost chipped away by souvenir hunters. A remnant still stands near the graves, which are marked by a new monument erected in 1924. Here on January 31, 1861, Lincoln and his stepmother visited his father's grave.

As the Lincoln Heritage Trail moves on the farms are not seen in logical succession, because Thomas Lincoln doubled back. Thus at 101 m. there is a marker indicating that here was the third Lincoln family home, where Thomas and Sarah Lincoln lived after Abraham had departed.

Then at 104 m. is the second Lincoln family home, whence Thomas and Sarah came in 1831 from Macon County. At 107 m. is a junction with Illinois 121, over which the Trail proceeds northward to MATTOON, 110 m. (19,681 pop. 1970) at a junction with US 45 *See Tour 3*. From Mattoon the Trail goes northwest on Illinois 121 to a junction with US 36, which it follows for 44 m.

DECATUR, 154 m. (683 alt., 90,397 pop.) *see Decatur*. Decatur is at a junction with US 51 (*see Tour 4*).

Decatur marked the end of the Lincolns' long journey from Indiana. They inquired here for the whereabouts of John Hanks, their kinsman, who had already selected for them a site high on the bluffs above the Sangamon River a short distance downstream. Seasoned logs lay ready for their use and they built a cabin, cleared ten acres of land, sowed it with corn, and split rails to fence it. Fall was mild and beautiful, but in December a two-day blizzard covered the ground with three feet of snow. On the open prairies it piled up in 15-foot drifts; in the fields it all but topped the corn shocks. Game was scarce, communication impossible. Immured in their lonely cabin, with no reserves of food but the corn from their first small crop, the Lincolns suffered acutely. In the spring the snow melted away in a flood. When the floods receded, Sarah and Thomas Lincoln moved to Coles County, while Abraham struck out for himself.

From Decatur it is an easy drive to MOUNT PULASKI, 24 *m.* on Illinois 121, where the Courthouse was in use from 1847 until 1853. *See Tour 17.* Continuing 24 *m.* northwest on Illinois 121, the trail leads to the town of Lincoln, which Abraham Lincoln helped to establish and which was named for him by his associates. *See Tour 17.*

The site of the first Lincoln farm home in Illinois, in LINCOLN TRAIL HOMESTEAD STATE PARK, off US 36 west of Decatur on Illinois 121, is marked by a huge red boulder with a bronze plaque, unveiled Nov. 10, 1956. The dedicatory speaker was Otto B. Kype, editor, and author of *Abraham Lincoln in Decatur.* The inscription reads:

In March, 1830, Abraham Lincoln came from Indiana with his family to settle here in Macon County at a place on the north side of the Sangamon River ten miles westerly from Decatur. The Lincolns built a log cabin and broke the sod to raise a crop of corn. On this site the family endured the famous terrible winter of deep snow until March of 1831 when Abraham left to take a flatboat down the Mississippi and Thomas Lincoln moved to Coles County.

CAMP BUTLER NATIONAL CEMETERY, 187 *m.,* opened in 1862, contains the bodies of many Union and Confederate soldiers. Still used, the cemetery accepts for burial the body of any honorably discharged U. S. soldier. During the Civil War the site, with adjacent lands, comprised a huge training camp and military prison. Here approximately one-third of the Illinois regiments that served in the Civil War were mustered into the Federal service and given preliminary training.

SPRINGFIELD, 194 *m.* (91,753 pop. 1970). This is the heart of Lincolnland. Here are located numerous private and public structures associated with Lincoln's career, from the time he came here as a young lawyer until he left his home for the inauguration as President and returned to be entombed. All sites are marked; all relics are carefully preserved; the whole city provides an opportunity for concentrated historical and biographical study that has no equal in the United States. Springfield is reached from Chicago on Int. 55 and US 66; Int. 57 and US 54. From Bloomington, US 66. From Champaign-Urbana, Int. 72, US 47, US 36. From Decatur, US 36. From East St. Louis, Int. 55, US 66. From Rockford, US 51 to Bloomington, then US 66. From Freeport and Peoria, Illinois 29. From Rock Island and Moline, US 67 to Beardstown, then Illinois 125. *See article on Springfield.*

From Springfield west on Jefferson St., Illinois 97, to NEW SALEM STATE PARK, in Menard County, 20 *m.* northwest of Springfield, the village of the young Abraham Lincoln, considered by many the most inspiring of all the Lincoln relics in Illinois. Located near the Sangamon River on part of the 488 acres of the park is a reproduction of the frontier village where Abe Lincoln, aged 22, arrived in April, 1831, with a flatboat of farm products that became stuck on the milldam. With him were three men: John Johnson, Lincoln's stepbrother; Dennis Hanks, his cousin, and Denton Offut, who owned the boat. Lincoln had helped build it in Sangamo Town, a settlement on the river that has disappeared. Offut hired the men to take the flatboat to New Orleans. This mission concluded, Lincoln returned to New Salem in July, 1831, after reaching St. Louis on a steamboat and walking the rest of the way.

Upon his return Offut engaged Lincoln to run a grocery store and a mill in New Salem. The village had been settled in 1828, but possessed fewer than 100 inhabitants. Lincoln strolled into town on election day and presently found himself on the edge of the voters. Voting was by acclamation, and the clerk, pressed for assistance, asked Lincoln to help him. Thus on his first afternoon in New Salem Lincoln came to know the names and faces of all the men in the district.

He quickly endeared himself to the community. Established in Offut's grocery, he measured off calico, weighed out tea and sugar, wrote letters, and arbitrated disputes. He became acutely aware of his educational shortcomings and remedied them by long hours of reading. On warm days customers found him outside the store reading under a tree in the door-yard, lying flat on his back, his feet high on the trunk, circling the tree as he followed the shade.

As in other frontier towns, sports in New Salem were crude—cock-fighting, horse racing, wrestling, and rough horse-play. Offut's loose tongue had spread stories of Lincoln's tremendous strength throughout the district, and one day the Clary Grove Boys roistered into town with Jack Armstrong, their champion, and challenged Lincoln to a wrestling match. He accepted cheerfully. A ring formed and for a time the match was even. Then Armstrong began to falter, and his friends rushed in. Lincoln, stung to anger, challenged any man in the crowd to single combat. None dared accept, and the match was called off. Finally tempers cooled, and Lincoln and Armstrong shook hands.

In the spring of 1832 Offut closed his store, and Lincoln volunteered for the Black Hawk War. He was elected captain of his company, but saw no action. Following the war he returned to New Salem, and became partner in a store that failed, leaving him burdened with debt. He was appointed postmaster, but the fees from the office were too small to provide a living. It was as a deputy surveyor of Sangamon County that he spent the balance of his residence in New Salem. Before the Black Hawk War Lincoln had announced himself candidate for the legislature. He was defeated at the time, but in 1834 he was elected, and in 1836 he was re-elected. Meanwhile, encouraged by his friend, John T. Stuart of Springfield, and aided by Stuart's books he was studying law.

From New Salem has come the romantic legend of young Lincoln's love for Ann Rutledge, daughter of James Rutledge, the tavernkeeper, with whose family Lincoln boarded after he arrived at New Salem. The basis for the legend is the account in the biography of Lincoln by his one-time law partner, William H. Herndon, whose accuracy has been questioned by historians. Ann was engaged to John McNamar, also known as McNeill, who went to New York, stayed a long time, and neglected to communicate with Ann. In August, 1835, Ann died of an acute fever and was buried in the old Concord cemetery about a mile south of the Concord Cumberland Presbyterian Church. Lincoln is supposed to have become so greatly affected that he gave way to melancholia, and Carl Sandburg in *Abraham Lincoln; the Prairie Years* describes him as sitting by her grave and weeping. But no one has found proof of this incident. Edgar Lee Masters has written: "Lincoln's interest in her pales into insignificance when the historical evidence is considered," but he admitted that her fame "rivals that of Emily Dickinson." (*See also Petersburg, below*).

Ann Rutledge's original grave was a small plot in the middle of a field, and according to the *Journal* of the Illinois State Historical Society, "one has to cross a meadow of stubble to reach it and climb over a wire fence to get into it. At once a large board design confronts the eyes of the visitor, which announces that Ann Rutledge was buried in this spot. Here for more than 50 years her dust reposed amid the silence of these meadows under moonlit skies, where the owls hooted and the field mice scampered over her grave. Not until 1890 did anyone pay any particular attention to it." According to one version there was mighty little to exhume when Petersburg made an enterprise of her reburial.

In the spring of 1837 Lincoln was admitted to the bar. In nearby Springfield, which had just been designated the State capital, his old friend Stuart was eager to take him into partnership. Thus it happened that one April day in 1837, Lincoln packed his few belongings in his saddle bags and rode out of the frontier village in which he had spent six eventful years.

New Salem, already declining, sank rapidly. Two years later, when Petersburg was made the seat of Menard County, it was practically deserted. In a few years only the crumbling ruins of a few cabins marked its site.

After 1897 the Old Salem Chautauqua held its summer tent meetings on the bank of the Sangamon River opposite the site of the village. In 1906 William Randolph Hearst spoke there and became so impressed with the history of New Salem that later he bought 62 acres that contained the site of the village for $11,000 and gave it to the Old Salem Lincoln League, which collected funds for its restoration. Much research preceded preparations to restore it. The original plat was found in the archives of Sangamon County, the locations of the lots were established and descendants of the settlers were consulted. The old cellar holes were found and original foundation stones were uncovered. The site was turned over to the State in 1918, but it was 1932 before rebuilding of the cabins was begun.

Only one cabin was still in existence—the Onstot Cooper Shop, and that had been moved to Petersburg. Its logs were returned to their original site and visitors may view it as a structure actually known to

Lincoln during his six years in New Salem. Houses, shops, and sheds were built of black walnut and red and white oak, as had been the originals. A search was made for original furnishings and many were recovered, including chairs, tables, spinning wheels, clocks, bootjacks, candle molds and churns. Wells were reopened and equipped with the windlass, ropes and buckets used by the pioneers. Even the rail-and-rider fences are back.

The center of interest is the Lincoln-Berry Store, with its meagre stock, its barrel of brooms, its wide fireplace. Other buildings include the Rutledge Tavern, home of Ann Rutledge; the Hill-McNeill Store, and Denton Offut's Store, where Lincoln first worked upon arriving at New Salem. In addition, there is a stone Museum, which contains the burrs from the Rutledge mill, an old covered wagon, and many other objects.

Governor Stratton accepted the Avard Fairbanks statue of Abraham Lincoln at New Salem State Park on June 21, 1954. It was presented by the Sons of Utah Pioneers. The Kelso Hollow Theatre, which seats 3,000, has frequent presentations of plays about Lincoln, including *Abe Lincoln in Illinois* by Robert Sherwood and *Prologue to Glory* by Abrams and Bentkover. A program called *Spoon River Speaks,* based on the *Spoon River Anthology* of Edgar Lee Masters also is presented occasionally.

PETERSBURG, 224 *m.* northwest of Springfield on Illinois 97 (2,632 pop. 1970; 2,359, 1960, inc. 11.6%) seat of Menard County, is less than 2 *m.* north of New Salem on the Sangamon River. After it became the county seat in 1839 it attracted new homeowners, some of whom came from New Salem. A farm town, it is incorporated as a city. It was first settled by Kentuckians and later attracted German immigrants. Its principal distinction today is as part of Lincolnland and gateway to New Salem State Park. Thousands of tourists who come to visit the park remain to visit Oakwood Cemetery in Petersburg and stand at the grave of Ann Rutledge, whose few remains were transferred here 50 years after her original burial in a country grave at Concord Cumberland Church. The site is distinguished by a granite boulder that bears the remarkable poem, "Ann Rutledge" from *The Spoon River Anthology* by Edgar Lee Masters.

In *The Sangamon* of the *Rivers of America Series* Masters described his connection with the epitaph:

"Henry B. Rankin of Springfield, who for many years specialized in Lincoln memorabilia, had much to do with the erection of this stone. He wrote me for permission to chisel upon it the epitaph from *The Spoon River Anthology* entitled 'Anne Rutledge'. I was very glad to grant the request. Then he or someone, changed the words of the poem, spoiling in one line the rhythm."

The folk history of Petersburg has been related in detail by Masters in *The Sangamon,* who wrote: "I know of no town in Illinois more attractive than Petersburg on the Sangamon." Now Masters also has become a Petersburg attraction, for when he died in 1950 he was buried in Oakwood Cemetery. Petersburg had been one of his boyhood homes; the other was Lewistown, which figures in the *Anthology*. The poem about Ann Rutledge with its lofty sentiments proved that Masters could rise above the bitterness and moroseness that fills most of his famous *Anthology*. Ironically, during his lifetime he was the outstanding author who refused to recognize greatness in Lincoln. Yet as a poet he contributed a masterpiece to the Lincoln legend.

Tour 22

THE ILLINOIS WATERWAY

Chicago River—Des Plaines River Valley—Lemont—Romeoville—Lockport — Channahon — Morris — Seneca — Marseilles — Ottawa —Starved Rock—Oglesby—La Salle—Peru—Spring Valley—Hennepin — Henry — Peoria — Pekin — Havana — Beardstown — Hardin —Grafton.

Lake Michigan to the Mississippi River, 327 *m.*

THE ILLINOIS WATERWAY, although essentially a commercial highway, is growing increasingly popular as an avenue of pleasure travel. Its historical associations are the richest of any of the traveled routes in the State. In beauty and variety its scenery rivals that of any part of Illinois; the opportunities it affords for hunting and fishing are exceeded only by the Mississippi in the southern part of the State. Along its course are some of the wildest and least populated sections of Illinois. The waterway has been, perhaps, the most significant single factor in the history of Illinois, and upon that factor emphasis is here laid. For this reason the larger cities and State parks along the route are treated briefly and only insofar as they pertain to the story of the river; their full descriptions are cross-referenced to other Tours.

Chicago is at the northern end of the Illinois Waterway. The CONTROL LOCKS, 0 *m.*, at the entrance to the harbor, mark the beginning of the Chicago River, which formerly emptied into Lake Michigan approximately a mile to the southwest. During the hundred years of engineering since the Illinois and Michigan Canal was begun, the flow has been reversed—the river has been made to drain out of the lake, rather than into it. The locks, opened in 1938, prevent the pollution of lake water, which sometimes resulted during storm periods when the river backed up into the lake.

At the South Fork, 5.5 *m.*, is the junction with the abandoned

Illinois and Michigan Canal, which the modern waterway parallels to La Salle. Opened in 1848, the canal was for 30 years a vital influence in the development of the State, and by linking Chicago with the Mississippi River helped the lake port to outstrip St. Louis as the dominant commercial center of the Midwest. Railroad competition in the latter half of the century reduced its traffic, but the canal continued to operate into the early 1900's. Its hundred-mile right-of-way has been developed by the State for recreational purposes, and old towpaths have been converted into pleasure drives.

At 6.1 *m.* the waterway leaves the river and enters the Sanitary and Ship Canal, which it follows for 30 miles to Lockport.

The canal, opened in 1900 as the Chicago Drainage Canal, serves the dual purpose implied in its new name: to remove the treated industrial and domestic waste of Chicago and some of its suburbs, and to replace the outmoded Illinois and Michigan Canal as a highway of commerce. Principal users of the canal are a few large independent companies and the Federal Barge Line, a Government owned and operated fleet of barges and towboats that carries freight between Chicago, Minneapolis, St. Louis, Kansas City, and New Orleans.

The channel, 20 ft. deep and 160 to 300 ft. wide, is cut through solid rock in its first seven miles. On calm days this stretch is easily navigated, but in stormy weather the passage is difficult, for a heavy wind can wreck a small boat upon the rocks. However, such winds are rarely experienced, since the canal lies in a deep valley and on either side is a high spoils bank, formed of the excavated rock through which the channel is cut. These high embankments screen the adjoining lands, which are utilized by railroads and varied manufacturing plants.

At 13.2 *m.* is the Old Chicago Portage Forest Preserve, a section of the once heavily traveled portage between the Chicago and Des Plaines Rivers; the route of Indians, explorers, missionaries, traders, trappers, and soldiers; the crossing between the waters that flowed eastward past Quebec and Montreal and those that found their way southward to New Orleans and the Gulf.

Jolliet crossed this low divide in 1673 and envisioned a canal that would link these two waterways. La Salle followed him, and a decade later, in reporting the geography of the region, noted the possibility of a canal through the portage. His enthusiasm for the project, however, was tempered by his experiences in traversing the portage. At times of high water, he noted, the floods of the Des Plaines so completely inundated the region that a canoe could pass from one river to another in water at least two feet deep. But during the low water stage the Des Plaines was often completely dry, and the Kankakee, with which it joined to form the Illinois, carried so small a volume of water that a canoe could not be floated above Starved Rock. In short, La Salle pointed out, a canal that would effectively link the Chicago and Illinois Rivers would have to be, not half a league in length, as Jolliet had optimistically reported, but the maximum length of the portage, nearly 100 miles. The Illinois and Michigan Canal, opened

165 years later, measured 96 miles, from Chicago to La Salle. The length of the modern Sanitary and Ship Canal, less than a third of this, is made possible only by the diversion of a considerably greater volume of water from Lake Michigan, and by the use of modern engineering in damming and dredging the channels of the Des Plaines and Illinois Rivers.

Immediately west of the portage the DES PLAINES RIVER enters the valley, and parallels the waterway for 23 miles to Lockport. Left is the old Illinois and Michigan Canal. On either side of the mile-wide valley the wooded bluffs rise sharply to the rolling upland. Between approximately 18 *m.* and 23 *m.* the Argonne Forest Preserve borders the valley—an extensive Cook County recreational area largely in its original wildland state. At the west end of the preserve Illinois 83 crosses the Des Plaines River, and at 23.5 *m.* is the Calumet Sag Channel, a tributary of the Sanitary and Ship Canal. This channel, leads southeast to Calumet and Indiana Harbor on Lake Michigan.

North of the Des Plaines River from Illinois 83 to the Lemont Road extend the 3,700 acres of the ARGONNE NATIONAL LABORATORY of the University of Chicago, a major installation for research in nuclear energy. The area extends about 3 *m.* to Int. 55.

LEMONT, 26.9 *m.* (605 alt., 5,080 pop. 1970; 3,397, 1960), last village in Cook County in this area, is located on the south bank opposite the southwest corner of Argonne Laboratory grounds. It has refineries and metal industries and a limestone quarry.

ROMEOVILLE, 31.3 *m.* (500 alt., 12,674, 1970; 3,574, 1960), in Will County, is located on both banks of the Des Plaines. The original settlement, on the east bank, was platted in 1833 by a developer who called it Romeo at the same time he named Juliet, which became Joliet. Romeoville was incorporated in 1895 and was credited with only 133 residents when the *Illinois State Guide* was issued in 1939. The Adlai Stevenson Expressway (Int. 55) with junction with Illinois 53 and new industries helped its population jump of 254% in 1960-70.

A Butterfly Dam occupies the center of the channel at 34 *m.* Its function is to serve as an emergency dam should the one at Lockport fail to function. Inasmuch as it remains open at all other times, it is not equipped with locks.

At LOCKPORT, 34.5 *m.* (582 alt., 9,985 pop. 1970; 7,500, 1960, inc. 32%) a city in Will County, once an important shipping and transfer point on the Illinois and Michigan Canal, is the lock that controls the volume of water withdrawn from Lake Michigan. Here were the offices of the canal company, among whose records are preserved many documents pertaining to the days of the canal's construction and operation. These include maps, field notebooks, correspondence, newspapers of a century ago in which bids for canal contracts are advertised, and such miscellaneous records of the disbursing office as the pork and flour contracts for 1838-39. Among the items is a prospectus of the Illinois Central Company offering for sale, in 1855, 2,400,000 acres of "selected proven farm and woodlands in tracts of any size to suit purchasers, on long credit at low rates of interest, situated on each side of the railroad, extending all the way from the extreme North to the South of the State of Illinois."

Lockport is reached by Ill. 171 (Archer Ave.) and Ill. 7, which crosses the river and ship canal to join Ill. 53. Left (north) on Ill. 53 to the Lewis College of Science and Technology and the Lockport Airport.

Right, at 35.5 *m.,* are the buff limestone buildings of Stateville State Prison (*see Tour 17*), set squarely among the varied greens and yellows of cultivated fields.

Lockport Lock and Dam, 36.1 *m.,* marks the end of the Sanitary and Ship Canal. The lock chamber is 110 ft. wide, 600 ft. long, has a lift of 41 ft. and can be filled or emptied in 12 minutes. The upper gates are of the vertical lift type, each 20 ft. high and weighing 190 tons. The lower gates are 60 ft. high, are of the mitering type, and weigh 315 tons apiece. Two emergency dams, of 50 and 75 tons, are part of the lock's equipment. They are for use in the event of damage to the lock gates. A feature of the Lockport development is a small chamber for locking pleasure craft.

Adjoining the locks is the Hydroelectric Power Plant of the Chicago Sanitary District, the only property retained by that authority when it surrendered title to the Chicago Drainage Canal, as the Sanitary and Ship Canal was known before it was acquired and improved by the Federal government. By measuring the amount of water passed through the turbines, and by computing the volume used for lockage purposes, Army engineers in charge of the waterway control the total amount of water diverted from Lake Michigan. This diversion, as established by the United States Supreme Court in 1930, averaged 5,000 cubic feet per second until December 31, 1938. At that time it was reduced to a maximum of 1,500 cubic feet per second, a volume of water that some shippers and canal authorities believe to be inadequate to maintain sufficient flow for sanitary purposes and adequate channel depths for navigation.

Downstream from the Lockport Dam the waterway follows the improved channel of the Des Plaines River for 18 miles to its junction with the Kankakee. JOLIET, 38.5 *m.* (545 alt., 78,887 pop.) (*see Joliet*), long an important shipping point on the river and waterway, is bisected by the canalized stream, which flows at street level in the northern part of town, but near the southern border of the city is actually at a higher elevation than the valley floor, so that boats sail along above the general level of the city. Only the residential districts on the wooded bluffs are high above the canal.

Brandon Road Lock and Dam, 41.2 *m.,* is the second of the series on the Illinois Waterway. The lock, 110 by 600 feet, has a lift of 31 feet. The dam, which has a retaining wall 2,000 feet in length, not only maintains the upstream level, but also confines the waters of Brandon Road Pool, a turning basin considerably above the level of the valley bottom.

At the southwest corner of the pool is one of the locks of the Illinois and Michigan Canal, now permanently closed and used as part of the retaining wall. Downstream, the old canal parallels the modern waterway, and seems by comparison a tiny ditch, with its trickle of water that seeps through the lock gates. Gone is the pageant of barge and packet, the holiday crowds on canal excursions, the drivers and horses along the towpaths. In its place is the modern waterway, sleek and efficient in its long graceful dams, its electrically operated locks, navy-trim in their bright coat of aluminum paint. Its modern steel barges, four, six, eight, ten at a time, locked in tow, pushed up or down the waterway by twin-screw, Diesel-powered boats, move in one tow more freight than the entire fleet operating on the old canal could have carried in a week.

At 50 *m.* the Du Page River enters the Des Plaines at the little village of CHANNAHON, (1,505 pop. 1970), an important shipping center in the days of the old canal. Three packets, the *China,* the *Whale,* and the *King Brothers,* carried flour to Chicago and Kankakee. The development of rail transportation put an end to Channahon's commercial activities.

At 54 *m.* the Kankakee River joins the Des Plaines to form the Illinois River, which the waterway follows for 273 miles to Grafton and the Mississippi. For 63 miles, between the junction of the Des Plaines with the Kankakee and the Great Bend, west of La Salle, the Illinois River flows in a westerly direction through a broad, deep valley carved thousands of years ago by the outpouring waters of a melting ice sheet. Even the improved river of today, which carries many times its normal volume of water, seems strikingly undersized as it flows through a gorge 100 to 200 feet deep and a mile and a half to two miles wide. It was at this point that La Salle, having descended the Kankakee, first entered the valley of the Illinois in the winter of 1679-80.

Dresden Island Lock and Dam, 55.6 *m.,* third of the series on the Illinois Waterway, has a lift of 17 ft. and a standard lock chamber, 110 by 600 ft. In this preliminary stretch of the river the valley sides are less steep than they are shortly downstream, and fields of corn often spill over the crest of the upland and descend to the river's bank, bringing to the waterway an agricultural scene that is generally out of view.

MORRIS, 63.7 *m.* (504 alt., 8,194, pop. 1970) (*see Tour 14*), important once as a grain shipping center, is now building and operating elevators. Here grain is stored and loaded onto the carriers. One or more of the 300-ft barges is commonly tied up at Morris.

SENECA, 74 *m.* (521 alt., 1,761 pop. 1970; 1,719, 1960), lies well within the gorge. A little town at the base of hundred-foot bluffs, astraddle the Illinois and Michigan Canal, Seneca is scarcely visible from the river. Seneca has a DuPont plant that makes explosives.

MARSEILLES, 80.1 *m.* (506 alt., 4,320, 1970) (*see Tour 14*), is at the head of a rapids that have contributed to its development as an important manufacturing city. Marseilles Dam, fourth on the water-way, is at the head of Marseilles Canal, through which traffic passes the two-and-a-half-mile rapids. MARSEILLES LOCK, of standard size, with a lift of 21 feet, is at the western end of the canal. Bells Island separates the waterway from the river; ILLINI STATE PARK a game refuge and bird haven, occupies 407 acres on the mainland.

At 87 m. is the junction with the FOX RIVER, at the northern limits of OTTAWA, 87.5 m. (486 alt., 18,716, 1970) (see Tour 14). Although an industrial city, Ottawa, as seen from the waterway, is one of the loveliest of Illinois River towns. Beautifully situated, the residential districts mount from the river to the encircling bluffs on both sides of the stream. Boats of the Federal Barge Line usually change their tows at Ottawa. Low bridges over the Sanitary and Ship Canal limit the use of the upper waterway to craft of low clearance.

In the 10 miles below Ottawa is the most rugged section of the valley. Here the sandstone bluffs rise precipitously 100 to 150 feet above the water. Tributary streams have carved deep canyons, and wind and water have eroded the soft rock into fantastic forms. At 92.5 m. is BUFFALO ROCK STATE PARK (see Tour 14), dominated by a pecularly shaped block of sandstone that rears its hump a hundred feet above the valley floor. Between the rock and the bluffs is a large turning basin of the Illinois and Michigan Canal.

On the left bank of the river is STARVED ROCK STATE PARK (see Tour 14), 1,451 acres of wildland as varied as any in Illinois. The body of water at this point is known as Lake Starved Rock. Two channels are marked: the one close to the south bank is for pleasure craft; the main channel leads to the lock.

Starved Rock Lock and Dam, 96.2 m., is the fifth of the modern installations on the Illinois Waterway. Immediately downstream the historic old promontory, STARVED ROCK rises 140 feet above the water's edge. Here in 1683 La Salle established a French fort, and here, according to legend, a band of the Illinois Indians later met the tragic death from which the Rock derives its name. West of the Rock is the boat entrance to Starved Rock State Park, marked by two mooring piers and two black buoys.

OGLESBY, 100 m. (465 alt., 4,175 pop. 1970) is at the mouth of Vermilion River. The Marquette Cement Company, a local industry, ships extensively by water, using its own boats and barges. A single tow often carries a load equivalent to 50 box-cars.

LA SALLE, 103 m. (448 alt., 10,376 pop. 1970) (see Tour 4), bears only slight resemblance, to the city once head of steamboat navigation and southern terminus of the Illinois & Michigan Canal. Docks and warehouses and other modern structures indicate that La Salle is again depending on the river for at least part of its economic life.

The Illinois & Michigan Canal, 104 m., today scarcely noticed from the waterway, was once the hub of commercial activity. Here cargoes were transferred between canal and river and as many as 100 canal boats and a dozen steamboats tied up.

Steamboating actively began on the Illinois in 1828, but not until several years later was the first organized steamboat line put in operation. It ran only as far upstream as Naples, 65 miles from Grafton. By 1841 60 boats were serving Peoria and by 1851 a regular, dependable trade was being carried on between St. Louis and La Salle. Fastest service of the day was that of the Five Day Line, which made the 250 miles between the two cities within that period, rather than the customary week. In La Salle rivermen often recalled the days when *Prairie Belle, Garden City, Amazon, Messenger,* and *Aunt Lettie* churned the river white with their great paddles.

PERU, 104 *m.* (459 alt., 11,772 pop. 1970) (*see Tour 4*), sister city of La Salle, turned its back on the river and developed the industries that came with the railroad. The revival of river traffic has effected the modern city only indirectly.

SPRING VALLEY, 108 *m.* (465 alt., 5,605 pop. 1970; 5,371, 1960), a manufacturing city in Bureau County, spreads over the bluffs and straggles out into the valley floor. Until recent decades the region was the scene of extensive coal mining.

At the Great Bend of the Illinois, 116 *m.,* where the river swings abruptly south, is the mouth of the Illinois and Mississippi Canal, a 75-mile channel opened in 1907 between the Illinois River and the Mississippi below Rock Island, generally called the Hennepin Canal. A feeder canal connects it with the Rock River at Sterling Rock Falls. The Canal follows the valleys of Bureau, Pond, and Cowcatcher Creeks, and when opened had 21 locks, which raised it by 196 ft. It was closed to commercial use July 1, 1951, because it had proved inadequate for navigation and the proposed cost for rebuilding it appeared prohibitive to the State. It has now become the responsibility of the State Board of Conservation, which has been converting it to park purposes, so that it can be utilized for fishing, boating, camping, hiking, horseback riding, and other outdoor activities, the longest park in the State.

HENNEPIN, 119.7 *m.* (505 alt., 535 pop. 1970 391, 1960; inc. 36.8%) on the Illinois River, is the seat of Putnam County, smallest county in the State (160 sq. *m.*). Hennepin can be reached by Interstate 180, which branches south from Interstate 80, the expressway between Chicago and Rock Island that passes 2 *m.* north of Princeton. Hennepin was a port on the Illinois & Mississippi Canal.

Putnam County had 5,007 pop. in 1970, down 9.6% from the 4,570 of 1960. Its largest village is Granville (1,232 pop. 1970; 1,048, 1960; inc. 17.6%).

Hennepin was named for Father Louis Hennepin, who accompanied LaSalle and Tonti on the Illinois River in 1680. Beaubien is said to have had a trading post here in 1817. Hennepin's prospects were considered good when it was made the county seat and erected a courthouse in 1835. Yet its real boost came only as recently as 1966, when the Jones & Laughlin Steel Co. opened one of its four major steel mills in Hennepin and created a new market for labor. It produces carbon steel products, cold rolled and galvanized sheet steel and tubular items and employs approx. 1,000 men. The corporation has 6,000 acres on the Illinois River.

PUTNAM COUNTY COURTHOUSE, said to be the oldest in continuous use in Illinois, is a two-story brick building with four white pillars reaching to the roof of the porch. It was erected in 1839 to replace an inadequate one built in 1835, and cost $14,000. In 1893 a wing was added at a cost of $4,780. Abraham Lincoln discussed political affairs with William and Madison Durley in Hennepin in September, 1845, and both he and Peter Cartwright, his opponent, are believed to have spoken in Hennepin during their 1846 campaign for Congress. In 1858 Stephen A. Douglas spoke at a rally on the village green west of the Courthouse.

Downstream from the Great Bend the character of the waterway differs sharply from that of the upper river. The narrow gorge of the Starved Rock section gives place to a broad valley, two to six miles in width. The bluffs remain equally steep, and rise to even greater heights, commonly 150 to 200 feet, occasionally 300 feet or more above the valley floor. The river winds lazily between its banks, for the drop in this lower 200 miles is so slight that there is scarcely a current. Oxbow lakes, sloughs, and marshes border the stream, and islands dot its channel. Sandbars alternate with marshlands, and extensive woodlands cover the valley floor and mount the gentler bluffs. These at times rise sharply from the water's edge, sheer cliffs of sandstone or limestone, or again are so far removed from the river as to be indistinct on the far horizon.

In early days the valley teemed with wild life, and today game fish and fowl, protected by conservation, abound in this lower region. Waterfowl inhabit the marshy bottom lands, upland birds are numerous on the prairies and in the woodlands back of the bluffs, and in the lakes, channel, and backwaters of the river are a variety of game fish.

Downstream from Hennepin the river passes SENACHWINE LAKE, which occupies a five-mile stretch of abandoned channel. The lake is named for the last of the Potawatomi chiefs in this region, who died about 1883. He is said to be buried in a mound overlooking the lake. Its mouth, at 128 m., is all but hidden in the wooded marshlands that separate the lake from the river. Islands are numerous. Boats should stay in the main channel; the chutes or sloughs, as river men call the passages behind the islands, are shallow and filled with sandbars and snags.

HENRY, 131 m. (491 alt., 2,610 pop. 1970; 2,278, 1960) is a city in Marshall County, on the crest of an extensive terrace. This long platform, which rises sharply a hundred feet above the valley floor, represents a level at which the river formerly flowed. Backing the terrace are the main valley bluffs, which rise another hundred feet to the upland level. The terrace is largely given over to stock farming.

A bridge, lock and dam were built here in 1869-71, the first bridge to span the Illinois River between LaSalle and Peoria.

At approximately 137 m. are the SPARLAND PUBLIC SHOOTING GROUNDS, one of several tracts along the river set aside for public hunting. Downstream are the river towns of LACON,

138 *m.* (501 alt., 2,147 pop. 1970; 2,175, 1960) in Marshall County and CHILLICOTHE, 146 *m.* (490 alt., 6,052 pop. 1970; 3,054, 1960, inc. 98%) in Peoria County. Opposite the latter are the Woodford County Public Shooting Grounds, 148 *m.,* at the north end of PEORIA LAKE, largest body of water on the river, a mile or more in width and 18 miles in length, in reality two lakes joined by a narrow strait. On the shores of the upper lake is the Illinois Valley Yacht and Canoe Clubhouse. On the banks of the strait La Salle first encountered the Illinois Indians. Here his men camped for 11 days in January, 1680.

PEORIA, 164 *m.* (608 alt., 126,963 pop. 1970) is a major industrial and commercial city. On the west bank of the lake is the River and Rail Terminal where cargoes are exchanged between freight cars, trucks, and river barges. *See article on Peoria.*

EAST PEORIA (478 alt., 18,455 pop. 1970) in Tazewell County (*see Tour 16*), situated for the most part on the valley floor, is built around the large Caterpillar Tractor Company Plant, visible from the waterways.

Peoria Lock and Dam, 169 *m.,* completed in 1938, is of the wicket type, a form of dam that can be laid down on the river bed during high water and raised and placed in operation during low water stage.

FORT CREVE COEUR STATE PARK, 172 *m.* (*see Tour 16*) marks the reputed site of the fort planned by La Salle in 1680 as a base for proposed exploration and eventual colonization of the Mississippi Valley. From here LaSalle started on his march of 1,500 miles to Fort Frontenac, and in 1682 on his journey of exploration of the Mississippi River, which ended in his murder near the Trinity River in Texas. A granite marker commerates the founding of the fort and tells its story of desertion.

PEKIN, 174 *m.* (470 alt., 21,375 pop. 1970) (*see Tour 16*), one of the earliest settlements in Tazewell County and its third county seat, was often visited by Lincoln when he traveled the eighth circuit. During steamboat days Pekin was a major port, with 1,800 arrivals and departures in 1850.

Copperas Creek Lock, 190 *m.,* one of the old river improvements, is now used as a coal-loading dock. The many lakes in this section afford excellent duck hunting.

LIVERPOOL, 199 *m.* (218 pop. 1970) is an early river town. It is linked by rail with Dunfermline and has two coal docks.

The Spoon River flows into the Illinois at 206.7 *m.* Along this stream, which drains a fertile, long settled region to the north, are the scenes of Edgar Lee Masters' Spoon River Anthology (*see Tour 16*).

HAVANA, 207 *m.* (451 alt., 4,376 pop. 1970) (*see Tour 5*), is one of the most popular places for duck hunting on the lower river.

GRAND ISLAND, six miles long, divides the river at 214 *m.* Two miles down the east channel is the village of BATH (462 alt., 422 pop. 1970) (*see Tour 5*) in Mason County, surveyed by Abraham Lincoln.

Below Grand Island lakes become more numerous as the river

meanders over a valley six to eight miles wide. At 229 *m*. The Sangamon River enters the Illinois. It seems a small stream, yet it has been navigated. In 1832 a steamboat, the *Talisman,* loaded with freight, put out from Cincinnati, Ohio, destined for Springfield. Down the Ohio it steamed to the Mississippi, up the Mississippi to the Illinois, up the Illinois to the Sangamon, and up the Sangamon to Springfield, there safely discharging freight and passengers. But the trip up the Sangamon had been difficult, and on the return voyage the captain of the *Talisman* put a young man of the vicinity at the wheel. This youthful pilot, who brought his boat safely down the river, was Abraham Lincoln. A replica of the *Talisman* takes visitors on river trips.

BEARDSTOWN, 238 *m*. (444 alt., 6,222 pop. 1970) (*see Tour 7*), in Cass County, lies low on the valley floor, and has at times suffered disastrous floods. Today it functions primarily as a trading center for an extensive agricultural region, and as the focus of hunting activities on the lower river.

La Grange Lock and Dam, 249.6 *m.,* is of standard size, 110 by 600 feet.

MEREDOSIA, 255 *m*. (446 alt., 1,178 pop. 1970, 1,034, 1960) in Morgan County, lies at the mouth of Meredosia Lake, a five-mile body of water that provides good fishing and hunting. Lake and town take their name from a corruption of the French marais d'osier, or "swamp of the basket reeds."

It was at Meredosia that the first railroad in Illinois, a section of the Northern Cross, met the river. That was in 1838, when steamboating was just getting under way. It was not until 1878, when receipts on the Illinois & Michigan Canal fell below operating costs, that the locomotive seriously threatened the supremacy of the riverboat. For 40 years the two systems of transportation developed side by side.

NAPLES, 261 *m*. (448 alt., 100 pop. 1970) in Scott County, a minor grain shipping point, is important in river history as the one place where a steamboat was built on the Illinois River. This was the *Olitippa,* which ran long before there was any regular steamboat service on the river.

The building of this and other Mississippi-type steamboats required no extensive plant or machine equipment. A man who wanted to build a boat had only to erect a shed or shelter on the bank in the early spring. A crude sawmill did the original cutting of logs; the rest of the work consisted of hand hewing or cutting with flitch saws. Skilled workers with drawknife, gauge, axe and adze shaped the hull timbers, fashioned the kelson and formed the stem. The long keel was laid down first. From this the ribs were extended out on either side. The hull was finished and floored over and sometimes the upper decks were added before the machinery, brought in by boat, was installed. So durable were the engines that they were often used over and over again, outlasting the life of several hulls.

GRIGGSVILLE LANDING, 266 *m*. (1,245 pop. 1970; 1,240, 160) in Pike County, was once a busy port. Today it is the landing for

VALLEY CITY, a short distance inland and not visible from the river. A local cement plant ships some of its product by water.

Downstream, in its southernmost 60 miles, the river spreads broadly over the valley floor. Past the Pike County towns of FLORENCE, 271 *m.* (438 alt., 65 pop.), MONTEZUMA 277 *m.*, BEDFORD, 278 *m.*, and PEARL, 284 *m.* (451 alt., 323 pop. 1970), the old stream winds its way among wooded islands. Pearl is on Illinois 100. Here are many small communities that have existed for a century or more, with the river as almost their sole contact with the outside world. Their names commonly carry the suffix of landing, as Buckhorn Landing, Retzers Landing and Lange Landing. They are quiet, picturesque reminders of days when the steamboat was a daily caller.

KAMPSVILLE, 295 *m.* (449 alt., 439 pop. 1970) a village in Calhoun County, is a major recreational point in southwestern Illinois. Bartholomew Beach is highly valued. At Kampsville there is a free ferry across the Illinois, and 4 *m.* west on Illinois 108 is ELDRED, a farm village gaining notice because here a dirt road turns south 6 *m.* to the KOSTER EXCAVATION, an Indian site in process of being uncovered. Tourists have spotted it as a desirable place to visit and the excavators provide student guides. There is a small collection of artifacts in Kampsville.

HARDIN, 305 *m.*, seat of Calhoun County, is the last town on the river. Beyond it, GRAFTON, 327 *m.* is on the Illinois bank where the two rivers meet. *See pages 540 and 541, Tour 7.*

A Selection of Recent Books about Illinois

For additional titles see Of the Making of Books

Jane Addams of Hull House, 1860-1935, by Margaret Tims. Macmillan, 1961.

Architecture of Skidmore, Owings & Merrill, 1963-1973, by Arthur Drexler. Hastings House, 1974.

The Autobiographies of the Haymarket Martyrs. Ed. with an introduction by Philip S. Fones. Humanities Press, 1969.

Black Chicago; the Making of a Negro Ghetto, 1890-1920, by Allen H. Spear. Chicago, 1967.

Bryan, A Political Biography of William Jennings Bryan, by Louis W. Koenig, Putnams, 1971.

Chicago, Growth of a Metropolis, by Harold Mayer and Richard C. Wade. University of Chicago Press, 1973.

Chicago Renaissance: The Literary Life in the Midwest, 1900-30, by Dale Kramer. Appleton-Century, 1964.

The Chicago Race Riots, by Carl Sandburg. Preface by Ralph McGill. Intro. by Walter Lippman. Harcourt, 1969.

City on Foot; an Architectural Walking Tour, by Ira J. Bach. Follett, 1969.

Created Equal? The Complete Lincoln & Douglas Debates of 1858, ed. by Paul M. Angle. University of Chicago Press, 1958.

The Croatian Immigrants in America, by George Pepic. Philosophical Library, 1971.

Stephen Douglas: The Last Years, 1857-1961, by Damon Wells. University of Texas Press, 1971.

The Dream and the Deal: The Federal Writers Project, 1935-43, by Jerre Mangione. Little, Brown, 1972.

John Buchan Eads, Master of the Great River, by Rosemary Yager. D. Van Nostrand Co., 1968.

Free But Not Equal: The Midwest and the Negro During the Civil War, by V. Jacque Voegeli. University of Chicago Press, 1967.

Free Soil, Free Labor, Free Men; The Ideology of the Republican Party Before the Civil War, by Eric Fones. Oxford University Press, 1970.

The Great Chicago Fire, Oct. 8-9, 1871, ed. by Paul M. Angle. Chicago Historical Society, 1971.

The Great Fire: Chicago, 1871, by Herman Kogan and Robert Cromie. Putnam's, 1971.

The Hodge Scandal: A Pattern of American Political Corruption, by George Thiem. St. Martin's Press, 1963.

Raymond Hood, Architect, Form Through Function in the American Skyscraper, by Walter H. Kilham, Jr. Hastings House, 1973.

Illinois Architecture, by Frederick Koeper. University of Chicago Press, 1968.

Illinois Fact Book and Historical Almanac, by John M. Clayton. Southern University Press, 1969.

Illinois, A History of the Prairie State, by Robert P. Howard. Erdman Publishing Co., 1972.

The Irreconcilables: The Fight Against the League of Nations, by Ralph Stone. Kentucky University Press, 1970.

Letters of the Lewis & Clark Expedition with Related Documents, 1783-1854, ed. by Donald Jackson. University of Illinois Press, 1962.

Abraham Lincoln, Prairie Lawyer, by John J. Duff. Rinehart & Co., 1960.

Marquette Legends, by Francis Borgia Stock, O.F.M. Pageant Press, 1960.

McClure's Magazine and the Muckrakers, by Harold S. Wilson. Princeton University Press, 1970.

Opera in Chicago: A Social and Cultural History, 1850-1965. by Ronald Davis. Appleton-Century, 1966.

Prairie Albion: An English Settlement in Pioneer Illinois, by Charles Boewe. Southwestern Illinois University Press, 1962.

Race Riot: Chicago in the Red Summer of 1919, by William Tuttle, Jr. Atheneum, 1970.

The State Universities and Democracy, by Allan Nevins. University of Illinois Press, 1962.

Adlai Stevenson, Patrician Among the Politicians, by Bert Cochran. Funk & Wagnalls, 1969.

Taxes and Politics: A Study of Illinois Public Finances, by Glenn W. Fisher. University of Illinois Press, 1969.

Frank Lloyd Wright, A Biography, by Finis Farr. Scribner, 1961.

CHRONOLOGY

1673 Father Jacques Marquette and Louis Jolliet pass down the Mississippi from the Wisconsin to the Arkansas, and return up the Illinois River over the Des Plaines portage to Lake Michigan via the Chicago River.

1674 In October Marquette started return; in December entered the Chicago. Stopped for winter near present Damen Ave.

1675 At Easter Marquette went to the Illini, founded Mission, returned with two companions to Lake Michigan, died May.

1680 La Salle, builds Fort Crevecoeur on the Illinois.

1682 Fort St. Louis built by La Salle on Starved Rock.

1699 Priests of the Seminary of Foreign Missions at Quebec establish Mission of the Holy Family at Cahokia.

1703 Jesuits establish Mission of the Immaculate Conception at Kaskaskia.

1717 By decree of French Royal Council, Illinois passes under government established for Louisiana.

1718 Construction of Fort de Chartres begun.

1731 Illinois area becomes royal province, governed by King.

1763 France cedes to Great Britain her North American possessions east of the Mississippi.

1765 British occupy Fort de Chartres.

1772 British abandon and destroy Fort de Chartres, but keep small garrison at Fort Gage in Kaskaskia, seat of government.

1774 By Quebec Act boundaries of Quebec are extended southward to the Ohio and westward to the Mississippi.

1778 George Rogers Clark captures Cahokia and Kaskaskia. Territory conquered by Clark becomes county of Virginia.

1779 John Todd, commissioned county lieutenant by Gov. Patrick Henry of Virginia, establishes civil government in Illinois County.

1783   By the treaty which concludes the War of Independence, the boundary of the United States is extended to the Mississippi.

1784   Virginia cedes Illinois Country to national government.

1787   Northwest Territory, including Illinois, organized by ordinance of Congress; prohibits slavery except as punishment for crime. Arthur St. Clair is governor.

1795   By Treaty of Greenville Indians cede large area to the states, including site of Fort Dearborn.

1800   Illinois included in newly organized Territory of Indiana.

1803   Fort Dearborn built. Indians cede vast tracts of land by treaties of Fort Wayne and Vincennes.

1804   Chiefs of Sauk and Fox tribes sign away all their lands east of the Mississippi.

1809   Western part of Indiana from Vincennes north to Canada organized as Territory of Illinois with Kaskaskia as capital.

1810   Population: 12,282. Mail route Vincennes to St. Louis via Kaskaskia, Prairie du Rocher, and Cahokia established.

1812   Illinois becomes territory of the second grade.

1812   Garrison evacuating Fort Dearborn massacred by Indians.

1816   Fort Dearborn rebuilt.

1818   Enabling act fixes northern boundary of Illinois at 42 degrees 30 minutes. First Constitutional Convention writes state constitution, which is submitted to Congress without popular vote. Illinois admitted as state, with seat at Kaskaskia.

1820   Population: 55,211. State capital moved to Vandalia.

1823   Rush to lead mines at Galena commences.

1824   People by vote refuse to amend constitution to permit slavery.

1825   First canal charter granted.

1827   Congress gives 224,322 acres to State to aid in building a canal.

1830   Population: 157,445. Lincoln family moves to Illinois.

1831   Governor John Reynolds calls out militia against the Sauk and Foxes, who are pushed into Iowa.

1832   Black Hawk returns to former home. Black Hawk War results in Indians driven into Wisconsin and defeated at Bad Axe.

1833   Chicago incorporated as town.

1834   Abraham Lincoln elected to State Legislature.

1836   Construction of Illinois & Michigan Canal begins.

1837   Elijah P. Lovejoy, editor of Alton *Observer*, murdered by a pro-slavery mob. State appropriates $10,000,000 for building railroads, etc. Chicago receives city charter.

1839   State capital moved to Springfield. Mormons come to Nauvoo.

1840   Population: 476,183. Liberty Party organized.

1844   Dissension over policies of Mormon Leaders causes armed clashes and murder of Joseph and Hyrum Smith.

1845   Free school law enacted.

1846   General exodus of Mormons begins: 2,000 cross the frozen Mississippi. Abraham Lincoln elected to Congress. George Donner leads 32 from Springfield to California; all but one perish in Sierras.

1847   Cyrus McCormick, reaper maker, opens Chicago plant.

1848   Illinois & Michigan Canal opened.

1850   Population: 851,470.

1851   Illinois Central Railroad granted charter.

1853   Illinois State Agricultural Society chartered and first state fair held. Illinois Wesleyan University opens in Bloomington.

1855   Northwestern University opens.

1856   Various elements opposed to Kansas-Nebraska bill organized as Republican Party. Illinois Central Railroad completed.

1857   Illinois State Normal University opens.

1858   Lincoln and Stephen A. Douglas debate Kansas-Nebraska bill.

1859   Lincoln defeated for Senate, Douglas reelected.

1860   Population: 1,711,951. Republican National Convention, Chicago nominates Abraham Lincoln for President.

1861   Civil War: Illinois furnishes 256,297 soldiers.

1865   Civil War ends; President Lincoln assassinated, d. Apr. 15. Buried at Springfield.

1866   First post of Grand Army of the Republic at Decatur.

1867   University of Illinois founded at Urbana.

1868   Republican National Convention (Chicago) nominates U. S. Grant for President. Construction of new state capitol begins. First river tunnel in U. S. completed under Chicago River.

1870   Population: 2,539,891. Third state constitution adopted. St. Ignatius College, later Loyola University, founded.

1871   Fire burns large section of Chicago Oct. 9.

1876   The right of the State to regulate business "clothed with a public interest" upheld by U. S. Supreme Court in case of Munn v. Illinois. Lake Forest University opened.

1880   Population: 3,077,871.

1881   Aurora, first city to light streets electrically.

1884   Knight of Labor meeting in Chicago demands eight hour day.

1886   Bomb thrown at labor protest meeting, Haymarket, Chicago, May 3, 1886, kills 8 policemen.

1888   State capitol completed.

1889   Illinois State Historical Library founded.

1890   Population: 3,826,351.

1892   University of Chicago opens. John P. Altgeld elected governor.

1893   World's Columbian Exposition held in Chicago.

1894   Workers in Pullman Car Company plant strike. American Railway Union calls general railroad strike in sympathy. President Cleveland sends Federal troops to Chicago in defiance of Gov. Altgeld. Strike is lost; Eugene V. Debs jailed.

1896   William Jennings Bryan, persuades Democratic National Convention at Chicago, to endorse silver as monetary standard; is nominated for President.

1898   Spanish-American War: Illinois raises nine regiments of infantry, one of cavalry, and battalion of artillery. St. Vincent College, later De Paul University, founded.

1900 Population: 4,821,550. Chicago Drainage Canal opened.

1902 People of Illinois vote for adoption of direct and popular election of United States senators.

1903 Fire in Iroquois Theatre, Chicago, causes 596 deaths.

1904 Theodore Roosevelt nominated for President by Republican National Convention at Chicago.

1906 State Highway Commission organized.

1907 Law permitting local option for consumption of alcoholic liquors passed. Hennepin Canal connecting the Illinois and Mississippi opened. Act provides new charter for Chicago.

1908 Republican National Convention, Chicago, nominates William Howard Taft for President.

1909 Ten hour law for women passed.

1910 Population: 5,638,591. Primary act passed.

1912 Republican National Convention, Chicago, renominates Taft for President. Theodore Roosevelt forces launch Progressive Party, nominate Roosevelt. US Senate votes seat of Wm. Lorimer, Illinois, vacant.

1915 Steamer *Eastland* capsizes in Chicago River, 812 drown.

1917 Race riots in East St. Louis.

1917 World War: *See page 39 for statistics.*

1918 Illinois celebrates centennial. Construction of State-wide system of hard roads approved by voters.

1919 Race riots in Chicago. Illinois ratifies 18th Amendment, prohibiting liquor. Also 19th Amendment, woman's suffrage.

1920 Prohibition becomes effective Jan. 16, 1920. Congress enacts Volstead Enforcement Act, Jan. 17, 1920. Woman's suffrage established.

1920 Population: 6,485,280. Warren G. Harding nominated for President by Republicans at Chicago and carries State.

1922 Mrs. Winifred Mason Huck elected Representative-at-large from Illinois succeeding father, William E. Mason.
　　　Striking United Mine Workers in Herrin, clashed June 22 with strikebreakers and 22 of the latter killed. Men accused of killings tried and acquitted.

1923 Road bond issue of $100,000,000 authorized by general assembly. Governor approves anti-Ku Klux Klan bill.

1926 Eucharistic Congress of Roman Catholic Church in Chicago.

1929 Children required to complete elementary grades before going to work. Obligatory school year raised from six to eight months.

1930 Population: 7,630,654.

1932 Franklin Delano Roosevelt nominated for President by Democratic National Convention, Chicago.

1933   General Assembly enacts general sales tax of 2 per cent. Mayor Cermak of Chicago dies of wound inflicted by assassin in attempt to kill President-elect Roosevelt. Century of Progress opens in Chicago, closes Nov. 1, 1934.

1936   General Assembly enacts old age security law, occupational disease compensation law, and permanent registration.

1937   General Assembly enacts 8-hr. day for women; requires medical examination for venereal disease before marriage. Ohio River flood inundates Shawneetown, causes removal to new town site. Governor Henry Horner dies and is succeed by John H. Stelle.

1939   Oil boom in central Illinois.

1940   Population: 7,897,241.

1941   World War II. Illinois contributes more than 900,000 men and women to Armed Forces and auxiliaries. Dwight H. Green governor, two terms, 1941-49.

1944   Illinois again gave a plurality for Franklin D. Roosevelt (D) over Thomas E. Dewey (R), and in 1948 Harry S. Truman carried the State by 33,612 over Dewey. General Eisenhower (R) carried Illinois in 1952 and 1956, in both campaigns defeating Adlai E. Stevenson (D), who had been governor of Illinois. In 1960 John F. Kennedy (D) won over Richard M. Nixon (R) by only 8,858 votes in Illinois. In 1964 Lyndon B. Johnson (D), President since Nov. 22, 1963, defeated Barry M. Goldwater (R) by 890,888; in 1968 Richard M. Nixon (R) won over Hubert Humphrey (D) by 134,960, and in 1972 Nixon carried Illinois over George McGovern (D) by 503,670.

1949   Adlai E. Stevenson (D) elected governor. Later governors: William G. Stratton (D) 1957; Otto Kerner, Jr. (D) elected 1961 and 1965, resigned 1968 to become judge of US Circuit Court of Appeals; Samuel H. Shapiro (D) 1968; Richard B. Ogilvie (R) 1969; Daniel Walker (D) 1972.

1950   Population: 8,712,170. 1960: 10,081,158. 1970: 11,113, 956.

1968   In 1968 the protests, demonstrations and agitations for social reform reached their peak, after a decade of unrest caused by Negro efforts to gain equality in civil life, student opposition to the draft and the Vietnam war, and police clashes with street gangs. Riots touched off by the murder of Martin Luther King, Jr. led to destruction by fire of 162 buildings and a loss of $13,000,000 in Chicago April 5-7, with the National Guard called out. The Democratic National Convention of Aug. 26-29 brought battles between adolescent protesters and police, this disorder being repeated Oct. 8-11. *See Chicago.*

1972   The Credentials Committee of the National Democratic Convention in Miami voted June 30 that the delegation of the Illinois Democratic organization under Mayor Richard M. Daley was not entitled to seats at the convention. A double-deck commutation train on the Illinois Central Gulf Ry. backing up to the 29th St. Station in Chicago Oct. 30, was run into by a speeding train, with 44 killed, 320 injured.

INDEX TO STATE MAP SECTIONS

(Roman numerals indicate sections)

735

Greenup	X	Le Roy	VI	Nauvoo	IV
Gridley	VI	Lewistown	V	Neoga	X
Griggsville	VIII	Lexington	VI	New Baden	IX
		Libertyville	III	Newman	VII
Hamilton	IV	Lincoln	V	Newton	V
Hampshire	III	Litchfield	IX	Nokomis	IX
Hanover	I	Lombard	III	Normal	VI
Hanna City	V	Louisville	X	North Chicago	III
Harrisburg	XII			Norris City	XI
Hardin	VIII	Macon	VI		
Hartford	VIII	Macomb	IV		
Harvard	III	Madison	VIII	Oak Brook	III
Hennepin	II	Mahomet	VI	Oak Forest	III
Herrin	XII	Manhattan	III	Oak Park	III
Heyworth	VI	Manteno	III	Oakland	X
Highland	IX	Marengo	III	Oakwood	III
Highland Park	III	Marion	VII	Oblong	X
Highwood	III	Marshall	X	Odell	VI
Hillsboro	IX	Marseilles	III	Odin	IX
Hinckley	III	Martinville	III	O'Fallon	VIII
Homer	VII	Mascoutah	IX	Oglesby	II
Homewood	III	Mason City	V	O'Hara	II
Hoopeston	VII	Mattoon	X	Old Shawneetown	XII
Huntley	III	McLeansboro	XII	Olney	X
		Mendota	II	Onarga	VI
Illiopolis	V	Meredosia	IV	Oquawka	IV
		Metamora	IV	Oregon	I
Jacksonville	VIII	Metropolis	XII		
Jerseyville	VIII	Milford	VII	Palatine	III
Jonesboro	XII	Milledgeville	II	Palestine	X
Johnston City	VII	Moline	I	Pana	IV
Joliet	III	Momense	III	Paris	X
		Monmouth	IV	Pawnee	IX
Kankakee	III	Monticello	VI	Paxton	VI
Kenilworth	III	Morris	III	Pekin	V
Kirkland	II	Morrison	II	Peoria	V
Knoxville	V	Morton	V	Peotone	III
		Mounds	XII	Peru	I
Lacon	V	Mound City	XII	Petersburg	V
La Grange	III	Mount Olive	IX	Philo	VI
Laharpe	IV	Mount Carmel	II	Pinckney Hills	XII
Lake Bluff	III	Mount Carroll	II	Pittsfield	VIII
Lake Forest	III	Mount Pulaski	V	Plano	III
Lanark	II	Mount Sterling	IV	Pleasant Hills	VIII
LaSalle	II	Mount Vernon	IX	Polo	II
Lawrenceville	X	Mount Zion	VI	Pontiac	VI
Lemont	III			Princeton	II
Lena	II	Naperville	III	Princeville	V
		Nashville	IX	Prophetstown	II

KEY

U.S. HIGHWAYS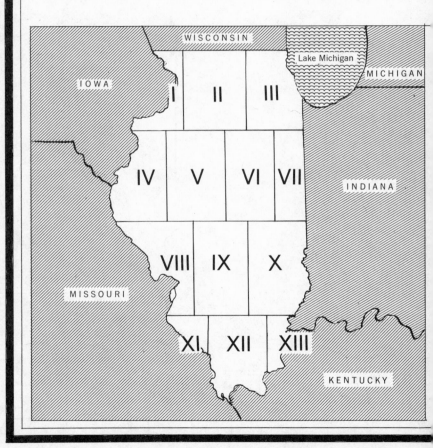
INTERSTATE HIGHWAYS
STATE HIGHWAYS

SECTIONAL DIVISION OF STATE MAP

Based on State Primary System of Highways map prepared by the Department of Transportation, Office of Planning, Programming, and Environmental Review of the State of Illinois, in cooperation with the U. S. Department of Transportation, Federal Highway Administration.

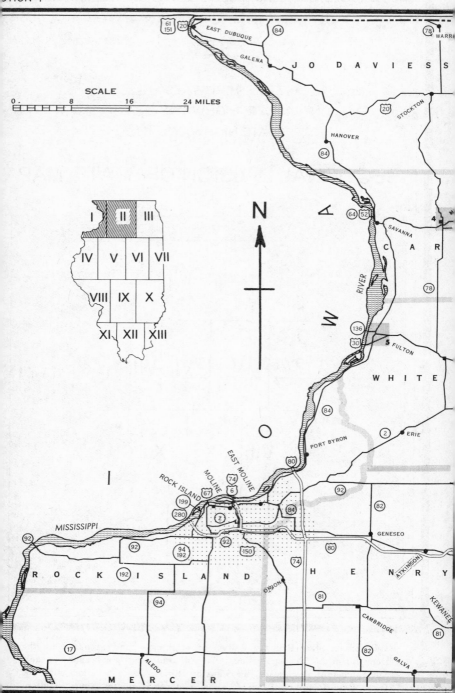

STEPHENSON

WINNEBAGO

BOON

ROCKTON

LENA

FREEPORT

CARROLL

LANARK

FORRESTON

MT. MORRIS

BYRON

OREGON

ROLL

OGLE

KIRKLAND

DE KALB

MILLEDGEVILLE

POLO

ROCHELLE

ASHTON

DE KALB

MORRISON

STERLING

DIXON

LEE

SIDE

ROCK FALLS

PROPHETSTOWN

AMBOY

EARLVILLE

WALNUT

MENDOTA

BUREAU

LA SALLE

SHEFFIELD

WYANET

PRINCETON

LADD

LA SALLE

UTICA

OTTA

DE PUE

SPRING VALLEY

PERU

HENNEPIN

GRANVILLE

OGLESBY

PUTNAM

ROCKFORD

BELVIDERE

ROCHELLE

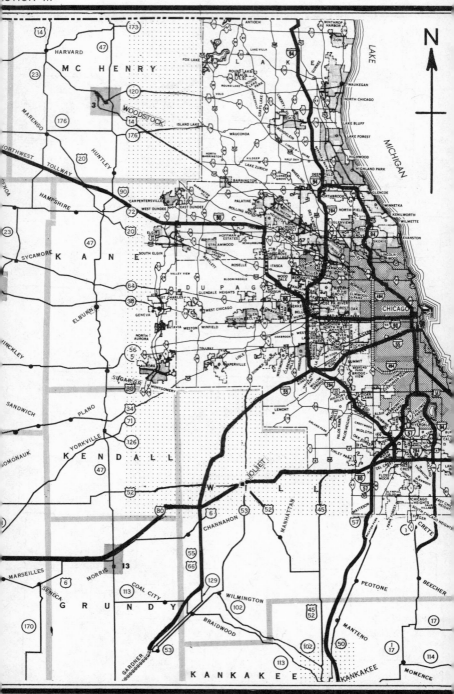

SCALE
0   8   16   24 MILES

I II III
IV V VI VII
VIII IX X
XI XII XIII

I

150

135
135
67
W A R R E N
94
135
MONMOUTH
164   16
34
41
OQUAWKA
164
34
ABINGDON
34
94
116
H E N D E R S O N
ROSEVILLE
AVON
96
94
9
LAHARPE
9
96
DALLAS CITY
9
BUSHNELL
9
94
MACOMB
67
41
CARTHAGE
COLCHESTER   136   19
HAMILTON
61
136
94
H A N C O C K
M C D O N O U G H
96
101
101
61
94
S C H U Y L E R
61
99
RUSHVILLE
67
A D A M S
94
BEARDSTOWN
24
CAMP POINT
MT STERLING
103
29
125
104
B R O W N
24
QUINCY
107
99
100
57
96
MEREDOSIA
67
104
104
57
67

W
A

MISSISSIPPI
NAUVOO

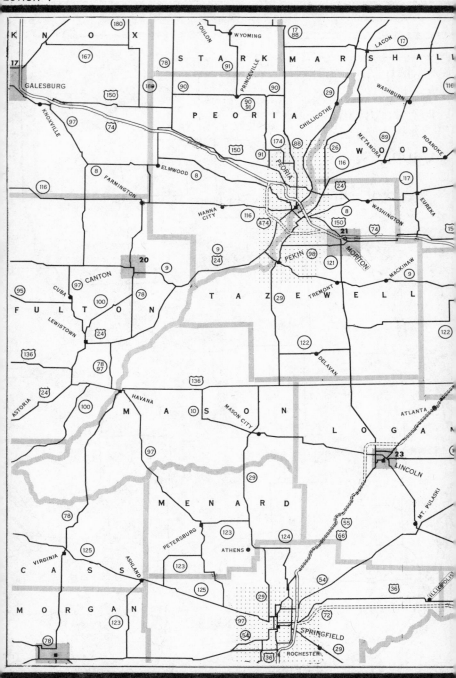

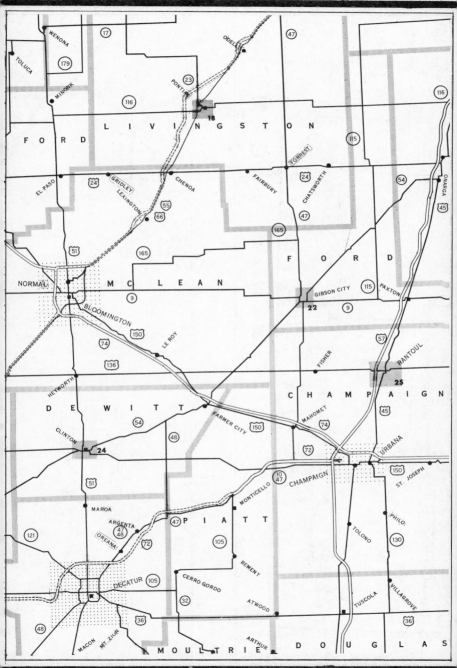

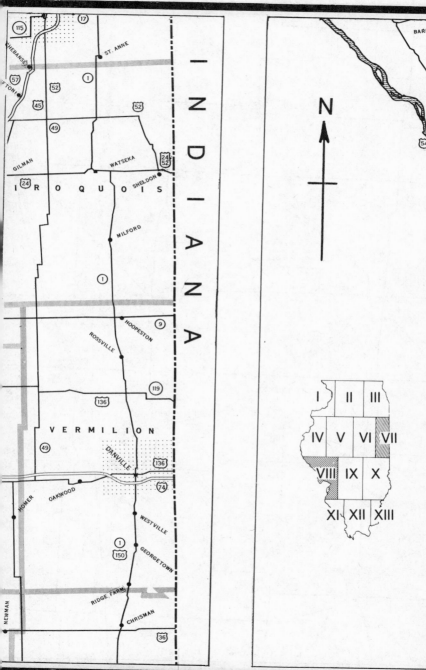

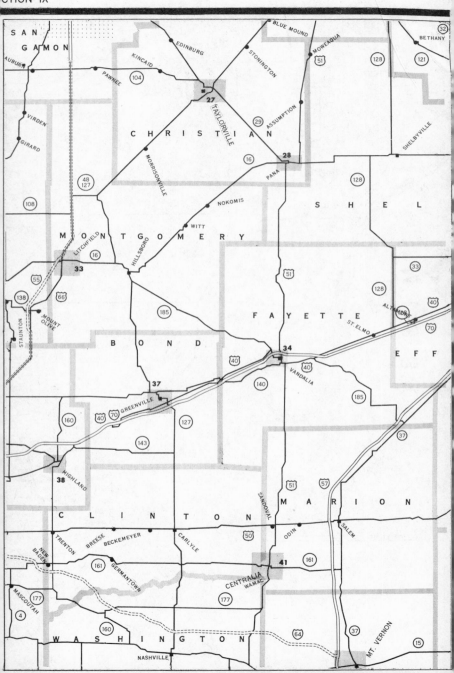

LOVINGTON · 133

SULLIVAN · 32

ARCOLA · 45

OAKLAND

E D G A R

133 · PARIS · 150

16 · 31 · 1

MATTOON · 316 · 30 · CHARLESTON

54 · 16

WINDSOR · 16

C O L E S

57 · 45 · 121 · 49 · 70 · 40 · MARSHALL

130

CUMBERLAND

NEOGA · TOLEDO · 36 · CASEY · MARTINSVILLE · C L A R K

B Y · 32 · 45 · 121 · GREENUP · 40

RIVER

32 · 33 · 40

35

EFFINGHAM · TEUTOPOLIS

J A S P E R

ROBINSON

PALESTINE

INGHAM · 33 · NEWTON · OBLONG

49 · WILLOW HILL · 33

C R A W F O R D

45

130

C L A Y

LAWRENCEVILLE · 1 · 33

LOUISVILLE

CLAY CITY · 250 · 39 · OLNEY · SUMNER · BRIDGEPORT · 40 · BR 50

FLORA · 50 · 250

R I C H L A N D · L A W R E N C E

WABASH

45

W A Y N E

W A B A S H

MOUNT CARMEL

15 · ALBION · 15

142 · FAIRFIELD · E D W A R D S · 1 · RIVER

N

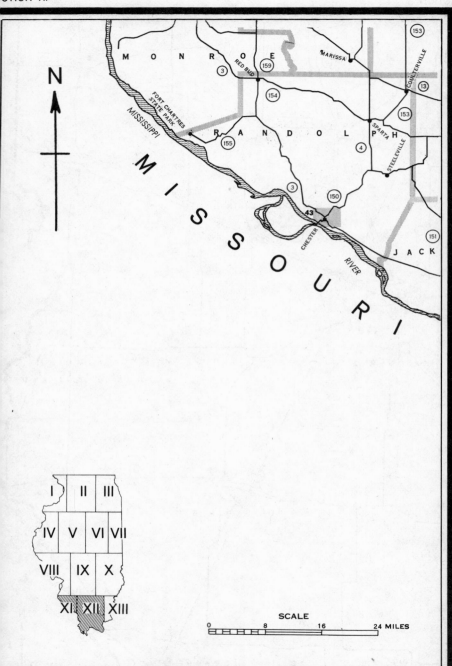

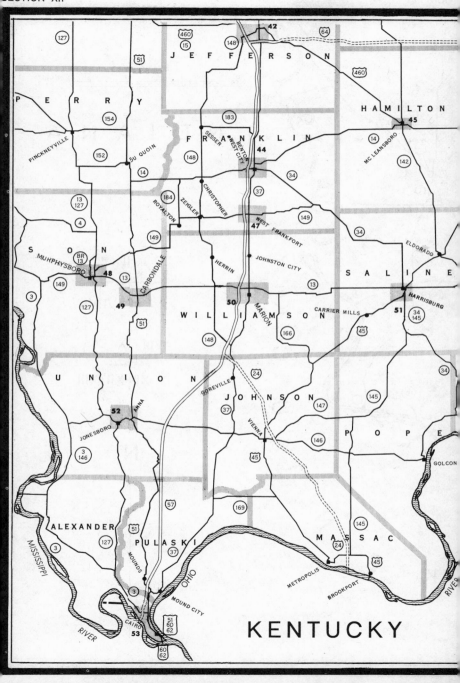

CHICAGO

CITIES AND TOWNS